W9-CKM-172

THE STORY OF
America

GEOGRAPHY CONSULTANT

Phillip Bacon
Professor Emeritus of Geography and Anthropology
University of Houston

Grateful acknowledgment is made to the scholars who read portions of *The Story of America* in manuscript.

Willard Bill
University of Washington

Ray A. Billington
Late of the Huntington Library

John Morton Blum
Yale University

John Bracey, Jr.
University of Massachusetts,
Amherst

Gloria Contreras
University of North Texas

Frank De Varona
Dade County Public Schools
Florida

Robert Farrell
Indiana University

Eric Foner
Columbia University

Thomas R. Frazier
Baruch College
City University of New York

William H. Harbaugh
University of Virginia

Asa G. Hilliard, III
Georgia State University

Michael Holt
University of Virginia

Ari Hoogenboom
Brooklyn College, CUNY

Arthur S. Link
Princeton University

Robert Middlekauff
University of California, Berkeley

Edmund Morgan
Yale University

Robert V. Remini
University of Illinois, Chicago

Timothy L. Smith
Johns Hopkins University

George C. Wright
University of Texas

In preparing *The Story of America* extensive discussions also were held with district administrators, faculty leaders, and teachers in California, Texas, Michigan, Illinois, Ohio, and Virginia

THE STORY OF
America

John A. Garraty

Gouverneur Morris Professor Emeritus of History
Columbia University

HOLT, RINEHART AND WINSTON
Austin • *New York • Orlando • Chicago • Atlanta • San Francisco • Boston • Dallas • Toronto • London*

A. GARRATY is a distinguished historian and writer and the
rneur Morris Professor Emeritus of History at Columbia University.
books include the widely adopted college textbook *The American
tion,* biographies of Henry Cabot Lodge and Woodrow Wilson, *The
reat Depression,* and the popular *1,0001 Things Everyone Should Know
About American History.* He has held Guggenheim, Ford, and Social
Science Research Council Fellowships. Professor Garraty is a former
president of the Society of American Historians, editor of the *Dictionary
of American Biography,* and coeditor of the *Encyclopedia of American
Biography.*

PHILLIP BACON is Professor Emeritus of Geography and Anthropology
at the University of Houston. He served on the faculties of Columbia University and the University of Washington and is former Dean of the Graduate
School of Peabody College for Teachers at Vanderbilt University.

Cover photograph: © *B. Gelberg, Sharpshooters.*

Maps: R.R. Donnelley Company Cartographic Services

Copyright © 1994, 1991 by Holt, Rinehart and Winston, Inc.

All rights reserved. No part of this publication may be reproduced or transmitted in any form or by any means, electronic or mechanical, including
photocopy, recording, or any information storage and retrieval system,
without permission in writing from the publisher.

Requests for permission to make copies of any part of the work should be
mailed to: Permissions Department, Holt, Rinehart and Winston, Inc., 8th
Floor, Orlando, FL 32887.

This work is derived in part from AMERICAN HISTORY, copyright ©
1986, 1982 by Harcourt Brace Jovanovich, Inc. All rights reserved.

Acknowledgments, see back matter.

Printed in the United States of America

ISBN 0-03-097559-X

34567   041   97 96 95 94

Contents

Unit One
THE AMERICAN COLONIES
Beginnings to 1770

Unit Two
THE AMERICAN NATION
1770-1798

Unit Three
A GROWING AMERICA
1790-1840

Contents

Unit Four
A WESTERING AMERICA
1816-1860

Unit Five
A DIVIDED AMERICA
1850-1877

Contents

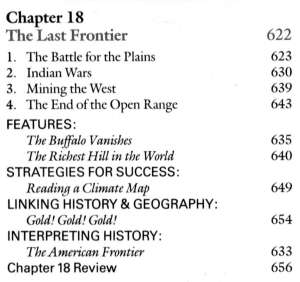

Contents

Unit Nine
A GLOBAL AMERICA
1940–1963

Unit Ten
MODERN AMERICA
1964 to the Present

Chapter 28
The Great Society

Chapter 29
The Vietnam Era

Chapter 30
Modern Times

REFERENCE SECTION

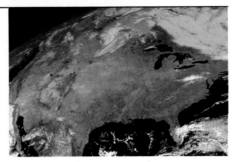

STRATEGIES FOR SUCCESS

FEATURES

CHARTS, GRAPHS, TABLES, & DIAGRAMS

The Story of America contains a vast amount of information. It has many useful features to help you understand and use this information. Some features help you preview what you are about to read. Others help you read for that information or find additional information. Still other features help you review what you have read. Using the features of *The Story of America* wisely will help you become a better student of history.

Using the Textbook's Features

To get the most from *The Story of America,* here are some guidelines.

1. **Use the Table of Contents.** Make yourself familiar with the **Table of Contents** (pages v-xvii). A quick skimming shows you how the book is organized and helps you anticipate **A** what you will be reading. It shows that *The Story of America* is organized into ten units, and the units are further divided into 30 chapters. As its name implies, the Table of Contents shows the content of each chapter, the special features the textbook contains, and the page on which each unit, chapter, and feature can be found. To the right is a sample.

2. **Study the unit opening pages.** Each unit gives a preview of its content with a unit title, an illustration, an introduction, and a list of chapters that are included. Take time to study the **B** unit opening page. It contains clues to what you are about to read. For example, after studying the opening page of Unit One on page 1, what can you tell about the people and times covered in this unit?

A Contents

New York Historical Association, Cooperstown
The prosperous Van Bergen farm at the foot of the Catskill Mountains was painted by a traveling artist in about 1735.

B THE AMERICAN COLONIES UNIT **1**

In Unit 1 of THE STORY OF AMERICA you will learn about the many peoples who contributed to the foundation of the United States and other nations of the Americas. Here are some main points to keep in mind as you read the unit.

• America was "discovered" at least three times: by Asian hunters—the ancestors of native Americans; by Vikings from Norway; and by Christopher Columbus.
• Native Americans, strongly influenced by their environment, developed many unique ways of life.
• Europeans came to America for many reasons. Among the most important were economic opportunity, religious freedom, and adventure. In contrast, most Africans were brought to the New World as enslaved people.
• Despite difficult beginnings, European colonies in the Americas prospered.
• In the 1760s, the British Parliament passed a series of taxes on the colonists, enraging many of them.

1

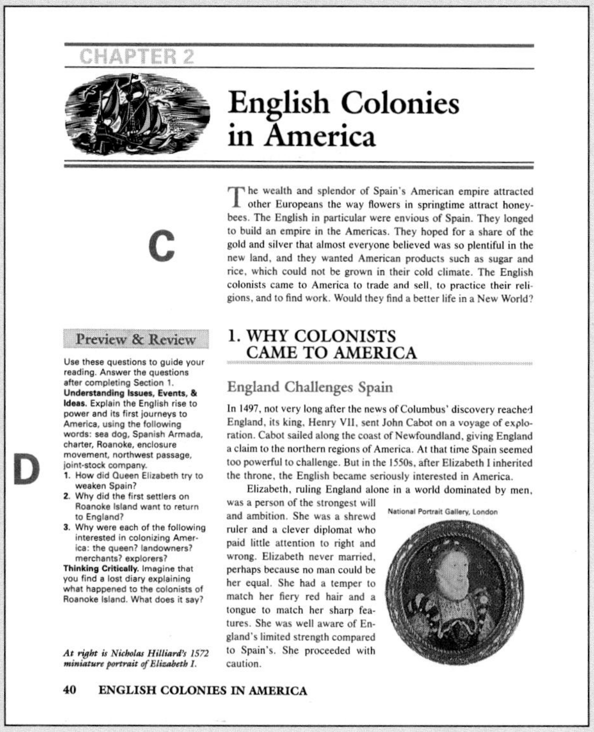

Reproduction of a textbook page spread

CHAPTER 2

English Colonies in America

C

The wealth and splendor of Spain's American empire attracted other Europeans the way flowers in springtime attract honeybees. The English in particular were envious of Spain. They longed to build an empire in the Americas. They hoped for a share of the gold and silver that almost everyone believed was so plentiful in the new land, and they wanted American products such as sugar and rice, which could not be grown in their cold climate. The English colonists came to America to trade and sell, to practice their religions, and to find work. Would they find a better life in a New World?

Preview & Review

Use these questions to guide your reading. Answer the questions after completing Section 1.
Understanding Issues, Events, & Ideas. Explain the English rise to power and its first journeys to America, using the following words: sea dog, Spanish Armada, charter, Roanoke, enclosure movement, northwest passage, joint-stock company.
1. How did Queen Elizabeth try to weaken Spain?
2. Why did the first settlers on Roanoke Island want to return to England?
3. Why were each of the following interested in colonizing America: the queen? landowners? merchants? explorers?
Thinking Critically. Imagine that you find a lost diary explaining what happened to the colonists of Roanoke Island. What does it say?

At right is Nicholas Hilliard's 1572 miniature portrait of Elizabeth I.

D

1. WHY COLONISTS CAME TO AMERICA

England Challenges Spain

In 1497, not very long after the news of Columbus' discovery reached England, its king, Henry VII, sent John Cabot on a voyage of exploration. Cabot sailed along the coast of Newfoundland, giving England a claim to the northern regions of America. At that time Spain seemed too powerful to challenge. But in the 1550s, after Elizabeth I inherited the throne, the English became seriously interested in America.

Elizabeth, ruling England alone in a world dominated by men, was a person of the strongest will and ambition. She was a shrewd ruler and a clever diplomat who paid little attention to right and wrong. Elizabeth never married, perhaps because no man could be her equal. She had a temper to match her fiery red hair and a tongue to match her sharp features. She was well aware of England's limited strength compared to Spain's. She proceeded with caution.

National Portrait Gallery, London

40   ENGLISH COLONIES IN AMERICA

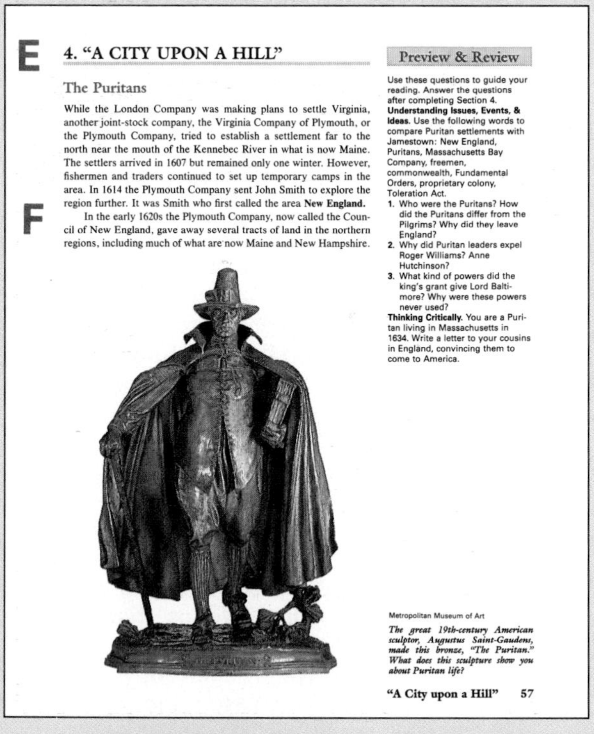

E

4. "A CITY UPON A HILL"

The Puritans

While the London Company was making plans to settle Virginia, another joint-stock company, the Virginia Company of Plymouth, or the Plymouth Company, tried to establish a settlement far to the north near the mouth of the Kennebec River in what is now Maine. The settlers arrived in 1607 but remained only one winter. However, fishermen and traders continued to set up temporary camps in the area. In 1614 the Plymouth Company sent John Smith to explore the region further. It was Smith who first called the area **New England**.

In the early 1620s the Plymouth Company, now called the Council of New England, gave away several tracts of land in the northern regions, including much of what are now Maine and New Hampshire.

F

Preview & Review

Use these questions to guide your reading. Answer the questions after completing Section 4.
Understanding Issues, Events, & Ideas. Use the following words to compare Puritan settlements with Jamestown: New England, Puritans, Massachusetts Bay Company, freemen, commonwealth, Fundamental Orders, proprietary colony, Toleration Act.
1. Who were the Puritans? How did the Puritans differ from the Pilgrims? Why did they leave England?
2. Why did Puritan leaders expel Roger Williams? Anne Hutchinson?
3. What kind of powers did the king's grant give Lord Baltimore? Why were these powers never used?
Thinking Critically. You are a Puritan living in Massachusetts in 1634. Write a letter to your cousins in England, convincing them to come to America.

Metropolitan Museum of Art

The great 19th-century American sculptor, Augustus Saint-Gaudens, made this bronze, "The Puritan." What does this sculpture show you about Puritan life?

"A City upon a Hill"   57

---

3. **Read the chapter introduction.** Every chapter of *The Story of America* begins with an introduction that provides an overview and states the main ideas of the chapter. When you read the introduction, begin forming questions you may have about the chapter's content.

C

4. **Use the section Preview & Review to guide your reading.** Every section of *The Story of America* begins with a **Preview & Review**. These contain key words and questions that can help guide your reading of the section. The questions are *the same ones* you use to review your mastery of the information in the section. The symbol shows you when you have reached the end of the section. A note in the margin tells you to return to the Preview & Review to begin your review of the section. By carefully reading the Preview & Review *before* beginning the section, you can identify important words or terms and major questions or ideas discussed in the section.

D

5. **Read the chapters and sections.** *The Story of America* has many features that make reading it easier. First, the headings and subheadings provide a kind of outline of the main ideas and important details.

E

Second, pay special attention to words printed in bold black type. These **boldfaced terms** call your attention to important history words. A definition follows most, right in that sentence or the next. You can also check a word's meaning in the glossary.

F

Third, study the illustrations and read the captions. Relate what you see to what you read. All of the pictures are chosen carefully to help you better understand what you are reading. One picture can be worth a thousand words.

A STRATEGIES FOR SUCCESS

READING GRAPHS

The successful student is able to gather information from a variety of sources, including graphs. *The Story of America* contains many graphs. Graphs present information visually. There are several types of graphs, each used to present a certain type of data. A *pie*, or *circle*, graph is used to show proportions. A *line* graph shows changes in two factors. It most often shows changes over time. A *bar* graph shows comparisons, making highs and lows stand out. A *picture* graph, or *pictograph*, uses pictures to illustrate amounts.

Because graphs can contain so much information and are so common in histories, it is important to know how to read them.

How to Read a Graph

Follow these steps to read a graph.

1. **Read the title**. The title will tell you the subject and purpose of the graph. It may also contain other information, such as dates.
2. **Study the labels**. Line and bar graphs show two sets of data, one set displayed on the horizontal axis and the other on the vertical axis. The *horizontal* axis is the line at the bottom of the graph that runs across the page. The *vertical* axis is at the left side of the graph and runs up and down. Labels on these axes identify the type of data and the unit of measurement, when appropriate.

3. **Analyze the data**. Note all trends, relationships, and changes among the data. Note increases and decreases in quantities.
4. **Put the data to use**. Use the information to form generalizations and hypotheses and to draw conclusions.

Applying the Strategy

You may have heard the expression, "A picture is worth a thousand words." The picture graph may also be worth a thousand words. Study the picture graph below. Note that small figures ⸸ are used to make a simple comparison of the population of the American colonies in 1730. Each symbol stands for 10,000 persons. A partial ⸸ figure represents a fraction of 10,000. For example, the population of Delaware in 1730 was 9,170 persons, so it is represented by part of a figure. What is the population of Virginia? New York? If you said 1,014,000 for Virginia and 48,000 for New York, you have read the graph correctly!

There also are examples of other types of graphs in this unit. The pie graph on page 89 shows the ethnic makeup of the colonial population. (For an example of a bar graph, turn to page 139 in the next chapter.)

For independent practice, see Practicing the Strategy on page 107.

COLONIAL POPULATIONS, 1730*

New Hampshire		Maryland	
Massachusetts		Virginia	
Connecticut		North Carolina	
Rhode Island		South Carolina	
New York			⸸ = 10,000 persons
New Jersey			⸸ = 8,000 persons
Pennsylvania			⸸ = 6,000 persons
Delaware			⸸ = 4,000 persons
			⸸ = 2,000 persons

Source: *Historical Statistics of the United States*

*Georgia not yet founded

78 LIFE IN COLONIAL AMERICA

HEROES OF THE REVOLUTION

B In the flush of victory Americans celebrated their first national heroes. Benjamin Franklin had been widely known for his experiments with electricity and for *Poor Richard's Almanack*. Now he was admired everywhere for his staunch support of the Revolution.

Thomas Jefferson had also become a national hero by the 1780s. American pride in the Declaration of Independence swelled when the Revolution succeeded and the courage of the document's signers could be fully appreciated.

The greatest hero of all was Washington. "The Father of His Country" was, by all accounts, a stern man who stood alone and said little. Yet all Americans admired his personal sacrifice and his careful use of power. One admirer called him "no harum

"John Paul Jones" by Charles Willson Peale.

Starum ranting Swearing fellow but Sober, steady, and calm."

A Scot, John Paul Jones, was revered as the founder of the strong United States naval tradition. In his little ship *Bon*

Homme Richard ("Poor Richard," named in admiration of Franklin), Jones came upon a British convoy led by the powerful *Serapis*. He lashed his ship to the *Serapis* and fought from sunset into moonlight until both ships were seriously damaged. Still Jones refused to surrender. "I have not yet begun to fight," he proclaimed. Finally the British vessel surrendered and was boarded by Jones as the *Bon Homme Richard* sank in a storm of fire.

All men and women who had been brave enough to take up arms against the British were now heroes. One, Andrew Jackson, was only a boy of nine when war broke out. For refusing to black the boots of a British officer, he was struck sharply in the face with the flat of a sword. He carried the scar to his grave.

INTERPRETING HISTORY: The American Revolution

C Historians study the past much like detectives solve crimes. Like a detective, an historian gathers evidence, such as letters, diaries, newspaper articles, and eyewitness accounts, interprets it, and reaches a conclusion. But different historians may interpret that evidence differently.

For example, historians have debated for nearly 200 years the reasons behind the American Revolution. Many historians, such as James Franklin Jameson, support the theory that the Revolution was an economic and social struggle. In his book *The American Revolution Considered as a Social Movement* he stresses that democratic ideals were growing among the colonists and the Revolution brought about significant economic and social changes. Historian Mary Beth Norton agrees in her

book *Liberty's Daughters: The Revolutionary Experience of American Women 1750–1800*. She points out that even the status of women in America improved after the Revolution.

Historian Gordon Wood in *The Creation of the American Republic 1776–1787* takes a contrasting view. He maintains that the colonists were motivated by patriotism. Historian Edmund S. Morgan supports this, arguing that the colonists were united by the principles expressed by Patrick Henry's "Give me liberty or give me death!"

Whether the Revolution was prompted by economic reasons or patriotic ones will always remain open to debate. Historians will continue to pursue the answers. This detective work makes history exciting.

132 GOVERNING THE AMERICAN COLONIES

Study the special features. *The Story of America* has many features that enrich history and help you develop the tools of the historian. These features appear on tinted backgrounds.

On blue pages are **Strategies for Success**. **A** These features appear in each chapter. They present additional information related to the specific chapter content and provide an opportunity for you to develop or sharpen your study skills.

Most chapters also contain one or more brief features that highlight an important person, event, or idea. These features are **B** easily identified by their three-column format and special heading. They are meant to give the reader a chance to pause and to consider their significance in our history.

A third feature, **Interpreting History,** teaches the historian's craft by discussing interpretations of events or ideas that have created historical controversy. Examples include the **C** causes of the American Revolution, the motives of the writers of the Constitution, and the importance of the frontier in the development of the American character.

Every chapter of *The Story of America* uses the words of historical figures whenever possible. Besides lengthy primary source quotations, marked with large red quotation marks, **D** you will often find a *Point of View* in the margin. This feature presents a brief statement about a key event, person, or situation. Sometimes opposing opinions are presented as *Points of View.*

Another key feature is the map program. The maps illustrate physical, cultural, and historical information clearly and accurately. Almost every map contains relief shading showing major **E** physical features, so you are constantly aware of the interplay of history and geography. Several Strategies for Success will help you hone your map-reading skills.

The Story of America highlights the ethnic and cultural contributions of different groups to American culture. To help you visualize **F** some of the many contributions, you will find four pictorial essays, or portfolios, that contain the art and artifacts of some of the groups that have come to America. These four portfolios are titled: America's Indian Heritage, America's

The Granger Collection, New York

John Smith was 27 years old when he took command of the Jamestown settlement. This engraving portrays him at the age of 33.

seen far more of the world than any of the other settlers. He had fought in a number of wars in eastern Europe against the Turks. In one war he was captured, taken to Constantinople, and sold into slavery. However, he managed to kill his master and escape. After many other remarkable adventures Smith found himself in the colony of Virginia.

In 1608 Smith was elected president of the Virginia council. Once in charge, he bargained with the Indians for food. He stopped the foolish searching for gold. Instead he put people to work building shelters and planting food crops. Hard work and strict discipline became the order of the day.

Reforms for Virginia

Virginia's difficulties finally convinced the merchant adventurers in England that the London Company needed to be reorganized. In 1609 Sir Edwin Sandys, a councilor who was also a member of Parliament, England's legislative body, obtained a new charter from King James. This charter called for the appointment of a governor who would rule the colony in Jamestown rather than from London.

The London Company then raised a good deal more money and outfitted a fleet of nine ships to carry about 600 new settlers across the Atlantic. Those who paid their own fare received one share of stock in the company. Those who could not pay agreed to work as servants of the company for seven years in return for their passage. Until 1616 everything the colonists produced was to be put into a common storehouse or fund. On that date the servants would have worked off their debt to the company. Then the profits of the enterprise were to be divided among the shareholders—both the investors back in England and the settlers. Every shareholder would also receive a grant of Virginia land.

These were fine plans but hard to put into effect. Conditions in Virginia got worse and worse. The first governor, Lord De La Warr, put off coming to Jamestown. Smith returned to England for supplies and colonists, and to convince company managers to invest more money in the colony. Without his firm hand, the organization and rules he had begun quickly fell apart. The years from 1609 to 1610 were a **starving time**. As Smith described it:

❝By their [the Indians'] cruelty, our Governours indiscretion [poor judgment] and losse of our ships, of five hundred [colonists] within six months after Captaine Smith's departure, there remained not past sixtie men, women and children, most miserable and poore creatures; and those were preserved for the most part, by roots, herbes, acornes, walnuts, berries, now and then a little fish . . . yea, even the very skinnes of our horses. . . . This was that time,

Return to the Preview & Review on page 116.

D

Point of View

An Algonquin leader asked John Smith why the colonists used force with the Indians.

❝Why will you take by force what you may have quietly by love? Why will you destroy us who supply you with food? What can you get by war? We can hide our provisions and run into the woods; then you will starve for wronging your friends. Why are you jealous of us? We are unarmed, and willing to give you what you ask, if you come in a friendly manner.❞

Powhatan, 1607

48   ENGLISH COLONIES IN AMERICA

And how was the new, larger empire in America to be governed? The old system of 13 separate colonies, each controlled from London, worked well enough when the colonies were separated from one another by thick forests. Now the wilderness was shrinking. Four colonies—Virginia, Pennsylvania, Connecticut, and Massachusetts—each claimed parts of the Ohio Valley just won from France. Each based its case on a royal charter drafted before anyone knew much about American geography. Who would untangle these conflicting claims?

There were also the Indians in the Ohio Valley. Everyone expected them to stop fighting when the French surrendered. Instead they organized behind Pontiac, a chief of the Ottawa, and tried to drive the settlers back across the Appalachians. How could an area claimed by so many different colonies be defended? Who would pay the cost if British troops were used?

These last questions were the most pressing in 1763. The answers were that the British put down **Pontiac's Rebellion** and paid the cost of doing so. To keep the peace the British stationed 6,000 soldiers in the land won from the French and closed the entire region beyond the Appalachian Mountains to settlers. This decision was announced in the **Proclamation of 1763**. Only licensed fur traders might enter the Ohio region. No one could purchase Indian lands.

Most American colonists did not like the Proclamation of 1763. It seemed to put the great West as far out of reach as it had been when the forts built by Governor Duquesne had first barred the way ten years earlier. 🔲

LEARNING FROM MAPS. *The French and Indian War significantly changed the face of North America. Study these maps. What changes can you discover?*

E

NORTH AMERICA IN 1754

British	Russian
French	Unexplored
Spanish	

Azimuthal Equal-Area Projection

NORTH AMERICA IN 1763

British	Russian
French	Unexplored
Spanish	
Proclamation Line of 1763	

Azimuthal Equal-Area Projection

America's Indian Heritage

F

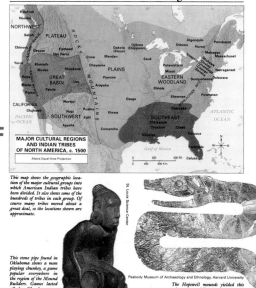

MAJOR CULTURAL REGIONS AND INDIAN TRIBES OF NORTH AMERICA, c. 1500

Albers Equal-Area Projection

This map shows the geographic location of the major cultural groups into which American Indian tribes have been divided. It also shows some of the hundreds of tribes in each group. Of course many tribes moved about a great deal, so the locations shown are approximate.

St. Louis Science Center

This stone pipe found in Oklahoma shows a man playing chunky, a game popular everywhere in the region of the Mound Builders. Games lasted all day. Chunky was a bit like bowling, a bit like the javelin toss.

Peabody Museum of Archaeology and Ethnology, Harvard University

The Hopewell mounds yielded this mica serpent. Mica is a mineral so very in color and so fine it is translucent—diffused light passes through.

10   THREE DISCOVERIES OF AMERICA

America's Pacific Heritage

F

Since ships first sailed or land caravans carried off its treasure, westerners have been fascinated by the East. Marco Polo was bedazzled even though he came from Venice, a western jewel. The art of the Orient is the oldest in the world, but it was hidden behind the walls of Forbidden Cities. Emigrants from Asia were too poor to own eastern treasures such as we see on these pages, but traders like John Ellerton Lodge filled the holds of the *Kremlin* and *Magnet* with china, silk, ivory, even fireworks that bloomed like chrysanthemums to bring Pacific culture to America.

The Metropolitan Museum of Art

This dragon comes from a Chinese embroidered chair of the 18th century. In Eastern art, dragons seldom breathed fire and were seen as protectors.

St. Louis Art Museum

Chinese porcelain has long been prized. The export ware above is an Orange platter in the "Fitzhugh" pattern.

Arnold Genthe/The Granger Collection, New York

Four children in holiday dress were photographed on the teeming streets of San Francisco's Chinatown before the earthquake of 1906.

America's Pacific Heritage   757

A

LINKING HISTORY & GEOGRAPHY

CROSSING THE ATLANTIC

By the 15th century Europe had two groups of sea powers. One, the Italian city states, located on the relatively calm and sheltered waters of the Mediterranean Sea, traded with China, the Indies, and India. The second group, the Hanse Towns, which later became the Hanseatic League, sailed the North and Baltic seas, carrying goods from Russia and Siberia to the towns of northern Europe. Both groups developed from unique geographic environments—the linking of great overland trade routes from the east with the indented coastlines of tideless seas. Captains and crews sailed in comparative security, knowing land lay not too far away.

Looking to the Atlantic

1. Why did the other nations of Europe begin to look for their own trade routes?

The merchants in Italy and the Hanse Towns charged other Europeans very high prices for the goods they traded. Because these merchants held monopolies, other nations had difficulty establishing their own trade routes. Slowly the leaders of the other European nations began to realize that their only realistic alternative was to look westward—to the Atlantic Ocean. But that meant facing a landless horizon and the vastness of an uncharted watery wilderness.

It is interesting to note that only those nations that actually faced the Atlantic—Spain, Portugal, England, France, and the Netherlands—actually met the challenge of the Atlantic (as Norway had centuries earlier). They, and they alone, took the knowledge of navigation, map making, and shipbuilding and applied it to a much sterner test of seamanship in the open Atlantic Ocean.

Geography of the Ocean Frontier

2. What manner of watery frontier did these early sailors find as they ventured westward?

We can get some sense of what lay ahead by looking at a map or globe. As you can see, the Atlantic covers one fifth of the earth's surface. And you can see it occupies a unique space on Planet Earth, separating Europe and Africa from the Americas and creating a barrier—or, for some, a highway—between those continents.

A map or globe shows you, too, that the Atlantic is a long body of water that resembles an hourglass. The widest part of the ocean, spanning some 4,150 miles (6,640 kilometers), stretches between Spain and Florida. It was precisely this expanse crossed by Columbus in 1492! The narrowest part lies between Norway and Greenland in the north. Here the distance is a mere 930 miles. Across this narrowest section, with islands scattered like stepping stones, the Vikings sailed around the year 1000.

Mixing the Waters of the Atlantic

3. How else is the Atlantic's geography unique?

Perhaps the most amazing aspect of the Atlantic's geography is its huge *drainage basin,* the area of land whose rivers flow into an ocean. Most of the world's great rivers empty their waters into the Atlantic.

In North American the Atlantic basin stretches all the way to the Rocky Mountains. There, in western North America, the many tributaries of the mighty Mississippi begin. At mid-continent they join to form the river that drains two thirds of the continent toward the Gulf of Mexico, an arm of the Atlantic.

In South America the Atlantic's drainage area extends across the continent to the soaring Andes Mountains. Among those towering peaks the world's greatest flow of water begins its journey to the Atlantic. So great is this rush of water—carried by the Amazon River—that the volume of water is greater than that of the Mississippi, Nile, and Yangtze rivers *combined.*

The Atlantic also gathers much of the water from Africa. Waters of the Nile, Congo, and Niger rivers eventually reach the Atlantic. The Atlantic also claims the Rhine and the other great rivers of Western Europe as well as many of those of Eastern Europe and central Russia.

The immense size of the drainage basin opened the way to yet-to-be-explored lands. In North America, the Gulf of St. Lawrence, Hudson Bay, and Gulf of Mexico carried sailing vessels from Europe to the continent's edge. Rivers carried explorers to its very heart.

Sailing West

4. What propelled the early sailing ships from Europe to the Americas?

One other aspect of the Atlantic's geography played a vital role in the discovery and exploration of the New World. Winds and ocean currents helped transport people and cargoes from Europe to the Americas and back.

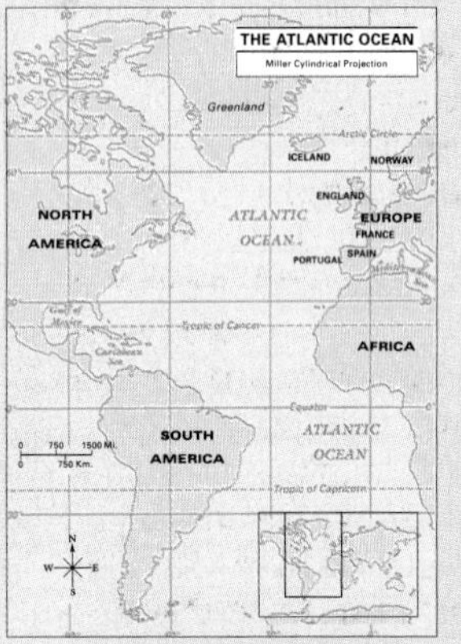

As you can see from the map on page 24, Columbus first headed south to the Canary Islands before turning westward. This was no accident. Early explorers voyaging southward along Africa's west coast found strong and steady winds from the northeast between 30° and 5° north of the equator. These winds carried the sleek sailing ships ever westward.

What causes these winds? Air always flows from centers of high atmospheric pressure to areas of lower pressure. The winds along the African coast result from air flowing from zones of high pressure near 30°N to a low-pressure zone always found near the equator.

Of course, if the world did not turn on its axis, the air would simply flow from north to south in the Northern Hemisphere and south to north in the Southern Hemisphere. The earth's rotation causes the winds to deflect, or bend.

These wonderful winds, among the steadiest and most reliable on earth, soon became invaluable for ships sailing westward. Within a remarkably short period of time they were known to sailors everywhere as the *trade winds.*

The Return Trip

5. Once in the Americas, how did people return to Europe?

Just as the trade winds carried ships westward, the Gulf Stream helped propel them back to Europe. The Gulf Stream begins in the eastern portions of the Gulf of Mexico. It flows northward along the eastern seaboard of the United States. At about 40°N the current swings eastward across the Atlantic toward the British Isles. It is one of the strongest and most consistent ocean currents. Coupled with the northeast trade winds, it provided knowledgeable navigators with the means to complete roundtrip voyages between Europe and the New World.

The geography of the Atlantic made it ideal as a pathway of discovery. Winds and currents moved the sailing ships on just the right paths. Plentiful bays and gulfs, fed by huge rivers, provided entrances into continents. Soon the forbiddingly vast waters of the Atlantic became one of the most heavily traveled routes in the world.

APPLYING YOUR KNOWLEDGE

Your class will work in three groups to create a profile map of the Atlantic Ocean. One group should map the major ocean currents. Another should identify and label on a map the major rivers eventually draining into the Atlantic. The third group should measure distances across the ocean from various spots (such as Virginia) in North America to Norway, Spain, and England. You will then combine the groups' findings to create your profile map of the Atlantic.

176 THE REVOLUTIONARY WAR

Linking History & Geography 177

B

CHAPTER 3 REVIEW

Enlightenment

Triangular Trade

1600 COLONIAL AMERICA 1650 1700 1750

1619 First Africans brought to America

1676 Bacon's Rebellion erupts

1706 Benjamin Franklin is born

1740 The Great Awakening

1750 Enlightenment in America

★ Settlement reaches the Appalachians

1754 Franklin's Albany Plan of Union

Chapter Summary

Read the statements below. Choose one, and write a paragraph explaining its importance.

1. The American land held many blessings for the first settlers.
2. Early colonists relied on rivers as transportation routes, and early cities grew on river banks.
3. Although colonial women could not vote and worked very hard, American life offered more opportunities than it did in Europe.
4. Most early settlers obtained land and worked hard to improve it, qualifying them to vote.
5. Africans were first brought to America to work as slaves.
6. Slavery was inhuman; educated slaves were more likely to run away or revolt.
7. Cash crops such as tobacco were the major southern products and required much labor.
8. Triangular trade became very profitable.
9. Intellectual movements such as the Great Awakening and the Enlightenment involved Benjamin Franklin and many Americans.
10. As settlers moved west, many controversies arose.

Reviewing Chronological Order

Number your paper 1-5. Then study the time line above and place the following events in the order in which they happened by writing the first next to 1, the second next to 2, and so on.

1. The Great Awakening
2. Bacon's Rebellion
3. Albany Plan of Union
4. First Africans brought to America
5. The Enlightment in America

Understanding Main Ideas

1. Why did the colonists have to be self-reliant? Give at least two examples of ways the colonists were self-reliant.
2. What hardships did women in colonial America face?
3. What geographical feature did all the large towns have in common?
4. Why did working people in the colonies earn more and get better treatment than workers in England? Why did indentured servants agree to come to America to work? How were African slaves usually treated by their owners in the American colonies?
5. How was American slavery different from slavery elsewhere?
6. Why was the Enlightenment welcomed in America?

Thinking Critically

1. **Synthesizing.** Imagine that you are the 26-year-old widow Martha Dandridge Custis. What advantages might you have over a European woman of your time? What major advantages does a twentieth-century American woman have over a colonial woman?
2. **Drawing Conclusions.** How did the availability of land and the scarcity of labor help make life in colonial America more democratic than it was in England?
3. **Evaluating.** Do you think "Yankee ingenuity" was a positive or a negative quality? Why? How did northern colonists use it to find a means of paying for the European goods they wanted? Do you think Americans still have "Yankee ingenuity"? Explain your answer.

Writing About History

An important point in this chapter is that the great amount of land in America affected the lives of the colonists. Suppose you are an American colonist. Write a letter to a friend in Europe explaining how the abundance of land affected one of the following: women, indentured servants, slaves, American Indians.

Practicing the Strategy

Review the strategies on pages 78 and 103.

Reading Graphs. Study the pie graph on page 89 and answer these questions.

1. What percentage of the colonial population was African? Where does that percentage rank?
2. The English, Scotch-Irish, and Scottish were all British. What percentage of the total population did the British make up?
3. What three groups represent the smallest percentages of the colonial population?

Creating a Graphic Representation. Reread the information on the Great Awakening on pages 95 to 98. Then create a word web of at least five terms centered on The Great Awakening.

Using Primary Sources

Being a freed slave in the South often meant being on your guard. Southerners began to fear the large number of freed slaves living in their midst. North Carolina and other states passed laws providing a reward for the capture and resale of "illegally" freed slaves. In 1797 Thomas Pritchet and three other freed slaves petitioned the House of Representatives for federal protection. After some debate the House voted to not accept the petition, leaving the fate of freed slaves to the individual states. Read the excerpt from the *Annals of the Congress of the United States,* 4th Cong., 2nd Sess. (1796–97) to get a sense of the struggle slaves faced. Then answer the questions.

> *I, Thomas Pritchet, was set free by my master Thomas Pritchet, who furnished me with land . . . where I built myself a house, cleared a sufficient spot of woodland to produce ten bushels of corn; . . . this I was obliged to leave . . . being threatened by Holland Lockwood, who married my said master's widow, that if I would not come and serve him, he would apprehend me, and send me to the West Indies; Enoch Ralph also threatening to send me to jail, and to sell me. . . . Being thus in jeopardy, I . . . escaped by night into Virginia. . . . where shipping myself to Boston, I was landed in New York, where I served as a waiter for seventeen months; but my mind being distressed on account of the situation of my wife and children, I returned to Norfolk in Virginia, with the hope of seeing them; but finding I was advertised in the newspaper, twenty dollars the reward for apprehending me, my dangerous situation obliged me to leave Virginia.*

1. Give two examples from the excerpt to show that Pritchet's freedom was often threatened.
2. How might you defend Pritchet's argument that he was a free person? How might you defend Holland Lockwood's belief that Pritchet was not a free person?
3. Why did Pritchet return to Virginia? Why did he leave again?

Linking History & Geography

Almost all of the early cities in America developed on a body of water. Research the location of the first colonial cities and draw a map showing their locations. Then in a brief essay explain why the first cities developed on bodies of water, using one city as a specific example.

Enriching Your Study of History

1. **Individual Project.** Some colonial business leaders advertised in England to persuade more European settlers to come to America. Draw an eye-catching poster with an attention-getting slogan for a group of these business leaders.
2. **Cooperative Project.** On page 99 there are examples of slogans or wise sayings from *Poor Richard's Almanack.* With your classmates write three of your own slogans. Consider such subjects as good health, friendship, and good study habits. Put your slogans on a poster and compare them with those of the rest of the class. What do you conclude makes a good slogan? Try to reach a class consensus in your discussion.

106 LIFE IN COLONIAL AMERICA

Chapter 3 Review 107

West African Heritage, America's Hispanic Heritage, and America's Pacific Heritage. The first contains unique works by American Indian artisans. The last three present beautiful and representative works of art from the native lands of their group's members.

A   **Linking History & Geography** features appear on beige pages. These two-page features are part of the narrative and appear in each unit. They highlight the importance of geography in the unfolding of America's history. Most contain beautifully detailed maps.

7. **Reviewing your study.** To check your understanding and to help you remember what you have learned, always take time to review.

B   When you finish a section, return to the Preview & Review and answer the questions. Complete the **Chapter Review** when you finish your study of the chapter. Do the same for the **Unit Review.**

8. **Use the Reference Section.** *The Story of America* provides a **Reference Section.** When you want to know the meaning of a boldfaced term, turn to the **Glossary,** which begins on page 1149. Entries are listed alphabetically, with page references for pages in the text where the word appears in boldface type. When you need to know on which page something is mentioned, turn to the **Index,** which begins on page 1181. Index entries are always in alphabetical order. Become familiar with the rest of the **Reference Section,** which contains an atlas and charts and graphs full of data about the story of America.

Studying Primary Sources

There are many sources of historical information. They include diaries, journals, and letters; memoirs and autobiographies; paintings and photographs; editorials and editorial cartoons. All of these are *primary sources.* They give firsthand eyewitness accounts of history.

Primary sources appear frequently in *The Story of America,* for they are the historian's most important tool. You should use primary sources, usually bracketed by large quotation marks, to gain an understanding of events that only eyewitness accounts can provide.

How to Study Primary Sources

To study primary sources, follow these guidelines.

1. **Read the material carefully.** Look for main ideas and supporting details. Note what the writer or speaker has to say about the atmosphere or the mood of the people.
2. **Ask yourself questions.** Ask *who* or *what* is described. If sources conflict, and they often might, *who* is speaking and *what special insights do they have?* You may also want to ask *why* an action took place.
3. **Check for bias.** Be alert for words, phrases, or information that present a one-sided view of a person or situation when it seems evident that more than one point of view is possible.
4. **When possible, compare sources.** Study more than one primary source on a topic if available. By comparing what they have to say, you can get a much more complete picture than by using only one source.

Also, remember that historians use *secondary sources* as well as primary sources. These are descriptions or interpretations of events written after the events have occurred. History books such as *The Story of America,* biographies, encyclopedias, and other reference works are examples of secondary sources.

Developing Historical Imagination

When we read history, we tend to form opinions about events in the past. Sometimes these opinions can keep us from fully understanding history. To judge people and events of the past using today's standards can lead to a false picture of history. We need instead to develop our historical imagination.

To develop historical imagination, we need to put ourselves in the place of those who lived in the past. In that way we can better see why they thought and acted as they did. Remember that science, education, and all other fields of endeavor have advanced greatly in a relatively short time. So it is important to keep in mind what people in the past knew and *what they did not know.* Throughout

The Story of America you will have the opportunity to use your historical imagination, to take yourself back to another time.

Writing About History

Writing is an important intellectual process. It helps us clarify our thoughts, learn information, and discover new ideas. *The Story of America* contains numerous writing opportunities. Although you may not always have time to use them all, the guidelines that follow can help you improve your writing. This is especially true of longer writing assignments.

How to Write More Effectively

To write more effectively, follow these guidelines.

1. **Prewrite.** Prewriting includes all the thinking and planning that you do before you write. Before you write, ask yourself these questions: Why am I writing? Who will read my writing? What will I write about? What will I say about the topic? How will I organize my ideas?

2. **Collect information.** Do research if necessary. You can write more effectively if you have many details to choose from.

3. **Write a first draft and evaluate it.** In your first draft, remember to use your prewriting plan as a guide. Write freely, but consider your purpose and audience.

   As you review and evaluate your first draft, note places where you need to add or clarify. It may help to read your draft aloud or to exchange it with a partner.

4. **Revise and proofread your draft.** Add, cut, replace, and reorganize your draft as needed to say what you want to say. Then check for proper spelling, punctuation, and grammar.

5. **Write your final version.** Prepare a neat and clean final version. Remember that appearance is important. Although it does not affect the quality of your writing itself, it can affect the way your writing is perceived and understood.

Many writing opportunities in *The Story of America* ask you to create a specific type of writing —a diary entry, a letter, an advertisement, a poem, or a newspaper editorial. Most of these opportunities ask you to use your historical imagination—to write from the point of view of a person living then rather than now.

A diary is a personal log of your experiences. Each entry is dated and is a brief statement of what has happened and your reactions. Your diary entries should be the personal recollections of a person *at a particular time in history*.

You are probably familiar with writing letters. When you write a letter, be sure to indicate to whom you are writing and include in your letter the specific details called for in the assignment.

You also are probably familiar with advertisements. An effective advertisement captures the attention and highlights an important feature of the "product." When you develop an advertisement, make it memorable and to the point.

Writing a poem often can seem difficult. Remember, however, that poems do not have to rhyme. An example of such free verse is Carl Sandburg's "Chicago" on pages 789-90. Notice that although the lines do not rhyme, they are organized in a specific way. That is what makes it poetry. When you write a poem, let the words flow but keep them focused.

A newspaper editorial is a statement of opinion or point of view. It states a stand about an issue and provides the reasons for that stand. You might wish to read the editorial page of your local paper to see how the editorials are written there.

Using the guidelines listed in this section together with those developed in the *Strategies for Success* should help you write with confidence as you study *The Story of America*. Remember to have a plan and to use historical imagination when it is called for. Now, enjoy *The Story of America*.

THE STORY OF

America

To the Student

The Story of America tells our story because it is important in itself. It is a great epic and the unique tale of how hundreds of millions of people came to live on this vast continent, while the original inhabitants lost their lands. There are other reasons for telling our story. It may be read as a grand lesson that permits us to understand how past affects present. Our story is composed of many pasts that allow us to explain how our present experiment in democracy has gone on for more than 200 years. Thus we read history knowing full well that those who study the past can come to understand who we are and how far we've come and are sometimes able to caution us about our present course toward the future. But we also realize that historians have never been any better at telling the future than politicians, economists, or fortune tellers.

The Story of America was written especially for you, young Americans born in the last half of the 20th century. It provides the background to help you know about the people and values that make America great. It also presents the many controversies and challenges that have faced Americans from time to time throughout history. You can learn from their successes—and failures.

The author of *The Story of America* is ever mindful that chronology is the spine of history. Events are presented in the order in which they occurred. Time lines at the end of each chapter help you see and remember the chronology of important events.

The Story of America contains many original documents and lengthy excerpts from primary and secondary sources. These include eyewitness accounts, poems, song lyrics, diary entries, and excerpts from a variety of other sources. These materials can give you special insight into the thinking and attitudes of Americans. *The Story of America* also is filled with striking and memorable illustrations. These paintings, photographs, and other illustrations may indeed be worth a thousand words. Each captures a bit of the history of its time. The illustrations in *The Story of America* also show changing aspects of American life such as dress, art, and architecture.

An integral part of the story of America is the relationship of people to the land. The beautifully detailed maps and special geography features in *The Story of America* illustrate this relationship and show its importance in the unfolding of our nation's story. The textbook also introduces you to the five themes of geography: location, place, relationships within places, movement, and regions. Charts, graphs, tables, and diagrams highlight the economic and sociological trends. Together, they portray a nation that has grown dramatically from such small beginnings.

When you have finished *The Story of America* you should understand the democratic values and ethical ideas that guide the American people and appreciate the civic responsibilities of all Americans to participate in American democracy. *The Story of America* will help you recognize the multicultural character of the American society and have empathy for the struggles of people to secure a place in society. With this information you will be able to take your place in society as an informed voter, more appreciative of the legacy that is the story of America.

New York Historical Association, Cooperstown

The prosperous Van Bergen farm at the foot of the Catskill Mountains was painted by a traveling artist in about 1735.

THE AMERICAN COLONIES

UNIT 1

In Unit 1 of THE STORY OF AMERICA you will learn about the many peoples who contributed to the foundation of the United States and other nations of the Americas. Here are some main points to keep in mind as you read the unit.

- America was "discovered" at least three times: by Asian hunters—the ancestors of native Americans; by Vikings from Norway; and by Christopher Columbus.
- Native Americans, strongly influenced by their environment, developed many unique ways of life.
- Europeans came to America for many reasons. Among the most important were economic opportunity, religious freedom, and adventure. In contrast, most Africans were brought to the New World as enslaved people.
- Despite difficult beginnings, European colonies in the Americas prospered.
- In the 1760s, the British Parliament passed a series of taxes on the colonists, enraging many of them.

Three Discoveries of America

A merica was discovered at least three times. The first time was between 20,000 and 60,000 years ago, when people from northern Asia touched foot on American soil in what is now Alaska. A second discovery of America occurred about the year 1000, but we know little about the Viking sailors who reached Newfoundland. The last discovery, 500 years ago, was made by a persistent Italian who sailed under the colors of Spain and claimed what he believed to be the Indies for King Ferdinand and Queen Isabella. Thus began the age of exploration and conquest of the Americas by Spain. Would Spain come to dominate the New World?

1. THE FIRST AMERICANS

The Ice Age

Today Asia is separated from America by the Bering Strait, a body of water between Alaska and Siberia more than 50 miles (80 kilometers) wide. When early people first came to America from Asia, the strait was dry land. The earth was then passing through a great **Ice Age,** a period when the weather was much colder than at present. What in warmer times would have fallen as rain and drained back into the oceans fell as snow instead. Gradually, enormous amounts of this snow piled up in the northern and southern regions of the earth, far more than could melt during the short summers. Vast ice fields called glaciers formed. So much water was trapped in these thick glaciers that the water level of the oceans dropped sharply, exposing a land bridge between Asia and North America.

Plants froze, but their seeds and spores lay dormant until warmer weather came. With each period of warmth the plants that grew from the seeds and spores spread to new areas. Eventually they spread across the land bridge into North America. The animals that fed on them followed. The bones of ancient Asian elephants, called mammoths, and of saber-toothed tigers have been found in dozens of places in the United States. Following the animals came people, the first Americans.

Preview & Review

Use these questions to guide your reading. Answer the questions after completing Section 1.
Understanding Issues, Events, & Ideas. Use the following words to compare early American Indians: Ice Age, historical imagination, society, culture, Stone Age, clan, generalization, environment, adobe, pueblo, Mound Builders, Five Nations, confederation, artifact, archaeologist, carbon-14 dating, anthropologist, folk tale.
1. How did the Ice Age lead Asian people to discover America?
2. Why did the first immigrants to America come in waves?
3. Give three examples of how environment influenced the customs of early American Indian societies.

Thinking Critically. 1. Compare the way of life of farmers with that of hunters and wanderers. **2.** You know that the peoples of North and South America spoke many different languages. Other than speaking, how could people from two different tribes communicate?

The exact year, decade, or century when the first Americans arrived will never be known, for no historian recorded the adventures of these pioneers. Their graves are unmarked. The ashes of their campfires have been scattered by the winds of the ages. These were accidental discoverers, hunters following wild game or herders driving their flocks over the next hill to find greener pastures.

The first American immigrants came in waves, for there were warmer periods when some of the ice melted and the water level rose. The last crossed about 10,000 years ago. At about that time the great glaciers began to melt, and the Bering land bridge was flooded over by the rising ocean.

The Great Migration

What did it feel like to be among the first people to reach this great, empty land? We know what the first astronauts experienced when they set foot on the moon. They were aware that they were doing something no one had ever done before. We do not know exactly what the first Americans experienced. They did not know that they were exploring a new continent. Understanding the difference calls for an act of **historical imagination.** Having a good historical imagination means being able to look at past events, keeping in mind what

Susan Middleton, © California Academy of Sciences

This jaw of a saber-toothed cat was found in the La Brea Tar Pits in Los Angeles. This and other fossils from the Pleistoscene era (between 2 million and 10,000 years ago) may be viewed today at the George C. Page Museum. How do fossils help us understand the past?

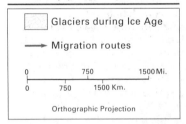

MIGRATION TO AMERICA
ca. **60,000 (?)–10,000** B.C.

☐	Glaciers during Ice Age
→	Migration routes

0   750   1500 Mi.
0   750   1500 Km.

Orthographic Projection

LEARNING FROM MAPS. *The Asiatic wanderers who came to the Americas spread slowly across the lands. What physical barriers hindered their spread to the east and west in North America?*

The First Americans   3

the people of the day knew, but at the same time remembering what they did not know.

Once in North America, the wanderers moved slowly southward and to the east, following the life-giving game. The distances they covered were enormous. It is 15,000 miles (24,000 kilometers) from their homeland in Asia to the southern tip of South America and 6,000 miles (9,600 kilometers) to what is now New England. Many thousand years passed before they had spread over all this land.

As they advanced and multiplied, the first Americans gradually changed their ways of life. Some made their homes in fertile valleys, others in tropical jungles. Some settled in mountainous regions or in deserts. Each group had different problems, and each learned to see the world in different ways. As a result each society created its own culture. A **society** is a group of people who live in a specific geographic area and who have a common culture. The **culture** of a society consists of those values and behavior patterns held in common: language, government, family relationships, how they make a living, how they educate their children, and the objects they create.

Some sense of how many different cultures developed comes from the fact that the peoples of North and South America spoke between 1,000 and 2,000 languages.

Early American Cultures

By the 1400s there were perhaps 50 million people living in North and South America. Only about 1 or 2 million of these inhabited what is now the United States and Canada. Partly because they were so few in number and spread over such a huge area, these people had developed a number of distinct cultures.

Many cultural differences stemmed from the ways groups dealt with the basic problem of scarcity. Like all societies these groups had to make choices about how best to use their limited resources to meet basic needs. Some hunted and gathered wild plants. Others turned to farming. Those who planted seeds and cultivated the land were able to develop a more secure and comfortable life than those who relied on hunting and gathering. People who had mastered farming, or agriculture, could settle in one place instead of roaming in constant search of food. They built permanent houses. Their societies grew to include more members.

None of the groups made much progress in developing simple machines or substituting mechanical or even animal power for their own muscle power. They had no wagons or other vehicles with wheels and no horses or oxen to help plow the land. Their tools and weapons were made of wood or stone or bone. Aside from a few copper objects and some gold and silver jewelry, they had no metals. Anthropologists call this stage of development the **Stone Age.** It ended with the arrival of Europeans and their technology.

This agate point was made into a weapon sharp enough to kill mammoths and bison. When the point was attached to a spear, and the spear was flung by an atlatl—a device for holding and throwing—it changed the way people hunted. Use your historical imagination to describe two hunts: one before these weapons existed and one after.

Lee Boltin, © American Museum of Natural History

© American Museum of Natural History

This water jar was one of the pieces of clay pottery made by the Zuñi who lived in the desert of the Southwest. After reading page 6 about the Zuñi environment, why do you think it was important that jars were watertight?

Most leaders, or chiefs, were chosen in a fairly democratic manner. That is, most chiefs ruled with the consent of their societies, not by force or written law. Life was mostly governed by tradition and custom. People tended to work in groups rather than alone. Usually they did not own their land as individuals. Their "hunting ground" or homeland was the general region in which the group lived. It was not an area with specific boundaries. This was true even of the farmers, who could not go far from the crops they tended.

These agricultural people were mostly peaceful, though they could fight fiercely to protect their fields. The hunters and gatherers, on the other hand, were quite warlike because their need to move about brought them frequently into conflict with other groups.

Some early American cultures were matrilineal, which means that kinship was traced through the female side. When a man and woman married in such a society, the man became a member of his wife's social group, or **clan.** A typical household might consist of an older woman, her daughters, and her granddaughters. Of course, the woman's husband, her sons-in-law, and her grandsons would also live in the household group. But only the female members were truly permanent members of the clan.

All of these statements are **generalizations,** broad statements that link loosely associated facts. They are true of most of the groups we are discussing. Yet every one of these communities was somewhat different from all the others. No generalization about them can be completely accurate. History is full of such "mostly but not entirely true" statements. This is unfortunate, but we must learn to live with this weakness. Remember, as you read, to add words like "usually" or "nearly always" when you spot a generalization.

Peabody Museum of Archaeology & Ethnology, Harvard University

What is this animal with horns? Nobody today seems to know. It was carved around the first century by the early residents of the Hopewell site in Ohio. The tail has a rattle, the head is horned, and little feet are pressed to the body. How do you suppose the early Americans used this carving?

The First Americans   5

© John Running

Early American Societies

Pueblo Bonito was the greatest Anasazi village in Chaco Canyon, New Mexico. At least 1,200 people lived there once. Drought ended most great pueblos in the last years of the 13th century. How might modern environmental studies have helped save Pueblo Bonito?

Land and climate strongly influenced the way the first Americans lived. They adjusted to nature—their **environment**—far more than they tried to change it. A brief look at some of the early American societies gives us an idea of the variety of American Indian cultures that evolved over hundreds of years.

The Southwest. As much as 1,000 years ago in the Southwest, the Hopi and Zuñi were building with **adobe**—sun-baked brick plastered with mud. Their homes looked remarkably like modern apartment houses. Some were four stories high and contained quarters for perhaps a thousand people, along with storerooms for grain and other goods. These buildings were usually put up against cliffs, both to make construction easier and for defense against enemies. They were really villages in themselves, as later Spanish explorers must have realized since they called them **pueblos.** *Pueblo* is Spanish for town.

The people of the pueblos were peaceful and gentle. They raised what they called the three sisters—corn, beans, and squash. They made excellent pottery and wove marvelous baskets, some so fine that they could hold water. The Southwest has always been a dry country, with water scarce. The Hopi and Zuñi brought water from streams to their fields and gardens through irrigation ditches. Water was so important that it played a major role in their religion. They developed elaborate ceremonies and religious rituals to try to bring rain.

The Great Basin. The way of life of less settled groups was simpler and more strongly influenced by nature. Small tribes such as the Shoshone and Ute wandered the dry and mountainous lands between the Rocky Mountains and the Pacific Ocean. They gathered seeds and hunted small animals such as rabbits and snakes.

The Far North. In Alaska and northern Canada the ancestors of today's Eskimos hunted seals, walruses, and the great whales. They lived in igloos built of blocks of packed snow. When summer came, they fished for salmon and hunted the lordly caribou.

The Northwest. Fishing was the mainstay of the Kwakiutl, Nootka, and Tlingit tribes. These people lived mostly on salmon and other fish caught in northwestern coastal waters. The magnificent forests of redwood, pine, and cedar that grew right down to the ocean supplied them with lumber to build their homes and canoes and to carve their ancestral totem poles.

The Great Plains. The Cheyenne, Pawnee, and Sioux tribes, known as the Plains Indians, lived on the grasslands between the Rocky Mountains and the Mississippi River. They hunted bison, commonly called buffalo. Its meat was the chief food of these tribes, and its hide was used to make their clothing and the covering of their tents and teepees. Every part of the animal was used, even its waste, which when dried served as fuel for cook fires in that treeless region. Little wonder that the buffalo was an important symbol in the religious life of the Plains Indians!

Field Museum of Natural History

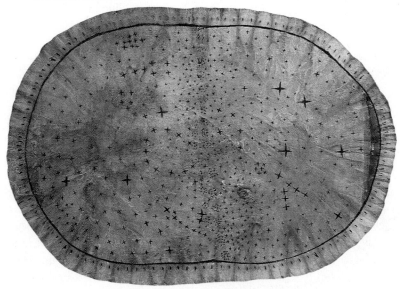

An early Pawnee astronomer painted this star chart on buckskin to show the stars and planets of the night sky. A reverence for the heavens was a part of the Pawnee tradition. How might the star chart have been used?

© American Museum of Natural History

This Kwakiutl ceremonial mask was carved from wood and painted. One head contains another. When opened, its heads look in three directions—perhaps to past, present, and future. Early Americans of the Northwest carved masks and totem poles to represent their ancestors. How many different works of art in this chapter would you classify as religious? How many are made for everyday use? Can you make a generalization about the kinds of artifacts that are usually preserved?

The Southeast. The Ohio Valley was once the home of the ancestors of such important tribes as the Choctaw and the Creek. They were called the **Mound Builders** because they buried their dead in elaborate earthen mounds built in the shape of birds or snakes, or in human form. These were very large, as high as an eight-story building, and one has been found that covers an area as large as 50 modern city blocks. We know that the people of the mounds traded with tribes as far away as the Rocky Mountains and the Gulf of Mexico because objects made of stone and ornaments made of the teeth of sharks and alligators have been found in their settlements. Tribes such as the Cherokee, Natchez, and Chickasaw gradually moved southeast from the Ohio Valley.

© Tony Linck

From the air we can see what no builder of the Hopewell effigy mounds could see. This mound is in the shape of a snake or serpent. Imagine that you were a visitor to this site while the great mound was being built. What would you tell others in your tribe on your return home?

8

The Eastern Woodlands. The Mohawk, Oneida, Onondaga, Cayuga, and Seneca made up a group of tribes that was later called the **Five Nations** or League of the Iroquois. They lived in the densely wooded central region of what is now New York State. The Iroquois **confederation,** a loose association of tribes, was very powerful because it could assemble many warriors. The Iroquois men were hunters, the women farmers. The Iroquois women also participated in tribal decision making, choosing new chiefs, for example.

For thousands of years these tribal societies knew nothing of the rest of the world. They were as isolated from their original homeland in Asia and from Europe and Africa as if they were on the moon.

Uncovering the Past

Since the first Americans did not record their history in books, we must reconstruct it from those objects they created that have survived the centuries. These include campsites and buildings, engraved stones, clay pots, tools and weapons, jewelry—what are known as **artifacts.** Putting together these fragments is like solving an enormous jigsaw puzzle with many missing pieces. It is a difficult but fascinating task.

Scientists called **archaeologists** search for and study artifacts. In America archaeologists have located and carefully dug up ancient camps, burial grounds, and entire cities. They have found hundreds of thousands of artifacts from arrowheads to huge stone statues.

We can estimate the age of these artifacts by using the technique called **carbon-14 dating.** Carbon is present in all living things, and some of this carbon takes a form called carbon-14. When a living thing dies, its carbon begins to break down at a very slow but steady rate. Thus, by measuring what remains of the carbon-14 in, say, a human bone or even a piece of charcoal from a campfire, an expert can tell about how long ago the person was alive or the fire put out. Carbon-14 dates are accurate only to within a few hundred years. They are not much use for studying recent events. But for learning the history of the peoples who first settled America, the method is most useful.

In addition to what archaeologists can tell us about the first Americans, we can also learn by studying their living descendants. The scientists who do this research are called **anthropologists.** Some anthropologists live with and observe the descendants of the first Americans. They ask how these peoples explain their relation to one another. What are their religious ideas and other values? Do they tell stories called **folk tales** that have been handed down from generation to generation? What are their habits and traditions? The answers to these questions throw light on how early Americans lived and thought. In such ways historians have been able to learn a great deal about these first settlers of America.

© John Running

The Anasazi of the Pueblo period around 1100 made this classic pottery in black on white. The vessels were painted with a dye.

Return to the Preview & Review on page 2.

America's Indian Heritage

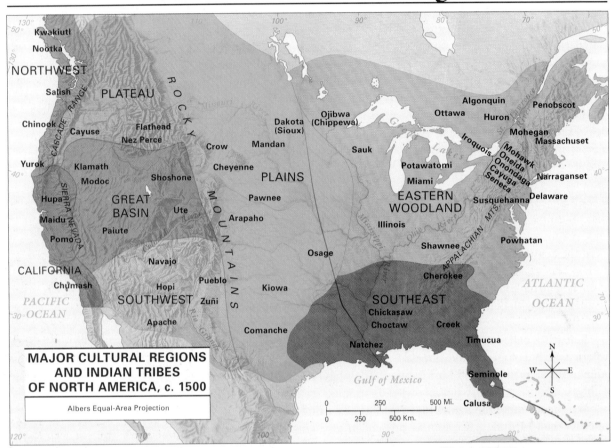

MAJOR CULTURAL REGIONS AND INDIAN TRIBES OF NORTH AMERICA, c. 1500

Albers Equal-Area Projection

Kwakiutl
Nootka
NORTHWEST
Salish
PLATEAU
Chinook
Cayuse
Flathead
Nez Percé
Yurok
Klamath
Modoc
Shoshone
Hupa
GREAT BASIN
Ute
Maidu
Paiute
Pomo
CALIFORNIA
Navajo
Chumash
Hopi
Pueblo
SOUTHWEST
Zuñi
Apache
Comanche

ROCKY RANGE
CASCADE RANGE
SIERRA NEVADA
MOUNTAINS

Crow
Mandan
Cheyenne
PLAINS
Pawnee
Arapaho
Kiowa

Dakota (Sioux)
Ojibwa (Chippewa)
Sauk
Osage
Natchez

Algonquin
Ottawa
Huron
Penobscot
Mohegan
Massachuset
Potawatomi
Miami
Mohawk
Oneida
Onondaga
Cayuga
Seneca
Iroquois
Narraganset
EASTERN WOODLAND
Susquehanna
Delaware
Illinois
Shawnee
Powhatan
APPALACHIAN MTS.
Cherokee
SOUTHEAST
Chickasaw
Choctaw
Creek
Timucua
Seminole
Calusa

Great Lakes
Missouri
Mississippi
Ohio River
Rio Grande

PACIFIC OCEAN
ATLANTIC OCEAN
Gulf of Mexico

N W E S

0   250   500 Mi.
0   250   500 Km.

This map shows the geographic location of the major cultural groups into which American Indian tribes have been divided. It also shows some of the hundreds of tribes in each group. Of course many tribes moved about a great deal, so the locations shown are approximate.

St. Louis Science Center

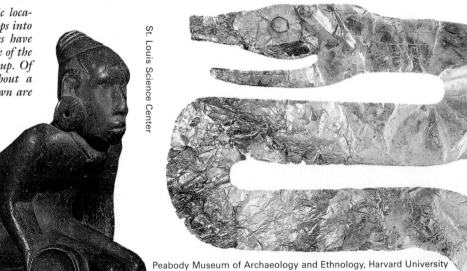

This stone pipe found in Oklahoma shows a man playing chunkey, a game popular everywhere in the region of the Mound Builders. Games lasted all day. Chunkey was a bit like bowling, a bit like the javelin toss.

Peabody Museum of Archaeology and Ethnology, Harvard University

The Hopewell mounds yielded this mica serpent. Mica is a mineral silvery in color and so fine it is translucent—diffused light passes through.

10   THREE DISCOVERIES OF AMERICA

Ashmolean Museum, Oxford

National Portrait Gallery

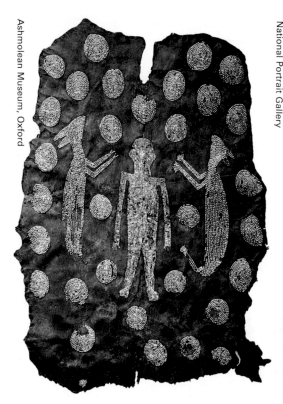

Matoaks als Rebecka daughter to the mighty Prince Powhatan Emperour of Attanoughkomouck als Virginia converted and baptized in the Christian faith, and Wife to the wor.ll M.r Tho. Rolff.

Ætatis suæ 21. A.º 1616.

Powhatan's Mantle was worn by the great leader of the Algonquins, who lived on the Virginia tidewater— lands just inland from the ocean. It is the oldest historical example of American Indian art. The cloak is made of tanned buckskin and decorated with shells.

American Museum of Natural History

Pocahontas, daughter of the great Powhatan, is seen here in a 1616 painting. She married John Rolfe of Jamestown and was taken to England. In 1617 she died of smallpox.

This painted fish bowl was made by the Mimbres, a Mogollon people of southern New Mexico. The Mogollon were among the first people of the Southwest to make pottery. They are best remembered for their black-on-white ware.

Utah Museum of Natural History

A fragment of a woven basket was found at Hogup Cave near the Great Salt Lake in Utah. The baskets were so tightly woven that they could hold water into which hot stones were lowered to boil stews.

America's Indian Heritage   11

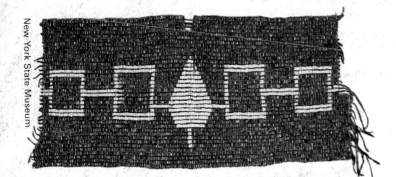

New York State Museum

Museum of the American Indian, Heye Foundation

The Hiawatha Belt shows the unity of the five Iroquois tribes. The squares are connected to a central tree, or heart. The beads from which the belt is fashioned were probably brought to America by Europeans.

The mask of painted wood below depicts the moon. It was carved by the Haida, a people of the Queen Charlotte Islands, which are west of British Columbia.

The men of the Hopi spun cotton yarn on a spindle. Weaving was also primarily man's work.

The wooden deer mask was made by inhabitants of Key Marco, off Florida's swampy coast.

University Museum, University of Pennsylvania

National Museum of Canada/Canadian Museum of Civilization

Field Museum of Natural History

A thunderbird—the mythical creator of the storms that rolled over the Great Plains—swoops out of the sky, hurling lightning flashes on this Pawnee ceremonial drum.

Joslyn Art Museum, Omaha

Those who knew the old ways wove this Navajo blanket.

Florence Curtis Graybill and Victor Boesen

The great photographer of the American West was Edward Sheriff Curtis. He photographed "A Piegan Dandy" (above), showing traditional Indian dress and hairstyle, in about 1855.

National Museum of American Art

George Catlin was one of America's greatest painters of western Indian life. His 1832 portrait of Black Rock shows Catlin's attention to detail. The chief of the Two Kettle tribe of the Blackfoot Nation wears a split-horn ermine cap with a trail of eagle feathers, the mark of the bravest of leaders.

America's Indian Heritage 13

Use these questions to guide your reading. Answer the questions after completing Section 2.
Understanding Issues, Events, & Ideas. Use the following words to describe the first European ventures outside Europe: Viking, saga, Vinland, manor, serf, feudal system, Crusades, Holy Land, Islam, Moslems, Indies, Commercial Revolution, compass, astrolabe.
1. What problems are there with using the Viking Sagas as a historical source?
2. Explain the relationship between serfs and lords.
3. How did Europe change during the Commercial Revolution?
4. What inventions made longer sea voyages possible? How?
Thinking Critically. 1. Imagine you are a member of Leif Ericson's crew. Describe what you see when you set foot on Vinland for the first time. **2.** Do you think the Crusades were successful? Why or why not?

National Archives of Norway, Oslo

A Norse ship such as the Vikings might have sailed to America is shown on the seal of the city of Bergen, Norway. It was carved in about 1300. Why do you think the Vikings crossed the ocean?

2. EUROPE AWAKENS

The Viking Sagas

A second discovery of America was much less important than the first. It occurred about the year 1000, less than a thousand years ago, but we know little for certain about the event or the European people who took part in it. The discoverers were Norwegian sailors who were called **Vikings.**

In 982 a redheaded Viking named Eric the Red sailed from Iceland and in 986 founded a settlement near the southern tip of the island of Greenland in the North Atlantic. The story of Eric and his family and their adventures was passed down from generation to generation in **sagas,** a traditional Scandinavian story form. These sagas were told and retold. They were not written down until 200 years after the events they describe.

The two major sagas about their adventures, *Eric the Red's Saga* and the *Greenlanders' Saga*, contradict each other at many points. They are obviously a mixture of fact and fancy. Nevertheless, it appears likely that either Leif Ericson, Eric's son, or another Viking sailor was the first European to set foot on the North American continent.

Archaeologists have discovered the remains of only one Viking camp in North America. It is at a place called L'Anse aux Meadows (the Creek of the Meadows) in Newfoundland. But the sagas speak of a land called **Vinland** (Wine Land) which must have been farther south since grapes do not grow as far north as Newfoundland. According to the *Greenlanders' Saga*, Leif sailed to Helluland (Baffin Island today) and Markland (Labrador). He then passed around a large island (Newfoundland) and reached a country "so choice, it seemed to them that none of the cattle would require fodder for the winter." There he found the grapevines. Leif and his crew loaded their boat with grapes and vines and timber before they sailed back to Greenland.

Next, the saga tells us, Leif Ericson's brother Thorvald sailed to Vinland. While exploring, he and his party encountered nine men in kayaks. A kayak is a kind of canoe. They killed eight of the men but the ninth escaped, soon to return with a larger force. Although the Vikings drove them off, Thorvald was killed in the battle.

According to the sagas, other expeditions followed, one led by Eric's daughter Freydis. The Vikings gathered grapes, traded for furs with the natives, whom they called *Skraelings*, and fought with them repeatedly. Sometime around the year 1010 the Vikings stopped visiting Vinland, perhaps because of these troubles with the Skraelings. Outside Norway and Iceland no one knew of their adventures. Nearly five hundred more years passed before the original Americans were again disturbed by outsiders.

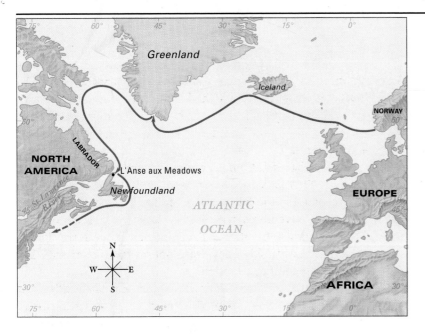

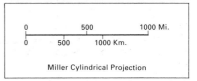

0   500   1000 Mi.

0   500   1000 Km.

Miller Cylindrical Projection

LEARNING FROM MAPS. *The Vikings crossed the Atlantic at one of its narrowest points. In what direction did they sail to reach Vinland?*

Europe in the Year 1000

If the Vikings could make their way to North America, why did no other Europeans attempt to explore the western seas for such a long time? There were several reasons for the delay. Life in Europe was slow paced. Little changed from one year to the next. The people were mostly poor and uneducated. Curiosity about the rest of the world was at a low point. Each village, or **manor,** was a tiny world in itself, ruled by a lord. The lord's fields were cultivated by peasants called **serfs.** Serfdom was a condition halfway between freedom and slavery. Serfs could not leave their village. They were said to be bound to the soil. They labored to feed themselves and their families, but a large part of what they produced went to the lord of the manor. In exchange the lord protected his serfs against enemies and acted as lawgiver and judge for the community.

Nations as we know them did not yet exist. True, there were kings of places called England and France, but these rulers had relatively little power. The lesser nobles, the lords of the manor, owed their power to a great duke or count, he in turn to a king. Under what was called the **feudal system** each lord owed certain payments or services to a higher authority. In return for these "feudal dues" the higher noble protected him. But the lords of the manors controlled the land and the people, which meant that more often than not they were practically independent.

There was little trade between one manor and the next. Nearly everything that was eaten, worn, or used was made right in the community. Such a life had advantages. Everyone knew what to expect of everyone else. Misunderstandings were rare. But it was a

Scala/Art Resource

This mural was painted on a castle wall in Trent, Italy. It is titled, "The Month of August." The 15th-century artist represented the feudal system with some ladies of the manor in the foreground, poor villagers going to market in the middle ground, and serfs harvesting grain in the background. Give a brief description of each of these three classes in the feudal system.

narrow existence in a small world. People lacked not only the wealth and free time to explore but even the urge to do so.

The Crusades

Outside pressures eventually ended Europe's slumber. One was a series of religious wars, the **Crusades,** organized by the Roman Catholic popes in order to get control of the city of Jerusalem and the rest of the **Holy Land** of Palestine. This region had been overrun by the followers of the Arab prophet Mohammed, founder of **Islam,** a new religion. *Islam* means "submission to God." Believers in Islam are called **Moslems.** The Moslems created a huge empire extending from India in the East through the Holy Land and across North Africa to the Atlantic Ocean. They also conquered most of Spain.

About the time that the Vikings were exploring the lands west of Greenland, the Moslem ruler of Palestine, the Caliph Hakam, began to persecute Christians in his domain. It became impossible for Europeans to visit the Holy Land.

Therefore, in 1095 Pope Urban II summoned Catholics to take up the cross (*crusade* means "marked with a cross") and drive the Moslems out of Palestine. All over Europe lords and serfs responded. Thousands sewed crosses to their garments and marched off, first to Constantinople, which is today the city of Istanbul in northwestern Turkey, and then on to Palestine. In 1099 the crusaders captured Jerusalem and founded the Christian Kingdom of Jerusalem. Crusaders sought not only a visit to the Holy Land but also the relics of the life and death of Christ—the Holy Grail used at the Last Supper, the Crown of Thorns, and the cross on which Christ was crucified.

The Moslems did not meekly submit to Christian control of a region that was equally holy to their faith. For the next 200 years war raged almost continuously. The sultan Saladin recaptured Jerusalem in 1187. Gradually the Moslems pushed the Christians back. Crusade after Crusade was organized in Europe to help the Christian Kingdom and regain the lost territory. Finally, in 1291, the last Christian stronghold, the city of Acre, was forced to surrender.

The Commercial Revolution

The Crusades caused great changes in the ways that Europeans thought and acted. The tens of thousands who traveled by land and sea to the Holy Land saw another world and heard new ideas. In the markets they tasted new foods such as dates and rice and oranges. They discovered pepper and cinnamon, ginger, nutmeg, cloves, and other spices to flavor and preserve foods. They bought garments made of silk and cotton, finer and more comfortable than the wool they wore. Jewels, rugs, and countless other beautiful objects excited them. Almost all of these treasures of the Orient came to the Holy

Bibliothèque Nationale

From a French manuscript hand colored in 1584 comes the "Capture of Alexandria." The crusaders in their armor are about to enter the ancient city in Egypt that once housed the world's greatest library. How does the artist show that this was a voyage on sea as well as on land?

> **"Stimulated by commerce, a surge took place in art, technology, building, learning, explorations by land and sea, universities, cities, banking and credit, and every sphere that enriched life and widened horizons. . . ."**
> Barbara Tuchman

Art Resource

Marco Polo, shown here in traditional Tartar dress, learned much about the Orient in his 17 years there. For much of the time, he served as an ambassador for Kublai Khan.

Land by old trade routes from India, China, and the islands off the east coast of Asia, the **Indies.**

When the crusaders returned to their homelands, they brought goods from Asia for others to see. Amidst this excitement, travelers from Venice—Marco Polo, his father, and uncle—set out for China in 1271. They returned 24 years later with riches and amazing stories. The desire for more Asian goods quickly spread. European society began to pass through what we call the **Commercial Revolution.** Imagine the excitement people felt when they read Marco Polo's descriptions of mysterious new Asian lands:

> **"** After going thirty miles in a westerly direction, through a country filled with fine buildings, among vineyards and many cultivated and fertile fields, we arrived at a handsome and considerable city, named Gouza. The townspeople lived by commerce and manual arts. They manufactured the finest kind of cloth.
>
> From the city of Gouza we journeyed ten days through Cathay [China]. . . . We saw many vineyards and much cultivated land. From here grapes were carried to Cathay, where the vine does not grow. Here we found an abundance of mulberry trees, the leaves of which allow the inhabitants [worms] to produce large quantities of silk. We noticed a degree of civilization which existed among all the people of this country, because of their frequent contacts with the towns, which are not far from each other. To these towns the merchants continually traveled carrying their goods from one city to another.
>
> At the end of ten days journey from the city of Gouza we arrived at the kingdom of Ta-in-fu, whose chief city, the capital of the province, bears the same name. Ta-in-fu is very large and beautiful. A great deal of trade is carried on in this city. A variety of articles are manufactured, including weapons which are used by the grand Khan's armies. There are many vineyards from which large quantities of grapes were gathered. Although this is the only district within the borders of Ta-in-fu that has vineyards, there is still enough supply for the entire province. Other fruits also grow here in plenty, as does the mulberry tree, together with the worms that yield the silk.
>
> Upon leaving Ta-in-fu, we traveled several days through a fine country in which there were many cities, where commerce and manufacturing prevailed. We reached a large city named Pi-an-fu, which is very famous. Like Ta-in-fu, this city contains numerous merchants and artisans. Silk is produced here also in great quantity.[1] **"**

[1]From *The Travels of Marco Polo: The Venetian*, edited by William Marsden

To pay for Asian goods, Europeans had to produce more goods of their own. They manufactured more woolen cloth, trapped more fur-bearing animals, cut more lumber. The isolated life of the self-sufficient manor ended. People left the manors. Towns grew into cities. Since townspeople produce no food, the remaining farmers increased their production to feed them. Lords of the manor cleared more land. To get their serfs to do more work, the lords had to grant them more privileges. In addition there were artisans of every sort to be housed and fed while they erected Europe's soaring cathedrals. By custom no serfs or slave laborers were used to build these mighty structures.

Life became more exciting—and more uncertain and dangerous, too. Trade between East and West made merchants and bankers more important. They needed strong rulers who would build roads, protect trade routes against robbers, and keep the peace. They willingly lent money to these rulers. The rulers used the loans to raise armies to protect their lands against foreign enemies and also against robbers who preyed on traveling merchants. Thus, merchants and kings helped one another. The kings became more powerful, the merchants richer. The European economy expanded.

The Granger Collection, New York

The print above shows how books were made in the late 16th century. On the left, typesetters pick movable type from trays called fonts. The press is on the right. Explain how printing broke down barriers between ordinary people and the rich.

Europe Stirs to New Ideas

The religious ideals that inspired the Crusades were not forgotten. But Europeans became more concerned about their own world, less about the hereafter. More people were buying and selling, enjoying luxuries, appreciating art, gaining scientific knowledge. Advances in printing made by Johannes Gutenberg of Germany in the 1450s did still more to break down barriers. With Gutenberg's press a printer could make any number of copies of a book simply by setting the type once. It was no longer necessary to copy books and manuscripts one at a time by hand. Books became much cheaper. As a result ordinary people as well as rich learned to read. They improved their minds with the powerful new knowledge found in books.

Great improvements were soon made in designing and sailing ships. The Vikings had crossed the Atlantic without navigation instruments. They steered by watching the stars and the sun, hoping for the best. By about 1100 the **compass** had been invented. Its magnetized needle always pointed north, which enabled sailors to know their direction even when sun and stars were hidden by clouds. By the 1400s sailors were also using the **astrolabe,** an instrument that measured a ship's latitude—that is, its distance north or south of the equator. These instruments made navigation more accurate.

Soon larger ships were designed and built. The stage was set for the third and final discovery of America and for the exploration and invasion of many other parts of the world by Europeans. 🖸

National Maritime Museum, Greenwich

This beautiful astrolabe and case from the 16th century probably made many sea voyages. It was used to reckon a ship's latitude. What other important navigational instrument had been invented about 1100?

Return to the Preview & Review on page 14.

Portuguese carracks combined European square foresails with aftermasts adapted from the Arabs.

National Maritime Museum, Greenwich

Preview & Review

Use these questions to guide your reading. Answer the questions after completing Section 3.

Understanding Issues, Events, & Ideas. Contrast the search for eastern routes with the Viking voyages, using the following words: middlemen, geography, navigation, San Salvador, Hispaniola, Line of Demarcation.

1. What made Europeans search for a new route to the Indies?
2. What contributions did Henry the Navigator make to the Age of Discovery?
3. What was Columbus' goal? In what way was he well qualified for his undertaking?

Thinking Critically. 1. Use your historical imagination to describe the arrival of Columbus and his crew as it appeared to the "Indians" living on San Salvador. **2.** Compare Columbus' reception when he first returned to Spain with the treatment he received in the last years of his life.

3. THE AGE OF DISCOVERY

The Search for Eastern Routes

All of the discoveries of America discussed in this chapter were made by accident. The third one was made by explorers who were looking for a better way to get to China.

Trade between Europe and the East was dominated by Italian merchants whose ships sailed from Venice, Naples, and other ports. Their ships carried cloth, furs, metals, and other European products to Constantinople and brought back the silks, spices, jewels, and other Oriental goods that Europeans craved. These goods were very costly.

The merchants of Constantinople justified their high prices by pointing out how dangerous and expensive it was to bring goods to Constantinople from places half the world away. Their caravans had to crawl through high mountain passes infested with bandits and cross burning deserts where bands of roving thieves might strike at any time. Goods passed through many **middlemen**. Each of these earned a profit, adding to the final cost. Local lords taxed the travelers and their goods. There were tolls to be paid at bridges and ferries. Little wonder that the people of western Europe were eager to find easier and less expensive routes to the East.

The obvious path east was by no means the shortest. It was the all-sea route around Africa to India, the Indies, and China. This longer route had many advantages. Ships sail day and night, while

READING A TIME LINE

Historians say that "the skeleton of history is chronology." The dictionary defines *chronology* as "the science that deals with measuring time by regular divisions and that assigns to events their proper dates." In other words, historians arrange events in *chronological order,* or the order in which they happened.

One of the best ways to show chronological order is by a *time line.* Time lines appear at the end of each chapter of *The Story of America.* These time lines show the order in which the events mentioned in each chapter happened and complement the written summary.

How to Read a Time Line

In reading a time line, follow these steps.

1. **Determine its framework.** Note the years covered and the intervals of time into which the time line is divided. The time lines in *The Story of America* are divided into years, except those in this first unit, which are divided by 100-year periods (centuries) because they cover such broad spans of time. Colored bars show long-term events.
2. **Study the sequence carefully.** A time line is proportional. The space between each date—the *interval*—is always the same. In this way you can visually see the span of time between events. Remember that sometimes the length of time between events is an important historical fact. (Also note that each year is marked on the time line, even when no event is listed.)
3. **Fill in the blanks.** Time lines usually list only key events. Study those listed. Think about the events and the people, places, and other events associated with them. In this way, you can "flesh out" the framework provided by the time line.
4. **Note relationships.** Ask yourself how each event relates to the other events. This will help you recognize cause-effect relationships.
5. **Use the time line as a summary.** Use the listed events to weave a summary of the time period.

Applying the Strategy

Study the time line below. Note that the years covered are 900 to 1500. The time line has intervals of 100 years. The time line lists events related to the Age of Discovery. As you know from your reading, each journey was built on the experiences of previous journeys. Eventually this spirit of exploration led to the discovery of a "New World." What other relationships among the events can you discover? Remember to "fill in" important events not listed on the time line.

For independent practice, see Reviewing Chronological Order on each Chapter Review page.

THE AGE OF DISCOVERY

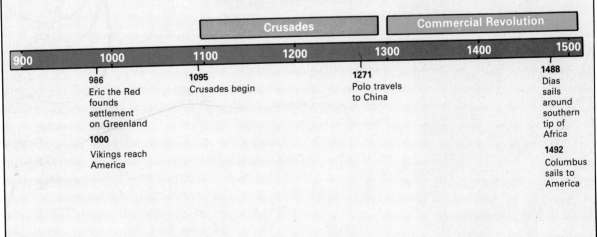

Prince Henry of Portugal led scholars in studying geography and navigation. He became known as Henry the Navigator. His portrait above was painted in the middle 15th century. Why did Henry establish his school?

This oil portrait is believed to be a likeness of Christopher Columbus, although none was painted during his lifetime. Why was Columbus more apt than most sailors to find a new route to the Far East?

Civico Museo Storico, Como

land travelers and the horses, donkeys, and camels that haul their belongings must stop each night to rest. The sea route would save time and labor. Once packed in a vessel's hold, goods would not have to be unloaded and reloaded until a port was reached. Still more important, only one shipper would profit from the sea voyage, and no tolls or taxes need be paid along the way.

No one had ever sailed from Europe all the way to the Orient. There were no maps or charts, little knowledge of winds and currents. Indeed, no European had even seen the west coast of Africa below the Sahara. Prince Henry of Portugal, who became known as Henry the Navigator, took the lead in finding a route around the continent of Africa.

Henry created a kind of research center for scholars to share their knowledge of **geography,** the study of the earth and its surface features, and **navigation,** the science of sailing ships. Experts came from many lands. Their information about tides and the position of the stars in different regions was of great value to Henry's captains. Armed with this information and financed by Henry, brave sailors gradually explored the African coast. In 1445 one of Henry's ships reached the site of present-day Dakar, in Senegal, where the great western bulge of Africa turns to the south and east.

By the 1470s, after Henry's death, Portuguese ships had reached the equator. In 1488 Bartolomeu Dias managed to sail around the southern tip of the continent, only to turn back when the crew panicked, afraid to venture into the unknown seas ahead. Finally, in 1498, Vasco da Gama sailed around Africa and on to India.

Christopher Columbus

Meanwhile, another explorer traveled in a different direction. His name was Christopher Columbus. Instead of sailing far to the south around Africa, he headed for Asia by sailing directly west. This possibility had attracted little attention. Educated people no longer believed that the world was flat. They did not think a ship sailing too far to the west would reach the edge and "fall off." But they believed that there was no land on the "other side" of the globe. Since it was at least 10,000 miles (16,000 kilometers) from western Europe to Asia, no ship could carry enough food and water to make the journey. The trip was out of the question.

Or was it? Columbus did not think so, and few captains knew the Atlantic Ocean as well as he. Columbus was a sturdily built man of above-average height, red-haired, and with a ruddy complexion. He was born in Genoa, in northern Italy, in 1451. He went to sea at an early age. While still a young man, he had sailed south to the Guinea coast of Africa and north to the waters around the British Isles. He may even have visited Iceland.

In 1476 Columbus was shipwrecked off Portugal. He settled in Lisbon and along with his brother Bartholomeo became a chart maker. Columbus studied every map and book of geography he could get his hands on. A doctor who knew him wrote that Columbus had a "noble and grand desire to go to the places where the spices grow." He was particularly fascinated by the famous tales of Marco Polo. If Columbus could get to China and the Indies by sailing west, fame and fortune would be his.

There were islands in the Atlantic—the Madeiras 350 miles (560 kilometers) from southern Portugal, the Azores 600 miles (960 kilometers) farther west. Columbus heard stories about an island called Antila, only 1,000 miles (1,600 kilometers) from Japan. He persuaded himself, moreover, that China was only 4,500 miles (7,200 kilometers) west of Spain and Portugal, Japan nearer still.

When he decided to sail westward, Columbus first sought the backing of the king of Portugal, John II. John believed, quite correctly, that Columbus was greatly underestimating the distance to be covered. He refused to invest in such a foolhardy expedition. Columbus, he said, was a "big talker and boastful . . . and full of fancy and imagination." The Columbus brothers then attempted to interest Henry VII of England, Charles VIII of France, and the Spanish monarchs, Ferdinand and Isabella. All rejected their proposals.

But Columbus persisted. Finally, early in 1492, Queen Isabella agreed to outfit three tiny ships. The *Santa María*, which Columbus personally commanded, was about 85 feet (about 26 meters) long and had a crew of 39. The *Pinta* and the *Niña* were smaller than the *Santa María*. The entire expedition consisted of 87 men.

On Friday, August 3, 1492, the little fleet set sail from Palos, Spain. After a stopover in the Canary Islands off northwestern Africa, the ships headed into the unknown. For over a month they sailed westward, always toward the setting sun, always alone, never another sail in sight. Columbus was a magnificent sailor. The *Santa María*'s compass guided him, but to judge his position he had only a sandglass that had to be turned each half hour to measure time and only his years of experience at sea to estimate his speed. Yet he reckoned the distance traveled each day with amazing accuracy.

As day followed day into mid-October, Columbus' men grew tense. They had sailed far beyond where land was supposed to be, and before them lay only the endless ocean. They demanded that Columbus turn back. He would not. Be of good hope, he urged them. Finally he promised to abandon the search if they failed to sight land by October 12.

The breeze freshened and the three ships picked up speed. Now broken branches, land birds, and other hopeful signs began to appear. At last, by moonlight at two o'clock in the morning of October 12, the lookout Rodrigo de Triana spotted the foam of waves breaking on a distant shore. "*Tierra! Tierra!*" he shouted. Land! Land!

Photo MAS

Why do you think Isabella, shown here, outfitted Columbus' tiny fleet when so many others had refused him?

Columbus in America

When day broke, Columbus approached the land, which was a small island. He was absolutely certain that he had reached the Indies. Now he had earned the title given him by Ferdinand and Isabella—Admiral of the Ocean Sea. He named the island **San Salvador,** or Holy Savior, out of gratitude for having reached it safely. He found no spices there, no silks or rugs. Except for tiny bits that some of the inhabitants wore in their noses, he found no gold.

The natives of the island of Guanahaní, for that was its name in their language, were astonished and awed by the Europeans. Columbus, certain in his belief that he was in the Indies, called them Indians. All native Americans would thereafter be thus mistakenly described. They came forth shyly, bearing gifts. "They invite you to share everything they possess," Columbus recorded. He in turn gave them small presents—beads, bits of cloth, and tiny brass bells that particularly delighted them. When Luis de Torres, a member of the crew who knew Arabic, tried to speak to these "Indians," not a one understood him. This seemed odd, for Arabic was a common language in the Indies.

By signs the Indians told Columbus that many other islands lay to the west and south. So he pushed on, taking a few Indians along

LEARNING FROM MAPS. *During his four voyages Columbus became quite familiar with the lands bordering the Caribbean Sea. Name the Caribbean lands he visited.*

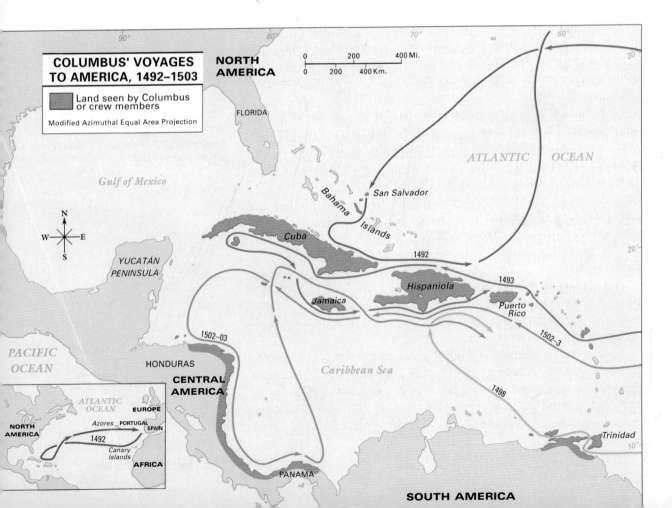

as interpreters. Everywhere he found the same charming, generous people. But he found no spices and no gold.

Soon the explorers reached Cuba. Perhaps this was China! At every harbor along this large landmass, Columbus expected to find a fleet of Chinese junks. Some of the local people told him that gold could be found at *Cubanacan,* by which they meant "in the middle of Cuba." Columbus thought they were saying *El Gran Can*—in Spanish, "the Great Khan"—and sent a delegation headed by de Torres to present his respects to the Emperor of China! Of course, the delegation found only tropical jungle.

Finally, in December 1492, Columbus reached an island which he named **Hispaniola,** the Spanish Isle. There the inhabitants had substantial amounts of gold; one chief gave him a belt with a solid gold buckle. The Spaniards could not find the source of the gold, but there was enough of it to convince them that there must be mines nearby. When the *Santa María* ran aground and had to be abandoned, Columbus decided to leave some of his crew on the island to look for the gold. He then sailed home in the *Niña,* still certain that he had reached the Far East.

Columbus Returns to Spain

Columbus landed a hero at Palos, Spain, on March 15, 1493. Everywhere crowds lined his route, gazing in wonder at the Indians he was bringing to show the king and queen. When he reached Barcelona, Ferdinand and Isabella showered honors upon him. They made him their personal representative, or viceroy, in the Indies and governor of the new territories.

No one yet had a very clear picture of where these new territories were. Columbus had made the Spanish claim, but Portugal, which already owned the Azores, claimed rights to lands farther into the Atlantic. The two Catholic countries turned to Pope Alexander VI to decide the issue. In May 1493 the Pope divided the ocean about 300 miles (480 kilometers) beyond the Azores. The dividing line was called the **Line of Demarcation.** New lands to the west of the line were to belong to Spain, those to the east to Portugal. The next year Spain and Portugal signed a treaty that moved the line somewhat farther west.

When Brazil, which extends well east of the Line of Demarcation, was discovered in 1500, it became Portuguese. This explains why today Brazilians speak Portuguese while most other South Americans speak Spanish.

Meanwhile, in September 1493 Columbus again sailed westward, this time with a fleet of 17 ships and 2,000 colonists. When he reached Hispaniola, he discovered that the crew members he had left there had been killed by the Indians. Columbus built a new settlement, named Isabella, then sailed off on a further futile search for China.

The Brooklyn Museum

A sorrowful Isabella and a sober court is the subject of "Columbus before the Queen." Emanuel Leutze did this oil painting in 1843. Columbus wrote of his experience in chains: "I am here and in such a state that even persons of the lowliest condition must despise me. Surely someone in the world will not allow this to be. If I had taken over the Indies and given them to the Moors, I should meet no greater hostility." What proved to be Columbus' fatal flaw?

Return to the Preview & Review on page 20.

When he returned to Isabella, he found the town in very bad condition. Many colonists were sick, others were squabbling with one another. More fighting had broken out with the Indians. Little gold had been collected. Much discouraged, Columbus sailed back to Spain.

Columbus was a great sailor and a brave and determined man. But he was not good at politics or business. He made two more trips across the Atlantic. On one he discovered the island of Trinidad off the north coast of South America. On the other he explored the coast of Central America from Honduras to Panama and spent more than a year on the island of Jamaica. He never obtained the wealth he had hoped for. The king took away most of his power. The great discoverer even spent a short time in jail. He died, almost forgotten, in 1506. He never accepted the fact that he had not reached the Indies. 🖎

4. SPAIN'S GOLDEN AGE

America: A New World

News of Columbus' voyage and the wonderful things he had brought back with him spread rapidly through Europe. Gradually more new lands were discovered as explorers ventured across the Atlantic. On one of these voyages an Italian named Amerigo Vespucci visited the northern coast of South America. Later he traveled along the coast of Brazil. The voyages were not in themselves path breaking, and Vespucci was more a tourist than an explorer. But he wrote a description of his adventures that attracted much attention. Europeans were beginning to realize that an entire new continent existed out there in the Atlantic Ocean. Amerigo Vespucci did not mention "the Indies." He wrote about a **New World.**

In 1507 a German geographer who had read Amerigo's account suggested that the New World should be called America in his honor. The idea caught on, and by the 1530s people in every European country except Portugal and Spain were calling the new regions **America.** But 300 years after Columbus, Spain still called the chief governing body for its colonies the Ministry of the Indies.

Balboa and Magellan

Vespucci showed that America was very large. Two Spanish explorers soon proved that it was nowhere near Asia.

The first was Vasco Núñez de Balboa. Balboa was the governor of a Spanish settlement in what is now the Republic of Panama, in Central America. In 1513 he set out with about 200 Spanish soldiers and several hundred Indians to explore the area. The party made its way through a thick jungle that was infested with insects and poisonous snakes. They crossed tangled swamps and climbed up rugged mountains. In three weeks they covered only about 60 miles (96 kilometers). Finally, when they neared the top of the mountains, Balboa ordered his men to stop. He climbed to the summit alone. There before him, glittering in the sun as far as the eye could see, stretched what seemed to be an endless ocean.

After giving thanks to God, Balboa and his men pushed onward until they reached the shore. Where breakers came roaring in over the sand flats, he waded in, sword in hand, and took possession of the new ocean for Spain.

Balboa had crossed the Isthmus of Panama, where the Panama Canal would be dug 400 years later. His discovery that another great body of water lay beyond America proved that it was a long way to the Indies. To get there by sailing west, one would have to find a passage through or around the land barrier.

Preview & Review

Use these questions to guide your reading. Answer the questions after completing Section 4.
Understanding Issues, Events, & Ideas. Use the following words to discuss Spanish adventures in America: New World, America, isthmus, strait, Pacific Ocean, circumnavigate, Aztecs, conquistadors, mission, Incas, immunity, economy.
1. What was the significance of Vespucci's voyages to the "New World"?
2. What did the voyage of Magellan and El Cano prove?
3. How did disease help the Europeans "conquer" the native Americans?
4. What made Spain's empire so rich? What drained away its riches? What brought Spain's Golden Age to an end?
Thinking Critically. 1. Predict what might have happened to Aztec culture and civilization if the Aztecs had not been conquered by the Spaniards. **2.** If you were a member of the party of any Spanish conquistador, which one would you choose to follow? Why?

The Granger Collection, New York

The inscription circling this 17th-century engraving reads: "This is Vasco Núñez de Zerez de Balboa who discovered the Sea of the South." What did Balboa's discovery tell the world?

Photo MAS

Ferdinand Magellan's portrait was probably made in the 16th century. Who was his partner in his round-the-world voyage?

Maritime Museum, Seville/Photo MAS

Juan Sebastian El Cano was able to complete Magellan's voyage around the world. Do you think this portrait shows the will power it must have taken to head home with the 17 survivors on the ship Victoria?

Since Balboa had shown that only a narrow neck of land, or **isthmus,** separated the oceans at Panama, surely somewhere there must be a narrow water passage, or **strait,** connecting the Atlantic to Balboa's ocean. In 1518 a Portuguese captain named Ferdinand Magellan presented Emperor Charles V of Spain with a plan to find such a route. Magellan was a short, stocky man, dark, bearded, and very, very tough. He was a veteran of several wars in the East and knew the area well. He approached Charles after his own king, Manuel I of Portugal, had refused to back his expedition.

Charles V agreed to finance Magellan's voyage. On September 20, 1519, the explorer set sail from Sanlúcar, Spain, with five ships and a crew of 237 men. Their first stop was in the Canary Islands. From there they sailed to Brazil, then southward along the coast of South America, searching always for a water passage to the west.

Off what is now Argentina Magellan's fleet ran into a terrible storm. One of the ships sank. This disaster so frightened the sailors that they urged Magellan to turn back. When he refused, some mutinied. Magellan crushed this rebellion before it could spread, and he put the leaders to death. Then he sailed on.

Finally the voyagers reached the southern tip of South America. As the fleet entered the narrow passage between the land and the island of Tierra del Fuego (Land of Fire), fierce storms and huge waves tossed the ships about wildly. The sailors on one ship, shaken and discouraged, turned tail before the tempest and fled homeward. Sadly, this vessel contained a large part of the expedition's supplies.

The three remaining ships battled head winds and powerful currents in the strait for 38 days. At last they made their way through the passage, which we now call the Strait of Magellan, into a broad and tranquil sea. Because it seemed so calm and safe after the long struggle with the turbulent strait, Magellan named it the **Pacific Ocean.** (*Pacific* means "peaceful.")

Magellan now happily pointed his fleet toward the west. But the greatest ordeal lay ahead. For 98 days the three ships sailed onward. They sighted only two uninhabited islands. When their food ran out, the hungry sailors ate the rats in the ships' holds, then leather from the rigging, then sawdust. Many died. Those who remained grew steadily weaker and weaker.

Finally, early in 1521, the fleet reached the island we call Guam. Magellan was now directly south of Japan. After seizing food and water from the peaceful inhabitants, he pushed on to the Philippine Islands. There, in a battle against local warriors, Magellan was killed. Following Magellan's death, Juan El Cano assumed command.

The fleet wandered about the Indies for many months. Two more ships were lost. Only the *Victoria* remained to sail across the Indian Ocean, around the tip of Africa, and home to Sanlúcar, Spain. On September 6, 1522, almost three years after they had set out, El Cano and the other 17 who were still alive set foot again on Spanish soil.

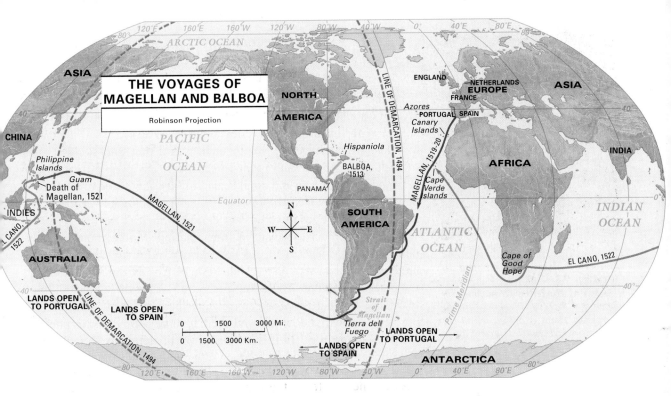

THE VOYAGES OF
MAGELLAN AND BALBOA

Robinson Projection

They were the first to **circumnavigate,** or sail around, the entire earth.

This was one of the greatest sea voyages of all time, which is reason enough for remembering it. But it brought few benefits to Spain. By proving that Asia was so far west of Europe, the expedition demonstrated that sailing there in that direction was much more dangerous and expensive than anyone had imagined. So ended Columbus' dream of capturing the rich trade of Asia by sailing west.

LEARNING FROM MAPS. *The circumnavigation of the earth by Magellan, El Cano, and their crew was an amazing feat. Why was the voyage across the Pacific Ocean the most trying part of the journey?*

Cortés and Montezuma

While Magellan and El Cano were making their great voyage, the Spaniards were extending their control in America. Colonies were founded on all the larger islands of the Caribbean Sea. By 1519 most of the coastline around the Caribbean had been explored, and some knowledge of the peoples of the interior had been gathered.

The most powerful nation was the **Aztec** empire of central Mexico. In 1519 Hernán Cortés and about 450 soldiers set sail from the Spanish colony of Cuba to make contact with the Aztecs. The Aztec society and culture was mighty and wealthy. They had built great stone temples. The capital city, Tenochtitlán, located on an artificial island in a shallow lake, housed 200,000 people. They had a written language and had mastered mathematics and astronomy.

The Aztecs were also warlike. They had conquered most of the other people of Mexico. According to their religion, human sacrifices had to be offered to the god of war to insure victory in battle. Each year thousands of people were slaughtered for this purpose. The

© American Museum of Natural History

This drawing from an early Aztec manuscript shows the meeting of Cortés and Montezuma. Montezuma is seated at the left with members of his court, Cortés at the right with his interpreter Doña Marina, whom the Aztecs called Malinche. In contrast to this peaceful greeting, what was the outcome of the conquistadors' discovery of the Aztecs?

victims were chosen from among the captives taken in earlier wars. The Aztecs also forced those they had conquered to pay heavy taxes.

As Cortés and his handful of Spanish soldiers marched inland from the coast, many local people eagerly joined forces with him. By the time he reached Tenochtitlán, he had an army of many thousands. With this army Cortés defeated the Aztecs.

The Aztec emperor, Montezuma, was a thin, fair-skinned man of about 40, delicate and refined in manner. His people treated him as a god. Members of the nobility had to bow low three times before approaching him. They addressed him as "Lord, my lord, great lord" and spoke with eyes lowered, not daring to look at his face.

Here we must use historical imagination. Montezuma probably believed that Cortés, with his steel armor, powerful weapons, and large war horses, was also a god. Perhaps Cortés was Quetzalcoatl, the chief rival of the Aztec war god. In any case the Aztecs did not resist the Spaniards. Montezuma gave them rich gifts of gold and precious stones, and he allowed them to take control of his empire. Why did he do this? In this excerpt from his letter to King Charles V of Spain, Cortés claimed among other things that the Aztecs willingly gave their treasure away:

      I spoke to Montezuma one day, and told him that Your Highness [Charles V] was in need of gold, . . . and I besought him to send some of his people, and I would also send some Spaniards to the provinces and houses of those lords who had there submitted themselves to your Highness to pray them to assist Your Majesty with some part of what they had. Besides Your Highness's need, this would testify that they began to render service, and Your Highness would the more esteem their good will; and I told Montezuma that he also should give me from his treasures, as I wished to send them to Your Majesty. He asked me afterwards to choose the Spaniards whom I wished to send, and two by two, and five by five, he distributed them through many provinces and cities. He sent some of his people with them, ordering them to go to the lords of those provinces and cities and tell them that I had commanded each one of them to contribute a certain measure of gold. Thus it was done, and all those lords to whom he sent gave very compliantly, as had been asked, not only in valuables, but also in bars and sheets of gold, besides all the jewels of gold, and silver, and the feather work, and the stones, and the many other things . . . so marvelous that, because of their novelty and strangeness, they have no price, nor is it probable that all the princes ever heard of in the world possess such treasures.[1]

[1]From *Fernando Cortes, his five letters of relation to the Emperor Charles V*, Vol. 1

Compare Cortés' claim with this view, taken from a written Aztec history of the conquest.

> Then Montezuma dispatched various chiefs to meet the Spaniards. They gave the 'gods' emblems of gold and feathers, and golden necklaces. And when they were given these presents, the Spaniards burst into smiles; their eyes shone with pleasure; they were delighted by them. They picked up the gold and fingered it like monkeys; they seemed to be transported by joy, as if their hearts were illumined and made new.
>
> The truth is that they longed and lusted for gold. Their bodies swelled with greed, and their hunger was ravenous; they hungered like pigs for that gold. They snatched at the golden emblems, waved them from side to side and examined every inch of them.
>
> They went to Montezuma's storehouse, where his personal treasures were kept. The Spaniards grinned like little beasts and patted each other with delight.
>
> When they entered the hall of treasures, it was as if they had arrived in Paradise. They searched everywhere and covered everything; they were slaves to their own greed. All of Montezuma's possessions were brought out: fine bracelets, necklaces with large stones, ankle rings with gold bells, the royal crowns and all the royal finery—everything that belonged to the king and was reserved to him only. They seized these treasures as if they were their own, as if this plunder were merely a stroke of good luck. And when they had taken all the gold, they heaped up everything else in the middle of the patio.[1]

For a time Cortés permitted Montezuma to remain as emperor while the Spaniards looted the Aztec treasure. But in 1520 the Aztecs suddenly revolted. They drove the Spaniards out of the city. Montezuma, however, was killed in the fight. The Spaniards quickly regrouped and, aided by their native allies, surrounded Tenochtitlán. In August 1521 they recaptured it. By 1540, when he returned to Spain, Cortés ruled over an empire that included all of modern Mexico and more.

The Conquistadors

Cortés was the most important of the Spanish **conquistadors,** or conquerors. There was no excuse for his invasion of Montezuma's empire. The conquistadors were greedy and ruthless. Yet the "Black Legend" of the conquistador is a generalization. The Spaniards were

[1]From *The Broken Spears, The Aztec Account of the Conquest of Mexico,* edited by Miguel Leon-Portilla

> I had [the Aztec] idols taken from their places and thrown down the steps. . . . I had images of Our Lady and of other saints put there, which caused [Montezuma] and the other natives some sorrow. . . . They believed that those idols gave them all their worldly goods.
>
> Hernan Cortés, c. 1520

Points of View

> Ixtlilxochitl [an Aztec ally] went to his mother . . . to bring her out to be baptized. She replied that he must have lost his mind to let himself be won over so easily by that handful of barbarians, the conquistadors. . . . He told her that she would receive the sacrament, even against her will.
>
> An Aztec account, c. 1519

READING MAPS

Your study of history is greatly enriched by geography. To fully understand geographic information, you must be able to read a map. All of the maps in *The Story of America* have four parts: a *title;* a *key,* or *legend;* a *scale;* and a global *grid.* If you understand the information provided by these four parts, you will be able to read a map with confidence.

How to Read a Map

To gather information from a map, follow these guidelines.

1. **Read the title.** The title of a map tells the subject of the map and what parts of the earth are shown. Some map titles include a date.
2. **Study the key, or legend.** The legend explains what the colors and special symbols on the map mean.
3. **Note the distance scale.** The map scale is used to measure distances. Maps in *The Story of America* have a bar scale. The length of the line on the scale represents that number of miles and kilometers on the earth's surface.
4. **Use the grid.** The grid of latitude and longitude helps you locate places on the earth through a special numbering system based on a unit of measure called a degree. Most of the maps in this textbook have grid "tics" around the map's border to indicate the presence of the complete grid.
5. **Note other map features.** Most maps show other information in special ways as well. The maps in *The Story of America* use a compass rose to indicate direction. *Italic* type marks physical features while regular type labels political features. Be sure to look for all the features of each map.

Applying the Strategy

Study the map below. The title, "Spanish Explorations and Conquests," tells you that the map illustrates the routes of Spanish explorers and areas of conquest in America. Although no special symbols are used on the map, colors mark the locations of the Aztec and Inca empires. You can use the compass rose to determine the directions the explorers moved. For example, Cabeza de Vaca and Esteban traveled first generally west, then south. You can use the scale to measure the distance the explorers traveled.

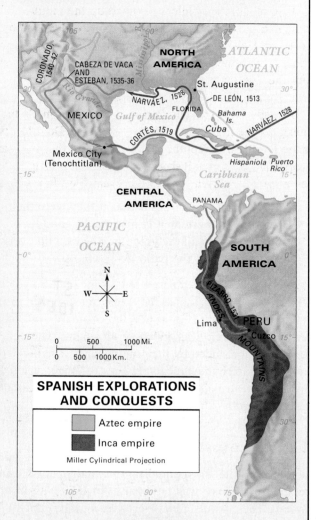

SPANISH EXPLORATIONS AND CONQUESTS

Aztec empire

Inca empire

Miller Cylindrical Projection

For independent practice, see Practicing the Strategy on pages 38–39.

no more greedy and ruthless than the British, French, or Dutch, nor did they cause more harm. Indeed, in their attempt to bring Christianity to America, the Spanish taught many Indians to read and write and helped them improve their arts and crafts.

Cortés and his men had mixed motives. Adventure for its own sake was one of these, and who can blame them? Uncovering the secrets of two vast, unknown continents was the greatest adventure in human history. Especially after gold and the other rich resources of America were discovered, most Spaniards believed that America was a paradise, a kind of Garden of Eden where they could live splendidly while also doing good. They developed a sense of special purpose, or **mission**—a belief that God had appointed them to do His work in this entirely new world. Here were people to be converted to Christianity, even if the task was a bloody one.

One of Cortés' soldiers summed up the motives of the conquistadors in a sentence: "We came here to serve God and the King, and also to get rich." The conquistadors were not only brave and ambitious but absolutely sure of the rightness of their beliefs. This gave them the energy to accomplish great deeds—and also to do great harm. By the 1530s they had created an empire.

Already, in 1513, Juan Ponce de León had made the first Spanish landing on the mainland of North America. De León was searching for the Fountain of Youth, a magical spring that was said to prevent anyone who bathed in it from growing old. Of course, he did not find such a magic fountain, but he did claim Florida for Spain.

The illustration below might be the earliest actual picture of the conquistadors in the Americas. It was made in about 1534. Using this picture as a guide, describe a conquistador in the words an Aztec might have used on first encounter.

The Granger Collection, New York

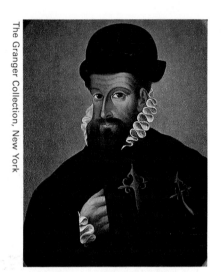

The Granger Collection, New York

The artist of this portrait of Francisco Pizarro is unknown. It was probably painted in the 16th century.

And in the same year that Cortés landed in Mexico, Alonzo Alvarez de Piñeda explored the coast of Texas. Piñeda's reports led Pánfilo de Narváez to mount another expedition. In 1528 Narváez sailed from Florida in search of treasure. He and his men became hopelessly lost in the wilderness. Only 15 survived the frigid winter of 1528. One survivor was an African named Esteban. Esteban's later expedition into the American Southwest led to further explorations by Coronado and others seeking gold.

In 1531 Francisco Pizarro marched into the snow-capped Andes Mountains of South America. There he found and overwhelmed the **Incas,** a people with a culture as rich and complex as the Aztecs. Pizarro and his men seized a huge treasure of silver. Then they forced the defeated Incas to work their silver mines for Spain's benefit.

The European Invasion

When Columbus stepped ashore on Guanahaní Island in October 1492, he planted the Spanish flag in the sand and claimed the land as a possession of Ferdinand and Isabella. He did so despite the obvious fact that the island already belonged to someone else—the "Indians" who gathered on the beach to gaze with wonder at the strangers who had suddenly arrived in three great, white-winged canoes. He gave no thought to the rights of the local inhabitants. Nearly every later explorer—French, English, Dutch, and all the others as well as the Spanish—thoughtlessly dismissed the people they encountered. What we like to think of as the discovery of America was actually the invasion and conquest of America.

In these new lands Europeans felt ten feet tall. Here were discoveries to be made, fame and fortune to be won. They were sure that the native people would offer little or no resistance. Of what use were spears and arrows against men clad in steel astride horses and armed with guns and cannon? How could "savages" who worshipped many different gods, even animals, resist good Christians, believers in the one true God, creator of the Universe?

Surely the natives at first thought the Europeans were superior in every way. With historical imagination it is not hard to see the Spanish conquerors as the first Americans must have seen them. Here were gods come from heaven to rule them. In the hands of these gods, flaming, roaring "firesticks" could strike down an animal or human, invisibly, across great distances. These gods looked down at frail canoes from enormous floating fortresses. How strong they seemed in their shining clothing, how rich in color!

In reality the Europeans were not so mighty, the Indians not so ignorant and powerless. The Europeans learned much from the native people—how to live, travel, hunt, and fight in tropical jungles and northern forests, what to plant and how to grow it. Of the dozens of products never before seen by Europeans, corn was by far the most important.

Of course the Indians also learned from the Europeans. Textiles, and metal tools of every sort from fish hooks to shovels, knives, guns, and steel traps were highly prized. But the Indians also learned that the visiting "gods" were all too human. When the Europeans tried to conquer and enslave them, they resisted bitterly. In the end they were defeated. But the main reason was not European firepower but disease. When Cortés invaded the land of the Aztecs in 1519, there were perhaps as many as 25 million people in Mexico. A hundred years later, there were barely 1 million! Smallpox, measles, and typhoid fever—not Spanish guns—accounted for so many deaths.

The germs that caused these diseases were brought to America from Europe, where people had suffered from them for countless generations. But while many Europeans died each year from diseases like smallpox, most people had developed considerable resistance, called **immunity.** The inhabitants of America lacked immunity. Measles was a "childhood disease" in Europe. Adults seldom caught it. But it struck down Americans by the thousands. No one can blame the Europeans for this terrible destruction. Indeed, the causes of the plagues were not then known. Nevertheless, this terrible loss of life was another tragic result of the third discovery of America.

The End of Spain's Golden Age

By 1536, when Pedro de Mendoza founded the city of Buenos Aires in Argentina, Spain had control of the mightiest empire in the world. The inhabitants of lands 20 times the size of Spain recognized the Spanish king as overlord. The red and gold Spanish flag flew on staffs all over the Caribbean islands and from Buenos Aires to the land of the Zuñi. This empire made Spain enormously rich. Gold and silver poured into the royal treasury. With this wealth and the weapons it could buy, Spain seemed all powerful.

But there were cracks in the Spanish armor. Spain's own ability to produce goods—its **economy**—was weak and inefficient. In the 1500s about 95 percent of the Spanish people were peasant farmers. Even so, because of poor soil and bad farming methods, they could not raise enough food to support the rest of the population. Spain had to import wheat from other parts of Europe. Manufactured articles had to be imported too, because Spain had almost no industry. Instead of using the gold and silver of America to improve farmland and finance manufacturing, the Spanish government bought what it needed abroad, paying for its imports with the treasure of America. While the flow continued, all was well. When the flow slowed to a trickle in the early 1600s, the Golden Age ended. 🖎

© Lee Boltin

Aztec metalworkers crafted beautiful works, such as this gold figure of the god of Regeneration. Their Spanish conquerors melted down many such pieces and used the precious metals in their own works.

Kunsthistorisches Museum, Vienna © Eric Lessing/Magnum

This 16th century Spanish bowl was shaped from captured Aztec silver. How did reusing these precious metals steal from our knowledge of the Aztec culture?

Return to the Preview & Review on page 27.

LINKING HISTORY & GEOGRAPHY

THE COLUMBIAN EXCHANGE

Imagine the excitement when Europeans first met American Indians. Curiosity seized both sides. Almost immediately a great exchange of material items and ideas, which we call the Columbian Exchange in honor of Christopher Columbus, began to take place.

Europeans dominated the exchange in many ways. Their plants and animals, styles, methods, and beliefs were brought to the New World by conquerers and colonists alike. Of course, plants and animals native to the Americas, such as tobacco and turkeys, new ideas, and even native people crossed the Atlantic to become established in Europe. But the greatest impact of the exchange was felt in the New World.

A Truly New World

1. How did the environment of the New World begin to change?

Not only people crossed the Atlantic Ocean to take up residence in the New World. A key aspect of the Columbian Exchange was a biological transfer. An entire collection of lifeforms was transported, both intentionally and unintentionally, by explorers, colonists, indentured servants, and slaves. What finally resulted from the mixing of these lifeforms created a unique environment in the Americas.

When Europeans first set foot on the western shores of the Atlantic, they found a biological world that was considerably different from the ones in their homelands. There were none of the Old World crops, such as wheat and peas, grasses, or even weeds that the Europeans recognized. They were unfamiliar with many of the trees, and there were absolutely no domesticated horses, sheep, goats, cattle, or even cats. Even such common creatures as rats, mice, sparrows, starlings, and honey bees were missing in the New World.

Europeans also brought with them germs that were totally new to America. Certainly the American Indians did not live in a germ-free paradise, but they had never known smallpox, measles, chickenpox, influenza, malaria, yellow fever, diptheria, whooping cough, scarlet fever, and a number of other diseases that plagued the inhabitants of the Old World. Accordingly, they had developed no immunities. European diseases soon ravaged the American Indians.

Impact on the New World

2. What was the impact of the new environment on the American Indians?

The Europeans brought many things to the New World that they hoped would help them— seeds of crops to provide food, horses for muscle and transportation. But did the native people benefit from what the Europeans brought?

There is no doubt that the American Indians did profit from European crops and livestock, especially the horse. Many tribes grew more food than they had ever known. But the toll exacted on the Indians in sickness and death from the new diseases, along with the destruction of their hunting grounds, farmland, and wild game far outweighed any of the benefits.

New Plants Take Root

3. Where and how were the first European plants introduced in the Americas?

It seems likely that the first Old World plants to spread to the New World found their first home in Newfoundland. It was here that European fishers put ashore to dry the cod and other fish taken from the waters of the Grand Banks. Before loading the dried and salted fish aboard their ships, sailors would clean out the holds of their vessels. Among the sweepings were the seeds of many European grasses, plants, and weeds that soon flourished in the new land.

Fishing vessels were putting into harbors along Newfoundland's coast nearly a century before the Jamestown and Plymouth colonies were established. In fact, in 1535, when Cartier "discovered" the St. Lawrence River, he found European fishing vessels already there! So Europe's plants began to spread on the new continent even before its people did.

A New Ecology Emerges

4. How rapidly and how far did new plants spread?

The European plants that spread most quickly over the widest area were white clover and what we call Kentucky blue grass. Mixed together they were known by the colonists as "English grass." They spread from Nova Scotia to the Carolinas and by the 1760s had crossed the Appalachians into Kentucky and Tennessee. Wherever white clover and blue grass encountered

Both, Photoresearchers

White clover, left, blue grass, right

native American grasses, they overpowered them. They grew westward to the 100th meridian, where lack of rainfall created an environment in which they could not survive.

So dramatic was the spread of white clover and blue grass that when the famous English naturalist Charles Darwin met Mr. Asa Gray, an American botanist, he teased Gray about the ability of European grasses and weeds to overtake the American landscape. Mr. Gray answered that American grasses and weeds were "modest, woodland, retiring things; and no match for the intrusive, pretentious, self-asserting foreigners." (Later historians would note that her comments also described the interactions of Europeans and American Indians!)

A Zoological Revolution

5. How did European animals cause a zoological revolution in the New World?

Mr. Gray's comments were true of animals as well. Regardless of their purpose—meat, milk, leather, power, or speed—European domesticated animals were quickly established in America. The only truly domestic animals raised by American Indians were the dog and turkey. As a result, a vast array of European livestock,

many of which were simply turned loose to fend for themselves, created a zoological revolution in America.

Swine, herds of cattle and horses, released or escaped from European masters, soon roamed the New World. Swine, probably brought by the Spanish in the 1540s, evolved into long-legged, sharp-snouted, vicious-tusked, "razorbacks."

Within a century they ranged from semitropical Florida to the cool French colonies in Canada. Within 30 years of the founding of Maryland, settlers there also were complaining about herds of wild cattle. In Virginia young men hunted wild cattle just as they hunted deer.

In Europe horses were expensive and worth taking care of. In America they were comparatively less expensive and wandered free. Wild horses were considered a nuisance in many of the colonies. The majority were unmarked and could legally be claimed by anyone who could catch them. Most, however, were so shy and swift that catching them was difficult.

Oddly, as with plants, only a few creatures native to America have ever been established in the wild in Europe. The list is confined to the grey squirrel, the muskrat, and a few insects like the Colorado potato beetle.

A New Environment

6. How was the environment in colonial America a new one?

Environments are always evolving. Within 100 years of the arrival of the first Europeans, a new environment had developed in the Americas. European plants and animals had spread, replacing or mixing with many native species. The children of colonists, indentured servants, and slaves—and of American Indians—grew up in a truly new world of plants and animals.

Applying Your Knowledge

Your class will create an encyclopedia of the flora and fauna of your local area. As a class, develop a list of the plants and animals living in your area. You will select or be assigned an item from the list to research. Write a brief insert for the class encyclopedia explaining where your item originated. You may wish to add a sketch to your article. Donate the encyclopedia to your school or community library.

CHAPTER 1 REVIEW

Crusades

60,000–20,000 years ago | 1000 A.D. | 1100 THE AGE OF DISCOVERY 1200

60,000–20,000 years ago
Great
Migration
begins

1000
Vikings sail
to America

1095
Crusades begin

1100
Compass invented

Chapter Summary
Read the statements below. Choose one, and write a paragraph explaining its importance.
1. The first Americans arrived in waves from Asia between 20,000 and 60,000 years ago.
2. Environment strongly influenced the American Indian cultures.
3. In about the year 1000 the Vikings made a second discovery of America.
4. The Crusades led to the Commercial Revolution, which caused Europeans to venture into the world outside of Europe.
5. Explorers looking for a better trade route to China made the last discovery of America.
6. The years between 1450 and the early 1600s became known as the age of discovery.
7. The Portuguese and the Spanish were the first European world explorers.
8. The Spanish led the early exploration of America, claiming vast areas and conquering the Indians.

Reviewing Chronological Order
Number your paper 1-5. Then study the time line above and place the following events in the order in which they happened by writing the first next to 1, the second next to 2, and so on.
1. The Crusades
2. Columbus comes to America
3. The Great Migration
4. Cortés conquers the Aztecs
5. Vikings sail to America

Understanding Main Ideas
1. Why did the first Americans develop so many cultures? Give three examples to support your answer.
2. What is a generalization? What words should the reader of history add?
3. What is our source of information about the Vikings?
4. How did Gutenberg's printing press help Europeans discover new ideas?

5. How did the native Americans view the Europeans when they first met them? How did their view change?
6. How did the conquistadors treat the American Indians? How did their "sense of mission" seem to excuse the conquistadors' behavior?

Thinking Critically
1. **Selecting Alternatives.** If you could have been one of the first Americans, would you rather have been one of the Indians of the Southwest, the Northwest, or the Great Plains? Why? (To support your reasoning, cite information you have learned about the effect of environment on these cultures.)
2. **Analyzing.** Why do you think it is important to use historical imagination when studying the past?
3. **Drawing Conclusions.** Which of the three discoveries of America discussed in this chapter do you think was the least important? Why?
4. **Evaluating.** Do you agree with the author's view that the discovery of America by Europeans was "actually the invasion and conquest of America"? Why or why not?

Writing About History
Imagine you are one of the following: one of the first Asians to arrive in America, a Viking explorer, a member of Columbus' crew, or an Indian witnessing Columbus' arrival in America. Write a letter to a friend describing what you see and your thoughts and feelings. Use the information in Chapter 1 to help you develop your letter.

Practicing the Strategy
Review the strategies on pages 21 and 32.
Reading a Time Line. Study the time line on page 21, then answer the following questions.
1. What are the intervals of time that divide this time line?
2. Name the first and last events on this time line and give their dates.

Commercial Revolution

1300	1400	1500	1600

271
Polo
ravels
o China

1291
Crusades end

1420
Henry
establishes
navigation
school

1450
Gutenberg
improves
printing
press

1492
Columbus
reaches
America

1513
Balboa
sights
Pacific
Ocean

★
De León
explores Florida

1519
Magellan's voyage begins

★
Hernán Cortés conquers the Aztecs

1522
El Cano completes circumnavigation

1528
Cabeza de Vaca, Esteban explore Texas

1531
Pizarro conquers the Incas

Reading Maps. Study the map on page 3. Then answer the following questions.

1. In what general direction did the first Americans crossing the Bering Strait travel?
2. In miles and kilometers, what is the distance from the coast of Asia to the coast of South America?

Using Primary Sources

On his first voyage, in 1492, Columbus kept a journal, which is now lost. Luckily a Spanish priest copied parts of it before it disappeared. As you read the following excerpt from *The Journal of Christopher Columbus (During His First Voyage, 1492–1493)* by Clements R. Markham, note Columbus' attitude toward the Indians. Then answer the questions to the right.

> **Friday, October 12** *At two hours after midnight the land was sighted. The vessels stayed in place, waiting for daylight. On Friday they arrived at a small island of the Lucayos Indians, called Guanahaní in the Indians' language. . . .*
>
> *The island was rather large and very flat with bright green trees, much water, a very large lake in the center, and without any mountains. The whole land was so green that it is a pleasure to look on it. The people are very friendly. They long to possess our things, but having nothing to give in return they take what they can get, and presently swim away.*
>
> *Still they give away all they have in return for whatever may be given to them, even broken bits of crockery and glass. I saw one of them trade 16 skeins of cotton for three small Portuguese coins, the skeins weighing as much as 25 pounds of cotton thread. . . . I think it is grown on this island, though my short stay did not allow me to find out for sure. Here also is found the gold that the people wear fastened in their noses. But in order not to lose time, I intend to depart from here and see if I can discover the island of Cipango*.*

*Present-day Japan

1. What evidence in this excerpt suggests that the Indians were unfamiliar with people from cultures and regions different from their own?
2. From Columbus' description of the geographic features of the island, what kind of foods do you think the Indians lived on?
3. What evidence indicates that Columbus did not realize he had discovered a land previously unknown to most Europeans?

Linking History & Geography

Many of the earliest explorers in the New World came from Spain, Portugal, England, France, and the Netherlands. Study the map on page 177 and note the location of each of these countries. Then in a brief paragraph explain how the geographic location of these countries helped them to lead the age of discovery and to be among the first to send sailors across the Atlantic to the Americas.

Enriching Your Study of History

1. **Individual Project.** Using the maps in this chapter as a guide, trace on an outline map of the world the explorations of Leif Ericson, Columbus, Balboa, Magellan and El Cano, Narváez and Esteban, Coronado, and De León.
2. **Cooperative Project.** With three of your classmates, choose one of the American Indian tribes mentioned in this chapter, and research its way of life. Your group might prepare a booklet about them including drawings and stories, or build a model of a typical village. If the tribe originally lived nearby, arrange a visit to a local museum.

Chapter 1 Review   **39**

English Colonies in America

The wealth and splendor of Spain's American empire attracted other Europeans the way flowers in springtime attract honeybees. The English in particular were envious of Spain. They longed to build an empire in the Americas. They hoped for a share of the gold and silver that almost everyone believed was so plentiful in the new land, and they wanted American products such as sugar and rice, which could not be grown in their cold climate. The English colonists came to America to trade and sell, to practice their religions, and to find work. Would they find a better life in a New World?

Preview & Review

Use these questions to guide your reading. Answer the questions after completing Section 1.
Understanding Issues, Events, & Ideas. Explain the English rise to power and its first journeys to America, using the following words: sea dog, Spanish Armada, charter, Roanoke, enclosure movement, northwest passage, joint-stock company.
1. How did Queen Elizabeth try to weaken Spain?
2. Why did the first settlers on Roanoke Island want to return to England?
3. Why were each of the following interested in colonizing America: the queen? landowners? merchants? explorers?
Thinking Critically. Imagine that you find a lost diary explaining what happened to the colonists of Roanoke Island. What does it say?

At right is Nicholas Hilliard's 1572 miniature portrait of Elizabeth I.

1. WHY COLONISTS CAME TO AMERICA

England Challenges Spain

In 1497, not very long after the news of Columbus' discovery reached England, its king, Henry VII, sent John Cabot on a voyage of exploration. Cabot sailed along the coast of Newfoundland, giving England a claim to the northern regions of America. At that time Spain seemed too powerful to challenge. But in the 1550s, after Elizabeth I inherited the throne, the English became seriously interested in America.

Elizabeth, ruling England alone in a world dominated by men, was a person of the strongest will and ambition. She was a shrewd ruler and a clever diplomat who paid little attention to right and wrong. Elizabeth never married, perhaps because no man could be her equal. She had a temper to match her fiery red hair and a tongue to match her sharp features. She was well aware of England's limited strength compared to Spain's. She proceeded with caution.

National Portrait Gallery, London

One way to weaken Spain without openly going to war was to attack Spanish merchant ships on the high seas. In those days a ship out of sight of land was at the mercy of any more powerful vessel. There was no way to call for help or even to send an alert. A fast, powerfully armed ship could overtake a clumsy Spanish galleon loaded with treasure. The crew would be easily overcome, the cargo taken off, and the ship sent to the bottom. No one could prove that the ship had not run on a rocky reef in a fog and been dashed to pieces, or gone down in a storm, as in fact frequently happened.

The Spanish considered such attackers pirates, and rightly so. Nevertheless, Elizabeth encouraged English captains to roam the trade routes between Spain and its colonies in America in search of such prey.

The most famous of what the English affectionately called their **sea dogs** was Francis Drake. In 1577 Drake began the most famous of his many escapades. From England he sailed his ship, the *Golden Hind,* across the Atlantic and through the Strait of Magellan. In the Pacific he captured the *Cacafuego,* a Spanish galleon carrying a fortune in silver from Peru. Then he sailed north to California, which he claimed for England.

National Portrait Gallery, London

Also by Nicholas Hilliard is this 1581 miniature of Sir Francis Drake. What might be some reasons for the popularity of such miniatures?

"Cabot Leaving the Port of Bristol" was painted in 1906 by Ernest Board. Which figures from religious life can you identify in this blessing of the ship?

City of Bristol Museum and Art Gallery

From California Drake crossed the Pacific and Indian Oceans, rounded Africa, and returned home. When he reached England in 1580, Drake presented Queen Elizabeth with a treasure worth twice her annual income. Little wonder that Elizabeth made him a knight of the kingdom right on the deck of the *Golden Hind*.

Drake sailed again into Spanish waters in 1585. This time he terrorized Spanish towns in the Caribbean islands. "Drake the Dragon," the Spanish called him. Philip II, the king of Spain, was furious. He collected the largest fleet the world had ever seen—130 ships carrying 30,000 men and armed with 2,400 cannon. In 1588 this mighty **Spanish Armada** sailed from Spain to invade England.

While Elizabeth and her troops awaited the Armada, she urged her men to fight for the glory of England:

> ❝ I know I have but the body of a weak and feeble woman; but I have the heart of a king, and of a king of England, too; and think foul scorn that Perma [the Spanish military leader] of Spain, or any prince of Europe, should dare invade the borders of my realms: to which, rather than any dishonor should grow by me, I myself will take up arms; . . . and by your valor in the field, we shall shortly have a famous victory over the enemies of my God, of my kingdom, and of my people.[1] ❞

Elizabeth's ships were fewer and smaller, but easier to maneuver and more powerful. They sank many of the attackers. Storms finished off still more. Not one Spanish sailor or soldier set foot on English soil, except as a captive. Only about half the Armada limped back to Spanish ports. With Spain's navy shattered, the stage was set for England to carve a place for itself in America.

False Starts in America

Even before the defeat of the Spanish Armada, English sailors were visiting North American waters in increasing numbers. By the 1570s about 50 vessels were catching fish on the Grand Banks off the coast of Newfoundland. Some of the fishermen established temporary camps ashore. In 1578 Queen Elizabeth issued a document called a **charter** to Sir Humphrey Gilbert. This charter gave Gilbert the right to establish and control a colony in America. Operating under the charter, Gilbert landed on Newfoundland with a party of 200. He officially claimed the island for England. This group did not stay, and Gilbert was drowned when his ship went down in a storm.

When Humphrey Gilbert was eight, his father had died. Later his mother married a man named Raleigh. They had a son, Walter, Humphrey's half-brother. He grew up to be the handsome and charm-

National Portrait Gallery, London

Another miniature by Nicholas Hilliard, this one is of Sir Walter Raleigh around 1585. He was a particular favorite of Elizabeth's at this time. Based on the three miniatures, what generalization can you make about clothing in Elizabeth's court?

---

[1]From *A Treasury of the World's Great Speeches,* selected and edited by Houston Peterson

ing Sir Walter Raleigh, a close adviser of Queen Elizabeth. Two years after Humphrey Gilbert's death, Raleigh sent seven ships carrying over a hundred men to America. Under Gilbert's charter they were to establish a colony and look for gold.

Raleigh did not accompany the group. Some said Queen Elizabeth was in love with him at this time and would not let him leave her court. His colonists passed the winter on an island called **Roanoke** off the coast of what is now North Carolina. One of them, an artist and mapmaker named John White, painted many watercolors of the Indians of the region and of the plants and animals there.

No gold was found at Roanoke. The colonists fought with the local Indians. Life was hard. When Sir Francis Drake arrived at Roanoke in June 1586 on his way back from his raid in the Caribbean, the colonists eagerly accepted his offer of passage back to England.

Ever hopeful, in 1587 Raleigh dispatched another hundred-odd colonists to Carolina, headed by John White. For the first time women were sent out, among them White's married daughter, Ellinor Dare. These colonists landed at Roanoke in July, and on August 18 Ellinor Dare gave birth to a daughter, Virginia, the first English child born in America.

A few days later John White sailed back to England for more supplies. He intended to return promptly, but he could not because of the national crisis caused by the attack of the Spanish Armada. Other delays followed and White did not get back to Roanoke until 1590. The island was deserted. No one has ever discovered what happened to the inhabitants of this "Lost Colony" of Roanoke.

All, The Granger Collection, New York

The Pyne frute.

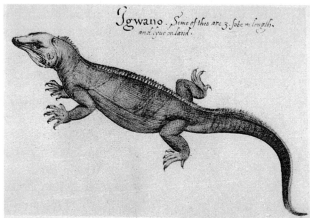

Jgwano. Some of thes are 3 fote in length, and lyue on land.

New Hopes in America

Despite the setbacks, many important people in England remained very interested in America. For the queen and other political leaders, a major attraction was the hope of finding gold and silver to increase England's wealth and power. Another was to reduce the power of Spain, which already controlled so much of the Americas. For upper-

Three of John White's watercolors made around 1585 are shown here. These may have been the first views the English had of the Atlantic loggerhead turtle, the iguana, and the pineapple. How do the watercolors show that White was a careful observer of nature?

class gentlemen like Raleigh and Gilbert, the chief goals were adventure, honor, and fame.

There were practical, down-to-earth reasons for more ordinary English people to colonize America. Many people were out of work in England. Because of a rising demand for woolen cloth, many landowners had stopped farming and begun raising sheep. They fenced in, or enclosed, their fields and planted them in grass for the sheep. This was known as the **enclosure movement.** Raising sheep took much less labor than growing grain, so many serfs and tenants had to look for work elsewhere. Some found jobs in the towns. Others wandered about the countryside, often disturbing the peace.

A nursery rhyme that appeared at about this time warned that homeless people, put out of work and home by the enclosure movement, were draining the strength of England:

> **"** Hark, hark, the dogs do bark;
> The beggars are coming to town,
> Some in rags and some in tags
> And some in velvet gowns. **"**

Perhaps they could be resettled and made useful workers again in America. People who thought this way saw America as a safety valve for troublemakers and to keep English jails from overflowing.

In addition, the expanding cloth industry in England gave a boost to foreign trade and made many merchants rich. These merchants were eager to invest their profits in colonial ventures. For them America was a new business opportunity. Finally, there was still the hope for a practical westward route to the Indies. Although the trip around South America was too long to be profitable, maybe sailors would discover a **northwest passage** through North America.

Merchant Adventurers

The experiences of men like Gilbert and Raleigh proved that founding a colony was expensive and risky. Most English merchants and manufacturers were shrewd and cautious in business, not daring adventurers or high-born court favorites. Instead of outfitting expeditions as individuals, they organized what they called **joint-stock companies.** These companies were the ancestors of our corporations. They were owned by many stockholders who shared in the profits and losses.

The London merchant Sir Thomas Smythe was typical of these merchant adventurers. Smythe backed the first English attempt to sail around Africa. In 1600 he helped found the British East India Company, which received exclusive rights from the English government to trade with the Indies. He also invested money in a number of expeditions into Arctic waters in search of the northwest passage. Smythe became the treasurer and guiding spirit of the Virginia Company of London, often called the London Company.

Giraudon/Art Resource

The true focus of this country scene is the fence. It separates the wheat field from the sheep who are yielding up their wool to the shearers. When the enclosure movement made work scarce, some Englishmen looked to America. What caused the landowners to enclose their fields and graze sheep?

The joint-stock Virginia Company was given charters by James I, who became king of England after his cousin Queen Elizabeth died in 1603. In l606 James gave the London Company the right to develop a huge area of North America. The region was named Virginia in honor of Queen Elizabeth, who because she never married was known as the Virgin Queen.

Virginia extended along the Atlantic Coast from about the latitude of New York City to what is now South Carolina, and west "from sea to sea"—that is, all the way to the Pacific Ocean! Obviously neither King James nor anyone else in England had the slightest idea of how enormous this grant was. The country had never been explored. The charter shows what big ideas the colonizers had, as well as their disregard for the rights of the native Americans. Because a few of his explorers had nosed their way along the Atlantic beaches, King James claimed the right to the whole continent. 🔳

Return to the Preview & Review on page 40.

Why Colonists Came to America 45

USING LATITUDE AND LONGITUDE

One of the basic tasks in both history and geography is to locate exactly what is where on the earth. To do this, you must identify the *absolute location* of each place, or its precise spot on the earth. Cartographers, or map makers, have created a grid system of imaginary lines to make this task easier.

Most maps are drawn with the North Pole at the top and the South Pole at the bottom. The *equator* is the line halfway between the North and South poles. Several shorter imaginary lines circle the earth parallel to the equator and on both sides of it. They are called *parallels,* or *lines of latitude.* Parallels are used to locate places north and south of the equator. They are numbered from zero degrees (0°) at the equator to 90 degrees (90°) north (N) at the North Pole and 90° south (S) at the South Pole.

A second set of imaginary lines called *meridians,* or *lines of longitude,* crisscrosses the parallels. In 1884, an international agreement set the meridian passing through the Royal Observatory in Greenwich, England, near London, as 0° longitude, or the *prime meridian.* The meridian directly opposite the prime meridian, on the other side of the globe, is the 180° meridian. Meridians are used to locate places east and west of the prime meridian. Meridians east of the prime meridian are numbered from 0°E at the prime meridian to 180°E and those to the west are numbered from 0°W to 180°W. By noting latitude and longitude, you can quickly find exact locations on earth.

How to Find Exact Location

To use latitude and location to find the exact location of a place, follow these guidelines.

1. **Use the global grid.** The grid provides lines of latitude and longitude marked with corresponding degrees.
2. **Find the equator.** Check the lines of latitude, those running from east to west, until you find 0°. This marks the equator.
3. **Locate the correct parallel.** Continue to check the lines of latitude until you find the one you are looking for. Remember that northern latitudes are above the equator and southern latitudes are below it.
4. **Find the prime meridian.** Check the lines of longitude by reading along the top or bottom of the map. The prime meridian is marked 0°.
5. **Locate the correct meridian.** Continue to read along the grid until you find the meridian you are looking for. Remember that west is to the left of the prime meridian and east is to the right.

Applying the Strategy

Study the map below. It shows the voyages of Cabot and Raleigh and the locations of the first colonies. You can note that Jamestown is located at about 37°N, 77°W while Plymouth is at about 42°N, 70°W. See if you can find the exact locations of other colonies as well.

For independent practice, see Practicing the Strategy on pages 70–71.

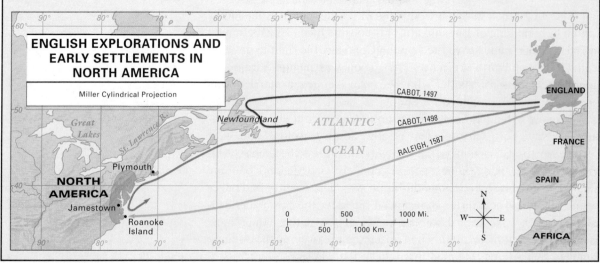

ENGLISH EXPLORATIONS AND EARLY SETTLEMENTS IN NORTH AMERICA

Miller Cylindrical Projection

2. THE SETTLEMENT OF VIRGINIA

Preview & Review

Use these questions to guide your reading. Answer the questions after completing Section 2.
Understanding Issues, Events, & Ideas. Use the following words to to describe events in Jamestown: Jamestown, soldier of fortune, starving time, headright, House of Burgesses, indentured servant.
1. Why did so many of the first settlers in Jamestown die?
2. What helped conditions in Jamestown begin to improve? What changes did John Smith make when he became president of the Virginia council?
3. How did wealthy settlers profit from the headright system?
4. How did the Indians help the Jamestown colonists? Why did they attack the colonists?
Thinking Critically. 1. You are an indentured servant in Virginia. Write a letter to a relative in England, telling about your life. **2.** You are a Virginia colonist in 1618. What crop would you plant in order to assure your success as a farmer? Why would you choose this crop?

Jamestown: The First Colony

A few days before Christmas 1606, the London Company sent off three ships, the *Discovery*, the *Susan Constant*, and the *Godspeed*, bearing 104 settlers. Their destination was Virginia, their purpose to build a town and search for gold, silver, and copper.

The three little ships reached Virginia on April 26, 1607. They sailed up a river, which they named after King James. A few days later they chose a place to build a fort on a peninsula jutting out into the river. They called this settlement **Jamestown.**

From the start life in Jamestown was an endless series of troubles. The site was easy to defend but swampy and infested with fever-bearing mosquitoes. By the end of summer half the colonists had died, and many of those who remained were sick with malaria. Because the planting season had ended before the colonists had finished building houses and walling the town, they were unable to plant a crop. Soon they were desperately short of food. When the first ship from England arrived the next spring, only 38 colonists were alive to greet it.

The colony also suffered from poor leadership. King James named a council to rule it. He appointed mostly stockholders in the London Company. They did not go to Jamestown and knew almost nothing about the difficulties the settlers faced. For example, there was no sign of gold in the area around Jamestown. Yet the London authorities insisted that the colonists spend much of their energy searching for the precious metal. The Londoners did create a local council in Virginia, supposedly to handle day-to-day problems, but they gave the councilors no real authority.

Still worse, the Virginia councilors quarreled among themselves and allowed the colonists to neglect the basic tasks of planting crops and making the settlement safe.

The Jamestown settlers were poorly prepared for the great challenge of living in the new country. The 36 so-called gentlemen among them had none of the skills needed by pioneers, such as carpentry and farming. They were unaccustomed to hard labor of any kind. As for the others, there were goldsmiths, perfumers, and jewelers, who were certainly skilled—but in the wrong trades. Not one of them had ever been a real farmer. Too many settlers apparently believed that in America wealth grew on trees. They did not realize that it was necessary to work hard if they wished to stay alive.

Fortunately, one man among these colonists had the courage to take command. He was John Smith. Smith was a swashbuckler, a **soldier of fortune,** who was ready to fight for whomever would pay him. He was a short, bearded fellow of 27, a man of action. He had

The Granger Collection, New York

John Smith was 27 years old when he took command of the Jamestown settlement. This engraving portrays him at the age of 33.

Point of View

An Algonquin leader asked John Smith why the colonists used force with the Indians.

Why will you take by force what you may have quietly by love? Why will you destroy us who supply you with food? What can you get by war? We can hide our provisions and run into the woods; then you will starve for wronging your friends. Why are you jealous of us? We are unarmed, and willing to give you what you ask, if you come in a friendly manner.

Powhatan, 1607

seen far more of the world than any of the other settlers. He had fought in a number of wars in eastern Europe against the Turks. In one war he was captured, taken to Constantinople, and sold into slavery. However, he managed to kill his master and escape. After many other remarkable adventures Smith found himself in the colony of Virginia.

In 1608 Smith was elected president of the Virginia council. Once in charge, he bargained with the Indians for food. He stopped the foolish searching for gold. Instead he put people to work building shelters and planting food crops. Hard work and strict discipline became the order of the day.

Reforms for Virginia

Virginia's difficulties finally convinced the merchant adventurers in England that the London Company needed to be reorganized. In 1609 Sir Edwin Sandys, a councilor who was also a member of Parliament, England's legislative body, obtained a new charter from King James. This charter called for the appointment of a governor who would rule the colony in Jamestown rather than from London.

The London Company then raised a good deal more money and outfitted a fleet of nine ships to carry about 600 new settlers across the Atlantic. Those who paid their own fare received one share of stock in the company. Those who could not pay agreed to work as servants of the company for seven years in return for their passage. Until 1616 everything the colonists produced was to be put into a common storehouse or fund. On that date the servants would have worked off their debt to the company. Then the profits of the enterprise were to be divided among the shareholders—both the investors back in England and the settlers. Every shareholder would also receive a grant of Virginia land.

These were fine plans but hard to put into effect. Conditions in Virginia got worse and worse. The first governor, Lord De La Warr, put off coming to Jamestown. Smith returned to England for supplies and colonists, and to convince company managers to invest more money in the colony. Without his firm hand, the organization and rules he had begun quickly fell apart. The years from 1609 to 1610 were a **starving time.** As Smith described it:

By their [the Indians'] cruelty, our Governours indiscretion [poor judgment] and losse of our ships, of five hundred [colonists] within six months after Captaine Smith's departure, there remained not past sixtie men, women and children, most miserable and poore creatures; and those were preserved for the most part, by roots, herbes, acornes, walnuts, berries, now and then a little fish . . . yea, even the very skinnes of our horses. . . . This was that time,

Virginia Museum of Fine Arts, Richmond. Collection of Mr. Paul Mellon

which still to this day (1624) we call the starving time; it were too vile to say, and scarce to be believed, what we endured. . . .[1] **"**

At one point the colonists almost decided to abandon the settlement and return to England.

Things began to improve in 1611 when the council appointed Thomas Dale, a soldier with a reputation for sternness, as governor. Dale arrived with fresh supplies and a new group of settlers in March. He promptly resumed the tough course set by John Smith. He soon became very unpopular because of his harsh rule. A man convicted of stealing some oatmeal was chained to a tree and allowed to starve to death. The colonists charged that Dale was a tyrant. Nevertheless, they began to plant corn, repair the fort, and work to make sure that the colony would survive.

Headrights and Indentures

In 1618 the London Company launched a campaign to attract more investors and settlers to Virginia. Colonists who paid their own way

"Good Times in the New World (The Hope of Jamestown)" was painted by John Gadsby Chapman in 1841. It depicts the arrival of the second group of Jamestown settlers.

[1]From *The General Historie of Virginia* by Captain John Smith

or that of others would receive 50 acres (20 hectares) of land for each "head" transported. This was called a **headright.** The company relaxed the rigorous discipline that Thomas Dale had imposed as governor of the colony. It guaranteed all settlers the same legal rights that English subjects had at home. It also gave settlers a voice in the local government of the colony. They would be allowed to elect representatives to an assembly known as the **House of Burgesses.** This was the first elected government body in America. Along with the governor's council, the House was given the power to make laws for the colony. It first met at Jamestown in 1619.

The London Company made an all-out effort to develop many kinds of products in the colony. But tobacco remained Virginia's most important commodity by far. As the price of tobacco rose, everyone rushed to plant more of it. The broad, green leaves of tobacco plants could be seen growing in the streets of Jamestown.

Growing tobacco required a great deal of labor. In Jamestown laborers to work the land were in short supply. Those settlers who had money had a tremendous advantage in obtaining workers because of the headright system. Poor people who wanted to come to Virginia signed contracts called indentures. They agreed to work for seven years to pay off the cost of getting to America. These contracts of indenture could be bought and sold. The newcomer, who was called an **indentured servant,** had to work without wages for the person who owned the indenture. The owner also received the headright issued by the colonial government for bringing the newcomer to Virginia. He could therefore claim 50 acres (20 hectares) of land. In other words, the person who paid the passage of the immigrant received for one price both land and the labor needed to farm it.

Treatment of indentured servants varied, as these letters written to parents back in England show[1]:

To Mr. John Sprigs White Smith in White Cross Street near Cripple Gate London

Maryland Sept'r 22d 1756

Honred Father

O Dear Father, believe what I am going to relate the words of truth and sincerity, and Ballance my former bad Conduct [to] my sufferings here, and then I am sure you'll pity your Distress[ed] Daughter. What we unfortunate English People suffer here is beyond the probibility of you in England to Conceive. Let it suffice that I, one of the unhappy Number, am toiling almost Day and Night, and very often in the Horses druggery . . . and then tied up and whipp'd to that Degree that you'd not serve an Animal.

[1]From Public Record Office, London, High Court of Admiralty, 30:258, no. 106, and 30: 258, no. 90

[There is] scarce any thing but Indian Corn and Salt to eat and that even begrudged. Nay, many Neagoes are better used. [I have] no shoes nor stockings to wear. . . . What rest we can get is to rap ourselves up in a Blanket and ly upon the Ground. This is the deplorable Condition your poor Betty endures. And now I beg, if you have any Bowels of Compassion left, show it by sending me some Relief. Clothing is the principal thing wanting, which if you should condiscend to, may easely send them to me by any of the ships bound to Baltimore Town, Patapsco River, Maryland. And give me leave to conclude in Duty to you and Uncles and Aunts, and Respect to all Friends,

Honred Father,

Your dutifull and Disobedient Child,

Elizabeth Sprigs

To Mr. Tuggey at Low Tewting in Surrey

Anoplis November 2, 1756

Honred Father and mother

I take this opertinewtey of riting to you to Lett you know that i am in Maryland and a footman to the Honrable Colnall Taskur and i am in a Good Place. . . . I live as well as aney one Can. But to be so Long fron hering or seeing from you, i think you are Ded. I shall be Glad to heer from you, but as i have sent 2 Letters to you and never Receved an Answer i Expect you are Ded.

I live [as] well as aney one Can in the world. I am marrad since i Come heer, and I hope to be in England in a bout 12 mounths and shall bring my wife with me. And Pray send to me som knives som buckls and Butins and Aney thing you think Proper for i Can make Good money heer. . . .

Pray send me a Letter by the first ship Com'g to maryland and Drict it to mr Toeggett att the Honrable Collnl. Taskers in Anoplis i Maryland

PS: I have marrad as sweat a gall [as] Ever was Born. Shee Is as trew to me as the verelle Sun an i [shall] bring hur to England will me plees God i Live. . . . Pray excuse the bad riting to you for you know i am a bad [scholar].

Your Dewtful Sun,

Richard Tuggeyy

The great tobacco boom did the London Company little good. By the time the boom began, the original colonists had already served their seven years and were no longer working for the company.

In the long run what made Virginia prosper was tobacco. When the colonists realized that there was no gold nor silver to be found, they looked for other sources of wealth. They tried to raise silkworms, to make glass, to grow wine grapes—all without success. Tobacco was a different story. Here was a plant native to America. The Indians prized it highly, using it for personal enjoyment and in their ceremonies. Sir Francis Drake brought tobacco to England from the West Indies after his raid, and Sir Walter Raleigh made smoking fashionable in high society. The habit spread quickly in England.

It is interesting that from the very start many people argued that smoking was unhealthy. King James himself opposed the use of tobacco. Although he

considered it beneath his dignity to engage in public debate, he published anonymously an essay on the subject. This "Counterblast to Tobacco" described smoking as a "vile and stinking" habit that would injure the lungs and the brain. Thousands of King James' subjects ignored his warning. Demand for tobacco soared in England.

The Indians of Virginia grew and smoked tobacco, but this local plant had a harsh and bitter taste. A colonist named John Rolfe, who came to Jamestown about 1610, solved the problem by bringing in tobacco seeds from the Spanish colonies. This variety of tobacco flourished in Virginia and produced a much milder smoke. In 1616 Virginia farmers exported about 2,200 pounds (1,000 kilograms) of tobacco to England. Two years later they exported more than 20 times that amount.

The Virginians now had a cash crop they could sell in England. They were able to purchase the manufactured items they could not yet produce themselves: cloth, tools, furniture, guns. Little wonder that King Charles I, who succeeded James I in 1625, joked that Virginia was "built upon smoke."

Bloodshed in Jamestown

The colonists treated their Indian neighbors far worse than they treated their indentured servants. In the early days Jamestown could not have survived without the Indians. They gave the starving colonists food. They taught them how to live in the wilderness. The land around Jamestown was a dense forest. Corn, a native American plant grown by the Indians, would not grow for the colonists in forest shade. It would take years to cut down the huge trees and root out their stumps. The Indians showed the colonists how to kill the trees by cutting a ring around the trunks. Sunlight could then shine through the dead and leafless branches, and corn planted by the colonists sprouted between the trunks.

The colonists accepted the Indians' help and advice and then tried to take control of their homelands! The Indians resisted. In a sudden attack in 1622 they killed about 350 colonists, almost one third of Virginia's European population. The bloodshed convinced King James that the colony, which was already being mismanaged, should be taken away from the London Company. In 1624 he canceled the charter and put Virginia under direct royal control. The Company was bankrupt, the stockholders' investment lost.

Return to the Preview & Review on page 47.

3. THE SETTLEMENT OF MASSACHUSETTS

Preview & Review

Use these questions to guide your reading. Answer the questions after completing Section 3.
Understanding Issues, Events, & Ideas. Describe the Pilgrim arrival in America, using the following words: Pilgrims, Separatists, Protestant Reformation, radical, Mayflower Compact, Plymouth, Thanksgiving Day.
1. Why were the Pilgrims called Separatists? Why did the Pilgrims leave Holland?
2. How were the experiences of the Pilgrims similar to those of the first Jamestown settlers?
3. How did the Pilgrims differ from the Jamestown settlers?
Thinking Critically. You are one of the Pilgrims who came to Plymouth on the Mayflower, and you are helping to write laws for your colony. Write the law you think is the most important. Explain why your law is the most necessary.

The Pilgrims

In 1617 Sir Edwin Sandys was trying to put Virginia's affairs in order. A community of people who were living in Holland asked him for permission to settle in America somewhere within the London Company's grant. These **Pilgrims,** as we now call them, had left England in 1608 to escape religious persecution. Pilgrims were **Separatists,** people who had "separated" themselves from the Anglican Church, the Church of England. The Anglican Church had been established when Henry VIII broke from the Pope in Rome and the Catholic Church. Separatists opposed the Anglican Church because it was sponsored by the state and seemed to them not to be accomplishing the true goals of the **Protestant Reformation** taking place in Europe.

In Holland the Dutch had not interfered with the Pilgrims' religious practice, but still the Pilgrims were not happy in their new home. They could not get good jobs. Their children were beginning to speak Dutch instead of English.

Sandys admired the Pilgrims, but other company officials considered them dangerous **radicals.** (Radicals are people who favor sudden and widespread changes.) There were long delays, but finally in 1619 the London Company and the king granted the Pilgrims permission to migrate. Because the Pilgrims were poor people without money to pay for their voyage, they accepted a proposal by a group of English merchant adventurers. The merchants would put up the money to found a new settlement. The Pilgrims would do the work. In September 1620 a party of 35 Pilgrims and 66 other colonists sailed from Plymouth, England, on the *Mayflower* bound for Virginia. They were the first English settlers who came to America for religious reasons.

Plymouth Plantation

The little party on the *Mayflower* never reached Virginia. On November 9 they sighted land on Cape Cod Bay, north of the London Company's territory. With winter so near, they decided not to test their ship any longer in the stormy waters of the Atlantic and to settle where they were.

Because Cape Cod was outside the region controlled by the London Company, there was no existing government. Therefore, the Pilgrims decided to draw up a document which would provide a legal basis for governing the area and themselves. This document is called the **Mayflower Compact.** Its signers first acknowledged the authority of King James. They were not seeking to create a new nation. They

This colored engraving of the May-flower at full sail was probably made in the 19th century. What do you suppose life was like for the more than 100 people aboard?

The Granger Collection, New York

then pledged "submission and obedience" to the officers they would themselves elect and to the laws they might pass. They wrote:

❝ In the name of God, Amen. We whose names are under-written, the loyal subjects of our dread sovereign Lord King *James,* by the grace of God, of Great Britain, France, and Ireland, King, Defender of the Faith, etc., having under-taken, for the glory of God, and advancement of the Christian faith, and honor of our king and country, a voyage to plant the first colony in the northern parts of Virginia, do by these Presents solemnly and mutually promise in the presence of God, and one of another, covenant and combine ourselves into a civil Body Politik for our better ordering and preservation and furtherance of the ends aforesaid; and by Virtue hereof, to enact, constitute, and frame such just and equal Laws, ordinances, acts, constitutions, and offices from time to time, as shall be thought most meet and con-venient for the Good of the Colony unto which we promise all due submission and obedience. ❞

The Mayflower Compact is a short and simple document. To us it might seem a rather obvious and unnecessary statement, made by decent and honest people about to settle in a new land. Yet the Compact tells us a great deal about life in America, then and later.

So far as any record shows, this was the first time in history that a group of people consciously created a government where none had existed before.

The Pilgrims decided to settle at a place they called **Plymouth.** The rock on which they are thought to have landed is now a national monument. They came ashore with almost nothing, no "butter or oil, not a sole to mend a shoe." They were true pilgrims, these wanderers, uncertain of what lay over the next hill.

In some respects the Pilgrims were like the first immigrants from Asia, people who owned little more than what they had on their backs, isolated in an unknown land. The Pilgrims were totally dependent on one another, but this was their strength. They recognized their common purpose and the need for unity. Above all they trusted in "the good providence of God." They were ready to give up the familiar world for the uncertain wilderness. One of the Pilgrims, William Bradford, described their lot:

     “ Being thus arrived in a good harbor, and brought safe to land, they fell upon their knees and blessed the God of Heaven who had brought them over the vast and furious ocean, and delivered them from all perils and miseries thereof, again to set their feet on the firm and stable earth, their proper element. . . .

      But here I cannot but stay and make a pause, and stand half amazed at this poor people's present condition; and so I think will the reader, too, when he well considers the same. Being thus passed the vast ocean, and a sea of troubles before in their preparation (as may be remembered by that which went before), they had now no friends to welcome them nor inns to entertain or refresh their weather-beaten bodies; no houses or much less towns to repair to, to seek for succor [relief]. It is recorded in Scripture as a mercy to the Apostle and his shipwrecked company [Acts: 28], that the barbarians showed them no small kindness in refreshing them, but these savage barbarians when they met with them (as after will appear), were readier to fill their sides full of arrows than otherwise. And for the season it was winter, and they that know the winters of that country know them to be sharp and violent, and subject to cruel and fierce storms, dangerous to travel to known places, much more to search an unknown coast. Besides, what could they see but a hideous and desolate wilderness, full of wild beasts and wild men—and what multitudes there might be of them they knew not. . . . Which way soever they turned their eyes (save upward to the heavens) they could have little solace or content in respect of any outward objects. For summer being done, all things stand upon them

The Pilgrim Society

"Signing the Compact" was painted by Percy Moran. What does this picture say about the roles of men and women in the Pilgrim society?

with a weather-beaten face, and the whole country, full of woods and thickets, represented a wild and savage hue. If they looked behind them, there was the mighty ocean they had passed and was now as a main bar and gulf to separate them from all the civil parts of the world.

What could sustain them now but the Spirit of God and His Grace? May not and ought not the children of these fathers rightly say: 'Our fathers were Englishmen which came over this great ocean, and were ready to perish in this wilderness; but they cried unto the Lord, and He heard their voice and looked upon their adversity.'[1] **""**

[1]From *History of Plimoth Plantation, 1620–1647* by William Bradford

Their early experiences were similar to those of the Jamestown settlers. Disease swept through the exhausted party. The survivors might well have starved to death if an Indian named Squanto had not befriended them. Squanto taught the Pilgrims how to grow corn. He showed them the best streams for fishing.

Things changed for the better in the spring. Unlike the first Virginians, the Pilgrims worked hard, planted their crops, and in the autumn gathered in a bountiful harvest. For this, in November 1621, the settlers came together to give thanks to God. Thus was established the American tradition of **Thanksgiving Day.**

However, Plymouth remained a very small colony. Life there was hard. The courage, determination, dignity, and piety of the Pilgrims—not wealth or power—has assured them a permanent place in our nation's history.

The Pilgrims came to America for very different reasons than the settlers of Virginia. Even at this early date it was clear that America attracted ordinary people. For nearly all, there was hope of finding a better life in the land of opportunity. 🖅

Return to the Preview & Review on page 53.

4. "A CITY UPON A HILL"

The Puritans

While the London Company was making plans to settle Virginia, another joint-stock company, the Virginia Company of Plymouth, or the Plymouth Company, tried to establish a settlement far to the north near the mouth of the Kennebec River in what is now Maine. The settlers arrived in 1607 but remained only one winter. However, fishermen and traders continued to set up temporary camps in the area. In 1614 the Plymouth Company sent John Smith to explore the region further. It was Smith who first called the area **New England.**

In the early 1620s the Plymouth Company, now called the Council of New England, gave away several tracts of land in the northern regions, including much of what are now Maine and New Hampshire.

Metropolitan Museum of Art

The great 19th-century American sculptor, Augustus Saint-Gaudens, made this bronze, "The Puritan." What does this sculpture show you about Puritan life?

Use these questions to guide your reading. Answer the questions after completing Section 4.
Understanding Issues, Events, & Ideas. Use the following words to compare Puritan settlements with Jamestown: New England, Puritans, Massachusetts Bay Company, freemen, commonwealth, Fundamental Orders, proprietary colony, Toleration Act.

1. Who were the Puritans? How did the Puritans differ from the Pilgrims? Why did they leave England?
2. Why did Puritan leaders expel Roger Williams? Anne Hutchinson?
3. What kind of powers did the king's grant give Lord Baltimore? Why were these powers never used?

Thinking Critically. You are a Puritan living in Massachusetts in 1634. Write a letter to your cousins in England, convincing them to come to America.

"A City upon a Hill" 57

Maine remained a part of Massachusetts until 1820, but in 1679 New Hampshire was proclaimed a separate royal colony. The most significant grant made by the Council of New England was to a group of religious reformers. Like the Pilgrims, these people were critical of the Church of England. But they were not Separatists. They had not given up hope of reforming the Church from within. They sought to purify it. Hence they were known as **Puritans.**

The efforts of the Puritans to reform the Church of England met strong resistance. Puritan ministers were even denied the right to preach. When they were persecuted, many Puritans began to think of moving to America. Perhaps there they could create a perfect church and community. As one of their leaders explained, they sought to build "a city upon a hill," a community other people could look up to and admire and eventually copy.

Before taking advantage of the council's grant, the Puritans obtained a new charter from the king and organized the **Massachusetts Bay Company.** Under the charter their colony was to be practically self-governing. They planned their venture carefully. Their first group was large—about a thousand people—and adequately supplied. In 1630 their 11-ship convoy reached Massachusetts.

The governor of Massachusetts Bay, John Winthrop, was well aware of the difficulties involved in founding a settlement in a wilderness. He was a practical person who preferred compromise and persuasion to force. The charter put all political power in the hands of the stockholders. But Winthrop feared that unless ordinary colonists had some share in governing the settlement, there would be trouble. Therefore he and the other stockholders decided to make about a hundred additional settlers **freemen**, which meant that they could vote for the governor of the colony and for members of its legislature, which was called the General Court. The new freemen were church members which violated the charter. Freemen were required to be church members until this was changed in 1664.

The Puritans were not democratic in the modern sense of the term. They did, however, try earnestly to create a **commonwealth,** a society devoted to the common welfare of all.

Within a year of their arrival the Puritans had "planted," as they called it, several communities centered around their chief town, Boston. During the next ten years, about 15 or 20 thousand people came, far more than to any earlier colony. Soon some groups, or congregations, were pushing out on their own. In 1636 the Reverend Thomas Hooker led his congregation from Massachusetts to the fertile valley of the Connecticut River. There in Connecticut they established the town of Hartford. Other "river towns" sprang up in the valley. These towns formed a common government and drafted a written constitution, the **Fundamental Orders.** The system outlined in the Fundamental Orders was not especially different from the government of Massachusetts Bay. Its main distinction was that it allowed male

Harvard University Portrait Collection

John Winthrop, the first governor of Massachusetts Bay, sat for this portrait in the 17th century. Compare this portrait with the miniatures of Sir Francis Drake and Sir Walter Raleigh at the beginning of the chapter. In what ways does Winthrop resemble an Englishman of Queen Elizabeth's court? How does he differ?

Wadsworth Atheneum, Hartford

residents who were not church members to become freemen. The document is very important historically because it was the first written frame of government in America, a kind of ancestor of all the state constitutions and of the Constitution of the United States.

Religious Conflicts

Because religion was so important to the Puritans, they would not tolerate anyone whose religious beliefs differed from their own. They believed theirs was the true faith and thought all others must be the work of the devil. Our concept of freedom of religion would have made little sense to them at all. Thomas Hooker left Massachusetts because of religious disagreements that now seem quite trivial. These differences were certainly unimportant compared with those of another minister, Roger Williams.

Williams was charming, the kind of person nearly everyone liked on first sight. But he was impulsive and easily excited. He was very stubborn about anything he considered a matter of principle, and he was a man of many principles. He was out of place in Massachusetts because he questioned many Puritan beliefs. He did not believe the government should have any power over religious questions, whereas the Puritans thought it should enforce all the Ten Commandments as well as civil law. He even insisted that, despite their charter, the colonists had no right to the land of Massachusetts until either they or the king purchased it from the Indians who lived there.

The oil painting above shows the journey of Thomas Hooker and company from Plymouth to Hartford in 1636.

Banished from Massachusetts, Roger Williams casts a dark look backward as he sets out to found Rhode Island. In what ways is his appearance like that of "The Puritan" on page 57?

Rhode Island Historical Society

By 1635 the members of the General Court had heard enough of Williams' criticisms. They ordered him to leave the Commonwealth. He went off with a few followers and the next year founded the town of Providence, on Narragansett Bay. There he put his theories about religious freedom and fair treatment of the Indians into practice. In 1644 he obtained a charter for the colony to be known as Rhode Island and Providence Plantations.

No sooner were the Puritans rid of Williams than they had to face another attack on their religious beliefs. This one came from Anne Hutchinson. Mrs. Hutchinson was one of the most remarkable of all the early colonists. She was both learned and deeply emotional. She and her husband William arrived in 1634, and soon she became known for her many acts of kindness and for her thorough knowledge of the Bible. She was very strong willed and, if possible, even more strict about matters of principle than Roger Williams. When she disagreed with some of the sermons delivered by her minister, she said so openly. She also began to hold meetings in her home to discuss religious questions. She told the people who attended these meetings that formal religion, church attendance, and prayer were less important than leading a holy life. One could go to Heaven without them.

These ideas horrified the Puritans. In 1637 Anne Hutchinson was brought to trial. Although she was able to defend her ideas brilliantly, she was found by the court to be "a woman not fit for our society." She too was banished, or expelled, from Massachusetts. Later, she and other exiles bought an island from the Narragansett Indians and founded Portsmouth, Rhode Island.

Anne Hutchinson is shown on trial in this 19th-century engraving. What impression does she seem to make on her all-male jury?

Maryland

By this time another English colony had been founded in the region immediately to the north of Virginia. It had a different origin than any of the others, being essentially the property of a single person. The English rulers claimed America as their private possession to do with as they wished. For this reason few people objected when Charles I gave 10 million acres (4 million hectares) of land around Chesapeake Bay to an important English nobleman, George Calvert, Lord Baltimore. The grant gave Calvert enormous power. He could found manors such as had existed in feudal times and hold the residents as serfs. He could act as the prosecutor and judge of anyone accused of breaking the law. He was known as the proprietor, or owner, of the area, and his colony was thus a **proprietary colony.**

Calvert died before the king's seal was attached to the charter making the grant. His son Cecilius Calvert became the first proprietor of the colony, which was called Maryland in honor of Queen Henrietta Maria, the wife of Charles I. The Calverts were Catholics and hoped to make Maryland a Catholic colony.

The first settlers landed in 1634 and founded the town of St.

Collection of the Maryland Historical Society, Baltimore

Mary's. Life was relatively easy for them because Virginia, now prosperous, was nearby. They could get food and other supplies without waiting for ships from distant England. They scarcely searched for gold. Instead they turned promptly to growing tobacco.

Despite the charter Cecilius Calvert soon realized that he could not rule Maryland like a feudal lord. In order to attract settlers, he had to allow people to own land and to have some say in the government. Although he encouraged Catholics to settle in Maryland, a majority of the people who came there were Protestants. The Catholics received large land grants and held most of the important positions in the colony. The Protestants resented this favoritism. To have made the Catholic Church the official church of Maryland might have caused a revolution.

Calvert dealt with this problem shrewdly. He encouraged the local legislature to pass the **Toleration Act** of 1649, which guaranteed freedom of religion to all Christians. On the surface the Catholics were "tolerating" the Protestants. In fact, the Catholic minority was protecting itself. 🖼

"Founding of Maryland" was painted by Emanuel Leutze. What does this scene say about religious life in Maryland? What does it say about relations between the colonists and the local Indians?

Return to the Preview & Review on page 57.

National Gallery of Art, Paul Mellon Collection

George Catlin was one of the greatest painters of the American West. In 1847 he painted the chief of the Taensa Indians receiving Robert La Salle in 1682. What ceremonial trappings of power do the Indians display?

Preview & Review

Use these questions to guide your reading. Answer the questions after completing Section 5.

Understanding Issues, Events, & Ideas. Compare the activities of European colonizers in America other than England, using these words: Quebec, New Netherland, patroon, New Sweden, Viceroy, New Spain.

1. What French claims were made in America at the time of the English claims?
2. What was the success of the early Dutch and Swedish settlements in America?
3. What were the geographic boundaries, east and west, of the Spanish colonies in the New World?

Thinking Critically. Did Peter Minuit pay a fair price to the Indians for Manhattan Island? Support your answer with sound reasoning.

5. EUROPEAN CHALLENGES TO ENGLAND

The French in America

In 1524, not long after John Cabot's voyage in the service of Henry VII of England, the French king, François I, sent an Italian explorer, Giovanni da Verrazano, along the Atlantic Coast from North Carolina to Nova Scotia in search of a northwest passage. Eleven years later Jacques Cartier sailed up the St. Lawrence River as far inland as the present site of Montreal. In 1608, while the English settlers were struggling at Jamestown, Samuel de Champlain founded the first permanent French settlement in America at **Quebec.**

In 1673 Father Jacques Marquette and Louis Joliet explored the upper Mississippi River. Soon after, in 1679, Robert La Salle set sail aboard the first vessel on the Great Lakes. By 1700 French explorers had sailed through the Great Lakes, down the Mississippi River to the Gulf of Mexico, and up the Missouri River to the Rocky Mountains. In addition to what is now Canada, France claimed the entire Mississippi valley, lands also covered by grants of the English king to Virginia. Many wars with England would be fought for control of these overlapping territories.

Dutch and Swedish Colonies

In 1620 the English had founded only two tiny settlements in America—Jamestown and Plymouth. Nevertheless, they claimed all the territory from Newfoundland to Florida. The claim, however, was impossible to enforce. The first to challenge it were the Dutch people of Holland, also called The Netherlands. The Dutch were excellent sailors and master shipbuilders. Like the English they were dependent for their prosperity on foreign trade. The English rightly considered them their greatest rival on the high seas.

The Dutch claimed the region drained by the Hudson River, basing their right to it on the discovery of the river by Henry Hudson in 1609. They called it **New Netherland.** In 1624 Dutch fur traders opened a post at Fort Orange, the site of present-day Albany. Two years later they founded New Amsterdam, on Manhattan Island at the mouth of the Hudson. Peter Minuit, the governor of the colony, bought Manhattan from its Indian inhabitants for some knives, beads, and trinkets. Eventually the island became the center of what is New York City, one of the most valuable pieces of property in the world. It has become fashionable to call Minuit's purchase the greatest real estate bargain of all time.

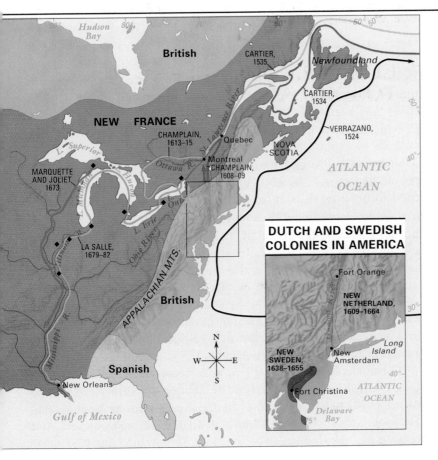

FRENCH EXPLORATIONS AND NON-ENGLISH SETTLEMENTS IN NORTH AMERICA

♦ French forts and trading posts

0   250   500 Mi.

0   250   500 Km.

Azimuthal Equal-Area Projection

LEARNING FROM MAPS. *French explorers traveled farther inland than explorers from other nations. What route did they follow? Why did this make it easier for them to explore inland areas?*

In 1629 Kiliaen Van Rensselaer, a jeweler from Amsterdam who owned stock in the Dutch West India Company, persuaded the company to issue a "Charter of Freedom and Exemptions" to encourage American settlement. A **patroon** was a landholder with powers like those of a feudal lord of the manor. Anyone who brought 50 new settlers to New Netherland was to receive a great estate in the Hudson River Valley and the powers to rule it. Rensselaer's patroonship, Rensselaerwyck, was the most successful one under the charter. Not many people came to New Netherland. The Dutch West India Company ruled it with an iron hand. The colonists had no voice at all in running the colony.

Two directors of the Dutch West India Company, Peter Minuit and Samuel Blommaert, were also involved in a New Sweden Company that founded **New Sweden** on the Delaware River near what is now the city of Wilmington. The Swedes built the first log cabins in America. These homes, so easy to build in a land covered with forests, were much copied.

The Swedes traded for furs with the Indians, but they did not prosper. When a Dutch force captured their settlement, Fort Christina, in 1655, New Sweden ceased to exist. The colonists, only about a hundred in all, were allowed to remain, and the region became a part of New Netherland.

The history of New Netherland was brief. The English saw the Dutch as intruders on English soil. Worse, Dutch merchants based in New Amsterdam were buying Virginia tobacco and selling it in Holland, much to the annoyance of English tobacco merchants. And the Dutch colony's excellent harbor at the mouth of the Hudson River was a tempting target.

In 1664 King Charles II sent four English warships carrying 400 soldiers to capture New Amsterdam. The town had only 1,500 inhabitants. The Dutch authorities had been too heavy-handed. The people had no will to fight. When their governor, Peter Stuyvesant, tried to organize a defense, they pushed him aside and turned the town over to the English without firing a shot.

Spanish Settlements

Spain was well established in the New World when the English colonists arrived. In 1565 the Spaniards had built at St. Augustine, Florida, a fort that became the first permanent European settlement in America. Over the next few years Spain built missions and *presidios,* or forts, as far up the Atlantic Coast as South Carolina.

Spanish influence also spread into the northern part of what was then Mexico. In 1598 Don Juan de Oñate, son of a wealthy mine owner in Mexico, set out to settle the area known as New Mexico. He took with him many soldiers and Catholic missionaries. After conquering the Indians who lived in the Acoma pueblo, Oñate

The Granger Collection, New York

Peter Stuyvesant appears smug and self-satisfied in this 19th-century engraving. Surely his appearance changed after he lost New Amsterdam to the English.

Daughters of the Republic of Texas Library

claimed New Mexico for Spain. In 1609 Sante Fe became the permanent capital of the area.

The Spanish influence spread slowly westward. In 1602 Sebastián Viscaíno explored the California coast. By 1700 many Spanish ranchers were living in southern California. Beginning in 1769 Gaspar de Portolá and Father Junípero Serra built a chain of missions and presidios up the Pacific Coast as far north as San Francisco.

Many Spanish colonists claimed large grants of land called *encomiendas*. To work the land, Spanish landowners claimed those Indians who lived on it. At best these Indians received meager wages. At worst they became slaves.

Roman Catholic priests and missionaries came to the colonies in large numbers. They built churches and cathedrals and set up the missions around which they gathered the local Indians. There the priests tried to teach the Indians Christianity, as well as agriculture, carpentry, masonry, and other skills. Some missionaries, most notably Friar Bartolomé de Las Casas, fought for freedom and justice for the Indians.

As with the English colonies, all power to govern the Spanish colonies was held by the king. His two representatives, or **viceroys,** ruled in his name. The viceroy for **New Spain**—Central America, the Caribbean, and Spanish North America—lived in Mexico City. The viceroy in Lima, Peru, ruled the Spanish colonies in South America. Lesser officials enforced the laws. This system often worked quite well, but, as we have seen, when Spain's Golden Age faded, its vast empire was weakened. Its influence lasts to this day, however, in the names given many western cities. And Spanish is the second most commonly spoken language in the United States. 🖰

Theodore Gentilz painted these Mexican couples dancing the fandango. The men hold candles aloft in their right hands. One enthusiast is firing his pistol into the ceiling.

The Granger Collection, New York

Bartolomé de Las Casas arrived in America in 1502. He became the first Catholic priest ordained in America. He fought enslavement of the Indians and worked to help them.

Return to the Preview & Review on page 62.

European Challenges to England 65

Use these questions to guide your reading. Answer the questions after completing Section 6.
Understanding Issues, Events, & Ideas. Use the following words in a description of the other colonies: Quakers, trustee.

1. Where did the proprietors of Carolina hope to find settlers?
2. How did the proprietors intend to run Carolina? Why did their plan fail?
3. Why did William Penn found a colony in America? Why was it unusual for someone like Penn to be granted a charter?
4. Why did many Europeans come to Pennsylvania?
5. Why was Georgia founded?

Thinking Critically. 1. Of the colonies described in this section, which would you have most liked to live in? Why? Which would you have least liked to live in? **2.** You know that New York was named for the Duke of York and Jamestown for King James I. If you could name a colony in honor of someone, who would it be and why? What name would you give the colony?

6. LATER COLONIAL SETTLEMENTS

The Carolinas

In 1663 Charles II gave the land between Virginia and Spanish Florida to eight noblemen, among them Sir George Carteret, who was probably the richest person in England, and Sir Anthony Ashley Cooper. The grateful proprietors named the region Carolina in honor of Charles I, whose name in Latin was *Carolus*. The Carolina proprietors hoped to attract settlers from the older colonies in order to avoid the expense of financing expeditions from England.

A number of Virginians did drift into the northernmost part of the grant, but settlement there was scattered and isolated. There were few roads and practically no villages, churches, or schools. Most of the colonizers became small farmers who grew food crops and a little tobacco.

When it became clear that settlers from the older colonies were not moving to the Carolinas in any number, Sir Anthony Ashley Cooper brought in people from the island of Barbados in the West Indies. In 1670 Charleston (originally Charles Town) was founded. Charleston soon became a busy trading center, as well as the social and political center of Carolina.

The proprietors of Carolina had broad political authority—on paper. They dreamed of creating a land of great estates where lords with feudal titles reigned over lowly tenants. Two fifths of the land was to be owned by the noble class.

The system was "almost unbelievably ill-suited to the American scene," as a modern historian has written. Most of the intended tenants quickly obtained land of their own. In 1719 the settlers rebelled against the proprietary government and asked the king to take over the colony. Ten years later the area was separated into North Carolina and South Carolina, each under a royal governor.

New York and New Jersey

When New Netherland was taken over by the English in 1664, the name of the colony was changed to New York in honor of the Duke of York, its new proprietor. The duke had control of the entire region between Connecticut and Delaware. He immediately began to hand out generous chunks of it to his friends. The largest prize was New Jersey, which included everything between the Hudson and Delaware Rivers. He gave this region to Sir George Carteret and another of the Carolina proprietors, John, Lord Berkeley.

To attract colonists, Carteret and Berkeley offered land on easy terms. They also promised settlers religious freedom and the right to elect a legislature. In 1674 Berkeley sold his half interest to two Quakers. **Quakers** were one of the Separatist groups. They were religious radicals. They believed that everyone could communicate directly with God. For this reason they did not depend upon ministers, church services, or even the Bible. They stressed religious tolerance, "brotherly love," and simplicity. They were opposed to warfare and any use of force.

Another group of Quakers bought the rest of New Jersey in 1681 from the heirs of George Carteret. In 1702 the two sections were reunited as one colony.

Pennsylvania and Delaware

Another large colonial grant was awarded to a very unlikely candidate, William Penn. Penn was a person of great wealth and high social status, the son of a much-decorated English admiral. While at Oxford University, he became a Quaker.

Because of their radical, anti-establishment beliefs, Quakers, both at home and in America, were often imprisoned, tortured, or even hanged. Penn himself spent some time in jail. To protect other Quakers from such persecution, Penn hoped to create a refuge in

Benjamin West, the most highly regarded artist of his day, went to Europe on the eve of the Revolution and never returned to America. He painted "Penn's Treaty with the Indians" around 1770. Do you think this painting gives an accurate picture of the meeting between Penn and the Indians? Explain.

The Pennsylvania Academy of the Fine Arts

William Penn's biographer tells of Penn's respect for American Indians.

> **"From what Penn had read or heard or seen of Indians, he had formed a highly favorable opinion of them. They were quiet folk, much like typical Quakers, serious, reserved, and taciturn, qualities Penn admired. . . ."**
> Harry Emerson Wildes

LEARNING FROM TABLES. *This table shows how the colonies are often grouped. Although there were no formal ties between the colonies in each group, geographical and cultural factors drew them together. What were the two most common reasons for founding colonies?*

America. Charles II was agreeable. He owed a large sum of money to Penn's father, who had died in 1670. To cancel this debt, in 1681 he gave William the region between New York and Maryland, suggesting that it be called Pennsylvania in honor of Penn's father.

William Penn was strongly religious and held to high ideals. He also had a solid understanding of the value of money and how to make it. Pennsylvania was to be "a holy experiment" in Christian living and self-government. Penn personally came to Pennsylvania to oversee the laying-out of Philadelphia, his city of "brotherly love." Like Roger Williams, he insisted that the Delaware Indians be paid for their land and treated fairly by the settlers.

Penn was shrewd in business. To attract settlers he wrote glowing accounts of Pennsylvania's soil and climate and circulated them throughout Europe. These, along with his promises of a voice in the government and religious liberty, lured settlers from many lands. Among these were large numbers of Germans, who were popularly known as the Pennsylvania Dutch. "Dutch" was the way English settlers pronounced the word *Deutsch,* which means German.

Pennsylvania prospered from the start. Farmers produced large crops of wheat and other foodstuffs. To obtain a port to export their surplus, Penn in 1682 obtained a grant of land on Delaware Bay. This region, known as Delaware, became a separate colony in 1704.

Georgia

The last of the English colonies in America, Georgia, was not settled until 1733. It was founded by a group of well-to-do, charitable En-

Colony	Founded	Reason for Founding
FOUNDING OF THE THIRTEEN COLONIES		
New England Colonies		
Massachusetts	1620	Religious freedom
New Hampshire	1622	Profit from trade and fishing; religious freedom
Connecticut	1636	Religious and political freedom; expand trade
Rhode Island	1636	Religious freedom
Middle Colonies		
New York (New Netherland)	1624	Expand trade (Dutch)
Delaware (New Sweden)	1638	Expand trade (Swedish)
New Jersey	1664	Investment by founders; religious and political freedom
Pennsylvania	1682	Investment by founders; religious and political freedom
Southern Colonies		
Virginia	1607	Expand trade and agriculture
Maryland	1632	Investment by founders; religious and political freedom
North Carolina	1663	Profit from trade and agriculture; religious freedom
South Carolina	1663	Profit from trade and agriculture; religious freedom
Georgia	1732	Investment; haven for debtors; buffer against Spanish

The Henry Francis du Pont Winterthur Museum

This formal portrait of the trustees of Georgia was probably painted in the 18th century. How were the motives of these trustees somewhat different than those of the founders of other colonies?

glishmen who hoped to provide a new start for English people who had been imprisoned for debt. Their leader was James Oglethorpe, a man deeply committed to helping victims of political, economic, and religious oppression.

Armed with a charter granting him and his associates the authority to manage Georgia as **trustees** for 21 years, Oglethorpe came to America in 1733 with about a hundred settlers. They founded the town of Savannah. Each settler was given 50 acres (20 hectares) of land, tools to work it with, and enough supplies for the first year. Oglethorpe was stubborn and very straitlaced. He tried to make the settlers grow things like olive trees and silkworms that would not flourish in Georgia. He demanded that no lawyers be allowed in the colony, insisting that all lawyers were born troublemakers. He attempted to ban liquor.

Georgia was an out-of-the-way colony. A hostile Spanish settlement in Florida on its southern border kept it from growing very fast. Few people lived there. The people who did come to Georgia resented the strict rules. They made it impossible to keep out liquor, or even lawyers. In 1752, a year before their charter was due to run out, the discouraged trustees turned the colony over to the king.

Return to the Preview & Review on page 66.

CHAPTER 2 REVIEW

Spain's Golden Age	

1500   **1550**   **1600**

1497
Cabot
explores
America

1585
Roanoke
founded

1607
Jamest
founde

1588
Spanish
Armada
defeated

1608
Quebe
settled
French

Chapter Summary
Read the statements below. Choose one, and write a paragraph explaining its importance.
1. Defeat of the Spanish Armada by the English led to Spain's decline and England's rise.
2. The first English settlements in America suffered severe setbacks.
3. People came to America to trade and sell, to practice their religion, and to find work.
4. Joint-stock companies invested in colonies such as Virginia.
5. John Smith's leadership and the popularity of tobacco saved Virginia.
6. The Pilgrims who settled Massachusetts came to America to escape religious persecution.
7. The Mayflower Compact represents the first attempt to create a government where none existed before.
8. The Puritans settled New England, where several religious conflicts eventually arose.
9. The French, Dutch, Swedes, and Spanish also established colonies in America.
10. The Middle Colonies and Georgia were established under royal grants and charters.

Reviewing Chronological Order
Number your paper 1-5. Then study the time line above and place the following events in the order in which they happened by writing the first next to 1, the second next to 2, and so on.
1. Jamestown founded
2. First Thanksgiving
3. Cabot explores America
4. Spanish Armada defeated
5. Penn granted Pennsylvania

Understanding Main Ideas
1. For what various reasons did the English want to establish colonies in America?
2. How did forming joint-stock companies help the English explore and colonize America?
3. Why are the Mayflower Compact and the Fundamental Orders important documents in American history?

4. By 1700, what French claims had been made in America? What Dutch claims? What Swedish claims? What was the extent of Spanish settlement in America?
5. How were colonists attracted to New Jersey? To Pennsylvania? To Georgia?

Thinking Critically
1. **Interpreting.** The English saw Sir Francis Drake as a hero; the Spanish saw him as a villain. In your opinion, which view was more accurate? Cite facts to support your point of view.
2. **Synthesizing.** Imagine that you are one of the colonists of Jamestown, Virginia—either a jeweler or an indentured servant. What is your attitude toward Captain John Smith as leader of your colony? Use information from this book, combined with historical imagination, to support your view of Smith.
3. **Evaluating.** How did Roger Williams, Anne Hutchinson, and William Penn differ from other colonists in their dealings with American Indians? Do you think their methods were more ethical or less ethical than those of the Jamestown colonists? Why?

Writing About History
Read about the Lost Colony of Roanoke in an encyclopedia or reference book. Then use your historical imagination to create a diary with at least ten entries that one of the settlers might have kept hidden in a tree.

Practicing the Strategy
Review the strategy on page 46.
Using Latitude and Longitude. Look at the map on page 29 and answer the following questions.
1. How many degrees are there between the parallels of latitude? Between meridians?
2. Which continent lies between approximately 40S° and 80W°?

70   **ENGLISH COLONIES IN AMERICA**

1634 Maryland settled	**1663** The Carolinas established	**1681** Penn granted Pennsylvania	**1704** Delaware becomes a separate colony	**1732** Georgia established
ower pact	**1635** Connecticut settled	**1664** England takes over New Netherland		
Thanksgiving **1636** Rhode Island settled				
achusetts founded				

3. What are the approximate coordinates of Plymouth? of Jamestown?

4. Approximately what is the latitude and longitude of Florida?

Using Primary Sources

In 1621 Edward Winslow, one of the Pilgrim settlers in Plymouth, wrote the first account of the settlement's beginnings, including this of the first Thanksgiving. Note that rather than blood-thirsty savages, Winslow describes a peaceful civilized people. To better understand life in these early colonies, read the excerpt from Winslow's *Relation or Journall, etc.* in Alexander Young's *Chronicles of the Pilgrim Fathers* and answer the questions that follow it.

Many of the Indians came to visit us, including their greatest king, Massasoit, who brought about 90 of his followers. We entertained and feasted them for three days. The Indians went out and killed five deer, which they presented to our governor. Although food is not always this plentiful, yet by the goodness of God we are so far from want that we often wish you were here to share our plenty.

We have found the Indians very faithful in their pact of peace with us, very kind, and ready to please us. We often go to them, and they come to visit us. Some of us have traveled 50 miles inland with them. We walk as peaceably and safely in the woods as on the roads of England. We entertain the Indians in our homes, and they give their deer meat to us.

1. Why do you think the Indian king presented the deer to the colonial governor?

2. How did the Indians demonstrate their commitment to peace with the colonists?

3. How do you think Winslow's account of colonial life may have influenced people in England? Support your answer with two specific examples from the excerpt.

Linking History & Geography

In the first two chapters you have read about trade routes and routes of exploration. Routes are paths by which people, goods, and culture travel from place to place. Routes usually develop where people can travel easiest and least expensively. Use the map of French Explorers in America on page 63 to answer the following questions.

1. By what route did the French explorers travel from Quebec to New Orleans?

2. European settlers often found natural waterways made the best routes. Why would lakes, rivers, and streams provide good routes?

3. What do you notice about the geographic location of all the French settlements, forts, and trading posts?

Enriching Your Study of History

1. Individual Project. The first Jamestown settlers had the wrong trades and skills needed for survival. Some were goldsmiths and jewelers. Use historical imagination to make a list of five occupations that would have made Jamestown stronger. Explain the reasons for each choice. Make a similar list for a group today going to an unexplored area. Are your lists similar? Why or why not?

2. Cooperative Project. In small groups, gather information on all the colonies and settlements in America described in Chapters 1 and 2. List the name of the colony, its date of founding, and other important information. Then pool your information with that of the other groups to create a large chart of all the colonies and settlements. Then work together to make a large map of North America that shows the Spanish, English, Dutch, and Swedish colonies, and the French settlements.

Chapter 2 Review 71

Life in Colonial America

The English colonies in North America were separate communities scattered along the Atlantic Coast from New England to Georgia. Few people in the Carolinas ever saw or spoke with a person from Massachusetts or New York or Pennsylvania. People did not often use the word "American" to describe themselves or their country. Most thought of themselves as English or Dutch or French—whatever their homeland was. Yet they and their children soon became more American than European, for they were changed by the land. Alas for others, the Africans first brought to America in 1619, there was slavery. What hope had the African American children born thereafter?

Preview & Review

Use these questions to guide your reading. Answer the questions after completing Section 1.
Understanding Issues, Events, & Ideas. Explain the influences of land and rivers on American settlers, using the following words: town common, public school, democracy, political equality, seaport.

1. How did the great amount of land in America influence the size of the family?
2. How did rivers shape life in the South? Why were seaports essential in the North?
3. What was the attitude toward women in colonial America?
4. In what ways were rural people self-sufficient?

Thinking Critically. 1. Why did most colonists believe that people who owned a country should have a say in running it? **2.** Suppose that you are a colonial person who does not own property. Make an argument for your right to vote. anyway.

1. AN AMERICAN CIVILIZATION

Land and People

In the beginning America was a very large country with a very small population. There was much work to be done and few people to do it. This situation had enormous effects on the colonists. For one thing it tended to make them more flexible. To succeed, one needed to be

New York State Historical Assn., Cooperstown

open-minded. Historical imagination can help us to see why this attitude was important. Everything was so different in America. Those who were willing to experiment, to try new ways of doing things, usually did better than those who insisted on following traditional paths. For the same reason, Americans had to be jacks-of-all-trades. Farming in the wilderness meant being one's own carpenter, tailor, butcher, even one's own doctor.

With so much land to farm and with the woods and streams full of game and fish, there was always plenty to eat. Children grew big and strong. Sons and daughters were usually taller than their parents. The grandchildren grew taller still. Because there was so much work to be done, another child was an asset, not merely another mouth to feed. A six-year-old could tend the chickens, a ten-year-old weed vegetables or milk cows. Large families were the rule. There was plenty of land. When they were grown, the children could have farms of their own.

Children were well treated and given much love by most American parents. Europeans claimed that American children were spoiled. Compared to how children were treated in Europe, this may have been so, but by modern standards it was far from true. American youngsters worked hard, and family discipline was quite strict.

Rivers Shape Life

In a country without roads the first colonists relied on rivers to get themselves and their goods from place to place. In Virginia, rivers like the James and the Potomac were broad, deep, and slow moving. Oceangoing vessels could sail up them for many miles. The ships brought the products of Europe to inland tobacco farmers and took away barrels of cured tobacco for sale in England. For this reason the population of Virginia was scattered thinly over the land. Farms

Point of View

Young Martha Dandridge of Virginia became a skillful rider. She once rode her horse Fatima up the stairs at her Uncle William's house. Her father called her by a pet name when he defended her.

"Let Patsy alone! She's not harmed William's staircase. And, by heavens, how she can ride."
   John Dandridge, c. 1745

For many years this painting of the Van Bergen farm in the Hudson Valley around 1735 hung over the fireplace mantle, so proud were those who lived on the prosperous farm. Where in the painting can you find the owner and his family?

Metropolitan Museum of Art

"The Plantation" was painted in about 1825. It reminds us of another great Virginia plantation, Mount Vernon. All roads run to the river's edge for easy shipping. How is this both a picture and a kind of map?

spread along the riverbanks. Land between the rivers lay untouched for many years. There were few towns because buying and selling could take place at each farmer's riverside dock.

In New England the rivers were shallow and full of rapids. Ships could not sail up them. Seaports were essential from the beginning. Boston, New Haven, Newport, and other coastal towns became quite large early in their histories. Inland transportation had to be by road.

Building roads was an expensive business. Settlers remained close together so that few had to be built. The New England village made its appearance. Around a small, parklike town square—the **town common**—the villagers built their church, meeting house, and school. Each family received a small plot of land for a house and a garden around this town common. Outside the village lay the fields where crops were grown. Workers went out each morning, tilled their strips of land, and returned at day's end to their snug homes.

Thus, people in New England were community minded. In Virginia and other southern colonies people were more family centered. There were more schools in New England, not only because Puritans believed that education was very important, but also because enough families lived within walking distance of the schools to support them. In 1647 Massachusetts began the first organized educational system in the colonies, requiring all towns with 100 families to set up the first **public schools.**

Colonists in the Middle and Southern Colonies also saw the value of an education. In the Middle Colonies churches and families started private schools. These schools charged fees so only children of wealthy colonists could attend. Wealthy southerners were more apt to educate their children at home with tutors, or private teachers. These children received an excellent education, but most other southern children received almost none. Southern education soon lagged far behind that of other sections, a condition that continued until after the Civil War. Also, perhaps because their lives were more isolated, southerners tended to welcome strangers with a special warmth. This was one origin of **southern hospitality.**

Women in Colonial America

Most of the first settlers were young men. Once a colony was established, however, it was important to these men and to the merchant adventurers or colonial proprietors that more women be recruited. The London Company shipped whole boatloads of unmarried women to Virginia. When the women married, their husbands would pay the cost of their passage. Women often came to America as indentured servants and frequently ended up marrying their masters. Colonists tended to take a practical rather than a romantic view of marriage.

Yet people familiar with European attitudes almost always noticed that American men were more respectful of women and more considerate of their wives than European men were. In America women were needed as workers and mothers—and companions too.

Essex Institute, Salem, Massachusetts

This oil painting shows "Abigail Gerrish and Her Grandmother" in about 1750. It was painted by John Greenwood, who with a handful of other New England painters broke with English traditions to create art that was truly American. Like Abigail, when colonial children were dressed up they appeared as miniature adults. How were most colonial children treated?

Metropolitan Museum of Art

Keturah Rawlins of Boston made this needlepoint around 1749. What are some other crafts made by colonial Americans?

Compared to their status today, women had few rights in colonial times. They were kept by law and custom under the thumb of men. Married women could not own property. If they earned any money, it belonged legally to their husbands. Almost none had the right to vote. Divorce was next to impossible. Needless to say, wives also worked very hard. In addition to keeping house, rearing children, and performing hundreds of farm chores, the typical colonial woman had to devote much time to teaching her children, to making clothing for the whole family, and to caring for anyone who was sick. If men were jacks-of-all-trades, women were surely jills-of-all-trades. The advantages of having many children in America were not weighed against the health of the mothers of these children. Constant childbearing caused many women to die at an early age.

Yet, when all these things have been said, it remains true that America offered women more opportunities than was common in Europe. Women learned to handle guns and to defend themselves against attack. Some women ran large farms and plantations because "the man of the house" was away or had died. Martha Dandridge Custis, still in her twenties when her husband died, became one of the wealthiest women in America. Women in America are known to have run newspapers, served as lawyers in colonial courts, and done other things that would have been almost impossible for women in Europe.

Washington and Lee University

Martha Dandridge Custis was one of the richest women in America. This detail is from an oil portrait painted by John Wollaston. In 1757 Mrs. Custis' husband died and she became the owner of the Custis lands in Virginia. She is the same "Patsy" Dandridge who rode her horse up her uncle's staircase. When she next appears in our story, she will be married to the commander in chief of the American army in the Revolutionary War.

Land and Labor

In Europe landowners were the kingpins of society. Membership in the nobility meant control of large territories and the people who lived in them. For lesser people, owning land brought prestige as well as whatever profit could be made from it. Except for highly skilled artisans, laborers in Europe tended to be poor.

In America there was so much unused land that without labor land was worth almost nothing. With labor it could be used productively. This meant that working people earned more than European workers and were better treated by their employers. In 1698 Gabriel Thomas, an English visitor, wrote of the value of labor and the abundance he saw in America:

❝ What . . . serves Man for Drink, Food and Rayment [clothes], is cheaper here than in *England*, or elsewhere; but the chief reason why Wages of Servants of all sorts are higher here than there, arises from the great Fertility and Produce of the Place; besides, if these large Stipends [payments] were refused them, they would quickly set up for themselves, for they can have Provision very cheap, and Land for a very small matter, or next to nothing in comparison of the Purchase of Lands in *England;* and the farmers there can better afford to give that great Wages than the farmers in England can, for several reasons very obvious.

At First, their Land costs them (as I said but just now) little or nothing in comparison, of which the Farmers commonly will get twice the encrease of [as much] Corn for every Bushel they sow, that the Farmers in *England* can from the richest Land they have.

In the Second place, they have constantly good price for their Corn, by reason of the great and quick vent [market] into the *Barbados* and other Islands; through which means Silver is become more plentiful there than here in *England*, considering the Number of People, and that causes a quick Trade for both Corn and Cattle; . . .

Thirdly, They pay no *Tithes*, and their Taxes are inconsiderable; the Place is free for all Persuasions [religions], in a Sober and Civil way, for the Church of *England* and the *Quakers* bear equal Share in the Government. They live Friendly and Well together; there is no Persecution for Religion, nor ever like to be; 'tis this that knocks all Commerce on the Head [in England], together with the high Imposts [duties], strict Laws, and cramping Orders. Before I end this paragraph, I shall add another Reason why Womens Wages are so exorbitant; they [women] are not yet very numerous, which makes them stand upon high terms for their several services, in *Sempstering* [seamstressing], *Washing, Spinning, Knitting, Sewing,* and in all other parts of their Imployments. . . .

Reader, what I have written, is not *Fiction, Flam, Whim,* or any sinister *Design,* either to impose upon the Ignorant, or Credulous [those tending to believe too easily], or to curry favour with the Rich and Mighty, but in meer pity and pure Compassion to the Numbers of Poor Labouring Men, Women, and Children in *England,* half starv'd, visible in their meagre looks, that are continually wandering up and down looking for Employment without Encouragement or reward for their Work. . . . Here there are no Beggars to be seen (it is a Shame and Disgrace to the state that there are so many in *England*) nor indeed have any here the least Occasion or Temptation to take up that Scandalous Lazy Life. . . .

What I have deliver'd about this *Province,* is indisputably true, I was an Eye-Witness to it all, for I went in the first Ship that was bound for England for that Countrey, since it received the Name of *Pennsylvania,* which was in the Year 1681.[1]

[1]From *An Historical and Geographical Account of the Province and Country of Pennsylvania* by Gabriel Thomas

An American Civilization   77

STRATEGIES FOR SUCCESS

READING GRAPHS

The successful student is able to gather information from a variety of sources, including graphs. *The Story of America* contains many graphs. Graphs present information visually. There are several types of graphs, each used to present a certain type of data. A *pie*, or *circle*, graph is used to show proportions. A *line* graph shows changes in two factors. It most often shows changes over time. A *bar* graph shows comparisons, making highs and lows stand out. A *picture* graph, or *pictograph*, uses pictures to illustrate amounts.

Because graphs can contain so much information and are so common in histories, it is important to know how to read them.

How to Read a Graph

Follow these steps to read a graph.

1. **Read the title.** The title will tell you the subject and purpose of the graph. It may also contain other information, such as dates.
2. **Study the labels.** Line and bar graphs show two sets of data, one set displayed on the horizontal axis and the other on the vertical axis. The *horizontal* axis is the line at the bottom of the graph that runs across the page. The *vertical* axis is at the left side of the graph and runs up and down. Labels on these axes identify the type of data and the unit of measurement, when appropriate.
3. **Analyze the data.** Note all trends, relationships, and changes among the data. Note increases and decreases in quantities.
4. **Put the data to use.** Use the information to form generalizations and hypotheses and to draw conclusions.

Applying the Strategy

You may have heard the expression, "A picture is worth a thousand words." The picture graph may also be worth a thousand words. Study the picture graph below. Note that small figures are used to make a simple comparison of the population of the American colonies in 1730. Each symbol stands for 10,000 persons. A partial figure represents a fraction of 10,000. For example, the population of Delaware in 1730 was 9,170 persons, so it is represented by part of a figure. What is the population of Virginia? New York? If you said 114,000 for Virginia and 48,000 for New York, you have read the graph correctly!

There also are examples of other types of graphs in this unit. The pie graph on page 89 shows the ethnic makeup of the colonial population. (For an example of a line graph, turn to page 139 in the next chapter.)

For independent practice, see Practicing the Strategy on page 107.

COLONIAL POPULATIONS, 1730*		
New Hampshire	Maryland	
Massachusetts	Virginia	
Connecticut	North Carolina	
Rhode Island	South Carolina	
New York	= 10,000 persons	
New Jersey	= 8,000 persons	
Pennsylvania	= 6,000 persons	
Delaware	= 4,000 persons	
	= 2,000 persons	*Georgia not yet founded

Source: *Historical Statistics of the United States*

High wages and cheap land meant that most Americans owned land. In Massachusetts and the other New England colonies the legislatures gave large tracts of land to groups of settlers who wanted to found new towns. The people then cleared as much of this land as they could farm and divided it up among the families. The rest, the commons, remained town property. As the town grew, newcomers were given some of the common land so that they could have farms of their own.

In other colonies people got land in many ways. Those with headrights received it for nothing. Others bought land or got large grants from the king or from colonial authorities. Indentured servants could get money to buy land by working for wages after their terms of service were completed. Those who were impatient and willing to live under crude and dangerous conditions moved west to the edge of the settled area. This region, vaguely defined and shifting always westward, was called the **frontier.** On the frontier a person could clear a tract of wild land, build a cabin, and plant a crop. Such people were called **squatters.** By the time settlement had expanded to their region, most squatters had made enough money to buy their property. If not, they usually sold their "improvements" to a newcomer and moved farther west to repeat the process.

Land and the Right to Vote

The fact that most Americans owned land affected in unexpected ways how the colonies were governed. Today we believe that all adult citizens should have the right to vote. One does not have to be rich or own property to participate in elections. This principle is known as **political equality,** a basic element of what we call **democracy.**

During the colonial era people did not believe in democracy as we now know it. For example, women were not allowed to vote. In addition, only men who owned a certain amount of land or had some other substantial wealth were considered qualified to vote.

There was almost no difference between the attitudes of the English and the Americans on this point. Most colonists believed that the people who *owned* a country should have a say in running it, not those who merely *lived* in a country. Yet, since a majority of the colonists owned land, having to meet a "property qualification" to vote did not disqualify many.

Thus, while the colonists did not believe in the idea of democracy, in practice their governments were quite democratic. In most of the colonies about as large a percentage of the adult men voted in elections as does today. With time, people became accustomed to voting. Since the property requirement had so little practical effect, it ceased to seem important. Gradually, the *idea* of democracy began to catch up with what was actually happening.

Yale University Art Gallery, Mable Brady Garvan Collection

"Burning Fallen Trees in a Girdled Clearing, Western Scene" is the title of this fine engraving by W. J. Bennett. The girdle is the band cut in the tree in the foreground. It was a way of killing trees learned from the Indians by the first settlers of Jamestown. What name was given settlers who cleared wild land and planted crops on it?

An American Civilization   79

In the early days settlers could remember England, where a handful of great landowners completely dominated elections. These settlers considered voting a privilege that they had gained by coming to America. Their grandsons, who grew up in a society where nearly every man voted, began to see voting as a natural right, not a privilege. This was one of the most important results of the ease of obtaining land in America.

Rural and Town Life in America

Both the northern colonies and the southern were mostly rural. In 1690 Boston was the largest town in North America, but it had a population of only about 7,000. A very large proportion of the colonists were farmers.

Despite the importance of trade and the foreign manufactured goods that trade made available, most farm families made many of the things they needed right in their own homes. They spun wool sheared from their sheep into thread. They wove the thread into cloth from which they made their coats and dresses and shirts and trousers. They used the skins of deer for "buckskin" leggings and moccasins. They carved buttons out of bone and made plates and spoons of wood. They built most of their own furniture, oftentimes using homemade tools. Instead of nails, they fastened things together with wooden pegs. All this was especially true of families on the frontier and those living in districts far removed from rivers and roads. These people had to be almost entirely self-sufficient.

The towns were centers of activity, really the hearts and minds of the colonies. In even the smallest villages there were group activities like discussion clubs and sewing circles that people enjoyed.

The largest towns, in addition to Boston, were New York, Philadelphia, Charleston, and Newport. All were **seaports,** their economy based upon sea trade and shipbuilding. Though small by modern standards, all were bustling, vital communities. Their harbors were forests of ships' masts and spars. Their docks were piled high with barrels, boxes, crates, chests, and bales of every sort. On the dockside streets one could hear many languages spoken. "We are a people thrown together from various quarters of the world," one proud citizen of Philadelphia explained.

In the shops and warehouses of the towns could be found fine English cloth and chinaware, tea from India, wine from Portugal and the Madeira islands, molasses from the sugar islands, as well as products from all the mainland colonies. Their taverns were crowded with sailors and dockworkers and artisans of all sorts. Every colonial town of any size had a weekly newspaper. Some had theaters too. The wealthy merchants built fine houses in the towns and filled them with good furnishings, some made by colonial cabinetmakers, silversmiths, and other artisans. 　🔲

National Gallery of Art

Mrs. Samuel Chandler, shown in an oil painted by Winthrop Chandler around 1780, was married to a merchant wealthy enough to supply her fine clothes from abroad. How does this painting show that Mrs. Chandler was wealthy?

Return to the Preview & Review on page 72.

America's West African Heritage

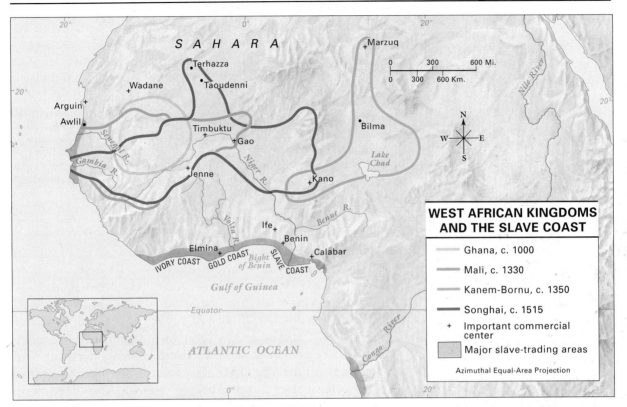

WEST AFRICAN KINGDOMS
AND THE SLAVE COAST

- Ghana, c. 1000
- Mali, c. 1330
- Kanem-Bornu, c. 1350
- Songhai, c. 1515
- + Important commercial center
- Major slave-trading areas

Azimuthal Equal-Area Projection

For more than a thousand years great civilizations rose and fell in West Africa south of the Sahara. Why these kingdoms came to be—the will of a powerful ruler, a favorable place to trade—and why so little of their grand architecture remains—is as much a mystery to us as why Egypt and Rome declined and fell, or, closer to home, what fate befell the Mayan civilization.

Our African heritage is not that of a "dark continent" but rather that of the place where civilizations developed and culture advanced. Consider Egypt, one of the world's greatest civilizations. Consider Ghana, Mali, and Songhai, in the Western Sudan. Each of these kingdoms had an elaborate court life with artisans organized into guilds before Europe's Renaissance.

Other West African kingdoms—Asante, Dahomey, the Yoruba, and Benin—flourished in the forest lands farther south toward the West African Coast. Trade was important to their economies, and travelers to Africa wrote descriptions of the regal courts, especially in Benin, where magnificent bronzes were cast. Only with the permission of the king could artisans cast brass.

In eastern Africa later kingdoms—Zimbabwe and Mwanamutapa—grew powerful. Recent research shows that slaves preserved many aspects of their culture. However, because slaves were forbidden to speak their own tongues and produce their own art, much of our African heritage was lost. But their voices still speak to us of Africa's past in the art we look at here.

West Africa was the site of several great trading kingdoms. For centuries they traded mostly with Arab merchants who traveled in camel caravans. When Europeans began to explore the coast in the early 1500s, many turned to coastal trade. They soon discovered that captured Africans, sold as slaves, were a valuable commodity.

The Brooklyn Museum

A hornblower from Benin summons us to our study of Western African culture. This figure was cast in brass in the 17th century.

81

Below is the figure of a king of the Asante culture in Ghana. He was carved from wood in the 19th century and wields the symbol of his authority.

Metropolitan Museum of Art

Royalty's pride is evident in this bronze altarpiece displayed in Benin City in Nigeria. To this day the king from this region of Nigeria wears a cap and choker similar to that in this 16th-century work.

Metropolitan Museum of Art

Again from the 19th century, this beaded stool, surely fit for a ruler, comes from the Cameroons. It may have been fashioned by workers from Benin or Yoruba.

These gold ornaments are possibly Asante from the Ivory Coast. They were fashioned in the 19th century. The artisan may have carried on this fine work without knowing that his comrades were captives bound for America in slave ships.

Metropolitan Museum of Art

Asante kings drank their palm wine from this 19th-century calabash vessel decorated with gold.

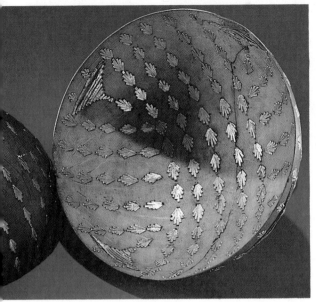

© Lee Boltin

Egypt produced this 12th-dynasty head of a sphinx made of polished stone in about 1900 B.C.

The Brooklyn Museum

Metropolitan Museum of Art

Metropolitan Museum of Art

This carved wood antelope head shows the bold use of line and pattern that influenced European and American artists in the 20th century. It would have been attached to a cap made of basketry for ceremonies commemorating tyi wara, who taught humans the secret of agriculture. The head comes from the Bambara culture of Mali.

An ivory spoon in the figure of a man was made in Sierra Leone (in the style of Portuguese explorers) in the 16th century.

America's West African Heritage   83

Photo by Don Renner, Courtesy of Folklorica

This woman's wrapper woven from costly threads was made by the Asante people of Ghana in the early part of this century.

These dolls, probably made between 1880–1900, consist of fabric, leather, ceramics, and metal. They may recall earlier dolls held secretly in slumber by slave children.

Colonial Williamsburg

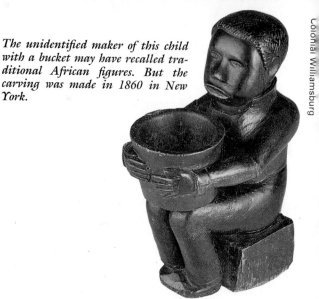

Colonial Williamsburg

The unidentified maker of this child with a bucket may have recalled traditional African figures. But the carving was made in 1860 in New York.

Romare Bearden used his African American heritage for inspiration to make this 1970 collage, SHE-BA. The artist has clothed the woman in a contemporary fashion but he also recalls the famous Queen of Sheba.

Wadsworth Athaeneum

2. SLAVERY AND THE ECONOMY

The Origins of Slavery

Indentured servants got land and eventually political power in America. Other laborers in America were cruelly used. These were the slaves brought from Africa. It takes a strong historical imagination to think as the European colonizers did about slavery. Most had certain deep-seated prejudices about people and their rights. Most believed that some people were better than others, that the values and customs of their society were better than any others. Being Christians, they felt certain that Christianity was the only true religion. Non-Christians were "heathens," sinful and evil by nature.

We have seen how this point of view affected the way other Europeans dealt with the Indians. In the English colonies, however, the newcomers were not often able to make the Indians work for them. The land was large, the Indian population small. In most cases the Indians—those who were not wiped out by warfare or disease—eventually gave up their lands and moved west. A few Indians were enslaved. A few took on European ways. Most simply melted into the forest rather than submit to white control. There was nothing the colonists could do to stop them from leaving.

Another source of labor then became available—that of African

Preview & Review

Use these questions to guide your reading. Answer the questions after completing Section 2.
Understanding Issues, Events, & Ideas. Explain why American slavery was a southern institution, using the following words: slave, British, peculiar institution, cash crops, tidewater, indigo, naval stores, fur trade, Yankee ingenuity, triangular trade.
1. Why did the colonists originally prefer indentured servants to African slaves? What caused a change in attitude?
2. What made growing cash crops profitable for the South?
3. Why did African slaves become the chief labor source in raising southern cash crops?
4. How was the triangular trade conducted? What were some variations of the triangular trade?

Thinking Critically. 1. Why do you think Africans brought to America as slaves were less likely to revolt than those born in America? **2.** Suppose that you are a Virginia tobacco planter. What similarities do you share with a South Carolina rice grower or a Pennsylvania wheat farmer?

The slave cabins of Mulberry Plantation stand in orderly rows behind the main house in this oil painting on paper by Thomas Coram. Do you think most slave cabins looked like the ones in this painting?

Gibbes Museum of Art

slaves. The story of how these innocent people were brought to America and compelled to work as slaves is the most tragic and shameful chapter in our history. It is even more shameful than the ill use of the Indians, who at least had the means of fighting back.

The Spaniards brought slaves from Africa to their American colonies before the founding of Jamestown. It may be that the English colonists got the idea of enslaving Africans from the Spanish example. In any case the first Africans were brought to the English colonies by Dutch traders, who sold them to the Jamestown colonists in 1619. Records are few, but these twenty Africans may have been treated as indentured servants rather than slaves because slavery was not legal according to English laws of the times.

At first few slaves were imported. Tobacco farmers and others in need of laborers much preferred indentured servants to Africans. Most indentured servants were **British**—from England, Scotland, or Wales—and were familiar with the English language and life style. The Africans could not speak English. Many lacked the skills needed by farmers. And it cost much more to buy a slave than to purchase the labor of a servant for a limited period of time.

For a long time there were plenty of indentured servants. When they completed their service, most of them became independent farmers. They then competed with their former masters. The more servants a tobacco planter hired, the more small farmers would be planting tobacco for themselves seven years later. The price of tobacco and other crops tended to fall as production increased. Under slavery this kind of competition did not occur.

Slave Life

By 1690 there were slaves in all the English colonies. The **peculiar institution,** as some slaveholders called it, was firmly fixed in American society. It was to last for another 175 years.

Slavery was not unique to America. Many societies—the Greeks, Romans, Arabs, some African tribes—enslaved prisoners of war. Many came to look on their slaves as members of the household. But American slavery was different. It was based on race. Americans considered Africans inferior, and slaves as property rather than human beings.

It is hard for persons in a free society to conceive of what it was like to be a slave. We must use historical imagination carefully. The idea that slaves were constantly beaten or worked to death like prisoners in a concentration camp is incorrect. Slaves were too valuable to be treated like that—unless they refused to work or rose up against their owners. They were usually given adequate food, clothing, and shelter, again because they were expensive property. But slaves had absolutely *no rights*. Not only could they not vote or own property, their owners had complete control over their lives. An owner could separate a husband and wife, or sell a child and keep the child's parents. Slaves worked for the exclusive benefit of their owners. Slavery was inhuman, but those who were enslaved were human beings.

Most who became slaves were prisoners taken in wars in Africa or unsuspecting villagers captured by African slave hunters. These people marched their captives in chains to prison pens on the coast, then sold them to slave traders. Venture Smith described his experiences when as a six-year-old boy he and his family were captured by slave hunters from a neighboring African tribe:

    " They then came after us in the reeds, and the very first salute I had from them was a violent blow on the back of the head with the fore part of a gun, and at the same time a grasp around the neck. I then had a rope put about my neck, as had all the women in the thicket with me, and was immediately led to my father, who was likewise pinioned [held down] and haltered for leading. In this condition we were all led to the camp. The women and myself being pretty submissive, had tolerable treatment from the enemy, while my father . . . was cut and pounded on his body with great inhumanity. . . . I thus saw him tortured to death. The shocking scene to this day fresh in my mind, and I have often been overcome thinking of it. . . .

The enemy army was large, I should suppose consisting of about six thousand men. . . . The enemy had remarkable success in destroying the country wherever they went. For as far as they had penetrated, they had laid the habitations [villages] waste and captured the people. . . . They pinioned the prisoners of all ages and sexes indiscriminately, took their flocks and all their effects, and moved on their way towards the sea. On the march the prisoners were treated with clemency [mercy], on account of their being submissive and humble. Having come to the next tribe, the enemy laid siege and immediately took men, women, children, flocks, and all their valuable effects. They then went on to the next district which was contiguous [next] to the sea, called in Africa, Anamaboo. . . . The enemies' provisions were then almost spent, as well as their strength. The inhabitants knowing what conduct they had pursued, and what were their present intentions, improved the favorable opportunity, attacked them, and took enemy, prisoners, flocks and all their effects. I was taken for a second time [by Africans]. All of us were put in a castle, and kept for market. On a certain time I and other prisoners were put on board a canoe, under our master, and rowed away to a

National Maritime Museum, Greenwich

A British warship captured a Spanish slaveship on its way to the West Indies in the 18th century. A young English naval officer, Lt. Francis Meynell, went below and made this watercolor sketch on the spot. In what ways do these prisoners appear more comfortable than other Africans who sailed the Middle Passage?

vessel belonging to Rhode Island, commanded by Captain Collingwood, and the mate Thomas Mumford. While we were going to the vessel, our master told us to appear to the best possible advantage for sale. I was bought on board by one Robertson Mumford, steward of said vessel, for four gallons of rum, and a piece of calico, and called VENTURE, on account of his having purchased me with his own private venture. Thus I came by my name. All the slaves that were bought for that vessel's cargo, were two hundred and sixty.[1] **99**

Next came the dreadful **Middle Passage,** the voyage across the Atlantic. The Africans were crowded below deck as closely as the captain thought possible without causing all to smother. How many died on the crossing was usually a matter of luck. If the winds were strong and favorable, the trip would be reasonably short. Most would survive. If the ship was delayed by bad weather, or if smallpox or some other contagious disease broke out, the death toll would be

[1]From *A Narrative of the Life and Adventures of Venture, A Native of Africa but Resident about Sixty Years in the United States of America* by Venture Smith

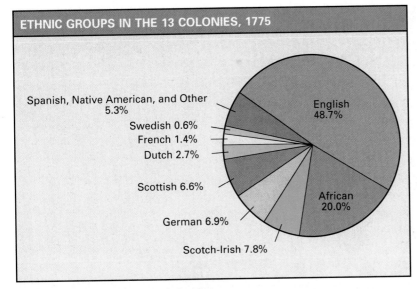

ETHNIC GROUPS IN THE 13 COLONIES, 1775

Spanish, Native American, and Other 5.3%
Swedish 0.6%
French 1.4%
Dutch 2.7%
Scottish 6.6%
German 6.9%
Scotch-Irish 7.8%
English 48.7%
African 20.0%

Source: *Historical Statistics of the United States*

LEARNING FROM GRAPHS.
Only nine ethnic groups had a sizeable number of people in the British colonies. What percentage of the total population did the British—English, Scotch-Irish, and Scottish—and their African slaves make up? What two other groups had the largest numbers?

enormous. Olaudah Equiano, a slave who later bought his freedom, described the Middle Passage thus:

> ❝ When the ship had loaded all its cargo, we were all put below deck. The number of people was so great that each person barely had room to move. The stale air and the heat almost choked us. Everyone was dripping sweat, so that the air became unfit to breathe, from a variety of foul smells. These conditions caused sickness among the slaves, and many died—in this way becoming victims to the short-sighted greed of their purchasers.
>
> This wretched situation was made even worse by the rubbing of the chains against the slaves' skin, which became unbearable, and by the filth of the tubs, into which the children often fell and were almost drowned. The screams of the women, and the moans of the dying, made this a scene of horror almost beyond belief.[1] ❞

Once in America, the slaves were put on public display and sold to the highest bidder. They were prodded and poked at by prospective buyers the way traders examine an old horse.

One can imagine how confused and depressed most new slaves were after these experiences. Separated from home and family, unable to communicate, drained of strength and hope, there was little likelihood that they would try to resist or run away. Where could they run to? You might think children born into slavery probably bore its weight with less pain, having never known freedom.

Not so. It is one of the many strange aspects of slavery that

[1]From *The Interesting Narrative of the Life of Olaudah Equiano, or Gustavus Vassa, The African,* vol. 1, by Olaudah Equiano

Slavery and the Economy   89

John Carter Brown Library

In the West Indies slaves refine sugar by boiling cane under the watchful eyes of the overseers who inspect the sugar drying in bins. An English artist made this colored lithograph in the 19th century. With your classmates, describe what you imagine these working conditions to be.

those who were born into slavery and particularly those who had the highest places in the system, such as those skilled at crafts like carpenters, were the ones who most frequently ran away or tried to organize slave revolts. Another puzzle is that by teaching slaves specific skills, their owners increased their usefulness but made them less willing to accept being slaves. Slaves who could read and write and practice a trade were far less willing to accept their condition than illiterate "field hands."

Southern Agriculture

What the colonists needed most were European manufactured goods. The money to buy these goods could be earned if the colonists raised crops that Europeans wanted but could not grow themselves. These were called **cash crops** because they brought the growers money to buy farm tools, furniture, clothing, guns and ammunition, pots and pans, books, glassware. The southern colonists had an advantage in the search for cash crops because of their warm climate. The island settlements in the West Indies, for example, raised sugarcane, a tropical plant that Europeans wanted badly but could not grow. By selling sugar refined from the sugarcane to their home countries, Spanish, English, French, and Dutch colonists in the West Indies could get money to buy European manufactured goods.

Tobacco provided a cash crop for the colonists of Maryland, Virginia, and the Carolinas. The seeds of tobacco are so small that a tablespoon will hold about 30,000 of them. The colonists planted these tiny seeds in beds of finely powdered soil. When the seeds sprouted, the little plants were moved to the fields. The best tobacco was made from the largest leaves. As the plants matured, the side shoots of each plant were cut off. At a certain point the top bud was clipped to stop growth. This pruning concentrated the plant's energies in the big leaves. In the fall these leaves were removed and carefully cured, or dried, in airy sheds. Then the tobacco was packed in barrels for shipping.

When tobacco first became popular in England, the price of American tobacco was very high. Anyone with even a small plot of land could make a good living growing it. More and more tobacco was planted as the tobacco colonies expanded. Gradually the price fell. The large planters could still live well enough earning a small profit on each barrel of tobacco. But many small farmers were forced to sell out and move west. When the news of this change reached Europe, poor people were less eager to come to America as indentured servants. With fewer Europeans coming to the tobacco colonies, African slaves became the chief source of labor on the tobacco plantations.

In parts of South Carolina and later in Georgia too, rice became the chief cash crop. Rice needs a warm climate and much water. It grew well in swamps and low-lying lands along the Atlantic Coast. The fields were flooded by building dikes and canals and trapping river water that was backed up by the incoming ocean tides. Coastal areas of the South were called the **tidewater** because their rivers were affected in this way by the ocean tides.

Malaria and other tropical fevers struck down many of the people who had to work in the rice fields. For this reason slave labor was used almost exclusively. Owners claimed that slaves were immune to these diseases because of their African origin. It may have been that they suffered less because of natural immunity, but large numbers of Africans caught malaria and many died. Working knee-deep in mud with the temperature in the nineties and humidity high, the air swarming with mosquitoes, was not good for anyone.

South Carolina farmers also grew indigo, a plant that produced a blue dye used by the English cloth manufacturers. Indigo was first grown in the English colonies by Eliza Lucas, who while still in her teens was running three large South Carolina plantations owned by her father, a colonial official in the British West Indies. An inventive person, Lucas also produced silk and experimented with other products, although without much success.

The great pine forests of the South yielded tall, straight logs that became the masts of ships in the Royal Navy. The sap, or resin, of pine trees was made into tar and pitch that were used to preserve rope and make the hulls of ships watertight. These products were called **naval stores.**

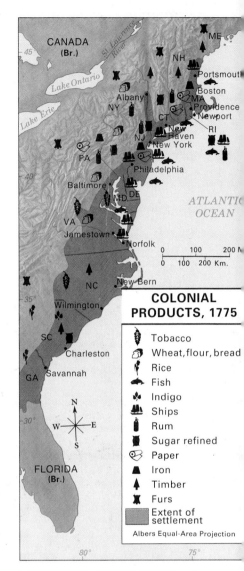

LEARNING FROM MAPS. *By 1775 the colonies produced an amazing number and variety of goods. What area was the manufacturing center? Why do you think manufacturing developed there?*

Northern Products

The northern colonies also produced naval stores, but the climate from Pennsylvania to Massachusetts Bay and New Hampshire was too cold to grow most of the southern cash crops. Put differently, the climate in these colonies was similar to the climate in England. And England already produced all it needed of the crops that grew best in the North—wheat, barley, and oats.

One American product, more northern than southern, highly valued in Europe was fur. Fur-bearing animals were scarce in Europe but abundant in the forest wildernesses of America. Americans hunted and trapped beaver, deer, and other animals and sent the skins to Europe, where they were made into coats and wraps or converted into felt for hats. The colonists also traded for furs with the Indians. The **fur trade** was essentially a frontier activity. As the colonies grew larger, fur traders and hunters had to go farther and farther west. And there the English often encountered angry French and unfriendly Indians, who claimed those lands and especially the fur trade for themselves.

Some northerners did a great deal of fishing, especially in the waters off Newfoundland. The English worked that area too, so there was no market in England for the American catch. The Americans instead exported large quantities of dried and salted fish to southern Europe.

Yet, not many northerners trapped fur-bearing animals or fished. Most had to find other means of paying for the European manufactured goods they craved. The problem turned out to be a great advantage, for it encouraged northerners to try different things. It stimulated their imagination, or what has come to be called **Yankee ingenuity**—a knack for solving difficult problems in clever and creative ways.

Since most people were farmers, the northern colonists produced much more food than they could eat. Where could they sell this surplus? The answer they came up with was the sugar-producing islands of the West Indies. These islands were all small. Every acre of fertile soil was devoted to raising sugarcane. Moreover, producing sugar requires a great deal of labor. The islands were densely populated, mostly by African slaves. The sugar planters worked their slaves very hard. They realized that the slaves had to have plenty to eat if they were to work well.

American merchants and sailors soon discovered that they could make excellent profits shipping grain and fish to the sugar islands, and also horses for plowing and hauling and barrels to pack sugar in. They could invest the profits of this trade in sugar and carry the sugar to England. When the sugar was sold, they could buy English manufactured goods and sell these at another fat profit when they returned to their home port.

The Triangular Trade

The trade between the northern colonies, the sugar islands, and England was called the **triangular trade** because three separate voyages were involved. The trade did not operate as neatly as its name suggests. There were many variations, some quite complex. American merchants frequently bought molasses in the sugar islands instead of sugar. Molasses is what is left over after the crystallized sugar has been boiled out of the sugarcane. It was almost a waste product in the islands, and very cheap. The Americans took it back to the mainland, most frequently to Rhode Island, where it was distilled into rum, a powerful alcoholic drink. The rum was then shipped to West Africa, where it was traded for slaves. The slaves, in turn, were taken to the West Indies, or perhaps to the colonies in America. Then the cycle might be repeated: slaves for molasses, molasses into rum, rum for slaves. If the African slaves were sold in Virginia, the captain of the vessel might buy tobacco and take that to England. He might then purchase manufactured goods for sale back home.

The triangular trade was extremely profitable. The Americans bought things where they were plentiful and cheap and sold them where they were in great demand. Each leg of the voyage added to the gain. The more complicated the route, the more money that could

Sea captains relax in port on a leg of their triangular trade. This oil painting on bed ticking was done by John Greenwood in the late 18th century. Called "Sea Captains Carousing in Surinam," its title shows that the artist disapproved of such behavior. Why do you think the artist painted a scene that doesn't meet with his approval?

The St. Louis Art Museum

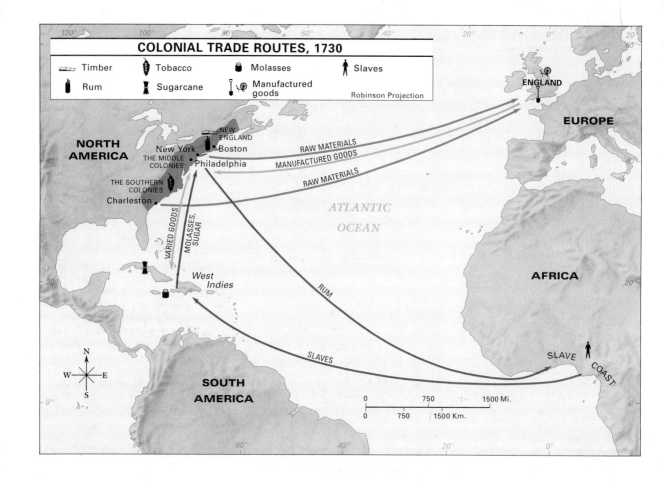

COLONIAL TRADE ROUTES, 1730

Timber · Tobacco · Molasses · Slaves

Rum · Sugarcane · Manufactured goods

Robinson Projection

NORTH AMERICA

NEW ENGLAND
New York · Boston
THE MIDDLE COLONIES
Philadelphia

THE SOUTHERN COLONIES
Charleston

RAW MATERIALS
MANUFACTURED GOODS
RAW MATERIALS

ATLANTIC OCEAN

ENGLAND

EUROPE

AFRICA

VARIED GOODS

MOLASSES, SUGAR

West Indies

RUM

SLAVES

SLAVE COAST

SOUTH AMERICA

N W E S

0   750   1500 Mi.
0   750   1500 Km.

LEARNING FROM MAPS. *This map of colonial trade routes helps us see how logical British economic policies were. Raw materials were sent to England to be transformed into finished products. Manufactured goods were sent to the colonies. Why did England discourage the growth of colonial industries?*

Return to the Preview & Review on page 85.

be made. Sometimes a ship was away from its home port for years. When it finally returned, the owners were rich indeed.

Thus what looked like a disadvantage—the fact that England did not need what northern colonists could produce—became an advantage, especially for the merchants and shipowners. A typical example was Thomas Amory, Irish born, who settled in Boston in 1720. Amory's ships traded with the West Indies, the Azores, England, and several European nations. He manufactured rum and naval stores and also built ships. He was so wealthy that when he married the daughter of a Boston tavern keeper, he could speak of his wife's fortune as *only* £1,500, although that was quite a large sum at the time. (£ is the symbol for the British monetary unit "pound.") Another Boston merchant, James Bowdoin, son of a French Protestant who came to America to escape religious persecution, acquired a fortune of over £182,000.

Trade was the key to prosperity in the northern colonies, just as cash crops were the key to prosperity farther south. For this reason merchants were the most admired people in the North, the leaders of society, and often the political leaders too. In the South the planter, owner of a large estate and many slaves, played a similar role.

3. AMERICANS SHARE NEW IDEAS

The Great Awakening

American colonists were deeply religious and made great efforts to maintain their churches. Particularly on the frontier where the population was spread over great distances, people would travel for miles to attend services. Frontier ministers also rode from place to place on horseback, preaching and holding church meetings wherever a group could be brought together.

Just how deeply most colonists felt about religion was revealed by what is called the **Great Awakening** of the 1740s. In November 1739 a young English preacher named George Whitefield arrived in Philadelphia. He was on his way to Savannah, Georgia, where the trustees had appointed him minister and where he intended to found an orphanage.

Whitefield was a small, fair-skinned man with sparkling, deep-blue eyes. While preaching, he radiated energy and enthusiasm, bounding about, waving his arms to emphasize his points. He would undoubtedly have made a brilliant actor had he chosen the stage as a career. In Philadelphia, and then while traveling south to Savannah, he spoke wherever he could find a church. Sometimes he held services outdoors. Later he returned to the northern colonies, again preaching almost daily. Everywhere he went, he stirred intense religious emotions in his listeners. Thousands of colonists came forward to confess their sins and resolve to lead blameless lives in the future.

Preview & Review

Use these questions to guide your reading. Answer the questions after completing Section 3.

Understanding Issues, Events, & Ideas. Explain the significance of the following words: Great Awakening, Enlightenment, Albany Plan of Union, orrery.

1. What was the Great Awakening? In what way was the Great Awakening a force for religious toleration?
2. What was the Enlightenment? Why was its spirit welcome in the colonies?
3. For what reasons was Benjamin Franklin the greatest American of the Enlightenment?
4. How did self-taught Americans add to the spirit of the Enlightenment in the colonies?

Thinking Critically. Imagine that you are attending a town meeting in North Carolina. One of the topics discussed is Benjamin Franklin's Albany Plan. Would you be for or against uniting the colonies? Why?

National Portrait Gallery, London

Salvation is in the hands of George Whitefield in this early painting done at the time of the Great Awakening. Reread the description of Reverend Whitefield on this page to see how well the oil painting matches the historical account.

95

Benjamin Franklin, a man of the Enlightenment, was surprised at the effectiveness of Whitefield's preaching. In his autobiography, Franklin wrote that he knew Whitefield would ask for money and that he was determined not to give any. But Franklin says:

> 66 I began to soften, and concluded to give the coppers. Another stroke of his iratory [speech] made me asham'd of that, and determin'd me to give the silver; and he finished so admirably, that I empty'd my pocket wholly into the collector's dish, gold and all.[1] 99

Dozens of other preachers followed in Whitefield's steps, the best known being Jonathan Edwards. On July 8, 1741, Edwards delivered his most memorable sermon, "Sinners in the Hands of an Angry God." Imagine how his listeners trembled as he said:

New-York Historical Society

Jonathan Edwards, Whitefield's disciple, has a surprisingly gentle appearance for the prophet of an "Angry God."

> 66 [T]here is nothing between you and Hell but the air; it is the only power of and mere pleasure of God that holds you up. . . .
>
> Your wickedness makes you as it were heavy as lead, and to tend downwards with great weight and pressure towards Hell; and if God should let you go, you would sink immediately and swiftly descend and plunge into the bottomless gulf, and your healthy constitution [body], and your own care and prudence [sensibility], and best contrivance [plans], and all your righteousness [good behavior], would have no more influence to uphold you and keep you out of Hell than a spider's web would stop a falling rock. . . . There are the black clouds of God's wrath now hanging directly over your heads, full of the dreadful storm, and big with thunder; and were it not for the restraining hand of God it would immediately burst forth upon you. The sovereign [supreme] pleasure of God for the present stays [holds back] his rough wind; otherwise it would come with fury, and your destruction would come like a whirlwind, and you would be like the chaff [seed coverings] on the summer threshing [process used to separate the grain from the useless pieces collected at harvest] floor.
>
> The wrath [anger] of God is like great waters that are dammed for the present; they increase more and more, and rise higher and higher, till an outlet is given; and the longer the stream is stopped, the more rapid and mighty is its course when once it is let loose. 'Tis true that judgment against your evil works has not been executed hitherto [recently]; the floods of God's vengeance have been withheld; but your guilt in the meantime is constantly increasing; and you are every day treasuring up more wrath; the waters

[1]From *Out of Our Past* by Carl N. Degler

are continually rising and waxing [growing] more and more mighty; and there is nothing but the mere pleasure of God that holds the waters back that are unwilling to be stopped, and hard press to go forward; if God should only withdraw his hand from the floodgate, it would immediately fly open, and the fiery floods of the fierceness and wrath of God would rush forth with inconceivable [unimaginable] fury, and would come upon you with omnipotent [unlimited] power; . . .

The bow of God's wrath is bent, and the arrow made ready on the string, and justice bends the arrow at your heart, and strains the bow, and it is nothing but the mere pleasure of God, and that of an angry God, without any promise or obligation at all, that keeps the arrow one moment from being drunk with your blood. . . .

The God that holds you over the pit of Hell, much as one holds a spider, or some loathsome insect, over a fire, abhors [rejects] you, and is dreadfully provoked [angered]; his wrath towards you burns like fire; he looks upon you as worthy of nothing else but to be cast into the fire; . . .

How dreadful is the state of those that are daily and hourly in danger of this great wrath and infinite misery! But it is the dismal [sad] case of every soul in this congregation that has not been born again, however moral and strict, sober and religious, they may otherwise be. Oh that you would consider it, whether you be young or old! There is reason to think that there are many in this congregation now hearing this discourse [sermon], that will actually be the subjects of this fiery misery to all eternity. . . .

Therefore let everyone that is out of Christ now awake and fly from the wrath to come! . . . 'Haste and escape for your lives, look not behind you, escape to the mountain, lest you be consumed [Genesis 19:17].'[1]**"**

The colonies from Georgia to New Hampshire were swept by repeated waves of religious excitement. Whitefield, Edwards, and most of the others played down the differences of doctrine that separated many of the Protestant sects. What mattered, they said, was to have sincere religious feelings. Philosophy and logic would get no one into Heaven.

The Great Awakening was one of the first truly national events in colonial history. It was a force for religious toleration because of its come-one-come-all spirit. Many people were carried away by the excitement in the crowd when they heard a dynamic speaker like Whitefield preach. They announced that they were converted. They

[1]From *Jonathan Edwards: Representative Selections, with Introduction, Bibliography and Notes,* edited by Clarence Faust and Thomas H. Johnson

swore to lead saintly lives in the future. They were perfectly sincere, but most of them could not change their old habits. In rural areas some of the people who gathered to listen were attracted more by the festival atmosphere that surrounded the meetings than by the desire to save their souls. Although the Awakening quietly faded after 1741, it had permanently changed American religious attitudes.

The Great Awakening also had important political consequences. The Christian and Jewish traditions of most Americans had always encouraged democracy. Religious teachings stressed that people were created equal in the eyes of God. The power of the state was not absolute because Jews and Christians believed they owed an important part of their allegiance to the "kingdom of God." The Protestant Reformation had emphasized the importance of individual conscience. Some congregational Protestant denominations were even set up according to democratic models of government. Now, the Great Awakening encouraged these democratic ideals. People experienced freedom of choice in their religious lives. Soon they sought the same in their political lives.

The Search for Knowledge

By the 1750s many people in the colonies were caught up by the spirit of what is known as the **Enlightenment.** The name describes a belief that in an orderly universe human reason will prevail. This time is sometimes called the Age of Reason because "enlightened" people believed that they could improve themselves and the world around them by careful study and hard thought.

Two great scientific advances set the stage for the Enlightenment. One was the invention of the telescope by the Italian scientist Galileo in 1609. Using his telescope, Galileo was able to arrive at a much better understanding of the size of the universe and makeup of our own solar system than was earlier possible. The other advance was Sir Isaac Newton's discovery of the laws of gravity, which explained why the stars and planets behaved as they did.

The work of Galileo and Newton and other scientists changed the way educated people thought and the value they gave to thinking. The orderliness of the movements of the planets seemed to suggest that the universe was like a gigantic watch, complicated but operating according to fixed laws. If laws or rules governed the universe, surely no mystery of nature was beyond human solution. Surely humans, once they had solved the mysteries of nature, were destined to march steadily forward to greater and greater achievements.

These ideas found a welcome home in the colonies. It was easy to believe in progress in America because the colonies were so obviously making progress. The dense forest was being pushed back. The people were growing richer and more numerous. It was easier still to believe that thought and study would push forward the frontiers of knowledge. Explorers and scientists were constantly finding new rivers and mountains, new plants and animals. Americans produced clever new ideas and ingenious ways of doing things.

Benjamin Franklin

The greatest American of the Enlightenment was Benjamin Franklin. The story of his life begins in Boston, where he was born in 1706. His father was a soap and candle maker. Benjamin was the fifteenth of 17 children. He had only two years of schooling. At ten he became an apprentice in his father's shop, but after two years he shifted to the printer's trade, working for one of his nine older brothers.

When he was 17, Benjamin left Boston to seek his fortune in Philadelphia. Soon he owned his own printing shop, then also a newspaper, the *Pennsylvania Gazette*. He published books and wrote the annual *Poor Richard's Almanack*, each volume full of practical advice, weather predictions, odd bits of information, and what he called "scraps from the table of wisdom." One of the best-known examples of these "scraps" was the slogan "Early to bed, and early to rise, makes a man healthy, wealthy, and wise." Other typical examples are "God helps them that help themselves," "One today is worth two tomorrows," and "When the well is dry, they know the worth of water." He was so successful that by the time he was 42 he had enough money to live comfortably for the rest of his life.

Harvard University Portrait Collection

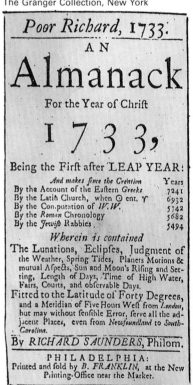

The Granger Collection, New York

Above is the title page from **Poor Richard's Almanack** *for 1733. At left is the earliest known portrait of Benjamin Franklin, painted around 1746 by Robert Feke. Look at this painting. Would you say Franklin is a successful man? Why?*

At this point Franklin retired from the printing business so that he could pursue his other interests. These were almost endless. He invented a cast-iron fireplace (the Franklin stove) which radiated most of its heat into the room instead of allowing it to escape up the chimney. He invented bifocal eyeglasses so that people who were both nearsighted and farsighted need have only one pair. His famous experiment with a kite in a thunderstorm proved his theory that lightning was a form of electricity. This alone made his reputation among the leading European scientists of the time.

In addition to his scientific discoveries, Franklin was an outstanding citizen and public servant. He helped found the first library in Philadelphia, and the first fire department, and the first hospital, and a school—the Academy for the Education of Youth, which became the University of Pennsylvania. He was the town postmaster and later, by appointment of the king, postmaster for all the colonies.

In 1754 Franklin drafted a scheme for uniting the colonies—the **Albany Plan of Union.** At this time he had no idea that the colonies might break away from England. Under his proposal England would still have had the final say about American affairs. But long before most other colonists understood the need, Franklin realized that the common interests of the different colonies were making it necessary for them to have some sort of common government. To make the point he drew a sketch of a snake divided into many pieces representing the different colonies. He attached to this drawing the title *Join, or Die.*

The Granger Collection, New York

In 1754 Franklin was already world famous. But, as we shall later see, the most important and exciting part of his life still lay ahead of him.

Self-Taught Americans

Colonial America had only a few colleges, such as Harvard in Massachusetts, William and Mary in Virginia, Yale in Connecticut, and the College of New Jersey, now called Princeton. But many colonists, caught up by the spirit of the Enlightenment, taught themselves.

David Rittenhouse was a clockmaker who made valuable contributions to the construction of telescopes and other instruments. He also built an **orrery,** a mechanical model of the sun and planets which copied their movements exactly.

John Bartram was a farm boy who had little formal education but a passionate interest in all growing things. He traveled far and wide in America, collecting strange plants for his garden outside Philadelphia. He sent carefully packed samples of his discoveries to the leading European naturalists and received from them their own unusual finds. Distinguished visitors from Europe made detours to see his collection, and prominent Americans like George Washington and Benjamin Franklin came frequently to his garden. 🖎

Princeton University Observatory

David Rittenhouse, a clockmaker, made this beautiful orrery which copied the movements of the sun and planets exactly. Why would a clockmaker have been particularly comfortable with the European ideas of the Enlightenment?

Return to the Preview & Review on page 95.

4. EAST-WEST DISPUTES

Conflicts over Land and Government

America was indeed a land of opportunity. In England the cities and highways were crowded with ragged beggars and tramps. Few free people in America were that poor and hopeless. Some colonists were rich by any standard, but none was nearly as rich as the great English noble families or the merchant princes of London. Most Americans had what was called "middling" wealth. They lived comfortably, not lavishly. And they worked hard. Even the rich were rarely idle rich.

Yet colonial society was not really the "peaceable kingdom" that the Quaker artist Edward Hicks liked to portray. Sharp conflicts frequently occurred. Some even led to bloodshed.

By about 1750 settlement in most colonies had reached the eastern slopes and valleys of the Appalachian Mountains—that long range that runs from Georgia to New York and New England. In those days this was "the West" to the English colonists. It was only 100 miles (160 kilometers) or so from the seacoast where settlement had begun. But travel was slow and difficult. Most people rarely saw anyone from outside their own communities.

Most colonists did not like Franklin's Albany Plan of Union. They were afraid of losing some of their independence to what seemed to them a "foreign" institution. The average person was loyal to only one colony and to only one village or county in particular. If the colonists had any common loyalty beyond that, it was to England or to the British Empire of which they were a part.

Colonial governments sometimes engaged in bitter disputes with each other over territory. Boundaries were vague, mostly because the original land grants were made before the territories involved had been explored. The boundary between Maryland and Pennsylvania caused endless disputes and court battles. The dispute was finally settled in the 1760s when surveyors Charles Mason and Jeremiah Dixon set the boundary at a line that came to be called the **Mason-Dixon line.** David Rittenhouse designed some of the instruments used by Mason and Dixon to survey this boundary. Disagreements of this type occurred so frequently that during his career Rittenhouse served on boundary commissions for more than half the English colonies.

Different interest groups in a single colony often came into conflict with one another. In areas already settled people tended to think that defense against attack was a local matter. They argued that frontier settlers were responsible for their own troubles and should have to face the consequences without outside help.

The Quakers of Philadelphia, who opposed war as a matter of principle, often blaming the "hotheaded" Scotch-Irish settlers in the frontier sections of Pennsylvania for conflicts with the local Indians.

Preview &

Use these questions reading. Answer the q after completing Section

Understanding Issues, E Ideas. Use the following w discuss colonial east-west disputes: Mason-Dixon Line; person, one vote; Bacon's Rebellion.

1. Why did colonial governments have so many disputes among themselves over territory?
2. Why did people in the frontier sections of most colonies resent the eastern sections?
3. What was the cause of Bacon's Rebellion?
4. Why did many Virginians consider Bacon a hero?

Thinking Critically. 1. Do you think our electoral system today is similar to that of our colonial past? Explain the similarities or differences and the reasons for them. **2.** Use your historical imagination to describe what nonviolent methods Nathaniel Bacon might have used to protest the Indians' attacks.

American Philosophical Society

David Rittenhouse designed many tools for surveyors. Why were his services so often in demand in the English colonies?

Edward Hicks painted "The Peaceable Kingdom" in the early 19th-century. He was a preacher and a painter who made over 100 views of wide-eyed animals living in harmony with settlers of America. William Penn's meeting with the Delaware Indians can be seen in the background. How did colonial society differ from the world that Hicks portrayed?

Whether the Quakers were correct or not, pioneers whose fields were burned or neighbors slain in surprise attacks were furious at the attitudes of these easterners, who were safe from such attacks.

People in the frontier sections favored policies that made it easy for them to get land cheaply. Eastern landowners usually objected to such policies. If land was cheap in the West, the value of their own property would go down. A seaport merchant in the fur trade might sell guns to the Indians because guns made them better hunters. Westerners opposed such sales because they were afraid the Indians might use the guns to shoot settlers rather than deer or bear.

There were many such honest differences between the West and the East. The problem was that easterners made the policies because they controlled the colonial governments. The Quakers were secure because they had a large majority in the Pennsylvania colonial legislature. They and similar groups in most colonies had more representatives than their numbers should have entitled them to.

STRATEGIES FOR SUCCESS

CREATING A GRAPHIC REPRESENTATION

Students are required to read and remember a great deal of information. One of the best ways to help you remember all you read is to develop a graphic representation. A graphic representation is a kind of diagram that links related words, terms, or concepts together, a visual illustration of a verbal statement.

There are many types of graphic representations. You are familiar with several: flow charts, pie charts, and even family trees. Other types include spider maps, continuum scales, and compare/contract matrices. One of the most useful in American history is a word web.

How to Develop a Word Web

To develop a word web, follow these steps.

1. **Identify the main ideas.** Read the information and list the heading or title of each major idea or topic. If no heading or title is given, create your own.
2. **Note supporting details.** Review the material to identify details that support each main idea.
3. **Structure the headings.** Form a word web by placing each main idea in a circle. Then place supporting details or related ideas in separate circles and connect them to the main idea. Continue to connect ideas and details to complete a web similar to the one below.
4. **Use the information.** Note the relationships among the data. Draw conclusions, make inferences, and form hypotheses.

Applying the Skill

Review Section 2 of this chapter on the origins of American slavery. Note that the section covers five main ideas: the origins of slavery, slave life, southern agriculture, northern products, and triangular trade. To make a word web, place those five ideas in circles.

What are the subtopics? Reread the section.

Note that under the origins of slavery, three topics are discussed: European prejudices, slaves as an improved labor source, and the arrival of the first slaves in 1619. Choose a term to indicate each of these topics, such as "prejudices," "labor source," and "first slaves." Place these terms in circles and connect them to your central term: origins of slavery. A word web for the first subsection would resemble the one below. You may wish to expand your web by finding additional terms to include on your web. (For example, "heathens" has been linked to prejudices in the web below.) Review the rest of Section 2 and create word webs for the other topics.

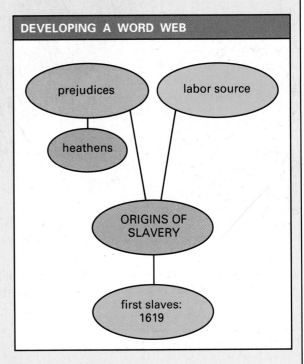

DEVELOPING A WORD WEB

prejudices — heathens

labor source

ORIGINS OF SLAVERY

first slaves: 1619

For independent practice, see Practicing the Strategy on page 107.

Museum of Fine Arts, Boston

Look carefully at this "Quaker Meeting," which took place in London. How does it differ from the religious paintings you saw in Chapter 2?

The American system was and still is to elect legislators by geographical districts. Today, under the principle **one person, one vote,** all election districts must have approximately the same number of residents. A city district may be very small in area, one in farm country quite large. But their populations must be about equal.

When the first assemblies were formed in any colony, the election districts were fairly even in population. As the colony grew, people moved westward beyond the boundaries of the original districts. Soon these western settlers were demanding the right to elect representatives. They asked the assemblies to create new election districts.

Because of the East-West disagreements, colonial assemblies were often reluctant to create new election districts, except in New England, where all the townships were the same size. Therefore, a western legislator would have to represent several times as many voters as an eastern legislator did. In this way the East continued to control the colonial government long after the western population greatly exceeded the eastern.

Because they were under-represented, westerners deeply resented laws regulating land, road construction, and other matters that conflicted with their interests. Sometimes they even resorted to force to correct the injustice.

Bacon's Rebellion

A good example of an East-West conflict occurred in Virginia in May of 1676. The trouble began along the Maryland-Virginia border when Indians killed a shepherd. Settlers responded by killing 24 Indians, including several of the Susquehanna tribe. Since the Susquehannas had not been involved in the murder, they were furious. Sweeping south out of Maryland, they killed at least 36 frontier settlers.

One of the men killed in this raid worked for a tobacco planter named Nathaniel Bacon. Not much is known about Bacon except that he was a thin, dark, rather sad-faced man who had come to Virginia from England only two years earlier. He had considerable money and was related to the wife of the governor of Virginia, Sir William Berkeley. Bacon promptly took charge of a large force of volunteers and marched them off to punish the Indians.

Governor Berkeley tried to stop the violence. When Bacon refused to heed his order to lay down his weapons, the governor proclaimed him a rebel. Bacon's force, in the meantime, had wiped out the Occaneechi, an Indian community that had nothing to do with the troubles. Indians, Bacon insisted, were "all alike." Then Bacon turned on the government. He drove the governor out of Jamestown and burned the town. He resumed his assaults on the Indians. In October 1676 Bacon died. The rebellion collapsed.

Nathaniel Bacon was not a pure villain, despite his slaughter of innocent people and his refusal to obey the governor's orders. Most of the western planters considered him a hero. Many people felt that the legislature—the House of Burgesses—was not responsive to their needs. There had not been an election in Virginia in 15 years.

Governor Berkeley had a long and distinguished career, but he had grown bad tempered in his old age. His wish to protect the Indians may not have been based entirely on his sense of justice. He seems to have had a considerable investment in the fur trade. If so, this would help explain why he did not want to see the Indians, on whom this profitable trade depended, killed or driven off.

After **Bacon's Rebellion** there were new elections in Virginia. The local Indians, most of whom had abandoned their lands when faced by Bacon's bloodthirsty army, were allowed to return after they agreed that they held the land under the authority of "the Great King of England." Some of their descendants still live on these lands. The conflict might have been avoided and many lives saved if the House of Burgesses had represented the interests of all the people.

Fortunately, incidents like Bacon's Rebellion were rare in the colonial period. Displacing the Indians, slavery, unfair representation, and other sources of conflict seemed to be balanced by the opportunities that a new country made possible. America was not paradise. Life was hard and often dangerous. Yet the future seemed promising. 📧

Return to the Preview & Review on page 101.

CHAPTER 3 REVIEW

1619
First Africans
brought to America

1676
Bacon'
Rebell
erupts

Chapter Summary

Read the statements below. Choose one, and write a paragraph explaining its importance.

1. The American land held many blessings for the first settlers.
2. Early colonists relied on rivers as transportation routes, and early cities grew on river banks.
3. Although colonial women could not vote and worked very hard, American life offered more opportunities than it did in Europe.
4. Most early settlers obtained land and worked hard to improve it, qualifying them to vote.
5. Africans were first brought to America to work as slaves.
6. Slavery was inhuman; educated slaves were more likely to run away or revolt.
7. Cash crops such as tobacco were the major southern products and required much labor.
8. Triangular trade became very profitable.
9. Intellectual movements such as the Great Awakening and the Enlightenment involved Benjamin Franklin and many Americans.
10. As settlers moved west, many controversies arose.

Reviewing Chronological Order

Number your paper 1-5. Then study the time line above and place the following events in the order in which they happened by writing the first next to 1, the second next to 2, and so on.

1. The Great Awakening
2. Bacon's Rebellion
3. Albany Plan of Union
4. First Africans brought to America
5. The Enlightment in America

Understanding Main Ideas

1. Why did the colonists have to be self-reliant? Give at least two examples of ways the colonists were self-reliant.
2. What hardships did women in colonial America face?
3. What geographical feature did all the large towns have in common?
4. Why did working people in the colonies earn more and get better treatment than workers in England? Why did indentured servants agree to come to America to work? How were African slaves usually treated by their owners in the American colonies?
5. How was American slavery different from slavery elsewhere?
6. Why was the Enlightenment welcomed in America?

Thinking Critically

1. **Synthesizing.** Imagine that you are the 26-year-old widow Martha Dandridge Custis. What advantages might you have over a European woman of your time? What major advantages does a twentieth-century American woman have over a colonial woman?
2. **Drawing Conclusions.** How did the availability of land and the scarcity of labor help make life in colonial America more democratic than it was in England?
3. **Evaluating.** Do you think "Yankee ingenuity" was a positive or a negative quality? Why? How did northern colonists use it to find a means of paying for the European goods they wanted? Do you think Americans still have "Yankee ingenuity"? Explain your answer.

Writing About History

An important point in this chapter is that the great amount of land in America affected the lives of the colonists. Suppose you are an American colonist. Write a letter to a friend in Europe explaining how the abundance of land affected one of the following: women, indentured servants, slaves, American Indians.

Triangular Trade

1700   1750

1706
Benjamin Franklin
is born

1740
The Great
Awakening

★

1750
Enlightenment in America

Settlement reaches the Appalachians

1754
Franklin's Albany Plan of Union

Practicing the Strategy
Review the strategies on pages 78 and 103.
Reading Graphs. Study the pie graph on page 89
and answer these questions.
1. What percentage of the colonial population was
African? Where does that percentage rank?
2. The English, Scotch-Irish, and Scottish were all
British. What percentage of the total population
did the British make up?
3. What three groups represent the smallest percentages of the colonial population?
Creating a Graphic Representation. Reread the information on the Great Awakening on pages 95 to
98. Then create a word web of at least five terms
centered on The Great Awakening.

Using Primary Sources
Being a freed slave in the South often meant being
on your guard. Southerners began to fear the large
number of freed slaves living in their midst. North
Carolina and other states passed laws providing a
reward for the capture and resale of "illegally"
freed slaves. In 1797 Thomas Pritchet and three
other freed slaves petitioned the House of Representatives for federal protection. After some debate the House voted to not accept the petition,
leaving the fate of freed slaves to the individual
states. Read the excerpt from the *Annals of the
Congress of the United States,* 4th Cong., 2nd
Sess. (1796–97) to get a sense of the struggle
slaves faced. Then answer the questions.

*I, Thomas Pritchet, was set free by my master Thomas
Pritchet, who furnished me with land . . . where I built
myself a house, cleared a sufficient spot of woodland to
produce ten bushels of corn; . . . this I was obliged to
leave . . . being threatened by Holland Lockwood, who
married my said master's widow, that if I would not
come and serve him, he would apprehend me, and send
me to the West Indies; Enoch Ralph also threatening to
send me to jail, and to sell me. . . . Being thus in
jeopardy, I . . . escaped by night into Virginia. . . .*

*where shipping myself to Boston, I was landed in New
York, where I served as a waiter for seventeen months;
but my mind being distressed on account of the situation
of my wife and children, I returned to Norfolk in Virginia, with the hope of seeing them; but finding I was
advertised in the newspaper, twenty dollars the reward
for apprehending me, my dangerous situation obliged
me to leave Virginia.*

1. Give two examples from the excerpt to show
that Pritchet's freedom was often threatened.
2. How might you defend Pritchet's argument that
he was a free person? How might you defend
Holland Lockwood's belief that Pritchet was not
a free person?
3. Why did Pritchet return to Virginia? Why did he
leave again?

Linking History & Geography
Almost all of the early cities in America developed
on a body of water. Research the location of the
first colonial cities and draw a map showing their
locations. Then in a brief essay explain why the
first cities developed on bodies of water, using one
city as a specific example.

Enriching Your Study of History
1. **Individual Project.** Some colonial business leaders advertised in England to persuade more
European settlers to come to America. Draw an
eye-catching poster with an attention-getting
slogan for a group of these business leaders.
2. **Cooperative Project.** On page 99 there are examples of slogans or wise sayings from *Poor
Richard's Almanack.* With your classmates
write three of your own slogans. Consider such
subjects as good health, friendship, and good
study habits. Put your slogans on a poster and
compare them with those of the rest of the
class. What do you conclude makes a good
slogan? Try to reach a class consensus in your
discussion.

Chapter 3 Review   **107**

Governing the American Colonies

As their colonies in America developed, the English worked out a system to govern and control them. The system applied to all the English colonies, not just those that eventually became the United States. Jamaica and Barbados in the West Indies, Bermuda, English possessions everywhere in the world, including its colonies in North America—all were part of one whole, the British Empire. The people of Massachusetts Bay may have felt a little closer to the people of Virginia than to the sugar planters of Jamaica, but the difference must have been small. All were British, and all were colonists. All recognized the same king, all flew the same flag. But how long could the English hold their far-flung colonies?

1. THE ENGLISH COLONIAL SYSTEM

Royal Grants and Charters

In theory the colonies belonged to the king himself, not to the English government. At one time the king owned all the land. He could dispose of it in whatever way he wished. Over the years, as we have seen, the kings established colonies in America in various ways. James I granted Virginia to the London Company in a kind of business deal. James gave the company the right to look for gold and silver, and in return the company was supposed to pay James one fifth of the gold and silver it found.

Charles II gave captured New Netherland to his brother, the Duke of York, as a present. He used Pennsylvania to pay off his debt to William Penn's father.

Each royal grant or charter was different from the others. But in every case the king remained the ruler, and his government supervised colonial affairs. The colonies remained English. They were not independent nations. England was an ocean away, but decisions made by the king and British lawmakers affected every colonist in one way or another.

Preview & Review

Use these questions to guide your reading. Answer the questions after completing Section 1.
Understanding Issues, Events, & Ideas. Describe the English colonial system, using the following words: Privy Council, Parliament, governor, assembly, legislature, town meeting, county court, justice of the peace.
1. Why could the king dispose of the American colonies as he wished?
2. Which groups made policies and passed laws that governed England's colonies in America?
3. Which groups assisted the governors of the English colonies?
4. Who handled local government in New England? Who handled local government in the southern colonies?
Thinking Critically. In your opinion, which benefitted more from the colonial system, the colonies or Britain? Explain your reasoning.

Franklin Institute, Boston (Photo: Gabor Demjen)

Of course, the kings did not personally manage the everyday affairs of the colonies. Ever since King John signed the Magna Carta, or Great Charter, in 1215 at Runnymede, the English rulers had shared power with lawmaking bodies. And it is important to keep in mind that colonial concerns were much less important to the kings and to the English government than dozens of local matters. Colonial policy was set by the king's principal advisers, who made up what was called the **Privy Council.** *Privy* originally meant "private." A subcommittee of the council, the Lords of Trade, made the major decisions and handled particular colonial problems as they arose. All were subject to the lawmaking body of England, **Parliament.** Parliament consisted of the king or queen, the House of Lords, and the House of Commons, which controlled government finances. Parliament passed the laws that applied specifically to the colonies.

Benjamin Franklin stands at the bar of the English House of Commons in 1766. Members of Parliament have assembled for Franklin's report from the American colonies. His red-robed questioner is former prime minister George Grenville. The members of Parliament include William Pitt and Edmund Burke, who both spoke for better treatment of the colonies. Compare this picture with those you can find of the present-day House of Commons in session.

Government in the English Colonies

There were also governments in each English colony. These carried out the policies and enforced the laws of England and attended to all sorts of local matters that were of no direct concern to England. The colonial governments were modeled after the government of England. At the head of each colony was a **governor.** The governor was the chief executive. He represented the king. He was supposed to oversee the colonial government and make sure that the laws were executed, or enforced. Some governors were American born but most were English. Governors received orders and policies from London and put them into effect. When local problems arose, they decided what was to be done. For example, when Nathaniel Bacon raised a force to attack the Indians in Virginia, Governor Berkeley, on his own authority, ordered Bacon to put down his arms.

Point of View

Free men in America were encouraged to carry arms. The governor of Virginia complained bitterly.

> **"How miserable that man is that Governes a People wher six parts of seaven at least are Poore Endebted Discontented and Armed."**
> Sir William Berkeley, c. 1676

Governors were assisted by councils, which had roughly the same powers and duties that the king's Privy Council had in England. In most of the colonies members of the council were appointed, not elected by the voters. Councilors tended to be picked from among the wealthiest and most socially prominent people in each colony. This was true also of colonial judges.

Local laws were made by elected bodies. These **assemblies,** or **legislatures,** were modeled on the House of Commons in England. On paper their powers were strictly limited. Both the colonial governor and the government in England could disallow, or cancel, any law passed by an assembly. In practice the assemblies, like the House of Commons, had a great deal of power because they controlled the raising of money by taxes and the spending of that money too. Governors could call the assemblies into session and dismiss them at their pleasure. They could order new elections, thus ending the terms of the legislators. A governor could not, however, make the legislators pass any law the legislature did not want to pass.

Because the assemblies had control over money, they could control the governor. They would refuse to spend money on projects the governor wanted unless he agreed to approve laws they wanted to enact. In extreme cases they could attach a sentence providing money for the governor's salary to a bill he had threatened to disallow. Then, if the governor disallowed the law, he got no pay!

Local Government

Each town or community also had a government of its own. In New England townships the inhabitants ran their affairs through what were called **town meetings.** Almost all citizens were entitled to take part in these gatherings. At the meetings they set the rate of town taxes, approved applications of new settlers, set aside land for the newcomers, hired teachers and ministers, and settled local issues.

In the Southern Colonies local government was in the hands of **county courts.** These courts decided when and where to build roads, license taverns, raise taxes, try criminals, and settle lawsuits. In general they oversaw all local matters. The chief officials of the county courts were **justices of the peace.** They were appointed by the governor.

The colonial system of government was quite well suited to the needs and wishes of all involved. The king and his advisers in London made the major decisions and appointed the people who put these decisions into effect. The colonists, however, were able to influence the decision makers in many ways. Purely local questions were left in the hands of the community. It was a complicated system, and often those who ran it were not efficient. But for about 150 years it worked reasonably well. The raw materials of America flowed to England in exchange for manufactured goods. The colonies grew and prospered. 🔖

Return to the Preview & Review on page 108.

Both, National Portrait Gallery, London

2. ENGLISH COLONIAL POLICIES

The Dominion of New England

Most colonists liked the fact that the British Empire was divided into so many separate parts. It allowed each colony a great deal of control over its own affairs. British leaders felt differently. If they could combine the colonies into a few regional groups, it would be easier to manage them.

The most serious attempt to unify a group of colonies occurred after the death of Charles II in 1685. Since Charles had no children, his brother James, the Duke of York, became king. James was already proprietor of the colony of New York. In 1686 he created the **Dominion of New England.** When organized, the Dominion included New York, New Jersey, Connecticut, Rhode Island, Massachusetts, and New Hampshire. Sir Edmund Andros, a soldier who had formerly been governor of New York, was appointed governor of the Dominion.

Each of the colonies in the Dominion resented the loss of its independence. Moreover, the new governor was given enormous power. He could make laws on his own, including tax laws. Indeed, he ruled like a dictator, deciding by himself all questions of importance. The colonial assemblies ceased to meet.

Fortunately for the citizens of the Dominion, Andros' rule did not last very long. James II proved to be extremely unpopular in England. He ignored laws that Parliament had passed and adopted a strongly pro-Catholic policy that alarmed the many powerful Protestant groups in the nation. When his second wife, Queen Mary of Modena, gave birth to a son who would be raised a Catholic, the leaders of Parliament staged what was soon known as the **Glorious Revolution.** They invited James' daughter Mary, who was a Protestant, and her Dutch husband, William of Orange, to become joint

Preview & Review

Use these questions to guide your reading. Answer the questions after completing Section 2.

Understanding Issues, Events, & Ideas. Use the following words to explain the economic benefits to Britain of the colonies: Dominion of New England, Glorious Revolution, favorable balance of trade, Navigation Acts, enumerated articles.

1. Why did the English government want to combine the colonies into a few regional groups? How did the colonists react?
2. What effect did the Glorious Revolution have on the Dominion of New England?
3. What was the overall purpose of the Navigation Acts?

Thinking Critically. How would our economy be different today if the British still controlled the American colonies?

When the news came to America that William and Mary were England's monarchs, the Glorious Revolution that brought them to power was already several months old. These portraits of William and Mary were painted in the late 17th century. What was the religious question that brought William and Mary to the throne?

English Colonial Policies 111

Source: *History of the American Economy, Fifth Edition*

GROWTH OF COLONIAL TRADE WITH ENGLAND

Value (in pounds sterling) — ☐ Exports ■ Imports

	1700	1763
Exports	395,000	345,000
Imports	1,100,000	1,630,000

LEARNING FROM GRAPHS. *Many British laws had a major effect on the colonial economy. How does the chart illustrate the growth of a favorable balance of trade for Britain and an unfavorable one for the colonies?*

Point of View

You read on page 91 of young Eliza Lucas' attempt to cultivate indigo. An historian took this view.

> **"Indigo proved more really beneficial to Carolina than the mines of Mexico or Peru were to Spain. . . . The source of this vast wealth . . . was the result of an experiment by a mere girl. . . ."**
>
> Edward McCrady

rulers of England. James was so unpopular that he could not raise an army to put down the revolution. It was won without a shot being fired. William and Mary crossed the English Channel from the Netherlands in November 1688 to take the throne.

When news of the Glorious Revolution reached Boston the next April—the delay provides a good example of the slowness of communication between England and America—an angry crowd gathered. Andros and other Dominion officials were arrested. A council of leading citizens took over the government. The other colonies in the Dominion also revolted. The Dominion quickly fell apart.

Thereafter the English authorities gave up trying to unify the colonies. The new king, William III, had little interest in America. He relied on the Lords of Trade to manage the colonies, but that committee was made up of weak and inefficient men. Local self-government once again flourished in America.

A Favorable Balance of Trade

The English did not give up the idea of regulating their American colonies. Colonies were supposed to be profitable. The English expected to add to their national wealth by developing and using American raw materials. They passed laws designed to control what the colonists produced and where they sold it. The object was to have the colonists concentrate on goods that England needed and to make sure that these goods were sold in England rather than in another country.

Another way of explaining English policy is to point out that all the European nations were trying to obtain as much gold and silver as possible. Gold and silver seemed at the time to be the true source of national power and wealth. Since neither England nor its colonies had gold or silver mines, England had to trade for these metals. Foreigners would pay gold and silver for English and colonial goods. The more the colonies could produce, the more there was to sell. Moreover, it was important to have what is called a **favorable balance of trade.** That is, England must sell more than it bought. A favorable balance was important because every English purchase of foreign goods reduced the amount of gold and silver that could be held in the country. Trading goods for gold and silver was the key to prosperity. Trade, said Daniel Defoe, the author of *Robinson Crusoe,* was "the Wealth of the World." Colonies were helpful in making trade grow. That is why the Lords of Trade had been put in charge of them.

The Navigation Acts

To make sure that the colonies raised the right products and sold them in the right places, Parliament passed many laws regulating colonial commerce, or the buying and selling of goods. These laws—the Acts of Trade and Navigation—were known as **Navigation Acts.** The first Navigation Act was passed in 1651. The last important one was enacted in 1733. We need not consider each law separately because they were all part of one system, known as the Old Colonial System.

The Navigation Acts provided that all goods passing between England and the colonies must be carried in ships that had been built either in Britain or in the colonies. The owners of these vessels must be British or American. The captain and most of the crew must be British or American too. For example, a Boston merchant could own a ship made in London or Philadelphia and carry goods from Virginia to New York or to any port in Britain. But the merchant could not use a French-made ship for these voyages or hire a Dutch or Portuguese captain.

Many British ships sailed from Bristol, shown in this painting, on their voyages to explore and colonize America. At this broad quay ships took on provisions or unloaded cargo from the colonies. After reading page 114, list some of the enumerated articles these ships might have brought from American colonies.

City of Bristol, Museum and Art Gallery

European goods could be brought into the American colonies *only* after being taken to England. American colonists could import French wine, for instance, but only after it had been brought to England. Once in England, of course, the wine could only be carried to the colonies in a British or colonial ship because of the first rule.

Colonial producers could sell certain products only within the British Empire. The names of these products were listed, or enumerated, in various ways. These items were known as **enumerated articles.** Only goods that England needed but could not produce at home were enumerated. Sugar, tobacco, furs, naval stores, cotton, and the dye indigo were the most important enumerated articles. Many very important colonial products, such as fish and wheat, were not enumerated because England already had adequate supplies. Colonists could sell these products anywhere they could find a buyer.

In addition, the British could buy enumerated products only from their own colonies. British sugar planters in the West Indies and tobacco planters in Virginia and Maryland could not sell their crops in France or Spain or Holland. In return British consumers could not buy sugar or tobacco raised in colonies controlled by the French, Spanish, or Dutch.

Parliament put restrictions on a few colonial manufactured products that competed with British goods. Although the manufacture of woolen cloth and fur hats for local sale was legal, their exportation was prohibited. Late in the colonial period the construction of any new forges, or shops to make iron products, was outlawed. The British believed that these laws were perfectly fair to the colonists. They were trying to make their empire self-sufficient. If the colonies concentrated on producing raw materials that England needed, and if England concentrated on manufacturing, each would benefit. No precious gold or silver would have to be spent for foreign goods. The favorable balance of trade could be maintained.

LEARNING FROM GRAPHS. *Compare the chart of the destinations of colonial exports with the map of colonial trade routes on page 94. What exports did the colonists send to the West Indies? What did they send to Great Britain and Ireland?*

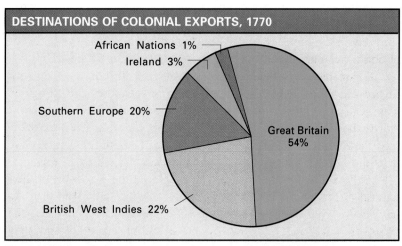

DESTINATIONS OF COLONIAL EXPORTS, 1770

African Nations 1%
Ireland 3%
Southern Europe 20%
Great Britain 54%
British West Indies 22%

Source: *Shipping, Maritime Trade and the Economic Development of Colonial North America*

The need to channel the flow of colonial raw materials into England—and to keep foreign goods and vessels out of colonial ports—became obvious in the 1650s when the Dutch built a magnificent merchant fleet of 10,000 ships. They dominated trade wherever they sailed: coastal France, the North Atlantic, South America, India, and the East and West Indies.

The Navigation Act system worked quite well for more than a hundred years. The complicated triangular trade described in Chapter 3 did not conflict with it. The laws followed the natural trends of trade. The colonies were not well enough developed at this time to produce large amounts of manufactured goods. England, on the other hand, was by far the most efficient producer of manufactured goods in the world.

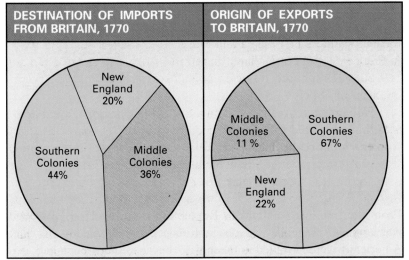

Source: *Shipping, Maritime Trade and the Economic Development of Colonial North America*

LEARNING FROM GRAPHS. *By comparing the two graphs at the left you can draw conclusions about the economies of the three colonial regions. Which region was the most self sufficient? Why did the Middle Colonies account for such a small proportion of the exports to Britain?*

Moreover, the Navigation Acts were not enforced very strictly. Smuggling was common. America was far from England. It had a long coastline with many isolated harbors and tiny coves where small ships could slip in under cover of night and easily unload their cargoes of contraband goods.

For many years the English government did not try very hard to prevent smuggling. Most Americans obeyed the laws. England was getting all the colonial products it needed. It hardly seemed worth the effort and expense to stop shippers who tried to sneak past the British navy with a cargo of tobacco bound for Amsterdam, or with French wine or silk that had not been taken first to England.

Although American smugglers considered the Royal Navy their natural enemy, most colonists believed that the British army and navy were vital to their safety and well-being. Like children, the colonists were under the control of a mother country, and they needed its protection. 🖳

Return to the Preview & Review on page 111.

Photo: Dan McCoy/Rainbow

In this watercolor France's Indian allies are shown attacking Deerfield, Massachusetts. Already much of the town is in flames in this scene. What do you suppose was the function of the red building in the center of town?

Preview & Review

Use these questions to guide your reading. Answer the questions after completing Section 3.
Understanding Issues, Events, & Ideas. Use the following words to cite the significance of French challenges to England in America: King William's War, Schenectady, Queen Anne's War, Deerfield, King George's War, Fort Pitt, Seven Years' War, Pontiac's Rebellion, Proclamation Line of 1763.
1. How were French colonies different from English colonies?
2. Why did France win most of the early battles in America?
3. What were the results of the French and Indian War?
4. What was the purpose of the Proclamation of 1763? How did most colonists react to it?
Thinking Critically. 1. Why did the building of forts by the French obstruct westward expansion of the British colonial frontier? **2.** Using your historical imagination, write Robert Dinwiddie's message, which young George Washington delivered, to Marquis Duquesne. Explain Dinwiddie's objection to building forts west of Virginia.

3. FRANCE CHALLENGES ENGLAND

The French and English Wars

From the time of the Glorious Revolution until the 1760s, England was almost constantly at war in Europe, always against France. Americans were involved in these wars because the French had also become a colonial power in North America.

The French, who had begun their explorations of America in 1524, did not build many permanent settlements in America. While the English were clearing land and planting crops along the Atlantic Coast, the French were ranging deep into the continent, hunting, trapping, and setting up trading posts where they bought furs from the American Indians.

Whenever war broke out in Europe between England and France, French and English colonists fought in America. It was difficult for them to get at each other because their posts and settlements in America lay far apart in the wilderness. Most of the battles consisted of sneak attacks and raids on frontier outposts. Relatively few colonists actually took up arms. Much of the fighting was done by Indians allied with one side or the other.

The first colonial conflict was known as **King William's War.** It went on with interruptions from 1689 to 1697. The French, with Indian support, attacked **Schenectady** in New York and a few villages in New England. American colonists responded by marching against

Port Royal in Nova Scotia, which they captured and then lost. An attempted invasion of Canada failed miserably. When the war ended, the treaty of peace returned all captured territories to their colonial owners.

Both sides followed a similar strategy in **Queen Anne's War,** which began in 1702 and ended in 1713. France's Indian allies attacked several New England settlements and destroyed **Deerfield,** Massachusetts. The English colonists responded by making raids on Nova Scotian villages. Once again they captured Port Royal. Far to the south a force of Carolinians struck a blow at France's ally, Spain, by burning St. Augustine, Florida. The outcome of this war was decided in Europe, where England won a series of decisive victories. The Treaty of Utrecht in 1713 gave England control of Nova Scotia, Newfoundland, and Hudson Bay.

The third English-French clash in America, **King George's War,** lasted from 1744 to 1748. Once again Indians friendly to France crossed the St. Lawrence and attacked settlements in New England. New Englanders sailed north and captured Louisbourg, a fort on Cape Breton Island that guarded the mouth of the St. Lawrence River. England fared badly in the European phases of this war. To the New Englanders' disgust Fort Louisbourg was given back to France at the peace conference ending the war.

The French and English wars involved few of the colonists. Still, they increased tensions between settlers from both nations, who blamed each other for their troubles on the frontier. We can easily see the attitudes of both sides from the following excerpts. The first is from a letter written in 1718 by Alexander Spotswood, deputy governor of Virginia to the British Board of Trade.

    ❝ The French have built so many forts that the British settlements almost seem surrounded by French trade with the numerous Indian tribes on both sides of the lakes. The French may, in time, take over the whole fur trade. But even if they do not they can, whenever they please, send bands of Indians to the outskirts of our settlements and greatly threaten His Majesty's subjects there. If the French should increase their settlements along these lakes, in order to join their lands in Canada to their new colony in Louisiana, they might take over any English settlements they please.

    Nature, it is true, has formed a defense for us with that long chain of mountains which runs from the west of South Carolina as far north as New York and which is passable only in a few places. But even this natural defense may become a danger to us, if we do not take over before the French do. Now, while both nations are at peace, is the time to prevent all such dangers caused by the growing power of the French which threaten His Majesty's holdings. While the French are still unable to seize all that vast area west of our lands, we should attempt to make some settlements along the Great Lakes. At the same time we should also take over the passes of the mountains in order to safeguard communications with such settlements. . . . We could also cut off or disturb the communication between Canada and Louisiana if a war should break out. Once such a settlement was made, I can't see how the French could dispute our right of possession. The law of nations recognizes the right of the first nation that settles an area. And if the French should try to make us leave the area by force, we are closer to our settlements and aid than they are to theirs.[1] **"**

The English acted on Spotswood's advice, building forts along the Great Lakes. But the French reacted strongly as we see in this excerpt from a letter written in 1750 by a French settler in Canada.

" The St. Lawrence River and the lakes which supply the waters of that great river stretch across the interior of Canada. Its navigation and trade can be halted more easily than people may think. One of the best ways to avoid this misfortune is further to strengthen not only Quebec and Montreal, but also Fort Frederic. It is essential to establish at that fort a large, well-fortified French village in time of peace and to attract an Indian village in time of war. This effort will cost little if we settle some farmers on Lake Champlain at the same time and form some villages there.

Fort Frontenac is at the outlet of Lake Ontario, on which the English have established a post or fort called Oswego. This is clearly illegal, and is a serious threat to Canada. This Oswego post is located on a lake that has long been claimed by France. And it has been built by the English during a period of peace. The Governor of Canada has protested but taken no further action. Although it ought to have been pulled down in the beginning by using force, the post is still there.

This post, which has been regarded as of little importance, can, in fact, destroy Canada, and it already caused the greatest harm. . . . It is there that the English hand out rum to the Indians, even though the King of France has forbidden this trade. It is there that the English try to win over all Indian nations. They not only try to corrupt them with gifts but also urge them to kill the French traders throughout the vast forests of New France.

[1]From *The Official Letters of Alexander Spotswood*, edited by R.A. Brock

As long as the English occupy Fort Oswego, we must distrust even those Indians who are most loyal to the French. . . . Shipping on the lakes will always be exposed to danger. Agriculture will make very slow progress, and will be limited to the heart of the colony. In short, we will face all the difficulties of war and none of its advantages. Everything possible, then, must be done to destroy this dangerous post.

We must also have free and dependable communication from Canada to the Mississippi. This chain, once broken, would leave an opening where the British would doubtless move in. . . .[1]**"**

The French Menace

Though considerable blood had been spilled between 1689 and 1748, neither England nor France had gained much from the other in America. In 1752 the French governor of Canada, the Marquis Duquesne de Menneville, ordered the construction of a new chain of forts running from Lake Erie south to the Ohio River, in what is now western Pennsylvania. These forts, Duquesne believed, would keep English fur traders and settlers from crossing the Appalachian Mountains into territory claimed by France.

Duquesne's action alarmed many people in the English colonies, none more so than Lieutenant Governor Robert Dinwiddie of Virginia. Dinwiddie was very interested in buying land beyond the frontier, which could later be sold to settlers at a big profit.

When Dinwiddie learned what the French were doing, he sent a young planter and land surveyor named George Washington to warn them that they were trespassing on Virginia property. Washington was only 21 years old, but as a surveyor he knew the western land well. In November 1753 he set out with a party of six to find the French commander. After weeks of tramping through the icy western forests, Washington delivered Dinwiddie's message. But Duquesne rejected it with contempt.

In the spring of 1754, Dinwiddie sent another group of Virginians to build a fort where the Monongahela and Allegheny join to form the Ohio River. He also appointed Washington as lieutenant colonel of the Virginia militia and ordered him to lead a force of 150 soldiers to protect the new post against a possible French attack.

Before Washington could reach the Ohio, the French drove off the construction party and completed the post on their own, naming it Fort Duquesne. They occupied it with a force of about 600 men.

Washington should have turned back at this point or at least called for reinforcements. But he was young, ambitious, and head-

[1]From *Documents Relative to the Colonial History of the State of New York,* Vol. X, edited by E.B. O'Callaghan

The war that started to shape North America began with a headstrong young colonel named George Washington holed up in a place called Fort Necessity.

Early in 1755 Major General Edward Braddock arrived in Virginia with two regiments of red-coated British soldiers. He was under orders to drive the French out of Fort Duquesne. Braddock was a veteran with over 40 years in the British army. But his long military experience proved a disadvantage in America. Instead of moving swiftly along forest trails, guided by Indian scouts, he carved a road through the wilderness so that he could haul heavy cannon for the attack on the French.

Under such conditions surprise was impossible. As the troops approached Fort Duquesne, the French were ready for them. When Braddock's force of 1,400 men was passing through a narrow gulch about 8 miles (13 kilometers) from the fort, the woods suddenly exploded with gunfire. Redcoats fell by the hundreds. Panic spread among the survivors. Braddock fought bravely but finally was shot in the lungs.

Colonel Washington, who was serving under Braddock, miraculously escaped injury. A big man, well over six feet, he must have presented a tempting target as he tried to rally and organize the British soldiers. Two horses were shot out from under him. After he had finally led the 500 survivors back to safety, he discovered four bullet holes in his coat.

Washington/Custis/Lee Collection, Washington and Lee University

strong. He marched straight toward Fort Duquesne. On the way he surprised a small French scouting party, killing their leader. The main French force then advanced against him. He set up a defensive post, Fort Necessity, but the French easily surrounded it. After an all-day attack Washington had to surrender. The French commander then allowed him and his men to go free. They returned to Virginia, leaving the disputed territory to the French.

The French and Indian War

With Washington's retreat the war began in earnest. In all North America there were no more than 90,000 French settlers. The population of the English colonies was about 1.5 million. Thousands of British soldiers took part in the struggle. Yet for about two years the outnumbered French won most of the battles. They were experts at forest warfare. Most of the Indians sided with them, for unlike the English the French colonists were mostly interested in the fur trade. They did not try to force the Indians to give up their lands or abandon their ways of life.

The British were not easily discouraged. The tide began to turn after a brilliant English politician, William Pitt, took over management of the war effort. In 1758 English troops finally captured Fort

Duquesne. They changed its name to **Fort Pitt,** which is why the modern city on the site is named Pittsburgh.

Gradually other key French posts were taken. The most decisive battle occurred at the city of Quebec in 1759. Quebec is located on a cliff overlooking the St. Lawrence River. The British attack force, led by General James Wolfe, could not at first find a way to get up the cliff without being exposed to murderous fire.

Then one day Wolfe noticed some women washing clothes on the bank of the St. Lawrence. The next day he saw the same clothes hung out to dry on the cliff above. There must be a hidden path up the cliff! Wolfe investigated, found the path, and in the dead of night moved his army up to the city. There on a field outside the city called the Plains of Abraham the battle took place. Both Wolfe and the French commander, General Louis Joseph de Montcalm, were killed in the fight, which ended with the surrender of the city to the English.

By this time the conflict had spread throughout the world, including Europe, where it has been called the **Seven Years' War.** Everywhere the British were victorious. French outposts in Asia and Africa were captured. Spain entered the conflict on the side of France in 1761, only to see its colonies in Cuba and the Philippine Islands overwhelmed by the British.

When the war ended in 1763, the British were able to redraw the map of the world. Outside North America they were remarkably generous. They returned most of the lands they had conquered.

LEARNING FROM MAPS. *Note that most of French lands were north and west of the British colonies. Despite this, a strong rivalry existed. Why were the British concerned with French control of this area?*

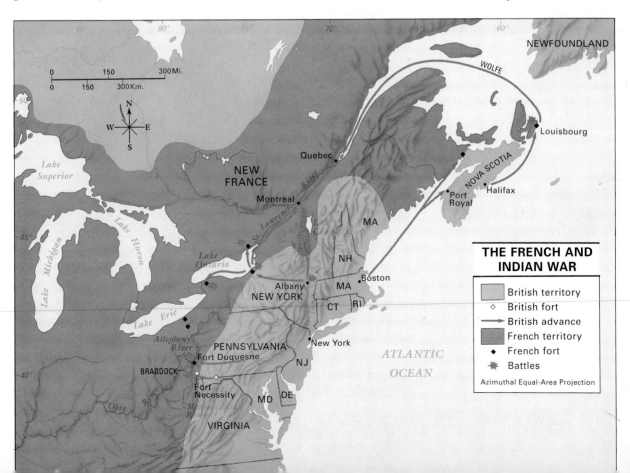

The National Gallery of Canada, Ottawa

Benjamin West painted "Death of General Wolfe" in 1771. The oil painting shows the general's last breaths on the Plains of Abraham, where he was the victor in 1759. The French commander Montcalm died in the same battle. Do you think battlefield deaths were really like the one shown here? How did they probably differ?

France had to surrender Canada and all claims to the Ohio and Mississippi Valleys. Spain turned over to the British Florida and the Gulf Coast as far west as the Mississippi River.

Nearly everyone in the English colonies in America was delighted with the outcome of the war. The French threat had been removed. Spain had been pushed back from the southern frontier. The way to the West lay open.

Although some of the colonies had contributed men and money to the conflict, British soldiers and sailors had done most of the fighting. The Royal Treasury paid most of the bills. Never did Americans feel more loyal to the king or more grateful to England than in 1763.

Postwar Problems

As often happens after wars, peace brought new problems and caused new conflicts. The British government had borrowed huge sums during the war to pay its heavy costs. The new, larger empire would also be more expensive to maintain and defend. Where was the money to come from?

And how was the new, larger empire in America to be governed? The old system of 13 separate colonies, each controlled from London, worked well enough when the colonies were separated from one another by thick forests. Now the wilderness was shrinking. Four colonies—Virginia, Pennsylvania, Connecticut, and Massachusetts—each claimed parts of the Ohio Valley just won from France. Each based its case on a royal charter drafted before anyone knew much about American geography. Who would untangle these conflicting claims?

There were also the Indians in the Ohio Valley. Everyone expected them to stop fighting when the French surrendered. Instead they organized behind Pontiac, a chief of the Ottawa, and tried to drive the settlers back across the Appalachians. How could an area claimed by so many different colonies be defended? Who would pay the cost if British troops were used?

These last questions were the most pressing in 1763. The answers were that the British put down **Pontiac's Rebellion** and paid the cost of doing so. To keep the peace the British stationed 6,000 soldiers in the land won from the French and closed the entire region beyond the Appalachian Mountains to settlers. This decision was announced in the **Proclamation of 1763.** Only licensed fur traders might enter the Ohio region. No one could purchase Indian lands.

Most American colonists did not like the Proclamation of 1763. It seemed to put the great West as far out of reach as it had been when the forts built by Governor Duquesne had first barred the way ten years earlier.

LEARNING FROM MAPS. *The French and Indian War significantly changed the face of North America. Study these maps. What changes can you discover?*

Return to the Preview & Review on page 116.

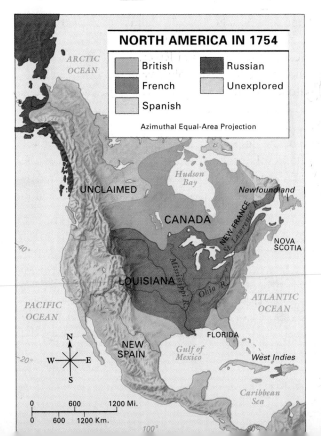

NORTH AMERICA IN 1754

- British
- French
- Spanish
- Russian
- Unexplored

Azimuthal Equal-Area Projection

ARCTIC OCEAN
UNCLAIMED
Hudson Bay
Newfoundland
CANADA
NEW FRANCE
NOVA SCOTIA
St. Lawrence R.
Mississippi R.
Ohio R.
LOUISIANA
ATLANTIC OCEAN
PACIFIC OCEAN
NEW SPAIN
FLORIDA
Gulf of Mexico
West Indies
Caribbean Sea

0   600   1200 Mi.
0   600   1200 Km.

NORTH AMERICA IN 1763

- British
- French
- Spanish
- Russian
- Unexplored
- —— Proclamation Line of 1763

Azimuthal Equal-Area Projection

ARCTIC OCEAN
ALASKA
DISPUTED
Hudson Bay
Newfoundland
CANADA
French
St. Lawrence R.
RESERVED FOR INDIANS
ORIGINAL 13 COLONIES
Mississippi R.
LOUISIANA
ATLANTIC OCEAN
PACIFIC OCEAN
FLORIDA
Gulf of Mexico
West Indies
Caribbean Sea
French

0   600   1200 Mi.
0   600   1200 Km.

Use these questions to guide your reading. Answer the questions after completing Section 4.
Understanding Issues, Events, & Ideas. Use the following words to describe colonial protests to British tax policies: Sugar Act, duty, taxation without representation, Stamp Act, Sons of Liberty, boycott, Declaratory Act, indirect tax, tariff, Townshend Acts, Circular Letter, Boston Massacre.
1. For what two reasons did colonists dislike the Sugar Act?
2. What caused the Stamp Act to be repealed?
3. What did Parliament say about taxation without representation?
4. How did the conflicts draw colonists together?
Thinking Critically. 1. Could conflicts between the British and the colonists before 1772 have been resolved peacefully? Explain your reasoning. **2.** You are a reporter who witnessed the Boston Massacre. Write an article and headline on it.

4. TAXATION WITHOUT REPRESENTATION

The Sugar Act

The Proclamation of 1763 made sense as a temporary policy designed to make peace with the Indians and to buy time to untangle complicated colonial claims in the Ohio Valley. The problem of governing the empire as a whole and paying the costs involved proved much more difficult to manage.

In 1763 the British prime minister was George Grenville. Grenville had the mind of a bookkeeper: he saw the colonies in terms of money taken in, money spent. Running the colonies was expensive. Most of the tax money collected in the colonies was also spent in the colonies. They were no longer so profitable for the mother country. In England taxes were high. In America taxes were low. To Grenville the conclusion was obvious: Parliament should raise the money to run the colonies by taxing the colonists.

The first of Grenville's tax measures was the **Sugar Act** of 1764. Under this law sugar, coffee, and a number of other products the colonists imported were to be taxed upon entry into any colonial port. These import taxes, called **duties,** were not high. One of the most controversial, the duty on foreign molasses, actually reduced the existing molasses tax from sixpence a gallon to threepence.

Although the Sugar Act resembled many of the earlier laws regulating colonial trade, it actually marked a drastic change in British policy. The old sixpenny tax on foreign molasses, put into effect by the Molasses Act of 1733, was not designed to raise money. It was passed to protect planters in the British sugar islands from foreign competition by making foreign molasses so expensive that no American would buy it. In other words, the tax was not supposed to be collected. The Molasses Act of 1733 was one of the Navigation Acts, part of the effort to make the Empire self-sufficient and hold down the importing of foreign products. A tax of only threepence a gallon would not be high enough to keep French molasses out of America, and England would receive duties from *all* imported molasses, regardless of where it came from.

Americans did not want to pay any new taxes. They were particularly alarmed by Grenville's determination to crack down on smugglers so that the new taxes could be collected. Remember that the Navigation Acts had never been strictly enforced. A merchant who wanted to import French molasses could slip into a remote cove at night and bring his kegs ashore. If caught and brought to trial, a local jury would probably set him free. Or, more likely, he could pay bribes of about a penny a gallon to the customs officials and in perfect safety unload at his own wharf in broad daylight.

The Granger Collection, New York

Sugar is being refined in this 1667 engraving by Jean Baptiste Duarte. Trace the steps from squeezing the juice from the cane, boiling it into sugar, and collecting the excess liquid as molasses.

The Sugar Act contained regulations requiring shippers to file papers describing their cargoes in detail. Persons accused of smuggling could be tried in admiralty courts, which had jurisdiction over all affairs of the sea. In British admiralty courts there were no juries and the judges were stern. If convicted, offenders lost both the cargo involved and the ship that carried it.

Americans disliked the Sugar Act, both for selfish reasons and because an important principle was involved. That they did not want to pay new taxes was understandable but hard to justify. The money raised was to be spent in the colonies and for the defense and development of the colonies. That the colonists should bear part of the expense of maintaining the Empire was certainly a reasonable thing for the English to ask, particularly since it was for the protection of the colonies.

The moral principle behind their objection, however, was very important. Did Parliament have the right to tax people who had no say in the election of its members? *No,* most Americans answered. It was **taxation without representation.** People should be taxed only by legislative bodies that they had themselves elected. The Sugar

The Granger Collection, New York

James Otis

Act violated the laws of God and nature. Taxing people without their consent was little different from outright robbery. A Boston lawyer named James Otis put the issue clearly in his essay *The Rights of the British Colonies Asserted and Proved.*

❝ I have waited for years to hear some friend of the colonies pleading in public for them [in England]. I have waited in vain. One privilege after another is taken away. Where we shall end up only God knows. I trust He will protect and provide for us, even if we are driven and persecuted—as many of our ancestors were driven to these once inhospitable shores of America. . . .

It is unjust that a heavy burden should be laid on the trade of the colonies to maintain an army of soldiers, customhouse officers, and fleets of guardships. All the wealth both from trade and the colonies themselves was not enough to support these groups last war. How can anyone suppose that all of a sudden the trade of the colonies alone can bear such a heavy burden? . . .

To say that the Parliament has absolute and arbitrary power does not make sense. Parliament cannot make two and two equal five. Parliament can declare that something is being done for the good of the whole, but this declaration by Parliament does not make it true. There must be a higher power—that is, God. Should any act of Parliament be against any of His natural laws, which are eternally true, such an act would be contrary to eternal truth and justice. Therefore, it would be void. . . .

We regard ourselves as happy under Great Britain's rule. We love, esteem, and revere our mother country, and honor our king. If the colonies were offered a choice between independence and subjection to Great Britain upon any terms other than absolute slavery, I am convinced they would accept subjection. The British government in all future generations may be sure that the American colonies will never try to leave Britain's rule unless driven to it as the last desperate action against oppression. It will be an oppression that will make the wisest person mad and the weakest strong. . . .

I hope these hints . . . will not be misunderstood. They are delivered in pure affection to my king and country, and are not a reflection on any individual. The best army and the best people may be led into temptation. All I know is that it is easier to prevent evil than to escape it once it is here.[1] ❞

[1]From "The Rights of the British Colonies Asserted and Proved," by James Otis

Not all colonists agreed with Otis' ideas. Martin Howard, a Rhode Island lawyer, spoke for those still loyal to Britain.

" Our personal rights of life, liberty, and property are guaranteed to us by the law of England. These form the birthright of every citizen, whether born in Great Britain, on the ocean, or in the colonies. The political rights of the colonies are more limited. The nature, quality, and scope of these political rights depend completely upon the charters which first established them.

I am aware that this reasoning will be argued against by quoting the saying ''No English subject can be taxed without his consent, or the consent of his representatives.''

It is the opinion of the members of the House of Commons that they are the representatives of all British subjects, wherever they may live. From their point of view, the saying about taxation is fully respected, and its benefit applies to the colonies. And indeed, the saying must be viewed in this way, for in a strict sense taxation with consent always was and always will be impractical. . . .

Believe me, my friend, it causes me great pain to see that the colonies are so ungrateful to the mother country, whose army and money have just rescued them from being ruled by a French government. I have been told that some colonists have gone so far as to say that, the way things are, they would even prefer a French government to an English one. Heaven knows I have little ill will for anyone. Yet for a moment I wish that those unworthy subjects of Britain could feel the iron rod of a Spanish inquisitor or a French tax agent. This would indeed be a punishment suited to their ungrateful feelings.[1] "

The Stamp Act

Most colonists did no more than complain about the Sugar Act. So Prime Minister Grenville moved ahead with his plans to raise money in America. In March 1765 Parliament passed another tax measure, the **Stamp Act.** This law taxed the use of all sorts of printed matter— deeds to land, marriage licenses, advertisements, newspapers, diplomas, customs documents, even packets of playing cards. Actual stamps or special stamped paper had to be purchased and attached before any of these items could be sold.

Seldom has a political leader been so wrong about what the public would accept. When the terms of the law became known in America, nearly all the colonists spoke out in opposition. The colo-

[1]From *A Letter from a Gentleman at Halifax, . . . The Rights of Colonies Examined,* by Martin Howard

The Granger Collection, New York

This is one of the hated stamps used to tax all kinds of goods in the American colonies. What items were taxed under the Stamp Act?

❝Exemption from the burden of taxes we have not passed ourselves must be a principle of every free state. Without this right there can be no liberty, no happiness, and no security.❞

General Assembly of New York, 1776

Points of View

❝The liberty of an Englishman, is a phrase of so various a signification . . . that I shall not here presume to define its meaning; but I will venture to assert what it cannot mean; that is, an exemption from taxes imposed by the Parliament of Great Britain, nor is there any charter, that ever pretended to grant such a privilege to any colony in America.❞

Soame Jenyns, Member of Parliament, 1765

nial assemblies wrote petitions urging that the law be done away with. They drafted stern resolutions denying Parliament's power to tax the colonies. A Stamp Act Congress attended by representatives of nine colonies met in New York and passed 14 polite but firm resolutions. Laws such as the Stamp Act, one resolution stated, "subvert the rights and liberties of the colonists."

The first open resistance to British authority now occurred. Groups calling themselves **Sons of Liberty** began to organize. These "Liberty Boys" believed in action rather than talk. Grenville had appointed a stamp master who was to receive the stamps and sell them to the public. In Boston the Liberty Boys stormed the house of stamp master Andrew Oliver even before he had received any stamps to sell. They broke his windows and made off with many of his valuables. Similar Stamp Act Riots erupted in other colonies. Many of the stamp masters found their very lives in danger. No one could safely distribute the hated stamps.

Colonists also began to refuse to buy anything English until the law was repealed. A thousand merchants agreed to **boycott,** or not import, British goods. This boycott was effective because it hurt the business of exporters in England. These exporters were soon urging Parliament to back down. Finally, since the law was not bringing a single penny into the treasury, Parliament repealed it.

The Declaratory Act

The issue was far from settled. The British were puzzled by the colonial argument against taxation without representation. Many older laws of Parliament applying to the colonies, such as the Molasses Act of 1733, had been tax laws. If representation was so important, what was the difference between the Stamp Act and any of the English laws that colonists had been obeying without argument for the past 150 years?

Furthermore, English leaders claimed, Parliament *did* represent the colonies. Every member of Parliament was said to represent every person in the Empire. The fact that no colonist sat in Parliament or voted for members seemed unimportant. Many thousands of people living in England could not vote for members of Parliament. Many parts of England, including some entire cities, were not represented in Parliament.

The members of Parliament did not think the colonists' objections were sincere. Nor did they want the repeal of the Stamp Act to seem like a surrender. They therefore passed the **Declaratory Act** at the same time that they repealed the Stamp Act. The act was only a statement of power, not an exercise of power. It had no specific effects. The colonies, it said, were "subordinate"—that is, under the control of Parliament. Parliament could pass *any* law regarding the colonies that it desired.

The colonists were so happy to learn that the Stamp Act had been repealed that they ignored the threat contained in the Declaratory Act. Still, they did not accept the principle that Parliament was supreme. When the colonies were tiny and isolated settlements struggling to survive, they had submitted to Parliament in return for aid and protection. By the 1760s the colonies were strong and solidly established. Like children, they were now growing up. The mother country no longer commanded their unquestioning obedience. If trouble was to be avoided, England would have to recognize that time had changed its relationship with its American offspring.

The Declaratory Act was not merely ill-advised. It was both untrue and unwise—untrue because the colonies were in fact no longer completely ''subordinate'' and unwise because by claiming that the colonies were subordinate, it was sure to encourage them to prove that they were not.

The Townshend Acts

The Declaratory Act did nothing about Great Britain's need for money. In 1767 Charles Townshend, the chancellor of the exchequer, or finance minister, made yet another attempt to tax the colonists.

Paul Revere's engraving of Boston in 1768 shows British troopships landing the Redcoats. To Bostonians unaccustomed to the presence of British soldiers, this seemed like an invasion.

Henry Francis du Pont Winterthur Museum

Museum of Fine Arts, Boston

Fiery radical Sam Adams is the subject of this 1771 oil by the great John Singleton Copley, who also painted Paul Revere below.

Silversmith, engraver, firebrand, later hero of the Midnight Ride, Paul Revere sat for this Copley portrait around 1770. He is musing over a piece of his handsome silver. This is one of the first portraits to celebrate the work of a tradesman rather than an aristocrat. Why is Revere a good subject for this new kind of portrait?

Museum of Fine Arts, Boston

Townshend was an attractive, witty person, the kind of man often described as clever. But he was short of common sense. Like many upper-class English of that time, he had a low opinion of colonists, whom he thought crude and rather dull.

If the colonists considered direct taxes like the stamp duties beyond Parliament's authority, Townshend reasoned, then let them pay **indirect taxes.** Taxes on imports collected from shippers and paid by consumers in the form of higher prices were indirect taxes. The Sugar Act taxes were an example. The colonists had not liked that law, but they had not done much about it but grumble.

Townshend therefore proposed a number of additional **tariffs,** or taxes, on colonial imports. The **Townshend Acts** of 1767 taxed glass, lead, paper, paint, and tea—all things in everyday use that were not produced by Americans. Like Grenville before him, Townshend also tried hard to collect the taxes. He appointed a Board of Customs Commissioners with headquarters in Boston to enforce the law. The commissioners turned out to be greedy racketeers.

Under the law the customs officials received a third of the value of all ships and cargoes seized for violations. But these commissioners were not satisfied with what they could collect by enforcing the regulations strictly. They trapped merchants by allowing minor technical violations to go unpunished for a time and then cracking down when the merchants had grown used to doing business this way. They brought false charges of smuggling against shippers and paid witnesses to testify falsely to obtain convictions. When their thievery caused local citizens to riot against them, they demanded that the British government send troops to Boston to protect them.

The colonists responded to the Townshend Acts and the greed of the customs commissioners by organizing another boycott. After all, no one could collect the taxes if no tea or glass or paint was imported. The Massachusetts legislature also sent a **Circular Letter** to the other colonial assemblies. No more taxation without representation, it said. Let us take action together.

The British minister in charge of colonial affairs, Lord Hillsborough, ordered Massachusetts to rescind, or cancel, the Circular Letter. When the legislature refused, he ordered the assembly dissolved by the governor. He also moved two regiments of British soldiers from the frontier to Boston.

The Boston Massacre

Before the French and Indian War, British troops had never been stationed in the colonies. Now, during peacetime, several thousand "Redcoats," so called because of their red uniforms, were suddenly quartered in Boston. Tensions mounted. Most people in Boston did not hesitate to show their dislike for the soldiers, but they avoided violence. On March 5, 1770, serious trouble erupted. A squad of

American Antiquarian Society

soldiers guarding the hated customs house was being taunted by a crowd of sailors, loafers, and small boys. The crowd threw snowballs and rocks and some attacked the British soldiers. Suddenly the Redcoats began to fire into the crowd. When order was restored, three Americans lay dead on the ground. Two others died later of their wounds.

The captain of the guards, Thomas Preston, and eight of his men were arrested and accused of murder. A few Boston radicals, led by Sam Adams, now began to hint that the colonies should declare their independence. Adams was a founder of the local Sons of Liberty and one of the authors of the Massachusetts Circular Letter. Another radical, the silversmith Paul Revere, made and distributed an engraving of this **Boston Massacre** that portrayed Captain Preston commanding his sneering soldiers to fire at unarmed American civilians.

Paul Revere quickly published "The Boston Massacre" after the Redcoats fired in March 1770. From your reading what are some ways in which this engraving may be considered to give only one point of view? What is art or printed matter of this type generally called?

Taxation Without Representation   131

STRATEGIES FOR SUCCESS

RECOGNIZING CAUSE AND EFFECT

Determining cause-and-effect relationships is crucial for the reader of history. A cause is a condition, person, or event that makes something happen. An effect is the outcome of a cause. A cause may have many effects. An effect may itself be the cause of other effects. For example, because of high costs of the French and Indian War, Britain levied taxes on the colonies. The costs were a cause and the taxes were the effect. But the taxes resulted in colonial unrest, becoming a cause of the Revolution. Visually, the relationship would look like this:

CAUSE	EFFECT/CAUSE	EFFECT
Cost of French and Indian War →	New taxes levied →	Colonial protests

To fully understand the reasons for an event, you must be able to recognize the cause-effect relationships.

How to Recognize Cause-Effect Relationships

Follow these steps to recognize cause-effect relationships.

1. **Look for cause-effect clues**. Certain words are immediate clues to cause and effect. Cause clues include *led to, brought about, produced, because, as a result of, the source of,* and *the reason why*. Some effect clues are the *outcome of, as a consequence, resulting in, gave rise to,* and *depended on*.

Remember, however, that writers do not always state the link between cause and effect. Sometimes you must read closely to see the relationship between the events.

2. **Check for complex connections**. Note that many cause-effect relationships have complex connections. A single cause may have many effects. Likewise, a single effect may have root in many causes. And remember that an effect may itself be a cause.

Applying the Strategy

Read pages 130–133 and identify at least one cause-effect relationship. Then draw a cause-effect diagram similar to the one in the first column.

There are numerous cause-and-effect relationships presented in the material. For example, the stationing of troops in Boston caused tensions to mount. The situation flared into the Boston Massacre. Can you find other relationships, both stated and unstated, in the excerpt?

For independent practice, see Practicing the Skill on page 134.

INTERPRETING HISTORY: The American Revolution

Historians study the past much like detectives solve crimes. Like a detective, an historian gathers evidence, such as letters, diaries, newspaper articles, and eyewitness accounts, interprets it, and reaches a conclusion. But different historians may interpret that evidence differently.

For example, historians have debated for nearly 200 years the reasons behind the American Revolution. Many historians, such as James Franklin Jameson, support the theory that the Revolution was an economic and social struggle. In his book *The American Revolution Considered as a Social Movement* he stresses that democratic ideals were growing among the colonists and the Revolution brought about significant economic and social changes. Historian Mary Beth Norton agrees in her book *Liberty's Daughters: The Revolutionary Experience of American Women 1750–1800.* She points out that even the status of women in America improved after the Revolution.

Historian Gordon Wood in *The Creation of the American Republic 1776–1787* takes a contrasting view. He maintains that the colonists were motivated by patriotism. Historian Edmund S. Morgan supports this, arguing that the colonists were united by the principles expressed by Patrick Henry's "Give me liberty or give me death!"

Whether the Revolution was prompted by economic reasons or patriotic ones will always remain open to debate. Historians will continue to pursue the answers. This detective work makes history exciting.

The Calm Before the Storm

Cooler heads took control. Sam Adams' cousin John Adams, a respectable lawyer, was a prominent Boston critic of British policy. Nevertheless, he came forward to defend the accused soldiers to make sure they had a fair trial. He eventually obtained their freedom.

Frustrated once again in its effort to raise money in America, Parliament repealed all the Townshend duties except the tax on tea. That tax was kept, not for the money it might bring, but to demonstrate that Parliament still claimed the right to tax the colonies.

The crisis seemed to have ended. Lord Hillsborough announced that the government would not try to raise any more money in America. Normal trade relations between the colonies and England resumed. Business was good. Colonial merchants even imported a good deal of tea, in most cases quietly paying the threepenny duty.

This period of calm hid a basic change in attitude in both Great Britain and in the colonies. Until the late 1760s few colonists had considered England unfair to them. Most were proud to be known as English. They might complain about this or that action of the government in London, but only in the way that citizens today may complain about their political leaders in Washington. Hardly anyone had thoughts of breaking away from England.

The conflicts resulting from the Sugar, Stamp, and Townshend Acts drew colonists together. Many began to fear that the English might try to take away their rights or destroy their liberty. This fear led them to cooperate more with people in other colonies. They recognized that they had common interests. During the calm following the repeal of the Townshend duties, the colonists were less fearful. Yet they remembered the heavy hand of the British. When new threats appeared, the colonists would readily join together to protect themselves.

The English leaders had failed to make Americans pay reasonable taxes for their own defense and administration. This struck a terrible blow to English pride. They could do nothing about it at the moment. Their frustration made them boil inside. They too would react differently—and forcefully—when a new crisis developed.

In the early 1770s most people who had lived through the turmoil of the previous ten years thought that the threat to the peace and stability of the British Empire had ended. Nearly all were genuinely relieved. Nearly all were convinced that no serious trouble would ever again disturb this happy state of affairs. Of course they were wrong. On both sides of the Atlantic people were ready in their minds for separation, whether they knew it or not. More and more they were thinking of those on the other side of the ocean as "them" rather than "us." John Adams had this idea in mind when he wrote, "The revolution was complete in the minds of the people, and the Union of the colonies, before the war commenced."

Return to the Preview & Review on page 124.

CHAPTER 4 REVIEW

1651
First Navigation Act passed

1686
Dominion of New England created

1688
Glorious Revolution

1689
English-French conflict in colonies begins

Chapter Summary
Read the statements below. Choose one, and write a paragraph explaining its importance.
1. English monarchs and their advisers felt they had complete control of the colonies.
2. Each colony was led by a governor, who represented the king or queen and who was assisted by a council and an assembly.
3. Town meetings in New England handled local matters while in the Southern Colonies county courts headed by justices of the peace were the local government.
4. The colonies were a key part of England's trade and economy.
5. Parliament passed many laws regulating colonial commerce.
6. European wars between France and England often spilled over into the colonies.
7. England's victory over France in the French and Indian War drove France from North America.
8. Postwar problems such as large debts and conflicting western claims created problems for England.
9. Taxation without representation led to serious conflicts between the colonists and the English government.
10. The first warning of upcoming violence erupted in the Boston Massacre.

Reviewing Chronological Order
Number your paper 1-5. Then study the time line above and place the following events in the order in which they happened by writing the first next to 1, the second next to 2, and so on.
1. The Boston Massacre
2. The first Navigation Act is passed
3. Parliament passes the Stamp Act
4. The French and Indian War ends
5. Dominion of New England created

Understanding Main Ideas
1. Explain how the colonies were governed from England.
2. What was the purpose of the Navigation Acts?
3. Why did most Indian tribes side with the French rather than the English?
4. What was the Declaratory Act? Why did Parliament pass this law?
5. How did the colonists respond to the Townshend Acts of 1767?

Thinking Critically
1. **Synthesizing.** Imagine that you are an American Indian at the time of the French and Indian War. Would you prefer to fight on the side of the French or the British? Support your choice with sound reasoning based on fact.
2. **Solving Problems.** If you were an American colonist in 1764, you probably would be opposed to the Sugar Act and similar new British tax laws. In your opinion, what could the British have done to appease the colonists and to avoid provoking their discontent?
3. **Evaluating.** In your own words, explain what John Adams meant when he wrote, "The revolution was complete in the minds of the people . . . before the war commenced."

Writing About History
Use your historical imagination to put yourself in the boots of one of the British soldiers accused of the Boston Massacre. Write a letter to your family in England to present your side of the story.

Practicing the Strategy
Review the strategy on page 132.
Recognizing Cause and Effect. Review "France Challenges England" on page 116–23 and answer these questions.
1. What caused the English and French colonists in America to start fighting.
2. What was the effect of Queen Anne's War on the French and English colonies?
3. What effects did Duquesne's decision to build forts have? What was the final outcome?

1752
French fortify
Ohio Valley

1754
French and Indian
War starts

1759
Quebec falls to
British troops

1763
French and Indian War ends

★
Proclamation of 1763

1764
Sugar Act passed

1765
Stamp Act enacted

★
Sons of Liberty formed

1767
Townshend Acts

1768
Circular Letter sent

1770
Boston Massacre

Using Primary Sources

Mercy Otis Warren's play *The Adulateur* was written to protest the Boston Massacre and other British acts. It was first printed in *The Massachusetts Spy* in 1773. Its heroes, Brutus and Cassius, were patriots opposed to a greedy ruler. Brutus has often been identified as Warren's brother, James Otis, and Cassius as Samuel Adams. Brutus and Cassius also were the Roman senators who assassinated Julius Caesar in hopes of preserving the Roman republic. As you read the excerpt, compare the sentiments of the characters to those of the Patriots. Then answer the questions.

Brutus: *I sprang from men who fought, who bled for*
          freedom:
         From men who in the conflict laugh'd at danger:
         Struggl'd like patriots, and through seas of blood
         Waded to conquest—I'll not disgrace them.
         I'll show a spirit worthy of my sire.
         Tho' malice dart her stings—tho' poverty
         Stares full upon me;—tho' power with all her thunder
         Rolls o'er my head,—thy cause my bleeding country
         I'll never leave—I'll struggle hard for thee,
         And if I perish, perish like a freeman.
Cassius: *You're not alone—there are, I know, ten*
          thousand,
         Ne'er bow'd the knee to idol power—Repeated insults
         Have rous'd the most lethargic [lazy].

1. Compare the speech of Brutus with Otis' essay on page 126.
2. Why might a play be an excellent form of propaganda for the Patriots' cause?

Linking History & Geography

In today's world of instant communications and supersonic flight, it takes historical imagination to understand what it was like when ships powered only by wind and ocean currents were the one way to travel between America and Europe. Then the geographic location of America meant that time and distance had a major effect on life. To understand how geographic location affected the colonists, complete the following activities.

1. Research how long it took to sail from England to America in 1750.
2. Then in a paragraph discuss some of the problems this travel time caused both rulers and colonists.
3. In a second paragraph, explain why time and distance helped foster a sense of independence in the colonies.

Enriching Your Study of History

1. **Individual Project**. Prepare a chart with a column headed *Cause* and a column headed *Effect* to show the consequences of British actions from the Proclamation of 1763 to the Boston Massacre of 1770. Include the following example in your chart:

Cause		*Effect*
Townshend Acts	→	Colonists organize a boycott

2. **Cooperative Project**. With four other classmates, write and perform a skit in which you attend a meeting of the Sons of Liberty. What actions of the British upset you? What actions might you take? Have at least one member argue for proceeding with caution.

Chapter 4 Review   135

UNIT ONE REVIEW

Summing Up and Predicting

Read the summary of the main ideas in Unit One below. Choose one statement, then write a paragraph predicting its outcome or future effects.

1. America was discovered at least three times— by Asian wanderers, by the Vikings, and by Columbus.
2. Early American Indian cultures were strongly influenced by the environment and developed many unique life styles.
3. Europeans came to America for many reasons—economic opportunity, religious freedom, and adventure among them.
4. Most Africans were brought to America as slaves.
5. At first life in the colonies was hard, but it improved as the colonies grew.
6. Royal grants and charters permitted colonial settlement, but the monarchs themselves had complete authority over the colonies.
7. The British defeated other European colonial threats in America, but postwar problems caused conflicts with the colonies.

Connecting Ideas

1. Contrast ways in which native Americans affected the environment with ways in which European colonists affected it.
2. Compare reasons that people first came to North America with reasons that people immigrate to the United States today.
3. If you could colonize another planet, name three things you would do to avoid mistakes made by the early colonists of America.

Practicing Critical Thinking

1. **Analyzing.** Explain how the Commercial Revolution in Europe after the Crusades led to Columbus' voyage to the New World.
2. **Synthesizing.** The year is 1606. You are in charge of leading a group of English people to America to start a colony. Name three types of skilled workers you would take with you, and three objects that you would pack, all to help assure your colony's survival. Explain your reason for each choice.
3. **Drawing Conclusions.** Benjamin Franklin was one of the greatest Americans of the Enlightenment, or Age of Reason, a time of belief in human progress. Which achievement in Franklin's life do you think is the best example of the Enlightenment's spirit of progress? Why?

4. **Evaluating.** You know that many of the tax laws that outraged colonists were made by Britain's prime minister, George Grenville, and the finance minister, Charles Townshend. If you could advise these men to change their attitudes in order to avoid conflict with the colonies, how would you recommend they behave?

Cooperative Learning

1. Study the time lines at the end of each of the chapters in Unit One. Then your group will create its own time line of the most important events in the unit. Members of your group may wish to illustrate the time line.
2. Your group will prepare a debate on taxation in the colonies. One side will explain the British reasons for taxing the colonists. The other side will give the American argument against taxation by Britain. After the debate, your class will vote on which side presents the best argument.
3. Your group will prepare a panel discussion to present to the class. Various members will portray John Smith, Anne Hutchinson, William Penn, and Pontiac. The topic of the discussion: "Life in the Colonies." Actors should conduct research to gain knowledge about their characters' lives and points of view.

Reading in Depth

Alderman, Clifford L. *Colonists for Sale: The Story of Indentured Servants in America.* New York: Macmillan. Provides a close-up view of indenture and the people who became indentured servants.

Curtin, Philip D., ed. *Africa Remembered: Narratives by West Africans from the Era of the Slave Trade.* Madison: University of Wisconsin Press. Presents personal accounts of Africans who were sold as slaves.

Hampden, John, ed. *New Worlds Ahead: First Hand Accounts of English Voyages.* New York: Farrar, Straus, & Giroux. Tells the story of the early voyages to America in the words of the people who made them.

Hooks, William H. *The Legend of White Doe.* New York: Macmillian. Tells a fictional tale about the fate of Virginia Dare and the small band of settlers with her.

Syme, Ronald. *La Salle of Mississippi; Champlain of the St. Lawrence.* New York: Morrow. Provides accounts of the journeys of these two great French explorers.

The Granger Collection, New York

"Raising the Liberty Pole" shows how excited the American colonists had become at the prospect of freedom.

THE AMERICAN NATION

UNIT 2

I n Unit 2 you will learn about the Revolutionary War and the establishment of the United States of America. Here are some main points to keep in mind as you read the unit.

- The colonists' objections to British policies led to the Declaration of Independence and the Revolutionary War.
- After early setbacks, the colonists won major victories at battles such as Saratoga and Yorktown. The defeated British agreed to give the colonies independence.
- After the war, American leaders drew up the Constitution to give the new country sound government.
- George Washington became the first president of the United States. During his term, the power of the federal government was strengthened. He also kept the United States out of wars in Europe brought about by the French Revolution.

CHAPTER 5

The Revolutionary War

Ordinary people rarely protest when the cost of living goes down. Yet such was the American character that its revolt from Britain began when the price of tea was lowered. For at the same time a British company was given nearly total control of the tea market. What did this mean for the future of American self-government? This chapter explains how the struggle for the colonists' rights as Englishmen became the American Revolution. The Declaration of Independence was published to explain to the world the complaints the colonists had with the British government and why they wanted to create a government of their own. Major persons and events of the Revolutionary War as well as the impact of war on everyday life are described here. Battles fought in the Northeast, South, and West gradually brought America its freedom. But what was the price of victory for the Americans who won this freedom in 1781?

Preview & Review

Use these questions to guide your reading. Answer the questions after completing Section 1.
Understanding Issues, Events, & Ideas. Use the following words to explain the beginning of the Revolution: Tea Act, East India Company, monopoly, Boston Tea Party, Coercive Acts, Intolerable Acts.
1. What was the purpose of the Tea Act?
2. Why did the British think the colonists would be pleased with the Tea Act? Why did the colonists resent it?
3. How did Great Britain react to the Boston Tea Party?
Thinking Critically. You wish to protest the Tea Act, but you disapprove of the method used by those involved in the Boston Tea Party. What would you do instead?

1. THE REVOLUTION BEGINS

The Tea Act

The calm before the storm of the revolution ended in 1773. In May of that year Parliament passed a law known as the **Tea Act.** This law was designed to help the British East India Company, which was in very bad shape. After its founding in 1690, the **East India Company** had prospered, bringing riches to its stockholders and employees by its trade with India. But by 1773 the company had fallen upon hard times. King George III and Parliament felt that something must be done to revive the company's fortunes.

One of the chief products of the East India Company was tea. In 1773 it had about 17 million pounds (7.65 million kilograms) of unsold tea stored in English warehouses. Normally the company sold its tea at auction in London to wholesale merchants. The merchants then sold the tea to English storekeepers or to American wholesalers, who in turn sold it to retail merchants in the colonies. These merchants sold the tea to the colonists. The tea was taxed first in England and then again—the threepenny Townshend duty—in the colonies.

138   THE REVOLUTIONARY WAR

The Tea Act authorized the East India Company to sell tea directly to American retailers. This would eliminate the handling charges and profits of both British and American wholesalers. In addition, the act repealed the English tax on tea so that only the Townshend tax remained.

Frederick, Lord North, who had become prime minister of England in 1770, assumed that the colonists would not object to the Tea Act. The cost of tea would be greatly reduced for Americans, and opposition to paying the Townshend duty had been gradually dying out. Now, with the price much lower because of the elimination of the middlemen's profits and the English tax, surely the colonists would not mind paying the threepenny charge. East India tea, even with the tax, would be as cheap as tea from the Dutch East Indies, which smugglers were selling in America. Many people thought the prime minister's reasoning made sense.

The East India Company promptly shipped 1,700 chests containing about 500,000 pounds (225,000 kilograms) of tea to its agents in Boston, New York, Philadelphia, and Charleston.

Contrary to Lord North's hopes, news of the Tea Act caused great resentment in the colonies. What bothered most people was not only the tea tax but the fact that Parliament had given an English company what amounted to a **monopoly** of the tea trade in America. A monopoly is the exclusive control of a product or service in a given market. American importers of English tea would be cut out of the business. Even smugglers of foreign tea could not beat the company's price. Both groups were furious.

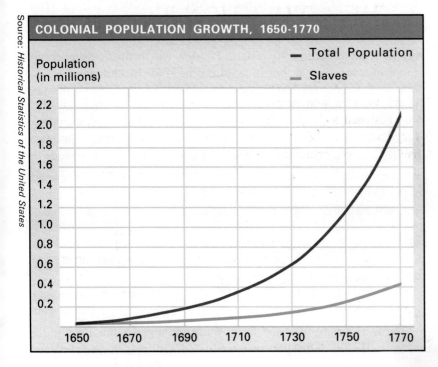

Source: Historical Statistics of the United States

COLONIAL POPULATION GROWTH, 1650-1770

Population (in millions)

— Total Population
— Slaves

2.2
2.0
1.8
1.6
1.4
1.2
1.0
0.8
0.6
0.4
0.2

1650   1670   1690   1710   1730   1750   1770

LEARNING FROM GRAPHS. *The colonial population grew very rapidly, almost doubling every 20 years! Artisans and craftsmen of every type came to America. By 1770 the colonies were no longer a wilderness and could produce the food and most of the goods they needed. How did this affect the move toward independence?*

The Revolution Begins   139

Other merchants were angry too. If Parliament could give the East India Company a monopoly of the tea business, could it not give other monopolies to the company or to any favored group? "Every Tradesman will groan under dire Oppression," warned one excited Philadelphian.

The American merchants were very influential people. No doubt their dislike of the Tea Act affected how other citizens responded to it. As we said earlier, ordinary people rarely protest when the cost of living goes down. Yet in this case they did. The strength of the public reaction showed how mistrustful the Americans were of the British by 1773.

The Tea Act seemed part of a devilish plot to make the colonies totally subordinate to England. Had not Parliament itself revealed that intention in the Declaratory Act back in 1766? Only recently, in 1772, the British government had begun to pay the salaries of colonial governors. Now the governors were no longer dependent upon the colonial assemblies, which had been able to threaten not to pay governors who disregarded colonial opinion. For years English leaders had been complaining about the high cost of governing the colonies. Why were they now taking on an additional expense? Many Americans believed that Lord North and his associates intended to crush local self-government in America.

The Boston Tea Party

When the ships carrying the East India Company's tea began to arrive in American ports, public protest rose to new heights. The ship *London* arrived in Charleston, South Carolina, on December 2. An angry crowd gathered and persuaded the company agent who was to receive the tea to resign. The tea was brought ashore and stored in a warehouse, but it could not be sold. In Philadelphia and New York public feeling was so strong that the captains of the tea ships did not dare unload. Instead they sailed back to England.

In Boston, however, an explosive situation developed when the tea ship *Dartmouth* tied up in the harbor on November 27. The governor of Massachusetts, Thomas Hutchinson, was determined to enforce the law. Hutchinson was American born. He had opposed all the British efforts to tax the colonies after the French and Indian War. But he believed that Parliament had the *right* to tax the colonies and to pass laws like the Tea Act.

Over the years Hutchinson had become the chief target of the Boston Sons of Liberty and of Sam Adams in particular. His house had been looted by rioters during the Stamp Act crisis. It was he who had announced, with obvious pleasure, the alarming news that the English had decided to pay the salaries of colonial governors.

Now Hutchinson stood firm. With his support the East India agents in Boston refused to resign. Customs officers denied the cap-

The Granger Collection, New York

tains of tea ships permission to leave the port. For more than two weeks tension mounted in the town. Crowds milled in the streets. Sam Adams and other radicals stirred public feeling at mass meetings.

Finally, on the night of December 16, Adams gave the signal to a group of townspeople disguised as Mohawk Indians. They boarded three tea ships and dumped the tea chests into the harbor. Tea worth about £15,000, a considerable fortune, was destroyed while a huge crowd watched silently from the shore.

Overboard go the chests of East Indies tea while Boston citizens watch from the harbor. Many probably recognized the thinly disguised "Mohawks."

The Coercive Acts

The **Boston Tea Party** was, as the name suggests, a kind of celebration in the eyes of those who participated in it. In British eyes (and, it must be admitted, to any neutral observer) it was a serious crime. Obviously it had been carefully planned. The ''Mohawks'' had gathered at the home of Benjamin Edes, editor of the Boston *Gazette,* to put on their costumes and await Sam Adams' signal.

When the news reached England, government leaders were furious. Parliament promptly passed a series of laws to force Massachusetts to pay for the tea.

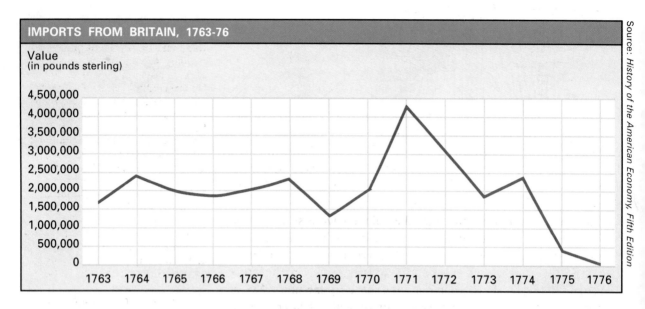

IMPORTS FROM BRITAIN, 1763-76

Value
(in pounds sterling)

Source: *History of the American Economy, Fifth Edition*

LEARNING FROM GRAPHS.
Much of the conflict between England and the colonies grew out of economic policies. What was the general trend of imports from England before 1771? What was the trend after 1771? What caused the change?

The first of these laws, known collectively as the **Coercive Acts,** was the Boston Port Act. It provided that no ship could enter or leave Boston harbor until the town had paid for the tea. The second, the Administration of Justice Act, gave the governor power to transfer the trials of soldiers and royal officials accused of serious crimes to courts outside of Massachusetts. This would be done when the governor felt that a fair trial could not be had in the colony.

The third law, the Massachusetts Government Act, further increased the governor's power by giving him control over town meetings, and it replaced the elected colonial council with a council appointed by the king. Another law, not directly related to the Tea Party but equally disliked by the colonists, ordered citizens to house British soldiers in their homes. A general, Thomas Gage, commander of British troops in America, replaced Thomas Hutchinson as governor of Massachusetts. Hutchinson promptly set sail for England to report to the king. He never returned to America.

Many Americans who had been critical of British policies spoke out against the Tea Party as an unnecessary act of violence. But the Coercive Acts angered and frightened everyone. To punish the entire community because some tea had been destroyed by extremists was the act of tyrants. Benjamin Franklin wrote that if the English government wanted to make up for the East India Company's loss, it ought to pay the money itself. It could subtract the sum from the far larger amount it had "extorted" from the colonies by its many illegal policies.

The Americans called the Coercive Acts the **Intolerable Acts.** The two names reflect the two views of the crisis. To the British the time had come to *coerce*, or force, the colonists into obedience. To the colonists the use of such force was *intolerable*—more than they could be expected to put up with.

Return to the Preview & Review on page 138.

2. SHOTS HEARD ROUND THE WORLD

Preview & Review

Use these questions to guide your reading. Answer the questions after completing Section 2.
Understanding Issues, Events, & Ideas. Use the following words to describe the outbreak of the Revolutionary War: Committee of Correspondence, First Continental Congress, Patriot, Minute Man, Concord, Lexington, Revolutionary War, Battle of Bunker Hill.
1. What did Lord North hope to accomplish by punishing Massachusetts so severely?
2. What actions did the First Continental Congress take?
3. When and why did Parliament declare Massachusetts to be in a state of rebellion?
4. Why were British troops sent to Concord?
5. Why did the Americans occupy Bunker Hill and Breed's Hill?
Thinking Critically. 1. After Lexington and Concord, could a peaceful solution to the problems between the colonists and the British government still have been found? Why or why not? **2.** Imagine that you are a resident of Boston. From your roof you are watching the Battle of Breed's Hill. In your diary, describe what you see and your reaction.

The First Continental Congress

Lord North hoped to accomplish two things by punishing Massachusetts so severely. One was to frighten the other colonies into accepting more British control over their affairs. The second was to tempt the other colonists to take advantage of Massachusetts' suffering. Ships that could not unload at Boston could unload at New York or Philadelphia or Baltimore to the benefit of those towns.

Lord North was assuming that the colonies were still separate societies. He was quite mistaken. Even before the Tea Act, radicals in Boston had formed a **Committee of Correspondence** to keep in touch with radicals elsewhere in Massachusetts and in the other colonies. A network of such committees existed by the time news of the Coercive Acts reached America. Almost without intending to, these committees were becoming an informal central government, a kind of United States waiting to be born.

The leaders of the other colonies did not even consider taking advantage of Massachusetts' misfortune. When the Massachusetts committee sent out a message in June 1774 calling for a meeting of colonial leaders, all but Georgia sent delegates. In September these delegates gathered in Philadelphia for what we now call the **First Continental Congress.**

The Congress took a firm but moderate position. It condemned the Intolerable Acts, and it urged full support for the citizens of Boston. It passed resolutions demanding the repeal of all the British laws aimed at raising money in the colonies. Only the colonial assemblies, it declared, had the right to tax Americans. The delegates denounced the British practice of maintaining an army in the colonies in peacetime. The Congress also set up a Continental Association to enforce a ban on importing British products of all kinds.

No one spoke openly about independence. Indeed, the delegates sent off a "loyal address" to George III, asking him politely to help them in their struggle for the rights of English subjects. Yet the Congress concluded its session in October with this stern warning: "We have *for the present* only resolved to pursue . . . peaceable measures." Then they adjourned, agreeing to meet again the following May if their demands had not been met.

Lexington and Concord

Meanwhile, in Massachusetts hatred of the Intolerable Acts had turned the colony into an armed camp. General Gage ruled in Boston, supported by his regiments of British Redcoats. Outside the city no

British law could be enforced. With the colonial legislature no longer functioning, local groups calling themselves **Patriots** took over. In the towns and villages citizens began to form militia companies. These civilian-soldiers could soon be seen drilling on town commons all over the colony. They were called **Minute Men** because they were supposed to be ready for action on a moment's notice.

Parliament now declared Massachusetts to be in a state of rebellion. The government decided to send more Redcoats to General Gage in Boston and ordered him to "arrest and imprison" the radical leaders. On the night of April 18, 1775, Gage sent a force of 700 men commanded by Lieutenant Colonel Francis Smith to seize a supply of weapons that the Patriots had gathered at **Concord,** a town about 15 miles (24 kilometers) west of Boston. On the way the troops could also arrest Sam Adams and the merchant John Hancock, another Patriot leader, who were at **Lexington.**

When the British troops set out, Paul Revere, who had made the engraving of the Boston Massacre, and another Patriot, William Dawes, rode ahead to rouse the countryside. Revere reached Lexington at midnight and warned Adams and Hancock to flee. Dawes reached the town about half an hour later. They then rode on toward Concord, accompanied by Dr. Samuel Prescott, a young man from Concord who had been visiting a lady in Lexington. Revere and Dawes were captured by a British patrol. Prescott escaped by jump-

This scene of the "Occupation of Concord" is taken from a larger engraving by Ralph Earl. Row upon row of Redcoats march past the Concord cemetery. How did this orderly march collapse when the Minute Men assembled?

The Butterick Collection

144

Albany Institute of History and Art

ing his horse over a stone wall, and he got to Concord in time to warn the people of the coming attack.

The British advance guard under Major John Pitcairn reached Lexington at dawn. Before them, lined up on the common, were some 70 Minute Men. The group included a number of men in their sixties as well as youngsters in their teens. Such a tiny force could not hope to stop the Redcoats.

Major Pitcairn rode forward and with a sneer ordered the Minute Men to move off. They were about to do so when someone fired a shot. British accounts say it was an American, American accounts blame a British soldier. More shots followed, and suddenly the Redcoats, "so wild," as one witness put it, "they could hear no orders," fired a volley directly into the American line.

When the smoke cleared, eight Minute Men lay dead. Ten other Americans and one Redcoat were wounded. The Britishers then marched on to Concord. They managed to occupy the town and destroyed whatever supplies the Americans had not carried off or hidden after the warning that the Redcoats were coming.

It was now mid-morning. The Redcoats had been on the march since midnight. Outside Concord, Minute Men from every nearby town were rapidly gathering. One group drove back three British infantry companies guarding Concord's North Bridge. Two more Americans were killed in this skirmish, but three Redcoats also fell. Colonel Smith decided to head back to Boston.

The march back was like a trip through the corridors of Hell. The Americans used their knowledge of the natural landscape to great advantage. All along the route they hid behind trees, along river banks, and in hollows. Snipers peppered the weary Redcoats with

The Minute Men at Lexington fall before the Redcoats led by Major John Pitcairn on April 19, 1775. This is the first of a series of hand-colored engravings made by Amos Doolittle. What is the response of the Minute Men here? How did it quickly change?

Shots Heard Round the World   145

STRATEGIES FOR SUCCESS

TRACING MOVEMENTS ON A MAP

Oftentimes a map shows routes of movement. Maps in Chapter 1, for example, show the migration of the first Americans (page 3) and the voyages of discovery of Columbus (page 24) and of Magellan and El Cano (page 29). Other maps in this book show the movement of troops in wartime. Studying routes on a map will give you a great deal of information about the course of events and will help you understand how the story unfolded.

How to Trace Movements on a Map

To trace movements on a map, follow these guidelines.

1. **Read the map's title.** The title will tell you what general information is shown on the map.
2. **Study the legend.** Lines indicate routes. Arrows indicate the directions of movement. In the case of troop movements, the routes and arrows may be colored differently to represent each army. Battle sites will be shown and will often indicate by color which army was victorious.

3. **Note the routes and related events carefully.** The routes tell you a great deal about the geography of an area as well as the overall picture of the historical event. For example, by studying troop movements closely you gain a sense of the sweep of an army from battle to battle—the victors in pursuit, the defeated in retreat. You can see where armies gathered strength and where desperate fighters played out their final hours.

Applying the Strategy

Like all good maps, the one on this page tells a story. But the story may be fully appreciated only by carefully reading the descriptions in your book on pages 143–47. Then turn to the map to see Revere, Dawes, and Prescott riding across Massachusetts ahead of the advancing British army. Note the site of the American victory at North Bridge near Concord and the retreat of the British troops to Boston.

For independent practice, see Practicing the Strategy on pages 178–79.

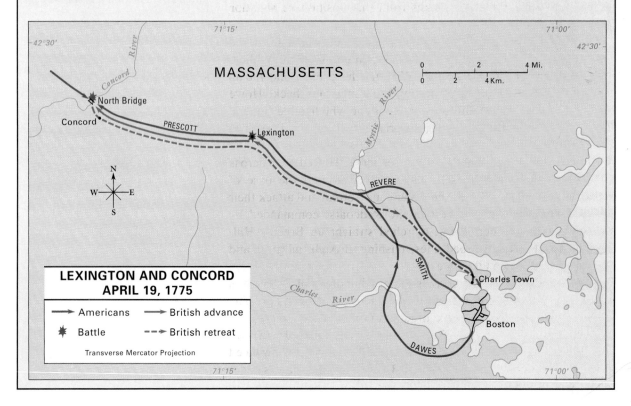

MASSACHUSETTS

LEXINGTON AND CONCORD
APRIL 19, 1775

→ Americans → British advance
✳ Battle --→ British retreat

Transverse Mercator Projection

bullets. Hundreds and hundreds of local citizens picked up their muskets and followed the sound of gunfire to join in the fight. By the time the British were safely back in Boston, they had suffered 273 casualties. American losses came to just under 100.

Breed's Hill

The **Revolutionary War** had begun. Within 48 hours nearly 20,000 angry American militiamen had gathered in and around Cambridge, across the Charles River from Boston. The new Massachusetts Provincial Assembly appointed Artemas Ward, a veteran of the French and Indian War, to command this large force. Ward, however, was not a good organizer. Militiamen from other New England colonies had their own commanders. Everywhere there was confusion.

Fortunately for the Americans the one important British force in America was penned up in Boston. In May Ethan Allen and the "Green Mountain Boys," militiamen from Vermont, took Fort Ticonderoga on Lake Champlain, capturing some valuable heavy cannon. Then, on June 16, the Americans occupied Bunker Hill and Breed's Hill, two high points near Charles Town, on the peninsula across the harbor from Boston. Working all night, they built an earthen *redoubt*, or fort, on Breed's Hill.

From this strong point cannon would be able to pound Boston and the British warships in the harbor. The British realized at once that they must clear the Americans from this position or abandon the city.

Three weeks earlier, three leading English generals had arrived in Boston to advise Gage. One of them, Major General William Howe, a veteran of King George's War and the French and Indian War, was assigned the task of driving the Americans back. Howe was a brave man and a skillful soldier. It was he who had led General Wolfe's advance guard during the surprise attack on the French at Quebec in 1759.

On the morning of June 17, Howe ferried 1,500 Redcoats across the bay on barges. He himself led one force around the base of Breed's Hill, hoping to cut off the Americans' retreat and attack their position from the rear. The rest of the Redcoats, commanded by Brigadier General Robert Pigot, marched straight up Breed's Hill. They advanced in three broad lines, pushing through tall grass and climbing over fences as they went.

It was a dramatic sight. Across the bay hundreds of Bostonians watched the brewing battle from their windows and rooftops. The Americans on Breed's Hill were tired and hungry after their night's labor with spades and shovels. Fresh troops were supposed to relieve them, but none arrived. The inexperienced civilian soldiers now faced hardened professional troops—skilled British bayonet fighters eager to avenge the bloody retreat from Concord.

The Americans knew how to shoot, and their commander, Colonel William Prescott, knew how to maintain discipline. Legend has it that the men were told not to fire until they could see the whites of the enemy's eyes. The British came on, firing with no effect against the earthen wall of the redoubt. They were prepared to take losses until they could scale the wall and end the battle with their bayonets. When the British were almost to the wall, Prescott gave the signal. A wall of flames erupted as the Americans fired. The heavy musket balls tore through the British lines. A second volley sent the Redcoats back down the hill in confusion. The field before the redoubt was littered with dead and dying men.

Meanwhile, General Howe's force had met a similar fate in front of an American defense line along the shore. Both British generals then regrouped and sent their brave soldiers forward once more against the American defenses. Once more they were thrown back.

Instead of landing behind the two hills as he could easily have done, Howe had probably attacked the Americans directly to shock them. He thought the untrained colonials would turn and run when faced by his disciplined veterans. Once the Redcoats had taken the

"Attack on Bunker Hill with the Burning of Charles Town" is the title of this oil painting. However, the real battle is being fought on Breed's Hill, to the right, which the orderly rows of Redcoats are attempting to scale. Can you spot the rockets being launched from Boston?

National Gallery of Art

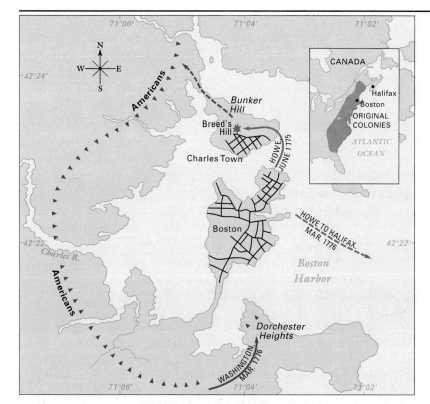

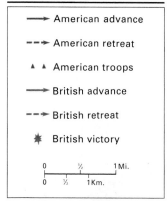

- → American advance
- ⇢ American retreat
- ▲ ▲ American troops
- → British advance
- ⇢ British retreat
- ✳ British victory

0   ½   1 Mi.

0   ½   1Km.

LEARNING FROM MAPS. *The Americans held a very strong position around Boston, forcing Howe to retreat to Halifax, Nova Scotia. What made the American position so strong? If Washington had been able to capture Howe and his retreating Redcoats, the war may have ended quickly. How did the British escape?*

hill by direct assault, the weakness and cowardice of the defenders would be exposed. The rest of the rebel army would melt away and the war would be over. After all, American militiamen had proved very poor soldiers in earlier wars. Howe's former commander, General Wolfe, had described the American soldiers attached to his command during the French and Indian War as "the dirtiest, most contemptible cowardly dogs you can conceive."

After two charges Howe knew that he had made a terrible mistake. Now he *had* to take the hill or face a defeat that would shatter morale. Reinforced by fresh troops, the Redcoats advanced up the hill for the third time. Inside the redoubt the Americans were almost out of ammunition. Those who had no more bullets loaded their muskets with nails and pieces of glass. Their last volley tore fresh holes in the British line. Then the Redcoats were over the wall.

Now American blood flowed freely as the veteran Redcoats proved their skill in hand-to-hand fighting. Among those killed was Dr. Joseph Warren, leader of the Massachusetts Patriot government.

The battle ended with the British in control of the vital high ground. For some reason it has been remembered as the **Battle of Bunker Hill** rather than Breed's Hill. Over a thousand English soldiers were dead or wounded, more than four out of every ten in the battle. About a hundred Americans were killed. Three hundred more were wounded or taken prisoner. Most of the American casualties came after the men had used up their ammunition. 🖼

Return to the Preview & Review on page 143.

The delegates attending the Second Continental Congress in 1776 were painted by Robert Pine and Edward Savage. A weary Benjamin Franklin is in the center.

Historical Society of Pennsylvania

Preview & Review

Use these questions to guide your reading. Answer the questions after completing Section 3.
Understanding Issues, Events, & Ideas. Contrast the divided sentiments of the Tories and the Whigs, using the following words: Second Continental Congress, Olive Branch Petition, Dorchester Heights, Loyalist, Tory, Whig.

1. What was the mood of the Second Continental Congress? Why?
2. What were Washington's major assets as a general?
3. What was the condition of the American army when Washington took command? What changes did he make?
4. Why was discipline of ordinary British soldiers so harsh?
5. Why did Washington allow Howe to leave Boston?

Thinking Critically. Compare the British and American soldiers during the Revolutionary War. From your comparison, predict who might be the winner.

3. "LIBERTY OR DEATH"

The Second Continental Congress

Lexington, Concord, and Bunker Hill had been fought by Massachusetts with some help from neighboring New England colonies. The rest of the colonies were now to enter the conflict. In May the **Second Continental Congress** met in Philadelphia. Some of the most important men in America had been elected delegates. Others not yet well known would soon become important. The Massachusetts radicals Sam Adams, John Adams, and John Hancock were there. So was Benjamin Franklin of Pennsylvania. Virginia sent its fiery orator Patrick Henry, who had just urged the arming of the Virginia militia in a speech ending:

    ❝ We are not weak if we make proper use of the means which the God of nature has granted us. Three million people, armed in the holy cause of liberty, and in such a country as ours, cannot be conquered by any force which our enemy can send against us. Besides, we shall not fight our battles alone. There is a just God who rules the fates of nations. He will raise friends to fight our battles for us.

    The battle is not won by the strong alone. It is won by the alert, the active, the brave. Besides, we have no choice. Even if we were cowardly enough to desire it, it is now too late to back down from the conflict. There is no retreat but in submission and slavery! Our chains are forged! Their clanking may be heard on the plains of Boston! The war is inevitable—and let it come! I repeat, let it come!

It is in vain to drag the matter out. Gentlemen may cry peace, peace. But there is no peace. The war is actually begun! The next gale that sweeps from the north will bring to our ears the resounding clash of arms! Our brethren are already in the [battle]field! Why stand we here idle? What is it that gentlemen wish? What would they have? Is life so dear, or peace so sweet, as to be purchased at the price of chains and slavery? Forbid it, Almighty God! I know not what course others may take; but as for me, give me liberty or give me death![1] 99

Virginia was also represented by George Washington, well known for his role in the French and Indian War, and by a young lawyer named Thomas Jefferson. Jefferson had recently attracted attention by writing a pamphlet, *A Summary View of the Rights of British America,* in which he argued that kings should be "the servants of the people," not their masters.

Mount Vernon Ladies' Association of the Union

Washington carried this miniature of his "dear Patsy" throughout the Revolutionary War. It was painted by Charles Willson Peale in about 1776. Below, Washington stands in 1782 with his horse Nelson. John Trumbull painted this picture in 1790.

proceeded cautiously. It sent an **Olive Branch Petition** asking the king to protect them against Parliament. (An olive branch is a symbol of peaceful intentions.) It issued a "Declaration of the Causes and Necessity of Taking Up Arms." Earlier, on June 15, two days before the Battle of Bunker Hill, Congress had created an official American army and appointed George Washington as its commander in chief.

Washington looked like a general. He was over six feet tall, strong, a fine athlete, yet dignified and reserved. His bravery had been demonstrated in the western wilderness on the day the French ambushed General Braddock. Yet Washington was also known for his sound judgment and his sense of responsibility. He was the kind of person people trusted and respected from the first meeting.

Actually, Washington had much to learn about warfare and running an army. The other possible commanders, however, knew still less. The fact that Washington was from Virginia, the most powerful of the southern colonies, was another reason why he was chosen. The appointment symbolized the union of the colonies that was rapidly taking place.

Washington accepted the assignment eagerly and, in fact, so expected it that he had arrived in his uniform. He set out at once for Massachusetts. It was typical of the man that he refused to take a salary. His conviction that a commander in chief should not profit from the war was so strong that he stood fast on the issue.

Henry Francis du Pont Winterthur Museum

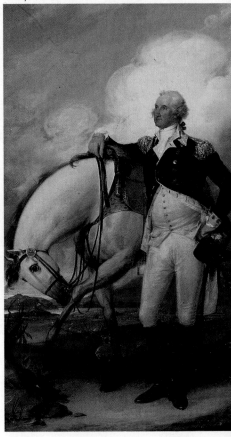

[1]From *Sketches of the Life and Character of Patrick Henry,* 3d ed., edited by William Wirt

"Liberty or Death"

The American Army

When Washington arrived outside Boston on July 3, 1775, he found himself in charge of an army of about 14,000 men. Some were living in dormitories on the campus of Harvard College. Others were in private homes. A few units had set up tents. Nearly all the men wore their ordinary outdoor clothing. There were no American uniforms. The soldiers even had to supply their own guns. Most of them were armed with muskets, a weapon that fired a round bullet with murderous effect at close range. Beyond 50 yards (about 46 meters) it was wildly inaccurate. Some soldiers had only spears or axes. Gunpowder and cannon were scarce.

There was very little discipline. Men commanded by leaders like Colonel Prescott, the hero of Breed's Hill, made good soldiers. Those with lazy or cowardly officers seldom performed well. Most units had elected their own officers and treated them as equals rather than as their superiors. This was not a force for military efficiency.

Washington was very unhappy with the army he found. As a southern planter and slave owner he was accustomed to ordering men about and being obeyed. He set out at once to turn what he called "this mixed multitude" into his own idea of an army. He made the men build barracks and taught them to march in step. He weeded out officers who could not maintain discipline. Any soldier found drunk was given a good whipping.

Then Washington sought to persuade the men to sign up for a year's service in the new Continental Army. Only about 10,000 did so. Many had families to support at home. Moreover, Washington's stern discipline was not popular with many units. Officers in this army were appointed, not elected. Washington chose mostly men like himself from the upper classes of society. He believed that ordinary soldiers would obey their "betters" more readily than people of their own level. There were 28 regiments, each with 8 companies of about 90 men. Units from the more distant colonies arrived, and gradually a national army emerged.

Rifle companies from the Southern Colonies were particularly impressive in Washington's army. Their guns, called "Pennsylvania rifles," had grooved barrels which set a bullet spinning when fired. In the hands of sharpshooters, these rifles were accurate at 150 yards (135 meters) or more. They were greatly feared by the British, especially when snipers began to pick off sentries at what seemed to be incredible distances. The British sent one captured rifleman back to England to demonstrate his weapon. His aim proved so deadly that the exhibition was said to have discouraged many English civilians from enlisting.

Pennsylvania rifles still had to be loaded and fired in the same slow and cumbersome way that muskets were. Gunpowder was poured down the barrel. Then the bullet and some kind of wadding

Anne S.K. Brown Military Collection, Brown University

The American "sharpshooter" on the left and Pennsylvania regular infantryman on the right were drawn in 1784. The figure on the right is wearing the brown that soldiers were encouraged to wear. Why would this have been a good color for soldiers fighting in America?

THE REVOLUTIONARY WAR

Delaware Art Museum

were packed in with a ramrod. Next a small amount of powder was sprinkled on the firing pan. When the marksman pulled the trigger, a sparking arrangement similar to that of a cigarette lighter ignited the powder in the pan. That flame entered a small hole in the barrel and exploded the main charge, firing the bullet. Occasionally the powder in the pan "flashed" without causing the gun to fire. This is the origin of the expression "a flash in the pan."

Obviously it was difficult and dangerous for a soldier to reload either a rifle or a musket while moving and under fire.

The British Army

In July 1775 the British had fewer than 4,000 soldiers in Boston. It was a force much different from the army Washington commanded. The generals were members of the aristocracy. Often they were prominent in politics too. William Howe and two other generals then in Boston—John Burgoyne and George Clinton—were members of Parliament. Such men paid little heed to instructions from London that did not please them.

Officers of lower rank normally obtained their commissions by buying them. Prices were high. A colonel's post might go for £5,000, a substantial fortune in the 1700s. This meant that only wealthy men

Howard Pyle illustrated the Battle of Bunker Hill with such attention to detail that we have a good idea of British fighting techniques. How is this picture a kind of closeup of the painting on page 148? Which do you find more helpful in picturing the battle in your mind?

"Liberty or Death"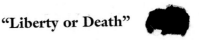

PRAISE TO WASHINGTON

In October 1775 George Washington received a remarkable poem that was written by Phillis Wheatley, a young slave who was brought to Boston from Africa when she was about seven. The Wheatleys, who gave her their name, taught her to read and write. Soon she began to write what became the first widely applauded American poems. Here are some lines from "To His Excellency George Washington," a poem written in the classical manner:

In bright array they seek the work of war,
Where high unfurl'd the ensign waves in air.
Shall I to Washington their praise recite?
Enough thou know'st them in the fields of fight.
Thee, first in peace and honours,—we demand
The grace and glory of thy martial band. . . .
Proceed, great chief, with virtue on thy side,
Thy ev'ry action let the goddess guide.
A crown, a mansion, and a throne that shine,
With gold unfading, WASHINGTON! be thine.[1]

Washington was greatly impressed. He wanted to publish the poem himself, but he was too modest to do so. Instead he wrote to Phillis to say he would "be happy to see a person so favored by the Muses" and invited her to visit him at the Continental Army camp. We know she made the visit, but we do not know what was said between the Father of the Country and the first African American poet.

New York Public Library Picture Collection

could hope to be officers. The gap between officer and enlisted man could not be bridged.

Ordinary soldiers were mostly drawn from the very bottom of society. Criminals were often allowed to enlist to avoid jail or execution. Vagrants and idle persons of all sorts were frequently "pressed" into service. Discipline was brutal, in part because it seemed the only way to control such types. A marine in the Boston garrison who was convicted of punching an infantry officer was sentenced to receive 800 lashes with a cat-o'-nine-tails. Nearly 1,000 slaves fought with the British for a promise of freedom.

The principal weapon of the British infantry was a musket similar to that used by colonial troops but heavier and equipped with a bayonet. Soldiers "leveled" their muskets before firing, but they did not really try to aim. The guns did not even have rear sights. If a whole line fired at once in the general direction of the enemy, some damage would be done. The smoke alone caused by the exploding gunpowder could screen the soldiers as they plodded methodically ahead. The object was to get close enough to the foe to go for him with cold steel. Their bright red uniforms made British soldiers easy

[1]From "To His Excellency George Washington" by Phillis Wheatley

THE REVOLUTIONARY WAR

targets for marksmen, but against the inaccurate muskets of the day what the men wore made little difference. The attack on Breed's Hill is an excellent example of the strengths and weaknesses of British tactics.

Despite the harsh treatment of enlisted men, the British army was an excellent fighting machine. Both officers and men were brave, enduring, effective. The system reflected English society just as the American system reflected American society. Conditions that today might seem cruel and mindless were accepted as normal and necessary by most of those on the bottom as well as by their leaders. Perhaps the typical soldier took a kind of pride in his ability to stand up to the punishing life he had to lead. All ranks could take pride in being English, members of the most powerful nation in the world.

Washington's First Victory

For long months after the Battle of Bunker Hill, the British army sat pinned down in Boston. The American forces ringing the city greatly outnumbered them. Washington was eager to attack, but he was persuaded not to assault the city directly. In January 1776 Colonel Henry Knox, a very stout but energetic and talented young artillery officer, reached camp with the heavy brass and iron cannon that had been captured at Fort Ticonderoga. Using sleds and teams of oxen, Knox and his men had dragged the cannon nearly 300 miles (480 kilometers), a tremendous achievement. In March Washington had these guns pulled up **Dorchester Heights,** south of Boston. He built strong defenses to protect them. From this position the cannon could have blown the British positions in the city below to bits.

General Howe realized at once that he must either capture Dorchester Heights, a task far more difficult than the capture of Breed's Hill, or abandon Boston. He had neither the men nor the desire to attack. He let the Americans know that if they did not allow him to leave peacefully, he would destroy the city. Washington wisely agreed to let Howe move his troops. On March 17, 1776, the British departed for their naval base at Halifax, Nova Scotia, there to await reinforcements and supplies from home. With the fleet went more than 1,500 Americans. These people preferred exile to rebellion against a king and country they considered their own. They and others like them, perhaps a fifth of the American population, were called **Loyalists,** or **Tories.** Americans who believed in the patriotic resistance to King George were called **Whigs.**

For the moment the thirteen colonies were entirely clear of British troops. But the struggle was just beginning. By July 1776 General Howe was back on American soil with a powerful army. By then the colonies had given up trying to persuade England to treat them more fairly. Instead they had declared their independence and become the **United States of America.** 🖻

Return to the Preview & Review on page 150.

"Liberty or Death"

4. INDEPENDENCE IS DECLARED

Use these questions to guide your reading. Answer the questions after completing Section 4.
Understanding Issues, Events, & Ideas. Use the following words to describe the sentiments of the colonists: tyranny, Declaration of Independence, Fourth of July, democracy.
1. What was the significance of Thomas Paine's *Common Sense*?
2. Why did Congress appoint a committee to prepare the Declaration of Independence?
3. What did the Declaration of Independence tell the world?
4. Why must we use historical imagination to understand the first "self-evident" truth of the Declaration?
Thinking Critically. **1.** What do you consider to be the two most important ideas of the Declaration of Independence? Why? **2.** If you had been one of the framers of the Declaration of Independence, name one other "unalienable right" that you would have included. Explain your choice.

The Movement for Independence

Once large numbers of Americans had been killed by British soldiers, the conflict was bound to turn into a war for independence. Bayonets had been used on the brave defenders of Breed's Hill after their ammunition had run out. Any peaceful solution seemed unlikely.

For many months the colonists had tried to believe that King George was their friend. He was being misled by evil advisers, the argument ran. Of course, this was not true, and eventually the colonists realized that it was not.

The person most responsible for opening the colonists' eyes was an Englishman who had just recently immigrated to America. His name was Thomas Paine. In January 1776 Paine published a pamphlet, *Common Sense*. In it he attacked not only George III, whom he called a "Royal Brute," but the whole *idea* of monarchy. *Any* king was a bad thing, Paine insisted. People have "a natural right" to rule themselves. Therefore, the colonies should throw off all connection with Great Britain and create a republic of their own.

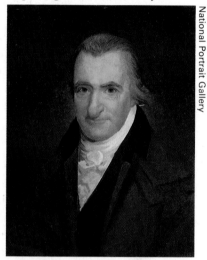

National Portrait Gallery

Paine opposed **tyranny,** which is the cruel and unjust use of power. He wrote:

> 66 Alas! We have been long led away by ancient prejudices and [have] made large sacrifices to superstition. We have boasted the protection of Great Britain, without considering that her motive was *interest* not *attachment* and that she did not protect us from *our enemies* on *our account,* but from *her enemies* on *her own account.* . . .
>
> But Britain is the parent country say some. Then the more shame upon her conduct. Even brutes do not devour their young, nor savages make war upon their families. . . . This New World has been the asylum [a place of security] for the persecuted lovers of civil and religious liberty from *every part* of Europe. Hither have they fled, not from the tender embraces of the mother, but from the cruelty of the monster; and it is so far true of England that the same tyranny which drove the first emigrants from home pursues their descendants still. . . .

A brooding Thomas Paine is shown in the portrait above by John Wesley Jarvis.

THE REVOLUTIONARY WAR

A government of our own is our natural right; and when a man seriously reflects on the precariousness [uncertainty] of human affairs, he will become convinced that it is infinitely wiser and safer to form a constitution of our own, in a cool, deliberate manner, while we have it in our power, than to trust such an interesting event to time and chance. . . .

O ye that love mankind! Ye that dare oppose not only the tyranny but the tyrant, stand forth! Every spot of the old world is overrun with oppression. Freedom has been hunted round the globe. Asia and Africa have long expelled her. Europe regards her like a stranger, and England has given her warning to depart. . . .

Wherefore, instead of gazing at each other with suspicious or doubtful curiosity, let each of us hold out to his neighbor the hearty hand of friendship, and unite in drawing a line, which like an act of oblivion [pardon], shall bury in forgetfulness every former dissension. Let the names of Whig and Tory be extinct; and let none other be heard among us, than those of a good citizen, and open and resolute friend, and a virtuous supporter of the RIGHTS OF MANKIND, and of the FREE AND INDEPENDENT STATES OF AMERICA.[1] **"**

Common Sense was an immediate best seller. Nearly everyone in the colonies read it or heard it discussed. Once the idea of independence was freely talked about, more people accepted it.

By June 1776 nearly all the members of the Second Continental Congress were ready to act. Richard Henry Lee of Virginia introduced a resolution for independence on June 7:

" RESOLVED: That these United Colonies are, and of right ought to be, free and independent States, that they are absolved from all allegiance to the British Crown, and all political connection between them and the State of Great Britain is, and ought to be, totally dissolved. **"**

Before passing this resolution, Congress appointed a committee to prepare a statement explaining why independence was necessary. The members of this committee were Benjamin Franklin of Pennsylvania, John Adams of Massachusetts, Roger Sherman of Connecticut, Robert Livingston of New York, and the youngest delegate, 33-year-old Thomas Jefferson of Virginia. The document they drafted, the **Declaration of Independence,** was written mainly by Jefferson. On July 2, voting by states, the delegates resolved to declare their independence. Then, on the **Fourth of July,** they officially approved the Declaration.

[1]From *Common Sense* by Thomas Paine

The Granger Collection, New York

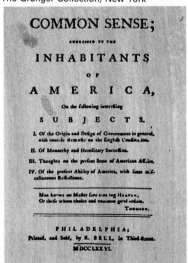

This is the title page of Paine's widely read Common Sense. *What was the main idea of Paine's essay?*

Yale University Art Gallery

"The Declaration of Independence" was painted by John Trumbull in 1786. Thomas Jefferson and Benjamin Franklin may be found near the center of the painting.

THE DECLARATION OF INDEPENDENCE
In Congress, July 4, 1776
The unanimous Declaration of the thirteen united States of America,

Thomas Jefferson wrote the first draft of the Declaration in a little more than two weeks. He was 33 years old.

In the first paragraph, the signers state that the colonists must break their political ties with Britain. They feel that it is important to justify why they are making the separation.

impel: force

endowed: provided

"Laws of Nature" and "Nature's God" refer to Isaac Newton's belief that certain patterns are invariable and predictable. Natural or "unalienable" rights (the rights to life, liberty, and the pursuit of happiness) cannot be taken away. This protection, reasoned the English philosopher John Locke, is called natural law. People created governments to protect their natural rights. A government, therefore, must have the consent of the governed. If a government abuses its powers, it is the right as well as the duty of the people to do away with that government.

When in the Course of human events, it becomes necessary for one people to dissolve the political bands which have connected them with another, and to assume among the powers of the earth, the separate and equal station to which the Laws of Nature and of Nature's God entitle them, a decent respect to the opinions of mankind requires that they should declare the causes which impel them to the separation.—

We hold these truths to be self-evident, that all men are created equal, that they are endowed by their Creator with certain unalienable Rights, that among these are Life, Liberty, and the pursuit of Happiness.—

That to secure these rights, Governments are instituted among Men, deriving their just powers from the consent of the governed,—

That whenever any Form of Government becomes destructive of these ends, it is the Right of the People to alter or to abolish it, and to institute new Government, laying its foundation on such principles and organizing its powers in such form, as to them shall seem most likely to effect their Safety and Happiness. Prudence, indeed, will dictate that Governments long established should not be changed for light and transient causes; and accordingly all experience hath shown, that mankind are more disposed to suffer, while evils are sufferable, than to right themselves by abolishing the forms to which they are accustomed. But when a long train of abuses and usurpations, pursuing invariably the same Object evinces a design to reduce them under absolute

Despotism, it is their right, it is their duty, to throw off such Government, and to provide new Guards for their future security.

Such has been the patient sufferance of these Colonies; and such is now the necessity which constrains them to alter their former Systems of Government. The history of the present King of Great Britain is a history of repeated injuries and usurpations, all having in direct object the establishment of an absolute Tyranny over these States. To prove this, let Facts be submitted to a candid world.—

He has refused his Assent to Laws, the most wholesome and necessary for the public good.—

He has forbidden his Governors to pass Laws of immediate and pressing importance, unless suspended in their operation till his Assent should be obtained; and when so suspended, he has utterly neglected to attend to them.—

He has refused to pass other Laws for the accommodation of large districts of people, unless those people would relinquish the right of Representation in the Legislature, a right inestimable to them and formidable to tyrants only.—

He has called together legislative bodies at places unusual, uncomfortable, and distant from the depository of their public Records, for the sole purpose of fatiguing them into compliance with his measures.—

He has dissolved Representative Houses repeatedly, for opposing with manly firmness his invasions on the rights of the people.—

He has refused for a long time, after such dissolutions, to cause others to be elected; whereby the Legislative powers, incapable of Annihilation, have returned to the People at large for their exercise; the State remaining in the meantime exposed to all the dangers of invasion from without, and convulsions within.—

He has endeavored to prevent the population of these States; for that purpose obstructing the Laws for Naturalization of Foreigners; refusing to pass others to encourage their migrations hither, and raising the conditions of new Appropriations of Lands.—

He has obstructed the Administration of Justice, by refusing his Assent to Laws for establishing Judiciary powers.—

He has made Judges dependent on his Will alone, for the tenure of their offices, and the amount and payment of their salaries.—

He has erected a multitude of New Offices, and sent hither swarms of Officers to harass our people, and eat out their substance.—

He has kept among us, in times of peace, Standing Armies without the Consent of our legislatures.—

He has affected to render the Military independent of and superior to the Civil power.—

He has combined with others to subject us to a jurisdiction foreign to our constitution, and unacknowledged by our laws; giving his Assent to their Acts of pretended Legislation:—

For quartering large bodies of armed troops among us:—

despotism: unlimited power

usurpations: wrongful seizures of power

tyranny: oppressive power exerted by a government

candid: fair

Here the Declaration lists the charges that the colonists had against King George III. How does the language in the list of grievances in the Declaration appeal to people's emotions?

relinquish: release, yield

inestimable: priceless

formidable: causing dread

Why do you think the king had his legislatures in the colonies meet in places that were hard to reach?

annihilation: destruction

convulsions: violent disturbances

naturalization of foreigners: the process by which foreign-born people become citizens

appropriations of land: setting aside land for settlement

tenure: term

a multitude of: many

What wrongful acts does the Declaration state have been committed by the king working with the British Parliament?

quartering: lodging, housing

Declaration of Independence 159

What was the rallying cry of the colonists to protest the king's tax policies?

The "neighboring Province" that is referred to here is Quebec.

arbitrary: not based on law

render: make

abdicated: given up

foreign mercenaries: soldiers hired to fight for a country not their own

perfidy: violation of trust

insurrections: rebellions

petitioned for redress: asked formally for a correction of wrongs

Notice that the Declaration has 18 paragraphs beginning with "He has" or "He is." What is the effect of this repetition?

unwarrantable jurisdiction: unjustified authority

magnanimity: generous spirit

conjured: called upon

consanguinity: common ancestors

acquiesce in: consent to

Most American people thought that completely breaking ties with Great Britain should be a last resort. Why do you think they felt that way?

For protecting them, by a mock Trial, from punishment for any Murders which they should commit on the Inhabitants of these States:—

For cutting off our Trade with all parts of the world:—

For imposing Taxes on us without our Consent:—

For depriving us in many cases, of the benefits of Trial by Jury:—

For transporting us beyond Seas to be tried for pretended offences:—

For abolishing the free System of English Laws in a neighboring Province, establishing therein an Arbitrary government, and enlarging its Boundaries so as to render it at once an example and fit instrument for introducing the same absolute rule into these Colonies:—

For taking away our Charters, abolishing our most valuable Laws, and altering fundamentally the Forms of our Governments:—

For suspending our own Legislatures, and declaring themselves invested with power to legislate for us in all cases whatsoever.—

He has abdicated Government here, by declaring us out of his Protection and waging War against us.—

He has plundered our seas, ravaged our Coasts, burnt our towns, and destroyed the Lives of our people.—

He is at this time transporting large Armies of foreign Mercenaries to complete the works of death, desolation and tyranny, already begun with circumstances of Cruelty & perfidy scarcely paralleled in the most barbarous ages, and totally unworthy the Head of a civilized nation.—

He has constrained our fellow Citizens taken Captive on the high Seas to bear Arms against their Country, to become the executioners of their friends and Brethren, or to fall themselves by their Hands.—

He has excited domestic insurrections amongst us, and has endeavored to bring on the inhabitants of our frontiers, the merciless Indian Savages, whose known rule of warfare, is an undistinguished destruction of all ages, sexes and conditions.

In every stage of these Oppressions We have Petitioned for Redress in the most humble terms: Our repeated Petitions have been answered only by repeated injury. A Prince, whose character is thus marked by every act which may define a Tyrant, is unfit to be the ruler of a free people.

Nor have We been wanting in attentions to our British brethren. We have warned them from time to time of attempts by their legislature to extend an unwarrantable jurisdiction over us. We have reminded them of the circumstances of our emigration and settlement here. We have appealed to their native justice and magnanimity, and we have conjured them by the ties of our common kindred to disavow these usurpations, which would inevitably interrupt our connections and correspondence. They too have been deaf to the voice of justice and of consanguinity. We must, therefore, acquiesce in the necessity, which denounces our Separation, and hold them, as we hold the rest of mankind, Enemies in War, in Peace Friends.—

We, therefore, the Representatives of the united States of America, in General Congress, Assembled, appealing to the Supreme Judge of the world for the rectitude of our intentions, do, in the Name, and by Authority of the good People of these Colonies, solemnly publish and declare, That these United Colonies are, and of Right ought to be Free and Independent States; that they are Absolved from all Allegiance to the British Crown, and that all political connection between them and the State of Great Britain, is and ought to be totally dissolved; and that as Free and Independent States, they have full Power to levy War, conclude Peace, contract Alliances, establish Commerce, and to do all other Acts and Things which Independent States may of right do.—

And for the support of this Declaration, with a firm reliance on the protection of divine Providence, we mutually pledge to each other our Lives, our Fortunes and our sacred Honor.

rectitude: rightness

In this paragraph, the signers stated their actual declaration of independence. What rights would the new United States of America now have as an independent nation?

Congress adopted the final draft of the Declaration of Independence on July 4, 1776. A formal copy, written on parchment paper, was signed on August 2, 1776.

The following is part of a passage that was taken out of Jefferson's original draft by the Congress: "He has waged cruel war against human nature itself, violating its most sacred rights to life and liberty in the persons of a distant people who never offended him, captivating and carrying them into slavery in another hemisphere, or to incur miserable death in their transportation thither." Why do you think the Congress wanted to delete this passage?

While on the committee to prepare the Declaration, John Adams received a letter from his wife, Abigail Adams. The last sentence said, "If particular care and attention is not paid to the ladies, we are determined to foment a Rebellion, and will not hold ourselves bound by any laws in which we have no voice, or Representation." Did the writers of the Declaration heed her advice?

John Hancock	Benjamin Harrison	Lewis Morris
Button Gwinnett	Thomas Nelson, Jr.	Richard Stockton
Lyman Hall	Francis Lightfoot Lee	John Witherspoon
George Walton	Carter Braxton	Francis Hopkinson
William Hooper	Robert Morris	John Hart
Joseph Hewes	Benjamin Rush	Abraham Clark
John Penn	Benjamin Franklin	Josiah Bartlett
Edward Rutledge	John Morton	William Whipple
Thomas Heyward, Jr.	George Clymer	Samuel Adams
Thomas Lynch, Jr.	James Smith	John Adams
Arthur Middleton	George Taylor	Robert Treat Paine
Samuel Chase	James Wilson	Elbridge Gerry
William Paca	George Ross	Stephen Hopkins
Thomas Stone	Caesar Rodney	William Ellery
Charles Carroll	George Read	Roger Sherman
of Carrollton	Thomas McKean	Samuel Huntington
George Wythe	William Floyd	William Williams
Richard Henry Lee	Philip Livingston	Oliver Wolcott
Thomas Jefferson	Francis Lewis	Matthew Thornton

The Declaration of Independence

Jefferson's Declaration of Independence is one of the best-known and most influential political documents ever written. No one has expressed so well the right of a people to overthrow a government they do not like and make a new one they do like. This idea comes from the thinkers of the Enlightenment. So does the phrase "Laws of Nature and of Nature's God," which refers to the belief that certain patterns follow natural law and do not change. Jefferson based this idea on the works of Isaac Newton and Francis Bacon, who hoped to develop a science of human and political behavior.

Jefferson originally wrote that the truths set forth in the Declaration were "sacred and undeniable." In polishing the Declaration, Franklin changed the phrase to read "self-evident"—that is, obvious. The truths make up only a small part of the document. Nevertheless, they are the part that makes the Declaration so important. For the first time in history, a group of revolutionaries were carefully explaining why they had the right to use force to change their government.

The Declaration of Independence is a superb statement of the principles on which democratic government is based. (Political power in a **democracy** comes from the people and is for the benefit of all.) Using historical imagination reminds us that the Declaration was also wartime propaganda. As a description of the causes of the Revolution, the Declaration is one-sided. Many of the charges made against George III were strongly exaggerated. Some were untrue. The king had many faults. But he was not a tyrant.

Those who put their names on the Declaration of Independence were burning bridges behind them. In English eyes they were now traitors. If they lost the war, they could expect the treatment commonly given traitors—death.

Self-Evident Truths

Over the years people have argued heatedly about what Jefferson meant by the first of his self-evident truths in the Declaration of Independence—"that all men are created equal." Historical imagination can help us understand. First of all, Jefferson surely meant by *men* "people," just as when he spoke of "the opinions of mankind," he meant the opinions of all people, women and men alike.

This is not to suggest that Jefferson or any other signer of the Declaration believed in equal rights for women as the term is used today. The delegates who signed the Declaration believed that women were entitled to life, liberty, and the pursuit of happiness so long as they behaved as men thought they should behave.

During the Revolution women held many jobs usually performed by men in peacetime. Many ran farms and shops while their husbands, fathers, and brothers were at war. Abigail Adams called herself a "farmeress" and really did manage the Adams farm. Some women served as nurses in the army. A few actually fired guns in defense of liberty. Martha Washington joined her husband in winter camp and encouraged other women to do war work. "Whilst our husbands and brothers are examples of patriotism," she wrote, "we must be patterns of industry." Women were not the legal equals of men, and no movement to improve the position of women grew out of the Revolution.

On the other hand, Jefferson certainly meant that only free men were created equal. Jefferson believed that for free men there were certain *unalienable* rights, God-given rights that no just government could take away for *any* reason. How could he, a slaveholder, claim that liberty was a God-given right of "all men"?

During the Revolutionary War about 5,000 Africans served in the American army and navy. Crispus Attucks fell in the Boston Massacre. Peter Salem, Caesar Ferrett, Samuel Craft, and Prince Estabrook were among the militiamen on the Lexington common when the first shots were fired. Salem Poor, Cato Howe, and Cesar Jabor were among the defenders of Breed's Hill. Indeed, Africans, slave and free, fought in every major battle. Still, most Americans tolerated slavery.

Nearly every European person in America of the 1770s was in some ways prejudiced against Africans by today's standards. Further, most men of all origins were "male chauvinists" by today's standards. We must use our historical imagination if we want to understand these men and their times. To condemn George Washington for owning slaves and taking control of his rich wife's property would only show that we did not understand Washington and the Revolution. We would be equally wrong if we took the Declaration so literally as to believe that the signers were perfect democrats.

Reaction to the Declaration

Many Americans, particularly the Patriots (also known as Whigs), rejoiced at the news that independence had been declared. Throughout the colonies Whigs celebrated, holding festive banquets and demonstrations to show their support of the Declaration. Some Americans greeted the news with indifference. These people did not care one way or another. The Loyalists (or Tories), strongly opposed the sentiments expressed in the Declaration and regarded the Whigs as traitors.

Despite Paine's plea to "let the names of Whig and Tory be extinct," arguments between the Whigs and the Tories continued throughout the Revolutionary War. In many cases, the Tories openly welcomed the British troops and did all they could to hurt the Patriots' cause. In other cases they fled to Canada or returned to England as the revolution and the war spread. 🖅

"I desire you would Remember the Ladies, and be more generous and favourable to them than your ancestors. Do not put such unlimited power into the hands of the Husbands. Remember all Men would be tyrants if they could. . . ."
Abigail Adams, 1776

Points of View

"Depend upon it, We know better than to repeal our Masculine systems. Altho they are in full Force, you know they are little more than Theory. . . . We have only the Name of Masters, and rather than give up this, which would compleatly subject Us to the Despotism of the Peticoat, I hope General Washington, and all our brave Heroes would fight."
John Adams, 1776

Return to the Preview & Review on page 156.

5. AMERICANS HOLD TOGETHER

Use these questions to guide your reading. Answer the questions after completing Section 5.
Understanding Issues, Events, & Ideas. Use the following words to describe the progress of the war: Battle of Long Island, sunshine patriot, mercenary, battles of Trenton and Princeton, Battle of Saratoga, treaty of alliance.
1. Why did the British want to capture New York?
2. What was the British strategy for 1777?
3. In what way was General Washington a victor in 1777?
4. What was the most important result of the Battle of Saratoga?
5. What did the French promise in the 1778 treaty of alliance?
Thinking Critically. 1. Why do you think the author refers to 1776–77 as "America's dark hour"? 2. Suppose you are a German mercenary serving under General Burgoyne at Saratoga. Write a letter to a friend describing this leader and telling what you think of him.

America's Dark Hour

The British were now determined to crush the American rebellion. General Howe had left Boston in March 1776 with 4,000 soldiers. He returned to New York City in July 1776 with 32,000. This army was supported by a huge fleet of over 400 warships and transports under the command of General Howe's brother, Richard, Lord Howe.

By capturing New York and patrolling the Hudson River with their warships, the British could split New England from the rest of what they still called "the colonies." General Howe first established a base on Staten Island. Then, late in August, he landed 20,000 soldiers on Long Island. Instead of attacking directly, he brilliantly outmaneuvered Washington's army. Then he struck from two directions. The **Battle of Long Island** revealed that Washington was inexperienced at managing a complicated operation. He barely managed to withdraw his battered troops across the East River to New York City.

The victory greatly heartened the British. Howe became a national hero. King George knighted him. Sir William, as he was thereafter called, again proceeded slowly and carefully. Apparently the losses he had suffered in the Battle of Bunker Hill had made him overly cautious.

After delaying several weeks, Howe finally moved his army across the East River. Once more the British troops routed Washington's force. The Americans fled to the northern end of Manhattan Island, leaving Howe in control of New York City. New York was not like Boston. A large proportion of the citizens were Loyalists. They welcomed the British with open arms.

This was one of the low points of the war for the Americans. If Howe had been more aggressive, he could probably have destroyed Washington's army completely.

Yet, after more fighting, Washington crossed the Hudson to New Jersey, where Howe could not use the British fleet to maneuver around him. Half of Washington's army had been captured by now, nearly 3,000 at Fort Washington at the northern end of Manhattan Island. Washington had left this garrison behind when he moved his main force to New Jersey. Through late November and into December, the disheartened army retreated in the direction of Philadelphia, followed by Howe. The Continental Congress, thoroughly alarmed, shifted its sessions from Philadelphia to Baltimore. In mid-December the exhausted American army retreated across the Delaware River into Pennsylvania.

In this dark hour Washington devised a daring and brilliant plan. Winter was closing in. The enlistments of most of his men were about to expire. Something had to be done to revive their spirits and raise

Yale University Art Gallery

the hopes of the people. As Thomas Paine wrote in another of his powerful pamphlets, too many Americans were **sunshine patriots,** enthusiastic for independence when things were going well, cowards and shirkers when the future looked grim.

Across the Delaware River in Trenton, New Jersey, 1,400 of General Howe's soldiers were encamped. These men were not English but Hessians—German troops from the principality of Hesse-Cassel. Americans hated and feared the Hessians, partly because they were tough soldiers known to be fond of looting and mistreating civilians, partly because they were **mercenaries,** hired soldiers, killing for money. Actually, the Hessians were not really mercenaries. The real mercenary was their ruler, Prince Frederick II of Hesse-Cassel. It was the prince who had ordered his soldiers to America, and it was he who pocketed the money paid by the British.

Washington decided to attack the Hessian camp. On Christmas night, amidst a snowstorm, he led his men back across the Delaware River, 9 miles (about 15 kilometers) above Trenton. The soldiers marched swiftly on the town. At dawn they overwhelmed their astonished foe. More than 900 Hessians were taken prisoner. So complete was the surprise that only 30 Hessians were killed before the brief **Battle of Trenton** was over. Not a single American was killed.

Washington quickly struck the British again, this time in the **Battle of Princeton,** where he drove two British regiments from the town, with heavy losses. Then he made camp for the winter at Morristown, New Jersey, only about 30 miles (48 kilometers) west of New York.

"The Death of General Mercer at the Battle of Princeton" was painted by John Trumbull in 1789. How did Washington spark his army with the battles of Trenton and Princeton?

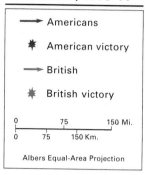

Americans

★ American victory

British

✸ British victory

0   75   150 Mi.

0   75   150 Km.

Albers Equal-Area Projection

LEARNING FROM MAPS. *The American army spent most of 1776 and 1777 retreating from the British. They won several key victories, however. What American victories are shown on this map? Burgoyne's troops were captured by the victorious Americans at Saratoga. Why was this a geographically important victory for the Americans?*

1777: The Year of Decision

When the snows melted, the war resumed. The British developed a complicated strategy for 1777. General George Clinton would hold New York with a small force while General Howe took the bulk of his troops by sea to Chesapeake Bay in order to attack Philadelphia from the south. At the same time another British army led by General John "Gentleman Johnny" Burgoyne would march down from Canada toward New York.

Howe carried out his part of the plan. He moved slowly, as usual, but effectively. He landed his men in Maryland on the Chesapeake in August. Washington hurried southward as soon as he learned where Howe was. The two armies clashed at Brandywine Creek, southwest of Philadelphia, on September 11.

The Battle of Brandywine near Philadelphia resembled the Battle of Long Island both in the tactics used and the result. Howe cleverly outmaneuvered Washington. He sent part of his force around the American right side and then struck from two directions. The Americans were badly defeated. On September 26 Howe marched into Philadelphia.

In October Washington staged a surprise counterattack. At the Battle of Germantown north of Philadelphia he gave a better account of himself than at Brandywine, but his battle plan was too complicated. A heavy fog led to much confusion. Once more the British held the field when the shooting stopped.

These losses were very discouraging. Nevertheless, at year's end Washington still held his army together. Its will to fight had not been broken. Howe won the battles, but he failed to smash the American army. With the approach of winter, Washington and his men retreated into camp at Valley Forge, northwest of Philadelphia.

The Battle of Saratoga

● The Frick Collection, New York

The English general John Burgoyne is the subject of this splendid oil portrait by Sir Joshua Reynolds. What five words would you choose to describe General Burgoyne after studying this painting?

The British were able to occupy and hold seaport towns and the surrounding countryside because of their powerful navy. However, it was gradually becoming clear that fighting in the interior was much more difficult for them. The fate of General Burgoyne illustrates this point effectively.

Burgoyne was a typical upper-class Englishman of his day—rich, pleasure loving, accustomed to having his own way. He was, however, more talented than most. He wrote a number of plays that were good enough to be performed in London. He had fought with distinction in Europe during the Seven Years' War. Ordinary soldiers loved him because he treated them as human beings, not as the scum of the earth.

Yet like General Braddock in the 1750s, Burgoyne did not adapt well to American conditions. He set out from Montreal in June 1777 with 6,000 regulars (half of them German mercenaries), a small force of Loyalists, and about 500 Indians. He also brought with him 138 pieces of artillery and an enormous amount of baggage of every sort. Burgoyne's personal baggage alone filled 30 carts.

A large crowd of peddlers and other civilians tagged along behind the army. Some of the officers brought their wives. Baron von Riedesel, commander of the German troops, and Frederika von Riedesel even brought their three small children, the youngest only a year old.

This cumbersome army sailed smoothly enough down Lake Champlain and recaptured Fort Ticonderoga on July 5. But thereafter, moving overland, the advance slowed to a crawl. The retreating Americans chopped down huge trees to block the forest paths. It took the army 24 days to reach Fort Edward, 23 miles (about 37 kilometers) south of Ticonderoga.

The Granger Collection, New York

This bronze medal was ordered struck by Congress to commemorate the surrender of the British at Saratoga. General Burgoyne is handing his sword to General Horatio Gates.

With every passing day more and more American militia gathered. Like the Minute Men at Concord, these were local farmers who picked up their rifles or muskets and gathered to defend their own districts. Burgoyne noted with dismay: "Wherever the King's forces point, three or four thousand [militiamen] assemble in twenty-four hours."

The commander of the regular troops facing Burgoyne was General Horatio Gates. Gates was very cautious. He avoided a major battle as long as possible. On September 19 the two armies finally clashed in the **Battle of Saratoga,** or Freeman's Farm. American units led by Colonel Daniel Morgan and Major General Benedict Arnold, dealt Burgoyne's army a smashing blow. The British advance was stopped. On October 7 Burgoyne was defeated again.

By this time Burgoyne's army was surrounded. Supplies were running low. On October 17 he surrendered at Saratoga. The Americans took 5,700 prisoners. British losses were heavy.

The Alliance with France

The Battle of Saratoga was probably the great victory that won the United States independence. It greatly increased the Americans' confidence.

But the most important result of the Battle of Saratoga occurred in France. When the news of the victory reached Paris, the French officially recognized the government of the United States. By March Benjamin Franklin and two other American diplomats negotiated a **treaty of alliance.** The proposed alliance discouraged the British so much that they offered to never again try to tax the colonists if they would lay down their arms. This offer was refused. In the treaty France promised to fight to protect the United States. France then declared war on Great Britain.

The French were eager to see the Americans win their independence because that would weaken their enemy, Great Britain. They had been helping the Americans with loans and war supplies from the start of the revolution. Many French officers had already come to America to fight. The best-known of these was the youthful Marquis de Lafayette, who was only 19 when he joined the American army. Now the French army and navy joined in the conflict directly. By the summer of 1778, a French fleet was operating in American waters. In 1780 an army of 5,000 men under Count Rochambeau landed in Rhode Island.

Spain entered the war against England in 1779. Bernardo de Gálvez, governor of Louisiana, sent gunpowder, guns, food, medicine, and money to the rebelling colonies. Later he captured the British fort at Pensacola. Spanish-born Jorge Farragut fought in both the Continental navy and army. Two Polish officers—Casimir Pulaski and Thaddeus Kosciusko—also served with great distinction.

Return to the Preview & Review on page 164.

The Valley Forge Historical Society

6. THE WAR IS WON

Winter at Valley Forge

We can see now that the American victory was almost certain after the Battle of Saratoga. This happy future was much less clear to Washington and the weary soldiers wintering at **Valley Forge.** Supplies of food and especially of clothing were scarce. According to Washington himself, 2,898 of his men were barefoot in December 1777. Many were ill.

The problem was bad organization and not enough horses and wagons to bring supplies to Valley Forge. Nearby, civilians had plenty to eat and adequate clothing. Knowing this made Washington boil with rage and discouraged his men. Thousands deserted.

The soldiers who did not leave were strengthened by their suffering. They also benefited from the training they got from a German volunteer, General Friedrich von Steuben. Von Steuben was something of a faker. He claimed to be a baron and a former lieutenant general in the army of King Frederick of Prussia. Actually, he had no noble title, and he had been only a captain in the Prussian army. He was perfectly sincere, however, in his wish to help the American cause. And he was an excellent soldier.

Von Steuben taught Washington's veterans how to maneuver in the field and how to use bayonets properly. He was a stern taskmaster who made the soldiers drill for hours. He lost his temper frequently, and since he knew very little English, he tended to shout at the Americans in a mixture of German and French, substituting curses for clear instructions. Nevertheless, the Americans came to love him. He worked himself as hard as the men he was drilling. His devotion

Preview & Review

Use these questions to guide your reading. Answer the questions after completing Section 6.
Understanding Issues, Events, & Ideas. Use the following words to report on the American victory in the Revolutionary War: Valley Forge; Battle of Monmouth Court House; King's Mountain; Battles of Cowpens and Guilford Court House; Vincennes; Yorktown.
1. Why were the conditions at Valley Forge so bad?
2. What were the American tactics in the war in the South?
3. In what area did George Rogers Clark fight the British?
4. Why was Washington able to defeat the British at Yorktown?
Thinking Critically. 1. In your opinion, what were the three most important reasons for the Americans' victory in the Revolutionary War? Explain. **2.** Who do you think is the most important American hero of the Revolutionary period? Why?

"The March to Valley Forge, December 16th," above, was painted by William B. Trego. Imagine that you are riding next to General Washington on his white horse. What are your impressions of the troops who pass before you?

The Granger Collection, New York

This fine engraving shows Francis Marion, the "Swamp Fox," crossing the Pee Dee River in South Carolina. How can you tell that his soldiers are "irregulars"?

to them was obvious. Despite his foreign background, he knew how to manage the Americans. And he understood something of American democracy. He said:

66 In Prussia, when an officer says, 'Do this,' the soldiers do it without argument. In America, I am obliged to say, 'This is the reason why you ought to do that.' 99

The War in the South and West

In May 1778 General Howe resigned his command. General Henry Clinton replaced him. Clinton marched the British army in Philadelphia back to New York. The Americans then put General Benedict Arnold, one of the heroes of the Battle of Saratoga, in charge of the American troops in reoccupied Philadelphia. While Clinton's troops were marching across New Jersey, Washington attacked. His action at the **Battle of Monmouth,** while not a clear victory, gave a valuable boost to American morale.

Thereafter the British concentrated their efforts in the South, where they hoped to find many Loyalists. Using the navy effectively, the British captured Savannah, Georgia, in 1778. In 1780 another naval expedition led by Clinton captured Charleston, South Carolina. Clinton took as many Americans prisoners in Charleston as the British had lost at Saratoga. He then returned to his base at New York, leaving General Charles Cornwallis in charge of the southern campaign. Later in 1780 Cornwallis routed an American army under the command of General Horatio Gates at Camden, South Carolina.

The British in the South counted on local support, but they soon found guerrilla bands picking away at them. These irregular soldiers, led by men like Francis Marion, the "Swamp Fox," and Thomas Sumter, continued to resist the Redcoats. Soon Cornwallis was in serious trouble in the South.

After Gates' defeat at Camden, Nathanael Greene was put in charge of the American forces in the South. General Greene used hit-and-run tactics against Cornwallis with brilliant results. A band of militiamen had already destroyed a Tory force at **King's Mountain** in South Carolina. Now Greene divided his forces and staged a series of scattered raids. At the **Battle of Cowpens** in South Carolina one flank soundly defeated the British. They then rejoined Greene and attacked Cornwallis' army at **Guilford Court House,** forcing the British to retreat to the coast. There Cornwallis would be supported and

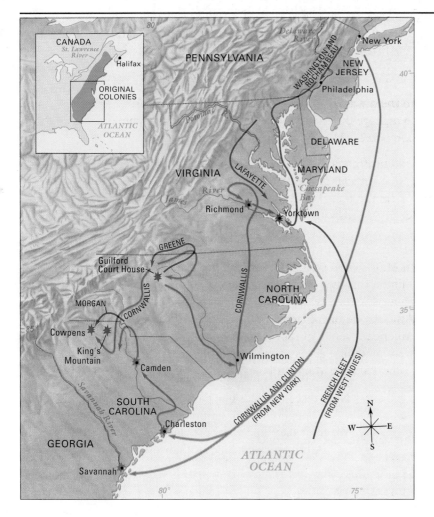

THE WAR IN THE SOUTH, 1778–81

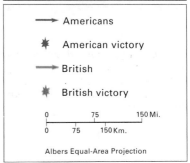

→	Americans
✳	American victory
→	British
✳	British victory

0   75   150 Mi.

0   75   150 Km.

Albers Equal-Area Projection

LEARNING FROM MAPS. *The British relied on the navy to move the army into strategic position. How is this illustrated on the map? Note the locations of the British and American victories. Do you think the American army intentionally avoided major confrontations along the coast? Why?*

supplied by the Royal Navy. But soon most of Georgia and the Carolinas were back in American hands.

The Patriots won control of the interior of South Carolina with the Battle of Eutaw Springs. In this battle, which was the last major encounter in South Carolina, the colonists attacked the British, who fell back to Charleston. The American poet Philip Freneau memorialized the sacrifices of the Americans who fought the battle in his poem, "To the Memory of the Brave Americans." Freneau wrote:

The Granger Collection, New York

Philip Freneau served as a soldier in the American Revolution. He was one of the first professional American journalists, and a great supporter of the Revolution and of the Jeffersonian democracy.

*Under General Greene, in South Carolina, who Fell in
the Action of September 8, 1781.*

At Eutaw Springs the valiant died;
 Their limbs with dust are covered o'er—
Weep on, ye springs, your tearful tide;
 How many heroes are no more!

If in this wreck of ruin, they
 Can yet be thought to claim a tear,
O smite your gentle breast, and say
 The friends of freedom slumber here!

Thou, who shalt trace this bloody plain,
 If goodness rules thy generous breast,
Sigh for the wasted rural reign;
 Sigh for the shepherds, sunk to rest!

Stranger, their humble graves adorn;
 You too may fall, and ask a tear;
'Tis not the beauty of the morn
 That proves the evening shall be clear.—

They saw their injured country's woe;
 The flaming town, the wasted field;
Then rushed to meet the insulting foe;
 They took the spear—but left the shield.

Led by thy conquering genius, Greene,
 The Britons they compelled to fly;
None distant viewed the fatal plain,
 None grieved, in such a cause to die—

But, like the Parthian, famed of old,
 Who, flying still their arrows threw,
These routed Britons, full as bold,
 Retreated, and retreating slew.

Now rest in peace, our patriot band;
 Though far from nature's limits thrown,
We trust they find a happier land,
 A brighter sunshine of their own.[1]

[1]From *American Literature Survey: Colonial and Federal to 1800*, edited by Milton Stern and Seymour Gross

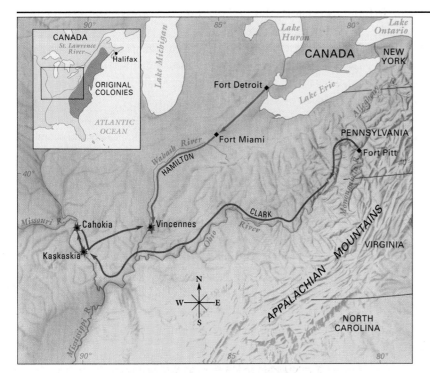

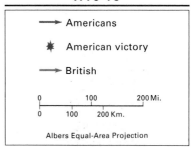

→ Americans

✳ American victory

→ British

| 0 | | 100 | | 200 Mi. |
| 0 | 100 | 200 Km. | | |

Albers Equal-Area Projection

LEARNING FROM MAPS. *As the map shows, few battles of the Revolutionary War were fought west of the Appalachian Mountains. Why? Most of Clark's military expenses were financed by the state of Virginia. Why do you think Virginia was interested in insuring American control of the Ohio Valley?*

The Americans' fortunes also improved in the West, while fighting in the North was at a standstill. George Rogers Clark, financed by Virginia's governor, Patrick Henry, swept into Illinois country. There he won several battles against the British and their Indian allies. He took **Vincennes,** on the Wabash River, in 1778 and recaptured it in February 1779. Clark built Fort Nelson, now Louisville, Kentucky, and planned a campaign to march upon Fort Detroit. But he was unable to proceed when adequate supplies did not arrive from Virginia.

In the North there was treason. Benedict Arnold had persuaded Washington to make him commander of the key American fort at West Point, on the Hudson River north of New York City. He had secretly agreed to turn over the fort to the British for a large sum of money and a commission in their army.

Fortunately for the United States, a British officer, Major John André, was captured while returning from West Point with papers confirming Arnold's treachery. André was hanged as a spy, but Arnold escaped to New York and later became a British general.

In May 1781 Cornwallis marched north into Virginia, hoping for a decisive victory. Again local militiamen and regular army units began to pick away at his army. Again he retreated to the sea. This time he fortified himself at **Yorktown,** a small tobacco port located where the York River flows into Chesapeake Bay. An American force under General Lafayette took up positions outside the town to keep the British under observation.

George Rogers Clark, the conqueror of the Northwest, was painted by James Barton Longacre.

National Portrait Gallery

The War Is Won 173

HEROES OF THE REVOLUTION

In the flush of victory Americans celebrated their first national heroes. Benjamin Franklin had been widely known for his experiments with electricity and for *Poor Richard's Almanack.* Now he was admired everywhere for his staunch support of the Revolution.

Thomas Jefferson had also become a national hero by the 1780s. American pride in the Declaration of Independence swelled when the Revolution succeeded and the courage of the document's signers could be fully appreciated.

The greatest hero of all was Washington. "The Father of His Country" was, by all accounts, a stern man who stood alone and said little. Yet all Americans admired his personal sacrifice and his careful use of power. One admirer called him "no harum

"John Paul Jones" by Charles Willson Peale.

Starum ranting Swearing fellow but Sober, steady, and calm."

A Scot, John Paul Jones, was revered as the founder of the strong United States naval tra-

dition. In his little ship *Bonhomme Richard* ("Poor Richard," named in admiration of Franklin), Jones came upon a British convoy led by the powerful *Serapis.* He lashed his ship to the *Serapis* and fought from sunset into moonlight until both ships were seriously damaged. Still Jones refused to surrender. "I have not yet begun to fight," he proclaimed. Finally the British vessel surrendered and was boarded by Jones and his crew.

All men and women who had been brave enough to take up arms against the British were now heroes. One, Andrew Jackson, was only a boy when war broke out. For refusing to black the boots of a British officer, he was struck sharply in the face with the flat of a sword. He carried the scar to his grave.

Independence National Historical Park

Surrender at Yorktown

Now came the final act of the long struggle. Washington had originally intended to assault New York City with the support of the French army that Count Rochambeau had brought to Rhode Island. Rochambeau urged a joint attack on Yorktown instead. Washington finally agreed. Leaving a small force to trick General Clinton into thinking the Americans intended to attack New York, the combined American and French armies marched swiftly south.

At the same time two French fleets, one from the West Indies, the other from Newport, Rhode Island, came together off Yorktown. The squadron from the West Indies landed 3,300 more French soldiers outside the Yorktown defenses. After Washington and Rochambeau arrived in early September 1781, there were 16,000 allied soldiers and 36 warships in position. Cornwallis had only 8,000 men, and many of them were ill. When a British fleet sought to relieve him, it was driven off by the French. Cornwallis' army was doomed.

Washington's grasp of the lay of the land at Yorktown was excellent. The Americans had pinned the British on a swampy peninsula with their backs to the Chesapeake Bay. On October 9 Washington began to batter Cornwallis' fortifications with heavy artillery.

Yale University Art Gallery

The assault was under the able direction of French gunners and of the same Henry Knox, now a general, who had brought the guns of Fort Ticonderoga to Boston to make possible Washington's first victory back in 1776. Cornwallis sent off a last message to General Clinton: "If you cannot relieve me very soon, you must be prepared to hear the Worst." No relief arrived.

Cornwallis had to surrender on October 19. His men marched out, their flags furled, while the band played "The World Turned Upside Down." The French troops, in beautiful white uniforms, were lined up on the right. On the left were the Americans. Only the front ranks wore the buff and blue uniform of the Continental Army. The rest were, in the words of General von Steuben, "a ragged set of fellows." As the British soldiers threw down their arms angrily in formal surrender, Lafayette told the band to strike up "Yankee Doodle." This dramatic scene took place on a field no more than 10 miles (16 kilometers) from Jamestown, where the first English settlers had landed 174 years before.

The last battle was over. The British still had control of New York City, Charleston, Savannah, and some frontier posts, but they no longer had the will to fight. Public opposition in England to the war was growing, and British Whigs were gaining strength against the Tories and the King. In March Parliament voted to give up "further prosecution of offensive war on the Continent of North America." A few days later Lord North resigned as prime minister. Although a peace treaty was still to be signed, the Revolutionary War had been won. 🖅

For Cornwallis' British troops this is "The World Turned Upside Down" as they surrender to the Americans at Yorktown in October 1781. At the center is General Benjamin Lincoln leading the Redcoats past the Americans, in buff and blue, on the right. General Washington is in front of the flag. On the left are French allies, in buff, with Polish and Prussian fighters behind. John Trumbull painted this oil titled "Surrender of Lord Cornwallis." How do you suppose regular American soldiers looked at the time of the surrender?

Return to the Preview & Review on page 169.

LINKING HISTORY & GEOGRAPHY

CROSSING THE ATLANTIC

By the 15th century Europe had two groups of sea powers. One, the Italian city states, located on the relatively calm and sheltered waters of the Mediterranean Sea, traded with China, the Indies, and India. The second group, the Hanse Towns, which later became the Hanseatic League, sailed the North and Baltic seas, carrying goods from Russia and Siberia to the towns of northern Europe. Both groups developed from unique geographic environments—the linking of great overland trade routes from the east with the indented coastlines of tideless seas. Captains and crews sailed in comparative security, knowing land lay not too far away.

Looking to the Atlantic

1. Why did the other nations of Europe begin to look for their own trade routes?

The merchants in Italy and the Hanse Towns charged other Europeans very high prices for the goods they traded. Because these merchants held monopolies, other nations had difficulty establishing their own trade routes. Slowly the leaders of the other European nations began to realize that their only realistic alternative was to look westward—to the Atlantic Ocean. But that meant facing a landless horizon and the vastness of an uncharted watery wilderness.

It is interesting to note that only those nations that actually faced the Atlantic—Spain, Portugal, England, France, and the Netherlands—actually met the challenge of the Atlantic (as Norway had centuries earlier). They, and they alone, took the knowledge of navigation, mapmaking, and shipbuilding and applied it to a much sterner test of seamanship in the open Atlantic Ocean.

Geography of the Ocean Frontier

2. What manner of watery frontier did these early sailors find as they ventured westward?

We can get some sense of what lay ahead by looking at a map or globe. As you can see, the Atlantic covers one fifth of the earth's surface. And you can see it occupies a unique space on Planet Earth, separating Europe and Africa from the Americas and creating a barrier—or, for some, a highway—between those continents.

A map or globe shows you, too, that the Atlantic is a long body of water that resembles an hourglass. The widest part of the ocean, spanning some 4,150 miles (6,640 kilometers), stretches between Spain and Florida. It was precisely this expanse crossed by Columbus in 1492! The narrowest part lies between Norway and Greenland in the north. Here the distance is a mere 930 miles. Across this narrowest section, with islands scattered like stepping stones, the Vikings sailed around the year 1000.

Mixing the Waters of the Atlantic

3. How else is the Atlantic's geography unique?

Perhaps the most amazing aspect of the Atlantic's geography is its huge *drainage basin,* the area of land whose rivers flow into an ocean. Most of the world's great rivers empty their waters into the Atlantic.

In North America the Atlantic basin stretches all the way to the Rocky Mountains. There, in western North America, the many tributaries of the mighty Mississippi begin. At mid-continent they join to form the river that drains two thirds of the continent toward the Gulf of Mexico, an arm of the Atlantic.

In South America the Atlantic's drainage area extends across the continent to the soaring Andes Mountains. Among those towering peaks the world's greatest flow of water begins its journey to the Atlantic. So great is this rush of water—carried by the Amazon River—that the volume of water is greater than that of the Mississippi, Nile, and Yangzte rivers *combined.*

The Atlantic also gathers much of the water from Africa. Waters of the Nile, Congo, and Niger rivers eventually reach the Atlantic. The Atlantic also claims the Rhine and the other great rivers of Western Europe as well as many of those of Eastern Europe and central Russia.

The immense size of the drainage basin opened the way to yet-to-be-explored lands. In North America, the Gulf of St. Lawrence, Hudson Bay, and Gulf of Mexico carried sailing vessels from Europe to the continent's edge. Rivers carried explorers to its very heart.

Sailing West

4. What propelled the early sailing ships from Europe to the Americas?

One other aspect of the Atlantic's geography

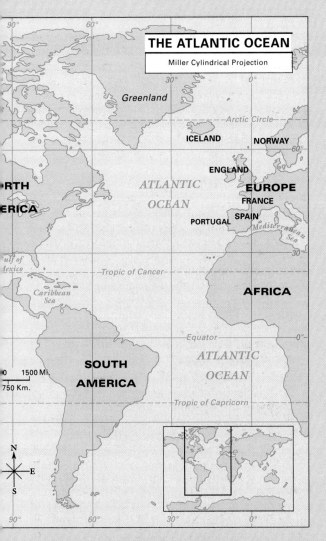

THE ATLANTIC OCEAN

Miller Cylindrical Projection

areas of lower pressure. The winds along the African coast result from air flowing from zones of high pressure near 30°N to a low-pressure zone always found near the equator.

Of course, if the world did not turn on its axis, the air would simply flow from north to south in the Northern Hemisphere and south to north in the Southern Hemisphere. The earth's rotation causes the winds to deflect, or bend.

These wonderful winds, among the steadiest and most reliable on earth, soon became invaluable for ships sailing westward. Within a remarkably short period of time they were known to sailors everywhere as the *trade winds*.

The Return Trip

5. Once in the Americas, how did people return to Europe?

Just as the trade winds carried ships westward, the Gulf Stream helped propel them back to Europe. The Gulf Stream begins in the eastern portions of the Gulf of Mexico. It flows northward along the eastern seaboard of the United States. At about 40°N the current swings eastward across the Atlantic toward the British Isles. It is one of the strongest and most consistent ocean currents. Coupled with the northeast trade winds, it provided knowledgeable navigators with the means to complete roundtrip voyages between Europe and the New World.

The geography of the Atlantic made it ideal as a pathway of discovery. Winds and currents moved the sailing ships on just the right paths. Plentiful bays and gulfs, fed by huge rivers, provided entrances into continents. Soon the forbiddingly vast waters of the Atlantic became one of the most heavily traveled routes in the world.

APPLYING YOUR KNOWLEDGE

Your class will work in three groups to create a profile map of the Atlantic Ocean. One group should map the major ocean currents. Another should identify and label on a map the major rivers eventually draining into the Atlantic. The third group should measure distances across the ocean from various spots (such as Virginia) in North America to Norway, Spain, and England. You will then combine the groups' findings to create your profile map of the Atlantic.

played a vital role in the discovery and exploration of the New World. Winds and ocean currents helped transport people and cargoes from Europe to the Americas and back.

As you can see from the map on page 24, Columbus first headed south to the Canary Islands before turning westward. This was no accident. Early explorers voyaging southward along Africa's west coast found strong and steady winds from the northeast between 30° and 5° north of the equator. These winds carried the sleek sailing ships ever westward.

What causes these winds? Air always flows from centers of high atmospheric pressure to

Linking History & Geography

CHAPTER 5 REVIEW

1773		1775		1777

1773
Parliament passes Tea Act
★
Boston Tea Party

1774
Intolerable Acts
★
First Continental Congress

1775
Battles of Lexington
and Concord
★
Battle of Bunker Hill
★
Second Continental Congress
★
Washington appointed
commander of Continental Army

1776
Common Sense published
★
Declaration of Independence
★
American victory
at Trenton

1777
American
at Princeto
★
Battle of
Saratoga
★
Winter at
Valley For

Chapter Summary

Read the statements below. Choose one and write a paragraph explaining its importance.

1. British economic policies and other attempts to control colonial life angered the colonists.
2. Lexington and Concord were the first battles of the Revolutionary War and ended chances for peaceful settlement.
3. The American Army was small, inexperienced, and ill-equipped to fight the British.
4. Washington's leadership and the cause of freedom helped Americans endure dark days.
5. The Declaration of Independence told the world of America's grievances.
6. Successes at Saratoga and elsewhere in 1777 turned the tide of war in America's favor.
7. Help from France and other Europeans bolstered the colonists.
8. The American victory at Yorktown convinced England to end the war.

Reviewing Chronological Order

Number your paper 1-5. Then study the time line above and place the following events in the order in which they happened by writing the first next to 1, the second next to 2, and so on.

1. The Battle of Saratoga
2. The British surrender at Yorktown
3. The Boston Tea Party
4. Lexington and Concord
5. The Declaration of Independence

Understanding Main Ideas

1. Why were the Committees of Correspondence important?
2. How did Lord North misjudge the other colonies when he punished Massachusetts?
3. Why was the Battle of Saratoga so critical to the American cause.
4. What was the last major battle of the war? Explain the role of the French in this battle.
5. Use your historical imagination to explain what "all men are created equal" meant to the leaders of the American Revolution.

Thinking Critically

1. **Evaluating**. It is the night of December 16, 1773. You, Samuel Adams, and several others disguise yourselves as Mohawks, board East India Company ships anchored in Boston Harbor, and dump English tea chests overboard. Are you committing a crime, or are you committing an act of political protest? Support your position with sound reasoning.
2. **Analyzing**. During the first years of the Revolutionary War, was George Washington a good general or a poor one? Why? Name three battles that support your answer.
3. **Seeing Connections**. You know that Thomas Paine's *Common Sense* had an important effect on the views of the colonists. Do you think Paine's ideas could have influenced Thomas Jefferson's writing in the Declaration of Independence? Cite examples from both works to support your opinion.

Writing About History

Write your own eyewitness account of the Boston Tea Party, either as a member of the Sons of Liberty or as a captain of one of the tea ships. Use the information in Chapter 5 to help you develop your account. Begin with a draft copy. Write freely. Then be sure to evaluate the content, organization, and style of your draft, taking care to check spelling and punctuation. After making any changes you feel necessary, write out your final copy.

Practicing the Strategy

Review the strategy on page 146.
Tracing Routes on a Map. Study the map on page 166 and answer the following questions.

1. From what city did Washington leave? What two battles did he win?

THE REVOLUTIONARY WAR

Revolutionary War	
1779 THE AMERICAN REVOLUTION	1781

778
reaty with France signed

★
merican victories in West

1781
British surrender at Yorktown

2. Along what route did British troops travel to reach Saratoga? How can you tell the Americans won?
3. In what general direction did Gates lead his troops from Albany to Saratoga?
4. What aspects of Howe's route are different from those of the other commanders shown on the map?

Using Primary Sources

It remains a mystery who fired the first shots of the revolution at Lexington. Even eyewitness accounts, such as those of militiaman Ebenezer Munroe of Lexington and British commander Colonel Francis Smith, contradict each other. To see how their accounts differ, read the following excerpts. Then answer the questions below.

About seventy of our company had assembled when the British troops appeared. Some of our men went into the meeting house where the town's powder was kept. . . . When the regulars had arrived within eighty or one hundred rods (438 to 547 yards), they . . . halted, charged their guns, and doubled their ranks, and marched up at quick step. Captain Parker ordered his men to stand their ground, and not molest the regulars unless they meddled with us. The British troops came directly in our front. The commanding officer advanced within a few rods of us and exclaimed, "Disperse, you . . . rebels! You dogs, run!—Rush on my boys!" and fired his pistol.

Corporal Ebenezer Munroe, Lexington militia

Our troops advanced toward them, without any intention of injuring them, further than to inquire the reason of their being thus assembled, and if not satisfactory, to have secured their arms; but they in confusion went off, principally to the left—only one of them fired before he went off, and three or four more jumped over a wall and fired from behind it among the soldiers; on which the troops returned it.

Colonel Francis Smith, British Tenth Infantry

1. What evidence in Munroe's account leads you to believe that the British approached the Lexington militia aggressively?
2. According to Colonel Smith's account why did the British troops approach the colonists?
3. Note the contradiction between the two accounts. Which version do you think is closer to the truth? Why do you think so?

Linking History & Geography

In every war geography plays a key role. It helps shape where battles are fought and often influences their outcomes. The Americans' familiarity with their native land was a major factor in their success against the British. Review the map on page 149 and read General Burgoyne's description of the Boston landscape. Then explain how geography helped and hindered each side in the fighting to control Boston.

Boston is a penninsula, joined to the main land only by a narrow neck. . . . Arms of the sea and the harbor surround the rest. . . . On one of these arms, to the north is Charlestown and over it is a large hill (Breed's Hill). . . . To the south is an even larger scope of land, containing three hils, joining also to the main by a tongue of land and called Dorchester Neck. The heights . . . north and south . . . command the town.

Enriching Your Study of History

1. **Individual Project.** Make a recruiting poster for Washington's army. Make up a slogan for your poster. (A slogan is a short phrase that catches people's attention and advertises a group's purpose.) Display your poster.
2. **Cooperative Project.** Prepare with your classmates a map of the major battles of the Revolutionary War. Make your map large enough to display in the classroom. Decide whether or not you will show troop movements and how you will distinguish on your map between American forces and British forces.

Chapter 5 Review 179

Creating the United States

Yorktown was the last battle of the Revolutionary War. Great Britain gave up its thirteen American colonies, and the fighting ended. But the Battle of Yorktown did not end the American Revolution that had begun in the early 1770s. Ending the Revolution was something only the Americans could do. The British had tried to stop the Revolution by force. When they failed, the Revolution went forward. In other words, there was more to the Revolution than the war. Breaking free from British control did not answer this question: What kind of government shall America have instead? Nor did it answer these questions: What kind of society should the people of America create? What kind of economic system?

Preview & Review

Use these questions to guide your reading. Answer the questions after completing Section 1.
Understanding Issues, Events, & Ideas. Use the following words in discussing plans to govern the new nation: constitution, legislature, executive, court, Bill of Rights, conservative, public servant.
1. What two tasks lay before the Americans who were creating a new system of government?
2. Why did the state constitutions give legislatures power?
3. Why was the creation of the state constitutions the most significant event of the Revolution?
4. In what ways was the Second Continental Congress the first central government of the United States?
Thinking Critically. Imagine that you are a state governor at the time a new state constitution has been written. What powers do you wish to be granted?

1. SELF-GOVERNMENT

A Central Government

The most obvious task facing Americans after the war was creating a new system of government. This task had two parts. One was to change the governments of the individual colonies into governments that were independent of England. The other was to find a substitute for the British colonial system—that is, to establish a new central government that could deal with common problems and advance the common interests of the new independent governments. Several political and intellectual traditions helped shape these governments. Some of these traditions were anchored in English history. In 1215, for example, English nobles had forced King John to sign the Magna Carta, which limited the power of the king and protected the liberties of the nobles. The document also dealt with the rights of the ordinary people. It established the principle that the king could not levy taxes without the consent of the Great Council, a body of nobles and church leaders who advised the king. It guaranteed an accused person a trial by a jury of peers, or equals. The Magna Carta provided the basis for establishing parliamentary democracy in England and later in the United States. American leaders also looked to the traditions of parliamentary government in England and to the English Bill of

Free Library of Philadelphia (Photo: Joan Broderick)

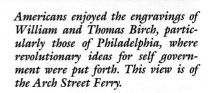

Rights of 1689, which declared that the monarch could not proclaim or suspend any law, impose any tax, or maintain an army in peacetime without Parliament's consent.

The Enlightenment (see page 98), with its emphasis on reason and the rule of law, also influenced American leaders. Many Americans believed, as Bacon, Newton, and other political philosophers had, in an orderly government based on the consent of the governed.

Other traditions rested on colonial practices. The Mayflower Compact (see page 54), for example, had established the people, not the government, as the ultimate source of authority. And the tradition that the people should play a major role in making and agreeing to laws had long been practiced in New England town meetings and the Virginia House of Burgesses.

Many Americans looked back even further to the democratic ideals of Greek and Roman governments and to the moral responsibilities taught by the early Jewish and Christian writers of the Bible.

All of these traditions, then, influenced Americans as they took the first steps toward forming lasting governments for the young nation. The first step was to create the states. The second was to create the United States. The first step was more important in those days because the state governments affected the lives of the people much more than the central government. The second step was more difficult because it meant deciding what power the United States should have over the separate states that made it up.

Americans enjoyed the engravings of William and Thomas Birch, particularly those of Philadelphia, where revolutionary ideas for self government were put forth. This view is of the Arch Street Ferry.

Self-Government

State Governments

Changing a colony into a state meant getting rid of all British controls on local government and then deciding what, if any, new controls should be substituted. The original colonial charters had been grants of power by the king. In place of these royal charters, the people of the states substituted **constitutions.** These constitutions were written descriptions of the system of government the people wanted and of the powers that each part of the government was to have.

The constitutions were all more or less alike, although each state made its own. They divided government into three parts: an elected **legislature,** where proposed laws were to be debated and either passed or rejected; an **executive,** who was to carry out the laws and manage the day-to-day operations of the government; and a system of **courts,** where the laws could be enforced.

The state legislatures replaced the colonial assemblies. The assemblies had always been the part of the colonial governments most influenced by public opinion. They had become centers of popular opposition to British control. Naturally the new constitutions gave the legislatures a great deal of power.

On the other hand, state governors were given very little power by the constitutions. They lost the right to dismiss the legislatures and the power to keep a particular legislature in office for years without its members having to stand for reelection. The powers to declare war, to conduct foreign relations, and to appoint government officials were generally assigned to the legislatures, not to the governors. Governors, in other words, were intended to be mere administrators, not rulers or even policy makers. This change was a natural result of the widespread resentment of the way colonial governors had tried to dominate the assemblies.

One state, Pennsylvania, decided not to have a governor at all. The work usually done by a governor was to be done by a supreme executive council of 12 persons elected by the people. Another state, Virginia, dealt with the problem of controlling the governor by having the legislature elect him. Even with this control the Virginia constitution went on to order that the governor's salary be "adequate *but moderate.*"

The powers of state judges were also limited by the constitutions. Even the legislatures were subject to strict checks. They were increased in size so that individual representatives would have less power. Terms of office were usually only one year, kept short so that voters could quickly get rid of representatives whose actions they disapproved of. Most of the constitutions also contained **Bills of Rights,** lists of what the state governments could *not* do and liberties that the people could not be deprived of. The troubles that led to the Revolution had made Americans suspicious of *all* government.

Some of the constitutions were more **conservative,** or less likely

CREATING THE UNITED STATES

to encourage change. Some made greater changes in the colonial patterns. Qualifications for voting varied. The Pennsylvania constitution gave the right to vote to all adult free men who paid taxes. In South Carolina property qualifications for voting were kept high, and a person running for office needed a considerable fortune.

What was common to all constitutions and what made them all fundamentally democratic was that the people were establishing the rules by which political life was to be organized and run. The constitutions were contracts, written legal agreements. They demonstrated that governments existed to do what the people wanted them to do, but no more. They made government officials **public servants,** not the public's masters.

The creation of these constitutions also proved that people could change their government peacefully. The American states were created in an orderly, legal manner. Making constitutions caused hot debates and sharp arguments, but there was no rioting and bloodshed, no use of any kind of force. It was particularly remarkable that governments could be changed in this peaceful and orderly way even while the people were fighting a war for survival. The creation of the state constitutions was the most significant event of the Revolution.

Representing the People

The new governments did not try to make radical changes. Many people worried about the government being controlled by a few "aristocrats." By aristocrats they meant the rich and socially prominent people of their communities. Other groups feared control by "the mob," meaning the artisans and manual laborers of the towns and other relatively poor people who owned little or no property. Since the great majority of the people were neither "aristocrats" nor members of "the mob," most of the constitutions tried to protect the owners of property and at the same time to prevent these well-to-do citizens from using their wealth and influence to take advantage of the poor. The result was usually to keep things more or less as they had been in colonial times.

In some cases the constitutions were written by special assemblies called conventions elected by the voters specifically for that purpose. This method made sure that the ideas and intentions of those who prepared the constitutions were known and approved of in advance. The convention system was one of the most original political ideas to come out of the Revolution.

Most of the new governments finally gave their western districts fairer representation in the state legislatures. Many did away with state support for one particular region. The constitutions did not attempt, however, to do away with slavery.

The high ideals of the times had led many owners to free their slaves, but they did so as individuals, not in response to state law.

Point of View

An English writer whose books take us backward *and* forward in time made this observation about the American Revolution.

"From the point of view of human history, the way in which the Thirteen States became independent is of far less importance than the fact that they did become independent. And with the establishment of their independence came a new sort of community into the world. It was like something coming out of an egg. . . . It had no dukes, princes, counts, nor any sort of title-bearers claiming to ascendancy or respect as a right. Even its unity was as yet a mere unity for defence and freedom. It was in these respects such a clean start in political organization as the world had not seen before. . . ."

From *The Outline of History,* H. G. Wells, 1920

Self-Government

However, in the northern states the legislatures gradually passed laws to free the children of slaves born after a certain date. These laws did not deprive owners of any existing human property. No such laws were passed in the South, where nine of every ten slaves were held. Indeed the Revolution had transformed slavery from a national to a sectional institution. The movement to free slaves was probably caused more by the high cost of maintaining slavery than by a belief in freedom for all inspired by the Declaration of Independence. Even in Virginia, for example, the price of tobacco was very low in the 1770s and 1780s, so owning slaves was not very profitable. When conditions changed, the attitudes of southern slave owners changed also, as we shall see later.

Forming a Central Government

Forming a central government for all the states was much more complicated. In a sense it began with the Plan of Union drafted by Benjamin Franklin at the Albany Congress in 1754. The Stamp Act Congress was another step. So were the colonial committees of correspondence and the informal organizations designed to enforce bans on importing British goods. The First Continental Congress followed. All these attempts at union were responses to the same pressures that led Benjamin Franklin to say, "we must indeed all hang together, or, most assuredly we shall all hang separately."

The Second Continental Congress was the first central government, the first true United States. It had a continuing existence, and it ran the country on a day-to-day basis. In the beginning this government had no constitution or specific duties. Then the new state constitutions provided for the regular election of representatives to the Congress, and it was firmly and legally established.

From the start the Congress assumed a great deal of power. It appointed Washington commander in chief of the army and selected other generals. It drafted the Declaration of Independence. It operated a postal service. It sent representatives to foreign countries to obtain support. The diplomats who negotiated the crucial treaty with France after the Battle of Saratoga were assigned by the Continental Congress. The Congress also figured out how much money would be needed each year to carry on the war and perform other government functions. It decided how much each state should contribute to this total. It then sent bills for these amounts, called requisitions, to the states. These were often ignored by the states and rarely paid in full. Congress had to borrow large sums of money to make up the difference. It even printed paper money.

The Congress was a kind of American parliament. But there was no American equivalent to the English king or the prime minister. Instead committees of Congress carried out the functions of the head of state and executive leader of the country. 🔲

Return to the Preview & Review on page 180.

 CREATING THE UNITED STATES

2. SETTING NEW BOUNDARIES

The Articles of Confederation

By November 1777 a committee of Congress had drafted a written constitution, the **Articles of Confederation.** This charter made no important change in the way what it called "The United States of America" was already operating. It put in writing the powers that the Continental Congress was already exercising. It stressed the independence of the separate states. The United States was to be only a "league of friendship"—that is, a kind of alliance. The Articles of Confederation provided that each state should have but one vote in Congress. All laws passed by Congress had to be approved by 9 of the 13 states. The Articles themselves could not be amended unless all the states agreed.

Limits were set on the power of the United States, even while the nation was fighting a war for its very survival. This reveals how suspicious people were of a central government. In particular they feared being taxed by the central government. This was obviously a result of their resentment of the Stamp Act and the other taxes that Parliament had tried to make them pay. Thus Section 8 of the Articles of Confederation said Congress should decide how much money had to be raised, but actual tax laws would have to be passed by the state legislatures.

Many states were reluctant to give Congress the authority that the Articles proposed, even though it was severely limited. However,

Preview & Review

Use these questions to guide your reading. Answer the questions after completing Section 2.
Understanding Issues, Events, & Ideas. Use the following terms to describe America's first government: Articles of Confederation, ratify, Peace of Paris, Land Ordinance of 1785, township, Land Ordinance of 1787 or Northwest Ordinance, territory, republican.
1. How did the Articles of Confederation stress the independence of the states?
2. How would new states come into being under the Land Ordinance system?
3. What two limitations did Congress place on states that were formed from territories?
Thinking Critically. You are John Jay negotiating Treaty of Paris. Before your meeting with Richard Oswald of Britain, write a list of the points you will try to make.

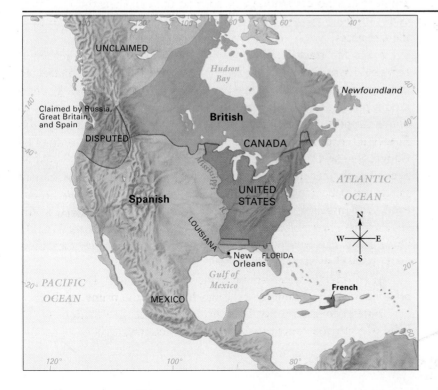

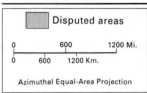

NORTH AMERICA IN 1783

Disputed areas

| 0 | 600 | 1200 Mi. |

| 0 | 600 | 1200 Km. |

Azimuthal Equal-Area Projection

LEARNING FROM MAPS. *The end of the war added a large area to United States control. What problems might this large area cause for the new nation?*

after a little more than a year had passed, all the states except Maryland had **ratified** the document. To ratify means to approve. Maryland's objections had nothing to do with the fear of a central government. In fact, it was demanding an increase in the power of Congress.

At issue was the old question of who should control the western lands. Maryland's colonial charter did not include a "sea-to-sea" land grant such as that of Virginia, Massachusetts, and other colonies. Maryland insisted, therefore, that all state claims to lands beyond the Appalachian Mountains be turned over to the United States. Some of the states agreed, but Virginia, which had enormous western claims, refused to do so. Maryland was equally stubborn. Therefore the Articles of Confederation could not go into effect. Finally, in January 1781, Virginia gave up its western claims, and Maryland ratified the Articles.

No one could have known this at the time, but the decision to put all western lands under the control of the central government was one of the most important in the entire history of the United States. The incident is an example of how the give-and-take of political compromise in a democratic system can have unintended results. In this case the results were all good.

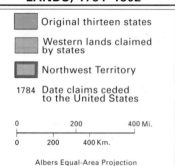

CLAIMS TO WESTERN LANDS, 1784–1802

- Original thirteen states
- Western lands claimed by states
- Northwest Territory

1784 Date claims ceded to the United States

0   200   400 Mi.

0   200   400 Km.

Albers Equal-Area Projection

LEARNING FROM MAPS. As the map shows, many of the original colonies claimed western lands. On what were these claims based? Why was it geographically and politically important for the new nation to settle these western claims immediately?

186   CREATING THE UNITED STATES

Maryland had held out for national control of the western lands for selfish reasons. People in the state seeking to make a fast profit buying and selling land, including the governor himself, hoped to get huge tracts of Indian land in the Ohio Valley. Virginia gave up its claims for equally selfish reasons. Benedict Arnold's raiders had invaded the state in December 1780. Cornwallis was preparing to march his powerful army north from the Carolinas. Virginia was obviously going to need the help of the other states. Giving up its western claims was a kind of goodwill gesture.

The Treaty of Paris

The importance of settling the western claims became fully clear only after a peace treaty was signed with Great Britain officially ending the Revolutionary War. Negotiating the treaty was complicated because the struggle had become another world war. Spain and France were deeply involved, and their interests were not always the same as America's. Spain, for example, wanted to extend its control in America into what are now Mississippi and Alabama. France was not eager to see the United States become too large and powerful either. Both these nations wished to settle many issues with the British. In the complicated negotiations they might sacrifice American goals to advance their own.

Another problem was that the British leaders resented having lost a war to colonists. Their pride was hurt. To have to negotiate with "rebels" was a bitter pill for them to swallow. They might prefer to give more to the French and Spanish to avoid giving in to the Americans.

The peace negotiations took place in Paris in 1782 and 1783. Congress appointed an extremely distinguished delegation consisting of Benjamin Franklin, Thomas Jefferson, John Adams, Henry Laurens, and John Jay. Franklin, Jefferson, and Adams were probably the best-known and most respected Americans of their generation. Henry Laurens had made a fortune as a merchant and planter in South Carolina. He had served as president of the Continental Congress. During the war he had been captured by the British while sailing to Holland on a diplomatic assignment. He had spent more than a year locked up in the Tower of London. Finally he was released in exchange for General Cornwallis, who had surrendered after the Battle of Yorktown.

John Jay, a New York lawyer and drafter of the first New York state constitution, had also been a president of the Continental Congress. Jay came to Paris directly from service as United States minister to Spain. He was a humorless person but extremely intelligent and a shrewd diplomat. Franklin tended to accept the suggestions of the French foreign minister, Count Vergennes. Jay did not trust Vergennes, and he was right not to.

Point of View

The king of England made his separate peace with John Adams after the Revolutionary War with these words.

"I wish you, Sir, to believe, that it may be understood in America, that I have done nothing in the late contest but what I thought myself indispensably bound to do by the duty which I owed my people. I will be very frank with you. I was the last to consent to the separation; but the separation having been made, and having become inevitable, I have always said, as I say now, that I would be the first to meet the friendship of the United States as an independent power."

George III

Fortunately for the United States, Jay did the most important negotiating with the chief British delegate, Richard Oswald. He persuaded Oswald that a strong United States in North America would be less of a threat to England than a strong France or Spain.

In the end Oswald accepted Jay's argument. In November 1782 he signed an agreement that gave the United States nearly everything it hoped for. Besides official recognition of the United States, the British accepted the Great Lakes as the northern boundary of the new nation and the Mississippi River as the western boundary. The southern boundary was set at 31° north latitude. Louisiana remained under Spanish control while the British returned control of Florida and the southern parts of present-day Alabama and Mississippi to Spain.

The British also agreed to remove their armies from American soil "with all convenient speed." In return the Americans promised not to seize any more property from American Loyalists. They would urge the state governments to give back property that had already been taken. Finally, they agreed not to try to prevent British subjects from recovering debts owed them from before the Revolution by Americans. This agreement, the **Peace of Paris,** was officially accepted by both sides in September 1783.

Benjamin West had to leave unfinished his portrait of the delegates to the Paris Peace Convention. The British delegates refused to pose. The Americans, from left, are John Jay, John Adams, Benjamin Franklin, Henry Laurens, and Franklin's grandson, who was secretary to the delegation. As you read this book, think how this picture symbolizes that the quarrel between the United States and Britain was also unfinished.

The Henry Francis du Pont Winterthur Museum

Courtesy, Cincinnati Historical Society

CINCINNATI-1800.

The Land Ordinances

With peace and with the United States recognized as a member of the family of nations, Congress turned to other problems. One of the most important was the organization of the territory beyond the Appalachian Mountains. As early as 1780 Congress had decided that western territories under its control should be "formed into distinct republican States which shall become members of the Federal Union." After the war was won, Congress put the policy into effect by passing two laws called Land Ordinances.

The first, the **Land Ordinance of 1785**, established a method of selling the land. This method combined the New England idea of carving up the wilderness into large townships and the southern practice of giving land in smaller units to individuals. Unsettled regions were to be surveyed into squares 6 miles (about 10 kilometers) on a side. Half of these **townships** would then be subdivided into 36 sections, each 1 square mile (640 acres, or 256 hectares) in area. The townships and sections were to be sold at public auction. The money would go into the treasury of the United States, but the money from the sale of one section in each township would be given to the local community for the support of its schools. Thus America committed itself early to an educated population as the foundation of a democratic society. In the words of Thomas Jefferson:

> ❝ If a nation expects to be ignorant and free, in a state of civilization, it expects what never was and never will be. ❞

The **Land Ordinance of 1787**, better known as the **Northwest Ordinance,** was a plan to govern the lands bounded by the Ohio and Mississippi Rivers and the Great Lakes while they were growing from territory to statehood. The new regions could have been carved up into colonies the way the English had done with their American possessions. But the American people had just fought a war to get

Cincinnati, on the Ohio River, lay in the new Northwest Territory. A. J. Swing painted this view in 1800. Fort Washington is in the background. If you can, compare this early view with a contemporary picture of Cincinnati. Another group might find out the origins of the name Cincinnati and try to decide why it was chosen for this frontier settlement.

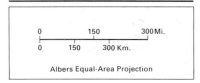

THE NORTHWEST ORDINANCE, 1787

0   150   300 Mi.

0   150   300 Km.

Albers Equal-Area Projection

LEARNING FROM MAPS. *Compare this map to the one on 186. Note that the ordinance settled claims to lands in the Northwest Territory. What states had claimed lands there? Why were the lands divided into townships and sections?*

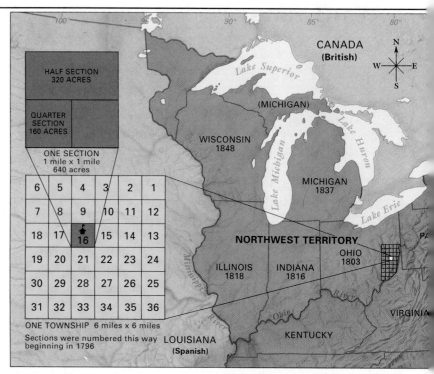

rid of colonialism. The Ordinance provided that the Northwest be divided into units called **territories.** Each territory was to be ruled by a governor, a secretary, and three judges appointed by Congress. When 5,000 men of voting age had settled a territory, they could elect a local legislature to deal with their own affairs and a nonvoting delegate to represent their interests in Congress.

When the population of the territory reached 60,000, the voters were to draft a state constitution. After Congress approved this document, the territory would become a state, equal to all the other states. The only limitations placed by Congress were that the state government must be **republican**—that is, its power must lie in representatives elected by the people—and that slavery must be prohibited in all land north of the Ohio River.

Under the Northwest Ordinance, the states of Ohio, Indiana, Illinois, Michigan, and Wisconsin were eventually formed. As the nation expanded westward, the same method was used again and again. Thus the original 13 states became the present 50. This development was not always smooth. Many controversies marked the history of westward expansion. Slavery, for example, was not ruled out in all new territories. Bitter conflicts erupted over this issue, as we shall see.

Without the Land Ordinance system there would surely have been far more bitter conflicts. If Congress had tried to give the West less power than the original states, the United States would almost certainly have become a number of separate nations. 🖃

3. PEACETIME TROUBLES

Hard Times

The end of the Revolutionary War was a great blessing. The bloodshed stopped. Normal life could resume. American ships could sail the seas without fear of attack. Merchants could buy and sell in markets such as China that formerly had been closed to them.

However, peace brought out the weaknesses of a government that was only a "league of friendship." When the need to "hang together" to save their necks ended, the states tended to go off in different directions. The great Land Ordinances could never have been passed if Virginia had not given up its western claims. And the Virginians would never have given them up if they had not felt threatened by the coastal invasions of General Cornwallis.

Once the war was over, rivalries between the various states became more troublesome. As every American sports fan knows, members of leagues, however friendly, can compete with one another fiercely! There was a brief economic downturn, or **depression.** War had disrupted both farming and trade. Farmers and merchants experienced hard times. This depression lasted from 1784 to 1786. During the hard times the states were stingier than ever about supplying the money that the United States needed to run its affairs. Each state would pay only for direct benefits and ignore national needs. States like North Carolina and Georgia had frontier districts where there could be fighting with the Indians or possible invasion by Spanish forces. These states were willing to contribute to national defense. South Carolina, geographically protected from danger by its neighbors Georgia and North Carolina, was unwilling to pay its share of national defense.

The Trade Problem

Many Americans were hurt by British regulations of trade with the United States after the war. To the British the United States had become a foreign country. They therefore applied the Navigation Acts to American commerce. They barred American dried and salted fish from the sugar islands in the British West Indies. This hurt New England fishermen. The British required that other American products be carried to the West Indies in British ships. This hurt American merchants and shipbuilders.

British manufacturers had not been able to sell their products in America during the war. Local manufacturing had begun to spring up to supply the needs of the people. With peace restored, the British began to sell goods in America at extremely low prices in order to win back the customers they had lost.

Preview & Review

Use these questions to guide your reading. Answer the questions after completing Section 3.
Understanding Issues, Events, & Ideas. Use the following words to explain the nation's problems under the Articles of Confederation: depression, tariff, Continental dollar, hard money, inflation, unconstitutional, Shays' Rebellion.

1. What were some of the peacetime troubles for the "league of friendship"?
2. How did British restrictions on trade hurt Americans after the war had ended?
3. Why did Congress begin to print paper money? Why did Americans prefer "hard" money to paper money? What was the fate of paper money in Rhode Island?
4. Why did the farmers in western Massachusetts rise up against their government?

Thinking Critically. 1. If you were a storekeeper at the end of the Revolutionary War, would you accept Continental dollars? Why or why not? 2. Of the problems discussed in this section, which do you think was the most difficult? Why?

This practice, called dumping, could have been checked by taxing British imports. High **tariffs,** or taxes on imports, might also have persuaded the British to remove the restrictions on American trade with the West Indies. But the United States government did not have the power under the Articles of Confederation to put tariffs on foreign goods.

One need only recall how Americans felt about the Townshend duty on tea to understand why the states had been unwilling to allow the central government to tax imports. And if one or another individual state taxed British goods, British merchants would simply ship their products to a port in a state that had not passed tariff laws.

Soon many Americans began to suggest that Congress be given the power to tax foreign goods. This could be done only if all the states agreed to change the Articles of Confederation. Despite many attempts this unanimous consent could not be obtained.

The Money Problem

Another power denied the United States under the Articles of Confederation was the power to tax. The system of asking the states for money never worked well, even during the war. To pay its bills Congress printed more and more paper money, called **Continental dollars.** This money fell in value because people had no confidence

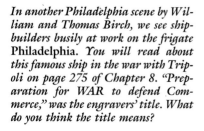

In another Philadelphia scene by William and Thomas Birch, we see shipbuilders busily at work on the frigate Philadelphia. *You will read about this famous ship in the war with Tripoli on page 275 of Chapter 8. "Preparation for WAR to defend Commerce," was the engravers' title. What do you think the title means?*

The John Carter Brown Library, Brown University

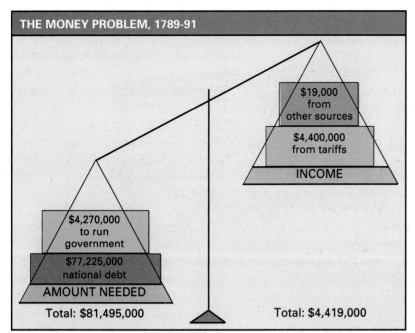

THE MONEY PROBLEM, 1789-91

$19,000
from
other sources

$4,400,000
from tariffs

INCOME

$4,270,000
to run
government

$77,225,000
national debt

AMOUNT NEEDED

Total: $81,495,000

Total: $4,419,000

Source: *Historical Statistics of the United States*

LEARNING FROM DIAGRAMS.
Part of the money problem for the young nation was the money borrowed during the Revolutionary War. According to the diagram, what was the national debt? In what ways could the United States bring the scales into balance?

in it. They preferred **hard money**—gold and silver coins that simply as metal were worth the value stamped on them. The lower the real value of the Continental dollar, the more dollars the government had to print. A vicious cycle developed. Soon people were using the expression "not worth a Continental" to mean "worthless."

The state governments did have the power to tax their citizens. They could issue paper money too, and all did so. This increase in the amount of paper money caused **inflation.** Inflation happens when prices rise because the amount of dollars in people's pockets is increased without an increase in the amount of goods available for sale. People lost confidence in state money for the same reason that they distrusted Continentals.

Some states therefore cut down on their paper money issues. To pay their expenses, they increased taxes. Money paid in taxes was money that otherwise might have been spent on goods, so the demand for goods declined. Sellers then had to lower their prices.

Not everyone benefited from lower prices, not even all the people who could buy things more cheaply. People who had borrowed money in the past preferred inflation, which made it easier for them to pay their debts. A farmer who borrowed $10 when wheat was selling for 25 cents a bushel would have to grow 40 bushels to pay his debt. If the price of wheat went up to 50 cents a bushel, he would only have to produce 20 bushels to pay it.

Popular pressure for "cheap" paper money was particularly strong in Rhode Island. That state had been hard hit by the postwar depression. Taxes were a heavy burden on the farm population.

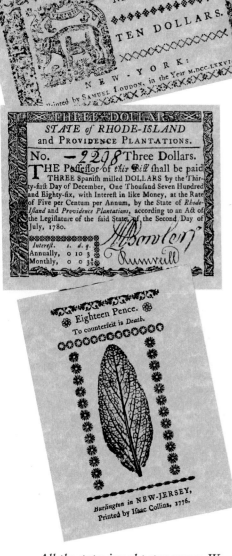

All the states issued paper money. We see that there once was a three dollar bill in Rhode Island and that "to counterfeit is Death" in New Jersey. Study the other bills carefully for their different messages.

In 1786 the Rhode Island legislature passed a bill allowing property owners to borrow fixed amounts of money from the government at a very low interest rate for 14 years. The state would simply print the money and hand it over to any Rhode Island landowner who applied. When lenders refused to accept this paper money in payment of debts, the legislature passed a law allowing the debtors to deposit the money with local judges, who would declare the loan repaid. When storekeepers refused to accept the paper at face value, the legislature passed a law to heavily fine them.

These laws caused business in Rhode Island to come to a standstill. Storekeepers closed their shops rather than sell goods for money they believed worthless. People who were owed money went into hiding. Some fled the state. One jokester suggested that instead of paper the state issue money made of rope. Then people who refused to accept it could be whipped with the rope, and if they continued to refuse, hanged with it.

One tough-minded butcher, John Weeden of Newport, Rhode Island, refused to accept paper money from a customer, John Trevett. When he was fined for refusing, Weeden went to court. In the case of *Trevett v. Weeden,* the Rhode Island Supreme Court refused to make Weeden pay the fine on the grounds, never before used by an American court, that the law was **unconstitutional.** It violated the state constitution. The constitution had not given the legislature the power to pass the law. After the court's decision people refused to accept Rhode Island paper money. It fell rapidly in value.

Shays' Rebellion

Cautious people in all the states had been greatly concerned by the actions of the Rhode Island legislature. Events in Massachusetts soon brought more cause for alarm. There the reverse of the Rhode Island situation existed. The Massachusetts legislators were determined to pay off the large state debt by raising taxes.

The Granger Collection, New York

Daniel Shays brought his protest against taxes to the steps of the state supreme court in Springfield, Massachusetts in 1786. Howard Pyle recreated the drama 100 years later. Study the engraving carefully. What differences do you see between Shays (on the porch, top right) and his opponents?

These taxes hit people in the western part of the state very hard. Poor farmers who did not have the money to pay them had their farms seized and sold. Resentment mounted. Crowds gathered to prevent local courts from meeting to condemn the property of debtors so that it could be sold to pay the taxes. In September 1786 a mob marched on Springfield, Massachusetts, to prevent the state supreme court from meeting.

The leader of the protesters was Daniel Shays, a veteran of the Revolutionary War. Shays had fought at Lexington, Bunker Hill, and Saratoga. Although he was uneducated, he had risen to the rank of captain. He was a poor man, much troubled by the determination of the state to prevent inflation and pay off the debt.

After breaking up the meeting of the supreme court, Shays tried to attack the Springfield arsenal in order to get more weapons. However, his force of 1,200 men was routed by militia units. A second battle with the militia in February 1787 had the same result. **Shays' Rebellion** collapsed and Shays fled to Vermont.

Return to the Preview & Review on page 191.

Peacetime Troubles

Independence National Historical Park

Preview & Review

Use these questions to guide your reading. Answer the questions after completing Section 4.

Understanding Issues, Events, & Ideas. Use the following words to report on the Constitutional Convention: Constitutional Convention, national government, Preamble, nationalism, federalism.

1. What surprising result came from the meeting to revise the Articles of Confederation?
2. Why did the delegates agree so quickly to a new Constitution?
3. What are some of the powers the Constitution gave to the United States government?

Thinking Critically. You are a supporter of having a strong central government. What arguments would you use to sway others to your side?

As a historical record of the signing of the Constitution, this painting is not a very good one. Even the tapestry of the sunburst that hangs behind Washington is fanciful. The actual sunburst was painted on the president's chair. Why do you suppose artists "touch up" history in this way?

4. "WE, THE PEOPLE"

The Constitutional Convention

The financial disturbances in Rhode Island and Massachusetts raised questions in the minds of many conservatives about the future of republican government. Was this what happened when the people were allowed to govern themselves? Would debtors always use their votes to cheat the rich when they had the votes to do it, as in Rhode Island, or resort to force when they did not, as in Massachusetts?

One result of such questions was to make people want to increase the power of the United States government at the expense of the states. Then it would be more difficult for a minority to frighten the majority or for one group to get control of the government.

A stronger central government could maintain order better. It could develop a unified policy for the whole country. Those who favored giving the national government control over foreign trade expected prosperity to result. These objectives—unity, order, and prosperity—made a powerful combination. The time had come to revise the Articles of Confederation.

In September 1786 delegates from five states met at Annapolis, Maryland, to discuss the foreign trade problem. They could do nothing about it unless all the states participated. One of the men present was Alexander Hamilton of New York, a young lawyer who had served on General Washington's staff during the war. He suggested that the group call another meeting. Delegates to this meeting should consider a plan for revising the entire Articles of Confederation.

Congress voted to recommend this proposal to the states. All the legislatures except Rhode Island's sent delegates to the meeting. The sessions began at the Pennsylvania State House in Philadelphia on May 25, 1787.

The delegates' first decision was to elect George Washington president, or chairman, of the conference. The presence of Washington, who was 55, and of Benjamin Franklin, who was over 80, added prestige to the group. But most of the work was done by much younger people like James Madison of Virginia, who was 36.

The next major step was the decision to try to draft a new constitution. The delegates had been authorized by the state legislatures only to try to patch up the Articles of Confederation. Instead they decided to wipe the slate clean. The meeting then became the **Constitutional Convention.** This was technically illegal. The delegates justified their action by pointing out that they were only recommending changes. The states could always reject their proposals.

The Supreme Law of the Land

On May 30, only five days after beginning their first discussion, the delegates agreed in principle to the most fundamental change. The Articles of Confederation had created a "league of friendship." A league is a kind of treaty signed by basically independent nations. The delegates at Philadelphia proposed a **national government** instead. Gouverneur Morris of Pennsylvania, one of the best speakers at the convention, explained the difference between the two. The "league of friendship" was "a mere compact resting on the good faith of the parties." A national government was "a complete and compulsive" authority, able to enforce its laws directly on the people.

This principle was spelled out in the famous first sentence of the Constitution, the **Preamble.** It reads: "We the *People* of the United States . . . do ordain and establish this Constitution," not "We the states . . ." In Article VI the Constitution further states that it is to be "the supreme Law of the Land." Judges in the states are to be bound by it without regard for anything in the state constitutions. Even the members of the state legislatures were to be required to take an oath to support the United States Constitution.

Such a drastic change was agreed upon so quickly because the delegates were determined to create a more effective central government. Of course, some Americans disapproved of the change. When Sam Adams, who was not a delegate, saw that the Preamble to the Constitution began "We the People" rather than "We the states," he remarked, "As I enter the Building I stumble at the Threshold." Nevertheless, the Philadelphia delegates had been appointed by *state* legislatures. The legislatures would not have selected them if they were not prepared to see the United States made stronger.

Historical imagination helps us to understand another reason why people were ready for a more powerful government. The Revolutionary War had stirred **nationalism,** a feeling of national pride. It had given people their first heroes and their first flags. Thousands of soldiers had traveled far from home and seen other parts of the country. They had fought alongside soldiers from other states. Their horizons had been broadened. Afterwards, they were less likely to think of themselves as Virginians or Pennsylvanians or New Yorkers. They had become first of all Americans.

No one wanted the central government to swallow up the states. The state governments should remain strong and active and independent. However, to the powers already possessed by the United States, the delegates now added several. The most important were the power to tax and the power to regulate trade between the states and between all the states and foreign countries. The Constitution also took away from the separate states the right to coin money and print paper money and the right to tax imports and exports. Such a system of shared powers is known as **federalism.**

Now the United States could raise money to pay its expenses without depending on the state legislatures. Therefore it could avoid printing too much money. The dollar would be worth a dollar, whether in silver or gold coins or in the form of a dollar bill.

Now the United States could place tariffs on imported goods, either to raise money or to regulate foreign trade. These were powers Parliament had tried to exercise before the Revolution. Now Congress was to exercise them.

Moreover, reducing the power of the states to "make" money meant that incidents like Rhode Island's paper money problems could no longer occur. Any future Daniel Shays could be checked by the power of the whole nation if necessary.

The states, however, would still have enough power to manage their local affairs. They could not print money, but they could obtain money by taxing their citizens. The states and the local communities within them could continue to have their own police, and state governors could call up militia units in emergencies.

LEARNING FROM CHARTS. *Federalism is the term used for the sharing of power by the national and state governments. "Delegated powers" are given to the national government. "Reserved powers" are held by the states. Why are delegated powers best held by the national government? Why are reserved powers best held by the states?*

FEDERALISM

Powers Delegated to National Government	Powers shared by National and State Governments	Powers Reserved to States
Declare war		Establish and maintain schools
Maintain armed forces		Establish local goverments
Regulate interstate and foreign trade	Maintain law and order	Conduct elections
Admit new states	Levy taxes	Create corporation laws
Establish post offices	Borrow money	Regulate business within the state
Set standard weights and measures	Charter banks	Make marriage laws
Coin money	Establish courts	Provide for public safety
Establish foreign policy	Provide for public welfare	Assume other powers not delegated to the national government or prohibited to the states
Make all laws necessary and proper for carrying out delegated powers		

THE ARTICLES OF CONFEDERATION AND THE CONSTITUTION	
The Articles	**The Constitution**
THE EXECUTIVE BRANCH	
No executive to administer and enforce legislation Executive committee to oversee government 　when Congress out of session Congress with sole authority to govern	President chosen by electors, who in turn are 　chosen by the states Administers and enforces federal laws
THE LEGISLATIVE BRANCH	
A unicameral legislature (one house) Each state with one vote, regardless of population Nine votes (of original 13) to enact legislation	A bicameral legislature (two houses) Each state having equal representation in the Senate Each state represented according to population in 　the House of Representatives Simple majority to enact legislation
THE JUDICIAL BRANCH	
No national court system Congress to establish temporary courts to hear 　cases of piracy	National court system, headed by the Supreme Court Courts to hear cases involving national laws, 　treaties, the Constitution; cases between states, 　between citizens of different states, or between 　a state and citizens of another state
OTHER MATTERS	
Admission to the Confederation by nine votes (of 13) Amendment of Articles must be unanimous	Congress to admit new states All states must have a republican form 　of government Amendment of the Constitution by two-thirds vote 　of both houses of Congress or by a national con- 　vention and ratified by three-fourths of the states

The Preamble of the Constitution neatly summarizes what these changes were meant to accomplish. "We the People" were creating "a more perfect Union" where "Justice" would be assured and order maintained (the founders used the term "domestic Tranquility"). The new system would "provide for the common defense" against foreign enemies too. It would "promote the general Welfare" and secure for Americans and their descendants "the Blessings of Liberty." In other words, the Constitution would supply the nation with the *unity, order,* and *prosperity* lacking under the Articles of Confederation.

The Constitution embodied the ideas and ideals of the European Enlightenment. That governments must be created by and subject to the will of the people was basic to the political philosophies of John Locke and Jean-Jacques Rousseau. Baron de Montesquieu proposed a government of three branches with the powers divided among them. Voltaire contributed the ideals of personal liberties and "unalienable rights" guaranteed by the government. The complete text of the Constitution, with commentary, follows on pages 201–18. 🖎

LEARNING FROM CHARTS.
This chart illustrates the weaknesses of the Articles of Confederation and the parts of the Constitution aimed at avoiding those weaknesses. Which of the weaknesses of the Articles do you think was the most serious? Why?

Return to the Preview & Review on page 196.

"We, the People"　　**199**

THE CONSTITUTION

"Although it had flaws and is still not perfect, our Constitution has allowed a system of government to flourish with freedom and opportunity unequaled anywhere in the world before or since. The United States has no need for walls or laws to keep people from moving elsewhere; and for over 200 years countless millions of people have come here from all parts of the globe, creating a society of pluralism and diversity resting on liberty.

For being an American and enjoying the fruits of our Constitution—the liberty and opportunity that our system of self-government makes possible—is a lifelong adventure. It is a privilege to be an American, and a privilege that carries responsibilities we must all fulfill.[1]"

Warren E. Burger

When the delegates arrived at the Constitutional Convention in Philadelphia, their instructions were to revise the Articles of Confederation. Instead they wrote a brilliant new document that has come to embody the true meaning of democracy. Even more astonishingly, what the framers wrote more than 200 hundred years ago still applies today. The United States is the only country in the world that has been governed under the same basic law for so long. The flexibility of the Constitution has allowed the United States to function smoothly through the past two centuries of tremendous change and growth while it developed into a great world power.

Most of the debates at the convention were about protecting the rights of the states from the powers of the federal government, the small states from large states, the powers of Congress from a strong president, and the rights of minorities from the will of the majority. Even though the Articles of Confederation gave the federal government no real power, the delegates still feared a central government that could become *too* powerful.

To restrict power, the men who wrote the Constitution devised ways to balance each branch of government against the others. They believed that if each branch of government could check, or put limits on, the other branches, then the central government would be efficient without taking away the liberties of the people. The writers also had foresight to provide a means of amending, or changing, the Constitution. They made the amendment process part of the Constitution. It was important that the amendment process not be made too easy. If it were, the Constitution would not be a basic law at all. So the amendment process was made diffi-

[1] From *The Constitution: Foundation of Our Freedom* by Warren E. Burger

cult but not impossible. As a result, the Constitution as originally written has been amended only 26 times in 200 years. The parts of the Constitution that are no longer in effect are marked in blue. Some of these have become inactive due to the passage of time. Others have been removed by amendments. As you read these changes, consider why they happened.

The first part of the Constitution consists of seven Articles. The Articles describe the three branches of government, discuss states' rights, and explain the amendment procedure, the concept of "national supremacy," and the ratification process. The second part of the Constitution consists of the 26 amendments.

CONTENTS

THE CONSTITUTION OF THE UNITED STATES OF AMERICA

The Granger Collection, New York

Preamble

We the People of the United States, in Order to form a more perfect Union, establish Justice, insure domestic Tranquility, provide for the common defense, promote the general Welfare, and secure the Blessings of Liberty to ourselves and our Posterity, do ordain and establish this Constitution for the United States of America.

Article I

Section 1. All legislative Powers herein granted shall be vested in a Congress of the United States, which shall consist of a Senate and House of Representatives.

Section 2. The House of Representatives shall be composed of Members chosen every second Year by the People of the several States, and the Electors in each State shall have the Qualifications requisite for Electors of the most numerous Branch of the State Legislature.

No Person shall be a Representative who shall not have attained to the Age of twenty-five Years, and been seven Years a Citizen of the United States, and who shall not, when elected, be an inhabitant of that State in which he shall be chosen.

Representatives and direct Taxes shall be apportioned among the several States which may be included within this Union, according to their respective Numbers, which shall be determined by adding to the whole Number of free Persons, including those bound to Service for a Term of Years, and excluding Indians not taxed, three fifths of all other Persons. The actual Enumeration shall be made within three Years after the first Meeting of the Congress of the United States, and within every subsequent Term of ten Years, in such Manner as they shall by Law direct. The Number of Representatives shall not exceed one for every thirty Thousand, but each State shall have at Least one Representative; and until such enumeration shall be made, the State of New Hampshire shall be entitled to choose three; Massachusetts eight; Rhode Island and Providence Plantations one; Connecticut five; New York six; New Jersey four; Pennsylvania eight; Delaware one; Maryland six; Virginia ten; North Carolina five; South Carolina five; and Georgia three.

When vacancies happen in the Representation from any State, the Executive Authority thereof shall issue Writs of Election to fill such Vacancies.

Preamble
The short and dignified Preamble explains the goals of the new government under the Constitution.

Legislative Branch
Article I explains how the legislative branch, called Congress, is organized. The chief purpose of the legislative branch is to make the laws. Congress is made up of the Senate and the House of Representatives. The decision to have two bodies of government solved a difficult problem during the Constitutional Convention. The large states wanted the membership of Congress to be based entirely on population. The small states wanted every state to have an equal vote. The solution to the problem of how the states were to be represented in Congress was known as the Great Compromise.

The number of members of the House is based on the population of the individual states. Each state has at least one representative. The current size of the House is 435 members, set by Congress in 1929. If each member of the House represented only 30,000 American people, as the Constitution states, the House would have more than 6,000 members.

The House of Representatives shall choose their Speaker and other Officers; and shall have the sole Power of Impeachment.

Section 3. The Senate of the United States shall be composed of two Senators from each State, chosen by the Legislature thereof, for six Years; and each Senator shall have one Vote.

Immediately after they shall be assembled in Consequence of the first Election, they shall be divided as equally as may be into three Classes. The Seats of the Senators of the first Class shall be vacated at the Expiration of the second Year, of the second Class at the Expiration of the fourth Year, and of the third Class at the Expiration of the sixth Year, so that one third may be chosen every second Year; and if Vacancies happen by Resignation, or otherwise, during the Recess of the Legislature of any State, the Executive thereof may make temporary Appointments until the next Meeting of the Legislature, which shall then fill such Vacancies.

No Person shall be a Senator who shall not have attained to the Age of thirty Years, and been nine Years a Citizen of the United States, and who shall not, when elected, be an Inhabitant of that State for which he shall be chosen.

The Vice President of the United States shall be President of the Senate, but shall have no Vote, unless they be equally divided.

The Senate shall choose their other Officers, and also a President pro tempore, in the Absence of the Vice President, or when he shall exercise the Office of President of the United States.

The Senate shall have the sole Power to try all Impeachments. When sitting for that Purpose, they shall be on Oath or Affirmation. When the President of the United States is tried, the Chief Justice shall preside: And no Person shall be convicted without the Concurrence of two thirds of the Members present.

Judgment in Cases of Impeachment shall not extend further than to removal from Office, and disqualification to hold and enjoy any Office of honor, Trust or Profit under the United States: but the Party convicted shall nevertheless be liable and subject to Indictment, Trial, Judgment and Punishment, according to Law.

Section 4. The Times, Places and Manner of holding Elections for Senators and Representatives, shall be prescribed in each State by the Legislature thereof; but the Congress may at any time by Law make or alter such Regulations, except as to the Places of choosing Senators.

The Congress shall assemble at least once in every Year, and such Meeting shall be on the first Monday in December, unless they shall by Law appoint a different Day.

Section 5. Each House shall be the Judge of the Elections, Returns and Qualifications of its own Members, and a Majority of each shall constitute a Quorum to do Business; but a smaller Number may adjourn from day to day, and may be authorized to compel the Attendance of absent Members, in such Manner, and under such Penalties as each House may provide.

Every state has two senators. Senators serve a six-year term, but only one third of the senators reach the end of their terms every two years. In any election, at least two thirds of the senators stay in office. This system ensures that there are experienced senators in office at all times. The framers wanted to make sure that changes in our government would only be made after careful study.

The only duty that the Constitution assigns to the vice president is to preside over meetings of the Senate. Modern presidents have given their vice presidents more and varied responsiblity.

The House charges a government official of wrongdoing, and the Senate acts as a court to decide if the official is guilty.

Congress has decided that elections will be held on the Tuesday following the first Monday in November of even-numbered years. The Twentieth Amendment states that Congress shall meet in regular session on January 3 of each year. The president may call a special session of Congress whenever it is necessary.

Each House may determine the Rules of its Proceedings, punish its Members for disorderly Behavior, and, with the Concurrence of two thirds, expel a Member.

Each House shall keep a Journal of its Proceedings, and from time to time publish the same, excepting such Parts as may in their Judgment require Secrecy; and the Yeas and Nays of the Members of either House on any question shall, at the Desire of one fifth of those Present, be entered on the Journal.

Neither House, during the Session of Congress, shall, without the Consent of the other, adjourn for more than three days, nor to any other Place than that in which the two Houses shall be sitting.

Section 6. The Senators and Representatives shall receive a Compensation for their Services, to be ascertained by Law, and paid out of the Treasury of the United States. They shall in all Cases, except Treason, Felony and Breach of the Peace, be privileged from Arrest during their Attendance at the Session of their respective Houses, and in going to and returning from the same; and for any Speech or Debate in either House, they shall not be questioned in any other Place.

No Senator or Representative shall, during the Time for which he was elected, be appointed to any civil Office under the Authority of the United States, which shall have been created, or the Emoluments whereof shall have been increased during such time; and no Person holding any Office under the United States, shall be a Member of either House during his Continuance in Office.

Section 7. All Bills for raising Revenue shall originate in the House of Representatives; but the Senate may propose or concur with Amendments as on other Bills.

Every Bill which shall have passed the House of Representatives and the Senate, shall, before it become a Law, be presented to the President of the United States; If he approve he shall sign it, but if not he shall return it, with his Objections to that House in which it shall have originated, who shall enter the Objections at large on their Journal, and proceed to reconsider it. If after such Reconsideration two thirds of that House shall agree to pass the Bill, it shall be sent, together with the Objections, to the other House, by which it shall likewise be reconsidered, and if approved by two thirds of that House, it shall become a Law. But in all such Cases the Votes of both Houses shall be determined by Yeas and Nays, and the Names of the Persons voting for and against the Bill shall be entered on the Journal of each House respectively. If any Bill shall not be returned by the President within ten Days (Sundays excepted) after it shall have been presented to him, the Same shall be a Law, in like Manner as if he had signed it, unless the Congress by their Adjournment prevent its Return, in which Case it shall not be a Law.

Every Order, Resolution, or Vote to which the Concurrence of the Senate and House of Representatives may be necessary (except on a question of Adjournment) shall be presented to the President of the United States; and before the Same shall take Effect, shall be approved

Congress makes most of its own rules of conduct. The Senate and the House each have a code of ethics that members must follow. It is the task of each house of Congress to discipline its own members. Each house keeps a journal, and a publication called the *Congressional Quarterly* records what happens in congressional sessions. The general public can learn how their representatives voted on bills.

The framers of the Constitution wanted to protect members of Congress from being arrested on false charges by political enemies who did not want them to attend important meetings. Neither did the framers want members of Congress to be taken to court for something they said in a speech or in a debate.

The power of taxing is the responsibility of the House of Representatives. Because members of the house are elected every two years, the framers felt that representatives would listen to the public and seek its approval.

The veto power of the president and the ability of Congress to override a presidential veto are two of the important checks and balances in the Constitution.

by him, or being disapproved by him, shall be repassed by two thirds of the Senate and House of Representatives, according to the Rules and Limitations prescribed in the Case of a Bill.

The framers of the Constitution wanted a national government that was strong enough to be effective. This section lists the powers given to Congress.

Section 8. The Congress shall have Power To lay and collect Taxes, Duties, Imposts and Excises, to pay the Debts and provide for the common Defense and general Welfare of the United States; but all Duties, Imposts and Excises shall be uniform throughout the United States;

To borrow Money on the credit of the United States;

To regulate Commerce with foreign Nations, and among the several States, and with the Indian Tribes;

To establish an uniform Rule of Naturalization, and uniform Laws on the subject of Bankruptcies throughout the United States;

To coin Money, regulate the Value thereof, and of foreign Coin, and fix the Standard of Weights and Measures;

To provide for the Punishment of counterfeiting the Securities and current Coin of the United States;

To establish Post Offices and post Roads;

To promote the Progress of Science and useful Arts, by securing for limited Times to Authors and Inventors the exclusive Right to their respective Writings and Discoveries;

To constitute Tribunals inferior to the supreme Court;

To define and punish Piracies and Felonies committed on the high Seas, and Offences against the Law of Nations;

To declare War, grant Letters of Marque and Reprisal, and make Rules concerning Captures on Land and Water;

To raise and support Armies, but no Appropriation of Money to that Use shall be for a longer Term than two Years;

To provide and maintain a Navy;

To make Rules for the Government and Regulation of the land and naval Forces;

To provide for calling forth the Militia to execute the Laws of the Union, suppress Insurrections and repel Invasions;

The last sentence in Section 8 contains the famous "elastic clause," which can be stretched (like elastic) to fit many different circumstances. The clause was first disputed when Alexander Hamilton proposed a national bank. Thomas Jefferson said that the Constitution did not give Congress the power to establish a bank. Hamilton argued that the bank was "necessary and proper" in order to carry out other powers of Congress, such as borrowing money and regulating currency. This argument was tested in the court system in 1819 in the case of *McCulloch v. Maryland,* when Chief Justice Marshall ruled in favor of the federal government. Powers given to the government by the "elastic clause" are called implied powers.

To provide for organizing, arming, and disciplining, the Militia, and for governing such Part of them as may be employed in the Service of the United States, reserving to the States respectively, the Appointment of the Officers, and the Authority of training the Militia according to the discipline prescribed by Congress.

To exercise exclusive Legislation in all Cases whatsoever, over such District (not exceeding ten Miles square) as may, by Cession of particular States, and the Acceptance of Congress, become the Seat of the Government of the United States, and to exercise like Authority over all Places purchased by the Consent of the Legislature of the State in which the Same shall be, for the Erection of Forts, Magazines, Arsenals, dock-Yards, and other needful Buildings;—And

To make all Laws which shall be necessary and proper for carrying into Execution the foregoing Powers, and all other Powers vested by this Constitution in the Government of the United States, or in any Department or Officer thereof.

Section 9. The Migration or Importation of such Persons as any of the States now existing shall think proper to admit, shall not be prohibited by the Congress prior to the Year one thousand eight hundred and eight, but a Tax or duty may be imposed on such Importation, not exceeding ten dollars for each Person.

The Privilege of the Writ of Habeas Corpus shall not be suspended, unless when in Cases of Rebellion or Invasion the public Safety may require it.

No Bill of Attainder or ex post facto Law shall be passed.

No Capitation, or other direct, Tax shall be laid, unless in Proportion to the Census or Enumeration herein before directed to be taken.

No Tax or Duty shall be laid on Articles exported from any State.

No Preference shall be given by any Regulation of Commerce or Revenue to the Ports of one State over those of another: nor shall Vessels bound to, or from, one State, be obliged to enter, clear, or pay Duties in another.

No Money shall be drawn from the Treasury, but in Consequence of Appropriations made by Law; and a regular Statement and Account of the Receipts and Expenditures of all public Money shall be published from time to time.

No Title of Nobility shall be granted by the United States: And no Person holding any Office of Profit or Trust under them, shall, without the Consent of the Congress, accept of any present, Emolument, Office, or Title, of any kind whatever, from any King, Prince, or foreign State.

Section 10. No State shall enter into any Treaty, Alliance, or Confederation; grant Letters of Marque and Reprisal; coin Money; emit Bills of Credit; make any Thing but gold and silver Coin a Tender in Payment of Debts; pass any Bill of Attainder, ex post facto Law, or law impairing the Obligation of Contracts, or grant any Title of Nobility.

No State shall, without the Consent of the Congress, lay any Imposts or Duties on Imports or Exports, except what may be absolutely necessary for executing its inspection Laws: and the net Produce of all Duties and Imposts, laid by any State on Imports or Exports, shall be for the Use of the Treasury of the United States; and all such Laws shall be subject to the Revision and Control of the Congress.

No State shall, without the Consent of Congress, lay any Duty of Tonnage, keep Troops, or Ships of War in time of Peace, enter into any Agreement or Compact with another State, or with a foreign Power, or engage in War, unless actually invaded, or in such imminent Danger as will not admit of delay.

If Congress has implied powers, then there also must be limits to its powers. This section lists powers that are denied to the federal government. Several of the clauses protect the people of the United States from unjust treatment. The *Writ of Habeas Corpus* means that people have the right to appear before a judge to determine if they are being held legally. This section prohibits a *bill of attainder,* a legislative act by which a person is declared guilty and punished before a trial has been held. Also prohibited is an *ex post facto law,* which is a law that retroactively punishes an act that was legal at the time the act was committed.

Section 10 lists the powers that are denied to the states. In our system of federalism, the state and federal governments have separate powers, share some powers, and are denied other powers. The states may not exercise any of powers that belong to Congress.

Article II

Section 1. The executive Power shall be vested in a President of the United States of America. He shall hold his Office during the Term of

Executive Branch
The president is the chief of the executive branch. It is the job of the president to enforce the laws. The framers wanted the president and vice president's term of office and manner of selection to be different from those of members of Congress. They decided on four-year terms, but they had a difficult time agreeing on how to select the president and vice president. The framers finally set up an electoral system, which varies greatly from our electoral process today. The Twelfth Amendment changed the process by requiring that separate ballots be cast for president and vice president. The rise of political parties has since changed the process even more.

In 1845 Congress set the first Tuesday after the first Monday in November of every fourth year as the general election date for selecting presidential electors.

The youngest elected president was John F. Kennedy; he was 43 years old when he was inaugurated. (Theodore Roosevelt was 42 when he assumed office after the assassination of McKinley.) The oldest elected president was Ronald Reagan; he was 69 years old when he was inaugurated.

four Years, and, together with the Vice President, chosen for the same Term, be elected, as follows.

Each State shall appoint, in such Manner as the Legislature thereof may direct, a Number of Electors, equal to the whole Number of Senators and Representatives to which the State may be entitled in the Congress: but no Senator or Representative, or Person holding an Office of Trust or Profit under the United States, shall be appointed an Elector.

The Electors shall meet in their respective States, and vote by Ballot for two Persons, of whom one at least shall not be an Inhabitant of the same State with themselves. And they shall make a List of all the Persons voted for, and of the Number of Votes for each; which List they shall sign and certify, and transmit sealed to the Seat of the Government of the United States, directed to the President of the Senate. The President of the Senate shall, in the Presence of the Senate and House of Representatives, open all the Certificates, and the Votes shall then be counted. The Person having the greatest Number of Votes shall be the President, if such Number be a Majority of the whole Number of Electors appointed; and if there be more than one who have such majority, and have an equal Number of Votes, then the House of Representatives shall immediately choose by Ballot one of them for President; and if no Person have a Majority, then from the five highest on the List the said House shall in like Manner choose the President. But in choosing the President, the Votes shall be taken by States, the Representation from each State having one Vote; A quorum for this Purpose shall consist of a Member or Members from two thirds of the States, and a Majority of all the States shall be necessary to a Choice. In every Case, after the Choice of the President, the Person having the greatest Number of Votes of the Electors shall be the Vice President. But if there should remain two or more who have equal Votes, the Senate shall choose from them by Ballot the Vice President.

The Congress may determine the Time of choosing the Electors, and the Day on which they shall give their Votes; which Day shall be the same throughout the United States.

No Person except a natural born Citizen, or a Citizen of the United States, at the time of the Adoption of this Constitution, shall be eligible to the Office of President; neither shall any Person be eligible to that Office who shall not have attained to the Age of thirty-five Years, and been fourteen Years a Resident within the United States.

In Case of the Removal of the President from Office, or of his Death, Resignation, or Inability to discharge the Powers and Duties of the said Office, the Same shall devolve on the Vice President, and the Congress may by Law provide for the Case of Removal, Death, Resignation or Inability, both of the President and Vice President, declaring what Officer shall then act as President, and such Officer shall act accordingly, until the Disability be removed, or a President shall be elected.

The President shall, at stated Times, receive for his Services, a Compensation, which shall neither be increased nor diminished during the

Period for which he shall have been elected, and he shall not receive within that Period any other Emolument from the United States, or any of them.

Before he enter on the Execution of his Office, he shall take the following Oath or Affirmation:—"I do solemnly swear (or affirm) that I will faithfully execute the Office of President of the United States, and will to the best of my Ability, preserve, protect and defend the Constitution of the United States."

Section 2. The President shall be Commander in Chief of the Army and Navy of the United States, and of the Militia of the several States, when called into the actual Service of the United States; he may require the Opinion, in writing, of the principal Officer in each of the executive Departments, upon any Subject relating to the Duties of their respective Offices, and he shall have Power to grant Reprieves and Pardons for Offenses against the United States, except in Cases of Impeachment.

He shall have Power, by and with the Advice and Consent of the Senate, to make Treaties, provided two thirds of the Senators present concur; and he shall nominate, and by and with the Advice and Consent of the Senate, shall appoint Ambassadors, other public Ministers and Consuls, Judges of the supreme Court, and all other Officers of the United States, whose Appointments are not herein otherwise provided for, and which shall be established by Law: but the Congress may by Law vest the Appointment of such inferior Officers, as they think proper, in the President alone, in the Courts of Law, or in the Heads of Departments.

The President shall have Power to fill up all Vacancies that may happen during the Recess of the Senate, by granting Commissions which shall expire at the End of their next Session.

Section 3. He shall from time to time give to the Congress Information of the State of the Union, and recommend to their Consideration such Measures as he shall judge necessary and expedient; he may, on extraordinary Occasions, convene both Houses, or either of them, and in Case of Disagreement between them, with Respect to the Time of Adjournment, he may adjourn them to such Time as he shall think proper; he shall receive Ambassadors and other public Ministers; he shall take Care that the Laws be faithfully executed, and shall Commission all the Officers of the United States.

Section 4. The President, Vice President and all civil Officers of the United States, shall be removed from Office on Impeachment for, and Conviction of, Treason, Bribery, or other high Crimes and Misdemeanors.

Article III

Section 1. The judicial Power of the United States, shall be vested in one supreme Court, and in such inferior Courts as the Congress may from time to time ordain and establish. The Judges, both of the supreme and inferior Courts, shall hold their Offices during good Behavior, and

Emolument means "salary, or payment." In 1969 Congress set the president's salary at $200,000 per year. The president also receives an expense account of $50,000 per year. The president must pay taxes on both.

The oath of office is administered to the president by the chief justice of the United States. Washington added "So help me, God." All succeeding presidents have followed this practice.

The framers wanted to make sure that an elected representative of the people controlled the nation's military. Today, the president is in charge of the army, navy, air force, marines, and coast guard. Only Congress can decide, however, if the United States will declare war. This clause also contains the basis for the formation of the president's cabinet. Every president, starting with George Washington, has appointed a cabinet.

Most of the president's appointments to office must be approved by the Senate.

Every year the president presents to Congress a State of the Union message. In this message, the president explains the legislative plans for the coming year. This clause states that one of the president's duties is to enforce the laws.

Judicial Branch
The Articles of Confederation did not make any provisions for a federal court system. One of the first things that the framers of the Constitution agreed upon was to set up

shall, at stated Times, receive for their Services, a Compensation, which shall not be diminished during their Continuance in Office.

Section 2. The judicial Power shall extend to all Cases, in Law and Equity, arising under this Constitution, the Laws of the United States, and Treaties made, or which shall be made, under their Authority;—to all Cases affecting Ambassadors, other public Ministers and Consuls;—to all Cases of admiralty and maritime Jurisdiction;—to Controversies to which the United States shall be a Party;—to Controversies between two or more States;—between a State and Citizens of another state;—between Citizens of different States;—between Citizens of the same State claiming Lands under Grants of different States, and between a State, or the Citizens thereof, and foreign States, Citizens or Subjects.

In all Cases affecting Ambassadors, other public Ministers and Consuls, and those in which a State shall be Party, the supreme Court shall have original Jurisdiction. In all the other Cases before mentioned, the supreme Court shall have appellate Jurisdiction, both as to Law and fact, with such Exceptions, and under such Regulations as the Congress shall make.

The Trial of all Crimes, except in Cases of Impeachment, shall be by Jury; and such Trial shall be held in the State where the said Crimes shall have been committed; but when not committed within any State, the Trial shall be at such Place or Places as the Congress may by Law have directed.

Section 3. Treason against the United States, shall consist only in levying War against them, or in adhering to their Enemies, giving them Aid and Comfort. No Person shall be convicted of Treason unless on the Testimony of two Witnesses to the same overt Act, or on Confession in open Court.

The Congress shall have Power to declare the Punishment of Treason, but no Attainder of Treason shall work Corruption of Blood, or Forfeiture except during the Life of the Person attainted.

Article IV

Section 1. Full Faith and Credit shall be given in each State to the public Acts, Records, and judicial Proceedings of every other State. And the Congress may by general Laws prescribe the Manner in which such Acts, Records and Proceedings shall be proved, and the Effect thereof.

Section 2. The Citizens of each State shall be entitled to all Privileges and Immunities of Citizens in the several States.

A Person charged in any State with Treason, Felony, or other Crime, who shall flee from Justice, and be found in another State, shall on Demand of the executive Authority of the State from which he fled, be delivered up, to be removed to the State having Jurisdiction of the Crime.

No Person held to Service of Labor in one State, under the Laws thereof, escaping into another, shall, in Consequence of any Law or Regulation therein, be discharged from such Service or Labor, but shall be delivered up on Claim of the Party to whom such Service or Labor may be due.

Section 3. New States may be admitted by the Congress into this Union; but no new State shall be formed or erected within the Jurisdiction of any other State; nor any State be formed by the Junction of two or more States, or Parts of States, without the Consent of the Legislatures of the States concerned as well as of the Congress.

The Congress shall have Power to dispose of and make all needful Rules and Regulations respecting the Territory or other Property belonging to the United States; and nothing in this Constitution shall be so construed as to Prejudice any Claims of the United States, or of any particular State.

Section 4. The United States shall guarantee to every State in this Union a Republican Form of Government, and shall protect each of them against Invasion; and on Application of the Legislature, or of the Executive (when the Legislature cannot be convened) against domestic Violence.

This section permits Congress to admit new states to the Union. When a group of people living in an area that is not part of an existing state wishes to form a new state, it asks Congress for permission to do so. The people then write a state constitution and offer it to Congress for approval. The state constitution must set up a representative form of government and must not in any way contradict the federal Constitution. If a majority of Congress approves of the state constitution, the state is admitted as a member of the United States of America.

Article V

The Congress, whenever two thirds of both Houses shall deem it necessary, shall propose Amendments to this Constitution, or, on the Application of the Legislatures of two thirds of the several States, shall call a Convention for proposing Amendments, which, in either Case, shall be valid to all Intents and Purposes, as Part of this Constitution, when ratified by the Legislatures of three fourths of the several States, or by Conventions in three fourths thereof, as the one or the other Mode of Ratification may be proposed by the Congress; Provided that no Amendment which may be made prior to the Year One thousand eight hundred and eight shall in any Manner affect the first and fourth Clauses in the Ninth Section of the first Article; and that no State, without its Consent, shall be deprived of its equal Suffrage in the Senate.

Amendments
America's founders may not have realized just how enduring the Constitution would be, but they did make provisions for changing or adding to the Constitution. They did not want to make it easy to change the Constitution. There are two different ways in which changes can be proposed to the states and two different ways in which states can approve the changes and make them part of the Constitution.

Article VI

All Debts contracted and Engagements entered into, before the Adoption of this Constitution, shall be as valid against the United States under this Constitution, as under the Confederation.

This Constitution, and the Laws of the United States which shall be made in Pursuance thereof; and all Treaties made, or which shall be made, under the Authority of the United States, shall be the supreme Law of the Land; and the Judges in every State shall be bound thereby, any Thing in the Constitution or Laws of any State to the Contrary notwithstanding.

The Senators and Representatives before mentioned, and the Members of the several State Legislatures, and all executive and judicial Officers, both of the United States and of the several States, shall be bound by Oath or Affirmation, to support this Constitution; but no

National Supremacy
One of the biggest problems facing the delegates to the Constitutional Convention was the question of what would happen if a state law and a national law conflicted. Which law would be followed? Who decided? The second clause of Article VI answers those questions. When a national and state law disagree, the national law overrides the state law. The Constitution is the supreme law of the land. This clause is often called the "supremacy clause."

religious Test shall ever be required as a Qualification to any Office or public Trust under the United States.

Article VII

The Ratification of the Conventions of nine States, shall be sufficient for the Establishment of this Constitution between the States so ratifying the Same.

DONE in Convention by the Unanimous Consent of the States present the Seventeenth Day of September in the Year of our Lord one thousand seven hundred and Eighty seven and of the Independence of the United States of America the Twelfth. IN WITNESS whereof We have hereunto subscribed our Names.

George Washington—
President and deputy from Virginia

Ratification

The Articles of Confederation called for all 13 states to approve any revision to the Articles. The Constitution required that the vote of nine out of the 13 states would be needed to ratify the Constitution. The first state to ratify was Delaware, on December 7, 1787. The last state to ratify the Constitution was Rhode Island, which finally did so on May 29, 1790, almost two and a half years later.

New Hampshire
John Langdon
Nicholas Gilman

Massachusetts
Nathaniel Gorham
Rufus King

Connecticut
William Samuel Johnson
Roger Sherman

New York
Alexander Hamilton

New Jersey
William Livingston
David Brearley
William Paterson
Jonathan Dayton

Pennsylvania
Benjamin Franklin
Thomas Mifflin
Robert Morris
George Clymer
Thomas FitzSimons
Jared Ingersoll
James Wilson
Gouverneur Morris

Delaware
George Read
Gunning Bedford, Jr.
John Dickinson
Richard Bassett
Jacob Broom

Maryland
James McHenry
Daniel of St. Thomas Jenifer
Daniel Carroll

Virginia
John Blair
James Madison, Jr.

North Carolina
William Blount
Richard Dobbs Spaight
Hugh Williamson

South Carolina
John Rutledge
Charles Cotesworth Pinckney
Charles Pinckney
Pierce Buttler

Georgia
William Few
Abraham Baldwin

Attest: *William Jackson,* Secretary

THE AMENDMENTS

ARTICLES in addition to, and Amendment of the Constitution of the United States of America, proposed by Congress, and ratified by the Legislatures of the several States, pursuant to the fifth Article of the original Constitution.

First Amendment

[The First through Tenth Amendments, now known as the Bill of Rights, were proposed on September 25, 1789, and declared in force on December 15, 1791.]

Congress shall make no law respecting an establishment of religion, or prohibiting the free exercise thereof; or abridging the freedom of speech, or of the press; or the right of the people peaceably to assemble, and to petition the Government for a redress of grievances.

Second Amendment

A well regulated Militia, being necessary to the security of a free State, the right of the people to keep and bear Arms, shall not be infringed.

Third Amendment

No Soldier shall, in time of peace, be quartered in any house, without the consent of the Owner, nor in time of war, but in a manner to be prescribed by law.

Fourth Amendment

The right of the people to be secure in their persons, houses, papers, and effects, against unreasonable searches and seizures, shall not be violated, and no Warrants shall issue, but upon probable cause, supported by Oath or affirmation, and particularly describing the place to be searched, and the persons or things to be seized.

Fifth Amendment

No person shall be held to answer for a capital, or otherwise infamous crime, unless on a presentment or indictment of a Grand Jury, except in cases arising in the land or naval forces, or in the Militia, when in actual service in time of War or public danger; nor shall any person be subject for the same offence to be twice put in jeopardy of life or limb; nor shall be compelled in any criminal case to be a witness against himself, nor be deprived of life, liberty, or property, without due process of law; nor shall private property be taken for public use, without just compensation.

Bill of Rights
One of the conditions set by several states for ratifying the Constitution was the inclusion of a Bill of Rights. Many people feared that a stronger central government might take away basic rights of the people that had been guaranteed in state constitutions. If the three words that begin the preamble—*We the people*—were truly meant, then the rights of the people needed to be protected.

The first ten amendments to the Constitution are called the Bill of Rights.

The First Amendment protects freedom of speech and thought, and forbids Congress to make any law "respecting an establishment of religion" or restraining the freedom to practice religion as one chooses.

A police officer or sheriff may enter a person's home with a search warrant, which allows the law officer to look for evidence that could convict someone of committing a crime.

The Fifth, Sixth, and Seventh Amendments describe the procedures that courts must follow when trying people accused of crimes.

The Fifth Amendment guarantees that no one can be put on trial for a serious crime unless a grand jury agrees that the evidence justifies doing so. It also says that a person cannot be tried twice for the same crime.

The Sixth Amendment makes several promises, which include a prompt trial and a trial by a jury chosen from the state and district in which the crime was committed. The Sixth Amendment also states that an accused person must be told why he or she is being tried and promises that an accused person has the right to be defended by a lawyer.

The Seventh Amendment guarantees a trial by jury in cases that involve more than $20, but in modern times, usually much more money is at stake before a case is heard in federal court.

The Ninth and Tenth Amendments were added because not every right of the people or of the states could be listed in the Constitution.

Sixth Amendment

In all criminal prosecutions, the accused shall enjoy the right to a speedy and public trial, by an impartial jury of the State and district wherein the crime shall have been committed, which district shall have been previously ascertained by law, and to be informed of the nature and cause of the accusation; to be confronted with the witnesses against him; to have compulsory process for obtaining witnesses in his favor, and to have the Assistance of Counsel for his defense.

Seventh Amendment

In Suits at common law, where the value in controversy shall exceed twenty dollars, the right of trial by jury shall be preserved, and no fact tried by a jury shall be otherwise reexamined in any Court of the United States, than according to the rules of the common law.

Eighth Amendment

Excessive bail shall not be required, nor excessive fines imposed, nor cruel and unusual punishments inflicted.

Ninth Amendment

The enumeration in the Constitution, of certain rights, shall not be construed to deny or disparage others retained by the people.

Tenth Amendment

The powers not delegated to the United States by the Constitution, nor prohibited by it to the States, are reserved to the States respectively, or to the people.

Eleventh Amendment

[Proposed March 4, 1794; declared ratified January 8, 1798]

The Judicial power of the United States shall not be construed to extend to any suit in law or equity, commenced or prosecuted against one of the United States by Citizens of another State, or by Citizens or Subjects of any Foreign State.

Twelfth Amendment

[Proposed December 9, 1803; declared ratified September 25, 1804]

The Electors shall meet in their respective states and vote by ballot for President and Vice President, one of whom, at least, shall not be an inhabitant of the same state with themselves; they shall name in their ballots the person voted for as President, and in distinct ballots the person voted for as Vice President, and they shall make distinct lists of all persons voted for as President, and of all persons voted for as Vice President, and of the number of votes for each, which lists they shall sign and certify, and transmit sealed to the seat of the government of the United States, directed to the President of the Senate;—The President of the Senate shall, in the presence of the Senate and House of Representatives, open all the certificates and the votes shall then be counted;—The person having the greatest number of votes for President, shall be the President, if such number be a majority of the whole number of Electors appointed; and if no person have such majority, then from the persons having the highest numbers not exceeding three on the list of those voted for as President, the House of Representatives shall choose immediately, by ballot, the President. But in choosing the President, the votes shall be taken by states, the representation from each state having one vote; a quorum for this purpose shall consist of a member or members from two thirds of the states, and a majority of all the states shall be necessary to a choice. And if the House of Representatives shall not choose a President whenever the right of choice shall devolve upon them, before the fourth day of March next following, then the Vice President shall act as President, as in the case of the death or other constitutional disability of the President;—The person having the greatest number of votes as Vice President, shall be the Vice President, if such number be a majority of the whole number of Electors appointed, and if no person have a majority, then from the two highest numbers on the list, the Senate shall choose the Vice President; a quorum for the purpose shall consist of two thirds of the whole number of Senators, and a majority of the whole number shall be necessary to a choice. But no person constitutionally ineligible to the office of President shall be eligible to that of Vice President of the United States.

The Twelfth Amendment changed the election procedure for president and vice president. This amendment became necessary because of the growth of political parties. Before this amendment, electors voted without distinguishing between president and vice president. Whoever received the most votes became president, and whoever received the next highest number of votes became vice president. A confusing election in 1800, which resulted in Thomas Jefferson's becoming president, caused this amendment to be proposed.

Thirteenth Amendment

[Proposed January 31, 1865; declared ratified December 18, 1865]

Section 1. Neither slavery nor involuntary servitude, except as a punishment for crime whereof the party shall have been duly convicted, shall exist within the United States, or any place subject to their jurisdiction.

Section 2. Congress shall have power to enforce this article by appropriate legislation.

Although some slaves had been freed during the Civil War, slavery was not abolished until the Thirteenth Amendment took effect.

In 1833 Chief Justice John Marshall ruled that the Bill of Rights limited the national goverment but not the state governments. This ruling meant that states were able to keep blacks from becoming state citizens. If blacks were not citizens, they were not protected by the Bill of Rights. The Fourteenth Amendment defines citizenship and prevents states from interfering in the rights of citizens of the United States.

Fourteenth Amendment

[Proposed June 13, 1866; declared ratified July 28, 1868]

Section 1. All persons born or naturalized in the United States, and subject to the jurisdiction thereof, are citizens of the United States and of the State wherein they reside. No State shall make or enforce any law which shall abridge the privileges or immunities of citizens of the United

States; nor shall any State deprive any person of life, liberty, or property, without due process of law; nor deny to any person within its jurisdiction the equal protection of the laws.

Section 2. Representatives shall be apportioned among the several States according to their respective numbers, counting the whole number of persons in each State, ~~excluding Indians not taxed~~. But when the right to vote at any election for the choice of electors for President and Vice President of the United States, Representatives in Congress, the Executive and Judicial officers of a State, or the members of the Legislature thereof, is denied to any of the ~~male~~ inhabitants of such State, being ~~twenty-one years of age, and~~ citizens of the United States, or in any way abridged, except for participation in rebellion, or other crime, the basis of representation therein shall be reduced in the proportion which the number of such ~~male~~ citizens shall bear to the whole number of ~~male~~ citizens ~~twenty-one years of age~~ in such State.

Section 3. No person shall be a Senator or Representative in Congress, or elector of President and Vice President, or hold any office, civil or military, under the United States, or under any State, who, having previously taken an oath, as a member of Congress, or as an officer of the United States, or as a member of any State legislature, or as an executive or judicial officer of any State, to support the Constitution of the United States, shall have engaged in insurrection or rebellion against the same, or given aid or comfort to the enemies thereof. But Congress may by a vote of two thirds of each House, remove such disability.

Section 4. The validity of the public debt of the United States, authorized by law, including debts incurred for payment of pensions and bounties for services in suppressing insurrection or rebellion, shall not be questioned. But neither the United States nor any State shall assume or pay any debt or obligation incurred in aid of insurrection or rebellion against the United States, ~~or any claim for the loss of emancipation of any slave;~~ but all such debts, obligations and claims shall be held illegal and void.

Section 5. The Congress shall have power to enforce, by appropriate legislation, the provisions of this article.

Fifteenth Amendment
[Proposed February 26, 1869; declared ratified March 30, 1870]

The Fifteenth Amendment extended the right to vote to black males.

Section 1. The right of citizens of the United States to vote shall not be denied or abridged by the United States or by any State on account of race, color, or previous condition of servitude.

Section 2. The Congress shall have power to enforce this article by appropriate legislation.

Sixteenth Amendment
[Proposed July 12, 1909; declared ratified February 25, 1913]

The Sixteenth Amendment made legal the income tax described in Article I.

The Congress shall have power to lay and collect taxes on incomes, from whatever source derived, without apportionment among the several States, and without regard to any census or apportionment among the several States, and without regard to any census or enumeration.

Seventeenth Amendment
[Proposed May 13, 1912; declared ratified May 31, 1913]

The Senate of the United States shall be composed of two Senators from each State, elected by the people thereof, for six years; and each Senator shall have one vote. The electors in each State shall have the qualifications requisite for electors of the most numerous branch of the State legislatures.

When vacancies happen in the representation of any State in the Senate, the executive authority of such State shall issue writs of election to fill such vacancies: *Provided,* That the legislature of any State may empower the executive thereof to make temporary appointments until the people fill the vacancies by election as the legislature may direct.

This amendment shall not be so construed as to affect the election or term of any Senator chosen before it becomes valid as part of the Constitution.

The Seventeenth Amendment required that senators be elected directly by the people instead of by the state legislature.

Eighteenth Amendment
[Proposed December 18, 1917; declared ratified January 29, 1919; repealed by the Twenty-first Amendment December 5, 1933]

Section 1. After one year from the ratification of this article the manufacture, sale, or transportation of intoxicating liquors within, the importation thereof into, or the exportation thereof from the United States and all territory subject to the jurisdiction thereof for beverage purposes is hereby prohibited.

Section 2. The Congress and the several States shall have concurrent power to enforce this article by appropriate legislation.

Section 3. This article shall be inoperative unless it shall have been ratified as an amendment to the Constitution by the legislatures of the several States, as provided in the Constitution, within seven years from the date of the submission hereof to the States by the Congress.

Although many people felt that Prohibition was good for the health and welfare of the American people, the amendment was repealed 14 years later.

Nineteenth Amendment
[Proposed June 4, 1919; declared ratified August 26, 1920]

The right of citizens of the United States to vote shall not be denied or abridged by the United States or by any State on account of sex.

Congress shall have power to enforce this article by appropriate legislation.

As you have read, Abigail Adams was disappointed that the Declaration of Independence and the Constitution did not specifically include women. It took almost 150 years and much campaigning by women's suffrage groups for women to finally achieve voting privleges.

Twentieth Amendment
[Proposed March 2, 1932; declared ratified February 6, 1933]

Section 1. The terms of the President and Vice President shall end at

In the original Constitution, a newly elected president and Congress did not take office until March 4, which was four months after the November election. The officials who were leaving office were called "lame ducks" because they had little influence during those four months. The Twentieth Amendment changed the date that the new president and Congress take office. Members of Congress now take office on January 3, and the president takes office on January 20.

noon on the 20th day of January, and the terms of Senators and Representatives at noon on the 3rd day of January, of the years in which such terms would have ended if this article had not been ratified; and the terms of their successors shall then begin.

Section 2. The Congress shall assemble at least once in every year, and such meeting shall begin at noon on the 3rd day of January, unless they shall by law appoint a different day.

Section 3. If, at the time fixed for the beginning of the term of the President, the President elect shall have died, the Vice President elect shall become President. If a President shall not have been chosen before the time fixed for the beginning of his term, or if the President elect shall have failed to qualify, then the Vice President elect shall act as President until a President shall have qualified; and the Congress may by law provide for the case wherein neither a President elect nor a Vice President elect shall have qualified, declaring who shall then act as President, or the manner in which one who is to act shall be selected, and such persons shall act accordingly until a President or Vice President shall have qualified.

Section 4. The Congress may by law provide for the case of the death of any of the persons from whom the House of Representatives may choose a President whenever the right of choice shall have devolved upon them, and for the case of the death of any of the persons from whom the Senate may choose a Vice President whenever the right of choice shall have devolved upon them.

Section 5. Sections 1 and 2 shall take effect on the 15th day of October following the ratification of this article.

Section 6. This article shall be inoperative unless it shall have been ratified as an amendment to the Constitution by the legislatures of three fourths of the several States within seven years from the date of its submission.

Twenty-first Amendment
[Proposed February 20, 1933; declared ratified December 5, 1933]

The Twenty-first Amendment is the only amendment that has been ratified by state conventions rather than by state legislatures.

Section 1. The eighteenth article of amendment to the Constitution of the United States is hereby repealed.

Section 2. The transportation or importation into any State, Territory, or possession of the United States for delivery or use therein of intoxicating liquors, in violation of the laws thereof, is hereby prohibited.

Section 3. This article shall be inoperative unless it shall have been ratified as an amendment to the Constitution by conventions in the several States, as provided in the Constitution, within seven years from the date of the submission hereof to the States by the Congress.

Twenty-second Amendment
[Proposed March 24, 1947; declared ratified March 1, 1951]

Section 1. No person shall be elected to the office of the President more than twice, and no person who has held the office of President, or acted as President, for more than two years of a term to which some other person was elected President shall be elected to the office of the President more than once. ~~But this Article shall not apply to any person holding the office of President when this Article was proposed by the Congress, and shall not prevent any person who may be holding the office of President, or acting as President, during the term within which this Article becomes operative from holding the office of President or acting as President during the remainder of such term.~~

Section 2. ~~This article shall be inoperative unless it shall have been ratified as an amendment to the Constitution by the legislatures of three fourths of the several States within seven years from the date of its submission to the States by the Congress.~~

From the time of President Washington's administration, it was a custom for presidents to serve no more than two terms of office. Franklin D. Roosevelt, however, was elected to four terms. The Twenty-second Amendment made into law the old custom of a two-term limit for each president, if reelected.

Twenty-third Amendment

[Proposed June 16, 1960; declared ratified April 3, 1961]

Section 1. The District constituting the seat of Government of the United States shall appoint in such manner as the Congress may direct:

A number of electors of President and Vice President equal to the whole number of Senators and Representatives in Congress to which the District would be entitled if it were a State, but in no event more than the least populous state; they shall be in addition to those appointed by the States, but they shall be considered, for the purposes of the election of President and Vice President, to be electors appointed by a State; and they shall meet in the District and perform such duties as provided by the twelfth article of amendment.

Section 2. The Congress shall have power to enforce this article by appropriate legislation.

Until the Twenty-third Amendment, the people of Washington, D.C., could not vote in presidential elections.

Twenty-fourth Amendment

[Proposed August 27, 1962; declared ratified February 4, 1964]

Section 1. The right of citizens of the United States to vote in any primary or other election for President or Vice President, for electors for President or Vice President, or for Senator or Representative in Congress, shall not be denied or abridged by the United States or any State by reason of failure to pay any poll tax or other tax.

Section 2. The Congress shall have power to enforce this article by appropriate legislation.

Twenty-fifth Amendment

[Proposed July 6, 1965; declared ratified February 23, 1967]

Section 1. In case of removal of the President from office or of his death or resignation, the Vice President shall become President.

Section 2. Whenever there is a vacancy in the office of the Vice Pres-

The illness of President Eisenhower in the 1950s and the assassination of President Kennedy in 1963 were the events behind the Twenty-fifth Amendment. The Constitution did not provide a clear-cut method for a vice president to take over for a disabled president or for the death of a president. This amendment provides for filling the office of the vice president if a vacancy occurs, and it provides a way for the vice president to take over if the president is unable to perform the duties of that office.

ident, the President shall nominate a Vice President who shall take office upon confirmation by a majority vote of both Houses of Congress.

Section 3. Whenever the President transmits to the President pro tempore of the Senate and the Speaker of the House of Representatives his written declaration that he is unable to discharge the powers and duties of his office, and until he transmits to them a written declaration to the contrary, such powers and duties shall be discharged by the Vice President as Acting President.

Section 4. Whenever the Vice President and a majority of either the principal officers of the executive departments or of such other body as Congress may by law provide, transmit to the President pro tempore of the Senate and the Speaker of the House of Representatives their written declaration that the President is unable to discharge the powers and duties of his office, the Vice President shall immediately assume the powers and duties of the office as Acting President.

Thereafter, when the President transmits to the President pro tempore of the Senate and the Speaker of the House of Representatives his written declaration that no inability exists, he shall resume the powers and duties of his office unless the Vice President and a majority of either the principal officers of the executive department or of such other body as Congress may by law provide, transmit within four days to the President pro tempore of the Senate and the Speaker of the House of Representatives their written declaration that the President is unable to discharge the powers and duties of his office. Thereupon Congress shall decide the issue, assembling within forty-eight hours for that purpose if not in session. If the Congress, within twenty-one days after receipt of the latter written declaration, or, if Congress is not in session, within twenty-one days after Congress is required to assemble, determines by two-thirds vote of both Houses that the President is unable to discharge the powers and duties of his office, the Vice President shall continue to discharge the same as Acting President; otherwise, the President shall resume the powers and duties of his office.

Twenty-sixth Amendment
[Proposed March 23, 1971; declared ratified July 5, 1971]

The Voting Act of 1970 tried to set the voting age at 18 years old. But the Supreme Court ruled that the act set the voting age for national elections only, not state or local elections. This ruling would make necessary several different ballots at elections. The Twenty-sixth Amendment gave 18-year-old citizens the right to vote in all elections.

Section 1. The right of citizens of the United States, who are eighteen years of age or older, to vote shall not be denied or abridged by the United States or by any State on account of age.

Section 2. The Congress shall have power to enforce this article by appropriate legislation.

INTERPRETING THE CONSTITUTION

You Be the Judge

Listed below are 6 fictional situations. Decide if each situation is allowed by the Constitution. Then, on a separate piece of paper, tell if each situation is allowed or not allowed and write the part of the Constitution that supports your decision.

1. You are a 33-year-old lawyer running for a seat in the House of Representatives. You immigrated to the United States 15 years ago and became a United States citizen five years later.

2. Because the state of New York has more people than Alabama, Congress has decided to tax the people of New York at a higher rate than the people of Alabama.

3. Congress has passed a law making it illegal to purchase or smoke cigarettes. In addition, the law states that anyone who smoked cigarettes before the law was passed will be sentenced in court to pay a $500 fine.

4. You were born in the United States and have lived here all your life. Now, at age 40, you decide to run for president of the United States.

5. You are a Supreme Court justice. A senator who disliked your ruling on a case is writing a bill to cut the salaries of the Supreme Court justices in half.

6. The states of Oregon and Washington declare that they are now one state named Orewash. The legislatures of both states agreed to the formation of the new state, as did Congress.

Classifying Amendments

Carefully read the 26 amendments. Then, classify the amendments according to the headings in the chart below.

Protect Rights   Extend Rights   Solve a Problem

Thinking Critically

Ratification of the Constitution was a long fight for public opinion. Much of the battle took place in newspapers. About 70 newspapers were for the new Constitution and about 12 newspapers were against it. Imagine that you are a newspaper editor in 1787. What would you say to your readers? Write a short editorial expressing your opinion— either for or against the Constitution.

INTERPRETING HISTORY: The Constitution

Did you know that the Constitution has been a source of continuing controversy among historians? Few people do. The debate centers on the reasons the United States Constitution was written as it was.

Times in America were perilous in the years from 1781 to 1787. Economic problems and interstate squabbles threatened the future of the weak new nation. But the Articles of Confederation established no central governing authority. Political power was divided equally among the states. Such a system had great difficulty dealing with these problems. So why from this setting did the Constitution emerge?

Historians disagree about the answer. The major theories focus on the same two motives—economics and patriotism—that historians debate in their study of the American Revolution. The traditional view holds that the Constitution was written by patriots who wanted nothing more than to help the struggling nation survive. These patriots recognized the weaknesses of the Articles of Confederation and felt if they were not revised the security of the nation—if not the nation itself—was at stake. They met to revise the Articles. But noting its basic weakness, they wrote a new document— the Constitution—creating a stronger central government. Historian John Fiske, who wrote *The Critical Period in American History,* insisted that the nation would not have survived under the Articles of Confederation.

Noted historian Charles A. Beard disagreed with Fiske. In his *An Economic Interpretation of the Constitution of the United States* Beard claimed that the writers of the Constitution were wealthy men who had loaned the government large sums of money. If the government failed, they would lose their investment. In writing the Constitution, with its stronger central government, Beard said they were protecting their economic interests. He called the Constitution "an economic document drawn with superb skill by men whose property interests were at stake."

In more recent years other historians with other interpretations have tried to solve the mystery. But the controversy continues. As historians quickly learn, people's motives are difficult to gauge accurately and are often open to interpretation.

5. "A MORE PERFECT UNION"

Use these questions to guide your reading. Answer the questions after completing Section 5.
Understanding Issues, Events, & Ideas. **a**. Create a word web around the word *Constitution* using the following words: Virginia Plan, New Jersey Plan, president, Congress, Senate, House of Representatives, judiciary, Supreme Court, Great Compromise.   **b**. Write a brief analysis of the Constitution using the following words: Three-Fifths Compromise, elector, advice and consent, district court, appellate court, checks and balances, veto, override, impeachment, ratifying, convention, Federalist, Antifederalist, Federalist Papers.
1. Why did the delegates give so much power to the president?
2. What was the reasoning behind the electoral system?
3. How does the Constitution guard against misuse of power?
Thinking Critically. If you were Alexander Hamilton, how would you persuade Samuel Adams and John Hancock to ratify the Constitution?

The Great Compromise

Giving new power to the United States was relatively simple. Deciding who should control and use the power was more difficult. The problem was complicated. Should the authority of the United States government remain concentrated in Congress? Or should it be separated into executive, legislative, and judicial branches as in most state constitutions? Further, should each state have an equal weight in electing representatives to the United States as was true under the Articles of Confederation? Or should representation depend upon population? That would give the larger states more representatives and thus more influence than the smaller ones.

Early during the Convention, Governor Edmund Randolph of Virginia, a member of that state's delegation, presented the **Virginia Plan.** It provided for a government with three separate branches and for representation by population. William Paterson then offered the **New Jersey Plan,** which would have left all power in Congress and continued the one-state, one-vote system.

The delegates adopted the basics of the Virginia Plan with little debate. There was to be an executive branch headed by a **president** of the United States; a legislative branch, the **Congress,** with two chambers, a **Senate** and a **House of Representatives;** and a system of courts, the **national judiciary,** including the **Supreme Court.**

The delegates from the smaller states, however, dug in their heels on the question of representation by population. The debate went on for weeks. Both camps realized they must find some way to agree or the entire Constitution would be defeated. Finally they worked out the so-called **Great Compromise.** Members of the House of Representatives would be elected on the basis of population. (In the first House, Virginia, the largest state, elected 11 representatives, New Hampshire chose 3, Pennsylvania 8, and so on.) But each state was to have two seats in the Senate. Further, to protect the influence of the state governments, the Constitution provided that senators were to be elected by the state legislatures, not by the people.

Slavery in the Constitution

When the delegates spoke of "the People," they were not talking about slaves. The delegates decided to allow each state to determine who could vote and who could not. The only limit they imposed was a clause saying that the same rules must apply to the elections to Congress as to the "most numerous" branch of the state's own legislature. Because they did not qualify to vote in Congressional elections, almost no Africans in America could vote, not even those who were free.

The Art Museum of Princeton University

Mrs. B. S. Church painted this fine oil portrait of William Paterson.

FRANKLIN'S ADVICE

The delegates to the Convention completed the Constitution on September 15, 1787. On September 17 they held their final meeting to sign the document. They were painfully aware that it was not perfect. Benjamin Franklin expressed the general attitude when he said, "There are several parts of this Constitution which I do not at present approve, but I am not sure that I shall never approve them."

Franklin urged doubters to accept the view of the majority. They should not, he said, be like the French woman who, during an argument with her sister,

Bradley Smith/Laurie Platt Winfrey

Benjamin Franklin by Duplessis

said, "I don't know how it happens, Sister, but I meet with nobody but myself that's always in the right." Nearly all of the delegates took Franklin's advice.

As the last of the delegates were adding their signatures, Franklin looked up at the now-empty president's chair, where George Washington had sat throughout the sessions. On its back was painted a rising sun. Turning to some of the others, Franklin said, "I have often looked at that without being able to tell whether it was rising or setting. But now I know that it is a rising and not a setting sun."

Northern and southern delegates did clash over whether slaves should be counted in determining the number of representatives a state should have in Congress. The issue was decided by what is called the **Three-Fifths Compromise**—three fifths of the slaves were counted in the population of a state. Actually, the delegates were very squeamish about slavery. They did not even mention the word in the final document. The Three-Fifths Compromise provided for counting "the whole Number of free Persons" and "three fifths of all other Persons." In another so-called compromise Congress was denied the power to outlaw bringing slaves from abroad until 1808. The ban was worded this way: "The Importation of such Persons as any of the States . . . shall think proper to admit, shall not be prohibited" before 1808. Still another clause required the free states to return any slave who managed to escape into a free state. It referred to slaves as persons "held to Service or Labor."

The ban on importing slaves did not effectively end slavery. Why did the delegates avoid deciding the fate of the peculiar institution? Historical imagination helps us here. Some of the delegates surely had guilty consciences about allowing slavery to exist in a nation where "all men" were supposed to be equal and where the government was committed to providing "the people" with "Blessings of Liberty." But their feelings of guilt did not prevent them from protecting the interests of slave owners in the ways just mentioned. Political considerations also influenced them. They believed that if slaves were banned, the southern states would not stay in the Union.

Other delegates in 1787 thought that slavery was a dying institution in North America. They agreed to the compromises because they felt slavery would not be a problem by 1808. But the framers of the Constitution were profoundly mistaken! Preserved by the constitutional compromises, slavery expanded and became more important to the South, and affected the lives of hundreds of thousands of African Americans. For more than seventy years the nation struggled with the moral and legal issues of slavery. Not until a bloody civil war erupted was slavery finally brought to an end.

Women and the Constitution

Just as the framers of the Constitution allowed slavery to exist in a nation where "all men were created equal," they provided no further guarantees for women. The enlightened political views expressed in the Declaration of Independence and Constitution did give women in America hope for future changes. But the Constitutional guarantees were not specific. Women were not specifically given the right to vote, or to hold office, or other rights seemingly reserved for men. As with slavery, this situation would create problems for America as the nation matured.

The Presidency

The most drastic change put into effect by the Constitutional Convention was the creation of a powerful presidency. As we have seen, under the Articles of Confederation there was no chief executive. In discussing the new office, the delegates were torn in two directions. They wanted a national leader. But they did not want to make the chief executive too powerful. Neither did they want a figurehead.

Some delegates wanted to give the executive power to a group. Others preferred a president sharing authority with an elected council. Some suggested that the state legislatures choose the president.

The delegates settled for one president—and a president with a great deal of power. Besides being responsible for administering the laws passed by Congress, the president was to be commander in chief of the army and navy. He alone was in charge of foreign relations. He was to appoint judges and other important government officials. And the president was also given the power to veto laws passed by Congress.

Everyone assumed that the first president would be George Washington. This was one reason why the office was given so much power. Washington was so admired and trusted that the delegates made the presidency worthy of his talents. For example, who but Washington could serve as commander in chief of the army?

Of course, Washington would not be president forever. Looking

© Grant Le Duc/Monkmeyer

In the heart of Wall Street stands this statue in bronze of Geroge Washington by J. Q. A. Ward. It marks the site where the first president took the oath of office.

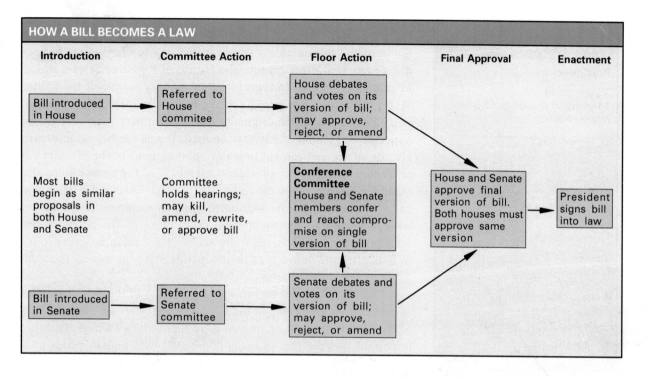

HOW A BILL BECOMES A LAW

Introduction	Committee Action	Floor Action	Final Approval	Enactment
Bill introduced in House	Referred to House commitee	House debates and votes on its version of bill; may approve, reject, or amend	House and Senate approve final version of bill. Both houses must approve same version	President signs bill into law
Most bills begin as similar proposals in both House and Senate	Committee holds hearings; may kill, amend, rewrite, or approve bill	**Conference Committee** House and Senate members confer and reach compromise on single version of bill		
Bill introduced in Senate	Referred to Senate committee	Senate debates and votes on its version of bill; may approve, reject, or amend		

ahead, the delegates worked out a complicated system for choosing his successors. Each state was to select in whatever manner its legislature wished as many **electors** as it had senators and representatives in Congress. The electors in each state would then meet to vote for president. Each elector would vote for two people, only one of whom could be a resident of that state. The votes would then be counted and the results forwarded under seal to the national capital. On an appointed day the ballots from the different states would be opened and counted in the presence of the Senate and the House of Representatives. The person with the largest number of votes would become president, the second largest, vice president. However, if the leading candidate did not receive a majority, the House of Representatives would choose a president from among the five persons with the largest number of votes. In this voting each state delegation in the House would have only one vote.

There were good reasons why the delegates created such a complicated system of election. The country was large. Communication was slow and limited. It seemed unlikely that any person less famous than a Washington could be well-known all over the country. Yet it was important that the president be a person of outstanding character as well as ability. If candidates were selected in each region by persons who knew them well, the high standard needed could probably be met. Then the people's representatives in Congress could discuss the merits of the best of these and make a final selection. The rule that the House of Representatives vote by states was another concession to the smaller states.

LEARNING FROM CHARTS. *A bill is sent to the president for approval or veto only after it passes both houses. Why must both houses approve the same version of a bill?*

"A More Perfect Union" 223

REQUIREMENTS FOR HOLDING FEDERAL OFFICE
President
35 years old
14 years in the United States
Native-born
Senator
30 years old
Must reside in state in which elected
9 years citizenship
Representative
25 years old
Must reside in state in which elected
7 years citizenship
Supreme Court Justice
No specific requirements

LEARNING FROM CHARTS. *The requirements to hold public office in the federal government vary depending on the office. Which office has the strictest requirements? Why might this be?*

The Congress

Some of the reasons for a two-branch Congress have already been discussed. The lower branch, the House of Representatives, was to be popularly elected to represent the ordinary people of the United States. It alone could introduce bills to raise money.

The Senate, which originally had 26 members, was seen as the upper house, a kind of advisory council. It was the Senate that must give its **advice and consent** to major appointments of the president or to treaties made by the president. Members of the Senate were also expected to represent the interests of what Alexander Hamilton called "the rich and the well-born," just as members of the House were expected to represent "the great mass of the people." But senators were not expected to be snobs. Their main task was to try to look after the interests of their separate states as well as the well-being of the United States.

The Congress, not surprisingly, is the first of the three branches of government described in the Constitution. After all, the members of the Constitutional Convention were themselves a Congress. More important was the fear of being dominated by a king or prime minister. The Americans who drew up the Constitution remembered vividly what had happened to the colonies under English rule.

The Judiciary

The Constitution also provided for a system of United States courts, separate from the courts of the individual states. It only mentioned specifically a **Supreme Court.** It left it to Congress to decide how many judges to have on the Supreme Court and how many lower courts to set up under the Supreme Court. (There are now nine Supreme Court Justices and two kinds of lower federal courts—the **district courts** and the **appellate courts,** or appeals courts.)

Under the Constitution all United States judges serve "during good Behavior." This means that they cannot be removed once appointed unless they commit a crime or are unable to perform their duties for some reason, such as insanity. The Constitution gives the federal courts the responsibility of hearing all cases involving the laws and treaties of the United States and also cases involving foreigners, two or more states, and the citizens of different states.

Checks and Balances

Although they were creating a more powerful government, the delegates at Philadelphia were very concerned about the possible misuse of power. They tried to prevent misuse by dividing power among many people and institutions and by a clever system of **checks and balances.** Here are a few examples of how the president's powers are checked. The other branches are subject to similar restraints.

The president can **veto,** or reject, bills passed by Congress. This is a check on the power of Congress, but Congress can **override** a veto. If both houses pass the bill again by two-thirds majorities, it becomes law.

The president is commander in chief of the army and navy. But Congress controls the raising of money to maintain the armed forces, and Congress alone has the power to declare war.

The president or representatives of the president can negotiate treaties with foreign countries. But such treaties become law only when approved by two thirds of the Senate.

The president has the power to appoint judges, ambassadors, and other important officials. But the Senate can vote to reject any of these appointments.

Finally, if the president commits a serious crime, he can be brought to trial by a process called **impeachment.** In such cases the House of Representatives brings the charges against the president, and the Senate acts as judge and jury. A two-thirds vote is necessary for conviction and removal from office.

LEARNING FROM CHARTS.
Two of the key aspects of the Constitution are its separation of powers and its checks and balances. Make a list of the checks each branch has on the others. Which check is the most powerful? Why?

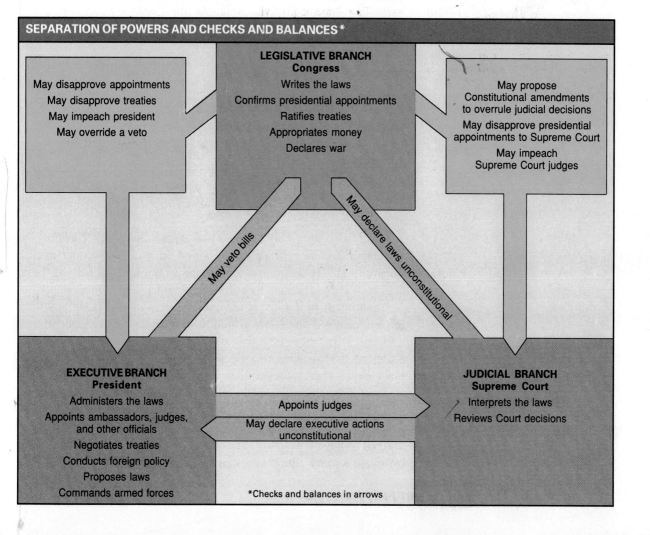

SEPARATION OF POWERS AND CHECKS AND BALANCES*

LEGISLATIVE BRANCH
Congress
Writes the laws
Confirms presidential appointments
Ratifies treaties
Appropriates money
Declares war

May disapprove appointments
May disapprove treaties
May impeach president
May override a veto

May propose
Constitutional amendments
to overrule judicial decisions
May disapprove presidential
appointments to Supreme Court
May impeach
Supreme Court judges

May veto bills

May declare laws unconstitutional

EXECUTIVE BRANCH
President
Administers the laws
Appoints ambassadors, judges,
and other officials
Negotiates treaties
Conducts foreign policy
Proposes laws
Commands armed forces

Appoints judges

May declare executive actions
unconstitutional

JUDICIAL BRANCH
Supreme Court
Interprets the laws
Reviews Court decisions

*Checks and balances in arrows

Ratifying the Constitution

The Constitution was to go into effect when nine states (two thirds) had approved it. Interest in the document was high. Everywhere citizens read and discussed the new form of government. They elected representatives to state **ratifying conventions** where the decision to approve or disapprove was to be made. Since it was complicated and involved many important changes, the Constitution did not win everyone's approval. Opinions were sharply divided.

Supporters of the Constitution called themselves **Federalists.** Those who opposed it are known as **Antifederalists.** The second name is confusing because a *federal* form of government is one that involves a combination of independent states. We speak of the United States today as the federal government. The so-called Antifederalists actually were federalists in this sense.

Both groups, in other words, wanted a federal form of government. They differed about how strong the federation known as the United States should be. Almost no one wanted to center all power in the federal government, and very few were satisfied with the old "league of friendship" the Constitution proposed to replace.

Since there was no nationwide vote on the Constitution nor public opinion polls to sample popular attitudes, it is impossible to know whether or not a majority of the people favored the new system. In some states there was little organized opposition. In others opinion was sharply divided. Those who disapproved of the Constitution did so mostly because they were afraid the new central government would be so powerful that it would soon destroy the independence of the states. The Constitution, one excited Antifederalist said, was "a beast, dreadful and terrible," which "devours, breaks into pieces, and stamps [the states] with his feet." Supporters of the Constitution did their best to persuade Antifederalists that the state governments would remain powerful and free to manage local affairs.

The first state to hold its ratifying convention was Delaware. On December 7, 1787, the delegates voted unanimously to accept the Constitution. By February four more states had ratified by large margins—Pennsylvania, New Jersey, Georgia, and Connecticut.

Sentiment in a number of other states was also running strong for ratification. Nine states would be enough to put the Constitution into effect, but how effective could the government of the United States be if Massachusetts, New York, and Virginia refused to join the Union? The Antifederalists in these important states were numerous and well organized.

The Massachusetts convention met in early January 1788 and debated the question for nearly a month. At first the Antifederalists seemed to have a majority. The memory of Shays' Rebellion was on everyone's mind. Representatives from the troubled districts were strongly against ratification. The men Paul Revere had gone to Lexington to warn in April 1775, Sam Adams and John Hancock, were delegates. They were believed to oppose the Constitution.

The Federalists, however, proved to be shrewd politicians. They organized a mass meeting in Boston in favor of ratification. This show of support in his home district persuaded Sam Adams to vote for the Constitution in spite of his doubts. The Federalist leaders promised Hancock, who was very ambitious, that they would not oppose him for governor in the next election if he would vote for the Constitution. They even hinted that he might be a good candidate for vice president if the new government was accepted.

Hancock then came out for the Constitution. He also made an important practical suggestion that helped persuade others in Massachusetts and other states to go along: once the Constitution was accepted, amendments should be submitted dealing with objections to it. The convention then voted 187 to 168 to ratify.

The contest was also close in Virginia, but again the Federalists won out. By the end of June ten states had ratified. Only Rhode Island, North Carolina, and New York had yet to act.

New York was crucial. Because of its geographical location the nation would be split almost in two if New York did not join. And 46 of the 65 delegates at the New York convention were Antifederalists. These Antifederalists had numerous supporters who wrote lively articles for New York newspapers. One such writer submitted his articles under the pen name "Brutus." Although historians are uncertain of Brutus' real identity, many people think that he was Robert Yates, a New York judge. In one essay Brutus wrote:

RATIFICATION OF THE CONSTITUTION	
State	Date
Delaware	1787
Pennsylvania	1787
New Jersey	1787
Georgia	1788
Connecticut	1788
Massachusetts	1788
Maryland	1788
South Carolina	1788
New Hampshire*	1788
Virginia	1788
New York	1788
North Carolina	1789
Rhode Island	1790
*Ninth state, guarantees ratification	

LEARNING FROM TABLES. *Delaware became the first state, ratifying the Constitution in December of 1787. Within the next year several other states joined Delaware. Why was New Hampshire's ratification especially important?*

“ Let us now proceed to enquire, as I at first proposed, whether it be best the thirteen United States should be reduced to one great republic, or not? It is here taken for granted that all agree in this, that whatever government we adopt, it ought to be a free one; that it should be so framed as to secure the liberty of the citizens of America, and such an one as to admit of a full, fair, and equal representation of the people. The question then will be, whether a government thus constituted, and founded on such principles, is practicable, and can be exercised over the whole United States, reduced into one state? . . .

History furnishes no example of a free republic, any thing like the extent of the United States. The Grecian republics were of small extent; so also was that of the Romans. Both of these, it is true, in process of time, extended their conquests over large territories of country; and the consequence was, that their governments were changed from that of free governments to those of the most tyrannical that ever existed in the world.

Not only the opinion of the greatest men, and the experience of mankind, are against the idea of an extensive republic, but a variety of reasons may be drawn from the reason and nature of things, against it. In every government, the will of the sovereign [supreme authority] is the law. In despotic governments, the supreme authority being lodged in one, his will is law, and can be as easily expressed to a large extensive territory as to a small one. In a pure democracy the people are the sovereign, and their will is declared by themselves; for this purpose they must all come together to deliberate, and decide. This kind of government cannot be exercised, therefore, over a country of any considerable extent; it must be confined to a single city, or at least limited to such bounds as that the people can conveniently assemble, be able to debate, understand the subject submitted to them, and declare their opinion concerning it. . . .

The territory of the United States is of vast extent; it now contains near three millions of souls, and is capable of containing much more than ten times that number. Is it practicable for a country, so large and so numerous as they will soon become, to elect a representation, that will speak their sentiments, without their becoming so numerous as to be incapable of transacting public business? It certainly is not.[1] 〞

Defeat seemed certain.

The leader of the Federalists at the convention was young Alexander Hamilton. Although he did not have a very high opinion of the Constitution—he thought it too weak rather than too strong—he was determined to see it ratified. He, John Jay, and James Madison had already written a series of newspaper articles explaining and defending the Constitution, the now-famous **Federalist Papers.** In Federalist Paper 9, for example, Hamilton wrote:

〞 A Firm Union will be of the utmost moment to the peace and liberty of the States as a barrier against domestic faction and insurrection. It is impossible to read the history of the petty Republics of Greece and Italy, without feeling sensations of horror and disgust at the distractions with which they were continually agitated, and at the rapid succession of the revolutions, by which they were kept in a state of perpetual vibration, between the extremes of tyranny and anarchy. If they exhibit occasional calms, these only serve as short-lived contrasts to the furious storms that are to succeed. . . .

[1]From *The Anti-Federalist Papers and the Constitutional Convention Debates,* edited by Ralph Ketcham

A distinction, more subtle than accurate has been raised between a *confederacy* and a *consolidation* of the States. The essential characteristic of the first is said to be, the restriction of its authority to the members in their collective capacities, without reaching to the individuals of whom they are composed. It is contended that the national council ought to have no concern with any object of internal administration. An exact equality of suffrage between the members has also been insisted upon as a leading feature of a Confederate Government. These positions are in the main arbitrary; they are supported neither by principle nor precedent. It has indeed happened that governments of this kind have generally operated in the manner, which the distinction, taken notice of, supposes to be inherent in their nature—but there have been in most of them extensive exceptions to the practice, which serve to prove as far as example will go, that there is no absolute rule on the subject. And it will be clearly shewn, in the course of this investigation, that as far as the principle contended for has prevailed, it has been the cause of incurable disorder and imbecility [stupidity] in the government.

The definition of a *Confederate Republic* seems simply to be, an "assemblage of societies" or an association of two or more States into one State. The extent, modifications and objects of the Federal authority are mere matters of discretion. So long as the separate organization of the members be not abolished, so long as it exists by a constitutional necessity for local purposes, though it should be in perfect subordination to the general authority of the Union, it would still be, in fact and in theory, an association of States, or a confederacy. The proposed Constitution, so far from implying an abolition of the State Governments, makes them constituent parts of the national sovereignty by allowing them a direct representation in the Senate, and leaves in their possession certain exclusive and very important portions of sovereign power. This fully corresponds, in every rational import of the terms, with the idea of a Federal Government.[1] 🍀

At the ratifying convention Hamilton advanced all the arguments developed in those essays and invented some new ones on the spot.

Although Hamilton probably did not change many minds, the Antifederalists were in a difficult position. If the United States needed New York, so did New York need the United States. Moreover, opinion in New York City was strong for the Constitution. Hamilton

[1]From *The Federalist Papers* by Alexander Hamilton, James Madison, and John Jay

STRATEGIES FOR SUCCESS

SQ3R—A HELPFUL STUDY PLAN

One of your most important tasks is to remember what you learn. SQ3R is a strategy that makes that task simpler. SQ3R stands for *Survey, Question, Read, Recite,* and *Review.* It is a study plan that can make you a more efficient reader. With practice it will save you time and help you remember important information.

How to Use SQ3R

To use the SQ3R method to study, follow these steps.

1. **Survey the sections.** When you begin a reading assignment in *The Story of America,* skim over the section titles, Preview & Review, boldface words, and illustrations and their captions. Surveying helps you prepare to read the assignment.
2. **Question what lies ahead.** Use the information from your survey to question what lies ahead. Turn section heads into questions. Ask who? what? when? where? why? and how? Write down your questions as a study guide for yourself.
3. **Read to answer the questions.** You needn't try to remember everything you read. Usually the answers to the questions you have formed will give you the main ideas and the most important details.
4. **Recite what you find.** Write down answers to your questions in your own words. This gives you an immediate check on your understanding and helps you not to forget what you read. Using your own words makes you think carefully about the material.
5. **Review your work.** There are two times for useful review—immediately and later. When you finish writing down answers to all your questions, *immediately* answer the questions a second time without looking at your written answers. Reread any parts of the chapter that give rise to questions you still find difficult to answer.

   A few days later, perhaps while preparing for a test, review again by answering your set of questions without looking back to your written answers. Again reread if necessary.

SQ3R GUIDELINES

STEP	WHAT TO DO
Survey	Read the Preview & Review. Read the headings. Scan for specific details. Skim for unfamiliar words. Look at illustrations and their captions.
Question	Make up a set of questions from your survey. Turn titles into questions. Ask who? what? when? where? why? how?
Read	Read to find answers to your questions.
Recite	Write the answers to your questions in your own words.
Review	Immediately answer your questions without looking at your earlier answers. Reread if necessary. Later answer your questions again. Reread if necessary.

SQ3R may seem to take a great amount of time and effort. But as you learn to use it, you will see that it actually saves both reading and study time. Use the chart on this page to help you organize your use of SQ3R.

Applying the Strategy

Use SQ3R to help you study "A More Perfect Union" on pages 220–31. The Preview & Review on page 220 introduces new words about the Constitution. The Preview & Review questions indicate the section focuses on the writing of the Constitution and its ratification. The section headings, such as "The Great Compromise," "Slavery in the Constitution," and others can be turned into questions such as "What was the Great Compromise?", "What did the Constitution say about slavery?", and other questions to help you understand the Constitution. Reviewing your answers to these questions and those in the Preview & Review will help you study the section.

For independent practice, see Practicing the Strategy on page 232.

The Granger Collection, New York

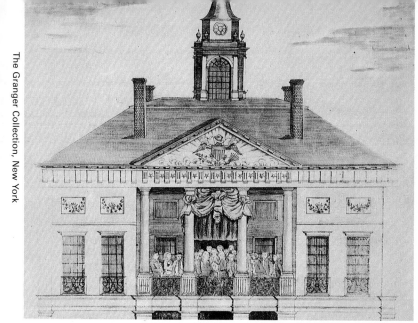

and other city leaders threatened to break away from the state and join the Union on their own if the Constitution was rejected. For practical reasons rather than because their minds had been changed, enough Antifederalists voted on July 26, 1788, to ratify the Constitution, 30 to 27.

The inauguration of George Washington at Federal Hall was engraved by Amos Doolittle in 1790.

The United States of America

Now the new system would have its chance. The first Congress was elected early in 1789. The state legislatures chose their presidential electors. On April 6, on order of the last Continental Congress, the new Congress gathered for the formal counting of the electoral votes in New York City, the temporary national capital. No one was surprised that George Washington was the unanimous choice of the 69 electors. John Adams, who received 34 votes, was declared vice president.

On April 30 Washington stood on the balcony of Federal Hall, at the corner of Broad and Wall Streets in New York City, and took the oath of office as president. A fine statue of Washington marks the site today. The oath he recited has been repeated by every president, for it is part of the Constitution:

❝ I do solemnly swear that I will faithfully execute the Office of president of the United States, and will, to the best of my ability, preserve, protect, and defend the Constitution of the United States. **❞**

Thus ended the Revolution. Thirteen English colonies in America had become one independent nation. That new nation was to be guided by a rare and special type of government—one based on consent of the governed. What would the Americans make of their independence and their new union? 🖅

Return to the Preview & Review on page 220.

CHAPTER 6 REVIEW

1777
Articles of
Confederation
drafted

1781
British
surrender
at Yorktown

Chapter Summary
Read the statements below. Choose one, and write a paragraph explaining its importance.
1. The first task Americans faced after the war was creating a new system of government. The system included both a central and state governments to represent the people.
2. At first the states formed a "league of friendship" under the Articles of Confederation.
3. The Treaty of Paris in 1783 gave lands in the Ohio Valley to the states, who settled troublesome colonial claims to the lands through land ordinances.
4. Hard times hit Americans after the war, making them realize they needed a stronger bond than the Articles of Confederation.
5. The Constitution of the United States is the supreme law of the nation.
6. The Constitution is in large part a document of compromises.
7. Debates between Federalists favoring the Constitution and Antifederalists opposing it took place throughout the country before the states voted on ratification.
8. The Constitution was approved as our plan of government when New Hampshire became the ninth state to ratify it.

Reviewing Chronological Order
Number your paper 1-5. Then study the time line above and place the following events in the order in which they happened by writing the first next to 1, the second next to 2, and so on.
1. Washington elected first president
2. Northwest Ordinance
3. Articles of Confederation drafted
4. Constitution ratified
5. Treaty of Paris

Understanding Main Ideas
1. Why did the new state constitutions give more power to the legislatures than to governors?
2. How might a tariff on British goods have helped Americans immediately after the war?
3. What are some of the major duties of each of the three branches of the federal government under the Constitution?
4. Explain the difference between the American Revolution and the Revolutionary War.

Thinking Critically
1. **Analyzing.** Explain in your own words what Benjamin Franklin meant when he said, "We must all hang together, or we shall surely all hang separately."
2. **Synthesizing.** Imagine that you are a poor Massachusetts farmer in 1786. Would you be likely to follow Daniel Shays to prevent the state supreme court from meeting? If so, why? If not, why not?
3. **Evaluating.** On the question of ratification of the Constitution, how would you vote if you were a ship's captain from Boston? A bank clerk from New York City? A plantation owner from Georgia? In each case, explain why you would vote for or against ratification.

Writing About History
Imagine you are a delegate at the Constitutional Convention. Write a letter to the people of your state explaining why you feel the Constitution is an improvement on the Articles of Confederation. Use the information in Chapter 6 to help you write your letter.

Practicing the Strategy
Review the strategy on page 230.
SQ3R—A Helpful Study Plan. SQ3R can be helpful in studying important documents. This is certainly true of the United States Constitution. Apply the strategy to the Constitution on pages 201–18. Then answer the following questions.
1. Into what major sections is the United States Constitution divided?
2. What questions would you use to review each of the sections of the Constitution?
3. How would you answer each of your questions?
4. How would this process help you study the Constitution?

1784 Economic depression hits America

1785 Land Ordinance of 1785

1786 Shays' Rebellion in Massachusetts

1787 Northwest Ordinance

★ Constitutional Convention meets

1788 New Hampshire ratifies Constitution

★ Constitution ratified

★ New York ratifies the Constitution

1789 Washington elected first president

Using Primary Sources

Review the following excerpts from the United States Constitution to understand the workings of the document. Then complete the activities below each.

> ARTICLE I, Section 8. *The Congress shall have the Power . . . To make all Laws which shall be necessary and proper for carrying into Execution the foregoing Powers, and all other Powers vested by this Constitution in the Government of the United States, or in any Department or Officer thereof.*

1. *Article I, Section 8* lists all the many powers assigned to Congress. The last entry on the list is called the "necessary and proper clause." Its intent and scope have been the subject of heated debate throughout the nation's history. What do you think the framers of the Constitution had in mind when they included this clause among the powers of Congress?
2. Give an example of a situation in which Congress might use the necessary and proper clause. (You may wish to review the other powers listed in *Section 8* on pages 204–05.)

> ARTICLE V. *The Congress, whenever two thirds of both Houses shall deem it necessary, shall propose Amendments to this Constitution, or, on the Application of the Legislatures of two thirds of the several states, shall call a Convention for proposing Amendments, which, in either Case, shall be valid to all Intents and Purposes, as Part of this Constitution, when ratified by the Legislatures of three fourths of the several States, or by Conventions in three fourths thereof, as the one or the other Mode of Ratification may be proposed by the Congress; Provided that no Amendment which may be made prior to the Year One thousand eight hundred and eight shall in any Manner affect the first and fourth Clauses in the Ninth Section of the first Article; and that no State, without its Consent, shall be deprived of its equal Suffrage in the Senate.*

1. *Article V* describes two methods for amending the Constitution. What are the basic steps in amending the Constitution?
2. Create a chart illustrating the steps in the two ways to amend the Constitution. What is the difference in the two methods?
3. Which method of amending the Constitution do you think is most often used? Why?

Linking History & Geography

The new United States of America faced a serious geographic problem at the end of the Revolutionary War. The country had new territory west of the Appalachian Mountains to govern. The new government faced conflicting colonial claims to these lands and decisions about their settlement. Study the map on page 186 and review the information about the land ordinances. Then in a brief paragraph, explain how the nation's leaders dealt with the serious geographic problem of settling the new territory.

Enriching Your Study of History

1. **Individual Project.** Clip articles from current newspapers and magazines that deal with activities of the three branches of the federal government. Group the articles that deal with each branch and add them to bulletin board charts. See how many different kinds of activities you can find for each branch of the government.
2. **Cooperative Project.** In your group, choose one branch of the federal government—legislative, executive, or judicial—and make a chart illustrating the duties of that branch. Combine your chart with charts from groups choosing the other branches to illustrate the system of checks and balances.

Chapter 6 Review 233

Governing the United States

Under the Constitution a federal government began to develop. As the first president, George Washington made decisions that to this day shape the highest office in the land. He set up a cabinet of advisers. His secretary of the treasury attempted to pay off the national debt and restore the credit of the United States. He avoided foreign wars and put down a small rebellion. When he left office, he delivered a famous Farewell Address urging national unity and neutrality. Would those who came after him be able to follow this advice?

Preview & Review

Use these questions to guide your reading. Answer the questions after completing Section 1.
Understanding Issues, Events, & Ideas. Use the following words to describe Washington's presidency: precedent, department of state, department of the treasury, department of war, attorney general, cabinet, amendment, Bill of Rights, natural rights, legal rights, human rights.
1. Why was Washington especially careful about the precedents he established?
2. What was Washington's view on the use of presidential power?
3. What is the purpose of the Bill of Rights?
Thinking Critically. Imagine that you live during the administration of George Washington. Which of his qualities as president do you admire most? Why?

1. A GOVERNMENT IS FORMED

Establishing Precedents

Like all later presidents, Washington's first task was to appoint officials to run the government departments. He also had to decide what jobs needed to be done and how the work should be organized and supervised. The task was complicated by the need to cooperate with the Congress. Of course, the Senate had to approve the major appointments. In addition, laws had to be passed to create the positions and provide money to pay salaries. Washington's government seems simple when compared to the enormous federal government of today. It was not so simple to design and staff it back in 1789.

Washington was extremely conscientious. He knew that as the first president he was establishing a **precedent,** a guide for later action, every time he made a decision. The Constitution had given him a great deal of power. He was a strong and determined person. He wanted to use his power to the full. Yet he wanted to assure citizens who were worried about the misuse of presidential power.

Washington sincerely believed in the separation of powers. In particular he was careful not to tread on the toes of Congress. It was the job of Congress to make the laws. His job was to execute, or carry out, the laws.

Congress created three main departments: the **department of state,** the **treasury,** and a **war department.** Each of these was headed by a secretary appointed by the president. Today the secretary of

The Granger Collection, New York

Washington probably never assembled his cabinet as a group, as is shown in this portrait. Henry Knox, secretary of war, is seated at left. Next to him stand Thomas Jefferson, secretary of state; Alexander Hamilton, secretary of the treasury; and Washington himself. How might a picture of a recent cabinet meeting with the president be different from this scene?

DEVELOPMENT OF THE CABINET	
Office	**Date Established**
State	1789
Treasury	1789
War[1]	1789
Attorney General[2]	1789
Navy[3]	1798
Postmaster General[4]	1829
Interior	1849
Agriculture	1889
Commerce and Labor[5]	1903
Commerce	1913
Labor	1913
Defense	1947
Health, Education, and Welfare[6]	1953
Housing and Urban Development	1965
Transportation	1966
Energy	1977
Health and Human Services	1979
Education	1979
Veterans Affairs	1989

◻ Original Members

[1]Lost cabinet status, 1947
[2]Not head of Justice Dept. until 1870
[3]Lost cabinet status, 1947
[4]Lost cabinet status, 1970
[5]Divided, 1913
[6]Divided, 1979

state has charge of the relations of the government with foreign countries. In 1789 the secretary also had to manage all domestic affairs except those handled by the war and treasury heads. Yet Jefferson, the first secretary of state, had a staff of only five persons.

The war department headed by General Henry Knox maintained a small army and navy, but in peacetime five people could carry out its functions. Only the treasury department, under Alexander Hamilton, had a fairly large staff. It collected taxes and tariffs and attempted to make a farsighted economic plan for the United States. By 1790 the treasury department had 70 persons. Washington made Edmund Randolph, presenter of the Virginia Plan at the Constitutional Convention, **attorney general.** Randolph, a part-time employee, was a legal adviser to the president.

Washington called upon the secretaries for advice, but he did not meet with them as a group. What we call the **cabinet,** a group of department heads meeting regularly with the president to discuss current issues, did not exist in Washington's day.

General Knox, who worshiped Washington, his former commander, ran the war department efficiently. He was mostly a follower who merely agreed with whatever decision Washington made. Jefferson was just the opposite. He disliked routine office details and sometimes neglected his duties as head of the state department. He

LEARNING FROM CHARTS. *This chart illustrates the steady growth in the size of the cabinet. Why do you think the president today has more advisers than the first presidents did?*

A Government Is Formed

often disagreed with Washington about important matters. Hamilton was a bundle of energy and wide ranging in his interests. He was eager to increase his own power. Gradually he became Washington's most influential adviser.

Washington as President

Washington would have preferred to serve without salary, as he had during the Revolutionary War, but Congress voted him a salary of $25,000. That was a very large sum for the time. Congress did not give him an expense account, however, so the salary was not as generous as it seemed. Washington actually spent about $5,000 a year of his own money on official business.

Congress did rent a fine three-story mansion near the federal building for the president. The house was, according to the first lady, Martha Custis Washington, ''handsomely furnished, all new.'' Washington supplied his own servants. He brought seven of his slaves up from Mount Vernon, his Virginia plantation. He hired another 14 servants locally. He served the best food and wines at official dinners. He drove about in a fine carriage drawn by six horses. At receptions he appeared in rich formal clothes and wore his dress sword.

On the other hand, the small size of the government made for simplicity. New York City, the nation's capital, was still a small town of about 30,000 people in 1789. On Tuesday afternoons from three to five o'clock, President Washington received guests. Every Friday evening Martha Washington gave a tea party. No invitations were necessary for these affairs. Anyone who was properly dressed could

Martha Washington received guests at tea parties on Friday evenings in the presidential mansion in New York City. This oil painted by Daniel Huntington turns the tea party into "The Republican Court." All eyes are on the first lady at left center. President Washington is near the center. Does this picture suggest that America had found its own style or does the gathering look more European?

The Brooklyn Museum

simply walk in. Washington particularly hated the afternoon affairs, which were for men only. The visitors tended to stand and stare in awe at the Great Man, or else they ignored him and spent their time gobbling up the refreshments.

The tea parties were different. Washington enjoyed chatting with the women at these affairs very much. The president was a tall, powerfully built man. Women often found him charming. According to Abigail Adams, the wife of the vice president, Washington was much more dignified and well mannered than King George III of England. Of course, Abigail Adams was an ardent patriot. She may have been prejudiced!

To many people of the time Washington seemed more like a statue on a pedestal than a human being. That is still the case. He seemed almost too formal and dignified to be a real person. This was because he was so aware of his responsibilities. He could hardly ever relax. Americans considered him the greatest hero of their Revolution. He felt that he had to live up to the almost godlike image the people had made of him.

This must have made life difficult for Washington at times. He frequently complained of the burdens of his office. He looked forward to the day when he could retire to his plantation at Mount Vernon. Yet he never neglected his duties. Although he only looked like a perfect man, he was as close to a perfect first president as the young nation could have hoped for.

The Massachusetts Historical Society

Abigail Smith Adams is shown as a young woman in this watercolor. She wrote wise and warm letters to her husband, John, during the Continental Congress.

The Bill of Rights

One of the first tasks Congress took up was preparing the **amendments** to the Constitution that the Federalists had promised the Antifederalists. The purpose was to reassure people who were afraid that the new government had too much power. About 80 proposed amendments had been suggested by one or another state. After debating through the summer of 1789, the Congress passed 12. Ten of these were ratified by the states.

These first ten amendments are known as the **Bill of Rights.** They did not give rights to the people or to the states. The rights already existed. The amendments stated simply and clearly that the government had no authority to take them away. The First Amendment begins, ''Congress shall make no law . . .'' That was the basic principle.

The First Amendment protects the freedoms of religion, speech, and the press, and the right of people to gather together in groups peacefully—that is, the right to assembly. The Second Amendment guarantees the rights of American citizens to own firearms. It prevents the government from absolutely prohibiting such ownership. It also protects the right and duty to serve in the armed forces. The Third Amendment provides that in peacetime no soldiers can be

A Government Is Formed

lodged in private homes without the consent of the owners. In war-time soldiers can be quartered in private homes only according to specific laws passed by Congress at the time. The Fourth Amendment protects the right to privacy—no "unreasonable searches and seizures" are permitted.

Several amendments deal with the rights of people accused of committing crimes. The Fifth Amendment prohibits forcing people to testify against themselves and bans "double jeopardy"—prosecuting again a person acquitted of a crime for the same crime, and guarantees "due process"—standard procedures applied in all cases to all accused persons. The Six, Seventh, and Eighth Amendments guarantee speedy trial, trial by jury, and protection from excessive bail and from torture. All accused persons are entitled to be told in advance what crime they are accused of. All have the right to be helped by a lawyer.

The Ninth Amendment says that the rights mentioned in the Constitution and the first eight amendments are not the only rights of the people. Civil liberties are not taken away from the people simply because they are not mentioned. The Tenth Amendment states that all powers not given to the United States government by the Constitution or denied by the Constitution to the States are "reserved" to the states or to the people as individuals.

Two points about the Bill of Rights are particularly important. One is that most of the amendments did not protect people's rights against violation by the state governments. The First Amendment says that *Congress* may not interfere with freedom of religion, speech, or the press. It did not prevent Massachusetts or South Carolina or any other state from doing so. Some states permitted and protected slavery, the most complete denial of human rights one can imagine.

The second point is that the rights protected were what the people of that day called **natural rights.** People also have **legal rights,** those given them by laws. For example, our present old-age pension law gives persons over a particular age fixed amounts of money each month. The people have a right to these payments. But the law can be and many times has been changed by Congress. If for some reason Congress voted to repeal the old-age pension law, that right would disappear. The right of free speech, however, is one of our natural rights, or **human rights.** Under the Constitution the government cannot take that right away.

The insistence of many Americans on the addition of the Bill of Rights illustrates how concerned Americans were with human rights and ethical behavior of government. Stating these ideals in the Constitution focused attention on principles which were becoming world-wide concerns. It also alerted all Americans to their civic responsiblities. If the nation were to remain free and democratic, each citizen would have to participate.

GOVERNING THE UNITED STATES

THE BILL OF RIGHTS	
AMENDMENT 1	Guarantees freedom of speech, religion, and the press, and the right to assemble peacefully, and to petition the government.
AMENDMENT 2	Guarantees the right to bear arms and to organize state militia.
AMENDMENT 3	Prohibits quartering of troops.
AMENDMENT 4	Prohibits searches and seizures of property without warrants.
AMENDMENT 5	Guarantees that no one may be deprived of life, liberty, or property without due process of law; prohibits forcing accused persons to testify against themselves; requires a grand jury for serious criminal charges; prohibits military trial for civilians.
AMENDMENT 6	Guarantees the right to a speedy trial in criminal cases, the right to know all charges, the right to obtain and question witnesses, and the right to have counsel.
AMENDMENT 7	Guarantees a trial in most civil cases.
AMENDMENT 8	Prohibits excessive fines and bail, and cruel and unusual punishment.
AMENDMENT 9	Gives rights not specifically mentioned in the Constitution to the people.
AMENDMENT 10	Reserves the powers not delegated to the national government for the states.

LEARNING FROM CHARTS. *The Bill of Rights grew out of the ratification debate. Its intent was to guarantee individual rights. Study the chart and refer to the amendments on pages 211–12. Then restate in your own words what is guaranteed by each of the first ten amendments.*

But how would Americans know what their responsibilities were? How could they be relied on to make intelligent and ethical decisions? That was the role of education. Educated voters were the key to preserving a democratic society. From the beginning leaders linked education to America's social and civic values—freedom, justice, self-reliance, and prosperity. Informed Americans could better solve economic and political problems and advance technologically. At the time, of course, formal education was still mostly limited to boys and young men. Girls and young women would struggle for more than 50 years to gain access to the educational system.

The Living Constitution

The writers of the Constitution had hoped to create a government that would guide the nation forever. But they were mindful that as America grew the needs of society might change. They believed that later generations of Americans should be able to change, or amend, the Constitution if they needed to. Therefore, they included the amendment process as part of the Constitution itself. It is this process that makes the Constitution flexible, allowing it to adapt to the tremendous changes in America over 200 years.

Return to the Preview & Review on page 234.

A Government Is Formed

Historical Society of Pennsylvania
(photo: Bradley Smith/Laurie Platt Winfrey)

Alexander Hamilton, the genius of finance who put the United States on a firm financial foundation, was painted by John Trumbull. With other class members, prepare a series of reports on how the United States is financed today. Then contrast today's financial arrangements with Hamilton's plan.

Preview & Review

Use these questions to guide your reading. Answer the questions after completing Section 2.
Understanding Issues, Events, & Ideas. Use the following words to explain the nation's early financial system: government bond, speculator, Bank of the United States, security, bank note, necessary and proper clause, elastic clause.
1. How did Hamilton propose to pay off the national debt?
2. How did speculators profit when the government paid its debts?
3. Why did Hamilton want a Bank of the United States?
4. Why did Jefferson oppose the bank bill?
Thinking Critically. 1. Which term, *necessary* or *proper,* would you emphasize to interpret the elastic clause? Why? 2. During Alexander Hamilton's term as secretary of the treasury, would you rather be a speculator or a war veteran? Why?

2. FINANCING THE NATION

Hamilton and the National Debt

One of the main reasons for strengthening the national government was the poor condition of the finances of the United States. Congress therefore acted quickly to use its new power to tax. In 1789 it placed a tariff, or tax, of 5 percent on all foreign goods entering the country. This law was quite similar to the measures Parliament had employed in the 1760s to raise money in America. Those laws had caused a revolution. The Tariff Act of 1789 was accepted by everyone. The vital difference was that the new taxes were agreed to by the people's own representatives. These taxes were not imposed by an outside power.

These taxes raised enough money to meet the day-to-day expenses of the government. They did not deal with the problem of paying off the large debts that the government had accumulated during and after the Revolutionary War. This debt included money lent by foreign governments and bonds sold to private citizens by the government to raise money during the Revolution. It included bonuses and other payments promised to soldiers. The government also owed money to merchants and manufacturers who had supplied it with various goods.

Because of the large national debt, investors were unwilling to lend the government more money. They considered the United States

GOVERNING THE UNITED STATES

a poor credit risk. The **government bonds,** certificates representing the money the national government had borrowed, had fallen far below their face value. A person who owned a $1,000 bond might not be able to sell it for even $500.

It was the responsibility of the secretary of the treasury, Alexander Hamilton, to find a way to pay off the debt and restore the credit of the government. Many people admired Hamilton extravagantly during his lifetime. Others considered him a villain. This division of opinion remains today.

Everyone recognizes that Hamilton was a genius of finance. But his ideas about government and about human nature remain controversial. Hamilton had a low opinion of the average person's honesty and judgment. He believed that most people were selfish and easily led astray by crafty, power-hungry leaders.

Hamilton did not trust the rich any more than he did what he called "the great mass of the people." If "aristocrats" had power, they would oppress the rest of society. If the poor controlled the government, they would use their power to seize the property of the rich. A good government, he thought, was one that balanced rival interests. This attitude was not unusual, as we have seen. However, Hamilton went beyond most political thinkers of his day. He thought that the selfish desires of the rich could be used to strengthen the government and thus the whole nation.

Many of the people who had bought government bonds had sold them at a loss. Others had been forced to accept the government's promises to repay them when the money owed them became available. They had sold these paper promises to investors for less than their face value. These investors were what we call **speculators.** They were gambling that some day the government would be able to pay off its bonds and other debts at full value. Speculators were wealthy or well-to-do people who had spare cash.

Hamilton proposed gradually raising enough money by taxes to pay off all the national government's debts. He also wanted the United States to assume, or take over, the debts of the states. He wanted to pay all at their face value. A speculator who had bought a $1,000 bond for $500 would receive $1,000. Hamilton reasoned that by doing this he would make the wealthy bond owners enthusiastic supporters of the national government. With such powerful people behind it, the government would be strong.

Some Americans felt that this policy was unfair to the former soldiers and other owners of bonds or government promises who had sold them cheaply. They wanted the original owners of these securities to receive at least some of their increased value. Hamilton refused. The speculators had paid what the bonds were worth at the time they bought them, he pointed out. They had taken the risks. Now they were entitled to the profits. After some hesitation Congress passed the necessary laws.

The John Carter Brown Library, Brown University

On Philadelphia's Third Street stood the Bank of the United States, shown in this 1799 engraving by William Birch. The building was a fine example of Greek revival architecture. Note its graceful columns and marble front. Explain how a bank is more than a building.

The Bank of the United States

The next step in Hamilton's plan was the establishment of a **Bank of the United States.** In 1790 there were almost no banks of any kind in the country. Hamilton argued that the government could use the bank to deposit the money it received from taxes. The bank would also be able to print new paper money, called **bank notes,** to represent the money it had on deposit. It could lend them to merchants and manufacturers, thus speeding the growth of business. For example, a manufacturer of shoes might ask the bank for a loan to buy leather. The leather and the shoes made from it would be **security** for the loan. If the shoemaker did not repay the loan, the bank would seize the goods. Thus the manufacturer would be able to produce more shoes, earn more money, and repay the loan. Without such a bank the shoe manufacturer and all sorts of other people in business would have to operate on a much smaller scale. Once again Hamilton's scheme would greatly benefit the nation, especially the rich.

In 1791 Congress passed a bank bill. But President Washington did not sign it immediately. He hesitated because he could find noth-

The First Bank of the United States issued this $10 bank note in 1796. The X-marks probably show that it was redeemed, or turned in to the Bank for gold or silver. Notice that at the bottom of the note the name of the holder and the date were written in by hand. Which branch of the government has the power to coin money and issue bank notes?

ing in the Constitution authorizing Congress to create a bank. So he asked Himilton and Secretary of State Jefferson if they thought the bill was constitutional.

Hamilton, naturally enough, said the bill was constitutional. Jefferson, however, insisted that it was not. What is most interesting about their arguments is that they relied on the *same* clause in the Constitution—**the necessary and proper clause.** Yet they reached opposite conclusions.

Besides spelling out the powers of Congress, such as the power to tax and the power to borrow money, the Constitution says that Congress can "make all laws which shall be necessary and proper" to put its powers into effect. This clause means, for instance, that since Congress has the power to coin money, it may also build and operate a mint. But the necessary and proper clause is vague. Hamilton concluded that the bank had "a natural relation" to the power to collect taxes and regulate trade. A bank was a *proper* way to make use of that power.

On the other hand, Jefferson claimed that Congress could only pass laws that were *necessary,* "not those which are merely '*convenient.*'" Since the government could function without a bank, a bank was "not *necessary* and consequently not authorized," Jefferson said.

Washington accepted Hamilton's argument. He signed the bank bill. In most cases since, government leaders have done the same. The necessary and proper clause is often called the **elastic clause** because it has been used so often to stretch the powers of Congress. Yet the clause can be read two ways. If only the Constitution had said "necessary *or* proper," many later arguments would have been avoided.

Critics of Hamilton's financial policies objected more to his desires to help already powerful interests than to the policies themselves. The policies were so effective that almost everyone approved of them. The credit of the United States was soon as good as that of any nation in the world. The Bank proved a most valuable institution, both to the government and to business. 🖳

Return to the Preview & Review on page 240.

Use these questions to guide your reading. Answer the questions after completing Section 3.

Understanding Issues, Events, & Ideas. Use the following words to explain America's dilemma in staying neutral: French Revolution, privateer, Battle of Fallen Timbers, Jay's Treaty, Treaty of Greenville, right of deposit, Pinckney's Treaty, special interest group.

1. How did Americans greet news of the French Revolution in 1789?
2. What reasons were there for America to side with France in the war?
3. What actions of "Citizen" Genet made Washington's neutrality policy harder to maintain?
4. What did the country gain from Jay's Treaty? Pinckney's Treaty?
5. What arguments did Washington make for unity in his Farewell Address? For neutrality?

Thinking Critically. 1. Predict the effect on future relations between Indians and settlers caused by the fate of the Indian Confederacy. Support your prediction with facts from the textbook. **2.** In your opinion, what was Washington's greatest achievement?

3. THE NATION IS TESTED

The French Revolution

The first serious political conflicts in the United States were not caused by Hamilton's schemes but by events that occurred on the other side of the Atlantic Ocean. The American Revolution had been very popular in France. Of course, it had weakened France's chief European rival, Great Britain. But the Revolution also seemed a great step forward to the liberal-minded French people. Washington and Jefferson were almost national heroes to them.

Thus the American Revolution was one of the causes of the **French Revolution,** which began in 1789. That revolution, in turn,

was greeted with enormous enthusiasm in America. Did it not prove that America's republican ideas were spreading?

This enthusiasm slackened, however, when the French Revolution took a more radical turn. By 1793 extremists were in control of France. They executed King Louis XVI and many members of the nobility. They began to put radical social changes into effect. Then, in 1793, war broke out between France and Great Britain.

The United States had signed a treaty of alliance with France in 1778. French help had made it possible for America to win its independence. The treaty was still in effect. Furthermore, the United States had not yet managed to get the British to live up to all the terms of the treaty that had ended the Revolutionary War. Was the United States duty bound to side with France?

Musée de Versailles

The French Revolution erupted in 1789. Here we see the revolutionaries storming the Bastille, where political prisoners were held. Hubert Robert painted the large oil from which this scene is taken. Why did Americans support the citizens of France in their uprising?

Point of View

The opening lines of *A Tale of Two Cities* capture the mood in France on the eve of its great revolution.

> "It was the best of times, it was the worst of times, it was the age of wisdom, it was the age of foolishness, it was the epoch of belief, it was the epoch of incredulity, it was the season of Light, it was the season of Darkness, it was the spring of hope, it was the winter of despair, we had everything before us, we had nothing before us, we were all going direct to Heaven, we were all going direct the other way—. . ."
>
> Charles Dickens, 1859

Edmond Genet preferred to call himself simply "Citizen" Genet. This oil portrait by Ezra Amos, a traveling painter, shows an older, less meddlesome Genet. Compare this portrait with the description of Genet at age 30 on this page.

Albany Institute of History and Art

The Neutrality Proclamation

Should the United States come to the aid of France by declaring war on Great Britain? Many Americans thought that was the honorable course the country should follow. But Washington felt otherwise. He issued a neutrality proclamation warning American citizens not to aid either side. The government would try to be "friendly and impartial" to both.

The revolutionary government in France paid little attention to this proclamation. It sent a special diplomatic representative, Edmond Charles Genet, to rouse support for France in the United States.

Genet was a charming, red-haired man of 30, an enthusiastic supporter of his country's cause. He spoke English fluently. Although the son of an important French diplomat, he called himself simply "Citizen" Genet. He arrived at Charleston, South Carolina, in April 1793. While making his way northward to present himself to President Washington, he persuaded a number of Americans who owned merchant ships to mount guns on their vessels and sail off to attack unarmed British ships on the high seas. These ships and the men who sailed them were called **privateers.** They flew the French flag and carried papers issued by the French government making them part of the French navy.

Privateering was a common practice at the time. Americans had often engaged in it under the British flag in earlier wars. Privateering was possible during the days of wooden sailing ships because the differences between a warship and a merchant vessel were slight. A small privateer was designed for speed and easy maneuvering. Armed with a few cannon, it could capture or destroy an unarmed cargo vessel. It could also escape large pursuing warships. Since Genet's privateers were entitled to keep two thirds of the value of the cargo and ships they captured, the business could be very profitable.

A privateer was certainly not acting in a neutral manner. When Washington learned what Genet was up to, he was furious. When Genet reached the capital, which had been moved to Philadelphia, Washington ordered him to stop these activities at once. Genet ignored the orders. Privately he called Washington *le vieillard,* which is French for "the old man." He continued to recruit and arm privateers. He tried to persuade several Americans to organize private armies to attack Spanish Florida and Louisiana, since Spain was also at war with France at this time. He even tried to raise an army to invade Canada. Washington finally demanded that the French replace him.

The removal of Genet did not stop the efforts being made to involve the United States in this latest European war. Washington and his advisers believed that neutrality was the proper policy for America. Maintaining neutrality was not easy. Both France and Great

Britain wanted to trade with the United States. Since they were at war with each other, each also wanted to prevent the other from getting American products. The navies of both began to seize unarmed American merchant ships on the Atlantic. In a single year several hundred American vessels loaded with valuable goods were captured. The British attacks were much more damaging than the French because Great Britain had a much larger navy than France.

The Indian Confederacy

Americans were also troubled by the refusal of the British to remove their troops from forts on American soil in the Great Lakes area. These outposts were not important in themselves, but American frontier settlers claimed that the British were supplying the Indians of the area with guns to use against them.

The Revolutionary War had not won the Indians of the country their independence. During the conflict Indians fought on each side. When the war ended, the British coldly betrayed those Indians who had helped them. They did so by signing the peace treaty granting all the land between the Appalachian Mountains and the Mississippi River to the United States. The Indians properly claimed that they, not the British, owned this land.

The tribes of the region north of the Ohio River resisted the invasion of American settlers who pressed into the area after 1783. They joined together in a confederacy and pledged not to sell any territory to the settlers. Unlike the tribes who lived by hunting, many of these Indians had taken up farming. For them, moving would mean more than having to find another hunting ground.

By the late 1780s 10,000 settlers were pouring into the Ohio Valley each year. They disregarded the fact that the land had always been owned by the Indians. These settlers demanded that the government protect them. Finally in 1790 an army of 1,400 led by General Josiah Harmar advanced against the Indian confederacy.

The leader of the Indian confederacy was Michikinikua, or Little Turtle, chief of the Miamis. Despite his mild name, Little Turtle was a brave and skillful fighter. He defeated Harmar's force badly. The next year Little Turtle and his warriors defeated an even larger army commanded by Major General Arthur St. Clair. They killed over 600 of St. Clair's 2,000 men and wounded 250 others. These battles were among the fiercest

The artist who drew Little Turtle is unknown but the likeness is thought to be accurate. His opponent Arthur St. Clair was painted by Charles Willson Peale.

Smithsonian Institution

Independence National Historical Park

The Henry Francis du Pont Winterthur Museum

General Anthony Wayne orders a charge at the Battle of Fallen Timbers where he routed Little Turtle.

and bloodiest in the entire history of warfare between settlers and Indians.

In 1792 Washington placed General "Mad Anthony" Wayne in command of the army. Wayne was "mad" only in the sense that he was a tough professional soldier. He loved a good fight, but he was certainly not crazy.

Wayne had more than 3,600 soldiers under his command. He spent months training and drilling them. In October 1793 he headed north from a base on the Ohio River near Fort Washington (present-day Cincinnati). As he advanced, he built a series of forts to protect his rear guard. Scouts ranged ahead and on each side to protect the army against surprise. The army passed the winter at Fort Greenville, about halfway between Fort Washington and Lake Erie.

Observing Wayne's careful preparations, Little Turtle decided that it would be hopeless to resist. "The Americans are now led by a chief who never sleeps," he warned his fellows. But hotter heads prevailed. Led now by Blue Jacket, a chief of the Shawnees, in June 1794 the Indians attacked part of Wayne's force near the place where St. Clair had been routed. They won a minor victory. Still, Wayne continued his slow, steady advance. The showdown battle occurred in August near Fort Miami, one of the British posts a few miles southwest of Lake Erie.

This **Battle of Fallen Timbers** was a great victory for Wayne. He had more men and he "outgeneraled" Blue Jacket. The Indians fled in disorder. When they sought safety in Fort Miami, the British commander refused to let them in. Wayne then set fire to the Indians' cornfields and homes. Their defeat was total, their spirits broken. Soon their ancestral lands were settled by whites.

The distrust between Indians and whites continued, and in many cases increased. Some people used the situation for profit. Swindlers became rich cheating government Indian agents. One ingenious method was to "create" an "Indian chief" to receive government goods and money.

> **“** You have heard of the Indian nations to the westward, that occasionally make war upon the frontier settlements? It has been the policy of government, to treat [sign treaties] with these, and distribute goods. Commissioners are appointed for that purpose. Now you are not to suppose that it is an easy matter to catch a real chief, and bring him from the woods; or if at some expense one was brought, the goods would go to his use; whereas it is much more profitable to hire substitutes and make chiefs of our own; and as some unknown gibberish [nonsense language] is necessary, to pass for Indian language, we generally make use of Welsh, or Low Dutch, or Irish [languages]; or pick up an ingenious fellow here and there, who can imitate a language by sounds of his own. . . . If your man is tractable [easily taught], I can make him a Kickapoo [Indian] in about nine days. . . . He must have a part of his head shaved, and painted, with feathers on his crown; but the paint will rub off, and the hair grow in a short time, so he can go about with you again.[1] **”**

Is it any wonder the great chief Tecumseh came to think most white men were evil? He said:

> **“** I admit that there are good white men, but they bear no proportion to the bad; the bad must be the strongest, for they rule. They do what they please. They enslave those who are not of their color, although created by the same Great Spirit who created them. They would make slaves of us if they could; but as they cannot do it, they kill us. There is no faith to be placed in their words. They are not like the Indians, who are only enemies [of each other] while at war, and are friends in peace. They [whites] will say to an Indian, "My friend; my brother!" They will take him by the hand, and, at the same moment, destroy him. . . . Remember that this day I have warned you to beware of such friends as these. I know the Long-Knives. They are not to be trusted.[2] **”**

[1] From *Modern Chivalry* by Hugh Henry Brackenridge
[2] From *A Century of Dishonor* by Helen Hunt Jackson

Jay's Treaty

Earlier in 1794 Washington had sent John Jay, chief justice of the United States, to England to try to work out a solution to all the conflicts that had developed between the two nations. Jay had done well in the negotiations leading to the treaty of 1783 ending the Revolutionary War. This time he was far less successful.

Jay got the British to agree to withdraw their troops from the western forts. They also agreed to let American ships trade with British colonies in Asia. And they promised to pay damages to the shipowners whose vessels they had illegally seized in the West Indies. But that was all.

The British refused to stop attacking American merchant ships elsewhere in the world. They would not allow American ships to trade with the British sugar islands in the West Indies. They rejected the American view of the trading rights of neutral nations during wartime. They would not pay for the slaves who had fled to their lines during the Revolutionary War.

Most Americans disliked **Jay's Treaty.** Many leading politicians urged Washington to reject it. Washington, however, decided to accept it, and he managed to persuade the Senate to ratify it. He considered it unfair and in some respects insulting. Americans had proper claims that the British had flatly refused to recognize. Nevertheless, he realized that the United States had some gains from the treaty. More important, the treaty made it possible to avoid going to war again. Washington knew that time was on the nation's side. Each year the United States was becoming larger, richer, and stronger. A war with Great Britain, or any other European nation, would cost much and could gain little.

The removal of the British troops and the defeat of the Indians at the Battle of Fallen Timbers opened the northwest to peaceful settlement. In August 1795 General Wayne and 92 leading chiefs signed the **Treaty of Greenville.** The Indians agreed to turn over the entire southern half of what is now Ohio to the American settlers.

America obtained an additional and unexpected benefit from Jay's Treaty. Relations between the United States and Spain were not good. The Spanish government had refused to recognize the boundary between Florida and the southern United States that had been fixed by the peace treaty ending the Revolutionary War. The Spanish also controlled the west bank of the Mississippi River and both sides of the mouth of the river, including the city of New Orleans.

The Spanish refused to allow Americans to load and unload cargo freely at New Orleans. This especially hurt the western farmers. They needed what they called the **right of deposit** at New Orleans in order to transfer their farm products from river craft to ocean-going ships.

When the Spanish read Jay's Treaty, they were greatly alarmed. They suspected that the published version was incomplete. Perhaps there was a secret clause outlining a joint British-American attack on Spain's possessions in North America. The / decided to try to make friends with the United States. In 1795 they signed a treaty accepting the American version of the Florida boundary line and granting Americans the right to ship goods freely down the Mississippi. This agreement is known as **Pinckney's Treaty** because it was negotiated for the United States by Thomas Pinckney, a son of Eliza Lucas Pinckney, who first cultivated indigo in America.

Washington's Farewell Address

By 1796 Washington could justly feel that he had set the United States well on its way as an independent nation. The Jay and Pinckney Treaties had assured the United States the boundaries first laid out in the treaty of 1783. The bloody fighting between settlers and Indians had been ended, at least for the moment. Settlers were pushing west across the Appalachian Mountains. Kentucky had enough people to become a state by 1792. Tennessee entered the Union in 1796. Ohio would soon follow.

Besides his sense of having completed his main tasks, Washington was tired after serving two terms as president. Political bickering was beginning to affect his reputation as a national hero. Although he could surely have been elected to a third term had he wished one, Washington decided to retire.

His Farewell Address of September 1796 announced his decision. It also contained his final advice to the American people. That advice can be boiled down to two ideas—unity at home, neutrality abroad. Washington said:

“ The name of American, which belongs to you in your national capacity, must always exalt the just pride of patriotism more than any appellation [name] derived from local discriminations. With slight shades of difference, you have the same religion, manners, habits, and political principles. You have in a common cause fought and triumphed together. . . .

In contemplating the causes which may disturb our union, it occurs as matter of serious concern that any ground should have been furnished for characterizing parties by *geographical* discriminations—*Northern* and *Southern, Atlantic* and *Western*—whence designing men may endeavor to excite a belief that there is a real difference of local interests and views. . . . You cannot shield yourselves too much against the jealousies and heartburnings which spring from these misrepresentations; they tend to render alien [unfriendly] to each other those who ought to be bound together by fraternal affection. . . .

THE WHISKEY REBELLION

Imagine the president of the United States, on horseback, leading an army westward across the United States, with the secretary of the treasury as second in command. In 1794 this surprising turn of events came about when western farmers rioted to protest a tax placed on the manufacture of whiskey. This was the so-called Whiskey Rebellion.

Congress had placed a tax of about 25 percent on the value of any whiskey distilled, or manufactured, in the United States. The tax was one of the measures designed by Hamilton to pay off the debts of the United States and the states. This very heavy tax angered frontier farmers, who usually distilled a large part of their corn and other grain into whiskey. They did so because land transportation was so difficult and expensive. There were few roads and they were rough and impassable in bad weather. It was much cheaper to ship whiskey than bulky farm products the long distances to market over these bad roads.

In 1794 farmers in western Pennsylvania rioted to protest the tax. They bullied tax collectors, prevented courts from meeting, and threatened to march on Pittsburgh. Washington promptly called up 12,900 militiamen to duty and marched westward. Alexander Hamilton was his second in command. When the soldiers reached the troubled area, not a single "rebel" could be found. No one dared to stand up before this huge force, which was actually larger than any army Washington had commanded during the war! The "rebellion" ended, or perhaps it would be more accurate to say it disappeared.

Some historians feel that Washington overreacted to the Whiskey Rebellion. Perhaps he did. Still, the contrast was sharp between his swift and painless enforcement of the law and the bloodshed of Daniel Shays' rebellion only eight years earlier. This time there was a strong central government backed by the new Constitution.

Observe good faith and justice toward all nations. Cultivate peace and harmony with all. . . .

Against the insidious wiles [sly tricks] of foreign influence (I conjure [beg] you to believe me, fellow citizens) the jealousy [suspicion] of a free people ought to be constantly awake, since history and experience prove that foreign influence is one of the most baneful foes of republican government. But that jealousy, to be useful, must be impartial, else it becomes the instrument of the very influence to be avoided, instead of a defense against it. . . .

The great rule of conduct for us, in regard to foreign Nations, is in extending our commercial relations, to have with them as little Political connection as possible. So far as we have already formed engagements let them be fulfilled with perfect good faith. Here let us stop. . . . **"**

Washington's advice was far-sighted. His main points bear repeating. First, *unity.* Washington disliked political squabbling, but his argument mostly concerned conflicts between **special interest groups** in different sections of the country. Too often northerners, southerners, and westerners thought only of what was best for their own region and tried to gain their objectives no matter what the effect on other sections. Washington called these rivalries "the jealousies and heartburnings" of "geographical discriminations." Such attitudes were shortsighted. Northern manufacturers needed southern raw

The Metropolitan Museum of Art

materials. Southern farmers sold their crops in northern markets. East and West had common interests. All sections of the country profited from the increase in trade that resulted. To understand why Washington put so much emphasis on so obvious a point, one must remember how new the United States was. Local pride remained strong. Washington stressed the argument that national unity was "a main pillar . . . of real independence."

As for *neutrality*, Washington urged a policy of avoiding "passionate attachments" to any foreign country. The United States was fortunate. Its "detached and distant" location meant that it did not have to become involved in European conflicts. To do so would be very costly. The "great rule of conduct" for America ought to be to encourage trade with the rest of the world but to "steer clear of permanent alliances."

Washington did not mean by this last statement that the United States should isolate itself from the rest of the world, as the Jay and Pinckney Treaties provided. He was against *permanent* ties with any particular nation but the president did not oppose evenhanded dealings with all foreign countries. 🖽

President Washington, on his white horse, rode to put down the Whiskey Rebellion in 1794. This oil painting is probably by F. Kemmelmeyer. How was the central government threatened by this rebellion?

Return to the Preview & Review on page 244.

The Nation Is Tested 253

Preview & Review

Use these questions to guide your reading. Answer the questions after completing Section 4.
Understanding Issues, Events, & Ideas. Use the following terms to explain the development of political parties: two-party system, Federalist, Democratic-Republican, reactionary, District of Columbia, XYZ Affair, Alien and Sedition Acts.
1. Why did Jefferson distrust Hamilton? Why did Jefferson distrust all government?
2. Explain the events of the election of 1796 to illustrate how the growth of political parties ruined the election process set up in the Constitution.
3. Why did President Adams send commissioners to France?
4. How was the Sedition Act motivated by politics?
Thinking Critically. You are a newspaper editor. Write an editorial expressing your opinion about French actions in the XYZ Affair.

4. THE TWO-PARTY SYSTEM

The First Political Parties

The election of a president to succeed Washington was the first in which political parties played a role. Today we think of political parties as the machinery by which office seekers work out programs and present issues to the voters. The **two-party system**—today the Democratic and Republican parties—makes it possible for this large country to have an effective national government. If every candidate or local group set up a different organization, no one would ever have a majority. No satisfactory decisions could be made.

The framers of the Constitution, however, disliked and distrusted political parties. They made no provision for them. They called parties *factions*. The word suggests fringe groups conspiring to dominate the rest of society. The framers believed that individuals representing small districts could arrive at agreements based on the national interest. In their eyes political parties meant corruption. Leaders, they thought, should take personal responsibility for their decisions.

Yet very soon after the Constitution was ratified, political parties began to form. They did so because the Constitution created a strong

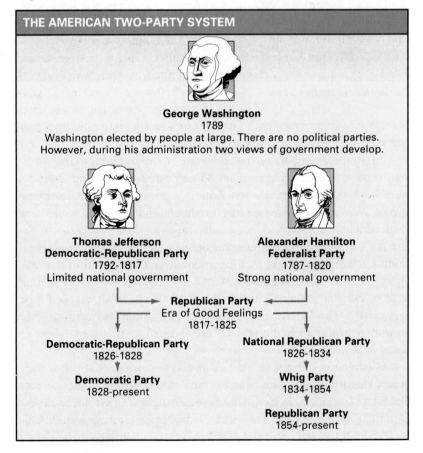

THE AMERICAN TWO-PARTY SYSTEM

George Washington
1789
Washington elected by people at large. There are no political parties. However, during his administration two views of government develop.

Thomas Jefferson
Democratic-Republican Party
1792-1817
Limited national government

Alexander Hamilton
Federalist Party
1787-1820
Strong national government

Republican Party
Era of Good Feelings
1817-1825

Democratic-Republican Party
1826-1828

National Republican Party
1826-1834

Democratic Party
1828-present

Whig Party
1834-1854

Republican Party
1854-present

LEARNING FROM DIAGRAMS. *This chart illustrates the development of the two-party system in America. Why did different political parties develop? How do the goals of the Republican party today differ from those of the Federalist party?*

national government. Because it was powerful, the government made important decisions. National politics therefore *mattered.* People joined together in parties to attempt to control the decisions of the government.

The first parties were influenced more by personalities than by issues. The principal figures were Secretary of the Treasury Hamilton and Secretary of State Jefferson. Members of Congress who favored Hamilton's financial policies took the name **Federalists.** They began to vote as a group on most issues, even those not related to Hamilton's programs.

Those who opposed Hamilton and his ideas began to call themselves **Democratic-Republicans.** James Madison, at the time a congressman from Virginia, was the chief organizer and manager of the Democratic-Republican party. Jefferson was its best-known leader. He was the person most responsible for the ideas it stood for.

Jefferson and Hamilton

Thomas Jefferson considered Alexander Hamilton to be a dangerous **reactionary.** A reactionary is one opposed to political or social change. Jefferson thought that Hamilton wished to undo the gains of the Revolution and go back to a less democratic form of government. He even thought that Hamilton wanted to make the United States into a monarchy, perhaps with George Washington as king.

Yet Jefferson himself was not a democrat in the modern sense. He distrusted human nature almost as much as Hamilton did. Because governments consisted of people, Jefferson distrusted *all* government. He wanted to keep the government as small as possible. Hamilton, on the other hand, wanted to use the government to control the weak and selfish elements in human nature.

In Jefferson's opinion the best way to keep government small was to keep society simple. The United States was a free country, he believed, because it was a nation of farmers. The population was spread out. Most families owned their own land. They managed their own affairs. Countries with crowded seaports and industrial towns needed more government controls to preserve order. City workers seldom owned land. They had less interest in protecting property and in having orderly government. "When we get piled upon one another in large cities," Jefferson said, "we shall become corrupt." Hamilton disagreed with all these ideas. He wanted the United States to have a strong and varied economy. He urged the government to do everything it could to encourage the growth of industry.

When Hamilton proposed paying off the national debt, Jefferson did not oppose him. Jefferson also went along with the plan to take over the state debts. In exchange Hamilton agreed that the permanent capital of the United States—the **District of Columbia**—should be located in the South, on land donated by Maryland and Virginia.

The Metropolitan Museum of Art

Thomas Jefferson wanted to keep government as small as possible. This fine miniature portrait is by John Trumbull. Later Jefferson stopped wearing powdered wigs.

Jefferson *did* object to Hamilton's Bank of the United States and to the Whiskey Tax. Those measures favored eastern merchants and other city interests. Southern and western farmers had little to gain from a national bank, and they were the ones who had to pay the Whiskey Tax.

The Election of 1796

The growth of political parties ruined the complicated system for choosing the president established by the Constitution. Instead of voting for local electors whose judgment they trusted, voters in 1796 were presented with lists of names. The party leaders drew up these lists. They picked persons who had promised to vote for the party's choice for president. Ballots containing the names of the party's electors were sometimes printed and handed out to voters in advance.

John Adams, who had been Washington's vice president, was the logical choice of the Federalists for president. Jefferson was the Democratic-Republican favorite. For vice president the Federalist party leaders decided to run Thomas Pinckney of South Carolina, who had negotiated the popular treaty with Spain. The Democratic-Republican candidate for vice president was Senator Aaron Burr of New York.

The campaign to succeed Washington was a bitter one. The election became a struggle for national power between the Federalists and the Democratic-Republicans. The following political broadside—a large sheet of paper printed on one side—urged Democratic-Republicans in Pennsylvania to vote for Jefferson and the other Democratic-Republicans. Such attacks on Adams and the Federalists would soon lead to the first challenge of the freedoms guaranteed by the first Amendment.

❝ FELLOW CITIZENS!
The first concern of freemen, calls you forth into action.— Pennsylvania was never yet found wanting when Liberty was at stake; she cannot then be indifferent when the question is, *Who shall be President of the United States?* The citizen who now holds the office of President [Washington], has publicly made known to his fellow citizens that he declines to serve in it again. Two candidates are offered for your choice, as his successor; THOMAS JEFFERSON of Virginia, and JOHN ADAMS of New England.—No other candidate is proposed, you cannot therefore mistake between them. THOMAS JEFFERSON is the man who was your late Secretary of State, and Minister of the United States to the French nation; JOHN ADAMS is the man who is now Vice President of the United States, and was the late Minister to the king of Great Britain.—THOMAS

The Museum of Fine Arts, Boston

John Adams, elected president in 1796, was painted by John Singleton Copley. In contrast to Washington, Adams was short and stocky.

JEFFERSON is a firm REPUBLICAN,—JOHN ADAMS is an avowed MONARCHIST. . . .

Thomas Jefferson first drew the declaration of American independence;—he first framed the sacred political sentence that all men are *born* equal. *John Adams* says this is all a farce and a falsehood; that some men should be Kings, and some should be born Nobles. Which of these, freemen of Pennsylvania, will you have for your President? Will you, by your votes, contribute to make the avowed friend of monarchy, President? or will you, by neglectfully staying at home, permit others to saddle you with Political Slavery?

. . . *Adams* is a fond admirer of the British Constitution, and says it is the first wonder of the world. *Jefferson* likes better our Federal Constitution, and thinks the British full of deformity, corruption, and wickedness. Once more, fellow citizens! Choose ye between these two, which you will have for your President, *Jefferson* or *Adams*. . . . Put in your tickets for fifteen good REPUBLICANS, and let the watch word be LIBERTY and INDEPENDENCE!¹ **"**

Independence National Historical Park

Elbridge Gerry was one of the three American commissioners who negotiated with the French in the XYZ Affair.

Hamilton, who was very influential in the Federalist party, disliked Adams. However, he dared not openly oppose him for president. Instead he worked out a clever, but very shady, scheme. The Federalists seemed likely to win a majority of the electors. If all these electors voted for Adams and Pinckney, both would have the same number of electoral votes. Since Adams was known to be the presidential candidate, he would be chosen president and Pinckney vice president. To prevent this from happening, Hamilton persuaded a few Federalist electors in South Carolina not to vote for Adams. If Pinckney got even one more vote than Adams, according to the rules he would be president and Adams vice president.

Unfortunately for Hamilton, news of his plan leaked out. A large number of Federalist electors who were friendly to Adams reacted by not voting for Pinckney. When the electoral votes were counted in the Senate, Adams had 71, Pinckney only 59. Jefferson, who had the united support of the Democratic-Republican electors, received 68 votes. He, not Pinckney, now became the new vice president!

The XYZ Affair

From the beginning of his presidency, John Adams had to deal with a serious problem with the French. France was still at war with Great Britain. French leaders were angry at the United States for agreeing to the Jay Treaty. French warships and numerous French privateers called picaroons were stopping American merchant ships on the high seas and seizing their cargoes. In 1795 alone they captured 316

¹From *The People Make a Nation* by Sandler, et al.

STRATEGIES FOR SUCCESS

SEPARATING FACT FROM OPINION

Being able to distinguish fact from opinion is a key strategy for the successful student. Reading history presents us with many facts. A *fact* is something known to be true. For example, you read on page 235: "By 1790 the treasury department had 70 persons." This is a statement of fact. It can be proven from records that exist. Also a fact is the statement on page 236: "Washington would have preferred to serve without salary, as he had during the Revolutionary War, but Congress voted him a salary of $25,000." Again, records verify this information.

But history also presents us with opinions. An *opinion* is a personal belief. When the facts are sorted through, it remains for the historian to offer an opinion about larger events. For example, in describing Washington's approach to his responsibilities as president, the author states: "Washington was extremely conscientious." This statement is the historian's opinion that Washington was very conscientious about his duties. People at the time and other historians might disagree with this assessment. It is important to know when the ideas you are reading are facts and when they are opinions.

How to Separate Fact from Opinion

To separate facts from opinions, follow these guidelines.

1. **Ask "can it be proven?"** Determine whether the idea can be checked for accuracy in other sources. If so, it is probably factual. If not, it probably contains an opinion.
2. **Look for context clues.** Opinions are sometimes signaled in writing by words like *believe* or *think*. Other clues that signal opinions include **loaded words** intended to stir your emotions, such as *extremely, ridiculous,* or *most important.*

Applying the Strategy

Read the following excerpt from *The Story of America*. List the sentences that contain the opinions of the historian who wrote the excerpt.

The election of a president to succeed Washington was the first in which political parties played a role. Today we think of political parties as the machinery by which office seekers work out programs and present issues to the voters. The two-party system—today the Demo-cratic and Republican parties—makes it possible for this large country to have an effective national government. If every candidate or local group set up a different organization, no one would ever have a majority. No satisfactory decisions could be made.

The framers of the Constitution, however, disliked and distrusted political parties. They made no provision for them. They called parties factions. *The word suggests fringe groups conspiring to dominate the rest of society. The framers believed that individuals representing small districts could arrive at agreements based on the national interest. In their eyes political parties meant corruption. Leaders, they thought, should take personal responsibility for their decisions.*

Yet very soon after the Constitution was ratified, political parties began to form. They did so because the Constitution created a strong national government. Because it was powerful, the government made important decisions. National politics therefore mattered. People joined together in parties to attempt to control the decisions of the government.

The first parties were influenced more by personalities than by issues. The principal figures were Secretary of the Treasury Hamilton and Secretary of State Jefferson. Members of Congress who favored Hamilton's financial policies took the name Federalists. They began to vote as a group on most issues, even those not related to Hamilton's program.

Those who opposed Hamilton and his ideas began calling themselves Democratic-Republicans.

You should note that the historian claims that the framers of the Constitution "disliked" and "distrusted" political parties. The author is basing his statements on a consensus of the sources he has studied. It is a valid interpretation of the situation, but it is an opinion because it cannot be proven with absolute certainty.

Continue to reread the discussion of the first American political parties. Note that the historian claims these early parties were more influenced by personalities such as Hamilton and Jefferson than by issues. Is this an example of an opinion? Why or why not? What other examples of opinions can you find in the section?

For independent practice, see Practicing the Strategy on page 263.

The Granger Collection, New York

vessels. When President Washington sent Charles Pinckney, Thomas Pinckney's brother, to France to try to settle these problems, the government refused to receive him. The French even ordered him out of the country.

When he became president, Adams decided to make another effort to reach an understanding with France. He sent three special commissioners to France: Charles Pinckney, the former ambassador; John Marshall, a Federalist from Virginia; and Elbridge Gerry of Massachusetts, a personal friend of his who happened to belong to the Democratic-Republican party.

In those days diplomats had much greater responsibilities than they do today. It took Marshall almost seven weeks to get from Philadelphia to Paris. Without radios or telegraphs diplomats could not send back home for new instructions. They had to make many important decisions on their own. This explains why the negotiations between the French and the three American commissioners developed as they did.

The French foreign minister, Talleyrand, was brilliant, but he could not be trusted. He was of noble birth and had been a bishop of the Catholic church before the French Revolution. During the revolution he became a leading diplomat of the new republican

The XYZ Affair is the subject of this American political cartoon of 1798. It is titled "Cinque-Têtes, or the Paris Monster." The five-headed monster stands for the Directory, the French government. The three American commissioners, Pinckney, Marshall, and Gerry, are on the left. A symbolic monster sits top right in front of a guillotined citizen. The interesting "Civic Feast" on the right seems to consist of live frogs. Why does the five-headed monster say, "Money, money, money"?

government. When the revolution became more radical, however, Talleyrand had to flee the country to save his life. He spent nearly two years in the United States. In 1796 he returned to France after a more conservative government, known as the Directory, took office. Soon thereafter he was named foreign minister.

The three Americans expected Talleyrand to be friendly because the United States had given him refuge. They were completely wrong. He had disliked America. "If I have to stay here another year," he had written to a French friend, "I shall die." Moreover, Talleyrand loved money. He would not discuss the issues unless he received a large bribe.

The Americans did not know what to do. For weeks they had a series of meetings and exchanged letters with three secret agents of Talleyrand—one a Swiss banker, another a German merchant, the third a French diplomat. Besides the outright bribe, Talleyrand expected the United States to make a large loan to France that would be practically a gift. The United States must also apologize to France for certain harsh remarks about the French nation that President Adams had made in a speech to Congress.

Bribing officials was not as frowned upon then as it later became. Yet Talleyrand wanted $250,000, a huge sum. (At today's prices it would have amounted to several million dollars.) He would not stop the attacks on American ships or even begin to negotiate until the money was promised. "It is money," the Swiss banker reminded the Americans. "It is expected that you will offer money." Pinckney, the only American commissioner who could speak French properly, burst out angrily, "No, no. Not a sixpence!" Finally the commissioners gave up. Pinckney and Marshall returned home very much discouraged by Talleyrand's greed.

Gerry remained in Paris because he feared that France would declare war on the United States if the negotiations were broken off. President Adams was very upset by the request for a bribe. He ordered Gerry to return to America. He published the letters of the commissioners, substituting the letters X, Y, and Z for the names of Talleyrand's secret agents.

The publication of the XYZ correspondence created a sensation. Congress ordered 10,000 additional copies distributed free in rural areas where there were few newspapers. When John Marshall reached Philadelphia, Federalist members of Congress gave a huge banquet in his honor. "Millions for defense, but not one cent for tribute"—that is, for bribes—became a Federalist slogan. Congress created a department of the navy and appropriated money for 40 new warships. It increased the size of the tiny United States army from 3,500 to about 10,000 men. It officially suspended the treaty of alliance with France.

War seemed unavoidable. Public feeling against France was bitter. Children in the streets played games of French against Americans. Washington came out of retirement to command the army. Suddenly Adams, who had been elected president by such a narrow margin, became a national hero.

The Alien and Sedition Acts

War with France would certainly have been popular in 1798. President Adams, however, wished to avoid it. He was right to do so. France had the most powerful army in the world. Its commander, Napoleon Bonaparte, was a military genius. The French navy completely outclassed the American navy. Although three powerful new warships called frigates were being built, the largest American warships ready for action were tiny coast guard patrol boats with crews of only six men. French privateers waited outside American harbors and picked off merchant ships almost at will.

Nevertheless, many Federalist leaders, including Hamilton, hoped for war. War would give them an excuse to destroy what they called their "internal enemies." Jefferson's Democratic-Republicans had long been supporters of France and some of the radical ideas of the French Revolution. Would they not side with France if war broke out? It was time to crack down on "Demo*crats* and 'all other kinds of rats,' " these Federalists claimed.

Taking advantage of the war scare and the public anger over the XYZ Affair, the Federalists pushed several laws through Congress in the summer of 1798. These laws are known as the **Alien and Sedition Acts** because they were aimed at foreigners in the United States and at people who were supposedly trying to undermine the government in order to help France.

One of these laws increased from 5 to 14 years the length of time foreigners had to live in the United States before they could become citizens. Another gave the president the power to jail or order out of the country foreigners who he thought were "dangerous to the peace and safety of the United States."

Still more severe was the Sedition Act, which outlawed conspiracies against the government and attempts to start riots or uprisings. The act made it a crime for anyone to "write, print, utter, or publish" even merely "scandalous" statements critical of the government, of either house of Congress, or of the president. So much for the First Amendment!

The Sedition Act was an attempt to frighten the Democratic-Republicans into silence. In practice it made criticism of the Federalists a crime but not criticism of the Democratic-Republicans. It was against the law to "defame" the president but not the vice president.

Such an attack on freedom of speech and of the press was a threat to everything the American Revolution had sought to protect. In 1798 the American experiment in republican government was little more than 20 years old. Was it about to end in a new tyranny? 🔳

Return to the Preview & Review on page 254.

CHAPTER 7 REVIEW

1785   ESTABLISHING AMERICAN PRECEDENTS 1790

1789
Washington inaugurated
as president

★
French Revolution begins

★
Tariff Act of 1789

1791
Bill of Rights
adopted

★
Bank of U.S.
is chartered

1
K
b
a

Chapter Summary
Read the statements below. Choose one, and write a paragraph explaining its importance.
1. Washington took great care in each decision because he realized that as the first president he was setting precedents.
2. The Bill of Rights, the first ten amendments to the Constitution, protect natural rights.
3. Hamilton and Jefferson disagreed over the interpretation of the ''necessary and proper clause'' of the Constitution.
4. Americans at first cheered the French Revolution but remained uninvolved as it took a radical turn.
5. Settlers crossing the Appalachians into the Ohio Valley faced conflicts with the Indians until General Wayne's victory at Fallen Timbers.
6. The Jay and Pinckney Treaties were beneficial to the young nation because they kept it out of war.
7. In his farewell address, Washington stressed unity and neutrality.
8. The country developed a political system with two opposing parties, leading to the unusual results of the 1796 election.
9. The XYZ Affair created a sensation and led to the Alien and Sedition Acts.

Reviewing Chronological Order
Number your paper 1-5. Then study the time line above and place the following events in the order in which they happened by writing the first next to 1, the second next to 2, and so on.
1. Bill of Rights adopted
2. Genet comes to the United States
3. The XYZ Affair
4. Washington becomes the first president
5. The Battle of Fallen Timbers

Understanding Main Ideas
1. Why were Washington and other Americans concerned about the precedents the first president established?
2. Why did Hamilton want the national government to assume state debts and pay state and national debts at face value?
3. Why did Washington want to avoid going to war against Great Britain or aiding the French?
4. What were Washington's accomplishments as president?
5. How did the views of Jefferson and Hamilton contrast on the uses of government?
6. What actions did Congress take after the XYZ correspondence was published? How did ordinary Americans respond?

Thinking Critically
1. **Interpreting.** Explain the difference between natural rights and legal rights. Which of these are protected by the Bill of Rights?
2. **Contrasting.** Contrast the views of Hamilton and Jefferson as they applied the ''necessary and proper clause'' to the bank bill.
3. **Analyzing.** Explain the two main ideas expressed in Washington's Farewell Address.
4. **Seeing Relationships.** Why did political parties begin to form so soon after the Constitution was ratified?
5. **Evaluating.** According to the treaty of alliance with France, the United States was to join France in the war against Britain. Washington, however, urged neutrality and the country refused to join France. Was that the proper action? Explain your answer.

Writing About History
Imagine you are an eyewitness to one of the following: a tea party with President Washington, Washington's meeting with Citizen Genet, the Battle of Fallen Timbers, or the negotiation between American diplomats and secret agents X, Y, and Z. In a brief essay describe what you see and your thoughts and feelings. Use the information in Chapter 7 to help you develop your essay.

	1795					1800

| comes | **1794**
Battle of
Fallen Timbers | **1795**
Treaty of
Greenville | **1796**
Two-party
system develops | **1797**
XYZ Affair | **1798**
Alien and Sedition Acts passed | |

d States

★
Jay's Treaty

★
Pinckney's
Treaty

★
Adams elected president

ality
mation
ed

★
Whiskey Rebellion

★
Tennessee enters the Union

Practicing the Strategy

Review the strategy on page 258.

Separating Fact From Opinion. Number your paper 1–5. Then read the following list of statements. If you think the statement is a fact, write an *F* next to the number. If you think it is an opinion, write an *O*.

1. Washington was America's greatest president.
2. By the late 1780s 10,000 settlers were pouring into the Ohio Valley each year.
3. Most Americans disliked Jay's Treaty.
4. Genet was a charming, young gentleman.
5. By 1796 Washington could justly feel that he had set the United States well on its way.

Using Primary Sources

Washington presented his farewell address on September 17, 1796. In it he stated his recommendations for the nation's future course. Read the following excerpt from Washington's Farewell Address and answer the questions in the next column.

> *The great rule of conduct for us, in regard to foreign Nations, is, in extending our commercial relations, to have with them as little* Political *connection as possible. So far as we have already formed engagements, let them be fulfilled with perfect good faith. Here let us stop.*
>
> *Europe has a set of primary interests, which to us have none, or a very remote relation. Hence she must be engaged in frequent controversies, the causes of which are essentially foreign to our concerns.*
>
> *Our detached and distant situation invites and enables us to pursue a different course. . . . 'T is our true policy to steer clear of permanent alliances, with any portion of the foreign world.*

1. Why did Washington recommend America avoid foreign alliances?
2. What advantages might "detached and distant" political relations provide to the United States? What disadvantages might have resulted from the situation?
3. Do you think Washington's views on trade with foreign nations would be acceptable policy for the United States government to follow today? Why or why not? Support your opinion with at least two reasons.

Linking History & Geography

Geography, as you have learned, influences people's actions. For example, it helps determine how they make their living and how they get their goods to market. Review the information about the Whiskey Rebellion on page 252 and study the map on 186. Then explain how geographic factors contributed to the Whiskey Rebellion.

Enriching Your Study of History

1. **Individual Project.** Do research in your library to prepare a short report on the life of one of the following persons: Thomas Jefferson, James Madison, Alexander Hamilton, Aaron Burr, Anthony Wayne, John Adams, John Jay, Thomas Pinckney.
2. **Cooperative Project.** Research with your classmates the Battle of Fallen Timbers. Then use your historical imagination to prepare interviews with members of both armies—the Indian confederacy and the United States. Questions and answers should explain why each side fought, describe the battle itself, and explain the results and consequences of the battle. Your group should present its interviews to the class as television interviews.

UNIT TWO REVIEW

Summing Up and Predicting
Read the summary of the main ideas in Unit Two. Choose one statement, then write a paragraph predicting its outcome or effect in the future.
1. Vast distance and the need for self-sufficiency separated the colonists from Britain.
2. Objections to British policies led to the independence movement.
3. Shots fired at Lexington and Concord started the Revolutionary War.
4. The Declaration of Independence stated American principles of democratic government and listed colonial grievances against Britain.
5. American forces suffered early setbacks but eventually defeated the British.
6. The major task after the war was establishing government—state and national. The Articles of Confederation failed to deal with serious problems, prompting development of the United States Constitution.
7. As the first president, Washington established many precedents.
8. Americans cheered the spirit of the French Revolution, but it caused them problems.

Connecting Ideas
1. You know that Thomas Jefferson did not mention women in the Declaration of Independence. In what ways have women's rights been expanded today?
2. James Madison said, "In framing a system which we wish to last for ages, we should not lose sight of the changes which ages will produce." In your opinion, why has the Constitution lasted for more than 200 years? How does the Constitution provide for changes?
3. If you could repeal an amendment to the Constitution, which one would it be? Why? If you could add an amendment to the Constitution, what would it be?

Practicing Critical Thinking
1. **Drawing Conclusions.** As you know, the American Revolution helped inspire the French people to revolt. From what you have learned, how was the French Revolution different from the American Revolution?
2. **Synthesizing.** You are a delegate to the Constitutional Convention in 1787. What do you think is the most serious flaw in the Articles of Confederation? How is it being corrected by the new Constitution? Cite the article and section of the Constitution that will correct this flaw.
3. **Evaluating.** You are a member of the ratifying convention for Rhode Island, the only state that has not yet ratified the Constitution. Write the speech that you would deliver to persuade your fellow members to ratify.

Cooperative Learning
1. Prepare a notebook or bulletin board display on the United States government today. Members of your group should collect newspaper and magazine clippings dealing with the activities of each branch of government.
2. Together with nine classmates, analyze the Bill of Rights. Have each member of your group study one amendment. Prepare a report, skit, or other presentation that explains the protections provided by that amendment. Use current examples whenever possible.
3. With several classmates, prepare and present a skit illustrating a key scene from the Revolutionary War, Constitutional Convention, or XYZ Affair. Review Unit Two to be sure you present accurate points of view.

Reading in Depth
Borden, Morton. *George Washington.* Englewood Cliffs, NJ: Prentice-Hall. Traces Washington's life as general and president.

Bowen, Catherine Drinker. *Miracle at Philadelphia.* Boston: Atlantic Monthly Press. Presents a dramatic account of the debates, quarrels, and compromises that resulted in the United States Constitution.

Chidsey, Donald Barr. *Valley Forge.* New York: Crown. Tells the gripping story of the Continental army at Valley Forge in the winter of 1777.

Davis, Burke. *Black Heroes of the American Revolution.* San Diego: Harcourt Brace Jovanovich. Recounts the many contributions of African Americans to the independence movement.

———. *Three for the Revolution.* San Diego: Harcourt Brace Jovanovich. Contains information about Patrick Henry, George Washington, and Thomas Jefferson.

Williams, Selma R. *Demeter's Daughter: The Women Who Founded America, 1587–1787.* New York: Antheneum. Describes the exploits of both famous and everyday women in the founding of America.

The Thomas Gilcrease Institute of American History and Art, Tulsa, Oklahoma
"Indian Village" by Jules Tavernier

A GROWING AMERICA

UNIT 3

I n Unit 3 you will learn how the United States gained vast territories and took part in the Industrial Revolution. Here are some main points to keep in mind as you read the unit.

• The Kentucky and Virginia Resolutions raised the issues of nullification and states' rights.

• The Louisiana Purchase and the Transcontinental Treaty more than doubled the area of the United States.

• Native Americans of the Ohio Valley resisted the wave of settlers from the east but were finally overwhelmed.

• The War of 1812 began after British ships interfered with American trade and impressed American seamen.

• Revolutions in Latin America prompted the Monroe Doctrine.

• The growth of industry, transportation, and immigration rapidly changed American society in the early 1800s.

The Age of Jefferson

In his inaugural address in 1801, Thomas Jefferson called the United States "the world's best hope." Since the people *were* the government, they were eager to protect and defend it. America's leaders realized this was a rare, indeed unique, form of government. Jefferson's greatest accomplishment was the purchase from France of the Louisiana Territory for $15 million. This chapter describes the expedition of Lewis and Clark to explore the Louisiana Purchase and concludes with troubles on the high seas with Britain. Would the young nation find itself at war again?

Preview & Review

Use these questions to guide your reading. Answer the questions after completing Section 1.
Understanding Issues, Events, & Ideas. Discuss reasons for the attacks on the Sedition Act, using the following words: First Amendment, unconstitutional, Kentucky and Virginia Resolutions, nullify, doctrine of nullification, repeal, states' rights, Convention of 1800, dictator, Twelfth Amendment.
1. What was the political purpose of the Sedition Act?
2. What was the historical importance of the Kentucky and Virginia Resolutions?
3. Why did the election of 1800 and the growth of political parties lead to the Twelfth Amendment to the Constitution?

Thinking Critically. 1. You are to fill in for Charles Holt while he is in jail for sedition. Write an editorial defending Holt, using the First Amendment to support your view. 2. Do you agree that Adams was heroic in reestablishing negotiations with the French? Why or why not?

1. THE FALL OF THE FEDERALISTS

Attacks on the Sedition Act

In 1798 the Federalists pushed the Sedition Act through Congress. Although the law was passed because of the war scare abroad with France, its real motives had to do with politics at home. The Sedition Act made it a crime to criticize the president, who was a Federalist, but not a crime to criticize the vice president, who was a Democratic-Republican. In that sense the act was purely political.

Only about ten people were convicted of violating the Sedition Act. Not one of these was accused of plotting against the government. All the convictions were for *criticizing* the government or some important Federalist leader. Charles Holt, a newspaper editor, published an article calling the United States army "a band of disorganized . . . ruffians, a burden, a pest, and a terror to the citizens." For this and similar statements he was sentenced to six months in jail and fined $200. James Callender, another editor, claimed that President Adams was "repulsive," a "fool," and "the blasted tyrant of America." His punishment was nine months in jail and a $200 fine.

Such statements were untrue and in very bad taste. Still, the right to make them was protected by the **First Amendment** of the Constitution, which guarantees freedom of speech and of the press. Moreover, equally unfair criticisms of Jeffersonian leaders were made by Federalist editors. These were ignored by the government.

The Granger Collection, New York

A Federalist editor strikes phrases from America's great documents in this 1799 political cartoon. 'Peter Porcupine' says, "I hate this country and will sow the seeds of discord in it." Liberty weeps at the tomb of Benjamin Franklin. At right the devil himself whispers, "Let us destroy this idol liberty," while the British lion purrs, "Go on, dear Peter, my friend, and I will reward you." How do you think those who favored the Sedition Act felt about this cartoon?

Vice President Jefferson reacted swiftly to the obvious political bias of the Sedition Act against his party. Above all, he believed that Congress did not have the power under the Constitution to pass any of the Alien and Sedition Acts. They were **unconstitutional,** in his opinion. That is, they violated the intent of the framers of the Constitution. He wrote out a series of statements called *resolutions* which explained his reasoning. A friend of his introduced these resolutions at a session of the legislature of the new state of Kentucky, where the Jeffersonians had a large majority. The legislature voted to approve them in November 1798.

At the time the public did not know that Jefferson had written the resolutions. They were called the *Kentucky Resolutions*. About a month later a similar set of resolutions was passed by the Virginia legislature. These were written by James Madison.

The **Kentucky and Virginia Resolutions** did not claim that the rights of free speech and free press had no limits. The issue was whether the federal government had the power to limit them. Jefferson and Madison argued that because of the First Amendment, it could not. Only the state legislatures could restrict these rights.

When Congress goes beyond its legal powers, what can be done? Jefferson had a simple answer. The Constitution, he wrote, was a contract. It was an agreement made by separate states. It gave certain powers to the federal government created by the states. What if Congress broke the contract by passing a law that the Constitution did not give it the power to pass? Jefferson argued that any state could **nullify,** or cancel, the law. The law would no longer exist within that state. Each state, said Jefferson, "had an equal right to judge for itself" whether or not a law of Congress was constitutional.

Bowdoin College Museum of Art

James Madison was author of the Virginia Resolutions. Gilbert Stuart painted Madison in the early 1800s.

The Fall of the Federalists   267

If put into practice, this **doctrine of nullification** would have meant the end of the United States as one nation. If any state could refuse to obey a law of Congress, the national government would soon collapse. Even the friendly Kentucky legislature found the idea of nullification too radical. It changed that resolution. Instead it urged Congress to **repeal,** or revoke, the unconstitutional law. The Virginia Resolutions took the same position.

The Kentucky and Virginia Resolutions had no practical effects. The other states did not respond favorably to them. Congress did not repeal the Alien and Sedition Acts. The resolutions are important, however, because they put forth an argument about **states' rights** that reappears many times in the story of America, most notably over the issue of slavery.

The Heroism of John Adams

The Federalists, of course, did not think that the Alien and Sedition Acts were unconstitutional. President John Adams had special reason for believing them both legal and desirable. The coarse personal attacks of Democratic-Republican editors like James Callender made him very angry. He was understandably delighted to see such people punished.

This engraving shows Georgetown, the Potomac River, and dimly in the distance the Federal City planned by Pierre Charles L'Enfant. Washington, D.C. was but a tiny village when this view was made in 1801.

Library of Congress

Adams also wanted to be reelected president in 1800. He knew that his strong stand against France at the time of the XYZ Affair had made him very popular. The people saw him as the defender of the nation's honor and security during a national crisis. The danger of war with France was a political advantage for him. If war actually broke out, he would almost certainly be reelected.

John Adams, however, was too honest and too patriotic to put personal gain ahead of duty. He learned that the French foreign minister, Talleyrand, was eager to repair the damage caused by the XYZ Affair. Adams decided to try again to solve the nation's difficulties with France by negotiation. Late in 1799 he sent three new commissioners to Paris.

This made Hamilton and his Federalist supporters furious. They wanted the conflict between America and France to continue. But they could not prevent Adams from acting.

The American commissioners were greeted "with a friendly dignity." After months of discussion the diplomats signed a treaty known as the **Convention of 1800.** Peace was restored between the two nations. France agreed to release the United States from its obligations under the treaty of alliance of 1778. Little else was gained, for the French would not agree to pay for the damages their warships and privateers had done to American vessels and their cargoes.

On October 4, 1800, Napoleon Bonaparte, who was now **dictator,** or absolute ruler, of France, gave an enormous party for the American commissioners. It took place at his brother's estate outside Paris. There were 180 guests, including all the high officials of the French government. A magnificent meal was eaten. Champagne toasts were drunk to "perpetual peace," to "freedom of the seas," and to President John Adams. Later there were fireworks and a concert.

The Election of 1800

President Adams had stopped the threat of war with France. He was quite rightly proud of what he had done. Many years later he said that the treaty was his greatest achievement—"the most splendid diamond in my crown" was the way he put it. Peace ended the crisis that had led to passage of the Alien and Sedition Acts. Equally important, it ended the threat to democracy these laws posed. It also lessened the fear of many Americans that the Jeffersonians preferred France to their own country. This helped Jefferson in his campaign for the presidency in 1800.

The Democratic-Republican party again nominated Jefferson for president and Aaron Burr for vice president. The Federalists ran Adams for president and Charles C. Pinckney of XYZ fame for vice president. In the campaign the Jeffersonians were united, the Federalists badly divided. Hamilton disliked Adams so much that he

Thomas Jefferson, top, and Aaron Burr, below, were the Democratic–Republican candidates for president and vice president in 1800. Jefferson was painted by Rembrandt Peale about the year of the election and Burr was painted by John Vanderlyn in 1809. Who were their Federalist opponents?

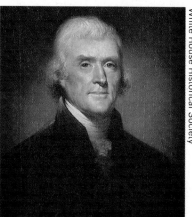

White House Historical Society

New-York Historical Society

The Fall of the Federalists   269

Jefferson was the first president to be inaugurated in the new capital city, which was named after George Washington, who had died in 1799. The land on which Washington was built, which is called the District of Columbia, had been chosen by President Washington himself. He selected a site a few miles down the Potomac River from his plantation, Mount Vernon. The land was surveyed by two former clockmakers, Andrew Ellicott and his assistant Benjamin Banneker, who was probably the first black civil servant employed by the federal government.

Washington also selected the designer of the capital, Pierre Charles L'Enfant, a French-born engineer who had come to America to serve in the Revolutionary Army. L'Enfant had remodeled Federal Hall, the first home of Congress, in New York City. Washington liked his work and asked him to design the permanent capital. It was a remarkable opportunity, and L'Enfant did a brilliant job.

L'Enfant's plan provided for broad avenues reaching out like spokes in a wheel from two main centers where the president and Congress would be located. The plan left generous room for parks as well. It has been widely regarded as one of the finest examples of city planning in the world.

In 1801, however, Washington was a tiny village. Only one

The New York Public Library

Benjamin Banneker, a clockmaker and scientist, assisted Andrew Endicott in surveying the District of Columbia.

wing of the Capitol building had been erected. The Treasury Department building and the still-unfinished president's mansion

published a pamphlet on "The Public Conduct and Character of John Adams," in which he described Adams as jealous, vain, and stubborn. According to Hamilton, John Adams was totally unfit to be president.

Once again Hamilton tried to manage the votes of the Federalist electors in order to make the Federalist candidate for vice president get more votes than Adams. Again this trick failed. The Democratic-

LEARNING FROM GRAPHS.
These charts show the electoral vote in the 1800 and 1804 presidential elections. According to the graphs, how had the balance of political power shifted by 1804?

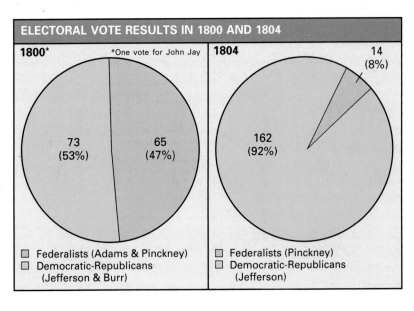

ELECTORAL VOTE RESULTS IN 1800 AND 1804

1800*   *One vote for John Jay

73 (53%)   65 (47%)

☐ Federalists (Adams & Pinckney)
☐ Democratic-Republicans (Jefferson & Burr)

1804   14 (8%)

162 (92%)

☐ Federalists (Pinckney)
☐ Democratic-Republicans (Jefferson)

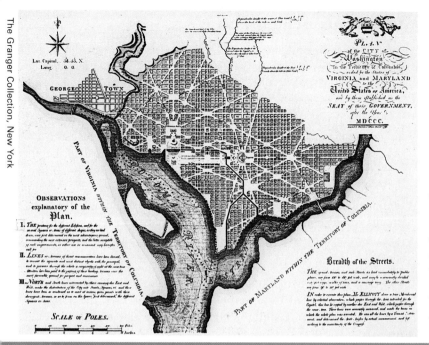

The Granger Collection, New York

were the only other solidly con-structed buildings. There were a few clusters of houses and shops. The streets were un-paved, dusty in dry weather, an-kle-deep in mud after every rain. Living was uncomfortable. Mem-bers of Congress slept and ate in rough hotels called boarding houses. A room and three meals a day in one of these places cost about $15 a week. There was lit-tle to do after sessions of Con-gress. Most senators and rep-resentatives hurried back to their home districts as soon as Congress adjourned. In summer the village was almost deserted. President Jefferson flatly re-fused to stay there in July and August because of the heat and humidity.

Republican party won the election. Jefferson received 73 electoral votes, Adams only 65.

Because the Democratic-Republicans were well organized, all their electors had voted for Burr as well as Jefferson. He, too, had 73 electoral votes! The electors intended, of course, that Burr be vice president. Nevertheless, the tie meant that the House of Rep-resentatives would have to choose between them. Under the Con-stitution each state, no matter how many representatives it had, would have one vote. Since there were 16 states, 9 were needed for a majority. The Democratic-Republicans controlled 8 states. The Federalists had 6, and 2 were divided evenly. The Federalists voted for Burr, partly to make trouble for the opposition, partly because they thought Burr less radical than Jefferson. Thus, on the first ballot Jefferson got 8 votes and Burr 6. The votes of the equally divided states cancelled each other. For an entire week all the delegates held firm. They voted 35 times without anyone changing his vote. Finally, Federalist James A. Bayard of Delaware, that small state's only representative, changed to Jefferson. That gave Jefferson the presi-dency, 9 states to 6. Burr became vice president.

Everyone now realized that the development of well-organized political parties meant tie votes between members of the same party would become common. The **Twelfth Amendment** was added to the Constitution. Thereafter the electors voted separately for president and vice president. 🗐

Return to the Preview & Review on page 266.

The Fall of the Federalists 271

2. JEFFERSON AS PRESIDENT

Use these questions to guide your reading. Answer the questions after completing Section 2.

Understanding Issues, Events, & Ideas. Use the following words to discuss Jefferson's presidency: *Marbury v. Madison,* Barbary pirate, right of deposit, Louisiana Purchase, secession.

1. What did Jefferson mean by "We are all Republicans—we are all Federalists"?
2. What was established by John Marshall's ruling in *Marbury v. Madison?*
3. Why was the United States at war with the Barbary States?
4. Why were New England Federalists upset over the Louisiana Purchase? What was their plan? How was Vice President Burr involved?

Thinking Critically. 1. You are a farmer in the Ohio River valley in 1802. Write a letter to President Jefferson that explains how the loss of the right of deposit has affected you and your fellow farmers. **2.** In your opinion, did Jefferson take his presidential powers too far? Explain your answer.

Jefferson's Inaugural Address

Jefferson's inaugural address, delivered in the Senate chamber of the Capitol on March 4, 1801, was a fitting beginning for the new city and his administration. Jefferson believed that his election was a kind of second American Revolution that had checked the Federalists' attempt to make the United States into a monarchy. The speech, however, showed that he intended to make few changes. The tone was similar to that of Washington's Farewell Address. Like that speech, its main themes were unity at home and neutrality abroad.

Majority rule was the first principle of democracy, Jefferson reminded his audience. But minorities also have rights and "to violate [them] would be oppression." His main point was that political differences could be smoothed over by discussion and compromise. He said:

66 Every difference of opinion is not a difference of principle. We have called by different names brethren of the same principle. We are all Republicans—we are all Federalists. 99

With this clever reference to the political parties, he was reminding people that everyone wanted America to be a *republic* rather than a monarchy, and also that everyone believed in a *federal* system, with power divided between the central government and the states.

As for the rest of the world, Jefferson tried to show that he did not intend to make the United States dependent on France, as the Federalists had claimed during the campaign. His policy would be "honest friendship for all nations, entangling alliances with none."

The United States Capitol with its handsome proportions was designed by a Quaker architect and doctor, William Thorton. He presented this drawing to President Washington in 1793. The building features a copper dome. Jefferson said that it "captivated the eyes and judgment of all."

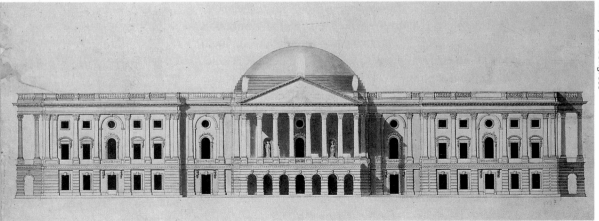

Library of Congress

He also spoke with deep feeling about American democratic ideals. The United States, he said, was "the world's best hope." It had "the strongest government on earth" because the people felt that they were part of the government. They were therefore eager to protect and defend it.

Jefferson's speech promised a moderate and reasonable program. The Alien and Sedition Acts were either repealed or allowed to expire. By 1802 all were gone. Jefferson got Congress to repeal the Whiskey Tax too. And he canceled the Federalists' program for expanding the army and navy. On the other hand, he continued Hamilton's policy of paying off the national debt and made no effort to do away with the Bank of the United States.

The author of the Declaration of Independence had no taste for pomp and ceremony in the White House. He sometimes wore a frayed coat and carpet slippers to greet the representatives of foreign nations who presented themselves in powdered wigs, bemedaled coats, and silver-buckled shoes. Plain citizens and foreign diplomats were each seen in their turn, for Jefferson told them all, "Nobody shall be above you, nor you above anybody."

Point of View

At a dinner honoring American winners of the Nobel Prize, the president made this toast, some 160 years after Jefferson's time in office.

"This is the most extraordinary collection of talent . . . that has been gathered together at the White House—with the possible exception of when Thomas Jefferson dined alone."
John F. Kennedy, 1962

Jefferson and the Judiciary

The only serious trouble Jefferson encountered in his first term involved the courts. He believed that judges must be independent. But he feared what he called their "habit of going out of the question before them, to throw an anchor ahead, and grapple further hold for future advances of power."

Jefferson, like many presidents, had to contend with a Supreme Court whose members had been appointed by his political opponents. The chief justice, John Marshall, whom Jefferson particularly disliked, was appointed by John Adams. Adams also appointed numerous other judges unfriendly to the Jeffersonians. Several of these appointees were known as "midnight justices" because Adams had signed the commissions appointing them during the final hours of his presidency.

In the confusion of Adams' last hours the commissions of a number of justices of the peace for the new District of Columbia were not distributed. When Jefferson found them, he refused to let them be released to the appointees. This led William Marbury, one of Adams' appointees, to ask the Supreme Court to order the secretary of state, James Madison, to issue the commissions. The case of **Marbury v. Madison** (1803) provided a great test for the court and Chief Justice Marshall. Marshall ruled against Marbury. The law allowing Marbury to sue, he announced, was not authorized by the Constitution. Thus, Jefferson had his way. But this case established the power of the Supreme Court to declare an act of Congress unconstitutional, which was much more important.

National Portrait Gallery

John Marshall was painted by Henry Inman in 1781. Why is Marshall's name so often linked to Constitutional law?

STRATEGIES FOR SUCCESS

INTERPRETING A PHYSICAL MAP

A *physical map* is a special-purpose map that shows the natural landscape, or *topography,* of an area. It shows the location and extent of physical features such as rivers and mountain chains. It also illustrates the relative locations of various features. Because elevation, access to water, and the "the lay of the land" often influence human activities, a physical map can help you better understand how the history of an area unfolded.

How to Understand a Physical Map

To understand a physical map, follow these guidelines.

1 **Use basic map reading skills.** Review the strategy on page 32. Study the title, key, scale, and grid for important information.

2. **Note the colors used to show elevation.** The distance above or below sea level is *elevation.* Look at the colors on the map to get a "feel" for the landscape. Check the elevation key to associate colors to elevations. Note also that special shading called "cartographic art" highlights mountain and valley areas.

3. **Study shapes.** Look closely at the shapes of the features shown on the map—how steep a mountain range is and how far it stretches, how wide and long a river is.

4. **Read the labels.** Learn the names of the key features.

5. **Note relative locations.** *Relative location* is the position of a feature in relation to other features. Note where each major feature appears in relation to other major features. Use this information to draw conclusions about the effect of the topography on movement, settlement patterns, and economic activity.

Applying the Strategy

Study the physical map to the right. It shows the topography of the lands of the eastern seaboard of the United States. Note that the Appalachian Mountains form a wall to the west of the region. What effect did they have on settlement? Note also that the area is drained by several rivers. What are the major ones? How did they affect settlement? Along which did important cities begin to grow? How did rivers affect farming and transportation for the early settlers? Note the physical features shown on the map of the Louisiana Purchase on page 285.

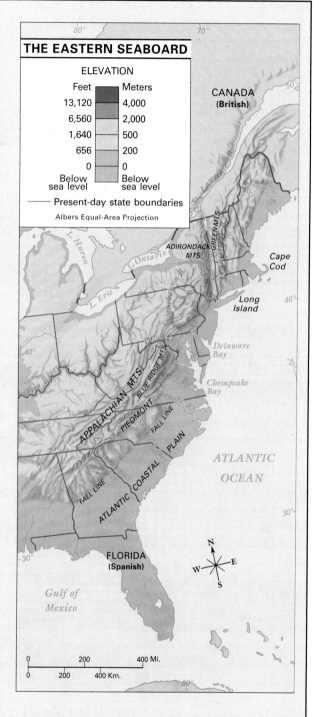

THE EASTERN SEABOARD

ELEVATION

Feet		Meters
13,120		4,000
6,560		2,000
1,640		500
656		200
0		0
Below sea level		Below sea level

—— Present-day state boundaries

Albers Equal-Area Projection

For independent practice, see Practicing the Strategy on pages 292–93.

The Barbary Pirates

Aside from his problems with the courts, Jefferson's first term was a parade of triumphs. Despite cutbacks he had made in the navy in order to save money, he managed to fight a small war with the **Barbary pirates.**

For decades the North African Arab states of Morocco, Algiers, Tunis, and Tripoli had made a business of piracy. They seized ships, crews, and passengers all over the Mediterranean Sea and held them for ransom. European countries found it simpler and cheaper to pay annual protection money called tribute than to crush the pirates. Under Washington and Adams, the United States had paid this tribute as well. However, the practice went against Jefferson's grain. "When this idea comes across my mind," he said, "my faculties are absolutely suspended between indignation and impatience." So when the pasha of Tripoli tried to increase the tribute, Jefferson refused to pay. Tripoli then declared war in May 1801, and Jefferson sent a naval squadron to the Mediterranean.

In the words of one historian, the action was "halfhearted and ill-starred." The pirates were not overwhelmed. The war dragged on for several years. In 1804 Lieutenant Stephen Decatur, who had captured two pirate ships, performed one of the boldest acts of the war. He and ten sailors secretly slipped into Tripoli harbor and set fire to the *Philadelphia,* an American warship that had been captured by the pirates. Their bravery is remembered in the famous phrase of the *Marine's Hymn:* "To the shores of Tripoli."

The navy then blockaded Tripoli harbor and forced the pasha to

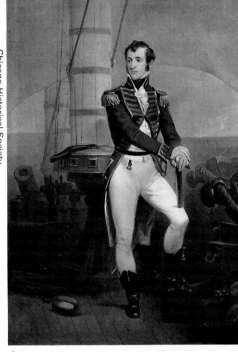

Chicago Historical Society

Stephen Decatur, after forcing Algiers to sign a peace treaty, stands on the deck of his man-of-war. Alonzo Chappel painted this portrait. Lord Nelson, England's greatest naval hero, called Decatur's secret burning of the Philadelphia *"the most bold and daring act of the age." Decatur was killed in a duel in 1820.*

THE BARBARY STATES

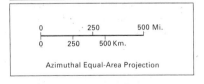

LEARNING FROM MAPS. *Although the Barbary states were tiny and far from the United States, they caused problems. How did their location make it possible for them to harm United States trade?*

Jefferson as President   275

"Decatur at Tripoli," by W. A. Martin, also celebrates the triumph of the American hero. Finally through Decatur's efforts the pasha of Tripoli and the rulers of Algeria and Tunisia left American vessels unharmed.

U.S. Naval Academy Museum

stop attacking American ships. The United States continued to pay tribute until 1815, but the firm action of the American government strengthened its reputation.

The Louisiana Purchase

Jefferson's most important accomplishment was adding a huge new western region to the nation. This came about in a most unexpected manner. The settlers who crossed over the mountains into Kentucky, Tennessee, and the lands north of the Ohio River cleared the land and planted crops. As the country developed, traffic on the Mississippi River increased rapidly. Frontier farmers floated their wheat, lumber, tobacco, and other produce down the river on log rafts. These goods had to be stored in warehouses and on docks in New Orleans while waiting to be reshipped to East Coast ports or to Europe on oceangoing vessels. As we have seen, Pinckney's Treaty of 1795 with Spain guaranteed Americans what was called the **right of deposit** at New Orleans. Without the right of deposit, western settlers could not get their produce to market.

All went well until 1800, when Spain, under pressure from the powerful Napoleon Bonaparte, agreed to give New Orleans and the rest of the land called Louisiana back to France. For more than a year Spain continued to govern New Orleans. But France was obviously preparing to take over the city as part of a general expansion of its overseas empire. Napoleon planned to use Louisiana as a breadbasket to feed the French West Indian sugar islands. France's most important island colony, Santo Domingo, had broken away during the French Revolution. Slaves led by Toussaint L'Ouverture

The Granger Collection, New York

Toussaint L'Ouverture astride his horse led so strong an uprising in Santo Domingo that it took 20,000 of Napoleon's French soldiers to quiet the rebellion. The French later seized him and he died a year later. Why was Napoleon determined to crush L'Ouverture's rebellion?

took control of the island. In 1801 Napoleon had sent 20,000 soldiers to put down the rebellion.

Jefferson had long been an admirer of France and of French civilization. He disliked the English. Yet the mere thought of France controlling New Orleans made him willing to consider an alliance with Great Britain against France. If France canceled the right of deposit, he wrote to his diplomatic representative in Paris, Robert R. Livingston, we must "marry ourselves to the British fleet."

Spain was a weak nation. It could not seriously threaten American interests. If Spain closed New Orleans to Americans, the city could probably be captured by a force of arms. With a great military power such as France in control, the result might be very different. To solve the problem, Jefferson instructed Livingston to offer to buy the city of New Orleans from France.

Livingston spent the greater part of 1802 trying to arrange a deal. Talleyrand, who was still in charge of French foreign relations, looked down his nose at him. He would not even tell Livingston whether or not Spain had also given Florida to France. Napoleon seemed to be the only person able to make decisions, and he was hard to reach. "He seldom asks advice," Livingston complained in a letter to James Madison, the secretary of state. "His ministers are mere clerks."

Louisiana State Museum

"Raising the Flag at New Orleans" shows the Stars and Stripes replacing the French tricolor after the Louisiana Purchase. The scene is the Vieux Carré (old square), now Jackson Square. In the background are the landmark St. Louis Cathedral built in 1795, and the Cabildo, the government headquarters built in 1794. Fire recently ravaged the third floor of the Cabildo but its contents were saved. Why was New Orleans so important to the United States?

In October 1802 Spain canceled the American right of deposit at New Orleans. The situation was at once critical. Much alarmed, Jefferson sent a trusted adviser, James Monroe, to join Livingston in France. He authorized Monroe to offer Napoleon $10 million for New Orleans. Meanwhile, the French expedition to Santo Domingo had been wasted by yellow fever and jungle warfare.

Now Napoleon needed money. Soon he planned to resume his long war with England. The French possessions in America would then be easy targets for Britain's powerful navy. Early in 1803 he ordered Talleyrand to offer to sell New Orleans and all the rest of Louisiana to the United States. The Americans quickly took the offer.

When Napoleon offered to sell Louisiana, he did not simply mean what is now the state of Louisiana. Rather he meant all the land between the Mississippi River and the Rocky Mountains! When Talleyrand, the French foreign minister, passed this news on to Robert Livingston, the American negotiator was dumbfounded. But he recovered swiftly. He offered $5 million for the territory. Not enough, said Talleyrand. He urged Livingston to think the matter over.

The very next day James Monroe arrived in Paris to represent President Jefferson. After considerable discussion he and Livingston decided to offer $15 million. If Jefferson thought $10 million a fair price for New Orleans, surely $15 million was not too much to pay for that city and the entire western half of the Mississippi Valley. Talleyrand accepted the offer.

This **Louisiana Purchase** was one of the greatest real estate bargains in history. When the Americans asked Talleyrand about the exact boundaries of Louisiana, he could not tell them. No one knew. "You have made a noble bargain for yourselves," Talleyrand said. "I suppose you will make the most of it."

Hamilton and Burr

Adding all this new territory to the United States alarmed many of the leaders of the Federalist party. Jefferson was popular with farmers and with western settlers in general. Federalist strength was greatest in New England and among merchants and other city residents. When people began to settle Louisiana, and new states were formed beyond the Mississippi, the power and influence of the Federalists in Congress seemed sure to decline.

A group of angry Federalists in the New England states, led by Timothy Pickering, a former secretary of state, began to scheme to withdraw their states from the Union. Such a withdrawal, the technical name for which is **secession,** would be more likely to succeed if New York joined the movement. Then a strong northeastern confederacy could be formed. Pickering and his friends therefore tried to persuade Vice President Aaron Burr of New York to join them.

Burr did not enjoy being vice president. He had decided to seek

The Granger Collection, New York

With steady aim Aaron Burr has just fired the fatal shot in his duel with Alexander Hamilton, who had fired his pistol into the air. What events led to this duel?

election as governor of New York. When he was approached by the Federalists, he did not agree to join the plot, but he did not reject the idea either. However, he was defeated in the New York election, which took place in April 1804. Without the support of New York, the secession scheme had to be abandoned.

During his campaign for governor, Burr had become very angry with Alexander Hamilton, who had criticized him in a most insulting manner. Hamilton had strongly opposed the idea of secession. He disliked Burr even more than he disliked Jefferson. After Burr had lost the election, Hamilton continued to make insulting remarks about him. Finally Burr challenged Hamilton to a duel.

Dueling was against the law in New York and in many other states. Hamilton had performed bravely during the Revolutionary War. Therefore no one could accuse him of cowardice. Like many Americans of his day, Hamilton believed that a challenge to duel could not honorably be refused. He accepted. On July 11, 1804, the two men met secretly in New Jersey, across the Hudson River from New York City. At the signal to fire, Hamilton discharged his pistol into the air. Burr aimed his gun carefully. Hamilton fell. The bullet had passed through his liver and come to rest against his backbone. Nothing could be done. The next morning, he died.

In a way, this senseless tragedy marked the decline of the Federalist party that Hamilton had created. The Louisiana Purchase was popular nearly everywhere. Jefferson was easily reelected president in 1804. Four years later his friend and adviser, James Madison, became president. Madison served two terms, and then another of Jefferson's friends, James Monroe, was president for eight more years. 🖅

Return to the Preview & Review on page 272.

Jefferson as President 279

Use these questions to guide your reading. Answer the questions after completing Section 3.
Understanding Issues, Events, & Ideas. Describe the Lewis and Clark expedition, using the following words: Corps of Discovery, continental divide.

1. What kinds of instructions were Lewis and Clark given for their expedition?
2. What was Sacagawea's surprise discovery when the Lewis and Clark Expedition met the Shoshone Indians?
3. How did Captain Lewis maintain harmony? Why was such harmony unusual?
4. What were some achievements of Lewis and Clark?
5. On what explorations did Pike travel?

Thinking Critically. 1. You are a soldier on the Lewis and Clark Expedition. Write a diary entry describing your visit to the Shoshone camp. 2. What is a modern voyage of discovery that you would consider to be as great as that of Lewis and Clark? Why?

3. THE LOUISIANA TERRITORY

The Lewis and Clark Expedition

President Jefferson began promptly to plan for the development of the Louisiana Territory. In fact, he first asked Congress for money to explore the region even before Spain had returned it to France. Congress supplied him with $2,500. He then appointed his private secretary, a young ex-soldier named Meriwether Lewis, to head the expedition. According to Jefferson, Lewis was brave, careful, and "habituated to the woods."

Lewis persuaded another soldier, William Clark, to become co-leader of the expedition. The two had met while both were fighting under General Anthony Wayne against the Indian confederacy in the Ohio Valley. These two experienced outdoorsmen made an excellent team.

Jefferson gave the explorers very detailed instructions. These instructions reflected his own interests, which were as varied as Benjamin Franklin's. Besides describing and mapping the country, Lewis and Clark were to keep careful records of its climate—the temperature, the number of rainy days, wind directions, and so on. They were to locate and map the course of all rivers in order to find "the most direct . . . water connection across this continent." In addition, Jefferson ordered them to take note of soil conditions and to look for traces of valuable minerals. They were to collect plant and animal specimens and even to bring back the bones of any "rare or extinct" animals they could find.

Jefferson was particularly interested in the many American Indian cultures. As a young man he had been one of the first people to find and excavate a settlement of the ancient civilization of the Mound Builders. He instructed Lewis and Clark to gather all sorts of information about the western Indians. He wanted to know about their languages, their clothing, what they ate, how they lived, their diseases. He gave Lewis and Clark a list of basic English words and told them to take note of the corresponding words in the languages of the Indians they met.

Lewis and Clark prepared for their journey carefully. They consulted with leading scientists. They gathered the necessary equipment, such as guns, warm clothing, gifts for Indians, and medicines. They even secured navigational instruments so that they could map the country accurately.

They chose with equal care the members of what they called their **Corps of Discovery.** They employed a half-French, half-Indian interpreter who was skilled in the sign language used by Indians of different tribes to communicate with one another. One member was an expert at repairing guns, another a carpenter. Twenty-one members of the Corps were army men. The secretary of war had authorized Lewis to "detach" from their military duties any volunteers he wanted. Only strong men used to living in the woods were chosen, for as Lewis said, hard work was "a very essential part of the services required of the party." The group finally chosen consisted of 45 people. One of these, an enormously strong man named York, became the first person of African descent to cross the continent. He was a slave owned by William Clark.

Both, Independence National Historical Park

Westward to the Pacific

On May 14, 1804, the explorers set out from their base at the junction of the Mississippi and Missouri Rivers. Up the Missouri they went. They traveled in three boats, the largest a 55-foot (about 17-meter) keelboat manned by 22 oarsmen. Their first objective was the "mountains of rock that rise up in the West."

By August they had reached what is now Council Bluffs, Iowa. There they had their first meeting with Indians belonging to the tribes of the Great Plains. Lewis and Clark put up the United States flag, which at the time had 17 stars. Through an interpreter Lewis told the Plains Indians that "the great Chief of the seventeen nations of America" wanted to live in peace and was eager to trade with them for their furs. He then gave out gifts and left them an American flag, but Jefferson's hopes for peace were doomed to disappointment.

By October the explorers were deep in the northern plains. Cold weather was fast approaching. They built Fort Mandan, and in this snug, easily defended post they passed a long, bitterly cold winter.

When spring came, Lewis and Clark shipped the many boxes of plants, Indian craft objects, and animal bones and skins that they had collected back to St. Louis in the keelboat. Everything was carefully labeled. Then they pushed on. A Canadian, Toussaint Charbonneau, accompanied them as an interpreter, as did Sacagawea (Bird Woman), a Shoshone Indian married to Charbonneau.

Sacagawea became a very important member of the party. High in the Rockies, near the present-day border of Montana and Idaho, the expedition met up with the Shoshone. Lewis had pushed ahead with Charbonneau and the guide who knew Indian sign language. Most Indians of the region were very wary and difficult to find, but the explorers came upon three Shoshone women. After giving them gifts, they persuaded these Shoshone to lead them to their camp. There they found 60 warriors on horseback. The Shoshone people greeted the explorers in friendly fashion, giving them food and smoking a ceremonial pipe of peace. When Sacagawea and the rest of the party reached the Shoshone camp, she discovered to everyone's delight that the chief was her brother!

The Shoshone sold Lewis and Clark 29 horses for the trip across North America's **continental divide,** the ridge of the Rocky Mountains that separates the streams that flow east into the Mississippi Valley

Some names in history—Lewis and Clark among them—seem forever paired. James Meriwether Lewis is at the top, William Clark is below. Both were painted by Charles Willson Peale. Lewis was Jefferson's secretary, an ex-soldier. Clark was also a soldier. As you read on, decide whether this team was well chosen.

from those that flow west to the Pacific Ocean. Equally important, one of the warriors, whom the explorers called Toby, guided them through the Bitterroot Mountains. Without Toby's help they might have become hopelessly lost in the rugged High Plateau country.

Lewis and Clark were the first outsiders to describe the Shoshone people and many of the other Indians of the mountain area. They obtained more horses from a tribe called the Flatheads. Eventually they reached the great Columbia River. In November 1805, having floated down the Columbia in dugout canoes carved from the trunks of great ponderosa pine trees, they reached the Pacific.

They settled for the winter near the mouth of the Columbia River. There they built Fort Clatsop, named after the local Indians. The fort was 50 feet (15 meters) square. It consisted of two rows of huts made of pine logs facing each other across a courtyard. During the rainy winter months when food was scarce, the men ate a good deal of dog meat and whale fat, called blubber. According to Captain Lewis, the men became "extremely fond" of dog meat. "For my own part," Lewis added, "I think it is an agreeable food and would prefer it vastly to lean venison or elk."

After a long, rainy winter the explorers began the trip back. They had been gone nearly two years. Most people, even President Jefferson, had lost hope of their return. The group reached St. Louis late in September 1806. Crowds lined the river to greet them. Their exciting but difficult adventure had been remarkable for its harmony. There had been no serious clashes with the many Indians they met along the way. The explorers had managed to get along with one another too, even when cooped up far from home with little to do during two winters.

Charles Marion Russell was a famous painter of the American West. Once a trapper and cowboy, Russell lived for a time with the same people whose ancestors had been visited by Lewis and Clark. In this Russell painting Sacagawea, who gave birth on the journey, greets her Shoshone relatives. The scene is set near the present-day border of Idaho and Montana.

The Thomas Gilcrease Institute of American History and Art, Tulsa, Oklahoma

Amon Carter Museum

In this Charles Russell painting, leaders of the Corps of Discovery encounter Indians—perhaps Clatsops— in the lower Columbia River. Sacagawea signs their greetings. Why do you think it was important that the corps members included a native American interpreter?

Captain Lewis deserves much of the credit for this harmony. He was a firm but considerate leader. He treated all members of the party fairly. He was careful not to exclude the slave York or Sacagawea, as when he called for a vote on where to build Fort Clatsop.

Lewis and Clark's Achievement

Besides giving the United States a claim to territory in the Northwest, this remarkable expedition produced an amazing amount of new information about the Great West. Lewis and Clark discovered the true course of the Missouri River. They proved that the continent was much wider than most people had thought. They found and mapped a number of passes through the Rockies. In later years their maps would help settlers make their way through the mountains and on to the Pacific. Hundreds of hunters, trappers, scientists, and ordinary settlers profited from Lewis and Clark's maps and reports.

Lewis and Clark also discovered and brought back many new plants. They saw animals in their natural habitats. They sent back large numbers of skins of animals as well as many live animals of the region for scientific study. The journals and diaries of the journey contained many fantastic stories and adventures. Lewis recounted a day that included a hair-raising encounter with a bear and the near-loss of the expedition's supplies:

> In an instant this monster ran at them with open mouth. The two who had reserved their fires discharged their pieces [guns] at him as he came towards them. Both of them struck him, one only slightly and the other fortunately broke his shoulder. This however only retarded [slowed] the bear's motion for a moment.
>
> The men unable to reload their guns took to flight, the

Missouri Historical Society
President Jefferson specifically asked for information on new flora (plants) and fauna (animals). One of William Clark's sketches is shown below.

bear pursued and had very nearly overtaken them before they reached the river. Two of the party betook themselves to a canoe, and the others separated and concealed themselves among the willows. Reloading their pieces, each discharged his piece at him as they had the opportunity. They struck him several times again but the guns served only to direct the bear to them.

In this manner he pursued two of them separately so close that they were obliged to throw themselves into the river altho' the bank was nearly twenty feet perpendicular [high]. So enraged was this animal that he plunged into the river only a few feet behind the second man he had forced to take refuge in the water. Finally one of those who still remained on shore shot him through the head and killed him. They then took him to shore and butchered him. They found that eight balls [bullets] had passed through him in different directions. The bear being old, the flesh [meat] was indifferent not tasty. They therefore only took the skin and fleece, [the fat] of the latter made us several gallons of oil.

It was after the sun had set before these [men] came up with us, where we had halted by an occurrence, which I have now to describe. Altho' the occurrence happily passed without ruinous injury, I cannot recollect it but with the utmost fear and horror. This is the upsetting and narrow escape of the white perogue [canoe].

It happened unfortunately for us this evening that Charbono was at the helm of this perogue, . . . Charbono cannot swim and is perhaps the most timid waterman in the world. Perhaps it was equally unluckey that Capt. C [Clark], and myself were both on shore at that moment. . . . In this perogue were embarked our papers, instruments, books, medicine, and great part of our merchandize and in short almost every article indespensibly necessary . . . to ensure the success of the enterprise in which we were now launched to the distance of 2200 miles [3520 kilometers]. . . . A sudon squal [sudden gust] of wind struck her obiquely [at an angle], and turned her considerably.

The steersman alarmed, instead of puting her before the wind, lufted her up into it. The wind was so violent that it drew the brace of the squarsail out of the hand of the man attending it, and . . . would have turned her completely topsaturva [upside down], had it not been for the resistence made by the oarning [sail] against the water.[1] **99**

[1]From *Original Journals of the Lewis and Clark Expedition,* edited by Ruben Gold Thwaites

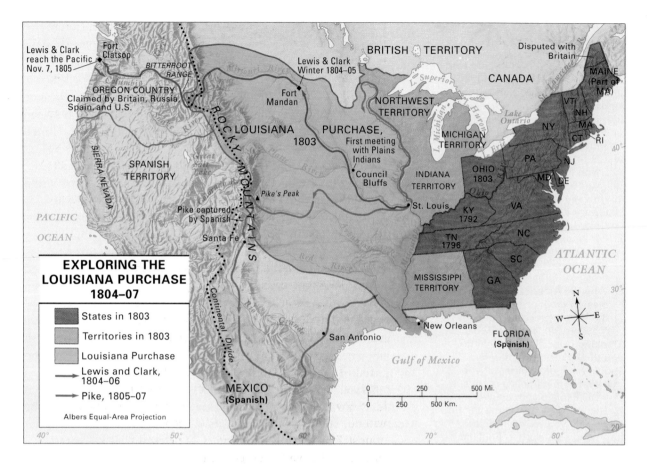

EXPLORING THE LOUISIANA PURCHASE 1804–07

Legend:
- States in 1803
- Territories in 1803
- Louisiana Purchase
- Lewis and Clark, 1804–06
- Pike, 1805–07

Albers Equal-Area Projection

Map labels: Lewis & Clark reach the Pacific Nov. 7, 1805; Fort Clatsop; BITTERROOT RANGE; OREGON COUNTRY Claimed by Britain, Russia, Spain, and U.S.; SIERRA NEVADA; SPANISH TERRITORY; ROCKY MOUNTAINS; Great Salt Lake; Pike's Peak; Pike captured by Spanish; Santa Fe; PACIFIC OCEAN; Continental Divide; Rio Grande; Red River; MEXICO (Spanish); San Antonio; LOUISIANA PURCHASE, 1803; Missouri River; Fort Mandan; Lewis & Clark Winter 1804–05; First meeting with Plains Indians; Council Bluffs; St. Louis; Platte River; Arkansas River; BRITISH TERRITORY; CANADA; NORTHWEST TERRITORY; L. Superior; Lk. Michigan; Lake Huron; MICHIGAN TERRITORY; Lake Ontario; Lake Erie; INDIANA TERRITORY; OHIO 1803; KY 1792; TN 1796; MISSISSIPPI TERRITORY; GA; New Orleans; Gulf of Mexico; FLORIDA (Spanish); Disputed with Britain; MAINE (Part of MA); VT; NH; MA; NY; CT; RI; PA; NJ; MD; DE; VA; NC; SC; ATLANTIC OCEAN; St. Lawrence

Scale: 0 250 500 Mi. / 0 250 500 Km.

Lewis and Clark's accounts of the Indian tribes they met, such as the one on page 293, provided much fresh information. In some cases the very existence of large tribes was unknown until the reports of Lewis and Clark were published. All in all, their expedition was one of the great voyages of discovery of modern times.

Pike's Adventures

The success of Lewis and Clark did not open wide the gates of Louisiana. But their discoveries spurred other explorations. In 1805, a year before the return of Lewis and Clark, Zebulon Pike led an expedition north from St. Louis. He traveled up the Mississippi, searching for the river's source. Although Pike was not successful, he learned much about the upper Mississippi region.

In 1806 Pike explored the southern part of the Louisiana Purchase. His party traveled up the Arkansas River, and in November Pike sighted the mountain in Colorado that was later named Pikes Peak. Pike then went on to Santa Fe and across the Rio Grande. He returned to Louisiana through Texas. Although Pike's notes added to the information being collected about the American West, he was not nearly so careful an observer as Lewis and Clark. 🔲

Return to the Preview & Review on page 280.

LEARNING FROM MAPS. *The Louisana Purchase almost doubled the size of the United States. Trace the route Lewis and Clark took. What were the major obstacles they encountered? Do the same for Pike's journey.*

Zebulon Pike is the subject of this Charles Willson Peale portrait.

Independence National Historical Park

4. THE THREAT OF WAR

Use these questions to guide your reading. Answer the questions after completing Section 4.
Understanding Issues, Events, & Ideas. Create a chronological outline of President Jefferson's foreign policy, using the following words: impressment, Embargo Act, Non-Intercourse Act, Macon's Bill Number Two.

1. How did the war between France and England affect the United States on the high seas?
2. For what purpose was impressment originally intended? Why were Americans sometimes victims of impressment?
3. Why did America still have troubles on the high seas even after the Non-Intercourse Act and Macon's Bill Number Two?

Thinking Critically. 1. What do you think President Jefferson should have done differently to make his foreign policy more successful? Explain your answer.
2. The year is 1807. Before the Embargo Act, you were a manufacturer who sold cloth to England. Now you are unemployed. Are you sympathetic toward a ship captain arrested for smuggling sugar? Why or why not?

Jefferson and the Navy

Only a few weeks after selling Louisiana to the United States, France was again at war with England. Once again the struggle between these two European nations had powerful effects upon the United States.

America's prosperity depended to a large extent on foreign trade. Americans still needed foreign manufactured goods, and farmers sold a great deal of their produce abroad. French and British warships and privateers hurt this trade by capturing American merchant ships bound for each other's ports.

During 1806 the British seized 120 American ships carrying cargoes to and from the French West Indies. The British also claimed the right to seize American ships headed for European countries that Napoleon had conquered, such as Holland and Belgium. Napoleon, in turn, issued orders to his captains to capture any neutral vessel that had allowed itself to be inspected on the high seas by a British warship. Such vessels "have become English property," Napoleon announced in his Milan Decree of 1807.

Jefferson had said in his inaugural address that he favored "honest friendship" with all nations. How could the United States be friendly with countries that attacked its ships in this manner? What could be done to prevent these attacks?

One obvious way to protect American shipping would be to build a navy powerful enough to escort convoys of merchant ships and drive off or sink privateers. When John Adams was president, a naval building program had been undertaken. The frigates *Constitution, Constellation,* and *United States* had performed well against French armed vessels in the late 1790s. They were without doubt the most powerful warships of that type afloat at the time. But frigates cost several hundred thousand dollars each and were expensive to maintain. Once peace with France had been reached, Jefferson saw no need to expand the navy further. He preferred to rely on small gunboats, which cost only about $10,000 apiece to build. These tiny gunboats were useless on the high seas or in combat with a large warship. This is one reason the war with the Barbary pirates had dragged on so long.

Jefferson's trouble was that although he was very upset when foreign powers threatened the rights of American citizens, he was unwilling to spend large sums of public money to defend those rights. In a way, the whole country suffered from the same confusion. War in Europe caused attacks on American ships. These attacks were a blow to American pride. Yet the war greatly increased the demand for American goods in Europe. Sales doubled between 1803 and 1805. The foreign war was making America prosperous.

The Granger Collection, New York

Trouble on the High Seas

Merchants could protect themselves against the loss of ships and their cargoes by insuring them. Insurance rates were high in wartime, but the prices merchants could get for their goods were high too. More alarming was the loss of men.

For hundreds of years the Royal Navy had claimed the right to *impress* any British civilian into the navy in a national emergency. **Impressment** was a hit-or-miss way of drafting men for military service. As the system developed in the 1700s, a ship's captain in need of sailors would send what he called a *press gang* ashore. Perhaps some of his crew had been killed in a battle at sea. More likely, some may have deserted when the vessel reached port.

The press gang, composed of members of the warship's crew, would go ashore armed. They would roam the waterfront area searching for men who looked as though they were experienced sailors. The press gang seized anyone they wanted and carried the men away to their ship. Sometimes they found it easiest just to drag off drunks from shoreside bars. The unfortunate men who were impressed received one shilling, called press money, to "compensate" them for having been forced to serve in His Majesty's navy.

Press gangs were not supposed to take anyone who was not a British subject. But sometimes they made mistakes. Particularly in British ports in the West Indies, American sailors on shore leave were often taken. These men naturally protested loudly that they were Americans. But Englishmen who wanted to avoid being impressed frequently claimed that *they* were Americans. Because they spoke the same language, it was not always easy to tell the difference.

The captain of H.M.S. Leopard is impressing four angry American seamen after capturing the U.S.S. Chesapeake in 1807. Howard Pyle made this illustration. Use historical imagination to think what it might have been like to be impressed—a long voyage ahead—in the navy of another country.

English sailors sometimes even carried false papers, pretending that they were Americans. Real Americans often did not have any way of proving they were citizens when grabbed by a press gang. The gangs seldom troubled to check carefully in any case. They took any man they wanted. When the captains of British warships sent press gangs ashore, they were not accustomed to having them come back empty-handed. By the time an American was reported missing, he would be far at sea, beyond reach of rescuers.

The United States government did not deny the right of the British to impress British sailors from American merchant ships. But most Americans considered the practice shameful, even if no sailors were taken. British naval officers were often arrogant and domineering. Sometimes they treated the Americans rudely and with contempt. "On board our good old ship *Leander*," one British officer later admitted, "we had not enough consideration for the feelings of the people we were dealing with."

The Embargo Act

In December 1807 Congress passed the **Embargo Act.** This law prohibited all exports from the United States. Jefferson reasoned that if

"You shall be king hereafter," says the emperor Napoleon, standing just behind President Jefferson. This English political cartoon is a satire on the Embargo Act and its effects on American merchants. The profits go to the French. Look closely. "My warehouses are full," says one man. Says another, "My family is starving." Yet Jefferson tells his audience: "This is a Grand Philosophical Idea. If we continue this Experiment for about fifteen or twenty years, we may begin to feel the good effects." This is all too much for one man, who remembers 'Great Washington.' Even the little dog is angry. What complaint do the merchants have?

The happy Effects of that Grand System of shutting Ports against the English!!

Thomas Jefferson Memorial Foundation

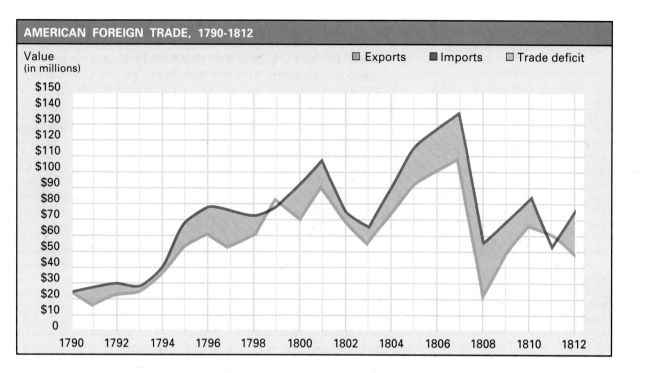

AMERICAN FOREIGN TRADE, 1790-1812

Value (in millions)

☐ Exports   ■ Imports   ☐ Trade deficit

merchant ships could not carry goods abroad, no American sailor could be forced into a foreign navy. This was, of course, a drastic way of dealing with the problem, like trying to kill a fly on a window by throwing a brick at it.

Stopping exports caused unemployment among sailors and among workers who had been making goods that were usually exported. The busy shipbuilding industry nearly came to a standstill. More workers were unemployed. Even more serious, foreign shipowners would not carry goods to America if they had to return to their home ports empty. The value of all the goods imported in 1808 was less than half that of 1807. The embargo policy was an economic disaster.

People in the New England states and in other areas where foreign trade was important deeply resented the Embargo Act. Josiah Quincy, a Massachusetts Federalist in Congress during the embargo crisis, was a vocal opponent of the embargo. Quincy and other opponents of the embargo felt it was doing great economic damage to the United States as a whole, and especially to trading interests in New England. In a speech before Congress Quincy explained his concerns:

❝ The entire nation is suffering under a most serious oppression, the embargo. All the business of the nation is in disorder. All the hopes of the people are frustrated. All the nation's industry is at a standstill. Its many products hastening to market are stopped in their course. With every

LEARNING FROM GRAPHS. *This line graph illustrates trends in American foreign trade. As you can see, Americans imported more than they exported even in the early 1800s. What general trend do you note for American trade between 1790 and 1807? Then what happens? Why?*

passing hour the desire of the citizens to resist the embargo increases.

The embargo, which holds in its crippling grip all the hopes of this nation, has two important characteristics: it hurts all Americans, and nothing like it has ever been tried before. Every interest in the nation is affected by the embargo. The merchant, the farmer, the planter, the craftsman, the laboring poor—all are sinking under its weight. The embargo especially hurts the poor. From those who have much, it takes something. But from those who have little, it takes all. What hope is left to the hard-working poor when they lose their jobs because of the embargo?

The embargo affects the hopes and interests of all people. But it is also remarkable because it has never been tried before. In fact it never before entered into human imagination! There is nothing like it in all of history or in the tales of fiction. All the habits of our mighty nation are at once frustrated. All property of our people sinks in value. Five million Americans are trapped by this embargo. They can neither travel nor trade outside our once free country.

I ask whether the embargo, which affects so many Americans and which is so new, and which interferes with the desires and interests of the whole nation, ought to be left in effect. Who can predict when the British and French will honor American trading rights and bring an end to the embargo? And who can guarantee that the patience of the citizens will not soon give out and lead them to resist the embargo?[1] **”**

Many people broke this law because they considered it unwise and unfair. There were many ways of doing so. Trade by sea between one American port and another was allowed. A captain could sail from Boston to New York or from Philadelphia to Charleston or to any other American port. Many announced that they were sailing on such a voyage and went instead to Europe or the West Indies. If caught, they claimed that a storm had driven them off course.

The captain of the merchant ship *Commerce,* supposedly headed for New Orleans, sailed to Havana, Cuba. The excuse he gave was that he had run out of water for his crew. At the same time that he filled his water barrels, he sold his cargo and bought sugar.

Besides tricks such as these, many Americans resorted to direct smuggling in order to sell their goods abroad. Large amounts of American products were carried illegally from the northern states to Canada. That long and still almost unsettled border was very difficult to patrol. When smugglers were caught and brought to trial, juries

[1]From "How Jefferson's Embargo Paralyzed Trade" by Josiah Quincy in *America: Great Crises in Our History Told by Its Makers,* Vol. V

made up of their fellow citizens usually found them not guilty. It was as hard to convict a merchant charged with violating the Embargo Act as it had been in the 1770s to convict someone of violating the Townshend Act by importing Dutch tea to avoid the tea tax.

America on the Eve of War

In the fall of 1808, James Madison, Jefferson's longtime friend, was elected to succeed him as president. After the election Jefferson gave up the struggle to enforce the Embargo Act. Early in 1809 Congress repealed it. Congress then passed a law to permit reopening trade with all foreign countries except France and Britain. Under this **Non-Intercourse Act** no English or French ship could enter an American harbor nor could Americans sell goods to those countries. The law also gave the president the power to end the boycott against either nation whenever it "shall cease to violate the neutral commerce of the United States."

The Non-Intercourse Act was even harder to enforce than the Embargo Act. A ship's captain could set out officially for Spain or Holland or any other nation and then land his cargo in whatever country he liked—including Britain or France. English and French attacks on American ships continued.

In desperation a congressman from North Carolina, Nathaniel Macon, proposed a bill allowing American ships to trade with England and France but prohibiting English and French ships from trading with the United States. How this would reduce attacks on American ships and sailors was hard to see. Congress did not pass Macon's bill. But in 1810 it did pass **Macon's Bill Number Two.**

This law removed all restrictions on trade with England and France. It also provided that if either nation stopped attacking American merchant ships, the president could cut off all trade with its rival nation unless it also stopped its attacks. For example, if the English would leave American ships alone, the Americans would boycott England's rival—France.

Macon's Bill Number Two seemed to treat England and France in exactly the same way. In fact, trade with England quickly became as great as it had been before the Embargo Act. But there was little trade with France because by 1810 the British navy dominated the Atlantic Ocean. Few neutral merchant ships dared try to get to French-controlled ports. And the British practice of impressing American sailors continued. The policies of Jefferson and Madison had failed. To more and more people it seemed that the only way to protect the right to trade freely was to go to war. 🔲

Return to the Preview & Review on page 286.

CHAPTER 8 REVIEW

Federalist Era	Adams Presidency	
1795	1800	THE AGE OF JEFFERSO

1798
Kentucky
and Virginia
Resolutions

1800
Convention
of 1800

★
Jefferson elected
president

1801
Tripoli declares
war on U.S.

Chapter Summary

Read the statements below. Choose one, and write a paragraph explaining its importance.

1. Federalist attempts to continue to control the government failed.
2. The Kentucky and Virginia Resolutions emphasized the idea of nullification and states' rights.
3. The first Democratic-Republican president, Thomas Jefferson, was elected in 1801.
4. Federalist attempts to control electors led to passage of the Twelfth Amendment, which provided for electors to vote separately for president and vice president.
5. *Marbury v. Madison* set a precedent for declaring an act of Congress unconstitutional.
6. The United States purchased the Louisiana Territory from France in 1803, doubling the nation's size.
7. New England Federalists were alarmed that the Louisiana Purchase would lessen the influence of their section.
8. Lewis and Clark explored the northern region of the new territory while Pike explored the southern reaches.
9. War between Britain and France caused serious problems for Americans.
10. The Embargo Act, Non-Intercourse Act, and Macon's Bill Number Two failed to protect American shipping and sailors.

Reviewing Chronological Order

Number your paper 1–5. Then study the time line above and place the following events in the order in which they happened by writing the first next to 1, the second next to 2, and so on.
1. Embargo Act passed
2. Jefferson elected president
3. *Marbury v. Madison*
4. Kentucky and Virginia Resolutions
5. Lewis and Clark expedition begins

Understanding Main Ideas

1. Why was the Twelfth Amendment needed? How did it improve national elections?
2. What was Jefferson's doctrine of nullification?
3. Why did Jefferson want to buy Louisiana? Why did Napoleon want to sell it?
4. Why was Sacagawea important to the success of the Lewis and Clark Expedition?
5. What was impressment? Why did it anger many Americans?
6. Why did many Americans break the Embargo Act of 1807?

Thinking Critically

1. **Seeing Relationships.** Write a note to Thomas Jefferson, explaining why you think his doctrine of nullification is dangerous to the Union. Explain your view of states' rights.
2. **Evaluating.** You know that Aaron Burr killed Alexander Hamilton in a duel. If dueling were still practiced today, would you be for or against legalizing it? Why?
3. **Synthesizing.** Imagine that you are either York, the slave of William Clark, or Sacagawea. From your point of view, what was the most important achievement of Lewis and Clark's famous expedititon?

Writing About History

Suppose you are one of the following: A Federalist supporting the Sedition Act or a Democratic-Republican supporting the Kentucky and Virginia Resolutions. Write a letter to a newspaper stating your views. Use the information in Chapter 8 to help you develop your letter.

Practicing the Strategy

Review the strategy on page 274.
Interpreting a Physical Map. Study the map on page 285 and answer the following questions.
1. Why were rivers so important to Lewis and Clark's expedition?

1804 Lewis and Clark begin expedition ★ Burr shoots Hamilton in duel		**1806** Pike explores southwestern territory	**1807** Embargo Act	**1809** Non-Intercourse Act	**1810** Macon's Bill Number Two

ury v.
son

purchases
ana

e and Britain go to war

2. Using your historical imagination and the map, describe the landscape Lewis and Clark encountered on the second half of their journey. How does the map show this?

Using Primary Sources

In the following entry from the *Original Journals of the Lewis and Clark Expedition,* Clark describes trading with a group of Indians. He compares these people to the other Indians he had described earlier in his journal. (Clark's original spelling and punctuation have been retained.) As you read the excerpt, think how you would interpret Clark's descriptions.

November 7th Thursday 1805

A cloudy foggey morning Some rain. we Set out early proceeded . . . under a high rugid hills with Steep assent the Shore boalt and rockey, the fog so thick we could not see across the river, two canoe[e]s of Indians met and returned with us to their village, they gave us to eate Some fish, and Sold us, fish, Wap pa to roots three dogs and 2 otter skins for which we gave fish hooks principally of which they were verry fond.

Those people call themselves War-ci-à-cun and Speake a language different from the nativs above with whome they trade the Wapato roots of which they make great use as food. their houses differently built, raised entirely above ground eaves about 5 feet from the ground Supported and covered in the same way of those above, dores about the Same size but in the Side of the house in one corner, one fire place and that near the opposit end, around which they have their beads [beds] raised about 4 feet from the flore which is of earth, under their beads they Store away Baskets of dried fish Berries & Wappato. . . . Their Canoes are of the Same form as those above.

1. What evidence in this excerpt from Clark's journal indicates that the Indians he met were peaceful?

2. In what ways did the Indians Clark met differ from the other natives he described?
3. In what ways do you think the geographic features of the area that Clark refers to limited the diet of the Indians?

Linking History & Geography

Lewis and Clark encountered many geographical obstacles in their quest to reach the Pacific. Using the information in this chapter and on the map on page 285, answer the following questions:
1. How long did it take Lewis and Clark to reach the Pacific Ocean? About how great a distance had they traveled?
2. What major physical obstacles made their trip difficult?
3. How did climate affect the expedition? Why?

Enriching Your Study of History

1. **Individual Project.** Read further about the Lewis and Clark expedition in an encyclopedia or other reference book. Then use historical imagination to prepare diary entries that you might have written as a member of the expedition. Try to describe one ordinary day and one very exciting day.
2. **Cooperative Project.** Using historical imagination, have your group prepare and present a skit for the class. The scene is a public meeting in an American port city. It is 1807. The British have seized 120 American ships. Now the French will capture any American ship that allows itself to be searched on the high seas by the British. Members of your group should explain why American ships must sail the Atlantic and offer several points of view about ways to protect America's shipping. Then your classmates will vote on which course of action is best.

Chapter 8 Review 293

War and Peace, 1812-1823

This Shoshone encampment is so vast that it fades into the horizon. Alfred Jacob Miller painted the scene in 1837. The Shoshone ranged as far east as the Rocky Mountains, where their meeting with the Lewis and Clark expedition occurred.

When America declared war on Great Britain in 1812, the people of the Northeast were bitterly opposed. Strangely enough, they were also the people most injured by British attacks on American ships and their crews. Those who favored the war were westerners and southerners, called War Hawks, many of whom had never even seen the Atlantic Ocean. If war broke out, these "hawks" hoped to gobble up British-owned Canada. They also expected to take Florida from Spain, because Spain had now taken the side of England in the long war the British were fighting against Napoleon. Trouble began on the frontier with fighting between settlers and American Indians. Then, when the War of 1812 broke out, Britain and America battled inconclusively at sea and on land. When peace was made in 1815, the Stars and Stripes still flew over the land. But how would the world react when put on notice that the United States now intended to police the whole Western Hemisphere?

The Thomas Gilcrease Institute of American History and Art, Tulsa, Oklahoma

1. WAR IN THE NORTHWEST

War Hawks on the Frontier

The **War Hawks** and other frontier settlers blamed England for the troubles between Indians and settlers in the Northwest Territory. They felt that the British in Canada kept the Indians riled up to make trouble. They correctly believed that if war broke out, the Indians in the Great Lakes region would side with the British. Henry Clay, a young senator from Kentucky was a leading War Hawk. The following is an excerpt from the speech Clay delivered in the Senate on February 22, 1810, expressing the attitude of the War Hawks:

“ No man in the nation wants peace more than I. But I prefer the troubled ocean of war, with all its disasters and desolation, to the calm decaying pool of dishonorable peace. If we can settle our differences with one of our enemies—Britain or France—I should prefer it be Britain. But if with neither, and we are forced into a selection of our enemy, then I choose war with Britain. I believe her first in aggression and her injuries and insults to us are extremely cruel in character.

Britain stands out in her outrage on us, by her violation of the sacred personal rights of American freemen, in the arbitrary and lawless imprisonment of our seamen.

But we [Congress] are asked for the means of supporting the war, and those who oppose it triumphantly appeal to the empty vaults of the Treasury. We have, I am credibly informed, in the city and vicinity of New Orleans alone, public property sufficient to pay off the debt noted in the Treasury report. And are we to regard as nothing the patriotic offers so often made by the States, to spend their last cent, and risk their last drop of blood, in the preservation of our neutral privileges?

It is said, however, that it is hopeless to go to war with Great Britain. If we go to war, we are to estimate not only the benefit gained for ourselves, but the injury to be done the enemy. The conquest of Canada is in your power. I trust that I shall not be thought to be bold when I state that I truly believe that the militia of Kentucky are alone competent to place Montreal and Upper Canada at your feet. Is it nothing to the pride of the King, to have the last of the immense North American possessions held by him in the beginning of his reign taken from him? Is it nothing to us to put out the torch of Indian warfare? Is it nothing to gain the entire fur trade connected with Canada? . . .

Use these questions to guide your reading. Answer the questions after completing Section 1.

Understanding Issues, Events, & Ideas. Use the following words to describe troubles on the frontier from the Indian point of view: War Hawk, Red Stick Confederacy, Battle of Tippecanoe.

1. Why was Tecumseh so opposed to the Indian land sale in 1809? What else did he oppose?
2. What did Tecumseh do to organize the tribes east of the Mississippi River?
3. Why was sentiment for declaring war on England stronger on the frontier than elsewhere in the country by 1812?

Thinking Critically. Imagine that you are a member of a hunting tribe in the early 1800s. Do you agree with Jefferson's theory that your standard of living will improve if you become a farmer? How will your way of life change?

STRATEGIES FOR SUCCESS

SYNTHESIZING INFORMATION

To synthesize information you must combine ideas from several sources. *The Story of America* is a synthesis. The author studied many historical sources and used that information to create this textbook. You, too, are asked to synthesize information in this and other courses. Each time you are directed to read information *and* study a map to gain a new understanding, you are synthesizing information.

How to Synthesize Information

To effectively synthesize information, follow these guidelines.

1. **Select sources carefully.** Make sure that the sources you are studying cover the same information and complement, or add to, each other.
2. **Read for understanding.** Identify main ideas and important supporting evidence in each source.
3. **Compare and contrast.** Note where sources agree or build on each other. More importantly, note where they differ.
4. **Interpret all the information.** Use what you have found to interpret the information. This is the key step in synthesizing.

Applying the Strategy

You know that after the end of the Revolutionary War, settlers moved into the lands beyond the Appalachian Mountains. Here troubles erupted. Study the map on this page and then reread "War in the Northwest" on pages 295–99.

By studying these two sources, you should be able to answer some key questions about these events. Why were so many settlers attracted to these lands? What would most of the settlers do with the land? The map shows the area beyond the Appalachians as gently rolling, with abundant streams and rivers. Could this be what many of the settlers were looking for? As you know, many of these pioneers were farmers. They were looking for fertile soil on which to start farms. Do you think they found what they were searching for?

This surge of land-hungry settlers across the mountains caused trouble with the Indians already there. Why? Synthesize the information by using your prior knowledge about how the Indians and settlers differed on their view of land

ownership and the information from your reading and the map to answer this question.

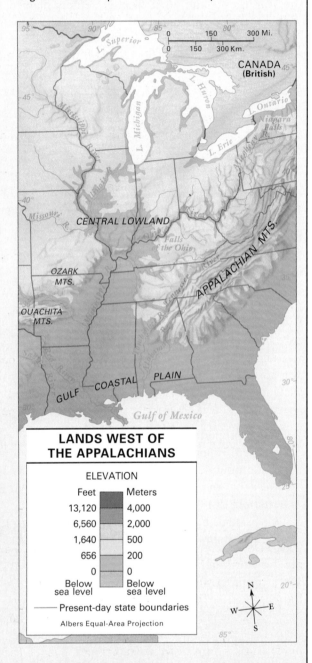

LANDS WEST OF THE APPALACHIANS

ELEVATION

Feet		Meters
13,120		4,000
6,560		2,000
1,640		500
656		200
0		0
Below sea level		Below sea level

— Present-day state boundaries

Albers Equal-Area Projection

For independent practice, see Practicing the Strategy on page 326.

If we surrender without a struggle to maintain our rights, we forfeit the respect of the world and (what is worse) of ourselves.[1] **99**

The huge area of land in southern Ohio that was turned over to the settlers by the Indians in the Treaty of Greenville in 1795 was not enough to satisfy the land-hungry pioneers for long. Their most cold-blooded leader was General William Henry Harrison. Harrison was governor of the Indiana Territory, the region directly west of the new state of Ohio. He considered the Indians "wretched savages" blocking the forward march of what he called "civilization." By "civilization" Harrison meant his own way of life.

Harrison used trickery, bribery, and military force to push Indians off more and more land. Other government leaders who seemed milder and more tolerant than Harrison did the Indians almost as much harm. They tried to get Indians to settle on farms and become "good Americans." They wanted Indians to give up their customs and religions and copy the largely European culture of the newly arriving settlers. They claimed that the change would be the best thing that could happen both to the Indians and to their new neighbors on the frontier. They did not care that this would destroy the Indians as a distinct group of people.

As President Jefferson put it, if the Indians farmed the land and gave up hunting, more land would be available for the new settlers. By becoming farmers, the Indians would increase what Jefferson called their "domestic comforts"—that is, their standard of living.

Many Indians found some parts of the European way of life attractive. Guns, for example, made them more efficient hunters and warriors. Knives and metal tools, bright-colored cloth, whiskey, cheap jewelry, and other trinkets appealed to them powerfully. Sharp-eyed traders took great advantage of the Indians' desire for these things, swapping nearly worthless goods or whiskey for their valuable furs.

Tecumseh and the Prophet

By about 1809 a brilliant leader was rising among the Indians of the Ohio Valley. He was Tecumseh, a Shawnee chief. Tecumseh is Shawnee for Panther Lying in Wait. He had fought under Chief Little Turtle against United States troops in the 1790s. He took part in the Battle of Fallen Timbers, where one of his brothers was killed.

Tecumseh was against all grants or sales of land to settlers. He believed that God, "the Great Spirit," had created the land for all Indians to *use,* not to own. He claimed Indians had no right to sell the land, even to one another. He asked:

[1]From *Annals of Congress,* 11th Congress, 1st Session (1809–10)

Field Museum

We believe this to be a portrait of Tecumseh, the great leader of the Red Stick Confederacy. What view did Tecumseh take on land ownership? Who did he believe "owned" the land?

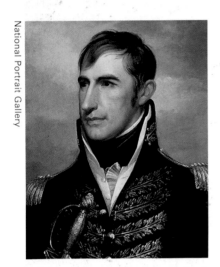

National Portrait Gallery

William Henry Harrison here is painted as a young soldier by Rembrandt Peale. In your opinion, which more describes Harrison—diplomat or warrior?

National Museum of American Art

The portrait in oil of Tenskwatawa, known as the Prophet, is by George Catlin. It was painted in the 1830s by the great 19th century painter of American Indians.

> **Why not sell the air, the clouds, and the great sea? . . . White people are never satisfied. . . . They have driven us from the great salt water, forced us over the mountains. . . . We are determined to go no farther.**

Tecumseh was also against torture and other forms of cruelty in warfare.

In September 1809 General Harrison signed a treaty with the chiefs of a number of tribes. The Indians gave up 3 million acres (1.2 million hectares) in return for about $10,000. That was not even half a cent an acre. The United States government was selling similar land for $2 an acre. Clearly, the Indians were being cheated.

Tecumseh was furious. No Shawnees signed the treaty. He went to see General Harrison. He warned the general not to try to take over the lands just purchased. The local "village chiefs" who had signed the treaty had no right to do so. "We are prepared to punish those chiefs who . . . sell their land," Tecumseh said. And he added sternly, "If you continue to purchase . . . it will produce war."

Tecumseh realized that war was likely to break out between the United States and Great Britain. He intended to organize the many Indian tribes south of the Great Lakes. Then he would threaten to side with the British forces in Canada. Perhaps that would persuade the Big Knives, as he called the soldiers because of their swords and bayonets, to allow the Indians to hold their land in peace.

Tecumseh made this promise to Harrison: If the United States would give up its claims to the Indian lands purchased by the 1809 treaty, the Indians would become loyal allies and help the United States in any war against the British in Canada.

Harrison told Tecumseh frankly that the president would never agree to this. Tecumseh then said that he hoped the Great Spirit would put some sense in the president's head. Otherwise, "he may sit still in his town and drink his wine," but "you and I will have to fight it out."

Tecumseh then set out to organize all the Indian tribes east of the Mississippi to resist expansion onto their land. The alliance he formed was called the **Red Stick Confederacy,** possibly after the Creeks, also known as Red Sticks, who joined the Confederacy.

Tecumseh was an inspiring leader. He was a tall, handsome man with a long, thin face. He wore simple deerskin clothing with few decorations. Usually he had a single eagle's feather in his hair. He was a marvelous speaker and very intelligent. Even General Harrison admitted that Tecumseh was "one of those . . . geniuses which spring up occasionally to produce revolutions."

All along the southern and western frontiers Tecumseh preached Indian unity and resistance to expansion onto Indian land. Resistance meant more than fighting with gun and tomahawk. Indians, he said, must cast off every sign of other cultures. Tecumseh was aided in

The Granger Collection, New York

his crusade by his brother Tenskwatawa, known as the Prophet. Tenskwatawa had been a heavy drinker and troublesome as a young man. He was sometimes called Laulewasikaw, which in Shawnee means Loud Mouth. In 1805 he experienced a religious vision. He dropped all his bad habits and began to preach against drinking and against copying other cultures. He claimed to have magical powers and to be able to see the future.

The Prophet attracted many Indians to the Red Sticks, but he was a poor leader. General Harrison marched against his headquarters at the village called Prophetstown in the fall of 1811. The Prophet ordered a night attack. The battle took place in Indiana, near where Tippecanoe Creek joins the Wabash River. On November 7 the battle raged among the tall oaks and thickets along the rivers. The fighting was fierce and extremely bloody. Harrison squeezed the Indians back against the streams until they fled. Harrison then destroyed their town, but almost a fifth of his own force of about a thousand men were killed or wounded.

The chief result of this **Battle of Tippecanoe** was to make Harrison a popular hero. Tecumseh had been away from Prophetstown recruiting more men for the Red Stick Confederacy. He was annoyed with his brother, who should not have started the fighting. But he did not think that the battle was very important. He referred to it as a "scuffle with the Big Knives."

No one could doubt, however, that the Red Sticks were preparing to fight the Big Knives. The British in Canada would probably help the Indians in such a contest. Because western settlers blamed the British for the Indians' warlike behavior, sentiment for declaring war on England was strong on the frontier by 1812.

The fierce fighting, much of it at close quarters in the Indiana woods, can be seen in this lithograph by Kurz and Allen. General Harrison, at far left, urges his men on in the bloody battle. According to the lithograph, why would it seem the soldiers had the advantage at Tippecanoe?

Return to the Preview & Review on page 295.

War in the Northwest   299

Preview & Review

Use these questions to guide your reading. Answer the questions after completing Section 2.
Understanding Issues, Events, & Ideas. Using the following words, describe the early United States navy: War of 1812, frigate, ship of the line, Old Ironsides.
1. Why did northeastern members of Congress vote against war with Britain?
2. In what European conflict was Britain involved in 1812?
3. Why were so many battles at sea won by the United States?
Thinking Critically. Imagine that you are a young American sailor aboard the *Constitution*. Write a letter to a relative in Great Britain, explaining how you and your crew defeated the *Guerrière*.

The War of 1812 Begins

In June 1812 Congress declared war on Great Britain. The vote was fairly close in both the Senate and the House of Representatives. Nearly all the members of Congress who voted against the war came from the northeastern states, where shipping and foreign trade were important. Although these people were angered by the impressment of sailors and by British attacks on American ships, they realized that war with England would seriously injure their trade. They would rather suffer the insults and losses and wait for the war in Europe to come to an end.

The War Hawks continued to defend the war, even after the fighting had begun. Henry Clay stated in Congress in 1813:

66 What cause, Mr. Chairman, which existed for declaring the war has been removed? . . . Indian hostilities, which were before secretly instigated [caused] now openly encouraged; and the practice of impressment . . . unceasingly insisted upon. . . . An honorable peace is attainable only by an efficient war. My plan would be to call out the ample resources of the country, give them a judicious [sensible] direction, prosecute [fight] the war with the utmost vigor, strike wherever we can reach the enemy, at sea or on land, and negotiate the terms of a peace. . . .[1] 99

Still opposition to the war grew. Newspaper editorials such as the following one appeared all over the Northeast. Compare the sentiments expressed in it to those in Clay's speeches urging war.

66 The feeling is growing by the hour that we are in a condition no better in relation to the South than that of a conquered people. We have been forced, without the least necessity, to give up our habits, occupations, means of happiness, and means of support. We are plunged into a war without feeling that there has been sufficient cause for it. We are obliged to fight the battles of a conspiracy which, while pretending to defend republican equality, aims at trampling into the dust the weight, influence, and power of trade.

We, whose ships were the training ground of sailors, are insulted with the pretense of a devotion to sailors' rights by those whose region knows nothing of navigation beyond the size of a ferryboat or an Indian canoe. We have no interest in fighting this sort of war, at this time and under these circumstances, under the command of Virginia.

[1] From *Annals of Congress*, 12th Congress, 2nd Session (1811–13)

THE WAR OF 1812

→ Americans

✳ American victory

→ British

✳ British victory

| 0 | 200 | 400 Mi. |

| 0 | 200 | 400 Km. |

Albers Equal-Area Projection

LEARNING FROM MAPS. *This map well illustrates the British strategy in the War of 1812. At what three points did they attempt to attack the United States?*

The consequences must be either that the southern states must drag the northern states farther into the war or we must drag them out of it, or the union of our nation will break apart. We must no longer listen to those foolish outcries against a separation of the states. It is an event we do not desire. But the states are separated in fact when one section continues in actions fatal to the interests and opposed to the opinions of another section because of a geographical majority.[1] 99

Probably those opposing the war were correct in thinking that this **War of 1812** was a mistake. The British were engaged in a life-and-death struggle with Napoleon, now emperor of France. Napoleon was seeking to conquer and control all Europe. French attacks on American commerce were fewer in number than British attacks only because France had a much smaller navy.

The British had no real quarrel with the United States. Nor could the United States gain anything by fighting Britain that it would not get anyway once the war between Great Britain and France was over. By forcing Britain to fight in America, the United States was obviously making it more difficult for the British to bring the war in Europe to an end.

[1]From *Columbian Sentinel* (Boston), Jan. 13, 1813

Victories at Sea

The first battles of the War of 1812 occurred at sea. They resulted in some spectacular American victories. The most powerful ships in the American navy were its seven **frigates.** These three-masted, square-rigged ships varied in length from about 140 to 175 feet (about 42 to 53 meters). The *Chesapeake* was one of the vessels in this class. Others bore such names as *Constitution, United States,* and *President.* The frigates were all quite new. They had been built as a result of the war scare following the XYZ Affair of 1797. They were beautifully designed—fast, easy to maneuver, and armed with 40 to 50 or more cannon. Their officers were young but highly skilled and experienced. Morale in the navy was very high.

The British fleet in the Atlantic was many times larger than the American. To begin with, there were seven **ships of the line.** Ships of the line were armed with 60 to 70 or more cannon. Then there were 34 frigates. These were somewhat smaller and less heavily armed than the American type. Dozens of smaller ships and transports completed the British force.

The British had excellent officers and sailors. Their one mistake was in not reckoning how able the American navy had become.

The Constitution, *America's prized frigate, commenced firing on the British* Guerrière *on August 12, 1812. Under the deadly blaze of its cannon the* Guerrière *was smashed. Thomas Birch is thought to have painted this scene. Can you explain in your own words the maneuver known as "crossing the T" that helped Americans in the battle?*

U.S. Naval Academy

In August 1812 the *Constitution* met with the British frigate *Guerrière* off the coast of Maine. The *Guerrière,* a French-built ship, had been captured by the British in 1806. Captain Isaac Hull of the *Constitution* held his fire until the two ships were side by side. Then he said to his gun crews, "Now, boys, pour it into them."

The *Constitution*'s first volley broke the *Guerrière*'s mizzenmast. With sails and rigging trailing over its stern, the *Guerrière* could not be managed. Captain Hull then crossed in front of the crippled ship. This maneuver, called crossing the T, enabled him to fire broadsides while the British ship's guns could not be aimed at the *Constitution*. The Americans' cannon fired again and again, splintering the Britishers' hull and smashing down masts, sails, and rigging. From above, perched high in the *Constitution*'s rigging, American riflemen picked off sailors on the *Guerrière*'s deck. After half an hour the British captain surrendered. His ship was a total wreck. Of its crew of over 270, 79 were killed or wounded. Only 14 Americans died.

The *Constitution* later defeated the frigate *Java* in another famous battle. **Old Ironsides,** as it is now called, is the most famous ship ever to have flown the American flag. It has been preserved as a museum and monument at the Boston Navy Yard.

In October 1812 the American frigate *United States* sighted H.M.S. *Macedonian* near the Azores. Captain Stephen Decatur of the *United States* was already famous for his exploits while fighting North African pirates when Jefferson was president. Now he outmaneuvered the captain of the *Macedonian* brilliantly. Taking advantage of the fact that he had more powerful, long-range guns, he pounded the *Macedonian* from a distance. When the *Macedonian* finally surrendered, 100 cannon holes were counted in her hull. Decatur put an American crew aboard the captured ship and sailed it to New York. There the vessel was sold for $200,000, the money going, according to the custom of the time, to the crew of the *United States.*

These and other victories at sea were won because the American frigates were better fighting machines than the British ships. The American sailors proved to be superior fighters too. The fire of their guns was extremely accurate, and the tactics of the American captains were often brilliant.

After early losses the British high command ordered captains to avoid single-ship battles with American frigates. Instead the huge British navy was used to bottle up most American warships in their home ports. By early 1813 the British fleet in American waters had been increased to 17 ships of the line, 27 frigates, and about 50 other warships.

The frigates *Essex* and *President* both got to sea, the latter to be defeated by a squadron of four British ships.

Dozens of American privateers roamed the oceans during the

The opening and closing stanzas of a 21-year-old scholar's first poem show how he fought to save the *Constitution* in 1830.

Old Ironsides

Ay, tear her tattered
   ensign down!
   Long has it waved on
   high,
And many an eye has
   danced to see
   That banner in the sky;
Beneath it rung the
   battle shout,
   And burst the cannon's
   roar—
The meteor of the ocean
   air
   Shall sweep the clouds
   no more.
 . . . .
   Oh, better that her
   shattered hulk
   Should sink beneath
   the wave;
Her thunders shook the
   mighty deep,
   And there should be
   her grave;
Nail to the mast her
   holy flag,
   Set every threadbare
   sail,
And give her to the god
   of storms,
   The lightning and the
   gale!

      Oliver Wendell
        Holmes, 1830

The War at Sea   **303**

A WOLF AGAINST SHEEP

National Archives

The Essex

Captain David Porter was one of the American naval captains whose tactics were particularly brilliant. One time, while captain of the frigate *Essex,* Porter saw a British ship approaching. He turned the *Essex* away and set more sails to make the enemy captain think he was trying to escape. At the same time he ordered weights dragged from the stern so that in fact the ship was moving more slowly.

The commander of the British ship, the 22-gun *Alert,* fell for this trick and sped after the *Essex.* Then, when the *Alert* was in range, Porter turned and let loose with his 46 cannon. Within eight minutes the battle was over, the *Alert* a wreck. In two months on the high seas, Captain Porter captured seven British ships.

The *Essex* later managed to slip past the British in the Atlantic and sail around South America into the Pacific Ocean. There it destroyed or captured many English ships that were hunting whales. The *Essex,* one historian writes, "was like a wolf in a pasture of unguarded sheep." Eventually, British "guardians" arrived. Then the *Essex* was trapped off the coast of Chile by three British warships and forced to surrender.

war. These privateers were fast, light, and beautifully designed. They could easily outsail the best frigates of the Royal Navy. One privateer, the *True-Blooded Yankee,* captured 27 British merchant ships off the coast of Ireland and Scotland in a little more than one month. By the war's end privateers were capturing an average of nearly two ships a day. All told, they took about 1,300 vessels during the war.

Return to the Preview & Review on page 300.

3. THE WAR ON LAND

The Fight for Canada

The fighting on land during the War of 1812 was a seesaw struggle. It seemed at the start that Canada would be an easy target. The population was small, and many Canadians sympathized with the United States. Yet when a force commanded by General William Hull, an uncle of Captain Isaac Hull of the *Constitution*, crossed the border from Detroit, it quickly ran into trouble. Indians under Tecumseh ambushed one militia unit. Confused, Hull retreated to Detroit without making a real fight. Far worse, he surrendered the fort to a small Canadian force commanded by General Isaac Brock. Brock then announced that Michigan had been annexed to the British Empire! And for the moment it had. Indeed, by the end of 1812, most of what are now Indiana and Illinois was also controlled by Canadian troops.

In 1813 the Indian-hater William Henry Harrison, who was a competent general, was put in charge of the war on the border. Before he could invade Canada, however, a British naval squadron had to be cleared from Lake Erie. The officer who accomplished this task was Oliver Hazard Perry.

Perry came from a navy family. His father, his four brothers, and two of his brothers-in-law were naval officers. To win control of Lake Erie, he built a fleet, including two 20-gun ships, right on the scene. Finally, in September 1813, in the bloody **Battle of Put-in-Bay**, he defeated the British squadron. ''We have met the enemy, and they are ours,'' he informed General Harrison. About a quarter of Perry's

Preview & Review

Use these questions to guide your reading. Answer the questions after completing Section 3.
Understanding Issues, Events, & Ideas. Explain the significance of the following words: Battle of Put-in-Bay, Battle of the Thames, Plattsburg, Creek War, Battle of Horseshoe Bend, Bladensburg, Fort McHenry, Battle of New Orleans.
1. Why were the British able to burn Washington in 1814?
2. Why was the defense of Fort McHenry so important?
3. Why were the British defeated at the Battle of New Orleans?
Thinking Critically.   1. You are a member of Jackson's frontier militia. Write a letter to a friend, describing your opinion of Jackson.
2. You are a reporter on the night of August 24, 1814, in Washington, D.C. From a safe hiding place you observe the events. Write your observations in a newspaper article.

Oliver Hazard Perry, 28 years old, is shown transferring the United States colors from his sinking ship, the **Lawrence,** *to the* **Niagara.** *William Powell painted this view of the "Battle of Lake Erie."*

U.S. Capitol Historical Society

brave men were African Americans, which led him to comment that "the color of a man's skin" was no more an indication of his worth than "the cut and trimmings" of his coat.

Harrison was then able to capture Detroit and advance into Canada. At the Thames River, which flows through southern Canada to Lake Erie, he defeated Canadian troops and their Indian allies in the **Battle of the Thames.** The victory won back the Great Lakes region for the United States. But the most significant result of the battle was the death of Tecumseh. Without the great chief it was easier for the United States to gain full control of the northwestern region.

American forces also turned back a combined land and naval attack from Canada. The Americans, anticipating an invasion from Montreal, built a fleet of ships on Lake Champlain. British troops swept into New York and reached **Plattsburg.** There they fought American forces while awaiting naval support that never came. In a hard-fought battle on Lake Champlain the Americans under Commodore Thomas Macdonough defeated the British. The invading British army then scurried back to Canada.

The Creek War

The southern Indians were also soon crushed. Tecumseh, it will be remembered, had traveled extensively in the South persuading the Indian tribes there to join his Red Stick Confederacy. He had won many supporters among the younger Creek warriors in Alabama and Georgia.

These Indians, with some support from both British and Spanish agents, began to attack southern frontier outposts. The most serious of their assaults during this **Creek War** occurred in August 1813 when Red Eagle, leader of the warring Creeks, surprised and overwhelmed the defenders of Fort Mims in western Alabama. Red Eagle's warriors killed between 400 and 500 persons, many of them women and children.

General Andrew Jackson, commanding a force of Tennessee militiamen, then marched into Creek country. Jackson had fought in the Revolutionary War while still a boy. After the Revolution he had moved to Tennessee, where he prospered as a lawyer and plantation owner. He served for a time in both houses of Congress, and he was a judge of the Tennessee Supreme Court.

Jackson was at heart a fighting man, a natural leader of soldiers. Most frontier militia units were hard to discipline. Being used to living on their own, frontiersmen disliked taking orders and being controlled in any way. Jackson's soldiers, however, accepted his orders without question. This was because they both feared and respected him. He had a reputation for being very tough. The men called him "Old Hickory" because the wood of the hickory tree is

The Granger Collection, New York

extremely hard. But he was also known for his loyalty to his men and for his concern for their welfare.

In a series of battles Jackson's army smashed the Creek forces. The climax came in March 1814 at the **Battle of Horseshoe Bend,** on the Tallapoosa River in Alabama. There 1,200 of Red Eagle's Red Sticks had dug in, protected, they thought, by the curve of the river and a wall of earth. Jackson's soldiers swept over the wall and killed 700 of the Indians, losing only 26 of their own men. Jackson forced the Creeks to surrender 20 million acres (8 million hectares) of their land. The Indians in the South could resist no longer.

Creek chief Red Eagle, also known as William Weatherford, surrenders to Andrew Jackson after the Battle of Horseshoe Bend. Red Eagle had escaped but surrendered when they realized that the Indian situation was hopeless. The Creeks agreed to leave southern and western Alabama. Why do you think they were asked to leave?

The Burning of Washington

The British had thus far depended mostly upon Canadian militia units and Indian allies to fight the United States. But by the spring of 1814 Napoleon had been defeated in Europe. The British then sent 14,000 soldiers to fight in America.

The British set out to destroy Washington. The capital city was supposed to be protected by a fleet of 26 gunboats on Chesapeake Bay. When a British squadron led by a 74-gun ship of the line entered the bay, the gunboats' commander hastily pulled his tiny ships back

Anne S.K. Brown Military Collection, Brown University

The British burned most federal buildings in Washington. They spared the Patent Office because the superintendent, Dr. William Thornton, in the second-story window, threatened to charge them with vandalism. The president's house nearby went up in flames. Dolley Madison, below, saved the now famous Stuart portrait of Washington from the burning White House.

New York Historical Society

into a shallow stream. There they were out of range of the British cannon but useless for the defense of Washington.

In August an army of 4,500 Redcoats came ashore south of Washington. It was commanded by General Robert Ross, who had fought against Napoleon under the great British general the Duke of Wellington. At the village of **Bladensburg,** Ross's troops attacked a large but poorly organized force of American militiamen. The Americans fled in panic. On the night of August 24 the British marched straight into Washington and set fire to all the public buildings. Even the president's mansion, the White House, was set afire. A British officer, George R. Glieg, wrote of the city's conquest:

❝ While the two brigades which had been engaged [at Bladensburg], remained upon the field to recover their order, the third, which had formed the reserve, and was consequently unbroken, took the lead, and pushed forward at a rapid rate towards Washington.

As it was not the intention of the British government to attempt permanent conquests in this part of America; and as the General [Ross] was well aware that, with a handful of men, he could not pretend to establish himself for any length of time, in an enemy's capital, he determined to lay it under contribution [destroy it], and return quietly to the shipping [British troop ships]. . . .

Such being the intention of General Ross, he did not march the troops immediately into the city, but halted them upon a plain in its immediate vicinity, whilst a flag of truce was sent in with terms. But whatever his proposal might have been, it was not so much as heard; for scarcely had the party bearing the flag entered the street, than they were fired upon from the windows of one of the houses, and the horse of the General himself, who accompanied them, killed. . . . All thoughts of accomodation [mercy for Washingtonians] were instantly laid aside; the troops advanced forthwith [immediately] into the town, and having first put to the sword [executed] all who were found in the house from which the shots were fired, and reduced it to ashes, they proceeded, without a moment's delay, to burn and destroy every thing in the most distant degree connected with government. In this general devastation were included the Senate-house, the President's palace, an extensive dock-yard and arsenal, barracks for two or three thousand men, several large store-houses filled with naval and military stores, some hundreds of cannon of different descriptions, and nearly twenty thousand stand of small arms. . . . The powder magazines were of course set on fire, and exploded with a tremendous crash, . . . whilst quantities of shot, shell, and hand-grenades, which could not otherwise be rendered useless, were thrown into the [Potomac] river. . . .

Had the arm of vengeance been extended no further, there would not have been room given for so much as a whisper of disapprobation [disapproval]. But, unfortunately, it did not stop there; a noble library, several printing offices, and all the national archives were likewise committed to flames, which, though no doubt the property of the government, might better have been spared.[1] **”**

President James Madison had been at the battlefield at Bladensburg. He escaped by fleeing up the Potomac River into Virginia. Dolley Madison, the first lady, protected by a slave named Jennings, got away from the White House only minutes before the British entered. All she could save was some silverware and an oil painting of George Washington.

The Defense of Baltimore

The British had no intention of remaining in Washington. Their next objective was Baltimore, Maryland, at the head of Chesapeake Bay.

[1]From *The Campaigns of the British Army at Washington and New Orleans* by George Robert Glieg

Maryland Historical Society

Typical of the battles of the War of 1812, bombs really did burst in air. Flags told of victory and loss. This is the bombardment of Fort McHenry, which Francis Scott Key made so memorable.

Transport ships of their fleet put General Ross' army ashore on September 12 about 14 miles (about 23 kilometers) south of the city. Then the ships advanced toward **Fort McHenry,** which guarded the entrance to Baltimore Harbor.

Unlike the assault on Washington, the attack on Baltimore was a failure. Ross' troops ran into stiff resistance about 7 miles (about 11 kilometers) from the city. When the general himself rode forward to investigate, he was killed by a sharpshooter. The Americans retreated a few miles, but their line held.

Meanwhile, the fleet could not get within cannon range of Fort McHenry. The water was too shallow for most of the warships. Five special ships armed with rockets and bombs did get to within 3 miles (about 5 kilometers) of the fort. At dawn on September 13 Admiral Sir Alexander Cochrane ordered these vessels to open fire.

After a day and night of firing on Fort McHenry, the British fleet withdrew. Baltimore was safe. Now the tide of the war was turning. The shame of having the nation's capital destroyed roused people to fight harder. The defense of Baltimore showed their new determination. Thousands of young men came forward to enlist in the army.

The Battle of New Orleans

Now the British were planning a still greater attack. This one came in the South, near the city of New Orleans. During the fall of 1814 they gathered an army of 11,000 veterans of the war against Napoleon

THE STAR-SPANGLED BANNER

The bombardment of Fort McHenry, which began at dawn, went on all that day and the following night. It had little effect. The distance was too great for accurate fire. Many of the bombs burst harmlessly in the air. Only four soldiers in the fort were killed. Its walls remained unbroken.

Francis Scott Key

The Granger Collection, New York

While the firing was in progress, Francis Scott Key, a Washington lawyer, was aboard one of the larger British vessels. He had been sent to try to obtain the release of an American doctor who had been arrested by the British after the Battle of Bladensburg. Admiral Cochrane had agreed to let the doctor go free, but he would not allow the Americans to go ashore until the battle was over.

Key watched the attack on Fort McHenry. Until darkness fell, he could see the fort's flag, an enormous banner 36 feet long and 29 feet wide (about 11 meters by 8 meters). During the night the continuing glare of the British rockets and the bursting bombs gave proof that the Americans were holding out. Then, when dawn came, Key could again see the flag, waving proudly over Fort McHenry. He was so inspired by the sight that he wrote "The Star-Spangled Banner." This poem, when set to

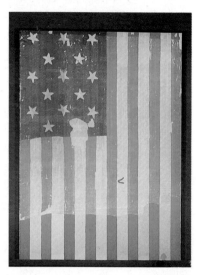

National Museum of American History
The flag that flew over Fort McHenry is now shown in a patriotic flourish at selected times of the day.

the music of an English song, became our national anthem (see page 327). The great flag, the original "star-spangled banner," hangs in the Smithsonian Institution in Washington.

---

at a base on the island of Jamaica in the Caribbean Sea. A fleet of 60 ships carried this force to the Louisiana coast.

The Redcoats landed east of the mouth of the Mississippi River and marched through the swampy country without being discovered. They were only 7 miles (about 11 kilometers) from New Orleans when muddied messengers with the news burst in upon the American general who was in charge of defending the city. The date was December 23, 1814.

The American general was Andrew Jackson, who had been put in command of southern defenses after his victories over the Creeks. He had marched south, captured Pensacola in Spanish Florida so the British could not use it as a base, and then prepared to defend New Orleans. Although surprised by the British advance, Jackson reacted at once. "Gentlemen," he announced, "the British are below. We must fight them tonight." Quickly he ordered every available unit forward. A force of cavalry advanced on the left. Down the Mississippi went a warship to bombard the enemy from the right. In the center went Jackson's regular troops along with hastily organized

Ladies' Hermitage Association

Andrew Jackson on the eve of his great national popularity is shown here in a portrait by Ralph Earl.

The War on Land   311

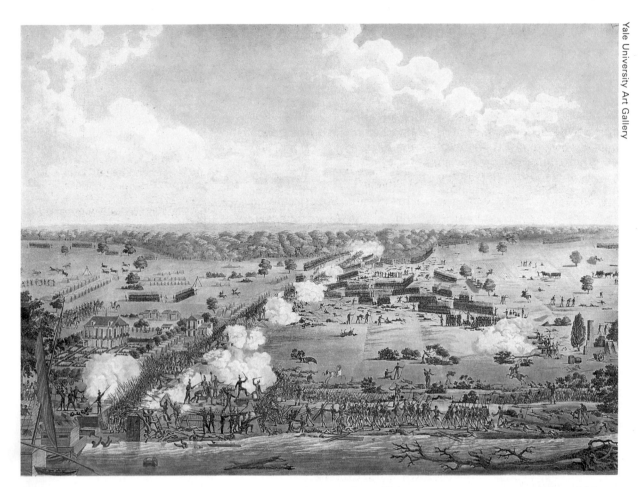

Yale University Art Gallery

Hyacinthe Laclotte went into the thick of the fighting to make this drawing of the Battle of New Orleans. Later it was colored. The British and Americans can be seen fighting hand-to-hand with sabers. Use your historical imagination to describe the sights and sounds of this battlefield.

militia units. Among the militiamen was a company of free African American citizens of New Orleans. A group of pirates came forward "patriotically" to defend the city in exchange for Jackson's promise not to arrest them.

The battle began at 7:30 that very evening. It lasted for two hours and ended in a draw. Jackson then retreated and began to build an earth-wall defense line behind a canal only 5 miles (8 kilometers) from New Orleans.

The sudden American attack made the British delay their advance. They should have abandoned it altogether. Jackson had brought up many cannon and had his men properly positioned to defend the wall. When the British commander, General Sir Edward Pakenham, finally attacked on January 8, 1815, his men were mowed down by a hail of iron and lead. They suffered over 2,000 casualties in about an hour. General Pakenham and both his second and third in command were killed. When the smoke cleared, even the toughest American veterans were stunned by the sight of the battlefield. "You could have walked a quarter of a mile . . . on the bodies," one of them reported. Only 71 Americans were killed, wounded, or missing in action in this **Battle of New Orleans.**

Return to the Preview & Review on page 305.

4. PEACE AND NEW BOUNDARIES

Preview & Review

Use these questions to guide your reading. Answer the questions after completing Section 4.
Understanding Issues, Events, & Ideas. Explain the importance of each of the following words: Peace of Ghent, Hartford Convention, Rush-Bagot Agreement, Negro Fort, Transcontinental Treaty.
1. What were the terms of the Peace of Ghent?
2. What did the Rush-Bagot Agreement provide?
3. Why did General Jackson march into Florida?
4. Why did Luis de Onis agree to negotiate the Florida question with John Quincy Adams?
5. What were the terms of the Transcontinental Treaty? What claims did the United States make for the territory west of the Louisiana Purchase?
Thinking Critically. 1. Why do you think the Federalist Party lost popularity after the War of 1812? **2.** Imagine that you are Luis de Onis in 1818. Write a journal entry that describes your negotiations with John Quincy Adams.

The Peace of Ghent

The loss of life at New Orleans was particularly tragic because the battle should never have been fought. Although the soldiers did not know it, the war was officially over!

Since August 1814 five American commissioners had been trying to negotiate a peace treaty with British diplomats at the city of Ghent in Belgium. The British demanded that the United States return most of the Northwest Territory to the Indians. The Americans wanted the British to give up the right to impress sailors from American ships. Neither side would compromise.

The discussions dragged on for months. Finally everyone realized that the reasons for fighting had simply disappeared. With Napoleon defeated, the British did not need to stop American ships from carrying goods to Europe. There was no longer any need to seize sailors and force them into the Royal Navy.

On December 24, 1814, the day after Jackson had rushed his men out from New Orleans to stop the British advance but two weeks before the final battle, the delegates signed the **Peace of Ghent.** The terms of this treaty were simple. Peace was restored. No territory changed hands. No promises were made. The United States did not get what it had set out for in 1812. As one witty historian has said, "It surrendered nothing except the right to shoot Englishmen." That was a right no one any longer wished to exercise.

Nowadays, of course, the whole world would have known about the treaty within hours after the signing. But in 1814 it took weeks for the news to reach Washington and more weeks for word to be sent to the troops around New Orleans. Thus, the brave men who fell before Jackson's defense wall died needlessly.

The Battle of New Orleans did serve some purpose. It restored American military morale, which had been badly damaged by the ill-organized battles along the Canadian border and by the burning of Washington. It also made a popular hero of Andrew Jackson.

The peace treaty itself was equally popular. In New England, where most people had been opposed to fighting Great Britain, some Federalist leaders had revived talk of seceding from the Union. Late in 1814 they held a meeting, the **Hartford Convention,** to consider this step. Fortunately, moderates at the convention managed to prevent such an extreme act. When the war ended without serious loss to the United States, the Federalist party suddenly seemed out of date and almost unpatriotic. Trade with Europe also picked up rapidly after the war. In the 1816 presidential election, Rufus King, the Federalist candidate, got only 34 votes in the electoral college to James Monroe's 183.

Solving Problems with England

Still another result of the War of 1812 was that it convinced Europe that the United States was here to stay. The British no longer dreamed of regaining their former colonies. This did not mean that England and the United States suddenly became allies or even particularly friendly. The new attitude was one of respect rather than friendship.

Many sore spots remained between the United States and Great Britain. After 1815, however, these conflicts were solved by diplomats, not by soldiers and sailors.

The first step was to negotiate a treaty in 1815 removing many restrictions on trade between the two nations. Then, in 1817 they signed the **Rush-Bagot Agreement,** which provided that neither would maintain a fleet of warships on the Great Lakes. Each was to have four small vessels on the lakes to act as a kind of police force, but the border between the United States and Canada—one of the longest in the world—was to remain forever unfortified.

A difficult problem was deciding on the exact boundary between Canada and the United States. Special commissions made up of American and British experts worked on this. In 1818 one of these commissions fixed the northern boundary of the Louisiana Purchase at 49° north latitude. At this time the two nations also agreed to joint control of the area west of the Louisiana territory, known as the Oregon Country.

Jackson's Invasion of Florida

Many westerners had hoped that the War of 1812 would pry Florida from Spanish control. They were disappointed. But soon after the war the United States got possession of both Florida and a huge chunk of Spanish territory west of Louisiana.

Settlers who lived along the southern frontier of the United States complained of raids by Seminoles from Florida, reinforced by many Creek warriors who had gone there after their terrible defeat by Andrew Jackson at the Battle of Horseshoe Bend.

The settlers also complained that many of their slaves were escaping into Florida. About 250 of these runaways controlled what was known as the **Negro Fort** on the Apalachicola River, about 60 miles (96 kilometers) south of the American border. Knowing there was a fort controlled by runaways encouraged other slaves to try to escape. In 1816 an American force marched into Florida—Spanish territory—and blew up the fort, killing most of its occupants.

Early in 1818 General Jackson was sent to crush the Seminoles. Again ignoring the boundary line, he boldly pursued them into Florida at the head of an army of 3,000 soldiers and 2,000 Indian allies. The Seminoles fell back, avoiding a battle.

Library of Congress

Jackson was furious. When two Indian chiefs were captured by trickery, he had them hanged. At the town of St. Marks on the Gulf of Mexico he seized Alexander Arbuthnot, a harmless, 70-year-old British trader. Arbuthnot's crime had been to warn the Seminoles that the army was coming. Shortly thereafter Jackson captured another British civilian, Robert Ambrister, a former British marine who was indeed working with the Seminoles.

Jackson believed that all the conflicts with the Indians were caused by foreign agents. He decided to put Arbuthnot and Ambrister on trial. It was obviously illegal to try English civilians before an American military court on territory belonging to Spain. Jackson nevertheless did just that. The two men were found guilty and sentenced to death. Arbuthnot was hanged. Because of his military background, Ambrister was executed by a firing squad.

Since he was unable to find any Indians to attack, Jackson next marched into West Florida and captured the capital, Pensacola, which had been returned to the Spanish by the Treaty of Ghent. He dashed off a letter to President Monroe explaining what he had done. Then he went home to Tennessee.

The Seminoles attacked an American fort in Florida in 1816. These raids brought Andrew Jackson in bold pursuit.

The Transcontinental Treaty

Jackson's invasion proved that Spain could no longer control Florida. In Washington the Spanish minister to the United States, Luis de Onis, bitterly protested the seizure of Pensacola. It was "an outrage," he said. Jackson must be punished.

President Monroe was embarrassed. He did not want to approve of what Jackson had done. But he did not want to give up the territory Jackson had taken. He dared not criticize the popular general publicly. So he told Onis that he agreed that Jackson had gone beyond his orders, but had done so because of military necessity.

Onis knew then that the United States was not going to give back West Florida. The rest of Florida was surely lost as well.

Onis was already negotiating with John Quincy Adams, the secretary of state, about the boundary between the Louisiana Purchase and Spanish Mexico. Perhaps he could get better terms in this discussion by agreeing to give up Florida.

John Quincy Adams, the son of ex-president John Adams, had been in public service since he was a teenager. Like his father he was very intelligent, hard-working, stubborn, and as shrewd as a Yankee trader. He suggested to Onis that Spain should give up Florida. The United States would then be willing to postpone settling the Louisiana boundary. As Adams well knew, this was exactly the opposite of what Onis wanted.

Onis was afraid that a delay would only increase American demands in the West. Already Adams was claiming that the Mexican province of Texas was part of the Louisiana Purchase. So Onis insisted that a "safe and permanent" line be agreed to quickly.

Adams pressed Onis to accept the Rio Grande as the line. Since this would have given Texas to the United States, Onis practically spat out his refusal. After further dickering Adams suggested a compromise. A western boundary would be drawn that left Texas in Spanish hands. But he added the idea that from a point north of Texas the boundary line should extend west *"straight to the Pacific Ocean."*

This would give the United States a boundary all the way across North America. Onis tried to get Adams to give up this claim. He failed. Finally he wrote his superiors in Spain: "If His Majesty . . . hasn't sufficient forces to make war on this country, then I think it would be best not to delay making the best settlement possible."

In October 1818 the Spanish government gave in. It agreed in principle to Adams' demand. In a few months the details were ironed out by Adams and Onis. Spain ceded Florida to the United States. In return the United States canceled $5 million in claims against the Spanish in Florida. The line between Mexico and the United States followed roughly the present eastern and northern boundaries of Texas, then went north to 42° north latitude, then west to the Pacific Ocean.

Adams drove such a hard bargain that he forced Onis to agree that where the boundary followed rivers, it would run along the Spanish side of the river, not the middle of the stream as most such boundaries do.

The **Transcontinental Treaty** was a great triumph for Adams and

Museum of Fine Arts, Boston

The young John Quincy Adams sat for this oil portrait by John Singleton Copley. Copley's paintings were said to mirror his subjects with great accuracy. What negotiation did Adams successfully complete?

316   WAR AND PEACE, 1812–1823

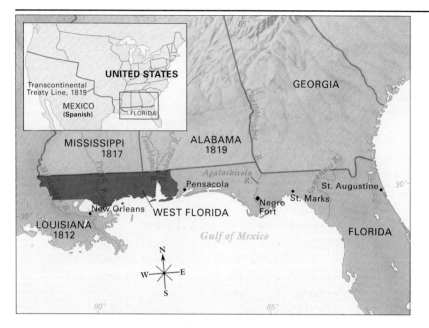

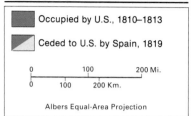
Occupied by U.S., 1810–1813

Ceded to U.S. by Spain, 1819

0   100   200 Mi.

0   100   200 Km.

Albers Equal-Area Projection

LEARNING FROM MAPS. *Florida, which was a British colony at the time of the Revolutionary War, had again become a Spanish possession. Why was it important for American defenses that Florida become part of the United States? Did the United States gain or lose land by signing the Transcontinental Treaty in 1819?*

for the United States. Great Britain's Proclamation of 1763 had set the western boundaries of the American colonies at the Appalachian Mountains. In 1783 the peace treaty ending the Revolutionary War extended that boundary to the Mississippi River. The Louisiana Purchase of 1803 extended the boundary to the Rocky Mountains. Now this treaty with Spain pushed the line on to the Pacific Ocean. In little more than 50 years the nation had grown from a string of settlements along the Atlantic Coast to a powerful country a continent wide. John Quincy Adams was not exaggerating when he said that the day he and Onis signed the treaty was "the most important day of my life."

The Whole Continent One Nation

When Adams first suggested extending the boundary line between Mexico and the United States west to the Pacific, Onis argued that there was no need for such a boundary. He insisted that the entire Pacific Coast belonged to Spain. He denied that the United States had a right to any territory west of the Louisiana Purchase.

Adams declared that Onis's argument was "nonsense." He reminded the Spaniard that Great Britain claimed the Oregon Country and was willing to share control of it with the United States. Russia also had a number of trading posts along the northern Pacific Coast.

Adams, of course, won the argument. But his success was more a sign of Spain's weakness than of the correctness of his argument. Aside from the explorations of Lewis and Clark, the United States had little on which to base its claims in the region beyond the Rocky Mountains. Jefferson had *purchased* Louisiana from France. Was

Shelburne Museum, Shelburne, Vermont

A Conestoga wagon on a Pennsylvania turnpike was painted by Thomas Birch in 1814. What are some other ways people moved westward?

this not proof that the nation had not owned that land before 1803? How could it claim a right to land still farther west?

The answer to this question was very simple. The people were pushing steadily westward. They assumed that the land beyond the mountains was eventually to be a part of the United States. John Quincy Adams, for example, was convinced that God intended the United States to control all of North America. He wrote in 1811:

❝ The whole continent appears to be destined . . . to be peopled by one nation. . . . The acquisition of a definite line of boundary to the [Pacific] forms a great epoch in our history. ❞

No European country was strong enough or determined enough to resist United States claims very vigorously. Of course, the native Americans of the Northwest were another matter. They fought hard to protect their own claims. But that came much later. When Adams and Onis divided the land by drawing a line on a map, the actual invasion of the region by white settlers lay far in the future.

Return to the Preview & Review on page 313.

America's Hispanic Heritage

The Prado, Madrid; Courtesy Art Resource

The "Maids of Honor" shows Princess Margarita surrounded by her friends. Velázquez himself stands to the left, holding a brush. The mirror at the back reflects the smiling king and queen. How do you think the artist was able to paint himself into the picture?

Courtesy Christie's, N.Y.

"Princess Margarita after Velázquez" was painted by Fernando Botero of Colombia in 1978. His figures with large heads recall the sculptures made by early Indian artisans.

More than 300 years pass before our eyes when we see these two paintings of the same little Spanish princess. The first is by Diego Rodriquez de Silva y Velázquez. In 1656 he painted *Las Meñinas* ("Maids of Honor") in the court of Philip IV of Spain. The second portrait of Princess Margarita was painted in 1978 by Fernando Botero of Colombia. His painting, like the others on these pages, shows our Hispanic heritage. Botero is modern and at the same time pays homage to the American Indians whose art and architecture flourished long before the painted sails of Columbus' ships hove into view.

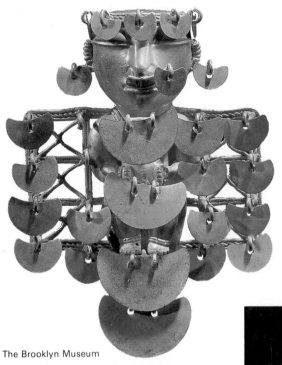

The Brooklyn Museum

From Colombia comes this Quimbáya gilded pendant fashioned between 500 and 1000 A.D. The medallions cover the likeness of a woman whose face we see but whose torso is modestly covered.

New Orleans Museum of Art

salamiel Paxdei

"Archangel with a Gun" was painted on cotton in the 17th century by a Peruvian disciple of an artist known as the Master of Calamarcha.

Photo: MAS

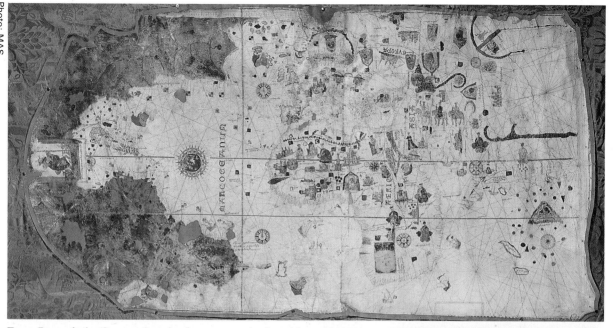

From Juan de la Cosa, a Spaniard, we have this world map published in 1500. It shows for the first time the islands and coasts of the Americas.

A Spanish-trained Indian artist made this Peruvian miniature of "Atahualpa, Last King of the Incas."

The Thomas Gilcrease Institute

Museo de Arte de Ponce

A TAHVALLPA INGA XIIII. Y vltimo El vencido Hijo de Mama Chachapoya Reyna de Quito aclamado por Rey del Cuzco Fue vencido y prezo el desdichado Monarca del Conquistador D.ⁿ Francisco Pizarro, y despues degollado en Cajamarca, Hallase que fue Bautizado y se llamo Donjuan ATAHUALLPA. El año de 1533.

The first great native-born Puerto Rican painter was José Campeche. His "Dama a Caballo" ("Lady on Horseback") shows how strong the Spanish influence was in 1785.

America's Hispanic Heritage   321

The Museum of Modern Art, N.Y.

Amelia Pelaez del Casal is a Cuban painter who studied for a time in Europe. There she was influenced by the Cubist style of Pablo Picasso of Spain and Georges Braque of France. To these influences she brought the vivid colors of her Caribbean homeland, as seen in "Fishes," on the left, painted in 1943.

One of Mexico's greatest artists was Diego Rivera, best known for his murals. "Women Washing Clothes in a River among Zopilotes" was painted in 1928.

Miguel Martinez, a contemporary Hispanic American who lives in Taos, New Mexico, is the artist of this contemporary painting entitled "Taos Mesa."

Courtesy Miguel Martinez

Collection of Frances de Santos, Courtesy Sotheby's

5. A LATIN AMERICA POLICY

Revolution in Latin America

Spain ceded Florida to the United States and signed the Transcontinental Treaty because it was no longer strong enough to protect its vast holdings in the Americas. The great Spanish empire was falling apart. Revolutionary leaders like Simón Bolívar in Venezuela, José de San Martín in Argentina, Bernardo O'Higgins in Chile, and Miguel Hidalgo y Costilla in Mexico inspired the people to break from their colonial masters. By 1822 most of Spain's colonies in South and Central America, often called **Latin America,** had revolted and declared their independence.

Just as the American Revolution had stirred revolutionary feelings in France, it had a profound effect on Latin America. More and more people were demanding the "natural rights" described in the Declaration of Independence and the Constitution. One by one the Spanish colonies in South and Central America threw off their colonial bonds and established governments based on their own values.

These Latin American revolutions delighted most people in the United States. The new nations seemed to be copying the example of their North American neighbor. As free countries they would be open to ships and goods from the United States. This had not been so under Spanish rule. President Monroe promptly established diplomatic relations with the new republics.

Great Britain also profited from Spain's declining influence. But it did not intend to recognize the new republics officially, as the United States had done. The British found themselves in a difficult position. On the one hand, they did not want to encourage revolutions or the formations of republics anywhere. British leaders feared that revolutionary ideas might spread and "infect" their own colonies. On the other hand, they did not want to see the South American republics destroyed. They were worried about other European powers that did not trade heavily with South America. Might they not help Spain regain control of its former colonies? Already there was talk of a large French army being sent to South America.

In 1823 George Canning, the British foreign minister, proposed that the United States and Great Britain issue a joint statement warning other nations not to try to restore Spanish control in America. The two countries themselves should promise not to try to take over these former colonies, Canning added.

This was most flattering for the United States—this opportunity to issue with Great Britain a joint statement of international policy. But this particular statement was not really one that the United States wished to make. Secretary of State Adams had two reasons for rejecting Canning's suggestion. The island of Cuba was still a Spanish

Use these questions to guide your reading. Answer the questions after completing Section 5.
Understanding Issues, Events, & Ideas. Compare Monroe's foreign policy with Washington's, using the following words: Latin America, Monroe Doctrine, historical significance.
1. Why did the revolutions in Latin America delight most people in the United States?
2. What joint statement did Great Britain want to issue with the United States? Why did the United States refuse?
3. What were the major principles of the Monroe Doctrine?
Thinking Critically. Why might nations of Latin America have supported the Monroe Doctrine? Why might they have opposed it?

OAS—Museum of Modern Art of Latin America

Simón Bolívar is the great revolutionary hero of South America. He is often called The Liberator. With his fellow patriots he drove the Europeans out of Latin America.

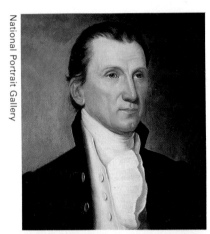

National Portrait Gallery

White House Historical Association

Thomas Jefferson said, "Monroe was so honest that if you turned his soul inside out there would not be a spot on it." To the Monroes fell the task of refurnishing the rebuilt White House, and when we visit the president's home today we are more apt to see their taste reflected than that of the earlier founders. Monroe was painted by John Vanderlyn. Elizabeth Monroe was painted by Benjamin West. Do you suppose she would draw criticism today for her ermine and velvets?

colony. Someday, Adams hoped, the United States might be able to take it over. Canning's plan would rule out this possibility. And why should the United States help the British increase trade with the new republics?

Why trail along like a rowboat in the wake of a warship? It would be better, Adams advised President Monroe, for the United States to issue a statement of its own. The statement, he added, should deal with the whole question of relations between the United States, the other countries of the Western Hemisphere, and the nations of Europe. After much discussion the president agreed.

On December 2, 1823, the members of Congress gathered to hear the president's annual State of the Union message. The message, like most such speeches, dealt with many subjects. What Monroe said about foreign relations made up a relatively small part of it. He did not stress the subject in any special way.

The Monroe Doctrine

What the president said in his State of the Union message came to be known as the **Monroe Doctrine.** It consisted of the following principles:

The United States would not interfere with any existing European colony in North or South America. In other words, the United States had no intention of trying to force Great Britain to give up Canada, or Spain to give up Cuba.

The colonial period of North and South American history was now over. No more colonies could be founded in the Americas.

The United States would consider any attempt to create a new colony "dangerous to [its] peace and safety." In other words, the United States might go to war to prevent such an attempt.

The United States and Europe had different political systems that should not be mixed. Therefore, the United States would not become involved in purely European affairs.

In 1823 no one realized how important this statement of principles was. It was many years before anyone referred to it as the Monroe Doctrine. Even the person most responsible for the statement, John Quincy Adams, thought it a small matter compared to the Transcontinental Treaty and many of the lesser diplomatic affairs he handled as secretary of state. In 1824, when Adams was running for president, he did not even list the Monroe Doctrine among his achievements.

European leaders were more amused than annoyed by Monroe's speech. If the United States could not even protect its capital city from a raiding party, how could it police the whole Western Hemi-

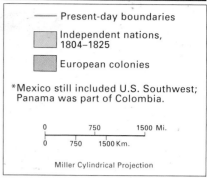

NEW NATIONS IN LATIN AMERICA, 1825*

— Present-day boundaries

Independent nations,
1804–1825

European colonies

*Mexico still included U.S. Southwest;
Panama was part of Colombia.

0   750   1500 Mi.

0   750   1500 Km.

Miller Cylindrical Projection

LEARNING FROM MAPS. *By the mid-1820s revolutions in Latin America modeled on the American Revolution produced many new countries. According to the map, what countries remained in the possession of Europeans?*

sphere? The new Latin American republics felt the same way. They approved of the ideas in President Monroe's statement. They hoped he was sincere. But could the United States really protect them in time of crisis?

Yet the Monroe Doctrine was one of the most important statements of American foreign policy ever issued. It provides a good example of how people closest to an event sometimes cannot appreciate its significance. The **historical significance** of events is seldom entirely clear when the events occur. This is because the significance usually depends upon the results of the event. These results occur over time and seldom can be predicted. The Declaration of Independence of July 4, 1776, for example, was a fine statement of principles. But its historical significance was clear only when the new nation fought and won the Revolutionary War.

Similarly, only after the United States had grown powerful enough to back its words with actions did it become clear that President Monroe had issued a kind of second Declaration of Independence. This one said to the nations of Europe: "Hands off the Western Hemisphere."

Return to the Preview & Review on page 323.

CHAPTER 9 REVIEW

1795	1800	1805

1795
Treaty of Greenville

Chapter Summary

Read the statement below. Choose one, and write a paragraph explaining its importance.

1. The War Hawks and frontier settlers blamed England for continuing troubles with the Indians in the Northwest Territory.
2. Tecumseh, the great Indian leader, organized many of the Indians in the Ohio Valley.
3. General William Henry Harrison defeated the Indians at Tippecanoe.
4. Many Americans, especially northeastern merchants, opposed the War of 1812.
5. The United States Navy was very successful, and despite the burning of Washington, D.C., land forces fought the British to a draw.
6. American pride was heightened by the defense of Fort McHenry and Andrew Jackson's heroic leadership at the Battle of New Orleans.
7. Negotiations after the war solved problems with England and added Florida and other territory to the United States.
8. Between 1804 and 1825 many nations in Latin America became independent. In the Monroe Doctrine the United States insisted that Europe no longer involve itself in the affairs of the Western Hemisphere.

Reviewing Chronological Order

Number your paper 1–5. Then study the time line above and place the following events in the order in which they happened by writing the first next to 1, the second next to 2, and so on.

1. British troops burn Washington
2. The Monroe Doctrine
3. The Transcontinental Treaty
4. Tecumseh organizes the Indians
5. War of 1812 begins

Understanding Main Ideas

1. In which region of the country was the War of 1812 bitterly opposed? Why was this opposition surprising?
2. What were the causes of conflicts between settlers and Indians on the frontier?

3. How did General Harrison try to gain land from the Indians? What method did other government leaders propose?
4. What were the major provisions of the Peace of Ghent? What were some outcomes of the war that were not part of the treaty?
5. Why had so many Latin American nations broken from Spanish rule by 1822?
6. What did the Monroe Doctrine state?

Thinking Critically

1. **Synthesizing.** Imagine that you are an African Amerian sailor serving under Oliver Hazard Perry. In your diary, write a personal account of the Battle of Put-in-Bay, including your appraisal of Perry and his treatment of you.
2. **Evaluating.** You know that when Dolley Madison fled the burning White House moments before the British arrived, she saved some silverware and a portrait of George Washington. If you were in the first lady's situation today and could save only two objects, which would you choose? Why?
3. **Analyzing.** If the telegraph had existed on December 24, 1814, how might the Battle of New Orleans have been different? Why?

Writing About History

You are one of the following: Dolley Madison escaping from the White House, Francis Scott Key watching the bombardment of Fort McHenry, an American soldier fighting at New Orleans. Write a diary entry describing what you see and your thoughts and feelings. Use the information in Chapter 9 to help you write your entry.

Practicing the Strategy

Review the strategy on page 296.
Synthesizing Information. Reread "Peace and New Boundaries" and study the maps closely. Then write a paragraph describing how and why the boundaries of the United States changed, using information from those two sources.

1812	1813	1814	1815	1817	1818	1819	1823
War of 1812 begins	Battle of Put-in-Bay	Battle of Horseshoe Bend	Battle of New Orleans	Rush-Bagot Agreement	Jackson enters Florida	Transcontinental Treaty	Monroe Doctrine

⭐ U.S. navy wins several victories

⭐ Battle of the Thames

⭐ Creek War begins

⭐ British troops burn Washington

⭐ Fort McHenry bombarded

⭐ Peace of Ghent signed

⭐ Hartford Convention

Using Primary Sources

On the night of September 13, 1814, Francis Scott Key watched the shelling of Fort McHenry. Deeply moved, Key composed a poem describing the events he had witnessed. The poem was later set to music and entitled "The Star-Spangled Banner." Ferdinand Durang first sang the tune in public in 1815. It was officially adopted as the national anthem by an act of Congress on March 3, 1931. As you read Key's words, note how they keep alive the image of the American flag. Then answer the questions.

> *"Oh, say can you see by the dawn's early light*
> *What so proudly we hail'd at the twilight's last gleaming*
> *Whose broad stripes and bright stars through the perilous fight*
> *O'er the ramparts we watched were so gallantly streaming?*
> *And the rockets' red glare, the bombs bursting in air*
> *Gave proof through the night that our flag was still there*
> *Oh, say does that star-spangled banner yet wave*
> *O'er the land of the free and the home of the brave?"*

1. Although Key watched the battle at night, he still could see the flag flying over Fort McHenry. What enabled him to see it? What does the flag symbolize?
2. What do the words "broad stripes and bright stars . . . were so gallantly streaming" suggest about Key's attitude toward his country?
3. Which line describes the United States and the American people?

Linking History & Geography

Relative location is a geographic term that refers to the positions of places in relation to other places on earth. The most common way to express relative location is in terms of distance and direction. For example, San Francisco is about 340 miles (544 kilometers) northwest of Los Angeles. The principles behind the Monroe Doctrine are based in part on relative location. Review the Monroe Doctrine on page 324 and study the map on page 325. Then in a brief paragraph, explain the geographic reason why the United States felt closely linked to the countries of Latin America.

Enriching the Study of History

1. **Individual Project.** Build a model or make a sketch of the U.S.S. *Constitution* ("Old Ironsides"). Use your model or sketch to illustrate a short oral report on this famous ship.
2. **Cooperative Project.** Create and present a half-hour biographical play about Tecumseh. Have six groups prepare and present five-minute scenes, with different classmates in the role of Tecumseh. Show Tecumseh (a) meeting with General Harrison after Harrison has made a treaty with other Indian tribes, (b) with the Prophet, planning the Red Stick Confederacy, (c) recruiting for the Redsticks on the frontier, (d) recruiting in the South, (e) meeting with the Prophet sometime after the Battle of Tippecanoe, and (f) with some of his warriors just after the Battle of the Thames.

Building America, 1790-1840

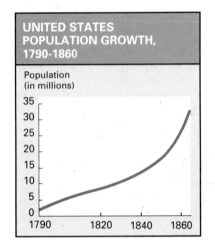

UNITED STATES POPULATION GROWTH, 1790-1860

Population (in millions)

35
30
25
20
15
10
5
0

1790   1820   1840   1860

Clayville, Rhode Island, as it appeared in 1850.

A mericans who lived between 1790 and 1840 must have been amazed by the changes that had taken place before their eyes. The population of the nation had grown from 4 million to 17 million. In 1790 the country was already larger in area than England, France, Spain, and several other European countries *combined*. By 1840 it had doubled its size. In 1840 America was still a rural society, a nation of farmers. But the picture was beginning to change. In 1790 nine out of ten people depended on the soil for their livelihood. Only about 5 percent lived in urban centers—that is, in places with a population of at least 2,500. By 1840 the percentage of Americans engaged in farming had dropped. Only about six out of ten made their living from the soil. The number of people living in towns and cities had risen to almost 11 percent. Nearly 10 percent of the labor force was working in factories in 1840. In 1790 the first factories were just being built. Clearly the nation was changing in significant ways. How would these changes come about and how would they affect American society?

Rhode Island Historical Society

After grazing in greener pastures the cows come home for the night. Asher Durand painted this picture about 1854.

Metropolitan Museum of Art

1. A DIVERSIFIED ECONOMY

Nature's Nation

What strikes us most today about the economic development of the United States is the speed with which the country changed from a land of farmers into a nation of factory workers and city dwellers. The change came about so swiftly that it seems there could have been no stopping it. But was it in fact unstoppable? If so, how can we explain the fact that most Americans of that time *opposed* the development of manufacturing and the growth of cities?

Ever since the first settlements were established in the 1600s, land had been the chief source of wealth in America. It was still so in the early 1800s. Most people wanted to own land, even if only a small plot. To own land was a sign that a person was free and independent and held a stable place in society.

Thomas Jefferson and countless other writers and speakers of the period sang the praises of the American farmer. "Those who labor in the earth," Jefferson wrote in 1785, "are the chosen people of God, if ever He had a chosen people. . . . " Little wonder that

Preview & Review

Use these questions to guide your reading. Answer the questions after completing Section 1.

Understanding Issues, Events, & Ideas. Describe changes in the American economy in the early 1800s, using the following words: diversified economy, protective tariff, duty.

1. Why did most people in America want to own land?
2. Why did some Americans want a diversified economy?
3. Why did American manufacturers want the government to place protective tariffs on imported goods?

Thinking Critically. Imagine that you are a British manufacturer in 1816. Write a letter to your cousin in America, explaining how the Tariff of 1816 has affected your business.

A Diversified Economy   329

Until they became extinct, passenger pigeons blackened the sky in flight. In the spring of 1794, in central New York, the fictional Leatherstocking—six feet tall, gray-eyed, sandy-haired, with but a single tooth left in his enormous mouth—foresees the birds' fate.

“This comes of settling a country!" he said—"here have I known the pigeons to fly for forty long years, and, till you made your clearings, there was nobody to scare or hunt them. I loved to see them come into the woods, for they were company for a body; hurting nobody; being, as it was, as harmless as a garter snake. But now it gives me sore thoughts when I hear the frighty things whizzing through the air, for I know it's only a motion to bring out all the brats in the village at them. Well! the Lord won't see the waste of his creatures for nothing, and right will be done to the pigeons, as well as others, by-and-by.”

From *The Pioneers*, James Fenimore Cooper, 1823

America was referred to as "Nature's nation." Agriculture was the foundation on which the nation was built. Most people believed that manufacturing and big cities would simply destroy the peaceful farming society that was the American ideal. Americans had only to follow the "laws of nature" heralded by the Enlightenment to be successful.

The Turn Toward Manufacturing

A small but determined group of Americans did see the need to develop manufacturing. Alexander Hamilton was the first to speak for them. They favored a **diversified economy,** one in which manufacturing existed side by side with agriculture. They argued that manufacturing would make America independent of European suppliers. Not surprisingly, the supporters of manufacturing first gained a wide audience during the crisis that led to the American Revolution.

Political freedom would mean little without economic independence. This was the warning of Dr. Benjamin Rush, who was the president of the United Company of Philadelphia for Promoting American Manufactures. Many people agreed when Rush said:

The Granger Collection, New York

Benjamin Rush

“ A people who are *entirely* dependent upon foreigners for food and clothes must always be subject to them.”

After the first battles of Lexington and Concord there was no argument against American manufacturing. It was now a necessity. The Continental Congress was especially anxious to encourage the production of weapons. But guns and ammunition remained scarce, as the soldiers at the Battle of Bunker Hill and in other early campaigns sadly learned. The Continental Army had to depend upon foreign supplies. The Americans could not have won the war without this assistance.

The American Revolution brought the nation political independence. But did it have economic independence? No sooner had the war ended than the British began selling cloth, chinaware, and every sort of manufactured product at bargain prices in order to win back American customers. Consumers purchased these goods eagerly. American producers lost business as a result. They wanted the government to place high taxes, called **protective tariffs,** on imported goods. Then those goods could not be sold so cheaply. As we have seen, the wish to have only one set of laws to regulate all trade and

A PROTECTIVE TARIFF

A protective tariff works this way: Suppose a hat manufacturer in Danbury, Connecticut, could make a hat for $3. After adding a profit the hat might be sold for $4. But an English hat manufacturer, having lower labor costs, might be able to make a similar hat for $2.50. Even after adding a dollar for profit, the English manufacturer could undersell the American. As a result the American manufacturer would be driven out of business.

The Tariff of 1816, therefore, put a tax of 30 percent on imported hats. Because 30 percent

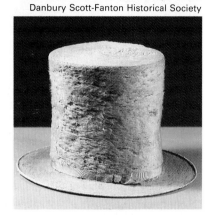

Danbury Scott-Fanton Historical Society

of $3.50 is $1.05, the English hat would now cost $4.55. The American manufacturer's business would be safe. Even if the

English hatmaker sold hats at cost, the duty—30 percent of $2.50—would raise the price to $3.25, still leaving the American with a small advantage.

Of course, American consumers had to pay higher prices because of the new tariff. But the theory was that the whole country would benefit. Business activity would increase because of the protection given to manufacturers. More people, for example, would be employed in making hats. And these hatmakers would spend their earnings, thus helping other businesses grow.

commerce was one of the most important reasons for revising the Articles of Confederation.

Americans continued to depend on foreign-made goods until Jefferson's Embargo Act of 1807 and the War of 1812 made importing them almost impossible. With European goods unavailable, quick

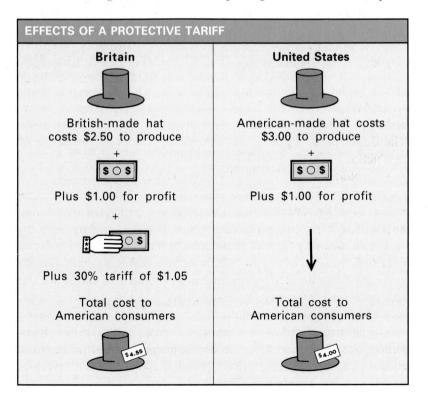

EFFECTS OF A PROTECTIVE TARIFF

Britain

British-made hat costs $2.50 to produce
+
Plus $1.00 for profit
+
Plus 30% tariff of $1.05

Total cost to American consumers

$4.55

United States

American-made hat costs $3.00 to produce
+
Plus $1.00 for profit

Total cost to American consumers

$4.00

LEARNING FROM PICTOGRAPHS. *What does the pictograph to the left illustrate? Why is the measure called a protective tariff?*

A Diversified Economy 331

Collection IBM Corporation, Armonk, N.Y.

The Yankee peddler was a welcome visitor in New England homes. His horse-drawn wagon carried an enormous variety of the goods essential for everyday life. What might each of the two women be thinking as they look at his wares?

profits could be made by anyone who could produce articles that were usually imported. People put money into manufacturing. Before 1808 there were only 15 cotton mills in the nation. In 1809 alone, 87 mills were built.

Most Americans became persuaded that manufacturing must become an important part of their economy. Even Thomas Jefferson, who had opposed government aid to industry while he was president, wrote in 1816:

> " To be independent for the comforts of life, we must make them ourselves. We must now place the manufacturer by the side of the agriculturalist. "

After the war the British again tried to dump manufactured products on the American market. Congress responded by passing the Tariff of 1816, which placed a tax on imports, or **duty,** of 20 to 30 percent on many foreign manufactured products. The purpose of these high duties was not to collect money. It was to make foreign goods cost more than the same American products. In other words, the duties were protective tariffs intended to protect American industry from foreign competition.

To aid manufactures with loans, Congress created a new Bank of the United States in 1816. The first Bank had gone out of business when its charter expired in 1811. The new Bank, like the first one, was given a 20-year charter. 🖘

Return to the Preview & Review on page 329.

2. THE INDUSTRIAL REVOLUTION

Mass Production

American manufacturers had a treasure store of natural resources to draw on. Abundant forests provided lumber for buildings and machines and also logs for fuel. There was iron for making tools and nails. Swift-running streams supplied waterpower to run machinery.

Still, American manufacturers had to overcome many obstacles. It was difficult to turn out goods in large quantities. The shoemakers of Lynn, Massachusetts, made boots one pair at a time for particular customers. The clockmakers of Philadelphia made timepieces only after individuals placed their orders. Americans did not yet have the manufacturing know-how to **mass produce,** or make large numbers of articles. Their **industrial technology**—that is, the tools, machines, and other things used to produce goods—was very inefficient.

One of the first Americans to improve the nation's industrial technology was Eli Whitney. When war threatened between the United States and France in the 1790s, Congress decided to purchase 7,000 muskets. Muskets were still in short supply in America. The new government arsenal at Springfield, Massachusetts, had turned out only about 1,000 muskets in three years.

Here in Whitneyville, Connecticut, Eli Whitney built his gun factory to make muskets with interchangeable parts.

Yale University Art Gallery

Use these questions to guide your reading. Answer the questions after completing Section 2.
Understanding Issues, Events, & Ideas. Describe early factory production in the United States, using the following words: mass produce, industrial technology, interchangeable parts, Industrial Revolution, spinning jenny, water-frame, putting-out system, Rhode Island system, Lowell system.

1. What assets did American manufacturers have? What obstacles did they have to overcome?
2. How did Eli Whitney set out to improve the nation's industrial technology?
3. What ws the benefit of the spinning jenny?
4. How did the British government try to protect the secrets of its Industrial Revolution?
5. Why did Lowell not want to copy British labor methods?

Thinking Critically. If you were a worker in the early 1800s, would you have preferred to work under the putting-out system, the Rhode Island system, or the Lowell system? Explain your answer.

Muskets were made by hand. A gunsmith shaped each barrel and fitted it with its own trigger and other parts. If a part broke, a new one had to be made and fitted to that particular gun. The barrel or trigger of one musket could not be substituted for another. It would not fit.

Whitney decided that he could manufacture muskets by the thousands if he could make them from **interchangeable parts.** If all triggers and barrels for a certain model of gun were exactly the same, the parts from any musket could be used with those of any other.

In 1798 Whitney wrote to Oliver Wolcott, the secretary of the treasury. He offered to turn out 10,000 muskets. His offer must have astonished Wolcott, but the government needed the guns badly. Whitney got the contract and an advance payment of $5,000 to get his business started.

It took Whitney two years to produce the grinders and borers and lathes that would enable him to produce identical parts. By September 1801 his shop in New Haven, Connecticut, had produced 500 muskets. He took ten of these to Washington. There he appeared before an amazed but delighted group of officials, which included President John Adams and Vice President Thomas Jefferson. Whitney took the muskets apart. He mixed the parts so that it was no longer possible to know which trigger went with which barrel, and so on. Then, choosing pieces at random, he reassembled the parts into ten muskets. Whitney's demonstration led to a revised contract. The new contract gave him an advance of $30,000.

James Hargreave's spinning jenny was first built in 1765. The one pictured is an improved model. At it a spinner could operate all the spindles at once by cranking the wheel. When the cotton fibers were stretched, fine thread was made. What were some advantages of the spinning jenny?

Machines Replace Hand Tools

While Whitney was developing his method of producing interchangeable parts, English manufacturers were shifting their work from hand tools to power-driven machinery. This was the **Industrial Revolution.**

The process began in the 1700s. In those days almost every home had a spinning wheel for making thread and a loom for weaving cloth. Families made a good deal of their own clothing, working in their spare time. But it took about six times as long to make thread as it took to weave the same thread into cloth. This meant that one weaver used all the thread that six spinners could produce.

In 1765 an English weaver and carpenter named James Hargreaves built a machine called the **spinning jenny.** (Some say the machine was named after his wife. Others say the name came from "gin," a short form of the word "engine.") The spinning jenny was a mechanical spinning wheel. It was small, cheap, and easy to build. It could be operated by hand. Soon Hargreaves's invention found its way into thousands of English homes.

The spinning jenny increased output, but it did not reduce the price of cotton cloth very much. Because cotton fibers are not very strong, cotton could only be used for the short threads running across the cloth. Linen had to be used for the thousands of threads running lengthwise. And linen, which was made from the flax plant, was much more expensive than cotton.

In 1768 Richard Arkwright, a barber, solved this problem. He invented a spinning machine that produced much stronger cotton thread. Now cloth could be made entirely of cotton. The price fell.

Arkwright's machine was much bigger and heavier than Hargreaves's jenny. It could not be kept in a home or operated by hand. It required a mechanical force, such as waterpower, to run it. Thus it was called the **water-frame.** In 1771 Arkwright formed a partnership and constructed what the English called a "mill." Americans sometimes called mills factories.

The Factory Comes to America

Arkwright's water-frames proved so successful that by the late 1780s over 100 cotton mills in England were using them. Cotton cloth production increased greatly. Soon English cloth was being exported to every part of the world.

The British government had no intention of sharing the secrets of its Industrial Revolution with other countries. It would not allow the export of textile-making machinery. Nor would it allow workers who were familiar with the machines to leave the country. But a number of these skilled workers, called mechanics, still made their way to America. The most important was Samuel Slater, who at one time had worked for Arkwright. When Slater decided to go to Amer-

Public Records Office, London

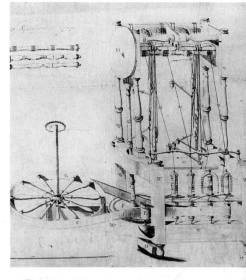

Here is the 1769 patent drawing for the spinning machine invented by Richard Arkwright. Cotton fibers were twisted between its rollers to produce strong thread. Why was Arkwright's spinning machine a product of the Industrial Revolution, but not Hargreave's spinning jenny?

Rhode Island Historical Society

Samuel Slater came to America in 1789 after memorizing plans for cotton-spinning machinery. Today he would be considered an industrial spy. Do you think it was right for him to memorize his employer's designs to take to another country?

Rhode Island Historical Society

Moses Brown is one of America's early benefactors of education. He built the factory to house Samuel Slater's spinning machines. Brown prospered and later gave large sums of money to the Quakers and to Brown University, which is named for his brother. You might inquire in your own state to see how much financial support must come from private sources for colleges and universities, large and small.

ica, he memorized the designs for the new cotton-spinning machinery.

Slater landed in New York in 1789, the year the new Constitution went into effect. He soon met up with Moses Brown of Providence, Rhode Island. Brown was a member of a family that had been engaged in commerce and small-scale manufacturing in Rhode Island for generations. Slater agreed to build cotton-spinning machines for Brown in Pawtucket, Rhode Island, on the Blackstone River. By 1791 the work was done. Slater's machines spun cotton thread, using waterwheels turned by the current of the Blackstone for power. This thread was both better and cheaper than homespun cotton. The day of the factory had arrived in America.

Slater's machines made only thread. Brown sold some of this thread in his Providence store. The rest he supplied to workers who wove it into cloth on looms in their own homes. This was known as *putting out* the thread. The weavers returned the cloth to Brown, who paid them so much a yard for their work. He then sold the cloth in his store.

The **putting-out system**—families producing finished items at home—was widely used in America. It persisted long after factories became common. Hats, shoes, stockings—many products as well as cloth—were made in this manner. The system made one workshop out of many homes. Brown's weavers worked for wages, but they did so at home. They were less dependent upon Brown than the workers in Slater's factory were on Slater. They owned their own tools and had control over when and how hard they worked.

The Changing Role of Women

The beginnings of industrialization had both positive and negative effects on women. Women had long been respected for their role in the family. Women in the colonies had worked at jobs ranging from shopkeepers and journalists to "doctoresses" and midwives. But by the late 1700s their opportunities had begun to slip. Medicine and other professions began requiring college training and licensing. Because women weren't permitted in college, they could not get a license. So they could no longer practice, no matter how much practical experience they had.

Generally speaking, American women accepted their lot in life. Most were content to marry, have children, and keep house. They realized the hard work and lack of status that being a housewife meant.

Industrialization meant many changes for women. The shift from homemade goods to factory-made goods changed women's economic role. In colonial America women on farms had worked side by side with their husbands as partners. As factories sprang up in towns and cities, more and more families left the farm and men entered the business world. Now instead of being a partner in producing what her family needed, a wife was dependent on her husband to buy factory-made goods and food. But with husbands away at work six days a week, wives began to assert control over day-to-day activities once shared with husbands.

As the American economy moved steadily from an agricultural base to manufacturing, as more and more people left the self-sufficiency of the farms, class distinctions in American society became more obvious: There were people with money and people without it. Women, as well as men, became increasingly identified with specific social classes: lower, middle, upper.

Women from the lower classes began to work in the factories of the early Industrial Revolution. For these women industrialization was an advantage. They were able to earn money and participate in the world of labor outside the home. Many later became involved in the push for better working conditions and workers' rights. Wives of wealthier men had more leisure time. It was these middle- and upper-class women who eventually became the leaders of the women's rights movements.

Beginning in the late 1700s there was also a growing interest in education for women. Several "Ladies Academies" were founded. Young girls who had brothers in school were allowed to study along side them and receive the same training. In 1787 Dr. Benjamin Rush, a professor at the University of Pennsylvania, spoke out on the need for education for women. Among the subjects he suggested they study were the English language and writing, geography, history, biography, travel, vocal music, dancing, and religious instruction. Then in the 1820s Boston opened an "experimental" high school for girls that taught the same subjects as the boys' schools.

Recruiting a Labor Force

Who wanted to work in factories? In England most factory jobs were filled by former tenant farmers who had been thrown out of work when owners fenced the land and planted grass in order to raise sheep. But there had been no enclosure movement in the United States. Most American farmers worked their own land for themselves. They were self-employed. So were most artisans, such as carpenters and shoemakers. Few people in America worked for wages. Still fewer were willing to work in factories.

American manufacturers tried to solve this problem in two ways. The **Rhode Island system** made much use of children. Slater's first spinning machines were operated by seven boys and two girls ranging in age from 7 to 12. Slater could use these young children because his machinery was relatively easy to operate. He could pay them much less than adults. Children in the Slater mills received between 33 and 67 cents a week, while adult workers in Rhode Island were earning between $2 and $3 a week. As late as 1820 more than half of the workers in the Rhode Island mills were children.

This gentle watercolor cannot reproduce the noisy waterfall from the Blackstone River which turned Samuel Slater's spinning machines at Pawtucket Falls, Rhode Island. By today's standards how is this an ecologically sound operation?

Rhode Island Historical Society

FAMILY WANTED,
To work in a Thread-Mill:

THE Mill is four miles and a half from Providence, on the Turnpike road leading from Providence to Chepachet, and one fourth of a mile from Messrs. Richard Anthony & Son's Cotton-Mill. For particulars, enquire of Asa Sayles, on the premises.   A. SAYLES & Co.
North-Providence, March 7. 13W.

Child labor seemed perfectly reasonable to most people. Farm children had always worked. In those days children were not required by law to go to school. Poor families were delighted to have any money their children could earn. Often entire families, parents and children together, worked in the early factories, answering advertisements like the one on the left from a Providence newspaper.

The second method of getting workers for the factories was invented by Francis Cabot Lowell, a prominent Boston merchant. In 1810 Lowell visited spinning and weaving mills in England. He was deeply impressed by their efficiency. Like Slater, he carefully memorized the layout of the mills. He hoped to be able to reproduce them in New England.

Lowell's opportunity to test his memory came sooner than he had expected. When he returned to America, the War of 1812 was under way. Foreign trade had come to a standstill. No English goods were available. Lowell therefore organized a group of investors called the Boston Associates and hired a brilliant young engineer named Paul Moody.

Lowell and Moody spent a year constructing power looms copied from English designs. Meanwhile, the Associates built a factory at Waltham, Massachusetts, where they could use the waterpower of the Charles River. By the end of 1813 the factory and machinery were ready to operate. This plant both spun cotton into thread *and* wove it into cloth by machine.

Lowell did not copy British labor practices. He and other manufacturers were disturbed by the poverty of English workers during the Industrial Revolution in England. Lowell was as much concerned with the well-being of his workers as with his own profits. He was determined not to use children and poor families, as was being done in England and Rhode Island.

Instead, the **Lowell system** employed young unmarried girls from neighboring farms. Many of these young women were willing to work for wages before settling down. Many found they were far better off than if they had stayed at home. Eben Jennison wrote to his daughter Elizabeth in Lowell:

Point of View

The women workers in Lowell, Massachusetts, published their own magazine. Here is the view of one of the millworkers.

> 66 The season with us has been very Dry and the Drough[t] verry severe. The crops are very light indeed and business verry Dull [slow]. If you should be blessed with your health and are contented I think you will do better where you are than you could do here.[1] 99

Many were able to save part of the wages, and some even sent money home. In a later letter Jennison thanked his daughters (Amelia had joined her sister in Lowell) for sending $5, and promised to repay them with interest "some day or other." He also instructed Elizabeth to "look out for" another younger sister, Emily, who was coming to Lowell:

> 66 A few words in relation to Emily. She had got about ready to come to Lowel. . . . I should not consent to hir coming at any rate if you was not there. She is young [16] and needs a mothers care and a mothers advise. You must se to hir and give hir such council as you thinks she needs. She may be homesick for a spell but if you comfort hir up she will soon get the better of it.[2] 99

And the young girls who had left their families and friends did get homesick! Sarah Hodgdon wrote to her mother Mary:

> 66 Give my love to farther. Tell him not to forget me and to my dear sister and to my brothers and to my grandmother. Tell her I do not forget her. And to my Aunts and to all my enquiring friends.
>
> I want to se you more I think
> Than I can write with pen and ink.
> But when I shall I cannot tell
> But from my heart I wish you well.
> I wish you well from all my heart

> Poor lone Hannah,
> Sitting at the window,
> binding shoes:
>   Faded, wrinkled,
> Sitting, stitching, in a
> mournful muse.
>   Bright-eyed beauty
> once was she,
>   When the bloom was
> on the tree:
>   Spring and winter,
> Hannah's at the window
> binding shoes.
>   Lucy Larcom, c. 1820

[1]From *The Underside of American History*, edited by Thomas R. Frazier
[2]*Ibid.*

The Industrial Revolution   339

Although we are so far apart.
If you die there and I die here,
Before one God we shall appear.[1] 〞

But homesick or not, the idea of life in the factory community seemed interesting and even exciting to most of the young girls. Most found, however, that their life was very hard.

Families sometimes moved to mill towns too. Making a living at farming was increasingly hard, especially in New England. Factories offered new hopes—and new frustrations. This letter, written by a New England farmer in 1843 to friends back home, explains why the family moved and what they encountered:

    ❝ You will probely want to know the cause of our moveing here. One of them is the hard times to get a liveing off the farm for so large a famely. So we have devided our famely for the year. We had left Plummer and Luther to care for the farm with granmarm and Aunt Polly. The rest of us have moved to Nashvill thinking the girls and Charles they would probaly worke in the Mill. But we have had bad luck in giting them in. Only Jane has got in yet. Ann has the promis of going to the mill next week. Hannah is going to school. We are in hopes to take in a few borders but have not got any yet.[2] 〞

Conditions varied from mill to mill. Some were far more pleasant than others. The English novelist Charles Dickens described several Lowell factories in his *American Notes for General Circulation,* written in 1842. In general, he felt conditions in these factories were much better than those in English factories, with which his readers were all too familiar. Dickens wrote:

    ❝ The girls were returning to their work; . . . They were all well dressed, but not to my thinking above their condition. . . . The rooms in which they worked, were as well ordered as themselves. In the windows of some, there were green plants, which were trained to shade the glass; in all, there was as much fresh air, cleanliness, and comfort, as the nature of the occupation would possibly admit of. Out of so large a number of females, many of whom were only then just verging on womanhood, it may be reasonably supposed that some were delicate and fragile in appearance; no doubt there were. But I solemnly declare, that from all the crowd I saw in the different factories that day, I cannot recall or separate one young face that gave me a painful impression, not one young girl whom, assuming it to be a matter of necessity that she gain the daily bread by the

[1]From *The Underside of American History*, edited by Thomas R. Frazier
[2]From *A History of the American People* by Stephen Thernstrom

labour of her hands, I would have removed from those works if I had had the power. . . .

In this brief account of Lowell . . . I have carefully abstained from drawing a comparison between these factories and those of our land [England]. . . . The contrast would be a strong one, for it would be between the Good and Evil, the living light and the deepest shadow. . . . But I only more earnestly adjure [urge] all those whose eyes may rest on these pages, to pause and reflect upon the difference between this town [Lowell] and those great haunts of desperate misery [in England].[1] "

Not all the "Lowell girls" would agree with Dickens. Not all thought their situation was "Good" or "the living light." The following lines are from a letter written in 1845 by a Lowell girl known simply as Julianna. In it she expresses the despair often felt by some of the factory workers. Compare her feelings with those expressed in Dickens' observations:

" THE EVILS OF FACTORY LIFE. NUMBER ONE
. . . All is hurry, bustle and confusion in the street, in the mill and in the overflowing boarding house. If there chance to be an intelligent mind in that crowd which is striving to lay up [learn] treasures of knowledge, how unfavorably it is situated! Crowded into a small room, which contains three bed and six females, all possessing the "without end" tongue of woman, what chance is there for *studying?* and much less so for thinking and reflecting? . . .

Incarcerated [imprisoned] within the walls of a factory, while as yet mere children—drilled there from five [A.M.] until seven o'clock [P.M.], year after year—thrown into company with all sorts and descriptions of minds, dispositions and intellects, without counsellor or friends to advise—far away from a watchful mother's tender care or father's kind instruction . . . what *must*, what will be the natural, rational result? What but ignorance, misery, and *premature decay* of both *body* and *intellect?* Our country will be but one great hospital filled with worn out operatives [Lowell girls] and colored slaves. . . . What we would ask, . . . will be the mental and intellectual character of the future generations of New England? What but a race weak, sickly, imbecile, both mental and physical? A race fit only for corporation tools and time-serving slaves. . . . "

JULIANNA

Lowell, October, 1845[2]

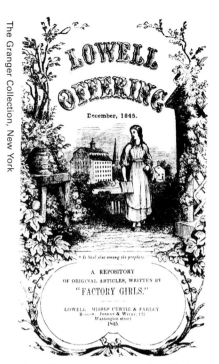

The Granger Collection, New York

Contributors to the Lowell Offering *were the young women who worked in the Lowell factories.*

[1]From *American Notes for General Circulation* by Charles Dickens
[2]From *America's Working Women: A Documentary History 1600 to the Present,* compiled and edited by Rosalyn Bauxhall, Linda Gordon, Susan Reverby

Yale University Art Gallery

The first mill operations spun wool and cotton into thread, but soon weaving was also done by machines. Do you think the child working under the spindles at left had a safe job?

Growth of the Factory System

Much of America's early industry developed in New England. The successes of Slater and Brown meant other Americans soon wanted to build factories. The locations of these factories, and later of the cities that would grow up around them, was influenced partly by America's unique geography and partly by history. The machinery in the first American factories was driven by water. These factories sprang up at waterpower sites in New England and the Middle Atlantic states. Especially ideal were sites on the fall line. Along this line rivers drop from the Appalachian foothills to the Atlantic Coastal Plain in small waterfalls. Water rushing over these falls provided the power to run the factory machinery. All along the eastern seaboard owners built factories to take advantage of this power source.

By 1812, however, steam-powered machines were replacing water-driven ones in America. Location directly on lakes, rivers, and streams remained important, however. Such waterways provided another advantage—cheaper water transportation. Bulky materials moved more easily on water in barges and ships than in wagons over land. Mills that used bulky raw materials such as iron, timber, or coal or that produced bulky products such as steel continued to open along the shores and banks of navigable waterways. Cities such as Pittsburgh, Buffalo, and Richmond soon spread from clusters of factories.

Return to the Preview & Review on page 333.

3. THE RISE OF THE CITIES

Immigration from Europe

Many women walked out of factories to protest wage reductions in 1834 and 1836. They were replaced by men and women recently come from Europe. These **immigrants** were very poor and willing to take any jobs they could find. The number of people coming to America was increasing yearly. Only about 250,000 immigrants had entered the United States between the end of the Revolutionary War and 1820. During the next 20 years more than 700,000 crossed the Atlantic.

The majority of these immigrants came from England, Ireland, and Germany. Most came as families. Nearly all came to the United States because they were poor and hoped to earn a better living in what Europeans considered "the land of opportunity."

No one rolled out the red carpet for these newcomers. Some Americans opposed unlimited immigration. These **nativists** believed that too much immigration would destroy American institutions. They wanted to keep the country for "native Americans." They conveniently forgot that the only real native Americans were the Indians! The 1835 *Annual Report* for the Bible Society of Essex County, New Jersey contained this challenge to its members:

❝ At a time when a vast foreign population is rushing in on us like a flood—when infidelity [unfaithfulness] on the one hand, in its protean [various] forms, and Romanism [Catholicism] on the other, with its determined and deadly hostility to God's truth and our free institutions—are assailing those truths, and endeavoring day and night to undermine those interests which are dear to our hearts, shall we be idle?❞

The nativists were members of various Protestant churches. They were particularly hostile to Irish Catholics, who were entering the country in large numbers. Disease had destroyed most of the potato crop in Ireland, and thousands of Irish, facing starvation, turned to America. In 1834 a nativist mob burned a Catholic convent near Boston. Similar shameful incidents occurred in other parts of the country. Andrew M. Greeley, a popular contemporary writer, scarcely conceals his anger at the typical nativist view of the Irish Catholics who came to America:

❝ It is no secret that the Irish were not especially welcomed when they entered the United States. One can understand this reaction. Most earlier immigrants were, if not wealthy, at least reasonably skilled workers or artisans. They were the most ambitious and vigorous of the Europeans seeking

Use these questions to guide your reading. Answer the questions after completing Section 3.
Understanding Issues, Events, & Ideas. Describe the growth of American cities, using the following words: immigrant, nativist, urban frontier, urban center, tenement.
1. Where did most immigrants come from between 1820 and 1840?
2. Why did nativists fear too much immigration?
3. In what sense were western cities an urban frontier?
4. What caused slums to develop in cities?
Thinking Critically. 1. Imagine that you are an immigrant in Boston in 1830. Use your historical imagination to describe the kind of job you would look for and the skills that would be necessary for that job. **2.** The year is 1835. You have decided you want to move to the urban frontier. What service would you most like to provide farmers? Why?

The Rise of Cities   343

The Granger Collection, New York

Blood flows in the streets of the City of Brotherly Love in this 1844 engraving of an anti-Catholic riot in Philadelphia. Why was the mob so threatened by new arrivals to America?

to make new lives for themselves in a richer country. But the famine Irish [people who left Ireland because disease destroyed the potato crop] were poor, uneducated, and confused. They fled not to a better life but from almost certain death. They were dirty, undernourished, disease-ridden, and incapable of anything but the most unskilled labor. That they arrived in great numbers and filled up whole sections of cities almost overnight did not go unnoticed by native Americans [Those already living there]. . . .

If the Irish were to be accepted into American society they must be sober, industrious, and ambitious, like the Protestant immigrants who had come before them. There, of course, was the heart of the problem. Not only were they poor, sick, dirty, and uneducated. They were also Catholic.

The Irish Catholics, with their unmarried clergy, had an equally strange tendency not to send their children to public schools, where every effort would be made to turn them into good Americans—this meant, of course, good Protestant Americans. From the nativist point of view, it was no wonder that churches were burned and that Catholics were occasionally murdered in riots.[1] 🙶

[1]From *That Most Distressful Nation: The Taming of the American Irish* by Andrew M. Greeley

Meanwhile people continued to leave their homes in Ireland, miserable and downtrodden. Many sang this farewell to their homeland:

    " Farewell to thee, Erin mavoureen [Ireland dear],
    Thy valleys I'll tread never more;
    This heart that now bleeds for thy sorrows
    Will waste on a far distant shore.
    Thy green sods lie cold on parents,
    A cross marks the place of their rest,
    The wind that moans softly above them
    Will waft [blow] their poor child to the West.[1] **"**

[1]From *The Irish in America* by James E. Johnson

City Life in America

Most of the immigrants who came to America between 1820 and 1840 settled in the cities of the Northeast. These were still communities where a person could easily walk from one end to the other in half an hour—places where church steeples stood out on the skyline and the masts and spars of ships at the wharves towered over the roofs of the houses, shops, and warehouses. There were no skyscrapers

LEARNING FROM GRAPHS. *These charts show the total number of immigrants coming to the United States between 1820 and 1860 and their places of origin. What are some trends in immigration during those years illustrated by the charts?*

Source: *Historical Statistics of the United States*

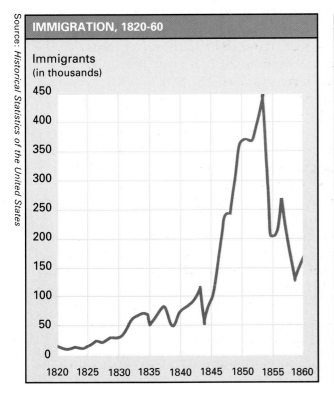

IMMIGRATION, 1820-60

Immigrants (in thousands)

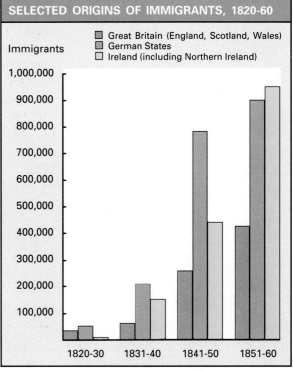

SELECTED ORIGINS OF IMMIGRANTS, 1820-60

Immigrants

- Great Britain (England, Scotland, Wales)
- German States
- Ireland (including Northern Ireland)

The Rise of Cities   **345**

or great factories. The largest manufacturer in New York City in the 1830s employed only about 200 people.

These eastern cities were mainly shipping centers. Manufacturing was not very important. Most industries which did exist, such as shipbuilding and barrel making, were linked to trade and commerce.

The cities to the west were also mainly commercial centers. We think of cities as developing in already settled areas, but these western cities developed on the edge of settlement. They made up what may be called an **urban frontier.** They were founded even before most of the surrounding forests were cleared by farmers. Indeed, they acted as outposts and depots from which settlers spread out. Many people went west not to farm but to live in these communities and supply the needs of farmers.

All American cities underwent similar growing pains in this period. Since few city streets were paved, there was always mud in rainy weather. This gave rise to a famous joke about the poor condition of city streets: A passing citizen offers help to a man who has sunk up to his neck in a huge mud puddle. "No need to worry," replies the man. "I have a horse under me."

Many a stockbroker may have lifted a cup to his lips at the Tontine Coffee House, right, since it also served as the Stock Exchange. Meanwhile, the life of New York City, as it always has, goes on in all its variety. Down Water Street is a forest of masts and spars from the wharves of the East River. Describe some of the problems of city life illustrated by this picture.

New–York Historical Society

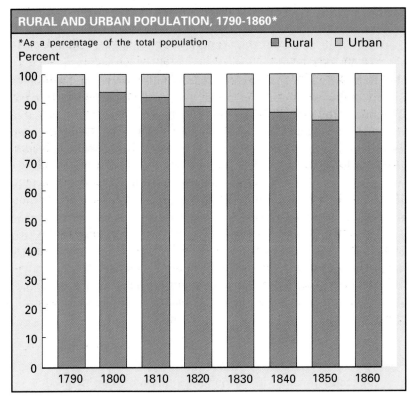

RURAL AND URBAN POPULATION, 1790-1860*

As a percentage of the total population ■ Rural ☐ Urban

Percent

Source: *Historical Statistics of the United States*

LEARNING FROM GRAPHS.
Originally the United States was a nation of farmers. But almost immediately that began to change. Why were people attracted to cities?

Garbage littered city streets. In all parts of the country, goats and hogs were allowed to roam about rooting through the waste. Charleston, South Carolina, passed a law against shooting turkey buzzards because these scavengers ate the dead cats and dogs and rotting food left lying about the town.

Polluted water and the lack of sanitation often led to epidemics of contagious diseases. The most dreaded was cholera. This terrible disease is caused by bacteria and is spread in polluted water, but no one knew this at the time. During cholera epidemics people living in dirty, crowded slums died by the hundreds. Many people, therefore, thought the disease was a punishment for poverty.

Many American cities had neither police nor fire departments. Even the largest cities had no more than a dozen police officers, and these were only part-time employees. They refused to wear uniforms, arguing that uniforms were for servants.

Fires were put out by volunteer fire companies. There was often much competition between these associations. When fires broke out, fire companies sometimes fought each other rather than the blaze. More than glory was at stake. Cash prizes were frequently awarded to the companies that responded most quickly to alarms.

In 1790 there were only 24 **urban centers** in the United States with a population of 2,500 or more. By 1840 there were 131. Many

The Rise of Cities   347

people moved into the cities, but many left them too. There was, in other words, a great deal of turnover among the urban population. Between 1830 and 1840, for example, 35,775 families either came into or left the city of Boston.

Rapid city growth caused crowded slums to develop. Most cities simply could not absorb people as fast as the newcomers arrived. The poor crowded into the attics and basements of houses. Large apartments were broken up into many small ones. Buildings with many families crowded together were called **tenements.** Rents were low. But because there were so many apartments in each, the profits made by owners of tenements could be very large. Little, if any, of the profit went to keep the tenement buildings in repair. They were unsanitary and unsafe. An American reformer declared in 1840: "One half of the world does not know *how the other half lives.*" The great crusader for housing reform, Jacob Riis, made the phrase popular some 50 years later, as we shall see.

Education also was a major concern in cities. Urban educators, especially those in Boston and other New England cities, came to see their schools as a "community in miniature." One historian says of these schools:

    “ There, the child could mature in an environment created especially for him, in surroundings tailored to fit his needs as separate from those of the adult community. There, . . . the schoolmaster could impart the moral instruction that had once come from the pulpit. . . . The public school was to be a classroom, a family room, a church house—all things to all children. The school was to nurture the child to adulthood, equip him with necessary skills of a livelihood, and familiarize him with the rigors and dangers of life in the city. In short, the school was to be the social incubator [a device providing a safe and controlled environment] of responsible citizens.[1] ”

[1]From *The Culture Factory: Boston Public Schools* by Stanley K. Schultz

By the late-1820s many cities had year-round primary schools. Nearly 45 percent of Boston's school-age population was in school. Boston provided a Latin high school for boys, an English high school for boys and a similar experimental school for girls (schools with less emphasis on the classics than the Latin schools), and two separate schools for African Americans. Other large cities soon followed Boston's lead.

Despite all of these problems, the cities remained the cultural centers of American life. Cities, with their theaters, cafes, taverns, and libraries, attracted people in large numbers—artists, writers, ordinary people searching for excitement and adventure.

Return to the Preview & Review on page 343.

CANADA

Lake Superior

MI

WI

MI

Lake Michigan

Lake Huron

Lake Erie

L. Ontario

NY

VT

NH

ME

Portland

MOHAWK TURNPIKE

Albany

Boston

CATSKILL TURNPIKE

MA

RI

Buffalo

CT

New York

SENECA ROAD

PA

NJ

Cleveland

Lancaster

Philadelphia

Pittsburgh

LANCASTER TURNPIKE

OH

Wheeling

Baltimore

IL

IN

NATIONAL ROAD

Cumberland

MD

DE

Washington, D.C.

Vandalia

Ohio River

VA

Louisville

Boonesborough

Richmond

KY

WILDERNESS ROAD

Cumberland Gap

NC

TN

ATLANTIC OCEAN

MS

AL

GA

Charleston

Savannah

To St. Augustine

BOSTON POST ROAD

COASTAL POST ROAD

Mississippi River

N
W   E
S

LEARNING FROM MAPS. *Note the pattern of America's earliest roads. Why do most of the roads run from east to west?*

4. IMPROVEMENTS IN TRAVEL

New Roads and Turnpikes

As the cities expanded, it was no longer easy to walk from one end to the other. A new means of transportation was necessary. In 1827 Abraham Brower began running a stagecoach up and down Broadway in New York City. By 1833 there were about 80 stagecoaches in New York. The coaches were drawn by two horses and seated 12 passengers. In the winter some drivers replaced their wheels with runners, turning them into sleighs. Stagecoaches could soon be found in every city, and service between many cities was also available.

Travel overland could be efficient only if there were good roads. America's roads were poor indeed. Most were unpaved. They turned into seas of mud after every heavy rain. In dry weather they were bumpy and rutted, and every passing wagon sent up clouds of dust. An inexpensive way to build weatherproof roads had not yet been found. Most roads were built by private companies that hoped to earn profits. The roads these companies built marched straight up and down hill and dale rather than around them in a more level but longer and more expensive way.

Builders collected tolls from people who traveled over their roads. The tollgate was usually a pole, or pike, blocking the road. When the traveler paid the toll, the pike was raised or turned aside to let the travelers pass. Hence these toll roads were called **turnpikes.**

Travel overland was both expensive and time-consuming. In the

Use these questions to guide your reading. Answer the questions after completing Section 4.
Understanding Issues, Events, & Ideas. Use the following words to discuss travel in the 1800s: turnpike, Cumberland Road or National Road, canal, Erie Canal, *Fulton's Folly, Tom Thumb,* Transportation Revolution.
1. In what ways were America's early roads poor? Why was the National Road built?
2. What problem was there in traveling inland?
3. What were some early uses of steam power?
4. What were some advantages of railroads? How did railroads boost the economy?

Thinking Critically. 1. You are a merchant in New York after the building of the Erie Canal. Write a letter to your brother in Georgia, explaining how the canal has improved your business. 2. Briefly explain how the railroad would affect you if you were: a farmer; a mine owner; a land owner in a remote area.

early 1800s it cost more to haul a ton of goods only 9 miles inland (about 14 kilometers) than to bring the same ton all the way across the Atlantic Ocean. Little wonder that in the 1790s the rebellious farmers of Pennsylvania had turned their corn into whiskey! In bulk form corn was far too expensive to ship to eastern markets.

During the War of 1812 a wagon drawn by four horses took 75 days to go from Worcester, Massachusetts, to Charleston, South Carolina. It would have been quicker to sail to Europe, stay a week or two, and return to America—and cheaper too. Any profits that might have been earned would have been eaten up by the four horses during the 75-day trip.

The roads of this period did not unite the country. In 1806 Thomas Jefferson took the first steps to link the eastern regions with the western. He authorized the building of the **Cumberland Road,** or **National Road.** Construction began in 1811 at Cumberland, Maryland. The route crossed over the mountains in southern Pennsylvania and ended at the site of present-day Wheeling, West Virginia. Later it was extended west to Vandalia, Illinois.

With the crack of a whip the driver of this stagecoach urges his horses westward. The wheels of the stagecoach sink into the muddy road, which is marked by the stumps of the trees probably felled to build the bridge at right. Whenever the horses galloped around a curve such as this, there was always the chance the overland travelers would "be stumped"—or stopped by stumps that broke the coach's wheels. How were America's first roads a good example of private enterprise in action?

Museum of Fine Arts, Boston, M. and M. Karolik Collection

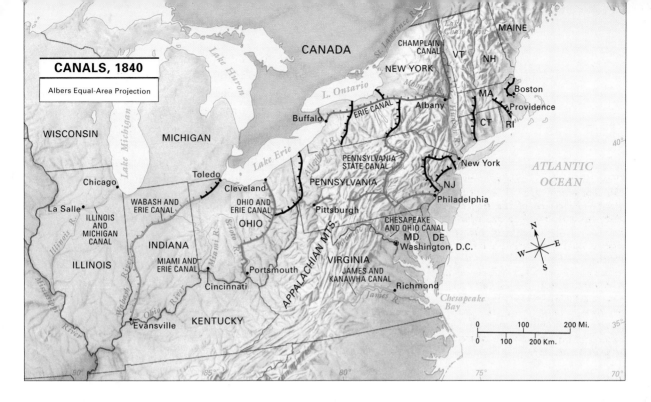

CANALS, 1840

Albers Equal-Area Projection

The National Road was a remarkable engineering achievement. It was built on a solid stone foundation with a gravel topping. Over it rolled an almost endless caravan of coaches, carts, and wagons. Its sturdy stone bridges still carry traffic today.

Canals

The easiest means of moving goods and people was by water. But like its roads, America's rivers and lakes were not connected. Fortunately many of them could be joined by digging **canals.**

Goods were carried through canals on barges towed by horses or mules. The animals plodded patiently along what were called towpaths on the bank of the canal. A mule could pull a load 50 times or more heavier on water than it could over any road. Thus, canal transportation was much cheaper than transportation by road.

Canals were very expensive to build. They could not be dug without government support. In 1816 De Witt Clinton, the canal commissioner of New York, persuaded the state legislature to build a canal running from the Hudson River across the state all the way to Lake Erie. This route offered the most attractive passage from the Atlantic Coast to the Great Lakes. It passed through the Mohawk Valley, a gap in the Appalachian Mountains. There the land was relatively level. The water did not have to be raised and lowered very much by canal locks. In 1817 work on Clinton's "Big Ditch" began. Much of the digging was done by European immigrants.

The first section was opened to traffic in 1819, and in 1825 the **Erie Canal** was completed. It was an engineering wonder: 363 miles

LEARNING FROM MAPS. *Canals helped form a transportation network that included the early roads. Why were canals particularly important to farmers and merchants?*

Samuel S. Spaulding Collection, Buffalo and Erie County Historical Society

This plate celebrates the building of the Erie Canal with its view of the entrance of the canal at the Hudson River.

Improvements in Travel   351

New York Public Library Print Room

long, 40 feet wide, and 4 feet deep (about 580 kilometers long, 12 meters wide, and 1 meter deep). It cost the state $7 million, an enormous sum for those days, but it attracted so much traffic that the tolls collected soon paid its cost. Because of this high volume, the rates charged for using the canal were very low. The cost of shipping a ton of goods fell from 19 cents a mile before the canal was built to 1 cent. The canal became the busiest route for goods and people moving between the Atlantic Coast and western cities and farms.

When other states saw how profitable the Erie Canal was, they hastened to build canals of their own. Soon a wave of canal building was under way. In 1816 there were only about 100 miles (160 kilometers) of canals in the entire nation. By 1840 there were more than 3,300 miles (5,280 kilometers). This meant that the combined length of the canals of the United States was greater than the distance across North America between the Atlantic and Pacific Oceans.

The canals created a network that united the different sections of the country and stimulated their economies. Bulky farm products could now be shipped cheaply to distant markets. Eastern manufactured products no longer had to be lugged over the Appalachians.

In 1849 when this scene was captured by its artist, Pittsburgh was often called the "Gateway to the West." From its crowded docks steamboats set out to carry settlers on the Ohio River as they began their journeys westward. In the years after Fulton sailed his Clermont, steamboats became huge floating palaces, gliding from city to city, practically cities in themselves. Read descriptions of steamboat travel. In what ways is travel today superior and in what ways is it not?

Steamboats

Travel by canal was slow. It still depended on animal power. Mules would only walk about 3 miles an hour (about 5 kilometers) pulling a barge. Keelboats, pulled by hand or pushed by the wind in a small sail, were not much faster. What was needed was a new source of power. Once again, British technology supplied the answer. In the 1760s a Scot named James Watt had invented a practical steam engine. Watt's invention used the energy of burning wood and coal to replace the energy of beasts and human beings. When the steam engine was used to run machines in factories, it replaced waterpower. This meant that factories did not have to be located near dams or swiftly moving rivers. They could be built anywhere.

If steam can move machines, can it not be used to move boats? One of the first Americans to ask this question was John Fitch, a silversmith and clockmaker. In 1787 Fitch launched a steamboat propelled by 12 paddles on the Delaware River. Among the many spectators who witnessed the launching of Fitch's smoke-belching monster were several of the delegates from the Constitutional Convention in nearby Philadelphia. Shortly afterwards, Fitch built a

AVERAGE FREIGHT RATES* BETWEEN LOUISVILLE AND NEW ORLEANS, 1810-59		
*per 100 pounds	**Upstream**	**Downstream**
1810-1819	$5.00	$1.00
1820-1829	$1.00	$0.62
1830-1839	$0.50	$0.50
1840-1849	$0.30	$0.25
1850-1859	$0.25	$0.25

Source: History of the American Economy

New York State Historical Association, Cooperstown

Robert Fulton's portrait is by Benjamin West. Fulton had himself been a Philadelphia portrait painter before he turned his mechanical aptitude to canal engineering and steamboats. What did Fulton's steamboat prove?

second boat which carried passengers between Philadelphia and Burlington, New Jersey. But this enterprise was a commercial failure.

For another 20 years steamboats were neither efficient nor reliable. Then, in 1807, Robert Fulton, an artist turned inventor, began building a steamboat on the East River in New York City. Fulton called it the *Clermont,* but those who had watched it being built called it **Fulton's Folly.** In August the boat made its first voyage up the Hudson River from New York City to Albany. The 300-mile trip (480 kilometers) took 62 hours, but the *Clermont* soon proved that a steam vessel could earn a profit.

In 1811 Nicholas Roosevelt, an associate of Fulton and a distant relative of two future presidents, built the *New Orleans* at Pittsburgh. In the winter of 1811–12 this boat made the 1,950-mile trip (3,120 kilometers) from Pittsburgh to New Orleans in only 14 days. Previously the journey had taken four to six weeks.

An even more dramatic breakthrough occurred in 1815 when the *Enterprise* was piloted up the Mississippi from New Orleans to Pittsburgh against the current. Before that time a trip upstream by sail or keelboat from New Orleans to Pittsburgh took more than four months. Soon dozens of steamboats were sailing up and down the western rivers. In 1817 there were only 17. By 1840 there were 536.

New forms of transportation such as the steamboat had a certain glamour about them. People, especially young boys, were fascinated by them. Here is how Mark Twain described his fascination:

    ❝ When I was a boy, there was but one permanent ambition among my comrades in our village on the west bank of the Mississippi. That was to be a steamboatman.

    After all these years, I can picture that old time myself now, just as it was then: the white town drowsing in the sunshine of a summer's morning; the streets empty, or pretty near so; . . . the great Mississippi, the majestic, magnificent Mississippi, rolling its mile-wide tide along, shining in the sun; the dense forest away on the other side; the 'point' [of land] above the town and the 'point' below. Presently a film of dark smoke appears above one of those remote 'points'; instantly a Negro drayman [wagon driver], famous for his quick eye and prodigious [mighty] voice, lifts up the cry, 'S-t-e-a-m-boat acomin'!' and the scene changes! . . . All in a twinkling, the dead town is alive and moving. Drays, carts, men, boys, all go hurrying from many quarters to a common center, the wharf. Assembled there, the people fasten their eyes upon the coming boat as upon a wonder they are seeing for the first time.

And the boat is rather a handsome sight, too. She is long and sharp and trim and pretty. She has two fancy-topped chimneys, with a gilded device of some kind swung between them, and a fanciful pilothouse, all glass and ''gingerbread'' [fancy wood designs] perched on the top of the ''texas'' deck [the deck with the largest cabins; steamboat decks were named after states, according to size]. The paddle boxes are gorgeous with a picture or with gilded rays above the boat's name; the boiler-deck, the hurricane-deck, and the texas deck are fenced and ornamented with clean white railings. There is a flag gallantly flying from the jack-staff; the furnace doors are open and the fires glaring bravely. The upper decks are black with passengers. The captain stands by the big bell, calm, imposing, the envy of all. Great volumes of the blackest smoke are rolling and tumbling out of the chimneys; . . . the pent steam is screaming through the gauge cocks [devices for measuring the steam pressure]. The captain lifts his hand, a bell rings, the wheels stop; then they turn back, churning the water to foam, and the steamer is at rest. . . .

Ten minutes later the steamer is under way again, with no flag on the jack-staff, and no black smoke issuing from the chimneys. After ten more minutes the town is dead again, . . .[1]99

Railroads

Soon after the canals and steamboats, there came a still more significant technological advance—the railroad. The first steam-driven locomotive, the *Tom Thumb,* was built by Peter Cooper for the Baltimore & Ohio Railroad in 1830. The track on which the *Tom Thumb* made its first run had been used by horse-drawn coaches. To demonstrate the engine, Cooper raced *Tom Thumb* against a horse-drawn coach. The locomotive swept ahead from the start. But it broke down before the finish line. The horse won the race.

[1]From *Life on the Mississippi* by Mark Twain

Point of View

Alexis de Tocqueville of France visited America in 1831. His observations about the young nation became the classic *Democracy in America.*

66The roads, the canals, and the mails play a prodigious part in the prosperity of the Union. . . . In the Michigan forests there is not a cabin so isolated, not a valley so wild, that it does not receive letters and newspapers at least once a week. . . . Of all the countries of the world, America is the one where the movement of thought and human industry is the most continuous and the most swift.99

Alexis de Tocqueville, 1831

STRATEGIES FOR SUCCESS

INTERPRETING A SPECIAL-PURPOSE MAP
Special-purpose maps, as their name tells you, contain specific information. The map on page 351 is a special-purpose map that illustrates the growth of the canal system in America. Interpreting the information contained on a special-purpose map will help you to understand that aspect of history or geography.

How to Interpret a Special-Purpose Map
To interpret a special-purpose map, follow these guidelines.
1. **Use map basics.** Read the title, check the legend, and scale. These map parts will tell you the subject of the map and its extent.
2. **Note special symbols.** Special-purpose maps often use symbols to illustrate information.

Study the key to make sure you understand what the symbols on the map represent.
3. **Read the labels.** Identify each feature portrayed on the map.
4. **Study the map as a whole.** Note the overall pattern of the information. Is it concentrated in one area? Does it seem to be influenced by geographic factors?

Applying the Strategy
Study the map below. Note that it illustrates the railroad network in the United States in 1860. The paths of railroads are marked by——and the main ones are labeled. What area of the country had the most railroad mileage? Why?

For independent practice, see Practicing the Strategy on page 360.

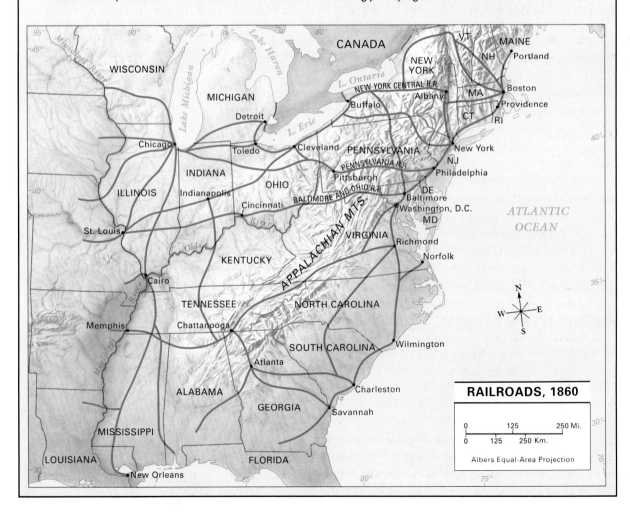

RAILROADS, 1860

0   125   250 Mi.
0   125   250 Km.
Albers Equal-Area Projection

The Chessie System, B & O Railroad Museum Archives

"The Race of the Tom Thumb" was painted as part of a series for the Fair of the Iron Horse held in celebration of 100 years of operation by the Baltimore & Ohio Railroad. The horse won this race. What does this tell us about making generalizations from too few instances?

Trains had many advantages over canals and steamboats. They could go practically anywhere. They were much faster. They could pull greater loads. And they could operate all year round in the northern states, where the canals and many rivers were frozen solid in the winter months.

In the beginning many Americans considered trains dangerous. The sparks from their engines set fields afire and frightened farm animals. The engines often jumped their tracks. But the advantages of railroads could not be resisted. In 1830 the Baltimore & Ohio, the nation's only railroad, had 13 miles (about 21 kilometers) of track. By 1840 there were dozens of lines operating more than 3,300 miles (5,280 kilometers) of track, most of it in the Northeast.

Railroads gave the economy a great boost. Besides reducing travel time and cost, they caused many other businesses to expand. The demand for iron for engines and rails greatly increased the mining and smelting of iron. Remote areas boomed once the railroads reached them. Farmers expanded output. Land prices rose.

The railroads completed the web of transportation which began with turnpikes. This **Transportation Revolution** brought about dramatic changes. It tied westerners to easterners. It made it easier for people in one region to know and do business with people in other regions. It made nearly everyone more prosperous. In a way, the Transportation Revolution had almost as much to do with creating the *United* States as the American Revolution itself.

Return to the Preview & Review on page 349.

LINKING HISTORY & GEOGRAPHY

HOMES FOR AMERICANS

It is easy to overlook the importance of houses in the study of history. They are so common, fulfilling a basic need—shelter. In today's cities and suburbs they seem to stretch for miles in no particular pattern, holding no historical clues. But to those who study such houses, they tell a great deal about us.

Houses and the Cultural Landscape

1. What is the cultural landscape? Why is housing of special interest to those studying the cultural landscape?

Every inhabited part of the earth has both a physical and a cultural landscape. Physical features such as the mountains, deserts, plants, and animals make up the *physical landscape.* The imprint or effect a group of people leaves on its *human habitat*—the place where it lives—creates the *cultural landscape.*

Housing interests geographers and other scientists because the design and construction of a house often shows how people adapt to their physical setting. The Hopi built pueblos, ancient apartment houses, in the cliffs. The Arapaho stretched buffalo hide on poles to make teepees to provide shelter on the treeless plains. Later settlers on the Plains cut chunks of sod to build their houses.

Housing also often reflects the cultural heritage of its builders. The Hopi were farmers and built permanent structures. The Arapaho were hunters. Their teepees could be quickly taken down as they pursued buffalo herds. Size and style made a statement about the owner's place in society. No one who saw a plantation mansion could mistake the wealth of a southern planter!

Housing and the Environment

2. How do houses reflect the environment?

Environment influenced European settlers as it had the Hopi and Arapaho. Builders developed many styles to deal with particular conditions. In places with heavy snowfall, settlers often sharply pitched the roof to cause the snow to slide off easily. In areas with long rainy seasons, such as the Pacific Northwest, Indians and later settlers frequently built roofs with a broad overhang or a porch to provide a dry walkway beside the house. Where there was little rainfall, as in the Southwest, rooflines were flat. There overhangs provided shade from the relentless sun and large windows caught every breeze.

The Log Cabin

3. Why was the log cabin the typical pioneer home east of the Mississippi?

Perhaps the best example of a house reflecting the American environment is the log cabin. When we think of houses on the early frontier, log cabins instantly come to mind. It was the most common housing for pioneers until the frontier reached the Great Plains, an area too dry to support the trees needed to build log cabins.

In many ways the log cabin was nearly perfect housing for the frontier environment. With its notched logs, joined at the corners, it was easy to construct. And the building material—trees—surrounded the pioneers. Often a family, using little more than an axe as a tool, could put together a simple log cabin in a few days.

Building a Log Cabin

4. How did settlers adapt log cabins to their needs?

Nature influenced the style and construction of log cabins. Pioneer families could handle only logs of a limited size. They could not lift or move the largest into place. The natural taper of the logs also created a built-in limit to the size of the cabin for a builder using only an axe.

The simplest cabins consisted of one room with a chimney at the end. To add space the family might put planks over part of the rafters to create a loft. Such lofts, reached by ladder from the main floor, often became the bedroom for the children. An ambitious family might also build a second log room attached to the first.

American Housing and European Culture

5. How does culture and tradition influence housing design?

Some architectural designs reflect cultural traditions rather than environmental concerns. As you might expect, European—especially British—influences dominated housing styles in the colonies in the 1700s and 1800s. The frame construction common to New England reflected European traditions. First, a heavy frame of vertical, horizontal, and diagonal timbers was

The Granger Collection, New York

raised. The open spaces of this skeleton were filled with materials such as mud and stone.

It did not take long before New England builders found that, unlike in their homelands, timber was abundant. Soon the framework was covered with horizontal sidings called clapboard. The New England frame house was born.

The plantation home characteristic of the South in the late 1700s evolved from the English cottage. American builders quickly adapted their cottages. It became common to add a front porch and rear shed with its own chimney as the kitchen. Later, as the wealth of the planters increased, porches surrounding the entire building were added along with balconies, a great number of rooms, and massive columns reaching upward to the overhanging roofline.

The "Shotgun House"
6. Why is the shotgun house unique?

One of the most unique designs in American homes is the long, narrow house found in many southern cities. It is called a "shotgun house." It is unique because it is of African origin and was brought to the United States from Haiti. It is a distinctive and significant African contribution to the American cultural landscape.

The shotgun house is a narrow, one-story house, one room in width, and three or four rooms deep. It has a narrow, frontward-facing gable. The term *shotgun* refers to the interior arrangement of the house. Each room is directly behind the room in front. The doorways are in a straight line so, as the story goes, "a shotgun can be fired in the front door and the bullet will travel out the back without hitting anything."

The first shotgun homes were probably built in New Orleans. Haitians began pouring into the city in the early 1800s. Many were the descendants of African slaves from the Yoruba area of West Africa, in modern-day Nigeria. The characteristic Yoruba house consists of two or three rooms, one directly behind the other. The Haitian descendants of the Yoruba brought the style to New Orleans.

By 1810 there were almost twice as many African Americans as Europeans in New Orleans, and most were free. Many were skilled craftsman, especially carpenters and stone masons. Slowly, New Orleans took on a distinctive flavor strongly influenced by African American styles. By the 1830s independent African American contractors were busily constructing shotgun houses throughout the city.

American Houses
7. Why did the American environment create unique houses?

As with most things brought from Europe, settlers found that their traditional housing styles did not quite fit the new environment. Trial and error helped them invent styles that were better for America. Soon new styles of houses, each reflecting both environmental and cultural aspects of their builders, dotted the American cultural landscape.

Applying Your Knowledge
Your class will create a display of traditional American houses. Each group will research a different housing style: New England, plantation, log cabin, shotgun, sod, and others. Reports should explain cultural links to housing style and descriptions of typical building materials. Groups should prepare a model or detailed drawing of the styles they research.

Linking History & Geography   **359**

CHAPTER 10 REVIEW

1765
Spinning jenny invented

1768
Water-frame developed

1787
Fitch's
steam-
boat

1789
Samuel Slater
comes to U.S.

1791
Slater a
Brown's
opens

Chapter Summary

Read the statements below. Choose one, and write a paragraph explaining its importance.

1. Americans recognized the need for a diversified economy during the wars with England.
2. In the early 1800s the government began to help American businesses with protective tariffs and the Bank of the United States.
3. In the early 1800s Americans imported and invented the technology to mass produce goods.
4. Finding industrial workers was often a problem until waves of immigrants began to arrive in the United States in the 1820s.
5. Despite nativist opposition, immigrants poured into growing American urban areas.
6. During the 1800s the United States gradually changed from a rural to an urban nation.
7. Rapid city growth caused slums to develop.
8. Building new roads, canals, and railroads led to a Transportation Revolution.

Reviewing Chronological Order

Number your paper 1–5. Then study the time line above and place the following events in the order in which they happened by writing the first next to 1, the second next to 2, and so on.

1. Whitney demonstrates interchangeable parts
2. Lowell develops Lowell system
3. Erie Canal completed
4. Samuel Slater comes to U.S.
5. National Road begun

Understanding Main Ideas

1. How does a protective tariff work? Use an example to illustrate your answer.
2. What were some of the major changes that occurred during the Industrial Revolution?
3. Why did some Americans fear the large number of immigrants that began to arrive in the United States in the 1820s?
4. Why was immigration important to both the Industrial and Transportation revolutions?

Thinking Critically

1. **Judging.** When Samuel Slater memorized designs for English cotton-spinning machinery and moved to America, was he committing a crime, or was he ignoring unjust laws? Explain your answer.
2. **Synthesizing.** The year is 1840. You have immigrated to New York, where you live in a tenement with your parents and four brothers. Compose a letter to your grandmother back in Ireland, describing your new home.
3. **Inventing.** You are one of the workers who helped build Clinton's "Big Ditch." Write a song or poem praising the wonders of the Erie Canal.

Writing About History

You are a newspaper reporter in 1801. Use your historical imagination to join the onlookers as Whitney takes apart and reassembles the ten muskets. Write a report of the event and the reactions of the audience. Use the information in Chapter 10 to help you develop your report.

Practicing the Strategy

Review the strategy on page 356.
Reviewing Special-Purpose Maps. Study the map on page 351, then answer the following questions.

1. This special-purpose map illustrates which specific mode of transportation? What time frame is indicated?
2. How would a shipment of coal be transported from Pittsburgh, Pennsylvania, to Chicago, Illinois? Name each part of the water route that would be used for the journey.
3. Which river is connected to the Great Lakes by five of these canals?

Using Primary Sources

One sign of America's economic growth was the development of improved methods of transpor-

American Industrial Revolution

Transportation Revolution

				1825	AGE OF AMERICAN INGENUITY	1850

1
tney's
rchangeable
s

1807
*Fulton's
Folly*

1811
National
Road
begun

1813
Lowell
starts
Lowell system

1816
Tariff
of 1816

★
Second
Bank of the United States

1820
Immigration
increases
dramatically

1825
Erie Canal
completed

1830
Tom Thumb built

tation. During the early 1800s water transportation was especially important. Timothy Flint, a missionary and writer, described a journey he took on a keelboat in his book *Recollections of the Last Ten Years*.

Our keelboat was between 80 and 90 feet [24 and 27 meters] in length, had a small but comfortable cabin, and carried 17 tons. It was an extremely hot afternoon when we left. The river was almost to the top of its banks, and the current was very rapid. We looked out over a deep, green forest with a richness of plants and trees and a grandeur of size and height, that characterizes the forest in this part of Ohio.

We started this trip under favorable signs. We experienced in a couple of hours what has so often been said of all earthly enjoyments—how near to each other are the limits of happiness and trouble. Banks of thunderclouds were on the horizon when we left Cincinnati. They gathered over us, and a violent thunderstorm followed. We had no time to reach the shore before it burst upon us, accompanied by strong gusts of wind. The gale [wind] was too violent for us to think of landing on a rugged, rockbound shore. We protected the open part of the boat as well as we could, and began scooping out the water the boat took in from the waves. We had women passengers on board, whose screams added to the uproar outside. . . . The patron [skipper], who had done this work for many years and who had been, as he said, "boatwrecked" half a dozen times, kept perfectly cool! . . .

1. From Flint's description of the keelboat, how do you think this craft helped in the settlement and trade of the West?
2. Why would a thunderstorm such as the one described be especially dangerous to a keelboat?
3. Use Flint's description to sketch what you think a keelboat looked like.

Linking History & Geography
As the nation developed, geography had less and less influence on transportation. To understand how the Transportation Revolution helped change even the direction goods were carried in the United States, answer the following questions.
1. Study the map on page 296. Into what major river do most of the rivers in the Ohio Valley flow? In what direction does that river flow?
2. Look at the map on page 351. Why had farmers in central Ohio begun to send their produce down the Ohio and Mississippi rivers? What general direction would their route follow?
3. Use the map on page 356. What two railroads might you use to move goods from central Ohio to New York City? In what general direction would your goods travel?
4. How did the development of canals and railroads change the *direction* of transportation in the eastern United States?

Enriching Your Study of History
1. **Individual Project**. Young women in the factories of Lowell worked 12 hours a day, six days a week. Each shared a bedroom with six other women. Although wages in Lowell were higher than women could earn in any other occupation, factories were hot, damp, and stuffy, and the work was usually boring. Use historical imagination to write a letter home to your family on the farm describing what you like and dislike about Lowell.
2. **Cooperative Project**. As a class project, prepare a bulletin board or multimedia display to show the scope of the Transportation Revolution in the United States. Each group will be responsible for one form of transportation. When completed, the display should show major rivers, canals, roads, and railroads that made up the American network by 1840.

Chapter 10 Review **361**

UNIT THREE REVIEW

Summing Up and Predicting
Read the summary of the main ideas in Unit Three below. Choose one statement, then write a paragraph predicting its outcome or future effect.
1. The *Kentucky and Virginia Resolutions*, in response to the Sedition Act, put forth the doctrine of nullification and states' rights.
2. The Louisiana Purchase in 1803 and the Transcontinental Treaty in 1819 more than doubled the area of the United States.
3. Troubles continued with England, pushing the countries to the brink of another war.
4. The Indians in the Ohio Valley attempted to resist the onslaught of settlers from the east but were eventually defeated.
5. Despite opposition to the War of 1812 by many Americans, a war was declared in which the United States fought Britain to a draw.
6. Revolutions throughout Latin America produced many independent countries and prompted the Monroe Doctrine.
7. The Industrial Revolution, European immigration, and the Transportation Revolution began to rapidly change American society in the early 1800s.

Connecting Ideas
1. John Adams called his part in the Convention of 1800 "the most splendid diamond in my crown." Would this statement have alarmed a Democratic-Republican? Why or why not?
2. How did the Louisiana Purchase, the death of Alexander Hamilton, and the War of 1812 weaken the Federalist Party?
3. Which idea expressed in the Monroe Doctrine do you think is the most important to the United States today? Why?

Practicing Critical Thinking
1. **Drawing Conclusions**. Soon after the Revolutionary War, the young United States had trouble with England and France. Which of these two countries do you think was the greater threat? Cite specific examples to support your answer.
2. **Evaluating**. In your opinion, which battle in the War of 1812 was the most important to the Americans? Why?
3. **Synthesizing**. Write a conversation between two twelve-year-olds: Jane, a thread mill worker, and John, a farm boy. Have Jane describe her job; have John describe his chores.

Cooperative Learning
1. In your assigned group, use historical imagination to present a skit in two acts. Act One depicts a visit by city dwellers to relatives in the country in the early 1800s. Act Two is a return visit by the country relatives to the city. Your skit should show the merits of city life and of country life.
2. You and members of your group will conduct research to create a display comparing problems faced by cities today with those in the years 1790–1840. Some students will find newspaper and magazine articles to show problems that have continued to the present. Others will report on solutions to city problems of the past and of today.
3. Have some members of your group research and prepare a bulletin board showing some of the problems faced by cities in 1790–1840. Add newspaper and magazine articles to illustrate problems which continue to this day. Other members may report on the solutions found to some city problems of 1790–1840 and of today.

Reading in Depth
Adams, Samuel H. *Chingo Smith of the Erie Canal.* New York: Random House. Relates the experiences of a homeless boy in the early days of the canal.

Blos, Joan W. *A Gathering of Days: A New England Girl's Journal, 1830–1832.* New York: Scribner's. Portrays the life of a young factory worker.

Chidsey, Donald Barr. *Lewis and Clark: The Great Adventure.* New York: G. P. Putnam's Sons. Contains a detailed description of the journey with many interesting sidelights.

Cooney, Barabara. *Island Boy.* New York: Viking. Traces New England's history, culture, and social changes through four generations of a local family.

Cooke, David C. *Tecumseh: Destiny's Warrior.* New York: Messner. Presents an account of the great Indian leader's life.

Leckie, Robert. *The War Nobody Won: 1812.* New York: Putnam. Describes events surrounding the war, including American opposition to it.

Tallant, Robert. *Louisiana Purchase.* New York: Random House. Investigates the politics of the purchase and the American reaction to the "Great Bargain."

Butler Institute of American Art

"The Oregon Trail" by Albert Bierstadt is an oil painting completed in 1869.
Its golden sunset captures the romance of a westering America.

A WESTERING AMERICA

UNIT 4

I n Unit 4 you will learn about the Age of Andrew Jackson. You also will witness life and culture in the mid 1800s and the growing conflict between North and South. Here are some main points to keep in mind as you read the unit.

- During the Era of Good Feelings, the nation prospered.
- The election of Andrew Jackson as president heralded the "era of the common man."
- The United States expanded its borders to the Pacific Ocean.
- The debate over slavery threatened national harmony.
- Some of America's greatest authors including Herman Melville and Emily Dickinson wrote during this period.
- A powerful reform movement sought to improve education, child care, and other aspects of American life.

The Age of Jackson

James Monroe's presidency came to be known as the Era of Good Feelings. The Republicans had little political opposition; the nation was prosperous, at peace, and growing rapidly. The era ended when regional differences between the Northeast, the South, and the West caused sectional conflicts. These conflicts set the stage for Andrew Jackson's rise to power. This chapter compares and contrasts the democratic ideals of Thomas Jefferson and Andrew Jackson. It describes the three main concerns of Jackson's presidency—the preservation of the Union, his battle against the Bank of the United States, and Indian removal. Finally the chapter raises questions about the new style of political campaigning started by Jackson's supporters and made traditional by the Whigs in the Log Cabin Campaign of 1840. Would such changes in politics be for the better?

1. THE ERA OF GOOD FEELINGS

Monroe's Presidency

President James Monroe was one of the luckiest persons ever to hold high office in the United States. He got on easily with most people, but he was really quite an ordinary fellow. He was little brighter than the next person. He seldom had an original idea. Nevertheless, in his long and happy life he advanced from one success to another. He achieved nearly every goal he set out after. Because the Federalists were so unpopular after the War of 1812, Monroe was elected president in 1816 without serious opposition.

In 1817 he made a goodwill tour of New England. That part of the country had been a Federalist stronghold. Yet everywhere the president went, enthusiastic crowds gathered. Local officials—Federalists and Republicans alike—greeted him warmly. As one Boston newspaper wrote, "an **Era of Good Feelings**" had begun. When Monroe ran for reelection in 1820, no one ran against him. Only one presidential elector refused to vote for him.

The country was at peace with all nations. It was prosperous and growing rapidly. There were 15 stars in the flag that Francis Scott Key saw waving over Fort McHenry in 1814 when he wrote "The

Preview & Review

Use these questions to guide your reading. Answer the questions after completing Section 1.
Understanding Issues, Events, & Ideas. How did the writings of Irving and Cooper reflect the American character and experience?
1. What was the Era of Good Feelings?
2. How did advances in technology improve Americans' lives?
3. What were advantages of regional specialization?
Thinking Critically. What characters in modern stories or movies does Deerslayer remind you of?

Pennsylvania Academy of Fine Arts

Star-Spangled Banner.'' By 1821 the flag that flew over the fort had 21 stars. Indiana, Illinois, Alabama, Mississippi, Missouri, and Maine had been admitted to the Union as states during that seven-year period. Ohio and Louisiana had also become states, but their stars had yet to be added to the flag.

American Literature

During the Era of Good Feelings Americans became more aware of the unique qualities of their own culture. At this time the first works of truly American literature were written. There had long been American writers and many books had been published in America. But they were more European in style and content. Now authors wrote about the unique American past, with an emphasis on nature, that was part of the American spirit.

The first American writer to receive worldwide literary acclaim

This Fourth of July celebration in Philadelphia's Centre Square around 1815 is certainly more formal than one imagines the frontier salutes to freedom that must have taken place the same day. Farmers would have come in from the fields and merchants closed up their shops to picnic and watch fireworks. During the Era of Good Feelings, there was probably little of the political speechmaking that later came to be a large part of Fourth of July celebrations.

was Washington Irving. Irving wrote books on a variety of American subjects: histories of the fur trade, a record of his personal tour of the West, and a four-volume biography of George Washington. Although Irving is often considered one of the early writers of the Romantic Age, he did not believe that a creative artist must be "original." In fact, he is most renowned for two stories from his

Washington Irving

The Granger Collection, New York

The Sketch Book of Geoffrey Crayon, Gent., published in 1819. Both "Rip Van Winkle" and "The Legend of Sleepy Hollow" draw on old German folktales. But their setting is all American: the Hudson River and Catskill Mountains of Irving's New York home.

Irving's writings are noted for their wit, their portrayal of the American spirit, and their wonderful descriptions of the American landscape. Notice the detailed geographic description in this excerpt from "The Devil and Tom Walker" from *Tales of a Traveler* (1824):

" One day that Tom Walker had been to a distant part of the neighborhood, he took what he considered a shortcut homeward, through the swamp. Like most shortcuts, it was an ill-chosen route. The swamp was thickly grown with great gloomy pines and hemlocks, some of them ninety feet high, which made it dark at noonday, and a retreat for the owls in the neighborhood. It was full of pits and quagmires, partly covered with weeds and mosses, where the green surface often betrayed the traveler into a gulf of black, smothering mud; there were also dark and stagnant pools, the abodes [homes] of the tadpole, the bullfrog, and the water snake; where the trunks of pines and hemlocks lay half drowned, half rotting, looking like alligators sleeping in the mire.

Tom had long been picking his way cautiously through this treacherous [dangerous] forest; stepping from tuft to tuft of rushes and roots, which afforded precarious footholds among the deep sloughs [a muddy, swampy area]; or pacing carefully, like a cat, along the prostrate [fallen] trunks of trees; startled now and then by the sudden screaming of the bittern [a bird], or the quacking of a wild duck rising on the wing from some solitary pool. At length he arrived at a firm piece of ground, which ran out like a peninsula into the deep bosom of the swamp. It had been one of the strongholds of the Indians during their wars with the first colonists. Here they had thrown up some kind of fort, . . . used as a place of refuge for their squaws and children. Nothing remained of the old fort but a few embankments, gradually sinking to the level of the surrounding earth, and already overgrown in part by oaks and other forest trees, the foliage [leaves] of which formed a contrast to the dark pines and hemlocks of the swamp. . . .[1]**"**

James Fenimore Cooper

Tales of a Traveler celebrated a truly American experience. So did the writings of another notable author of this period, James Fenimore Cooper. Cooper's best-known work, the Leatherstocking tales, is five related novels written about the American frontier. The series includes *The Pioneers, The Last of the Mohicans, The Prairie, The Pathfinder*, and *The Deerslayer*. They portray the life of Natty Bumpo as he journeys westward with the frontier.

Cooper's views of the first Americans is not realistic. Historians have criticized his distortion of historical fact about the Indians. They are either too good or too vicious to be believable. His portraits of conditions on the frontier are more accurate. They represent the first descriptions of the frontier read by a large segment of the American public. His novels also present a range of social conflicts faced by Americans—conflicts between the individual and society, between civilization and the wilderness, and between two different societies (settlers and Indians).

In *The Deerslayer* (1841), the last of the Leatherstocking tales, Bumpo, who was raised by the Delaware Indians, is passing from adolescence to manhood. In this excerpt he has been captured by the Huron Indians and charged with killing one of their warriors. He suddenly makes a daring escape and is chased by the Hurons. Note that although much of the story has the unrealistic quality of a folk tale, the descriptions seem real enough:

" Deerslayer had thrown a bit of dead branch in the canoe, and this was within reach of his arm. Removing the cap he wore, he put it on the end of this stick, and just let it appear over the edge of the canoe, as far as possible from his own person. This ruse [trick] was scarcely adopted before the young man had a proof how much he had underrated the intelligence of his enemies. In contempt of an artifice [trick] so shallow and commonplace, a bullet was fired directly

[1]From *Tales of the Traveler* by Washington Irving

Yale University Art Gallery

through another part of the canoe, which raised [caused a welt on] his skin. He dropped the cap, and instantly raised it immediately over his head, as a safeguard. It would seem that this second artifice was unseen, or what was more probable, the Hurons, feeling certain of recovering their captive, wished to take him alive.

Deerslayer lay passive a few minutes longer, his eye at the bullethole, however, and much did he rejoice at seeing that he was drifting further and further from the shore. When he looked upward, the treetops had disappeared, but he soon found that the canoe was slowly turning, so as to prevent his getting a view of anything at his peephole but the two extremities of the lake. He now bethought him of the stick, which was crooked, and offered some facilities for rowing, without the necessity of rising. The experiment succeeded on trial, better even than he had hoped, though his great embarrassment [test] was to keep the canoe straight. That this present maneuver was seen soon became apparent by the clamor [loud noise] on the shore, and a bullet entering the stern of the canoe, traversed [traveled] its length, whistling between the arms of our hero, and passed out at the head [of the canoe]. This satisfied the fugitive that he was getting away with tolerable speed and induced [caused] him to increase his efforts. . . . As the sound of voices seemed to grow more distant, however, Deerslayer determined to leave all to drift, until he believed himself beyond the reach of bullets. This was nervous work, but it was the wisest of all the expedients [ways] offered; and the young man was encouraged to persevere [continue] in it by the circumstance that he felt his face fanned by the air, a proof that there was a little more wind.[1] **99**

Technology and Progress

American creativity and ingenuity in technology also soared. Many of America's first technological advances had been borrowed from Great Britain. But soon Americans were innovating on their own. Eli Whitney's revolutionary new method of making muskets with interchangeable parts was used to produce watches, clocks, sewing machines, farm machinery, and even the famed Colt revolver.

Technological breakthroughs seemed to advance every possible activity but none more than farming and manufacturing. Plows made from the new alloys (a mixture of metals) and shaped for differing soil conditions helped farmers cultivate more land. New and better crop varieties and breeds of livestock, the use of crop rotation, and the

[1]From *The Deerslayer* by James Fenimore Cooper

development of fertilizers—such as the marl and guano used by southern tobacco growers—allowed farmers to grow crops on worn out land or in areas that were marginally fertile. Contour plowing and improved drainage techniques protected the topsoil in many areas. These and other advances contributed to the farming boom in America before the Civil War.

American industry enjoyed similar successes. Oliver Evans built a high-pressure steam engine that could be adapted for many purposes. Within a few years it was being used not only in steamboats but to run sawmills and printing presses. Evans also used his engine to power an amazingly modern flour mill he designed. Charles Goodyear discovered vulcanization, a process that toughened rubber. Jacob Perkins developed a nail-making machine. Furnaces and rolling mills replaced local forges in Pennsylvania's iron industry, and the shoe industry was mechanized. Of this burst of American creative genius an English visitor said:

66 We find Americans producing a machine even to peel apples; another to beat eggs; a third to clean knives; a fourth to wring clothes; in fact there is scarcely a purpose to which human hands have been ordinarily employed for which some ingenious attempt is not made to find a substitute in a cheap and efficient labor-saving machine.[1] 99

[1]From *A History of the American People* by Stephan Thernstrom

He did not exaggerate! Only 41 patents were granted to American inventors in 1800; in 1860, 4,357—more than 100 times as many—were issued.

As mechanical devices and innovation played increasingly important roles in the lives of Americans, the study of applied science became part of American education. Beginning in Boston in 1795 a network of mechanics' institutes spread through American cities to train men to build and repair machines. President Madison urged the creation of a national university as a "temple of science." At Harvard and Yale lectures on the exciting frontier of technology became increasingly popular with students. And in 1824 Rensselaer Polytechnic Institute opened "for the purpose of instructing persons who may choose to apply themselves in the application of science to the common purpose of life."

As the United States grew larger and richer, people noticed more differences between one region and another. These differences were in many ways for the good. People in one section produced one thing, those in another section something else. A large percentage of the nation's shoes were made in or near Lynn, Massachusetts. Fairfield County, Connecticut, especially the town of Danbury, was a center of hat manufacturing. Such **specialization** meant that there was a great deal of trading, not only of goods but also of ideas.

Point of View

An English poet viewed America's vigor and self sufficiency with some sorrow.

In the States
With half a heart I
  wander here
    As from an age gone
    by,
A brother—yet though
  young in years,
    An elder brother, I.
You speak another tongue
  than mine,
    Though both were
    English-born.
I toward the night of
  time decline;
    You mount into the
    morn.
Youth shall grow great
  and strong and free,
    But age must still
    decay;
Tomorrow for the
  States—for me,
    England and
    Yesterday.
  Robert Louis Stevenson,
  1887

Return to the Preview & Review on page 364.

Use these questions to guide your reading. Answer the questions after completing Section 2.
Understanding Issues, Events, & Ideas. Explain the issues of the election of 1824, using the following words: American system, internal improvements.
1. What caused sectional conflicts? Into which sections did the nation seem divided?
2. Describe differences among the regions.
3. How was the outcome of the election of 1824 determined?
4. What kind of government did the second President Adams believe in?
Thinking Critically. 1. Of the four candidates for president presented in the section, for whom would you have voted? Why? 2. You are heading westward in a Conestoga wagon in 1817. Describe the benefits and drawbacks of this method of travel.

2. SECTIONAL CONFLICTS

Regional Differences

The Industrial Revolution helped strengthen and diversify the nation's economy and the Transportation Revolution tied its far-flung parts together. Americans were developing a sense of their national identity. Yet regional differences persisted. As American author Thomas Kettell explained in 1860:

❝ The Northern or New England States are endowed [given] by nature with a mountainous and barren soil, which poorly rewards the labor of the farmer. However, its wooded slopes, and tumbling streams, which fall into spacious harbors, showed the first settlers the direction in which their industry [hard work] was to be employed. Shipbuilding and navigation at once became the leading industry, bringing with it wealth.

The harsh rule of the mother country forbade a manufacturing development, and that branch of industry never got a footing in the colonies. Independence from Britain opened up manufacturing, and also provided a large market for the sale of manufactures to the agricultural laborers of the more fertile fields of the Middle and Southern States.

The genius of Northern industry was quick in applying profits earned in commerce to the development of manufacturing. With every increase in population, and every extension of national territory, the New England States gained a larger market for their wares, while the foreign competing supply has been restricted by high duties on imports.

The mountain rivers of New England have become motors, by which annually improving machinery has been driven. These machines require only the attendance of females, but a few years since a non-producing class, to turn out immense quantities of textile fabrics. In the hands of the male population, other branches of industry have multiplied, in a manner which shows the stimulant of an ever-increasing demand.

At about the time that New England became free to manufacture, . . . Charleston, S.C., was no longer regarded as the nearest port to Europe, and New York assumed its proper position, as the leading seaport. The commerce of the Middle States rapidly increased, and with that increase a larger demand for the manufactures of New England was created.

When population spread west of the Allegheny Mountains, and the annexation of Louisiana opened up the Mississippi River to a market for western produce, a new demand for New England manufactures was felt. This was further enhanced by the opening of the Erie Canal. In later years, the vast foreign immigration, pouring over new lands opened up by railroads, has given a further stimulus to the demand for New England manufactures.[1]❞

These regional differences came to cause conflicts and arguments over government policies. New leaders emerged who tended to represent their own sections of the country rather than the country as a whole. The Era of Good Feelings ended, to be replaced by an era of **sectional conflicts.** The nation seemed divided into three geographic regions: the Northeast, the South, and the West.

The Northeast

The northeastern section, consisting of the New England states, New York, New Jersey, and Pennsylvania, became the major manufacturing area of the United States. Most of the important seaports were also located in this section.

These seaports and other towns were growing rapidly. New York City had 200,000 people by 1830. Europeans began coming to the United States in increasing numbers about 1830, and many settled in New York City and other eastern cities. The hustle and bustle of city life was exciting. Theaters and concert halls were built, book and magazine publishing flourished. But overcrowding turned older neighborhoods into slums. The rich seemed to get richer while the poor grew poorer.

But this was not really the case. Although the rich seized a larger share of the pie than before, the pie itself was larger. The poor were actually getting richer too, in terms of their purchasing power. Wages rose for most people, even laborers and servants. There was a greater variety of consumer goods than ever before.

So the industrial changes in the Northeast brought dramatic improvements in the standard of living of the average family. By 1840 the industrial surge had lifted income per person in the region 35 percent above the national average and almost double the southern average.

These gains made life for people in the Northeast more comfortable and satisfying in many ways. People had a far more varied diet: less bread and more meat, fruit and vegetables most of the year, and more milk for growing children. Homes were larger, warmer, and better lighted. Machine-made clothing fit better and was easier to launder than homespun garments. More low-cost books, magazines, and newspapers were available.

[1]From *Southern Wealth and Northern Profits* by Thomas P. Kettell

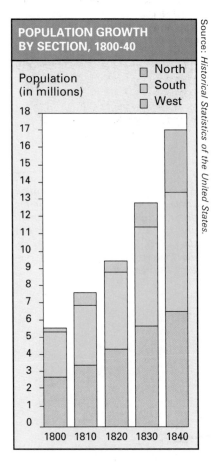

POPULATION GROWTH BY SECTION, 1800-40

Population (in millions)

☐ North
☐ South
☐ West

Source: *Historical Statistics of the United States.*

LEARNING FROM GRAPHS. *The American population grew rapidly in the 19th century. This graph reflects how much of that growth happened in the nation's three major sections. How does the graph illustrate the increasing attraction of the West?*

But who was the average resident of the Northeast—a Boston merchant who collected fat dividends on textile stocks, a young woman who toiled 72 hours a week in a mill in Lowell, the owner of a large tenement in New York or Philadelphia, or an immigrant laborer living in the slum? In this region there really was no typical, average resident. And because city life had such variety, it is not possible to describe a typical city resident, particularly the poor. Far more is known about a well-to-do family like that of John Ellerton Lodge and Anna Cabot Lodge of Boston.

The Lodges of Boston. The Lodges lived in a big, square stone house in a quiet residential neighborhood. Their home was surrounded by a beautiful garden. There were stables where the Lodge horses and carriage were kept. The house was full of fine English and early American furniture. John Lodge was a merchant whose ships were mostly engaged in trading with China. His business was located on Commercial Wharf. From his office overlooking the harbor, he could see the masts and spars of his many ships. These vessels brought in varied Chinese goods—tea, silk, chinaware, ginger and other spices, even fireworks.

John Ellerton Lodge was an extremely hard worker who was also active in charitable affairs. Private charity was especially important in those days, for there were few government welfare programs. Lodge was interested in the cultural life of Boston too. He was president of the board of directors of the local opera house.

Despite the growth of cities in the Northeast, agriculture remained the occupation of a large majority of the people. Farmers grew wheat, corn, and other grains and raised cattle, sheep, and hogs. Farms tended to be small, run by a single family with perhaps one or two "hired hands." Since most people had large families, many sons and daughters of farmers moved to the towns and cities when they grew up. Others headed west to seek their fortunes.

Massachusetts Historical Society

John Ellerton Lodge and his wife Anna Cabot Lodge are among those remembered in the popular Boston ditty: "Cabots speak only to Lowells and Lowells speak only to God." But the Lodges, founders of a political dynasty, were great supporters of Boston's cultural life.

The South

The aristocratic traditions and plantation economy of the South made life there dramatically different from life in the Northeast or West. By the South we mean the states south of Pennsylvania and east of the Mississippi River. These were the states where slavery was still legal. As in colonial times, tobacco was the most important cash crop in Maryland, Virginia, and North Carolina. By 1815 and after, cotton replaced rice as the main crop of South Carolina, Georgia, and, as the country grew, of Alabama, Tennessee, and Mississippi too. Southern farmers also grew grain and other food crops and raised hogs and cattle.

Tobacco and cotton were especially important to the South. There was a great demand for these crops in Europe and in the northern states. Southerners did not develop much manufacturing.

The Abbey Aldrich Rockefeller Folk Art Center, Colonial Williamsburg

They could buy the clothing, tools, and other manufactured goods they needed with the money earned by exporting cotton and tobacco.

Cotton was grown on small family farms of a few dozen acres and on large plantations worked by a hundred or more slaves. There were far more small farms than plantations, but the great cotton plantation was the ideal of southern society. The planters were the most influential leaders of the region.

These planters were rich and influential indeed. They had big houses, dozens of slaves, and thousands of acres of prime land. In 1860 only 22 percent of the white population lived in the South, yet two thirds of all the men with estates valued at $100,000 were southerners. Three quarters of the white families had no slaves. Most did own their own small farms. But the most fertile lands with access to transportation were controlled by the planters. Slaveless white families scratched out a living on the less-desirable lands. The richest 10 percent of the farmers in the South owned almost 65 percent of the farm wealth. In addition, the average slaveholder was five times as wealthy as the average northerner and more than ten times richer than the average slaveless southern farmer. Slave labor was the basis of almost every southern fortune.

Planters liked to think of themselves as aristocrats. They proved to be as dominant politically as they were economically. They held more political offices than the slaveless majority. The more powerful the office, the more likely it was held by a planter. Generally nonslaveholders supported the planters politically. As you have read, there were few southern schools and not everyone could attend. The children of wealthy families usually attended college. Few others had a good chance to go to school. Only about 15 percent of school age whites attended school, averaging a mere 11 days of school each year! Half of the white people of South Carolina were unable to read or write in 1850. No wonder the planters controlled politics as well as economics.

Greenville, South Carolina, in 1825 shows the prosperity of the plantation economy with two-story and three-story buildings. Notice how these early southern buildings differed from those in the rest of the country. What were some reasons that the southern people adopted a different architecture from that of the Northeast or the West?

National Portrait Gallery

John C. and Floride Calhoun managed a 550-acre plantation called Fort Hill; the mansion is now part of the Clemson College campus. Since Calhoun was usually in Washington, it fell to Floride Calhoun to attend to the daily life at Fort Hill. Describe what you imagine a typical day in her life was like.

But the planter was not the typical southerner. Only 16,000 families—one percent of the southern population—had plantations with 40 or more slaves. As in the North, life styles varied so from group to group that no typical southerner emerged. Still, the South was identified with its planters.

The Calhouns of South Carolina. A good example of an important planter was John C. Calhoun, master of Fort Hill plantation in South Carolina. Fort Hill is in the northern part of the state, in hilly country within sight of the Blue Ridge Mountains. John and Floride Calhoun built their place in 1825, after he had been elected vice president of the United States.

Despite their wealth, their many slaves, and his importance as vice president, the Calhouns' life was not that of the idle rich. Floride was responsible for managing the entire household. Besides raising her nine children, she had to make sure that any slave who was ill or injured was properly cared for. She made some of the clothing worn by women slaves. She rarely had a free moment.

When not in Washington, the vice president worked at dozens of farm chores. He was up at dawn and in the fields by 7:30. He checked with his plantation manager, the **overseer.** He experimented with new varieties of crops. He had to keep his eye on every detail of a very large operation.

The West

The West had an amazingly important influence on America's politics, economy, and culture. The flow of people west changed the nation's perspective.

In the early 1800s so many families were moving west that an Englishman on the way to Ohio in 1817 wrote:

“ Old America seems to be breaking up and moving westward. We are seldom out of sight as we travel . . . of family groups, behind and before us. ”

People of every sort were on the move. In the South well-to-do planter families accompanied by a dozen or more slaves shared the roads with poverty-stricken farmers who had nothing more than the clothes on their backs and a few tools. Along the National Road, which crossed the mountains, individuals on horseback passed weary couples pulling handcarts. Many discontented or poor people actually walked all the way from the eastern states to Ohio and Indiana.

Sometimes several families banded together for the trip. One traveler described a group that included 42 children crowded into three wagons. The **Conestoga wagon** was developed to handle the heavy loads of the pioneers. It was built with strong, wide wheels to withstand the ruts and mud and bumps of unpaved roads. A canvas cover protected the travelers from rain and snow and sheltered them

Maryland Historical Society

at night. The wagons were not known for speed or comfort. But they were tough, roomy, and not very expensive. A good one cost less than the horse that pulled it.

Of course, after the opening of the Erie Canal across New York in 1825, traveling west became far less difficult. But the trip was never easy. Soon wagons and canals had carried enough people west to populate vast new markets for eastern merchants.

What attracted the hundreds of thousands of settlers—most of them farmers, and some artisans—away from the cleared fields and established towns and cities of the East? The chief answer is: the seemingly unlimited land and opportunity offered by the West.

Throughout the West nearly everyone began as a farmer. For the settlers of Indiana or Alabama the work of clearing land and building a house was little different from what it had been 200 years earlier. Huge trees had to be chopped down, or at least killed by stripping their bark, so that sunlight could shine on the pioneers' first crops. Their first houses were usually made of logs. No one could spare the time or energy to saw logs into boards. The kitchen was often an open shed or lean-to on the side of the cabin. The rugged self-reliance of these frontier settlers has become part of America's self-image.

Historians have long noted the importance of the West on the American character. Westerners seemed the model of self-sufficiency, a trait most Americans considered part of the national identity. There was also a community spirit—everyone pitched in to help out. This made economic, social, and political arrangements more democratic. One settler boasted that "a pleasing feature of western life is the perfect social equality."

Weary travelers were glad to stop their Conestoga wagons at the Fairview Inn on Old Frederick Road. There they could swap stories and get supplies before beginning again on their long journey west. Surely an overnight stay was a luxury. How much do you think a Conestoga wagon or a span of horses cost? Where would you find the answer?

The Fine Arts Museums of San Francisco, M. H. DeYoung Memorial Museum

Mission San Gabriel Arcangel was founded in 1771.

By 1820 there were almost as many people west of the Appalachian Mountains as there had been in the original 13 states at the time of the American Revolution. Settlers thought of this area between the Appalachians and the Mississippi River as the West. It was indeed the western frontier of the United States. By 1850 the land called the Northwest Territory lay in the eastern half of the Middle West. Its location, like other areas of the growing nation, was redefined by the rush west. In this way the meaning of the term "the West" kept changing as the United States grew westward.

The first Americans had lived in western America for perhaps 30,000 years or more. By the 1770s there were many Spanish and Russian settlements, mostly trading posts and missions, in the Far West along the Pacific coastline. These western peoples either had separate societies or were colonists of Spain, Russia, or Great Britain. Some would later come to refer to themselves as Americans. But they did so only after the United States had grown to include them at the western edge of the continent. Then the West came to mean the land between the Rockies and the Pacific Ocean.

Even the present-day use of the terms "West" or "Far West" is not particularly accurate when talking about the nation. What of those most western of all the states—Alaska and Hawaii?

Most western residents owned and operated their own family farms. And although wealth was not evenly distributed, it was not as unequal as in southern agriculture or northern business. Because the price of land was cheaper in the West, it was easier to work one's way up from hired hand to farm owner. In the West it seemed a man, through hard work and ingenuity, could succeed faster than in other sections of the country. This was the American way!

The American frontiersman was a rugged individualist, venturing into the unknown wilderness. He moved often, clearing new land and building new shelters. His mobility and self-sufficiency preserved his freedom and independence. These values, those most cherished by Americans, seemed to be fading elsewhere. Society and the economy had changed. In the settled parts of the country few people produced all they needed. Few could pick up at will and move. The westerner was a reminder to all Americans of the strength and determination of the American character.

Natty Bumpo, the hero of James Fenimore Cooper's immensely popular Leatherstocking tales, and Daniel Boone are perfect examples of the westerner. Their amazing mobility was a unique characteristic of the American West. Restless movement from place to place was common. Most people moved to find more fertile land or to take advantage of rising land values. But almost always they moved to "get ahead."

Such mobility often affected western community life. Wrote one pioneer:

    “ Everything shifts under your eye. The present occupants sell, pack up, and depart. Strangers replace them. Before they have gained the confidence of their neighbors, they hear of a better place, pack up, and follow their neighbors.[1]”

And though the environment was new and unique, the earliest settlers built institutions they had been familiar with. Small western towns often resembled much larger eastern cities in this respect. When 22-year-old Abraham Lincoln arrived in New Salem, Illinois, in 1831, the town had fewer than 150 residents but already supported a school, a Sunday school, even a debating society.

Western life held some advantages for women. They had no more political and legal rights than their eastern sisters. But in general they were more accepted in the roles formerly reserved for men. Why was this so? Frontier life was a physical challenge, and more so for women. Aside from helping in the field, women did all the cooking, making and repairing of clothing, and laundering. They cut firewood, carried water, tended the garden and chickens, and made cheese, butter, soap, and candles. And they had children, whom they looked after. An 1862 report by the commissioner of agriculture stated that "on three out of four farms, it is safe to say, the wife works harder, endures more, than any other on the place; more than the husband, more than the farm hand, more than the hired help of the kitchen." Frontier men respected women who were up to such a challenge. So in the West it was easier for women to manage large farms, open shops, run general stores, and undertake other activities usually defined as men's work in other parts of the country.

The Lincolns of Indiana. A famous example of the hardships faced by these pioneers is the story of Thomas and Nancy Lincoln, who settled with their two children in Indiana in the winter of 1816. The land was covered with dense forest. Thomas Lincoln, a carpenter as well as a farmer, began by building a "half-faced camp." This was a crude, three-sided shelter of logs and branches, entirely open on the south. It was December when Thomas Lincoln built his camp.

[1]From *A History of the American People* by Stephan Thernstrom

Joslyn Art Museum, Omaha

"Settler's Farm in Indiana" is the work of Karl Bodmer, a Swiss artist, who left his sketch unfinished. But we clearly see the rustic cabin, a spring house for storing provisions in the cool earth, and split rail fences. Lincoln the Rail Splitter would have been at home here. What were some of the hardships of getting settled in the West?

The family survived only by keeping a roaring fire going day and night in front of the camp. Thomas hastened to build a more permanent log cabin, complete with a stone fireplace and chimney.

That winter the family lived on deer, turkey, and other forest animals shot by Thomas Lincoln. The Lincolns' young son Abraham, who was only seven when they arrived, had to fetch their water from a spring some distance from the cabin. Once the cabin was finished, Abraham helped his father clear land for their first crop. He soon became expert with an axe. (Later, when Abraham Lincoln became a politician, he was known as "the Rail-Splitter" because of his skill at splitting long logs into fence rails.)

The Lincolns suffered many hardships of the frontier. Nancy Lincoln died of a mysterious disease called "the milk sickness." Abraham had almost no formal schooling. He loved to read, but there were few books to be bought or borrowed. After ten years of backbreaking labor, Thomas sold the farm for only $125.

Abraham Lincoln was an exceptional person who would surely have made his mark in any situation. He rose easily in the rough-and-tumble frontier world. He was able to become a lawyer and make an excellent living, despite his humble origins and lack of education. Westerners respected ability and paid little mind to a person's origins.

Corn was usually the first crop planted in the West. It was easy to grow and could feed both the pioneers and their farm animals. After the work of clearing and fencing the land was finished, wheat, tobacco, and cotton would be grown in one place or another. And although the West remained mostly agricultural, small-scale manufacturing of all kinds soon sprang up everywhere. Transportation was so expensive at first that westerners made all kinds of goods for themselves. Everything from nails and pots and stoves to paper and barrels and clocks was made in shops and small plants in dozens of western communities.

The Election of 1824

By 1824 the three sections of the United States had produced strong leaders, each of whom was favored by a particular section. No one had opposed Monroe for president in 1820. Four candidates, each strong in his section of the country, competed for the office when Monroe retired four years later.

One candidate was John Quincy Adams. He seemed the logical choice in 1824 because he was Monroe's secretary of state. Monroe had been Madison's secretary of state before becoming president, and Madison had been Jefferson's. Adams had also been very successful as secretary. The Adams name and his long career of public service were other advantages. But he had few supporters outside New England and the other northeastern states.

The favorite in the southern states was William H. Crawford of Georgia. Crawford was Monroe's secretary of the treasury. Like Adams he had been a diplomat. He had served in the Georgia legislature and in the United States Senate.

Crawford was a tall, attractive man who got on easily with all sorts of people. He was a politician's politician, a master of all the ins and outs of that craft. Although his support was mainly southern, some important northern leaders backed him for president. He seemed likely to be elected, until he suffered a stroke that left him partly paralyzed.

The other two candidates were westerners. One was General Andrew Jackson. He was one of the few nationally popular persons of the time. He was not much of a politician, and he had relatively little interest in sectional issues like roads and tariffs. The second western candidate was Henry Clay of Kentucky. Like Crawford, Clay was handsome and charming. He loved the give-and-take of political debate and the behind-the-scenes negotiations that were necessary to get important bills through Congress.

Chicago Historical Society

Clay had been a prominent War Hawk in 1812, but he was best known for his superb ability to solve sectional conflicts by working out clever compromises. Clay was the father of a plan for sectional cooperation that he called the **American System.** Easterners wanted the government to place high tariffs on foreign manufactured goods that competed with their own

Three times Henry Clay saved the Union when sectional conflict led to crisis. For his efforts he was known as the Great Compromiser. Why is it sometimes hard for people to reach a compromise?

products. Westerners wanted the government to help pay for what were called **internal improvements**—the roads and canals needed to get western goods to market cheaply.

Clay proposed that western members of Congress vote for high tariffs in exchange for eastern votes for internal improvements. By helping each other, he explained, both sections would profit. In 1824 Clay was well known throughout the country because he was speaker, or presiding officer, of the House of Representatives. But his support in the election was only in the West.

When the electoral votes were counted, Jackson had 99, Adams 84, Crawford 41, and Clay 37. Since no one had a majority, under the Constitution the House of Representatives had to choose the president from among the three candidates with the most votes. This meant that Henry Clay was eliminated. But although he could not hold the office himself, Clay decided who would be president. He urged his supporters to vote for Adams, who was then elected.

The Second President Adams

National Portrait Gallery

John Quincy Adams, like his father, President John Adams, was intelligent, strong willed, energetic, and totally dedicated to serving his country. Naturally he had been brought up a Federalist. But in the early 1800s he realized that Federalist ideas were out of date. He switched to the Jeffersonian Republican party.

Adams believed firmly, like Alexander Hamilton, that the federal government should encourage the development of manufacturing and stimulate all kinds of economic activity. He considered Clay's American System an excellent idea. He also hoped to establish a national university in Washington, and he urged Congress to spend large sums on scientific research and exploration.

Like his father, President John Adams, John Quincy Adams put service to country ahead of personal gain. He lacked the common touch, and critics found him hard and stern. You might be interested in researching Adams' political career and contributions after he left the presidency.

Adams favored big government that would look after national interests, but the country was still sharply divided. People were mostly caught up in their own sectional interests. Even as brilliant a politician as Clay or Crawford would have found it difficult to bring the people together. And Adams was a very poor politician. His administration was a disaster.

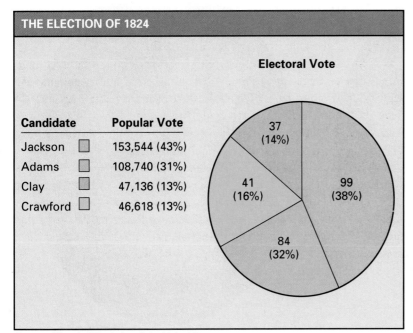

THE ELECTION OF 1824

Electoral Vote

Candidate	Popular Vote
Jackson ☐	153,544 (43%)
Adams ☐	108,740 (31%)
Clay ☐	47,136 (13%)
Crawford ☐	46,618 (13%)

37 (14%)
41 (16%)
99 (38%)
84 (32%)

Source: *Historical Statistics of the United States*

LEARNING FROM GRAPHS. *The figures from the 1824 presidential election show that none of the candidates gained a majority of either the electoral or popular votes, although clearly Jackson received the most of each. Why did Adams become president? How do you think most Americans felt about that outcome?*

Adams was extremely hardworking. Every morning he got up at five o'clock. In the dead of winter he would throw open his window and take a sponge bath with ice-cold water to prepare for his day's work. He assumed that everyone in government was as devoted to duty and as energetic as he was. When his associates did not live up to his expectations, he managed, without intending to, to make them feel guilty.

An example of Adams' clumsiness as a politician was his appointment of Henry Clay as secretary of state. Clay was certainly able, and he had some diplomatic experience. But naming him looked like a political payoff. It had been Clay's friends in the House of Representatives who had cast the votes that made Adams president. Furthermore, the last four secretaries of state had moved up from that office to the presidency. The supporters of Andrew Jackson were outraged. They charged Adams with making a "corrupt bargain" with Clay by promising to try to make Clay his successor in return for votes in the election.

Once in office, Adams quickly showed that he did not know how to use the power of the presidency to get his program adopted. He would not replace government officials who resisted his policies with people who supported them. When he was sure he was right, he was rigid and stubborn. And he was nearly always sure that he was right.

His plan for a national university had no chance of being accepted by Congress. "Let us not recommend anything so unpopular," the practical-minded Henry Clay suggested. But Adams made the recommendation anyway. "I feel it is my indispensable duty," he explained to Clay. 🔲

Return to the Preview & Review on page 370.

nal Gallery of Art

Ladies' Hermitage Association

Andrew Jackson and his wife, Rachel, who died shortly before his inauguration.

Preview & Review

Use these questions to guide your reading. Answer the questions after completing Section 3.
Understanding Issues, Events, & Ideas. Describe Jacksonian democracy, using the following words: Democrats, common man, popular vote, nominating convention, spoils of office, spoils system, rotation in office.

Write a newspaper editorial explaining the conflict over protective tariffs, using some of the following terms: tariff question, Tariff of Abominations, ordinance, ordinance of nullification, ticket, Nullification Crisis.

1. Why did Jackson win in 1828?
2. Why did some people argue that protective tariffs were unconstitutional?
3. Why did Jackson oppose the South Carolina Ordinance of Nullification?

Thinking Critically. Would you have been a supporter of Jeffersonian democracy or Jacksonian democracy? Give reasons for your answer.

3. JACKSON AS PRESIDENT

The Election of Andrew Jackson

By 1828 Adams was discouraged and depressed. None of his policies had succeeded, but he was determined to seek reelection. This time he faced only one opponent, Andrew Jackson. The Jacksonians were now calling themselves simply **Democrats** instead of Democratic-Republicans. This was the formal beginning of the Democratic party.

In those days candidates for president did not themselves campaign. To do so was considered undignified. Their supporters were not so restrained. The campaign of 1828 was bitterly fought and mean spirited.

The Jacksonians said little about issues like the tariff and internal improvements. They again accused Adams of having made a "corrupt bargain" in 1824. When they discovered that he had bought a chess set and a billiard table for the White House, they charged him with wasting public money on gambling devices. One Democratic newspaper claimed that Adams was so pro-British that he intended to move to England and buy a noble title when he retired.

The president's supporters replied with lies of their own. Jackson was a gambler and a murderer, they said. They told shady stories about his mother and his wife, Rachel. Understandably, by the end of the campaign Jackson and Adams were furious with each other.

These lies and wild charges probably had little effect on the election, nor did any of the real issues. Jackson won the election chiefly because he was so popular, while Adams was so ramrod straight and remote from ordinary voters.

Jacksonian Democracy

Jackson's victory marked a turning point in American history. Although he was neither poor nor ordinary in any sense, he presented himself as being in tune with the **common man.** (Women were not counted in politics at that time because they could not vote.) Jackson's position was shrewd politically, and there was some truth to it. He was not an ignorant man, but he was poorly educated. He wrote with a terrible scrawl. His spelling was even worse. He had the manners of a gentleman, but he was capable of behaving like a rowdy. He was utterly unlike any earlier president.

Jackson was also the first "westerner" to occupy the White House. His election signified the beginning of a shift of political power to the West.

After Jackson delivered his inaugural address on March 4, 1829, he held an open house at the White House. Anyone could come. The mansion became so crowded that Jackson was almost crushed to death. Furniture was broken, mud tracked over expensive carpets.

In the Era of the Common Man the White House was open to all. Robert Cruikshank made this clever caricature titled "The President's Levee, or all Creation going to the White House." How did Jackson finally escape his well wishers on inauguration day? Do you think such events should be open to everyone?

Library of Congress

Huge amounts of food and drink were consumed. Jackson finally had to escape out a side door and spend the night in a hotel.

This was a new kind of democracy, quite different from that of Thomas Jefferson. Jefferson had tried to teach people that public officials were their servants. No person had *rights* superior to those of anyone else. The Jeffersonians believed that the people should have the right to choose their leaders. Yet they assumed that the people would choose exceptional persons to lead them.

The Jacksonians claimed that any ordinary person could be a leader. The common sense of the common man was all that was required to handle public office or a government job.

This faith in ordinary people led to a number of democratic reforms. State property qualifications for voting and holding office were dropped, allowing more people than ever to vote. More and more, presidential electors were chosen by **popular vote,** or by the people, not by the state legislatures.

Soon national meetings of party leaders began to be held. These **nominating conventions** were attended by delegates from all over the nation. The delegates chose the party's presidential and vice presidential candidates. Then, at the presidential election, voters cast

In this political cartoon called "Office Hunters for the Year 1834," Jackson is a devilish puppet master pulling the strings attached to a crowd of political office seekers. What is the cartoonist's view of those who seek to ride their candidate's coattails for political gain? Do you agree?

The Granger Collection, New York

ballots for the electors in their states who were pledged to vote for the candidates selected at the party conventions. Both the Democrats and their opponents adopted this method of choosing candidates.

Not all results of this new faith in the good sense of the common man were for the good. Politicians soon learned to attract voters by slogans and flattery rather than by discussing the issues. Probably this was bound to come with the spread of democratic ideas and the pressures of closely fought elections.

In Jackson's case there was no way to avoid making personality more important than issues. No party had been led by as popular and colorful a figure as "Old Hickory" Jackson, ex-Indian fighter and Hero of New Orleans. Since then, "personality"—and sometimes the lack of it—has decided many an election.

Election campaigns were becoming a spectator sport with voters watching from the sidelines while office seekers competed for what became known as the **spoils of office.** The Jacksonian Democrats went further. They made politics a team sport which a great many ordinary citizens could play. When they won an election, elected officers appointed as many supporters as possible to government jobs. This became known as the **spoils system.**

The Jacksonians then added the idea known as **rotation in office.** After a certain length of time, usually four years, most jobholders were replaced by other members of the team. The purpose was to get as many people as possible involved in party politics by holding out to all loyal party workers the possibility of a government job.

Southerners did not share as fully as those from other sections in the egalitarian urge of Jacksonian democracy and later political reforms. Aristocratic traditions held that only the planter class was qualified to hold office. Few, if any, outside their ranks were ever elected or appointed.

The Idea of Nullification

Jackson was popular in all parts of the country, but sectional disagreements did not end when he was elected president. The **tariff question** was particularly troublesome. Many members of Congress represented districts whose products had to compete with foreign-made goods, such as cotton and woolen cloth. These districts, mostly in the northeastern states, favored high protective tariffs. The southern states produced few such products. They opposed tariffs that would raise the prices of goods they had to buy.

A few months before the presidential election, Congress had passed a tariff law with very high duties. People who opposed it called it the **Tariff of Abominations.** They considered it abominable, or disgusting. Most southerners were among this group.

What made the tariff argument so serious was the belief of some experts that protective tariffs were unconstitutional. They argued

Point of View

A lifetime studying Andrew Jackson led one modern historian to this view.

"At one time in the history of the United States, General Andrew Jackson of Tennessee was honored above all living men. And most dead ones, too. The American people reserved to him their total love and devotion. . . . Nothing within their sovereign power did they deny him. Nothing satisfied the need to acknowledge his greatness or the enormous debt they owed him. As a mark of their devotion and confidence—if not the mark of madness—some men continued to vote for him for President of the United States nearly fifteen years after his death. As the nation stumbled toward the crisis of the Civil War these voters desperately sought to summon him from his tomb to rescue once again his beloved country.[1]"
    Robert Remini, 1976

[1]*Andrew Jackson and the Course of the American Empire,* Copyright © 1977 by Robert V. Remini. Harper & Row.

that the Constitution gave Congress the power to tax imports only in order to raise money. To tax imports to keep foreign goods out of the country was an abuse of power and therefore illegal, they said.

One person who considered the Tariff of Abominations unconstitutional was Vice President John C. Calhoun, whose South Carolina cotton plantation we have described. In 1828 Calhoun wrote an essay insisting that a state had the right to prevent an unconstitutional law from being enforced within its territory.

Jefferson and Madison had made a similar argument in the Kentucky and Virginia Resolutions in 1798. But Calhoun went further. He described an orderly way for a state to be free of a law it found unconstitutional. When a state legislature considered a law of Congress unconstitutional, he wrote, it could order a special election to choose delegates to decide the question. If the delegates agreed, they

The Granger Collection, New York

"Sun of Intellectual light & liberty, stand ye still, in Masterly inactivity, that the Nation of Carolina may continue to hold Negroes & plant Cotton till the day of Judgment!"

This caricature of John C. Calhoun shows him as the biblical Joshua commanding the sun to stand still. He wants to hold back time so that "The nation of Carolina may continue to hold Negroes and plant cotton till the day of Judgment." What position of Calhoun's was the cartoonist attacking? What clause in the Constitution would have contributed to Calhoun's distress?

could pass an act, or **ordinance,** called an **ordinance of nullification.** The law would then be *nullified*—that is, cease to exist—in the state.

Neither South Carolina nor any other state tried to nullify the Tariff of Abominations. Calhoun believed that Jackson agreed with him about tariffs. He supported Jackson for president in 1828 and was himself elected to a second term as vice president, running this time with Jackson on the Democratic **ticket,** as the list of candidates is called. He assumed that after the election Congress would pass a new law lowering the tariff.

But the influence of manufacturers in Congress was growing steadily. When a new tariff was finally passed in 1832, it lowered the duties only slightly. Southerners were disappointed and angry.

The Nullification Crisis

The South Carolina legislature decided to put Calhoun's theory of nullification into practice. It ordered a special election. The delegates chosen by the voters met in November 1832 and passed an ordinance nullifying the tariff laws. After February 1, 1833, the collection of tariffs would be prohibited in South Carolina. (The delay was decided upon in hopes that Congress would avoid a showdown by lowering the tariff before the deadline.) When the ordinance was passed, Calhoun resigned as vice president and returned to South Carolina. The legislature then elected him a United States senator.

President Jackson was not particularly interested in tariffs. Unlike Calhoun, he was not brilliant at political theory. But he knew the United States would fall apart if a state could refuse to obey any federal law it did not like. As president he had sworn to protect and defend the Constitution. He therefore acted as decisively as he had acted in 1815 when he learned that General Pakenham's Redcoats were approaching New Orleans.

First Jackson issued a *Proclamation to the People of South Carolina.* This warned them that he would use the army if necessary to enforce tariff laws if nullification was actually tried. Then he announced that he would march personally into South Carolina at the head of his troops and hang the leading nullifiers. "Union men, fear not," he said. *"The Union will be preserved."*

If other southern states had supported South Carolina by nullifying the tariff, civil war would probably have resulted. But most southerners were not ready to break up the Union over tariffs. Northerners were also eager to avoid a fight. In Congress, Calhoun and Henry Clay worked out a compromise tariff bill with a gradual lowering of duties. When it passed and was signed by Jackson, the South Carolina legislature repealed the Ordinance of Nullification.

The **Nullification Crisis** was over. But the question remained unanswered. Did a state have the right to refuse to obey a federal law that it considered unconstitutional? 🖅

Return to the Preview & Review on page 382.

4. JACKSON AND THE ECONOMY

The Bank of the United States

Use these questions to guide your reading. Answer the questions after completing Section 4.
Understanding Issues, Events, & Ideas. Explain the significance of the following words: Second Bank of the United States, bank note, hard money, bankrupt, "pet bank," inflationary spiral, boom, Panic of 1837, depression.

1. Why did state-chartered banks dislike the Bank of the United States? Why did Jackson dislike it?
2. Why was Jackson's bank veto so popular?
3. How did Jackson try to close the Bank of the United States?
4. What was the result of reckless lending and putting more bank notes into circulation?

Thinking Critically. 1. You are a student of economics in 1830. Do you agree with Jackson's "hard money" theory? Why or why not? **2.** Imagine that you are Nicholas Biddle. Write a letter to the president of a state bank, explaining the dangers of his issuing too many bank notes. Warn him of what you will do if he persists.

The Nullification Crisis showed Andrew Jackson at his best. He was determined, coolheaded, and confident. He stood firm for the great principle of saving the Union. Yet he was willing to compromise on the particular issue of the tariff. The same cannot be said for his handling of another controversy of his presidency. This was the question of whether or not to renew the charter of the **Second Bank of the United States.**

After the Second Bank of the United States was founded in 1816, many state-chartered banks lost business to it. Several states therefore passed laws placing heavy taxes on branches of the Bank within their borders. The Bank refused to pay these taxes. In the case of *McCulloch v. Maryland* (1819), the Supreme Court declared that the Bank was constitutional and therefore that no state could tax it. That appeared to answer the constitutional question first raised by George Washington when Alexander Hamilton proposed the first Bank of the United States in 1790. After 1819 the new Bank prospered.

The president of the Bank, Nicholas Biddle, was an excellent financier. He used the resources of the powerful Bank to stimulate the nation's economy by lending money to businesses to expand their operations. At the same time he tried to prevent state banks from lending money too recklessly.

Banks made loans by issuing paper money to borrowers who put up some sort of security, such as a deed to land, to guarantee that the loan would be repaid. Each bank created its own paper money, with its name printed on the bills. This paper money, called **bank notes,** was supposed to represent gold or silver coins in the bank's safe. These bank notes passed from hand to hand, as money does today. Anyone who received any bank's note had the right to go to that bank and exchange the note for coins, called **hard money.**

So long as people were sure a bank would exchange hard money for bank notes, few would trouble to make the exchange. For this reason banks issued far more notes than they had gold and silver in their vaults. Up to a point this was reasonable and safe.

But some banks were tempted to issue very large amounts of

Courtesy Nicholas Biddle, Jr.

Nicholas Biddle is shown in a fine miniature painted by Henry Inman, c. 1831.

notes. The more notes issued, the more loans there were earning interest for the bank. This was dangerous, for if people suddenly began turning in these notes, the bank would not have enough gold and silver. It would then be **bankrupt,** and people who owned its paper money or who had deposited their savings in it would be hurt.

However, Nicholas Biddle had a way to force state banks to be conservative about making loans. He could threaten to turn in all of the state bank notes that the Bank of the United States received in the course of its far-flung activities and demand payment in gold or silver in return.

Many state bankers objected to Biddle's policies. They wanted the government to let the Bank go out of business when its 20-year charter ran out in 1836. Then they would be able to make loans more freely and thus earn larger profits.

Andrew Jackson also wanted to do away with the Bank of the United States. His reasoning, however, was far different from that of the state bankers. Jackson was what was called a hard-money man. His reasoning went this way: Bank notes were supposed to represent gold and silver coins. A bank that issued more notes than it had gold and silver in its vaults was committing a fraud. Since *all* banks did so, including the Bank of the United States, Jackson considered them all dangerous. "I do not dislike your Bank any more than all banks," the president told Biddle. And he added that he was "afraid of banks." For this tough old frontier fighter to admit that he was afraid of anything was most unusual. The Bank of the United States was in deep trouble.

Jackson also had more logical reasons for disliking the Bank. He believed that its conservative policies had caused a depression in 1819. And he was convinced that a private corporation ought not to have so much power over the nation's economy. The fact that Biddle had used the Bank to influence political events angered him further. Biddle had employed Senator Daniel Webster and other opponents of Jackson, and he made loans to newspaper editors who supported anti-Jackson candidates.

The Bank Veto

Biddle and supporters of the Bank in Congress knew that Jackson hoped to destroy it. They decided to introduce a bill in Congress to recharter the Bank in 1832, four years before its charter would expire. This would extend the charter before campaigning began for the presidential election of 1832.

Jackson could sign the bill if he believed the Bank was popular, or he could veto it. If he signed it, the Bank would be safe. If he vetoed it, his decision could be used against him in the election. Perhaps he would be defeated. Then Congress could pass another recharter bill which the new president would sign.

New York Historical Society

President Jackson in a cloak attacks the many-headed Bank of the United States. Nicholas Biddle in his top hat is at the center. The heads of the 24 bank directors spring up from the "nasty varmit." Jackson defends himself with his "veto stick," aided by Vice President Van Buren, who is choking Massachusetts and Delaware. Research the story of the Hydra, the many-headed monster of mythology, to see how it was the inspiration for the monster in this cartoon.

Source: *Historical Statistics of the United States*

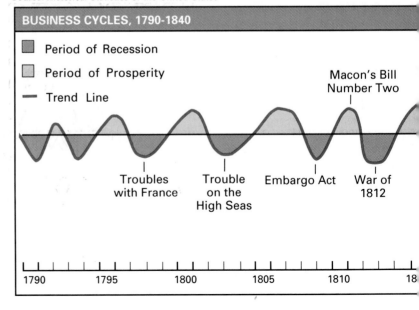

BUSINESS CYCLES, 1790-1840

- Period of Recession
- Period of Prosperity
- Trend Line

Troubles with France

Trouble on the High Seas

Embargo Act

War of 1812

Macon's Bill Number Two

1790   1795   1800   1805   1810   18

Jackson vetoed the bill. He gave reasons: The Bank was unconstitutional. It was a dangerous financial monopoly. The arguments defied the Supreme Court's ruling in *McCulloch v. Maryland*. This was one of several confrontations between Jackson and the Court.

He also claimed the Bank had allowed a few wealthy investors to make profits from "the earnings of the American people." Many of its stockholders were foreigners.

Some of these arguments made little sense. But most ordinary people were impressed by Jackson's attack on monopoly and uncontrolled wealth. The veto was very popular. The Bank was still in business, but its charter was running out. In the election Jackson defeated his opponent, Henry Clay, by 219 electoral votes to 49.

Boom and Bust

Jackson then set out to close down the Bank of the United States. He began to withdraw the government money that was already in the Bank to pay bills. At the same time he stopped depositing government money in the Bank. Instead he ordered that the income from taxes and land sales be deposited in various state banks. Jackson's opponents charged that the government was showing favoritism in this matter. They called banks that received these deposits "Jackson's pets" or **"pet banks."** This was somewhat unfair because the money was soon spread out among nearly 100 different state banks.

Biddle tried to fight back by forcing state banks to convert their paper money to gold. This was done to limit the number of business loans they could make. His policies only turned more people against the Bank. Many of the banks began to lend money recklessly. More and more bank notes were put into circulation.

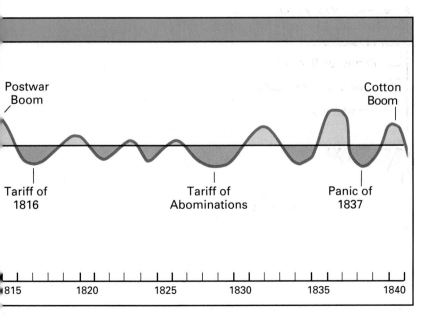

Postwar
Boom

Cotton
Boom

Tariff of
1816

Tariff of
Abominations

Panic of
1837

1815   1820   1825   1830   1835   1840

LEARNING FROM GRAPHS.
American business continually goes through a series of ups and downs known as the business cycle. This graphic shows the cycles between 1790 and 1840. How many recessions did the nation experience in those years? What is one generalization you can make about periods of prosperity?

New York Historical Society

The Panic of 1837 has brought hard times to this family with its starving children.

With so much paper money available, prices began to rise rapidly. Many people borrowed money in order to buy land. The price of city lots soared. As the price of land rose, more people hastened to buy land. The federal government sold undeveloped western lands in enormous amounts. In 1832 government land sales came to $2.6 million. Four years later the total was nearly $25 million.

Jackson's battle with the Bank outlasted his time in office. In 1837 there was an **inflationary spiral**—that is, a continuous rise in prices when the higher cost of one product or service causes the prices of other goods and services to go up too. This inflationary spiral, called a **boom,** ended as most booms do in a sudden collapse of prices and business activity. This collapse, the **Panic of 1837,** was followed by a period when economic activity generally slowed down. This is called a **depression.** Worried depositors all over the country suddenly began rushing to the banks to change their bank notes into gold or silver. Banks swiftly ran out of coin and had to close their doors.

Return to the Preview & Review on page 388.

5. JACKSON'S INDIAN POLICY

Preview & Review

Use these questions to guide your reading. Answer the questions after completing Section 5.
Understanding Issues, Events, & Ideas. Describe Jackson's policy to remove the southern Indians, using the following words: Cherokee Nation, Removal Act, Treaty of Dancing Rabbit Creek.

Write a political analysis of the election of 1840, using the following terms: Whig, Independent Treasury System, Log Cabin Campaign.

1. In what sense did the southern Indians have governments within governments?
2. What did Jackson offer in an attempt to persuade the southern Indians to move west?
3. What was the outcome of the Treaty of Dancing Rabbit Creek?
4. What tactic did the Whigs use to win the election of 1840?

Thinking Critically. **1.** You are a Choctaw Indian making the trip west from Mississippi during the winter of 1831–32. Tell about your experiences. **2.** In your opinion, did the Log Cabin Campaign of 1840 present General Harrison as a man qualified to be president? Give reasons for your answer.

The Southern Indians

The third great issue of Jackson's presidency was the removal of the southern Indians to undeveloped territory west of the Mississippi River. In 1830 about 120,000 Indians still occupied parts of Florida, Georgia, Alabama, and Mississippi.

Few Americans at the time knew much about these or any Indians beyond what they read in novels such as the Leatherstocking tales and stories they heard. These often portrayed Indians as savages on the warpath. Most people had little or no idea about what the Indians valued. The Cherokee stressed honor, dedication, and bravery. The Shawnee lived by two basic rules: "Do not injure or kill your neighbor, for it is not him or her you injure but yourself," and "Do not wrong or hate your neighbor, for Moneto, the Grandmother, the Supreme Being, loves him or her also as she loves you." To the Shawnee, absolute honesty was the basis for all character. Dishonesty was a crime, the greatest dishonor. These same values were shared by many Indian societies. Surely many Americans would have been surprised at how similar those rules are to the Ten Commandments honored by Christians and Jews.

Ordinary people knew little about Indian religions. Most Indian societies were guided by shamans, or religious leaders. Cherokee shamans conducted religious ceremonies and ministered to the special needs of families. They also reminded the people of Cherokee traditions and the examples set by their ancestors. Shamans continually told Indian parents to teach their children the importance of tribal ideals such as honesty, the rights of others, and bravery. Miami Indian shamans took the boys of the village on vision quests. During these four-day fasts the young braves waited for visions of their personal guardian spirits. The values of their personal guardians were to guide them through life. Girls also had visions of spirits.

Few people realized how the Indians lived. Some Indians east of the Mississippi continued to hunt regularly after settlers began crossing the Appalachians in the 1790s. But most were farmers, tending tribal lands. The Cherokee lived in houses grouped in small settlements or towns. They farmed fields owned by the community. Families were assigned specific farm plots in the field. The entire Cherokee family worked at farming. Even the children had certain tasks, such as cleaning harvested crops or helping to carry tools or produce. Indian societies that wanted to retain a culture based on hunting and gathering asked the United States government to be permitted to move west. By 1807 the Shawnee, Wyandot, Delaware, and Miami had made such requests. The Miami adapted to their new home in an interesting way. Each summer they would leave their forest villages and go west to the prairies to hunt buffalo.

Woolaroc Museum, Bartlesville, Oklahoma

Travelers on the Trail of Tears surely hadn't such warm blankets and sturdy ponies. Yet this is how a later artist came to romanticize the relocation of the Cherokees. Read the excerpt on page 403 for an eyewitness account.

The most tragic story of Indian removal was that of the Cherokees of Georgia. Of all the American Indians, the Cherokees made the greatest effort to accept new customs. They developed a written language and published their own newspaper. They drafted a written constitution for the Cherokee Nation. Many took up farming. Some built houses in the style of southern plantation owners. They even copied their southern neighbors by buying a considerable number of slaves!

The Cherokees would not surrender their independence. They fought against removal in the federal courts. When the Supreme Court upheld their claims, President Jackson ignored the court's decision. In 1835 a small group of Cherokees agreed to go west, but the vast majority still refused.

In 1838 Martin Van Buren, Jackson's successor as president, sent General Winfield Scott to Georgia with orders to round up the Cherokees and force them to leave the area. Seven thousand soldiers swiftly herded together 15,000 Cherokees and marched them off. They were forced to leave nearly all their possessions behind. About 4,000 of them died on the long Trail of Tears to Oklahoma. It was, one white soldier later recorded, "the cruelest work I ever knew."

The southern Indian tribes would not agree to blend into the United States. They insisted on keeping their tribal governments, so there were what amounted to governments within governments in these states. The Indians' attitude was understandable. The southern states treated Indians almost as harshly as they did slaves. They did not allow Indians to vote or testify in court. Yet they wished to tax them and make them serve in the state militia. They refused to recognize the existence of tribal governments.

Jackson backed up the states in these matters. In the opinion of Chief Justice John Marshall in the case of *Worcester v. Georgia* (1832), Georgia law did not extend to the **Cherokee Nation,** which was located entirely within that state. Jackson refused to enforce the Court's decree. "John Marshall has made his decision," the president is supposed to have said. "Now let him enforce it."

Although he had been a fierce Indian fighter, Jackson did not hate Indians. He respected their courage and fighting ability. But since they were unwilling to give up their ancient customs and way of life, he believed they should move to open territory west of the Mississippi River.

This seemed a reasonable proposal to the president. After all, he explained, every year thousands of Americans left family and friends "to seek new homes in distant regions."

But since it would be unfair and maybe dangerous to try to force the Indians to move, Jackson set out to persuade them to go. He offered to pay for their present lands, to transport them west at government expense, and to give them new land beyond the frontier. The place chosen was west of Arkansas in what is now Oklahoma.

Not all Americans favored Jackson's removal policy. State laws passed by Georgia, Alabama, and Mississippi shattered the terms and spirit of treaties between the Indians and the United States. Many Americans felt it was unfair and unjust to break the treaties that granted these Indians the right to live on their lands *forever*. These people blamed Jackson for not protecting the rights of Indians guaranteed by the treaties. Edward Everett, a Massachusetts congressman, was a strong defender of Indians' rights. In a speech to Congress in 1831 Everett expressed the feelings of many of those who opposed removing the Cherokee and other Indian tribes from lands granted to them by treaty. Everett said:

> **"** I cannot disguise my impression that it [the cancellation of the previous Indian treaties] is the greatest question which ever came before Congress, short of the question of peace and war. It concerns not an individual, but entire communities of men, whose fate is wholly in our hands, . . . As I regard it, it is a question of inflicting the pains of banishment [exile] from their native land on seventy or eighty thousand human beings, the greatest part of whom are fixed and attached to their homes in the same way that we are. . . .
>
> The Indians, as was natural, looked to the Government of the United States for protection. It was the quarter [place] whence they had a right to expect it—where, as I think, they ought to have found it. They asked to be

protected in the rights and possessions guaranteed to them by numerous treaties, and demanded the execution [making], in their favor, of laws of the United States governing the intercourse [interactions] of our citizens with the Indian tribes. They came first to the President, deeming [claiming], and rightly, that it was his duty to afford them this protection. They knew . . . he had but one constitutional duty to perform toward the treaties and laws—the duty of executing [enforcing] them. The President refused to afford the protection demanded. . . .

The President acquiesces [accepts passively] in this course, on the part of the States, although it is his sole duty, in reference to this matter, to enforce the law, of which these treaties are a part. Congress last winter made express provision against their violation. They are violated. Let us either make provision to execute [the treaties], or let us abrogate [abolish] them.[1] "

Of course, many Indians also spoke out against the policy. Speckled Snake, a Creek more than 100 years old, responded in 1829 to Jackson's announcement:

" Brothers! I have listened to many talks from our great father [American leaders]. When he first came over the wide waters, he was but a little man . . . very little. His legs were cramped by sitting long in his big boat, and he begged for a little land to light his fire on. . . . But when the white man had warmed himself before the Indians fire and had filled himself with their hominy, he became very large. With a step he bestrode the mountains, and his feet covered the plains and the valleys. His hand grasped the eastern and western sea, and his head rested on the moon. Then he became our Great Father. He loved his red children, and he said, 'Get a little further, lest I tread [step] on thee. . . .'

Brothers I have listened to a great many talks from our great father. But they all begin and ended in this: 'Get a little further; you are too near me.'[2] "

Indian Removal

In 1830 Congress passed a **Removal Act** providing money to carry out Jackson's policy of Indian removal. The first Indians approached were the Choctaws, who lived in central Mississippi. In September 1830 government agents organized a great conference at Dancing Rabbit Creek in Mississippi. Between 5,000 and 6,000 Choctaws

[1]From *Congressional Debates*, 21st Congress, 2nd Session
[2]From *Red Men Calling on the Great White Father* by Katherine C. Turner

attended. The agents supplied food for this huge gathering. They distributed cloth, soap, razors, and other gifts. They promised the Choctaws land in the West, free transportation, expense money for a year while they were settling in their new home, and annual grants to support the tribal government. Any Choctaw who wished to remain in Mississippi as an individual farmer would be given a plot of land. Failure to move, agents warned, could mean destruction of their society. The federal government could offer them no protection.

In the **Treaty of Dancing Rabbit Creek** the Choctaws accepted these terms. The Indians gave up a battle they could not win. Most were filled with a sadness we cannot feel. George M. Harkins, a district chief of the Choctaw Nation, expressed the sadness of his people and the hope that this would be the last injustice toward his tribe:

Council members from 17 tribes have been assembled in 1843 at Tahlequah, the new Cherokee capital in Oklahoma. About 10,000 delegates attended this meeting. Cherokee chief John Ross called upon his people to promote friendship between the southern exiles and the Plains Indians, their new neighbors.

National Museum of American Art

❝ TO THE AMERICAN PEOPLE:
I ask you in the name of justice for repose [rest], for myself and my injured people. Let us alone—we will not harm you, we want rest. We hope, in the name of justice that another outrage may never be committed against us. . . .

Friends, my attachment to my native land is strong—that cord is now broken; and we must go as wanderers in a strange land! I must go—let me entreat [beg] you to regard us with feelings of kindness, and when the hand of oppression is stretched against us, let me hope that every part of the United States, filling the mountains and valleys, will echo and say stop. . . .[1] ❞

[1]From *Touch the Earth: A Self-Portrait of Indian Existence* by T.C. McLuhan

Colonel Cobb, another Choctaw chief, expressed similar feelings. His was one of the last groups to head westward. Here he addresses a government agent who has come to prepare the tribe for removal:

66 Brother! We have listened to your talk, coming from our father, the Great White Chief, at Washington, and my people have called upon me to reply to you. . . .

Brother! we have, as your friends, fought by your side, and have poured out our blood in your defense, but our arms are now broken. You have grown large. My people have become small, and there are none who take pity on them.

Brother! my voice is become weak—you can scarcely hear me. It is not the shout of a warrior, but the wail of an infant. I have lost it in mourning over the desolation and injuries of my people. These are their graves which you see scattered around us, and in the winds which pass through these aged pines we hear the moanings of their departed Ghosts. Their ashes lie here, and we have been left to protect them. Our warriors are nearly all gone to the West, but here are our dead. Will you compel us to go too, and give their bones to the wolves?

Brother! . . . you speak the words of a mighty nation. I am a shadow, and scarcely reach to your knee. My people are scattered and gone; when I shout, I hear my voice in the depths of the forest, but no answering voice comes back to me—all is silent around me! My words therefore must be few. I can now say no more.[1] 99

Not many Americans heard or read these sad speeches, or knew to what they referred. Indians as Americans' allies? Few realized that the Oneida and Tuscarora had fed Washington's starving men at Valley Forge when white settlers refused supplies because the army had no money. Few knew Washington had once said: "If these Indians had been our enemies instead of our friends, the war would not have ended in American independence."

So removal proceeded. Jackson was eager to carry out the removal smoothly. As one government agent put it, if the removal could be handled well, it would "break the ice and pave the way for future removals." A full year was devoted to preparations. Still, the move was badly managed.

The first group of Indians set out during the winter of 1831–32. That winter turned out to be bitterly cold, even in Mississippi and Arkansas. Many died of exposure and starvation. Later groups in 1832 and 1833 fared better. All in all, about 15,000 Choctaws settled

[1]From "A Chieftain's 'Farewell Letter' to the American People" in *The American Indian*, vol. 1, no. 3

STRATEGIES FOR SUCCESS

USING PHOTOGRAPHS AS PRIMARY SOURCES

Photographs are important primary sources. Studying them for details can tell you much about a person, event, or time.

On this page are the photographs of the first three presidents of the United States to sit before the camera: John Quincy Adams, *upper right,* Andrew Jackson, *below,* and Martin Van Buren, *lower right.* It is hard today to believe that the camera lets us see so far into the past. In fact, we are able to view the actual images of all but five of the presidents.

How to Use Photographs as Primary Sources

Follow these steps to use photographs as primary sources.

1. **Study the subject.** Identify the person, event or location in the photograph.
2. **Check for details.** Note the expression, action, or setting. Look closely at the style of dress and other details.
3. **Don't be misled.** Remember that many scenes are posed and exclude more than is included. Remember also that early photography took such a long time for the exposure that subjects appear unnaturally stiff.

Applying the Strategy

Study the photographs on this page. What do they tell you about these former presidents? About the early and mid 1800s?

For independent practice, see Practicing the Strategy on pages 402–03.

Metropolitan Museum of Art

National Portrait Gallery

George Eastman House

beyond the Mississippi. The federal government had cut costs of the relocation wherever possible. Sometimes the Indians were supplied with spoiled meat and other bad food. Even so, the move still cost much more than had been expected. Nevertheless, Jackson went ahead with the Indian removal policy. More than 45,000 southern Indians were resettled.

The Seminoles refused to sign a treaty of removal. Led by their great chiefs Phillip and Osceola, the Seminoles fought. Joseph Hernández, Florida's first congressional delegate and the first Hispanic in Congress, raised an army of volunteers. Within a few short months, Hernández had captured all the Seminole leaders. By 1842 the Seminole resistance, called the Second Seminole War, was over.

By the 1840s scarcely an Indian remained in the southern states. The tribes that were removed had suffered heavy losses. For the moment the survivors were free to go their own way, but not for long.

The Log Cabin Campaign of 1840

Martin Van Buren had been secretary of state during Jackson's first term and vice president during his second. Van Buren came from New York. He was a small, red-haired man, one of the shrewdest politicians of his day. He was so clever at political dealing that he was frequently called "the Little Magician" or "the Red Fox."

In 1836, with Jackson's approval, the new Democratic party nominated Van Buren for president. When the opposition, now calling itself the **Whig** party, put up three different presidential candidates, Van Buren won the election easily. He got 170 electoral votes, while his closest opponent, General William Henry Harrison, received only 73.

As president, Van Buren was hurt by the economic depression that followed the Panic of 1837. Many state banks closed. Others had shaky finances. The federal government had no safe place to store tax payments and other income. At Van Buren's urging, Congress established an **Independent Treasury System.** Thereafter, all money due the government was to be paid in gold or silver. This money was simply stored in government vaults until needed.

In 1840 Van Buren sought reelection. This time the Whigs united behind General Harrison. They correctly guessed that this old Indian fighter would have an appeal to voters similar to that of Andrew Jackson. Their strategy was the **Log Cabin Campaign.**

In 1828 the Democrats had ignored most issues and concentrated on describing the virtues of that friend of the common man and savior of his country, Andrew Jackson. Now the Whigs sang the praises of "Old Tippecanoe," the conqueror of Tecumseh. Harrison was a simple man of the people, the Whigs claimed. He lived in a log cabin and always had a warm welcome for strangers. He drank that won-

Library of Congress

Part of the hoopla of the 1840 presidential campaign is this sheet music, "General Harrison's Log Cabin March and Quick Step." If you're musical you might try to play this song to hear how a tune sung at a political rally might have sounded over 100 years ago.

derful beverage of the people, homemade hard cider, right out of the jug. On the other hand, the Whigs insisted, Van Buren was an aristocrat who dined off gold plates in the White House and misused the people's money on expensive French wines. When Van Buren tried to discuss issues such as the tariff and banking policy, they shouted, "Van, Van, is a used-up man." Then they launched into speeches describing the Battle of Tippecanoe. At every Whig gathering cider flowed freely.

These tactics worked perfectly. The campaign was mindless but very exciting. Voters by the thousands were fascinated. In the election of 1836, 1.5 million citizens had gone to the polls. In 1840 the total soared to 2.4 million. Harrison won by a big margin, 234 electoral votes to 60. The ideas set in motion by the Jacksonians in 1828 had proved unbeatable. American politics would never be the same. 🖅

Return to the Preview & Review on page 393.

CHAPTER 11 REVIEW

Era of Good Feelings

1815   1825

1816   **1817**
Era of Good Feelings begins   First Seminole War begins

★
American System adopted

1824
John Quincy Adams elected

Chapter Summary
Read the statements below. Choose one, and write a paragraph explaining its importance.
1. The Era of Good Feelings after the War of 1812 was brought to an end by sectional quarrels.
2. The nation became divided into the Northeast, South, and West by regional interests.
3. President John Quincy Adams was not very successful at ending sectional conflicts.
4. The election of Andrew Jackson, champion of the common man, in 1828 was a turning point in American history.
5. After 1828 elections and government in general were more democratic, involving more people than ever before.
6. The Tariff of Abominations led to the Nullification Crisis, which Jackson forcefully ended.
7. Jackson's opposition to the Bank of the United States and his banking policies led to a depression called the Panic of 1837.
8. Jackson hoped to move the southern Indians to open western lands, but removal attempts were disasters.
9. The Log Cabin Campaign of 1840 changed election campaigning.

Reviewing Chronological Order
Number your paper 1–5. Then study the time line above and place the following events in the order in which they happened by writing the first next to 1, the second next to 2, and so on.
1. Tariff of Abominations
2. Jackson elected president
3. Trail of Tears
4. Log Cabin Campaign
5. Ordinance of Nullification

Understanding Main Ideas
1. Why were the years after 1817 known as the Era of Good Feelings? Why did it end?
2. How was Henry Clay's American System intended to help both westerners and easterners?
3. Describe the major economic differences among the Northeast, the South, and the West.
4. How did the Tariff of Abominations lead to the Nullification Crisis?
5. Why did Jackson veto the rechartering of the Second Bank of the United States?
6. Describe Jackson's removal of the southern Indians to western lands.
7. Who was "Old Tippecanoe"? Describe his campaign in the election of 1840.

Thinking Critically
1. **Synthesizing.** Imagine that you are Abraham Lincoln at age 18. Write the brief part of your autobiography beginning with the winter of 1816 and ending with the sale of the farm.
2. **Defending a Point of View.** Do you agree or disagree with the Jacksonians' claim that the "common sense of the common man" was the only requirement necessary for working in government? Why?
3. **Solving Problems.** If you had been Van Buren's campaign manager before the election of 1840, how would you attempt to win? Cite specific examples of tactics you would use.

Writing About History
A Cherokee named Sequoyah invented what is called a syllabary—a system that permitted writing the sounds of spoken Cherokee with 85 different characters. By 1828 a weekly newspaper was published in the Cherokee language. Use your historical imagination and the information in Chapter 11 to write reports for the Cherokee newspaper about events leading to Indian removal.

Practicing the Strategy
Review the strategy on page 399.
Reviewing Photographs as Primary Sources. Study the photographs on page 399, then answer the following questions.

of inations	**1830** Congress passes Removal Act	**1831** First group of Choctaws removed	**1832** Jackson vetoes Bank charter	**1833** Compromise tariff passed	**1836** Martin Van Buren elected	**1837** Financial Panic sweeps country	**1838** Trail of Tears	**1840** Log Cabin Campaign
w Jackson d president			★ Ordinance of Nullification					★ Harrison elected president

1. How do years of military service and battle show on Andrew Jackson's face?
2. What do John Quincy Adams' posture, clothing, and furnishings tell you about his status and way of life? About the time in which he lived?
3. How would you have felt in the presence of Martin Van Buren if you had been granted an interview with him in 1836?

Using Primary Sources
Many Americans were upset by the removal of the Indians. Among the most outspoken were missionaries who had lived and worked among these Indians. As you read the following excerpt—written by Mr. Jones, a Baptist missionary—think about why the route was called the Trail of Tears. Then answer the questions.

> Camp Hetzel, near Cleveland (Miss.), June 16 [1838]. *The Cherokees are nearly all prisoners. They have been dragged from their houses, and encamped at forts and military posts, all over the nation. In Georgia, especially, multitudes were allowed no time to take anything with them, except the clothes they had on. Well-furnished houses were left a prey to plunderers, who like hungry wolves, follow in the train of the captors. These wretches rifle the houses, and strip the helpless, unoffending owners of all they have on earth. Females, who have been habituated to comforts and comparative affluence are driven on foot before the bayonets of brutal men. . . . It is a painful sight. The poor captive . . . his weeping wife almost frantic with terror, surrounded by a group of crying, terrified children . . . is in most cases stripped of the whole [of his property], in one blow.*

1. According to Mr. Jones, what way of life did the Cherokee Indians have before they were taken captive?

2. If you had been a soldier assigned to help capture the Cherokees, why might you not allow the captives to take their belongings with them?
3. Do you think Mr. Jones viewed the American soldiers any differently than he viewed the plunderers? Support your opinion with two examples from the excerpt.

Linking History & Geography
Completion of the National Road gave the economy of the West a boost. By 1853 the road had almost reached the Mississippi River. In order to understand the importance of the National Road, complete the following activities.
1. Draw a map showing the route of the National Road and the cities through which it passed.
2. Write a brief statement relating each of the following to the National Road: carrying freight became cheaper and easier, more people moved to the west, cities in the Ohio Valley grew larger, and land values west of the Appalachians rose.

Enriching Your Study of History
1. **Individual Project.** Prepare a brief campaign speech to endorse John Quincy Adams, William H. Crawford, Andrew Jackson, or Henry Clay for the presidency in 1824. Present your speech to the class, which will hold a mock election after all the speeches have been given.
2. **Cooperative Project.** Work as a team to prepare multimedia presentations. Each team will cover one region—Northeast, South, or West—in the early 1830s. Give an accurate picture of work and home, reporting on as many details as you can find through research.

Chapter 11 Review   **403**

Manifest Destiny

This chapter describes the popular attitude of the 1840s that the United States was destined to dominate the entire continent, all the way west to the Pacific. First, Texas joined the Union. After war with Mexico, California and the territories of the Southwest became part of the United States. Oregon was settled and the boundary dispute with the British was resolved by compromise in 1846. Early settlers in the West included Spanish missionaries and the *rancheros* in California, the people who followed the Oregon Trail in caravans of covered wagons, the Mormons of Utah, and the Forty-Niners who flocked to California during the Gold Rush of 1849. As new territories came into the Union, the old question of slavery again arose: Which lands should be free, which slave?

1. THE TEXAS QUESTION

A Troubled President Eyes Texas

William Henry Harrison took the oath of office as president on March 4, 1841. He was 68 years old, then the oldest man elected president. Exactly one month later, on April 4, he died of pneumonia. His successor, Vice President John Tyler of Virginia, was 51, the youngest president up to that time.

John Tyler was the first vice president to become president because of the death of his running mate. He was not a success as president. The Whig party had nominated him only because he was a former Democrat who had opposed the policies of Andrew Jackson. They had not studied his position on important issues. One of these was adding Texas to the Union, which Tyler favored but most Whigs opposed.

John Tyler

National Portrait Gallery

Preview & Review

Use these questions to guide your reading. Answer the questions after completing Section 1.
Understanding Issues, Events, & Ideas. Briefly describe Texas history from 1820 to 1844, using the following words: dark horse, annexation, *ranchero, rancho, presidio, empresario,* Alamo, Goliad, Republic of Texas, San Jacinto.
1. How was life in New Spain somewhat different than life elsewhere in the United States?
2. How did the issue of annexing Texas affect the presidential election of 1844?
3. Why did immigrants to Texas from the United States feel little loyalty to Mexico?
4. Why did President Jackson oppose statehood for Texas?
Thinking Critically. Imagine that you are Stephen F. Austin in 1834. You are in Mexico City to explain the feelings of the Texans about Texan–Mexican conflicts. What would you say to the Mexican leaders.

Tyler's troubles first began when Henry Clay and other Whigs in Congress attempted to push through a bill creating a new Bank of the United States. The Whigs discovered that Tyler considered a federal bank unconstitutional. He vetoed the bill.

The Whig politicians were furious. They referred to Tyler as "His Accidency" instead of "His Excellency." Unfortunately, neither they nor later political leaders learned from this experience. Even today much less attention is paid to the qualifications of vice presidential candidates than presidential ones. Yet eight vice presidents have become president after the death or resignation of their running mates.

Should Texas Join the Union?

Since they disliked him so much, the Whigs did not nominate Tyler for a second term in 1844. Instead they chose Henry Clay, even though he had been defeated for that office twice before, in 1824 and 1832. The Democrats were expected to nominate former president Van Buren.

But a new issue had developed by 1844 that caught even experienced politicians like Clay and Van Buren by surprise. This issue caused Van Buren to lose the Democratic nomination to James K. Polk, a former governor of Tennessee. Polk was what is called a **dark horse** candidate. A dark horse is one who seems to have no chance at the start of a convention but wins the nomination when the favored candidate or candidates cannot obtain the required majority of the delegates.

The new issue was **annexation.** Should the Republic of Texas be annexed, or added to the Union as a state? As we have seen, Texas lay on the Spanish side of the boundary negotiated in the Transcontinental Treaty of 1819. Two years later, Texas became part of independent Mexico when that nation revolted against Spain.

At that time hardly any United States citizens lived in Texas, but pioneers were beginning to trickle in. Their arrival set off a chain of events that eventually led the United States to acquire the vast area of the American Southwest.

Texas' Roots in New Spain

The northern lands of Mexico were mostly inhabited by Spanish missionaries and *rancheros*—wealthy ranchers who worked the large *ranchos* (ranches) awarded them by the Mexican government. American Indians lived there also. These were the lands that we know today as Texas, New Mexico, Arizona, California, Nevada, Utah, and part of Colorado and Wyoming. Americans were just beginning their trek west.

Interestingly, the people from the United States were called

Polk Home, Columbia, TN

This daguerreotype of James K. Polk and his wife, Sarah, is the first taken of a president and first lady. Sarah Polk often advised the president on speeches and correspondence.

Americans, but their neighbors in Mexico were not. This made about as much sense as Columbus calling the first Americans Indians.

The Spaniards based their claim to northern Mexico on the explorations of Coronado and other early travelers. This meant little to the Indians, who tended to send the Spanish on wild goose chases for the Seven Cities of Cibola and other lands of dubious wealth. Yet the Spanish armies were strong enough to hold the land. They called it New Spain, and its capital was Mexico City.

Mexico City lay so far from the new Spanish territory that a nothern capital was created in Santa Fe. The Spanish also began the complicated task of connecting the towns and missions of New Spain by building *El Camino Real* (the King's Road), which joined Mexico City with Veracruz, Santa Fe, and many of the missions in California. Travelers today still follow *El Camino Real*.

The labors and movements of the Spanish did not go unnoticed by the French, Russians, and British in the area. For protection the Spanish began an ambitious program of building forts called ***presidios***, missions, and settlements of various sizes.

The center of life in the colonies of New Spain lay in the missions and the *ranchos*. Franciscan priests of the Catholic Church hoped to bring the message of Christianity to the local Indians. To attract followers, they built their missions as cities unto themselves, the church at the center. The influence of this architecture of adobe and tile is much with us today. Covered walkways connected the various buildings. They led to the priests' simple living quarters and to work-shops where the Indians were taught to weave, blacksmith, and farm. In the fields outside the mission walls the Indians grew grain and grapes and tended sheep and cattle. Trusted Indians had their own farms nearby.

For the Franciscan priests the one true religion was Catholicism. It was also the state religion of Spain. Patient missionaries explained the mysteries of the church and taught the Indians to remember the feast days which commemorated saints of the church. Surely all at Mission San Juan Capistrano could recall that the swallows returned every year on the Feast of St. Joseph. But for many Indians mission life was forced labor. They fled to return to the old ways.

The *ranchos* placed as deep an imprint on the Spanish communities as the missions. Here strong, self-sufficient communities developed far from Mexico City. These were powerful estates with thousands of cattle and sheep to tend. On the *ranchos* the young men learned to ride and developed nearly all the tools of the American cowhands who came later to the Great Plains.

All settlers of New Spain were loyal to the Spanish flag and to Catholic teachings. Yet, like the English colonists along the Atlantic Coast, the Spaniards found themselves a far distance from their capital and rulers. They began to think that the lands they worked belonged to them, not to the wealthy governors who mounted horses on saddles trimmed in silver and rode with beautiful wives wearing jeweled combs in their hair. They also feared outsiders and forbade trade with Americans.

Hispanics had a strict class system which they wished to keep intact. Highest were Spaniards born in Spain. Next came Creoles, Spanish born in America. These groups held all the power of New Spain. Mestizos, people of Spanish and Indian ancestry came next, with the Indians last. They were treated as children by the missionaries and abused by the foremen of mines and ranches where they worked.

Revolution in New Spain

Like the American colonists, the settlers of New Spain came to deeply resent the heavy hand of their government in Mexico City. When revolutions began to topple governments in Europe late in the 1700s and early in the 1800s, the Spanish and Portuguese colonies in America also revolted. In 1821 New Spain successfully won its independence from Spain. New Spain became the independent Republic of Mexico. But sadly in the flush of these victories, the original purpose of the revolution—to free those who were oppressed by the class system—was forgotten.

Most Spaniards returned to Spain, leaving the leadership of the Republic to Creoles. The struggle to organize the government took three years. Finally Mexico's republic was organized and a constitution proclaimed in 1824. It strictly outlawed slavery, a change that would come to have important consequences when American settlers began to stream into northern Mexico.

Life in Northern Mexico

By 1830 perhaps as many as 50,000 Mexicans, mostly mestizos, lived in the northern part of the new territory. Already living on these lands were more than 250,000 Indians. Some, such as the Hopi and Zuñi, married newcomers and merged their ways of life. Others, the Ute and Apache especially, moved or did battle for their ancestral territories with the new arrivals.

Life in northern Mexico was not much different than life elsewhere in Mexico. Rich landowners still controlled vast *ranchos* and large herds of sheep or cattle, as well as silver or copper mines. Most people worked for the landowners. The missions also owned huge tracts of land and large herds. Here, Indians did most of the work.

There were not many large towns in northern Mexico. Ranches were far apart and most settlements had only a few buildings. People counted on each other. Men headed the households. They handled the trading and worked outside the home. Women did not usually go out in public except to go to market or to church. But inside the home the mother was in charge. She made most of the decisions, and her children helped and obeyed her. A Mexican boy or girl was expected to be *respeto* and *bien educado*—to be respectful of others and to do well the work others depended on.

Before he was very old, a boy joined his father in the fields or mines, or rode beside him as he gave orders to his workers. A girl helped her mother go to market, bake, weave, and take care of the younger children. If the family was wealthy, servants might do many of these jobs. Quite often many members of the same family—grandparents, aunts and uncles—lived close together. A large family meant more hands to help do the work. People learned to work with others and to do what was best for the family. They also learned that when one member of the family did something wrong, all members were disgraced.

Americans in Texas

Into this setting came settlers from America. Moses Austin of Missouri, after losing his money overnight in a financial panic, struck out for Texas. He respected and admired the Mexicans and felt his future lay with them. He was granted a colony in 1821 in what is now Texas, but he died of pneumonia the same year. On his deathbed Moses Austin asked his son Stephen to carry out his dream of colonizing Texas.

Some Mexican leaders opposed American settlement. Others thought settlers should be attracted to Texas, where they could eventually become Mexican citizens. Trade would increase, particularly over what came to be known as the Santa Fe Trail. The second group won the argument and Stephen Austin was given a renewal of his father's grant. He thus became an *empresario*—the Mexican term used to describe business people who brought in settlers. Each empresario received 23,000 acres (9,315 hectares) of land for every 300 families brought into Texas. Austin and his group, the "Old Three Hundred," joined about 6,000 Tejanos—Texans of Mexican descent—living near San Antonio and other small Texas towns. They were loyal Sons of Mexico who were taken with the notion of colonizing Texas. Austin and Juan Sequín, the Tejano leader, became friends at once.

The families who followed Austin each received a grant of land. Most grew cotton on it. They prospered. By 1830 about 20,000 Americans had come to Texas, bringing 2,000 slaves with them.

Stephen Austin became a citizen of Mexico and urged that Catholicism be the religion of the colony. For several years he was the governor of Texas, which by then was a Mexican province. But

Texas State Capitol (Photo: TexaStock)

Texans see this painting of Stephen F. Austin at their capitol in Austin. He is shown in his cabin in 1824. Why is Austin considered a hero in Texas? What makes a person a hero?

Austin, whose heart was in America, had difficulty inspiring loyalty to Mexico when most of his settlers had come from America. The friendship with the Tejanos aside, most Americans came to feel that Texas was *their* country and that they were the real Texans. Few troubled to learn Spanish. When the Mexican government abolished slavery, the Texans found legal ways to keep their slaves.

The trickle of colonists from the United States and the third-generation Tejanos in Texas gave people a feeling of independence and nationalism. Why should they report to a foreign capital as far away as Mexico City? Hadn't they earned the land by farming and ranching as others had in the westward-moving United States?

Texas Wins Its Independence

Government leaders in Mexico City naturally disliked the Texans' attitude. They tried to stop further immigration to Texas. When

Library of Congress

This painting by Theodore Gentilz is thought to be the most accurate view of the final Mexican assault on the Alamo. The original 1885 oil painting is lost. Can you locate the Mexican soldiers and the Texas defenders of the Alamo?

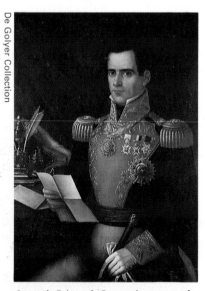

De Golyer Collection

Antonio López de Santa Anna was the general who called himself the Napoleon of the West. In 1836 he led the Mexican army's siege of the Alamo. Why did Santa Anna feel he was right in leading the Mexican army into Texas? Do you think he was right?

Austin came to Mexico City to explain the feelings of the Texans, he was thrown in jail and held for a year without trial. Finally, in 1835, the Texans revolted.

The president of Mexico, Antonio López de Santa Anna, marched northward at the head of his army to put down the rebellion. In February 1836 he captured the town of San Antonio. But 155 Texans in the town retreated into the **Alamo,** the stronghold built by Spanish missionaries. They refused to surrender. Others joined them.

Santa Anna's army attacked the Alamo again and again. Repeatedly his men were driven back with heavy losses. But after ten days of fighting, they broke into the Alamo. Every one of the defenders, even the wounded, were killed on the spot. Among the dead were Davy Crockett, a colorful frontier character who had represented Tennessee in Congress, and James Bowie, who designed the Bowie knife. A similar massacre occurred at **Goliad** when some 350 Texans were shot by firing squads.

Enraged Texans now declared themselves an independent country—the **Republic of Texas.** They appointed Sam Houston commander of the Texas army. For a time Houston retreated eastward. Then, at **San Jacinto,** he turned and attacked the Mexicans. It was a small battle. Houston had only 783 soldiers, Santa Anna about 1,300. Yet this battle determined who would win the war. On the afternoon of April 21, 1836, Houston surprised the Mexican soldiers. The Texans broke through Santa Anna's defenses, firing "the Twin Sisters," their two cannon. "Forward!" Houston shouted. "Charge! Remember the Alamo! Remember Goliad!"

The Texans rushed into the Mexican camp, this slogan on their lips. The Mexicans fought bravely but were soon defeated. Many died. The others fell back in disorder, calling out fearfully *"Me no*

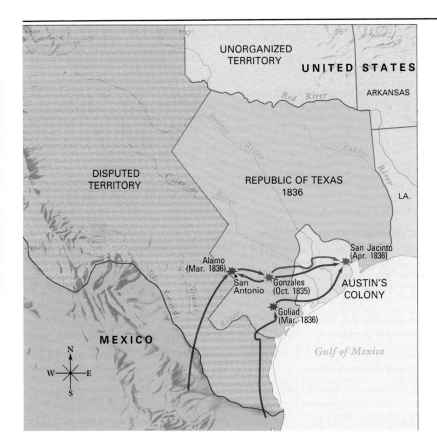

TEXAS WAR
FOR INDEPENDENCE,
1835–36

→ Texan army

✶ Texan victory

→ Mexican army

✶ Mexican victory

0   200   400 Mi.

0   200   400 Km.

Albers Equal-Area Projection

LEARNING FROM MAPS. *Although Texas was still part of Mexico, many Texans viewed Santa Anna's campaign as an invasion. Where did the Texans win battles?*

San Jacinto Museum Association

Sam Houston commanded the Texas army. He sits astride his horse in this oil painting by Steven Seymour Thomas. Why did Houston grant Santa Anna his freedom in 1836?

Alamo,'' although in fact these were the very men who had slaughtered the defenders of the mission.

The victory was total. ''The fierce vengeance of the Texans could not be resisted,'' Houston later explained. Santa Anna was captured. But instead of killing him, Houston wisely gave him his freedom in exchange for his promise to take his army out of Texas. The Republic of Texas then elected Houston its first president.

The people of the republic, however, were eager to see Texas become one of the United States. Andrew Jackson, who was still president at the time, was unwilling to accept Texas. He was worried about the political problem that might result if another slave state were admitted to the Union. The next president, Van Buren, took the same position. That is why the Democrats rejected Van Buren as their 1844 presidential candidate.

President Tyler, being a southerner, favored admitting Texas. He had his secretary of state negotiate a treaty of annexation in 1844. The Senate refused to ratify this agreement. In 1844 the Democrats nominated Polk, who favored both slavery and the annexation of Texas. To balance this pro-southern policy, Polk proposed ending the agreement with Great Britain for joint control of the Oregon country. The United States would take over all that area, which extended far beyond the present northern boundary of the nation.

Return to the Preview & Review on page 404.

The Texas Question   **411**

Preview & Review

Use these questions to guide your reading. Answer the questions after completing Section 2.
Understanding Issues, Events, & Ideas. Use the following words to describe the westward movement: manifest destiny, Willamette Valley, Sutter's Fort, Oregon Trail.

1. What obstacles faced westward travelers seized with the spirit of manifest destiny?
2. How was the Willamette Valley region in Oregon settled? Why did Sutter's Fort in California attract settlers?
3. How were the wagons moving westward on the Oregon Trail a "community on wheels"?
4. How did Texas and the Oregon Territory enter the Union?

Thinking Critically. 1. You know that many easterners had "Oregon fever" in the 1830s. What do you think attracted pioneers to the Willamette Valley in Oregon? **2.** How does the verse from the song on page 414 express the settlers' view of manifest destiny?

Manifest Destiny

In the 1840s westward expansion became a hot political issue. For 200 years moving west had seemed like climbing up a steep incline—slow and difficult work. It was as though North America were an enormous plank balanced just west of the Mississippi River like a seesaw. Once the midpoint was passed, the balance tilted. The road ahead now seemed downhill, therefore easy.

People rushed westward eagerly. Suddenly it appeared possible that the entire continent might be theirs! This new attitude was given a name by a writer named John L. O'Sullivan. It was, O'Sullivan announced, **manifest destiny**—that is, the obvious future role of the people of the United States—"to overspread the continent."

The way west only seemed easy. Wild animals and mighty forests lay in the path of eastern travelers. John Adams had written of "conquering" the West "from the trees and rocks and wild beasts." The pioneers of the 1840s had to cross rugged and dangerous country to reach the Pacific Coast. But neither the Rocky Mountains nor the great western desert could stop them. One enthusiastic speaker referred to the Rockies as "mere molehills."

Beyond the Rocky Mountains lay an enormous land of towering mountains, magnificent forests, and fertile valleys drained by rivers teeming with fish. This area is now called the Pacific Northwest. In the 1800s it was known as the Oregon Country or simply as Oregon. Oregon stretched northward from 42°N—the northern border of California—to 54°40'N—the southern boundary of Alaska.

Until the early 1820s Oregon had been claimed by four countries—Spain, Russia, Britain, and the United States. Spain gave up its claim in 1819 in the Transcontinental Treaty. Russia, which had built several forts to protect its fur trappers, withdrew in 1825. The United States and Great Britain, noting that Oregon was far from either, agreed to what they called joint occupation. Britons, Canadians, and Americans slowly trickled in.

Fur traders were the first Americans interested in Oregon. Soon after the Lewis and Clark expedition the Rocky Mountain Fur Company started business. It hired rugged "mountain men" who roamed the West collecting animal skins, or pelts. These mountain men followed Indian trails or cut new ones through the mountains, establishing paths that were later used by settlers moving west. Another successful venture was the American Fur Company, started by John Jacob Astor, a German immigrant. By the 1820s it controlled most of the western fur trade.

The movement west began in the 1830s when a few Christian missionaries settled in the **Willamette Valley** in Oregon. Among the first to make the six-month journey was Jason Lee, a Methodist sent

New York Public Library Picture Collection

William Henry Jackson, who painted this view of Sutter's Fort in 1941, was a photographer who 'painted in' the historical additions of mules and mounted horsemen. What are some reasons pioneers might have been attracted to Sutter's Fort?

to preach to the Indians. Samuel Parker, a Presbyterian minister, followed a year later. Then in 1836 four Presbyterian missionaries— Marcus Whitman, Narcissa Prentice Whitman, Henry Spalding, and Elizabeth Spalding—made the long, hard trip across the mountains to minister to the Flathead Indians. In 1840 Father Pierre de Smet, a Jesuit priest, arrived in the Oregon country.

The missionaries had little success in persuading the local Indians to become Christians. But their descriptions of the country began to attract more easterners. They described a fertile valley, sheltered on the west by the Coastal Ranges. Water was plentiful. Abundant rain fell on the western slopes of the Cascade Range, feeding numerous streams and the Willamette River. By 1840 about 120 families were living there. As you will read, such availability of water was crucial to western settlement.

Others were making their way to the Mexican province of California. John A. Sutter was one of the first from the United States to do so. Sutter had immigrated to New York City from Switzerland in 1834. From New York he had made his way to Oregon. Then he sailed to the Hawaiian Islands. In Hawaii he purchased a ship and transported a cargo of local produce to San Francisco.

Somehow Sutter persuaded the Mexican governor of California to grant him a large tract of land in the Sacramento River valley. He settled on the American River, a branch of the Sacramento, in 1839. Gradually he built a fortified town, which he called **Sutter's Fort.** The entire place was surrounded by a thick wall 18 feet high (about 6 meters) topped with cannon for protection against unfriendly Indians. Sutter's Fort attracted weary, westward-moving pioneers the way a magnet attracts iron.

The Oregon Trail

From small beginnings there came a mass movement westward in 1843. All over the eastern states people caught what they called

"Oregon fever" and prepared to move west. They gathered in groups in western Missouri to make the 2,000-mile voyage (3,200-kilometer) over the **Oregon Trail.** This trail followed the Platte River to Fort Laramie in Wyoming and then crossed the Rockies by way of South Pass before descending to Oregon along the Snake and Columbia rivers.

One such group set out on May 21, 1843. One of its guides was Marcus Whitman, the early missionary settler in Oregon who had returned east on church business. Almost a thousand people were involved. They rode in 120 canvas-covered wagons pulled by oxen. About 5,000 cattle and a small army of dogs accompanied them.

Such a large group was really a community on wheels. Because much of the trail crossed Indian territory, the caravan had to be ruled like an army. An elected council of ten settled disputes. A guide or pilot planned the route and decided where and when to stop for food and rest. Each wagon had its special place in the caravan. A bugler summoned everyone to rise at dawn and signaled the time to settle down for the night. Each night the wagons were formed in a great circle as protection against possible Indian attack.

The group traveled 15 or 20 miles (24 to 32 kilometers) on an average day. Getting the entire company across a river could take as long as five days, for there were no ferries or bridges along the way. Nevertheless, progress was steady. On October 27, 1843, the caravan reached the Willamette Valley safely.

The next year five groups made the trip overland to Oregon and California. Although California belonged to Mexico and control of Oregon was in dispute with the British, these pioneers gave no thought to the fact that they were going to foreign countries. In this respect they were like the people who were settling Texas. On the Oregon Trail people sang:

> " The hip-hurrah for the prairie life!
> Hip-hurrah for the mountain strife!
> And if rifles must crack, if swords we must draw,
> Our country forever, hurrah, hurrah! "

Still, leaving home was a bittersweet experience for many of the pioneers. Elizabeth Goltra wrote in her diary as she was leaving Kansas for Oregon in 1853:

> " Today we started across the dreary plains. Sad are the
> thoughts that steal over the reflecting mind. I am leaving
> my home, my early friends and associates never to see them
> again, exchanging the disinterested solicitude [attention] of
> fond friends for the cold and unsympathetic friendship of
> strangers. . . . Hard indeed that heart that does not drop a
> tear as these thoughts roll across the mind.[1] "

[1] From "Diaries and Reminiscences of Women on the Oregon Trail: A Study in Consciousness," an unpublished essay by Amy Kesselman

STRATEGIES FOR SUCCESS

LEARNING FROM ART

Many books you study, as *The Story of America* does, contain reproductions of famous paintings and other artwork. Gathering information from these sources is a key strategy to understanding history. An engraving such as Currier & Ives' "Westward the Course of Empire Takes Its Way," shown below, can provide a great deal of historical information. This engraving, made by Fanny Palmer and James M. Ives in 1868, gives the artists' view of manifest destiny. More importantly, such a work of art can help shape the ideas of a nation. This Currier & Ives print has appeared in more history books than any other and greatly influenced the way Americans in the 1870s and 1880s viewed westward expansion.

How to Gather Information from Art

To effectively gather information from art, follow these steps.

1. **Determine the subject of the work.** Check its title or caption. Study the people, objects, and actions it depicts.
2. **Examine the details.** If it is a painting or drawing, study the background. Remember that *all* the visual evidence is important to understanding the historical event or period.
3. **Note the artist's point of view.** If possible, determine whether the events are portrayed favorably or unfavorably. Ask what impact the work might have on other viewers.
4. **Use the information carefully.** Remember that a work of art may be an artist's *interpretation* of an event. Try to determine how accurately it depicts the event before deciding how to use the information.

Applying the Strategy

James M. Ives and Nathaniel Currier were America's most popular makers of hand-colored prints (pictures from engravings). Carefully study their print below. The main title is "Across the Continent." Close study discloses a picture full of clues to the artists' optimistic view of the westward movement. Note the locomotive puffing on its endless tracks, hardworking men and women building their community, covered wagons heading for further frontiers, and the vast open spaces of yet-to-be-settled America. See if you can spot other historical details.

For independent practice, see Practicing the Strategy on page 446.

Museum of the City of New York

People were leaving their families, their friends behind. Most had a great sense of loss. Imagine what Mary Stewart felt when she began the following poem as her first diary entry:

To Martha

“ Oh friend, I am gone forever, I cannot see you now
The damp comes to my brow
Thou wert [You were] my first and only friend, the hearts best treasure thou;
Yet in the shades of troubled sleep my mind can see you now,
And many a time I shut my eyes and look into the past.
Ah, then I think how different our fates in life were cast,
I think how oft we sat and played
Upon some mossy stone,
How we would act and do when we were big girls grown
And would always live so near
That I could always come to you,
And you would come to me, and this we would always do
When sickness came in fevered brow and burning through each vein . . .[1] ”

The trip was long, tiring, and hazardous. Men drove the wagons, herded the cattle, scouted the trail for Indians, and made the decisions on where to camp. Women did the cooking and washing and much more. Martha Ann Morrison, a girl of 13, remembered:

[1]From ''Diaries and Reminiscences of Women on the Oregon Trail: A Study in Consciousness,'' an unpublished essay by Amy Kesselman

Benjamin Franklin Reinhart painted "The Emigrant Train Bedding Down for the Night" in 1867. Pioneers did not use cumbersome Conestoga wagons to cross the country nor find water this easily. What does the painting suggest about the roles of women and children in wagon trains?

The Corcoran Gallery of Art

"The women helped pitch the tents, helped unload, and helped yoking up the cattle. Some of the women did nearly all the yoking; many times the men were off [away from camp, usually scouting for Indians]. One time my father was away hunting cattle driven off by the Indians, and that left Mother and the children to attend to everything. . . .[1]"

Children were also called upon to do their share of heavy jobs. Most, when they stayed healthy, saw the trip as a great adventure. But along the way thousands of people died, many of them children. Lodisa Frizzel, headed to California in 1852, remarked:

"That this journey is tiresome no one will doubt, that it is perilous, the deaths of many will testify, and the heart has a thousand misgivings, and the mind is tortured with anxiety, and often as I passed the freshly made graves, I have glanced at the side boards of the wagon, not knowing how soon it might serve as the coffin for some one of us; but thanks for the kind care of Providence [God], we are favored more than some others.[2]"

[1] From *Women's Diaries of the Westward Journey* by William Schlissel
[2] From "Diaries and Reminiscences of Women on the Oregon Trail: A Study in Consciousness," an unpublished essay by Amy Kesselman

Taking Texas and Oregon

The mood of the country was aggressive and confident. In such an atmosphere the presidential election of 1844 was held. James K. Polk emerged the winner.

Polk had promised to bring both Texas and Oregon into the Union. He was soon able to do so.

Congress voted to annex Texas by joint resolution a few months after the election. In December 1845 Texas became a state. At the same time Polk began diplomatic negotiations with the British about Oregon. He made it clear that if England did not agree to a satisfactory settlement, he was ready to take the territory by force. The British had no stomach for a fight over Oregon. But they were unwilling to surrender all of the area. In 1846, after considerable discussion, the negotiators reached a compromise. The territory was divided by extending the already existing boundary between the United States and Canada to the West Coast.

Polk also had hoped to take New Mexico and California. Unfortunately, he could not claim, as he had with Texas and Oregon, that the lands were already peopled by Americans. There were almost none in New Mexico and less than 700 in California, compared with 11,000 Mexicans. General Santa Anna, back in power in Mexico City, refused to discuss the sale of the two provinces. To gain those territories would take a little longer.

Archives Division, Texas State Library

The Lone Star flag was adopted as the national banner of Texas in 1839. It is today the state flag. By what process did Texas become a state in 1845?

Return to the Preview & Review on page 412.

Westward Movement 417

Preview & Review

Use these questions to guide your reading. Answer the questions after completing Section 3.
Understanding Issues, Events, & Ideas. Describe the war with Mexico, using the following words: Rio Grande, Nueces River, Battle of Buena Vista, Santa Fe, Bear Flag Revolt, Republic of California, Veracruz, Cerro Gordo, Puebla, Mexico City, Treaty of Guadalupe Hidalgo.

1. Why did the United States go to war with Mexico?
2. How did California respond to the Mexican War?
3. Why did Polk put General Scott in command of the army sent to capture Mexico City?

Thinking Critically. You are Nicholas P. Trist in the midst of negotiating a treaty with Mexico when you receive Polk's message to break off discussions. Why do you ignore Polk's message?

3. WAR WITH MEXICO

Message to Congress: "War Exists"

Annexing Texas led to war. Although Mexico had not been able to prevent Texas from becoming independent, the Mexicans did not accept the Texans' claim that the new republic extended all the way to the **Rio Grande,** the "Great River." They insisted that the **Nueces River,** a river farther to the north and east, was the boundary between Mexico and Texas.

After Texas was annexed, President Polk sent troops com-

Chicago Historical Society

manded by General Zachary Taylor across the Nueces River. Then he sent a diplomatic representative, John Slidell, to Mexico City. The Mexican leaders were unwilling even to discuss the boundary question. National pride was involved. The Mexicans again stated their claim for all of Texas. Polk then ordered General Taylor to march straight to the Rio Grande. When he did so, a Mexican force crossed the river and attacked one of his patrols. When word of this skirmish reached Washington, Polk informed Congress: "War exists." Congress promptly declared war on Mexico on May 13, 1846.

At right is General Zachary Taylor's 1847 portrait by artist William Garl Brown, Jr. It is a detail of a larger painting.

Despite the vigor of manifest destiny and the Texas and Oregon gains, war with Mexico was instantly unpopular with easterners. Polk had deliberately provoked the war, critics argued—and many historians today agree. They thought the true cause of the war was Polk's determination to have New Mexico and California for the United States. Abraham Lincoln, a young Illinois lawyer serving his only term in Congress, introduced his Spot Resolutions. In them he questioned whether the "spot" on the north bank of the Rio Grande where American blood had been shed was actually United States soil. If we were going to declare war, he said, we'd better be sure.

Not even everyone in the army agreed with the war. Years later, in his autobiography, then Captain Ulysses S. Grant remembered, "I was bitterly opposed to the measure [war], and to this day regard the war . . . as one of the most unjust ever waged by a stronger against a weaker nation."

The Early Fighting

United States forces fought the Mexican War on land and sea. They had the easiest time in California and New Mexico, which included present-day Arizona. For one thing, the Mexicans had not kept strong forces at their presidios in this region. Equally important, many wealthy Mexican families had political, economic, even ties by marriage with American settlers. Many did not resist the invaders.

In the summer of 1846 troops led by General Stephen Kearny marched southwestward from Fort Leavenworth on the Missouri River. They took Santa Fe, winning control of New Mexico. Kearny then pushed on to sourthern California. There Mexican resistance was stiff, but Kearny managed to get the upper hand. From San Diego he advanced his army up the coast to Los Angeles and Santa Barbara.

In California John C. Frémont joined the U.S. naval squadron and a militia force raised by residents of the area around Sutter's

"The Battle of Buena Vista," painted in 1847 by Carl Nebel, shows General Zachary Taylor astride 'Old Whitey' at the center.

New York Public Library Picture Collection

Fort to defeat the local Mexican forces. For this **Bear Flag Revolt,**

California Printing Office

they designed a simple flag, a grizzly bear on a plain background and proclaimed themselves the **Republic of California.** By February 1847 the important towns of San Francisco, Los Angeles, and San Diego had been won from Mexico.

The war did not go quite as smoothly in Mexico. Mexico was a large country far from the supply depots of the United States. The fighting was often fierce, especially in the region just south of the Rio Grande. Yet the U.S. forces quickly defeated the Mexicans. General Taylor was not a brilliant commmander, but his well-trained troops were devoted to him. By autumn of 1846 they had won three major battles. In February 1847, in the **Battle of Buena Vista,** they routed the last important force in northern Mexico.

The Capture of Mexico City

These early victories posed a political problem for President Polk. General Taylor had become a national hero. He was a plain, unassuming soldier made in the mold of William Henry Harrison and Andrew Jackson. His troops affectionately called him "Old Rough and Ready." Taylor belonged to the Whig party. Polk was afraid that Taylor might decide to run for president in 1848. The president had no intention of seeking a second term himself, but as a loyal Democrat he did not want Taylor to be too successful on the battlefield. He therefore put a different general, Winfield Scott, in command of the army which had the task of capturing Mexico City.

General Scott, a powerful man nearly six feet, six inches tall, was also a Whig. He lacked Taylor's easy-going style. He was stuffy and rather vain. Behind his back his troops called him "Old Fuss and Feathers." Scott therefore seemed less of a threat to the Democrats than Taylor. Fortunately for the nation, Scott was an excellent general, actually far more competent than Taylor.

Scott approached Mexico City from the sea. In March 1847 his fleet of 200 ships put 10,000 men ashore near the city of **Veracruz** on Mexico's east coast. The United States army captured Veracruz easily and then marched inland. They won an important battle at **Cerro Gordo** and another at **Puebla.** By September they were at the outskirts of **Mexico City.**

There the showdown clash occurred. It was hard fought with 1,000 United States soldiers and 4,000 Mexican soldiers killed or wounded. But again Scott's troops were victorious. The capital city was occupied, the Mexicans forced to surrender.

The Anne S.K. Brown Military Collection, Brown University

The Treaty of Guadalupe Hidalgo

Polk had attached a state department official, Nicholas P. Trist, to Scott's army. Trist's task was to negotiate a peace treaty once the Mexicans had been defeated. In addition to insisting on the Rio Grande boundary of Texas, he was told by Polk to offer as much as $30 million if Mexico would sell California and the rest of the Southwest to the United States.

Trist proved to be an excellent negotiator. He persuaded the defeated Mexicans to turn over all that territory for a little more than $18 million. The negotiations took a great deal of time, however, because there was great confusion in Mexico City as weary soldiers returned from battle.

The Stars and Stripes flies over the shore near Veracruz as an artist of the day depicts the landing of some of the 200 ships and 10,000 men who came ashore in eastern Mexico. Explain how this painting might be considered patriotic.

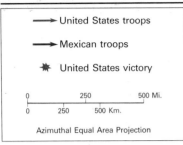

- → United States troops
- → Mexican troops
- ✹ United States victory

0 ——— 250 ——— 500 Mi.
0 ——— 250 ——— 500 Km.

Azimuthal Equal Area Projection

LEARNING FROM MAPS. *Notice the disputed area between the Nueces River and the Rio Grande. Judging from the map, how did the United States navy contribute to the victory?*

President Polk became impatient and also somewhat greedy. Mexico had been so thoroughly beaten that he began to think of demanding even more territory. He sent Trist a message ordering him to break off the discussions and return to Washington. Trist ignored the order. He completed the negotiations with the Mexican government and sent the resulting **Treaty of Guadalupe Hidalgo** back to the United States.

President Polk was furious. Out of pure spite he had Trist fired from his state department job. He would not even pay Trist his salary for the time he had spent in Mexico.

Nevertheless, Polk found that he had to agree to the Treaty of Guadalupe Hidalgo. The terms, after all, were better than he had hoped for. And the war had become extremely unpopular in some parts of the country. Particularly in the North, many people felt that there had been no reason for seizing so much of Mexico over what was really a minor boundary dispute. In Congress Senator Thomas Corwin expressed their feelings:

❝ Mr. President, . . . I voted for a bill somewhat like the present at the last session—our army was then in the neighborhood of our line [border]. I then hoped that the President

did sincerely desire peace. Our army had not then penetrated far into Mexico, and I did hope, that with the two
millions [dollars] then proposed, we might get peace, and
avoid the slaughter, the shame, the crime, of an aggressive,
unprovoked war. But now you have overrun half of Mexico—you have exasperated and irritated her people— . . .
and boldly ask her to give up New Mexico and California;
and as a bribe to her patriotism, seizing on her property,
you offer three million [dollars] to pay the soldiers she has
called out to repel your invasion, on condition she will give
up to you at least one-third of her whole territory. . . .

What is the territory, Mr. President, which you propose
to wrest from Mexico? It is consecrated to the heart of the
Mexican by many a well-fought battle with his old Castilian
master [against the Spanish in the Mexican Revolution].
His Bunker Hills, and Saratogas, and Yorktowns, are there!
The Mexican can say, "There I bled for liberty! and shall I
surrender that consecrated home of my affections to the
Anglo-Saxon [descendants of the English] invaders? What
do they want with it? They have Texas already. They have
possessed themselves of the territory between the Nueces
and the Rio Grande. What else do they want? . . .

What would be the response? . . . The Senator from
Michigan says he must have this. Why, my worthy Christian
brother, on what principle of justice? "I want room!"

Sir, look at this pretense [unsupported claim] of want of
room. With twenty millions of people, you have about one
thousand millions of acres of land, inviting settlement by
every conceivable argument, bringing them down to a quarter of a dollar an acre, and allowing every man to squat
where he pleases. But the Senator from Michigan says we
will be two hundred millions in a few years, and we want
room. If I were a Mexican I would tell you, "Have you not
room in your own country to bury your dead men? If you
come into mine, we will greet you with bloody hands, and
welcome you to hospitable graves. . . .[1]"

Adding more territory where slavery might be established was
another concern in the North. Polk therefore swallowed his anger
and submitted the treaty to the Senate, which ratified it after heated
debate.

A Blending of Cultures

After the treaty had been signed, more and more Americans moved
into the Southwest. They brought their own language, laws, and ways

[1]From *Appendix to the Congressional Globe*, 29 Congress, 2nd Session

Was the Mexican War fought to
protect the border of the U.S.?
Or was it waged to gain California and New Mexico? These famous lines have outlasted the
controversy.

"I heartily accept the
motto,—'That
government is best which
governs least,' . . . Witness
the present Mexican wars,
the work of comparatively
a few individuals using
the standing government
as their tool; for, in the
outset, the people would
not have consented to
this measure."
From *Civil Disobedience*,
Henry David Thoreau,
1848

of behaving. Differences in the cultures of the Americans and the Mexicans—75,000 or more in the new U.S. lands—created problems at first.

For families with ties to Americans, adjusting was usually fairly easy. Other Mexicans did not do as well. Many lost their property. To get the prime land held by Mexicans, Americans challenged land titles that had been granted by Spanish or Mexican authorities and held for years. This started long and costly court battles. Whatever the decision, hard feelings resulted.

Under the treaty Mexicans were granted all the rights of American citizenship. Yet their culture, which blended Spanish, Mexican, and Indian ways of life, often was viewed as inferior. Traditions of family loyalty, personal honor, and devout Catholicism were not respected by the newcomers. Poor Mexican Americans suffered most. Many of these newcomers were forced to take low-paying jobs on American ranches, railroads, or in American mines. Mexican American bandits, many of them trying to recover their stolen property or livestock, raided American settlements.

In time, though, the two groups helped change each other's way of life. They borrowed ideas from each other. The Americans learned from the Mexicans how to mine the rich hills of the Southwest. Because they had no mining laws of their own, Americans also used Mexican laws to form their own. They also learned sheep ranching. The tough *churros* of the Mexicans were well-adapted to thrive in dry lands of the Southwest. These sheep had already changed the lives of some of the Indian tribes in the area. Navajo women learned to weave their wool into beautiful, warm blankets colored with Navajo dyes and woven into traditional patterns. Seeing that they could trade their blankets for horses and other things they needed, the Navajo decided to settle down and raise sheep. Now the Americans began to raise sheep too. As you will read later, American cowhands also learned their craft from Mexican *vaqueros*.

The Americans brought tools, seeds, and livestock with them. They had the latest inventions and business techniques. They established a legal system that preserved the rights of the accused. Mexicans adopted the best of these and many other things. Slowly a new way of life was formed in the Southwest, a system of values and behavior shared by most of the people there. You can see this special way of life today throughout the Southwest. You see it in the music of Santiago and Flaco Jiménez and Laura Canales and in the art of Diego Rivera, José Clementé Orozco, Amado Peña, Joan Miró, Carmen Lomas Garza, and Julio Gonzalez. You can also see the blending of cultures in the clothes the people wear, in their laws, and in the words they use. It is a way of life with deep roots in three cultures—Indian, Mexican, and American.

Return to the Preview & Review on page 418.

Thomas Gilcrease Museum of History and Art, Tulsa, Oklahoma

The pride of the Spanish rancheros is evident in this color lithograph titled "Hacendado y Su Mayordomo," "The Landowner and His Foreman." The Mexican artist is Julio Michaud. Judging from these riders, were most rancheros wealthy people? How can you tell?

4. THE GOLDEN WEST

California and the Rancheros

The great prize that the United States won in the Mexican War was the province of California. In the 1840s most of the region beyond the Rocky Mountains was untouched by any other than its native Indians. But, as we have seen, the Spanish had been living in California and New Mexico since the late 1700s. By the 1830s there were 21 mission settlements in a kind of broken string from San Diego to Sonoma, north of San Francisco. The landholdings of the missions were enormous.

Around the missions founded by the Spanish were clustered large Indian villages, for Father Junípero Serra and other priests had converted thousands of Indians to Christianity. These Indians were practically slaves. They did all the work that supported the missions. They tended large herds of cattle and grew corn, grapes, and other crops. They also made cloth, leather goods, wine, soap, and many other manufactured products.

The missions were so prosperous that other Mexicans demanded that the government open mission lands to settlers. In the early 1830s it did so. Thereafter any Mexican citizen with cattle could obtain a huge *rancho* free. These landholders were called *rancheros*. Within a few years 700 *ranchos* were established in California, most of them

Preview & Review

Use these questions to guide your reading. Answer the questions after completing Section 4.

Understanding Issues, Events, & Ideas. Contrast the settlement of Utah with that of California, using the following words: Mormons, Nauvoo, Salt Lake City, Mormon Trail, Law of Riparian Rights, Law of Prior Appropriation, prospector, Gold Rush, Forty-Niner, clipper ship, stake a claim, mining camp, Negro Hill, ghost towns.

1. Compare life in a California mission with life on a *rancho*.
2. How were Mormons able to move so many people westward?
3. Define two laws of water rights.
4. What were some of the means of travel used by the Forty-Niners?

Thinking Critically. You are a prospector who has struck gold in California. Write a letter persuading a relative to join you.

The Golden West   425

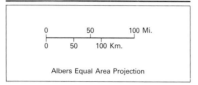

SPANISH MISSIONS IN CALIFORNIA, 1830

0   50   100 Mi.

0   50   100 Km.

Albers Equal Area Projection

San Francisco Solano (Sonoma) 1823

San Rafael 1817

San Francisco (Mission Dolores) 1776

San José de Guadalupe 1797

Santa Clara 1777

Santa Cruz 1791

San Juan Bautista 1797

San Carlos 1770

La Soledad 1791

CALIFORNIA

San Antonio de Padua 1771

San Miguel 1797

PACIFIC OCEAN

San Luis Obispo 1772

Santa Inés 1804

La Purísima Concepción 1787

San Fernando 1797

Santa Bárbara 1786

San Buena Ventura 1782

San Gabriel Arcángel 1771

San Juan Capistrano 1776

NEVADA

CALIFORNIA

PACIFIC OCEAN

MEXICO

San Luis Rey 1798

San Diego 1769

N W E S

LEARNING FROM MAPS. *The missions were located no more than one day's travel apart. Why are most near the coast?*

about 50,000 acres (20,000 hectares) in area. Each *ranchero* had an enormous amount of land.

Life on one of these great ranches was rich but simple. People ate enormous quantities of meat at every meal. Horses were so plentiful that travelers merely lassoed a new one when their own mounts became tired. Most of the hard work of caring for the herds and raising crops was still done by the Indians, who were even worse off than when they had lived outside the missions.

Yet in spite of their wealth, the ranchers had few comforts and conveniences. Their homes were unheated and poorly furnished. Window glass was scarce. Most homes had dirt floors. People lived so far apart that they had few visitors. There were no newspapers. The days stretched out one after another.

The Mormons of Utah

The signing of the Treaty of Guadalupe Hidalgo increased interest in westward expansion. During the Mexican War one of the most re- markable migrations of American history had taken place into what is now Utah. This was the settlement that spread out next to the

Great Salt Lake. It consisted of members of a uniquely American religious sect, the **Mormons.**

The Mormon religion was begun in 1830 by Joseph Smith, a young farmer in western New York. According to Smith, an angel named Moroni gave him golden tablets on which was written the *Book of Mormon.* Smith's English version of the book was published in 1830. It became the basis of the Mormon Church.

Smith attracted many followers, and in 1831 he founded a new community in Ohio. In 1837 the Mormons moved to Missouri. In 1839 they moved again to a town they called **Nauvoo,** in Illinois. The close-knit, cooperative society that the hard-working Mormons developed enabled them to prosper. Nauvoo grew rapidly. By 1844 it was the largest city in Illinois, with a population of 15,000.

The Mormons adopted religious practices that tended to set them apart. One was polygamy, which permitted a man more than one wife at the same time. Smith also became quite domineering as the church grew. He organized a private army, the Nauvoo Legion. He refused to allow critics of his group to publish a newspaper in Nauvoo. By 1844 opposition to the Mormons in Illinois led to Smith's arrest. Then a mob formed. Smith was dragged from jail and lynched.

"Handcart Pioneers" was painted on linen about 1870 by C.C.A. Christensen, who himself pulled his belongings westward. He later traveled with his paintings to portray the Mormon Exodus. What is an exodus?

The Church of Jesus Christ of Latter-Day Saints Museum

A DESERT IN BLOOM

Amon Carter Museum

"View of Great Salt Lake City" is an 1867 toned lithograph by Christian Inger.

The valley near the Great Salt Lake was almost a desert. It was here upon the salt flats under the strong sun that the Mormons made their home. The streams running down from the nearby mountains were ordered dammed by Brigham Young. Irrigation ditches were dug so that fields could be watered and crops planted.

As more groups of Mormons arrived, the place became a beehive of activity. Indeed, a beehive is one of the symbols of the Mormon religion. Everything was organized to serve the common good.

Salt Lake City was a planned community. By 1849 it had broad streets lined with neat houses that were set off by well-tended gardens. The surrounding fields were rich with wheat, corn, and potatoes. There were large herds of cattle, horses, and sheep.

Passing travelers marveled at the Mormons' prosperity and at the speed with which they made the desert bloom and caused their mighty temple and tabernacle to rise.

After the murder of Smith the Mormons decided that to practice their religion they would have to find a place far removed from other people. Brigham Young became their new leader. Young was devoutly religious, handsome, and tremendously strong. He was also an excellent organizer. He realized that moving 15,000 people across the country would require very careful planning.

First he divided the Mormons into small groups. He himself led the first group west in 1846. The party proceeded slowly across Iowa, stopping to build camps and to plant crops at several points so that those who followed would have food and shelter. In western Iowa they built a large camp on the Missouri River. It contained nearly a thousand cabins.

Then, in April 1847, Young led a small advance party west. Now they moved swiftly. In July they reached a dry, sun-baked valley near Great Salt Lake. There they established **Salt Lake City,** their permanent home. Their route, followed by many later pioneers, came to be known as the **Mormon Trail.** The ruts worn by their wagons may still be seen today.

The Mormons' success was possible because Brigham Young had almost total control over the community. He headed both the church and the government. Most Mormons believed that Young was inspired by God. They considered him all-wise and devoted to their happiness. They accepted his leadership without questions.

Regulating Water Rights

Even today we wonder why the Mormons chose to build Salt Lake City in a desert where the available water conditions could best be described as *semiarid*—that is, very dry. We know, after the lynching of Joseph Smith in Nauvoo, that the Mormons wanted to go as far away from "civilization" as possible. And we know that the Mormons were not simply led to their destination by seagulls: too much careful planning had been ordered by Brigham Young to leave such matters to chance. No, there were two reasons for the Mormon's success: their industry and the regulation of water rights.

Water is essential to life. Without it, no crops can be grown, no cattle and sheep grazed, no shade trees planted. Most of the earlier settlers of the West put down roots beside river banks or mountain streams. Hardly anyone ventured out of the river valleys.

Settlers of the eastern United States had developed a law that governed the use of water. There rainfall and rivers were abundant, yet the easterners wanted to be sure water ran freely. They applied what is known as the **Law of Riparian Rights.** The term *ripa* comes from the Latin for "riverbank." Basically the law says that property owners whose land borders a stream or river have the right to a steady flow of water in the stream and may use its water reasonably. But the landholders may not decrease or increase the flow of water by changing its direction, nor may they alter its quality. Imagine the consequences of doing so for those living downstream! This law applied to manufacturing as well as farming. A waterwheel could turn the lathes and looms of factories, but the water must pass freely to the next location.

For the Mormon settlers in Utah here was a terrible dilemma. To survive they had to dam streams, flood land, and create a system of canals and irrigation ditches. In doing so, they violated the Law of Riparian Rights. Yet this was the only way to make their desert blossom and attract passersby to an oasis where fresh fruits and vegetables could be bought for the hungry children of the wagon caravans.

Since water resources were so different in the West, the Mormons began to develop a new law to govern the use of water. Brigham Young insisted that land set aside for farming adjoin an irrigation ditch connected to a stream from a nearby mountain. Church councils

The Granger Collection, New York

Brigham Young sat for this daguerreotype in his later years. How would you describe his appearance?

The Golden West 429

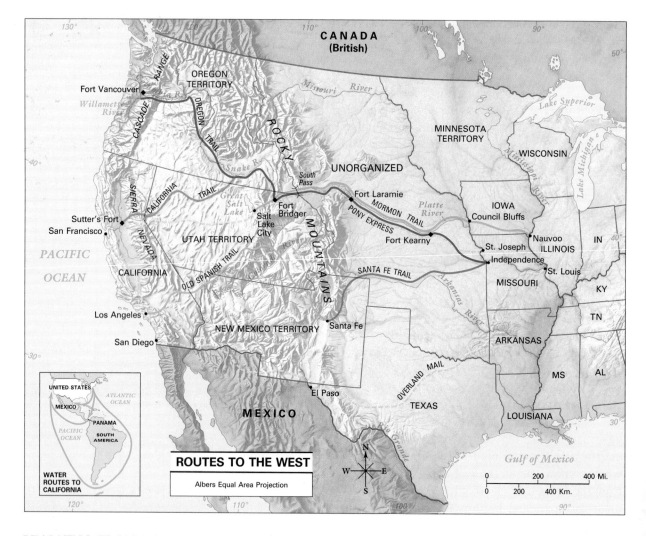

ROUTES TO THE WEST

Albers Equal Area Projection

LEARNING FROM MAPS. *Note from the inset map that there were three water routes to the west. Why did most people travel one of the land routes?*

supervised the ditches. Within two years the system was working smoothly and there seemed to be water for all.

The Law of Prior Appropriation

Brigham Young understood that he was violating the law by irrigating. He set about developing a new legal concept that would meet the realities of the West. This he called the **Law of Prior Appropriation.** The law says that rights to water use belong to the person who first uses the water, as long as it is for beneficial purposes such as farming, mining, manufacturing. It also says that the community good outweighs the good of individuals. A limited resource such as water must be divided among as many people as have need of it. It is the basic water law in all western states.

Water laws are as important to California fruit growers as range watering holes are to ranchers. Today even easterners must rethink their water laws, but in their case it is because so much free-running water has been polluted.

Gold in California

By 1848 the Oregon travelers, the Mormons, and other westward-moving pioneers had made crossing the continent a fairly common experience. The trip was still long and tiring. Sometimes it could be dangerous. But the routes were well marked, and there were a number of forts and settlements along the way where travelers could rest and obtain fresh supplies.

After the Mexican War California attracted more easterners. Many of them settled in and around John A. Sutter's well-known fort on the American River. As the area developed, Sutter, with an eye to new business, expanded his activities. To supply lumber for new settlers, he decided to build a sawmill about 40 miles (64 kilometers) up the river from Sutter's Fort.

First the river bed next to the mill had to be dug out so that a large water wheel could be installed to produce power to run the saws. James W. Marshall was in charge of building the mill. During the digging he noticed bits of shiny yellow metal shimmering in the water. He collected some of them and had them tested. They were pure gold.

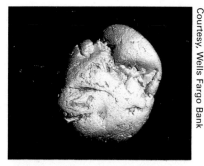

Courtesy, Wells Fargo Bank

How did the discovery of gold nuggets like this one set the nation abuzz in 1848?

The golden hills of California rise above Sutter's Mill in this colored drawing. The site may be visited today. What was the result of the surprise discovery made here?

Robert Honeyman Collection

What name is given people such as the miner panning for gold?

Thomas Gilcrease Institute, Tulsa

This discovery took place in January 1848. Soon other people began to prospect, or search for, gold. When they found gold, they told friends about their good luck. More people became **prospectors.** By May the town of San Francisco was buzzing with the news. "Gold! Gold! *Gold* from the American River!"

By the end of the year the whole country had the news. Then, in December 1848, President Polk himself announced that the gold was "more extensive and valuable" than had been thought.

The Forty-Niners

After the President's announcement the **Gold Rush** was on. In 1849 at least 80,000 people came to California to look for gold. The historian Samuel Eliot Morison described "the gold-fever of '49" this way:

> **66** Farmers mortgaged their farms, workmen downed their tools, clerks left counting-rooms, and even ministers abandoned their pulpits. **99**

Most of these **Forty-Niners** followed the overland trails across the Rocky Mountains. Some, however, took longer but more comfortable water routes. Some sailed from the East to Panama, crossed the isthmus on foot, and then sailed north to San Francisco. Others took the all-water route around South America.

Sometimes it took half a year to make the long ocean voyage. But for those who could afford the fare (about $1,000), **clipper ships** made the trip around in much less time. The sleek, three-masted clippers were incredibly fast. Several are known to have sailed over

The Marine Arts Collection, Seamen's Bank for Savings

The fleet clipper ship "Flying Cloud" was painted by Frank Vining Smith. What advantages did these ships offer western travelers?

Charles Christian Nahl and August Wenderoth painted "Miners in the Sierras" in 1851. What does this view tell you about the physical features of California's gold-mining areas?

National Museum of American Art, Smithsonian Institution

400 miles (640 kilometers) in 24 hours. The best modern racing yachts have rarely approached their records.

The clipper ships were 200 to 300 feet (60–90 meters) or more in length. Their towering masts supported clouds of sails. Their sharp, graceful bows knifed through the seas smoothly. The most famous clipper ship was *Flying Cloud* designed by Donald McKay. In 1851 *Flying Cloud* sailed from New York to San Francisco in 89 days, less than three months. Remember that it had taken Magellan 38 days just to sail through the Straits of Magellan!

Mining Camps

Gold was worth $16 an ounce in 1849. About 10 million ounces (28 million grams) were mined in California that year. Production increased in 1850 and 1851. By 1852 100,000 prospectors were mining in California. They found 81 million ounces (2.3 billion grams) during that one year. Some miners became millionaires. Others made smaller fortunes. But most made very little.

When a miner found gold, he would **stake a claim** by driving wooden stakes in the ground to mark the spot. Then no one else could legally work that place. Soon dozens of other prospectors would flock to the surrounding area to stake out claims. Disputes about boundaries and other rights frequently broke out.

Villages called **mining camps** sprang up wherever gold was found. These camps were given colorful names such as Whiskey Flat, Hangtown, Roaring Camp, and Volcano. Life in the camps was uncomfortable, expensive, and sometimes very dangerous. A person could be flat broke one day and worth thousands of dollars the next. Such an up-and-down life, combined with the hardships the miners faced, encouraged a devil-may-care attitude. Many miners were heavy drinkers and reckless gamblers. This situation attracted all sorts of thieves and tricksters, as well as shrewd business dealers, saloon-

Charles Christian Nahl of Rough and Ready painted "Sunday Morning in the Mines" in 1872. This is an allegorical painting. It shows evil on the left and good on the right. The bad miners break the Sabbath by rough riding to the gambling tent. But the good miners hear the Bible read and wash clothes. Do you suppose mining camp life was more like that on the left side of the picture or the right?

© Crocker Art Museum, Sacramento

Sutter's Fort State Historical Monument

At the head of the Auburn Ravine in 1852, American and Chinese miners posed for this rare picture. How might the sluice that divides the miners be a symbol of a deeper division?

keepers, and merchants who sold the miners everything from pick-axes and tents to fancy clothes and fine horses at extremely high prices. These types made far more money than the miners. Fighting in the mining camps—with fists, knives, and guns—was common.

People from all over the United States, from Mexico and South America, from Europe, and from as far away as China and Australia flocked to the gold regions. With so many people crowding into the camps, disputes of all kinds occurred. Mexican Californians were badly treated and often prevented from prospecting. The Chinese and free African Americans were also mistreated, although none of the gold seekers were more hard working. The local Indians were driven off by brute force, although as always they were the original settlers of the land.

Nevertheless, some from these various groups found gold, and a few became rich. Two African American miners, digging in a most unpromising spot, hit a deposit so rich that the site was named **Negro Hill.** These two men found gold worth $80,000 in four months. By 1852 there were 2,000 African Americans in California, half of them working in the mining area.

Despite the problems of camp life the majority of the prospectors and storekeepers in the mining country were decent people eager to build schools and churches and live at peace with one another. The difficulty was that most of the camps sprang up too quickly to establish orderly governments. Prospectors abandoned them when the gold ran out and rushed off to other strikes in other regions. The old camps became **ghost towns,** inhabited only by a stray cat or two or a few hermits or vagabonds. 🖐

California State Library

Perhaps 1,000 of the prospectors in California were African Americans. How were they treated by the majority of the miners?

Return to the Preview & Review on page 425.

The Golden West   435

Preview & Review

Use these questions to guide your reading. Answer the questions after completing Section 5. **Understanding Issues, Events, & Ideas.** Explain the issue of the spread of slavery, using the following words: free state, slave state, Missouri Compromise, popular sovereignty, Free-Soil, Wilmot Proviso, secede, Compromise of 1850.

1. What had the Missouri Compromise decided about free and slave states? What problems would arise if California were added to the Union?
2. Why did northern Democrats form the Free-Soil party?
3. Why did southerners oppose the Wilmot Proviso?
4. What did the Compromise of 1850 seem to accomplish?

Thinking Critically. You are a reporter witnessing the debates between Clay, Calhoun, and Webster. In a newspaper article, describe the arguments of each man, the attitude of the audience, and the atmosphere in the room.

5. FREE AND SLAVE TERRITORIES

Slavery in the Southwest

Adding California to the Union caused new problems. In the past the movement of white settlers into new lands had forced most of the native Indian population to retreat westward. But the California Indians had their backs to the ocean. As a result those who had not been forced to labor on the great California ranches were practically wiped out by the invading white settlers.

In earlier times most new territories had been added to the United States before many settlers had entered them. But California already had a well-established Spanish population. Then the Gold Rush, as we have just seen, greatly increased the population. Everyone realized that California did not need to go through the territorial stage of development. Like Texas, it would enter the Union directly as a state. But should California be a **free state** prohibiting slavery or a **slave state** allowing it?

Always in the past, northern territory had become free, southern slave. The Northwest Ordinance of 1787 had declared that the land north of the Ohio River and east of the Mississippi should be free. Kentucky and the territory south of the Ohio became slave states.

"Slaves Escaping Through the Swamp" was painted in 1863 by Thomas Moran.

Philbrook Art Center

In 1820 a sharp conflict had developed over the admission of Missouri as a state. Missouri, which was part of the Louisiana Purchase, extended far north of any slave state. But most of its citizens wanted slavery. The **Missouri Compromise** of 1820 allowed Missouri to become a slave state. Congress balanced this decision by creating a free state, **Maine,** which had been part of Massachusetts.

The Missouri Compromise also divided the rest of the Louisiana Purchase into free and slave territory. The land south of Missouri's southern border—latitude 36° 30'—was opened to slavery. The land west and north of Missouri was to be free.

After the Treaty of Guadalupe Hidalgo some people favored extending this line dividing free territory from slave all the way to the Pacific. That would have split California in two. The people who were living in California did not want any of it to become a slave state. The Spanish in California had no wish to hold slaves. The gold miners were opposed because they were afraid that big mining companies would bring in large numbers of slaves to compete.

If California became a free state, what would the eastern slave states expect in return? And what about slavery in the rest of the territory obtained from Mexico? These questions led to a great debate in Congress and throughout the country.

The Election of 1848

The debate over free and slave territories began even before the discovery of gold. It played an important part in the presidential election of 1848. Since President Polk did not seek a second term, the Democrats nominated Senator Lewis Cass of Michigan. Cass had been secretary of war in Andrew Jackson's cabinet. He favored a system known as **popular sovereignty.** This system would let settlers in new territories make their own decision about slavery.

Many northern Democrats were unhappy about the nomination of Cass. They considered popular sovereignty a victory for slavery because it would allow southerners to bring their slaves into new land. These Democrats founded a new organization, the **Free-Soil** party. Their candidate was former president Martin Van Buren.

The Whig party chose General Zachary Taylor as its candidate. President Polk's worst fears had come true. "Old Rough and Ready" had no political experience, but he was very popular. He refused to express an opinion on any of the controversial issues of the day. During the campaign the Whigs stressed his victories in the war, his courage, and his personal honesty. As had been the case with General Harrison in 1840, this tactic worked perfectly. In the election Taylor got 163 electoral votes to Cass's 127. Van Buren received about 10 percent of the popular vote but no electoral votes because he did not get a majority in any state.

National Portrait Gallery

Zachary Taylor, twelfth president, was the popular 'Rough and Ready' of the Mexican War. This lithograph is by Francis D'Avignon, made while Taylor was president. What qualities did the Whigs stress when Taylor campaigned? Are these the same qualities you would look for in a president? Explain your reasoning.

The Compromise of 1850

After the election the debate continued. Besides the future of California and the other new territory, every aspect of the slavery issue was discussed. There were lengthy arguments on the question of the slave trade in Washington, D.C., and on the question of how to force northern officials to return slaves who had escaped into their states.

On each issue there was a northern and a southern position. Many northerners hoped to keep slavery out of all the new territory. In August 1846, long before the end of the Mexican War, Congressman David Wilmot of Pennsylvania introduced the **Wilmot Proviso** in the House of Representatives. The proviso called for prohibiting slavery "in any territory [taken] from the Republic of Mexico."

Southerners, of course, wanted to be able to take their slaves into all such territory. They controlled enough votes in Congress to defeat the Wilmot Proviso. But for both groups slavery was becoming a moral question—that is, a question of right and wrong.

As we shall see in the next chapter, many northern people believed strongly that it was sinful for one person to own another. Few of these northerners believed that it was legally possible to abolish slavery in states where it already existed. But large numbers were determined that it should not spread into new lands. Since Congress had always had the power to decide whether or not to allow slavery in new territories, people who felt this way were urging their representatives and senators to support measures like the Wilmot Proviso that would ban slavery in the entire Southwest.

Congress also controlled the city of Washington because the District of Columbia was not part of any state. Those who disliked slavery urged Congress to abolish the institution there. At the very least they wanted Congress to prohibit the buying and selling of slaves in the capital.

The more extreme southerners wanted a law guaranteeing the right of owners to bring their slaves into all the new territories. Even moderate southerners would not agree to the abolition of slavery in Washington. Some were not opposed to a law which would prohibit buying and selling of slaves there. In return they demanded that Congress pass a stricter fugitive slave law. They argued, with considerable truth, that many northern police officials and northern judges were refusing to help in the capture and return of slaves who had escaped into the free states.

All the important members of Congress took part in the debate over these issues. Old Henry Clay, three times an unsuccessful candidate for president and now senator from Kentucky, worked out the compromise that was eventually accepted.

Congress should admit California as a free state, Clay urged. The rest of the land obtained from Mexico should be organized as New Mexico Territory. Slavery should neither be prohibited nor

The Granger Collection, New York

specifically authorized there. In other words, Clay supported Lewis Cass's popular sovereignty plan for this territory.

To please antislavery northerners, Clay suggested that the buying and selling of slaves in the District of Columbia be prohibited. To please southerners, he proposed a very harsh fugitive slave bill. Another of Clay's bills provided that some lands claimed by Texas were to be transferred to New Mexico Territory. In exchange the debts that Texas had built up while it was an independent republic were to be paid by the United States.

Clay's proposals caused one of the most famous debates in American history. The bitterest attack came from John C. Calhoun, the father of nullification. Calhoun, old and ill, his once-powerful voice broken by the throat cancer that would soon kill him, sat grim and silent as another senator read his words:

66 How can the Union be saved? There is but one way by which it can with any certainty; and that is, by a full and final settlement, on the principle of justice, of all the ques-

Henry Clay, 72 years old and ailing, pleads with the Senate to reach the Compromise of 1850. Seated at left, head in hand, is Daniel Webster, who supported Clay. His attackers are John C. Calhoun, standing third from right, and William Seward, seated in the left front. Vice President Fillmore presides. What was debated?

"The South asks for justice, simple justice, and less she ought not to take. She has no compromise to offer but the Constitution, and no concession or surrender to make."
John C. Calhoun, 1850

Points of View

"I speak today for the preservation of the Union .... for the restoration to the country of that quiet and that harmony which make the blessings of the Union so rich and dear to us all."
Daniel Webster, 1850

tions at issue between the two sections [North and South]. The South asks for justice, simple justice, and less she ought not to take. She has no compromise to offer but the Constitution; and no concession or surrender to make. She has already surrendered so much she has little left to surrender. Such a settlement would go to the root of the evil, and remove all cause of discontent, by satisfying the South she could remain honorably and safely in the Union, and thereby restore the harmony and fraternal feelings between the sections which existed anterior to [before] the Missouri agitation [compromise in 1820]. Nothing else can, with any certainty, finally and forever settle the question, terminate the agitation, and save the Union.

But can this be done? Yes, easily; not by the weaker party [the South], for it can of itself do nothing—not even protect itself—but by the stronger. The North has only to will it to accomplish it—to do justice by conceding to the South an equal right in the acquired territory, and to do her duty by causing stipulations [rules] relative to fugitive slaves to be faithfully fulfilled [followed]—to cease the agitation of the slave question, and to provide for the insertion of a provision in the Constitution, by an amendment, which will restore the South in substance [reality] the power she possessed of protecting herself, before the equilibrium [balance] between the sections was destroyed by the action of this Government. There will be no difficulty in devising [creating] such a provision—one that will protect the South and which at the same time will improve and strengthen the Government, instead of weakening and impairing it.

But will the North agree to this? It is for her to answer the question. But, I say she cannot refuse, if she has half the love of the Union which she professes [claims] to have, . . . At all events, the responsibility for saving the Union rests on the North, and not on the South. The South cannot save it through any act of hers, and the North may save it without any sacrifice whatever, unless to do justice and to perform her duties under the Constitution should be regarded by her as sacrifice. . . .[1]**"**

Calhoun claimed the North now controlled the government, which was making laws that took away the rights of southerners. All citizens had the right to take their property into all the territories of the United States. Unless Congress allowed owners to bring their slaves into the territories, the southern states would **secede,** or leave the Union. There was nothing evil or immoral about slavery, Calhoun argued. Northerners must accept the fact that it exists. If they want

[1]From the *Congressional Globe,* 31st Congress, 1st Session

to live at peace with the South, they must stop criticizing slavery. The South would compromise no more. Calhoun would die on March 30, croaking sadly, "The South, the poor South!"

Also attacking the compromise was Senator William Seward of New York. He spoke against making any concessions to the slave interests. Clay's fugitive slave bill must not pass, said Seward. Although the Constitution of the United States required the return of fugitives, a "higher law," the law of God, would keep decent people from helping to capture an escaped slave.

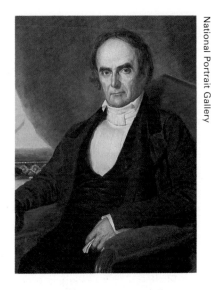

National Portrait Gallery

Daniel Webster of Massachusetts sat for this oil painting done in 1846 by G.P.A. Healy. How did Webster support Clay's Compromise of 1850?

Then, on March 7, three days after Calhoun's speech, Daniel Webster, the important and famous senator from Massachusetts, rose to answer Calhoun's remarks. He delivered a powerful speech in support of Clay's compromise proposals. In part he said:

> " Mr. President, I wish to speak to-day, not as a Massachusetts man, nor as a northern man, but as an American, and as a member of the Senate of the United States. . . . It is not to be denied that we live in the midst of strong agitations, and are surrounded by very considerable dangers to our institutions of government. The imprisoned winds are let loose. The East, the West, the North, and the stormy South, all combine to throw the whole ocean into commotion [noisy confusion], to toss its billows to the skies, and to disclose its profoundest depths. I do not affect [pretend] to regard myself, Mr. President, as holding, or as fit to hold, the helm [a steering device for a ship] in this combat of political elements; but I have a duty to perform, and I mean to perform it with fidelity [faithfulness]. . . . I speak to-day for the preservation of the Union. "Hear me for my cause" I speak to-day out of a solicitous [concerned] and anxious heart, for the restoration to the country of that quiet and that harmony which makes the blessings of this Union so rich and so dear to us all. . . .
>
> There has been found in the North, among individuals and among legislators, a disinclination [unwillingness] to perform fully their constitutional duties in regard to the return of persons bound to service [fugitive slaves] who have escaped into the free States. In that respect, the South, in my judgment, is right, and the North is wrong. . . .

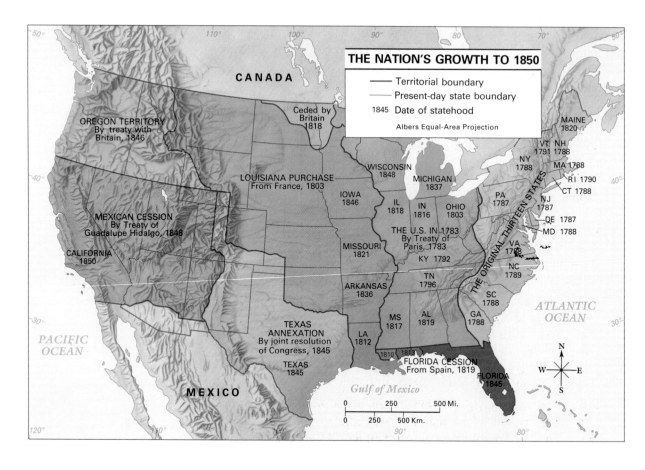

THE NATION'S GROWTH TO 1850

— Territorial boundary
— Present-day state boundary
1845 Date of statehood

Albers Equal-Area Projection

CANADA

Ceded by
Britain
1818

OREGON TERRITORY
By treaty with
Britain, 1846

MAINE
1820

VT NH
1791 1788
NY
1788   MA 1788
RI 1790
CT 1788

WISCONSIN
1848

LOUISIANA PURCHASE
From France, 1803

MICHIGAN
1837

IOWA
1846

PA
1787   NJ
1787

MEXICAN CESSION
By Treaty of
Guadalupe Hidalgo, 1848

IL
1818   IN
1816   OHIO
1803

DE 1787
MD 1788

CALIFORNIA
1850

THE U.S. IN 1783
By Treaty of
Paris, 1783

MISSOURI
1821

VA
1788

KY 1792

NC
1789

ARKANSAS
1836

TN
1796

SC
1788

ATLANTIC
OCEAN

PACIFIC
OCEAN

TEXAS
ANNEXATION
By joint resolution
of Congress, 1845

LA
1812

MS
1817   AL
1819   GA
1788

THE ORIGINAL THIRTEEN STATES

TEXAS
1845

1810 1813

FLORIDA CESSION
From Spain, 1819

N
W E
S

FLORIDA
1845

MEXICO

Gulf of Mexico

0   250   500 Mi.
0   250   500 Km.

LEARNING FROM MAPS. *By 1853 the continental United States was complete. How was the land in your state acquired?*

Now, as to California and New Mexico, I hold slavery to be excluded from these territories by a law even superior to that which admits and sanctions Texas—I mean natural law—of physical geography—the law of the formation of the earth. That law settles forever, with a strength beyond all terms of human enactment, that slavery cannot exist in California or New Mexico. . . . I look upon it, therefore, as a fixed fact, to use an expression current at this day, that both California and New Mexico are destined to be free, so far as they are settled at all, which I believe, especially in regard to New Mexico, will be of very little for a great length of time—free by the arrangements of things by the Power Above us [God]. . . . I will say further, that if a resolution, or a law, were now before us, to provide a territorial government for New Mexico, I would not vote to put any prohibition [of slavery] into it whatever. . . . I would not take the pains to reenact the will of God. . . . I would put into it no evidence of the votes of superior power [the North], . . . to wound the pride of the gentlemen who belong to the Southern states. I have no such object—no such purpose. They would think it a taunt [insult]—an indignity. They would think it to be an act of taking away from them what they regard as a proper equality of privilege; and whether they expect to realize any benefit from it or not, they would think a theoretic wrong—that something more or less derogatory [insulting] to their character and their rights had taken place. I propose to inflict no such wound on any body, unless something essentially important to the country, and efficient to the preservation of liberty and freedom, is to be effected. . . .

And now, Mr. President, instead of speaking of the possibility or utility [usefulness] of secession, instead of dwelling in these caverns of darkness, instead of groping with those ideas so full of all that is horrid and horrible, let us come out into the light of day; let us enjoy the fresh air of liberty and union; let us cherish those hopes which belong to us; let us devote ourselves to those great objects that are fit for our consideration and our action; let us raise our conceptions [thoughts] to the magnitude [high level] and importance of the duties that devolve upon [pass to] us; let our comprehension be as broad as the country for which we act, our aspirations [goals] as high as its certain destiny; let us not be pigmies in a case that calls for men. Never did there devolve, on any generation of men, higher trusts than now devolve upon us for the preservation of this Constitution, and the harmony and peace of all who are destined to live under it.[1] **99**

[1]From the *Congressional Globe*, 31st Congress, 1st Session

In the midst of the debate on Clay's bills, President Taylor fell ill and died. Vice President Millard Fillmore of New York succeeded him. Fillmore favored Clay's compromise. Nevertheless, the arguments dragged on into the summer months.

Finally the various proposals came to a vote. California was admitted to the Union as a free state. The rest of the former Mexican lands were organized into two large territories, Utah and New Mexico, where slavery was not restricted. Texas was given $10 million to pay its debts. The slave trade in the District of Columbia was abolished. A new Fugitive Slave Act was passed.

Few Americans, North or South, approved of all these laws. But nearly all who followed the debate were pleased with the result as a whole. The **Compromise of 1850** appeared to finally put an end to the conflict between the free and slave states. All the territory owned by the United States had now been organized. Never again would Congress have to decide the future of slavery on American soil. As Senator Stephen A. Douglas of Illinois put it, a "final settlement" had been reached. At least that was how it seemed in 1850. 🖹

National Portrait Gallery

Millard Fillmore completed Zachary Taylor's term as president. This daguerreotype was taken about 1850. What stand did Fillmore take on the Compromise of 1850?

Return to the Preview & Review on page 436.

Free and Slave Territories   443

LINKING HISTORY & GEOGRAPHY

THE NATION MOVES WEST

During the mid-1800s hardy pioneers, looking ever westward, ventured beyond the Mississippi into an entirely new frontier. The West was an enormous land of many physical regions—grass-covered but treeless plains, parched deserts, and towering snowcapped mountains.

Each region was different in landforms, climate, soil, and vegetation from anything the pioneers had seen east of the Mississippi. These were lands whose mysteries had to be probed and tested before permanent settlements could be fully undertaken.

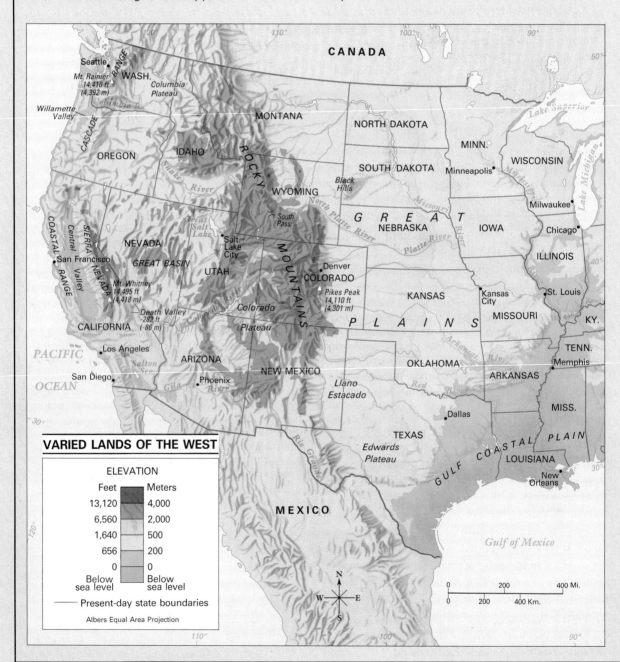

VARIED LANDS OF THE WEST

ELEVATION

Feet		Meters
13,120		4,000
6,560		2,000
1,640		500
656		200
0		0
Below sea level		Below sea level

— Present-day state boundaries

Albers Equal Area Projection

The Great Plains

1. How did the pioneers view the Plains? Why?

The first geographic region the pioneers encountered was a grassy region that became known as the Great Plains. The Plains feature level to rolling land with few trees. The dry region receives too little rain to support forests, but enough for a carpet of low-growing grasses to flourish.

Travelers who crossed the Great Plains reacted in many different ways to the vast empty space. Pioneers raised in the eastern United States were struck by the lack of trees and apparent worthlessness of its dry landscape. Familiar with abundant rainfall and thick forests, they agreed with Major Stephen H. Long, who labeled the region the Great American Desert. Days and weeks of dry weather greeted travelers. Because many sought farmland, few stayed to farm the seemingly too-dry plains. In fact, the Great Plains would be the last area of the United States to be fully settled—awaiting farming advances such as the steel plow and the windmill that would help make the dry land of the plains productive.

A Geographic Explanation

2. What natural forces created the Plains?

The geographic explanation for this broad, dry grassland lies in the nature of the western landscape. In the United States the prevailing wind blows from west to east. This wind crosses the Pacific Ocean, picking up moisture. As the rain-bearing air blows onto North America, it runs headlong into the towering Cascade and Sierra Nevada mountain ranges. The mountains force the air to rise and cool. Because cool air cannot hold as much moisture as warm air, the now-cool air drops its moisture as rain or snow. Thus, rain or snow falls frequently on the western slopes of the Cascades and Sierra Nevadas.

The drier and lighter air crosses the peaks and slides down the eastern slopes. With its downward rush, the air warms, snatching whatever moisture it can from the land between the Pacific Ranges and the Rocky Mountains. The warming air thus dries the landscape as far as the western slopes of the Rockies. Then the air is once again forced to rise, cool, and lose its moisture. The air slides down the eastern slopes of the Rockies, becoming the warm dry winds that cross the western Great Plains.

The Rocky Mountains

3. Why did the trails west follow irregular routes rather than straight lines?

Looming in the path of the pioneers who crossed the plains rose the great masses of the Rocky Mountains. This mountain range extends from Alaska into Texas and southward. Rain and snow, available from the air that was forced to rise over the mountain peaks, support the dense forests of pine, fir, and spruce covering the mountainsides. Most of the precipitation, however, occurs as snow during the late winter and early spring. Depths of 25 feet (7.6 meters) or more are common. Pioneers trapped in such snows faced death from cold and starvation, so journeys were planned to cross the Rockies before winter. To the early pioneers, the Rocky Mountains seemed more suited to trappers and miners than farmers, so they pushed on.

The Intermountain Region

4. Why did most of the pioneers find the Intermountain landscape forbidding?

Travelers now crossed the vast desert area that fills the entire country between the Rockies and the Pacific ranges. Jagged rocks and dry sands characterize this Intermountain Region. It is hardly a landscape that the early pioneers found attractive, especially the farmers used to the lush green of the lands east of the Mississippi. Hardy prospectors, however, soon uncovered the region's valuable treasury of minerals.

The Pacific Coast

5. What attracted settlers to the Pacific Coast?

Near the western edge of the continent the pioneers discovered many fertile valleys. In the northwest, sheltered by the Cascades from winter blasts, lie valleys watered by broad rivers and streams. To the south in California, between the Sierra Nevada and the Coastal Ranges, stretch great valleys of rich soil and water for irrigation. The pioneers, their descendants, and other newcomers turned this westernmost edge of the United States into a land of great abundance.

Applying Your Knowledge

You will work in groups to plan a trip by wagon train across the West. Your group should prepare a list of items you will need on the journey. Create a class list by combining the items on individual group lists.

CHAPTER 12 REVIEW

1820	**1821**	**1824**	**1828**	**1834**
Congress ratifies Missouri Compromise	Austin leads settlers into Texas	Adams elected president	Jackson elected president	Settlement of Oregon begins

Chapter Summary
Read the statements below. Choose one, and write a paragraph explaining its importance.
1. Texas independence focused the nation's attention on expansion and the West.
2. Manifest destiny encouraged eager pioneers to head west.
3. Victory in the Mexican War gave the United States a huge new territory that included most of present-day California, Arizona, Nevada, Utah, and New Mexico.
4. The Mormons and other pioneers followed established trails to western destinations.
5. The discovery of gold in California caused a rush of people to the West.
6. The acquisition of new territory raised questions about the spread of slavery.
7. First the Missouri Compromise, then the Compromise of 1850, attempted to solve the problems surrounding slavery's spread.

Reviewing Chronological Order
Number your paper 1-5. Then study the time line above and place the following events in the order in which they happened by writing the first next to 1, the second next to 2, and so on.
1. California Gold Rush begins
2. Mormon found Salt Lake City
3. Compromise of 1850
4. Republic of Texas proclaimed
5. Missouri Compromise

Understanding Main Ideas
1. Describe the events that led Texans to declare their independence from Mexico.
2. In your own words, explain what manifest destiny meant to Americans in the mid-1800s.
3. What was the chief cause of the war with Mexico? What were the major outcomes?
4. What events led the Mormons to move from western New York to Utah?

5. How did the Gold Rush add to the push of Americans westward?
6. How did the Compromise of 1850 differ from the Missouri Compromise?

Thinking Critically
1. **Drawing Conclusions**. When Travis and the other defenders of the Alamo refused to surrender to Santa Anna, were they brave or foolish? Why do you think so?
2. **Synthesizing**. You and your family are part of a wagon train headed for Oregon in 1843. What is your greatest fear as you journey from your Missouri home? What tasks will you take on in order to help your family arrive safely in the Willamette Valley?
3. **Evaluating**. Several presidents—Jackson, Harrison, and Taylor, for example—were elected because of their popularity as military leaders. In your opinion, does war experience qualify a person for the presidency? Why or why not?

Writing About History
Imagine you are a newspaper reporter. Prepare a news article that explains point by point the provisions of the Compromise of 1850. Finish your article with a paragraph that tells why most people felt this was the final settlement of the slavery question. Review the information on the compromise on pages 438–43.

Practicing the Strategy
Review the strategy on page 415.
Learning from Art. Study the painting on page 425 and answer the following questions.
1. What is the subject of the painting?
2. What, in your opinion, is the artist's point of view about the subject of the painting?
3. Do you feel that this painting is a fairly accurate representation? Explain your answer.

1836
Mexican army
defeats Texans
at the Alamo
★
Republic
of Texas
proclaimed

1840
Harrison
elected
president

1841
Tyler
succeeds
Harrison
as president

1844
Polk
elected
president

1845
Texas
enters
the
Union

1846
Oregon
boundary
dispute
settled
★
Republic
of
California
declared

1847
Mormons
found
Salt Lake
City

1848
Treaty of
Guadalupe
Hidalgo
★
Free-Soil party
runs presidential
candidate
★
Taylor elected
president

1850
Fillmore
succeeds
Taylor
★
Compromise
of 1850
★
California
enters the
Union

Lt. Col. Travis

Using Primary Sources

On February 23, 1836, a large Mexican army surrounded the Alamo. Inside was a force of fewer than 200 Americans, mostly Texans, under the command of William Barret Travis. A messenger carrying a letter from Travis slipped through Mexican lines in the darkness of the night after the siege began. As you read Travis' message, think how historians might judge his words and actions. Then answer the questions that follow it.

COMMANDANCY OF THE ALAMO
*BEJAR, Feb. 24, 1836

To the people of Texas & all Americans in the world

Fellow Citizens & Compatriots:

I am besieged, by a thousand or more of the Mexicans under Santa Anna. I have sustained a continual bombardment & cannonade for 24 hours & have not lost a man. The enemy has demanded a surrender at discretion, otherwise the garrison is to be put to the sword, if the fort is taken. I have answered the summons with a cannon-shot and our flag still waves proudly from the walls. I shall never surrender or retreat. Then I call on you, in the name of Liberty, of Patriotism, & of every thing dear to the American character, to come to our aid with all dispatch. The enemy is receiving reinforcements daily & will no doubt increase to three or four thousand in four or five days. Though this call may be neglected, I am determined to sustain myself as long as possible, and die like a soldier, who never forgets what is due to his honor & that of his country.

VICTORY OR DEATH

William Barret Travis

Lieutenant Colonel, Commanding

---

* The Mexican name for the area surrounding present-day San Antonio.

P.S. The Lord is on our side. When the enemy appeared in sight, we had not three bushels of corn. We have since found in deserted houses 80 or 90 bushels, and got into the walls 20 or 30 head of beeves.

T.

1. Why do you think Travis addressed his letter not only to the people of Texas but to all Americans in the world?
2. What do you think Travis meant by his reference to the "American character"?
3. What evidence in Travis' letter suggests that he was willing to make every sacrifice for the liberty of Texas?

Linking History & Geography

On an outline map of the United States, label with their names and dates of admission to the Union the states carved out of the lands won from Mexico, and trace the major trails to the West.

Enriching the Study of History

Individual Project. Prepare a report on the Alamo, telling its history from the time of its founding to 1836. You might include brief biographies of Davy Crockett, James Bowie, Antonio López de Santa Anna, or one of the Tejano fighters at the Alamo. You might also make a sketch or model of the Alamo to illustrate your report.

Cooperative Project. Your class will hold a Mexican American festival highlighting Mexican contributions to American culture. The festival should include Mexican foods, games, stories, art, music, and other contributions. Each group will research a different category for the festival.

Chapter 12 Review 447

Slavery and Abolition

While slaves wait on benches, the white men make their bids to the auctioneer, with his arm outstretched. Yet surely this 1852 oil painting by Eyre Crowe is unrealistic—the freshly starched aprons, the smiling mother, the boy in his dress-up clothes. In actuality, children commonly were separated from their parents, and husbands from their wives.

After the American Revolution slavery seemed to be dying out. The northern states passed laws gradually doing away with it. Many individual southerners gave up slavery voluntarily. Methodists north and south were expected to free their slaves. In 1808 Congress prohibited bringing any more slaves into the country. Yet slavery persisted. Southerners argued that slavery was essential for their economy based largely on growing cotton. When cotton production increased after the invention of the cotton gin, the demand for slaves and land grew. Was this a time when southerners would listen to arguments for the abolition of slavery?

Bradley Smith/Laurie Platt Winfrey

1. COTTON AND SLAVERY

200 Years of Slavery

Since no African slaves could be brought into the United States after 1808, by 1850 most of the slaves in America were native born. Nevertheless these slaves struggled to preserve their African heritage.

Some people who thought that slavery was bad for the country proposed freeing the slaves and sending them back to Africa. In 1817 they founded the **American Colonization Society.** They purchased land in Africa for former slaves to settle on. Most free African Americans were not interested in living in Africa. However, the American Colonization Society did persuade several thousand to make the move to what became the nation of **Liberia,** on the west coast of Africa.

Few of the sponsors of colonization genuinely wanted to help freed slaves. The colonization movement was mostly aimed at getting rid of the former slaves. Nevertheless, the movement was another sign that many people in the South, as well as the North, were unhappy with slavery.

Free African Americans

Most of the free African Americans lived in the North. There they found opportunities in almost every field of endeavor. Many joined the armed forces. Almost half the seamen aboard U.S. ships in 1850 were African Americans. Others blazed trails west. James Beckwourth, Pierre Bonza and his son George, and two African American missionaries—John Marrant and John Stewart—helped lead the westward movement.

Several became notable inventors and writers. Benjamin Banneker, an expert surveyor and mathematician, contributed to science, medicine, and politics. He also wrote a popular almanac that included antislavery essays as well as information about the tides, the moon, crops, and the weather. Lewis Temple invented a harpoon that was hailed as the most important invention in the history of whaling. James Forten, a veteran of the U.S. navy and of the Revolutionary War, invented a device for controlling sails. Thomas Jennings developed a process for cleaning clothes and became wealthy. William Wells Brown became the first African American novelist and playwright. He also wrote three travel books and several short histories of the African American people.

But most free African Americans in the North faced prejudice and discrimination. Northern laws kept them from voting and serving on juries and from becoming judges and law officers. In Ohio they could not even testify in court. Laws also barred them from schools in many states and from being buried in most "whites-only" cemeteries.

Use these questions to guide your reading. Answer the questions after completing Section 1.
Understanding Issues, Events, & Ideas. Tell what a slave and a slaveowner might have said about the following words: American Colonization Society, Liberia, cotton boll, Sea Island cotton, upland cotton, cotton gin.

1. What was the purpose of the American Colonization Society?
2. Why did the demand for cotton suddenly increase in the 1790s?
3. How did the cotton gin make it profitable to grow cotton?
4. Why did cotton increase the demand for slave labor but not the supply of slaves?

Thinking Critically. 1. As a free African American in 1817, you have the choice of moving to Liberia or staying in America. What do you decide? Why? 2. Imagine that you are Eli Whitney's father. Write a letter to your son agreeing or disagreeing with Eli's claim that the cotton gin would be a "great thing" for the country.

They were forced to ride in separate railway cars and sit in separate parts of the theaters, usually at the back of the balcony. Finding work was even more discouraging. In 1819 one teenager asked classmates in his graduating class:

❝ What are my prospects? To what shall I turn my hand? Shall I be a mechanic? No one will employ me; white boys won't work with me. Shall I be a merchant? No one will have me in his office. Can you be surprised at my discouragement?[1] ❞

He and other African Americans struggled in the decades before the Civil War for opportunities and rights available to other Americans.

And what of the more than 100,000 free African Americans in the South? A few rose to fame and importance. Norbert Rillieux helped revolutionize sugar refining. Henry Blair patented a seedplanter for corn. Daniel A. Payne established a school for free African Americans with a curriculum that included arithmetic, literature, science, chemistry, zoology, astronomy, and geography as well as reading and writing.

Many southern whites saw free African Americans as a threat. They watched them carefully and blocked many of their attempts to achieve. Like their brothers in the North, southern free African Americans could not vote or participate in the legal system. They could not own businesses in many places or secure loans or otherwise use banks. Despite these frustrations most southern free African Americans chose to stay in the South to help others—free and slave.

The Importance of Cotton

Southern attitudes about slavery changed after the discovery of a new crop that greatly increased the need for slave labor. This crop was cotton. In the 1790s cotton was in great demand in many parts of the world because of the new spinning machinery that had been invented in England. It was just at this time that Samuel Slater was building the first spinning machines in America. These machines could produce thread so rapidly that they were soon using up cotton faster than the world was producing it.

Most cotton came from Egypt. Egyptian cotton was of very high quality. It had long, soft fibers that grew around and protected the seeds of the plant. When the plant ripened, the **cotton boll** burst open. Then the fluffy white fibers could easily be separated from the shiny black seeds.

A little of this cotton was grown in America on the Sea Islands along the coast of Georgia and South Carolina. The winters there were very mild. But **Sea Island cotton** would not grow on the mainland. The plants were so tender that they were killed by the slightest spring frost.

[1]From *Eyewitness: The Negro in American History* by William Katz

New York Public Library Picture Collection

In a single engraving we see the blossom of a cotton plant and the boll ripe for picking.

Another variety of cotton, called **upland cotton,** could withstand colder temperatures. It was hardy enough to be grown almost anywhere in the southern states. Unfortunately, the fibers of this plant were short and tightly woven about the seeds. It took a whole day for a skilled person to remove the seeds by hand from a single pound of this cotton.

If only someone would invent a machine for removing the seeds from upland cotton! Many farmers in South Carolina and Georgia were expressing this hope in one way or another in the 1790s. Rice cultivation could not be increased much in those states. Rice needed a great deal of water. It could only be grown where the fields could be flooded. Indigo, the plant introduced in the 1740s by Eliza Lucas, was not worth growing after the Revolution because the British government no longer paid a bounty for producing it.

Eli Whitney and the Cotton Gin

In 1793 Eli Whitney was visiting a friend on a plantation near Savannah, Georgia. Whitney had just graduated from Yale College. He had learned about metalworking from his father, a nail maker. He had not yet turned his inventive mind to thinking about making guns from interchangeable parts.

During his visit he talked with a number of Georgia farmers. They mentioned their interest in growing cotton and showed him how difficult it was to remove the seeds from upland cotton bolls. Young Whitney had never seen a cotton plant before. Perhaps that was an advantage. He studied the plant carefully. He wrote to his father in Connecticut:

66 If a machine could be invented that would clean the Cotton, it would be a great thing both to the Country and to the inventor. 99

After a few days of thinking, Whitney designed a machine that he called a **cotton gin.** It consisted of a box that opened at the top and had rows of narrow slits down one side. The box was stuffed with cotton, seeds and all. Against the side of the box Whitney set a roller or cylinder. The cylinder had rows of wire teeth around it. These rows of teeth were arranged so that when someone turned the cylinder, the teeth passed into the box through the slits. The cotton in the box caught on the teeth as they turned. As the teeth came out of the box, they pulled the cotton fibers with them.

But the seeds, which were wider than the slits in the box, could not pass through with the fibers. The fibers therefore pulled free of the seeds. A second cylinder, turning in the other direction, brushed the fibers from the teeth. As the first cylinder continued to turn, the teeth reentered the box to catch up more of the cotton.

One person turning the handle of a cotton gin could remove the

Yale University Art Gallery

Eli Whitney was just graduated from Yale College when he designed and tested the cotton gin. How do you think he would have reacted if he had known the cotton gin would increase the demand for cotton and make slavery more economically desirable for the white South?

The Granger Collection, New York

This sketch of Eli Whitney's 1793 cotton gin shows how easily one slave could operate the rollers while others emptied baskets of newly picked cotton. What do the drawings in the border show you about cotton and slavery?

seeds of not one pound of cotton in a day but of fifty! A gin was easy to make and cheap. Even a small farmer could afford one. The owners of large plantations soon were building large gins powered by horses or mules. Quickly it became profitable to grow cotton.

Effects of the Cotton Gin

All over the South farmers began to plant cotton. In 1793 they grew about 10,000 bales, each containing 500 pounds (225 kilograms) of cotton. In 1801 American production reached 100,000 bales. By 1835 it had passed a million bales. Cotton was worth about 25 cents a pound in the 1790s. The price remained in the 15- to 20-cent range even after supply of cotton had increased enormously. Cotton planters prospered.

Most of the people who flocked westward into Alabama, Mississippi, Arkansas, Louisiana, and on into Texas became cotton planters. Of course they also raised large quantities of corn, wheat, cattle, and other food products. But cotton was their most important crop. Indeed, it became the key to prosperity for the South and almost as important for the rest of the country.

Cotton cultivation made possible the rapid growth of the northern cotton cloth industry. Citizens everywhere benefited from cheap cotton clothing, which was cool in summer and much easier to keep clean than woolen garments. Exports of cotton to England and other countries paid for badly needed foreign imports of all kinds.

The great cotton boom increased the need for workers to cultivate the fields and to pick and gin the fluffy white fibers when the crop was ripe. Cotton growing seemed especially well suited for the institution of slavery because it kept the slaves busy the year round. (Slaveowners always feared that if their workers had too little to do, they would get into trouble!)

The year began with spring planting, whether on a small farm worked by a single family and one or two slaves or on a large plantation with a hundred slaves. First, corn and other food crops were planted in March. When these were in the ground, the cotton seeds were sown. Once sprouted, the corn needed little care, but the small, tender cotton plants required much labor. The young shoots had to be thinned out. As the plants grew, the soil had to be hoed and cultivated frequently to keep down weeds. Insect pests had to be killed before they could do serious damage to the crop. This work kept all hands busy during the long southern summers.

By September it was time to harvest the corn. The cornstalks were gathered and stored away to make winter food for cows and pigs. Picking the cotton took up the rest of the fall because the cotton bolls did not all ripen at the same time. Unless the white fluff was gathered as soon as the bolls burst open, rain and dust would dirty it and thus reduce its value. The slaves had to go through the fields almost daily.

Picking took skill and patience but not a great deal of strength. Women and children worked the fields side by side with the men. A skilled worker could gather 200 pounds (90 kilograms) in a day. Solomon Northrup, a free African American kidnapped and sold into slavery, describes cotton picking on a Louisiana plantation in late August:

66 When a new hand, one unaccustomed to the business [of picking cotton], is sent for the first time into the field, he is whipped up smartly and made for the day to pick as fast as he possibly can. At night it is weighed so that his capability in cotton picking is known. He must bring in the same weight each night following. If it falls short, it is considered evidence that he has been laggard [lazy], and a greater or less number of lashes [with the whip] is the penalty.

An ordinary day's work is two hundred pounds. A slave who is accustomed to picking, is punished, if he or she brings in a less quantity than that. . . . The hands are required to be in the cotton field as soon as it is light in the morning, and, with the exception of ten or fifteen minutes, which are given them at noon to swallow their allowance of cold bacon, they are not permitted to be a moment idle until it is too dark to see, and when the moon is full, they often times labor till the middle of the night. They do not

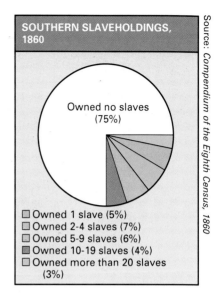

SOUTHERN SLAVEHOLDINGS, 1860

Owned no slaves (75%)

- ☐ Owned 1 slave (5%)
- ☐ Owned 2-4 slaves (7%)
- ☐ Owned 5-9 slaves (6%)
- ■ Owned 10-19 slaves (4%)
- ☐ Owned more than 20 slaves (3%)

Source: Compendium of the Eighth Census, 1860

LEARNING FROM GRAPHS. *We often think that all southerners owned slaves. How does this graph change that notion?*

Cotton and Slavery   453

dare to stop even at dinner time, nor return to the quarters, however late it be, until the order to halt is given by the driver [overseer].

The day's work over in the fields, the baskets are 'toted,' or in other words carried to the gin-house, where the cotton is weighed. . . . This done, the labor of the day is not yet ended, by any means. Each one must then attend to his respective chores. One feeds the mules, another the swine—another cuts wood, and so forth, beside, the packing [of the cotton] is all done by candlelight. Finally, at a late hour, they reach the quarters, sleepy and overcome with the long day's toil. Then a fire must be kindled in the cabin, the corn ground in the small hand-mill, and supper, and dinner for the next day in the field, prepared. All that is allowed them is corn and bacon, which is given out at the corncrib and the smoke-house every Sunday morning. Each one receives, as his weekly allowance, three and a half pounds of bacon, and corn enough to make a peck [8 quarts; 8.9 liters] of meal. That is all—no tea, coffee, sugar, and, with the exception of a scanty sprinkling now and then, no salt. . . .[1]**"**

[1]From *Twelve Years a Slave* by Solomon Northrup

"Cotton Plantation on the Mississippi" shows slaves picking cotton while their overseer watches from his mule. It is typical of Currier & Ives that this scene shows no more passion than a Sunday outing. Yet what does historical imagination suggest was truly the case?

The Granger Collection, New York

The Granger Collection, New York

After picking, the cotton had to be put through the gin to remove the seeds. Then it was packed in bales. This was done in a cotton press, a box-like affair with a heavy screw-down top. The bales were bound in burlap and tied with wire or twine.

Harvesting was usually over by Christmas time. Then, for about a week, all work stopped. During this brief period the harsh and cruel side of slavery was put aside, if not forgotten. There were feasts, singing and dancing, a Christmas tree bright with candles. One South Carolina slave described a tree he remembered as "a picture of beautifulness." There were also small presents for everyone. Some masters even dressed up as Santa Claus and distributed gifts to the slave children.

After this brief holiday it was time to clear new land. Fences had to be repaired, tools sharpened. Thus the winter passed. Soon it was time for the next spring planting.

Although cotton increased the demand for slave labor, there could be no sudden increase in the supply of slaves. Congress had forbidden bringing any more slaves into the country. Farmers therefore competed with one another for American-born slaves. The natural increase of the population could not satisfy the demand. The price of slaves rose rapidly. By 1850 slaves were selling for three or four times as much as they had cost before the invention of the cotton gin. 🖎

Cotton is packed into bales under pressure from the screw-down top of this cotton press. A mule can turn the heavy screw by patiently plodding its circular path. Where would the baled cotton most likely be sent?

Return to the Preview & Review on page 449.

Cotton and Slavery   **455**

Use these questions to guide your reading. Answer the questions after completing Section 2. **Understanding, Issues, Events, & Ideas.** Use the following words to describe a visit to a southern plantation: "Cotton is King," Fourth of July.
1. How did the cotton gin make life more difficult for slaves?
2. How did some southerners justify slavery?
3. What did southerners mean by boasting that "Cotton is King"?
4. Why did southerners believe that criticism of slavery was unpatriotic and dangerous?

Thinking Critically. 1. Plan a film that shows life for a slave on a cotton plantation. What props and details will you include on your "set"? 2. You are a northern newspaper reporter at a Fourth of July celebration in the South in 1830. Write an interview with a slave who saw the celebration.

2. "COTTON IS KING"

How Cotton Affected Slaves

In some respects the fact that slaves were becoming more valuable meant that their owners treated them better. Prosperous owners could afford to feed, clothe, and house slaves adequately. Probably most did so, if only because it made sense to take good care of such useful property.

The slaves ate simple food. It consisted mainly of corn, pork fat, and molasses. This did not make a balanced diet, for no one at that time understood the importance of vitamins and minerals for good health. Fortunately, most slaves were allowed to have small vegetable gardens of their own. They could fish in the streams and hunt and trap small forest animals, such as opossums and raccoons. They got enough to eat, even if their food was plain and simple.

The slaves wore clothing that was also simple but sufficient—overalls, cotton and woolen shirts, a pair of heavy work shoes, a hat for protection against rain and summer heat.

Slave cabins were small and poorly furnished. Most families lived in a single room. The cabins had fireplaces for cooking and to provide heat in winter. Some had board floors, but many were built directly on the earth. Windows rarely had panes of glass. These

Hampton University Archives

This photograph of the remains of a slave cabin in Georgia reveals little of the life—and death—that would have taken place inside. Imagine the voices once heard here—and perhaps the whispered longings for freedom.

STRATEGIES FOR SUCCESS

COMPARING STATISTICS

Statistics are numerical facts. They are often organized into tables, charts, or graphs so they are easier to analyze. Comparing statistics from two or more sources will help you understand relationships among the statistics.

How to Compare Statistics

To effectively compare statistics, follow these guidelines.

1. **Identify the types of data being compared.** Read the titles, headings, labels, and footnotes of each source (chart, graph, or table.)
2. **Examine the data.** Note the specific statistics for each heading.
3. **Be sure you know what is being compared.** Check quantities and values. They may vary from column to column or source to source and may be misread if not noted carefully.
4. **Notice both similarities and differences.** Observe how the numbers are alike or how they differ.
5. **Look for relationships.** Note *trends*—if quantities seem to increase or decrease at the same time or rate. Make inferences and draw conclusions. Form hypotheses to explain the trends you discover. Consider cause and effect relationships.

Applying the Strategy

Study the bar graphs below. The bottom graph shows cotton production and the top graph measures the size of the slave population of the United States. Both contain statistics for the years 1820 to 1860. How do the statistics compare? Note that both graphs show a steady increase during the years they cover. How might the statistics for cotton production and the size of the slave population be related? Would increasing cotton production require more slaves? Would more slaves increase production? Are both possible?

The map below shows the major cotton-producing areas in 1839 and in 1859. Note that this area has increased. How is the information on this map related to the statistics on the graphs? What are some conclusions you can draw from the information shown on the map and charts on this page?

For independent practice, see Practicing the Strategy on page 474.

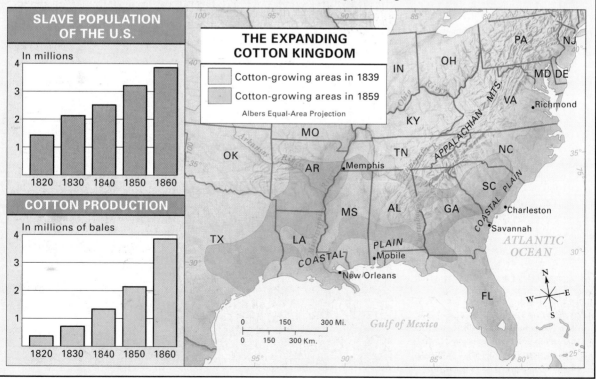

SLAVE POPULATION OF THE U.S.
In millions

| 1820 | 1830 | 1840 | 1850 | 1860 |

COTTON PRODUCTION
In millions of bales

| 1820 | 1830 | 1840 | 1850 | 1860 |

THE EXPANDING COTTON KINGDOM

Cotton-growing areas in 1839
Cotton-growing areas in 1859
Albers Equal-Area Projection

living conditions were primitive by modern standards. They were not, however, unhealthy. They tended to improve as time passed. Poor farm people, in the North as well as in the South, were not much better off in these respects.

However, the cotton gin also made life much more difficult for most slaves. When slaves were worth more, owners changed their attitude toward slavery. The number of slaves who were freed by their owners declined after 1800. Most southern state governments even passed laws making it difficult for owners who wanted to release their slaves to do so. Owners also tended to try to make their slaves work harder. The high price of cotton encouraged them to increase production by any possible means.

The westward expansion of cotton cultivation was extremely hard on thousands of slaves. Owners and slaves moved west together from Virginia and the Carolinas to Alabama, Mississippi, and Texas. But they made the move under very different circumstances.

American pioneers endured the dangers and hardships of the frontier willingly. They hoped to obtain a better way of life. They were prepared to take risks and suffer inconveniences to do so. The slaves whom they brought with them faced the same dangers and hardships. But they had no hope of benefiting as a result.

At a Slave Auction

No aspect of slavery brought home the inhumanity of it more than the slave auction. Slaves waited as buyers looked them over, deciding their fate and often that of their families. Josiah Henson recalled:

Culver Pictures

This is one half of a stereopticon slide, once very popular, that would show a three-dimensional image of these slaves picking cotton. Imagine viewing the slide in the comfort of your northern home in 1850. How might your future life be different from the lives of these children held as slaves?

" The crowd collected round the stand [auctioneer's platform], the huddling group of Negroes, the examination of muscle, teeth, the exhibition of agility, the look of the auctioneer, the agony of my mother—I can shut my eyes and see them all.

My brothers and sisters were bid off first, and one by one, while my mother, paralyzed by grief, held me by the hand. Her turn came, and she was bought by Isaac Riley of Montgomery County. Then I was offered to the assembled purchasers. My mother, half distracted with the thought of parting forever from all her children pushed through the crowd, while the bidding for me was going on, to the spot where Riley was standing. She fell at his feet, and clung to his knees, entreating [begging] him in tones that a mother could only command, to buy her baby as well as herself, and to spare to her one, at least, of her little ones. Will it, can it be believed that this man, thus appealed to, was capable not merely of turning a deaf ear to her supplication [request], but of disengaging himself from her with such violent blows and kicks, as to reduce her to the necessity of creeping out of his reach, and mingling the groan of bodily suffering with the sob of a breaking heart? As she crawled away from the brutal man I heard her sob out, "Oh, Lord Jesus, how long, how long shall I suffer this way!" I must have been then between five and six years old.[1] "

New Orleans claimed one of the largest slave markets in the South. Solomon Northrup recounted what he called a typical scene at an auction:

" David and Caroline were both bought by a Natchez planter. They left us, grinning broadly. They were happy because they had not been separated. Lethe was sold to a planter of Baton Rouge, her eyes flashing with anger as she was led away. The same man also purchased Randall. The little fellow was made to jump and run across the floor, and to perform many other acts to show his activity and condition. All the time the trade was going on his mother Eliza was crying aloud and wringing her hands. She begged the man not to buy him unless he also bought her and her daughter. . . . The man answered he could not afford it, and then Eliza burst into sobs. Freeman [the auctioneer] turned around to her savagely, with his whip in his uplifted hand, ordering her to stop her noise or he would whip her. Unless

Point of View

The master of Tombee, a cotton plantation of St. Helena Island, South Carolina, made this entry in his diary.

" I will be compelled to send about ten prime Negroes to town next Monday, to be sold. . . . I never thought I would be driven to this very unpleasant extremity. Nothing can be more mortifying and grieving to a man than to select out some of his Negroes to be sold. You know not to whom, or how they will be treated by their new owners. And Negroes that you find no fault with—to separate families, mothers & daughters, brothers & sisters—all to pay for your own extravagances. People will laugh at your distress, and say it serves you right, you lived beyond your means. . . . "
Thomas B. Chapin, May 3, 1845

SOLD DOWN THE RIVER

Kennedy Galleries

"Slave Auction at Richmond," above, is also by Eyre Crowe. With the rap of the autioneer's hammer the young woman on the platform will become the property of the highest bidder in this close, narrow hall.

Pioneers often left loved ones behind. Young men and women setting out for the West had to bid farewell to parents and friends knowing they would probably never see them again. It was very sad. For slaves these separations were cruel rather than sad. They had no choice in the matter. Since few could read or write, they did not even have the possibility of writing letters to those left behind.

It was bad enough for slaves whose owners took their human property west along with the farm tools, furniture, and other goods. Much worse was the fate of those who were sold to professional slave traders. These traders made a business of buying slaves wherever they could find them. They herded the poor captives together, chained them, and carted them off to regions where their labor was in great demand. Busy markets developed in cities like New Orleans, where slaves from the Upper South were collected.

At these markets the slaves were sold at auction, one by one, to the highest bidder. Mothers were often separated from their children, wives from their husbands—all by the fall of the auctioneer's gavel. To be sold down the river in this way was a terrible fate.

she stopped that minute, he would not have such whining, he said. He would take her out into the yard and give her a hundred lashes. Yes, he would take the nonsense out of her pretty quick.

Eliza cringed and tried to wipe away her tears, but it was all in vain. She wanted to be with her children, . . .[1] **99**

Slaves never stopped trying to locate and rejoin their families. Many slaves ran away in an effort to join loved ones sold away. Reward notices printed in many southern newspapers described these

[1]From *Twelve Years a Slave* by Solomon Northrup

attempts. Theodore Dwight Weld, a leading abolitionist, collected hundreds of such notices in his book *American Slavery As It Is. Testimony of A Thousand Witnesses*. Weld used the book to counter southern claims that slaves were basically happy. Many notices such as these appeared:

> **"** *Macon (Ga.) Messenger,* November 23, 1837. $25 Reward—Ran away, a Negro man, named Cain. He was brought from Florida, and has a wife near Mariana, and probably will attempt to make his way there.
>
> *Richmond (Va.) Compiler,* September 8, 1837. Ran away from the subscriber, Ben. He ran off without any known cause, and I suppose he is aiming to go to his wife, who was carried [moved] from the neighborhood last winter.
>
> *Richmond (Va.) Enquirer,* February 20, 1838. Stop the Runaway!!!—$25 Reward. Ran away from the Eagle Tavern, a Negro fellow named Nat. He is no doubt attempting to follow his wife, who was lately [recently] sold to a speculator named Redmond. The above reward will be paid by Mrs. Lucy M. Downman, of Sussex County, Va.
>
> *Lexington (Ky.) Observer and Reporter,* September 28, 1838. $50 Reward.—Ran away from the subscriber, a Negro girl, named Maria. She is of copper color, between 13 and 14 years of age—bare headed and bare footed. She is small of her age—very sprightly and very likey. She stated she was going to see her mother at Maysville.[1] **"**

The Peculiar Institution

By the 1830s most southerners were convinced that slavery—"the peculiar institution"—was absolutely necessary to their well being. They thought their whole way of life depended upon their ownership of slaves. They even persuaded themselves that slavery was good for the slaves as well as for the owners. They wrongly argued that their slaves were childlike by nature and of lower intelligence. They reasoned that under slavery they could protect and guide these "inferior" people. Compare the life of the slave with that of the northern free worker, they urged. Did slaves ever have to worry about where their next meal was coming from? Did anyone ever see a slave begging in the South? Sick slaves were cared for by their masters. Old slaves were certain of support as long as they lived and a decent burial when death finally came.

Southerners especially liked to compare the living conditions of plantation workers with those of poor immigrants and low-paid factory workers in northern cities. They insisted that the workers who

[1]From *American Slavery As It Is. Testimony of a Thousand Witnesses* by Theodore Dwight Weld

Point of View

While growing up in Hannibal, Missouri, Sam Clemens, the future Mark Twain, once saw an angry overseer strike a clumsy slave.

> "He was dead in an hour. Nobody in the village approved of murder, but of course no one said much about it. . . . Considerable sympathy was felt for the slave's owner, who had been bereft of valuable property by a worthless person who was not able to pay for it."
>
> Mark Twain

planted and picked cotton were better fed, better housed, and better clothed than the workers in the northern textile factories who spun the cotton into thread and wove it into cloth.

Yet even in the South people were still debating the evils and merits of slavery. In 1831 and 1832 delegates to the Virginia legislature held a year-long debate. Those who supported slavery used many arguments—economic, social, even religious. One of the most unusual was this one entered in the record of the debate:

> "We have no hesitation in affirming [claiming to be true], that throughout the whole slaveholding country, the slaves of a good master are his warmest, most constant, and most devoted friends; they have been accustomed to look up to him as their supporter, director and defender. Every one acquainted with southern slaves, knows that the slave rejoices in the elevation and prosperity of his master. . . . Have no doubt that they form the happiest portion of our society. A merrier being does not exists on the face of the globe, than the negro slave of the United States. . . .[1]"

Of course, every debate has two sides, as this one did. Those opposed to slavery pointed to its many "evils." Speaking during the Virginia debates, one delegate focused on the economic and social problems slavery caused for the South.

> "Slavery is ruinous to whites—retards improvement—roots out industrious population, banishes [throws out] the yeomanry [farmers] of the country—deprives the spinner, the weaver, the [black]smith, the shoemaker, the carpenter of employment and support. The evil admits no remedy—it is increasing, and will continue to increase, until the whole countryside will be inundated with one black wave, covering the whole extent, with a few white faces here and there floating on the surface. The master has no capital to invest but what is invested in human flesh—the father instead of being richer for his sons, is at a loss how to provide for them; there is no diversity of occupations, no incentive to enterprise. Labor of every species is disreputable because performed mostly by slaves . . . and the general aspect [look] of the countryside marks the curse of a wasteful, idle, reckless population who have no interest in the soil, . . .[2]"

Few southerners, however, spoke of the negative effects of slavery on the slaves. Their cause would be championed by northerners—white and black.

[1] From *Review of the Debate on the Abolition of Slavery in the Virginia Legislature of 1831 and 1832* by Thomas R. Dew
[2] From *Niles' Weekly Register*, vol. 43, Sept. 8, 1832

AFRICAN AMERICANS IN THE U.S. POPULATION, 1790-1860				
Year	African Americans in the U.S. Population	Percentage of Total U.S. Population	Free African Americans	Percentage of Total African Americans
1790	757,208	19.3	59,527	7.9
1800	1,002,037	18.9	108,435	10.8
1810	1,377,808	17.9	186,446	13.5
1820	1,771,656	17.8	233,634	13.2
1830	2,328,642	17.6	319,599	13.7
1840	2,873,648	16.9	386,293	13.4
1850	3,638,808	15.6	434,495	11.9
1860	4,441,830	14.0	488,070	11.0

Source: *Historical Statistics of the United States*

LEARNING FROM TABLES. *This chart contains data about African Americans—both free and slave—in the U.S. population. What surprising trend can you note in the percentage of the total population made up of slaves from 1790 to 1860? What do you think might have caused this?*

Pride and Prejudice

Slaveholders also took pride in the importance of American cotton to the whole world. **"Cotton Is King"** was a southern slogan. Southerners meant by this slogan that their cotton was essential to the prosperity of the United States and to most of Europe as well. Since cotton depended on slavery, criticism of slavery seemed to them unpatriotic and downright dangerous.

Of course, cotton was *not* king in the sense that southerners imagined. It was the nation's most valuable export, but the national economy would not have collapsed if no cotton were grown. Still, southerners were hardly alone in boasting about the importance of their system. Like Americans in all sections, they were proud of their country and their way of life.

That pride was understandable. The United States was a rich and growing country. The American experiment in republican government was proving a success. Most ordinary people in other nations greatly admired America. European reformers studied the Declaration of Independence and the Constitution. They looked forward to a time when they might create similar governments in their own lands. Each year more and more foreigners were crossing the Atlantic Ocean hoping to find wealth and happiness in the United States.

Noticing these things, Americans tended to sing the praises of their country and of themselves. Frontier settlers in particular liked to brag about their own abilities. One western character explained:

“ I am a real ring-tailed roarer . . . from the thunder and lightning country. I make my breakfast on stewed Yankee and pork steak and rinse them down with spike nails. I can lick my weight in wildcats or raccoons. . . . I can out-eat, out-drink, out-work, out-grin, out-snort, out-run, out-lift, out-sneeze, out-lie anything in the shape of man or beast from Maine to Louisiana. ”

The sketch shows a ring-tailed roarer on his diet of spike nails, an image that comes from the bragging voices of the American frontier.

Art Collection of the Boatmen's National Bank of St. Louis

"Stump Speaking" shows a politician campaigning in rural Missouri. His speech may have lasted hours and genuinely interested his attentive listeners. George Caleb Bingham, who painted this picture in 1854, was a politician himself as well as a fine American painter.

It was this kind of thinking that explains the foolish confidence of the western War Hawks who had expected to conquer Canada so easily when war broke out with Great Britain in 1812.

Most easterners and southerners were more restrained than western types like the War Hawks and the "ring-tailed roarer." But Americans in every section felt deep national pride. Each **Fourth of July** people gathered in towns and villages to celebrate the anniversary of the signing of the Declaration of Independence. There were fireworks, parades, brass bands, and many stirring speeches by politicians, ministers, and war veterans. The words of the Declaration were sometimes read aloud, reminding listeners that "all men are created equal." On the outskirts of plantation lawns and city parks slaves heard these words as they tended the horses and waited for their owners. How did they feel? As Frederick Douglass, a former slave, said:

> ❝ What to the American slave is your Fourth of July? I answer, a day that reveals to him, more than all the other days of the year, the injustice and cruelty of which he is the constant victim. . . .[1] ❞

[1] From *The Life and Writings of Frederick Douglass*, vol. 2, edited by Philip Foner

Americans of the day were quite pleased with their achievements. This was often harmless enough. But among the slaveholders this pride had very serious effects. They could not accept even the mildest criticism of "the peculiar institution."

Return to the Preview & Review on page 456.

3. ABOLITIONISM

The Movement to Abolish Slavery

Gradually, a small number of Americans, mostly but not entirely people from the free states, began to argue that slavery was wrong and ought to be **abolished,** or ended. These **abolitionists,** as they were called, were influenced by the same typically American pride and self-confidence that led so many southerners to insist that slavery was the best possible social system. The abolitionists believed in the ideal of freedom. They insisted that America was the land of liberty. They were impatient with any imperfection in their society. It was sinful, they said, to stand by idly while a flaw like slavery existed.

Abolitionists quoted the Declaration of Independence to show that slavery was contrary to American principles. They also put forth religious arguments stressing that all human beings are equal in the eyes of God. It was hard to disagree with these arguments. Nevertheless, most people, even non-slaveholders, considered the abolitionists to be dangerous radicals.

This was so because there seemed no legal way to do away with slavery in the United States. Under the Constitution each state could decide whether or not to allow slavery to exist within its borders. The northern states had abolished it after the Revolution. But nearly all voters in the southern states favored the slave system. There was no chance that the citizens of Virginia or Georgia or Mississippi would ever voluntarily agree to free their slaves.

Slavery could, of course, be abolished by amending the Constitution. But an amendment would require the approval of three fourths of the states. In 1850 half of the 30 states in the Union permitted slavery. No antislavery amendment could possibly be ratified. To campaign for abolition under these circumstances seemed like urging revolution and civil war.

Nevertheless, some important foes of slavery demanded action. One of the prominent early ones was Benjamin Lundy, a saddle maker from New Jersey. Lundy probably became interested in abolition because he was a Quaker. Even during the colonial period many Quakers had spoken out against slavery. In 1821 Lundy began to publish an antislavery newspaper, *The Genius of Universal Emancipation.*

Lundy's paper never had more than 700 subscribers. His influence, however, was quite large. He worked tirelessly for the cause. He urged Congress to abolish slavery in the District of Columbia and to prohibit its spread into the western territories. He bitterly attacked the plan to annex slaveholding Texas. He also demanded that free blacks in the North be treated fairly.

At first Lundy favored granting freedom to the slaves gradually. Perhaps if the children of all slaves born after a certain date were set

Preview & Review

Use these questions to guide your reading. Answer the questions after completing Section 3.
Understanding Issues, Events, & Ideas. Give the significance of the following words in the movement to end slavery: abolish, abolitionists, emancipation, *Appeal to the Colored Citizens of the World,* Underground Railroad.
1. What arguments did the abolitionists make against slavery?
2. How did the following work for abolition: Benjamin Lundy? William Garrison? Angelina and Sarah Grimké? Theodore Weld?
3. How did the following fight slavery: Paul Cuffe? Henry Garnet? Harriet Tubman? Gabriel Prosser? Denmark Vesey? Nat Turner? Frederick Douglass?
4. How did the abolitionists influence opinion in the North?
Thinking Critically. 1. You are a member of the American Anti-Slavery Society. Do you think that William Lloyd Garrison is too radical? Why or why not? **2.** As a volunteer on the Underground Railroad, write a letter describing the escaped slaves.

Benjamin Lundy was an early leader in the movement to abolish slavery.

Abolitionism 465

The Granger Collection, New York

William Lloyd Garrison, publisher of The Liberator, *proclaimed, "I will be heard." Whom did he blame for the institution of slavery? Do you agree with his argument?*

The Granger Collection, New York

Angelina Grimké Weld, shown above, and Sarah Grimké appealed to women of the South to reject slavery. Why did they urge its overthrow?

free, the South could accept abolition. When this idea of gradual **emancipation,** or freedom, attracted no southern support, Lundy became more radical. He began to demand immediate emancipation.

Radical and Moderate Voices

In 1829 Benjamin Lundy appointed a young man from Massachusetts, William Lloyd Garrison, as assistant editor of *The Genius of Universal Emancipation.* Garrison turned out to be much more radical than Lundy. Lundy had always hoped to persuade owners to free their slaves. He tried, for example, to show them that slavery was neither efficient nor economical. Garrison simply insisted that it was criminal and sinful to own a human being. He denounced not only slaveholders but all Americans who allowed slavery to exist.

Garrison soon disagreed with Lundy. He left his job as editor and in 1831 began publishing a paper of his own, *The Liberator.* He announced in the first issue:

> *I will be* as harsh as truth, and as uncompromising as justice. . . . I am in earnest—I will not equivocate—I will not excuse—I will not retreat a single inch—And *I WILL BE HEARD!*

Garrison's position was so radical that even most northerners who disliked slavery turned against him. He blamed *everyone* who tolerated slavery for the existence of the institution. He urged the northern states to secede from the United States. "No Union with Slaveholders," was one of his slogans. Garrison publicly set fire to a copy of the Constitution. The Constitution, he said, was a "compromise with tyranny" and an "agreement with Hell."

In 1833 Garrison and other abolitionists founded the American Anti-Slavery Society. But Garrison's radical position caused conflict in the organization. The first president of the Society was Arthur Tappan, a well-to-do New York merchant. He helped to finance the abolitionist movement, but eventually he broke with Garrison. So did Tappan's brother Benjamin, and so did two important southern abolitionists, the sisters Sarah and Angelina Grimké. The Grimké sisters were two of a number of Quakers who opposed slavery.

In 1836 Angelina Grimké published a pamphlet, *Appeal to Christian Women of the South.* The *Appeal* urged southern women to "overthrow this horrible system of oppression and cruelty." Next she made speeches attacking slavery before small groups of women in private homes. As her reputation grew, she began to lecture in public to larger groups. Her sister, Sarah Grimké, also spoke and wrote for the cause of abolition.

In 1838 Angelina Grimké married Theodore Dwight Weld, a clergyman who was a leader of the more moderate opponents of slavery. When Garrison demanded "immediate emancipation" of the slaves, he meant exactly that—right now and entirely free. Weld spoke in favor of what he called "immediate abolition gradually achieved." By this he meant that his *goal* was complete freedom for all slaves but that it would take time to change the minds of slave-holders and to persuade northerners to take a stand.

To attract recruits, Weld and his group collected and published stories showing how slaves were being mistreated. They organized support for members of Congress who sympathized with their views. They ran candidates of their own in many elections.

Slave Uprisings

It is surely correct to assume that every slave was at least a silent abolitionist. A few were so outraged by slavery that they rose in rebellion against it. The chances of success were slight. Slaveholders feared slave uprisings so much that they reacted to them with terrible brutality. When captured, rebellious slaves were always killed.

One rebel slave was Gabriel Prosser. Every Sunday morning in the spring and summer of 1800 he slipped into Richmond, Virginia. He studied the town, noting the layout and locations of buildings and streets. Quietly, secretly, Prosser planned and gathered followers. Late in August he was ready to strike. Everyone in and around Richmond except known friends of the rebels would die.

Two things stopped Prosser. Two of his followers felt loyalty to their masters. When they learned of the plan to kill everyone around Richmond, they warned their owners. These slaveowners alerted city officials. Still Prosser might have succeeded. More than 1,000 slaves and ex-slaves were ready to strike. But just as they were gathering, a violent storm came up. Heavy rains washed away the roads and bridges into Richmond. Before the group could reorganize, officials seized Prosser. He and 36 others were hanged.

Denmark Vesey of Charleston, South Carolina, was another rebel. Vesey had purchased his freedom after winning some money in a lottery. Yet he was not satisfied with escaping from bondage himself. For years he planned his uprising, gradually gathering a group of slaves and former slaves ready to take up arms. In 1822 he was ready to act. At the last moment one of his men lost his nerve and betrayed the plot. Although the rebellion never took place, Vesey and 35 others were hanged.

The bloodiest slave uprising was that organized by Nat Turner, a slave in Southampton County, Virginia. To those who knew him, Turner had seemed the last person who might be expected to resort to violence. He was mild mannered and deeply religious. Yet in 1831 he and his followers murdered 57 people before they were captured. Historians still argue about whether or not Turner was insane. The point is that nearly every slave hated bondage. Nearly all were eager to see something done to destroy the system.

"Nat Turner and His Confederates in Conference" was engraved in 1863. Turner leans on a pole, his face drawn with anger. When Turner rebelled, what bloody fate befell Southhampton County?

Turner's revolt had important results. In an attempt to quiet the growing antislavery clamor, proslavery people now claimed "Negro slavery, as it exists in the United States, is neither a moral nor a political evil." The revolt also spread fear throughout the white population of the South. Because Turner was a preacher and an educated man, southern states passed stricter laws to control African American preachers and the education of slaves. A member of the Virginia legislature admitted how far they would go to keep slaves from learning.

    66 We have, as far as possible, closed every avenue by which light might enter their minds. If you could extinguish [put out] the capacity to see the light, our work would be completed; they would be on the level of the beasts in the fields, and we would be safe.[1] 99

A few slaves learned to read before Turner's revolt. Almost none did after it. Indeed, in most states it was illegal to teach a slave to read. You could be put to death if you were caught. People feared that slaves who could read would be more rebellious. Of course slaves could no longer read the Bible. But as *De Bow's Review,* a southern magazine, stated:

    66 If a judgment may be formed from the known conduct of white readers, we may reasonably conclude that the great majority of blacks would prefer other books than the Bible. Is there any great moral reason why we should incur [cause] the tremendous risk of having our wives and children slaughtered in consequence of our slaves being taught to read incendiary [those that stir the emotions] publications? Religion is as important to the slave as to the master but is the ability to read essential to salvation? . . . Millions of those now in heaven never owned a Bible. To read is a

[1]From *Eyewitness: The Negro in American History* by William Katz

The Granger Collection, New York

valuable accomplishment, but it does not save the soul. . . .[1]"

A few slaves taught themselves to read through heroic efforts or the help of others who could read. On the eve of the Civil War only one or two percent of the slaves were able to read or write. On plantations illiteracy among slaves was almost complete. This illiteracy was one of the worst handicaps of slavery.

Slave Culture

Historians know too little about slave culture. A group of people who cannot read or write leave behind few documents to study. Fortunately, during the 1930s a federally funded writers' project collected an oral history of slavery through interviews with hundreds of ex-slaves. Most were very old when interviewed, and their memories had faded somewhat. But their recollections, along with surviving slave songs, folktales, proverbs, and stories, tell of a rich and complex slave culture.

Slaves managed to shape their own lives within the harsh guidelines of slavery. Most lived in small communities—the quarters—with fellow slaves. There they developed institutions separate from those of white southerners. Their spirituals, slave songs, and tales told of anger and undying hope for freedom and played a central part in the slave culture. Slaves sang not because they were happy or content but because they were told to. And as Frederick Douglass explained in this excerpt, it was the words and the tone of the songs that carried the message of sadness and anger. Slave songs, he said:

" . . . were mostly of a plaintive cast [one expressing suffering], and told a tale of grief and sorrow. In the most boisterous outbursts of rapturous sentiment, there was ever a tinge of deep melancholy [sadness]. . . .

I did not, when a slave, understand the deep meaning of those rude, and apparently incoherent songs. I was myself within a circle so that I neither saw nor heard as those without might see and hear. They told a tale which was then altogether beyond my feeble comprehension; they were tones, loud, long, and deep, breathing the prayer and complaint of souls boiling over with the bitterest anguish. Every tone was a testimony against slavery, and a prayer to God for deliverance from chains. The hearing of those wild notes always depressed my spirits and filled my heart with ineffable [unspeakable] sadness. The mere recurrence, even now, afflicts my spirit, and while I am writing these lines, my tears are falling. . . .[2]"

[1]From *De Bow's Review*, 1856
[2]From *My Bondage and My Freedom* by Frederick Douglass

Of course, any direct expression of slaves' feelings might have been suppressed by powerful owners and overseers. But within their communities and amongst themselves in the fields slaves did sing openly of their despair and suffering.

Slaves also developed other aspects of culture that gave them a sense of pride and humanity. Religion among slaves thrived. But it too was often practiced in secret. At night, deep in the woods behind their quarters, slaves would meet to pray. As more and more restrictive laws were passed, this became both more dangerous and more important. It uplifted the tired, beaten spirits of the slaves. It gave them hope.

Other aspects of culture did not develop as fully under the strict codes of slavery. Slave marriages were not recognized by southern law. But most owners encouraged stable marriages on their plantations. Of course, owners had the unquestioned right to break up families. Slaves had to live with this threat. Yet most were able to form lasting marriages and strong families.

Slaves had no legal status. In all southern states they were considered property. They could not own property themselves, marry freely, make contracts, or testify against a white person in court. They could not travel without a pass, or legally possess whiskey or guns. It was against the law for an owner to murder a slave. But severe punishments for disobedience by a slave were legal. Should such a punishment result in death, it was nearly impossible to gain a conviction because slave testimony was inadmissible in court.

Yet by bits and pieces a unique slave culture grew. This amazing achievement has been called by Ralph Ellison, an African American novelist, "one of the great triumphs of the human spirit in modern times."

African American Abolitionists

African Americans in the northern states could speak openly against slavery. Many did so before abolitionism became an important movement. They organized a large number of antislavery societies long before the creation of the American Anti-Slavery Society. The American Society of Free Persons of Color, formed during the National Negro Convention of 1830, was at the forefront of the abolition movement.

These abolitionists varied in their specific ideas. One of the first whom we know much about was Paul Cuffe. Cuffe was born free in Massachusetts Bay in 1759. As a youth he went to sea. Gradually he saved enough to buy a ship. He prospered. Eventually he owned a fleet of six merchant vessels. By 1800 he was probably the richest African American in the United States.

Cuffe favored the return of African Americans to Africa. Most colonizationists wanted to send former slaves to Africa to get rid of them. Cuffe saw colonization as a way for people to free themselves from prejudice and mistreatment. He transported 38 volunteers to West Africa in 1815 at his own expense. He intended to bring a new group each year, but he died before he could carry out his plan.

Henry Highland Garnet was more bitterly antislavery than Paul Cuffe. Garnet was born a slave in 1815 but escaped to the North with his parents when he was a small boy. His father became a shoemaker in New York City. Garnet managed to get a high school education. He went to sea and lost a leg as a result of an accident.

Garnet was a man of fierce determination. He had an eye, a friend said, "that looks through you." During the 1830s and 1840s he preached abolition in these tones:

Abolitionist Henry Highland Garnet is shown in this 1881 engraving.

> **❝** Brethren arise, arise! Strike for your lives and liberties. Now is the day and the hour. Let every slave throughout the land do this and the days of slavery are numbered. . . . *Rather die freemen than live to be slaves.* **❞**

He was soon joined by Charles Remond and others. Remond, a well-educated African American from Massachusetts, carried the anti-slavery crusade throughout the United States and to Great Britain.

Yet Garnet was moderate when compared to David Walker. In Boston in 1829 Walker published an angry ***Appeal to the Colored Citizens of the World***. He began his *Appeal*:

> **❝** We (the coloured people of the United States) are the most degraded, wretched, and abject [cast down in spirit] set of beings that ever lived since the world began. . . .
>
> The Indians of North and South America—the Greeks—the Irish, subjected under the king of Great Britain—the Jews, that ancient people of the Lord—the inhabitants of the islands of the sea—in fine [in total]; all inhabitants of the earth, (except however the sons of Africa) are called *men,* and of course are, and ought to be free. But we, (coloured people) and our children are brutes [beasts]!! and of course are, and *ought to be* Slaves to the American people and their children forever!! to dig their mines and work their farms; and thus go on enriching them, from one generation to another with our *blood* and our tears!!!![1] **❞**

Walker's essay was a powerful call for bold action by African Americans. African Americans in the South—free and slave—must strike for their freedom—violently, if necessary. If white Americans wanted to prevent racial war, insisted Walker, they had to immediately recognize the rights and humanity of black Americans.

Northerners, even some abolitionists, condemned Walker's essay as dangerous. Southerners put a price on Walker's head and tried to halt circulation of his *Appeal*.

[1]From *Appeal to the Colored Citizens of the World* by David Walker

Bradley Smith/Laurie Platt Winfrey

"On to Liberty" by Theodor Kaufmann shows escaping slaves surge forward as they realize that the prize of freedom lies just ahead of them.

Library of Congress

Harriet Ross Tubman helped between 200 and 300 escaped slaves make their way to freedom.

A number of African American women joined the attack on slavery. Sojourner Truth was a forceful speaker for abolition and women's rights. Harriet Ross Tubman escaped from Maryland into Pennsylvania when faced with the threat of being "sold down the river" after the death of her owner. She got a job as a cook in Philadelphia. But she was not satisfied merely to be free or even to make speeches urging the abolition of slavery. She became a specialist at the highly dangerous task of helping slaves escape into the northern states. She made 19 trips into the South and helped between 200 and 300 escaped slaves make their way to freedom.

Tubman was a "conductor" on the **Underground Railroad,** an informal organization that helped escaped slaves to make their way to Canada. Here and there along the route were "stations"—barns, stables, and safe houses—where the escaped slaves could hide. Angry slaveholders offered a reward of $40,000 for Tubman—dead or alive. Robert Purvis, a free African American in Charleston, worked tirelessly for the railroad. His zeal in helping slaves to freedom earned him the title "President of the Underground Railroad."

Frederick Douglass

The most famous African American who became an abolitionist was Frederick Douglass. Douglass had been a slave in Baltimore. In 1836 he ran away but was captured. Two years later he tried again, this time succeeding. He settled in Massachusetts.

One day in 1841 Douglass attended a meeting of the Massachusetts Anti-Slavery Society. Garrison himself was present. Without preparation Douglass stood up and delivered a powerful speech. The members of the society were so impressed that they urged him to become an agent of the society and work full time for abolition.

Abolitionists found that former slaves, like Frederick Douglass, were the best possible advertisements for their cause. These former slaves understood the horrors of slavery as no other person could.

Frederick Douglass proved to be the most moving and persuasive of all the African American abolitionists. He was a big, handsome man with what would today be called a magnetic personality. He was an excellent speaker. At first he followed the lead of Garrison, demanding instant abolition and refusing to make the slightest compromise. Eventually he decided that the only way to change the system was to work within it. He then began to engage in political activity. He also published his own abolitionist paper, *The North Star*. In it in 1849 he stated his position in clear, direct, and simple language:

National Portrait Gallery

Frederick Douglass was the much-admired speaker who, once a slave, now spoke out against the injustices of the peculiar institution with particular conviction. Why do you think people listened so attentively to an abolitionist who was once a slave?

66 The white man's happiness cannot be purchased by the black man's misery. Virtue cannot prevail among the white people, by its destruction among the black people, who form a part of the whole community. It is evident that white and black 'must fall or flourish' together. In the light of this great truth, laws ought to be enacted, and institutions established—all distinctions founded on complexion [skin color] ought to be repealed, repudiated, and forever abolished—and every right, privilege, and immunity, now enjoyed by the white man, ought to be as freely granted to the man of color.[1] 99

[1]From *The North Star*, November 16, 1849 by Frederick Douglass

These were words he would use time and again in his most famous essay and speech titled *What the Black Man Wants*, and in many other speeches before, during, and after the Civil War.

The Influence of the Abolitionists

In the 1840s and 1850s American abolitionists were a small minority in every part of the country. The followers of William Lloyd Garrison were a small minority of this minority. Nevertheless, the abolitionists had a large influence on public opinion, and Garrison and his followers had a large influence on other abolitionists.

Even people who considered abolitionists dreamers who threatened the peace of the Union were affected by their arguments against slavery. Such people were unwilling to act. But their dislike of slavery grew. Their consciences bothered them. Moderate abolitionists found themselves listening more closely to Garrison. Their own efforts to persuade others to support gradual change had come to nothing.

Many abolitionists became discouraged by their apparent lack of success in ending slavery. But in one important sense they were succeeding better than they knew. They were convincing the people of the North that slavery was a bad institution. They still had to convince them it was possible to free the nation of slavery. 🔲

Return to the Preview & Review on page 465.

CHAPTER 13 REVIEW

| **1793** | **1800** | **1808** | **1817** |
| Whitney invents cotton gin | Gabriel Prosser plans revolt | Congress bans slave importation | Amer Colon Socie |

Chapter Summary

Read the statements below. Choose one, and write a paragraph explaining its importance.

1. Soon after the American Revolution slavery in the United States seemed to be dying out.
2. The increasing importance of cotton to the southern economy revitalized slavery.
3. Many southerners convinced themselves that slavery was good for the slaves.
4. Gradually some Americans began to argue that slavery was wrong and ought to be abolished.
5. Slaves and ex-slaves protested their bondage by revolting or escaping along the Underground Railroad.
6. Although many Americans felt abolitionists were radicals, more and more people grew to dislike "the peculiar institution."

Reviewing Chronological Order

Number your paper 1–5. Then study the time line above and place the following events in the order in which they happened by writing the first next to 1, the second next to 2, and so on.

1. Importation of African slaves banned
2. Whitney's cotton gin
3. Garrison publishes *The Liberator*
4. Prosser plans slave revolt
5. Frederick Douglass joins abolition movement

Understanding Main Ideas

1. Describe the yearly cycle of life on a cotton plantation.
2. How did the lives of the slaves change as cotton production increased?
3. What arguments did some southerners use to defend slavery? What were arguments used by abolitionists to attack slavery?
4. Why did most people consider the abolitionists to be dangerous radicals?
5. Why did William Lloyd Garrison split with many other abolitionists?

Thinking Critically

1. **Determining Cause and Effect**. How did the cotton gin benefit southern farmers? Northern cloth manufacturers? Slaves? How did the cotton gin make life more difficult for slaves?
2. **Analyzing**. Write a script for an argument about slavery between a southern plantation owner and a northern factory owner.
3. **Synthesizing**. You are Frederick Douglass, writing an editorial for your newspaper, *The North Star*. Persuade your readers that in order to achieve the abolition of slavery, they must work within the system, rather than outside it.

Writing About History

Write an imaginary interview with Harriet Tubman based on one episode in her life. Use the information in Chapter 13 and in other reference books to prepare your interview.

Practicing the Strategy

Review the strategy on page 457.

Comparing Statistics. Study the graph on page 453, and answer the following questions.

1. What is significant about the date in the title of the graph?
2. What percentage of the white southern population owned no slaves at all?
3. Of the 25 percent who owned slaves, what percentage owned 10 or more? In what kind of occupation do you think these owners were engaged?
4. Why do you think the vast majority of southern whites supported slavery although only a small minority owned slaves?

1831
First issue of *The Liberator*
★
Nat Turner's revolt
1833
American Anti-Slavery Society

enius of Universal Emancipation

plans slave revolt

1841
Douglass joins
abolition movement

Using Primary Sources

English-born Frances Anne Kemble was a well-known actress. After a successful stage career, she married an American and moved to Georgia, where her husband and his brother owned several plantations. Read the following excerpt adapted from *Journal of a Residence on a Georgia Plantation in 1838–1839* by Fanny Kemble. As you read, notice how Mrs. Kemble's views differed from those of the plantation owner. Then answer the questions below.

> *But teaching the slaves is a finable offense. . . . The first offense of the sort is heavily fined, and the second more heavily fined. For the third, one is sent to prison. . . . I certainly intend to teach Aleck to read. I certainly won't tell Mr. Butler [the plantation owner] about it.*
>
> *I began to see one great advantage in this slavery: you are the absolute ruler on your own plantation. No slave's testimony counts against you, and no white testimony exists but what you choose to admit. Some owners injure their slaves, some brand them, some pull out their teeth, some shoot them a little here and there (all details gathered from ads for runaway slaves in southern papers). They do all this on their plantations, where nobody comes to see.*

1. Why was Fanny Kemble afraid to tell the plantation owner that she was teaching Aleck to read?
2. Why do you think plantation owners did not want their slaves to be educated?
3. What evidence from the excerpt suggests that plantation owners could mistreat slaves without fear of punishment by law?

Linking History & Geography

Because of the great distance to Canada, escaped slaves faced many hardships. Below are lists of typical routes. Refer to a map of the United States to help you develop a map showing each route and indicating the number of miles from the first point to the Canadian border. Then describe the hardships an escaped slave might encounter on one of these routes.

1. Charleston, Philadelphia, New York City, Albany, Canada
2. Evansville, Indiana; Indianapolis; Toledo; Detroit; Canada
3. Percival, Iowa; Des Moines; Chicago; Milwaukee; Canada
4. Norfolk, Boston, Montpelier, Canada

Enriching Your Study of History

1. **Individual Project.** Complete *one* of the following projects: make a model or a large-scale drawing of a southern plantation and explain its importance in the economy of the South; *or* make a model or large-scale drawing of a cotton gin and explain how it works and its importance.
2. **Cooperative Project.** In groups, your class will write and present skits showing how the North viewed the South and vice versa. Plot ideas: You return to your plantation from a visit to relatives in a northeastern city, where you attended an abolitionist meeting. Tell your southern friends about the attitudes you encountered. Or, while visiting relatives in the South, you were taken to the cabin of an elderly slave who worked for their family. Describe your impressions to your northern friends.

CHAPTER 14

Reform and Romanticism

F rom the 1830s through the 1850s the effort to get rid of slavery was only one of many reform movements. This was truly an **Age of Reform.** The rapid growth of the country was causing changes of all sorts. These changes were mostly good for the average person. But sometimes they had undesirable side effects. Using machines for mass production reduced the price of goods. But the introduction of machinery often caused skilled workers to lose their jobs. The growth of cities opened up a number of opportunities for thousands of people. But it also led to crowded, unhealthy living conditions. Since Americans were so proud of their society, they found any flaw or weakness in it frustrating and annoying. Because they were so self-confident, they took these imperfections as a challenge. At every hand they could see signs of growth and progress. This made them optimistic about the future. Something *could* be done. Therefore something *must* be done. That was the dominant attitude of the reformers.

State Street in Albany leads to the New York Capitol in 1848. In the center of the street, vendors are selling flowers and fresh fruit from their horse-drawn carts.

Albany Institute of History and Art

Above we see the Jacksonian view of women: to serve men. The women, unless they are very old or very young, serve the meal and stand aside. Do you think the painter meant to comment on women's role in society?

1. WOMEN AND REFORM

Women in Jacksonian America

One of the strangest things about the movement to free slaves was that many of its most active supporters were themselves not entirely free. When women came forward to speak out against slavery, they were attacked by people who believed that it was "unfeminine" for a woman to speak in public to a mixed audience. Even many male abolitionists took this position. At an international antislavery convention held in London in 1840, the men in charge refused to allow women delegates to participate. Two American delegates, Lucretia Mott and Elizabeth Cady Stanton, had to watch the proceedings from the balcony.

Nowhere were women placed in more lofty positions than in America. Nowhere were they more respected. But they were still treated as second-class citizens. They could not vote, hold public office, or sit on juries. Married women had no control over their own property. In the eyes of the law they were in the same position as children. They were subject to control by their husbands. Single women fared slightly better. At least they could manage their own property.

Women also had few opportunities to get a good education or have an interesting career. They could not be admitted to most high schools and colleges. People of the time believed that women's brains

Use these questions to guide your reading. Answer the questions after completing Section 1.
Understanding Issues, Events, & Ideas. Using the following words, describe the women's rights movement: Age of Reform, Women's Rights Convention, Seneca Falls Declaration.
1. What were some of the things women could not do in America in the early 1830s and 1840s?
2. What purpose was given for women's education?
3. In what field were the overwhelming majority of professional women?
4. For what did Susan B. Anthony campaign?
Thinking Critically. 1. Imagine that you are a delegate to the Women's Rights Convention in Seneca Falls, New York. Which right do you consider to be the most important for women to obtain? Why? 2. Write a letter to the editor of a newspaper in 1840, defending a woman's right to speak in public to a mixed audience.

Karolik Collection, Museum of Fine Arts, Boston

A woman's education was thought a good preparation to "protect women from the dangers with which democratic manners surround them," according to Alexis de Tocqueville.

The Museum of Fine Arts, Boston

and nervous systems could not stand the strain of studying difficult subjects such as chemistry and mathematics!

Even most women who tried to improve women's education believed this to be true. Emma Hunt Willard's *Plan for Improving Female Education,* published in 1819, called for teaching young girls religion, housekeeping, literature, and music. The goal was to prepare them for marriage and motherhood, not for a "masculine" career. Willard established the Troy Female Seminary, the first women's high school in America, in 1821. When Catherine and Mary Beecher decided to teach chemistry at their Female Seminary in Connecticut, they assured parents and prospective students that knowledge of chemistry would make their graduates better cooks.

But what of higher education for women? College was still an all-male institution, the final polishing of an educated man, the foundation for public life and the practice of a profession. Most people still viewed the role of women as domestic and private and questioned their need for a college education.

Then in 1833 Ohio's Oberlin College began to admit women. A few colleges and universities followed its lead. But real educational opportunities for women came with women's colleges. The first of these was Mount Holyoke Female Seminary (now Mount Holyoke College), founded by Mary Lyon in 1837.

Mary Lyon was an energetic woman, with red hair and bright blue eyes. She had attended and taught at several coeducational schools and had started the Buckland Female Seminary (a high school) in 1824. After touring several female high schools and visiting with Emma Willard in 1833, Lyon was driven to start a college for women. As she said in 1834, "My heart has so yearned over the adult female youth in the common walks of life, that it has sometimes seemed as if there were a fire shut up in my bones." Mount Holyoke Female Seminary was a rousing success. Soon women's colleges were opening in several states.

Women in the Professions

The ideal woman was expected to be religious, mild mannered, obedient, and totally domestic—nothing more. Practically all careers but marriage and teaching school were considered unfeminine. To be married and "live happily ever after" was supposed to be the goal for every young girl.

Nevertheless, a few women made their careers in male-dominated fields. Elizabeth Blackwell, a teacher, was determined to be a doctor. She read medical books at night. A sympathetic doctor gave her private lessons so that she could qualify for the Geneva Medical College in New York. She graduated first in her class in 1849 and became the first woman licensed to practice medicine in the United States.

Elizabeth Blackwell went on to establish her own hospital, the New York Infirmary for Women and Children, and a medical college for women. Her sister-in-law, Antoinette Brown Blackwell, became the first woman to be ordained a minister. Antoinette Blackwell was also active in many reform movements. Yet she found time to raise six children and to write no fewer than ten books.

Schlesinger Library, Radcliffe College

Elizabeth Blackwell established a medical college for women. Imagine some arguments she had to make to the all-male staff of Geneva Medical College to pursue her goal of practicing medicine.

> **"I do not wish to see the day come when women of my race in my state shall trail their skirts in the mire of partisan politics. I prefer to look to the American woman as she has always been, occupying her proud estate as the queen of the American home, instead of regarding her as a ward politician."**
> Congressman Frank Clark, 1915

Points of View

> **"Men call us angels, and boast of the deference they pay to our weakness! They give us their seats in church, in cars and omnibusses, at lectures and concerts, and in many other ways show us great respect where nothing but form is concerned. . . . But at the same time they are defrauding us of our just rights by crowding us out of every lucrative employment, and subjecting us to virtual slavery."**
> Amelia Bloomer, 1851

The Granger Collection, New York

Illustrations from Godey's Lady's Book, *edited by Sara Hale, show the modest dress of the age. If you wish, make a fashion sketch of a well-groomed and well-dressed woman of today (or tomorrow).*

Another such professional, Sara Josepha Hale, became the editor of the leading women's magazine of the day, *Godey's Lady's Book*. Hale worked to improve the education of women. She also wrote poetry for children, including "Mary Had a Little Lamb."

The overwhelming majority of professional women of the period were elementary school teachers. By the 1850s Philadelphia had 699 women and 82 men teaching in its school system. Brooklyn, New York, had 103 women and only 17 men. Yet nearly all the school principals were men, and male teachers were paid higher salaries.

Woman as Guardian of the Home

Elementary school teaching fit in neatly with women's role as mother. Child-rearing had always been their responsibility. In the 1830s and 1840s it seemed more important than ever. People were beginning to leave the farms for the cities. Instead of the whole family working on one plot of land, the father became the "breadwinner," the mother guardian of the home.

Factory work kept fathers away from home from early morning to late evening, six days a week. The mother had almost complete charge of rearing the children. Men no longer shared in most household chores. That was "woman's work."

The Women's Rights Movement

City life and increasing prosperity meant more leisure time for middle- and upper-class women. These women had household servants to help them with their domestic chores. Therefore they could develop new interests and activities. Many became involved in reform. In particular, many became abolitionists.

UNDERSTANDING SEQUENCE

Many times history unfolds as a sequence of events. Social progress in the United States from the 1820s through the 1850s provides a good example. Recognizing sequence and relationships among the events will help you understand such periods in the nation's history.

How to Understand Sequence

To understand sequence, follow these guidelines.

1. **Check for dates.** The most obvious clues to a sequence of events are dates.
2. **Look for key words and phrases.** Note terms such as *then, gave rise to, next,* and *finally* that indicate a sequence of events.
3. **Identify relationships among the events.** Determine if one event leads directly to others, and if they in turn lead to still others.
4. **Notice the larger picture.** Remember events in one area might spur events in other areas.

Applying the Strategy

Review Section 1, "Women and Reform." Create a sequential list of the key events mentioned in the section. When completed, your list should resemble the following one.

WOMEN AND REFORM

Plan for Improving Female Education published

Catherine and Mary Beecher open the Female Seminary in Connecticut

Sarah Grimké writes *Letters on the Equality of the Sexes and the Condition of Women*

Women banned from London antislavery conference

Women's Rights Convention in Seneca Falls, New York

Seneca Falls Declaration of Sentiments and Resolutions issued

Sara Josepha Hale becomes editor of *Godey's Lady's Book*

Elizabeth Blackwell becomes first woman licensed to practice medicine (1850)

Antoinette Brown Blackwell is first woman to become a fully ordained minister

Note that educational opportunities for women were the first steps in the women's rights movement. Sarah Grimké's book and the exclusion of Lucretia Mott and Elizabeth Cady Stanton from the London antislavery conference led directly to the Seneca Falls Conference. The declaration of women's rights issued at Seneca Falls quickly led to reforms by several states in laws concerning women.

For independent practice, see Practicing the Strategy on page 506.

The Granger Collection, New York

One African American woman and leading abolitionist also spoke out for women.

"The man over there says women need to be helped into carriages and lifted over ditches and over puddles, and have the best place everywhere. Nobody helps me into carriages and over puddles, or gives me the best place—and ain't I a woman? I have ploughed and planted and gathered into barns, and no man could head me—and ain't I a woman?"

Sojourner Truth, 1851

The Granger Collection, New York

Elizabeth Cady Stanton

Women who protested against slavery soon became aware of their own lowly position in society. One argument against slavery was the statement in the Declaration of Independence that all men were created equal. If slaves were entitled to equality, surely "free" women were too. Yet women who tried to speak out against slavery were often prevented from doing so by most male abolitionists.

Both Sarah and Angelina Grimké experienced so much resistance when they made public speeches attacking slavery that they became militant feminists. In *Letters on the Equality of the Sexes and the Condition of Women* (1838), Sarah Grimké wrote that "history teems with women's wrongs" and "is wet with women's tears." In 1838 she wrote:

"It will be scarcely denied, I presume, that, as a general rule, men do not desire the improvement of women. . . . As *they* have determined that Jehovah [God] has placed woman on a lower platform than man, they of course wish to keep her there; and hence the noble faculties of our minds are crushed and our reasoning powers are almost wholly uncultivated [undeveloped]. . . .

Within the last century, it has been gravely asserted [seriously claimed] that, 'chemistry enough to keep the pot boiling, and geography enough to know the location of the different rooms in her house, is learning sufficient for a woman.'[1]"

Women abolitionists began to believe that besides trying to free the slaves, they must try to free themselves from forms of bondage based on sex. Elizabeth Cady Stanton, one of the women who had not been allowed to participate in the London antislavery conference of 1840, wrote:

"I now fully understood the practical difficulties most women had to contend with. . . . The wearied, anxious look of the majority of women impressed me with the strong feeling that some measures should be taken."

In 1848 Stanton, with Lucretia Mott, organized a **Women's Rights Convention** at Seneca Falls, New York. Mott delivered the opening and closing addresses. The delegates to the convention issued a *Declaration of Sentiments* modeled on the Declaration of Independence. What better model could they select? Certainly the purposes of the colonists in writing the Declaration of Independence had been similar to those of the delegates. Both sought greater independence.

Often the delegates chose words that echoed the Declaration of Independence: "When in the course of human events" and "We hold these truths to be self-evident." But they also created a document that stated their views and purposes: "it becomes necessary for one

[1]From *The Liberator*, January 26, 1838

The Granger Collection, New York

portion of the family of man to assume among the people of the earth a position different from that which they have hereto occupied" and "all men *and women* are created equal."

Just as the first part of the Declaration of Independence had listed grievances of the colonists, the first part of this **Seneca Falls Declaration** listed the grievances of women. The history of mankind, it said, "is a history of repeated injuries . . . on the part of man toward woman." These injuries included denials of the right to vote, the right to equal educational opportunity, and the right to own property. The second part contained resolutions aimed at righting the wrongs listed in the first part. It closed with the demand that women be given "all the rights and privileges which belong to them as citizens of the United States."

Similar meetings were soon being held throughout the nation. In the 1850s several national feminist conventions took place. Women were on the move. Their cause won many new supporters. The most important of these was Susan B. Anthony of New York.

In the 1850s Anthony organized campaigns on behalf of equal pay for women teachers and for equal property rights. Her efforts encouraged other feminists to continue the struggle. Soon Massachusetts and Indiana passed more liberal divorce laws. In 1860 New York gave women the right to sue in court and to control their earnings and property. But nowhere were women able to win the right to vote. They made some progress during the Age of Reform, but the vote was not yet theirs. 🔽

A newspaper cartoonist sketched the Women's Rights Convention with the men in the balconies yawning, stretching, and jeering while many of the women hold up their heads and scowl. Below is Lucretia Mott, who organized and led the convention.

National Portrait Gallery

Return to the Preview & Review on page 477.

Women and Reform 483

2. REFORMS IN EDUCATION

Use these questions to guide your reading. Answer the questions after completing Section 2.
Understanding Issues, Events, & Ideas. Describe early education in the United States, using the following words: home school, church school, dame school, adventure school, normal school, *McGuffey's Eclectic Reader,* "the three R's," Lancasterian system.
1. For what reforms in education did Horace Mann work?
2. Why did educators and politicians like the Lancasterian system of education?
3. How did reformers like Mann want to change education?
Thinking Critically. Do you agree with educational reformers of the mid-1800s who said that "democracy could not exist unless all people could read and write"? Why or why not?

Education in Early America

As you have read, each section of the country developed a distinctive educational system. In each case education was viewed as the responsibility of the family rather than the government. Parents or other relatives taught children at home. In most of these **home schools,** education was restricted to studying the Bible or an almanac to master reading and writing and to learning basic arithmetic. Children who had no relatives who could read and write received little or no education.

As the nation grew, rural children and those on the frontier continued to learn at home or in **church schools,** where they were taught by the minister and his wife. Children in towns and cities often attended **dame schools.** Women instructors taught basic reading and writing skills in these schools and charged a nominal fee. The teachers in the dame schools often could barely read and write themselves, so the quality of instruction remained low.

"New England Country School" was painted in about 1878 by Winslow Homer. By then the movement for free public schools had placed schooling in the hands of men and women who were prepared to help children rise in the world.

Addison Gallery of American Art, Phillips Academy, Andover, Massachusetts

Young girls in towns and cities often attended **adventure schools** after completing dame schools. Located in the homes of the instructors, adventure schools stressed music, dancing, drawing, needlework, and handicrafts. In contrast, boys went to private or public grammar schools where they studied Latin and Greek. Boys from wealthier families then enrolled in a college or university where they often trained to become ministers or lawyers.

Free Public Schools

Unlike the women's rights movement, the fight for public education made a great deal of progress during the Age of Reform. Before the 1820s only a handful of communities maintained free schools. By the 1850s villages, towns, and cities all over the nation had established such schools. Education had become a public responsibility.

Educational reformers argued that a democracy could not exist unless all people could read and write. Schools would train students to be patriotic, hardworking, law-abiding citizens. In addition, ordinary working men and women supported public education because they hoped that schools would enable their children to rise in the world. The growth of public education for all had far-reaching effects. By 1860, 90 percent of all free adults in America could read and write.

This was largely due to the immense success of the textbooks of Noah Webster, later famous for his American dictionary. His first *Spelling Book* was published in 1783 when Webster was a young schoolteacher in Goshen, New York. Webster emphasized American forms of usage rather than British and wrote a patriotic preface urging Americans to read their own literature. Webster's *Reader* included speeches of the leaders of the Revolution. Some 15 million copies of the *Speller* were sold in the next five decades. The *Reader* was also a best seller.

Another textbook used in many early American schools was Caleb Bingham's *The Columbian Orator.* It was a collection of "original and selected pieces, calculated to improve youth and others in the ornamental and useful art of eloquence," or the art of public speaking. It taught specific speaking skills such as pronunciation, gesturing, and inflection (changes in the loudness and pitch of the voice). It also emphasized the values important to all Americans— freedom, hard work, and respect for human rights. Students read aloud the selections, such as Washington's speech to the French ambassador in 1796.

66 Born, Sir, in a land of liberty; having early learned its value; having engaged in a perilous [dangerous] conflict to defend it; having, in a word, devoted the best years of my life to secure it [liberty] a permanent establishment in my own country; my anxious recollections, my sympathetic feel-

National Portrait Gallery

Noah Webster declared in 1783, "America must be as independent in literature as she is in politics, as famous for arts as for arms." He spent his life molding an American language as part of a growing American culture. How did Webster's work help Americans feel pride in themselves?

ings, and my best wishes are irresistibly excited, whensoever, in any country, I see an oppressed nation unfurl [open] the banners of freedom. But above all, the events of the French revolution have produced the deepest solicitude [fondness], as well as the highest admiration. To call your nation brave, were to pronounce but common praise. WONDERFUL PEOPLE! ages to come will read with astonishment the history of your brilliant exploits. . . .[1] **99**

The first American history textbook was published by John M'Culloch in 1787, when the ink was scarcely dry on the Constitution. Jedidiah Morse soon followed with textbooks on American geography. His geographies described the nation's physical features and told the story of American life. Such textbooks helped students feel great pride in being Americans. They also helped shape Americans' view of what it was to be an American.

In 1836 William McGuffey published the first of *McGuffey's Eclectic Readers,* which taught moral lessons as well as reading. The following lessons are from the reader used by eighth graders[2]:

LESSON VII

RULE.—Be careful to pronounce every syllable distinctly and not join the words together.

EXERCISES UNDER THE RULE. To be read over several times by all the students.

We constructed *an arc* and began the problem.

The *surf beat* heavily.

Arm! warriors, arm!

Return to thy dwelling, *all lovely return.* . . .

The Whale Ship.—PROV. LIT. JOURNAL

1. They who go down to the sea in ships pursue a perilous vocation, and well deserve the prayers which are offered for them in the churches. It is a hard life—full of danger, and of strange attraction. The seaman rarely abandons the glorious sea. It requires, however, a pretty firm spirit, both to brave the ordinary dangers of the deep, and to carry on war with its mightiest tenants [whales]. . . .

QUESTIONS.—1. What is the character of the seaman's profession? Particularly of whalemen? 2. What are the most common accidents to which whalers are liable? . . .

ERRORS.—*Ord-na-ry* for or-di-na-ry; *pur-ty* or *per-ty* for pretty; *vict-ry* for vic-to-ry.

SPELL AND DEFINE.—(1) zealously, indisputably, glowingly, . . . (2) proximity, vanquished, leviathan. . . .

[1]From *The Columbian Orator* by Caleb Bingham
[2]From *The Eclectic Fourth Reader* by William H. McGuffey

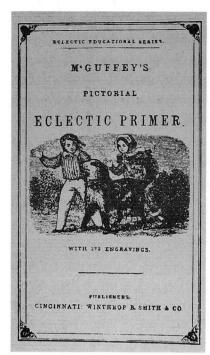

The Granger Collection, New York

Canajoharie Library & Art Gallery,
Canajoharie, New York

Winslow Homer was best known for his watercolors. "Homework" offers this portrait of a young pupil reading his lessons while the sun is still strong. Perhaps he is reading a lesson from a McGuffey's Reader such as the one on the left.

LESSON LXXVII

RULE.—Be careful to pronounce the little words, like *a, the, and, in,* etc., distinctly, and not to join them to the next word.

No Excellence without Labor.—WIRT.

1. The education, moral and intellectual, of every individual, must be, chiefly, his own work. Rely upon it, that the ancients were right—both in morals and intellect—we give their final shape to our characters, and thus become, emphatically, the architects of our own fortune. . . .

LESSON CVI

RULE.—When similar sounds come at the end of one word, and at the beginning of the next word, they must not be blended into one.

EXERCISE.—He sink*s s*orrowing to the tomb.
　　　　Man love*s s*ociety. . . .

Anthony's Oration over Caesar's Dead Body
　　　　SHAKESPEARE.

1. Friends, Romans, countrymen! Lend me your ears
   I come to bury Caesar, not to praise him.
   The evil that men do, lives after them;
   The good is oft interred with their bones. . . .

Reforms in Education　487

Generations of textbooks were modeled on McGuffey. Each lesson taught a specific skill, and students answered questions at the end. Each skill built on those already taught. The readers were "eclectic," by which McGuffey meant "selected from the best of various sources." They contained Bible quotations, excerpts, poetry, essays, and articles. Each was chosen partly for the skill it taught and partly for the message it carried. Eventually McGuffey sold some 122 million copies of these books.

Horace Mann

National Portrait Gallery

Horace Mann was a great leader in the efforts to improve public education. How did he use the Age of Reform to build on Massachusetts' tradition for education?

The effort to improve public education was particularly strong in Massachusetts. The early Puritans had established elementary and secondary schools in all but the smallest of their towns. Now, in the Age of Reform, the state built on this strong Puritan foundation.

Much of the credit belongs to Horace Mann, a lawyer and state legislator. When Massachusetts established a state board of education in 1837, Mann became its secretary. He worked for laws that required school attendance. He called for special schools to train teachers. He favored higher teacher salaries and better school equipment. Nowhere is his vision better stated than in his 1848 annual report to the Massachusetts Board of Education:

❝ Our means of education are the grand machinery by which the 'raw material' of human nature can be worked up into inventors and discoverers, into skilled artisans and scientific farmers, into scholars and jurists [judges], into the founders of benevolent institutions [those organized for the purpose of doing good], and the great expounders of ethical and theological science [philosophers]. By means of an early education, those embryos of talent may be quickened [made alive], which will solve the difficult problems of political and economical law; . . .[1] ❞

Mann alerted Americans to the importance of free public education. His tireless efforts earned him the proud title of "the Father of American public schools."

[1]From *Annual Reports on Education, 1837—49* by Horace Mann

In 1839 Mann founded the first teacher training institute in the United States. Similar schools were soon established throughout the country. These institutes were called **normal schools,** the word coming from *norm,* meaning a "model" or "standard."

Before 1839 teachers had rarely received any direct training. There were no established qualifications a teacher had to meet. One man being interviewed for a job in a mining town was asked only, "Do you retain a clear recollection of the twenty-six letters of the alphabet?" Apparently that was all he was expected to know to "educate" the local children.

Mann was also interested in building new schools. He was exaggerating only a little when he said that "there is more physical suffering endured by our children" in badly constructed schoolhouses "than by prisoners in our jails."

Down through the 1840s wood-frame, one-room "little red schoolhouses" were the rule. In these small buildings 60 or more children of all ages were crowded into one classroom. A single teacher had to deal with first graders and teenagers at the same time. It was difficult to learn with so many distractions. But in the Boston of Horace Mann's day there were few schoolhouses of any kind. Most classes were held in stores and cellars.

By modern standards the best schools of the 1830s and 1840s were very uncomfortable. They had no washrooms. Students sat on narrow, backless benches. Yet, thanks to Horace Mann, by 1848 Massachusetts had built 50 well-equipped and comfortable public schools. Other states soon followed Massachusetts' lead.

The School Curriculum

The main subjects students of the early 1800s learned were known as **"the three R's"**—reading, writing, and 'rithmetic. They were taught quite differently than they are today. Before the 1840s most American schools used a teaching method developed in England by Joseph Lancaster. Lancaster used a monitor system in which teachers instructed older students who, in turn, taught younger pupils their lessons.

The **Lancasterian system** appealed to American educators and politicians because it provided instruction at the lowest possible cost. It did nothing, however, to encourage individual growth or to open the imagination.

In the 1840s and 1850s some educators began to question the Lancasterian system. Reformers like Horace Mann wanted to make education more exciting. Students should be encouraged to give free play to their imaginations. But like all educators, the reformers agreed that the schools' main purpose should be to build character and train children to become good citizens. 🖅

Return to the Preview & Review on page 484.

Use these questions to guide your reading. Answer the questions after completing Section 3.
Understanding Issues, Events, & Ideas. Use the following words to explain religious reform movements: ideal community, Shakers, Amana community, Oneida community, transcendentalism, Second Great Awakening.
1. How did most Americans view ideal communities?
2. What was life like in a Shaker community?
3. How was God as portrayed by the preachers of the Second Great Awakening different from God as portrayed in the First Great Awakening?
Thinking Critically. In his essay "Self-Reliance" Emerson said, "Nothing is at last sacred but the integrity of your own mind." Find in the dictionary any words that you do not know. Then, explain what you think this sentence means.

3. RELIGION AND REFORM

Ideal Communities

Relying on education to improve society was likely to be a slow process. Few educational leaders were calling for drastic change. Yet many reformers were dreaming of totally reorganizing society. Some thought it wrong that a few people were much richer than all the others. They hoped to create a world where wealth would be shared equally.

Others thought that family life drew people into a small, closed circle and shut others out. They believed that people should live in community houses and that children should be reared and trained in common, not by their individual parents.

Most Americans considered such schemes foolish and unworkable, if not downright dangerous. Some reformers tended therefore to establish small communities in thinly settled parts of the country. The huge tracts of cheap, undeveloped land still to be found in the United States made it relatively easy to do so. Between 1820 and 1850 at least 58 **ideal communities** were founded.

Many of these were very short-lived. Some lasted many years. A few evolved into institutions that still survive. The Mormons went west to Utah for much the same reason that the Puritans had come to Massachusetts Bay. Both groups wished to practice their religion without interference from people in their country who considered them dangerous and wrongheaded. The settlement on the Great Salt Lake was the Mormons' ideal community, organized according to their distinct beliefs.

Many other ideal communities were created by religious sects. One of the first to do so was the **Shakers.** This sect was founded by an Englishwoman, "Mother Ann" Lee. Mother Ann believed that she was God. She predicted that the world would soon come to an end. There was no point, therefore, in anyone having children.

Life in Shaker communities, which were called "families," was strictly regulated by a group of elders, half of them men, half women. Members wore simple black clothes. The two sexes lived separately. Everyone was expected to work very hard. All money belonged to the group. Contacts with the outside world were few.

Despite these strict rules the Shakers seemed to enjoy life. Singing, listening to sermons, work itself were all seen as serious religious activities and profoundly satisfying group experiences. New recruits entered the sect. When time passed without the world coming to an end, the Shakers began to adopt orphans in order to renew the membership. By the 1840s there were 20 Shaker communities in America.

The **Amana community,** founded by a German immigrant, Christian Metz, and the **Oneida community,** founded by John Humphrey

The Granger Collection, New York

Noyes, were two other important communities of this type. Metz founded his settlement in western New York and later moved it to Iowa. The Noyes group began in Vermont and eventually settled in Oneida, New York. Both prospered. They owned much rich farmland and also developed manufacturing.

People who joined these communities made large personal sacrifices. Obviously most of them were deeply committed to the goals of the group. They were hardworking and skillful. Shaker furniture, simple and graceful, is still highly prized. The handiwork of both Oneida and Amana has evolved into modern manufacturing companies, Oneida making silverware, Amana electrical appliances.

These colonial Shakers at worship trembled and chanted wordless songs. A church leader claimed that he had seen this form of worship in a vision of Heaven.

The Transcendental Spirit

Literature and philosophy, rather than religion, were what most interested a group of New Englanders who called themselves the Transcendental Club. Ralph Waldo Emerson, who began his career as a Unitarian minister, was the best known of the group. One of his followers was Henry David Thoreau, the author of *Walden* (1854), which recounts Thoreau's attempt to live simply and in harmony with nature at Walden Pond in Massachusetts. Another follower, Bronson Alcott, became the founder of a cooperative vegetarian community called Fruitlands. When it failed he became largely

The Bettman Archive

National Portrait Gallery

National Portrait Gallery

Three leaders in the Transcendental movement, from left, Bronson Alcott, Ralph Waldo Emerson, and Henry David Thoreau. What meaning do you give to their phrase, "Hitch your wagon to a star"?

dependent on the success of his daughter, Louisa May Alcott, author of *Little Women.*

Transcendentalism is hard to define. Its central idea was that people could transcend, or rise above, reason by having faith in themselves. "Hitch your wagon to a star," was the advice of one of the transcendentalists.

In Emerson's most famous essay, "Self-Reliance," he made these and many other observations:

> **"**Trust thyself: every heart vibrates to that iron string.
> Whoso would be a man must be a nonconformist.
> A foolish consistency is the hobgoblin of little minds. . . .
> We are afraid of truth, afraid of fortune, afraid of death, and afraid of each other.
> Nothing is at last sacred but the integrity of your own mind.**"**

The transcendentalists were idealists, warm and affirmative, who believed in the power of reason and in basic human goodness. They celebrated aspects already so much a part of the American character—individualism and self-reliance.

Yet although they were optimists, the transcendentalists did not ignore the problems in American society. They criticized governments, laws, and social institutions. They did not join reform associations, but they did contribute to the spirit of reform. They believed people knew right from wrong, good from bad, and would seek the right and the good if given the chance. Asked Emerson, "What is man born for but to be a Re-former, a Re-maker of what man has made; a renouncer of lies; a restorer of truth and good? . . ."

The Second Great Awakening

The religious views of the first American colonists changed very little with time. The North was still overwhelmingly Protestant. But most

Protestant sects took a more tolerant view of those who disagreed with them than had the Puritans. Early in the 1820s a **Second Great Awakening** broke out in various sections of the country. The First Awakening had been a force for toleration. Although preachers like George Whitefield and Jonathan Edwards were hard on sinners, all believers were invited to hear their message.

The preachers of the Second Great Awakening were even more tolerant because their message was more optimistic. The most influential preacher of the movement was Charles Grandison Finney. Finney believed revivals were essential to spreading the word of God. He claimed:

The Granger Collection, New York

Charles Grandison Finney stirred his listeners with a vision of a democratic Heaven. How did the Second Great Awakening differ from the first?

❝ Almost all the religion in the world has been produced by revivals. God has found it necessary to take advantage of the excitability there is in mankind, to produce powerful excitements among them, before he can lead them to obey. Men are so spiritually sluggish, there are so many things to lead their minds off from religion, and to oppose the purpose of the Gospel, so that it is necessary to raise an excitement among them, till the tide rises so high as to sweep away the opposing obstacles. . . .[1]❞

In his sermons Finney described a democratic Heaven not unlike the United States of America. "God always allows His children as much liberty as they are prepared to enjoy," he declared. He preached of the duty of people to take the "right ground . . . on all subjects of practical morality which come up for decision from time to time." Finney inspired Theodore Dwight Weld and other revivalists who preached the gospel while speaking out against slavery, an institution they felt was morally wrong. Another leading revivalist, William Ellery Channing, a Boston Unitarian, did not preach about an angry God but spoke instead about what an exceptionally fine being Christ was.

These ministers preserved the Puritans' concern for high moral standards and social improvements, but played down the passions that had once driven men and women to found new colonies. They advanced the comforting belief that God would provide salvation for all.

The Second Great Awakening swept through the West with special force. James McGready preached that sin was wrong but all who repented could be saved. Yet McGready's visions were as frightening as Jonathan Edwards' before him. One description says:

❝ He could so array Hell before the wicked that they would tremble and quake, imagining a lake of fire and brimstone yawning to overtake them.❞

[1]From *Lectures on Revivals of Religion* by Charles G. Finney

The Granger Collection, New York

At camp meetings the speaker drew his listeners forward with visions of heaven until some were overcome by shame for their present lives. The evangelism of these meetings is still widely popular, although the greatest audience now watches on cable television stations.

During the Second Awakening frontier people flocked to religious camp meetings, which often lasted for days. Men wept and cried to Heaven. Disciples of McGready, such as Finis Ewing, traveled endlessly through the West bringing their message to isolated farms as well as large camp meetings. They converted sinners by the thousands. Others, like Peter Cartwright, a Methodist, traveled the revival circuit in the West. One biographer wrote of Cartwright:

“ His self-reliance, his readiness with tongue and fist, his quick sense of humor, all made him dear to the hearts of the frontier. If . . . intruders attempted to break up his meetings, he was quick to meet force with force and seems to have been uniformly victorious in these physical encounters. ”

Converts flocked to several Protestant sects, most notably the Presbyterian, Baptist, and Methodist, during this period of religious enthusiasm. Others joined one of the new religious groups—such as the Mormons and the Adventists—that arose. Throughout the country church attendance increased. This Second Great Awakening also advanced the cause of moral and social reform, which became a vital function of churches all over America. As Finney said, "Away with the idea that Christians can remain neutral and keep still, and yet enjoy the approbation [approval] and blessing of God."

Return to the Preview & Review on page 490.

4. THE ROMANTIC AGE

By the second quarter of the 19th century American writers and painters had become part of the Romantic movement. The Romantic movement had begun in Europe as a revolt against the cold-blooded logic of the Age of Reason and its view of nature governed by fixed scientific laws. Romantics emphasized their feelings and natural instincts over reason and logic. Romantics often viewed nature as a beautiful mysterious teacher. One of the founders of the Romantic movement, the English poet William Wordsworth, wrote:

> **"** One impulse from a vernal wood
> May teach you more of man,
> Of moral evil and of good,
> Than all the sages can.**"**

The **Romantic Age** began in Europe but seemed particularly American in its praise of ordinary people, individualism, and emotion.

Edgar Allan Poe

Edgar Allan Poe was born in Boston in 1809 and became in his short lifetime a living example of the anguished genius that Romantics often liked to portray. An orphan who had been raised and then rejected by a wealthy Virginian, John Allan, Poe spent much of his life trying to regain Allan's favor. He won appointment to West Point but was discharged for "gross neglect of duty." He sometimes drank to excess, and once attempted to poison himself. Yet he proved to be a marvelous editor, critic, and poet. In the opinion of many, he invented the detective story. His classics include "The Murders in the Rue Morgue" and "The Purloined Letter." He was one of the first to write what we today call science fiction, and he was a master of the horror tale with such works as "The Pit and the Pendulum," and "The Cask of Amontillado." Poe's poetic description of his childhood reveals much of the romantic in him:

> **"** From childhood's hour I have not been
> As others were—I have not seen
> As others saw—I could not bring
> My passions from a common spring—
> From the same source I have not taken
> My sorrow—I could not awaken
> My heart to joy at the same tone—
> And all that I loved—*I loved alone*—**"**

Nathaniel Hawthorne and Herman Melville

Nathaniel Hawthorne was born in Salem, Massachusetts, where women were executed as witches in the early days of America. He

Use these questions to guide your reading. Answer the questions after completing Section 4.
Understanding Issues, Events, & Ideas. In your own words, explain the historical significance of the Romantic Age.
1. How had artists during the Age of Reason viewed nature? How was the view of the Romantics different?
2. How did the experiences of Hawthorne and Melville influence their works?
3. What made Whitman's *Leaves of Grass* startling and original? How did Whitman and Dickinson differ?
4. Who were the writers responsible for "the flowering of New England"?
Thinking Critically. 1. If you had the opportunity to meet and talk with Poe, Hawthorne, Melville, Whitman, or Dickinson, who would you choose? Why? **2.** Write a biographical sketch one of the authors discussed in this section.

The Bettman Archive

Edgar Allan Poe, whose poems and stories told of mystery and horror, was the Stephen King of the 1840s. He is also credited with inventing the detective story, another popular literary form today.

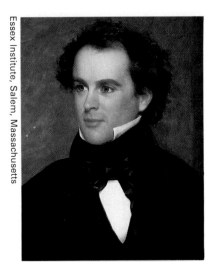

Essex Institute, Salem, Massachusetts

Berkshire Athenaeum

Nathaniel Hawthorne in 1840 was a handsome young author yet to make his reputation. His friend Herman Melville, shown in 1847, would soon begin his masterpiece Moby Dick.

was fascinated by the Puritan past of New England and its continuing influence on the people of his own generation. One of his greatest novels was *The Scarlet Letter* (1850), in which he urged his readers to condemn not sin so much as those who presume to judge the sinner. Another was *The House of the Seven Gables* (1851), a gripping account of the decay of an old New England family. The house in Salem may be visited today. One of his best-known short stories is "My Kinsman, Major Molineux," in which a young man learns to make his way in the world on his own merit.

In 1850, while writing *The House of the Seven Gables,* Hawthorne was introduced by his publisher to another writer in the midst of a novel. This was Herman Melville, who was writing *Moby Dick.* The two became good friends. Melville's life was quite unlike Hawthorne's quiet New England upbringing. As a boy Melville went to sea on a whaler, but jumped ship in the South Seas, where he lived among a tribe of cannibals. Later he became a beachcomber in Tahiti. When he returned to the United States in 1844 he began writing about his adventures. His first book was *Typee* (1846), a description of the South Seas. A sequel, *Omoo* (1847), quickly followed.

Melville's most famous work is *Moby Dick* (1851). Against the background of a whaling voyage—and nobody has described whaling better—he dealt with the problems of good and evil, courage and cowardice, faith, stubbornness, and pride. In the character Captain Ahab—driven to destroy the great white whale, Moby Dick, Melville created one of the greatest figures of American fiction.

Wall Street, not the sea, is the setting of Melville's best-known short story, "Bartleby the Scrivener." In this tale a mild-mannered law clerk finds the courage to tell his employer, "I prefer not to be a little reasonable"—a perfect response for the Romantic Age.

Walt Whitman and Emily Dickinson

The two great romantic poets of the 19th century are Walt Whitman and Emily Dickinson. Whitman, who was born in 1819, was truly a "common man," a supporter of Andrew Jackson, thoroughly at home with tradesmen and laborers. But he was surely not an ordinary man. His collection of poems, *Leaves of Grass* (1855), the last great outpouring of the American romantic movement, was startling and original in form and content with its free verse and plain language. In the poet's words:

> **“** I celebrate myself, and sing myself,
> And what I assume you shall assume,
> For every atom belonging to me as good belongs to
> you. **”**

His remarkable gift of catching everyday speech and making it

The Granger Collection, New York

poetic is evident in lines like these in which even the Earth is an equal to this celebration of democracy.

> Earth! you seem to look for something at my hands
> Say, old top-knot, what do you want?
>
> I bequeath myself to the dirt to grow from the grass
> I love,
> If you want me again look for me under your boot-
> soles.

What a contrast is Emily Dickinson, who was born in Amherst, Massachusetts, in 1830. Shy, reclusive, she would say to Whitman's celebration of self: "I'm nobody! Who are you?/ Are you—Nobody too?" Yet these words betray the wondrous gifts of the poet. Only after her death were her poems published, giving us images of America that will be remembered forever. She wrote:

> This is my letter to the world
> That never wrote to Me—
> The simple news that Nature told
> With tender Majesty.
>
> Her Message is committed
> To hands I cannot see—
> For love of her—Sweet—countrymen—
> Judge tenderly—of me.[1]

[1]In *The Poems of Emily Dickinson,* edited by Thomas H. Johnson

The Flowering of New England

Besides Emerson, Thoreau, Hawthorne, and Dickinson, many of the great figures of American literature before the Civil War were New Englanders. Henry Wadsworth Longfellow's fame came from poems like "The Village Blacksmith," "Paul Revere's Ride," *The Courtship of Miles Standish,* and *The Song of Hiawatha.* His galloping verses have been recited by generations of schoolchildren: "Listen, my children, and you shall hear/ Of the midnight ride of Paul Revere."

Also prominent in this "flowering of New England," as one critic put it, was John Greenleaf Whittier, a poet as popular in his own day as Longfellow. Whittier was an abolitionist and active in politics. But his poetry is little quoted nowadays. "The Barefoot Boy" was one of his most popular. "Blessings on thee, little man," it begins, "Barefoot boy with cheek of tan."

More weighty was James Russell Lowell, the first editor of the *Atlantic Monthly.* He wrote humorous stories to satirize the Mexican War. Another widely known poet and essayist was Oliver Wendell Holmes, remembered for "The Chambered Nautilus" and "Old Ironsides," a poem about the U.S.S. *Constitution.*

The Granger Collection, New York

Walt Whitman in about 1850 (top) scarcely resembles the bearded poet we know from many later photographs. Emily Dickinson kept to herself so much that we are fortunate to have her likeness at all.

Return to the Preview & Review on page 495.

The Romantic Age 497

The Granger Collection, New York

Brown Brothers

Dorothea Lynde Dix, left, and Helen Keller and Anne Sullivan, right.

Preview & Review

Use these questions to guide your reading. Answer the questions after completing Section 5.
Understanding Issues, Events, & Ideas. Using the following words, cite the important attempts to improve society: Perkins Institution, juvenile delinquency, almshouse, house of refuge, Children's Aid Society, temperance, total abstinence, prohibition, National Trades' Union.
1. How did Samuel Howe help blind people? How did Dorothea Dix work to help the insane?
2. Why did reformers want children taken out of almshouses?
3. What was the high point of the temperance campaign?
4. What reforms did Seth Luther seek for factory workers?
Thinking Critically. 1. Charles Brace said, "The best of all Asylums for the outcast child is a farmers's home." Do you agree with Brace? Do you think Brace's statement applies today? 2. If you were a reformer in the mid-1800s, what aspect of society would you reform? Why?

5. IMPROVING SOCIETY

Helping the Disadvantaged

Many people were unwilling to live in isolated communities and abandon all the customs and patterns of ordinary life. They were nonetheless sincerely interested in improving society. Some devoted their energies to helping people in need. Samuel Gridley Howe, a Boston doctor, specialized in the education of the blind. In the 1830s he founded a school, the **Perkins Institution.** He developed a method for printing books with raised type so that blind people could learn to "read" with their fingertips. Howe's greatest achievement was teaching Laura Bridgman, a child who was both blind and deaf, to read in this way and to communicate with others through signs called a manual alphabet. Another of his pupils, Anne Sullivan, learned the manual alphabet to communicate with Laura. She later became the teacher of Helen Keller, a remarkable woman who lost her sight and hearing as an infant but became a famous writer and lecturer.

Another Massachusetts reformer, Dorothea Dix, practically revolutionized the treatment of the mentally ill. Dix was a schoolteacher. One day in 1841 she was asked to teach a Sunday school class in a jail in Cambridge, Massachusetts. When she went to the jail, she discovered to her horror that insane and feeble-minded people were being kept there and treated like ordinary criminals. She launched a crusade to improve their treatment. In 1843 she completed her investigation by presenting to the Massachusetts legislature a shocking but true testimony on the conditions she found.

> **"** I come as the advocate of helpless, forgotten, insane, and idiotic men and women. I proceed, gentlemen, to briefly call your attention to the present state of insane persons confined in this Commonwealth [Massachusetts], in cages, closets, cellars, stalls, pens! Chained, naked, beaten with rods, and lashed into obedience.[1] **"**

Thereafter, Dix devoted her life to improving the care of prisoners and of the insane. She visited prisons all over the country and wrote reports describing conditions and exposing their faults. Dix insisted that insanity should be treated as a disease and that it could be cured. Through her efforts many states set up asylums for the care of the mentally ill.

Her crusade also lent force to that of prison reformers. These reformers feared social unrest and believed criminals could be rehabilitated to become useful members of society. They successfully called for prisons where first offenders were separated from hardened criminals and for detention schools for juvenile delinquents. But these new prisons stressed solitary confinement and strict discipline, and they probably did little to rehabilitate people who found themselves inside. Over the years the debate on the purpose of prisons would rage. Do they exist solely to separate wrongdoers from society? Or should they be places where criminals are reformed, to be returned to society? The debate continues today. Nonetheless, the prison system that evolved became a model for prison systems throughout the world; Alexis de Tocqueville, for example, came to examine American prisons for the French minister of justice.

Child Care

The social problem of **juvenile delinquency** was also attacked by reformers. As cities grew larger, an increasing number of children and teenagers began to get into trouble with the law. When a boy or girl was caught stealing, for example, the "criminal" was handled the same way that adult thieves were. If convicted, they were thrown into the same jails where older convicts were kept.

Many other children who had not committed crimes wandered homeless about the cities. They were orphans or runaways or youngsters who had been abandoned by their parents. When found, these children were often put into the local poorhouse, called an **almshouse.** Again they were kept along with adults, many of them tramps, drunkards, and similar types.

Reformers realized that this system only increased the chances that young delinquents and wanderers would become dangerous criminals when they grew up. As one put it, the jails turned "little Devils" into "great ones." Instead, the delinquent children should

[1]From Old South Leaflet No. 148 in *Old South Leaflets,* vol. VI

be reformed and the homeless ones protected and taught a trade so that they would be able to earn their livings.

To accomplish these goals, **houses of refuge** were founded as early as the 1820s in New York, Boston, and Philadelphia. Life in these houses was hard, discipline strict. The children rose at dawn, dressed, and were marched off to the washroom. After passing inspection to make sure they were neat and clean, they had an hour or so of lessons. Only then was there a recess for breakfast.

The rest of the day, except for the noon break, was spent working in shops. The boys made such things as cane chair seats, nails, and candles. The girls spent the time sewing. Work ended at about five o'clock. Then, after a light supper, the children marched back to school. The evening classes went on until bedtime.

This system was very harsh by modern standards. Children who violated the rules were often beaten, even put in solitary confinement. But it was a true reform. These houses of refuge represented the first attempt to treat delinquent children differently from adult criminals.

Gradually some of the people who studied juvenile delinquency began to realize that in many cases the children were more victims than criminals. The terrible poverty of the slums made it difficult for them to lead decent, normal lives.

One such person was Charles Loring Brace, one of the first American social workers. Brace founded the **Children's Aid Society** of New York in 1853. The society opened lodging houses where homeless boys and girls could live without actually being confined as they were in a house of refuge. It also established trade schools.

Brace persuaded manufacturers to give some of the children jobs. But his main goal was to be able to relocate homeless children with farm families. He believed that the terrible conditions of slum life in the cities was the main reason why delinquent children were getting into trouble. "The best of all Asylums for the outcast child," he said, is a "farmer's home."

The Attack on "Demon Rum"

Some reformers worked to improve the training of the deaf. Others worked for world peace. Still others tried to get citizens to give up what the reformers considered bad habits, such as drinking or playing games on Sundays. (Many critics considered these people not reformers but busybodies.)

The campaign against alcohol was the most important attempt made to control the personal behavior of citizens. The effort to restrict drinking began as a call for **temperance.** It was a fight against drunkenness, not against drinking in moderation. But it soon became a campaign for **total abstinence**—drinking no alcohol at all—and the **prohibition,** or outlawing, of the manufacture and sale of alcoholic beverages. Those who favored prohibition called drinkers sinners

Albright-Knox Art Gallery, Buffalo

"Buffalo Newsboy" was painted in 1893. At this time boys and girls in trouble with the law were jailed with adults. Homeless children wandered city streets. Have we solved these problems of the Age of the Reform in the 1990s?

The Granger Collection, New York

and potential criminals. Again it was Reverend Charles G. Finney who led the effort.

The members of the American Temperance Union, which was founded in 1826, went about the land lecturing and distributing pamphlets. Despite the name they were outright prohibitionists. They urged drinkers to "sign the pledge"—that is, to promise in writing that they would give up alcohol completely. They also formed youth temperance groups to educate young people to the "evils" of alcohol. These clubs, similar to today's Students Against Drunk Driving (S.A.D.D.) groups, even sang a song that carried their message:

A popular series of engravings made in the 19th century showed a family destroyed by alcohol. In the pleasant family scene on the left we watch as the husband invites his wary wife to join him in a friendly drink. In the scene at right, the bottle has taken its toll. While the children huddle together their father dozes drunkenly. Meanwhile the mother trades household goods to buy more liquor. Now the table is bare, the cupboard empty, the cat scrawny, and the fireplace cold. Would these engravings be good propaganda for members of the Temperance Society to take "the pledge"? Why?

> " This youthful band
> Do with our hand
> The pledge now sign—
> To drink no wine,
>
> Nor brandy red
> To turn the head,
> nor whiskey hot,
> That makes the sot [drunkard],
>
> Nor fiery rum
> To turn our home
> Into a hell
> Where none can dwell
> Whence peace would fly
>
> Where hope would die
> And love expire
> 'Mid such a fire:—
> So here we pledge perpetual hate
> To all that can intoxicate.[1] "

[1]From *A History of the American People* by Stephen Thernstrom

The campaign reached a high point in 1851 when the state of Maine outlawed the manufacture and sale of alcoholic drinks. The person most responsible for the passage of this law, Neal Dow, was a manufacturer who became alarmed because many of the men who worked for him were ruining their lives with drink.

Economic Reform

There were also reformers who wished to change the American economic system. Most people in the nation were better off by far than the average European. But some were not. Many who worked hard had not been able to rise above poverty. Furthermore, as the economy expanded, some people were growing very rich. The gap between wealthy merchants and manufacturers and people of ordinary income seemed to be widening.

Reformers found these trends to be alarming. William Leggett, a New York newspaper editor, asked:

> 66 Does a man become wiser, stronger, or more virtuous and patriotic because he has a fine house? Does he love his country the better because he has a French cook and a box at the opera? 99

Leggett blamed the growing gap between rich and poor on what he somewhat vaguely called "concentrated money power." He supported Andrew Jackson's attack on the Second Bank of the United States. And he favored reducing tariffs because high tariffs increased the profits of the manufacturers and caused prices to rise.

Leggett's policies were less drastic than those put forth by some other economic reformers. Thomas Skidmore, for example, proposed that rich people not be allowed to leave their wealth to their children. He even proposed that all the personal property of all the people in the country be taken over by the government. It would then be spread among the people in equal shares.

George Henry Evans, publisher of a newspaper called *The Working Man's Advocate,* had a more practical suggestion. Evans's slogan was "Vote Yourself a Farm." He wanted the government to limit the amount of land that any one person could own. He urged Congress to stop the sale of unoccupied land in the West. Publicly owned lands should be divided up into farm plots and given to citizens who were willing to cultivate them. One land reform statement ran:

> 66 Are you an American citizen? Then you are a joint owner of public lands. Why not take enough of your property to provide yourself a home? Why not vote yourself a farm? 99

William Leggett was one who struggled to close the gap between rich and poor in Jacksonian America. And what of today? Has the gap between rich and poor widened or narrowed, in your opinion?

Efforts to Help Workers

One of William Leggett's favorite proposals was that workers should organize into unions. Although there were some labor organizations during the colonial period, unions had always been considered illegal. They were thought to be conspiracies, plots organized by workers to "control" wages at the expense of employers and the public. Yet by the 1830s many skilled workers were founding unions. In 1834 several trade groups even managed to create a national organization, the **National Trades' Union.** Finally, in 1842, a Massachusetts judge, Lemuel Shaw, ruled in the case of *Commonwealth v. Hunt* that labor unions were not conspiracies unless the members engaged in specific criminal activity. "For men to agree together to exercise their . . . rights," is no crime, Judge Shaw declared. Thereafter, the courts of other states accepted this argument.

Few factory workers organized unions during these years. But the hard conditions and long hours of factory work caused a number of reformers to try to improve the lives of these workers.

Seth Luther, a carpenter and cotton textile worker, was one of the most radical critics of the factory system. Most of the reformers came from farms or from well-to-do city families. They had no actual experience as laborers. Unlike these types, Luther knew what life in the factories was like. He criticized the system vigorously. In particular he denounced the employment of children in factories. Instead of laboring all day over a loom, every child in the nation, he said, should receive a good education at public expense. He called for shorter work hours for all laborers and for better working conditions. He compared the New England textile mills to prisons, the workers to slaves. The employers, he said, "wish to control their men in all things; to enslave their bodies and souls, make them think, act, vote, preach, pray, and worship, as it may suit 'We the Owners.'"

Many less radical reformers supported the movement to reduce the working day from the usual dawn-to-darkness routine to ten

LEADING UNITED STATES INDUSTRIES BY EMPLOYMENT, 1860		
Rank	Industry	Number of Employees
1	Boots and shoes	123,026
2	Cotton goods	114,955
3	Men's clothing	114,800
4	Lumber	75,595
5	Iron	48,975
6	Machinery	41,223
7	Woolen goods	40,597
8	Carriages, wagons, and carts	37,102
9	Flour milling	27,682
10	Tanning (leather)	22,679

Source: *Eighth Census of the United States, Manufactures, 1860.*

LEARNING FROM TABLES. *This chart shows which American industries had the largest number of workers. Into what business category could you group the top three on the list? Is it surprising that they have the largest number of workers? Explain your reasoning.*

The Granger Collection, New York

Alexis de Tocqueville is best known for his Democracy in America. *He wrote his observations after an extensive tour of young America in the 1830s.*

hours. Unfortunately, the ten-hour movement made little progress. But in 1840 the federal government set a ten-hour limit on the workday of its own employees.

De Tocqueville's America

As you have read, Alexis de Tocqueville came to America in 1831 to examine its prisons. But he saw much more, and thus became the most famous foreign observer of America as it was swept by the spirit of reform. His book, *Democracy in America*, was full of insights about America. His description, however, is somewhat idealized, rarely mentioning slavery or the other problems facing Americans in the decade before the Civil War.

Perhaps the aspect of America that most amazed de Tocqueville was the high level of involvement of the American people in reform and in politics. He wrote:

" No sooner do you set foot upon American soil than you are stunned by a kind of tumult; a confused clamour [noise] is heard on every side; and a thousand simultaneous [at the same time] demand immediate satisfaction of their social wants. . . .

Everything is in motion around you; here, the people of one quarter [neighborhood] of the town meet to decide upon building a church; there, the election of a representative is going on; a little farther the delegates of a district are posting [hurrying] to the town in order to consult upon some local improvements; or in another place the labourers of a village quit their plows to deliberate [decide] upon the project of a road or a public school.

Meetings are called for the sole purpose of declaring their disapproval of the line of conduct pursued [followed] by the Government; . . .

The cares of political life take a most prominent place in the occupation of a citizen of the United States, and almost the only pleasure of which an American has any idea is to take part in Government, and to discuss the part he has taken. . . .[1] "

Certainly the Americans described by de Tocqueville were more involved in government and politics than Americans today. As the country has grown into an industrial nation, fewer and fewer people have voted or exercised their civic rights and duties. But then that is one of the virtues of democracy. All are free to choose their levels of participation.

The workings of American democracy fascinated de Tocqueville.

[1]From *Democracy in America* by Alexis de Tocqueville, translated by Henry Reeve

It was far different than the democracy he had observed in France and elsewhere in Europe, where the elite still held most of the power. In America democracy extended to a far greater number of people. The election of Jackson as president had signaled the start of this trend that would continue through the 1800s. De Tocqueville wrote:

66 The Americans have formed a high idea of political rights because they have some political rights. They do not attack those of others, because they do not want their own attacked. Whereas the same person in Europe would be prejudiced against all authority, even the highest, the American obeys the lowest officials without complaint.

Democratic government makes the idea of political rights spread to all citizens, just as the division of property puts the general idea of property rights within reach of all. That, in my view, is one of its greatest advantages.

I'm not saying that it is an easy matter to teach all people to make use of political rights; I only say that when that can happen, the results are important. . . .

In America the people were given political rights at a time when it was difficult for them to misuse them because the citizens were few and their ways of life simple. As they have grown more powerful, the Americans have not greatly increased the powers of democracy. Rather they have extended their democracy by increasing the number of people who have political rights. . . .

Democracy does not confer the most skilful kind of government upon the people, but it produces that which the most skilful governments are frequently unable to awaken, namely, an all-pervading [one that exists throughout] and restless activity, a superabundant force, and an energy which is inseparable from it, and which may, under favourable circumstance, beget [cause] the most amazing results.[1] 99

[1] From *Democracy in America* by Alexis de Tocqueville, translated by Henry Reeve

The End of the Age of Reform

The Age of Reform was a time of high hopes. Today some of the reformers' suggestions seem either undesirable or totally impractical. Others seem quite moderate. At the time the volume and variety of the proposals gave a special excitement to life. But the hectic urge to improve everything at once could not go on forever. What ended it was the conflict between North and South over the future of slavery. 🖻

Return to the Preview & Review on page 498.

CHAPTER 14 REVIEW

Chapter Summary

Read the statements below. Choose one, and write a paragraph explaining its importance.

1. From the 1830s through the 1850s the United States experienced an Age of Reform.
2. Reformers fighting for women's rights wanted greater opportunities for women in education and the professions. The Seneca Falls Declaration emphasized the goals of the movement.
3. Textbooks by Noah Webster, John M'Culloch, and William McGuffey helped a distinctly American educational system develop. Horace Mann and others sought to improve education through better teacher training and constructing schools.
4. Some reformers established ideal communities to practice their principles. But most Americans considered such communities foolish.
5. A Second Great Awakening swept the country, revitalizing American religion.
6. The Romantic Age, which began in Europe, seemed particularly American in its celebration of individualism.
7. Reformers also focused their attention on the blind, the insane, juvenile delinquents, orphans, and the poor. Others campaigned against alcohol and for improved working conditions and hours.

Reviewing Chronological Order

Number your paper 1–5. Then study the time line above and place the following events in the order in which they happened by writing the first next to 1, the second next to 2, and so on.

1. Elizabeth Blackwell licensed
2. Seneca Falls Declaration
3. Webster publishes his *Spelling Book*
4. Mann founds first normal school
5. National Trades' Union founded

Understanding Main Ideas

1. How were women treated as second-class citizens in Jacksonian America?
2. What were some of the reforms Horace Mann sought for public education?
3. For what reasons did people try to establish ideal communities between 1820 and 1850?
4. What were some reforms in the treatment of juveniles from 1820 through the 1850s?
5. How did the general public view labor unions?

Thinking Critically

1. **Synthesizing.** Imagine that you are a new teacher in a "little red schoolhouse" in 1840. Write an entry in your diary after your first day of teaching, describing your students, your classroom, and your reactions to them.
2. **Inventing.** Create your own ideal community, basing it on others described in this chapter. Then compose a list of at least seven rules by which members of your community must live.
3. **Editorializing.** Make a list of what you consider necessary to make working conditions "good." Next to each condition on your list, explain why it is important for "good working conditions." Which items on your list could workers in the 1840s hope for? Why?

Writing About History

Write a newspaper advertisement for an ideal community you are founding. Your advertisement should inform readers about life in your community and persuade them to join it. Use the information in Chapter 14 and in reference books to prepare your advertisement.

Practicing the Strategy

Review the strategy on page 481.
Understanding Sequence. Review pages 484–89. Then make a list showing the sequence of developments in American education from colonial times to the 1840s.

THE AGE OF REFORM				1840				

...wakening	**1826** American Temperance Union	**1830** Mormon religion founded	**1834** National Trades' Union	**1837** *McGuffey's Eclectic Reader*	**1840** Shakers grow to 20 communities		**1848** Seneca Falls Convention	**1853** Brace founds Children's Aid Society
		1831 Howe starts Perkins Institute		**1838** *Letters on the Equality of the Sexes and the Condition of Women*	**1841** Dix begins crusade to help mentally ill		**1849** Elizabeth Blackwell licensed to practice medicine	
				1839 First normal school			**1850** *The Scarlet Letter*	**1855** *Leaves of Grass*
							1851 *Moby Dick*	

Using Primary Sources

On July 19, 1848, the delegates at the women's rights convention at Seneca Falls adopted a *Declaration of Sentiments and Resolutions*. As you read the following excerpt, see if you can get a sense of what the delegates were saying. Then answer the questions below.

We hold these truths to be self-evident: that all men and women are created equal; that they are endowed by their Creator with certain unalienable rights. . . . Such has been the patient suffering of women under this government, and such is now the necessity which forces them to demand the equal position to which they are entitled.

The history of mankind is a history of repeated injuries and usurpations on the part of man toward woman, having as its direct object the establishment of an absolute tyranny over her. To prove this, let facts be given to a candid world:

He has never permitted her to exercise her unalienable right to vote.

He has forced her to submit to laws she had no voice in forming.

He has withheld from her rights which are given to the most ignorant and degraded men—both natives and foreigners. . . .

He has made her, if married, in the eye of the law, civilly dead.

He has taken from her all right to property, even the wages she earns. . . .

He has denied her the opportunity of obtaining a thorough education, all colleges being closed to her.

1. Why do you think the women at the convention used words of the Declaration of Independence as the framework of their *Declaration of Sentiments and Resolutions?*

2. Of the rights that the declaration lists as having been denied to women, which do you think has been the most important for women to gain? Why?

3. Do you think that holding a convention and issuing a declaration is an effective way to change the system? If so, why? If not, how would you do it differently?

Linking History & Geography

Organizers of ideal communities soon realized that their communities were best located in somewhat isolated areas. Locate and label the following areas that contained ideal communities on an outline map of the United States: Indiana (New Harmony), Iowa (Amana), western New York (Oneida and Shakers), and Utah (Mormon). What were the advantages of locating these communities in out-of-the-way places? What disadvantages?

Enriching the Study of History

1. **Individual Project**. In the Age of Reform some people realized that they could improve society by helping the disadvantaged. Find out and report on the efforts made by the government or volunteers in your community to help disadvantaged people. If possible, observe some of these efforts and add your own observations in your report.

2. **Cooperative Project**. In the Lancasterian system of education, older students called monitors, taught younger pupils. Your group will select one student to be a monitor and to teach a topic from this chapter to other group members. Then your group will prepare a report discussing the advantages and disadvantages of this method of education.

Chapter 14 Review   507

UNIT FOUR REVIEW

Summing Up and Predicting

Read the summary of the main ideas in Unit Four below. Choose one statement, then write a paragraph predicting its outcome or consequence in the future.

1. All parts of the country prospered during the Era of Good Feelings. Then regional issues began to threaten the nation's harmony.
2. Jackson's election was a victory for the common man, and a key turning point in American history.
3. Between 1820 and 1850, a feeling of manifest destiny swept the country, and large numbers of people moved westward.
4. The U.S. acquired huge territories, raising serious questions about the spread of slavery.
5. Even as slave labor became an integral part of the southern economy and way of life, a unified abolition movement grew.
6. Reformers sought to improve many aspects of American society.

Connecting Ideas

1. If the presidential election of 1828 could have been televised, do you think that Adams' and Jackson's campaigns would have been different? If so, how? If not, why not?
2. You know that Eli Whitney's cotton gin made life better for some Americans while making it more difficult for others. Name a twentieth-century invention that has had both positive and negative effects on people, and explain your answer.
3. The Seneca Falls Declaration of Sentiments and Resolutions stated, "We hold these truths to be self-evident: that all men and women are created equal." Do you think that women are treated as equals of men in America today? Give evidence to support your point of view.

Practicing Critical Thinking

1. **Making Inferences.** Suppose you were a teenager in the early 1800s. What would your daily life be like if you lived in the Northeast? the South? the West?
2. **Synthesizing.** Imagine that you are a Mormon following Brigham Young to the West. In your travel journal, describe your impressions of your leader.
3. **Evaluating.** You are a slave attempting to persuade your fellow slaves to revolt against your cruel master. What would you say to convince them? Include examples of your mistreatment that justify this action.
4. **Defining Problems.** From the beginnings of your country's history, Americans have believed that educated people make the best citizens in a democracy. If you were unable to read and write, how would your ability to perform your duties as an American citizen be affected?

Cooperative Learning

1. Have your group make a map of the United States as it appeared in 1841. Label major states and territories, physical features, and roads, railroads, canals, etc.
2. Imagine that the members of your group are newspaper reporters. Each reporter should write an article about a different American reform movement of the mid-1800s. When the articles are finished, organize them into sections as a newspaper would be.
3. Imagine that your group is the national committee of a major political party. Prepare a "platform" that states how your party stands on the important issues described in this unit. Be sure that your platform addresses each of the major political issues of the 1840s and 1850s.

Reading in Depth

Blassingame, John W. *The Slave Community*. New York: Oxford University Press. Describes the life and culture of American slaves.

Clarke, Mary S. *Bloomers and Ballots*. New York: Viking. Offers a well-documented story of the life of Elizabeth Cady Stanton.

Eggleston, Edward. *The Hoosier School Master*. Evanston, IL.: McDougal-Littell. Studies the life of an Indian teacher in the 1840s.

Johnson, Philip and Carmen Maldonado de Johnson. *A Probe into the Mexican American Experience*. Orlando: Harcourt Brace Jovanovich. Presents in both English and Spanish a brief history of Mexico and southwestern United States.

Petry, Ann. *Harriet Tubman: Conductor on the Underground Railroad*. New York: Archway. Presents an exciting biography of the former slave called the "Moses of her people."

Remini, Robert G. *The Life of Andrew Jackson*. New York: Harper & Row. Provides a dramatic account of the man and his times.

Gettysburg National Military Park/Photography by Henry Groskinsky

Visitors to Gettysburg can view this large circular mural called a cyclorama to see the famous battle waged there.

A DIVIDED AMERICA

UNIT 5

I n Unit 5 you will learn about the Civil War and the period called Reconstruction that followed. Here are some main points to keep in mind as you read the unit.

- The conflict between the North and South over the issue of slavery was a leading cause of the Civil War.
- Many southern states feared the election of Abraham Lincoln as president and seceded from the Union.
- The Confederate bombardment of Fort Sumter started the Civil War.
- The Confederates won many victories early in the war. Eventually, however, Union numbers, Union leadership, and Union strategy prevailed.
- During the period of Reconstruction, President Johnson and the radical Republicans battled over plans to reshape the South and restore it to the Union.
- Amendments to the Constitution of the United States were ratified to protect the rights of African Americans.

Causes of the Civil War

The conflict between the North and South over the future of slavery sputtered and grew into the threat that the southern states would leave the Union if the next president was a Republican. The stage was set by the publication of *Uncle Tom's Cabin*, a novel about slavery that was widely read. Then came the struggle over the Kansas Territory—would it be free or slave?—and the Supreme Court ruling in the Dred Scott case that slaves were a form of property and had "none of the rights and privileges" of citizens of the United States. With the election in 1860 of Abraham Lincoln, the southern states were prepared to secede. Would the secession crisis tear apart the 85-year-old United States of America?

1. THE NORTH AND SLAVERY

Slave Catching

Most Americans had expected the Compromise of 1850 to put an end to the slavery controversy. Events quickly proved that it had not done so. The Fugitive Slave Law was very strict. Anyone caught helping a slave escape faced six months in jail and a $1,000 fine. As soon as the new law went into effect southerners began to try to reclaim slaves who had escaped into the free states. Slaves who had escaped to the North found themselves in grave danger of recapture. Persons accused of being runaways could not testify in their own defense. Many blacks in the North who had not run away also felt threatened.

Thousands pulled up stakes and moved to Canada. Among those who left the country were many of the more outspoken African American leaders. "We have lost some of our strong men," Frederick Douglass mourned. He himself did not flee. "The only way to make the Fugitive Slave Law a dead letter," he wrote, "is to make half a dozen or more dead kidnappers." By kidnappers Douglass meant the men who sought to reclaim runaways under the Fugitive Slave Law.

During the next few years about 200 people were captured and

Preview & Review

Use these questions to guide your reading. Answer the questions after completing Section 1.
Understanding Issues, Events, & Ideas. Using the following words, explain how northerners felt about slavery during the 1850s: Fugitive Slave Act, segregation, *Uncle Tom's Cabin.*
1. Why did many northerners support runaway slaves?
2. Why did many northerners object to the Fugitive Slave Law?
3. What point did Stowe try to make in *Uncle Tom's Cabin?* In what way was *Uncle Tom's Cabin* something new in American fiction?
Thinking Critically. You are a northerner living in Massachusetts in 1852 and opposed to the Fugitive Slave Law. Compose the handbill you would pass out at a town meeting to persuade members of your community to protest the law.

The Brooklyn Museum

New York Public Library Picture Collection

Eastman Johnson painted "A Ride for Liberty—the Fugitive Slave" in about 1862. Johnson was a famous genre *painter—that is, his frequent subject was everyday life. But this is no everyday event for the family riding fearfully north to freedom. What message to fugitives can you find in the* Anti-Slavery Almanac *below?*

sent back into slavery under the new law. This was a small percentage of the number that had escaped. Even these cases, however, had a powerful effect on northern public opinion.

Most northerners were prejudiced against people of African descent, free or slave. Only five states, all in New England, permitted the handful who resided there to vote freely. Some states prohibited them from settling within their borders. Nowhere could they mix with white people. They sat alone on trains or in restaurants, theaters, or hotels. Except in Massachusetts, this **segregation** extended to public schools.

Yet in spite of their prejudices, many northerners were sympathetic to the plight of runaway slaves. Runaways had risked their lives to win freedom. It was hard not to be impressed by them, especially when they had gone on to raise families, learn trades, and become hard-working, law-abiding citizens.

When northerners saw such people seized and dragged off without being given a chance to defend themselves in court, thousands were outraged. In Indiana, for example, a man named Mitchum was arrested and turned over to a southerner who claimed that Mitchum was a slave who had run away 19 years earlier. Whether or not Mitchum had really run away, it seemed cruel and unjust to separate him from his wife and children after so many years.

—VOL. I. NO. 5.—
THE
AMERICAN
ANTI-SLAVERY
ALMANAC,
FOR
1840,
BEING BISSEXTILE OR LEAP-YEAR, AND THE 64TH OF AMERICAN INDEPENDENCE. CALCULATED FOR NEW YORK; ADAPTED TO THE NORTHERN AND MIDDLE STATES.

NORTHERN HOSPITALITY—NEW YORK NINE MONTHS' LAW.
The slave steps out of the slave-state, and his chains fall. A free state, with another chain, stands ready to re-enslave him.

Thus saith the Lord, Deliver him that is spoiled out of the hands of the oppressor.

NEW YORK:
PUBLISHED BY THE AMERICAN ANTI-SLAVERY SOCIETY,
NO. 143 NASSAU STREET.

The North and Slavery 511

A Philadelphia woman, Euphemia Williams, escaped a somewhat different fate. She was arrested, but a judge released her at the last moment. Had he not, her six children, all born in Pennsylvania, would have been enslaved with her. Under southern law whether or not a child was a slave depended on the status of the mother, not the father.

Even northerners who were unmoved by the way the new fugitive slave law affected escaped slaves objected to it. It required citizens of the northern states to help capture runaways when ordered to do so by a law enforcement officer. Thousands considered this a violation of their rights. The abolitionists led the attack on the law.

As you have read, the abolitionist crusade was carried in large part by northern religious leaders. The Quakers had been foremost in the antislavery movement since colonial days. They had been joined by northern ministers and preachers such as Theodore Dwight Weld and Henry Ward Beecher.

In Boston a group headed by the respected clergyman Theodore Parker rescued a runaway couple, William and Ellen Craft. The group so threatened the man who had arrested the Crafts that he fled the city in fear for his life. In Syracuse, New York, a fugitive named Jerry McHenry was freed when a crowd of 2,000 people broke into the jail where he was being held. In Pennsylvania a mob actually killed a slave catcher.

Not many of the runaways who were arrested were freed by force. In most cases they were brought to trial as the law provided. Some were released. Others were sent back into slavery without the public taking much notice. The law was disliked throughout the North, even though little was done to stop it from being enforced. More and more northerners were becoming "uncomfortable" about the existence of slavery in the country.

A Novel About Slavery

Discomfort in the North increased when people began to read *Uncle Tom's Cabin,* a novel about slavery published in 1852. The author, Harriet Beecher Stowe, was not an active abolitionist. In her book she tried to make the point that the slave system was at fault, not the people who owned slaves and profited from their labor. She made the villain of her story, Simon Legree, a northerner.

The plot of *Uncle Tom's Cabin* is as hard to believe as that of a modern soap opera. The main character is the slave Uncle Tom, who accepts slavery with "patient weariness." He speaks to his owners in a soft voice and has "a habitually respectful manner." He is content to remain a slave as long as his master is kind. Indeed, most of the slaves in the book quietly accept slavery and all its injustices.

Tom is first owned by a kindly Kentucky planter named Shelby.

National Portrait Gallery

Harriet Beecher Stowe sat for this oil portrait in 1853, one year after publication of Uncle Tom's Cabin.

Next he becomes the property of a noble gentleman from New Orleans named St. Clare. All goes well. Then St. Clare dies. Tom is sold to the Yankee-born Simon Legree, who owns a cotton plantation in Louisiana.

Simon Legree is one of the arch villains of American literature. He enters and exits twirling his moustaches, his lips curled in a sneer. Legree cares only for money. He drives his slaves unmercifully, whipping them repeatedly to make them work harder. He controls them with fierce bulldogs who would "jest as soon chaw one of ye up as eat their dinner," and by Sambo and Quimbo, evil slave overseers whom "Legree had . . . trained in savageness and brutality as systematically as he had his bulldogs." At one point the saintly Tom refuses to whip a slave woman who is too tired to pick as much cotton as Legree wishes. Legree has Tom brutally beaten by Sambo and Quimbo. One lashing follows another. Finally Tom dies of his injuries. As Stowe described the scene:

" Scenes of blood and cruelty are shocking to our ear and heart. What man has the nerve to do, man has not nerve to hear. What brother-man and brother-Christian must suffer, cannot be told us, even in our secret chamber, it so harrows [torments] the soul. And yet, oh my country! these things are done under the shadow of thy laws! Oh Christ! thy church sees them, almost in silence. . . .

'He's almost gone [dead], Mas'r,' said Sambo, touched in spite of himself by the patience of his victim [Tom].

'Pay away, till he gives up! Give it to him!—give it to him!' shouted Legree. 'I'll take every drop of blood he has, unless he confesses!'

Tom opened his eyes, and looked upon his master. 'Ye poor miserable critter!' he said, 'there an't no more ye can do! I forgive ye, with all my soul!' and he fainted entirely away.

'I believe, my soul, he's done for, finally,' said Legree, stepping forward, to look at him. 'Yes, he is! Well, his mouth's shut up, at last,—that's one comfort.'

Yes, Legree; but who shall shut up that voice in thy soul? that soul past repentance [to ask for forgiveness], past prayer, past hope, in whom the fire that never shall be quenched [hell] is already burning.[1] "

The first and last paragraphs are Stowe's voice. Her words echo the feelings of most abolitionists. She, and they, could not understand how America could allow slavery to continue. Why had the reform movement not boldly tackled the slavery issue? And what of the slaveholders themselves? Why could they not see that slavery was

[1]From *Uncle Tom's Cabin* by Harriet Beecher Stowe

Point of View

To the author of *Uncle Tom's Cabin* Oliver Wendell Holmes wrote these lines after John Brown had been awarded sainthood by northern abolitionists.

" All through the conflict, up and down
Marched Uncle Tom and Old John Brown,
     One ghost, one form ideal,
And which was false and which was true,
And which was mightier of the two,
The wisest sibyl° never knew,
     For both alike were real. "
Oliver Wendell Holmes

°**sibyl**: a woman prophet

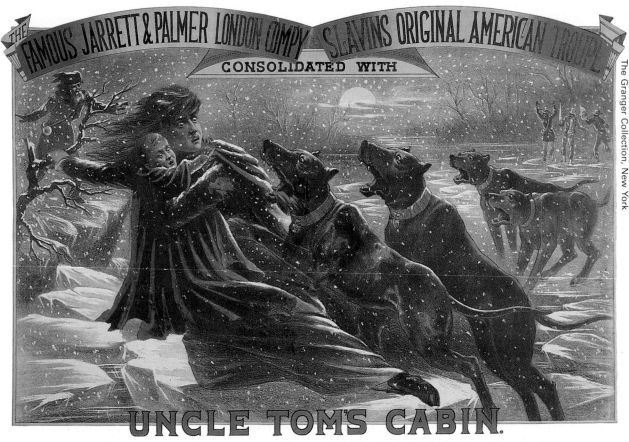

The Granger Collection, New York

Uncle Tom's Cabin was applauded widely in the North, both the novel and a traveling melodrama (a type of play) based on it. Many people saw no spectacle to rival the pursuit of Eliza Harris by bloodhounds on the icebound Ohio River. The poster below praises "the greatest book of the age." Do you think this might be so, or is the publisher simply a good advertiser?

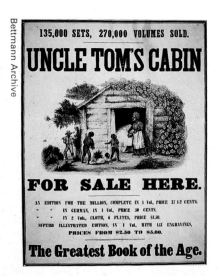

Bettmann Archive

Return to the Preview & Review on page 510.

wrong? *Uncle Tom's Cabin* now thrust those questions in front of all Americans.

Stowe's description of slavery was not very realistic. She had grown up in Connecticut and Ohio. She had seen slaves only once, during a visit to a plantation in Kentucky. Many angry African Americans rejected the patient, submissive Uncle Tom. But while the characters in *Uncle Tom's Cabin* are all either saints or the worst of sinners, the slaves are shown as human beings with deep feelings. This was something new in American fiction.

The book was an immediate popular success. Within a year of publication 300,000 copies were sold. It was made into a play and presented before packed houses in theaters all over the northern states. We cannot know how many of the millions of people who read the book or saw the play became abolitionists as a result. But the historian David Potter was unquestionably correct when he wrote, "The northern attitude toward slavery was never quite the same after *Uncle Tom's Cabin*."

2. THE STRUGGLE FOR KANSAS

The Kansas-Nebraska Act

The concern of northerners about slavery increased dramatically in 1854. In 1853 Senator Stephen A. Douglas of Illinois had introduced a bill setting up a territorial government for the frontier west of Missouri and Iowa. On the surface it was a routine measure. As settlers pushed the frontier westward, Congress always organized the districts they were entering by setting up governments for them. This had been done repeatedly, beginning with the Northwest Ordinance of 1787.

Douglas' bill, however, ran into trouble. Once California entered the Union, plans for building a railroad to the West Coast sprang up everywhere. Being from Illinois, Douglas favored a route running west from Chicago. No such line could be built until the land beyond Missouri and Iowa had a territorial government.

Southern interests wanted the railroad to run west from New Orleans or some other southern city. All the lands such a route would cross had already been organized. In 1853 the United States had bought from Mexico a tract on the border known as the **Gadsden Purchase.** This land contained a pass through the mountains. A

Engravings such as "The Express Train" were an ever-popular subject for Currier & Ives. What might you have felt as this train passed by?

The Granger Collection, New York

Preview & Review

Use these questions to guide your reading. Answer the questions after completing Section 2.
Understanding Issues, Events, & Ideas. Use the following words to explain events in Kansas during the 1850s: Gadsden Purchase, Wilmot Proviso, popular sovereignty, Kansas-Nebraska Bill, Ostend Manifesto, free soiler, Beecher's Bibles, Pottawatomie Massacre, guerrilla, "Bleeding Kansas."

1. For what two reasons had Senator Douglas introduced a bill to establish the new territories of Kansas and Nebraska?
2. How did antislavery forces hope to prevent slavery in Kansas? How did proslavery groups influence the Kansas territorial election in 1855?
3. How did northern newspapers report the events in Kansas?

Thinking Critically. You are a free laborer in 1854, planning to move to Kansas. Write a letter to the editor of your local newspaper, explaining why you oppose the Kansas-Nebraska Bill.

National Portrait Gallery

Franklin Pierce was elected to the presidency in 1852. He served one unhappy term as president, the Pierces grieving at the loss of their son, who was killed in a train wreck before the inauguration.

railroad could be constructed over this pass and on to the Pacific Ocean. Southerners in Congress did not want to encourage the building of a northern rail line. They refused to vote for the Douglas bill.

Stephen A. Douglas was extremely ambitious. In 1852, when he was only 39, he announced himself a candidate for the Democratic presidential nomination. Other party leaders considered him much too young for that office. They nominated Franklin Pierce of New Hampshire. Pierce went on to defeat the Whig candidate, General Winfield Scott, in the 1852 election.

Douglas did not let this failure discourage him. All his life he had gotten what he wanted. He had made a fortune as a lawyer and real estate investor. He had been a state legislator, a judge, and a member of the House of Representatives before being elected to the Senate. Although he was very short, people spoke of him with awe as the "Little Giant." He seemed to give off energy and determination. He once boasted:

66 I live with my constituents, drink with them, lodge with them, pray with them, laugh, hunt, dance, and work with them. I eat their corn dodgers and fried bacon and sleep two in a bed with them. 99

Douglas was a shrewd politician. When he realized that southern congressmen were opposed to his bill, he looked for a way to change their minds. He knew they had held up for two years the passage of a bill creating the Oregon Territory because it contained a clause excluding slavery. He knew they had also defeated the Wilmot Proviso. As you read, in 1846 Congressman David Wilmot of Pennsylvania proposed that slavery be excluded from the lands acquired from Mexico after the Mexican War. The proviso passed the House of Representatives in both 1846 and 1847. But it was defeated in the Senate. Southern senators, led by John C. Calhoun, claimed that the Constitution forbade Congress from passing such a law. It was up to the citizens of each state or territory to decide.

Douglas now came up with a scheme. Why not open the new territory to slavery? To prevent an uproar in the North, however, no new slave territory would be specifically created. Instead, settlers of the area would themselves decide whether or not to permit slavery.

This was the principle of **popular sovereignty** that had already been applied to New Mexico and Utah territories by the Compromise of 1850. As a further compromise the area would be split into two territories—Kansas, west of the slave state of Missouri, and Nebraska, west of the free state of Iowa.

Douglas knew that many northerners would dislike this **Kansas-Nebraska Bill.** But he thought most of them would merely grumble. The possibility of slavery actually being established in the new territories was small. The climate was unsuitable for growing cotton or any other plantation crop. Douglas himself considered slavery a

STRATEGIES FOR SUCCESS

COMPARING MAPS

One of the most important ways to learn history through geography is by comparing maps. You have already been introduced to many of the strategies you need to compare maps. Review the strategies for reviewing map basics, interpreting physical maps, and comparing and contrasting ideas.

How to Compare Maps

To effectively compare maps, follow these guidelines.

1. **Select the maps to be compared carefully.** Make sure the areas covered, the dates of the information, and other important pieces of information provide a reliable picture.
2. **Note similarities and differences.** Examine the patterns and symbols closely.
3. **Apply critical thinking skills.** Make inferences, draw conclusions, and state generalizations about the evidence you find.

Applying the Strategy

The question of extending slavery into the western territories was hotly debated for more than half a century. Three times Congress acted to settle the matter. But it was not resolved by the Missouri Compromise (Compromise of 1820) or the Compromise of 1850. Four short years later Congress once again struggled with the problem before passing the Kansas-Nebraska Act of 1854.

Such a complex matter as the attempts to settle the slavery issue may be better understood by comparing maps of the compromises. Study the maps on this page. Note that they show the changing status of the territories as Congress passed each new compromise. How did the status of California change with the Compromise of 1850? How did the status of Nebraska change with the Kansas-Nebraska Act? What other details can you compare? Based on these maps, what generalizations can you state about the issue of extending slavery?

For independent practice, see Practicing the Strategy on pages 540–41.

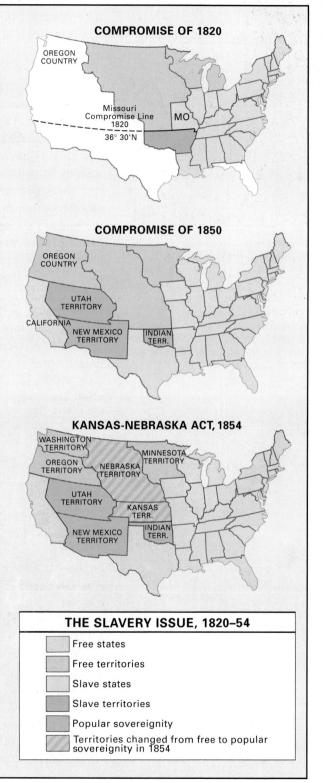

COMPROMISE OF 1820

COMPROMISE OF 1850

KANSAS-NEBRASKA ACT, 1854

THE SLAVERY ISSUE, 1820–54

- Free states
- Free territories
- Slave states
- Slave territories
- Popular sovereignty
- Territories changed from free to popular sovereignty in 1854

terrible institution. But he did not think the development of the West should be held up over the principle of whether or not to permit it. On January 4, 1854, he introduced the bill in the Senate.

The Struggle for Kansas

By 1854 antislavery northerners were outraged. News of the **Ostend Manifesto** (see page 541) had leaked out and was published. Shocked Americans read that President Pierce, pressured by influential southerners, had begun negotiations with Spain to buy Cuba. Northerners saw this as an obvious attempt to add to southern territory. The secrecy surrounding the talks added to their anger.

Now they responded to the Kansas-Nebraska Bill with roars of protest. Although it did not do so specifically, Douglas' bill repealed the ban on slavery in that region which had been imposed by the Missouri Compromise. It was a "criminal betrayal" of the interests of free laborers eager to settle in the new land. It was "an atrocious plot" to make the territory "a dreary region . . . inhabited by masters and slaves."

For months the Kansas-Nebraska Bill was debated in Congress. Finally, with the votes of southerners who approved of the slavery provision, it passed both houses and was promptly signed by President Pierce.

These Missourians are crossing into Kansas by ferry. What side must they have been on in the struggle for control of Kansas?

The Granger Collection, New York

Douglas had hoped that northerners who opposed his bill would quiet down once the issue was settled. Instead they grew more bitter. Antislavery critics were determined to prevent slavery from gaining a foothold in Kansas. Senator William H. Seward of New York said:

> " Gentlemen of the Slave States, we will engage in competition for the virgin soil of Kansas, and God give the victory to the side which is . . . right. "

Eli Thayer, a member of the Massachusetts legislature, organized the Massachusetts Emigrant Aid Company to help pay the moving expenses of antislavery families willing to settle in Kansas.

And what of these lands so furiously fought for? Broad and flat, they rose gently from east to west to a plateau and the foothills of the Rockies. Tall prairie grass stretched as far as the eye could see. Rainfall was scarce, especially to the west, and trees were few. Shallow rivers flowed east across the rich soils—the Platte and Niobara in the north and the Kansas and Arkansas in the south—to the Missouri and Mississippi rivers.

Hundreds of **free soilers**—those opposed to slavery—might now rush to Kansas and use popular sovereignty to keep slaves out. Alarmed proslavery groups in Missouri therefore hastened across the state line to Kansas. When the first territorial governor took a census of Kansas late in 1854, he found fewer than 3,000 adult males in the territory. But when a territorial legislature was elected in March 1855, more than 6,300 votes were cast! About 5,000 Missourians had crossed over into Kansas to vote. Their ballots were illegal since they were not residents of the territory. Still their votes were counted. As a result a large majority of the men elected to the territorial legislature were proslavery.

The new legislature moved quickly to pass laws authorizing slavery in Kansas territory. It even passed one that provided the death penalty for anyone giving help to runaway slaves. Free Soil Kansans were furious. They refused to recognize the right of this legislature to govern them. Instead they set up their own government at the town of Topeka.

With two governments claiming to rule the same territory, it is not surprising that fighting broke out. Abolitionists in the East began to send guns to the antislavery forces. One such abolitionist was the Reverend Henry Ward Beecher of Brooklyn, New York, a brother of Harriet Beecher Stowe. He was so active and successful in collecting money for guns that people began to speak of the weapons as **Beecher's Bibles**.

Fighting was common in most rough-and-ready frontier communities. In Kansas tension between northern and southern settlers made the situation explosive. Ruffians on both sides armed themselves. In November 1855 a free soil settler was killed by a proslavery man in an argument over a land claim. The dead man's friends then

National Portrait Gallery

Reverend Henry Ward Beecher's photograph was taken by Napoleon Sorony in about 1880.

burned down the killer's cabin. A proslavery sheriff, Samuel Jones, arrested one of these men. *His* friends promptly attacked the sheriff and forced him to release his prisoner. Sheriff Jones, backed by a force of 3,000 Missourians, then set out to track down the rescuers. Luckily the territorial governor put a stop to this activity before more blood could be spilled.

"Bleeding Kansas"

Trouble broke out again in Kansas the following spring. The town of Lawrence had become the headquarters of the antislavery settlers. Bands of armed men marched about the town much the way the Minute Men had paraded about the towns of Massachusetts in 1775. A United States marshal tried to arrest some of the leaders, but they fled before he could do so.

Then, on May 21, Sheriff Jones, again at the head of an army of Missourians, marched into Lawrence. In broad daylight they threw the printing presses of two newspapers into a river. They burned down the Free State Hotel and other buildings. Antislavery Kansans

How would a scene like the one below, titled "Marais des Cygnes Massacre," have fueled the fires raging between North and South over Kansas? The Marais des Cygnes is a river near Topeka. In English its name would be Swamp of the Swans—not quite as musical as Swan Lake.

Bettmann Archive

A CANING IN CONGRESS

The Granger Collection, New York

While fighting went on in Kansas, angry legislators in Congress traded insults and threats. Words like "liar" were freely tossed about. Prominent among the new personalities engaged in these outbursts was Senator Charles Sumner of Massachusetts. The handsome and well-spoken Sumner was popular in New England as a reformer and abolitionist. His ego was large; his sense of humor poor.

In the debates over Kansas Sumner showed such icy disdain for his foes that he became the most hated man in the Senate. Southern colleagues called him a "filthy reptile" and a "leper."

One day in May 1856 Sumner began a bitter personal attack on Senator Andrew P. Butler of South Carolina, who was not present. Congressman Preston S. Brooks of South Carolina, a nephew of Senator Butler, re-solved to uphold his uncle's honor. Two days after Sumner's speech, Brooks entered the Senate as it adjourned. Sumner remained at his desk writing. Brooks walked up to Sumner and rained blows upon his head with a cane until Sumner fell, bloody and unconscious, to the Senate floor. "I . . . gave him about 30 first-rate stripes," boasted Brooks. "Towards the last he bellowed like a calf. I wore my cane out completely but saved the head which is gold."

Such was Congress on the eve of secession.

seethed with rage. Here is how one eyewitness described the attack:

“ The newspaper offices were the first objects of attack. First the office of the *Free State* was destroyed, then that of the *Herald of Freedom*. The presses were broken down to pieces and the type carried away to the river. The papers and books were treated the same way, until the soldiers became tired of carrying them to the river. Then they piled them in the street, and burned, tore, or otherwise destroyed them.

From the printing offices the attackers went to the hotel. By evening, all that remained . . . was a part of one wall. The rest was a shapeless heap of ruins.

The sack of Lawrence occupied the rest of the afternoon. Sheriff Jones, after looking at the flames rising from the hotel and saying that it was "the happiest day of his life," dismissed the troops, and they began their lawless destruction. . . .[1]”

[1]From *The Englishman in Kansas* by Thomas H. Gladstone

The Struggle for Kansas   521

Yale University Art Gallery

These travelers from Missouri have crossed the Kansas border to make trouble for antislavery settlers. How does the artist of "Border Ruffians Invading Kansas" make clear in the men's faces which side he is on?

A few days later a man named John Brown set out to avenge the attack on Lawrence. During his 56 years Brown had moved restlessly from place to place. He tried many businesses but failed time after time. His behavior had often been on the borders of the law, if not outside it. Yet he was sincerely opposed to slavery and devoted to the cause of racial equality. He had come to Kansas in October 1855.

When Brown learned of the attack, he led a party of seven men, four of them his own sons, to a settlement near Pottawatomie Creek, south of Lawrence. In the dead of night they entered the cabins of three unsuspecting families. For no apparent reason they murdered five people. They split open their skulls with heavy, razor-sharp swords. They even cut off the hand of one of their victims.

The **Pottawatomie Massacre** brought Kansas to the verge of civil war. Free soilers and proslavery men squared off to fight as irregular soldiers, or **guerrillas.** Brown was one of many of these. Very few people were killed. But politicians played up the unrest to win support. Soon horror-stricken citizens in the Northeast were reading exaggerated newspaper reports about **"Bleeding Kansas."**

Return to the Preview & Review on page 515.

3. NEW POLITICAL PARTIES

Preview & Review

Use these questions to guide your reading. Answer the questions after completing Section 3.

Understanding Issues, Events, & Ideas. Explain how two new political parties formed in the 1850s, using the following words: nativist, Native American party, Know-Nothings, Republican party.

1. How did the Democratic party suffer from passage of the Kansas-Nebraska Act? Why was the Whig party shattered?
2. In what ways was the political situation unsettled in 1856?
3. What were Buchanan's qualifications for the presidency? Why did the Democrats nominate him?

Thinking Critically. Imagine that you arrived in America from Ireland in 1850. Write a letter to your family in Ireland, explaining why you would *not* join the Native American party or the Republican party.

Political Breakups

The controversy over slavery in the western territories once again became a major political issue. It brought about major shifts in the nation's political parties. The Kansas-Nebraska Act had been a Democratic party measure. Its passage caused that party to lose thousands of supporters in the North. The Whig party, however, was shattered completely. Southern Whigs and their northern allies—known as "Cotton" Whigs—could not remain in the same organization with Northern "Conscience" Whigs. Most of the southerners and "Cotton" Whigs supported the Kansas-Nebraska Act.

The northern Whigs went in two directions. The huge increase of immigration in the 1840s and 1850s hurt the Whig party greatly. For various reasons about 90 percent of the new Irish citizens became Democrats. The tendency of German immigrants to vote Democratic was almost as strong. Most of these immigrants were Catholic, while most Whigs belonged to one or another of the Protestant churches. So the Whigs disagreed in both politics and religion with the new Democrats. As a result many Whigs became **nativists.** They favored strict controls on the admission of foreigners into the country. They joined a new political organization, the **Native American party.** Many former Democrats also joined this new party. Members of the Native American party were often called **Know-Nothings** because when asked about the organization, they replied, "I know nothing."

Perhaps without realizing it, the nativists were trying to make the slavery issue go away by ignoring it. They were also bucking a tide that could not be stemmed without ruining the country. A steady flow of immigrants was essential if the United States was to expand. The very people who joined the Native American party benefited from the work the new immigrants did. By spending their wages, the immigrants stimulated the whole national economy. Fortunately most American-born citizens realized this. The Know-Nothings won some important local elections in the 1850s, but they never replaced either of the two major political parties.

The other new organization that northern Whigs and Democrats joined was the **Republican party.** It sprang up in many northern states immediately after passage of the Kansas-Nebraska Act.

The Republican platform was simple: Keep slavery out of the western territories. Dislike of slavery was not the only reason the party took this stand. Indeed, many Republicans shared the common racial prejudice of most northerners. But they feared that small farmers in the territories could not compete with southerners who could bring their slaves there.

The ranks of voters swelled with newcomers from Ireland, nearly

Milwaukee County Historical Society

all of whom joined the Democratic party. They were poor and unskilled. These Irish interpreted Republican talk about free soil and free men as threatening their jobs. While not in favor of slavery, the Irish found Democratic politics more to their liking.

The Election of 1856

The political situation in 1856 was most unsettled. Neither President Pierce nor Senator Douglas could get the Democratic nomination for the presidency. Their support of the Kansas-Nebraska Act convinced party leaders that these men could not win in the northern states. Instead the Democrats chose James Buchanan of Pennsylvania.

National Portrait Gallery

Why did James Buchanan seem well qualified to be president of the United States?

Buchanan seemed well qualified for the presidency. He had been a congressman and also a senator. He was an experienced diplomat, having been minister to both Russia and Great Britain. He had been President Polk's secretary of state. But the chief reason the Democrats picked him was that his service as minister to Britain had kept him out of the country during the bitter fight over the Kansas-Nebraska Act.

The Republicans nominated John C. Frémont, "the Pathfinder." Unlike Buchanan, who was 64, Frémont was a relatively young man in his early forties and something of a national hero. As his nickname indicates, he was an explorer. He had also played an important role in taking California during the Mexican War. A strong, silent type, Frémont had almost no political experience. With voters so divided, that too was a political advantage. Former president Millard Fillmore was also a candidate in 1856. He received the nomination of the Native American party and also was the candidate of the rapidly declining Whig party.

National Portrait Gallery

Why was John C. Frémont something of a national hero when he ran for president?

The Republicans did not even attempt to campaign in the South. Fillmore got many northern votes that might otherwise have gone to Frémont, but he did not even come close to winning a single free state. So the contest was between Buchanan and Frémont in the North and between Buchanan and Fillmore in the South. Buchanan's strength in both sections gave him a great advantage among undecided voters and people who put sectional peace ahead of any particular issue.

Buchanan proved to be much more popular than Fillmore in the South. He lost only Maryland. Frémont was the stronger of the two in the North. But Buchanan won narrow victories in Illinois, Indiana, New Jersey, and his home state, Pennsylvania. These gave Buchanan a majority of the electoral vote, 174 to Frémont's 117. Fillmore gained only 8.

Again the danger of the Union breaking up over slavery seemed to have been avoided. Buchanan's conservatism and his long political experience encouraged people to believe that he would proceed cautiously and with good judgment.

Return to the Preview & Review on page 523.

4. A CONTROVERSIAL COURT

The Dred Scott Case

Before Buchanan had a chance to demonstrate his abilities, a new crisis erupted. This one was produced by the Supreme Court. For nearly 20 years American courts had struggled with various legal questions surrounding the rights of free blacks and former slaves. In 1841 the nation's attention had been riveted on the Supreme Court as it prepared to issue its decision in the *Amistad* case (page 526). The surprising outcome of that case had heartened abolitionists and given hope to blacks. Abolitionists ignored what was implied in the decision: slaves have no legal rights. Now Americans anxiously awaited the Court's ruling in a case involving a slave named Dred Scott.

We know very little about Dred Scott, the man. He was short and had a dark complexion. He could neither read nor write. He must have been a very determined person because he carried on a long struggle for his freedom.

In 1833 Scott had been purchased by John Emerson, an army doctor in St. Louis, Missouri, who used him as a servant. When the army assigned Doctor Emerson to duty at Fort Armstrong in Illinois, he took Scott with him. Then, in 1836, Emerson was transferred to Fort Snelling, a post in the western part of Wisconsin Territory, now Minnesota. Again Scott accompanied him. While there, Scott met and married a slave named Harriet Robinson.

After further moves Emerson was transferred to Florida. He sent the Scotts to St. Louis with his wife. When Emerson died in December 1843, his wife inherited them. Exactly what happened next is not clear. But in 1846, with the help of the family that had originally sold Scott to Emerson, the Scotts sued for their freedom in a Missouri court.

Scott argued that since slavery had been banned in Illinois by state law, he had become free when Emerson brought him to that state. Furthermore, slavery was also illegal in Wisconsin Territory because Wisconsin was in the northern part of the Louisiana Purchase. Slavery had been banned there by Congress in the Missouri Compromise of 1820. In other words, Scott claimed that when he returned to the state of Missouri, he was no longer a slave. Since he had not been reenslaved, he was still free.

This complicated case shuttled from one Missouri court to another for many years. In 1852 the Missouri Supreme Court ruled against Scott. The matter did not end there, however. In 1851 Mrs. Emerson had moved to Massachusetts and remarried. She either sold or gave the Scotts to her brother, John Sanford.

Sanford lived in New York. This offered fresh hope for Scott. Again with the support of friends, he started a new suit for his freedom, this one in the federal courts.

Preview & Review

Use these questions to guide your reading. Answer the questions after completing Section 4.
Understanding Issues, Events, & Ideas. Explain the Supreme Court's decision in its controversial 1857 case, using these words: *Dred Scott v. Sandford*, void.
1. What argument did Dred Scott make for his freedom?
2. What did the Supreme Court rule in *Dred Scott v. Sandford?* What argument did Chief Justice Roger Taney make?
3. How was precedent important to the Court's decision?
4. Why was the Court's decision strongly criticized?

Thinking Critically. 1. As a newspaper reporter assigned to cover the Dred Scott case, you have obtained an interview with Scott. Write an article that describes the case from his point of view. **2.** As a justice on the Supreme Court in 1857, you disagree with Taney in *Dred Scott v. Sandford*. List your reasons for disagreeing with his ruling.

Missouri Historical Society

Although little is known about Dred Scott, we do have this portrait made in 1858. It was painted from a photograph of Scott taken earlier.

A Controversial Court   525

THE *AMISTAD* MUTINY

One of the most dramatic and widely publicized court cases before *Dred Scott v. Sandford* was the *Amistad* case that began in 1839. In June 1839 a Spanish slaver named the *Amistad* sailed from Havana bound for a plantation in eastern Cuba. The *Amistad* carried four crew members and two Spanish slaveowners with their cargo of fifty-three African slaves. After three days at sea the Africans, led by Joseph Cinqué, revolted. They killed the captain, took control of the *Amistad*, and ordered one of the slaveowners to sail the ship home to Africa. The Spaniard tricked Cinqué and his men for months by sailing a zigzag course up the American coastline. Finally with sails shredded and tattered, the *Amistad* lay becalmed and anchored in Long Island Sound near New London, Connecticut. American naval authorities towed the *Amistad* to New London, where Cinqué and the other Africans were jailed. Here legal proceedings began on behalf of the Spanish owners who demanded that their ship and cargo of slaves be returned to them. Abolitionists immediately took up the Africans' cause, providing them with lawyers and an African interpreter by the name of James Covey.

In September legal proceedings began in the United States Circuit Court in Connecticut and in January moved to the United States District Court. Here Cinqué testified, through Covey, that he had been recently kidnapped in his homeland of Mende in Western Africa. His captors had carried him and others aboard a slaver where they were chained below decks

Cinqué

New Haven Historical Society

until the ship reached Havana. There they were sold and put on the *Amistad* where, fearing for their lives, they mutinied and took command of the ship.

Meanwhile, President Van Buren had begun to fear that the *Amistad* case could make slavery a major issue in the 1840 election. He decided that the best way to avoid this possibility was to return the Africans to Cuba for trial by the Spanish. In violation of his presidential power he secretly dispatched a ship to Connecticut with orders to take the Africans into custody and transport them to Cuba. At the last moment Van Buren retracted his order, and by February 1841 the matter had been appealed to the United States Supreme Court under Chief Justice Roger B. Taney. John Quincy Adams defended the Africans. He argued that they were freemen who had been kidnapped and that Van Buren had defied the Constitution's separation of powers by interfering with the judicial system. United

States Attorney General Henry Gilpin headed the prosecution, which argued that the Africans were criminals because they had killed the ship's captain and that they were property as proved in documents carried by their Spanish owners.

On March 9 Justice Joseph Story read the Court's decision: The prosecution had failed to prove the Africans were slaves; therefore, they were free to return home. Freemen had the right to mutiny and to defend themselves if kidnapped; therefore they could not be considered criminals. What were Cinqué's thoughts on hearing the Court's decision? In *Echo of Lions*, novelist Barbara Chase-Riboud has Cinqué speak these prophetic words:

I, too, have become a dangerous man. The war of the Amistad *has become a rallying point for emancipators and the abolitionists and an example to the colored men of America. I am the symbol of insurrection, the amalgamation and lurking violence the slaveholder will not tolerate: that of self-emancipation. I am some marvelous phenomenon, a black man who has defied the courts of America, who has been recognized as having natural as well as legal rights in the highest court of the land. I am a hero. I am a revolutionary.*

What the Court also implied was that had the Africans been slaves, they would have had no rights as human beings. As property, slaves could be legally transported from one state to another. This proved to be the case in 1857 when Taney issued his decision in *Dred Scott v. Sandford*.

The Court and the Constitution

The case of **Dred Scott v. Sandford** began in 1854. Eventually it came to the Supreme Court for final settlement. (The case is incorrectly cited as *Sandford* because of a court clerk's error.) On March 6, 1857, only two days after the start of James Buchanan's term as president, the Court announced its decision.

Chief Justice Roger B. Taney ruled against Scott. "Negroes," he said, were "a subordinate and inferior class of beings." They had "none of the rights and privileges" of citizens of the United States. Scott was not a citizen. Therefore he had no right to bring a suit in a federal court even if he had been free! This amazing statement was enough to keep Scott a slave.

Taney had more to say. Living in Illinois and Wisconsin Territory had not made Scott free. Going to Wisconsin Territory could not have made Scott free because Congress did not have the right to keep slaves out of a federal territory. Taney's argument ran as follows: Slaves were property. Any law which prevented owners from bringing their slaves into a territory would deprive them of property. Since the Fifth Amendment to the Constitution states that "no person shall be . . . deprived of life, liberty, or property without due process of law," the Missouri Compromise was in violation of that amendment. It was unconstitutional and therefore **void**—the law was no longer in force. Of course, Congress had already canceled the Missouri Compromise by passing the Kansas-Nebraska Act.

Taney's argument was particularly annoying to people who were opposed to opening western territories to slavery. The Court was using part of the Bill of Rights to keep people in chains! Furious abolitionists were joined in their outcry by thousands of other people who considered slavery wrong.

Only once before the Dred Scott case had the Supreme Court declared a law passed by Congress to be unconstitutional. That had occurred in 1803, in the case known as *Marbury v. Madison*. Without this precedent to look back to, the justices might not have dared declare that an important law was unconstitutional.

The Dred Scott decision was greeted with a storm of criticism, and with good reason. Whether or not free African Americans were citizens of the United States, many states treated such people as citizens. Everyone agreed that a citizen of one state could sue a citizen of another in the federal courts. Still worse, why was the Supreme Court declaring the Missouri Compromise unconstitutional? That law no longer existed. The Republicans simply had to come out against this part of the decision. It made their reason for existence—keeping slavery out of the territories—illegal.

The justices had acted as they did in hopes of settling the question of slavery in the territories once and for all. Instead they only made the controversy more heated. 🖼

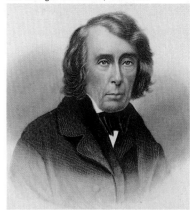

The Granger Collection, New York

Roger B. Taney was the chief justice in both the Amistad *and Dred Scott cases. What shocking reason did he give for his ruling against Scott?*

Return to the Preview & Review on page 525.

A Controversial Court   527

Preview & Review

Use these questions to guide your reading. Answer the questions after completing Section 5. **Understanding Issues, Events, & Ideas.** Describe the events of the Illinois election of 1858, using the following words: Lecompton Constitution, Lincoln-Douglas Debates, Freeport Doctrine.

1. Why did Senator Douglas speak out against acceptance of the Lecompton Constitution?

2. Why did the Republican party promote Abraham Lincoln's candidacy for the Senate?

3. What position did Senator Douglas take in his debates with Lincoln? What position did Lincoln take?

4. What was Douglas' argument in the Freeport Doctrine? How did it help him in Illinois but hurt him nationally?

Thinking Critically. **1.** Lincoln compared slavery to a cancer and said that abolishing slavery might cause the country to "bleed to death." Do you agree or disagree with Lincoln? Give reasons for your answer. **2.** You have been assigned to cover the Lincoln-Douglas debates for a Chicago newspaper. In your article, explain the issues presented in the debates.

Senator Douglas' Dilemma

Conditions in Kansas Territory grew still worse. Meeting at the town of Lecompton, the proslavery convention in Kansas had drawn up a proposed state constitution authorizing slavery. The delegates represented only a minority of the people of the territory. But since they were Democrats, President Buchanan supported them. He urged Congress to accept this **Lecompton Constitution** and admit Kansas as a state. Of course, antislavery forces in Kansas and throughout the nation objected strongly.

These developments put Senator Stephen A. Douglas in a difficult position. He was a Democrat. (But he was clearly no friend of the president's. Indeed he often used his skills as an orator to express his open contempt for Buchanan.) The president had made the matter a party issue. On the other hand, Douglas sincerely believed in popular sovereignty. And it was obvious that a majority of the people in Kansas were opposed to the Lecompton Constitution and to the opening of the territory to slavery.

To complicate his problem, Douglas had to stand for reelection to the Senate in 1858. If he went against the Democratic party, he would suffer. If he supported the Lecompton Constitution, he might lose his Senate seat, for thousands of Illinois Democrats objected bitterly to that document.

Douglas did not hesitate for long. He announced that he opposed the Lecompton Constitution. When President Buchanan tried to put pressure on him to change his mind, he flatly refused.

When a vote was finally taken on the Lecompton Constitution, the people of Kansas rejected it by a huge majority, 11,300 to 1,788. Southern Democrats and President Buchanan were furious. They blamed Douglas for this defeat.

In Illinois the Democratic party split into factions, one group pro-Buchanan, the other pro-Douglas. Illinois Republicans were of course delighted. It gave them a chance to defeat Douglas and win his seat in the United States Senate.

In those days senators were still chosen by the state legislatures, not by popular vote. Ordinary citizens often had no idea who would be chosen senator when they cast their ballots for their representatives to the state legislature. The 1858 Illinois election did not follow this pattern. Douglas was too important and his quarrel with the president too public. Illinois voters were very much aware that the state representatives they chose would reelect or defeat Douglas. Douglas campaigned hard for his seat. Technically, he and his Republican opponent were speaking in behalf of local candidates for the legislature. But everyone knew that their votes—Democratic or Republican—would decide who Illinois would send to the Senate.

The Lincoln-Douglas Debates

The Republican candidate for the Senate was Abraham Lincoln, a lawyer and former member of the Illinois state legislature. He had served a term in Congress in the 1840s. Lincoln had moved to Illinois in 1830 when he was 21 years old. He had little formal education. As a youth he had attended school only during the few winter weeks when he was not needed to work on his father's farm. But he had read widely on his own. He was a hard worker, and very ambitious.

Lincoln also had a reputation for honesty. Early in his life people began to call him "Honest Abe." He had an excellent sense of humor. Once he saw a woman who was wearing an enormous feathered hat slip and fall in a mud puddle. "Reminds me of a duck," he said to a friend he was with. "What do you mean?" asked the friend. "Feathers on her head and down on her behind," Lincoln replied. These qualities helped him in politics. In 1834 he was elected to the Illinois legislature.

Although Lincoln had prospered as a lawyer, his political career had been only modestly successful. After his term in Congress ended in 1849, he had held no further public office. He had always been a loyal member of the Whig party, but people in Illinois thought of him as a rather ordinary local politician.

All this changed when the Kansas-Nebraska Act revived the question of slavery in the territories. "If slavery is not wrong," Lincoln said, "nothing is wrong." Still, he was not an abolitionist. Slavery was like a cancer, he said, but cutting it out might cause the patient—the United States—to "bleed to death." However, there must be no further extension of slavery in the West. By 1856 Lincoln had joined the new Republican party.

Lincoln expressed his ideas well. He had a remarkable gift for words. What called him to the attention of Republican leaders, however, was his conservatism and good judgment. Although he hated slavery, he did not hate slave owners. He did not blame them for the existence of the institution. He admitted that he did not know how to do away with slavery in states where it already existed.

These views appealed to moderates in the North. To survive as a party, the Republicans had to attack the Dred Scott decision. Their problem was that they did not want to appear to be abolitionists or to favor racial equality. Lincoln seemed the kind of candidate who could manage this difficult task. His good mind and clever tongue were also important because Stephen A. Douglas was a brilliant orator and a master of every detail of the issues of the day.

Lincoln challenged Douglas to debate the issues with him in different sections of Illinois. Douglas agreed. Their meetings attracted large crowds, for each debate was a great local occasion. Because of the importance of the election, newspapers all over the country reported on the debates in detail.

Perhaps Lincoln and Douglas stated their views most clearly in their last debate, at Alton, Illinois, on October 15, 1858. Lincoln said:

> On the point of my wanting to make war between the Free and the Slave States, there has been no issue between us. So, too, when he assumes that I am in favor of introducing a perfect social and political equality between the black and white races. These are false issues. . . . The real issue in this controversy—the one pressing upon every mind—is the sentiment on the part of one class [the Republicans] that looks upon the institution of slavery as a *wrong*, and of another class that does not look upon it as wrong. . . . They [the Republicans] look upon it as being a moral, social, and political wrong; and . . . they insist that it should, as far as may be, *be treated* as a wrong; and one of the methods of treating it as a wrong is to *make provision that it shall not grow larger*. . . .
>
> That is the issue that will continue in this country when these poor tongues of Judge Douglas and myself shall be silent. It is the eternal struggle between these two principles—right and wrong—throughout the world. They are the two principles that have stood face to face from the beginning of time; and will ever continue to struggle. . . .[1]

Lincoln did not want war to settle the slavery issue, and he did not claim complete racial equality. But he did cautiously agree that he, like other Republicans, felt slavery was wrong. And he supported the Republican stand that slavery should not spread to the new territories. Douglas then responded in this meeting that is often called The Great Debate. He said:

> We ought to extend to the negro race . . . all the rights, all the privileges, and all the humanities which they can exercise consistently with the safety of society. Humanity requires that we should give them these privileges; Christianity commands that we should extend those privileges to them. The question then arises. What are those privileges, and what is the nature and the extent of them? My answer is, that that is a question each State must answer for itself. . . . If the people of all the States will act on that great principle, and each State mind its own business, attend to its own affairs, take care of its own negroes, and not meddle in with its neighbors, then there will be peace throughout the North and the South, the East and the West, throughout the whole Union.[2]

National Portrait Gallery

The "Little Giant," Stephen A. Douglas, was the Henry Clay of his generation. He was able to put the needs of the nation above self-interest. If you need help to recall Henry Clay, reread pages 438–43.

[1]From Speech at Alton, Illinois, October 15, 1858 by Abraham Lincoln
[2]From Speech at Alton, Illinois, October 15, 1858 by Stephen A. Douglas

Douglas tried to persuade the voters that Lincoln and the Republicans were dangerous radicals. He accused them of being abolitionists and of favoring equality. Lincoln "thinks the Negro is his brother," the Little Giant sneered. As for the western territories, Douglas claimed that all were destined by climate and soil conditions to become free. *Allowing* slave owners to settle in Kansas would not in fact mean that they would do so.

It was obvious that most Illinois voters shared the Little Giant's low opinion of African Americans. Lincoln's own feelings were less extreme but not essentially different. But, Lincoln insisted, all people had the "natural rights" described in the Declaration of Independence: the right to life, liberty, and the pursuit of happiness.

The Freeport Doctrine

On the question of slavery in the territories Lincoln took a firm stand. He put Douglas in a difficult political position by asking him if the people of a territory could exclude slavery *before* the territory became a state. After all, did not the Dred Scott decision mean that slavery could not be banned in any territory?

Lincoln asked Douglas these questions during their debate at Freeport, Illinois. Douglas's answer is now known as the **Freeport Doctrine.** He said:

❝ It matters not what way the Supreme Court may . . . decide. . . . The people have the lawful means to introduce or exclude [slavery] as they please, for the reason that slavery cannot exist . . . unless it is supported by local police regulations.❞

Obviously, Douglas was correct. If local authorities did not back up the owners, all the slaves could simply walk off and do as they pleased. This being the case, the people of a territory could effectively prevent slaves from being brought into their regions merely by doing nothing.

This argument helped Douglas in Illinois, where many voters were eager to believe that popular sovereignty could work in the territories despite the Dred Scott decision. It hurt him in the slave states, however. Thus it reduced his chances of winning the Democratic presidential nomination in 1860.

On election day in November the voters gave the Democrats a small majority in the state legislature. Douglas was therefore reelected to the Senate. But Lincoln was helped by the campaign too. The publicity and his effective speeches attracted much national attention. His own account of his feelings is worth recording. "It gave me a hearing," he said. "I believe I have made some marks." But he also said, "I feel like the boy who stumped his toe. I am too big to cry and too badly hurt to laugh." 🖳

Library of Congress

The "Rail Splitter," Abraham Lincoln, is beardless in this early photograph. Reread pages 377–78 to recall Lincoln's early life in Indiana.

Return to the Preview & Review on page 528.

Above, Harpers Ferry lies peacefully in the Shenandoah Valley.

Use these questions to guide your reading. Answer the questions after completing Section 6.
Understanding Issues, Events, & Ideas. Using the following words, explain the events that led to secession: Harpers Ferry, Homestead Act, border state, Constitutional Unionist party, states' rights, southern regionalism.
1. Why did John Brown and his small army raid Harpers Ferry?
2. How did Brown's raid further divide North and South?
3. How did the four-way race for president help Lincoln get elected?
4. What event prompted the Deep South to secede? What was the southerners' legal argument for their secession?
Thinking Critically. 1. Was John Brown a hero, or was he insane? Cite evidence to support your opinion. **2.** For which candidate would you have voted in 1860? Why?

6. THE THREAT OF SECESSION

The Attack on Harpers Ferry

At this point John Brown again appeared on the national scene. Brown was never punished for his part in the Pottawatomie massacre. He believed that God had commanded him to free the slaves by force. Kansas had seemed the best place to wage this battle. But violence was no longer necessary to keep slavery out of Kansas, and its settlers had little interest in fighting to get rid of it anywhere else.

Brown had to develop a new scheme. He decided to organize a small band of armed followers, march into the South, and seize land in some remote area. What would happen next he never made clear. Apparently he expected slaves from all over the region to run away and join him. With their help he would launch raids throughout the South aimed at rescuing more slaves.

Brown managed to persuade six important Massachusetts abolitionists to give him enough money to organize and supply his attack force. The goal of his tiny 18-man army was a United States government armory in the town of **Harpers Ferry**, Virginia, on the Potomac River northwest of Washington.

On the evening of October 16, 1859, Brown and his commandos crossed the Potomac. They overpowered a watchman and occupied the armory and a government rifle factory. Brown then sent some of his men off to capture two local slaveholders as hostages. One of these was Lewis Washington, a great-grandnephew of George Washington. When workers began to arrive in the morning, Brown also took some of them prisoner. Then he sat back to wait for local slaves to rise up and join his rebellion.

Not one slave did so. But the local authorities reacted promptly. In a matter of hours Brown's force was under siege, pinned down in the armory. A detachment of marines commanded by Lieutenant Colonel Robert E. Lee arrived from Washington. Brown refused to surrender. On October 18 Lee sent the marines forward with fixed bayonets. They quickly overwhelmed the rebels.

Ten of Brown's men were killed, but Brown was taken alive. He was charged with murder, conspiracy, and treason. After a fair but swift trial he was convicted and sentenced to be hanged.

John Brown was almost certainly insane. He was so disorganized that he did not even attempt to let the slaves know that he had come to free them. The affair might have been dismissed as the act of a lunatic if Brown had acted like a disturbed person after his capture, but he did not do so. Indeed, he behaved with remarkable dignity and self-discipline. Shortly after his capture he was interviewed. Clement L. Vallandigham, a congressman from Ohio, and James M. Mason, a senator from Virginia, were among those present. A *New York Herald* reporter wrote notes during the interview and they were later published. Judge for yourself if Brown sounds insane in the following part of the interview:

" *Mr. Vallandigham*. Mr. Brown, who sent you here?

Brown. No man sent me here; it was my own prompting and that of my Maker, or that of the Devil—whichever you please to ascribe it to. I acknowledge no master in human form. . . .

Mason. What was your object in coming?

Brown. We came to free the slaves, and only that. . . .

A Volunteer. How many men, in all, had you?

Brown. I came to Virginia with 18 men only, besides myself. . . .

Mason. How do you justify your acts?

Brown. I think, my friend, you [slaveholders] are guilty of a great wrong against God and humanity,—I say it without wishing to be offensive—and it would be perfectly right for any one to interfere with you so far as to free those you wilfully and wickedly hold in bondage. I do not say this insultingly.

Mason. I understand that.

Brown. I think I did right, and that others will do right who interfere with you at any time and at all times. I hold that the Golden Rule, 'Do unto others as ye would that others should do unto you,' applies to all who would help others gain their liberty.

Lieutenant Stuart. But don't you believe in the Bible?

Brown. Certainly I do. . . .

A Bystander. Do you consider this a religious movement?

Brown. It is, in my opinion, the greatest service man can render to God.

Bystander. Do you consider yourself an instrument in the hands of Providence [God]?

Brown. I do.

Bystander. Upon what principle do you justify your acts?

Brown. Upon the Golden Rule. I pity the poor in bondage that have none to help them: that is why I am here; not to gratify any personal animosity [resentment], revenge, or

Metropolitan Museum of Art

"The Last Moments of John Brown" is the way northerners imagined the leader of the raid on Harpers Ferry being led to his execution. Horace Greeley wrote for his newspaper a description of the woman waiting with her little child: "He stopped a moment, and stooping, kissed the child." But Greeley was not present and in fact only soldiers met Brown. Why would the North have taken such a generous view of John Brown?

vindictive [vengeful] spirit. It is my sympathy with the oppressed and the wronged, that are as good as you and as precious in the sight of God. . . .

    Bystander. Brown, suppose you had every [slave] in the United States, what would you do with them?

    Brown. Set them free. . . .'**

Even Brown's judge and jailors admired his calm courage. When he was condemned to death, he said that he had acted in the name of God:

    To have interfered as I have done . . . in behalf of His despised poor, is not wrong, but right. Now, if it is . . . necessary that I should forfeit my life for the furtherance of the ends of justice . . . I say, let it be done. I feel no consciousness of guilt.

Brown became a hero to the abolitionists and to many other northerners. They considered him a noble freedom fighter. His bloody murders in Kansas and his reckless assault at Harpers Ferry were conveniently forgotten. When northerners made Brown a near saint, southerners in the slave states became even more concerned. They began to think that northerners intended to destroy slavery, not merely limit its expansion. Once again, northerners and southerners looked at each other with suspicion, fear, and even hatred.

The Election of 1860

As the 1860 presidential election drew near, the Democrats became even more sharply divided. The northern faction supported Senator Douglas. The southern wing was led by President Buchanan, although he was not a candidate for a second term. The party's nominating convention was held in April 1860 at Charleston, South Carolina. Douglas controlled a small majority of the delegates, but the rules of the convention required a two-thirds majority for nomination. This he could not get. The convention then adjourned.

The delegates gathered again in June in Baltimore. Once more they failed to agree. This time the party broke formally in two. The northerners nominated Douglas for president. The southerners selected Buchanan's vice president, John C. Breckinridge of Kentucky.

In the meantime the Republican presidential convention had taken place in Chicago. To broaden their appeal, party leaders drafted a program of economic reforms to go along with their demand that slavery be kept out of the territories. They called for a **Homestead Act** giving 160 acres (64 hectares), enough land for a family farm, to anyone who would settle on it. They urged government support for a railroad to the Pacific and higher tariffs on manufactured goods in

'From *The Life and Letters of John Brown* edited by F.B. Sanborn

John Brown's assault in Shenandoah Valley prompted this poem which foretells Brown's hanging and the coming Civil War.

The Portent

**Hanging from the
  beam, Slowly swaying
  (such the law),
Gaunt the shadow on
  your green,
    Shenandoah!
The cut is on the crown
(Lo, John Brown),
And the stabs shall heal
  no more.

Hidden in the cap°
  Is the anguish none
  can draw;
So your future veils its
face,
    Shenandoah!
But the streaming beard
  is shown
The meteor of the war.**
  Herman Melville, 1859

° A cap was placed over the head of a man being hanged.

Thomas Cole's "Home in the Woods" was painted in about 1845. Family farms sprang up everywhere, especially after the Homestead Act of 1862 made land available to anyone who would settle it. After studying this painting closely, what can you say about daily life on the frontier?

order to protect producers from foreign competition. They rejected the idea of nativist support. They promised not to restrict immigration into the country.

Before the convention Senator William H. Seward of New York seemed the person most likely to get the Republican presidential nomination. However, to win the election, the Republicans would have to carry Pennsylvania, Indiana, and Illinois—the northern states that Buchanan had carried in 1856. Seward was thought to be too antislavery to persuade doubtful voters in those states. After much political "horse-trading" the delegates nominated Abraham Lincoln.

Many proslavery radicals had threatened that the southern states would secede from the Union and set up an independent country of their own if a Republican was elected president. This possibility was particularly alarming to many people in the Upper South, the so-called **border states** of Maryland, Delaware, Kentucky, and Missouri. Should civil war break out, it would surely be fought on their soil.

These people formed still a fourth party, the **Constitutional Unionist party,** in 1860. The Constitutional Unionist's platform was simple: They stood for "the Constitution and the Union." In other words, they tried to ignore the controversial issues that were dividing the country. If the party had lived long enough to develop a symbol like the Democratic donkey and the Republican elephant, the symbol should have been an ostrich with its head buried in the sand.

The Constitutional Unionists nominated John Bell, for many years a congressman and senator from Tennessee. Bell was a stiff, rather colorless person. He was chosen because of his long record as a conservative and the fact that although he was a slave owner, he had voted against the Kansas-Nebraska Act.

With four candidates running, no one could hope to get a majority of the popular vote. Lincoln received 1,866,000, nearly all in the northern states. Douglas got 1,383,000, also mostly in the North. Breckinridge received 848,000 and Bell 593,000. But Lincoln won a solid majority of the electoral votes, 180 of the 303 cast.

What had happened was this: In the free states the election was between Lincoln and Douglas. It was a fairly close contest, but Lincoln won in every state. Despite his large popular vote, Douglas got only 12 electoral votes, Missouri's 9 and 3 from New Jersey.

In the slave states Breckinridge and Bell divided the votes. Breckinridge had a majority in all the states of the Deep South. Bell carried the border states of Tennessee, Kentucky, and Virginia.

The Secession Crisis

Although he got much less than half the popular vote, Lincoln had been legally elected president. Even the southerners recognized that this was so. The more radical of them therefore prepared to take their states out of the Union.

LEARNING FROM MAPS. *The outcome of the election of 1860 had long-range consequences. Where was each candidate strongest? How can you explain these regional strengths?*

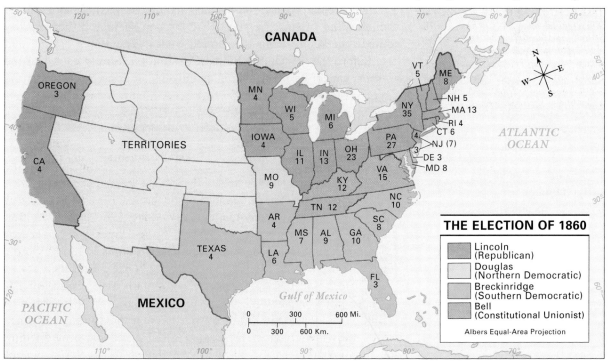

THE ELECTION OF 1860

Lincoln (Republican)
Douglas (Northern Democratic)
Breckinridge (Southern Democratic)
Bell (Constitutional Unionist)

Albers Equal-Area Projection

For several years there had been much talk of the South seceding if a "black Republican" was ever elected president. Lincoln and other northerners had convinced themselves that this talk was merely bluff. Stephen A. Douglas, however, recognized how serious the threat was. As the campaign progressed, he sensed the trend of popular opinion. A month before the election he realized that Lincoln was almost certainly going to win. "Mr. Lincoln is the next president," he told his secretary. "We must try to save the Union. I will go South." During the remaining weeks he campaigned in Tennessee, Georgia, and Alabama. Everywhere he spoke not for himself but for preserving the Union.

His noble effort failed. Within days of the news of Lincoln's election, the legislature of South Carolina summoned a special convention to consider the question of secession. Before the end of the year the delegates to that convention voted to take the state out of the Union. Other southern states followed quickly. Only the states of the Upper South held back, and leaders in these states were seriously considering leaving the Union.

The reasons why the South seceded have puzzled historians for more than a hundred years. Probably no completely satisfactory explanation is possible. But this much can be said: The slave system was at the root of the difficulties between the sections. Southerners felt that the security of their peculiar institution was being threatened. By leaving the United States and setting up a country of their own, they hoped to protect not only slavery but what they considered their whole way of life.

The southern states based their right to leave the Union on the fact that the original 13 states had existed separately before they joined together to form the United States. The states drafted and then approved the United States Constitution. Surely each had the right to cancel its allegiance if its citizens so desired. This was the

LEARNING FROM TABLES. *These tables show the status of American manufacturing in 1860. What was the South's leading product? What problems would leaving the Union cause for southern consumers?*

LEADING U. S. MANUFACTURES, 1860		
Rank	Product	Value
1	Cotton goods	$54,671,082
2	Lumber	$53,569,942
3	Boots and shoes	$49,161,124
4	Flour and meal	$40,083,056
5	Men's clothing	$36,680,803
6	Iron	$35,689,276
7	Machinery	$32,565,843
8	Woolen goods	$25,032,489
9	Carriages, wagons, carts	$23,654,560
10	Leather	$22,785,715

Source: *Eighth Census of the United States, Manufactures, 1860*

MANUFACTURING BY SECTIONS, 1860		
Section	Number of Establishments	Value of of Products
North	73,958	$1,270,937,679
New England	20,671	$468,599,287
Middle Atlantic	53,287	$802,338,392
West	45,562	$455,836,519
Midwest	36,785	$384,606,530
California	8,777	$71,229,989
South	20,631	$155,531,281
Territories	282	$3,556,197

Source: *Eighth Census of the United States, Manufactures, 1860*

The Granger Collection, New York

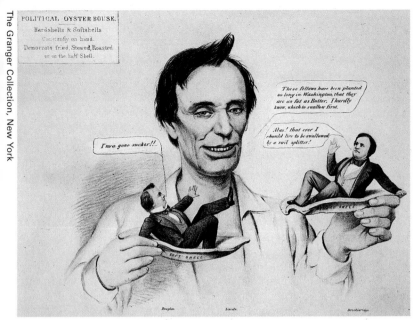

POLITICAL OYSTER HOUSE.
Hardshells & Softshells
Constantly on hand.
Democrats fried, Stewed, Roasted
or on the half Shell.

These fellows have been planted so long in Washington, that they are as fat as Butter, I hardly know, which to swallow first.

Alas! that ever I should live to be swallowed by a rail splitter!

I'm a gone sucker!!

In this caricature of Abraham Lincoln we see how easily he downed his opponents. "Honest Abe Taking Them on the Half Shell" shows Douglas on the left and Breckinridge on the right. How does this cartoon capture the outcome of the 1860 election?

doctrine of **states' rights,** first argued by Jefferson in the 1790s. It was given its most complete expression by John C. Calhoun in the 1820s and 1830s when he argued that a state could nullify a federal law it did not consider constitutional.

The ideas of nullification and secession were a challenge to the basic tenets of the Constitution. The Constitution bound all the states together by mutual consent. States agreed to recognize the Constitution as the supreme law of the land. They also recognized federalism–the sharing of power by the national and state governments— and the responsibility of the national government to oversee certain government functions. Now the southern states proposed to cast aside the Constitution in favor of states' rights.

Belief in states' rights was the legal justification of secession, but it was not the reason why the southern states seceded. That was more a matter of **southern regionalism**—loyalty to the region and to the slave system. The national controversy over slavery had weakened the southerners' loyalty to the entire United States. For a person like Lincoln to say, "If slavery is not wrong, nothing is wrong," was a slap in the face to most southerners. No matter that Lincoln and other moderates had no intention of trying to destroy slavery where it already existed, southern defenders of slavery could not accept the idea that the system was "wrong." When Lincoln's point of view triumphed and he became president of the United States, southerners no longer wished to be part of the Union.

Return to the Preview & Review on page 532.

CHAPTER 15 REVIEW

1850	**1852**	**1854**
Compromise of 1850 (Fugitive Slave Act)	*Uncle Tom's Cabin* published	Kansas-Nebraska Bill

Chapter Summary
Read the statements below. Choose one, and write a paragraph explaining its importance.
1. The Fugitive Slave Act and *Uncle Tom's Cabin* increased northerners' discomfort with slavery.
2. The violent and bloody struggle for Kansas between pro- and antislavery groups gave a preview of the Civil War.
3. The controversy over slavery helped end the Whig party and start both the Know-Nothings and the Republican party.
4. The decision in *Dred Scott v. Sandford* continued to focus attention and criticism on slavery.
5. The Lincoln-Douglas debates summarized feelings of both sides of the slavery question and put Lincoln's name before the public.
6. The view of John Brown as a hero after his raid on Harpers Ferry angered southerners.
7. The election of Lincoln rekindled threats of secession based on states' rights and, in fact, several states voted to secede.

Reviewing Chronological Order
Number your paper 1–5. Then study the time line above and place the following events in the order in which they happened by writing the first next to 1, the second next to 2, and so on.
1. Brown's raid on Harpers Ferry
2. *Uncle Tom's Cabin*
3. Lincoln elected president
4. Kansas-Nebraska Bill
5. *Dred Scott v. Sandford*

Understanding Main Ideas
1. How did Douglas hope to persuade southerners to support his Kansas-Nebraska Bill? How did he hope to avoid a northern uproar?
2. How did proslavery and antislavery forces square off in Kansas?
3. What was the Republican platform? In what section of the country was it strongest?
4. What did the Supreme Court decide in the case of *Dred Scott v. Sandford?* Why was the decision strongly criticized?

5. Who were the four candidates for president in 1860, and which was the party of each?
6. How did the Republican party try to broaden its appeal in the election of 1860?

Thinking Critically
1. **Synthesizing.** Imagine that you are a northern abolitionist. Compose a fiery letter criticizing slavery to send to the editor of your local paper.
2. **Creating.** Write the copy for a handbill advertising the play based on *Uncle Tom's Cabin*, to be presented at the Abolition Theatre of Boston, Massachusetts, in 1853. Choose dates and time of performance. Create names of actors for the leading roles.
3. **Evaluating.** In your opinion, what did Lincoln mean when he said every person has a right "to the bread . . . which his own hand earns"? Do you agree or disagree with this statement? Why?
4. **Identifying Issues.** Take the part of a senator from South Carolina after the 1860 election of Abraham Lincoln. In a letter to your closest friend, a senator from New York, explain why your state has chosen to secede from the Union.

Writing About History
Use your historical imagination to write a news story about of one of the Lincoln-Douglas debates. Be sure to describe the setting and to summarize each candidate's position. Also describe the crowd's reaction to the speakers. Use the information in Chapter 15 and in reference books to prepare your story.

Practicing the Strategy
Review the strategy on page 517.
Comparing Maps. Study the maps on pages 457 and 551, then answer the following questions.
1. On the map on page 457, what states included cotton-growing areas by 1859?

1857	1858	1859	1860
ner caned e Senate	*Dred Scott v. Sandford*	Lincoln-Douglas debates ★	Brown's raid on Harpers Ferry	Lincoln elected president ★

awatomie Massacre

Lecompton Constitution rejected ★

South Carolina votes to secede

anan elected president

Douglas states Freeport Doctrine

2. How had these areas of cotton growing changed since 1839?

3. On the map on page 551, which states belonged to the Confederacy? Which states were considered "border states," on the side of the Union?

4. Locate the border states on the map on page 457. Why do you think that those states joined the Union side rather than the Confederacy?

Using Primary Sources

Southerners had long wanted to obtain Cuba, arguing that a slave rebellion there might cause American slaves to revolt. In 1854 the United States began negotiations with Spain to buy Cuba. From these talks came the Ostend Manifesto, a secret state department proposal to act if Spain refused. When news of the manifesto leaked out, northerners were outraged, seeing it as a "slaveholder's plot" to add to southern territory. As you read the excerpt from the manifesto, see if you agree with its logic. Then answer the questions below.

> *Self-preservation is the first law of nature, with states as well as with individuals. . . . After we shall have offered Spain a price for Cuba far beyond its present value, and this shall have been refused, it will then be time to consider the question, does Spain, in possession of Cuba, seriously endanger our internal peace and the existence of our cherished Union?*
>
> *Should this question be answered in the affirmative, then, by every law, human and divine, we shall be justified in wrestling it from Spain if we possess the power; and this upon the very same principle that would justify an individual in tearing down the burning house of his neighbor if there were no other means of preventing the flames from destroying his own home.*

1. What evidence in the excerpt suggests that the states were more concerned with their own in-

terests than with maintaining peace with foreign nations?

2. According to the excerpt, what is the justification for taking Cuba by force? Do you think this logic applies to foreign affairs today? Why or why not?

3. If you were a historian, how might you use the Ostend Manifesto to support the argument that the causes of war develop gradually? Explain your answer.

Linking History & Geography

The Missouri Compromise (1820), the Compromise of 1850, and the Kansas-Nebraska Bill (1854) all revised the geographic limits of slavery. Use the maps on page 517 and the information in Chapters 12 and 15 to answer these questions.

1. Which territories remained free under the Compromise of 1850? Which permitted slavery?

2. What physical features of the West might have limited the spread of slavery naturally?

3. Why do you think southerners continued to fight for the right to bring slavery into the new territories?

Enriching the Study of History

1. **Individual Project**. Prepare a chart to show the political parties that came into being in the 1850s. Include information about the party platforms, candidates, and region of strongest support. Your teacher may wish to display the charts.

2. **Cooperative Project**. Your teacher will divide your class into four teams. Each team will be assigned one of the 1860 presidential candidates: John Bell, John C. Breckinridge, Stephen A. Douglas, or Abraham Lincoln. Each team will prepare and present to the class a short campaign speech to endorse its candidate. Then your class will hold a mock election.

Chapter 15 Review   541

The Civil War

Abraham Lincoln's election sent a signal to southerners to take their states out of the Union. When the Confederacy fired on Fort Sumter, the Civil War began. For four years North and South were locked in battle. Southerners fought the war for the right of self-determination, northerners to keep the Union whole. This chapter relates the major battles and strategies of the war and its burden upon the economies of the North and South. It shows something of the lives of typical Union and Confederate soldiers, as well as of the men and women who came to care for the wounded. The chapter concludes with General Sherman's total war and March to the Sea and the surrender at Appomattox by General Lee to General Grant. And as weary soldiers wended their way home, many wondered "What is lost? What is won?"

Connecticut Historical Society

The American eagle guards its nest of states in this 1861 cartoon. But while the eagle warns against traitors, the southern states in the foreground are hatching rebellion. This war propaganda cartoon leaves no doubt as to the artist's position: "The Union: It Must and Shall be Preserved." Make a poster or draw a picture that shows the breakup of the Union in a different way.

1. THE WAR BEGINS

Between Peace and War

The states of the Deep South left the Union during a time when the United States government was particularly weak. President-elect Lincoln would not take office until March 4, 1861. Furthermore, he showed no interest in dealing with the problem of secession or taking responsibility of any kind before that date. The outgoing president, James Buchanan, seemed paralyzed by the crisis. He announced that secession was illegal. Then he added that it would also be illegal for the federal government to try to prevent a state from seceding!

Matters drifted throughout the winter. Several members of Congress tried to work out compromises that would satisfy the fears of southerners without stirring up northern foes of slavery. None succeeded. More southern states withdrew from the Union. Each seceding state tried to take over federal property within its borders—post offices, army forts, courthouses.

Buchanan did not try to hold on to government property in the states that left the Union. But there were three forts in Charleston, South Carolina, that did not fall into local hands. One of these, **Fort Sumter,** was on an island in Charleston harbor. The others were on the mainland. They were held by about 100 soldiers commanded by Major Robert Anderson.

Gradually, national attention focused on these forts. Would South Carolina use force to seize them? If so, would Buchanan try to defend the forts? Major Anderson was a southerner. But he was also a patriotic soldier who had taken an oath to protect the flag of the United States. Anderson realized that he could not protect all the forts with his tiny force. One night in December 1860 he moved his men to the more easily protected Fort Sumter.

South Carolina troops then occupied the abandoned forts on the mainland. When Buchanan sent an unarmed ship with men and supplies to Fort Sumter, the South Carolinians drove it off with cannon fire from the shore. For the first time shots were fired in anger. Yet no one was injured. Anderson remained in control of Fort Sumter.

The Confederate States of America

On February 4, 1861, 37 delegates representing six southern republics met at Montgomery, Alabama, to create a central government. Southern leaders knew that the seceding states had to design a strong union if they were to stay independent. They had to work fast. They wanted to have the new government in operation before Abraham Lincoln became president of the United States on March 4.

The delegates began work on February 5 and adopted a constitution only three days later. This was possible because the document

Preview & Review

Use these questions to guide your reading. Answer the questions after completing Section 1.
Understanding Issues, Events, & Ideas. Using the following words, explain how the war between the North and South began: Fort Sumter, confederacy, Confederate States of America, Civil War.

1. Why was there no strong presidential reaction in the winter of 1861 to the secession of the Deep South?
2. How did the Confederate constitution reflect the South's belief in states' rights?
3. What was Lincoln's message to the Confederacy in his first inaugural address?
4. What reasoning did President Lincoln give for going to war?

Thinking Critically. 1. Imagine that you are a secretary for President Davis. In your journal, describe Jefferson Davis and explain what you think are his strengths and weaknesses as president of the Confederacy.
2. You are the messenger sent by President Davis to give the order to fire on Fort Sumter on April 12. Write a letter to your cousin in the North, explaining why you think Davis should or should not have issued this order.

was almost a copy of the United States Constitution. The differences were small but significant. The new nation was to be a **confederacy** of independent states, not a union. Hence the delegates called it the **Confederate States of America.** The constitution also specifically mentioned slavery and guaranteed the rights of citizens to own slaves. Congress was forbidden to pass any law "denying . . . the right of property in negro slaves."

Despite a stress on the rights of the separate states, the Confederate constitution, like the United States Constitution, was to be the "supreme law of the land." The president was to hold office for six years instead of four. But he could not be reelected. Congress could not spend money unless two thirds of the representatives approved. The constitution could be amended if two thirds of the states approved, not three fourths as under the United States Constitution.

The Confederacy Chooses Jefferson Davis

Jefferson Davis' portrait was made halfway through the war, after he had served two of the six years of his term.

Museum of the Confederacy, Richmond, VA
Photography by Katherine Wetzel

The day after finishing the constitution, the delegates elected Jefferson Davis of Mississippi to be president of the newly formed Confederate States of America. They chose Alexander Stephens of Georgia as vice president.

Davis was in the rose garden at his plantation, Brierfield, overlooking the Mississippi, when a telegram announcing his election was delivered. The president was a tall, slender man with high cheekbones, fair hair, and blue-gray eyes. He was 52 years old, the tenth child of a pioneer family in Todd County, Kentucky. He attended Transylvania University in Lexington, Kentucky, and was graduated from the United States Military Academy in 1828. He resigned his commission in 1835 to become a cotton planter in Mississippi.

Davis had long and varied experience in public life before becoming president of the Confederacy. He was elected to the House of Representatives in 1845. The next year the Mexican War broke out. He gave up his seat in Congress to serve as a colonel in the army. He was wounded in the foot at the Battle of Buena Vista. The wound was quite serious because the bullet drove pieces of his brass spur into his foot. He came back to Mississippi on crutches but recovered fully. In 1847 he was elected to the United States Senate. When Franklin Pierce became president in 1853, he named Davis secretary of war.

Southerners rally for the inauguration of Jefferson Davis, who stands on the balcony of the capitol in Montgomery, Alabama. Judging from the clock, he probably took office at high noon. How was this moment a turning point for the South?

In his inaugural address President Davis insisted that he desired to maintain peaceful relations with the United States. His speech was not very inspiring. Davis was an extremely hard worker, but he did not get on well with people. He often quarreled with members of his cabinet and with other government officials. He could be very stubborn. His feelings were easily hurt by criticism. He wasted far too much of his time handling unimportant details. Once he spent a whole day dictating one 4,000-word letter.

The Granger Collection, New York

Lincoln Becomes President

In 1861 Jefferson Davis's strengths were much more obvious than his weaknesses. Indeed, when Abraham Lincoln was inaugurated as president of the United States on March 4, many people thought him a far less inspiring leader than the president of the new Confederacy.

Lincoln had chosen a cabinet that reflected a wide variety of attitudes and regions. This was understandable at a time of national crisis. Yet would this backwoods lawyer be able to control such a group? Or would he become a figurehead, a kind of homespun master of ceremonies? He had appointed the best-known Republican in the United States, William H. Seward, as secretary of state. Seward did not resent Lincoln's having defeated him for the Republican presidential nomination. But he did not think Lincoln competent to be president. He was ready, he told his wife, "to save freedom and my country" by making the major government decisions himself.

Lincoln, however, did not intend to be dominated by Seward or anyone else. People like Seward misunderstood him. They took his slow, deliberate, rather uncertain manner to mean confusion and lack of intelligence. Nothing could have been further from the truth.

Lincoln seemed a strange figure, six feet, six inches tall without his stovepipe hat. His voice was thin and high-pitched. He was awkward. At a dance he told his future wife, "I want to dance with you in the worst possible way." "And he certainly did," added Mary Todd Lincoln. She was convinced her husband would one day be president. She had once been courted by Stephen A. Douglas, but after marriage she made Lincoln a fine home and raised his sons in Springfield and Washington.

Lincoln first publicly revealed his depth and determination in his inaugural address. He told the troubled American people:

Library of Congress

Mary Todd married Abraham Lincoln in 1842. She was from Kentucky but met Lincoln while visiting relatives in Illinois. How might her Kentucky origins have troubled some people after the Civil War began?

    66 Apprehension [fear] seems to exist among the people of the Southern states that by the accession [coming into office] of a Republican administration their property and their peace and their personal security are to be endangered. There has never been any reasonable cause for such apprehension. Indeed, the most ample evidence to the contrary has all the while existed and been open to their inspection. It is found in nearly all the published speeches of him who now addresses you [Lincoln]. I do but quote one of those speeches when I declare that "I have no purpose, directly or indirectly, to interfere with the institution of slavery in the states where it exists. I believe I have no lawful right to do so, and I have no inclination [desire] to do so. . . .

    Before entering upon so grave a matter as the destruction of our national fabric, with all its benefits, its memories, and its hopes, would it not be wise to ascertain precisely why we do it? . . .

All profess to be content in the Union if all constitutional rights can be maintained. Is it true, then, that any right, plainly written in the Constitution, has been denied? I think not. . . .

One section of our country believes slavery is right, and ought to be extended, while the other believes it is wrong, and ought not to be extended. This is the only substantial [major] dispute. . . .

Physically speaking, we cannot separate. We cannot remove our respective sections from each other, nor build an impassible wall between them. . . . They cannot but remain face to face, and intercourse [dealings], either amicable [friendly] or hostile, must continue between them. . . .

In your hands, my dissatisfied countrymen, and not in mine, is the momentous issue of civil war. The government will not assail [attack] you. You can have no conflict without being yourselves the aggressors. . . .

We are not enemies, but friends. We must not be enemies. Though passion may have strained, it must not break, our bonds of affection. **99**

Lincoln hoped his words would soothe raw emotions. He assured the South that he would not send troops into the region to prevent secession. He promised again not to interfere with slavery in the states. Nevertheless, secession was illegal, even "revolutionary," he said. "No state upon its own mere notion can lawfully get out of the Union." In any case, secession would not end any of the existing disagreements between the North and South. Conflicts of interest would remain. The only sensible solution was to negotiate as friends. Thus the new president held out every hope that the Union might be preserved.

The Firing on Fort Sumter

The immediate problem Lincoln faced was what to do about Fort Sumter, a problem he inherited from President Buchanan. Major Anderson and his men could not hold out forever without fresh supplies. After considering the question for about a month, Lincoln decided to send food to the besieged garrison but no troop reinforcements or ammunition. He informed the governor of South Carolina of his intention.

The Confederates would not accept even this small "invasion" of what they considered their territory. On April 12, acting on orders from President Davis, they began to bombard Fort Sumter. By the next day the fort was in ruins. When his ammunition was almost exhausted, Major Anderson and his weary troops laid down their arms in surrender.

New York Public Library Picture Collection

A direct hit on Fort Sumter signals the beginning of the Civil War. Judging from the engraving, how would you describe the weapons of this war?

The **Civil War** had begun. Southerners felt that they were fighting for what we would call the right of self-determination. They believed that the people of a state ought to be able to decide what kind of government they wanted for themselves. They had no intention of injuring the states that remained in the Union. What right had the United States to prevent them from going their own way?

Lincoln's answer to this argument was simple: A nation has the right to protect itself against destruction. If one part could separate itself from the rest whenever it disapproved of the result of an election, or the passage of a controversial law, the nation would swiftly break up into many tiny fragments.

Lincoln's reasoning made it possible to go to war for patriotic reasons. Slavery was obviously the major cause of the war. But the war was not fought to abolish slavery. People in the northern states did not suddenly become abolitionists when Confederate cannon began to pound Fort Sumter. They fought "to save the Union," not "to free the slaves."

Return to the Preview & Review on page 543.

Richmond, Virginia, became the capital of the Confederacy, the capitol itself visible at the center.

New York Library, Stokes Collection

2. RAISING THE ARMIES

Robert E. Lee

After the attack on Fort Sumter, Lincoln called for 75,000 volunteer soldiers to put down the rebellion. Recruits came forward enthusiastically all over the North. But news that Lincoln intended to use force against the Confederacy caused Virginia, North Carolina, Tennessee, and Arkansas to secede and join the other Confederate states. When Virginia joined the Confederacy, the government shifted its capital from Montgomery, Alabama, to Richmond, Virginia.

In both North and South, recruiting was left to the states. Young men enlisted with high hopes for an exciting adventure that would take them far from farm or factory. A passion for "Zouave" units swept both sides. Prospective soldiers joined these Zouave companies to wear their broad sashes and baggy red breeches.

Since northern and southern soldiers were so much alike, any differences had to come from their generals. Lincoln's first choice for commander of the Union army had been Colonel Robert E. Lee, the officer who captured John Brown. Although Lee was a Virginian, he owned no slaves and was known to have opposed secession. His great hero was George Washington, and he was married to the first president's step-great-granddaughter.

Lee had been a top student in his class at the United States Military Academy. He always had high grades and graduated second

Preview & Review

Use these questions to guide your reading. Answer the questions after completing Section 2.

Understanding Issues, Events, & Ideas. Describe your experiences as either a Confederate or Union soldier, using the following words: Bull Run, Army of the Potomac, Battle of Seven Pines, Army of Northern Virginia, Seven Days Before Richmond.

1. Why did Lincoln wish Lee to command his army?
2. What advantages did the North have at the beginning of the Civil War? What advantages did the South have?
3. What did the Battle of Bull Run reveal about both sides?
4. In what ways was the Civil War the first modern war?

Thinking Critically. 1. Imagine that you are General Robert E. Lee. In a letter, tell President Lincoln that you cannot lead the Union forces and why. 2. You are a Union soldier under the command of General McClellan. In your diary, record your opinion of McClellan as a man and as a leader.

Raising the Armies 549

Robert E. Lee sits astride his horse Traveller. Lee was a true national hero because of his strong personal character. Traveller was nearly as celebrated. Visitors after the war pulled the hairs from his tail for souvenirs. Lee's home is today part of the Arlington National Cemetery. Do you think it is unusual for a rebel leader to be respected by friend and foe alike? Why?

Virginia Historical Society

in his class. As a young officer in the Mexican War, he had performed brilliantly. If he had accepted Lincoln's offer, the Civil War might not have lasted as long as it did.

Unfortunately for the United States, Lee put loyalty to his home state of Virginia above the Union. He resigned from the army and joined the Confederates. Lincoln then turned to General Irvin McDowell, who was an efficient officer but without battle experience.

By July 1861 30,000 Union soldiers were training in camps outside Washington. Twenty miles (32 kilometers) to the south other thousands of Confederate soldiers were gathered at Manassas railroad junction, on a small stream called Bull Run. The southern troops at Manassas were commanded by General Pierre Beauregard of Louisiana. Beauregard had also seen action in the Mexican War. In the attack on Mexico City he was twice wounded. It was Beauregard who had commanded the guns that battered Fort Sumter.

North Versus South

In numbers the Confederacy seemed no match for the United States. The North had about 22 million people, the South only 9 million. Nearly 4 million of the southerners were slaves. Since southerners were unwilling to put guns in the hands of slaves, the Confederate army could draw upon only 1,280,000 men between the ages of 15 and 50 to fill its ranks.

In 1860 over 90 percent of the nation's factories were in the northern states. New York, Pennsylvania, and Massachusetts each manufactured more goods than the entire Confederacy. There were only two gunpowder factories in the South, both small. There was not one factory capable of handling orders for uniforms and shoes.

The North also had more than twice as many miles of railroad tracks as the South and twice as many horses, donkeys, and mules. The government had little trouble moving its troops and supplies from the farms and the cities to its armies in the field. Since the United States was already in existence, it had an army, a navy, and ways of raising money. The South had to create these from scratch.

Just to begin operations, Confederate officials were forced to borrow from the state of Alabama and from bankers in New Orleans. The Confederate treasury was originally located in the back room of a bank in Montgomery. The secretary of the treasury and his one assistant had to use their own money to furnish the office.

On the other hand, the Confederacy had certain advantages over the Union. Like the colonists during the Revolutionary War, the southerners were defending their homeland. The invading northern armies had to maintain longer and longer lines of communication as they advanced. The southerners' homes and their whole way of life were at stake. This added to their determination and helped make up for the shortage of men and supplies.

LEARNING FROM MAPS. *This map shows the Union torn apart by the Civil War. Why do you think the border states were so called?*

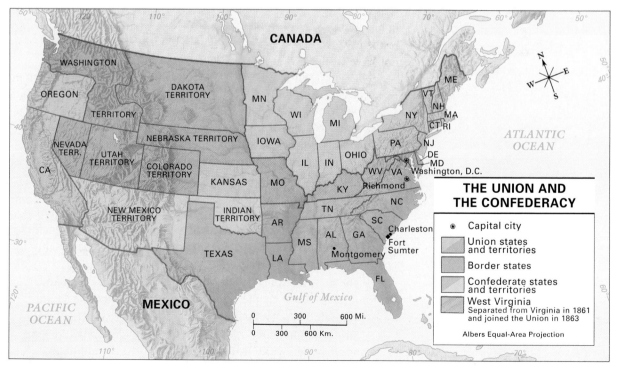

THE UNION AND THE CONFEDERACY

* Capital city

Union states and territories

Border states

Confederate states and territories

West Virginia
Separated from Virginia in 1861 and joined the Union in 1863

Albers Equal-Area Projection

At the beginning of the Civil War, most Union and Confederate soldiers carried the musket, a gun that was only accurate up to about 80 yards. Gradually, the musket was replaced by rifles that had much greater range and accuracy. The result was to put attacking troops in much greater danger and strengthen those in definitive positions. To advance in mass formation against forces armed with these rifles was to invite wholesale slaughter.

Army food ranged from fair to awful. It consisted mostly of salt or pickled beef or pork and bread—cornbread for the Confederate troops and hardtack for the Union. Hardtack was a solid cracker made from wheat. It came in thick, square chunks. The men generally soaked it in their coffee and ate it with a spoon. Coffee was therefore especially important to the Union soldiers.

In camp Confederate "Johnny Reb" and Union "Billy Yank" passed the time playing cards, organizing horse races, and taking care of their equipment. Baseball was popular. When bats and balls were not available, the men made do with a board or a section of some farmer's fence rail for a bat. A walnut or stone wrapped with yarn made a usable ball.

Music was a popular pastime in both armies. Soldiers gathered around campfires in the evening to sing songs like "Home, Sweet Home." "I don't believe we can have an army without music," said Robert E. Lee. Even northerners found themselves whistling "Dixie," the Confederate anthem.

"Johnny Reb" Meets "Billy Yank"

The Civil War was the bloodiest war Americans have ever waged. Americans fought Americans, yet the diaries and journals of soldiers on both sides described many friendly encounters. Alexander Hunter, a young Confederate soldier, wrote of one such meeting in Virginia. Consider how you would feel fighting the "friendly enemy" he describes here:

    " It was the latter part of August [1863]; orders were given to be prepared to go on [guard] early in the morning; and until a late hour the men were busy cooking rations and cleaning equipment.

Before the mists had been chased by the rising sun, the company in close column of fours marched down the road. Man and animals were in perfect condition, brimful of mettle [excited] and in buoyant spirits.

The route lay along the banks of the river; upon the winding course of which, after several hours riding, the regiment reached its destination and relieved the various [guards]. A sergeant and squad of men were left at each post . . . to watch the enemy on the other side of the Rappahannock [River].

The next day our squad, Sergeant Joe Reid in command, sauntered down to the bank, but seeing no one we lay at length under the spreading trees. . . .

The Rappahannock, which was at this place about two hundred yards wide, flowing oceanward [to the southeast], its bosom [surface] reflecting the roseate-hued [pink] morn, was as lovely a body of water as the sun ever shone upon. The sound of the gentle ripple of its waves upon the sand was broken by a faint 'halloo' which came from the other side.

'Johnny Reb; I say, J-o-h-n-n-y R-e-b, don't shoot!'

Joe Reid shouted back, 'All right!'

'What command are you?'

The spoken words floated clear and distant across the water, 'The Black Horse cavalry. Who are you?'

'The Second Michigan Cavalry.'

'Come to the bank,' said our spokesman, 'and show yourself; we won't fire.'

'On your honor, Johnny Reb?'

'On our honor, Billy Yank.'

In a second a large squad of blue-coats across the way advanced to the water's brink. The Southerners did the same; then the former put the query [question].

'Have you any tobacco?'

'Plenty of it,' went our reply.

'Any sugar or coffee?' they questioned.

'Not a taste nor a smell.'

'Let's trade,' was shouted with eagerness.

'Very well,' was the reply. '. . . meet us here this evening.'

'All right,' they answered; then added, 'Say, Johnny, want some newspapers?'

'Y-e-s!'

'Then look out, we are going to send you some.'

'How are you going to do it?'

'Wait and see.' . . .

Eagerly he watched. . . . Presently he shouted:

'Here they come!' and then in a tone of intense admiration, 'I'll be doggoned if these Yanks are not the smartest people in the world.'

On the other side were several miniature boats and ships—such as school-boys delight in—with sails set; the gentle breeze impelled [pushed] the little crafts across the river, each freighted with a couple of newspapers. . . .

Drawing lots, Joe Boteler, who found luck against him, started to town, with a muttered curse, to buy tobacco, . . .

Joe returned in the evening with a box of plug tobacco about a foot square; but how to get it across was the question. The miniature boats could not carry it, and we shouted across to the Yanks that we had about twenty pounds of cut plug, and asked them what we must do? They hallooed back to let one of us swim across, and declared it was perfectly safe. . . . I volunteered. Having lived on the banks

A typical young recruit posed for this picture at the beginning of the war.

of the Potomac all my life, I was necessarily a swimmer. . . .

As I approached the shore the news of my coming reached camp, and nearly all the Second Michigan were lined up along the bank.

I felt a little queer [strange], but had perfect faith in their promise [not to shoot] and kept on without missing a stroke. . . . The blue-coats crowded around me and gave me a hearty welcome, . . . and heaped offerings of sugar, coffee, lemons, and even candy . . .

Bidding my friends the enemy good-by, I swam back with the precious cargo, and we had a feast that night.[1] 99

This aspect of the Civil War is sometimes the hardest to remember: countrymen fought countrymen, brother fought brother. Friends faced each other in battle. And "brother against brother" was not just a writer's image. At the Union attack on Hilton Head, South Carolina, Percival Drayton commanded the U.S.S. *Pocahontas*, one of the Union vessels attacking Confederate troops under Brigadier General Thomas F. Drayton, his brother. Both were South Carolinians. Such confrontations were not uncommon, and they made the conflict sadder and more costly to the American people.

The First Modern War

What made the Civil War modern was the change in warfare itself. In earlier times wars had been fought by professional armies—not masses of quickly trained citizen-soldiers. Mercenaries fighting for pay often far outnumbered the patriots in such an army. But that had begun to change during the Revolutionary War. Ordinary Americans swept up by a cause battled the professional British army. The Americans were unwilling to abandon their cause even in the face of heavy losses. This was even more true of both sides in the Civil War.

Battlefield tactics had also changed. In traditional battles armies of nearly equal strength sent long lines of soldiers marching slowly toward each other. But new tactics were developed during the American Revolution and the Napoleonic wars. Virtually all Civil War generals on both sides had been trained in these new strategies at West Point. The basic tactic of modern war was to look for the enemy's weakest point and break through it with superior force. Commanders also now considered geographic, economic, and political aspects of the battle, trying to control the high ground or capture economically or politically important places. Winning generals were often those who were best prepared. They made the best use of the

[1]From *The Blue and the Gray: The Story of the Civil War as Told by Participants*, vol. 1, edited by Henry Steele Commager

SOLDIERING IN THE CIVIL WAR

The typical soldier in the newly formed armies of the North and South had no previous military experience. Most knew how to handle guns, but the rest of soldiering was a mystery to nearly all. To teach recruits how to march, their drill sergeants sometimes tied a piece of hay to each man's left foot and a piece of straw to the right. Then, lining the men up on the drill field, the sergeant would chant, "Hay-foot, straw-foot, hay-foot, straw-foot," until the troops caught on.

Most ordinary soldiers joined the armies with no idea of what actual warfare was like. Some were looking for personal glory. Others joined in hopes of visiting distant places and getting to know Americans from other parts of the country. For North and South, however, love of country was the main motive. The names of volunteer companies reflected this patriotism

Courtesy of the Cooper-Hewitt Museum, Smithsonian Institution/Art Resource NY

and sought to inspire fear in the enemy ranks. Confederate regiments had names like the Southern Avengers, Rejectors of Old Abe, and Barton Yankee Killers. Northern regiments took names like Detroit Invincibles and Union Clinchers.

Most regiments were made up of men from one town or county. Since the soldiers elected their own officers, popularity rather than ability often determined who would be leaders. One Confederate regiment picked a colonel who gave the men two jugs of whiskey.

This system did not make for strict discipline. In one Union regiment drilling on a hot parade ground, a private was heard saying to the company commander, "Tom, let's quit this foolin' around . . . and get a drink."

Winslow Homer caught the youth and innocence of this Union soldier in a watercolor sketch.

geography of the battlefield and concentrated their troops skillfully. For this reason, armies put great effort into collecting information. Planning and reconnaissance—exploring enemy territory—became essential.

The armies were organized and deployed much as an army is today. They were divided into three separate units: cavalry, artillery, and infantry. Each had its particular purpose. The rapidly-moving cavalry gathered information, often riding far behind enemy lines to observe troop movements and the availability and location of supplies and reinforcements. They also studied the lay of the land so that the generals could take the geography of the area into account in designing their strategy and tactics. During a battle, cavalry units might be rushed forward to reinforce weak points, but their basic task was to help in overall planning.

Artillery units manned the big guns. It was hot, noisy, dangerous work. But Civil War leaders knew these guns were crucial in major battles. The artillery pounded away at enemy fortifications, making them vulnerable to attack. Artillery fire also sheltered retreating troops from pursuers. Large numbers of accurate guns could be swiftly moved into position to smother the enemy infantry with heavy fire. The importance of artillery signaled the dawn of modern war.

Cavalry and artillery units were essential parts of a Civil War army. But as always the infantry, or "foot soldiers" as they were called, did most of the fighting. Infantry units consisted of regiments of 1,000 soldiers each. Four regiments composed a brigade.

Even the infantry approached the battle differently from previous wars. Cannon and accurate rifle fire were deadly for troops in the open. So opponents dug trenches and fired at each other from the protection of earthworks. To overwhelm the enemy, the front lines charged toward the trenches into enemy fire, ear-shattering noise, and clouds of dense smoke. At close quarters it was nearly impossible to aim and fire, so soldiers used their bayonets or battered each other with their rifle butts. Often the final stage of the assault was brutal hand-to-hand combat.

War had fundamentally changed. Strategy built on information about enemy positions and the geography of the site determined the outcome of most battles. The tools of war—artillery, shells, and rifles—were more accurate and therefore more deadly. Modern war had become total war. Armies sought to destroy the entire productive capacity of the enemy and the will to fight, not just of its troops but of its civilians too. As the noted Civil War historian Bruce Catton wrote:

> " In the Civil War it was all or nothing. . . . Once a little blood had been shed, there was no halfway point at which the two sides could get together and compromise. So the stakes were greatly increased. This too affected the way in which people fought. If you are fighting a total war, the enemy's army is not your own target. What you are really shooting for is the ability to carry on the fight. This means you will hit wherever you can with any weapon that comes into your hand.
>
> Probably it is this more than any other thing that distinguishes modern war: anything goes.[1] "

From Bull Run to Richmond

It took time to raise and train an army. The northern people were impatient. "On to Richmond" was the popular cry in Washington. In July 1861, long before the troops were ready, General McDowell ordered them forward. Laughing and joking along the way, the northern soldiers were joined by a parade of carriages filled with congressmen, newspaper reporters, and the curious. The crowd carried picnic lunches and made plans to eat a late supper in Richmond.

[1]From "The First Modern War" by Bruce Catton in *America Goes to War*

On July 21 at **Bull Run** this poorly trained force of 30,000 met the Confederate army, which was not much better prepared. The Confederates, 22,000 strong, had dug into the high ground above Bull Run. McDowell circled west, correctly guessing that the Confederate line was weakest on the left. He was right, and at first the Confederates fell back.

The Yankees almost cracked the southern line. Behind the Rebels lay an open road to Richmond, less than 90 miles (144 kilometers) away. But troops under Thomas J. Jackson stopped the Union advance cold. At the peak of the battle an officer rallied his men with the cry, "There stands Jackson like a stone wall," winning for Jackson the nickname "Stonewall." Then the southerners counterattacked. The Union army was thrown into confusion and panic. Hundreds of soldiers threw down their guns and fled northward toward Washington. If the Confederate soldiers had not been so green, they might have captured the capital before the northern army could regroup. As southern general Joseph E. Johnston commented, "The Confederate Army was more disorganized by victory than that of the United States by defeat."

After this disgraceful defeat President Lincoln put General George B. McClellan in command of the army. McClellan was an excellent organizer. He was also popular with rank-and-file soldiers. He soon whipped the **Army of the Potomac** into excellent shape.

The Granger Collection, New York

Stonewall Jackson surveys his men and the lay of the land at the First Battle of Bull Run. How did he win his nickname in this battle?

Raising the Armies   557

READING A STATISTICAL CHART

As you learned in the strategy on page 457, statistics are often organized into chart form. An example is below. A chart is especially valuable for use in organizing several sets of numbers. Exact or round numbers may be used in any number of columns to show growth or change. The data shown on a chart is often related, helping you compare the numbers, recognize relationships, and see trends.

How to Read a Statistical Chart

To effectively read a statistical chart, follow these steps.

1. **Identify the type of data.** Read the chart's title. Note headings, subheadings, and labels.
2. **Examine the chart's components.** Study the specific statistics given under each heading. Read across rows and down columns.
3. **Relate numbers and values.** Note quantities. Often a chart will contain a note in parentheses that indicates if the data is to be read in thousands, millions, billions, tons, dollars, or other units. (Be sure to read any footnotes or other special notes at the bottom of the chart as well.)
4. **Use the information.** Ask "what do these statistics tell me?" Draw conclusions and form hypotheses. Compare and contrast the data to note trends and changes.

Applying the Strategy

Study the chart below. Note that it contains information about the Union and the Confederacy on the eve of war. Look at the left column. It lists nine categories of statistics on which you can compare the North and South. Reading across the row for each of these categories gives you both the total number and the percentage of the total for both sides. What was the population of the North? Of the South? As you can see from the chart, the North had more people, nearly three quarters of the total population of the United States.

The North also had more than 10 times the value of manufactured goods and produced more than 10 times the steel as the South. What do these two statistics mean in wartime? The North also had nearly three times the railroad mileage and bank assets as the South, and twice as many farms. Again, what might each of these figures mean on the eve of war? The South did have a small but significant advantage in the value of exports. How might this affect southern war strategy? Review all the statistics, and ask yourself what they meant to each side as the war erupted.

For independent practice, see Practicing the Strategy on page 588.

COMPARING THE NORTH AND THE SOUTH, 1860	North		South	
	Total	%	Total	%
Land Area (square miles)	2,250,000	75.0	750,000	25.0
Population	21,800,000	71.3	8,800,000*	28.7
Farms	1,360,000	67.3	681,000	32.7
Factories	119,500	85.2	20,850	14.8
Value of Manufacturing	$1,730,000,000	91.5	$156,000,000	8.5
Iron Produced (long tons)	2,720,000	94.6	155,000	5.4
Railroad Mileage	21,500	71.0	8,500	28.7
Bank Assets	$345,900,000	72.0	$76,000,000	18.0
Value of Exports	$175,000,000	43.6	$226,000,000	56.4
			*Southern population included 3.8 million slaves	

Yet McClellan had a number of serious weaknesses as a leader. He was very vain and had too high an opinion of his own abilities. He thought President Lincoln stupid and incompetent. He even had vague visions of taking over control of the government in order to save the Union single-handedly.

These flaws alone would have been bad enough. But McClellan was also overly cautious when it came to fighting. Despite his dashing appearance and bold talk, he never seemed ready to march against the enemy. When he was first appointed, caution was the right policy. The army had to be trained and disciplined. Yet even when this task had been accomplished, McClellan still delayed. Finally, in March 1862, he prepared to attack.

McClellan's plan for capturing Richmond was complicated but sensible. Instead of marching directly south, he moved his army by boat down the Potomac River and through Chesapeake Bay to the mouths of the York and James Rivers, southeast of the Confederate capital. He then advanced up these streams. By the middle of May he had over 110,000 men, a huge force, within 25 miles (40 kilometers) of Richmond.

Instead of striking swiftly at the Confederate capital, McClellan delayed. On May 31 he was moving his army across the Chickahominy River, a branch of the James. While his troops were divided by the river, the Confederate commander, General Joseph E. Johnston, launched a fierce attack. The loss of life in the **Battle of Seven Pines** was heavy on both sides. Yet neither side gained an advantage.

General Johnston was wounded in this battle and had to give up his command. The new leader of the **Army of Northern Virginia** was Robert E. Lee.

The North quickly learned how much it had lost when Lee decided to fight for the Confederates. Although outnumbered, Lee realized how cautious McClellan was. He therefore reduced his force by ordering General Stonewall Jackson and his men in the Shenandoah Valley north and west of Richmond to attack small Union forces stationed there.

Jackson specialized in the swift movement of troops. Soon his force was closer to Washington than to Richmond. This caused alarm in Washington. President Lincoln ordered large numbers of Union troops to the Shenandoah region. These units were in the wrong place to help McClellan. This was exactly what Lee had hoped for. While the Union soldiers were marching westward, Jackson was hurrying back toward Richmond!

The moment Jackson's brigades had rejoined his own, Lee ordered an all-out attack. What followed is known as the **Seven Days Before Richmond.** The Union army fell back to Harrison's Landing, a base on the James River. Over 15,000 Union soldiers were killed or wounded. The Confederates lost nearly 20,000 men. Neither side could be said to have won the battle. 📧

Chicago Historical Society

As a general, George B. McClellan thought he could save the Union single-handedly. He was sharply critical of President Lincoln. Why is a general who doesn't support his commander in chief unlikely to succeed? Give several reasons.

Return to the Preview & Review on page 549.

Raising the Armies   559

The popular McCormick Reaper helped farmers feed the armies of the North.

National Archives

3. WAR AND THE ECONOMY

Behind the Northern Lines

By the summer of 1862 northern leaders realized that the Civil War would not be won quickly. It was sure to cost many more thousands of lives and great sums of money. It would affect everyone in the nation—women and men, civilians and soldiers.

The early months of the war brought a business depression and much confusion to many parts of the North and West. The loss of southern trade injured many businesses. Hundreds of millions of dollars owed by southern borrowers could not be collected. Many banks in the North collapsed. About 6,000 companies went bankrupt.

The demands of the army and navy for uniforms, guns, and other supplies soon caused business to pick up again. Union soldiers wore out about 1.5 million uniforms and about 3 million pairs of shoes a year. The clothing and shoe industries boomed. Between 1860 and 1865 the consumption of wool more than tripled.

The Union forces also needed enormous amounts of everything from coal and nails to soap and writing paper. The demand for horses, ambulances, and wagons rose steadily. An army ambulance cost the considerable sum of $170. By October 1862 the army had purchased 3,500 of them.

An army marches on its stomach. But food had to be raised by fewer people because so many young farmers were in uniform. Fortunately, the **mechanical reaper** came into general use at just this

Preview & Review

Use these questions to guide your reading. Answer the questions after completing Section 3.
Understanding Issues, Events, & Ideas. It is 1862. Explain why you believe the Civil War will not end quickly, using the following words: mechanical reaper, inflation, Copperhead, blockade runner, cotton diplomacy, conscript, contraband.
1. Why was the mechanical reaper so important during the war?
2. How did Lincoln treat critics of the war?
3. How successful was the naval blockade of the South? What goods were exchanged by the blockade runners?
4. What did southerners believe cotton diplomacy would bring?
5. Why did southerners dislike the draft?
Thinking Critically. **1.** You are an economics reporter. Write a column for the business section of a newspaper, describing the economic effects of the Civil War. **2.** You are a woman whose husband is a Confederate soldier. What do you do during the war?

time. One reaper could harvest as much wheat as five field hands using scythes and cradles. Cyrus Hall McCormick, the inventor of the reaper, sold about 165,000 of these machines during the war.

The wartime boom caused **inflation.** Prices rose rapidly. The wages of the men and women of the North who produced war supplies and other goods did not keep pace with the rising cost of living. However, work was plentiful. Nearly all people were able to take care of themselves.

Northern Opponents of the War

Many people in the North and West were not willing to fight a war to prevent the southern states from seceding. Some believed that the United States would be better off without the South. Others had no objection to slavery. Still others felt that the southern states had a right to secede.

People who opposed the war came to be popularly known as **Copperheads.** Most of the Copperheads supported the Democratic party. They were sympathetic to the South and argued that it was not worth the cost to force the Confederacy to surrender.

Radical Copperheads organized secret societies with such names as Knights of the Golden Circle and Sons of Liberty. They tried to persuade Union soldiers to desert, and they helped Confederate prisoners to escape. Some Copperheads even smuggled guns and ammunition into the South.

The most important Copperhead leader was Clement L. Vallandigham, a congressman from Ohio. Vallandigham charged that

The Granger Collection, New York

THE COPPERHEAD PARTY.—IN FAVOR OF A VIGOROUS PROSECUTION OF PEACE!

Liberty with her Union shield draws back from the Copperheads in this 1863 cartoon. Copperheads are snakes that strike without warning. These all resemble Clement Vallandigham, the Copperhead leader. What message do you think the cartoonist meant to send?

War and the Economy   561

Lincoln intended to abolish slavery if the United States won the war. He demanded that the government try to negotiate a reunion with the South. In 1863 he was thrown in prison by the military authorities. President Lincoln, however, ordered him released and deported to the Confederacy. Vallandigham went from the South to Canada, and in 1864 he came back to Ohio. Although he resumed his criticisms of the government, Lincoln decided it would be better not to silence him.

Lincoln did not let all critics off so easily. In 1861 he suspended the right of people to *habeas corpus* (from the Latin for "you shall have the body"). This is the legal process for ensuring that an accused person is not imprisoned unlawfully. It is a right guaranteed by the Constitution. But during the war over 13,000 Americans were held in jail without formal charges made against them.

Lincoln insisted that his first duty was to protect the Union. He exercised more power than any earlier president. But Lincoln did not try to be a dictator. The government did not censor newspapers or prevent citizens from voting as they wished in elections. When Union soldiers were sentenced to death for running away during a battle, Lincoln tended to pardon them. He called them "leg cases" rather than cowards, adding, "It would frighten the poor fellows too terribly to kill them." In a more serious mood, while pardoning one deserter, he said, "This boy can do us more good above ground than below ground."

Shortages in the South

Unlike the North the Confederate economy was injured by the war. Paying for the war was the South's most difficult task. It could not raise enough by borrowing or taxing to meet all its bills. As a result the government had to print money that it could not back with gold or silver. It issued over $1 billion in bank notes of questionable value during the war.

The South promised to pay off these notes in gold or silver after the war ended. When the South began to lose the war, people doubted that it would be able to pay its debts. Confederate paper money then fell rapidly in value. By early 1865 50 Confederate paper dollars were worth less than one gold dollar. Prices of goods in the South skyrocketed. In 1864 eggs cost six Confederate dollars a dozen. In the North eggs cost about 25 cents a dozen.

Almost every kind of manufactured product was scarce in the South because the region had been almost entirely agricultural. Shortages of clothing sent people rummaging in their attics in search of spinning wheels and hand looms that their grandparents had used. Soldiers marched in ragged uniforms. Sometimes they had no shoes. For civilians thorns took the place of pins. The blank side of wallpaper served as a substitute for writing paper.

Museum of the Confederacy, Richmond, VA, Photography by Katherine Wetzel

The Blockade

Union leaders eventually developed a war strategy that included several military objectives. First was a blockade of southern ports. The navy remained loyal to the Union. After the fall of Fort Sumter President Lincoln ordered the navy to blockade all southern harbors. This blockade gradually choked off the South's foreign trade. About 6,000 ships had entered and left southern ports in 1860. The next year only 800 managed to slip past northern warships. Thereafter almost none escaped.

Many southern captains tried to break through the blockade. Their ships, like the privateers of earlier wars, were small and fast. These **blockade runners** operated out of Charleston or Savannah or out of Mobile, Alabama, on the Gulf of Mexico.

The British island of Bermuda, only 400 miles (640 kilometers) off the North Carolina coast, was the blockade runners' favorite destination. There they exchanged cotton or other farm products for guns, medicines, blankets, and coffee, as well as for fancy silks and other luxuries. The blockade runners brought in whatever they thought would sell for the best price. Since they were private citizens, the government could not control their activities or order them to import only war supplies.

Quakers do not fight. That is why the artist titled this scene "Quaker Battery." Look closely at the cannon. Or are they really cannon? What damage could these soldiers do? What does this painting by Conrad Wise Chapman tell us about the South's fortunes of war after the northern blockade became effective?

Peabody Museum of Salem

Winning a victory for the South, the C.S.S. Nashville *is shown burning the ship* Harvey Birch *in this painting by D. McFarlane. Research other naval engagements of the war, including the one between the* Monitor *and the* Merrimack.

Cotton Diplomacy

At the start of the war southern leaders thought that the economies of England and France would collapse without southern cotton. Those nations imported immense amounts of cotton for their textile factories. If their mills were forced to shut down, thousands of workers would lose their jobs. The southerners believed that England and France would enter the war on the side of the Confederacy to prevent this from happening.

Southerners who believed that **cotton diplomacy** would work tried to increase the pressure on England and France by preventing the export of cotton. "We have only to shut off your supply of cotton for a few weeks," one boasted to an English journalist, "and we can create a revolution in Great Britain."

These southerners were wrong. When the war broke out, English warehouses were bulging with cotton. By the time the supply had been used up, the British had discovered that they needed northern wheat more than southern cotton. Most British and French government leaders wanted the Confederacy to win the war. But they were unwilling to enter the war themselves.

Cotton was of little use to the South itself during the war. Planters shifted to growing corn and wheat and to raising pigs and cattle.

The Draft in the South

Another difficulty faced by the Confederacy was raising a large enough army to defend its borders. Thousands of men enlisted. But because the population was small, it became necessary in 1862 to **conscript,** or draft, men to serve as soldiers by law.

This draft law was very unpopular. It favored the rich, because a man who was conscripted could hire a substitute. Anyone who owned 20 or more slaves was exempted. The government believed that these owners of many slaves were needed at home to control the slaves. Many southerners complained that the draft law made the conflict "a rich man's war and a poor man's fight."

Slaves in the War

By 1865 the southern government decided to use slaves as soldiers. Slaves had been used by the Confederate army throughout the war as laborers, bakers, blacksmiths, shoemakers, and nurses. Slaves also worked in factories. Half of the 2,400 employees of the Tredegar Iron Works in Richmond, the largest factory in the South, were slaves.

Many persons thought that the slaves would riot or run off by the thousands during the war. Few did. But whenever northern armies invaded a district, some slaves slipped away and crossed the Union lines. Often northern officers put them to work building fortifications. These men became known as **contrabands.**

Slaves also tried to help the Union army whenever possible. The following account tells of two daring and ingenious slaves who spied on the Confederate army:

" There came into the Union lines a Negro from a farm on the other side of the river, known by the name of Dabney, who was found to possess a remarkably clear knowledge of the topography [lay of the land] of the whole region. . . . When he saw our system of army telegraphs, the idea interested him intensely, and he begged the operators to explain the signs to him. They did so, and found that he could understand and remember the meaning of the various movements as well as any of his brethren of the paler hue [white color].

Not long after, his wife, who had come with him expressed great anxiety to be allowed to go over to the other side as servant to a 'secesh [secessionist, or southern] woman.' The request was granted. Dabney's wife went across the Rappahannock, and in a few days was installed as laundress at the headquarters of a prominent rebel General. Dabney, her husband, on the north bank, was soon found to be wonderfully well informed as to all the rebel plans. Within an hour of the time that a movement of any kind was projected, or even discussed, among the rebel generals, Hooker [the Union commander] knew all about it. . . . And all this knowledge came through Dabney, and his reports always turned out to be true.

Yet Dabney was never absent, and never talked with the scouts. . . .

How he obtained his information remained for some time a puzzlement to the Union officers. At length, upon much solicitation [asking], he unfolded his marvellous secret to one of our officers.

Taking him to a point where a clear view could be obtained at Fredericksburg, he pointed to a little cabin in the suburbs near the river bank, and asked him [the officer] if he saw that clothes-line with clothes hanging to dry. 'Well,' he said, 'that clothes-line tells me in half an hour just what goes on at Lee's headquarters. You see my wife over there . . . moves the clothes on that line so I can understand it in a minute. That there gray shirt is Longstreet [a southern general]; and when she takes it off, it means he's gone down to Richmond. That white shirt means Hill [another southern general]; and when she moves it up to the west end of the line, Hill's corps has moved up stream. That red one is Stonewall. He's down on the right now, and if he moves, she will move the red shirt.' . . .[1]"

The War and Free African Americans

The outbreak of the war filled free African Americans with hope— and with fear. Most could not imagine northerners fighting southerners let alone whites fighting whites over slavery. But now it had happened! The war meant an end to the hated Fugitive Slave Law, and if the North won maybe an end to slavery itself. Men and boys rushed to join the Union army. Many later distinguished themselves in battle. Sixteen African Americans won the Medal of Honor for their bravery.

But what if the North lost? Certainly a Union victory was not assured. Thoughts of a Confederate victory brought fear to free African Americans' hearts, along with many questions. Would they be forced into slavery, even those whose families had never been slaves? They held special prayer meetings in their churches for a Union victory.

And what was the status of free "people of color" *during* the war? There was frightening word that Union soldiers had returned slaves seeking refuge in the Union lines to their owners. President

[1]From *The Blue Coats*, edited by John Truesdale

Library of Congress, Brady Collection

Lincoln's hesitation to make the abolition of slavery an aim of the war added to the confusion of free African Americans.

Urging their oxen onward, fugitive slaves ford the Rappahannock River in this 1862 photograph taken by Timothy O'Sullivan. They are following the retreat of General Pope's army as it makes its way back to Washington after the Second Battle of Bull Run. What probably lies ahead for these so-called contrabands?

Women and the War

Women were not soldiers in the Civil War, but many on both sides took over the management of businesses and farms, while continuing to hold together families. Especially in the South women had great responsibilities. They ran plantations, oversaw slaves, arranged for loans, and collected food and supplies for their families and for the army. They had to do all this in the midst of severe wartime shortages. Many found the experience the most vital incident of their lives. Women in the North were just as captivated by the great turmoil swirling around them.

Some women found jobs in new occupations. More than 400 women—the first to serve in the federal government—were hired as clerks. Women staffed Confederate government offices as well. By the end of the war women had done so well in clerical positions that they were not replaced by men returning from the war. Women on both sides also worked in factories and arsenals. Most of these women were underpaid. Seamstresses received as little as four cents for making a shirt.

Hundreds of women also became nurses. Despite the depressing conditions of wartime work, nursing offered tremendous new opportunities for women. Clara Barton, who was one of the first women attracted to nursing, believed the war had created employment opportunities for women that normally would have taken 50 years. More importantly, women held on to many of the gains after the war.

Return to the Preview & Review on page 560.

Understanding Issues, Events, & Ideas. Using the following words, explain the important moments of the war in the East: Second Battle of Bull Run; Battle of Antietam; emancipate; Emancipation Proclamation; Battles of Fredericksburg, Chancellorsville, and Gettysburg; Gettysburg Address.

1. What did General Lee believe he must do to end the war?
2. What were the conditions of the Emancipation Proclamation? What was necessary to actually free slaves?
3. What led to the draft riots in 1863?

Thinking Critically. 1. You are a Confederate soldier who survived the Battle of Antietam. Explain the importance of this battle in a letter to your family. **2.** Of Fredericksburg, Chancellorsville, or Gettysburg, which battle do you think was the most important to the North? To the South? Give reasons for your answer.

4. THE WAR IN THE EAST

The Second Battle of Bull Run

Northern attention remained focused on a second objective of the war: the capture of Richmond. In the summer of 1862, under orders from Lincoln, McClellan began to withdraw the Union army from its positions near Richmond. The plan was to combine his veterans with a new army being organized south of Washington by General John Pope. As soon as the northerners pulled back, Lee moved northward. He was determined to destroy General Pope's army before McClellan could join with it. He knew that it was not enough simply to defend Richmond. To end the war, he had to deliver such a stinging defeat that the people of the North would lose the will to fight.

In a daring maneuver Lee sent 25,000 men commanded by Stonewall Jackson to hit Pope's army from the rear. Once again Jackson marched swiftly, then struck silently. He cut off the railroad running from Washington to the Union front and set fire to most of Pope's supplies.

In desperation, on August 29 Pope attacked Lee. This **Second Battle of Bull Run** was fought on almost the same ground as the first. The Army of Northern Virginia halted the Union assault and then drove Pope's troops back toward Washington. Dismayed by Pope's failure, Lincoln dismissed him and again gave McClellan command of the Army of the Potomac. Ben Wade, a congressman from Ohio, objected strongly to McClellan's appointment. Lincoln asked him whom he should appoint instead. "Anybody," Wade answered impatiently. "Wade," said Lincoln calmly, "anybody will do for you, but I must have somebody."

Antietam

Lee now marched around the defenses of Washington. On September 4 he crossed the Potomac River to Maryland. McClellan was unsure of Lee's exact position. So he too crossed the river. On September 13 one of McClellan's soldiers found a copy of Lee's battle plans wrapped around some cigars in an abandoned Confederate camp. With this information McClellan was able to track down Lee's army. The armies met in battle on September 17 at Sharpsburg, a town on a branch of the Potomac called Antietam Creek. Lee had fewer than 50,000 men, McClellan about twice that number.

It was a foggy, gray morning when this **Battle of Antietam** began. When the bloody struggle ended at twilight, the Confederates had lost 13,000 men, the Union forces 12,000. One historian wrote:

    At last the sun went down and the battle ended, smoke heavy in the air, the twilight quivering with the anguished cries of thousands of wounded men.

Missouri Historical Society

This is ever the price of war. Here lie Confederate soldiers who have fallen in front of Dunker Church at Antietam in September 1862. Explain from your reading how someone's carelessness led to this loss of life.

For yet another time in this bloody war neither side had won much of an advantage. All next day the exhausted armies faced each other silently. Then, that night, the Confederates retreated back across the Potomac. The North had finally won a battle.

The Emancipation Proclamation

The cost of the war in blood and money was changing the way ordinary people in the North felt about slavery. Anger at southerners more than sympathy for the slaves caused this change. The first result of it came in April 1862 when Congress abolished slavery in the District of Columbia.

Gradually Lincoln came to the conclusion that the United States should try to free all the slaves. He would have preferred to have the states buy the slaves from their owners and then **emancipate** or free them. This idea was known as compensated emancipation.

But Lincoln was a clever politician. He knew that many citizens would oppose paying anything to rebels and slave owners. Others still objected to freeing the slaves for the sake of doing away with an evil institution. Lincoln therefore decided to act under his war powers. He would free slaves not because slavery was wrong but as a means of weakening the rebel government.

Lincoln hesitated until after the Union victory at the Battle of Antietam. Then he issued the **Emancipation Proclamation.**

The Emancipation Proclamation was reprinted in this elaborate poster, the corner of which has been damaged. Tell briefly why true emancipation could not come from a beautiful scroll or even a presidential order while the war was waged. An excerpt appears on page 589.

Library of Congress

The War in the East   569

This proclamation stated that after January 1, 1863, "all persons held as slaves within any States . . . in rebellion against the United States shall be . . . forever free."

Notice that the Proclamation did not liberate a single slave that the government could control. It applied only to areas ruled by the Confederates. Slaves in Maryland, Kentucky, Missouri, and even in those parts of the Confederacy that had been captured by Union armies, remained in bondage.

Yet when the armies of the United States advanced into new territory after January 1, 1863, the slaves there were freed. At last the war was being fought for freedom, not only to save the Union. Lincoln also ordered that freed slaves should be encouraged to enlist in the army. In August 1863 Lincoln wrote to Grant that enlisting them "works doubly, weakening the enemy and strengthening us." In December 1863, upon hearing of the bravery of these segregated units, Lincoln said, "It is difficult to say they are not as good soldiers as any." All told, about 180,000 African American soldiers fought for the United States during the Civil War. More than 38,000 lost their

THE WAR IN THE EAST, 1861–63

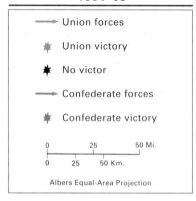

→ Union forces

✴ Union victory

★ No victor

→ Confederate forces

✴ Confederate victory

0   25   50 Mi.

0   25   50 Km.

Albers Equal-Area Projection

LEARNING FROM MAPS. *Most of the early battles were fought in the East. Why do you think so many battles took place in eastern and northern Virginia?*

National Portrait Gallery

The Granger Collection, New York

Notice that the composer of the sheet music "Hymm of the Freedman" at left is identified only as "A Contraband." It was probably a tune used to recruit soldiers. Above is Major Martin R. Delany, who was promoted right on the battlefield for bravery. How many African Americans fought for the Union? How many Hispanic Americans?

lives in the struggle. Several thousand Hispanic Americans fought on both sides. Union admiral David Farragut was the best known.

The Draft Riots

The benefits of the Emancipation Proclamation were slow in coming. Its disadvantages appeared at once. Probably it made southerners more determined than ever to maintain their independence. Many poor northerners resented it because they feared that slaves liberated under the Proclamation would flock into the North to compete with them for jobs. As a result the Democratic party made large gains in the 1862 Congressional elections.

Michigan Department of State Archives

RALLY ROUND

THE UNION — FOREVER

THE FLAG, BOYS!

100 MEN WANTED!!

For the 23d Mich. Infantry.

Enlist before April 1st, secure the Government Bounty of $300 00,

AND "KEEP OUT OF THE DRAFT!"

Government Bounty, $300; State Bounty, $100; Town Bounty, $100.

Apply to WM. SICKELS, St. Johns, or

O. L. SPAULDING,

Lieut. Col., 23d Mich. Infantry, Corunna.

March   , 1864.

("REPUBLICAN" PRINT, ST. JOHNS.)

"Rally Round the Flag, Boys!" says this 1864 Michigan recruiting poster. And "Keep Out of the Draft!" which passed the month the poster went to press.

A few months after the Proclamation went into effect, Congress passed a conscription law. Like the Confederate draft, this measure allowed men who were drafted to hire substitutes. They could even avoid military service by paying the government $300.

Poor men could not possibly raise $300, which was as much as a laborer could earn in a year. Many made a connection between the draft law and emancipation. They resented having to risk their lives in order to free slaves who could then compete with them for work.

Draft riots broke out in many parts of the country in the spring and summer of 1863. The worst occurred in New York City, where Irish-born workers ran wild for four days in July. The rioters burned buildings, looted shops, and terrorized innocent local African Americans. Over a hundred African Americans in New York were murdered. These riots should have been a warning. The war might free the slaves, but it was not likely to produce racial harmony, either in the North or South.

Fredericksburg

Meanwhile the Emancipation Proclamation had little effect on the battlefields. When McClellan failed to attack the Confederates as they retreated after the Battle of Antietam, Lincoln again removed him from command of the Army of the Potomac, choosing General Ambrose E. Burnside to succeed him. Unlike McClellan, Burnside was a bold, even reckless officer. He decided to push directly toward

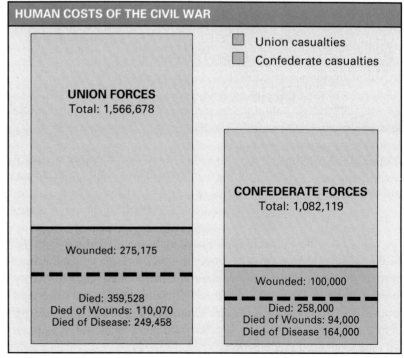

HUMAN COSTS OF THE CIVIL WAR

Union casualties
Confederate casualties

UNION FORCES
Total: 1,566,678

Wounded: 275,175

Died: 359,528
Died of Wounds: 110,070
Died of Disease: 249,458

CONFEDERATE FORCES
Total: 1,082,119

Wounded: 100,000

Died: 258,000
Died of Wounds: 94,000
Died of Disease 164,000

Source: *Encyclopedia Britannica*

LEARNING FROM CHARTS. *Unlike other wars all the casualties of the Civil War were Americans. Of total Union forces, more than 40 percent were casualties, and nearly 23 percent died. About 33 percent of the Confederate forces were casualties, and almost 24 percent died. Why did such high casualty rates actually favor the North?*

Historical Society of Pennsylvania

Richmond. In December 1862 he crossed the Rappahannock River over pontoon bridges and occupied the town of Fredericksburg, about 50 miles (80 kilometers) north of Richmond.

The Confederate army was entrenched on a ridge behind Fredericksburg called Marye's Heights. It was an extremely strong position. Looking across the field that lay before the Confederate lines, General E. P. Alexander, Lee's chief of artillery, remarked, "A chicken could not live in that field when we open on it."

Burnside nevertheless attacked. He had 120,000 men to Lee's 75,000. The **Battle of Fredericksburg** was fought on December 13. It began in heavy fog. About eleven o'clock in the morning the fog lifted. The Confederates could see the Union soldiers coming across the frozen plain. They commenced firing.

Burnside sent his blue-coated soldiers charging at Lee's position six separate times. Each time they were driven back by musket and cannon fire, leaving the field littered with their dead. At the end of the day they had suffered 12,000 casualties. Utterly defeated, Burnside crossed back across the Rappahannock. Shortly afterwards, at his own request, Burnside was relieved of command.

Chancellorsville

Lincoln next turned the Army of the Potomac over to General "Fighting Joe" Hooker. General Hooker concentrated his units at Chancellorsville, a village in the densely wooded area of Virginia known

Only the bayonet would do. Firing was useless. These were the instructions to raw recruits from Pennsylvania in this 1862 assault on Marye's Heights. Why did Confederate troops have a strong geographical position in this Battle of Fredericksburg?

The War in the East   573

Medical treatment in the Civil War was terribly crude by modern standards. Thousands of soldiers died of blood poisoning. Operations were performed without anesthetics. Still worse, about twice as many soldiers died of disease as of wounds.

Typhoid fever took countless lives. No one knew its cause or how to cure it. Army doctors treated pneumonia by bloodletting, a procedure which surely increased the chances that the sick soldier would die.

The best military hospital in the South was run by Sally L. Tompkins in Richmond. President Jefferson Davis made Tompkins a captain. She and

Bettmann Archive

Clara Barton is shown at the time she ministered to the wounds of war suffered by northern soldiers. Who was her counterpart in the South?

Loreta Velásquez were the only women officers of the Confederate army. Like her many counterparts in both North and South, Tompkins saw thousands of amputations performed to halt deadly gangrene.

On the Union side heroic work was performed by the nurse Clara Barton. She cared for sick and wounded soldiers at Antietam and Fredericksburg. By wagon caravan she carried supplies from one Union hospital to another, calming the frightened horses when cannon shells exploded in their pathway. In 1864 she was appointed superintendent of nurses for the Union army. Later Barton founded the American Red Cross Society. She served as president of the Red Cross from 1882 to 1904.

as "the Wilderness." While he was preparing to advance, Lee attacked him. This **Battle of Chancellorsville** on May 1–5, 1863, showed Lee at his best. Although he had only 60,000 soldiers to Hooker's 125,000, he divided his army again. Stonewall Jackson's troops slipped quietly around the right side of the Union army. Then Jackson and Lee attacked at the same time. After days of bloody fighting, Hooker retreated. Lee had won another brilliant victory.

The victory was a costly one. General Jackson was wounded by stray bullets from his own lines. Three bullets hit him, one in the right hand and two in the left arm. Nowadays such wounds would not be fatal. But the bone in his arm was badly broken. The arm had to be amputated. Stonewall died from shock and loss of blood.

Gettysburg

A month after the battle of Chancellorsville, Lee again invaded the North. He still hoped that a decisive victory on northern soil would cause the United States to give up the struggle.

As gray-clad Confederates marched through Maryland and into Pennsylvania, Union forces raced cross-country to intercept them. General George G. Meade was now in command, the fifth officer to hold this post in less than a year.

On July 1, 1863, one of Meade's units made contact with a Confederate detachment at the town of Gettysburg, in southern Pennsylvania. Lee's soldiers had wandered into the town looking for

Historical Picture Service

Stonewall Jackson is shown shortly before his death at Chancellorsville. Study his face. Does Stonewall seem a good nickname for him?

shoes. Meade's men were looking for Lee. Lee's army was spread out across the rolling southern Pennsylvania farmland, traveling in three separate columns. Now he quickly concentrated his forces. Meade placed his Union troops outside the town on a ridge shaped like a fishhook. A hill called Cemetery Ridge was the center of their position. Lee's Confederate forces occupied another ridge half a mile away. The center of the Confederate line was on Seminary Ridge.

For two days the battle raged. As the sun set on the second day, Union troops still held a steep knoll called Little Round Top. From there they cut the Rebel ranks to ribbons. That night Lee made the fateful decision to charge the center of Meade's line.

That same night a few miles away, Meade planned for an attack on his center. He moved his strength there. The afternoon of July 3 proved him right. Between one and two o'clock, while Confederate artillery pounded Cemetery Ridge, General George E. Pickett led a charge at the Union position. Howling the eerie "rebel yell," 15,000 infantrymen started to trot across the open ground. For a brief moment some of these Confederates reached the Union trenches on Cemetery Ridge. But Union reserves counterattacked quickly. Pickett's surviving men were driven off. Pickett wrote this account of the battle to his wife:

> 66 Over on Cemetery Ridge the Federals saw a scene never before witnessed on this continent. . . . an army forming in line of battle in full view of the enemy, under their very eyes—charging across a space of nearly a mile [1.6 kilometers] in length over fields of grain and then a smooth expanse—moving with the steadiness of a dress parade, the pride and the glory soon to be crushed by an overwhelming heartbreak.
>
> Well, it is over now. The battle is lost, and many of us are prisoners, many are dead, many wounded, bleeding and dying. Your soldier lives and mourns. If it were not for you, my darling, he would rather, a million times rather, be back there with his dead, asleep for all time in an unknown grave.[1] 99

The battle was over. Lee retreated back into Virginia. Had Meade pursued the Confederates quickly, he might have destroyed them and ended the war. Instead he delayed, and the war dragged on for nearly two more years.

Some months after the **Battle of Gettysburg**, President Lincoln dedicated a cemetery there where thousands of Union soldiers were buried. He delivered a speech so short it left his listeners disappointed. Lincoln's **Gettysburg Address** attracted little attention at

Point of View

A senator from California wrote this impression of Lincoln's delivery of *The Gettysburg Address.*

> 66 Mr. Lincoln arose, and laying aside his famous cloak, delivered his celebrated address. It was listened to, I need not say, with the greatest attention, as indeed was everything Mr. Lincoln said on any occasion, but no one at the time regarded it as anything very unusual. . . . There was an impression that his speech was cut short by his emotions. . . . It seemed to me the very least in length, or substance, that might be expected from the President of the United States on such an occasion. . . . 99
> From *Memoirs of Cornelius Cole,* 1908

[1]From "Pickett's Account" in *Sources in American History*

State Museum of Pennsylvania, Pennsylvania Historical and Museum Commission

"Pickett's Charge at the Battle of Gettysburg" by Peter F. Rotnermel shows the Union forces on the left, the Confederates on the right. Use your reading and this painting to help you write a description of the battle.

the time. It is now recognized as his noblest expression of the purpose of the Civil War and of the ideals of American democracy. Lincoln said:

66 Four score and seven years ago our fathers brought forth on this continent a new nation, conceived in liberty, and dedicated to the proposition that all men are created equal.

Now we are engaged in a great civil war, testing whether that nation, or any nation so conceived and so dedicated, can long endure. We are met on a great battlefield of that war. We have come to dedicate a portion of that field as a final resting place for those who here gave their lives that that nation might live. It is altogether fitting and proper that we should do this.

But, in a larger sense, we cannot dedicate—we cannot consecrate—we cannot hallow—this ground. The brave men, living and dead, who struggled here, have consecrated it far above our poor power to add or detract. The world will little note nor long remember what we say here, but it can never forget what they did here. It is for us, the living, rather, to be dedicated here to the unfinished work which they who fought here have thus far so nobly advanced. It is rather for us to be here dedicated to the great task remaining before us—that from these honored dead we take increased devotion to that cause for which they gave the last full measure of devotion; that we here highly resolve that these dead shall not have died in vain; that this nation, under God, shall have a new birth of freedom; and that government of the people, by the people, for the people, shall not perish from the earth. 99

Return to the Preview & Review on page 568.

576   THE CIVIL WAR

5. THE WAR IN THE WEST

Cutting the South in Two

In the West the Union objective was to control the Mississippi River. Then it would be impossible for the Confederates to bring men and supplies to the eastern front from Arkansas, Louisiana, and Texas. The South would be cut in two.

The struggle for the river began in 1862. It was long and bitter. Out of it came the great general that Lincoln had been searching for since the beginning of the war. His name was Ulysses S. Grant.

Unlike Robert E. Lee, Grant had done poorly at West Point. He served well enough in the Mexican War. But he found army life boring in peacetime. He began to drink too much. In 1854 he resigned his commission in the army. He tried a number of businesses but succeeded in none. He seemed a totally undistinguished person.

When the Civil War broke out, Grant was working in a leather shop in Galena, Illinois. He joined an Illinois regiment. Since experienced officers were scarce, he was made a brigadier general.

Preview & Review

Use these questions to guide your reading. Answer the questions after completing Section 5.
Understanding Issues, Events, & Ideas. Using the following words, explain the important moments of the war in the West: Fort Henry, Fort Donelson, Battle of Shiloh, Siege of Vicksburg, Port Hudson, Chattanooga.
1. Why was General Grant called "Unconditional Surrender"?
2. What tactics did Grant use to lay siege to Vicksburg?
3. What was General Grant's strategy to end the war?
Thinking Critically. You fought with General Grant at the Battle of Shiloh. In your journal, record the details of the battle, and what happened to Grant afterward.

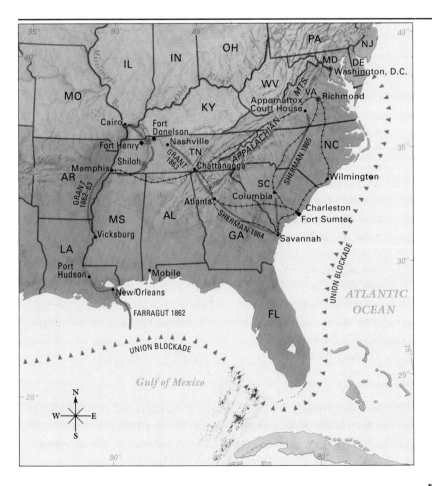

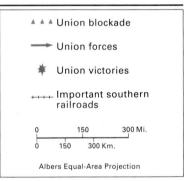

THE BLOCKADE AND THE WAR IN THE WEST, 1862–65

▲ ▲ ▲ Union blockade

→ Union forces

✳ Union victories

┼┼┼┼ Important southern railroads

0   150   300 Mi.

0   150   300 Km.

Albers Equal-Area Projection

LEARNING FROM MAPS. *The war in the West was actually fought in the Mississippi and Tennessee river valleys, where Union forces sought to control the rivers and rail lines. How would Union success there cripple the South?*

National Portrait Gallery

The generals of the Union Army flank U. S. Grant, who is hatless at the center below the flag.

Grant was a shy, slight man. He did not look like a soldier, much less a general. He was constantly chewing a cigar. He rarely stood up straight. His uniforms were rumpled and ill fitting. Often Grant did not wear his officer's insignia. Yet he was brave and determined, and he turned out to be an excellent military strategist.

In February 1862 Grant organized a successful land-and-river attack on **Fort Henry,** a Confederate stronghold on the Tennessee River. After the Confederates surrendered the fort, he laid siege to **Fort Donelson,** on the Cumberland River. When the Confederate commander asked Grant what terms he would offer for the surrender of the fort, Grant replied, ''immediate and unconditional surrender.'' With this brief remark U. S. Grant won the nickname ''*U*nconditional *S*urrender'' Grant.

Shiloh

Grant next marched his men up the Tennessee River. He intended to destroy railroad lines near Corinth, Mississippi. On April 6, 1862, about 30 miles (48 kilometers) from Corinth, his army was surprised by Confederates under General Albert Sidney Johnston. The resulting **Battle of Shiloh** caught Grant completely off guard. During the first day's fighting, his army was forced back to the river.

Fortunately, 25,000 fresh Union troops arrived during the night. The next day they drove the Confederates back. But Shiloh was an extremely costly victory. In two days about 13,000 Union soldiers were killed or wounded. Grant was so shaken by the surprise attack that he allowed the Confederates to escape. He was relieved of his command. His reputation seemed ruined.

The Siege of Vicksburg

Gradually other Union forces gained control of the Mississippi River. In April 1862 a fleet commanded by Captain David Farragut battered the forts defending New Orleans and Baton Rouge and captured the cities. Farragut's father, Jorge, was one of the many Spaniards who fought against the British in the Revolutionary War. And

David Farragut, to the right leaning from the side of his ship, led Union forces in the 1864 capture of the forts guarding Mobile Bay. The artist, William Heysham Overend, with tongue in cheek, titled this picture "An August Morning with Farragut: the Battle of Mobile Bay." How does the title make clear the artist's admiration for Farragut?

Wadsworth Atheneum, Hartford

Chicago Historical Society

Ulysses S. Grant posed for this picture during the Battle of the Wilderness in 1864. What are some reasons Lincoln's critics believed the president had not found his general?

Return to the Preview & Review on page 577.

both David, who was 13 at the time, and his father fought for the United States in the War of 1812. In honor of his outstanding service, David Farragut became the nation's first admiral.

By autumn only a 250-mile stretch (400 kilometers) of the river between Vicksburg, Mississippi, and Port Hudson, Louisiana, was still in Confederate hands. At this point Lincoln put Grant back in command of a powerful army. Grant decided to attack Vicksburg. The town was located high on cliffs overlooking a bend in the Mississippi. It was defended by the southern army commanded by General John C. Pemberton.

Grant approached Vicksburg from the north in November 1862. His artillery pounded Vicksburg's fortifications. But marshy land around the city made an infantry attack impossible. Grant therefore moved his entire army to the other side of the Mississippi. Then he marched past the Vicksburg fortifications at night and recrossed the river south of the city.

After driving off a Confederate army east of Vicksburg, Grant began the **Siege of Vicksburg,** pinning down Pemberton and his army. The siege began in mid-May. For weeks the Confederates held out. Eventually they ran short of food and ammunition. On July 4, 1863, Pemberton surrendered. Shortly afterwards, the remaining southern stronghold on the river, **Port Hudson,** was also captured. The Confederacy had been snipped in two.

Lincoln Finds His General

Lincoln now put Grant in command of all Union troops west of the Appalachian Mountains. In November 1863 a series of battles was fought around **Chattanooga,** Tennessee, an important railway center and another Union military objective. There Grant defeated a Confederate army under General Braxton Bragg. Bragg retreated into northern Georgia. A few months later, in March 1864, Lincoln called Grant to Washington. He was promoted to lieutenant general and named general-in-chief of all the armies of the United States. Together they planned the war's end.

Grant decided to try to end the war by mounting two great offensives. He himself would lead the Army of the Potomac against Lee, seeking a showdown battle in northern Virginia. A western army commanded by General William Tecumseh Sherman would march from Chattanooga into northern Georgia. Its immediate objective was to capture Atlanta.

Grant had given command of the western army to General Sherman because he was a tough soldier. Sherman had served under Grant at the bloody battle of Shiloh and in the fighting around Chattanooga, and was someone Grant could count on. Sherman's father, an Ohio lawyer and judge, had named his son after the Shawnee leader Tecumseh, whom he admired greatly.

Virginia Historical Society

6. THE FINAL BATTLES

Grant Versus Lee

In May 1864 Grant crossed the Rappahannock and Rapidan Rivers and marched into the tangled forest of the Wilderness, where Lee had defeated Hooker one year earlier. This time Lee was reluctant to fight. He had only 60,000 men. Grant had more than 100,000.

Grant made Lee fight. For two days Union and Confederate forces hammered away at each other in the **Battle of the Wilderness.** The Army of the Potomac suffered 18,000 casualties, far more than its Confederate enemy.

Scarcely had this battle ended when Grant pressed stubbornly on. He was trying to march around Lee's smaller army and get between it and Richmond. At **Spotsylvania Court House** the two armies clashed again. This time 12,000 Union soldiers fell in a single day.

Again Grant advanced. In another bloody clash, at Cold Harbor, 7,000 Union soldiers died in less than an hour. In one month of fighting Grant had lost 55,000 men, Lee 31,000.

Despite the tremendous human cost, Grant was gaining his objective. Lee was running short of equipment. Union factories were turning out almost unlimited amounts of supplies. The larger population of the North was beginning to tip the scales toward the Union. Lee could not replace all his casualties. But bolstered by a steady stream of volunteers and draftees, the Army of the Potomac was larger after the **Battle of Cold Harbor** than at the start.

In June 1864 Grant crossed the James River in order to strike at **Petersburg,** a town a few miles south of Richmond. Petersburg was an important railroad junction. If Grant could capture it, supplies to Richmond and to Lee's army would be cut off.

Lee's weary veterans managed to stop the Union army outside Petersburg. Grant had to place the city under siege. Both sides dug in. The trenches stretched for miles around the city. For nine months the Confederate defenses held.

Preview & Review

Use these questions to guide your reading. Answer the questions after completing Section 6.
Understanding Issues, Events, & Ideas. Describe the final battles of the Civil War, using the following words: battles of the Wilderness, Spotsylvania Court House, Cold Harbor, Petersburg, Atlanta, Savannah; total war; Appomattox Court House.
1. What was Grant's objective in pressing Lee to battle?
2. How did the capture of Atlanta help Lincoln be reelected?
3. Why did Sherman engage in total war?
4. What were the terms of surrender at Appomattox? Tell whether or not you think these terms were generous.
Thinking Critically. 1. You are a Confederate soldier at Petersburg, which has been under siege for eight months. In your diary, record your impressions of the battle.
2. You are a reporter at Lee's surrender to Grant at Appomattox Court House. Write a headline and front-page news story describing this momentous occasion.

Above, "Summer" shows Robert E. Lee on Traveller with some of his generals at his side in 1863.

Point of View

Despite his use of total war to bring the South to its knees, Sherman despised war.

❝ It is only those who have neither fired a shot nor heard the shrieks and groans of the wounded who cry aloud for more blood, more vengeance, more desolation. War is hell. ❞

William Tecumseh Sherman, 1865

Sherman's March to the Sea

While Grant was stalled outside Petersburg, General Sherman advanced toward **Atlanta** at the head of a force of 100,000. The Confederate general resisting him, Joseph E. Johnston, had only 60,000 men. He tried to avoid a showdown battle. President Jefferson Davis did not approve of this. He replaced Johnston with General John B. Hood. An aggressive officer, Hood twice attacked Sherman's much larger army. Both attacks failed. On September 2 the Union army marched triumphantly into Atlanta. Hood retreated northward into Tennessee.

News of Sherman's victory reached Washington just before the presidential election of 1864. Lincoln had been renominated by Republicans and pro-war Democrats on a National Union ticket. The vice presidential candidate was Andrew Johnson, a Tennessee Democrat who had remained loyal to the Union. The Democratic candidate was General McClellan. With the war dragging on and on,

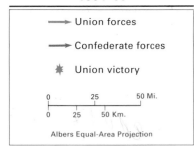

THE FINAL BATTLES, 1864–65

→ Union forces

→ Confederate forces

✳ Union victory

0   25   50 Mi.
0   25   50 Km.

Albers Equal-Area Projection

LEARNING FROM MAPS. *The war once again focused on northern Virginia in its closing days. What was the North's primary military objective in that area? Were they ever successful?*

582   THE CIVIL WAR

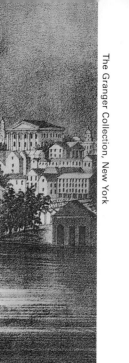

The Granger Collection, New York

Lincoln had expected to lose the election. Now, Sherman's victory helped him and his party immensely. Lincoln was reelected in a landslide, 212 electoral votes to 21.

After capturing Atlanta, Sherman burned the city to the ground. The next day, November 15, his army set out eastward toward the city of **Savannah** on the Atlantic Coast.

As Sherman's army went "marching through Georgia," as the song goes, "from Atlanta to the sea," it left a path of destruction behind it 60 miles wide (96 kilometers). On Sherman's order his troops destroyed or consumed everything in their path.

The Union soldiers slaughtered chickens and cattle. They burned barns and houses. When the men crossed a railroad line, they tore up the rails, piled up and set fire to the ties, and placed the rails on the roaring fire. When the rails were red hot, they bent and twisted them so that they were useless. Sometimes they wound the rails around tree trunks. These were known as "Sherman's neckties."

Sherman was carrying out what is now called **total war.** He sought to destroy the resources of the civilian population as well as the opposing army. He was trying to break the southerners' will to resist. When his harsh policy was questioned, Sherman simply said, "War is cruelty."

On December 21 the Union army entered Savannah. Next Sherman marched north, destroying large sections of South Carolina and North Carolina with the same cold-blooded efficiency.

The entire South was savaged by the war. Two thirds of its railroad mileage was destroyed. The Confederate capital at Richmond met the same fate as the cities in Sherman's path. On April 3, 1865, fires raged through its shattered streets.

Currier & Ives, comfortable with happier subjects, show "The Fall of Richmond" in 1865 as the capital city goes up in flames.

National Archives

This photograph of William Tecumseh Sherman was taken in 1865 by Mathew Brady, one of the greatest photographers of the Civil War.

The Final Battles   583

Only a month earlier, on March 4, 1865, Lincoln had begun his second term as president. Americans were still fighting Americans. But it was now evident the long and tragic war was drawing to a close. In his second inaugural address Lincoln outlined the policy toward the South he intended to follow. It closed with the words:

> 66 With malice [ill will] toward none, with charity for all, with firmness in the right as God gives us to see the right, let us strive on to finish the work we are in, to bind up the nation's wounds, to care for him who shall have borne the battle and for his widow and his orphan, to do all which may achieve and cherish a just and lasting peace among ourselves and with all nations. 99

Surrender at Appomattox

In April 1865 Grant finally cut the railroad line to Petersburg. Lee abandoned Petersburg and Richmond and retreated westward. His army was now thinned to 30,000 men. His last hope was to escape into North Carolina and join with the army that Sherman was driving before him. But Grant's pursuing troops sealed off this escape route. On April 8 Lee made the painful decision to surrender.

Lee and Grant met at the home of Wilmer McLean in the village of **Appomattox Court House** on Sunday, April 9. Lee wore his best dress uniform. Grant had on a muddy officer's coat and an ordinary private's shirt, unbuttoned at the neck. Seth M. Flint, a Yankee bugler, described the two men:

> 66 Grant looked like an old and battered campaigner as he rode into the yard. His blue blouse was unbuttoned and underneath could be seen his undershirt. He was unlike Lee.
>
> What a brave pair of thoroughbreds Lee and Traveler were. That horse would have attracted attention anywhere. General Lee's uniform was immaculate and he presented a superb martial [military] figure. But it was the face beneath the gray felt hat that made the deepest impression on me. I have been trying to find a single word that describes it and I have concluded that 'benign' is the adjective I'm after, because it means kindly and gracious. There was something else about him that aroused my deep pity that so great a warrior should be acknowledging defeat. . . .[1] 99

It was a moving scene. Lee was dignified in defeat, Grant gracious in victory. "I met you once before, General Lee, while we were serving in Mexico," Grant said after they had shaken hands. "I think I should have recognized you anywhere."

[1]From "I Saw Lee Surrender" by Seth M. Flint in *Saturday Evening Post*, vol. 248, no. 5 (April 1940)

Appomattox Court House National Historical Park, Photography by Russ Finley

At Appomattox Courthouse, in the quiet of a parlor, the Civil War is ended. How did each great general react to this moving scene?

The two great generals talked briefly about that war of long ago when they had been comrades. Then Grant sat down at a little table and wrote out the terms of surrender. The terms were generous. The Confederates must merely surrender their weapons, promise to be loyal to the Union, and depart in peace. When Lee hinted that his men would benefit greatly if allowed to keep their horses for the spring planting, Grant said, "Let all the men who claim to own a horse or mule take the animals home with them to work their little farms." Both men signed the surrender paper. Flint described what happened next:

> "Four o'clock—the door opened. Out came General Lee, his soldierly figure erect, even in defeat. We stiffened and gave him a salute, and the man in gray courteously [politely] returned it. At the moment his soul must have been heavy with sorrow—the years of desperate struggle fruitless—and yet he could return the salute of some Yankee troopers.
>
> After the departure of General Lee, we quickly learned the happy news of the surrender and it spread like wildfire through the army. That night was one of the happiest I have ever known.
>
> When I sounded taps, the sweetest of all bugle calls, the notes had scarcely died away when from the distance—it must have come from General Lee's headquarters—came, silvery clear, the same call. The boys on the other side welcomed peace.
>
> Soldiers don't carry hatred; . . .[1]"

[1]From "I Saw Lee Surrender" by Seth M. Flint in *Saturday Evening Post*, vol. 248, no. 5 (April 1940)

The war was over.

Return to the Preview & Review on page 581.

LINKING HISTORY & GEOGRAPHY

GEOGRAPHY AND WAR

One of the key influences on war strategy, today as well as yesterday, is geography. In the past, in fact, geography often was more important than strategy—actually determining the outcome of a battle or war. Control of a mountain pass or the high ground gave one side a distinct advantage over another. Can you think of other geographic features that would have a major effect on the progress and outcome of a battle?

Geography and the Civil War

1. How did geography influence the war strategy of the Union?

Lincoln and his military advisers developed a war strategy based on geography. Glance at the map on page 587. What geographic features might influence Union military strategy?

You can see that one key feature of the southern landscape is its long coastline. It stretches from Virginia around Florida to Texas, and is dented with inlets and harbors. Another feature that stands out is the Appalachian Mountains. Note how they effectively divide the Confederacy into east and west. A third prominent physical feature is the Mississippi River, which divides the Confederacy further.

The Union Blockade

2. Why did the Union blockade the southern coastline?

The long southern coastline concerned northern strategists. It concerned them because they knew it would be important to keep the South from getting needed supplies. Remember that most American manufacturing was located in the North. The Confederacy would have to depend on imports carried by ship to replenish their supplies.

What could the Union do? They decided to blockade the entire southern coastline. Union naval ships patrolled the offshore waters, capturing Confederate merchant ships bound for Europe for supplies or returning with them. The blockade, which stretched for 3,500 miles, became increasingly successful. At first, the Union navy could not effectively block the mile upon mile of coastline because Confederate ships were too numerous. As ships were added to the Union navy and lost from the Confederate one, the blockade grew more effective.

The Southern Landscape

3. Why was the Southern landscape a major influence on both war strategy and the war's outcome?

Virtually all the battles of the war were fought on Confederate land. Therefore, the geography of the South was of vital importance to both sides. Why did most of the war unfold in the South?

Remember that although the South fired the first shots of the war, southern strategy was not aggressive. To restore the Union, northern armies had to invade and defeat the Confederacy. The goal of the Confederacy, on the other hand, was to defend itself until the Union tired of fighting. The Confederacy need not invade the North because it sought no Union territory.

Divide and Conquer

4. How did the Union plan to fight the war on Confederate land?

Knowing their armies must invade, Union military advisers devised a plan to divide the South. Remember that the Appalachian Mountains and Mississippi River system already physically divided the South. Control of both would divide Southern armies and block supply routes. It would also require the outmanned Confederate army to fight on two fronts, stretching their limited manpower thin in certain places.

In the West control of the Mississippi and then its major tributaries—the Tennessee and Cumberland rivers—would further divide the South. It would be more and more difficult for reinforcements and supplies to reach Confederate forces. In fact, the Union was so conscious of the importance of geography and of rivers, they named many battles after nearby streams. (The Confederacy named the same battle after the nearest town.) The Battle of Bull Run (the Union name for a battle near a stream in northern Virginia) was also the Battle of Manassas (the Confederate name for the same battle near a small town in the area).

In the East, the North realized that controlling the mountainous spine of the Appalachians would isolate the tidewater South from vast lands of the Confederacy to the west. Union forces could then swiftly surround and capture Richmond and end the war.

A Successful Strategy

5. Did Union strategy work?

Lincoln had the confidence in his plan to stick with it. He knew that it was based on the geography of the land. Each part of the plan capitalized on a different physical aspect. And the war actually unfolded according to the plan Lincoln and his advisors had created.

The blockade eventually crippled the South. Shortages of almost every item became common. Neither southern industry nor southern agriculture could keep up with military or civilian needs. The Union army and navy gained control of the Mississippi and Tennessee river valleys, splitting the Confederacy. From that point on, Union victories divided the Confederacy into smaller and smaller isolated pieces. As the end of the war drew closer, Union troops surrounded Richmond, which was cut off from western reinforcements. Lincoln's confidence in the plan paid off. Strategy built on geography was one of the major keys to northern success in the Civil War.

Applying Your Knowledge

Your class will plan military strategy based on local geography. One group will plan an attack; the other should plan a defense. Consider all the geographic features that might influence a battle taking place in your area. Sketch maps to illustrate the strategies. If possible, visit the site you have selected and note the geographic features in person.

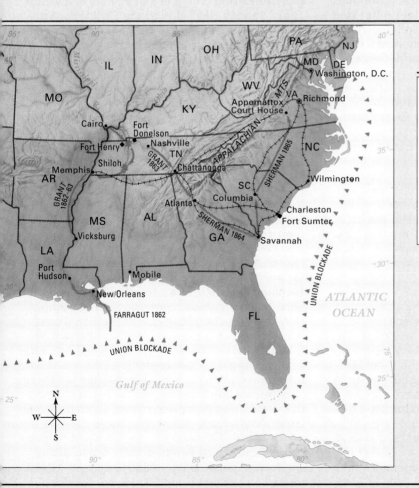

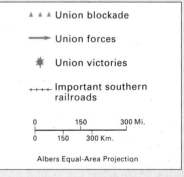

THE BLOCKADE AND THE WAR IN THE WEST, 1862–65

▲ ▲ ▲ Union blockade

→ Union forces

✳ Union victories

++++ Important southern railroads

0   150   300 Mi.

0   150   300 Km.

Albers Equal-Area Projection

CHAPTER 16 REVIEW

1860
Abraham Lincoln elected president

1861
Confederate States of America formed
★
Firing on Fort Sumter
★
Union blockade begins

1862
Union victory
at Antietam
★
Vicksburg Campaign

Chapter Summary
Read the statements below. Choose one, and write a paragraph explaining its importance.
1. In 1861 the states that seceded from the Union formed the Confederate States of America.
2. The Civil War started with the firing on Fort Sumter in Charleston harbor.
3. In numbers the Confederacy was no match for the Union, which had more people, railroads, and manufacturing. The South, however, had a cause and was fighting on its own land.
4. Although both sides were poorly trained for war, the South dominated the early battles.
5. The war had a major impact on the economies of both sides. Northern industrial output and employment boomed even as inflation rose. The South had shortages of many items.
6. The Union army finally won important victories at Antietam and Gettysburg.
7. Draft riots showed that many northerners opposed the Emancipation Proclamation.
8. Union control of the Mississippi River cut the Confederacy in two.
9. Union victories in Virginia forced Lee to surrender in April 1865.

Reviewing Chronological Order
Number your paper 1-5. Then study the time line above and place the following events in the order in which they happened by writing the first next to 1, the second next to 2, and so on.
1. Gettysburg
2. Lee surrenders at Appomattox
3. Confederates fire on Fort Sumter
4. Lincoln appoints Grant
5. Southern leaders form a confederacy

Understanding Main Ideas
1. Describe the life of a typical Civil War soldier.
2. What did the draft riots show about northern attitudes toward African Americans?
3. Why was the Battle of Vicksburg a turning point of the war?
4. How were Grant and Lee similar? How were they different?
5. What were the two parts of General Grant's plan to end the war?

6. Why did General Sherman use total war in his March to the Sea?

Thinking Critically
1. **Analyzing.** Compare and contrast Abraham Lincoln and Jefferson Davis as leaders. From what you have read in this chapter, who do you think was the better leader? Why?
2. **Evaluating.** Choose five Civil War generals and rank them from 1 to 5, according to their military performance. Then explain why you ranked them in this order.
3. **Synthesizing.** Imagine that you are "Billy Yank" or "Johnny Reb" during the Civil War. Write a letter to your parents or to your sweetheart, describing your life as a soldier.
4. **Drawing Conclusions.** Do you think President Lincoln issued the Emancipation Proclamation for ethical reasons, political reasons, or both? Explain.

Writing About History
Use your historical imagination to write a letter home as a soldier or nurse in either the Confederate or Union army. Include a description of a general you might have glimpsed in camp, or describe conditions in a hospital for the war wounded. Use the information in Chapter 16 and in other reference books to prepare your letter.

Practicing the Strategy
Review the strategy on page 558.
Reading a Statistical Chart. Study the chart on page 572, then answer the following questions.
1. What is meant by the words "Human Costs" in the title?
2. What kinds of data are being compared in the two columns of this chart?
3. Exactly how many more soldiers did the Union have than the Confederacy?
4. The Union won the war, but who paid the greatest price in casualties? How do you know?

Using Primary Sources
On New Years' Day, 1863 President Lincoln greeted guests at the annual presidential reception

1863
Emancipation Proclamation
★
Draft riots erupt in North
★
Gettysburg

1864
Grant controls Chattanooga
★
Lincoln appoints Grant
★
Sherman burns Atlanta; begins March to the Sea
★
Lincoln reelected

1865
Lee surrenders to Grant

at the White House. Then he slipped away to his private office where, in the presence of a few friends, he prepared to sign the Emancipation Proclamation. Pen in hand, he leaned forward to write his name, and then pausing a moment, said, "I never in my life felt more certain that I was doing right. . . ." With that he wrote his name in bold letters across the bottom of the document. As you read the following excerpt, see if you can feel the turmoil within Lincoln caused by conflicting political and moral values. Then answer the questions that follow it.

Whereas on the twenty-second day of September, A.D. 1862, a proclamation was issued by the President of the United States, containing among other things, the following, to wit:

On the first day of January, A.D. 1863, all persons held as slaves within any state or designated part of a state, the people whereof shall then be in rebellion against the United States, shall be then, thenceforward, and forever free; and the executive government of the United States, including military and naval authority thereof, will recognize and maintain the freedom of such persons and will do no act or acts to repress such persons or any of them, in any efforts they make for their actual freedom. . . .

And by virtue of the power and for the purpose aforesaid, I do order and declare all persons held as slaves within said designated states and parts of states are, and henceforward shall be, free; . . .

And I hereby enjoin the people so declared to be free to abstain from violence, unless in necessary self-defense; and I recommend to them that, in all cases when allowed, they labor faithfully for reasonable wages.

And I further declare and make known that such persons of suitable condition will be received into the armed service of the United States to garrison forts, positions, stations, and other places, and to man vessels of all sorts in said service.

And upon this act, sincerely believed to be an act of justice, warranted by the Constitution upon military necessity, I invoke the considerate judgment of mankind and the gracious favor of Almighty God.

1. Why do you think the Emancipation Proclamation did not specify that slaves in the border states be freed?
2. How do you think the Emancipation Proclamation affected slaves in the Confederate states during the Civil War? Why?
3. If you had been a slave on a southern plantation in 1863, what reasons might you have had to remain on the plantation?

Linking History & Geography

The geography of the South's transportation system helped Union leaders shape their strategy. Use the map on page 577 and the information in the chapter to answer the following questions.
1. What major southern ports were affected by the blockade? Why was control of the Mississippi River an important Union objective?
2. What were three cities connected to Chattanooga by railroad? What seems to be the relationship between railroads and Sherman's march from Atlanta to the sea?
3. About how far apart were the Union and Confederate capitals? How might Union strategy have been different if the Confederate capital had remained in Montgomery, Alabama?

Enriching the Study of History

1. **Individual Project.** Prepare a bulletin board to show the major battles of the Civil War. Give both southern and northern names when there are two. Arrange the battles in the order in which they were fought. Choose appropriate symbols for North and South, northern and southern victories, fighting on land and water, troop movements in the South and West.
2. **Cooperative Project.** Working in two teams, your class will present a newscast following the Battle of Gettysburg. One team will conduct interviews with the commanding generals and surviving soldiers from both armies. The other team will interview spectators who have just heard Lincoln deliver his *Gettysburg Address*. If possible, videotape your program.

Chapter 16 Review   589

Reconstruction

When the Civil War was ended and the slaves were set free, the problem of racial prejudice in the United States was not solved. When the slaves were freed, few thought of returning to Africa. In many cases America had been home for their families for 200 years. Yet African Americans still did not enjoy full citizenship during Reconstruction. Instead, they were now systematically excluded in the clearest form of prejudice, based on race. So-called "Jim Crow laws" and "Black Codes" passed after the Civil War greatly restricted the movement of former slaves. Amendments to the Constitution attempted to do away with race or skin color as a condition of voting, but "separate but equal" facilities, then permitted by the Supreme Court, effectively segregated black people from white. What long night of injustice and terror lay ahead?

Courtesy of The Library of Congress

In this portrait taken by a photographer from Brady Studio, we see President Lincoln in a quiet moment with his son Tad. Lincoln had valued reading from the time that he too was just a boy.

1. RADICALS AND MODERATES

Lincoln is Assassinated

On the evening of April 9, 1865, President Lincoln received a telegram from General Grant: "GENERAL LEE SURRENDERED THE ARMY OF NORTHERN VIRGINIA THIS MORNING." Next day the whole country had the news. Bells rang out, bands played, flags and banners flew everywhere in the North. A crowd gathered outside the White House. "Tad" Lincoln, the president's 12-year-old son, appeared at the window happily waving a captured Confederate flag. Everyone cheered.

Unfortunately, this happy national mood did not last. On the evening of April 14 Abraham and Mary Todd Lincoln were attending a play at Ford's Theater in Washington. Suddenly a shot rang out. John Wilkes Booth, a little-known actor who sympathized with the South, had slipped into the president's box and fired a bullet into his head. A popular writer described the assassination with these words:

> Booth kept his eye to the gimlet hole. The head in front of him barely moved. The universe seemed to pause for breath. Then Trenchard [a character on stage] said:' 'Don't know the manners of good society, eh?' Booth did not wait to hear the rest of the line. The derringer was now in his hand. He turned the knob. The door swung inward. Lincoln, facing diagonally away toward the left, was four feet from him. Booth moved along the wall. . . .
>
> The derringer was behind the President's head between the left ear and the spine. Booth squeezed the trigger and there was a sound as though someone had blown up and broken a heavy paper bag. It came in the midst of laughter, so that some people heard it, and some did not. The President did not move. His head inclined toward his chest and he stopped rocking. . . .
>
> A chrysanthemum of blue smoke hung in Box 7. Booth, with no maniacal [crazy] gleam, no frenzy, looked at the people who looked at him and said, 'Sic semper tyrannis! [Thus always to tyrants!] . . . Revenge for the South!'[1]

The next day the president died.

Booth escaped from the theater in the confusion and fled to Virginia. He was hunted down and trapped in a barn. The barn was set on fire, but Booth was killed by a bullet. Whether he was shot by someone else or killed himself is not clear.

The people of the North were shocked and grief-stricken. The Confederacy had surrendered, but the nation was still badly divided.

[1] From *The Day Lincoln Was Shot* by Jim Bishop

Preview & Review

Use these questions to guide your reading. Answer the questions after completing Section 1. **Understanding Issues, Events, & Ideas.** Describe the political problems after the Civil War, using the following words: assassination, Moderates, amnesty, Radicals, watershed, freedmen, Thirteenth Amendment, Black Codes, Reconstruction, Freedman's Bureau, veto, Civil Rights Act, override.

1. What did the Moderate Republicans think should be done to the South after the Civil War? What did the Radical Republicans think?
2. Why was the Thirteenth Amendment passed? What was the purpose of the Black Codes?
3. Why did Congress pass the Civil Rights Act?
   Thinking Critically. Write a newspaper obituary for Abraham Lincoln. Include what you consider to be his greatest accomplishment.

Lincoln lay for nine hours in a boarding house near Ford's Theater before he expired from his assassin's bullet. Alexander Hay Ritchie made this etching.

Few people realized the tremendous task of binding the nation's wounds that lay ahead. But now the leader who had guided them through the war was gone. Walt Whitman wrote a memorial to the dead president:

    ❝ O Captain! my Captain! our fearful trip is done,
        The ship has weathered every rack, the prize we sought
           is won,
        The port is near, the bells I hear; the people all
           exulting.
        While follow eyes the steady keel, the vessel grim and
           daring;
          But O heart! heart! heart!
          O the bleeding drops of red,
             Where on the deck my Captain lies,
               Fallen cold and dead.[1] ❞

The president's death left a terrible void at such a critical time. No one knew it yet, but another great struggle—this one over control of the defeated South—would extend the bitterness of the war for several more years.

President Andrew Johnson

Much now depended on Andrew Johnson, who became president after the **assassination** of President Lincoln. Before the Civil War Johnson had served in both houses of Congress and as governor of Tennessee. The Republicans had picked him to run for vice president in 1864, even though he was a Democrat. He was one of the few

[1]From "O Captain! my Captain!" by Walt Whitman

pro-Union politicians who came from a Confederate state. His home state of Tennessee was not even a member of the Union when he became president!

All through his career Johnson had been a champion of the small farmer. He favored laws to improve public education and provide free farms, or homesteads, for families who would settle on the public lands. He was always critical of great wealth. This helps explain his hatred of the southern planters he called "traitorous aristocrats."

Most Republican politicians expected Johnson to make a fine president. Moderate Republicans believed that "malice toward none" was the best policy and hoped he would extend it to the South. They hoped, as Lincoln had put it in his moving speech at his second inauguration, "to bind up the nation's wounds" quickly.

Johnson pleased the **Moderates** by issuing an **amnesty,** or pardon, to most former Confederates. Those who would take an oath of loyalty to the United States would regain full citizenship. The states of the former Confederacy could hold elections and send representatives and senators to Congress.

On the other hand, Republicans who were determined to protect the rights of the newly freed slaves, called **Radicals,** expected Johnson to act on his well-known dislike of the southern planter class and force the planters to accept the new ways. Congressman Thaddeus Stevens of Pennsylvania was one of the Radical leaders. He demanded that the United States seize the property of the large slaveholders and give it to the ex-slaves. There would be plenty of "rebel land," he said, to give a 40-acre farm (16 hectares) to every adult male ex-slave in the South.

The Aftermath of War

The American Revolution had been a **watershed,** or turning point in history, bringing great political changes. The new nation forged out of that revolution was unique, a government based on the consent of the governed. The Civil War also was a watershed. The secession of the southern states had challenged the very existence of the nation. From the ashes of war a dramatically different society emerged. The Civil War, historian Bruce Catton pointed out, destroyed "the old bases on which society stood. . . . The Civil War was a beginning, rather than an end, simply because it ended forever one of the things on which American society had been built." All Americans had to face the moral and legal questions of slavery. Had the war to end slavery in the United States succeeded? What would now happen to the former slaves?

War's end freed more than 4 million Americans from slavery. But the social and economic conditions of their newly gained freedom were undefined. The war also demolished the life style white southerners had enjoyed before the war. Plantations could no longer rely on slaves for labor, and the war had virtually destroyed the wealth of many planters. The very structure of southern society was questioned. Had it been fair that a few planters had controlled so much of the southern wealth and power? Everyone in the South, rich and poor, now found themselves in a world as new as that encountered by the first colonists.

Who in the South gained from the changes? Certainly the slaves gained their freedom. But their society had been torn apart too. They now entered a social and economic situation totally unlike any they had ever known. Some got land to farm; some got jobs. Most were merely confused and desperate at first. Poor southern whites also gained something. Although they now had to compete with the freed slaves for jobs and status, many were able to claim farmlands from the shattered plantations. This gave them hope for a better future.

Northerners' views of southern society changed too. Many people seemed to forget that most southerners were not rich and had owned no slaves. Myths about a land of prosperous plantations, fatherly masters, and contented slaves began to emerge. Such a South became the setting for many books and plays published in the years after the war. But the southerners, black and white, knew that these tales were of a South "gone with the wind."

Finally, the war cost the nation 600,000 lives. It caused enormous property losses, especially in the Confederacy. The total war just ended had ravaged farms and factories throughout the South. How long would it take to rebuild what the war had destroyed and at what cost?

The Black Codes

The Radicals were also concerned about the way former slaves, called **freedmen,** were being treated in the South. By the end of 1865, most of the southern state governments set up under Johnson's amnesty plan had ratified the new **Thirteenth Amendment** to the Constitution, which officially abolished slavery. But white people formed the majority in most parts of the South. They were powerful and well organized. Southern blacks could not protect their new rights without northern help. The new southern governments did not allow black people to vote. Their legislatures swiftly passed regulations called **Black Codes** designed to keep blacks in a condition of semi-slavery.

These codes barred blacks from any kind of work except farming and household service. Some states forced blacks to sign labor contracts with landowners at the beginning of each year. If they left their work, they received no pay. If they refused to sign, they were arrested and charged with being tramps. The "sentence" was to work for one of the landowners for the year.

These Black Codes alarmed most northerners. The results of the new southern elections alarmed them even more. Southern voters,

The Granger Collection, New York

all of them white, chose as leaders many of the same people who had led them during the rebellion. Several Confederate generals were elected to Congress. The Georgia legislature picked Alexander H. Stephens, vice president of the Confederacy, to represent the state in the United States Senate. Stephens had recently been paroled from prison after being charged with treason for his role in the Confederacy.

The newly elected representatives were members of the Democratic party. Admitting them was too much even for Moderate Republicans to accept. Both houses of Congress voted not to admit the new southern representatives. Johnson's plan for **Reconstruction**—bringing southern states back into the Union—was rejected.

Johnson and the Republicans

The Republicans in Congress then began to reconstruct the South according to their own ideas. Before the end of the war Congress had created a **Freedmen's Bureau** run by the army to care for refugees. Early in 1866 a new bill was passed increasing the power of the Bureau to protect southern blacks.

President Johnson decided to **veto,** or refuse to approve, this Freedmen's Bureau Bill. He claimed that he approved of the purpose of the bill. He was eager, he said, "to secure for the freedmen . . . their freedom and property and their entire independence." But he argued that it was unconstitutional to apply military law to civilians in peacetime.

Congress therefore attacked the Black Codes by passing a **Civil Rights Act.** This law made blacks citizens of the United States. It

Life for many freed slaves did not seem to improve after the Civil War. Such is the plight of these Virginia farmers in about 1900. The butchered hogs had to be lowered into scalding water until their bristles could be scrubbed off. What must have been the joys of freedom? What the sorrows?

Radicals and Moderates   595

INTERPRETING HISTORY: Reconstruction

Reconstruction is one of the most controversial topics considered by historians. Lincoln hoped Reconstruction would "bind up the nation's wounds" caused by the Civil War. Lincoln based his plan on "malice toward none." But his plan was doomed to failure. As historian Eric Foner said, "What remains certain is that Reconstruction failed, and that for blacks its failure was a disaster whose magnitude cannot be obscured by the genuine accomplishments that did endure."

Why did it fail? The traditional view, represented by historian William A. Dunning, holds that white southerners suffered greatly at the hands of radical Republicans. They imposed a harsh rule on the South, including enforcement of the Civil War Amendments which freed the slaves and gave them the right to vote. Suddenly, according to Dunning, black southerners were given too much political power. Carpetbaggers were able to invade the South to rob it, and black voters and corrupt politicians passed laws only to benefit themselves. African Americans were unprepared for their role, and white southerners reacted strongly to most of these measures, blocking the ultimate chances for success of Reconstruction.

The first historian to challenge this view was W.E.B. DuBois. He claimed in his book *Black Reconstruction* that Reconstruction was an effort by both whites and blacks to create a "true democratic society." It failed because it did not go far enough. DuBois remarked: "One fact and one alone explains the attitude of writers toward Reconstruction; they cannot conceive of Negroes as men." Then in the 1960s, during the intense civil rights movement, historians began to further revise the traditional view. Kenneth Stampp, in *The Era of Reconstruction,* insisted Reconstruction failed not because of what it did to southern whites but what it failed to do for southern blacks. It did not implement the reforms necessary to ensure African Americans equal rights, and in fact, blacks were not much better off than before the Civil War.

Stampp and other revisionist historians also reexamined the role of the radical Republicans. These historians point to the efforts to build schools and churches as evidence of their positive contributions. Most black elected officials were not corrupt, but rather had long and distinguished careers as public servants.

The debate continues today. Which interpretation do you think is closest to the truth?

was necessary to state this specifically because the Dred Scott decision had declared that even free blacks were not American citizens. The bill also forbade the southern states from restricting the rights of freedmen by special laws like the Black Codes.

President Johnson vetoed this bill too. It was a mistake to make blacks citizens, he now insisted. They needed to go through a period of "probation" before receiving this "prize." It was unconstitutional to give blacks "safeguards which go infinitely beyond any that the . . . Government has ever provided for the white race," he said.

As this veto made clear, Johnson's dislike of southern planters did not keep him from being prejudiced against blacks. Great wealth in the hands of a few plantation owners was what he really hated, not slavery. Before the war he once said that he wished every white family in America could have one slave "to take the drudgery" out of life!

In April 1866 both houses of Congress again passed the Civil Rights Act. They obtained the two-thirds majority necessary to **override** the president's veto. This was the first veto of an important law ever to be overridden. Thus the Civil Rights Act became law a year after the war ended.

Return to the Preview & Review on page 591.

2. THE CIVIL WAR AMENDMENTS

The Reconstruction Acts

Next, Congress passed and sent to the states for ratification what became the **Fourteenth Amendment** to the Constitution. In many ways this measure was even more important than the Thirteenth Amendment. The Republicans in Congress drafted it in order to put the terms of the Civil Rights Act directly into the Constitution.

"All persons born or naturalized in the United States," the amendment said, "are citizens of the United States *and of the State wherein they reside*." This made blacks citizens no matter where in the nation they lived. Then the amendment struck down the Black Codes. "No State shall . . . abridge the privileges and immunities of citizens of the United States; nor shall any State deprive any person of life, liberty, or property, without due process of law."

The Fourteenth Amendment guaranteed equal protection of the laws to all Americans. It did not make racial **segregation,** or separation, illegal. It did not even tell states to allow blacks to vote. It did provide blacks with equal access to the courts, and it forbade laws that applied only to blacks but not whites. Nevertheless, most white southerners objected to it strongly. Since the southern states refused to ratify the amendment, it was impossible to get the approval of three fourths of the states, which was necessary to make it part of

Use these questions to guide your reading. Answer the questions after completing Section 2.
Understanding Issues, Events, & Ideas. Using the following words, explain how the rights of African Americans were affected after the Civil War: Fourteenth Amendment, segregation, Reconstruction Act, impeachment, Tenure of Office Act, Fifteenth Amendment, Civil War Amendments.
1. Why was the Fourteenth Amendment passed?
2. How did Republicans use the Reconstruction Act to force southerners to give blacks the right to vote?
3. Why did the Republican leaders of Congress want to remove President Johnson from office?
4. How would northern blacks have influenced the election of 1868 if they had been allowed to vote?
Thinking Critically. 1. How would you view the Fourteenth Amendment if you were a conservative white southerner? A Radical Republican? An ex-slave in the South? **2.** Which of the Civil War Amendments do you think is the most important? Why?

The Granger Collection, New York

"The First Vote" is the title of this drawing. Discuss whether or not elections such as these counted—or whether the votes were even tallied.

Andrew Johnson's course toward the South was watched with special interest by Ulysses S. Grant.

> **"But for the assassination of Mr. Lincoln, I believe the great majority of the Northern people, and the soldiers unanimously, would have been in favor of a speedy reconstruction on terms that would be least humiliating to the people who rebelled against their government. . . ."**
>
> From *Personal Memoirs,*
> Ulysses S. Grant, 1885

Copyright by the White House Historical Association; photographed by the National Geographic Society

Although cartoonists often poked fun at him, there was a kindliness about Lincoln that his photographers captured. Andrew Johnson, shown here in his presidential portrait, lacked this trait. Was it his manner or his policies that riled his critics, according to what you've read?

the Constitution. These amendments became the legal basis of the Civil Rights movement of the 1960s.

President Johnson made his conflict with the Republicans an issue in the Congressional elections of November 1866. He campaigned back and forth across the country, arguing for his own approach. He failed to change many minds. Indeed, most historians believe that Johnson's angry speeches probably lost more votes for his policies than they gained. The Republicans easily maintained their large majorities in both houses of Congress.

After the failure of the southern states to ratify the Fourteenth Amendment, Congress passed the **Reconstruction Act** of March 1867. This stern measure divided what it called "the rebel states" into five military districts. "Sufficient military force" to "protect all persons in their rights" was stationed in each district. To end army rule, each former state would have to draw up a new constitution that guaranteed blacks the right to vote. The state would also have to ratify the Fourteenth Amendment.

In other words, Congress ordered a military occupation of the South. Lincoln's hope that the nation could bind up its wounds in harmony had come to nothing.

White southerners hated military rule, but they hated the idea of racial equality even more. They still refused to ratify the Fourteenth Amendment. A second, and a third, and finally a fourth Reconstruction Act were passed by Congress. Each put more pressure on "the rebel states." At last, in June 1868, southern governments in which blacks participated began to be formed. These governments ratified the amendment. The final state to complete the process was Georgia, in July 1870, more than five years after the end of the Civil War.

President Johnson Is Impeached

Radical Republicans blamed President Johnson for much of the stubborn resistance of white southerners to the Reconstruction Acts. He had urged the states not to accept the Fourteenth Amendment. He had vetoed each of the Reconstruction bills, even though their repassage by large majorities was certain. In February 1868 angry Congressional leaders decided to try to remove the president from office by impeaching him.

The Constitution provides that the House of Representatives, by majority vote, can bring charges against a president. This is called **impeachment.** The charges are judged by the Senate, with the chief justice of the United States presiding over the trial. A two-thirds majority vote is required for conviction and removal from office.

The Radicals brought 11 charges against the president. Most of them were totally without merit. The most serious accusation was that he had violated the **Tenure of Office Act** of 1867 by dismissing Edwin M. Stanton, the secretary of war. This law prohibited the

The Granger Collection, New York

president from *discharging* appointed officials without the consent of Congress.

Johnson believed that the Tenure of Office Act was unconstitutional. The Constitution states only that Senate approval is necessary for the *appointment* of high officials. In the past no one had challenged the right of a president to remove an appointee without consulting the Senate.

Johnson dismissed Stanton deliberately to bring the issue before the Supreme Court, where it could properly be decided. Impeaching the president was clearly not justified by the facts. Indeed, his term was almost over. But many members of Congress believed that Reconstruction would never be successful unless Johnson were removed from office.

The Senate sits as a court to judge whether or not Andrew Johnson will be convicted in his impeachment trial in 1868. Below is a ticket to the Senate chamber. What is the difference between impeachment and conviction?

The Granger Collection, New York

U. S. SENATE
Impeachment of the President
ADMIT THE BEARER
MARCH 13, 1868

Geo. T. Brown
Sergeant-at-Arms.

To be taken up at MAIN ENTRANCE
CARD No. U. S. SENATE

Philp & Solomons, Wash. D.C.

The Civil War Amendments   599

The president was spared conviction by a single vote. On each charge the Senate failed to obtain a two-thirds majority by only one vote.

Andrew Johnson remained in office until March 1869. He was a poor president. All his life he had been a valuable public servant when he was battling for reform, a lone "outsider" stubbornly attacking "the Establishment." When fate made him the head of that Establishment, he proved unable to adjust. He could not work well with other people. He made a dreadful mess of his time in the White House.

Yet Johnson was not an evil man. His Reconstruction policies seem wrong to us today, but he did not deserve to be accused of committing crimes against the nation. His problem was his inability to think of blacks as equal members of society.

The Election of 1868

A majority of the white people of his generation shared Andrew Johnson's low opinion of the character and intelligence of blacks. As we have seen, most northern states did not allow blacks to vote. However, the results of the presidential election of 1868 led to a dramatic change in this situation.

Blacks in the southern states *had* voted in that election. Federal troops stationed there under the Reconstruction Act prevented whites from keeping blacks from the polls. Eager to exercise their civic duty for the first time, many voted, and they naturally cast their ballots overwhelmingly for the Republican party.

The Republican presidential candidate, General Grant, won an easy victory in the electoral college, 214 votes to 80 for the Democratic candidate, Horatio Seymour. But in many northern states the popular vote was extremely close.

Republican politicians also felt that guaranteeing the right to vote for blacks was necessary. Maybe in future elections they could make an important difference. They reasoned that blacks could not have much power in the North. Blacks made up only about one percent of the population in that section. Why not allow them to vote? Certainly blacks would vote solidly Republican. Perhaps the hated Democrats could be kept out of power forever.

Early in 1869 the overwhelmingly Republican Congress drafted still another Constitutional amendment: "The right of citizens of the United States to vote shall not be denied . . . on account of race, color, or previous condition of servitude." Within about a year this **Fifteenth Amendment** was ratified by the states. With the Thirteenth and Fourteenth Amendments, it is one of the **Civil War Amendments** which later formed the basis of the civil rights movement of the 1960s.

Ulysses S. Grant posed for this portrait as president. After leaving the White House, poor and suffering from cancer, Grant wrote his **Personal Memoirs,** *which became a national best seller. Was Grant as good a president as he was a general?*

Return to the Preview & Review on page 597.

3. FREEDOM AFTER SLAVERY

The Privileges of Freedom

The Civil War Amendments did bring certain freedoms to black Americans. Freedom meant first of all the right to decide what to do with one's own time, from minute to minute and day to day. It meant lifting a terrible weight off the *minds* of nearly 4 million former slaves. It meant freedom to move about.

With freedom from slavery, most blacks had to work less hard. Now they could put down their hoes and stretch their tired muscles for a few minutes without fear of a blow or a harsh word. Parents did not send the youngest children into the fields as their former owners would have done. Old people labored less and rested more. Mothers devoted more time to their homes and children, less to planting, hoeing, and harvesting.

Another use that blacks made of freedom was to seek education. Very few slaves could read and write. There had been no schools for slave children, and indeed it was against the law in most southern states even to teach a slave to read.

The Freedmen's Bureau began to oversee schools in the South as soon as the war ended. Many religious and private groups from the North also contributed time, money, and teachers.

Blacks responded eagerly to this opportunity for schooling. In South Carolina, for example, a school for blacks was set up in

Preview & Review

Use these questions to guide your reading. Answer the questions after completing Section 3.
Understanding Issues, Events, & Ideas. What was the significance during Reconstruction of the following words: "Black Republican," Carpetbagger, Scalawag, sharecropping, lien, crop-lien system, world market.
1. What were some of the privileges of freedom for blacks?
2. What were some reasons Carpetbaggers and Scalawags sought public office?
3. Why was it difficult for freedmen to begin farming under the Homestead Act of 1862?
4. What were the unfortunate side effects of the crop-lien system?
Thinking Critically. 1. Imagine that you are a former slave who is now attending school. In your diary, tell why you think education is important for all blacks.
2. Compare and contrast black politicians with white politicians of the Reconstruction period.

The preacher comes to call, making the children watchful and shy. All here are former slaves. In what ways did freedom change their lives?

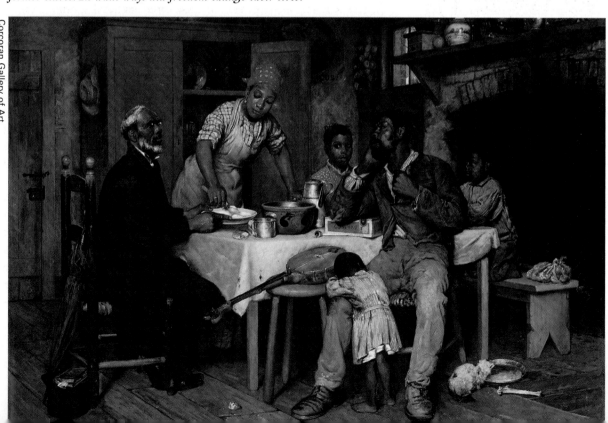

Corcoran Gallery of Art

Rufus S. Willard Saxton Papers, Yale University Library

In one of the Freedmen's Bureau schools, eager pupils gather around their teacher, who probably came from the North as a volunteer. What lie told by prejudiced whites did these schools put to rest?

Charleston as soon as the Union army captured the city. By 1867 there were about 20,000 blacks attending school in that state. All over the South elderly ex-slaves could be seen learning their ABC's alongside their grandchildren.

At first most white southerners sneered at the very idea of educating the freedmen. Remember that there had not even been state-supported public schools for whites in the prewar South. But many came to admit that blacks could learn as well as whites. Most blacks who were educated became useful citizens. Thus all but the most prejudiced whites changed their minds. These whites continued, however, to oppose teaching black and white children in the same schools.

Blacks in Government

While the United States army occupied the South, blacks voted and held office in all the states of the former Confederacy. Nothing made white southerners more bitter and resentful than to be "ruled" by the very people they had totally dominated for so long.

"Rule" is not, however, the proper word to describe the role of blacks in southern politics during Reconstruction. Only 22 ever served in Congress and only a handful were elected to high state office during the period. Blacks held many local offices, but they seldom controlled any branch of a local government. The only state legislature that ever had a black majority was South Carolina's between 1868 and 1877.

Most of the members of the **"Black Republican"** governments, as their opponents called them, were whites. Those who came from the northern states were called **Carpetbaggers** because travelers of the period usually carried their belongings in soft-sided bags made of carpeting. The name implied that these "invaders" had no stake in the South but to get rich. Southern white Republicans were referred to scornfully by their Democratic neighbors as **Scalawags**— runty, poorly bred cattle. Southerners strongly despised both groups.

Carpetbaggers and Scalawags came from all walks of life—military personnel, planters, businessmen, and speculators. Some genuinely wanted to help blacks achieve political influence. Others intended to win power for themselves by controlling black votes. Some were plain thieves. Black politicians in the South also varied widely in ability and devotion to duty. There were fewer Carpetbaggers than Scalawags and blacks in Reconstruction governments. But their undoubted loyalty to the Union and connections in Washington gave them great influence.

During the 1870s white people who objected to blacks holding office emphasized the numerous examples of black corruption and incompetence that came to light. A northern observer, James S. Pike, reported that the 1873 session of the South Carolina legislature was

The Granger Collection, New York

The Solid South staggers under the weight of the carpetbag carrying General Grant in an 1880 cartoon from the British magazine Puck. *The South is chained to two Union soldiers, whose bayonets support the unusual presidential chariot. What other signs of a fallen South can you find?*

marked by total confusion. "No one is allowed to talk five minutes without interruption," Pike complained. There was "endless chatter" and much "gush and babble." Pike said of one speaker:

66 He did not know what he was going to say when he got up . . . and he did not know what he had said when he sat down. 99

A black politician in Arkansas collected $9,000 for repairing a bridge that had cost the state only $500 to build in the first place. The black-controlled South Carolina legislature spent $16,000 a year on paper and other supplies. The average spent on these materials before the war was $400. The black South Carolina senators had a kind of private club in the capitol building where fine food and wines and the most expensive cigars were always available. Many black legislators routinely accepted money in exchange for their votes on important issues.

Such things did indeed happen. What white critics failed to mention was that many white politicians were just as corrupt and inefficient. In fact most of the corruption during this time can be traced to whites. One commentator watched the disorderly behavior of members of the United States House of Representatives at about this time. He said that trying to make a speech in the House was like

Chicago Historical Society

Robert B. Elliott of South Carolina addresses his fellow state legislators on civil rights in 1874. What influence do you suppose this well-educated African American had in the state legislature?

trying to speak to a crowd in a passing trolley while standing on the curb of a busy city street.

As for corruption, the main difference between white and black thieves was that the white ones made off with most of the money. After studying the actions of black and white officials during Reconstruction, the historian Joel Williamson concludes that "the most gigantic steals" were engineered by white politicians like "Honest John" Patterson, a Carpetbagger who systematically bribed South Carolina legislators to vote for a bill worth nearly $2 million to a railroad Patterson controlled.

However, the southern state governments also accomplished a great deal of good during these years. They raised taxes in order to improve public education, which had been badly neglected before 1860. They also spent large sums on roads, bridges, railroads, and public buildings damaged during the war. They also expanded public support for medical care and orphans. They began to rebuild the southern economy. And in many cases they established civil rights laws.

STRATEGIES FOR SUCCESS

INTERPRETING A GRAPH OF BUSINESS CYCLES

As you have learned, the United States has a free enterprise economy. This means that businesses are privately owned and operated with little interference by the government. American business is directly affected by the needs and wants of consumers—or the *market.* Prosperity goes in cycles. Events that influence consumers cause the economy to expand or recede. Graphs throughout *The Story of America* illustrate these cycles.

How to Read a Graph of Business Cycles

To read a graph of business cycles, follow these guidelines.
1. **Read the title**. The title identifies the time period illustrated by the graph.
2. **Check the key**. The key explains what the colors and special symbols on the graph mean.
3. **Study the trends**. The graph shows the ups and downs of the business cycle. Periods of expansion rise above the trend line (which may also be called the base line). Periods of recession, or slowdowns, dip below the trend line.
4. **Note the labels**. Historical events that strongly influence economic cycles help explain the reasons for the surge or sag of the economy.

5. **Compare the fluctuations**. The highs and lows differ in intensity and duration (length of time). Compare them to understand the business situation at that time in American history.

Applying the Strategy

Study the graph below. The title, "Business Cycles, 1840–1870" tells you that it illustrates the ups and downs of business from just before the Civil War to immediately after it. Note that the graph shows a period of general expansion, or business growth, from 1840 to 1857. What events helped spur this growth? What happened in 1857 to slow the growth? The Civil War strongly affected American business. Secession caused a recession. Why would this happen? Business recovered to expand during the war as businesses began producing for the war. You can see a brief primary recession immediately after the war as war production ended. Soon however, the economy began to grow again as businesses replaced what was lost in war. What do you think the business cycle from 1870 to 1900 would show?

For independent practice, see Practicing the Strategy on page 619.

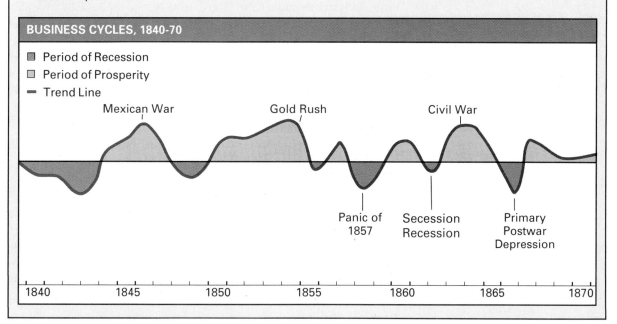

BUSINESS CYCLES, 1840-70

- ▨ Period of Recession
- ☐ Period of Prosperity
- ▬ Trend Line

Mexican War — Gold Rush — Civil War — Panic of 1857 — Secession Recession — Primary Postwar Depression

1840 1845 1850 1855 1860 1865 1870

In her diary the mistress of Mulberry Plantation wrote in Sherman's wake.

> **"**Nothing but tall blackened chimneys to show that any man has ever trod this road before. This is Sherman's track. It is hard not to curse him. I wept incessantly at first. The roses of the garden are already hiding the ruins. My husband said Nature is a wonderful renovator. He tried to say something else and then I shut my eyes and made a vow that if we were a crushed people, crushed by weight, I would never be a slave.**"**
>
> Mary Boykin Chesnut, May 2, 1865

The Ravaged Land

Economic ruin and social chaos swept the South. Wherever armies had clashed, houses and barns were shattered or burned, crops ruined, and livestock taken or killed. After the war seed to plant new crops and horses or mules to plow the land were scarce. Even labor was scarce. A quarter of a million southern soldiers had died and many former slaves did not want to work for their former masters.

Many southern industries also were badly damaged, and loans to rebuild or restart them were unavailable. Rubble littered cities that had stood in the path of invading armies.

Southerners set about working their land as best they could. Many whites felt relieved that slavery had ended. But they wondered what lay ahead. Some feared vengeance from former slaves. Others could not adjust to dealing with a free labor force. They had always been members of a group that viewed itself as superior and that thinking continued. In the late spring of 1865, however, both groups knew that unless food crops were planted, there would be nothing to eat in the winter, and unless cash crops were raised, there would be no money to buy seed for next year's crop.

Sharecropping

Nearly all the slaves had been farm workers and nearly all continued to work on the land after they became free. The efforts of Radicals like Thaddeus Stevens to carve up the large plantations and give each black family "forty acres and a mule" never attracted much support among northern whites. In theory, a freedman could get a 160-acre farm (64 hectares) under the Homestead Act of 1862. Only a handful of blacks were able to do so. They lacked the tools, seed money, and the means of getting to the distant frontier. The price of land was only a small part of the cost of starting a farm. As one congressman reported from Georgia in 1866:

> **"** The blacks own absolutely nothing but their bodies; their former masters own everything, . . . If a black man draws even a bucket of water from a well, he must first get permission of a white man. . . . If he asks for work to earn his living, he must ask it of a white man.**"**

Most of the former slaves therefore continued to cultivate land owned by whites. At first they worked for cash wages. But the South was poor after the war. Most landowners were very short of cash. So a new system called **sharecropping** was worked out.

Sharecropping means sharing the crop. Under this system the landowner provided the laborers with houses, tools, seeds, and other supplies. The sharecroppers provided the skill and muscle needed to

Los Angeles County Museum of Art

grow the crops. When the harvest was gathered, it was shared, half to two thirds for the landowner, the rest for the sharecropper.

This system allowed black workers to be free of the close daily control they had endured under slavery. Each black family had its own cabin and tilled its own land as a separate unit. Sharecroppers could at least hope that by working hard and saving they might some-day have enough money to buy a farm of their own. Then they would be truly free. For this reason most blacks much preferred sharecrop-ping to working for wages.

A long time passed before many sharecroppers owned their farms. Partly this was because most whites tried to keep blacks from obtaining land of their own. The landowners wanted to make sure they had enough workers for their own farms. And they wanted to keep all the blacks dependent upon them.

Some landowners cheated the sharecroppers when the harvest was divided. Local storekeepers also cheated them. Share-croppers had to buy supplies on credit. They ran up bills at the general store during the growing season. When the crop was sold in the autumn, they used the money to pay off this debt. Frequently the merchant added items to the bill the farmers had never purchased. Blacks who objected were threatened with the loss of credit in the future, or with violence. During Reconstruction, with blacks on local

Winslow Homer painted the cotton pickers whose pricked fingers some-times stained the cotton red with blood. In the engraving below, a freedman stands by his sack of cotton. Has freedom made this work easier?

Bettmann Archives

Freedom After Slavery   607

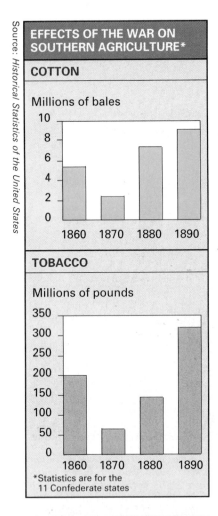

Source: Historical Statistics of the United States

EFFECTS OF THE WAR ON SOUTHERN AGRICULTURE*

COTTON

Millions of bales

TOBACCO

Millions of pounds

*Statistics are for the 11 Confederate states

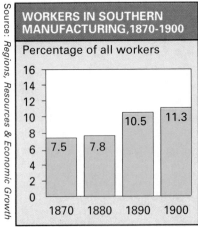

Source: Regions, Resources & Economic Growth

WORKERS IN SOUTHERN MANUFACTURING, 1870-1900

Percentage of all workers

LEARNING FROM GRAPHS. *What generalization about the southern economy can you draw from these graphs?*

juries, there was some hope for justice. After the end of Reconstruction, with blacks once again barred from juries, the local courts were not likely to give justice to blacks who sued any white person.

Even when dealing with honest landowners and merchants, it was hard to make much more than a bare living as a sharecropper. Prices were high in the stores because the storekeepers also had to borrow to get the goods they sold. They paid high interest rates because money was so scarce in the South. They had to charge high prices to cover that expense. So it was lack of money more than cheating by whites or racial prejudice that kept black sharecroppers from getting farms of their own. White sharecroppers hardly fared better.

The whole system seemed strangely similar to slavery. Blacks were again tied to the land they worked, with little hope of leaving. This time the bonds were more clearly economic, but their effects were similar. Southern state courts upheld the legality of the new arrangement. Their rulings seemed to undermine the spirit and effect of the Thirteenth Amendment, which had ended slavery. Finally in 1911 the Supreme Court ruled in *Bailey v. Alabama* that the new system, which it called black peonage, was unconstitutional.

The Crop-Lien System

The shortage of money made everyone dependent on bankers and other people with funds to invest. These investors wanted to be sure that the loans they made in the spring were repaid in the fall after the crops had been harvested. They demanded that the landowners pledge the future crop as security for the loan. This meant that they had a claim on the crop, called a **lien,** before it was even planted. If the borrower failed to pay when the loan fell due, the lender could take possession of the crop.

This **crop-lien system** was fair enough on the surface. However, it had an unfortunate side effect. The lenders insisted that the borrowers grow one of the South's major cash crops, such as cotton or tobacco. These were products for which there was a **world market.** They could be converted into cash anywhere and at any time. If the price was low, they could be safely stored until market conditions improved.

The landowners and sharecroppers of the South would have been better off if they could have grown many different things—vegetables and fruits as well as cotton and the other cash crops. By concentrating on one crop, they exhausted the fertility of the soil more rapidly. If they had a larger-than-normal harvest, the price of the cash crop fell steeply because supply was greater than demand.

Everyone was caught up in the system. The bankers put pressure

Brown Brothers

on the landowners and storekeepers. They, in turn, forced the sharecroppers to plant what the bankers wanted. The tendency is to blame the bankers. The charge is that they were greedy and shortsighted. But the bankers really had little choice. It would have been extremely risky, for example, to lend a farmer money to grow tomatoes, for they had to be sold locally when they were ripe or they would rot and become worthless within a few days.

So most southern black people stayed poor. The South itself stayed poor. It took about 20 years for the region to get production back to where it had been when the Civil War broke out. As we shall see, during those years the rest of the country was increasing its output at a rapid rate.

Yet for black southerners the Reconstruction era was a time of genuine progress. Any change from slavery had to be an improvement. They had power over many aspects of their life for the first time. Gradually their standard of living improved. They had more to eat, better clothes, and more comfortable houses. When they supplied these things for themselves by their own labor, they were better off than when they got only what their owners chose to give them. 🗐

Sharecroppers stand in front of their cabin, the cotton growing right up to the back porch. What do you suppose the man in the buggy has come for?

Return to the Preview & Review on page 601.

Freedom After Slavery 609

Use these questions to guide your reading. Answer the questions after completing Section 4.
Understanding Issues, Events, & Ideas. Describe how white southerners resisted Reconstruction, using the following words: Ku Klux Klan, Amnesty Act of 1872, Compromise of 1877.

1. Why was the outcome of the 1876 presidential election in doubt? How was the president finally selected?
2. Why did another Civil War threaten the nation in 1877?
3. What were the terms of the Compromise of 1877?
Thinking Critically. 1. You are a black living in the South. Write a letter to the editor of your local newspaper, explaining why you have decided not to vote in the presidential election of 1876. 2. Write a magazine article describing the events that led to the Compromise of 1877.

4. TROOPS LEAVE THE SOUTH

Resistance to Reconstruction

It is safe to say that the great majority of white southerners strongly resisted the changes forced upon them during Reconstruction, sometimes openly, sometimes in the dead of night. The Black Codes were one attempt to keep blacks in a lowly status. In 1866 the whites also began to form secret organizations to hold blacks down by terror.

The most important of these organizations was the **Ku Klux Klan.** Klan members were determined to keep blacks from voting and thus influencing political events. Klansmen tried to frighten blacks by galloping through the night dressed in white robes, hoods, and masks. They claimed to be the ghosts of Confederate soldiers. They burned crosses on the hillsides, a hint of the terrible tortures that awaited blacks who tried to vote. When blacks refused to be frightened, the Klan often carried out its threats. Hundreds of black southerners were beaten, other hundreds actually murdered by the Klan.

The federal government managed to check the Klan by about 1871. It sent troops to areas where violence had broken out. Many Klan leaders were arrested. Gradually, more white southerners joined in efforts to keep blacks from voting. They joined the Democratic

Blacks attempting to vote are halted by the sharp-featured election judge who keeps his gun at the ready. The man at the door holds a "Republican ticket," but it will not be used in this election. The Republican ticket won in no southern elections. What chance of voting do you think the freedman believed he had?

New York Public Library Picture Collection

party. In 1874 groups in Mississippi began an organized effort, its aim printed prominently in several newspapers, "Carry the election peacefully if we can, forcibly if we must." They formed military companies and marched about in broad daylight. They gave merciless beatings to those blacks they found "uppity" or rebellious. Many blacks fought back against this kind of violence. In some areas small-scale but bloody battles broke out between armed bands of whites and blacks.

The Election of 1876

Since blacks were in the minority in the South and had fewer weapons than whites, they lost most battles when they clashed. Northern whites, meanwhile, began to lose interest in controlling the South by means of the army. They became satisfied that southern whites did not actually intend to reenslave blacks. They began to put the South's problems out of their minds. Gradually the number of troops stationed in the southern states was reduced. Many blacks then chose not to risk voting and exercising their other rights.

In state after state during the 1870s Conservative parties, made up entirely of whites, took over the government from the Republicans. These parties resisted the changes proposed for the South. Many of the members of the parties were former Confederate officials and soldiers. They had been barred from holding office by Section 3 of the Fourteenth Amendment, but the **Amnesty Act of 1872** ended the disability for all but the highest Confederate officials. Former Confederates flocked to the Conservative parties and ran in almost every southern election.

The Republican party was further hurt by the failure of President Grant to live up to expectations as president. The military hero was honest and a true democrat, but he was a poor chief executive. He became the innocent victim of scandals and corruption in his administration. Although he was reelected in 1872 by 800,000 votes more than the Democratic party nominee, Horace Greeley, his party grew weaker. By 1876 the Republicans controlled only three southern states—Louisiana, Florida, and South Carolina. They rejoined their former Confederate partners after the election of 1876. In South Carolina, the last state to be reclaimed politically, the Red Shirts, a band patterned after similar groups in Mississippi, secured the election of a former planter and Confederate general, Wade Hampton.

The presidential election of 1876 pitted Governor Samuel J. Tilden of New York, the Democrat, against Governor Rutherford B. Hayes of Ohio, the Republican. Tilden won in his home state, New York, in neighboring New Jersey and Connecticut, in Indiana, and in all the southern states. This gave him a substantial majority of the electoral vote, 203 to 165. In the popular vote he won by 250,000 votes—4.28 million to 4.03 million.

National Portrait Gallery

Switched votes by three southern states kept the story of America from telling of the presidency of Samuel J. Tilden. Tilden won the election but it was Rutherford B. Hayes who became president in 1877. Tilden is above, Hayes below.

Copyright by the White House Historical Association; photographed by the National Geographic Society

Republican leaders saw that by switching the electoral votes of the three southern states they still controlled, plus the disputed vote from Oregon, Hayes would win 185 to 184! Republican officials threw out enough Democratic ballots in the southern states to change the result, and had the decision overturned in Oregon. They forwarded new results to Washington showing Hayes the winner.

Of course the Democrats protested loudly. They filed another set of "official" results that showed Tilden the winner in the three disputed states.

For weeks no one knew who the next president would be. The Constitution did not provide a clear method for solving the problem. According to the Constitution the votes had to be counted. But by whom? Certainly not the Republican-controlled Senate or the Democratic-controlled House of Representatives. Instead, Congress appointed a special commission to settle the issue. It was made up of ten members of Congress—five Democrats and five Republicans, and five members of the Supreme Court. The Supreme Court justices were supposed to be nonpolitical, but three were Republicans, the other two Democrats.

The commission held an investigation and heard evidence from both sides. It soon became clear that both parties had behaved in a completely corrupt manner in the states in dispute. In the South, more Democrats had almost certainly voted than Republicans. But large numbers of blacks who would surely have voted Republican had been kept away from the polls by force and threats.

The Compromise of 1877

When the commissioners finally voted, they split 8 to 7 on each of the disputed states. Every Republican voted for Hayes, every Democrat for Tilden. Obviously they had not paid much attention to the evidence. The Democrats felt cheated. Many were ready to fight to make Tilden president. For a time another Civil War seemed about to break out.

In this crisis the leaders of the two parties worked out what is known as the **Compromise of 1877.** Hayes agreed to recall all the remaining federal troops stationed in the South. He promised to appoint a conservative southerner to his Cabinet. He said also that he supported a proposal sponsored by southerners to build a railroad from Texas to southern California.

In exchange the Democrats promised to guarantee blacks their own rights and not to use their power in the southern states to prevent blacks from voting. After all these details had been settled in a series of informal, behind-the-scenes discussions, the Democrats agreed to go along with the electoral commission's decision. On March 4, 1877, Hayes was inaugurated as president in an orderly, entirely peaceful ceremony.

Return to the Preview & Review on page 610.

5. THE LONG NIGHT BEGINS

Second-Class Citizens

After the Compromise of 1877 the white citizens of the North turned their backs on the black citizens of the South. Gradually the southern states broke their promise to treat blacks fairly. Step by step they deprived them of the right to vote and reduced them to second-class citizens. Thus began the **Long Night** of racial segregation.

The first step was to pass **poll tax** laws. A poll tax is a charge made for voting. It can be avoided simply by not going to the polls. For poor people, paying a poll tax was a great sacrifice. Many preferred to spend what little money they had in other ways. In most southern states the tax *accumulated* when not paid. That is, a person who skipped one election would have to pay double if he wished to vote at the next year's local election. A person who voted only in presidential elections would pay four times the regular tax.

Another technique for keeping blacks from the polls was to require a **literacy test** for voting. People who could not read could not vote. And those blacks who could read were usually asked to read a difficult, technical legal passage of some kind. Poll taxes and literacy tests did not violate the Fifteenth Amendment because they were not directly based on ''race, color, or previous condition of servitude.''

These measures prevented many poor white people from voting too. But when they wanted to, the authorities could find ways of allowing whites to vote anyway. One method was to permit people who could not read to vote if they could ''understand'' and explain a passage that an election official read to them. A white person might be asked to explain a clause in the state constitution that said: ''The term of the governor shall be four years.'' A black person who sought to qualify would then be asked to explain a more complicated passage. And whatever the black said, he would be told his explanation was incorrect and that he had not ''understood.''

Another technique was the so-called **grandfather clause.** Grandfather clauses provided that literacy tests and poll taxes did not apply to persons who had been able to vote before 1867, or to their children and later descendants. Of course most whites came under this heading, but no blacks did at all. By about 1900 only a handful of black citizens were voting in the southern states. Not until 1915, in *Guinn v. U.S.*, did the Supreme Court rule that grandfather clauses were unconstitutional.

The Court and Segregation

When blacks ceased to have an influence on elections, elected officials stopped paying much attention to their needs and desires. The segregation of blacks and whites in public places became widespread.

Preview & Review

Use these questions to guide your reading. Answer the questions after completing Section 5.
Understanding Issues, Events, & Ideas. Using the following words, discuss the segregation of black Americans: Long Night, poll tax, literacy test, grandfather clause, Civil Rights Act of 1875, Jim Crow law, Civil Rights Cases, *Plessy v. Ferguson,* separate but equal, Tuskegee Institute, Atlanta Compromise, accommodation.
1. Why did southern whites want to keep blacks from voting?
2. What was the result of the Civil Rights Cases decided by the Supreme Court in 1883?
3. What was the importance of the decision in *Plessy v. Ferguson?*
4. What happened to blacks in the 1890s who protested against injustice?
Thinking Critically. 1. You have just read of the Court's ruling on *Plessy v. Ferguson.* Write a letter to your state representative, protesting the ruling. 2. Imagine that you are a black person in the South in 1895. Do you agree or disagree with Booker T. Washington's Atlanta Compromise? Why or why not?

Frederick Douglass had this to say about the plight of blacks in the South after the Civil War.

66 No man can be truly free whose liberty is dependent upon the thought, feeling, and actions of others, and who has himself no means in his hands for guarding, protecting, defending, and maintaining that liberty. 99
Frederick Douglass, 1882

There had always been a good deal of segregation in the North and South alike. In part it had been based on economics. Poor people could not afford to eat in the same restaurants as rich people, for example, and most blacks were poor. On the other hand, in the decades before the Civil War blacks and whites had often met together informally. This happened perhaps even more in the South than in the North.

After the destruction of the Confederacy, Congress had ruled out segregation in the South. The **Civil Rights Act of 1875** provided specifically that "citizens of every race and color" were entitled to "the full and equal enjoyment" of restaurants, hotels, trains, and all "places of public amusement."

But after 1877 whites began to ignore this law. In part they were more eager now for segregation because blacks were now unquestionably free. Separation had seemed less important to whites when blacks were clearly in lowly positions and under white "command." The typical southern white did not object to sitting next to a black on a streetcar if the black was a nursemaid caring for a white child. The same woman entering the car alone would cause the white to bristle if she tried to occupy the next seat. It became the common practice throughout the South to separate the races in schools, hospitals, orphanages, and other public and private institutions. But this practice was not the law.

That began to change in 1881, when Tennessee passed the first **Jim Crow law.** This law required blacks to ride in separate railroad cars. Florida in 1887 and Texas in 1889 passed similar laws. The laws were named after the black-faced characters in 19th-century song and dance acts. In time Jim Crow laws extended separation of the races to all places where it had become practice—and beyond.

When blacks began to be turned away from public places like theaters in cities all over the country, some went to court to seek their constitutional rights. In one case, W. H. R. Agee protested against being denied a room in a hotel in Jefferson City, Missouri. In another, Sallie J. Robinson sued because she was forced to ride in a second-class railroad car while traveling from Tennessee to Virginia, even though she had a first-class ticket.

These and other suits, known as the **Civil Rights Cases,** were decided by the Supreme Court in 1883. The majority of the justices ruled that the Civil Rights Act was unconstitutional. It was therefore not illegal for private businesses to practice racial segregation. The guarantees of the Fourteenth Amendment were protections against actions by state governments, not by private persons.

After this, segregation became more and more the rule, especially in the South. Then, in 1896, the Supreme Court heard the case of *Plessy v. Ferguson.* Homer Adolf Plessy, a light-skinned Louisiana black man, was arrested for sitting in a railroad car reserved by Louisiana law for whites. His attorneys argued that the law under

New York State Historical Association, Cooperstown

which he was arrested was unconstitutional. Judge John H. Ferguson ruled against Plessy on the grounds that the railroad provided separate but equally good cars for blacks, as required by law. The Supreme Court upheld this reasoning.

  🖌 The Court's decision permitted other "separate but equal" facilities. Thus segregation was legal, even in public schools, provided the schools for black children were equal to those for whites. The majority ruling stated in part:

> 66 We consider the underlying fallacy [faulty reasoning] of the plaintiff's argument to consist in the assumption that the enforced separation of the two races stamps the colored race with a badge of inferiority. If this be so, it is not by reason of anything found in the act, but solely because the colored race chooses to put that construction upon it. . . . The argument also assumes that social prejudices may be overcome by legislation, and that equal rights cannot be secured to the negro except by an enforced commingling [mixing] of the two races. We cannot accept this proposition. . . . If the civil and political rights of both races be equal one cannot be inferior to the other civilly or politically. If one race is inferior to the other socially, the Constitution of the United States cannot put them upon the same plane.[1] 99

[1]From *Plessy v. Ferguson,* 163 U.S. 537, 1896.

"Kept In" is the title of this painting. One sorrowful little girl remains after school, perhaps until she finishes her lessons. Her loneliness is a reminder of the physical barriers of segregation. Where else besides schools was segregation practiced?

The Long Night Begins   615

Brown Brothers

Justice John Marshall Harlan came from a family that once kept slaves in Kentucky. But he believed that segregation was in violation of the Constitution. What did he mean by "Our Constitution is color-blind"?

One justice, John Marshall Harlan, born in Kentucky, a slave state, objected to this **separate-but-equal** argument. Harlan's family had owned slaves. But the experiences of Reconstruction had caused him to change his mind about race questions. In his dissent he said:

66 The white race deems itself to be the dominant race in this country. And so it is, in prestige, in achievements, in education, in wealth and power. . . . But in view of the Constitution in the eye of the law, there is in this country no superior, dominant, ruling class of citizens. There is no caste here. Our Constitution is color-blind, and neither knows nor tolerates classes among citizens. In respect of civil rights, all citizens are equal before the law. The humblest is the peer of the most powerful. The law regards man as man, and takes no account of his surroundings or of his color when his civil rights as guaranteed by the supreme law of the land are involved.[1] 99

But in 1896 Harlan's was the minority view both of the Court and among white citizens in all parts of the country.

Efforts to prevent segregation practically ended as a result of these court decisions. Blacks could not stay at hotels used by white travelers. Theaters herded them into separate sections, usually high in the balcony. Blacks had to ride in the rear sections of streetcars. They could not enter "white" parks or swim at "white" public beaches. Even cemeteries were segregated.

The schools, parks, and other facilities open to blacks were almost never as good as those open to whites. The separate-but-equal rule was ignored everywhere. In 1876 South Carolina spent the same amount on the education of each child, black or white. By 1895, when school segregation was complete in South Carolina, the state was spending three times more on each white child.

The Atlanta Compromise

It is easy to imagine how depressed and angry American blacks must have been in the 1890s. Segregation was only the visible surface of the way they were mistreated. In almost any conflict between a black person and a white, the white had every advantage. Blacks were punished more severely when they were convicted of crimes. Many kinds of jobs were entirely closed to blacks. When they did the same work as whites, they received lower pay. If they refused to act humbly and politely to whites, they were insulted or even beaten. If they wanted to adjust to white ideas of how they ought to act, they had to behave like children or clowns.

ᴕ Some blacks protested violently against all this injustice. Those

[1] From the Dissent of Mr. Justice John Marshall Harlan, *Plessy v. Ferguson*, 163 U.S. 537, 1896.

who did were dealt with still more violently by the white majority. Lynchings, the killing without trial of supposed criminals by mobs, became ever more frequent, especially in the southern states.

Faced with these handicaps, many black Americans adopted the strategy proposed by Booker T. Washington, the founder of a trade school for blacks in Alabama, **Tuskegee Institute.** Washington had been born a slave. He obtained an education by working as a janitor at the school he attended. His experiences convinced him that a person of lowly origins could rise in the world by a combination of hard work and a willingness to go along with the wishes and prejudices of powerful people. He had seen firsthand what happened to black people, especially in the South, who openly fought the prejudices of whites.

Culver Pictures

Booker T. Washington founded Tuskegee Institute. What reason did he give for starting his famous school?

This classroom scene at Tuskegee Institute was photographed in about 1900. What form of segregation does this classroom reveal?

Washington was expert at obtaining the support of well-to-do whites who wanted to help blacks without actually treating them as equals. His school prospered. He was already well known when, in a speech at Atlanta, Georgia, in 1895, he proposed what became known as the **Atlanta Compromise.**

Blacks should accept the separate-but-equal principle, Washington said. They should learn skilled trades so that they could earn more money and thus improve their lives. And there was nothing shameful about working with one's hands. "There is as much dignity in tilling a field," he said, "as in writing a poem." Furthermore, it would be "the extremest folly" for blacks to demand truly equal treatment from whites. The way to rise in the world was to accept the system and try to get ahead with it.

Washington asked whites only to be fair. Help blacks who went along with segregation, he argued, by making sure that what was separate was really equal.

Most important white southern leaders claimed to be delighted with the Atlanta Compromise. In fact they made very little effort to change the attitude and behavior of average white citizens.

Today Washington seems to have buckled under with the Atlanta Compromise. Yet the failure of Reconstruction had awakened old fears and suspicions about blacks. Once again blacks had to move with caution. Historical imagination helps us see the Atlanta Compromise as a desperate effort to hold on to a few gains. For black people who had to live through those postwar years, going along, **accommodation,** was not cowardice but survival.

Brown Brothers

Return to the Preview & Review on page 613.

The Long Night Begins 617

CHAPTER 17 REVIEW

1865	THE AFTERMATH OF WAR	1875	

1865
Lee surrenders to Grant
★
Lincoln assassinated
★
Reconstruction begins
★
Thirteenth Amendment
1866
Civil Rights Act

1867
Reconstruction Act passed
1868
Johnson impeached and acquitted
★
Fourteenth Amendment
★
Grant elected president

1870
Fifteenth Amendment ratified

1875
Civil Rights Act of 1875
1876
Presidential election disputed

1877
House elects Hayes
★
Compromise of 1877 ends Reconstruction
★
Long Night begins

Chapter Summary

Read the statements below. Choose one, and write a paragraph explaining its importance.

1. Andrew Johnson succeeded to office after the assassination of Lincoln but had trouble working with Congress, which impeached him.
2. Moderate congressmen wanted quick Reconstruction, while Radicals were less forgiving.
3. The Thirteenth Amendment abolished slavery.
4. Congress established the Freedman's Bureau to help newly freed slaves with schools, food, and medical needs.
5. The Fourteenth Amendment guaranteed equal protection of the laws to all Americans. The Fifteenth Amendment made it illegal to deny the right to vote based on race, color, or previous condition of servitude.
6. Organizations such as the Ku Klux Klan were formed to keep blacks in check.
7. The last federal troops were removed from the South under the Compromise of 1877, which made Hayes president.
8. White southerners used many methods to keep blacks as second-class citizens.

Reviewing Chronological Order

Number your paper 1-5. Then study the time line above and place the following events in the order in which they happened by writing the first next to 1, the second next to 2, and so on.

1. Reconstruction Act passed
2. *Plessy v. Ferguson*
3. Grant elected president
4. Atlanta Compromise proposed
5. Lincoln assassinated

Understanding Main Ideas

1. How did the three Civil War Amendments attack the Black Codes?
2. What were the provisions of the Reconstruction Act of 1867? Why did President Johnson veto it? How did Congress react to his veto?
3. How did the election of 1868 show Republicans the importance of the black vote?
4. What were the motives of some Carpetbaggers and Scalawags in the "Black Republican" governments of the South?
5. What situation was resolved by the Compromise of 1877? What were the terms of this agreement?

Thinking Critically

1. **Analyzing.** You are the one senator whose vote is needed to obtain the conviction of President Andrew Johnson on impeachment charges. Why would you vote against removing him from office?
2. **Synthesizing.** If you were a former slave living in the South in 1870, how would your life change if you were a 58-year-old man? A 22-year-old woman? A 6-year-old boy?
3. **Hypothesizing.** Compose a brief dialogue between a southern banker and a landowner with sharecroppers, discussing which crops the landowner should order grown this year.

Writing About History

You are a newspaper reporter in Washington, D.C. Write a news report on either the assassination of Lincoln or the impeachment trial of Johnson. Your report should include both a description of the events and the reactions of participants and observers. Use the information in Chapter 17 and in reference books to prepare your report.

The Long Night

1885	1895

1883
Civil Rights Cases decided

1895
Atlanta Compromise proposed

1896
Plessy v. Ferguson

Practicing the Strategy

Review the strategy on page 605.

Interpreting a Graph of Business Cycles. Study the two charts on page 608, then answer the following questions.

1. What kinds of agriculture are represented in the top chart?
2. What event occurred between 1860 and 1870 that badly damaged the South's agricultural production?
3. How many years passed before southern agricultural production recovered and surpassed the pre-war levels?
4. In the bottom chart there is a sudden jump in the percent of southern workers in manufacturing between 1880 and 1890. What does this suggest about the nature of manufacturing in the South during that time?

Using Primary Sources

For many years after the Civil War Frederick Douglass remained a leading African American spokesman. He continued to encourage blacks to struggle, now against the effects of Reconstruction and the Long Night. In this excerpt from John W. Blasingame's *Frederick Douglass: The Clarion Voice*, Douglass explained why active struggle was necessary. As you read the excerpt, imagine the conditions blacks were struggling against. Then answer the questions that follow it.

> *The whole history of the progress of human liberty shows that all concessions yet made to her august [mighty] claims have been born of earnest struggle.... If there is no struggle, there is no progress. Those who profess to favor freedom, and yet deprecate [say bad things about] agitation, are men who want crops without plowing up the ground, they want rain without thunder and lightning. They want the ocean without the awful roar of its many waters.*

1. According to the excerpt, what had caused all progress in human liberty?

2. Do you agree that "If there is no struggle, there is no progress"? Use examples to support your point of view.
3. If you were a government leader during Reconstruction, what plan might you have suggested to help freed slaves begin a new life? Would your plan have been difficult to establish? Why or why not?

Linking History & Geography

Reconstruction meant more than just rebuilding southern governments. It also meant reconstructing land devastated by four years of war. To understand why this aspect of Reconstruction was so important to the South's recovery, answer the following questions.

1. A Virginia farmer in the Shenandoah Valley said soon after the war: "We had no cattle, hogs, sheep, or horses or anything else. The fences were all gone.... The barns were all burned; chimneys standing without houses; and houses standing without roofs or doors or windows." What are three things this farmer will have to do to make the farm productive again?
2. Destruction of southern railroads had been a prime Union military objective during the war. How had this isolated the South? What problems would such isolation cause?

Enriching the Study of History

1. **Individual Project**. Imagine you are traveling through the South in 1867. Use your historical imagination to write five diary entries describing Reconstruction.
2. **Cooperative Project**. Members of your group will present a debate of the Atlanta Compromise. Half the group will argue for following Washington's suggestions. The other half will argue against the compromise. After you present your debate, the class will act as a convention and vote on the issue.

Chapter 17 Review   619

UNIT FIVE REVIEW

Summing Up and Predicting
Read the summary of the main ideas in Unit Five below. Choose one statement, then write a paragraph predicting its outcome or future consequence.
1. The failure of the Missouri Compromise and the passage of the Kansas-Nebraska Bill caused even more sectional conflicts over slavery.
2. The election of Abraham Lincoln in 1860 led several southern states to secede. These states formed the Confederate States of America.
3. The firing on Fort Sumter started the Civil War.
4. The Confederacy won most of the early battles, but the Union advantage of sheer numbers and a successful strategy eventually led to victory.
5. Lincoln's plans for a moderate Reconstruction were ended by assassination and Johnson's difficulties with Congress.
6. Although the Civil War Amendments—the Thirteenth, Fourteenth, and Fifteenth—guaranteed civil rights to blacks, white southerners found ways to continue to deny those rights.
7. The Compromise of 1877 ended Reconstruction and several key court decisions led to the start of the Long Night of racial segregation.

Connecting Ideas
1. *Uncle Tom's Cabin* had a strong impact on American attitudes toward slavery and led, in part, to the Civil War. What other book, film, or television program has affected your attitude toward war? How has it affected you?
2. The author says, "When the Civil War was ended and the slaves were set free, the problem of racial prejudice in the United States was not solved." Do you think racial discrimination is still a problem in America? Explain.
3. In 1867 Congress ordered a military occupation of the south. Almost 100 years later, President Eisenhower ordered federal troops to Little Rock, Arkansas, to enforce a Supreme Court ruling on integration. Cite the articles, sections, and paragraphs of the Constitution that give Congress and the president this power.

Practicing Critical Thinking
1. **Evaluating.** Shortly after the news of Lincoln's election, southern states began seceding. If you had been a southerner at that time, would you have been for or against secession? Why?
2. **Synthesizing.** You are Robert E. Lee on April 8, 1865. Your last hope of victory has been dashed. Compose a letter to Jefferson Davis, explaining your decision to surrender.
3. **Analyzing.** In Lincoln's second inaugural address, he called for Americans to act "with malice toward none, with charity for all." How do you think the Reconstruction period would have been different if Lincoln had not been assassinated? Explain.

Cooperative Learning
1. Your group will make a diorama or model of a Civil War battlefield. Consult reference books to be sure that your details are accurate. Describe the battle in class, using chess pieces or toy soldiers to show troop movements.
2. Your group will prepare an illustrated chart to show the seesaw struggle for guaranteed rights for blacks during and just after Reconstruction. Include the Black Codes, the Civil Rights Act, the Civil War Amendments, the Long Night, the Civil Rights Act of 1875, the Supreme Court rulings on the Civil Rights Cases and *Plessy v. Ferguson,* and the Atlanta Compromise.
3. Working in groups, your class will research the impeachment trial of Andrew Johnson and act out scenes for and against the president. As Johnson did not appear at his trial, you may wish to set some scenes in the White House. Members of the class acting as the Senate should then decide the case.

Reading in Depth
Beatty, Patricia. *Turn Homeward, Hannalee.* New York: Morrow. Tells the fictional story of a poor southern family during the Civil War, as seen by the sensitive and brave 14-year-old heroine.

Hamilton, Virginia. *Anthony Burns: The Defeat and Triumph of a Fugitive Slave.* New York: Knopf. Tells the story of a runaway slave.

Hansen, Joyce. *Out of This Place.* Houston: Walker. Describes the challenges faced by ex-slaves during the Civil War and Reconstruction.

Kantor, MacKinlay. *Lee and Grant at Appomattox.* New York: Random House. Contains a dramatic account of the surrender.

Miers, Earl and Paul M. Angle. *Abraham Lincoln in Peace and War.* New York: American Heritage. Provides a brief glimpse of Lincoln's life.

Sandburg, Carl. *Abraham Lincoln: The Prairie Years and the War Years.* San Diego: Harcourt Brace Jovanovich. Contains the classic work on the political life of Lincoln (one of six volumes).

The Fine Arts Museum of San Francisco

The arrival of the daily train to Sacramento, California, is the subject of "Sacramento Railway Station."

A CHANGING AMERICA

UNIT 6

I n Unit 6 you will learn why Native Americans of the Plains lost their lands to white settlers and how the United States became one of the world's great industrial nations. Here are some main points to keep in mind as you read the unit.

- After the Civil War, thousands of Americans from the East moved westward to the Great Plains and other regions of the West.
- Andrew Carnegie, John D. Rockefeller, and others built huge industrial empires.
- Immigrants from Northwestern European lands such as Germany and Scandinavia poured into the United States.
- Mark Twain wrote *Tom Sawyer*, and James McNeill Whistler painted *Mrs. George Washington Whistler*, now known as "Whistler's Mother."
- The populist movement championed the interest of farmers and labor.

The Last Frontier

The Great Plains is strewn with skulls in Albert Bierstadt's 1889 oil painting, "The Last of the Buffalo." But would Plains Indians have been such wasteful killers?

The history of the Plains Indians shows that truth is often stranger and more interesting than fiction. A favorite subject of American books and movies is the "Winning of the West," or the plunder of the prairie and the end of the American Indian way of life, depending on your point of view. For about a hundred years, from around 1780 to 1880, the Plains Indians lived in the midst of an immense grassland, feeding upon the numberless buffalo and moving freely on their fleet ponies. Yet much of their culture was a direct result of the Indians' adopting such elements of European civilization as horses, guns, and metal tools. And in the end the European lust for land, the diseases spread by the conquerors and settlers, and the deadly efficiency of America's mechanical genius ended the Plains civilization. With the discovery of vast gold, silver, and copper deposits on the Indian lands—and the buffalo's grazing lands taken by the ranchers of the cattle kingdom—could there be much hope for the first Americans and their independent way of life?

In the collection of The Corcoran Gallery of Art, Gift of Mrs. Albert Bierstadt, 1909

1. THE BATTLE FOR THE PLAINS

Preview & Review

Use these questions to guide your reading. Answer the questions after completing Section 1. **Understanding Issues, Events, & Ideas.** Using the following words, trace the history of the Plains Indians: Great Plains; "Great American Desert"; Apache; Comanche; Pawnee; Sioux; Cheyenne; Arapaho; concentration; divide and conquer; Pacific Railway Act; right of way; Promontory, Utah; transcontinental railroad; Mexican American.
1. Why did farming on the Great Plains seem impossible?
2. What was the purpose of the system of concentration?
3. How did Congress encourage the building of a transcontinental railroad?
4. Why were settlers in the Southwest able to gain much of the land held for many years by Mexican Americans?

Thinking Critically. **1.** Imagine that you are a member of the Dogmen Band. Describe a typical day in your life. **2.** It is 1865. You are a Chinese worker on the Central Pacific railroad line. Write a letter to your family in China, describing your job.

The Great Plains

The vast region we call the **Great Plains** extends from western Texas north to the Dakotas and on into Canada. Endless acres of grassland roll westward from the Mississippi, gradually rising until they reach the towering ranges of the Rocky Mountains. Explorers and hunters once described this region and the mountains beyond as the **"Great American Desert,"** although it was *no* desert. Before the 1850s the Spanish Americans in the Southwest and the Mormons in Utah had made the only permanent settlements in this huge area with its few lonely travelers.

The land of the Great Plains is mostly level. There are few trees. Winter blizzards roar unchecked out of the Arctic. Temperatures fall far below freezing. In summer the thermometer can soar halfway to the boiling point when hot winds sweep north from Mexico.

Until well after the Civil War, farming on the plains seemed impossible. There was too little rain to raise crops and no wood to build houses or fences. Most people thought the desert was home only for the donkey-eared jackrabbit, the prairie dog, the antelope, the wolflike coyote, and the great, shaggy buffalo. The buffalo in particular seemed the lords of the Great Plains, by their numbers alone. About 12 million of them grazed on the seemingly arid prairie there at the time the Civil War ended.

The Plains Indians

Long before the European settlement of America, many people lived on the Great Plains. They knew it was not really a desert. These were the Plains Indians. They had survived and prospered there for thousands of years.

There were 31 Plains tribes. The **Apache** and **Comanche** lived in Texas and eastern New Mexico. The **Pawnee** occupied western Nebraska, the **Sioux** the Dakotas. The **Cheyenne** and **Arapaho** were the principal tribes of the central plains. In 1850 these tribes contained about 175,000 people. Although they spoke many different languages, all could communicate with one another. They had developed a complex and efficient sign language.

The Plains Indians differed from tribe to tribe. Some were divided into several groups, or bands, of about 500 people each. The Cheyenne, for example, consisted of ten bands with names like the Aorta Band, the Hairy Band, the Scabby Band, and the Dogmen Band. Although each band was a separate community, bands joined together for religious ceremonies and to fight other tribes or the European invaders. Their chiefs and councils of elders acted mostly as judges. Their decisions were enforced by small groups of warriors called soldier bands. The soldier bands settled disputes between band members, punished those who broke tribal laws, and protected the group against surprise attacks.

Within the circle of their band, warriors tried to prove their courage and daring on the battlefield. To touch an enemy or capture his weapon was proof of highest bravery, called counting coup.

The Plains Indians, as we have seen, had always depended heavily on the buffalo. After the European invasion of America they also captured and tamed wild horses. Spanish explorers had brought the first horses with them to America. Some of these animals escaped and ran wild. Eventually, large herds roamed the West.

The Indians quickly became expert riders. On horseback they were better hunters and fighters. They could cover large distances swiftly and run down buffalo and other game. Horses became so

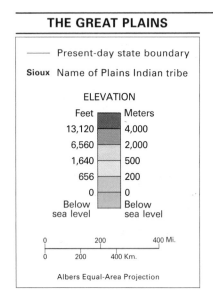

THE GREAT PLAINS

— Present-day state boundary

Sioux Name of Plains Indian tribe

ELEVATION

Feet		Meters
13,120		4,000
6,560		2,000
1,640		500
656		200
0		0
Below sea level		Below sea level

0 — 200 — 400 Mi.
0 — 200 — 400 Km.

Albers Equal-Area Projection

LEARNING FROM MAPS. *Many of the first European explorers of the Great Plains considered it a desert. Today, however, it is a region of rich agricultural production. Why did some of the first explorers consider it a desert? What has made it productive today?*

Courtesy Colorado Historical Society

important to the Plains Indians that many tribes went to war against their neighbors for them. Many counted their wealth in horses. Some paid their debts with horses. Some men swapped horses for wives.

Indians wore many kinds of clothing. In some tribes the men wore breechcloths and long leggings which went from hip to ankle. During the winter they wore buffalo robes. Women might wear sleeveless dresses made of deerskin. In desert regions Indians wore moccasins with double leather soles for protection against the heat or the hard ground.

The typical Plains warrior carried a bow about three feet long (nearly one meter). It was usually made of bone or ash wood. His arrows had points made of bone, flint, or metal. Some warriors were armed with long, stone-tipped lances and carried round shields made of buffalo hide. These buffalo-hide shields were smoked and hardened with glue made from buffalo hooves. They were so tough that bullets striking them at an angle would not go through.

In battle an Indian warrior could fire off half a dozen arrows from his stubby, powerful bow while an enemy was cramming a single bullet into his muzzle-loading rifle. Galloping on horseback at full speed, a warrior could shoot arrows so fast that the next would be in the air before the first found its target. These arrows struck with great force. At short range an Indian could sink the entire shaft of an arrow into the body of a buffalo.

The simplicity of the lives of Plains Indians is depicted in S.C. Stobie's "Indian Camp." From your other reading and observations, how much can you find in this camp that is already familiar to you—in lodging, family roles, child care, food preparation, and so on?

The Battle for the Plains 625

Mabel Brady Garvan Collection, Yale University Art Gallery

*Fort Laramie, shown in this water-
color sketch by Alfred Jacob Miller,
was a fur-trading post built in 1834.
The army bought it in 1849 to protect
travelers on the Oregon Trail. How
does this picture add to the description
of Indian life begun on page 623?*

Removing the Plains Indians

The Plains Indians rarely came into conflict with settlers before the
1850s. They usually traded in peace with hunters. The pioneers who
crossed the plains on their way to Oregon avoided the Indians.

In the early 1850s settlers began moving into Kansas and Nebraska. After the Mexican War, promoters planned to build railroads
to the Pacific through the newly won territory. They demanded that
the government remove the Plains Indians from this territory.

In 1851 agents of the United States called a meeting of the
principal Plains tribes at Fort Laramie, in what is now Wyoming.
The agents persuaded the Indians to sign the Fort Laramie Treaty.
The Indians agreed to stay within limited areas. In exchange the
government would give them food, money, and presents.

This new system was called **concentration.** It was a way of
dividing the Indians so that they could be conquered separately.
Divide and conquer is a very old military strategy. Once a tribe had
agreed to live in a particular region, it could be forced to give up its
holdings without arousing the others. Neither side fully realized that
this would mean the end of the Plains culture.

As soon as Senator Stephen A. Douglas pushed the Kansas-
Nebraska Act through Congress, settlers and storekeepers came
pouring into lands that had been reserved for the Indians. The Indians
were pushed into even smaller areas. By 1860 there were very few
native Americans left in Kansas and Nebraska.

Railroads in the West

In 1862 Congress passed the **Pacific Railway Act.** This law granted a charter to the Union Pacific Railroad Company to build a line westward from Nebraska. Another company, the Central Pacific Railway of California, was authorized to build a connecting line eastward from the Pacific.

The government granted each company the **right of way**—the thin strip of land on which the tracks were actually laid. In addition it gave them large amounts of land for every mile of track built. This land could be sold and the money used for construction. Or it could be held in reserve and sold later when the land became more valuable. The government also lent the companies large amounts of money at low interest. Private fortunes were to be had here.

The Central Pacific employed thousands of Chinese immigrants to lay its tracks. Most of the Union Pacific workers came from Ireland. All were underpaid. Construction got under way in 1865.

Building the railroad was tremendously difficult. The Central Pacific had to cross the snow-capped Sierra Nevada range. Omaha, Nebraska, where the Union Pacific began, had not yet been connected to eastern railroads. Thousands of tons of rails, crossties, and

While Chinese railroad workers watch, the Central Pacific train enters a snow shed in the Sierra Nevada. Snow sheds kept tracks clear and gave some protection to the wooden cars in the event of an avalanche. Why is it so appropriate that the workers pictured are Chinese Americans?

Thomas Gilcrease Institute

other supplies had to be shipped up the Missouri River by boat or hauled across Iowa by wagon.

The two companies competed with each other in order to get the lion's share of the land and money authorized by the Pacific Railway Act. Charles Crocker, manager of the Central Pacific's construction crews, drove his men mercilessly. During one winter they dug tunnels through 40-foot (12-meter) snowdrifts high in the Sierras in order to lay tracks on the frozen ground.

The two lines met on May 10, 1869, at **Promontory,** Utah. The Union Pacific had built 1,086 miles of track (1,738 kilometers), the Central Pacific 689 miles (1,102 kilometers). There was a great celebration. Leland Stanford of the Central Pacific was given the honor of hammering home the last spike connecting the two rails. The spike was of gold, the hammer of silver.

Soon other **transcontinental railroads** were built. These included the Atchison, Topeka & Santa Fe and the Southern Pacific in the Southwest and the Northern Pacific, which ran south of the Canadian border. The transcontinentals connected with the eastern railroads at Chicago, St. Louis, and New Orleans. Once they were completed, a traveler could go from the Atlantic Coast to San Francisco and other Pacific Coast cities in a week's time. The swiftest clipper ship had taken three months to make the journey from New York to San Francisco.

This painting shows "East and West Shaking Hands" in the 1869 meeting of the Union Pacific and Central Pacific at Promontory, Utah. Why was this a day to celebrate?

Union Pacific Railroad

Larry Sheerin

Theodore Gentilz, whose paintings capture much of our Spanish heritage, called this scene "Selling of the Cardinals on the Plaza." Research the layout of a typical Spanish settlement with its plaza, church, and workshops.

Settling the Southwest

During these same years settlers poured into the Southwest—western Texas, New Mexico, Arizona, and southern California—to look for gold, raise cattle, and claim land. When they arrived, they found the land occupied by Mexican Americans. These people were the descendants of the Mexicans who found themselves in United States territory after the Treaty of Guadalupe Hidalgo. Rather than learn Spanish, most settlers looked down on the Mexican Americans. The newcomers treated the old settlers like foreigners.

This was unjust. Many Mexican Americans had lived on their land long before it became United States territory. The land-hungry settlers discovered that most of the land was not registered. Often they simply claimed the already occupied land or bought it from the territorial government. By the 1880s Mexican Americans owned but one fourth of the land they had owned in 1848.

Return to the Preview & Review on page 623.

Preview & Review

Use these questions to guide your reading. Answer the questions after you complete Section 2.
Understanding Issues, Events, & Ideas. Use the following words to explain the tragedies of the Indian Wars: Fifty-Niners, Chivington Massacre, Washita, Bozeman Trail, ambush, Battle of the Little Bighorn, Nez Perce, Wounded Knee, Dawes Severalty Act.
1. Why did the Sioux try to stop prospectors from using the Bozeman Trail?
2. What finally forced the Sioux to surrender?
3. How did Helen Hunt Jackson and Sarah Winnemucca help Indians?
4. How did the Dawes Act show lack of understanding of Indian ways of life?
Thinking Critically. 1. Write a newspaper obituary for Chief Joseph. 2. Write a diary entry about Wounded Knee from the point of view of either an Indian or a member of the 7th Cavalry.

Red Cloud, the Oglala Sioux chief, and his grandaughter Burning Heart were painted by Henry Cross. From your reading or a cooperative research project, what statements can you make to describe the family life of the Plains Indians?

The Thomas Gilcrease Institute of American History and Art, Tulsa, Oklahoma

2. INDIAN WARS

"Pikes Peak or Bust"

The transcontinental railroads brought many more settlers into the West. Wherever they went, fighting with the Indians followed. Even before the Civil War there was trouble in the Pikes Peak area of Colorado, where gold was discovered. By 1859 a seemingly endless stream of wagons was rolling across the plains. Many had the slogan "Pikes Peak or Bust!" lettered on their canvas covers. The attraction of the West remained the same: a new start for discontented Americans, mostly easterners.

About 100,000 of these **Fifty-Niners** elbowed their way onto Cheyenne and Arapaho land. The Indians fiercely resisted this invasion. Between 1861 and 1864 they rode several times into battle against army units. Then, in November 1864, Colonel John M. Chivington attacked a peaceful Cheyenne encampment at Sand Creek without warning. The Cheyenne, under Chief Black Kettle, tried to surrender by first raising an American flag and then a white flag of truce.

Chivington ignored these flags. "Kill and scalp all, big and little," he ordered. His soldiers scalped the men, ripped open the bodies of the women, and clubbed the little children to death with their gun butts.

During this **Chivington Massacre** about 450 Cheyenne were killed. The Cheyenne answered with equally bloody attacks on undefended white settlements. In 1868 the Cheyenne and Arapaho were defeated at **Washita,** in present-day Oklahoma. They were forced to settle on reservations, one in the Black Hills of Dakota, the other in Oklahoma.

Meanwhile, the Pikes Peak boom had become a bust. Little gold was found. About half the miners returned to their homes. This time the signs on their wagons read "Busted, By Gosh!"

Yet if Colorado had proved a bust, many prospectors still believed that gold could be found elsewhere. New prospectors crossed the Great Plains and spread through the mountains in the 1860s. Many followed a route pioneered by John M. Bozeman, a prospector from Georgia. This **Bozeman Trail** ran from Fort Laramie in Wyoming north to Montana. It cut through the rolling foothills of the Big Horn Mountains, the hunting grounds of the western Sioux.

The Sioux pitched their teepees beneath the sheltering mountains. There they hunted the plentiful game—deer, buffalo, elk, antelope, and bear. The Sioux chief, Red Cloud, protested strongly when prospectors and settlers began to use the new Bozeman Trail. He warned that the Sioux would fight to save their hunting grounds.

In 1865 Red Cloud's warriors made repeated attacks on white parties. The United States army responded by building forts along

Courtesy of The Library of Congress

the trail. In December 1866 an army supply caravan approaching one of the forts was attacked. When a small troop of soldiers commanded by Captain W. J. Fetterman appeared, Red Cloud's warriors quickly dashed off into the wilderness. Captain Fetterman foolishly followed them. He blundered into a trap, or **ambush.** Fetterman and all 82 of his soldiers were killed. A few months later John Bozeman himself was killed crossing the Yellowstone River on the very trail he had marked.

At this point prospectors stopped crossing the Sioux country. A new treaty was signed in 1868. The Sioux agreed to live on a reservation in the Dakota Territory west of the Missouri River.

Custer's Last Stand

Still the fighting went on. Between 1869 and 1875 over 200 clashes between Indians and army units took place. In 1876 the territory of the Sioux was again invaded, this time by the construction crews of the Northern Pacific Railroad and by prospectors looking for gold in the Black Hills. War broke out.

This historic photograph of a Sioux camp was taken in 1891 near Pine Ridge, South Dakota. Make an estimate of the size of the encampment.

Courtesy of The Library of Congress

Above is "Custer's Last Stand," the situation already hopeless for his cavalry troops. How is the artist's view similar to the real battle described on these pages?

The Thomas Gilcrease Institute of American History and Art, Tulsa, Oklahoma

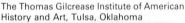

This is one of many portraits we have of George Armstrong Custer, with his flowing yellow hair and moustache. Do you agree with critics who found him a vain man searching for glory?

At this time Lieutenant Colonel George Armstrong Custer made his famous last stand in the **Battle of the Little Bighorn** in southern Montana. George Custer looked more like an actor than a soldier. He had long, flowing yellow hair. He wore buckskin trousers, red-topped boots, and a broad-brimmed hat. He was a good soldier, a graduate of the United States Military Academy at West Point. During the Civil War he fought at Bull Run and Gettysburg, and he accepted a Confederate flag of truce on the battlefield near Appomattox. But he sometimes deliberately led his men into dangerous situations in hopes of winning what he called "glory."

On June 25, 1876, Custer led a cavalry troop of 264 men toward what he believed to be a small Sioux camp. Instead, at the Little Bighorn River, his tiny force stumbled upon between 2,500 and 4,000 Sioux, commanded by chiefs Sitting Bull, Crazy Horse, and Rain-in-the-Face.

Sitting Bull helped prepare for battle. He had become chief of his band nine years earlier. He was a solid, muscular man, 42 years old in 1876. He had a slightly hooked nose and piercing black eyes. Deep lines marked his weather-beaten brow. His dark hair hung in two heavy braids in front of his shoulders.

INTERPRETING HISTORY: The American Frontier

During the late 19th century millions of Americans headed westward into vast frontier lands. As each area along the frontier became "settled," the next wave of pioneers pushed the frontier farther west. What role did the frontier play in the development of America and the American character? Was it merely a safety valve for an ever-increasing population? Or did Greeley write "Go west, young man!" because America was a land of unlimited opportunity?

Frederick Jackson Turner is the historian most closely linked to theories about the American frontier. In 1893 Turner published his theories in "The Significance of the Frontier on American History." In it he claimed that the seemingly inexhaustible frontier, more than the country's European heritage, shaped America. He wrote that frontier life spurred the development of independence and rugged individualism. He even suggested that the growth of democracy in America could be directly traced to the frontier experience. Simply put, he felt that the most important values and characteristics of the American spirit—courage, determination, democracy, independence, and others—grew out of people's trials on the frontier. Many generations of Americans experienced frontier life as they moved westward, and they drew on their experiences as they continually refined American values. This national experience officially came to an end, according to Turner, with the 1890 census. Maps in that census no longer carried a frontier line showing where population was less than two persons per square mile. "Now four centuries from the discovery of America, at the end of a hundred years of life under the Constitution, the frontier is gone, and with its going, has closed the first period of American history," wrote Turner.

Historians have since debated the validity of Turner's "frontier thesis." Professor Robert E. Riegal accused Turner of placing too much emphasis on the impact of the physical environment on the American people. He and many other historians attacked Turner's idea that the frontier was the "seedbed of democracy." He carefully traced America's democratic ideals to their roots in European life. He added, "Turner's feeling that each new frontiersman shed his old customs, started anew and became a real American appears to have been more a hope than a fact. Several historians have demonstrated very clearly the extent to which national characteristics were retained in western settlement."

The noted historian Ray Allen Billington disagreed with many of Turner's conclusions. But he agreed that the frontier indeed endowed its inhabitants with "characteristics and institutions that distinguished them from other nations." In other words, the frontier made Americans uniquely American.

Historians studying American society continue to argue to what degree the frontier shaped American life.

Sitting Bull was a fiercely proud and independent man. He resisted all efforts to get his people to give up their ancient customs. He would never sign a treaty with the whites, no matter how favorable the terms might seem. More than most Indians, he believed that no compromise with the whites was possible.

Now Sitting Bull faced Custer. Swiftly the Sioux warriors surrounded Custer's little force. Racing round and round on their ponies, they poured a deadly fire upon the troops. Desperately the soldiers dismounted and tried to use their horses as shields. Their situation was hopeless. A hail of bullets and arrows poured upon them from every direction. One bullet struck Custer in the temple, another in the chest. Within half an hour the entire company was wiped out.

This great victory at the Little Bighorn only delayed the final defeat of Sitting Bull and the rest of the Sioux. The chief held out until 1881. Then, his people near starvation, he surrendered to army units. In 1883 he was placed on the Standing Rock reservation in the Dakotas.

The Thomas Gilcrease Institute of American History and Art, Tulsa, Oklahoma

This portrait of Sitting Bull is by Henry Cross.

National Portrait Gallery, Smithsonian Institution

Chief Joseph was the subject for Cyrenius Hall in 1878, just after the chief's flight for Canada. Although there is no evidence of his pierced nose—hence the tribal name in French, Nez Perce—can you find other decorations in this portrait?

Point of View

Plains Indians were divided and conquered by disease as well as by soldiers.

"How many Indians from the Missouri tribes died of smallpox within the next few years can hardly be estimated. Possibly one hundred thousand. Some who recovered from the plague committed suicide after seeing their faces in a mirror. Vacant lodges stood on every hilltop. Starving people wandered aimlessly back and forth. 'No sound but the raven's croak or the wolf's howl breaks the solemn stillness. . . .''

From *Son of the Morning Star,*
Evan S. Connell, 1984

Chief Joseph

The search for gold also drew miners to Indian lands in the mountains of western Idaho. The whites called the Indians of this region the **Nez Perce,** or "pierced nose," because they wore nose ornaments made of shell. They were a peace-loving people. They claimed that no member of their tribe had ever killed a white. When Lewis and Clark traveled through Nez Perce lands on their expedition to the Pacific Coast, the explorers had been treated as honored guests.

The Nez Perce chief was a man the whites called Joseph. His real name was Hinmaton-Yalaktit, which means "Thunder coming out of the water and over the land." Like Tecumseh, the great Shawnee leader, Joseph believed that Indians had no right to sell the land they lived on. Joseph had promised his father that he would not surrender the lands to white settlers. It was his father's dying wish. Joseph was one of the greatest Indian spokesmen. Oratory was a fine art among the Nez Perce. Much of the power and prestige of the chiefs depended on their ability to speak. Perhaps when you read his words you can understand why he fought so hard.

" My father sent for me. I saw he was dying. I took his hand in mine. He said: 'My son, my body is returning to my mother earth, and my spirit is going very soon to see the Great Spirit Chief. When I am gone, think of your country. You are the chief of these people. They look to you to guide them. Always remember that your father never sold his country. You must stop your ears whenever you are asked to sign a treaty selling your home. A few years more, and white men will be all around you. They have eyes on this land. My son, never forget my dying words. This country holds your father's body. Never sell the bones of your father and your mother.' I pressed my father's hand and told him I would protect his grave with my life. My father smiled and passed away to the spirit-land.

I buried him in that beautiful valley of winding waters. I love that land more than all the rest of the world. A man who would not love his father's grave is worse than a wild animal.[1] **"**

Now the government insisted that Joseph make way for the whites and move his band to the Lapwai Reservation in Idaho. Joseph had only 55 men of fighting age. He decided to yield. He selected land on the reservation in May 1877. Then the government gave him only one month to move his people to the reservation.

While on the march to Idaho, a few angry Nez Perce killed some white settlers. Troops were sent to capture them. Chief Joseph and the other chiefs decided to take their people to Montana and

[1]From *Touch the Earth: A Self-Portrait of Indian Existence* by T.C. McLuhan

THE BUFFALO VANISHES

Courtesy of The Library of Congress

The Granger Collection, New York

William Cody

What finally put an end to Indian independence was the killing off of the buffalo. Thousands had been slaughtered to feed the gangs of laborers who built the western railroads. In one 18-month period the scout William Cody shot some 4,000 buffalo for the Kansas Pacific Railroad construction camps. This won him the nickname Buffalo Bill.

Once the railroads were built, shooting buffalo became a popular sport for tourists and hunters from the East. Bored rail passengers sometimes opened their windows to blast away at the grazing buffalo.

In 1871 a Pennsylvania tanner discovered that buffalo hides could be made into useful leather. Hides that were once worthless now brought $1 to $3 each. Buffalo hunting then became a profitable business. Between 1872 and 1874, 9 million buffalo were killed. By 1900 there were fewer than 50 buffalo left in the entire United States! The buffalo had been nearly sacred to many Indian tribes. It gave them food, clothing, and shelter. Without it, the Indians were powerless to resist the advance of the whites.

Wyoming and later into Canada instead of Idaho. For months the band slipped away from thousands of pursuing troops in the rugged country along the border between Oregon and Montana. In September 1877 they reached the Bear Paw Mountains, only 30 miles (48 kilometers) from Canada.

Joseph thought they were safe at last. He stopped to rest. Many of his people were starving. Children were dying. This is when army cavalry units suddenly attacked. Joseph and his warriors held out for four days. Finally they surrendered.

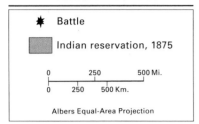

★ Battle

Indian reservation, 1875

```
0        250        500 Mi.
0    250    500 Km.
```

Albers Equal-Area Projection

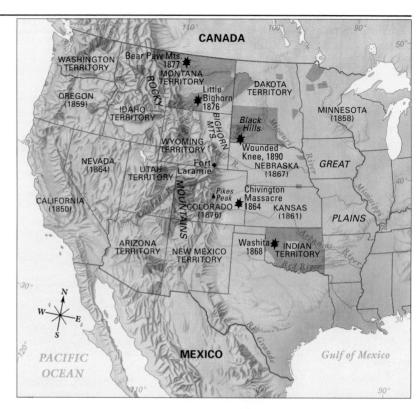

LEARNING FROM MAPS. *As settlers moved westward they pushed the Indians off much of the land they once held. In what states and territories were the largest reservations in 1875? Why do you think they were located in those places?*

Joseph's speech upon surrender is one of the most famous and admired of all such speeches. He hoped his words would carry a message to the warriors who were still fighting. He told his captors:

> ❝ I am tired of fighting. Our chiefs are killed. Looking Glass is dead. It is the young men who say yes or no. He who led the young men is dead. It is cold and we have no blankets. The little chidren are freezing to death. My people, some of them have run away to the hills and have no blankets, no food; no one knows where they are—perhaps freezing to death. I want to have time to look for my children and see how many I can find. Maybe I shall find them among the dead. Hear me my chiefs. I am tired; my heart is sick and sad. From where the sun now stands, I will fight no more forever.[1] ❞

Wetatonmi, widow of Ollokot, Joseph's brother, spoke of leaving the tribe's lands the night of Joseph's surrender. Compare her words and Joseph's to those of the Choctaw chiefs on pages 397 and 398. Imagine the sadness of being torn from your home as the Indians were. Wetatonmi said:

> ❝ It was lonesome, the leaving. Husband dead, friends buried or held prisoners. I felt that I was leaving all that I had but

[1]From *Touch the Earth: A Self-Portrait of Indian Existence* by T.C. McLuhan

did not cry. You know how you feel when you lose kindred [family] and friends through sickness—death. You do not care if you die. With us it was worse. Strong men, well women and little children killed and buried. They had not done wrong to be so killed. We had only asked to be left in our own homes, the homes of our ancestors. Our going was with heavy hearts, broken spirits. . . . All lost, we walked silently into the wintry night.[1]

The Nez Perce were settled on a barren reservation in Oklahoma. Far from the mountains of Idaho, this land was "the malarial bottom of the Indian Territory." Joseph, however, was sent to a reservation in Washington state. There he lived in exile, separated from his people and removed from the land he loved. When he died in 1904, the official cause of his death was listed as a broken heart.

The Ghost Dance

The final bloody battle in this chapter of the story of America was fought on the northern plains. In 1889 a religious revival swept through the Indian tribes. Chiefs and medicine men called their people to what whites called the "Ghost Dance." The celebration was based on the vision that an Indian leader would come to drive the whites from Indian lands and the buffalo would again roam the plains.

The Ghost Dance was not a call to war but a celebration of treasured Indian ways of life. Settlers and miners were alarmed at the energy and the mystery of the celebration. They demanded the army put an end to it.

The end came at **Wounded Knee** in South Dakota in December 1890. The 7th Calvary arrested a band of Sioux men, women, and children who were traveling in search of food and shelter as winter came. Suddenly a shot rang out. Without warning the troops opened fire with rifles and Hotchkiss guns, a type of small cannon. They poured a deadly hail of lead into the Indian band, killing 90 men and 200 women and children. The massacre ended armed Indian resistance to white demands.

The End of Indian Independence

All of the wars between the Indians and the army were hard fought. Yet many of the soldiers sympathized with their enemies. They understood why the Indians were fighting. Even Colonel John Gibbon, who discovered the bodies of Custer's men after the Battle of the Little Bighorn, blamed the wars on the settlers. Another officer said, "If I had been a red man . . . I should have fought as bitterly."

The way the government treated Indians shocked a great many

[1]From *Touch the Earth: A Self-Portrait of Indian Existence* by T.C. McLuhan

Point of View

An Oglala Sioux holy man told John G. Neihardt, a poet of the Middle West, of the coming of a new world.

"They saw the Wanekia ["One Who Makes Live"], who was the son of the Great Spirit, and they talked to him. . . . He told them that there was another world coming, just like a cloud. It would come in a whirlwind out of the west and would crush everything on this world, which was old and dying. In that other world there was plenty of meat, just like the old times; and in that world all the dead Indians were alive, and all the bison that had ever been killed were roaming around again."

Black Elk, 1930

Courtesy of The Library of Congress

Head held in his hand, the Hunkpapa Sioux Sitting Bull squints at the camera in this 1882 photograph. Here at Standing Rock reservation in the Dakota Territory the chief is living in exile. What clues in the photograph tell you that Sitting Bull's wars have all been waged?

Culver Pictures

Helen Hunt Jackson's novel Ramona *told the plight of the Indian people when the frontier closed. How did many Americans react to the government's treatment of the Indians?*

Return to the Preview & Review on page 630.

Americans. They were particularly upset when the government broke treaties it had made with the tribes. In *A Century of Dishonor*, published in 1881, Helen Hunt Jackson showed how the government broke promises to Indians. In her novel *Ramona* she tried to do for the Indians what Harriet Beecher Stowe's *Uncle Tom's Cabin* had done for the slaves.

Another fighter for Indian rights was Sarah Winnemucca, the daughter of a Paiute chief. Winnemucca wrote a book and gave lectures describing how unjustly the Indians had been treated. She demanded that the United States return much of the land it had taken from her people.

Congress finally responded by passing the **Dawes Severalty Act** of 1887. This law broke up reservation lands into individual family units. Each family got 160 acres (64 hectares). To protect the owners against speculators, they were not allowed to sell the property for 25 years. Only then did they have full rights to the land. And only then were they allowed to become citizens of the United States.

The Dawes Act was supposed to protect and help the Indians. However, it was written entirely from a white point of view. It ignored the Indians' culture and traditions. Its aim was to turn them into farmers, which would destroy their tribal organizations. It was well meant, but it simply showed once again that most white Americans had little understanding of or sympathy for the plight of the Indians. In this sense it was typical of most of the laws that Congress passed affecting the lives of the original Americans. 🗐

3. MINING THE WEST

The Comstock Lode

The Dawes Act spoke of encouraging the Indians to adopt "the habits of civilized life." The lawmakers apparently wanted them to copy the life styles of their white neighbors. How "civilized" those life styles were is another question!

The miners of the West offered one model. They carried their "civilization" into the mountains of Colorado, Nevada, Arizona, Idaho, Montana, and Wyoming. In each case they struck the region like a tornado.

The first important strikes after the California discovery of gold in 1848 came in Nevada in 1859. The center of this activity was Gold Canyon, a sagebrush-covered ravine on the southern slope of Mt. Davidson. At first the miners panned for gold in the gravel beds of streams. When their yields began to decline, the prospectors moved farther up the mountainside. Among these miners was Henry Comstock, known to his friends as "Old Pancake." His partner, James Fennimore, was called "Old Virginia." They began digging at the head of Gold Canyon on a small rise called Gold Hill. Another pair, Peter O'Riley and Patrick McLaughlin, started digging at Six Mile Canyon, a ravine on the northern slope of Mt. Davidson.

O'Riley and McLaughlin soon came upon a dark, heavy soil sprinkled with gold. Just as they were shouting news of their discovery, Henry Comstock came riding by. Jumping from his horse, he made a quick examination of the find. "You have struck it, boys!" he announced.

Then the old prospector bluffed his way into a partnership. "Look here," he said, "this spring was Old Man Caldwell's. You know that. . . . Well, Manny Penrod and I bought this claim last winter, and we sold a tenth interest to Old Virginia the other day. You two fellows must let us in on equal shares."

At first O'Riley and McLaughlin said no. Then they were afraid they might lose everything, so they said yes.

The partners went to work at once. They found very little gold. Instead they struck large deposits of heavy, bluish sand and blue-gray quartz. Not knowing what that "blasted blue stuff" was, they simply piled it beside the mine. Another miner, however, gathered up a sack of the blue quartz and had it tested, or **assayed.** The assayers' reports went beyond anyone's wildest dreams. The "blue stuff" was rich in silver and gold. The partners had hit upon what was known as a **bonanza**—a large find of extremely rich ore.

News of the discovery caused 15,000 people to swarm into the region in the next few months. Henry Comstock gained everlasting fame by giving the find his name. The enormous **Comstock Lode** ran along the eastern face of Mt. Davidson. It crossed the heads of Gold

Preview & Review

Use these questions to guide your reading. Answer the questions after completing Section 3.
Understanding Issues, Events, & Ideas. Describe mining discoveries in the West, using the following words: assayed, bonanza, Comstock Lode, Virginia City, boom town, vigilance committee, vigilante.

1. Where was the Comstock Lode struck?
2. What was life in a mining camp like? How was life in these camps similar to life in California mining camps in 1849?
3. How did vigilantes keep the law?

Thinking Critically. The author says that the Dawes Act encouraged the Indians to "adopt 'the habits of civilized life.' . . . How 'civilized' those life styles were is another question!" Suppose you are a native American who has been displaced under the Dawes Act. What is your opinion of your neighbors, the miners? Explain your answer.

Culver Pictures

"Old Pancake"

Mining the West   639

THE RICHEST HILL IN THE WORLD

Montana Historical Society

"Main Street will run north and south in a direct line through that cow," said the planners of Anaconda in 1887.

In Montana and Arizona the mining riches were in copper, not gold and silver. In the late 1870s Marcus Daly bought a small silver mine in Butte, Montana, for $30,000. For some reason this silver mine was named Anaconda. An anaconda is a large snake like a boa constrictor. Perhaps the silver ore ran in a curved, snakelike vein.

To finance the Anaconda, Daly turned to George Hearst, a millionaire California developer who had already invested in many western mines. Daly began operations in 1880.

The silver of Anaconda soon gave out. Beneath it, however, Daly found a rich vein of copper.

Hearst supplied the huge sums needed to mine and smelt this copper. By the late 1880s the Anaconda Copper Corporation had become the greatest producer of copper in the world. Eventually, Daly and his associates took over $2 billion worth of copper out of the "richest hill in the world."

Nevada Historical Society

"Old Virginia"

and Six Mile Canyons and dipped underneath the crowded mining camps.

Most of the gold and silver the prospectors sought was buried deep in veins of hard quartz rock. Heavy machinery was needed to dig it out. Huge steam-powered drills, tested in California, chiseled away massive chunks of earth. Newly developed steam shovels moved the chunks to waiting wagons, which carried them to smelters. The smelters, some like giant blast furnaces and some like huge rock crushers, separated the ore from the rock. By 1872 a railway wound through the mining communities, bringing coal to the smelters. But mine owners soon realized that large smelters, located in Golden or Denver, were more efficient. So the railroad hauled raw ore—rich with silver, copper, lead, and gold—to these plants. Tunneling operations called for experienced mining engineers. Powerful pumps were needed to remove groundwater that seeped in as the shafts grew deeper. Prospectors like Comstock, O'Riley, and McLaughlin did not have the skill or the money such operations required. Comstock eventually sold his share of the mine for a mere $10,000.

The real "bonanza kings" were John W. Mackay, James G. Fair, James C. Flood, and William S. O'Brien. All were of Irish ancestry. All had been born poor. All had come to California during the Gold Rush. In 1868-69 these four men formed a partnership. They used the profits of one strike to buy up other mines. Eventually they took precious metals worth over $150 million from the rich Nevada lode.

Mining Camp Life

Whenever a strike was made, mining camps seemed to sprout out of the surrounding hillsides like flowers after a desert rain. The camps were ramshackle towns of tents and noisy saloons. The most famous was **Virginia City,** Nevada. It was given its name by Henry Comstock's partner, "Old Virginia." While on a spree, "Old Virginia" tripped and fell, smashing his bottle of whiskey. Rising to his knees he shouted drunkenly, "I baptize this town Virginia Town."

Virginia City was a typical **boom town,** so crowded that a horse and wagon could take half an hour to cross the main street. The life of miners, shopkeepers, and others in these mining towns was sometimes as difficult as life on the open range. In these towns it was difficult to keep the peace. Smooth-talking gamblers, gunslingers, and other outlaws sidled alongside claim jumpers, shifty types who specialized in seizing ore deposits that had been staked out by others. Some camps were taken over by these outlaws, who ruled the terror-filled citizens at gunpoint. Such communities provided rich material for American writers. Mark Twain in *Roughing It* and Bret Harte in "The Luck of Roaring Camp" told of life in California mining camps. Charles Farrar Browne wrote this somewhat fictionalized account of a Nevada silver-mining town:

66 Shooting isn't as popular in Nevada as it once was. A few years since [ago] they used to have a dead man for breakfast every morning. A reformed desperado [bandit] told me that he supposed he had killed enough to stock a grave-yard. 'A feeling of remorse,' he said, 'sometimes comes over me! But I'm an altered man now. I hain't killed a man for over two weeks! What'll you poison yourself with?' he added, dealing a resonant [noisy] blow to the bar.[1] 99

Compare Browne's description to the following remembrances of some Virginia City residents. Which seems to be closer to the image of the "Old West" you have?

66 The men who worked in the mines . . . were [a] happy-go-lucky set of fellows, fond of good living, and not particularly interested in religious affairs. . . .

As regarded deportment [behavior], everyone was a law unto himself. . . . Most of the men employed in the

[1]From *Artemus Ward: His Travels* by Charles Farrar Browne

mines were unmarried and enjoyed none of the refining, humanizing influences of home life. They boarded at a restaurant, slept in a lodging-house, and, as a general rule, spent their leisure time on the street or at the gambling-tables.

During the flush times [when there was plenty of money] as many as twenty-five faro games [a gambling game in which players bet on cards drawn from a box] were in full blast night and day. When sporting men . . . sat down of an evening to a friendly game of poker it was no uncommon occurrence for five or six thousand dollars to change hands in a single sitting. Some idea of the amount of money in circulation may be inferred from the fact that every working-man's wages amounted to at least 120 dollars per month.

From what has already been written there is no desire to convey the impression that a low standard of morality was the rule in the Comstock mining district. Men quarreled at times and firearms were discharged [fired] with but slight provocation [cause]. Nevertheless they all had an acute instinct of right and wrong, a high sense of honor, and a chivalrous feeling of respect for the gentler sex. . . .

One of the most prominent traits of character as regarded the miners was their generous response to any worthy object. If a man of family lost his life in the mines thousands of dollars would be contributed to those dependent on him. Each miner contributed regularly one or two days' wages for benevolent causes [those for the public good]. . . .[1] 99

[1]From *The Mining Frontier: Contemporary Accounts from the American West in the Nineteenth Century,* edited by Marvin Lewis

When conditions in a mining camp got too bad, the respectable residents took action. They formed **vigilance committees** to watch over their towns. Sometimes they even drew up formal constitutions, pledging their members, called **vigilantes,** to restore order.

As soon as enough vigilantes had been signed up, the worst troublemakers were hunted down. These villains were given speedy trials before judges and juries made up of the same vigilantes who had run them down. The trials, of course, were not legal. The usual punishment for the guilty was death by hanging. In one six-week period Montana vigilantes hanged 22 outlaws.

Once a town was properly governed, more and more settlers moved in. Some opened stores. Others turned to farming. Lawyers, ministers, teachers, and doctors moved in. The people built schools and churches, started newspapers and opened hospitals. They built roads to other communities. They put down solid roots. 🖹

Return to the Preview & Review on page 639.

4. THE END OF THE OPEN RANGE

Preview & Review

Use these questions to guide your reading. Answer the questions after completing Section 4. **Understanding Issues, Events, & Ideas.** Describe the work on a cattle drive, using the following words: cattle kingdom, Texas longhorns, Abilene, Chicago, cattle towns, long drive, Chisholm Trail, open range, range rights, cattle baron, round up, brand, *vaquero*, Dodge City, boot hill, range war, sod house, drought, dry farming, bread basket of America.

1. How did Joseph G. McCoy plan to ship Texas longhorns to eastern cities?
2. Why was the open range so important to cattle ranchers?
3. What caused range wars?
4. What was the importance of the windmill, barbed wire, the steel plow, and the twine binder?

Thinking Critically. 1. You are a magazine reporter in 1875. Compose an article titled "A Day in the Life of a Cowhand." 2. It is the late 1800s. You can be a rancher, a cowhand, or a farmer. Which occupation will you choose? Why?

The Cattle Kingdom

While the miners were searching the mountains for gold and silver, other pioneers were seeking their own fortunes on the grasslands of the High Plains. The land that formed the **cattle kingdom** stretched from Texas into Canada and from the Rockies to eastern Kansas. This area made up nearly one quarter of the entire United States.

Spanish explorers had brought the first European cattle into Mexico in the early 1500s. Over the years their cattle had grown to enormous herds. Many ran wild. New breeds developed. These great herds spread northward as far as Texas.

By 1860 about 5 million wild cattle were grazing in Texas. These were the famous **Texas longhorns,** so named because their horns had a spread of as much as seven feet (over two meters). After the Civil War, cattle that were worth from $3 to $5 a head in Texas could be sold for $30 to $50 a head in the cities of the eastern United States. The problem was how to get them there. Joseph G. McCoy, an Illinois meat dealer, thought he knew the answer. He could make a fortune, he believed, if he could establish a convenient meeting place for eastern buyers and Texas cattle ranchers.

McCoy chose **Abilene,** Kansas, as this meeting place. There he put up a hotel for the cowhands and dealers and built barns, pens, and loading chutes for the cattle. He persuaded officials of the Kansas Pacific Railroad to ship cattle to **Chicago,** the meat packing center of the United States, at special low rates.

To get Texas longhorns to Abilene and other **cattle towns** meant herding them slowly northward over the empty plains. This **long drive** was a two-month journey. On the first drive Texans herded 35,000 longhorns over the **Chisholm Trail** to Abilene. During the next 20 years about 6 million head of cattle were driven north over the grasslands crossed by trails such as the Goodnight-Loving, Western, and Shawnee.

Open-Range Ranching

The key to the success of the long drive was the grass and water along the trail northward from Texas. Cattle ranchers discovered that prairie grass made an excellent food for their cattle. Then they discovered that the tough, rangy longhorns got along very well in the harsh winters of the northern plains. Soon millions of cattle were grazing on land belonging to the government. Ranchers could fatten their herds on this **open range** of lush grass without paying a cent for it. The cattle roamed freely across the unfenced plains.

Of course the cattle also needed water. It was a very dry region, almost a desert. Water rights, or **range rights,** along a stream meant

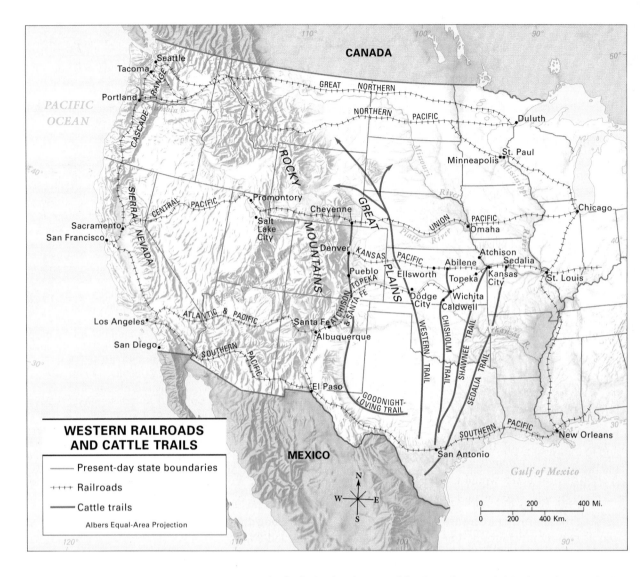

WESTERN RAILROADS AND CATTLE TRAILS

— Present-day state boundaries
+++++ Railroads
— Cattle trails

Albers Equal-Area Projection

LEARNING FROM MAPS. *Extension of the railroads across the nation meant many economic changes. One of the most important was the development of the cattle industry in Texas. Cattle were driven along established trails to railroad depots. How far was a long drive from the southern end of the Sedalia Trail to Sedalia? How long was the Chisholm Trail?*

control of all the land around it. Ranchers quickly bought up all the land around their water supply. By owning a few acres along a small river, a rancher could control thousands of acres of surrounding grasslands without actually owning it.

One Colorado **cattle baron,** John F. Iliff, had the use of an area the size of Connecticut and Rhode Island. Yet he owned only about 15,500 acres (6,200 hectares). His land consisted of 105 small parcels on which there was running water.

To secure adequate range rights, a number of ranchers would band together into an association. They would buy up all the land along the banks of a stream or claim it under the Homestead Act. Only *their* cattle would be allowed on this private property. Only *their* cattle could drink from the stream. Although the rest of the range was public property, no other rancher for miles around could graze cattle without water.

The Thomas Gilcrease Institute of American History and Art, Tulsa, Oklahoma

Under this system the cattle belonging to the ranchers who owned the banks of the stream became thoroughly mixed. Each spring and fall, cowhands would **round up** all the animals to a central place. The cowhands would fan out across the range, each riding up a canyon or hill. Each would return driving all the cattle in the area before him.

Next the cowhands sorted each rancher's cattle from the rest by checking every animal's marking, called a **brand.** The brand mark was a scar made by pressing a red-hot branding iron onto the animal's hide. Each rancher's brand had a distinct shape, so it was easy to determine who owned which cattle. Those that were ready for market were penned up and shipped off by rail. The rest were turned loose, free to roam the range again until the next roundup.

Of course, newborn calves had not been branded. But calves always trailed close beside their mothers, so it was easy to tell whose property they were. They were branded and sent bawling back to their mothers.

The Cowhand

That colorful western figure, the cowhand, was the master of the long drive and the roundup. Mexican Americans were the first cowhands. These *vaqueros* invented almost all the tools of the cowhand's trade, from his broad-brimmed felt hat, his cotton bandana, and his

Charles Marion Russell painted "Jerked Down." These cowhands rope a steer while scrambling to get free of its sharp hooves and horns. How does a great painter like Russell tell an entire story with his brushes and oil paints?

The Anschutz Collection

Above are "California Vaqueros" by James Walker. How did Mexican Americans influence the life of every cowhand?

rope lariat to his special western saddle. The word *rodeo* is the Spanish word for "roundup."

A cowhand's life was a hard one. The men worked sunup to sundown and received lower wages than most factory workers. Their legs became bowed from long days in the saddle. They developed permanent squints from peering into the glaring sunlight of the treeless plains. Their faces were lined and leathery, their hands calloused from constantly handling coarse ropes.

Not all cowhands were the strong, silent types portrayed in the movies by white actors. Many came from poor families or from groups outside the mainstream. About one third of the men who worked cattle on the open range were either Mexican Americans or African Americans.

Every item of the cowhand's clothes and equipment served a necessary function. The wide brim of his "ten-gallon hat" could be turned down to shade his eyes or drain off rainfall. His bandana could be tied over his nose and mouth to keep out the dust raised by the pounding hooves of countless cattle. The bandana also served as a towel, a napkin, a bandage, and a handkerchief. Cowhands sometimes wore leather trousers, called chaps, over regular overalls. Chaps were fastened to a broad belt buckled at the back. They protected a rider's legs from injury if he fell from his horse or when he had to ride through cactus, sagebrush, or other thorny plants.

The cowhand's western saddle had a sturdy horn, or pommel, for help in roping powerful steers and horses. These western saddles were heavy but comfortable. A weary cowhand could doze in the saddle while he rode. At night his saddle became a pillow and his saddlecloth a blanket when he stretched out beside the campfire and settled down to sleep. Around the campfire cowboys sang—to relax themselves and the herd. Their songs, such as "Home on the Range," have become a rich part of American music.

To the riders, the trail cook was the most important member of the team! Cowhands drank potfuls of thick, strong coffee to stay awake on the trail. They ate mostly stews, kidney beans, biscuits, and corn bread.

It was a lonely life. This explains why cowhands were famous for letting off steam when they reached cattle towns such as **Dodge City,** Kansas, the "Cowboy's Capital." Many cowhands were big drinkers and heavy gamblers when they came to town. Sometimes there were brawls and gunfights, but the violence and disorder have been exaggerated. Life in the West was much calmer and more orderly than it is usually pictured in the movies. Nevertheless, many cattle towns did have **boot hills**—cemeteries for those who "died with their boots on," either from overwork or on a spree.

The End of the Open Range

The cowhand rode tall on the open range. In the 1880s, however, the days of the open range were ending. By 1884 there were more than 4.5 million head of cattle roaming free on the Great Plains. The range was becoming overstocked. Good grazing land was scarce. In the foothills of the Rockies sheepherders squared off against local cattle

Montana Historical Society, Helena

Cowboy F.H. Corbin prepares to mount a "bronc" in a Montana corral.

> **"I have two miles of running water. That accounts for my ranch being where it is. The next water from me in one direction is 23 miles; now no man can have a ranch between these two places. I have control of the grass, the same as though I owned it."**
> Testimony Before Public Laws Commision, c. 1880s

ranchers. Cattle ranchers believed that sheep cropped the grass right down to the roots so that cattle could no longer find it. Many **range wars** broke out between cattle ranchers and sheep ranchers for control of the grasslands.

Farmers also competed with ranchers for land. Longhorns trampled their crops. The farmers feared the free-roaming herds would infect their cattle with a dread disease called "Texas fever."

Then came two terrible winters. In 1885-86 and in 1886-87 blizzards howled across the plains. Theodore Roosevelt, then a "gentleman rancher" in Dakota Territory, wrote:

> **"** Furious gales blow down from the north, driving before them the clouds of blinding snow-dust, wrapping the mantle of death around every unsheltered being. . . .**"**

When the spring came in 1887, ranchers discovered that the storms had all but wiped out their herds.

The boom times were over. Cattle ranchers could no longer count on the free grass of the plains. They had to fence in their herds and feed them hay and fodder in the winter. Cattle ranchers became cattle feeders, their work, like mining, less risky but also less adventurous. This change was important, especially to farmers on the Great Plains. Demand for corn, grains, and hay soared, as did the prices paid for them. Now economics urged Americans to find ways to farm the hard, dry soil of the plains.

Farming on the Great Plains

The soil of the Great Plains was fertile, but farming there proved to be very difficult. Still, settlers came by the thousands to claim their 160 acres under the Homestead Act or to buy land from the railroads. Some were the sons and daughters of farmers in states like Illinois and Iowa and Arkansas. Others were emigrants from Norway, Sweden, and a dozen other lands. O. E. Rölvaag wrote of several Norwegian families and the land they settled. Imagine the plains they saw as he describes them:

> **"** Bright, clear sky over a plain so wide that the rim of the heavens cut down on it around the horizon. . . . Bright, clear sky, to-day, to-morrow, and for all time to come.
> . . . And sun! And still more sun! It sets the heavens afire every morning; it grew with the day to a quivering golden light—then softened into all the shades of red and purple as evening fell. . . . Pure colour everywhere. A gust of wind, sweeping across the plain, threw into life waves of yellow and blue and green. Now and then a dead black wave would race across the scene . . . a cloud's gliding shadow . . . now and then. . . .

READING A CLIMATE MAP

Like election maps, climate maps are special-purpose maps. They show the climate of an area. *Climate* is the average daily weather conditions over a long period of time. Climate often influences human activity and decision making.

There are 13 major climate types. *Tropical wet* areas are hot and rainy all year. *Tropical wet-and-dry* areas are hot, with most rain falling in the summer. *Desert* regions receive little or no rain, while *semiarid* areas receive between 10 and 20 inches (25 and 50 centimeters) of rain a year. *Mediterranean* areas are mild and dry in the winter and hot and dry in the summer. *West coast marine* climates have cool summers and abundant rain all year. *Humid subtropical* areas have mild winters, hot and rainy summers. Regions with *continental* climates vary. All have severely cold winters, but some have cool summers while others have scorching ones. *Polar* climates—boreal, subarctic, and ice cap—are very cold. *Mountain* climates vary depending on elevation.

How to Read a Climate Map

To read a climate map, follow these guidelines.
1. **Study the key.** The key explains what the colors and special symbols on the map mean. Generally different colors will indicate different climatic regions.
2. **Note the map's patterns.** Climatic regions often follow a predictable pattern.
3. **Use the information.** The information on the climate map can help you form hypotheses and draw conclusions about economic activities and life styles in each climate area.

Applying the Strategy

Study the climate map of the United States below. Note that there are nine major climate regions in the United States. What generalization can you make about climate and human activity after studying the map?

For independent practice, see Practicing the Strategy on page 657.

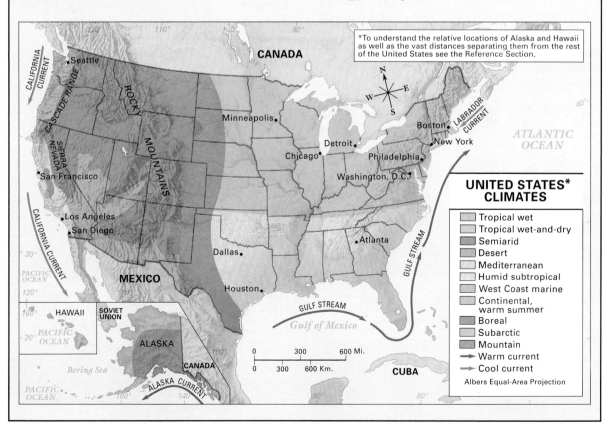

*To understand the relative locations of Alaska and Hawaii as well as the vast distances separating them from the rest of the United States see the Reference Section.

UNITED STATES* CLIMATES

- Tropical wet
- Tropical wet-and-dry
- Semiarid
- Desert
- Mediterranean
- Humid subtropical
- West Coast marine
- Continental, warm summer
- Boreal
- Subarctic
- Mountain
- → Warm current
- → Cool current

Albers Equal-Area Projection

It was late afternoon. A small caravan was pushing its way through the tall grass. The track that it left behind was like the wake of a boat—except that instead of widening out astern it closed in again.

'Tish-ah!' said the grass. . . . 'Tish-ah, tish-ah!' . . . Never had it said anything else—never would it say anything else. It bent resiliently under the trampling feet; it did not break, but it complained aloud every time—for nothing like this had ever happened to it before. . . . 'Tish-ah, tish-ah!' it cried, and rose up in surprise to look at this rough, hard thing that had crushed it to the ground so rudely, and then moved on. . . .

This was the caravan of Pers Hansa, who with his family and all his earthly possessions was moving west from Fillmore County, Minnesota, to Dakota Territory. There he intended to take up land and build himself a home; he was going to do something remarkable out there, which should become known far and wide. No lack of opportunity in that country, he had been told![1] **99**

On the treeless plains the pioneers built their first homes out of the earth itself. The thick roots of the wild grasses made it possible to cut sod into bricklike chunks. Only the roofs of these **sod houses** were made of wood. Sod houses were smoky and damp, but they provided shelter until the railroads reached the frontier. Then lumber could be brought in at reasonable rates.

This sod house is typical of those built in the land where few trees grew. Use historical imagination to ask what the boy will do next.

[1]From *Giants in the Earth* by O.E. Rölvaag

Kansas State Historical Society

Fencing was a more difficult problem. Farmers had to protect their crops. But nothing they used stood up to the pounding of the cattle and other farm animals. The problem was solved by Joseph Glidden, who invented barbed wire in 1873. Barbed-wire fences soon crisscrossed the open range.

In the East farmers got water from bubbling springs or from wells. They hauled ground water to the surface in buckets or pumped it up easily by hand. But on the Great Plains water flowed deep beneath the surface. Farmers needed powerful pumps to get it. Fortunately, the winds of the plains blew steadily enough to turn windmills. These powered the pumps that drew up the water.

The biggest problem facing the farmers of frontier Nebraska, Kansas, and the Dakotas was the lack of rainfall. In some years there was plenty of rain to grow wheat and other grain crops. But often there were dry years, even **droughts,** when almost no rain fell. Well water could be used to irrigate a small plot or a vegetable garden, but it was not enough for any large-scale farming.

Hardy W. Campbell, a Nebraska farmer, developed a technique called **dry farming** that made it possible to raise certain crops when as little as 15 or 20 inches (37 to 50 centimeters) of rain fell a year. Campbell plowed the land deeply and repeatedly until the soil was almost as absorbent as blotting paper. The idea was to make sure that all the rain that did fall was absorbed directly into the soil where the roots of the plants could use it. Campbell also planted special varieties of wheat that did not need as much water as other types. Using dry-farming methods, farmers could raise crops in drought years.

Despite such advances farming the plains remained tremendously hard work. Willa Cather captured this in her widely read *My Ántonia.* In this excerpt Jim Burden, the narrator, tells of a visit with his friend Ántonia Shimerda, the only daughter of immigrant parents from Czechoslovakia. Remember as you read that Ántonia's day is fairly typical.

The Bettmann Archive

The windmill above might have pumped water for the thirsty pony.

❝ The Shimerdas were in their new log house by then. The neighbors had helped them to build it in March. It stood directly in front of their old cave, which they used as a cellar. The family were now fairly equipped to begin their struggle with the soil. They had four comfortable rooms to live in, a new windmill—bought on credit—a chicken-house and poultry. Mrs. Shimerda had paid grandfather ten dollars for a milk cow, and was to give him fifteen more as soon as they harvested their first crop. . . .

When the sun was dropping low, Ántonia came up the big south draw with her team. How much older she had grown in eight months! She had come to us a child, and now she was a tall, strong young girl, although her fifteenth

Brown Brothers

Willa Cather, a Nebraskan, wrote her novels set in the Midwest after she herself moved to New York City. Her novels include O Pioneers!, One of Ours, A Lost Lady, *and* Death Comes for the Archbishop—*her masterpiece, set in colonial New Mexico.*

birthday had just slipped by. I ran out and met her as she brought her horses up to the windmill to water them. She wore the boots her father had so thoughtfully taken off before he shot himself, and his old fur cap. Her outgrown cotton dress switched about her calves, over the boot-tops. She kept her sleeves rolled up all day, and her arms and throat were burned as brown as a sailor's. Her neck came up strongly out of her shoulders, like the bole [trunk] of a tree out of the turf. One sees that draught-horse neck among the peasant women in all old countries.

She greeted me gaily, and began at once to tell me how much ploughing she had done that day. Ambrosch, she said, was on the north quarter, breaking sod with the oxen.

'Jim, you ask Jake how much he ploughed to-day. I don't want that Jake get more done in one day than me. I want we have very much corn this fall.'

While the horses drew in the water, and nosed each other, and then drank again, Ántonia sat down on the wind-mill and rested her head on her hand.

'You see the big prairie fire from your place last night? I hope your grandpa ain't lose no [hay] stacks?'

'No, we didn't. I came to ask you something, Tony. Grandmother wants to know if you can't go to the term of school that begins next week over at the sod school-house. She says there's a good teacher, and you'd learn a lot.'

Ántonia stood up, lifting and dropping her shoulders as if they were stiff. 'I ain't got time to learn. I can work like mans now. My mother can't say no more how Ambrosch do all and nobody to help him. I can work as much as him. School is all right for little boys. I help make this land one good farm.'

She clucked to her team and started for the barn. I walked beside her, feeling vexed. Was she going to grow up boastful like her mother, I wondered? Before we reached the stable, I felt something tense in her silence, and glancing up I saw that she was crying. She turned her face from me and looked off at the red streak of dying light, over the dark prairie.

I climbed up into the loft and threw down the hay for her, while she unharnessed her team. We walked slowly back toward the house. Ambrosch had come in from the north quarter, and was watering his oxen at the tank.

Ántonia took my hand. 'Sometime you will tell me all those nice things you learn at the school, won't you, Jimmy?' she asked with a sudden rush of feeling in her voice. 'My father, he went much to school. He know a great deal; how to make the fine cloth like what you not got here.

National Archives

He play horn and violin, and he read so many books that the priests in Bohemie [Bohemia, a district now in southern Germany] come to talk to him. You won't forget my father, Jim?'

'No,' I said, 'I will never forget him.' . . .'**"**

[1]From *My Ántonia* by Willa Cather.

This farmer was photographed while turning the soil of the prairie. The picture is titled "Mares of Percheron," which is the type of work horse pulling the plow. What time of year do you suppose this photograph was taken? Explain your answer.

The gigantic "bonanza farms" of the Red River Valley of North Dakota and Minnesota were the most spectacular farms on the plains. These farms spread over thousands of acres. One big wheat farm in Dakota Territory was managed by Oliver Dalrymple. He ran the farm like a factory. Everything possible was mechanized. When the wheat was ripe, he used 155 binders and 26 steam threshers to harvest it. In 1877 Dalrymple's workers harvested 75,000 bushels of wheat.

Farms of this type were unusual. Still, by the 1880s the average plains farmer was using a great deal of machinery. In 1868 James Oliver of Indiana began manufacturing a cast iron plow. This plow could easily slice through the tough sod of the plains. In the 1870s John Appleby invented a twine binder. This machine gathered up bundles of wheat and bound them with twine or string automatically. Soon an acre of wheat that had taken 60 hours to harvest by hand could be harvested in only 3 hours by machine.

By the 1890s the land west of the Mississippi Valley was no longer thought of as a desert. It had become the **breadbasket of America** and the greatest wheat-producing region in the world. By 1890 about 5 million people were living on the Great Plains. There was still unsettled land, but there was no longer a frontier separating settlement from wilderness. The march westward that had begun in Virginia in 1607 had overrun the continent.

Return to the Preview & Review on page 643.

The End of the Open Range   653

GOLD! GOLD! GOLD!

Prospectors differed from typical pioneers. They dreamed not of fertile valleys and rich farmlands. They sought steep mountainsides where roaring streams covered beds of ore, deserts where shifting sand hid precious metal, or highlands where jagged rock outcroppings protected great veins of mineral wealth.

Prospecting in California

1. What were the chief methods of mining used by prospectors and miners?

Gold! The word was magic. Like a magnet it attracted hopeful prospectors from all over the world to California in 1849. These Forty-Niners used simple devices—usually a pan or sluice box—to wash the ore to separate the particles of gold.

Once the easily obtained surface gold was gone, however, more sophisticated mining methods were necessary. Gold still remained but it was often locked in hard rock called quartz and was typically found deep beneath the earth's surface. To extract this gold, shafts had to be dug to reach the beds of ore. Crushing mills then separated the unyielding ore from the quartz. But shafts and crushing mills were too expensive for most miners. As a result, eastern bankers furnished the money to develop California's mining industry. Individual prospectors had to look elsewhere if they were to realize their dream of striking it rich on their own.

Searching the West

2. What attracted miners to Colorado?

Throughout the late 1850s and 1860s prospectors scoured the West, ranging from the Pacific to the Rockies. Every likely stream was panned and every promising outcropping of rock was examined in their quest to find pay dirt. Whenever a strike was made, a horde of hopeful miners swarmed in. A handful quickly became rich. Most were lucky if they found enough gold to pay their expenses.

Then in 1858 a number of important discoveries were made, all the way from British Columbia to Colorado. The Colorado strike was the most exciting. Rumors of gold in the region had persisted for years. These rumors were kept alive by the tales of an occasional trapper who would emerge from the mountains with a leather pouch filled with gold nuggets and of Indians who were said to fire bullets made of yellow metal. Add these rumors to the very real presence of water available from the many mountain streams and Colorado had all of the makings of a prospector's paradise.

The site of the original Colorado discovery was on the Cherry Creek near its junction with the Platte River—the very site of Denver, a dozen miles east of the Rockies. A number of small strikes were made during the summer of 1858 and news of each discovery was carried in newspapers throughout the country. By the spring of 1859 more than 100,000 hopeful prospectors flocked to what was known as Pikes Peak Country.

Most of Colorado's gold seekers came from California rather than from the settled lands of the Mississippi Valley. They had learned the basic elements of mining in California, and they attacked the Colorado gold fields with the same techniques. But by 1865 the day of the lone prospector in Colorado had ended, as it had 10 years earlier in California.

The Colorado Mining Industry

3. How did mining develop in Colorado?

Although Pikes Peak gold turned out to be a disappointment to most individual miners, mining continued to grow in Colorado. Large mining companies soon arrived, sinking deep mine shafts and feeding hungry milling machinery. Boom towns such as Central City and Blackhawk were squeezed into narrow ravines. Buildings appeared to be glued to steep slopes and jammed into gulch bottoms. Diggings and test pits were as thick as anthills.

As the miners burrowed deeper and deeper in their search for gold, new mining, milling, and smelting techniques were developed. A railroad wound its way to the communities by 1872, bringing coal to fuel the smelters. But people soon realized smelting was done more efficiently in Golden or Denver, nearer both coal and labor. So the railroad carried heavy machinery into the mining communities and the raw ore—rich with silver, copper, and lead as well as precious gold—out. By 1880 the population of the Central City-Blackhawk area had soared to 10,000. The area became known around the

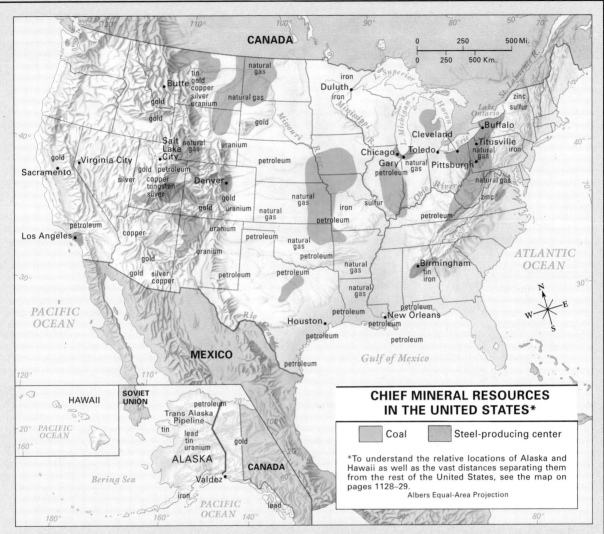

CANADA

natural gas

tin
gold
copper
silver
uranium

Butte

gold

gold

natural gas

gold

natural gas

Salt
Lake
City

uranium

petroleum

uranium

gold
copper
tungsten
silver

Virginia City

Sacramento

gold

silver

Denver

gold

gold
uranium

Los Angeles

petroleum

copper

uranium

natural
gas

gold

gold
silver
copper

uranium

petroleum

petroleum

petroleum

natural
gas

natural
gas

petroleum

petroleum

natural
gas

Houston

petroleum

petroleum

natural
gas

petroleum

PACIFIC
OCEAN

MEXICO

Rio Grande

iron
Duluth
iron

Mississippi R.

L. Superior

L. Michigan

L. Huron

Chicago

Gary
petroleum

Cleveland

Toledo

natural
gas

Pittsburgh

Lake Ontario

L. Erie

Buffalo

Titusville
natural
gas

zinc
sulfur

St. Lawrence R.

iron

natural gas

iron

sulfur

Ohio River

zinc

petroleum

natural
gas

petroleum

natural
gas

Birmingham
tin
iron

petroleum
New Orleans
petroleum

petroleum

petroleum

Gulf of Mexico

ATLANTIC
OCEAN

N
W E
S

0   250   500 Mi.
0   250   500 Km.

HAWAII

PACIFIC
OCEAN

SOVIET
UNION

Trans-Alaska
Pipeline

tin

petroleum

lead
tin
uranium

gold

ALASKA

Valdez

CANADA

iron

lead

Bering Sea

PACIFIC
OCEAN

**CHIEF MINERAL RESOURCES
IN THE UNITED STATES***

| | Coal | | Steel-producing center |

*To understand the relative locations of Alaska and
Hawaii as well as the vast distances separating them
from the rest of the United States, see the map on
pages 1128–29.
Albers Equal-Area Projection

world as the richest square mile on earth. The future of Colorado gold mining seemed assured.

The Decline of Mining
4. Why did the large-scale mining industry in Colorado decline?

The ultimate decline of the mining industry would have been difficult to foresee during its heyday of the 1870s and 1880s. But decline did come. Mining costs continued to rise as shafts got deeper. The quality of the ore lessened. Problems with ground water became very real. It seeped into the mines as miners penetrated below the water table. Costs of pumping were enormous. Ventilation also became increasingly complex and costly as the shafts angled deeper

and deeper. Finally, the market value of the minerals, with the exception of gold, began a downward slide. In time, copper, lead, and silver could be mined far more inexpensively in other parts of the country.

Applying Your Knowledge
Your class will create an exhibition of America's mineral wealth. Each group will select or be assigned a mineral to display in the exhibition. The display should include a description (or sketch) of the mineral (and a sample if available), a list of its uses, and a map of the locations of major deposits. Your class may wish to set up the exhibition in an appropriate place in the school or community.

CHAPTER 18 REVIEW

1845				1860		

1848
Treaty of
Guadalupe
Hildago

1849
California Gold Rush

1851
Treaty of Fort Laramie

1859
Fifty-Niners
surge to
Colorado

1860
Cattle kingdom
established on Plains

1862
Pacific
Railway
Act

1864
Chivin[
Massa[

Chapter Summary
Read the statements below. Choose one, and write a paragraph explaining its importance.
1. Before the 1850s only Indians, Spanish Americans, and Mormons lived on the Great Plains. Until then it was considered a desert.
2. Plains Indians developed unique ways of life, even adapting European items such as the horse and metal tools to their life-styles.
3. As settlers and railroads sought land on the Plains the Indians were removed to reservations. This process led to brief but bitter battles between the Indians and government troops. Settlers also seized land from Mexican Americans living in the Southwest.
4. Rich ore deposits west of the Plains brought a flurry of prospectors who built ramshackle mining camps.
5. The grasslands of the High Plains soon became the cattle kingdom. Thousands of cattle grazed on the open range and were then shipped to Chicago.
6. The open range closed as technical improvements made it possible to farm the Great Plains. Chief among these was dry farming, barbed wire, the steel plow, and the twine binder.

Reviewing Chronological Order
Number your paper 1–5. Then study the time line above and place the following events in the order in which they happened by writing the first next to 1, the second next to 2, and so on.
1. Treaty of Fort Laramie
2. Dawes Act
3. Wounded Knee
4. Transcontinental Railroad completed
5. Cattle kingdom established

Understanding Main Ideas
1. How was the system called concentration used to remove the Plains Indians?

2. How did the government encourage the building of transcontinental railroads?
3. Describe life in a typical mining town.
4. Describe the life of a cowhand. What were some inventions of the *vaqueros* used by cowhands?
5. What ended the open range? Why?
6. Describe the inventions and farming techniques that helped turn the Great American Desert into the breadbasket of America.

Thinking Critically
1. **Analyzing.** Putting yourself in the place of a Plains Indian of the early 1800s, make a list of the animals that are important to your tribe. Alongside the name of each animal, list the uses you make of it.
2. **Synthesizing.** Imagine that you are Leland Stanford writing your autobiography in June 1869. Describe your company's part in building America's first transcontinental railroad. Then tell of the important role other such railroads will play in the nation's future.
3. **Problem Solving.** You are a member of a vigilance committee in a rowdy boom town. You have called a meeting with other vigilantes to make plans for bringing law and order to your town. To prepare for your opening remarks at the meeting, outline the problems facing you. Then outline two or three ideas for how to solve these problems.

Writing About History
Use historical imagination to place yourself in one of the mining boom towns of the 1860s or as a cowhand on a long drive. Write a letter home to your family in the East telling about your life in the West. Describe your life as a miner and the town where you trade or a typical day on the drive as a cowhand. Use the information in Chapter 18 and in reference books to prepare your letter.

	1875	SETTLING THE GREAT PLAINS		1890

	1874	1876	1881	1887	1890
iron plow developed	Barbed wire patented	Battle of the Little Bighorn	Sitting Bull surrenders	Dawes Act	Wounded Knee
scontinental oad completed		1877 Chief Joseph surrenders	★ *A Century of Dishonor*	★ Blizzards end open range	

Practicing the Strategy

Review the strategy on page 649.

Reading a Settlement Map. Study the settlement map in the Reference Section and answer the following questions.

1. Into what three states of the Ohio Valley had settlement spread by 1790?
2. Large parts of Wyoming, Montana, western Texas, and several other states were not fully settled until after 1880. Why?
3. Oklahoma was not considered settled until much later than most of its neighbors. What fact in Oklahoma's history explains this?
4. Compare the settlement map to the population distribution map below it. How are the patterns similar? How would you explain this similarity?

Using Primary Sources

The winter of 1884–85 was one of the most disastrous in America's cattle-ranching history. As you read the following excerpt from J. Frank Dobie's *The Longhorns,* think about how people and animals struggled to survive on the Great Plains. Then answer the questions that follow.

> *When a terrible blizzard struck in late December, cattle from southwestern Kansas and No Man's Land [a geographic area in northern Oklahoma] went with it. The grass lay under a pavement of sleet and ice. The plains afforded no harbor or shelter. As endless strings of cattle going with the wind crowded up to the first drift fence, the leaders stopped, stiffened and went down, to be trampled on by followers until piles of dead made overpasses. In places the posts were shoved over and cattle struggling through cut themselves to pieces on the barbed wire. . . . After the storm the fence lines were marked by tens of thousands of frozen bodies. In the spring cattle from the upper ranges were found five hundred miles south in Texas.*

1. How do you think cowboys might have described "No Man's Land?"

2. Although the drift fences presented problems for trail drivers during a blizzard, what purpose does the reading suggest the fences served?
3. How do you think the harsh winters during the mid-1880s affected the cattle industry economically? Use evidence from the excerpt to support your opinion.

Linking History & Geography

As you read in this chapter, water is an especially valuable resource on the Great Plains. In 1820 Major Stephen Long led an army expedition through the region. Noting the dry, treeless plain, he labeled it the "Great American Desert." Except for reservoirs, there are no lakes on the Great Plains. Rivers are generally fewer and shallower than back east. On the eastern plains, precipitation—rain and snow together—averages 25 inches (64 centimeters) or more; on the western plains it is as little as 10 inches (25 centimeters). How did this lack of water affect the settlement of the Great Plains?

Enriching Your Study of History

1. **Individual Project.** A *diorama* is an exhibit of lifelike figures in natural settings in the foreground with a painting in the background. Make a diorama of an Indian camp on the Great American Desert, of a mining boom town, or of a farm on the Great Plains in the 1880s.
2. **Cooperative Project.** Your class will prepare a special section for a newspaper. Each group will use historical imagination to be newspaper reporters assigned to cover the Battle of Little Bighorn. Some of you will write biographical sketches of the key figures. Others will create illustrations, and still others will prepare a relief map of the battle site, showing the topography.

Chapter 18 Review   657

The Rise of Industrial America

Between 1860 and 1900 the United States went through one of the most dramatic periods of change in its entire history. In 1860 about 80 percent of the nation's 31 million inhabitants lived on farms. About 1.5 million, less than 5 percent, worked in factories. By the 1890s about 5 million Americans worked in factories. America's manufactured products were worth almost as much as the manufactured goods of Great Britain, France, and Germany combined. By the end of the century the new industrial growth was visible nearly everywhere. Railroads crossed and recrossed the continent. Small towns had been changed as if by magic into great cities. In 1900 about 40 percent of America's 76 million people lived in towns and cities. The steel, oil, and electrical industries, tiny in 1865, had become giants. Imagine how the United States would have seemed in 1900 to a person who had been out of the country since the Civil War!

An appropriate symbol for America in the 19th century is the ironworks at Pittsburgh. What can you say about the forms of transportation in this engraving? How would environmentalists today appraise this scene?

The Granger Collection, New York

1. THE POWER OF THE RAILS

The Railroad Network

Americans were fascinated by railroads. Poets celebrated the "pant and roar" of the locomotives, so powerful as to shake the ground, and the elaborate decorations painted on their sides. They even praised the "dense and murky" clouds that belched from the locomotives' smokestacks. To all sorts of people railroads symbolized the boundless energy of the nation. In 1879 the great American poet Walt Whitman traveled by rail west from Philadelphia to the Rocky Mountains and back. He then wrote this prose poem in tribute to railroads:

66 What a fierce weird pleasure to lie in my berth at night in the luxurious palace-car, drawn by the mighty Baldwin [a make of locomotive]—embodying, and filling me, too, full of the swiftest motion, and most resistless strength! It is late, perhaps midnight or after—distances join'd like magic—as we speed through Harrisburg, Columbus, Indianapolis. The element of danger adds zest to it all. On we go, rumbling and flashing, with our loud whinnies thrown out from time to time, or trumpetblasts, into the darkness. Passing the homes of men, the farms, barns, cattle—the silent villages. And the car itself, the sleeper, with curtains drawn and lights turn'd down—in the berths the slumberers, many of the women and children—as on, on, on, we fly like lightning through the night—how strangely sound and sweet we sleep! . . .[1] 99

When the Civil War began, there were only 30,000 miles (48,000 kilometers) of railroad track in the United States. Most railroads were very short, averaging only about 100 miles (160 kilometers). They had been built to serve local needs. Few direct lines connected distant cities. Passengers and freight traveling between New York and Chicago, for example, had to be transferred from one line to another 17 times! The trip took at least 50 hours.

The main task of the postwar generation was to connect these lines into one network. "Commodore" Cornelius Vanderbilt was a pioneer in this work. Vanderbilt could barely read and write, but he was aggressive and hard-nosed. He had made a fortune in shipping, but when river traffic fell during the Civil War, he invested in railroads. By 1869 he had control of the New York Central Railroad, which ran between Buffalo and Albany, and two other lines that connected the Central with New York City.

[1]From *The Collected Prose* (1891–1892) by Walt Whitman

Preview & Review

Use these questions to guide your reading. Answer the questions after completing Section 1.
Understanding Issues, Events, & Ideas. Using the following words, describe the economic changes in the United States after 1870: railroad baron, corporation, stock certificate, stockholder, board of directors, limited liability, partnership, Bessemer converter, Mesabi Range, smelt, division of labor, mass production, oil refining, "Drake's Folly," wildcatter, "black gold."
1. How did railroads stimulate the national economy?
2. Why did the railroad boom lead business leaders to set up corporations?
3. What effect on the production of steel did the Bessemer converter have?
4. What created the demand for kerosene? How did the discovery of oil lead to a boom?
Thinking Critically. 1. The year is 1870. You have just seen a passing locomotive for the first time. Write a brief description of your impressions. **2.** Which do you think was the most important scientific achievement in the 1800s: mass production of steel or the process of oil refining? Why?

The Granger Collection, New York

In 1870 Vanderbilt bought the Lake Shore and Michigan Southern Railroads. His growing New York Central system then extended 965 miles (1,544 kilometers) from New York to Chicago by way of Cleveland and Toledo. Passengers could travel between New York and Chicago in less than 24 hours without leaving their seats. When Vanderbilt died in 1877, he left a railroad system of over 4,500 miles (7,200 kilometers) serving a vast region. He left a personal fortune of $100 million.

In much the same way J. Edgar Thomson, head of the Pennsylvania Railroad, built up direct routes from Philadelphia to St. Louis and Chicago by way of Pittsburgh. In 1871 the Pennsylvania Railroad extended its tracks to New York City. Other lines were extended by wealthy developers such as Jay Gould, Jim Fisk, and James J. Hill.

Besides combining railroads to make through connections, the **railroad barons,** as the men who financed and profited from railroads were called, built many new lines. By 1900 the United States had about 200,000 miles (320,000 kilometers) of railroad track. This was more than were in all the nations of Europe combined.

In addition to speeding the movement of goods and passengers, the railroads supplied thousands of jobs for laborers, train crews, repair workers, and clerks. By 1891 the Pennsylvania Railroad alone employed over 110,000 workers. The largest United States government employer, the post office, had only 95,000 on its payroll in 1891.

Railroads stimulated the national economy in countless ways. They were great users of wood, copper, and steel. They made it possible to move bulky products like coal and iron ore cheaply over long distances. This made such products available at reasonable prices in regions where they had formerly been very expensive. Railroads enabled farmers in California to sell their fruits and vegetables in New York. Flour milled in Minneapolis could be purchased in Boston. Wherever railroads went, new towns sprang up almost overnight, and older towns grew to be big cities.

Travelers to ancient Greece saw the bronze Colossus of Rhodes, over 100 feet (30.5 meters) high. It was one of the seven wonders of the ancient world. Ships were said to have sailed between its legs, but in truth the Colossus stood on a hillside. "The Colossus of Roads" by Joseph Keppler makes Cornelius Vanderbilt a modern colossus with his empire of railroads. Explain how a man barely able to read and write amassed a fortune of 100 million dollars.

LEARNING FROM TABLES. *This table illustrates the growth of railroads between 1870 and 1900. Why was the extension of the railroad network essential to the development of the American economy?*

RAILROADS, 1870-1900			
Year	Miles of Track	Capital Invested (Millions)	Total Income (Millions)
1870	52,922	$ 2,476	NA
1880	93,262	$ 5,402	$ 503
1890	166,703	$10,122	$1,092
1900	193,346	$12,814	$2,013
NA= Not Available			

Source: *Historical Statistics of the United States*

The Corporation

Railroads were very expensive to build and operate. The sums needed to build even a small one were far larger than the amount John C. Calhoun had to raise to buy his South Carolina plantation, more than John Ellerton Lodge had invested in his fleet of merchant ships, greater than Francis Cabot Lowell and the Boston Associates needed when they built their first textile mill.

One person or family or even a group of partners rarely had enough money to construct and operate a railroad. Railroad developers had to raise money from other investors. To do this, they set up their businesses as **corporations.**

When a corporation is formed, the organizers sell shares called **stock certificates.** People who buy shares are called **stockholders.** These stockholders own the corporation, which is usually run by a **board of directors.** Stockholders can sell their shares to anyone for whatever price they can get. If the business is doing poorly, the value of the shares will fall.

For the organizers of big businesses the chief advantage of the corporation is that it brings together the money of many investors. For the investors the chief advantage is **limited liability.** This means that the individual investors risk only the money they have paid for their stocks. In a **partnership,** on the other hand, all the partners are responsible for the debts of the firm. For example, a partner who had invested only $100 could be held responsible for a $5,000 debt of a partnership. The same person investing $100 in the stock of a corporation could lose only that $100, no matter how much money the corporation owed.

Changing Iron into Steel

The railroad industry could not have grown as large as it did without steel. The first rails were made of iron. But iron rails were not strong enough to support heavy trains running at high speeds. Railroad executives wanted to replace them with steel rails because steel was 10 or 15 times stronger and lasted 20 times longer. Before the 1870s, however, steel was too expensive to be widely used. It was made by a slow and expensive process of heating, stirring, and reheating iron ore.

Then an English inventor, Henry Bessemer, discovered that directing a blast of air at melted iron in a furnace would burn out the impurities that made the iron brittle. As the air shot through the furnace, the bubbling metal would erupt in showers of sparks. When the fire cooled, the metal had been changed, or *converted,* to steel. The **Bessemer converter** made possible the mass production of steel. Now three to five tons of iron could be changed into steel in a matter of minutes.

Metropolitan Museum of Art

"Forging the Shaft: A Welding Heat" was painted in 1877 by John F. Weir. It captures the glow of molten metal that filled American steel mills in the 19th century. Use your historical imagination to describe the sensations you would have felt working in front of a blast furnace.

Just when the demand for more and more steel developed, prospectors discovered huge new deposits of iron ore in the **Mesabi Range,** a 120-mile-long region (192 kilometers) in Minnesota near Lake Superior. The Mesabi deposits were so near the surface that they could be mined with steam shovels.

Barges and steamers carried the iron ore through Lake Superior to depots on the southern shores of Lake Michigan and Lake Erie. With dizzying speed Gary, Indiana, and Toledo, Youngstown, and Cleveland, Ohio, became major steel-manufacturing centers. Pittsburgh was the greatest steel city of all. The large coal fields near Pittsburgh supplied cheap fuel to **smelt** the ore—that is, to melt it down to remove impurities.

Steel was the basic building material of the industrial age. After steel rails came steel bridges. Next came steel skeletons for tall buildings. Nails, wire, and other everyday objects were also made of steel. Production skyrocketed from 77,000 tons in 1870 to over 11 million tons in 1900.

Andrew Carnegie was by far the most important producer of steel. Born in 1835 in Scotland, he came to the United States at age 12 and settled with his parents in Allegheny, now a part of Pittsburgh. At 14 he was working 12 hours a day as a bobbin boy in a cotton mill for $1.20 a week. He studied hard and at 16 had progressed to a telegraph clerk earning $4.00 a week—a fair salary in those days. At 17 Carnegie became the private secretary to the president of the Pennsylvania Railroad.

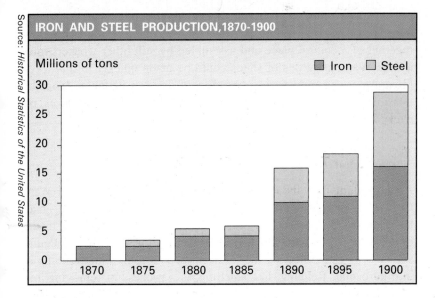

IRON AND STEEL PRODUCTION, 1870-1900

Millions of tons

Iron Steel

Source: *Historical Statistics of the United States*

LEARNING FROM GRAPHS.
Note the rapid increase in the production of iron and steel shown on this graph. Iron and steel, like railroad and communication networks, were necessary for modern industrial growth. Why?

Carnegie then invested in an oil well and began to make money in the new oil industry. But he soon turned to the steel industry. He frankly admitted he knew nothing about making steel when he started. Early in his career as an ironmaster, he visited a plant in England where the Bessemer process was being used. This new process made large quantities of steel cheaply. Now Carnegie became convinced that the day of cheap steel had arrived. He rushed home and built the largest Bessemer plant in America. He did so in the midst of the worst depression in the history of the United States. Labor and materials were cheap. Thus Carnegie got a large, up-to-date steel mill at a bargain price.

But Carnegie's true success was as a promoter and seller. He captured the largest share of the railroad business—the nation's largest steel users—with several shrewd deals. He also knew how to gather specialists and manage them. He was a relentless boss. By 1900 Andrew Carnegie, who came to America as a poor immigrant boy, was the second richest man in the world. In 1901 he sold his steel property for nearly $500 million!

Brown Brothers

Andrew Carnegie came to America from Scotland and began work in the factories as a bobbin boy. How did this hard-working immigrant make his fortune?

Mass Production

The rapidly growing production of steel formed the foundations of an industrial system that would eventually make the United States the most productive country in the world. Besides rails, bridges, and steel-framed buildings, steel went into heavy machines, factories, and mills. Businesses expanded and factories grew larger. Owners and managers developed more efficient production methods.

You have read about Eli Whitney's development of interchangeable parts. This led to a **division of labor.** A shoemaker no longer made an entire shoe. Instead, in large shoe factories one worker might run a machine that cut only heels. Another might run a machine that cut out the soles, and so forth. All the parts were then brought together at a central place and assembled by still other workers into a shoe. Vast quantities of shoes could be made quickly in this way. Most American industries soon adopted division of labor. It made possible the **mass production** of large quantities of products of every kind.

"Black Gold"

An important new industry, **oil refining,** grew after the Civil War. Crude oil, or petroleum—a dark, thick ooze from the earth—had been known for hundreds of years. But little use had ever been made of it. In the 1850s Samuel M. Kier, a manufacturer in western Pennsylvania, began collecting the oil from local seepages and refining it into kerosene. Refining, like smelting, is a process of removing impurities from a raw material.

Kerosene was used to light lamps. It was a cheap substitute for whale oil, which was becoming harder to get and therefore more expensive. Soon there was a large demand for kerosene. People began to search for new supplies of petroleum.

The first oil well was drilled by E. L. Drake, a retired railroad conductor. In 1859 he began drilling in Titusville, Pennsylvania. The whole venture seemed so impractical and foolish that onlookers called it **"Drake's Folly."** But when he had drilled down about 70 feet (21 meters), Drake struck oil. His well began to yield 20 barrels of crude oil a day.

News of Drake's success brought oil prospectors to the scene. By the early 1860s these **wildcatters** were drilling for **"black gold"** all over western Pennsylvania. The boom rivaled the California gold rush of 1848 in its excitement and Wild West atmosphere. And it brought far more wealth to the prospectors than any gold rush.

At first oil was shipped to refineries in barrels. The barrel was replaced first by railroad tank cars and then by oil pipelines. Crude oil could be refined into many products. For some years kerosene continued to be the principal one. It was sold in grocery stores and door-to-door. In the 1880s refiners learned how to make other petroleum products such as waxes and lubricating oils for new industrial machines. The discovery of these oils and the invention by Elijah McCoy, the son of runaway slaves, of a lubricating cup that fed the oil to parts of a machine while it was operating were important industrial breakthroughs.

Not until the 1890s was petroleum used to make gasoline or heating oil. The development then of the internal combustion engine, which burned gasoline or diesel fuel, finally turned oil into one of the nation's major sources of power. By the turn of the century modern factories were turning to oil as their source of energy.

Return to the Preview & Review on page 659.

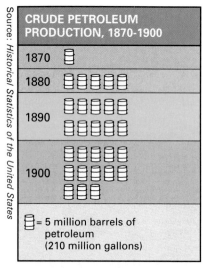

Source: *Historical Statistics of the United States*

CRUDE PETROLEUM PRODUCTION, 1870-1900

1870	
1880	
1890	
1900	

= 5 million barrels of petroleum (210 million gallons)

LEARNING FROM CHARTS. *Petroleum production boomed during the second half of the 19th century, as you can see from this chart. What were its main uses in American industry?*

2. THE COMMUNICATIONS REVOLUTION

The Telegraph and Telephone

Rapid, cheap communication over long distances is an essential part of modern industrial society. The **communications revolution** began in 1837 when Samuel F. B. Morse invented the **telegraph** to send electronic signals over wire. By 1861 telegraph lines connected all parts of the country. One line stretched all the way across the still-unsettled Great Plains to the Pacific Coast.

The telegraph made it possible for people to communicate over great distances in seconds. It took much of the guesswork out of business. Managers could know when supplies would arrive, where demand was greatest for their products, and what prices were being charged across the country.

In 1866 the Western Union Telegraph Company obtained control of the national telegraph network. The same year Cyrus W. Field succeeded in laying the first successful telegraph cable across the Atlantic Ocean to Europe. Not long after that, a telegraph network gave the United States almost instant communication with countries all over the world.

Next came the **telephone.** The telephone was invented in 1876 by Alexander Graham Bell, a teacher of the deaf in Boston. Work

Brown Brothers

Chicago Historical Society

Preview & Review

Use these questions to guide your reading. Answer the questions after completing Section 2. **Understanding Issues, Events, & Ideas.** Using the following words, summarize how inventions in the late 1800s changed the nation: communications revolution, telegraph, telephone, quadruplex telegraph, phonograph, electric light, suspension bridge, skyscraper, department store, chain store.

1. How did the communications revolution affect business?
2. How did Samuel F. B. Morse contribute to the communications revolution? How did Alexander Graham Bell contribute?
3. What did Thomas Edison say was the secret of his success as the great inventor of the era?
4. How did new marketing techniques help business grow?

Thinking Critically. It is 1880. Write and send a telegram to your family, telling them what you think is the most important invention of the late 1800s.

Cyrus Field, above, made the world a little smaller with his Atlantic cable. Mathew Brady was his photographer. Left is Alexander Graham Bell demonstrating a long-distance call from New York to Chicago for a group of businessmen in 1892.

with the deaf had led to the study of *acoustics,* the science of sound. His telephone turned sound waves into an electrical current. The current passed through a long wire and was then changed back into sound in a distant receiver.

Bell first demonstrated the telephone in 1876. When he offered Western Union the right to use his invention, the telegraph company turned him down. President William Orton of Western Union called the telephone an "electrical toy."

Fortunately, other people realized the telephone's usefulness. By 1880, 85 towns and cities had telephone systems. Five years later, more than 100 telephone companies were combined to create the American Telephone and Telegraph Company. Telephone wires soon wove spidery webs across the skies of America.

A web of wires—electric and telephone—crisscrosses Broadway in New York City. Perhaps no scene better illustrates the coming of the electrical age than this 1880s lithograph. But the wires came tumbling down when the wet snows fell during the Blizzard of 1888. Where are most electric and telephone lines in cities today?

Courtesy of The New York Historical Society

Edison National Historic Site, National Park Service, Department of the Interior

The Wizard of Menlo Park

In the same year that Bell invented the telephone, Thomas Alva Edison established the nation's first industrial research laboratory, at Menlo Park, New Jersey. Edison was the greatest inventor of the age. He was an inspired tinkerer and a hard worker, not a great thinker. "Sticking to it is the genius," he once said. He had only four years of off-and-on schooling.

Edison's first major invention, the **quadruplex telegraph,** was a machine that could send four messages over one wire at the same time. At Menlo Park he made several improvements on Bell's telephone. He invented the **phonograph** in 1877. But the **electric light** was his most important invention.

Using electricity to make light was not a new idea. In 1867 the boulevards of Paris were illuminated with arc lights. Arc lights, in which an electric discharge passed continuously between electrodes, were noisy and smoky. They could only be used outdoors. Edison was able to design a small light for indoors. His basic idea was to pass electricity through a fine wire inside an airless glass globe. The electricity heated the wire white hot, causing it to glow brightly. The wire could not burn up because there was no oxygen in the globe.

Edison spent two years experimenting with different filaments,

This photograph of Thomas Edison was taken on June 16, 1888, after he had spent an intense 72 hours at work on perfecting the phonograph. What did Edison say made him successful?

A biographer of Thomas Edison writes about what great expectations the public had for the inventor.

66On April 1 the *New York Daily Graphic* bannered: "Edison Invents a Machine that will Feed the Human Race—manufacturing Biscuits, Meat, Vegetables, and Wine out of Air, Water, and Common Earth." It was, of course, an April Fool's story, but other newspapers around the country picked it up and ran it straight. Nothing seemed impossible for a man who could make a machine that talked. . . .99

From *A Streak of Luck*, Robert Conot, 1979

or wires, that would glow for long periods without breaking. In December 1879 he found one. Soon "the Wizard of Menlo Park" was setting up city lighting companies and power stations to generate electricity and selling light bulbs by the millions. In 1900 only about 2 percent of America's manufacturing plants were powered by electricity. But soon it would join oil as the most important sources of energy for industry.

More American Inventiveness

The telegraph, the underwater cable, the telephone, and the discoveries of Thomas Edison were landmarks in the history of communications. But other important inventions and developments also reshaped American life. Engineers and architects tackled the most difficult problems. **Suspension bridges,** their roadways held by heavy cables, crossed broad bays and rivers. **Skyscrapers** poked their steel fingers into the sky. New machines for making cheap paper from wood pulp for printing newspapers, books, and magazines contributed to more effective communications. The typewriter, developed in the 1860s, and adding machine, invented in the 1870s, both soon became essential tools of American business. George Eastman's roll film and "Kodak" camera provided new forms of recreation as well as new techniques for industry and research.

Inventors of all races were caught up in the creative spirit. An African American inventor, Granville T. Woods, developed the automatic air brake for trains and was called "the greatest electrician in the world." Lewis Howard Latimer, who worked with both Bell and Edison, was the only African American member of the famous Edison Pioneers. That famous group of inventors issued a statement of their high regard upon his death in 1928.

66 It was Mr. Latimer who executed the drawings and assisted in the preparing the application for the telephone patents of Alexander Graham Bell. In 1880 he entered the employ of Hiram S. Maxim, Electrician of the United States Electric Lighting Co., then located at Bridgeport, Connecticut. It was while working in this employ that Mr. Latimer successfully produced a method of making carbon filaments for the Maxim electric incandescent lamp, which he patented. His keen perception of the possibilities of the electric light and kindred [related] industries resulted in his being the author of several other inventions. . . . Broadmindedness, versatility in the accomplishment of things intellectual and cultural, a linguist, a devoted husband and father, all were characteristic of him, and his genial presence will be missed from our gatherings.[1]99

[1]From "Statement of the Edison Pioneers," December 11, 1928

Courtesy of The Woolworth Corporation

Surely most Americans have shopped in the five- and ten-cent stores that spread across the country at the turn of the century. Pictured at left is the first Woolworth store, opened in 1879.

New Ways of Selling Products

Businesses came up with creative new ways to market their products. Just as factories and businesses grew bigger, so did stores. The small general store became less important. New types of stores arose to handle the ever-growing number of products.

The specialty store carried a single line of goods—hardware, clothing, groceries, shoes, and so forth. The **department store** combined many specialty stores under one roof. John C. Wanamaker opened the first department store in the United States in Philadelphia. Marshall Field opened another in Chicago in 1881. Soon others opened in larger cities.

Chain stores—stores with branches in many cities—also began to appear. The Great Atlantic and Pacific Tea Company (A & P) stores and Woolworth's were the first chain stores. Like department stores, they bought large quantities of goods at lower prices and passed the savings on to shoppers. And since women were both the major customers and commonly were paid less than men, managers gladly hired women as clerks.

Specialty stores, department stores, and chain stores were part of cities. In 1872, Aaron Montgomery Ward started a mail-order business aimed at the rural market. A few years later the Sears, Roebuck mail-order company started business. Customers received catalogs picturing goods for sale. They placed orders and paid for goods by mail; their goods were shipped to them by mail or railway express. Catalogs from the two companies became prized possessions in rural areas, helping bring the outside world to isolated parts of America.

Professional advertising also began to appear in the 1880s. It introduced new products and helped create large national markets for the streams of new manufactured products becoming available almost weekly. 🖎

Return to the Preview & Review on page 665.

Use these questions to guide your reading. Answer the questions after completing Section 3.

Understanding Issues, Events, & Ideas. Defend government regulation of big business, using the following words: entrepreneur, fixed cost, overhead, rebate, monopoly, pool, Standard Oil Company, trust, Interstate Commerce Act, regulatory agency, antitrust movement, interstate commerce, Sherman Antitrust Act, free enterprise.

1. In what ways were new American business leaders pioneers?
2. What practice did railroads use to reduce competition?
3. How did Rockefeller accomplish his objective of combining the country's oil refineries?
4. Why were the Interstate Commerce Act and Sherman Antitrust Act ineffective?

Thinking Critically. You are a farmer in a small "one-railroad town" in 1887. Write a letter to the Interstate Commerce Commission, complaining of the problems you are having.

3. REGULATION OF BIG BUSINESS

American Business Pioneers

The people who presided over new worlds of throbbing machines, noisy factories, and crowded cities were business leaders and financiers called **entrepreneurs.** They invested their money in new businesses. Although they varied greatly in personalities, abilities, and business methods, they were all pioneers. Some were rough, some were refined. All were eager to seize the seemingly unlimited opportunities of the new industrial world emerging around them. Some were fabulously successful. Others, the small business owners, never gained a huge fortune or power. But all of them—big-business leaders and small-business owners alike—shared the American ideal of self-reliant individualism. The men as well as the women of this group such as Nettie Fowler McCormick in farm machinery, Lydia Pinkham in patent medicine, and Kate Gleason in machine tools became the most influential people in America.

What motivated these people to take the risks of investing their money in business? See if you can feel his excitement as Andrew Carnegie describes receiving his first dividend:

66 Adams Express stock then paid monthly dividends of one per cent, and the first check for five dollars arrived. I can see it now, and I well remember the signature of 'J.C. Babcock, Cashier'. . . .

The next day being Sunday, we boys—myself and my ever-constant companions took our usual Sunday afternoon stroll in the country, and sitting down in the woods, I showed them this check, saying, 'Eureka! We have found it.'

Here was something new to all of us, for none of us had ever received anything except from toil. A return from capital was something strange and new.

How money could make money, how, without any attention from me, this mysterious golden visitor should come, led to much speculation upon the art of the young fellows, and I was for the first time called a 'capitalist.'

You see, I was beginning to serve my apprenticeship as a business man in a very satisfactory manner.[1] 99

Many of America's business leaders—Vanderbilt, Rockefeller, and others—told the same story: poor boy works hard and gets rich. Horatio Alger, Jr. made this "rags to riches" theme the most popular reading of the day. Alger, the son of a Massachusetts minister, had been the chaplain of a shelter for orphaned youth in New York City.

[1]From *The American Society* by Kenneth S. Lynn

He wrote over 130 books for boys, each preaching the rewards of hard work and good fortune. In his most famous, *Ragged Dick and Mark, the Match Boy*, he wrote:

> " 'I hope, my lad [said Mr. Whitney], you will prosper and rise in the world. You know in this free country poverty in early life is no bar to a man's advancement. I haven't risen very high myself,' he added, with a smile, 'but have met with moderate success in life; yet there was a time when I was as poor as you.'
>
> 'Were you, sir?' asked Dick, eagerly.
>
> 'Yes, my boy, I have known the time when I have been obliged to go without my dinner because I didn't have enough money to pay for it.'
>
> 'How did you get up in the world?' asked Dick, anxiously.
>
> . . .
>
> 'A taste for reading and study. During my leisure hours I improved myself by study, and acquired a large part of the knowledge which I now possess. Indeed, it was one of my books that first put me on the track of the invention, which I afterwards made. So you see, my lad, that my studious habits paid me in money, as well as in another way.
>
> 'I'm awful ignorant,' said Dick, soberly [seriously].
>
> 'But you are young, and, I judge, a smart boy. If you try to learn, you can, and if you ever expect to do anything in the world, you must know something of books.'
>
> 'I will,' said Dick, resolutely [determined]. 'I ain't always goin' to black boots for a livin'.'
>
> 'All labor is respectable, my lad, and you have no cause to be ashamed of any honest business; yet when you can get something to do that promises better for your future prospects, I advise you to do so. Till then earn your living in the way you are accustomed to, avoid extravagance, and save up a little money if you can.'[1] "

The new American hero was the successful entrepreneur. One minister even crossed the country telling people that "acres of diamonds" lay at their feet. He said, "It is your duty to get rich" and assured Americans that "Money is power, and you ought to be reasonably ambitious to have it." He preached his "gospel of wealth" over 6,000 times. The people heard his message.

The American economy began to shift into high gear. Fine transportation and communication networks had been completed. New sources of energy were developed and used to run the new machines of industry. Business leaders and investors created bigger businesses,

[1]From *Ragged Dick and Mark, the Match Boy* by Horatio Alger, Jr.

The Granger Collection, New York

This political cartoon is titled "A Tournament of Today—A Set To Between Labor and Monopoly." Which side represents monopoly? Which labor?

One observer of Industrial America called the period the "Great Barbecue." Everyone seemed to be rushing to get a share of the national inheritance. People were like hungry picnickers crowding around the roasting pit at one of the popular political outings of the time.

Yet one should not take too dark a view of Industrial America. At this time, perhaps more than any other, the American people showed their greatest vigor, imagination, and confidence in themselves and in the future of their country.

For some, especially the new arrivals from Eastern Europe and those crowded into teeming cities, this was an age of "survival of the fittest." This notion is sometimes called Social Darwinism, the argument that if left to themselves without government regulations or other restrictions, the most efficient would survive in every field—farming, commerce, industry. When a Yale student asked his professor, "Don't you believe in any government aid to industries?," the response was, "No! It's root, hog, or die."

A sugar baron added to the barnyard metaphor. "Let the buyer beware; that covers the whole business. You cannot wetnurse people from the time they are born until the time they die. They have to wade in and get stuck, and that is the way men are educated."

Fortunately few practical people held such extreme views. Yet the notion of Social Darwinism was sometimes used to excuse child labor, unregulated working conditions, and hands-off policies of government toward big business.

and developed new methods of producing, distributing, and selling their products and services. Everywhere it seemed that creative Americans were improving ways of doing things. Businesses, both agricultural and industrial, sprang up throughout the land, each playing its part in the ever-expanding, interlocking economic system.

Competition Among the Railroads

The railroad industry had extremely heavy **fixed costs.** Track and stations had to be maintained. Cars had to be cleaned and painted. It cost almost as much to run an empty train as one crowded with passengers or freight. These fixed costs, or **overhead,** were the same whether business was good or bad.

To attract more business, railroads often used what was called "cutthroat competition"—using any means to shoulder aside rival companies. Railroads often reduced rates. Between February and July 1869 the cost of sending 100 pounds (45 kilograms) of wheat from Chicago to New York fell from $1.80 to 25 cents.

Railroads also gave large shippers illegal kickbacks called **rebates.** In return for their business they would give these shippers lower rates than those charged their smaller competitors. In this way railroad competition was a force leading to **monopoly** in other fields. Monopoly is the total control of a product, service, or trade in a region.

Sometimes railroads tried to make up for low, competitive rates by charging high rates for shipping goods from places where no other railroad existed. It often cost more to ship a product from a small "one-railroad town" a short distance from the market than from a large city much farther away. This "long haul" versus "short haul" pricing also led to monopoly because it favored producers in large cities where railroads competed for traffic.

Railroads tried to reduce competition by making agreements called **pools.** Those who joined the pool agreed to divide up available business and charge a common price for shipments. Pools rarely worked very long. Whenever business fell off, the railroads could not resist the temptation to cut rates. There was no way to enforce pooling agreements when individual companies broke them.

John D. Rockefeller

Most industries were eager to keep business steady and to avoid costly struggles for customers. A new way of doing this was developed in the oil industry by John D. Rockefeller. The method helped Rockefeller become the richest man in the United States, possibly in the entire world.

Rockefeller was born in Richford, New York, in 1839. After

Culver Pictures

This photograph of John D. Rockefeller brings to mind the lines of Edward Arlington Robinson: "He was a gentleman from sole to crown, / Clean-favored, and imperially slim." Do you think a man can be deeply religious and at the same time a deadly competitor, as Rockefeller was said to be?

making a modest fortune in the wholesale food business in Cleveland, he decided to go into the oil business. He bought his first refinery in 1865. In 1870 he organized the **Standard Oil Company.** Soon he expanded from refining into drilling for oil and selling kerosene and other oil-based products to consumers. By the late 1870s Rockefeller controlled 90 percent of the oil business in the United States.

Rockefeller was a deeply religious person. Even before he became wealthy, he made large contributions to charity. But he was a deadly competitor. He forced railroads to give him rebates on his huge oil shipments. He sold below cost in particular communities to steal business from local refiners. Then he gave the refiners a choice: sell out to Standard Oil or face bankruptcy. He hired spies and paid bribes to informers to tell secrets about other refiners' activities.

Rockefeller was also an excellent businessman. His plants were so efficient that he could undersell competitors and still make sizable profits. He detested waste. He kept close track of every detail of Standard Oil's complicated affairs.

Rockefeller wanted to buy all the refineries in the country and combine them. Then the industry could develop without petty business squabbles. He always gave competitors a chance to join Standard Oil. Only if they refused did he destroy them.

The man who designed Rockefeller's supercompany was Samuel C. T. Dodd. Dodd's creation was called a **trust**—a legal agreement under which several companies group together to regulate production and eliminate competition. To do this, stockholders of the separate oil companies turned their stock over to a group of directors called trustees. By controlling the stock of all the companies in the supercompany, the trustees could control the industry.

The Antitrust Movement

The trust idea soon spread to other businesses. By 1900 almost every branch of manufacturing was dominated by a small number of large producers. The size and power of these trusts alarmed many Americans. They were afraid that the trusts would destroy small companies and cheat consumers by charging high prices once competition had been eliminated. In the following excerpt from his article, one journalist warned Americans of what he called "the dangers of the age of combination:"

    “ On the theory of 'too much of everything' our industries, from railroads to workingmen, are being organized to prevent milk, nails, lumber, freights, labor, soothing syrup, and all these other things from becoming too cheap. The majority have never yet been able to buy enough of anything. The minority have too much of everything to sell. Seeds of social trouble germinate fast in such conditions. Society is letting these combinations become institutions without compelling them to adjust their charges to the cost of production, which used to be the universal rule of price. . . . The change from competition to combination is nothing less than one of those revolutions which march through history with giant strides. . . .[1]"

Rockefeller, the leader most responsible for business combinations, often defended the practice. His defense was simple. He was in business to make money, and combinations were more profitable. He told a government commission:

" *Question.* What are . . . the chief advantages [of] industrial combinations?

Answer. It is too late to argue about the advantages of industrial combinations. They are a necessity. And if Americans are to have the privilege of extending their business in all the states of the Union, and into foreign countries as well, they are a necessity on a large scale, and require the agency of more than one corporation. Their chief advantages are:

(1) Command of necessary capital.

(2) Extension of limits of business.

(3) Increase in the number of people interested in business.

(4) Economy in business.

(5) Improvements and economies which are derived from knowledge of many interested persons of wide experience.

(6) Power to give the public improved products at less prices and still make a profit for stockholders.

(7) Permanent work and good wages for laborers. . . .

I speak from experience. . . . Our first combination was a partnership and afterwards a corporation in Ohio. That was sufficient for a local refining business. But dependent solely upon local business we should have failed years ago. We were forced to extend our markets and to seek for export trade.

We soon discovered as the business grew that the primary method of transporting oil in barrels could not last. . . . Hence we . . . adopted the pipe-line system, and found capital for pipe-line construction. . . . To perfect the pipe-line system required fifty millions in capital. This could not be obtained or maintained without industrial combination.
. . .

[1]From "Lords of Industry," by Henry D. Lloyd in *North American Review*, CXXXVIII (June 1884)

Every step taken was necessary in the business if it was to be properly developed, and only through successive steps and by such an industrial combination is America to-day enabled to utilize the bounty which its land pours forth, and to furnish the world with the best and cheapest light ever known.[1] **99**

The demand for government regulation of the economy increased steadily. The first target was the railroad industry. In 1887 Congress passed the **Interstate Commerce Act.** This law stated that railroad rates must be "reasonable and just." Rates must be made public and could not be changed without public notice. Pools, rebates, and other unfair practices were declared unlawful. To oversee the affairs of railroads and to hear complaints from shippers, the law created the Interstate Commerce Commission (ICC), a board of experts. This was the first of the many **regulatory agencies**—government commissions charged with protecting the public interest—that came to control so many aspects of American life.

The ICC had to overcome many difficulties. The Interstate Commerce Act was vague. How was it possible to decide what a "reasonable and just" freight rate was? The Commission did not have a large enough staff to handle the more than 1,000 complaints it received in its first few months of operation. Nor did the Commission have the power to enforce its decisions. It could only sue violating railroads in court. Of the 16 cases it brought to trial between 1887 and 1905, it won only 1.

The Interstate Commerce Act was supposed to *regulate* competition—that is, to make certain that railroads did not cheat the public. It did not attempt to *control* the size of any railroad company. The way of dealing with the monopoly problem was to break up large businesses into smaller businesses which would compete with one another. This approach was called the **antitrust movement.**

In the late 1880s several states tried to restore competition by passing laws prohibiting trusts. These laws were difficult to enforce because industrial combinations usually did business in more than one state. Under the Constitution only the federal government could regulate such **interstate commerce.**

Then, in 1890, Congress passed the **Sherman Antitrust Act.** This law banned combinations "in the form of trust or otherwise" that restricted interstate trade or commerce. Anyone "who shall monopolize, or attempt to monopolize" such commerce could be fined or sent to jail for up to a year. This law was also difficult to enforce. It did not define "restraint of trade" or monopoly. Every attempt the government made to break up a trust resulted in a lawsuit.

[1]From "Report of the United States Industrial Commission, I," December 30, 1899 in *Government and the American Economy, 1870-Present* by Thomas G. Manning and David M. Potter

The Granger Collection, New York

The courts usually sided with the business combinations. The first important Supreme Court case involving the Sherman Act was *U.S. v. E. C. Knight Co.* (1895). It involved an attempt to break up the American Sugar Refining Company. This trust had obtained control of about 90 percent of the sugar refining of the country by buying up four competing companies. The Court ruled that this combination was not illegal because it did not restrain trade. Since the trust refined its sugar in one state, interstate commerce was not involved. How it could dispose of all its sugar without selling it in many different states, the Court did not say.

The Interstate Commerce Act and the Sherman Antitrust Act had little effect on big business at this time. Most judges still put great stress on the right of individuals to run their affairs more or less as they pleased. Nevertheless, these two laws were extremely important. Both are still in effect and have been greatly strengthened over time. They established the practice of the federal government attempting to control the way American companies do business. After 1890 totally **free enterprise** was diminished in the United States. Free enterprise is the private operation of business with no government interference. The Industrial Revolution had made the power of business so great that some public control over business practices came to be increasingly accepted. 🖅

When Congress began to debate the Sherman Antitrust Act, Joseph Keppler drew this cartoon for Puck, *a popular humor magazine. Titled "Bosses of the Senate," the cartoon shows bloated trusts symbolized by bulging money bags entering the Senate through a door marked "Monopolists." The "People's Entrance" at the left is padlocked shut. With what opinion of the Senate does this artist leave us?*

Return to the Preview & Review on page 670.

Regulation of Big Business   677

Understanding Issues, Events, & Ideas. Explain how industrial growth affected American workers in the 1800s. Use the following words: specialization, Knights of Labor, strike, Haymarket bombing, American Federation of Labor, bread and butter issue, collective bargaining, Homestead Strike, lockout, yellow-dog contract, blacklist.

1. Why was the Knights of Labor organized? How was it changed under the leadership of Terence Powderly?
2. Who were the members of the American Federation of Labor?
3. What caused the Homestead Strike? How did Henry Frick respond? What was the outcome?

Thinking Critically. Imagine that you are a worker in a large factory in 1900. Describe your typical day at work, and explain how the increased use of machines has affected your job.

4. WORKERS AND WORK

Specialization

Post-Civil War industrial changes also greatly affected the men and women who worked in the factories of the United States. Division of labor changed the way things were made. Factory jobs became steadily more specialized. More and more workers tended machines. Usually they performed one task over and over, hundreds of times each day. In a steel plant, for example, some laborers shoveled coke and ore. Others loaded furnaces. Still others moved the finished steel. No single worker could make steel alone. This division of labor was called **specialization.**

Machines greatly increased the amount a worker could produce. This tended to raise wages and lower prices. Machines brought more goods within the reach of the average family. But they made work less interesting because it took little skill to operate most machines.

Manufacturing corporations grew larger and larger. In 1850 Cyrus McCormick's reaper manufacturing plant in Chicago employed 150 workers. By 1900 it had 4,000.

Such large factories had to be run like armies. The boards of directors were the generals. They set policy and appointed the people who carried it out. Next in the chain of command were the plant superintendents. Like the colonels of regiments, they were responsible for actually running the operation. They issued instructions to the foremen of the various departments, who were like army sergeants. The foremen in turn issued orders to the men and women who did the actual work.

LABOR FORCE BY SEX AND AGE*, 1870-1900					
YEAR	TOTAL LABOR FORCE	SEX		AGE	
		Male	Female	10-15 Years	16 and Older
1870	12,925	11,008	1,917	765	12,160
1880	17,392	14,745	2,647	1,118	16,274
1890	23,318	19,313	4,006	1,504	21,814
1900	27,640	22,641	4,999	4,064**	23,576†

* in thousands of workers
** 16 to 19 Years
† 20 and Older

Source: *Historical Statistics of the United States*

LEARNING FROM TABLES. *One of the most important needs of American business and industry was a large labor force. This chart contains data about those workers. In what ways did the labor force change between 1870 and 1900?*

Bettmann Archives

Factory workers by the hundreds use lathes and presses to create their product. What do you suppose the wires are for? What hazards do you see in this workplace?

These workers were expected to follow orders as obediently as army privates. In a Rochester, New York, carriage factory each worker had a number. To get a drink of water, a worker had to get the foreman's permission. To make sure that the rule was followed, the water faucets were locked up. In a Massachusetts tannery, guards patrolled the shop and reported any worker who talked during the workday. These were extreme examples. Workers hated all such rules. Many did not meekly submit to them. Instead, they sought ways to get around overly strict regulations.

Conditions in the clothing industries often were among the worst. In cities like New York and Chicago much of the work was done in "sweatshops," with the labor done mostly by women and children. Imagine the lives of those who toiled in the shop described in this excerpt.

❝ The *sweat-shop* is a place where, separate from the tailor-shop or clothing-warehouse, a "sweater" (middleman) assembles journeymen tailors and needle-women to work under his supervision. He takes a cheap room outside the dear [expensive] and crowded business center, and within the neighborhood where the work-people live. Thus is rent saved to the employer, and time and travel to the employed. The men can do work more hours than was possible under the centralized system [in a factory], and their wives and children can help. . . . For this service, at the prices paid, they cannot earn more than twenty-five to forty cents a day, and the work is largely done by Italian, Polish, and Bohemian women and girls. . . .

Girls, hand-sewers, earn nothing for the first month, then as unskilled workers they get $1 to $1.50 a week, $3 a week, and (as skilled workers) $6 a week. . . .

The 'sweat-shop' day is ten hours; but many take work home to get in overtime; and occasionally the shops themselves are kept open for extra work, from which the hardest and ablest workers sometimes make $14 to $16 a week. . . . The average weekly living expenses of a man and wife, with two children . . . are as follows: Rent (three or four small rooms), $2; food, fuel, and light, $4; clothing, $2; and beer and spirits, $1. . . .

A city ordinance enacts that rooms provided for workmen shall contain space equal to five hundred cubic feet of air for each person employed; but in the average 'sweat-shop' only about a tenth of that quantity is found. In one such place there were fifteen men and women in one room, which contained also a pile of mattresses on which some of the men sleep at night. The closets [toilets] are disgraceful. In an adjoining room were piles of clothing, made and unmade, on the same table with the food of the family. Two dirty children were playing about the floor. . . .[1]"

Unionization

In part because large corporations had so much power over their labor force, more workers began to join unions after the Civil War. This was especially true of skilled workers. In 1869 the **Knights of Labor** was founded in Philadelphia by Uriah Stephens, a tailor. At first it was a secret organization, with an elaborate ritual. Soon it expanded and began to work openly to organize workers into a "great brotherhood." By 1879 the Knights claimed to have 9,000 members. In that year Terence V. Powderly, a Pennsylvania machinist and one-time mayor of Scranton, Pennsylvania, became its head.

Under Powderly the Knights admitted women, African Americans, immigrants, and unskilled workers. This was a radical step. Most unions would not accept these workers. But Isaac Myers, the leading African American labor leader of the time, told the group: "American citizenship for the black man is a complete failure if he is proscribed [barred] from the workshops of the country." After his speech a majority of the delegates voted to admit all workers to the union. The Knights advocated the eight-hour workday and strict regulation of trusts. They hoped to avoid **strikes,** the refusal of laborers to work until their demands are met. Cooperation between

[1]From "Among the Poor of Chicago" by Joseph Kirkland in *The Poor in the Great Cities*

Collection, Lee Baxandall, Laurie Platt Winfrey, Inc.

owners, workers, and consumers should be possible, Powderly insisted.

Powderly was a good speechmaker but a very poor administrator. He had little patience with anyone who disagreed with him. He tried to supervise every detail of the union's business.

In the 1880s local leaders of the Knights organized and won several important strikes against railroads. Membership soared. By 1886, 700,000 workers belonged to the organization. This was more than the central leadership could manage. Local units called strikes, which failed. Workers became discouraged and dropped out of the union.

Then the Knights were blamed, quite unfairly, for a terrible bombing incident in Haymarket Square in Chicago in 1886. When the police tried to break up a meeting called by radicals during a strike, someone threw a bomb that killed seven policemen. Public opinion turned against unions after the **Haymarket bombing.** Thousands of workers dropped out of the Knights of Labor as a result.

In 1881, long before the Knights of Labor began to decline, representatives of a number of craft unions founded the Federation of Organized Trades and Labor Unions of the United States and Canada. In 1886 this group changed its name to the **American Federation of Labor** (AFL).

The AFL was led by Samuel Gompers, a cigar maker. Unlike the Knights, the AFL was made up exclusively of skilled workers, organized by particular crafts such as printers, bricklayers, and plumbers. The AFL concentrated on **bread and butter issues**—higher

Angry workers bring their grievances to the top-hatted factory owner in "The Strike" by Robert Koehler. Use historical imagination to tell what argument is making tempers flare.

He may look like a sheriff sent to break up a strike, but this is Samuel Gompers, head of the AFL. The photograph was taken during a drive to organize West Virginia coal miners. Report on any accounts of strikes you may find in today's newspapers.

The George Meany Archives, AFL-CIO

Workers and Work   681

wages, shorter hours, better working conditions. The way to obtain these benefits, Gompers and other leaders of the AFL insisted, was **collective bargaining** with employers. In collective bargaining union officials, representing the workers, negotiate with management about wages, working conditions, and other aspects of employment. If negotiation fails, workers may strike to support union demands.

The Homestead Strike

One of the most violent strikes in American history involved an AFL union, the Amalgamated Association of Iron and Steel Workers. In the early 1890s the Amalgamated was the most powerful union in the country. It had 24,000 dues-paying members. Some worked at the Carnegie steel plant in Homestead, Pennsylvania. In 1892, when the company reduced wages because of a slump in its business, the union called a strike.

Carnegie was in Scotland when the **Homestead Strike** began. The company was being run by one of his partners, Henry Clay Frick. Frick was a tough executive and a bitter opponent of unions. He decided to resist the strike and to try to destroy the Amalgamated with a **lockout**. With Carnegie's approval he closed the mill. He then announced that he would hire strikebreakers—nonunion workers—and reopen the Homestead mill. To protect the new workers, he hired private police from the Pinkerton Detective Agency, a company known to specialize in strikebreaking.

The Pinkerton Agency sent 300 armed men—Pinkertons—to Homestead. They approached the plant on barges on the Monongahela River in the dead of night. The strikers had been warned of their coming. They met them at the docks with gunfire and dynamite. A small-scale war broke out. When it ended, seven Pinkertons and nine strikers were dead. The governor of Pennsylvania then sent 8,000 National Guard troops to Homestead to keep the peace. The strike went on for more than four months. Finally the union gave up the struggle. The workers went back to the plant on Frick's terms.

Frick won the contest, but public opinion turned against him. Then a Russian immigrant, Alexander Berkman, attacked Frick in his Homestead office. To protest the use of Pinkertons, Berkman shot Frick three times in the neck and shoulder. He then stabbed him once in the leg and after that tried to chew a percussion capsule, an explosive device, which guards pried from his mouth. Frick survived, Berkman went to prison, and the public's attitude softened.

Employers looked for ways to keep their workers from forming or joining unions. Some used **yellow-dog contracts,** a written agreement not to join a union. An employee who broke the contract was fired. Others used **blacklists.** These were lists of workers who were members of unions and therefore undesirable employees. Blacklisted workers often found it impossible to get jobs.

Return to the Preview & Review on page 678.

5. THE GROWTH OF CITIES

Preview & Review

Use these questions to guide your reading. Answer the questions after completing Section 5.
Understanding Issues, Events, & Ideas. Use the following words to describe how American cities changed between 1860 and 1900: Gilded Age, Statue of Liberty, ethnic neighborhood, New Immigration, literacy test, Chinese Exclusion Act, settlement house, Hull House, cable car, electric trolley, Brooklyn Bridge.
1. How did the immigrants coming to the United States after the 1880s differ from those who had come earlier?
2. How were Chinese immigrants treated? Mexican immigrants?
3. What problems were faced by cities during their rapid growth? What were some solutions?
Thinking Critically. In 1890 you arrive in New York City from Poland. Write a letter to your cousin back home, describing your new life in the United States.

The New Immigration

About three quarters of the workers in the Carnegie steel mills had been born in Europe. Like most immigrants, including Carnegie himself, they had come to America to find work. To millions of poor people in other parts of the world, industrial expansion had made the United States seem like the pot of gold at the end of the rainbow. Mark Twain used a similar metaphor when he called this era the **Gilded Age.** The surface was dazzling, but only base metal lay below.

It was as though the country were an enormous magnet drawing people into it from every direction. Between 1860 and 1900 about 14 million immigrants arrived. Most settled in large cities. In 1880, 87 percent of the residents of Chicago were either immigrants or the children of immigrants. The situation was similar in New York, San Francisco, Milwaukee, Cleveland, Boston, and most other cities.

Before the 1880s most immigrants had come from western and northern Europe, especially from England, Ireland, Germany, and the Scandinavian countries. We have already noted that established Americans frequently resented the newcomers of this ''Old Immigration.'' However, people from western Europe had certain advantages that helped them to adjust in their new homeland. British and Irish immigrants spoke English. Many German immigrants were well educated and skilled in one or another useful trade. Scandinavians were experienced farmers and often came with enough money to buy land in the West. Except for the Irish, most of these immigrants were Protestants, as were most Americans.

In the 1880s the trend of immigration changed. Thousands of Italians, Poles, Hungarians, Greeks, and Russians flocked in. People believed in the golden dream of opportunity. America was the ''golden door.'' One Jewish girl living in Russia, 13 years old at the time, waited for her father already in America to send for the family. When the letter arrived, she wrote:

> 66 So at last I was going to America! Really, really going, at last! The boundaries burst. The arch of heaven soared. A million suns shone out for every star. The winds rushed in from outer space, roaring in my ears, 'America! America!'[1] 99

The trip to America was still a trial. But all were buoyed by hopes of a better life. Anzia Yezierska, a sixteen-year-old Jewish girl from Poland, remembered:

> 66 [We traveled in] steerage [the cheapest section of the ship] dirty bundles—foul odors—seasick humanity—but I saw and

[1]From *The Promised Land* by Mary Antin

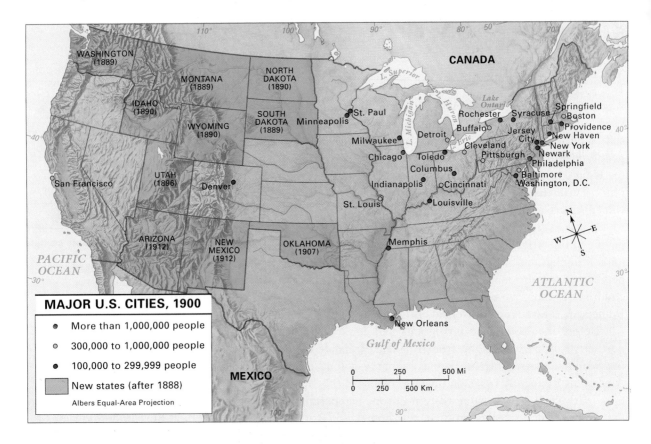

MAJOR U.S. CITIES, 1900

- ● More than 1,000,000 people
- ◉ 300,000 to 1,000,000 people
- ● 100,000 to 299,999 people
- ▢ New states (after 1888)

Albers Equal-Area Projection

LEARNING FROM MAPS. *The second half of the 19th century saw the growth of many of America's largest cities. Still, even by 1900 few of the largest cities are west of the Mississippi River. Why do you think this is true?*

heard nothing of the foulness and ugliness around me. I floated in showers of sunshine; visions upon visions of the new world opened before me.

From lips to lips flowed the golden legend of the golden country:

'In America you can say what you feel—you can join your friends in open streets without fear. . . .'

'In America is a home for everybody. The land is your land. . . .'

'Everybody is with everybody alike in America. . . .'

'Everybody can do what he wants with his life in America. . . .'

'Plenty for all. Learning flows free like milk and honey.'[1] **99**

After 1886 the immigrants' first sight of America was often the **Statue of Liberty.** At the base of the statue were the words written by the poet Emma Lazarus:

66 Give me your tired, your poor,
     Your huddled masses yearning to breathe free,

[1] From *Hungry Hearts* by Anzia Yezierska

Museum of the City of New York

The colossal Statue of Liberty raises the torch of freedom in New York Harbor. It was first known as "Liberty Enlightening the World." Here we see the dedication of the magnificent gift from France. The sculptor, F. A. Bartholdi, wished to pay tribute to the alliance of France with the American colonies during the Revolution. What does the statue symbolize today?

> The wretched refuse of your teeming shore,
> Send these the homeless, tempest-tossed, to me:
> I lift my lamp beside the golden door. . . . "

But although America was a vast improvement in most cases, it had a hard time living up to the dreams of most immigrants. Their first experiences were not what they had expected. Anzia Yezierska wrote:

" Between the buildings that loomed like mountains, we struggled with our bundles. . . . Up Broadway, under the bridge, and through the swarming streets of the ghetto [a segregated neighborhood], we followed Gedalyeh Mindel [a friend].

I looked about the narrow streets of squeezed-in stores and houses, ragged clothes, dirty bedding oozing out of the windows, ashcans and garbage cans cluttering the sidewalks. A vague sadness pressed down on my heart—the first doubt of America.[1] "

[1] From *Hungry Hearts* by Anzia Yezierska

The Growth of Cities   685

For many immigrants it was sail the crowded ships to America or starve. The author of *The Fitzgeralds and the Kennedys* explains the Irish exodus

❝As anybody who knows the history of Ireland knows, the potato failed. . . . The failure of four successive crops sentenced one out of every six peasants to death by starvation and forced more than a quarter of the Irish population to emigrate. . . . Before the Great Famine, as it came to be called, the Irish had regarded the idea of leaving their country as the most appalling of fates. But now, terrified and desperate in the wake of starvation and fever, they made their way out of Ireland by the tens of thousands. . . . burrowing their way onto the great "coffin ships," so named because of the great numbers who died on board. . . .❞

Doris Kearns Goodwin, 1987

Most immigrants were indeed poor. They had little or no education and no special skills. They knew no English. Their habits and cultures were very different from those of native-born Americans. The majority were Roman or Greek Orthodox Catholics or Jews.

Many of these immigrants came from areas where money was seldom used. People there exchanged food for cloth, a cow for a wagon, and so on. It was difficult for such people to adjust to life in a large industrial city. Most took the lowest-paid jobs. Whole families toiled to earn enough to survive. As Yezierska recalled:

❝I felt a strangling in my throat as I neared the sweatshop prison; all my nerves screwed together into iron hardness to endure the day's torture.

For an instant I hesitated as I faced the grated window of the old dilapidated building—dirt and decay cried out from every crumbling brick.

In the maw of the shop, raging around me the roar and the clatter, the clatter and the roar, the merciless grind of the pounding machines. Half maddened [crazy], half deadened, I struggled to think, to feel, to remember—what I am—who am I—why was I here?

I struggled in vain—bewildered and lost in a whirlpool of noise.

'America—America—where was America?' it cried in my heart.[1]❞

The immigrants from each country or district tended to cluster together in the same city neighborhood. In 1890 a New York reporter wrote that a map of the city showing where different nationalities lived would have "more stripes than the skin of a zebra, and more colors than any rainbow." These **ethnic neighborhoods** were like cities within cities. They offered people newly arrived in the strange new world of America a chance to hold on to a few fragments of the world they had left. There the immigrants could find familiar foods, people who spoke their language, churches and clubs based on old-country models.

Many native-born Americans resented this **New Immigration.** They insisted that the newcomers were harder to assimilate, or "Americanize" than earlier generations. Workers were disturbed by the new immigrants' willingness to work long hours for low wages. American Protestants believed the mass immigration would weaken their political and social clout. A new nativist organization, the American Protective Association, blamed the hard times of the 1890s on immigration. Nativists charged that the new immigrants were physically and mentally inferior. They were dangerous radicals, the nativists said, who wanted to destroy American democratic institutions.

[1]From *Hungry Hearts* by Anzia Yezierska

Museum of the City of New York

"The Battery, New York" was painted about 1855 by Samuel B. Waugh. This detail shows a shipful of immigrants arriving in New York. Immigrants were processed at Castle Garden, at the left in the background. Why did some Americans resent the new immigration?

One poet expressed these fears in this excerpt.

> " Wide open and unguarded stand our gates,
>   And through them presses a wild motley throng—
>   Men from the Volga and the Tartar steppes [Russia],
>   Featureless figures from the Hwang Ho [China],
>   Malayan, Scythian [Greek], Teuton [German], Celt [Irish],
>   and Slav,
>   Flying the Old World's poverty and scorn;
>   These bringing with them unknown gods and rites,
>   Those, tiger passions, here to stretch their claws,
>   In street and alley what strange tongues are loud. . . .[1] "

In the 1890s the Immigration Restriction League called for a law preventing anyone who could not read and write some language from entering the country. The League knew that such a **literacy test** would keep out many immigrants from southern and eastern Europe. In that part of the world many regions did not have public school systems.

Congress passed a literacy test bill in 1897, but President Grover Cleveland vetoed it. He insisted that America should continue to be a place of refuge for the world's poor and persecuted. Many

[1]From "Unguarded Gates" by Thomas Bailey Aldrich in *The Works of Thomas Bailey Aldrich, Poems, vol. II*

The Growth of Cities   687

STRATEGIES FOR SUCCESS

READING A TABLE

Tables, like charts, are ways visually to organize statistics. (Review the strategy on page 558.) Tables are most often used to show the changes in numbers over time. In a table, statistics are usually listed side-by-side in columns for easy reference. Effectively using a statistical table can tell you a great deal about a particular topic.

How to Read a Statistical Table

To read a statistical table, follow these guidelines.

1. **Note the title.** As in all graphics, the title of a table will tell you the subject for which statistics are given. Remember that all the numbers are related in some way to the subject of the table. Part of the skill of reading a table is understanding how all its parts are related. (As with charts, be sure to read any footnotes or other special notes.)
2. **Read the headings.** Quickly skimming the headings will show you how the data is organized and into what categories it has been divided.
3. **Study the information.** Read across each row. Note the statistical trends.
4. **Apply critical thinking skills.** Compare the numbers. Ask questions about the trends. Form hypotheses, make inferences, and draw conclusions.

Applying the Strategy

Study the statistical table above. It provides population statistics for major United States cities for three years—1860, 1880, and 1900. Note that these are at 20-year intervals. Why do you think that is so? The equal intervals give you a clearer picture of the rate of growth than random years

GROWTH OF MAJOR U.S. CITIES, 1860–1900

City	1860	1880	1900
New York City	1,174,800	1,912,000	3,437,000
Philadelphia	565,500	847,000	1,294,000
Boston	177,800	363,000	561,000
Baltimore	212,400	332,000	509,000
Cincinnati	161,000	255,000	326,000
St. Louis	160,800	350,000	575,000
Chicago	109,300	503,000	1,698,000

might. As you read across each row you can see how the population of a given city changed. New York City grew from 1,174,800 to 3,437,000 during that time period. Reading down the columns allows you to compare the statistics among the cities. In 1880 847,000 people lived in Philadelphia while 255,000 lived in Cincinnati. Based on what you have read in *The Story of America*, what is one reason why Philadelphia was larger than Cincinnati in 1880? Can you think of other reasons? Studying the chart as a whole gives you the opportunity to note trends and ask questions. What generalizations can you state about the growth of United States cities in the second half of the 19th century based on the seven cities in this table? Note that all the cities more than doubled in population between 1860 and 1900. Which ones grew the fastest? Note that Chicago grew much faster than Baltimore. Why do you think that happened? What other trends do you notice? Which ones can you explain from your reading of *The Story of America* and other books on American history?

For independent practice, see Practicing the Strategy on page 694.

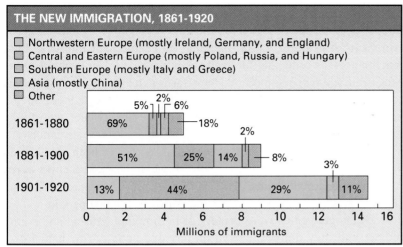

THE NEW IMMIGRATION, 1861-1920

☐ Northwestern Europe (mostly Ireland, Germany, and England)
☐ Central and Eastern Europe (mostly Poland, Russia, and Hungary)
☐ Southern Europe (mostly Italy and Greece)
☐ Asia (mostly China)
☐ Other

1861-1880: 69%, 5%, 2%, 6%, 18%
1881-1900: 51%, 25%, 14%, 2%, 8%
1901-1920: 13%, 44%, 29%, 3%, 11%

Millions of immigrants (0 to 16)

Source: *Historical Statistics of the United States*

LEARNING FROM GRAPHS. *Before 1900, most immigrants to the United States came from Northwestern Europe, particularly England, Ireland, and Germany. In the last decades of the 1800s, the proportion of immigrants from this region began to decline. By the early part of the 20th century, Northwestern Europe accounted for only a small share of newcomers to America. According to the graph, from which regions did most immigrants come after 1900?*

employers opposed any check on immigration for less humane reasons. They knew that unlimited immigration would assure them a steady force of low-paid but hard-working laborers.

Congress *did* exclude one type of immigrant during this period—the Chinese. By 1880 there were about 75,000 Chinese immigrants in California. They were extremely hard-working people. Most were Buddhists, a religion little understood in America. Because of language and cultural differences, the Chinese tended even more than most immigrants to stick together. They seemed unwilling to try American ways. Older residents feared and resented them. When a depression swept the country, California workers worried that Chinese workers would steal their jobs at lower wages. In 1882 Congress responded to the demands of Californians by passing the **Chinese Exclusion Act.** It prohibited Chinese workers from entering the United States for a period of ten years. Later the ban was extended. It was not lifted until 1965.

By 1900 about 80,000 Mexicans had emigrated to the United States. Increasingly they provided the labor force that developed the southwestern part of the nation. Unlike most other immigrants, these newcomers seldom settled in large cities. Many had to move continually from place to place. They encountered many social, economic, and political handicaps. Yet Mexican American communities survived and even thrived, strengthened by their cultural traditions and community life. Some Mexican Americans found jobs as laborers building the Southern Pacific and Santa Fe Railroads. When the lines were completed, they became section hands—men whose job it was to maintain the railroad right-of-way and repair damaged tracks and ties. Many families had to live in railroad boxcars. Other Mexican immigrants worked as cowhands on cattle ranches. Still others became farm laborers. Like so many immigrants, most were poorly paid and oftentimes badly treated.

66Not everyone was equally poor. When an immigrant family could occupy a two- or three-room apartment without several boarders, they were considered lucky. Boarders were a natural institution, particularly in the early years when most immigrants came without their families. But even the privilege of being a boarder was not enjoyed by every greenhorn.

There were various categories of boarders. A star boarder slept on a folding bed. But I knew a printer who every night unscrewed a door, put it on two chairs; he couldn't pay as much as the one who had the bed.99

From *The World of Our Fathers,* Irving Howe, 1976

Problems of City Life

American agriculture was expanding with American industry. But machinery was reducing the need for human labor on farms. Cyrus McCormick's reapers and other new farm machines were displacing thousands of farmhands who had previously plowed, planted, hoed, and harvested the nation's crops. For every city dweller who took up the plow between 1860 and 1900, 20 farmers moved to the city.

The growth of cities after the Civil War was both rapid and widespread. In 1860 places like Denver, Memphis, and Seattle were no more than small towns. By 1900 they were major urban centers. In that same year there were 50 cities of over 100,000 people.

The largest cities were centers of both manufacturing and commerce, and they did not depend on any one activity for their prosperity. Some smaller cities specialized in making a particular product. Dayton, Ohio, manufactured cash registers. Minneapolis, Minnesota, became a flour-milling center.

People moved to cities far more rapidly than housing and other facilities could be built to care for their needs. City land values soared. A New York City lot selling for $80 in the early 1840s sold for $8,000 in 1880. Because of the high cost of property, builders put up tenement apartments on plots only 25 feet (about 8 meters) wide. They were crowded so closely together that light and moving air were blocked out.

A five- or six-story tenement usually had four apartments on each floor. Front apartments contained four rooms, rear apartments three. Many of the rooms had no windows. In most cases two families had to share a single toilet located in a dark and narrow hallway. Dark, musty, garbage-cluttered ''air shafts'' separated one tenement building from the next. One resident described the air shaft of his tenement to the New York State Tenement House Commission in 1900:

66 **The Secretary:** How long have you lived in tenement houses?

Mr. Moscowitz: Seventeen years. . . .

The Secretary: What have you to say about the air shaft; do you think it is a good thing?

Mr. Moscowitz: I think it is decidedly a bad thing. I must confirm the statements made by other witnesses that the air shaft is a breeder of disease, and especially that there can be no fresh air in any building with an air shaft, from my experience, because of the refuse [garbage] thrown down the air shaft, the stench is so vile and the air is so foul that the occupants do not employ the windows as a means of getting air. . . .

The Secretary: Are there any other objections to the air shaft?

Mr. Moscowitz: It destroys privacy.

The Secretary: How does it do that?

Mr. Moscowitz: I know where I lived in a house where there was a family opposite, the windows which are usually diagonal, I heard everything, especially loud noises, and when the windows are not covered one sees into the house. . . .[1]"

Police and fire protection remained inadequate in most cities. Garbage collection was haphazard at best. City water was often impure. Sewers were smelly and often clogged. Disease could spread quickly under these conditions. In one crowded Chicago neighborhood three out of every five babies born in 1900 died before they were three years old. Jacob Riis, who wrote *How the Other Half Lives*, the most famous book on the tenements, described similar conditions in New York City:

"There are tenements everywhere. Suppose we look into one on Cherry Street. Be a little careful, please! The hall is dark and you might fall over the children pitching pennies back there. Not that it would hurt them. Kicks and punches are their daily diet. They have little else. . . .

Here is a door. Listen! that short hacking cough, that tiny helpless cry—what do they mean? They mean that the soiled bow of white you saw on the door downstairs [when someone died, a bow was hung on the door—black for an adult, white for a child] will have another story to tell—oh, a sadly familiar story—before the day ends. The child is dying of measles. With half a chance it might have lived. But it had none. That dark bedroom killed it. . . .[2]"

Of course, many people worked hard trying to solve the cities' problems and improve urban living conditions. Boards of health made studies and established standards for sewage and garbage disposal. Elaborate systems of pipes and reservoirs brought pure water from distant lakes and rivers. Social workers established community centers called **settlement houses** in poor neighborhoods. Settlement houses had something for everyone—day nurseries for little children, gymnasiums and social activities for young and old, English classes for immigrants.

The most famous of the settlement houses was **Hull House** in Chicago, founded in 1889 by Jane Addams. Many of the settlement

Jane Addams Memorial Collection, The University Library, The University of Illinois at Chicago

This photograph of Jane Addams as a young woman was taken in about 1890. She founded Hull House in Chicago with Ellen Gates Starr. In 1931, Addams was awarded the Nobel Peace Prize. In your own words, describe life for a poor person before and after settlement houses.

[1]From "Testimony of a Tenant" by Dr. Henry Moscowitz in *The Tenement House Problem*, edited by Robert W. DeForest and Lawrence Veiller

[2]From *How the Other Half Lives* by Jacob Riis

workers were young women who had graduated from college. They lived in the settlement houses and tried to become part of the community. They believed that they could grow personally by involving themselves in local political and social affairs. At the same time they were helping local people.

As cities grew larger, transportation became a problem. In 1865 most large cities had streetcars drawn by horses. Horses were slow and needed a great deal of care. In 1873 Andrew S. Hallidie installed **cable cars** on the steep hills of San Francisco, which horses could not climb. Hallidie used a long wire cable attached to a stationary steam engine to pull the cars.

Then, in the late 1880s, Frank J. Sprague designed the first electrified street railway in America. In 1887 he opened a 12-mile line (about 19 kilometers) in Richmond, Virginia. By 1890, 51 American cities had **electric trolley** systems.

As time passed, hundreds of bridges, paved roads, parks, and grand public buildings improved the appearance of cities and the

The Brooklyn Bridge is a fitting symbol of the rise of industrial America. The bridge opened in 1883 with fireworks and a water parade.

Metropolitan Museum of Art

quality of city life. The most famous symbol of the modern city was the **Brooklyn Bridge** in New York City. The Brooklyn Bridge took 13 years to build. It was designed by John A. Roebling and built by his son Washington. Washington Roebling was disabled during the construction and unable to walk about. He supervised the project from a nearby apartment, keeping track of progress with binoculars and a telescope. The bridge is now more than 100 years old and heavily

Culver Pictures

Watching from his window is the son of the designer of the Brooklyn Bridge, Washington Roebling, who was disabled for life by working in the compressed air caissons—watertight chambers used in construction work under water.

traveled by commuters moving between Brooklyn and Manhattan. New Yorkers remain fiercely proud of their bridge.

Thus arose industrial America. In 1865 most people lived much the same way as their parents and grandparents had. The lives of the people of 1900 were far different—closer to what we know today. 🖅

Return to the Preview & Review on page 683.

CHAPTER 19 REVIEW

1860	THE RISE OF INDUSTRIAL AMERICA	

1861
Telegraph wires span nation

1865
Civil War ends

1866
Field lays transatlantic cable

1869
Knights of Labor founded

★
Vanderbilt begins railroad empire

1870
Standard Oil Company

1876
Bell demonstrate: telephone

Chapter Summary
Read the statements below. Choose one, and write a paragraph explaining its importance.
1. Soon after the Civil War railroads and a communications network linked the nation.
2. The expense of developing railroads led to the new business arrangement of the corporation.
3. The growth of the steel industry paralleled the growth of railroads. At the same time, the oil industry began to develop.
4. Eventually the government banned business practices that harmed the public.
5. Workers fought to improve their conditions, eventually turning to unionization.
6. Immigrants from new regions—southern and eastern Europe, China, and Mexico—provided many of the workers for the industrial surge.
7. Most of the new immigrants crowded into ethnic neighborhoods in the growing cities.

Reviewing Chronological Order
Number your paper 1–5. Then study the time line above and place the following events in the order in which they happened by writing the first next to 1, the second next to 2, and so on.
1. Chinese Exclusion Act
2. Sherman Antitrust Act
3. Homestead Strike
4. Knights of Labor founded
5. Standard Oil Company

Understanding Main Ideas
1. What were some of the major changes in the United States in the years between the Civil War and 1900?
2. How did the railroads and the steel industry help each other grow?
3. What is a monopoly? How did railroad competition lead to monopoly in other fields?
4. What were some problems faced by growing cities between 1860 and 1900? What were some attempts to improve city life?

Thinking Critically
1. **Analyzing.** Suppose you have $500 to invest. Your choices are: a corporation with shares whose value has risen slowly but steadily for six years, or a partnership that stands a 50-percent chance of doubling your money in two years. In which business would you invest? Why?
2. **Judging.** You are a Supreme Court judge in 1895. The case before you involves a salt manufacturing trust in Louisiana. It has purchased five competing companies in its own state and three competing companies in the adjacent state of Texas. Would you rule that this trust violated the law? If so, which law or laws, and how? If not, why not?
3. **Evaluating.** If you were a member of Congress in the late 1800s, would you have voted for the literacy test bill? The Chinese Exclusion Act? Why or why not?

Writing About History
Write a story on the following idea: An ordinary citizen who lived in 1800 returns for a look at America in 1900. What are the reactions of this traveler from the time of Jefferson's "nation of farmers" to the sprawling cities and industries of 1900? Which changes impress your time traveler, and which might be upsetting? Use the information in Chapter 15 and in other reference books to prepare your story.

Practicing the Strategy
Review the strategy on page 688.
Reading a Table. Study the table on page 678, then answer the following questions.
1. What is the interval between the years in this table? What information is contained in the headings?

1882
Chinese Exclusion Act

1886
Haymarket
Square bombing

★
American
Federation of Labor

1887
Interstate Commerce Act

1889
Hull House
founded

1890
Sherman Antitrust Act

1892 Homestead Strike

2. Between 1870 and 1900, what was the rate of increase of the male workers as compared to the female workers?
3. Which 10-year interval saw the greatest increase in the total number of workers?
4. In 1900, the table shows a new age group: 16–19. What changes may have resulted in this new age group for workers?

Using Primary Sources
In the late 1800s people began arriving in America from eastern Europe. The following excerpt is from an essay that was submitted in a competition organized by the Committee for Immigrants in America. The essay appeared in a journal called *Immigrants in America Review*. As you read the excerpt from "What America Means to a Russian Jewess," think about an immigrant's point of view of "Americanization."

America means for an Immigrant a fairy promised land that came out true, a land that gives all they need for their work, a land which gives them human rights, a land that gives morality through her churches and education through her free schools and libraries. The longer I live in America the more I think of the question of Americanising the immigrants. At first I thought that there is not such a question as that, for the children of immigrants naturally are Americans and good Americans. America is a land made up of foreigners and the virtues of American life is the best Americaniser. The first generation of American immigrants can't be Americanized much for they were raised in different ways the mode of living is different. And yet how much it is when they love America and are such patriots.

1. According to the excerpt, what has America given the new immigrants?

2. The author thinks that "the virtues of American life is the best Americaniser." What do you think the author means by this statement?
3. What might the use of grammar and spelling tell you about the author of the article?
4. Think about recent immigrants to the United States. Do you think that "Americanization" is necessary? Why or why not?

Linking History & Geography
Immigration has been an important aspect of the development of the United States. To understand immigration, reread "The New Immigration" on pages 683–89 and on an outline map of the world, color the countries from which most of these new immigrants came. Then review "Immigration from Europe" on page 343. Mark the countries from which these earlier immigrants came in a different color.

Enriching Your Study of History
1. **Individual Project**. Complete one of the following projects. Use historical imagination to place yourself in a telegraph office in Homestead, Pennsylvania, in 1892. Prepare a telegraph message that reports on the clash of strikers and Pinkertons. Include the views of both sides in the Homestead strike. Or using historical imagination, place yourself in the year 1890. A few months ago, on your twenty-first birthday, you moved from your parents' farm to find work in the city. Write a letter to the folks at home telling them about city life.
2. **Cooperative Project**. Your class will prepare a multimedia presentation on the railroad network that was built after the Civil War. Various groups will use pictures, stories, and songs to show the development and effects of railroads.

Chapter 19 Review   695

CHAPTER 20

National Politics and Culture, 1867–1896

The Civil War and the rapid expansion of the economy that followed it had important effects on American government and politics. So did the great social changes, especially the flood of new immigrants and the shift of population from the farms to the cities. New issues arose as conditions changed. Older political questions had to be reconsidered too. The Democratic and Republican parties had to deal with difficult and confusing social, economic, and human rights issues. By and large, they failed to find clear solutions. Their efforts are worth studying closely if we are to understand how industrialization, the rise of cities, and the new immigration affected American politics and culture.

The Democratic donkey and the Republican elephant were the creation of the great political cartoonist Thomas Nast, who also gave us the plump bearded image of Santa Claus. Do you think the elephant and donkey are good symbols of the parties they represent?

Culver Pictures

The Granger Collection, New York

1. POLITICS AFTER THE WAR

Republican North and Democratic South

From a political point of view the Civil War did not end in 1865. Nor did it end in 1877 when the North gave up trying to control the South by force. Indeed, the war affected American politics for more than a century.

In the 1850s the controversy over slavery in the territories led most white southerners to become Democrats. When the war ended, most stayed Democrats. After southern whites regained control of their local governments in the 1870s, they voted Democratic in national elections almost to a man. With southern blacks not permitted to vote, the Republican party had no chance at all in any southern state. People spoke of the **Solid South.** Every state that had seceded from the Union cast its electoral votes for the Democratic candidate in every presidential election from 1880 until 1928.

The Republican party had become the leading party in the North and West by 1860. It remained so throughout the decades after the Civil War. Memories of the war stirred up strong emotions and had a great influence on how people voted. Tens of thousands saw the Republicans as the saviors of the Union, the Democrats as the disloyal dividers of the United States. These views held long after slavery had been done away with and the idea of secession abandoned by even its most extreme southern supporters.

After the war Congress had dozens of important issues to decide. Few of these issues had any connection with the geographical division that separated Democrats from Republicans. Yet Republican politicians constantly made emotional appeals to voters by reminding them that the Democrats were "ex-rebels."

This tactic was called "waving the bloody shirt." It got the name in 1866. During a speech in Congress, Benjamin Franklin Butler of Massachusetts displayed the blood-stained shirt of a carpetbagger official who had been beaten by a mob in Mississippi. The incident, according to Butler, proved that the South was still disloyal and must not be trusted.

Here is a famous example of the bloody shirt oratory of the period:

66 Every man that tried to destroy this nation was a Democrat. . . . Soldiers, every scar you have on your heroic bodies was given you by a Democrat. 99

Waving the bloody shirt helped keep northerners voting Republican. Yet Republicans never dominated the northern states as completely as the Democrats controlled the South. New England and most states west of the Mississippi River were Republican strongholds. So were Pennsylvania, Wisconsin, and Michigan. But New

Use these questions to guide your reading. Answer the questions after completing Section 1. **Understanding Issues, Events, & Ideas.** **1.** Create a word web about politics after the Civil War, using these words: Solid South, close state, native son, political machine, Tammany Hall, boss, franchise, kickback, sitting on the fence. **2.** Briefly describe the domestic issues such as the tariff, money crisis, and government jobs, using these words: monetary policy, greenback, hard money, deflation, inflation, civil service reform, merit system, patronage, Pendleton Act, Civil Service Commission.
1. What was "waving the bloody shirt"? How did it influence elections?
2. How did the political machines in northern cities attract the votes of recent immigrants?
3. Why were political parties afraid to take a stand on controversial issues?
4. How were farmers hurt by deflation after the Civil War?
Thinking Critically. **1.** If you were a member of Congress in 1875, would you have voted for or against protective tariffs? Why? **2.** The year is 1882. Write a newspaper editorial explaining the need for civil service reform.

Doris Kearns Goodwin has written this description of Matthew Keany—the North End boss in Boston. John Fitzgerald goes to Keany for help after his father's death.

"Fitzgerald found the bluff and genial Keany in his usual position, behind his desk in the back room of the red brick grocery store. . . . Into this low-ceilinged room which served as his headquarters, thousands of men and women had entered over the years in search of assistance. By Keany's word, a man's son could be liberated from prison, a widow provided with food, an aspiring peddler issued a permit and a destitute father given a coffin to bury his infant child. . . . [There] Fitzgerald reported all summer long in order to help the boss dispense the hundred and one favors regularly awarded in the course of a day, favors which spread the boss's influence, like a huge spider, over the entire district. . . ."

From *The Fitzgeralds and the Kennedys*, 1987

York, New Jersey, and Connecticut were a cluster of states where Democrats could sometimes win. Ohio, Indiana, and Illinois made another group where elections were usually very close.

In nearly every presidential election after the Civil War, the party that won the majority of the electoral votes of the "close" northern states won the presidency. For this reason both parties usually chose presidential and vice presidential candidates from these **close states.** These candidates were called **native sons.** Their names on the ballot could increase the chances of carrying the candidates' home states and perhaps winning the election.

Every president from Rutherford B. Hayes, elected in 1876, to William Howard Taft, elected in 1908, came from either Ohio, Indiana, or New York. Of the 27 men who were nominated for president or vice president by the Democrats and Republicans between 1876 and 1908, 19 came from these three states. Not a single southerner was nominated by the major parties for either office during the period. This shows how the Civil War continued to affect politics.

Ordinary people paid a great deal of attention to politics. A much larger proportion of eligible voters actually voted than has been true in recent times. Did they do so because the campaigns were so intense and colorful? Or were the campaigns intense and colorful because the people were so interested in politics? Unfortunately, these are questions almost impossible for historians to answer!

The Poor and Political Machines

One reason why elections were close in northern industrial states like New York and Ohio was that large numbers of recent immigrants lived in them. These immigrants, as we have noted, tended to settle in the cities. They were "outsiders," poor and without much influence. Most people with wealth and social position looked down upon them. And in the northern states the wealthy and socially prominent were nearly all Republicans.

This explains why most immigrants in the cities joined the Democratic party. Their position was somewhat like that of blacks in the southern states. Each group supported the minority party of its part of the country. Northern immigrants voted Democratic, southern blacks Republican. Northern blacks, on the other hand, while definitely not part of the majority, supported the Republican party. They were mindful that it was the Republican party that had abolished slavery.

In most northern cities local politicians took advantage of the immigrants' preference for the Democratic party to build up **political machines.** These organizations nominated candidates for local office and turned out large numbers of loyal voters on election day. One such machine was **Tammany Hall,** which was run by New York City Democrats.

Culver Pictures

The leaders of the machines, called **bosses,** provided many benefits to poor city dwellers. Well-to-do residents and most political reformers disliked the machines. The bosses used shady and even clearly illegal methods to win votes. But they certainly helped new people, especially immigrants, to make the adjustment to city life. They helped immigrants find jobs. When neighborhood workers were ill or out of work, the bosses would supply their families with food and small sums of money. The machines ran community picnics on holidays. They helped local youngsters who got in trouble with the law.

In return for their help the bosses expected the people to vote for the machine's candidates. By controlling elections, the bosses could reward their friends or line their own pockets. For example, companies that wanted to operate streetcar lines or sell gas or electricity for lighting homes or businesses needed city permits called **franchises.** Bosses often demanded bribes before they would have these franchises issued by the local officials they controlled. They also made deals with contractors who put up public buildings or did other work for the city. The bosses agreed to pay needlessly high prices for the work in return for large **kickbacks,** the illegal return to them of part of the payment made to contractors.

Politics for profit seemed to be the method of operation. This made politics and politicians the target of many reformers. Lincoln

"New York's New Solar System" was drawn by Joseph Keppler in 1898. Here Richard Croker, the head of the Tammany machine, is the sun. Around him revolve lesser corrupt politicians. Why are these figures definitely not heavenly bodies?

The Granger Collection, New York

Thomas Nast first drew a Tammany tiger in 1871. When this cartoon appeared in Harper's *magazine, the city bosses threatened to cancel all orders of Harper Brothers' textbooks. "The Tammany Tiger" upset Boss Tweed, who controlled Tammany Hall and who had said, "As long as I count the votes, what are you going to do about it?" Nast asked the same question in the cartoon's subtitle, "What Are You Going to Do About It?" On what ancient Roman practice is this cartoon based?*

Steffens, the leading reformer of political corruption, wrote:

66 There is hardly a government office from United States Senator down to alderman in any part of the country to which some business leader has not been elected. Yet politics remains corrupt and government pretty bad. Business leaders have failed in politics as they have in good citizenship. Why?

Because politics is business. . . . The commercial spirit is the spirit of profit, not patriotism; of credit, not honor; of individual gain, not national prosperity; of trade, not principle. . . .

We cheat our government and we let our leaders rob it. We let them persuade and bribe our power away from us. True, they pass strict laws for us, but we let them pass bad laws too, giving away public property in exchange. Our good, and often impossible, laws we allow to be used for oppression and blackmail. And what can we say? We break our own laws and rob our own government—the woman at the tax office, the lyncher with his rope, and the captain of industry with his bribe and his rebate. The spirit of graft and of lawlessness is the American spirit.

We Americans have failed. We may be selfish and influenced by gain. . . . [But] there is pride in the character of American citizenship. This pride may be a power in the land. So this record of shame and yet of self-respect, disgraceful confession, yet a declaration of honor, is dedicated, in all good faith, to the accused—to all the citizens of all the cities in the United States.[1]**"**

The machines did both good and harm in their day. Not all of them were associated with the Democratic party. The powerful Philadelphia machine, for example, was a Republican organization. So were many of the machines in middle-sized cities. But most of the big-city machines were run by the Democrats. They were very useful to the national Democratic party in presidential elections in close states like New York.

Sitting on the Fence

Extremely important social and economic problems were being discussed and settled after the Civil War. There were problems caused by industrial expansion and technological change. Other problems resulted from the growth of cities. Still other problems related to racial questions and to immigration. Logically, the parties should have fought their campaigns on these issues.

They rarely did so. Each was afraid that a strong stand on any controversial question would cost votes. It seemed politically safer to make vague statements that everyone could accept, even if no one entirely agreed with them. This was called **sitting on the fence.**

Still, the issues remained, and politicians had to deal with them in one way or another. For example, the need to regulate railroads and other big businesses resulted in the Interstate Commerce Act and the Sherman Antitrust Act. The Indian lands of the West were seized and divided up. During these years Congress and the presidents struggled with high protective tariffs on imported manufactured goods. They tried to solve what was known as "the money question." And they attempted to reform the way government employees were hired and fired.

The Tariff Issue

When the United States first began to develop manufacturing about the time of the War of 1812, a strong case could be made for tariffs that heavily taxed foreign manufactured goods. American "infant industries" needed protection in order to compete with larger, more efficient producers in Europe.

After the Civil War the need for protection was much less clear. America was rapidly becoming the greatest manufacturing nation in the world. Its factories were efficient. The costs of doing business were lower than in many foreign countries. Manufacturers did not, however, want to give up the extra profits that the protective tariffs made possible.

[1]From the *The Shame of the Cities* by Lincoln Steffens

HBJ Photo

This cartoon captured the plight of the American farmer. Its title tells all: "The Tariff Cow—the Farmer Feeds Her—the Monopolist Gets the Milk." Hasn't the artist made the farmer a hayseed and the rich man a gentleman? But whose side is he on?

High tariffs raised the prices that farmers and other consumers had to pay for manufactured goods. Many, therefore, were opposed to the policy of protection. A number of tariff laws were passed by Congress between 1865 and 1900. Democrats and Republicans devoted much time to arguing about tariff policy. Neither party took a clear stand on the question. The rates of various imported products were raised and lowered, then lowered and raised, then raised again. No firm decision was ever made about whether protective tariffs were good for the nation as a whole.

The Democrats tended to be for lowering the tariff, the Republicans for keeping it high. But so many members of Congress from each party voted the other way that it is impossible to say that the tariff was a clear-cut party issue.

The Money Question

From the days of Andrew Jackson to the Civil War, the United States had followed a **monetary policy** that was conservative and cautious. All paper money in circulation could be exchanged for gold or silver coins at a bank. Yet during the Civil War, as we have seen, the government could not raise enough money by taxing and borrowing to pay all its expenses. It had to print $431 million in paper money called **greenbacks,** which could not be exchanged for coin. The back sides of these bills were printed in green ink. Paper money printed in yellow ink, popularly called **hard money,** could be exchanged for gold.

The question after the war was what should be done about the greenbacks? Most people believed either that they should be able to exchange greenbacks for gold or silver or that greenbacks should be withdrawn from circulation entirely.

People who had bought government bonds during the war had paid for them with greenback dollars, which were worth much less than gold or silver coins of the same face value. If these purchasers were paid back in gold when the bonds fell due, they would make very large profits. If the greenbacks were withdrawn by the government, the amount of money in circulation would decline. This would cause **deflation.** Prices of all goods would fall. Every dollar would buy more. Once again, those with money on hand would make large gains. But those people who had borrowed greenbacks would have to repay their loans with more valuable money. They would lose.

Farmers in particular tended to be hurt by deflation after the Civil War. During the war they had borrowed money to buy more land and machinery. They had paid high prices because of the wartime inflation. If the price level fell, the money they paid out to cancel their debts would be more valuable than the money they had borrowed. If wheat sold for $1.50 a bushel when the money was borrowed and for only 50 cents a bushel when it had to be repaid, the farmer would have to produce three times as much wheat to pay off the debt.

Beginning in 1866, the government gradually withdrew greenbacks from circulation. This was called "retiring the greenbacks." The fewer greenbacks in public hands, the less people would fear that the government would print more and cause **inflation.** As the secretary of the treasury explained, the purpose of retiring the greenbacks was to end uncertainty about the money supply and encourage people to be "industrious, economical [and] honest."

However, reducing the money supply alarmed many business leaders. Early in 1878 Congress decided not to allow any further retirement of greenbacks. The argument continued until 1879 when the remaining greenbacks were made convertible into gold. Thereafter, greenbacks were the same as other American bank notes.

Cooper-Hewitt Museum

Peter Cooper was the candidate of the National Greenback party in 1876. He received 81,000 votes for president. He was the builder of the Tom Thumb *(page 355) and* Cooper Union, *where working folks could get an education. His party supported currency inflation. Explain the difference between inflation and deflation.*

Civil Service Reform

As the United States grew larger, the number of people who worked for the government increased rapidly. There were about 27,000 postmasters in 1869 and over 75,000 in 1900. In the same period the treasury department payroll grew from about 4,000 persons to over 24,000. In the 1830s the entire government had employed fewer than 24,000 people.

Much of the work done by the government became increasingly technical. This meant that federal workers needed more skills and experience to perform their jobs efficiently. The new department of agriculture, created in the 1860s, employed chemists and biologists in large numbers. Even so-called routine jobs required people with

The Granger Collection, New York

The good ship Democracy *tosses in stormy seas while its captain, Grover Cleveland, cuts away at mutineers who promote a silver purchase bill. On deck is the Tammany tiger gorging itself. The message of this cartoon from an 1894* Harper's Weekly *is that reforms in civil service and tariffs are about to be "deep sixed," or tossed overboard to drown. Explain how the cartoonist shows this.*

specialized skills. The introduction of the typewriter in the 1880s, for example, affected the training needed to become a government secretary or clerk.

These developments made the spoils system and the Jacksonians' idea of rotation in office badly out-of-date. The dismissal of large numbers of government workers each time a new president took office caused much confusion and waste. The president and other officials had to spend weeks deciding who of the tens of thousands of employees was to be kept, who fired, and who hired.

At the same time it became difficult to recruit properly trained people for government service. Men and women of ability did not want to give up good jobs to work for a government department. They knew that they might be fired after the next election no matter how well they had done their work.

After the Civil War many thoughtful people began to urge **civil service reform.** Most government jobs below the level of policy makers like cabinet members and their assistants should be taken out of politics, the reformers said. Applicants should have to take tests, and those with the best scores should be selected without regard for which political party they supported. Once appointed, civil service workers should be discharged only if they failed to perform their duties properly. This was known as the **merit system.**

President Rutherford B. Hayes was a leading advocate of reform. In his inaugural address in 1877 he stated his support:

    ❝ I ask the attention of the public to the paramount [most important] necessity of reform in our civil service—a reform not merely as to certain abuses and practices of so-called official patronage which have come to have the sanction of usage in several Departments of Government, but a change in the system of appointment itself; a reform that shall be thorough, radical, and complete; a return to the principles and practices of the founders of the Government. They neither expected nor desired from public officers any partisan [favoring one political party] service. They meant that the officer should owe their whole service to the Government and the people. They meant that the officer should be secure in his tenure as long as his personal character remained untarnished and the performance of his duties satisfactory. They held that appointments for office were not to be made nor expected as rewards for partisan services. . . .[1]**"**

[1]From *Inaugural Addresses of the Presidents of the United States*

The problem with civil service reform was that the political parties depended upon the spoils system for rewarding the organizers who ran political campaigns. Presidents and state governors used their powers of appointment, called **patronage,** to persuade legislators to support their programs. They would promise to give government jobs to friends and supporters of the legislators in exchange for the legislators' votes on key issues.

Civil service reform was not an issue that a particular party favored. When the Republicans were in office, the Democrats called for reform. When the Democrats won elections, the Republicans became civil service reformers. The party that controlled the government tended to resist reform. Its leaders needed the jobs to reward their supporters. Nevertheless, the need for government efficiency could not be ignored much longer.

Then came the tragic assassination of President James A. Garfield. Shortly after he took office in 1881, Garfield was shot in a Washington railroad station by Charles Guiteau, a Republican who had been trying without success to get a job in the state department. Chester A. Arthur succeeded to the presidency. A great public cry went up for taking government jobs out of politics. Finally, in 1883, Congress passed the **Pendleton Act,** which created a **Civil Service Commission.** Its charge was to make up and administer examinations for applicants seeking certain government jobs. Those with the best scores on the tests were to get the appointments. The Pendleton Act also outlawed the practice of making government employees contribute to political campaign funds.

At first only 15,000 jobs were classified, or placed under civil service rules, by the 1883 law. But the number of posts covered was steadily increased over the years. By 1900 about half of all federal employees were under the civil service system. 🖼

Both, Copyright by the White House Historical Association; photographs by the National Geographic Society

James Garfield, above, was assassinated in 1881 and Chester A. Arthur, below, succeeded him.

Return to the Preview & Review on page 697.

Use these questions to guide your reading. Answer the questions after completing Section 2.
Understanding Issues, Events, & Ideas. In your own words, explain the historical importance of the Age of Realism.
1. What was the source of inspiration for American realists?
2. How would working as a newspaper reporter serve as good training for a realist?
3. What subjects did realistic painters illustrate?
Thinking Critically. Write a character description of a boss of a political machine, a cowhand, or a factory worker as if you were a realist writer.

2. THE AGE OF REALISM

Changes in American Literature

American literature was still dominated by the romantics after the Civil War. Poe, Hawthorne, Melville, and the New England poets Longfellow, Whittier, and Holmes still held sway. As today, many of the most popular offerings were by women. Susan Warner's *The Wide, Wide World* (1850) was the sad tale of a meek and pious little girl who cried "more readily and steadily than any other tormented child." "Tears on almost every page" could have been her advertising slogan.

But the great changes of industrial America—the cities teeming, the family farmland no longer worked by its children—brought about a new style of writing, known as Realism. Novelists treated such problems as slum life, labor unrest, and political corruption. They created three-dimensional characters and wrote about persons of every walk of life. The period came to be known as the **Age of Realism.** Dialect and slang helped capture the flavor of local types. A good example is Joel Chandler Harris, whose "Uncle Remus" stories reproduced the dialect of the black people of Georgia so faithfully that some critics today think the stories make fun of the southern traditions they relate.

Mark Twain

The outstanding figure of western literature, the first great American realist, was Samuel Clemens, who wrote under the name Mark Twain. Clemens was born in 1835 and grew up in Hannibal, Missouri, on the banks of the Mississippi. He worked for a time as a riverboat pilot and in 1861 went west to Nevada to look for gold. Soon he began publishing humorous stories about the local life. In 1865, while working in California, Twain wrote "The Celebrated Jumping Frog of Calaveras County," a story that made him famous. He then toured Europe and the Holy Land and published *Innocents Abroad*.

In Mark Twain we find all the zest and enthusiasm of the Gilded Age—and its materialism, as well. Twain pursued the almighty dollar with his pen and lost a fortune in foolish business ventures. He wrote tirelessly about America and Europe and created some of America's most famous characters. From *The Gilded Age* there was eyewash salesman Colonel Beriah Sellers and his "Infallible Imperial Oriental Optic Liniment." From the classic *Huckleberry Finn* (1884), came the slave Jim, loyal, patient, yet above all a man. When Huck takes advantage of Jim, the slave turns from him coldly and says: "Dat trick duh is *trash;* and trash is what people is dat puts dirt on de head er ey fren's en makes 'em ashamed." And, of course, there is

Mark Twain papers, The Bancroft Library

Here we see Samuel Clemens as a printer's apprentice. How might the newspaper office have provided a good training for the future Mark Twain?

Huck Finn himself on a raft with Jim floating down the Mississippi River. Through Huck's voice, Twain criticizes a corrupt society overrun with violence and brutality. It contrasts with the tranquility of the river.

> 66 It was kind of solemn, drifting down the big, still river, laying on our backs looking up at the stars, and we didn't ever feel like talking loud, and it warn't often that we laughed—only a little kind of a low chuckle. We had mighty good weather as a general thing, and nothing ever happened to us at all—that night, nor the next, nor the next.

From *The Adventures of Tom Sawyer,* 1876.

This is the frontispiece of the original 1876 edition of Tom Sawyer. *From your reading could you produce a similar illustration for the front of* Huckleberry Finn?

Every night we passed towns, some of them away up on black hillsides, nothing but just a shiny bed of lights; not a house could you see. The fifth night we passed St. Louis, and it was like the whole world lit up. In St. Petersburg they used to say there was twenty or thirty thousand people in St. Louis, but I never believed it till I see that wonderful spread of lights at two o'clock that still night. There warn't a sound there; everybody was asleep. **"**

Twain's other works include *Tom Sawyer* (1876), *Life on the Mississippi* (1883), and *A Connecticut Yankee in King Arthur's Court* (1889). "The truth is," he once wrote, "my books are mainly auto-biographies." A story, he said, "must be written with the blood out of a man's heart." His works catch the spirit of the Age of Realism more than those of any other writer.

William Dean Howells

Mark Twain's long-time friend William Dean Howells of Ohio, born in 1837, was self-educated. He learned the printer's trade, then became a newspaper reporter. In 1860 he wrote a campaign biography of Abraham Lincoln. After the Civil War he became editor of the *Atlantic Monthly* and then, in 1886, of *Harper's*. Both these magazines are still published today.

Howells wrote many novels, one of which, *The Rise of Silas Lapham* (1885) dealt with the ethics of business in a competitive society. But Howells' greatest impact on American literature was as a critic. He encouraged important young novelists such as Stephen Crane, Frank Norris, and Theodore Dreiser. Like Twain and Howells, many novelists of the Age of Realism began as reporters, a job that provided an excellent training for any realist. They wrote about the most primitive emotions—fear, lust, hate, and greed. Crane's best-known work is *The Red Badge of Courage* (1895), which captures the pains and horrors of a young soldier in the Civil War. You can almost feel the youth's fear as those around him flee the battle:

" He slowly lifted his rifle and catching a glimpse of the thick-spread field he blazed at a cantering cluster [trotting group of enemy]. He stopped then and began to peer as best he could through the smoke. He caught changing views of the ground covered with men who were all running like pursued imps and yelling.

To the youth it was an onslaught of redoubtable [fearful] dragons. He became like a man who had lost his legs at the approach of the red and green monster. He waited in a sort

[1]From *The Adventures of Huckleberry Finn* by Mark Twain

Brown Brothers

Brown Brothers

Stephen Crane Collection,
Syracuse University, Manuscript Division

Brown Brothers

of horrified, listening attitude. He seemed to shut his eyes and wait to be gobbled.

A man near him who up to this time was working feverishly at his rifle suddenly stopped and ran with howls. A lad whose face had borne an expression of exalted courage, the majesty of he who dares to give his life, at an instant, smitten abject [struck down with degrading fear]. He blanched [turned white] like one who has come to the edge of a cliff at midnight and is suddenly made aware. There was a revelation. He, too, threw down his gun and fled. There was no shame in his face. He ran like a rabbit.[1] 99

Norris' *McTeague*, published in 1899, is the story of a brutal, dull-witted dentist and his miserable wife Trina, the winner of $5,000 in a lottery. Dreiser's *An American Tragedy* (1925) is the account of a young man's seduction by the apparent wealth and beauty of a social circle to which he does not belong.

Clockwise from top left are Frank Norris, Theodore Dreiser, Stephen Crane, and William Dean Howells. How did these "realists" portray America?

Realism in Art

American painters after the Civil War also treated more "realistic" subjects. The most prominent realist was Thomas Eakins. He mastered human anatomy and painted graphic illustrations of surgical operations. He experimented with early motion pictures to capture the attitudes of humans and animals in motion. Like his friend Walt Whitman, whose portrait is one of his greatest achievements, Eakins gloried in the ordinary.

Realism was also characteristic of the work of Winslow Homer, a Boston-born painter best known for his watercolors. He worked during the Civil War as a reporter for *Harper's Weekly,* and he

[1]From *The Red Badge of Courage* by Stephen Crane

Metropolitan Museum of Art

Thomas Eakins, "Max Schmitt in a Single Scull," 1871.

Winslow Homer, "The Croquet Game."

Art Institute of Chicago

Cliche des Musées Nationaux, Paris   Art Institute of Chicago

James McNeill Whistler, "Arrangement in Gray and Black."

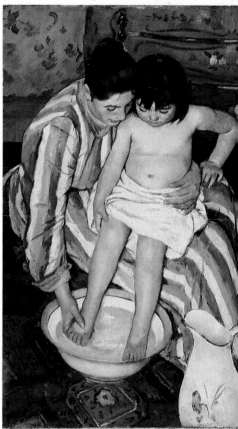

Mary Cassatt, "The Bath."

continued to create illustrations for some years thereafter. He roamed America, painting scenes of southern life, Adirondack camps, and magnificent seascapes.

At least two of America's great painters of the era abandoned their country for Paris. James A. McNeill Whistler left the United States when he was 21. His best-known painting, *Arrangement in Gray and Black* ("Whistler's Mother"), is probably the most famous canvas ever painted by an American. It hangs in the Orsay Museum in Paris.

A second expatriate artist was Mary Cassatt. (An expatriate is one who rejects and leaves the country of his—or her—birth.) The daughter of a wealthy Pittsburgh banker, she went to Paris as a tourist and remained, caught up in the Impressionist movement. Her studies of women, particularly mothers and daughters, hang in the finest museums in the world, including the Art Institute in Chicago.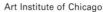

Return to the Preview & Review on page 706.

The Age of Realism   711

Use these questions to guide your reading. Answer the questions after completing Section 3.
Understanding Issues, Events, & Ideas. Describe the issues faced by farmers in the late 1800s, using the following words: third party, mandate, National Grange, Crime of 1873, Bland-Allison Act, Sherman Silver Purchase Act, free coinage, Farmers Alliance, co-op, People's party, Populist party.

1. Why did the presidents elected after the Civil War have little influence? Why was Congress inefficient?
2. How were Granger Laws supposed to help farmers?
3. Why did farmers favor coining silver money? What did the ratio of 16 to 1 mean in coinage?
4. How did the Populists differ from Republicans and Democrats in the election of 1892?
5. Why were Hispanic communities often able to thrive despite economic troubles and discrimination?

Thinking Critically. 1. Write an article for the business section of an 1890 newspaper, explaining how the coinage of silver will change the economy. **2.** Compose a note to a friend, explaining why you will or will not vote for the Populist candidate in the 1892 election.

3. POPULISM

Political "Musical Chairs"

Since neither Democrats nor Republicans took firm stands on the real issues, there were few real differences between them. This helps explain why elections were usually close.

In 1880 James A. Garfield got 48.3 percent of the popular vote for president. He defeated the Democrat, Winfield Scott Hancock, by only 7,000 votes out of nearly 9.2 million cast. Four years later, Grover Cleveland, a Democrat, won with 48.5 percent of the popular vote. His margin over Republican James G. Blaine was 4.87 million to 4.85 million.

In 1888 Cleveland was defeated by Benjamin Harrison. Although President Cleveland got more popular votes, Harrison had a majority of the electoral vote, 233 to 168. In the next presidential election Cleveland defeated Harrison and returned to the White House. Yet he got only 46 percent of the popular vote to Harrison's 43 percent.

In all of these elections no one got a majority of the popular vote because third-party candidates were in the field. A **third party** is a political party competing with the two major parties. Third-party candidates *did* stand for "real issues." There were Greenback party candidates running in 1880 and 1884, for example. They demanded that more rather than fewer greenbacks be put in circulation. Other candidates ran on platforms calling for prohibition of liquor.

The presidents were elected by such narrow margins that they had relatively little influence while in office. They could not claim to have a **mandate**—the backing of a solid majority of the people—when they presented their programs to Congress.

Ewing Galloway   National Portrait Gallery

Presidents Grover Cleveland, left, and Benjamin Harrison played political leapfrog with the White House. Explain how. Harrison's portrait is by the distinguished photographer Eastman Johnson, c. 1889.

The Granger Collection, New York

"His grandfather's hat was too big for his head," sang the opponents of Benjamin Harrison when he became president. A bust of President William Henry Harrison, his grandfather, is above the door. Joseph Keppler drew this caricature. What seems to be his opinion of the man who was elected president in 1888? Can you identify the poem to which Keppler refers?

In Congress the Democrats had a majority of the House of Representatives from 1874 to 1880 and from 1882 to 1888. But they had a majority of the Senate for only two years during this entire period. Turnover among representatives was extremely rapid. Often more than half the members of the House were in their first terms. Without experienced members, Congress was inefficient. With narrow, shifting majorities, controversial measures seldom were passed.

Hard Times for the Farmer

The times were particularly frustrating for farmers. Falling agricultural prices hurt them badly. So did the protective tariffs which raised the prices of the manufactured goods they purchased. But neither party was willing to work for laws that would bring much relief. The farmers found themselves left behind in American society's pursuit of wealth and status. Between 1860 and 1891 the number of farms rose from 2 million to 4.5 million. But farmers lacked the political clout of industry. So some farmers turned elsewhere in their agonizing search for help.

Courtesy of The Library of Congress

"I Pay for All" says the legend below this sturdy Granger. Rural scenes in this 1873 poster include the biblical Ruth and Boaz, lower right; a harvest dance, lower left; and the Grange in session, upper right. Study the picture to find other scenes of agrarian life.

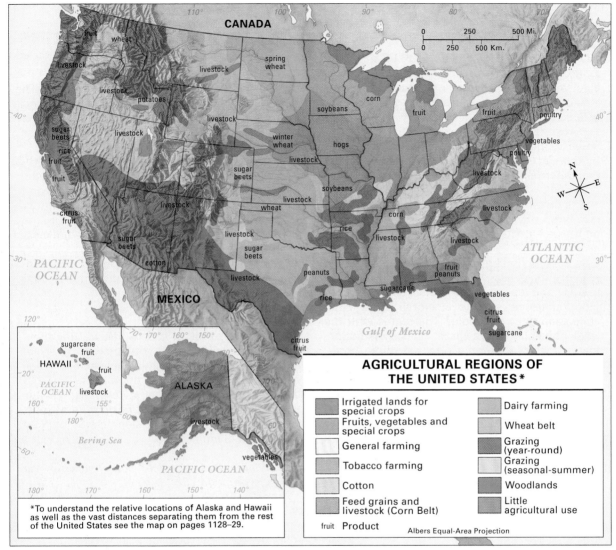

AGRICULTURAL REGIONS OF THE UNITED STATES *

Irrigated lands for special crops	Dairy farming
Fruits, vegetables and special crops	Wheat belt
General farming	Grazing (year-round)
Tobacco farming	Grazing (seasonal-summer)
Cotton	Woodlands
Feed grains and livestock (Corn Belt)	Little agricultural use

fruit Product

Albers Equal-Area Projection

*To understand the relative locations of Alaska and Hawaii as well as the vast distances separating them from the rest of the United States see the map on pages 1128–29.

In the 1870s many farmers joined the **National Grange.** The Grange was originally a kind of social club. It soon became a political organization as well. Many branches sprang up, especially in New York, Pennsylvania, Ohio, and the Middle West.

Granger leaders believed that railroad freight charges were too high. Because railroads had a monopoly on moving bulky goods to distant markets, Granger leaders demanded government regulation of rates. Their efforts led to the passage of Granger laws in many states. These measures set the rates that railroads and grain warehouses could collect so farmers would not be overcharged.

This raised the question of whether businesses like railroads could be regulated "in the public interest." Yes, ruled the Supreme Court in the case of *Munn v. Illinois* (1877). Granger laws were constitutional. Businesses like railroads that provided broad public services could not be considered completely private.

LEARNING FROM MAPS. *The United States has long been noted for its agricultural abundance. Note the wide variety and the productiveness of such a large percentage of the land. Compare this map to the one on page 649 and state a generalization about agriculture and climate in the United States.*

Populism   715

STRATEGIES FOR SUCCESS

INTERPRETING ELECTION RESULTS

Every four years the people of the United States elect a president. Or more correctly they elect electors who choose the president. This group of electors is called the *electoral college.* Election results are given for both *popular votes*—votes by the people—and *electoral votes*—votes by the electoral college. It is the electoral votes that determine which of the candidates becomes president.

The members of the electoral college are faceless and, in two thirds of the states, nameless on the ballot. They never assemble as a national group but meet instead in their respective states after each general election to cast their votes.

Every state has one electoral vote for each senator and representative. Thus, the more populous states have more electoral votes. What state today has the most? The states with the least population have three votes. In addition, the District of Columbia now has three votes. Today there are a total of 538 electoral votes. In order to be elected, a candidate must receive a simple majority, or 270, of those 538 votes.

The electoral system has often been criticized for its *unit rule.* That is, in each state the winner takes all. A candidate who receives one more vote than the closest rival gets all the state's electoral votes. Why do you think such a result would be controversial?

How to Interpret Election Results

To interpret election results, follow these steps.
1. **Check the figures**. Note both popular and electoral vote totals. In some elections the result of the popular vote is extremely close but the electoral vote is not.
2. **Note the trends**. See which states and regions voted for which candidate. Candidates have learned to effectively use the electoral system to their benefit. They spend a majority of their campaign time and money in the states with the largest populations—and electoral votes.
3. **Study the results**. Consider what factors influenced the election's outcome and resulted in the voting figures.

Applying the Strategy

Study the map and pie graphs below. They show the electoral and popular vote totals for the election of 1888. The map shows the electoral votes held by each state. Which three states had the largest totals? The close states have always played an important part in deciding elections. Which candidate won the close states of New York and Indiana in 1888?

For independent practice, see Practicing the Strategy on page 732.

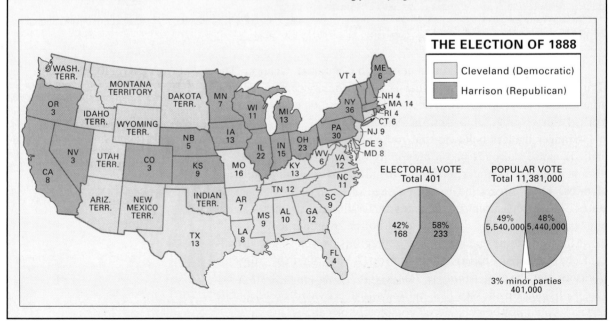

THE ELECTION OF 1888

Cleveland (Democratic)

Harrison (Republican)

ELECTORAL VOTE
Total 401
42% 168
58% 233

POPULAR VOTE
Total 11,381,000
49% 5,540,000
48% 5,440,000
3% minor parties 401,000

Other farmers, especially Hispanics, African Americans, and new immigrants, had nowhere to turn. As in other occupations, they faced prejudice and discrimination. They were not welcomed in many of the local granges and they had even less political clout than established white farmers.

Yet though life was shockingly hard for these people, in many places their communities thriyed. In the West and Southwest Mexican American communities grew, strengthened by cultural traditions. As you have read, one of the most important of those traditions was the spirit of community—everyone pitching in to help. See if you can get a feeling for life in the Southwest through the following excerpt, written by Jovita Gonzalez about her life in Texas:

> **"** In August, down towards the Rio Grande, the rays of the sun beat vertically upon the sandy stretches of land, from which all tender vegetation has been scorched, and the white, naked land glares back at the sun; the only palpitating [moving] things discoverable between the two poles of heat are heat devils. The rattlesnakes are as deeply holed up and as quiet as in midwinter. In the thickets of brush the roadrunners, rusty lizards, mockingbirds, and all other living things pant. Whirlwinds dance across the stretches of prairie interspersed between the thickets of thorn. At six o'clock it is hotter than at midday. Seven o'clock, and then the sun, a ball of orange-pink, descends below the horizon at one stride. The change is magical. A soft cooling breeze, the pulmotor [breathing apparatus] of the Border lands, springs up from the south.
>
> Down in the *cañada* [brook between mountains], which runs by the ranch, doves coo. Out beyond, cattle are grazing and calves are frisking. In the cottonwood tree growing beside the dirt "tank" near the ranch house the redbird sings. Children shout and play. From the corrals come the voices of vaqueros [cowboys] singing and jesting. Blended with the bleatings of goats and sheep are the whistles and hisses of the *pastor* (shepherd). The locusts complete the chorus of evening noises. Darkness subdues them; then, as the moon rises, an uncounted mob of mongrel curs [mixed-breed dogs] set up a howling and barking at it that coyotes out beyond mock.
>
> It was on a night like this that the ranch folk gathered at the Big House to shell corn. All came: Tío Julianito, the *pastor,* with his brood of sunburned half-starved children ever eager for food; Alejo the fiddler, Juanito the idiot, called the Innocent, because the Lord was keeping his mind in heaven; Pedro the hunter, who had seen the world and spoke English; the vaqueros; and, on rare occasions, Tío

Esteban, the mail carrier. Even the women came, for on such occasions supper was served.

A big canvas was spread outside, in front of the kitchen. In the center of this canvas, ears of corn were piled in pyramids for the shellers, who sat about in a circle and with their bare hands shelled the grains off the cobs.

It was then, under the moonlit sky, that we heard stories of witches, buried treasures, and ghosts. . . . Then the *pastor* told of how he had seen spirits in the shape of balls of fire floating through the air. They were souls doing penance for their past sins. As a relief to our fright, Don [a title of respect] Francisco suggested the Tío Julianito do one of his original dances to the tune of Alejo's fiddle. A place was cleared on the canvas, and that started the evening's merriment. . . .[1]”

The Silver Issue

Lower freight and storage charges did not help farmers as much as the Grangers had hoped. Costs were not reduced much. So farmers tried instead to raise the prices of their produce. The best way to push up prices seemed to be by causing inflation. Farmers looked for a way to put more money in circulation so their prices would rise. One way was by coining silver money.

Throughout the period before the Civil War both gold and silver had been minted into coins and used to back bank notes. But in 1873 Congress had voted to stop coining silver. That seemed a terrible mistake to those who favored inflation.

Many new silver mines had been discovered. If miners could bring their silver to the United States mint for coining, more money would be created. With more money in circulation, prices would rise. Yet silver was a relatively scarce metal. The amount that could be mined would place a limit on the amount of new money that could be put into circulation. This would prevent "runaway" inflation, which might result if there was no limit on how much paper money could be printed.

Farmers and silver miners joined to make a powerful political force. People began to refer to the law that had discontinued the coining of silver as the **Crime of 1873.** They demanded that the government once again coin all the silver brought to the mint.

The result of their pressure was a political compromise. In 1878 Congress passed a bill sponsored by Representative Richard Bland of Missouri and Senator William B. Allison of Iowa. Bland was a Democrat who believed sincerely in coining both gold and silver.

[1]From *Among My People* by Jovita Gonzalez

The Granger Collection, New York

A silverite runs away with the Democratic donkey pursued by a sound money Democrat. Which side of the pursuit does this 1896 cartoon seem to favor? The sign can help you answer.

Allison, a Republican, was a shrewd political manipulator. (It was said of Allison that he would make no more noise walking across the Senate floor in wooden shoes than a fly made walking on the ceiling.)

The **Bland-Allison Act** ordered the secretary of the treasury to purchase and coin between $2 and $4 million in silver each month. In 1890 another coinage law, the **Sherman Silver Purchase Act,** increased the amount of silver bought to 4.5 million ounces a month. This came to about the total being mined at that time.

The price of silver was usually expressed by comparing it to the price of gold. In 1873, when the mint had stopped coining silver, an ounce of gold was worth about 16 times as much as an ounce of silver. By 1890, when the Sherman Silver Purchase Act was passed, an ounce of gold was worth 20 times as much. This was because the

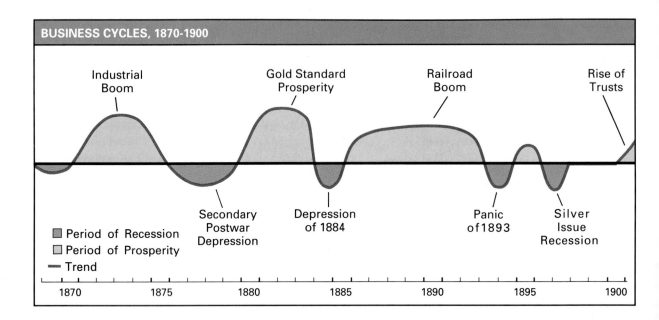

BUSINESS CYCLES, 1870-1900

Industrial Boom

Gold Standard Prosperity

Railroad Boom

Rise of Trusts

Secondary Postwar Depression

Depression of 1884

Panic of 1893

Silver Issue Recession

■ Period of Recession
□ Period of Prosperity
— Trend

1870 1875 1880 1885 1890 1895 1900

LEARNING FROM GRAPHS. *As you can see, the United States economy had extended ups and downs between 1870 and 1900. Why might there have been little change in the economy between 1898 and 1900?*

price of silver was falling steeply at the same time as the supply was increasing from new mines in the West.

Farmers and others who favored inflation wanted as much silver coined as possible in order to increase the money supply. If the United States would coin all the world's silver, the price of other products would rise because more money would be in circulation. Those who favored inflation therefore urged **free coinage**—that is, a law requiring the mint to turn all the silver offered it into silver dollars.

The silver miners were more interested in driving up the price of their silver than in what was done with it. They wanted the United States to exchange an ounce of gold for 16 ounces of silver. Thus, farmers and silver miners combined their interests. They demanded free coinage of silver at a ratio of 16 to 1 with gold.

The Populist Party

While the demand for free silver was developing, farmers were looking for other ways out of their hard times. First in Texas, and then elsewhere in the South, a new movement was spreading. It was the **Farmers Alliance.**

Like the earlier National Grange, the Alliance began as a social organization. In many areas local Alliance clubs formed cooperatives, or **co-ops,** to sell their crops at better prices. These co-ops set a single price for produce and purchased goods wholesale to save money for their members. By 1890 the Alliance movement had spread northward into Kansas, Nebraska, and the Dakotas.

Like the Grange, the Alliance became an important political

force. Its leaders campaigned against high railroad freight rates and high interest rates charged by banks for mortgages and other loans. Alliance members began to run for local offices, promising if elected to help farmers.

An angry rural editor wrote in 1890:

“ There are three great crops raised in Nebraska. One is a crop of corn, one is a crop of freight rates, and one is a crop of interest. One is produced by farmers who by sweat and toil farm the land. The other two are produced by men who sit in their offices and behind their bank counters and farm the farmers.”

In 1890 several southern states elected governors backed by the Alliance. More than 45 ''Alliancemen'' were elected to Congress. Alliance officials were encouraged by these results. They decided to establish a new political party and run a candidate for president in 1892. To broaden their appeal, they persuaded representatives of labor unions to join with them. They named their new organization the **People's party,** but it is usually referred to as the **Populist party.**

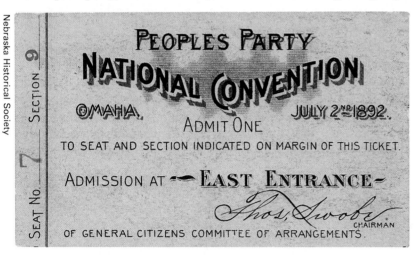

Nebraska Historical Society

In July 1892 the first Populist nominating convention met in Omaha, Nebraska. The delegates adopted a platform that called for a long list of specific reforms. One was government ownership of railroads and of the telegraph and telephone network. Another was a federal income tax. Still another was a program of government loans to farmers who would store their crops in government ware-houses as security for the loans.

To win the support of industrial workers, the Populist platform called for the eight-hour workday and for restrictions on immigration. It also demanded the ''free and unlimited coinage of silver and gold at . . . 16 to 1.''

The Populists chose James Baird Weaver of Iowa as their candidate for president in 1892. He had fought bravely for the Union in

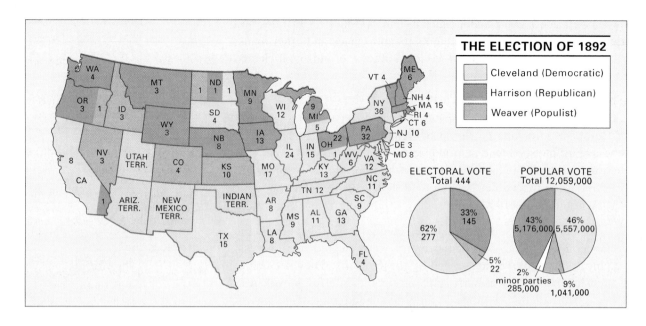

THE ELECTION OF 1892

- Cleveland (Democratic)
- Harrison (Republican)
- Weaver (Populist)

WA 4
OR 3 / 1
ID 3
NV 3
CA 8 / 1
UTAH TERR.
ARIZ. TERR.
NEW MEXICO TERR.
MT 3
WY 3
CO 4
ND 1 / 1 / 1
SD 4
NB 8
KS 10
INDIAN TERR.
TX 15
MN 9
IA 13
MO 17
AR 8
LA 8
MS 9
AL 11
GA 13
FL 4
WI 12
IL 24
MI / 9 / 5
IN 15
KY 13
TN 12
OH 22
WV 6
VA 12
NC 11
SC 9
PA 32
NY 36
VT 4
ME 6
NH 4
MA 15
RI 4
CT 6
NJ 10
DE 3
MD 8

ELECTORAL VOTE
Total 444

- 62% 277
- 33% 145
- 5% 22

POPULAR VOTE
Total 12,059,000

- 46% 5,557,000
- 43% 5,176,000
- 2% minor parties 285,000
- 9% 1,041,000

LEARNING FROM MAPS. *Compare the results of the election of 1892 shown on this map with the results of the 1888 election shown on the map on page 716. What major differences do you see? What major similarities?*

HBJ Collection

James B. Weaver was the nominee of the People's party at its convention in Omaha in 1892. How did the party balance its ticket?

Return to the Preview & Review on page 712.

the Civil War, rising from lieutenant to brigadier general. Their candidate for vice president was James G. Field of Virginia, a former general in the Confederate army.

The Populists created "a multi-sectional institution of reform," according to historian Lawrence Goodwyn. But they were not revolutionaries. They felt betrayed by what we today call "the establishment." They did not share the national passion for free enterprise, and they felt their problems were created by clever and selfish interests who used the American system to their advantage. As one Populist writer stated it:

> ❝The farmer has been the victim of a gigantic scheme of plunder. Never has such a vast combination of brains and money forced people into labor for the benefit of a few. . . .[1]❞

[1] From *The Farmer's Side: His Troubles and Their Remedy* by William A. Peffer

The Populists took clear stands on controversial issues, seeking voters who agreed with their ideas. Democratic and Republican leaders continued to duck controversial questions. In the South the Populists tried to unite black and white farmers. There were many blacks in the Alliance movement in the southern states, although their groups were segregated from the whites.

The 1892 presidential election was an exciting one. General Weaver got over a million votes, a large number for a third-party candidate. The Populist party won many local contests. On balance, however, the results disappointed the Populists. They lost many votes in the South because large numbers of their white supporters refused to vote for candidates who appealed openly for black support. 🖫

4. UNEMPLOYMENT AND UNREST

Preview & Review

Use these questions to guide your reading. Answer the questions after completing Section 4.
Understanding Issues, Events, & Ideas. Using the following words, describe the key instances of labor unrest during the Depression of 1893: gold standard, Coxey's Army, Pullman Strike.
1. Why did President Cleveland want the nation to return to the gold standard?
2. How would Coxey's plan have put people to work and caused prices to rise?
3. Why did many people turn against President Cleveland after the Pullman Strike? Why was the president hurt by Governor Altgeld's criticism?
Thinking Critically. Which amendment in the Bill of Rights might Jacob Coxey have used to protest his arrest in March 1894? Why?

The Depression of 1893

Shortly after the presidential election, which Grover Cleveland won, the country entered into the worst period of hard times in its history. Business activity slowed down. Unemployment increased. By the end of 1893 more than a hundred railroads had gone bankrupt. People hoarded money, withdrawing their savings in gold from the banks.

As usual the depression hurt African Americans, Hispanics, and recent immigrants worst of all. Many held the lowest-paying jobs and were therefore the first to be laid off. Others barely scraping out a living as farmers now could not sell their produce. One historian wrote of "the absolute destitute condition of the colored people of the South." It was as bad if not worse elsewhere.

The long period of deflation that began in the 1870s was an important cause of this depression. Farmers and wage earners blamed the depression on "tight money." They felt the Sherman Silver Purchase Act had not gone far enough. They demanded that the government coin even more money.

President Cleveland believed the business decline was caused by the uncertainty people had about the safety of their money. The government should stop coining silver, he insisted, and go back to the single **gold standard.** This meant that only gold would be used to back the currency. In October 1893 he persuaded Congress to repeal the Sherman Silver Purchase Act.

This action angered those who favored coining silver as well as gold. It split the Democratic party. And it did not end the depression. During 1894–1895, economic conditions got worse rather than better.

Other people blamed the depression on the government's failure to regulate business. Unsafe working conditions, child labor, low wages, and unfair pricing policies had gone on for most of the century. Government on all levels had ignored these and other effects of industrialization. Even more, they seemed to support business leaders in their pursuit of profit. These people claimed the depression of 1893 was another result of the lack of government regulation of American business.

Coxey's Army

As the depression dragged on, large numbers of unemployed men took to wandering about the countryside. These people were called tramps. Some thought them dangerous troublemakers, perhaps even revolutionaries who wanted to overthrow the government. In truth, they only wanted work.

Small groups of unemployed workers began making protest marches to seek government relief. This increased fear of the "tramp

The Granger Collection, New York

Jacob Coxey seems to be a timid, mild sort of man in this 1894 photograph. But appearances can be deceiving. You know him as the leader of Coxey's Army. How successful was he?

problem." The most important of these marches was headed by Jacob Coxey, who was himself a prosperous business leader.

Coxey's Army marched from Massillon, Ohio, to Washington, attracting an enormous amount of attention. One observer claimed that for every two marchers there was at least one newspaper reporter tagging along to describe the happenings.

Coxey's Army set out in March 1894 and reached Washington in May. There were only a few hundred marchers, most of them obviously harmless people. But when Coxey tried to present a petition to Congress, he was arrested for trespassing on the grounds of the Capitol. The police then broke up Coxey's followers and sent the marchers straggling home. Their march came to nothing.

What makes Coxey's Army important historically is the plan that Coxey worked out for dealing with the depression. The federal government should spend $500 million improving rural roads, he said. It should also lend money to state and local governments for other public works projects. The work itself should be done by the unemployed. Anyone without a job should be put to work.

Coxey further proposed that both the $500 million spent by the federal government and the money lent to local governments should simply be printed by the treasury. Like the Civil War greenbacks, this money would not be backed by gold or silver. This inflation of the money supply would cause prices to rise. That would help farmers and debtors of all sorts. Coxey's program seemed radical and impractical in 1894. Forty years later it appeared a perfectly reasonable way to deal with deflation and unemployment in a depression.

The Pullman Strike

Since he was president when the depression struck, Cleveland was blamed for the hard times. Emergency soup kitchens were set up to feed the long lines of hungry people who could not find work. Critics unfairly called them "Cleveland Cafes." But Cleveland did little to help the jobless or to stimulate the lagging economy.

More people turned against Cleveland when a great strike broke out in May 1894, shortly after the arrest of Jacob Coxey. The strike had begun in the factory of the Pullman Palace Car Company in Illinois, which manufactured and operated sleeping and dining cars for the railroads. After the strike had gone on for several weeks, engineers, conductors, and other workers of the American Railway Union, in sympathy with the strikers, voted not to handle trains to which Pullman cars were attached. This paralyzed the railroads in and around Chicago. It threatened to disrupt the nation's already depressed economy.

A federal judge ordered the railroad workers back to work. When they refused, President Cleveland sent troops into Chicago to make sure that the United States mail was not held up. The union was

The Granger Collection, New York

willing to operate mail trains. However, railroad officials insisted on attaching Pullman cars to these trains. The **Pullman Strike** continued.

Rioting broke out when blue-coated soldiers entered the Chicago rail yards. The violence turned public opinion against the union. Its president, Eugene Victor Debs, was arrested and thrown in jail. The strike collapsed.

Conservatives praised Cleveland's defense of "law and order." But thousands of union members were alarmed by his use of the army to break a strike. The governor of Illinois, John Peter Altgeld, had bitterly objected to the use of federal troops in his state. Altgeld claimed that Chicago police and state militia units could preserve order. He accused Cleveland of being a strikebreaker. Altgeld's opposition weakened Cleveland politically since Altgeld, like Cleveland, was a Democrat. 🖙

Illinois national guardsmen are firing on striking Pullman Company workers in this artist's sketch. Their fortress is the equipment brought in to get the train back on track. Describe this scene from both points of view—that of the guardsmen and that of the strikers.

Return to the Preview & Review on page 723.

Unemployment and Unrest   725

Use these questions to guide your reading. Answer the questions after completing Section 5.
Understanding Issues, Events, & Ideas. Give a brief eyewitness account of William Jennings Bryan's Cross of Gold speech.
1. What stand did the Republicans take on the money issue in their platform of 1896?
2. How did the Republican campaign of 1896 differ from the Democratic campaign?
3. How did McKinley's victory in 1896 mark the end of the post-Civil War era?
Thinking Critically. From the point of view of either a Republican or a free-silver Democrat, write a brief campaign pamphlet about the money issue for the election of 1896.

The Bettmann Archive

In a wicker rocker on his front porch William McKinley waits for visitors during his presidential campaign in 1896.

5. GOLD VERSUS SILVER

The Democrats Choose Silver

As the election of 1896 drew near, the Democrats had to make a difficult decision. President Cleveland was extremely unpopular. Rightly or wrongly, he was being blamed for the continuing depression. Furthermore, the public knew he was totally opposed to measures that would stimulate the economy by raising prices, especially the coining of silver.

In the southern states where the Democrats were in control, the Populist party was making large gains by calling for the free coinage of silver. Southern farmers were hard hit by the depression. If the Democrats again chose Cleveland, who defended the gold standard, they seemed sure to be defeated in the national election. They might even lose the South to the Populists.

The 1896 election was one which gave the Democrats a chance to hold the presidency and to take Republican seats in Congress. This was because the Republican party convention in June 1896 had nominated Congressman William McKinley of Ohio as its candidate for president. McKinley would be running on a platform that declared squarely for the gold standard. "We are . . . opposed to the free coinage of silver," the platform stated.

Many normally Republican farmers in the Middle West and nearly all the miners in the Rocky Mountain states were in favor of free silver. The Republican platform made them furious. States like Nebraska and Colorado, traditionally Republican, might go Democratic if that party would come out for free silver.

The Democratic convention met in St. Louis in July. Before picking a candidate, the delegates had to adopt a platform. The key issue to be decided was the money question. A formal debate took place. Three speakers defended the gold standard. Three others spoke in favor of the free coinage of silver.

The final debater was William Jennings Bryan, a young ex-congressman from Nebraska. Bryan was not a particularly thoughtful person, but he had a deep faith in democracy. He believed that legislators should represent the ideas of the people who elected them. As early as 1892 he said, "The people of Nebraska are for free silver, and [therefore] I am for free silver. I will look up the arguments later."

Bryan had served two terms in Congress. But few people outside Nebraska had ever heard of him. He was only 36, barely a year older than the minimum age set by the Constitution for becoming president. Nevertheless, he decided that he had a good chance of getting the 1896 presidential nomination.

Bryan's speech on the silver question was his great opportunity to attract attention. He succeeded brilliantly. Bryan was one of the

The Granger Collection, New York

William Jennings Bryan's "Cross of Gold" speech inspired this caricature. He is seen here as one who abuses the Bible, but Bryan was actually a very religious person who based courtroom arguments on the Bible. In what other ways does this cartoonist criticize Bryan?

greatest political orators in American history. He did not make any new economic arguments for free silver. Instead, like a skillful musician, he played upon the emotions of the delegates. His voice rang through the hall like a mighty organ in a great cathedral. As he approached the climax of his appeal, almost every sentence brought forth a burst of applause.

He likened those who favored coining silver to the Crusaders who had freed Jerusalem from the Moslems. He praised western farmers as "hardy pioneers who have braved the dangers of the wilderness" and "made the desert bloom." The country could exist without the cities, Bryan said, but without the nation's farms, "grass will grow in the streets of every city in the country." He concluded by likening the silver forces to Jesus Christ, saying to the defenders of the gold standard:

  ❝ You shall not press down upon the brow of labor this crown of thorns, you shall not crucify mankind upon a cross of gold. ❞

Gold Versus Silver   **727**

After cheering this **Cross of Gold speech,** the Democratic convention adopted a platform calling for "the free and unlimited coinage of both silver and gold at the . . . ratio of 16 to 1." The next day the delegates nominated the "Nebraska Cyclone," William Jennings Bryan, for president.

The Election of 1896

The presidential campaign of 1896 roused people throughout the nation. When it was over, many Republicans and Democrats had changed sides.

Nearly all business people and manufacturers supported McKinley. Like most other wealthy citizens, these people felt that the issue of silver inflation versus the gold standard and "sound money" was more important than party loyalty. They believed that if Bryan were elected, their businesses would collapse and their wealth would vanish.

Beyond question these people were wrong. There was nothing magical about the gold standard, and Bryan was no threat to their wealth. But they misunderstood the situation. They saw the campaign as a crusade. They thought that McKinley was a great patriotic hero, almost a Washington or a Lincoln, who would save the nation in an hour of terrible danger.

Free silverites have unhitched their wagon from the Democratic donkey as they roll out of control. This is the view of C. J. Taylor, who made this lithograph in 1896. Bryan has his arms stubbornly crossed while Governor Altgeld of Illinois waves a firebrand. Explain why the red banner says "Repudiation."

The Granger Collection, New York

THE FRONT-PORCH CAMPAIGN

McKinley ran what was called a front-porch campaign for the presidency. He stayed home in Canton, Ohio, partly to be near his wife, Ida, who had epilepsy. Groups from all over the country came to hear his views.

These visits were carefully planned. Each delegation was greeted at the railroad station by the "Canton Home Guards" mounted on horses. The visitors then marched to McKinley's modest house. The town took on the appearance of one long Fourth of July celebration. The streets were lined with flags and banners. Pictures of McKinley were everywhere. Stands along the route sold hot dogs, lemonade, and souvenirs.

When a delegation reached McKinley's house, the candidate came out to meet them, usually with his wife and mother at his side. He called their leaders by name and seemed to show keen interest in their problems. A member of the delegation would make a speech while McKinley listened to him "like a child looking at Santa Claus."

Ida McKinley

McKinley's responses showed how well he knew his audience. To a group of Civil War veterans he might speak about pensions. To manufacturers or factory workers he might stress the importance of the protective tariff. Always he pictured himself as a patriot defending America and the gold standard against the dangerous free-silver Democrats. "Patriotism," he would say, "is above party and National honor is dearer than party name. The currency and credit of the government are good, and must be kept good forever."

Newspaper reporters covered each of these visits. They wrote articles describing the crowds. They quoted the remarks of the candidate in detail. In this way McKinley reached voters all over the country without stepping off the front porch of his house.

Copyright by the White House Historical Association; photograph by the National Geographic Society

Actually, McKinley was a rather ordinary person. He was hard working, forward looking, and politically shrewd. But he was not especially intelligent, imaginative, or creative. His greatest advantage in the election was the solid support of his business backers.

The Republican campaign was organized by Marcus Alonzo Hanna, an Ohio industrialist. Mark Hanna and his assistants raised enormous amounts of money for the contest. Some of the contributions came from wealthy individuals, many of whom were normally Democrats. But most of the money came from large corporations. As one bank president explained, "We have never before contributed a cent to politics, but the present crisis we believe to be as important as the [Civil] war." It was not then illegal for corporations to give money to political candidates.

Hanna used this money very cleverly. Republican speakers spread across the country. At one point 250 Republican orators were campaigning in 27 states. Pamphlets explaining the Republican program were printed and 250 million distributed. Over 15 million pamphlets on the money question were handed out in two weeks.

Committees were set up to win the support of all kinds of special groups. One committee tried to influence German American voters, another those of African descent, and so on. There was even a committee assigned to campaign among bicycle riders, for bicycling was an especially popular sport in the 1890s.

The Democrats had very little campaign money, in part because so many wealthy Democrats were supporting the Republican candidate. The party organization was also weak. In many of the industrial states Democratic politicians would not support free silver. These "Gold Democrats" formed a National Democratic party and nominated Senator John M. Palmer of Illinois for president.

The Democrats did have one very valuable asset—Bryan himself. His magnetic personality and his brilliance as a speaker made him a great campaigner. He traveled constantly, speaking all over the nation. Sometimes he addressed huge crowds in city auditoriums. Sometimes he spoke to only a handful of listeners at rural railroad stations from the back platform of his train. All told, he made over 600 speeches between August and election day in November.

Most important newspapers supported McKinley. Their reporters frequently misquoted Bryan in order to make him appear foolish or radical. *The New York Times* even suggested that he might well be insane. But the papers did report Bryan's speeches in detail. In this election voters could readily learn where both candidates stood on all the issues of the day.

The election caused major shifts in voting patterns. After much debate the Populists nominated Bryan instead of running a candidate of their own. The effect was to end the Populist movement. Yet if the Populist party had run someone else, the free-silver vote would have been split. Then McKinley would have been certain to win the election.

Populist strongholds in the South and West went solidly for Bryan in November. So did the mountain states, where silver mining was important. But thousands of formerly Democratic industrial workers voted Republican. City people did not find Bryan as attractive as did farmers and residents of small towns. McKinley was popular with workers, despite his close connections with big business. He convinced workers that free silver would be bad for the economy. And he argued that a high tariff would protect their jobs by keeping out goods made by low-paid foreign laborers.

Boston, New York City, Baltimore, Chicago, and many other cities that had gone Democratic in the presidential election of 1892 voted Republican in 1896. Chicago, for example, had given Grover Cleveland a majority of over 35,000 in 1892. In 1896 McKinley carried the city by more than 56,000 votes.

The Election Ends an Era

The election was a solid Republican triumph. The electoral vote was 271 for McKinley, 176 for Bryan. Looked at one way, McKinley won

Courtesy Museum of Fine Arts, Boston, Gift of Miss Maude E. Appleton

simply because his party spent more money and was better organized than the Democrats. He carried all the crucial close states of the Northeast by relatively small margins. If Bryan had won in New York, Ohio, Indiana, and Illinois, he would have been president.

In a larger sense, however, McKinley's victory marked the end of the post-Civil War era. Within a year or two, new gold discoveries and improved methods of refining gold ore ended the money shortage. Free silver was no longer an issue. But the changes in voting patterns caused by the Depression of 1893 and the free-silver fight continued long after those problems were settled.

The farm states voted for Bryan, the industrial states for McKinley. But the election was not a victory for industry nor a defeat for American farmers. Agriculture remained important. As Bryan had said in his Cross of Gold speech, the cities and their industries could not prosper unless farmers were prosperous too.

The election marked the birth of the modern industrial age. To most people of that day, Bryan seemed to be pressing for change, McKinley defending the old, established order. In fact, McKinley was far more forward looking than Bryan. His view of the future was much closer to what the reality of the 20th century would be. 🔳

The century ends with the glow of lamplight on Boston Common. Childe Hassam painted this twilight scene in the early 1900s. But what lies ahead in the story of America? How do you imagine this scene will appear in 1920? 1960? 2000?

Return to the Preview & Review on page 726.

CHAPTER 20 REVIEW

| 1866 Tammany Hall | 1870 National Grange movement | 1872 Eakin's *The Agnew Clinic* 1873 Coining of silver discontinued | 1876 *Tom Sawyer* 1877 Hayes elected president ★ Reconstruction ends ★ *Munn v. Illinois* 1878 Bland-Allison Act |

Chapter Summary

Read the statements below. Choose one, and write a paragraph explaining its importance.

1. The United States remained politically divided after the Civil War into the Republican North and Democratic South.
2. Political machines controlled many local elections. These machines helped the poor and immigrants, and then counted on their votes.
3. Tariffs, the money question, and civil service reform posed important issues for Americans after the Civil War.
4. American writers and artists turned to a movement called Realism after the Civil War.
5. Presidential elections during the last half of the 19th century were very close. This happened because few candidates took a real stand on the issues.
6. After the war, times were hard for American farmers. They created the Grange and the Farmers Alliance to help them deal with their problems.
7. Farmers and consumers wanted free coinage of silver. Many wealthy people wanted to remain on the gold standard.
8. The Depression of 1893 led to severe unemployment and unrest such as Coxey's Army and the Pullman Strike.
9. McKinley's defeat of Bryan in 1896 ended the post-Civil War era.

Reviewing Chronological Order

Number your paper 1–5. Then study the time line above and place the following events in the order in which they happened by writing the first next to 1, the second next to 2, and so on.

1. Pendleton Act
2. Cross of Gold speech
3. National Grange formed
4. Coxey's Army marches to Washington
5. Garfield assassinated

Understanding Main Ideas

1. Why did the Democrats and Republicans nominate so many national candidates from close states after the Civil War?
2. What reforms were made in civil service after Congress acted in 1883?
3. What was the money question? How were greenbacks a part of it?
4. Which groups supported the Populist party? What was its platform in 1892?
5. Which groups supported the Republicans in 1896? Which supported the Democrats? Why did the Republicans win?

Thinking Critically

1. **Evaluating.** Suppose you are a political reformer in 1898. You will publish a pamphlet exposing the corruption of your local political machine. Write the introduction to the pamphlet, explaining various wrongs that the machine has committed in your community.
2. **Analyzing.** Although the Populist party lost the election of 1892, several reforms listed in the party's platform were later put into effect. Of these reforms, which do you think was the most important? Why?
3. **Synthesizing.** It is 1896. Write a letter to a friend, giving your eyewitness account of either (a) a meeting of the local Grange discussing farmers' concerns or (b) a Congressional debate on the pros and cons of civil service reform.

Writing About History

Use historical imagination to write a letter to a friend describing what you saw and heard at the Democratic convention in July 1896 when Bryan delivered his "Cross of Gold" speech. Or describe a visit to McKinley during his front-porch campaign. Use the information in Chapter 20 and in reference books to prepare your letter.

Practicing the Strategy

Review the strategy on page 716.

1882
Homer paints *Harvest Moon*

1883
Pendleton Act passed

1884
Cleveland elected president

1888
Harrison elected president

1890
Sherman Silver Purchase Act

★
Farmers Alliance formed

1892
Populist party enters national election

★
Cleveland again elected president

1893
Depression sweeps nation and world

1894
Coxey's Army marches on Washington

★
Pullman Strike

1895
Red Badge of Courage

1896
Bryan's Cross of Gold speech

★
McKinley elected president

★
Post-Civil War era ends

Interpreting Election Results. Compare the election maps on pages 716 and 722, then answer the following questions.

1. In which part of the country were the Democrats strongest in 1888? In 1892?
2. In which part were the Republicans strongest in 1888? In 1892?
3. In which part of the country were the Populists strongest?
4. How would you explain the geographic location of each party's strength?
5. How can you tell that the unit rule was in effect in 1888 but not in 1892?

Using Primary Sources

The following excerpt from Richard Hofstadter's book *The Age of Reform* examines the controversy that arose from the Populist movement. As you read the excerpt, note differences in the two points of view presented. Then answer the questions that follow.

> On the one hand the failure of the revolt has been described . . . as the final defeat of the American farmer. John Hicks, in his history of the movement, speaks of the Populists as having begun "the last phase of a song and perhaps a losing struggle—the struggle to save agricultural America from the devouring jaws of industrial America," while another historian calls Populism "the last united stand of the country's agricultural interest . . . the final attempt made by the farmers of the land to beat back an industrial civilization whose forces had all but vanquished them already."

1. According to the excerpt, how did the perspectives of the two historians differ?
2. Which of the views presented by the two historians reveals bias against industrial America? Quote from the reading to support your answer.
3. How might American farmers today agree or disagree with the views of Populism presented in the excerpt? Support your answer with specific examples.

Linking History & Geography

Agricultural land use is in part determined by a number of natural factors. Topography, rainfall, length of growing season, and other variables influence what is produced in an area. Study the maps on pages 624, 649, and 715 and answer these questions.

1. Why is the Great Plains topography well suited to growing grain?
2. What factors limit the agricultural use of land in Alaska? Wyoming?
3. What natural features help make the Central Valley of California so productive?

Enriching Your Study of History

1. **Individual Project** In your library and other American history books find examples of the cartoons of Thomas Nast. It was Nast who created the symbols of the Tammany Hall tiger, the Republican elephant, and the Democratic donkey. Study a copy of a Nast cartoon from this era and explain his use of one of these symbols. You also may wish to draw your own cartoon to express your view of a key point in the chapter.
2. **Cooperative Project** Presidential campaigns after the Civil War were hard fought and much discussed. Yet time seems to drop a veil over the occupants of the White House during this period, to say nothing of the candidates they defeated. Various members of your group will research and report on each of the following campaigns:

   1868 Grant v. Seymour
   1872 Grant v. Greeley
   1876 Hayes v. Tilden
   1880 Garfield v. Hancock
   1884 Cleveland v. Blaine, Butler
   1888 Harrison v. Cleveland
   1892 Cleveland v. Harrison, Weaver

UNIT SIX REVIEW

Summing Up and Predicting

Read the summary of the main ideas in Unit Six below. Choose one statement, then write a paragraph predicting its outcome or future effect.

1. The tremendous growth of America brought it to the last frontier—the Great Plains. Settlers eventually displaced the Plains Indians who, after several bloody battles, were placed on reservations.
2. A cattle kingdom thrived on the open range of the southern plains.
3. Discoveries of great mineral resources brought increased mining to the West. Many of the resources bolstered American industry.
4. Completion of railroad and communications networks prepared the nation for the rise of industry.
5. American industry became so large that new business organizations, such as corporations and trusts, were developed.
6. Workers turned to unionization to make their demands for improved conditions heard.
7. The "New Immigration" brought people from southern and eastern Europe to American cities and factories.
8. After the Civil War political machines controlled many of the nation's cities.
9. Farmers, workers, and the poor formed organizations to represent them.

Connecting Ideas

1. Ethnic neighborhoods developed in cities in the late 1800s and still exist in many cities. List some advantages and disadvantages of living in an ethnic neighborhood today.
2. What problems might immigrants to the United States today face? How are these problems like those faced by immigrants in the late 1800s? How are they different?
3. Does the author's description of what happened to the Indians in the late 1800s differ from what you have seen in movies and on television? Why or why not?

Practicing Critical Thinking

1. **Drawing Conclusions.** It is the late 1800s. How has the Homestead Act changed your life if you are a Plains Indian? A railroad baron? A farmer? A cattle baron?
2. **Synthesizing.** You know that cartoonist Thomas Nast created the elephant to represent the Republican party and the donkey to represent the Democratic party. Create two new symbols for these political parties and explain why you chose these symbols.
3. **Evaluating.** Of Thomas Edison, Alexander Graham Bell, Henry Bessemer, Jane Addams, John D. Rockefeller, and Cornelius Vanderbilt, who do you think made the greatest contribution to the world? Why?

Cooperative Learning

1. Have your group use the library or other American histories to report on the life of each of the following figures in industrial America:

Cornelius Vanderbilt	Samuel F. B. Morse
Andrew Carnegie	Alexander Graham Bell
John D. Rockefeller	Thomas A. Edison
Cyrus W. Field	Samuel Gompers
Terence V. Powderly	Jane Addams

2. The two great artists of the West were Frederic Remington and Charles Marion Russell. Members of your group will report on these popular artists and show reproductions of their works. Then make one or more poster-size drawings of the cowhands of the Old West.
3. Your group will make a scale model of an Indian village or a sod house that might have stood on the Great Plains. Design a roof that will lift off so you can show how the inside of the house might have been furnished.

Reading in Depth

Durham, Philip and Everett L. Jones. *The Adventures of the Negro Cowboys.* New York: Dodd Mead. Contains stories about the most famous African American cowboys.

Harvey, Brett. *Cassie's Journey: Going West in the 1860s.* New York: Holiday House. Describes the dangers and struggles of Cassie and her family as they migrate westward to California.

Hoexter, Corinne. *From Canton to California: The Epic of Chinese Immigration.* New York: Four Winds Press. Portrays the immigration of Chinese to California and their reception there.

Josephy, Alvin. *The Patriot Chiefs.* New York: Viking. Contains biographies of great Indian leaders such as Chief Joseph and Crazy Horse.

Wolfson, Evelyn. *From Abenaki to Zuñi: A Dictionary of Native American Tribes.* Includes discussions of tribal customs, foods, clothing, and means of travel.

U.S. Naval Academy

Ships of the U.S. Fleet, a symbol of what a mighty power America had become by the turn of the century, enter San Francisco's Golden Gate.

AN EXPANDING AMERICA

UNIT 7

I n Unit 7 you will learn how the United States acquired an overseas empire and how the Progressive movement fought to improve the lives of the American people. Here are some main points to keep in mind as you read the unit.

- American expansionism led the United States to win control of Alaska and Hawaii.

- As a result of the Spanish-American War of 1898, Cuba was freed from Spanish rule and the United States annexed Puerto Rico, Guam, and the Philippines.

- The Panama Canal was built by the United States and opened in 1914. The Canal drastically cut travel time between the Atlantic and Pacific oceans.

- Journalists called muckrakers attacked corruption and the terrible conditions in cities and industry.

- As president, Theodore Roosevelt led the charge for reform, earning the nickname *trustbuster*.

CHAPTER 21

America in World Affairs, 1865–1912

E ven those who thought manifest destiny a bold American notion might have been surprised by what happened after the Civil War. The parade of settlers marching "from sea to shining sea" stopped only to catch its breath before pressing on. Americans seemed to forget George Washington's warning to avoid foreign involvements. The country began to expand its influence in Latin America. Alaska and Hawaii were acquired. After the war with Spain, fought to free Cuba, the Philippines and Puerto Rico were taken by the United States. By the time Theodore Roosevelt became president at the turn of the century, America's influence in the Western Hemisphere was great. But how far could America stretch itself in world affairs?

Preview & Review

Use these questions to guide your reading. Answer the questions after completing Section 1.
Understanding Issues, Events, & Ideas. Describe American expansion overseas, using the following words: isolationism, American expansionism, Midway Islands, Alaskan Purchase, Seward's Folly, Hawaiian Islands, archipelago, McKinley Tariff, absolute monarch.
1. What was isolationism?
2. Why did the Japanese agree to open trade with the U.S.?
3. How did "Seward's Folly" turn out to be an immense bargain?
4. Who were the first Americans to reach Hawaii? Who followed?
Thinking Critically. 1. You are with Perry in Tokyo harbor. Describe your reactions. 2. You are a member of Congress. Would you vote for or against the purchase of Alaska? For or against the acquisition of Hawaii? Why?

1. EXTENDING AMERICA'S INFLUENCE

Isolationism

For many Americans longtime suspicions of Europe had increased during the Civil War. Great Britain and France had sympathized with the Confederate government. British companies had built ships for the southerners. This had enabled the Confederacy to get around the United States blockade of southern ports. The *Alabama*, a British-built warship flying the Confederate flag, destroyed many American merchant ships during the rebellion. For a time Great Britain even considered entering the war on the side of the Confederacy.

While the United States was fighting its desperate struggle, France boldly sent an army into Mexico. The French then named a European prince, Maximilian of Austria, as Emperor of Mexico. This was a direct challenge to the Monroe Doctrine, which had stated that no European colonies were to be established in the Americas.

Once the Civil War ended, the United States sent 50,000 soldiers to the Mexican border to aid the Mexican patriots who were fighting Maximilian and demand that France withdraw its army. The French pulled out. In June 1867 Mexican patriots led by Benito Juárez entered Mexico City. Maximilian was captured and put to death.

These events demonstrated that European powers were eager to take advantage of any weakness of the United States. Americans wanted nothing from Europe except the right to buy and sell goods. They considered European governments undemocratic. They also believed that European diplomats were tricky and untrustworthy. To get involved with a European diplomat meant the risk of becoming involved in the wars and rivalries of Europe. Better, believed the average American, to have as little as possible to do with Europe.

This was the popular view. American political leaders never took such an extreme position. But the policy of American relations with the European powers was **isolationism.** The United States should keep pretty much to itself, as Washington had cautioned in his Farewell Address. It should not meddle in European affairs. And it should not permit Europeans to meddle in American affairs. This latter point had been most strongly stated in the Monroe Doctrine.

Americans who were isolationists were taking no serious risks. As the nation grew in wealth and numbers, the possibility that any European country might attack it rapidly disappeared.

Culver Pictures

Benito Juárez was the high-minded leader of the Mexican people when France attempted to make Mexico its colony.

The Closing of the Frontier

Manifest destiny had carried the American people more than three thousand miles across the North American continent. They had conquered all obstacles as they spread from "sea to shining sea," from the Atlantic to the Pacific. But by the late 19th century the frontiers of the continent had virtually disappeared. The lands of the Great Plains and the Southwest were filling with people and within two decades—by 1912—all would become states. Only Alaska in the frigid north still represented an American frontier.

What did the closing of the frontier mean to America? To what would that boundless energy that had fueled manifest destiny be

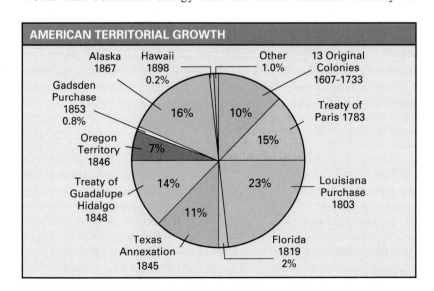

AMERICAN TERRITORIAL GROWTH

Alaska 1867
Hawaii 1898 0.2%
Other 1.0%
13 Original Colonies 1607-1733
Gadsden Purchase 1853 0.8%
Treaty of Paris 1783
16%
10%
15%
Oregon Territory 1846
7%
Treaty of Guadalupe Hidalgo 1848
14%
23%
Louisiana Purchase 1803
11%
Texas Annexation 1845
Florida 1819 2%

LEARNING FROM GRAPHS. *This chart shows how the United States has added to its territory throughout its history. During which century did the country add the most territory?*

turned? Certainly there were problems and challenges to be solved within the United States. Yet manifest destiny was something else, a part of the adventurous restlessness that was so much a part of the American character. Had the first period of American history ended with the closing of the frontier, as Frederick Jackson Turner claimed? Or would Americans turn their restless spirits elsewhere and continue to expand the nation's boundaries?

Expansionism

Americans never adopted an isolationist attitude toward the rest of the world. Many people believed that the same manifest destiny that had brought the Great West into the Union would eventually bring all of North and South America under the control of the Stars and Stripes—and the islands of the Pacific Ocean as well. This attitude was known as **American expansionism.**

Remember that the Monroe Doctrine had stated that no more *European* colonies should be established in the Americas. It said nothing about the United States extending its control in the Western Hemisphere.

In the years after the Civil War Americans began to extend their influence in Latin America and in the Pacific Ocean. In August 1867 the United States navy occupied the **Midway Islands,** located about 1,000 miles (1,600 kilometers) northwest of Hawaii. Most Americans then gave not another thought to these uninhabited flyspecks on the map of the vast Pacific until a great American-Japanese naval battle was fought there in World War II.

What convinced Americans to look beyond their boundaries? Writers such as Josiah Strong, a Congregational minister, claimed America had an ''Anglo-Saxon'' mission to expand overseas. These writers based their views on two ideas. The first was the concept of an Anglo-Saxon ''race,'' which to Americans meant the people of Great Britain and their descendants. This concept of race is scientifically inaccurate. Although Anglo Saxons share certain physical characteristics, they are actually part of the Caucasoid race. The other idea, called Social Darwinism, applied the theories of scientist Charles Darwin—especially the theory of the ''survival of the fittest''—to people and nations. According to Social Darwinism, the energetic, strong, and fit should rule everyone else. As you have read, people had used Social Darwinism to justify unsafe and unsanitary working conditions, child labor, and the exploitation of workers by American business leaders. Now the same argument claimed that the American people—the energetic, strong, and fit—should rule the other peoples of the earth, or at least teach them what was ''right.'' As Strong stated it:

“ The Anglo-Saxon is the representative of two great ideas, which are closely related. One of them is that of civil liberty.

Nearly all the civil liberty in the world is enjoyed by Anglo-Saxons. . . . The other great idea represented by the Anglo-Saxon is that of pure, spiritual Christianity. It follows, then, that Anglo-Saxons, as the great representatives of these two ideas, have a special relationship to the world's future. They are divinely commissioned to be, in a sense, their brother's keeper. . . .[1]"

The Opening of Japan

The first example of this mood of global expansion took place in Japan. For centuries Japan had kept itself isolated from the rest of the world. Except for Chinese and Dutch traders, Japan did not permit any foreigners to enter the country. Then, quite suddenly, their peaceful harbor was invaded.

On July 8, 1853, a crowd of astonished Japanese watched a fleet of ships move into Tokyo harbor. These ships had no sails or oars and belched black smoke from their funnels. The "black dragons," as the Japanese called them, were the coal-powered steamships of the American fleet.

[1]From *Our Country: Its Possible Future and Its Present Crisis* by Josiah Strong

The British Library

Point of View

In the opening lyric for *Pacific Overtures,* a musical based on the opening of Japan, a reciter sings:

"In the middle of the
   world we float
In the middle of the sea.
The realities remain
   remote
In the middle of the sea.
Kings are burning
   somewhere.
Wheels are turning
   somewhere,
Trains are being run,
Wars are being won,
Things are being done
Somewhere out there, not
   here.
Here we paint
   screens. . . ."
from *Pacific Overtures,*
Music and lyrics by
Stephen Sondheim, 1975

This detail from a Japanese painted scroll shows one of Commodore Perry's four ships in Edo (Tokyo) Bay. His arrival by steamship in July 1853 was described by the Japanese as "four black dragons" entering their tranquil harbor. Imagine you are aboard one of the small Japanese boats, or sampans, in the foreground. What would be your impression of Perry's steamship?

Commodore Matthew Perry commanded the American fleet. President Millard Fillmore had sent him to ask the Japanese emperor to open several Japanese ports to American trade. Perhaps frightened by American technology and naval power, the Japanese signed a treaty of friendship with the United States.

The Purchase of Alaska

Americans also knew little to nothing about Alaska, then called Russian America, until William H. Seward, secretary of state, purchased it from Russia in March 1867. Russian explorers, fur trappers, and merchants had been in the area since the 1790s. But Alaska had never brought them the riches they sought. The Russian government decided to sell the vast land. The United States seemed the logical customer. Seward jumped at the opportunity to add more territory to the United States. He agreed to a purchase price of $7.2 million.

News of this **Alaskan Purchase** surprised everyone in America. Congress knew little about the negotiations until the treaty was presented to it, along with the bill for $7.2 million.

To win support, Seward launched a nationwide campaign. Alaska was worth far more than $7.2 million, he claimed. Its fish, furs, and lumber were very valuable. By controlling it, America would increase its influence in the North Pacific. These arguments convinced the senators to accept the treaty by a vote of 37 to 2.

The House of Representatives, however, hesitated to provide the $7.2 million. Seward again ran through his arguments about the virtues of this land in the frozen North. The Russian minister to the

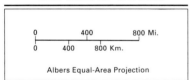

ALASKA AND THE UNITED STATES

```
0        400        800 Mi.
|----|----|----|----|
0    400    800 Km.
```

Albers Equal-Area Projection

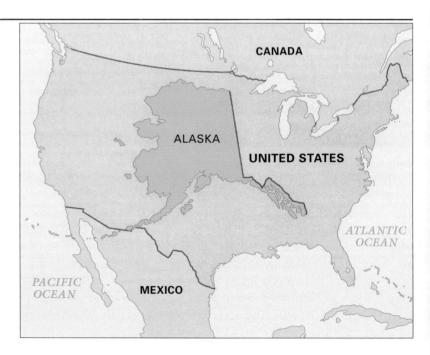

LEARNING FROM MAPS. Alaska's size is truly amazing. It is by far the largest state. This map compares the size of Alaska to that of the continental United States. In your own words, state how they compare in size.

United States, Baron Edouard de Stoeckl, wined, dined, and probably bribed a number of House members. Stoeckl later claimed that he had spent almost $200,000 getting the House to appropriate the money.

Many Americans thought buying Alaska was a mistake. They called the territory **"Seward's Folly,"** "Frigidia," and "President Andrew Johnson's Polar Bear Garden." One joke said that in Alaska a cow would give ice cream instead of milk. But most people were pleased. What a bargain Seward made! For about two cents an acre he obtained nearly 600,000 square miles (1,560,000 square kilometers) of land, a region twice the size of the state of Texas. The land contained immense resources of lumber, gold, copper, and other metals. A gold rush in the 1890s brought thousands of eager Americans to Alaska and led to the development of Seattle as a major Pacific port. More recently, rich deposits of oil and natural gas have been discovered there.

Hawaii

After the Civil War Americans also became interested in the **Hawaiian Islands.** This **archipelago,** or island group, is located in the Pacific about 2,000 miles (3,200 kilometers) southwest of San Francisco.

The first Americans to reach these beautiful, sunny islands were New England whalers and traders. Beginning in the late 1700s, they stopped there for rest and fresh supplies on their lonely voyages. These sailors were followed by missionaries who came to Hawaii hoping to convert the inhabitants to Christianity.

The foreign missionary movement, long important to both Catholics and Protestants, offered many Americans their first glimpse of the world beyond American shores. These Americans felt that the spread of Christianity around the world must precede the spread of democracy and social justice. The Hawaiian missionaries, besides spreading the gospel, settled down, built houses, and raised crops. In the 1840s and 1850s their children and grandchildren were beginning to cultivate sugar.

By the time of the American Civil War, the missionary families dominated the Islands' economy and government. Sugar was the Hawaiians' most important export. They sold most of it in the United States.

The Hawaiians were ruled by a king who made all the decisions and owned all the land. But in 1840 King Kamehameha III issued a constitution modeled after the United States Constitution. This was not surprising since many of Kamehameha's advisers were Americans. In 1875 the two countries signed a treaty which allowed Hawaiian sugar to enter the United States without payment of a tariff. In exchange the Hawaiian government agreed not to give territory or special privileges in the islands to any other nation.

HAWAII

Refer to map on pages 1128–29 for relative location to the United States.

Albers Equal-Area Projection

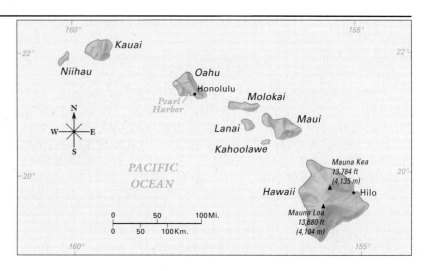

LEARNING FROM MAPS. *The Hawaiian Islands lie like a string of pearls in the Pacific Ocean. What are the three largest islands?*

The Bishop Museum

Queen Liliuokalani took the throne in 1891. She wrote the popular song "Aloha Oe" or "Farewell to Thee." Read these pages and Queen Liliuokalani's letter on page 779 to decide whom she might wish to bid farewell.

The 1875 treaty greatly encouraged sugar production. The missionary families formed corporations and imported thousands of low-paid Chinese and Japanese immigrants to work on the plantations. Most of these laborers signed long-term contracts similar to the ones that indentured servants had signed with Virginia tobacco planters 250 years earlier.

Between 1875 and 1890 the amount of Hawaiian sugar shipped to the United States jumped from 18 million to 160 million pounds (about 8 million to 72 million kilograms). But the Hawaiian sugar boom came to a sudden end when Congress passed the **McKinley Tariff** of 1890, a law that took away the special advantage of the Hawaiians. Their sugar now had to compete with sugar grown in the United States and also with sugar produced in Cuba and other countries. Prices fell, and the economy of the Hawaiian Islands suffered a serious depression.

Along with Hawaii's economic crisis came a political crisis. In 1891 the government changed hands. The new ruler was Queen Liliuokalani. She was intelligent and fiercely patriotic. She resented the influence of American planters and merchants in her country. Her attitude was expressed in the slogan "Hawaii for the Hawaiians."

Queen Liliuokalani was determined to break the power of the foreign-dominated Hawaiian legislature. In January 1893 she proclaimed a new constitution making her an **absolute monarch**—a ruler who holds all power. The constitution never went into effect.

The Americans responded by organizing a revolution. John L. Stevens, the American minister to Hawaii, supported the rebels. He ordered 150 marines ashore from an American warship in Honolulu harbor. They did not have to fire a shot to persuade Liliuokalani and the Hawaiians not to resist. The revolutionaries promptly raised the American flag.

Stevens announced that Hawaii was now under the protection of the United States. A delegation hurried off to Washington to

Peabody Museum of Salem

The Hawaiian Island of Oahu seems a paradise in this 1821 watercolor. The ship lying at anchor in the foreground flies the U.S. flag. What do you predict the U. S. presence will mean to Oahu and the rest of the Hawaiian Islands?

negotiate a treaty of annexation to bring Hawaii under American control. In February 1893 President Benjamin Harrison sent this treaty to the Senate for approval. But Harrison's term was about to end. President-elect Cleveland asked the Senate not to vote on the treaty until he had a chance to consider it. The Senate therefore postponed action.

After taking office, Cleveland withdrew the treaty. He sent a special commission headed by James H. Blount of Georgia to investigate conditions in the islands. Blount reported that the Hawaiian people did not want to be annexed to the United States.

After reading Blount's report, Cleveland decided to scrap the treaty. He called Stevens back to Washington and sent a new representative to the islands. This new United States minister met with the president of the revolutionary government, Sanford B. Dole, and urged him to resign. Cleveland wanted to return control of the islands to Queen Liliuokalani, who by this time was popularly known in America as "Queen Lil."

Dole (whose pineapples would soon be well-known in the United States) refused to resign. If the United States did not want Hawaii, the revolutionaries would remain independent. On July 4, 1894, they proclaimed Hawaii a republic. 🖅

Brown Brothers

Sanford B. Dole was born in Hawaii to American missionaries. He was president of the government that overthrew the queen. He later became first governor of the Territory of Hawaii. What hint can you find in the last paragraph on this page that pineapples as well as politics may have been behind Dole's motives?

Return to the Preview & Review on page 736.

Extending America's Influence   743

Use these questions to guide your reading. Answer the questions after completing Section 2.
Understanding Issues, Events, & Ideas. Use the following words to explain American attempts to police the Western Hemisphere: Pan-American Conference, Chilean Crisis, arbitration, Venezuela Boundary Dispute.
1. Why did Secretary of State Blaine want to bring the nations of the Western Hemisphere together?
2. Why did President Cleveland want to arbitrate the Venezuela Boundary Dispute?
3. What was the United States' notice to Europe and Latin America in the Venezuela Boundary Dispute?
Thinking Critically. Americans in the 1800s enjoyed "twisting the British lion's tail." Name a country or foreign group that recently has done the same thing to the United States. Why do you think they did it?

2. AMERICA AND ITS SOUTHERN NEIGHBORS

Pan-Americanism

American interest in the nations of Latin America also increased after the Civil War. Again American missionaries led the way. These countries sold large quantities of coffee, bananas, fertilizer, and many other products to the United States. But they bought most of their manufactured goods in Europe. In the 1890s James G. Blaine, who was secretary of state under Presidents Garfield and Harrison, set out to develop closer trade ties with Latin America. His strategy was simple but one-sided.

Blaine wanted all the nations of the Western Hemisphere to see themselves as belonging to a group with common interests. In his opinion the United States would obviously dominate such a group. This was one reason why many Latin American nations hesitated to cooperate with Blaine. In 1889 Blaine invited the Latin American countries to send representatives to Washington for a meeting. After a whirlwind tour of 41 cities, these representatives assembled for the first **Pan-American Conference.**

The conference did not accomplish much. The delegates rejected Blaine's suggestion that they lower their tariffs on American goods. Still, it was the first time the nations of North and South America had come together. They began to sense that the common interests of the Western Hemisphere were in many ways different from those of other nations.

The Chilean Crisis

Any goodwill that the Pan-American Conference generated suffered a setback in the **Chilean Crisis** of 1891-92. During a civil war in Chile between a faction supporting its president and one backing its congress, the United States supported the presidential side. Unfortunately for the United States, the other side won the war. The Chileans called people from the United States *Yanquis.* Anti-*Yanqui* feeling was now high.

In this heated atmosphere some sailors from the U.S.S. *Baltimore,* on shore leave in the city of Valparaiso, got in a fight outside the True Blue Saloon. Apparently the fight started when a local civilian spat in the face of one of the sailors. A mob attacked the sailors, and the Valparaiso police did nothing to stop the fighting. Two sailors were killed and 16 injured.

President Harrison threatened to break diplomatic relations unless the Chilean government apologized. A war scare resulted. Fortunately, the Chilean government did apologize. It also paid $75,000 in damages to the injured sailors and to the families of the dead.

The Venezuela Boundary Dispute

In 1895 the United States again flexed its muscles in South America. For decades Great Britain and Venezuela had haggled over the boundary line separating Venezuela and British Guiana, a small British colony on the north coast of South America. Venezuela had tried to settle the dispute in the past, but Great Britain had always refused to permit an outside judge to draw the boundary. Tensions increased in the 1880s when one of the largest gold nuggets ever found—509 ounces (14,252 grams)—was discovered in the territory both countries claimed.

President Grover Cleveland was afraid that if the British took any more territory in the Western Hemisphere, other European powers might follow. Then the economic and political interests of the United States in Latin America would be injured. He was determined to make Great Britain agree to settle the argument of who owned the territory by **arbitration**—that is, to allow a neutral judge to decide. President Cleveland ordered Richard Olney, his secretary of state, to send a stern message to the British government.

Olney's note of July 20, 1895, was extremely strong and quite insulting in tone. Cleveland described it as a "20-inch gun." The United States, said Olney, was the supreme power in the hemisphere. The Monroe Doctrine prohibited further European expansion in the Western Hemisphere. The United States would intervene in disputes between European and Latin American nations to make certain that the Monroe Doctrine was not violated.

Despite the harsh tone of Olney's message, the British prime minister, Lord Salisbury, dismissed it as a bluff. He thought Cleveland was playing the political game called "twisting the British lion's tail." The game's goal was to try to anger Great Britain. Any statement threatening Great Britain was sure to be popular with Americans of Irish origin. Most Irish Americans hated the British because they refused to give Ireland its independence. Instead of answering the note promptly, Salisbury delayed nearly four months.

When he did reply, Salisbury rejected Olney's argument that the Monroe Doctrine applied to the boundary dispute. Britain's dispute with Venezuela, he said politely but firmly, was no business of the United States.

This response made Cleveland "mad clean through." The Monroe Doctrine *did* apply to the situation. The United States would "resist by every means in its power" any British seizure of Venezuelan territory. The president asked Congress for money to finance a United States commission that would investigate the dispute. If the British refused to accept its findings, the United States would use force.

Nearly all people seemed to approve of Cleveland's tough stand. Venezuelans were delighted. When the news reached the capital of

The Granger Collection, New York

President Grover Cleveland twists the tail of an outraged British lion while his supporters cheer him on. Judging from the president's supporters, had the old feelings against England cooled over a hundred years?

Venezuela, Caracas, a cheering crowd of at least 200,000 people gathered at the home of the United States representative.

For a brief time war between the United States and Great Britain seemed possible. But neither government wanted war. Cleveland was mainly interested in reminding the world of the Monroe Doctrine. Great Britain had too many other diplomatic problems to be willing to fight over what they considered a relatively unimportant piece of land in South America.

As soon as he realized that the situation had become dangerous, Lord Salisbury agreed to let an impartial commission decide where to place the boundary. In 1899 this commission gave Britain nearly all the land in question.

On the surface the United States seemed to be defending a small Latin American nation against a great European power in what came to be known as the **Venezuela Boundary Dispute.** In fact, it was putting both Europe and Latin America on notice that the United States was the most important nation in the Western Hemisphere. Throughout the crisis Cleveland ignored Venezuela. Its minister in Washington was never once consulted.

Return to the Preview & Review on page 744.

3. THE SPANISH-AMERICAN WAR

Cuba and Spain

Early in 1895, shortly before Secretary Olney fired his "20-inch gun" over the Venezuela boundary, real gunfire broke out in Cuba. The Spanish had called their colony in Cuba the "Ever-Faithful Isle." Cuba was one of Spain's few colonies in America that had not revolted in the early 1800s. It was Spain's last important possession in the Americas.

In 1868 there had been a revolution in Cuba which lasted for ten years. It had failed, but now, in 1895, Cuban patriots again took up arms. Independence was their objective. The rebels engaged in the surprise attacks of **guerrilla warfare.** They burned sugar cane fields, blocked railroads, and ambushed small parties of Spanish soldiers. By the end of 1896 they controlled most of rural Cuba.

The Cuban patriots were led by José Martí, a poet, statesman, and essayist. Martí was a tireless critic of Spanish rule in Cuba. His poems, articles, and speeches were carried in many American newspapers. They helped focus America's attention on the brutality taking place in Cuba. When fighting broke out, Martí returned to Cuba. He was killed in the fighting a few days after his arrival. Martí became a national hero. Although he died three years before Cuban independence, he is often credited with doing more than any other individual to win his Cuba's freedom. An excerpt from one of Martí's patriotic poems is followed by the English translation.

> " **Dos patrias**
> Dos patrias tengo yo: Cuba y la noche.
> ¿O son una las dos? No bein retira
> su majestad el Sol, con largos velos
> un clavel en la mano, silenciosa
> Cuba cual viuda triste me aparece.
> ¡Yo sé cuál es ese clavel sangriento
> que en la mano le tiembla! Esté vació
> mi pecho, destrozado está y vació
> en donde estaba el corazón. Ya es hora
> de empezar a morir. La noche es buena
> para decir adiós. La luz estorba
> y la palabra humana. El universo
> habla mejor que el hombre.
>   Cual bandera
> que invita a batallar, la llama roja
> de la vela flamea. Las ventanas
> abro, ya estrecho en mí. Muda, rompiendo
> las hojas del clavel, como una nube
> que enturbia el cielo, Cuba, viuda, pasa. . . . "

Preview & Review

Use these questions to guide your reading. Answer the questions after completing Section 3.
Understanding Issues, Events, & Ideas. Discuss the Spanish-American War, using the following words: guerrilla warfare, *reconcentrado, junta,* yellow journalism, Teller Amendment, ultimatum, Spanish-American War, Manila Bay, Rough Riders, expeditionary force, Santiago, El Caney, San Juan Hill, Puerto Rico.
1. Why had the Spanish called Cuba their "Ever-Faithful Isle"?
2. Why did General Weyler place farm people in concentration camps?
3. Why was the *Maine* sent to Cuba? How did the explosion of the *Maine* bring the United States and Spain to the brink of war?
4. How did President McKinley try to prevent war with Spain? In general, what was the attitude of Congress?

Thinking Critically. 1. If you were an ambassador to Cuba in the 1890s, would you have urged the United States to go to war? Explain your reasoning. 2. Yellow journalists wrote very persuasive articles that influenced many people. Imagine that you are a journalist. Select a current issue about which you feel strongly and write a persuasive article about it.

José Martí

The Granger Collection, New York

The Spanish-American War 747

The Granger Collection, New York

The inspiration for this 1898 cartoon is the old saying, "Out of the frying pan and into the fire." The young woman who represents Cuba must decide between "Spanish Misrule" (the pan) and the flame of "Anarchy" burning on the isle of Cuba. Explain the artist's caption: "The Duty of the Hour—To Save Her Not Only from Spain, but from a Worse Fate."

" **Two Motherlands**

I have two homelands: Cuba and the night.
Or are they both one? No sooner has the sun
withdrawn its grandeur than Cuba appears
beside me in silence, a mournful widow
who clasps a carnation to funeral robes.
I know the bloody carnation
that trembles in her hand. My breast
is now hollow, the niche that once held my heart
is empty and shattered. Now is the hour
to start dying. Night is a good time
for bidding farewell. Human words and the light
only stand in our way. The universe
speaks more clearly than man.
                                    Like a banner
that calls us to battle, the flame of the candle
is burning red. My body no longer contains me,
I open the window. In silence, as she crushes
the carnation's petals, like a cloud
that darkens the sky, Cuba, the widow, passes. . . .[1] "

[1]Both versions from "Two Motherlands" by José Martí in *The Canary Whose Eye Is So Black,* edited and translated by Cheli Duran

In an effort to regain control of the countryside, the Spanish Governor-General, Valeriano Weyler, began herding farm people into what were called *reconcentrados*—concentration camps. He penned up about 500,000 Cubans in these camps. Weyler did this for two reasons. First, Cubans in the camps could not supply the rebels with food. Second, anyone outside the camps could be considered an enemy of Spain and arrested or shot on the spot.

Conditions inside the concentration camps were unspeakably bad. About 200,000 Cubans died in the camps, victims of disease and malnutrition.

Most people in the United States sympathized with the Cubans' wish to be independent. They were horrified by the stories of Spanish cruelty. Cuban revolutionaries fanned these fires. They established committees called *juntas* in the United States to raise money, spread propaganda, and recruit volunteers.

Explosion in Havana

Both President Cleveland and President McKinley had tried to persuade Spain to give the Cuban people more say about their government. They failed to make much impression. Tension increased. Then, in January 1898, President McKinley sent a battleship, the U.S.S. *Maine,* to Cuba. There had been riots in Havana, the capital city. McKinley sent the *Maine* to protect American citizens there against possible attack.

On February 15, while the *Maine* lay at anchor in Havana Harbor, a tremendous explosion rocked the ship. Of the 350 men aboard, 266 were killed. The *Maine* quickly sank.

To this day no one knows for sure what happened. Many Americans jumped to the conclusion that the Spanish had sunk the ship with a mine, a kind of underwater bomb. The navy conducted an investigation. It concluded that the *Maine* had indeed been destroyed by a mine. Another American investigation in 1911 also judged that an explosion from outside destroyed the ship.

The Spanish government claimed the disaster was caused by an explosion inside the *Maine*. This is certainly possible. A short circuit in the ship's wiring might have caused the *Maine*'s ammunition to explode, for example. It is difficult to imagine that the Spanish would have blown up the ship. The last thing Spain wanted was a war with the United States.

Emotions were inflamed on all sides. The Spanish government, or some individual officer, may indeed have been responsible. Or it is possible that the Cuban rebels did the job, knowing that Spain would be blamed.

In any case, a demand for war against Spain swept the United States. In New York City a man in a Broadway bar raised his glass and proclaimed, ''Remember the *Maine!*'' This became a battle cry

Point of View

A selected list of speeches delivered in 1898 by graduating high school seniors in Black River Falls, Wisconsin.

Girls:
   A Woman's Sphere
   Home Training
   Our Duty to Unfortunates
   A Modern Reformer
Boys:
   Individual Independence
   Is the Cuban Capable of Self-Government?
   The Stars and Stripes
   Spain's Colonial System
   Should the United States Extend Its Territory?
   War and Its Effects on the Nation.
   From *Wisconsin Death Trip,*
   Michael Lesy, 1973

The Granger Collection, New York

In strong detail this 1898 lithograph shows the explosion of the Maine *in Havana Harbor. What are two theories that might explain such a terrible explosion?*

similar to "Remember the Alamo!" during the Texas Revolution of the 1830s.

As tension mounted, the publisher of the New York *Journal*, William Randolph Hearst, had sent the artist Frederic Remington to Cuba to draw pictures of the Cuban Revolution. When Remington complained that there was no revolution and asked to come home, Hearst telegraphed:

❝ PLEASE REMAIN. YOU FURNISH THE PICTURES AND I'LL FURNISH THE WAR. ❞

War Is Declared

President McKinley wanted to avoid war. He told a friend:

❝ I have been through one war. I have seen the dead piled up, and I do not want to see another. ❞

McKinley did not let the sinking of the *Maine* cause a break with Spain. But he also wanted to stop the bloodletting in Cuba. He believed the Spanish must do away with the concentration camps and negotiate a truce with the Cubans. He also felt that more self-government should be granted Cuba.

Spain was willing to do this. However, the rebels demanded total independence. The Spanish government did not dare to give in completely. The Spanish people were proud and patriotic. Any government that "gave away" Cuba would surely be overthrown. Perhaps the king himself would be deposed. These unsettling thoughts made Spain stand firmly against Cuban independence.

Still, some peaceful solution might have been found if all sides had been patient. McKinley knew that Spain was earnestly exploring several possible compromises. He had also been promised that in time all his demands would be met. But he finally made up his mind that Spain would never give up Cuba voluntarily.

On April 11, 1898, the president told Congress that he had "exhausted every effort" to end the "intolerable" situation in Cuba. He asked Congress to give him the power to secure in Cuba "a stable government, capable of . . . insuring peace."

Congress had been thundering for war for weeks. By huge majorities it passed a joint resolution stating that the people of Cuba "are, and of right ought to be, free and independent." If the Spanish did not withdraw "at once" from the island, the president should use "the entire land and naval forces of the United States" to drive them out. Then Congress protected itself against being accused of going to war for selfish reasons. Its members approved a resolution

This elaborate 1898 cartoon shows President McKinley in a plumed hat, like Shakespeare's Hamlet, who also was unable to make up his mind. McKinley has several choices: heed the pleas of Uncle Sam to protect Cuba and close down the concentration camps, or revenge the watery ghosts who have risen from the Maine *by going to war or compensating the victims' families. How did he decide? What had Congress already decided?*

Culver Pictures

proposed by Senator Henry M. Teller of Colorado. This **Teller Amendment** stated that the United States had no intention of taking Cuba for itself or trying to control its government.

McKinley gave the Spanish government three days to accept his terms or face war. Unwilling to yield to McKinley's **ultimatum**—do this or face the consequences—the Spanish broke relations with the United States.

The Battle of Manila Bay

The first important battle of the **Spanish-American War** was fought not in Cuba but rather in the Far East on the Spanish-held Philippine Islands. The United States had a naval squadron stationed in Hong Kong, China, under the command of Commodore George Dewey. When war was declared, Dewey's ships sailed for instant action. He had been ordered weeks earlier to prepare for battle by Theodore Roosevelt, the assistant secretary of the navy.

Dewey steamed swiftly from Hong Kong across the China Sea to Manila, capital of the Philippines. His fleet entered **Manila Bay** on the night of April 30. Early the next morning, he gave the captain of his flagship, the cruiser *Olympia*, the famous command "You may fire when ready, Gridley." The American fleet far outgunned the

A great cheer rises from the crowds who have come to see the 10th Pennsylvania Volunteers set sail for Manila. What signs of patriotism are apparent in this lithograph?

The Granger Collection, New York

The Granger Collection, New York

YELLOW JOURNALISM

In the 1890s two popular New York newspapers, the *Journal*, owned by William Randolph Hearst, and the *World*, owned by Joseph Pulitzer, were competing bitterly for readers. Both played up crime and scandals to increase sales. This type of writing was called yellow journalism because the *World* printed a comic strip called "The Yellow Kid."

Both the *World* and the *Journal* supported the Cuban revolution. General Weyler's policy of *reconcentrado* provided the raw material for many of their stories about Spanish brutality. The actual conditions in Cuba were bad enough. But Hearst and Pulitzer made the camps seem even more shocking. Their exaggerated and untrue stories were topped by screaming headlines and accompanied by spine-chilling drawings and ugly cartoons.

This one-sided picture of the revolution no doubt influenced the United States' decision to go to war with Spain. How much influence the newspapers had is not an easy question to answer. It had some effect on many people. What is more clear is that Hearst and Pulitzer favored war partly for selfish reasons. They knew it would produce exciting news that would help them sell more papers.

Spanish warships guarding Manila. By noon the Spanish fleet had been smashed. Not one American sailor was killed. It was a marvelous triumph.

Dewey's victory made him an instant hero in the United States. Many people named babies after him. A chewing gum manufacturer came out with a gum named "Dewey's Chewies." However, until troops arrived from America, Dewey did not have enough men to occupy Manila or conquer any other part of the Philippine archipelago. So he set up a blockade of Manila harbor. When reinforcements reached him in August, he captured the city.

Moving an Army to Cuba

The war in Cuba did not begin so quickly. McKinley called for volunteers and received an enthusiastic response. In two months 200,000 recruits enlisted. Theodore Roosevelt, for example, promptly resigned as assistant secretary of the navy. Although he was nearly 40, he announced that he would organize a regiment and go off to fight in Cuba. He was commissioned a lieutenant colonel in the First Volunteer Cavalry.

Roosevelt led people as easily as the fabled Pied Piper of Hamelin. He came from a wealthy New York family of Dutch origin. He had been a sickly child with poor eyesight, but he had enormous determination. He built up his scrawny body and became a skillful boxer. He loved hunting, hiking, and horseback riding. He also loved

The Spanish-American War   753

Courtesy Frederic Remington Art Museum, Ogdensburg, New York

Frederic Remington painted this masterful "Charge of the Rough Riders Up San Juan Hill" in 1898. The scene is as Remington imagined it, for although he was a war correspondent in Cuba he did not witness the charge. Roosevelt leads the charge on horseback. Note that the man wearing a red bandanna in the center of the painting is probably African American. You and your classmates might take turns describing Roosevelt's Rough Riders, about whom you have just read.

politics and scholarship. While still in college, he wrote an excellent history of the naval side of the War of 1812.

Roosevelt had served in the New York state legislature. He had been police commissioner of New York City. And he had run a cattle ranch on the open range of the Dakota Territory until the terrible winter of 1885-86 wiped out his herds.

Roosevelt's call for volunteers brought forth no fewer than 23,000 applicants. The colorful colonel chose a remarkable collection of soldiers from this mass. He enlisted several hundred cowboys, many of whom he had known in his ranching days, and 20 American Indians. Several well-known athletes and some police who had worked for him in New York City also joined up. The chaplain of the regiment was a former football player. The outfit became known to the public as the **Rough Riders.**

With men like Roosevelt recruiting, the army soon had more volunteers than it could efficiently organize in so short a time. Dozens of new units were shipped off to Tampa, Florida, where the invasion force was to be trained and supplied. That city became a near madhouse.

All the railroad lines around Tampa were clogged by long lines of unopened freight cars jammed with guns and ammunition, uniforms, and food. The trainees sweated in heavy blue woolen uniforms while the temperature climbed into the humid 90s. Lightweight summer uniforms for the **expeditionary force** did not arrive at Tampa until after the soldiers had sailed off for Cuba. Tropical fevers and other diseases raged through camp. Spoiled foods caused outbreaks of diarrhea and more serious illnesses. The longer the army remained at Tampa, the worse conditions became. Roosevelt raged:

    ❝ No words could describe . . . the confusion and lack of system and the general mismanagement of the situation here.**❞**

The Capture of Santiago

The slow-moving transport ships that would carry the army to Cuba could not put to sea until the Spanish fleet in the Atlantic had been located. That fleet could not stand up against American warships, but it could raise havoc with the transports.

The Spanish commander, Admiral Pascual Cervera, had tried to avoid the American navy by putting into the harbor of **Santiago,** a city on the southern coast of Cuba. In late May an American squadron discovered his fleet there and blockaded the entrance to the harbor. It was then safe for the army transports to set out.

In mid-June 17,000 men boarded ship in Tampa. There was incredible confusion. Many lost contact with their units. Fearful of being left behind, dozens simply climbed aboard whatever ship they could find. At last the expedition managed to set sail.

Courtesy of the Library of Congress

Colonel Roosevelt and some of his Rough Riders posed for this picture atop San Juan Hill shortly after taking the strategic point. Compare and contrast this photograph with the painting on the opposite page.

755

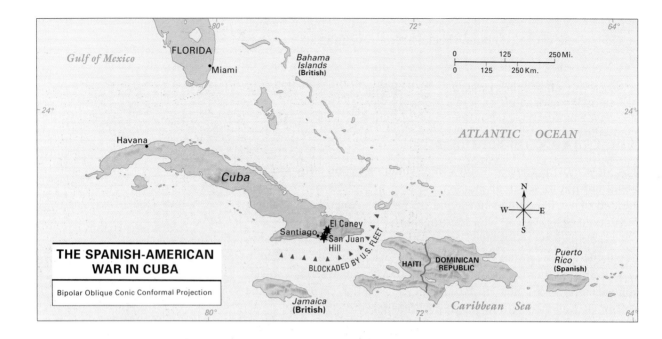

THE SPANISH-AMERICAN
WAR IN CUBA

Bipolar Oblique Conic Conformal Projection

LEARNING FROM MAPS. *Most of the Spanish-American War in the Caribbean was fought on Cuba. Where were the important battles?*

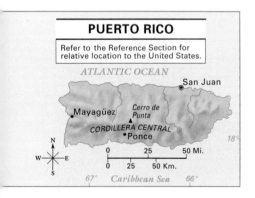

PUERTO RICO

Refer to the Reference Section for relative location to the United States.

LEARNING FROM MAPS. *Puerto Rico, the only American commonwealth, lies in the Caribbean. Mountains slope from the center to sandy beaches along the sea. Puerto Ricans are American citizens. Why did the United States value control of Puerto Rico in the early 1900s?*

Return to the Preview & Review on page 747.

American strategy called for an attack on Santiago. The army, commanded by General William R. Shafter, landed at Daiquiri, a town to the east of Santiago. Once ashore, it began its advance. The Spanish put up a stiff resistance.

Major battles were fought at **El Caney** and **San Juan Hill.** At El Caney a member of the Second Massachusetts regiment complained:

> 66 [The Spaniards] are hidden behind rocks, in weeds and in underbrush, and we just simply can't locate them. They are shooting our men all to pieces. 99

The Rough Riders and African American soldiers of the Ninth Cavalry took San Juan Hill by storm on July 1. In this battle Colonel Roosevelt seemed to have no care for his own safety. He galloped back and forth along the line, urging his men forward. Luckily, Roosevelt was not hit. Many of his men were not so fortunate. Most were firing bullets charged with black powder. Each time they fired, a puff of black smoke marked their location for Spanish gunners on top of the hill.

After the capture of San Juan Hill the American artillery could be moved within range of Santiago harbor. Admiral Cervera's fleet had to put to sea. When it did, the powerful American fleet swiftly blasted it. Every one of the Spanish vessels was lost. Only one American sailor was killed in this one-sided fight.

On July 16 the Spanish army commander surrendered Santiago. A few days later another American force completed the occupation of the Spanish island of **Puerto Rico,** about 500 miles (800 kilometers) east of Cuba. The Spanish-American War was over.

America's Pacific Heritage

Since ships first sailed or land caravans carried off its treasure, westerners have been fascinated by the East. Marco Polo was bedazzled even though he came from Venice, a western jewel. The art of the Orient is the oldest in the world, but it was hidden behind the walls of Forbidden Cities. Emigrants from Asia were too poor to own eastern treasures such as we see on these pages, but traders like John Ellerton Lodge filled the holds of the *Kremlin* and *Magnet* with china, silk, ivory, even fireworks that bloomed like chrysanthemums to bring Pacific culture to America.

The Metropolitan Museum of Art

This dragon comes from a Chinese embroidered chair of the 18th century. In Eastern art, dragons seldom breathed fire and were seen as protectors.

St. Louis Art Museum

Chinese porcelain has long been prized. The export ware above is an Orange platter in the "Fitzhugh" pattern.

Arnold Genthe/The Granger Collection, New York

Four children in holiday dress were photographed on the teeming streets of San Francisco's Chinatown before the earthquake of 1906.

The Metropolitan Museum of Art

Fernand Bourges/LIFE Magazine © Time Warner, Inc.

"Four black dragons spitting fire" is how Japanese artists described Commodore Perry's ships landing at Yokohama, above.

A gilded bronze Buddha from 10th-century Thailand reminds us that Buddhism has nearly 245 million followers in the East.

Soames Summerhays/Photo Researchers

St. Louis Art Museum

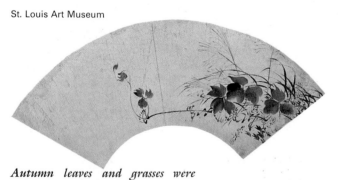

Autumn leaves and grasses were painted c. 1850 for this Japanese fan by Shibata Zeshiu.

A Filipino woman shows her considerable skill at weaving from Manila hemp fibers, right.

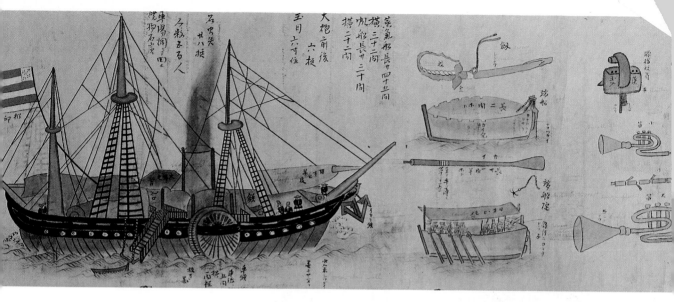

Birds and flowers are the subjects of this 18th-century silk embroidery from Korea (right).

Lee Boltin

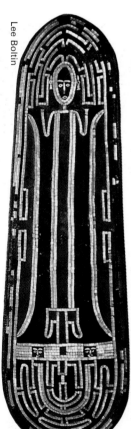

Little known before World War II, the Solomon Islands were home to artisans who produced the prized mother-of-pearl inlay for this mid-19th-century ceremonial shield (left).

The Metropolitan Museum of Art

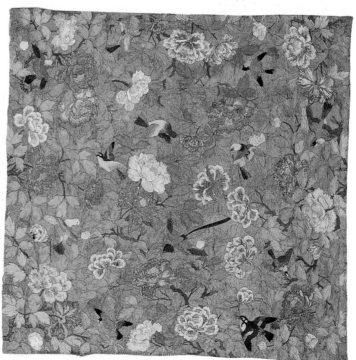

Bernice Pauahi Bishop Museum, Honolulu

Hawaiians have a tradition of creating and wearing leis, garland necklaces usually made of flowers. Leis made from the feathers of birds have adorned the nobility of Hawaii even before the rule of Kamehameha III or his successor.

America's Pacific Heritage   759

Gary Kinia/The Isamu Noguchi Foundation, Inc.

Isamu Noguchi, one of the greatest sculptors of the 20th century, was born in Los Angeles but taken to Japan when he was two. He called the sleek sculpture environment at right "California Scenario." It was completed in 1982 and covers 1.6 acres in Costa Mesa, California.

In the shadow of the Capitol is the east building of the National Gallery of Art. I.M. Pei, a Chinese American, designed this streamlined structure. Other works by Pei and his partners include the John F. Kennedy Library in Boston and the glass pyramid that is now part of the Louvre museum in Paris.

Ezra Stoller © Esto/Courtesy Pei Cobb Freed and Partners

4. AMERICA EXPANDS FURTHER

Preview & Review

Use these questions to guide your reading. Answer the questions after completing Section 4.
Understanding Issues, Events, & Ideas. Use the following words to first explain America's expansion and then the opposition to it: Guam, imperialism, anti-imperialist, anarchist, sphere of influence, Open Door Note, Boxer Rebellion, Second Open Door Note.

1. What peace terms did President McKinley demand of the Spanish? Why had he increased his demands?
2. What did the U.S. gain by its victory in the war?
3. How would ruling the Philippines make the United States an imperialist nation? What position did anti-imperialists take on annexing the Philippines?
4. What two principles were stated by the Open Door Notes?

Thinking Critically. **1.** Often public sentiment can influence political decisions. The Filipinos and the Boxers opposed American involvement in their countries. Why did America get involved anyway? Do you agree with the American decision? Explain. **2.** Imagine that you are William Jennings Bryan in 1901, and you are writing your memoirs. Explain your reasons for supporting the Treaty of Paris of 1898.

The Treaty of Paris

On July 30 President McKinley sent the Spanish government his peace terms. Spain must leave Cuba. It must give Puerto Rico and an island in the Pacific midway between Hawaii and the Philippines to the United States. American troops would continue to hold the city of Manila until the future of the Philippine Islands could be settled at a peace conference.

These demands were far greater than the original aim of winning independence for Cuba. The excitement of military victory caused McKinley and many other Americans to forget why they had first gone to war.

There was little the Spaniards could do. They accepted McKinley's preliminary terms. Representatives of the two nations then met in Paris in the autumn of 1898. There they framed a formal treaty of peace.

McKinley appointed five American peace commissioners. Three of these were United States senators. The president put the senators on the commission because he expected them to influence their fellow senators. Under the Constitution the treaty would be submitted to the Senate for its approval.

The Spanish commissioners agreed to give up Cuba and to turn Puerto Rico and the island of **Guam** in the Pacific over to the United States. The Americans, acting on McKinley's order, also demanded possession of the Philippines. The Spaniards objected strongly. The United States had not conquered the islands, they argued. Even Manila had not been captured until after the preliminary terms of peace had been agreed to. McKinley said this of his decision to annex the Philippines:

66 I walked the floor of the White House night after night until midnight, and I am not ashamed to tell you . . . that I went down on my knees and prayed Almighty God for light and guidance more than one night. And one night late it came to me this way—I don't know what it was, but it came . . . that there was nothing left for us to do but to take them all, and to educate the Filipinos, and uplift them and civilize and Christianize them, and by God's grace do the very best we could by them, as our fellow-men for whom Christ died. And then I went to bed, and went to sleep, and slept soundly. . . .[1] 99

The Spaniards had to give in. To make it easier for them, the Americans agreed to pay $20 million for the islands. This Treaty of

[1] From *In the Days of McKinley* by Margaret Leech

Paris was signed on December 10, 1898, only eight months after the war was declared.

At relatively little cost in money and lives, the United States had accomplished its objective of freeing Cuba. It had also won itself an empire. No wonder that McKinley's secretary of state, John Hay, called the conflict ''a splendid little war.'' Of course, it was splendid only if one put aside the fact that the United States had defeated a country that was much smaller and poorer than itself. Nor was it splendid for the brave soldiers who died or were injured or for their families.

The Fight Against the Treaty

Many people in the United States opposed the treaty with Spain. They insisted that owning colonies, or **imperialism,** was un-American. Taking Puerto Rico was bad enough, but it was one small island. It might be needed for national defense in case of another war. However, ruling the Philippine Islands without the consent of the Filipinos would make the United States an imperialist nation like Britain, France, Germany, and other European countries that owned colonies in Africa and Asia.

The Filipinos certainly would not consent to American rule. They wanted their independence. After his victory at Manila Bay, Commodore Dewey had returned the exiled leader of the Filipino patriots, Emilio Aguinaldo, on an American warship. Dewey encouraged Aguinaldo to resume his fight against the Spanish. Aguinaldo did so. He assumed that the United States was there to help liberate his country from Spanish rule, just as it had promised to free Cuba.

The **anti-imperialists,** as they were called, included many important Americans. Among the best-known were Andrew Carnegie, the steel manufacturer; Samuel Gompers, the labor leader; Jane Addams, the social worker; and Mark Twain, the author of *Tom Sawyer, Huckleberry Finn,* and many other novels. The anti-imperialists in the Senate were led by George F. Hoar of Massachusetts. Hoar argued:

> 66 [The United States was] trampling . . . on our own great Charter, which recognizes alike the liberty and the dignity of individual manhood. 99

Many anti-imperialists were not opposed to expansion. Senator Hoar, for example, voted for the annexation of Hawaii, which was finally approved during the Spanish-American War. Andrew Carnegie always favored adding Canada to the United States. But they all believed that it was morally wrong to annex the Filipinos without their consent.

Brown Brothers

Emilio Aguinaldo was the popular Filipino patriot whom the United States returned from exile to fight the Spanish. Later he opposed the U.S. occupation of his country and fought for Filipino freedom.

Few issues have erupted into such a national debate as the fate of the Philippines. The issue bitterly divided the American people. Like slavery, most of the arguments, pro and con, centered on right and wrong. Still, the success of the United States in the Spanish-American War led some Americans to dream of a colonial empire. One enthusiastic supporter stated his position in a Senate campaign speech in 1898. Note how close his argument is to that of Josiah Strong on pages 738–39.

> It is a noble land God has given us—a land that can feed and clothe the world; a land set like a guard between the two oceans of the globe. It is a mighty people that God has planted on this soil. It is a people descended from the most masterful blood of history and constantly strengthened by the strong working folk of all the earth. It is a people imperial by virtue of their power, by right of their institutions, by authority of their heaven-directed purposes. . . .
>
> Shall the American people continue their restless march toward the commercial supremacy of the world? Shall free institutions extend their blessed reign until the empire of our principles is established over the hearts of all humanity?
>
> We have no mission to perform, no duty to discharge to our fellow humans? Has the Almighty Father given us gifts and marked us with His favor, only to rot in our own selfishness? . . .
>
> We cannot escape our world duties. We must carry out the purpose of a fate that has driven us to be greater than our small intentions. We cannot retreat from any soil where Providence has placed our flag. It is up to us to save that soil for liberty and civilization. For liberty and civilization and God's purpose fulfilled, the flag must from now on be the symbol of all mankind.[1]

In 1899 Rudyard Kipling, a British writer, penned a poem called ''The White Man's Burden.'' On quick reading, the poem seems to state the expansionist attitude well. It immediately became a popular defense of American expansion. But Kipling meant the poem to be a satire and is actually critical of America's determination to civilize childlike and untamed captive people. Can you see the satire in this first stanza of Kipling's seven-stanza poem?

> Take up the White Man's burden—
>   Send forth the best ye breed—
> Go bind your sons to exile
>   To serve your captives' need;

[1]From *Modern Eloquence*, vol. 10, by Albert J. Beveridge, edited by Ashley H. Thorndike

Point of View

To the American peace commissioners looking into freedom for Filipinos, one prominent American wrote.

> You seem to have about finished your work of civilizing the Filipinos. About 8,000 of them have been civilized and sent to Heaven. I hope you like it.
> Andrew Carnegie, 1899

> To wait in heavy harness,
>   On fluttered folk and wild—
>   Your new-caught sullen peoples,
>   Half-devil and half-child.'**"**

The anti-imperialists even started a national organization, the American Anti-Imperialist League in 1899. Carl Schurz, a former senator from Missouri and secretary of the interior in President Hayes' cabinet, was its spokesman. Schurz stated the league's view:

" We hold that the policy known as imperialism is hostile to liberty and tends toward militarism, an evil from which it has been our glory to be free. We regret that it has become necessary in the land of Washington and Lincoln to reaffirm that all men, of whatever race or color, are entitled to life, liberty, and the pursuit of happiness. We maintain that governments derive their just powers from the consent of the governed. We insist that the subjugation of any people is 'criminal aggression' and open disloyalty to the distinctive principles of our government. . . .

We earnestly condemn the policy of the present national administration [McKinley's presidency] in the Philippines. It seeks to extinguish the spirit of 1776 in those islands. We deplore [hate] the sacrifice of our soldiers and sailors, whose bravery deserves admiration even in an unjust war. We denounce the slaughter of Filipinos as a needless horror. . . .

We hold with Abraham Lincoln, that 'no man is good enough to govern another man without the other's consent. When the white man governs himself, that is self-government, but when he governs himself and also governs another man, that is more than self-government—that is despotism [rule by an absolute authority].' 'Our reliance is in the love of liberty which God has planted in us. Our defense is in the spirit which prizes liberty as the heritage of all men in all lands. Those who deny freedom to others deserve it not for themselves, and under a just God cannot long retain it.'[2]**"**

Albert J. Beveridge, now a senator, led the imperialists in Congress. He responded to the Anti-Imperialist League statement:

" The opposition tells us that we ought not to govern a people without their consent. I answer, the rule of liberty that all just government derives its authority from the consent of the governed, applies only to those who are capable of self-

---

[1]From "The White Man's Burden" by Rudyard Kipling
[2]From "The Policy of Imperialism" by Carl Schurz in *A History of the American People,* vol. 2, by Stephan Thernstrom

The Granger Collection, New York

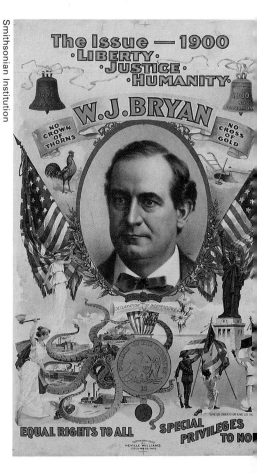

Smithsonian Institution

government. We govern the Indians without their consent; we govern our Territories without their consent; we govern our children without their consent. I answer, would not the natives of the Philippines prefer the just, humane, civilizing government of the Republic to the savage, bloody rule of pillage [ruthless plunder] and extortion [forcible theft] from which we have rescued them? Do not the blazing fires of joy and the ringing bells of gladness in Puerto Rico prove the welcome of our flag? And . . . do we owe no duty to the world? Shall we turn these peoples back to the reeking hands from which we have taken them? . . .[1]❞

Campaign posters for the 1900 presidential election show the Republican "ticket" of McKinley and Roosevelt on the left and William Jennings Bryan, the Democratic nominee, above. Which patriotic symbols can you find in these posters?

The anti-imperialists needed the votes of only one more than one third of the Senate to defeat the treaty. They seemed likely to succeed. Many Democratic senators would vote against the treaty to embarrass President McKinley and the Republican party.

But the McKinley administration received unexpected help from William Jennings Bryan. Although Bryan was against taking the Philippines, he believed that the Senate should consent to the treaty in order to bring an official end to the war.

Bryan planned to run for president again in 1900. He would make imperialism an issue in the campaign. He was convinced that a majority of the people were opposed to annexing the Philippines. After winning the election, he intended to grant the Filipinos their independence.

Bryan persuaded enough Democratic senators to vote for the

[1]From "The March of the Flag" by Albert J. Beveridge in *A History of the American People*, vol. 2, by Stephan Thernstrom

treaty to get it through. The vote was 57 to 27, only one vote more than the two thirds necessary. Senator Henry Cabot Lodge of Massachusetts, a leading supporter of the treaty, described the Senate debate this way:

66 [It was] the closest, most bitter, and most exciting struggle I have ever known. 99

Fighting in the Philippines

William Jennings Bryan's strategy backfired. He was nominated again for president in 1900, and he did make the Philippines a prominent issue in the campaign. But McKinley, running for reelection, defeated him easily. The electoral vote was 292 to 155.

The Republican ticket had been strengthened by the nomination of the popular Rough Rider Theodore Roosevelt for vice president. After returning from Cuba in triumph, Roosevelt had been elected governor of New York. He had intended to run for reelection as

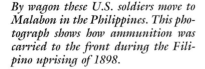

By wagon these U.S. soldiers move to Malabon in the Philippines. This photograph shows how ammunition was carried to the front during the Filipino uprising of 1898.

Courtesy of the Library of Congress

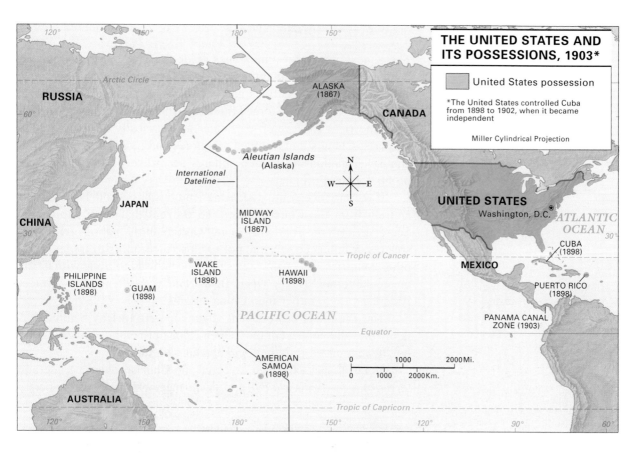

THE UNITED STATES AND ITS POSSESSIONS, 1903*

☐ United States possession

*The United States controlled Cuba from 1898 to 1902, when it became independent

Miller Cylindrical Projection

RUSSIA

Arctic Circle

ALASKA (1867)

CANADA

Aleutian Islands (Alaska)

International Dateline

JAPAN

CHINA

UNITED STATES
Washington, D.C.

ATLANTIC OCEAN

MIDWAY ISLAND (1867)

Tropic of Cancer

CUBA (1898)

MEXICO

WAKE ISLAND (1898)

HAWAII (1898)

PHILIPPINE ISLANDS (1898)

GUAM (1898)

PUERTO RICO (1898)

PACIFIC OCEAN

PANAMA CANAL ZONE (1903)

Equator

AMERICAN SAMOA (1898)

AUSTRALIA

Tropic of Capricorn

0   1000   2000Mi.
0   1000 2000Km.

governor in 1900. However, in November 1899 McKinley's vice president, Garret A. Hobart, had died. Roosevelt was persuaded to accept the Republican vice presidential nomination.

Then, less than a year after the election, President McKinley was shot and killed by an anarchist named Leon Czolgosz. An **anarchist** is one who believes that all government should be done away with. Theodore Roosevelt had been a mere assistant secretary of the navy two and one-half years earlier. Now he was president of the United States! This was the third time in the young nation's history that an assassin's bullet thrust the vice president to the seat of power in the White House.

There was still another unforeseen result of the Treaty of Paris. Even before the Senate voted for the treaty, the Filipino leader Emilio Aguinaldo had organized a revolution against American rule. Bloody jungle fighting broke out.

Peace was not restored until 1902. By that time more than 4,000 Americans and tens of thousands of Filipinos had been killed, a great many more wounded.

The United States continued to have great influence in many regions. Often it acted in ways that the local people resented. But opposition to imperialism was growing. Most Americans quickly lost their taste for owning colonies in distant parts of the world.

LEARNING FROM MAPS. *This map shows the extent of United States territory in 1903. How far is it from Washington, D.C., to the Philippines? To American Samoa? How could this distance create problems?*

America Expands Further   767

The Open Door Notes

The annexation of the Philippines made the United States a power in the Far East. For many years Great Britain, France, Germany, and other European nations had been seizing **spheres of influence** in China. This meant they forced the weak Chinese government to grant them the right to develop particular areas, mostly around Chinese seaports. China's undeveloped resources and its huge population of about 400 million made such spheres seem likely to bring in large profits for the Europeans.

If the practice continued, American businesses might be cut off entirely from the China market. To prevent that from happening, Secretary of State John Hay in 1899 asked all the nations with such spheres of influence to agree not to close their doors to traders from other countries. All businesses should be allowed to trade with China on equal terms. Hay's **Open Door Note** was intended to protect America's trade rather than China's rights.

The European powers sent vague answers to Hay's note. Certainly they did not accept the "Open Door" principle. However, Hay boldly announced that they *had* agreed with him.

None of this exchange involved the Chinese, whose trade and territory were being carved up. Then, members of a secret society

Fogg Art Museum

Tz'u-Hsi was the dowager empress of China who encouraged the Boxer Rebellion. This detail comes from her portrait.

Courtesy of the Library of Congress

of Chinese nationalists known as the "Righteous, Harmonious Fists," or Boxers, launched an attack on foreigners in Peking, the capital, and in other parts of China.

Armed with swords and spears, the Boxers destroyed foreign property and killed missionaries and business people. Frightened foreigners fled for protection to the buildings which housed their governments' representatives in Peking (Beijing). They remained there for weeks, virtual prisoners cut off from the outside world.

The western nations quickly organized an international army to put down this **Boxer Rebellion** of 1900. A force of 20,000, including 2,500 Americans, was rushed to the area. They rescued the trapped foreign civilians and crushed the Boxers.

Meanwhile, Hay feared that the European powers would use the Boxer Rebellion as an excuse to expand their spheres of influence. He sent off a **Second Open Door Note.** This one stated that the United States opposed any further carving up of China by foreign nations. The Open Door thus included two principles: equal trade rights for all in China and a guarantee of independence for China.

None of the European nations officially accepted these principles. In practice, however, Hay got what he wanted. American business interests were able to trade freely in the spheres and throughout the sprawling Chinese Empire. 🖰

An international army of Americans, British, French, Germans, Russians, and Japanese storm into Peking to free their diplomats trapped inside by the Boxer Rebellion in China.

Return to the Preview & Review on page 761.

America Expands Further   769

5. ROOSEVELT AND HIS CANAL

Use these questions to guide your reading. Answer the questions after completing Section 5.
Understanding Issues, Events, & Ideas. Describe American efforts to build the Panama Canal, using the following words: Clayton-Bulwer Treaty, Hay-Pauncefote Treaty, isthmus, canal zone, Republic of Panama, Hay-Bunau-Varilla Treaty, lock, Roosevelt Corollary, dollar diplomacy, gunboat diplomacy.

1. Why did the U.S. feel a canal was needed?
2. What were the arguments for and against building a canal across Panama? Across Nicaragua?
3. Why did Bunau-Varilla's "revolution" in Panama succeed?
4. Why did dollar diplomacy replace gunboat diplomacy?

Thinking Critically. **1.** Imagine that you are Dr. Walter Reed, just returned from Cuba. Explain how you wiped out yellow fever in Cuba and the influence of your work on Major Gorgas. **2.** If you had been a Cuban tobacco farmer in 1910, how would Taft's dollar diplomacy change your way of life? How would you view this change? Why?

The Panama Canal

The United States needed to link the Atlantic and Pacific Oceans. The Spanish-American War and the expansion of the United States into the Pacific made it obvious that a canal across Central America would be extremely valuable.

During the war the new American battleship *Oregon* had to steam 12,000 miles (19,200 kilometers) from the West Coast around South America in order to help destroy Admiral Cervera's fleet at Santiago. It took the *Oregon* 68 days, traveling at top speed. A canal would have reduced the *Oregon*'s voyage to 4,000 miles (6,400 kilometers) or one third the distance.

The United States government was eager to build a canal. The first step was to get rid of the **Clayton-Bulwer Treaty** of 1850 with Great Britain. That agreement stated that any such canal would be controlled by *both* nations.

The treaty had made sense in 1850 when the United States had barely reached the Pacific. It did not make sense in 1900. Therefore, in 1901, Secretary Hay negotiated a new agreement with the British. This **Hay-Pauncefote Treaty** gave the United States the right to build and control a canal by itself. In return the United States promised that all nations would be allowed to use the canal on equal terms.

There were two possible canal routes across Central America. One roughly followed the path the explorer Balboa had taken across the Isthmus of Panama when he discovered the Pacific in 1513. An **isthmus** is a narrow neck of land connecting two landmasses. This route was short, but it passed through mountainous country covered by dense tropical jungles. The other was in the Republic of Nicaragua. There the land was more level, and part of the route could make use of Lake Nicaragua, which was 50 miles (80 kilometers) wide. The total distance was much longer, but Nicaragua was closer to the United States.

A private French company had obtained the right to build a canal across Panama, which was then part of the Republic of Colombia. This company had spent a fortune but made little progress. Thousands of its laborers had died of yellow fever and malaria. The company was now bankrupt. There was no chance that it would ever be able to complete a canal. In an effort to regain some of its losses, the company offered to sell its right to build a canal to the United States for $40 million.

A representative of the bankrupt company, Philippe Bunau-Varilla, worked to persuade Congress to take over the canal project. His campaign succeeded. By 1903 President Roosevelt had made up his mind to build the canal in Panama. Congress went along with this decision.

To persuade Congress to choose Panama over Nicaragua for the new canal, Philippe Bunau-Varilla depended heavily on 90 one-centavo stamps. Bunau-Varilla was the representative of the bankrupt French company that had begun the canal.

Bunau-Varilla had mailed out 13,000 copies of a pamphlet, *Panama or Nicaragua?* One of his arguments against a Nicaraguan canal was that there were volcanoes there. No matter that nearly all had long been inactive. He wrote, "What have the Nicaraguans chosen to characterize their country . . . on their postage stamps? Volcanoes!"

The Senate was about to begin debate on the canal site. Far from Washington (and from Nicaragua) rumblings began coming from Mount Pele, a long-dormant volcano on the island of Martinique. On May 8, 1902, the entire mountain exploded,

killing nearly 30,000 people in two minutes. "What an unexpected turn of the wheel of fortune," wrote Bunau-Varilla. He thought again of the Nicaraguan stamp.

Bunau-Varilla went to every stamp dealer in Washington until he had 90 of the one-centavo Nicaraguan stamps. Each one showed a puffing locomotive in the foreground and an erupting volcano in the background. Bunau-Varilla pasted the stamps on sheets of paper. He mailed one to each of the 90 United States senators with the neatly typed caption: "An official witness of the volcanic activity on the isthmus of Nicaragua."

The Panama "Revolution"

Next, Secretary of State Hay and the Colombian representative in Washington negotiated a treaty in which Colombia leased a **canal zone** across Panama to the United States. Colombia was to receive $10 million and a rent of $250,000 a year. The United States Senate promptly consented to this treaty.

But the Colombian senate rejected it. The reason was simple. The Colombians wanted more money. The bankrupt French company was being offered four times as much for its rights in Colombia. And Colombia had granted those rights in the first place.

When Colombia rejected the treaty, Bunau-Varilla organized a revolution in Panama. There had been many such uprisings against Colombia there in the past. All had been easily put down. But this time the rebels had the support of the United States. Their "revolution" therefore succeeded.

The small rebel army was made up of railroad workers and members of the Panama City fire department. But when Colombian troops, sent by sea, landed at the port of Colón, they were met by the powerful U.S.S. *Nashville*. The Colombians were forced to return to their home port.

Thus was born the **Republic of Panama.** Only three days later, on November 6, 1903, the United States government officially recognized Panama. On November 18, in Washington, Secretary Hay signed a canal treaty with a representative of the new nation. This

Point of View

Just how massive a project was the Panama Canal is revealed in this study.

> **"To build the Great Pyramid or the Wall of China or the cathedrals of France, blocks of stone were set one on top of the other in the age-old fashion. But the walls of the Panama locks were poured from overhead, bucket by bucket, into gigantic forms. . . ."**
> From *The Path Between the Seas,*
> David McCullough, 1977

Both, Brown Brothers

Death took a holiday (right) in the fever-ridden swamps of Panama when William Gorgas, top, drained the swamps to eliminate yellow fever. Below him is Colonel George Goethals of the Army Engineers who led the canal builders.

representative was none other than Philippe Bunau-Varilla. The **Hay-Bunau-Varilla Treaty** granted the United States a ten-mile-wide Canal Zone (16 kilometers). The financial arrangements were the same ones that Colombia had turned down.

Building the Canal

Before work on the Panama Canal could begin, malaria and yellow fever had to be stamped out. Carlos Juan Finlay, a Cuban doctor trained in Philadelphia, had first suggested that yellow fever was spread by a certain kind of mosquito. The United States sent a delegation headed by Doctor Walter Reed to Cuba to find a way to wipe out the disease. Reed studied Finlay's experiments and agreed with his findings. The United States army under the direction of Major William Gorgas then proceeded to eliminate yellow fever in Cuba. Gorgas was now sent to Panama to rid the area of the mosquitoes which carried the disease. He drained the swamps and ponds where the mosquitoes laid their eggs.

Now the actual construction could begin. Colonel George Goethals of the Army Engineers had charge of the project. The level of the canal had to be raised as high as 85 feet (over 25 meters) above the sea. Water-filled chambers called **locks** would raise and lower ships from one level to another.

For ten years, from 1904 to 1914, a small army of workers drilled and blasted, dug and dredged. They had to cut a 9-mile-long channel (over 14 kilometers) through mountains of solid rock. In this

The Granger Collection, New York

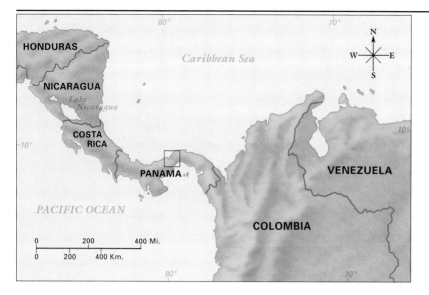

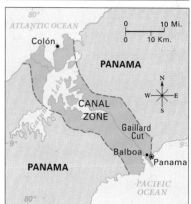

Modified Azimuthal Equal-Area Projection

excerpt a writer captured the problems of cutting through a particularly stubborn spot near the middle of the canal.

❝ Culebra Cut! Here the barrier of the continental divide resisted to the utmost the attacks of the canal army; here disturbed and outraged Nature conspired with gross mountain mass to make the defense stronger and stronger; here the mountain must be moved. . . .

Grim, now, but still confident, the attackers fought on. The mountain was defeated.

Now stretches a man-made canyon across the backbone of the continent; now lies a channel for ships through the barrier; now is found what Columbus sought in vain—the gate through the West to the East. Men call it the Culebra Cut.

Nine miles long, it has an average depth of 120 feet (37 meters). At places its sides tower nearly 500 feet (152 meters) above the channel bottom, which is nowhere narrower than 300 feet (91 meters).

It is the greatest single trophy of the triumph of man over the terrestrial arrangement of the world. . . . It is majestic. It is awful. It is the Canal. . . .

No one had the remotest idea of the actual difficulties that would beset the canal builders; no one dreamed of the avalanches of material that would slide into the cut. . . . No less than 26 slides and breaks were encountered in the construction of the Culebra cut.

To remove the 105,000,000 cubic yards of earth from the backbone of America required about 6,000,000 pounds of high-grade dynamite each year to break up the material, so

LEARNING FROM MAPS. *Completion of the Panama Canal meant a new route to the West Coast. How had ships traveled before the canal? American control of the canal also involved the United States more deeply in Latin American affairs. What are the advantages for the United States of that involvement? What are the disadvantages?*

Culver Pictures

The Cut of Las Cascadas, shown above, and the Gaillard Cut were two of the engineering wonders that made it possible to complete the Panama Canal in just ten years. Do you think such a project could be completed so quickly today? Why or why not?

that it might be successfully attacked by the steam shovel. . . . So carefully was the dynamite handled that during a period of three years, in which time some 19,000,000 pounds were exploded in Culebra Cut, only eight men were killed. . . .

Today Culebra Mountain bows its lofty head to the genius of the American engineer and to the courage of the canal army. . . . Through it now extends a ribbon of water broad enough to permit the largest vessels afloat to pass one another under their own power and deep enough to carry a ship with a draft [depth in the water] beyond anything in the minds of naval constructors today. . . . It is the mightiest deed the hand of man has done.[1] **99**

The channel was named the Gaillard Cut after Colonel David Gaillard, the engineer in charge of this part of the project.

The canal was finally finished in 1914. It was a truly magnificent

[1]From "The Culebra Cut" by Frederic Haskin

STRATEGIES FOR SUCCESS

INTERPRETING EDITORIAL CARTOONS

Editorial cartoons are drawings that present points of view on particular issues. They are usually found in the editorial sections of newspapers and magazines and have been used throughout history to influence public opinion. Although some cartoons present a positive point of view, most are critical of a policy, situation, or person.

The two most important techniques cartoonists use to express their message are caricature and symbolism. A caricature is a drawing that exaggerates physical features. Symbolism is the use of one thing to represent another idea, feeling, or object. Common symbols for the United States, for example, are the bald eagle and Uncle Sam. Cartoons also use titles, labels, and captions to get their message across.

How to Interpret Editorial Cartoons

To interpret editorial cartoons, follow these steps.

1. **Identify the caricatures.** Note the people or objects being characterized and note what is exaggerated.
2. **Identify the symbols.** Determine the meaning of each of the symbols used.
3. **Read the title, labels, and caption.** Check the title, labels, and caption to help you understand the artist's message.
4. **Analyze the information.** Decide if the cartoonist's point of view is positive or negative. Determine what events or situation led to the cartoon.

Applying the Strategy

President Theodore Roosevelt was a favorite of editorial cartoonists. Study the cartoon of him at the top of the next column. Does the cartoonist use caricature? If so, what features are exaggerated? Is there symbolism? If so what symbols are used and what do they stand for? Does the cartoonist present a positive or negative point of view? How can you tell? In your own words, state the cartoonist's message. Now answer the same questions for the cartoon at the lower right.

For independent practice, see Practicing the Strategy on page 778.

NO MOLLY-CODDLING HERE

Both, The Granger Collection, New York

achievement. President Roosevelt took full credit for the project and for its swift completion:

> "I am interested in the Panama Canal because I started it. If I had followed traditional conservative methods . . . debate would have been going on yet. But I took the Canal Zone and let Congress debate, and while the debate goes on the canal does also."

Roosevelt blamed Colombia for the revolution in Panama. He once told a friend that trying to make a deal with that country was like trying to nail jelly to a wall. Yet many Americans at that time and many more in later years felt that Roosevelt's behavior had been entirely wrong. In 1921, after Roosevelt was dead, Congress gave Colombia $25 million to make up for the loss of Panama. And in 1978 a new treaty provided that at the end of this century the Canal Zone itself would be turned back to Panama.

White House Historical Association

This portrait of Theodore Roosevelt was painted by John Singer Sargent. Portraits of all former presidents and first ladies hang in the White House and are worth a tour of the president's house. Your representative in Congress can get you tickets in advance.

The Roosevelt Corollary

President Roosevelt was eager to prevent any European country from interfering in the affairs of the small nations of the Caribbean. These countries were all poor, and most of them were badly governed. Their governments frequently borrowed money from European banks and investors and did not repay them when the loans fell due. Sometimes, European governments sent in warships and marines to force them to pay their debts.

Before he became president, Roosevelt did not object. "If any South American state misbehaves toward any European country," he wrote, "let the European country spank it." After Roosevelt became president, he had second thoughts. Any European interference in the affairs of Latin American nations violated the Monroe Doctrine, he decided.

Debts, however, must be paid. If a nation in the Western Hemisphere did not pay its debts, the United States must make it do so. That way justice could be done to the lenders, but there would be no European interference in the hemisphere. This policy became known as the **Roosevelt Corollary** to the Monroe Doctrine. *Corollary* means "what naturally follows from."

Roosevelt always said that he applied the Corollary with the greatest reluctance. When he sent marines into the Dominican Republic in 1905, he insisted that he had no more desire to make that nation a colony of the United States than a snake would have to swallow a porcupine backwards. Many Americans always protested the use of force in such situations.

After William Howard Taft became president in 1909, it seemed shrewder to try to control the nations of the region indirectly. By

The Granger Collection, New York

The American eagle stretches all the way to the Philippines in this 1904 cartoon by Joseph Keppler. He called it "His 126th Birthday—'Gee, But this Is an Awful Stretch.'" Do you agree, particularly when you use historical imagination to put yourself back to the beginning of this century?

investing money in countries like Cuba, Nicaragua, and the Dominican Republic, more stable economies would result. Then the governments of these countries would also be more stable. This policy came to be known as **dollar diplomacy** to distinguish it from the **gunboat diplomacy** of the Roosevelt Corollary.

The difficulty with dollar diplomacy was that, without meaning to, it often injured the people of the countries involved. An American company might purchase a number of small tobacco farms in Cuba. Then it might convert the land into a vast sugar plantation. The plantation would be more efficient. Its crops could be sold for larger amounts of money. But the Cubans who had been independent tobacco farmers now became hired plantation laborers. They were forced to change their entire way of life.

At this time people were just beginning to realize how heavy-handed the United States had become in the Western Hemisphere. Most people still assumed that the Latin American nations shared the values of the United States. Later they would understand that they were seriously mistaken.

Return to the Preview & Review on page 770.

Roosevelt and His Canal 777

CHAPTER 21 REVIEW

1867
U.S. occupies the Midway Islands
★
Alaskan Purchase

1875
U.S. and Hawaii sign sugar treaty

Chapter Summary
Read the statements below. Choose one, and write a paragraph explaining its importance.
1. Manifest destiny led many Americans to look beyond the nation's borders, especially across the Pacific and into the Caribbean.
2. Spanish rule in Cuba had become increasingly harsh. When the fight for Cuban independence finally erupted, the United States backed the rebels, leading to the Spanish-American War.
3. Spanish and American forces fought in the Philippines and in the Caribbean.
4. As a result of the U.S. victory in the Spanish-American War, the country gained Puerto Rico, Guam, and the Philippines.
5. Despite strong anti-imperialist opposition, the U.S. continued to expand. The Open Door Notes secured American trading rights in China and the Panama "Revolution" cleared the way for the American-controlled Panama Canal.
6. The Roosevelt Corollary to the Monroe Doctrine further warned against foreign interference in the Western Hemisphere. Dollar diplomacy soon replaced the gunboat diplomacy of the Corollary as America sought to help its neighbors pay their foreign debts.

Reviewing Chronological Order
Number your paper 1–5. Then study the time line above and place the following events in the order in which they happened by writing the first next to 1, the second next to 2, and so on.
1. Open Door Notes
2. U.S.S. *Maine* explodes
3. Alaskan Purchase
4. Panama Canal completed
5. Chilean Crisis erupts

Understanding Main Ideas
1. What events during the Civil War caused Americans to be suspicious of Europe?
2. What was the purpose of the Pan-American Conference? How was its goodwill set back by the Chilean Crisis?
3. What did John Hay call for in the Open Door Notes?
4. Explain the steps the U.S. took to build and control the Panama Canal?
5. What was the Roosevelt Corollary? Why did the president issue this policy?

Thinking Critically
1. **Synthesizing.** Suppose you are an American farmer or business owner in the 1890s. Would you have favored an American policy of isolation or expansion? Why?
2. **Evaluating.** Was the United States justified in going to war against Spain in 1898? Explain your reasoning. Would the same circumstances cause the United States to go to war today? Why or why not?
3. **Analyzing.** Some people criticized Theodore Roosevelt for extending American influence and for his aggressive foreign policy. State and support your view of his actions.

Writing About History
Imagine you are in Alaska in 1890, Manila Bay with Dewey, San Juan Hill with Roosevelt, or in Panama during the building of the Panama Canal. Use your historical imagination to write a letter describing what is happening. Use the information in Chapter 21 to help you develop your letter.

Practicing the Strategy
Review the strategy on page 775.
Interpreting Editorial Cartoons. Study the cartoon at the bottom of page 797 and answer the following questions.
1. What symbols are used by the cartoonist? What caricatures?
2. Why do you think the cartoonist chose those symbols? Why did the cartoonist caricature those particular features?
3. What is the message of the cartoon?

1891
Chilean
Crisis
erupts

1893
American
revolt in
Hawaii

1894
Republic
of Hawaii
declared

1895
Cuban
Revolution
begins

★

Venezuela
Boundary
Dispute

1898
U.S.S.
Maine
explodes
in Havana

★

U.S.
declares
war on
Spain

★

Treaty
of Paris
ends war

1899
Open Door Notes

1900
Boxer
Rebellion

★

McKinley
reelected
president

1901
McKinley assassinated

★

Roosevelt becomes president

★

Fighting in the Philippines

1903
Republic of Panama

1904
Roosevelt Corollary
proclaimed

★

Building of Panama
Canal begins

1909
Dollar diplomacy begins

★

Taft becomes president

1914
Panama
Canal
completed

Using Primary Sources

One of the most eloquent voices raised in opposition to American expansion was that of Queen Liliuokalani of Hawaii. Read the following excerpt from *Hawaii's History By Hawaii's Queen* to understand her argument. Then answer the questions below.

> *Perhaps there is a kind of right, depending on the precedents of all ages, and known as the "Right of Conquest," under which robbers and marauders may establish themselves in possession of whatsoever they are strong enough to ravish for their fellows. I will not pretend to decide how far civilization and Christian enlightenment have outlawed it. But we have known for many years that our Island monarchy has relied upon the protection always extended to us by the policy and the assured friendship of the great American republic.*
>
> *Oh, honest Americans, . . . hear me for my downtrodden people! Their form of government is as dear to them as yours is precious to you. Quite as warmly as you love your country, so they love theirs. With all your goodly possessions, covering territory so immense that there yet remain parts unexplored . . . do not covet the little vineyard of Naboth's [Hawaii], so far from your shores.*

1. According to Queen Liliuokalani, what is the "Right of Conquest"? Do you think a country should be allowed to take what it is strong enough to control? Why or why not?
2. In the second paragraph of the excerpt, the Hawaiian queen appeals directly to "honest Americans." What argument does she use? Do you agree or disagree with her? Why?

Linking History & Geography

Building the Panama Canal was a great engineering feat. Panama is a land of rugged mountains and dense jungles. To help understand the difficulty of building the canal and how the canal works, make a model of the Isthmus of Panama, using clay or plaster of paris. Show the route of the Panama Canal and label the locks. Use the model to explain the stages by which a ship passes through the canal.

Enriching Your Study of History

1. **Individual Project.** Choose one of the nations of Latin America and present a short report in class on its historical and present-day relationships with the U.S. Choose from among these countries:

Argentina	Guatemala
Bolivia	Haiti
Brazil	Honduras
Chile	Mexico
Colombia	Nicaragua
Costa Rica	Panama
Cuba	Paraguay
Dominican Republic	Peru
Ecuador	Uruguay
El Salvador	Venezuela

2. **Cooperative Project.** Less than 20 years after the Spanish-American War the American flag flew over many new lands. To illustrate the extent of the expansion, different groups in your class will research the following information: the lands that came into U.S. possession between 1865 and 1918, how America gained control of these lands, and the present political status of each. Then your class will create a three-column chart illustrating this information.

Chapter 21 Review   779

Reformers and the Progressive Movement

Hopeful and expectant at the turn of the century, these strollers in New York's Central Park were painted in about 1905 by William Glackens. His art is impressionistic. Rather than try to paint a photographic likeness, impressionists seized upon a detail of light or shadow that played on their subjects. What parts of this scene would you say are more impressionistic than realistic?

A round the turn of the century a new mood spread through the nation. People seemed to be full of hope about the future. This mood lasted for about 15 years in the early 1900s and was known as the Progressive Era. It was a time when large numbers of people were working to improve society. These reformers were called progressives. They were trying to make progress. They hoped to make a better world. This belief in progress was part of the American character. Thomas Jefferson and nearly every westward-moving pioneer had shared it. During the Progressive Era the feeling was especially strong. People consciously spoke of themselves and the times as "progressive." Some progressives belonged to the Republican party, some to the Democratic. Theodore Roosevelt, one of the two great presidents of the era, was a Republican. The other, Woodrow Wilson, was a Democrat. Progressivism was a point of view about society and politics, not a political organization.

The Cleveland Museum of Art

1. THE PROGRESSIVE IDEA

The Turn of the Century

What causes shifts of public feeling such as the **Progressive Movement** is a mystery. There were several reasons, but no one can say exactly how they were related to one another.

People looked forward because they were beginning the 20th century. They sensed they were at the beginning of new and probably better times. The return of prosperity after the long depression of the 1890s changed their mood. The easy victory in the Spanish-American War increased their self-confidence. They seemed likely to accomplish whatever they set out to do. These **progressives** felt stronger and more important because the war had added new territory to the nation in many parts of the world. When Senator Albert J. Beveridge of Indiana made a speech describing "the march of the flag" in the Carribbean and Pacific, he was cheered to the rafters.

Many Americans looked back on the time after the Civil War as good years. Tremendous technological changes had advanced life. The telephone, the camera, and other scientific breakthroughs had a positive effect on people's lives. So did changes in the educational system. Individual schools had been consolidated into district systems. A manager, usually the superintendent, oversaw its operations and consulted with professional educators. Curriculum changed with the times. Less attention was paid to "the classics," to Latin and Greek. More was spent on mathematics, science, and the mechanical arts. High school enrollments soared. No longer was high school the reserve of the wealthy few. More and more families were making enough money to allow their children to attend.

Problems of Growth

Yet the same Americans who were so confident and hopeful were aware that conditions in the country were far from perfect. Many serious problems remained unsolved. Speaking broadly, these problems were produced by the Industrial Revolution.

In the great cities of the United States lived both the richest and poorest people in the country. The mansions of millionaire manufacturers stood only a few blocks from ugly, unhealthy districts that housed the poor families who labored in their factories. Few Americans objected to the Carnegies and Rockefellers and Morgans being so wealthy. But sometimes the rich seemed too powerful, the poor too weak. What power the poor did have was in the control of the big-city political machines, which used their votes to steal from the rich and the middle class.

The continued growth of great corporations and trusts was

Preview & Review

Use these questions to guide your reading. Answer the questions after completing Section 1.
Understanding Issues, Events, & Ideas. Explain the goals of the reforms in the late 1800s and early 1900s, using the following words: Progressive Movement, progressives.
1. What changes were there in the national mood at the turn of the century?
2. How did the world's first billion-dollar corporation come into being?
3. How did the progressives differ from reformers of the past?
4. What was the role of the government as progressives saw it?
Thinking Critically. Why do you think the national mood of America changed around 1900? What might cause a change today?

AVERAGE RETAIL PRICE OF SELECTED ITEMS, 1905*	
Item	Price
Beef (per pound)	$0.10
Butter (per pound)	$0.19
Bacon (per pound)	$0.11
Eggs (per dozen)	$0.13
Oranges (per dozen)	$0.20
Ice cream cone	$0.10
Men's suit	$9.50
Ladies' shoes (per pair)	$1.65

*in Omaha, Nebraska

LEARNING FROM TABLES. *Compare the 1905 prices for the listed items with their prices today. How would you explain the differences?*

John Sloan, who painted "Women's Work" in 1911, is another American impressionist. He and his contemporaries painted common scenes from everyday life rather than fancy formal pictures. Critics called their group the "Ashcan School," but today these paintings give us valuable views of life at the turn of the century. Compare this painting with the one on page 780. In what ways is this painting impressionistic?

Oil on canvas, The Cleveland Museum of Art. Gift of Amelia Elizabeth White, 64.160

another cause of concern. The revival of the economy increased business profits. This encouraged businesses to expand their operations. Big companies bought out small ones. In the year 1899 alone, over 1,000 firms were swallowed up.

The largest corporations were merging with each other to form giant monopolies. In 1901 the banker J. P. Morgan bought Andrew Carnegie's huge steel company. He then combined it with corporations that made finished steel products like pipe and wire and rails. He called the result the United States Steel Corporation.

U.S. Steel became the world's first billion-dollar corporation. Because it was so large and powerful, many people considered such a supercompany dangerous no matter what the policies of its owners and managers.

Many people asked how, in America, these problems could have grown so large. Working conditions in factories and living conditions in parts of most cities were unsafe and unsanitary. The nation's wealth seemed to belong to a few very rich people. Why didn't governments—national, state, and local—do something? Why did they seem to pass laws that favored what was called "big business."

As you have read, Social Darwinism was the excuse most often given for the hands-off approach of governments. Charles Darwin had used certain theories to explain the development of animals. One, survival of the fittest, became a theory of social change as well. The most energetic and aggressive people would rise to the top of society and take control. And that is just what was happening. Business leaders were transforming America into an economic and industrial power. Government should do everything it could to help. Often that meant looking the other way!

It was just that attitude the progressive set out to combat. Social Darwinism was based on incorrect assumptions, they said. Perhaps survival of the fittest did apply to animals and plants in the wild. But Americans lived in a society, not the wilderness. And further, the United States was a democracy. And a democracy, as Theodore Parker had written and Abraham Lincoln had paraphrased in his *Gettysburg Address,* "is government of all the people, by all the people, for all the people." American government should work for *all* Americans, not just the fit. Many progressive reformers realized that changing American attitudes toward industrial growth and progress would be as hard as tackling the problems caused by it.

The Progressive Mood

The concerns of the reformers did not suddenly come in with the 20th century. The problems of the Industrial Revolution existed long before 1900. Reformers had been fighting political bosses and machine politics for years. Efforts had been made to improve conditions in the slums. Many state laws had been passed to protect workers. The federal government had tried to check the growth of monopolies by the Sherman Antitrust Act. It had regulated the great railroad corporations through the Interstate Commerce Act. In the 1890s the Populists had vigorously attacked the evils they saw in the industrial age.

What was different about progressives was their new mood. They were happy, cheerful reformers. Most Populists had seen themselves as underdogs being taken advantage of by powerful bankers and railroad tycoons. Progressives attacked bankers and tycoons of all sorts. But they did so more to protect others than to help themselves. Good times made it possible for people to be more generous.

Point of View

A fictional family feels the sting of society in this brief excerpt from the novel *Ragtime.*

"One Sunday, in a wild impractical mood, they spent twelve cents for three fares on the streetcar and rode uptown. They walked on Madison Avenue and Fifth Avenue and looked at the mansions. Their owners called them palaces. They had all been designed by Stanford White. Tateh [the father] was a socialist. He looked at the palaces and his heart was outraged. The family walked quickly. The police in their tall helmets looked at them. On these empty sidewalks in this part of the city the police did not like to see immigrants. Tateh explained that this was because an immigrant some years before had shot the steel millionaire Henry Frick in Pittsburgh...."

E. L. Doctorow, 1975

The Granger Collection, New York

On a paper horse, William Jennings Bryan rides to rouse his longtime Populist followers. "The Populist Paul Revere" was made in 1904. The horse is made of The Commoner, *a newspaper read by Populists. What does the age of Bryan's followers suggest was the status of the Populists in the early 1900s?*

Progressives wanted to share their prosperity with people less fortunate than themselves.

Like Thomas Jefferson, the progressives believed that if the people knew the truth, they would do what was right. Like Alexander Hamilton, they believed that the government should act forcefully to increase the national wealth and to improve the standard of living for all.

This is how the typical progressive reasoned. First of all, most ordinary people are basically decent and public spirited. When they realize what needs to be done to improve society, they will do it. Informing the people is the first step toward reform.

Next, the political system must be thoroughly democratic. If the wishes of the people are to be carried out, the government must respond to public opinion. Government officials must be both honest and efficient. It must be easy to remove dishonest or lazy officials and replace them with good public servants.

Then, with the will of the people behind it, the government should take action. It should check and control greedy special interests seeking selfish benefits at the expense of the people. It should try to improve the condition of weaker members of society—children, old people, the poor. And as one progressive put it:

Return to the Preview & Review on page 781.

❝ That would change all of us—not alone our neighbors, not alone the grafters [dishonest people], but you and me. ❞ 🖼

2. REFORMERS

The Muckrakers

Progressives depended heavily on newspapers and magazines to get their messages to the people. They placed more stress on describing what was wrong with society than on offering specific plans for reform. They assumed that once the people knew what was wrong, they would do something to correct the problem.

A small army of writers and researchers was soon engaged in what later came to be called investigative journalism. These writers dug into public records. They talked to politicians and business people, to city clerks and police officers, to factory workers and recent immigrants. Then they published their results in hard-hitting articles and books. They were specific. They named names. They demanded that "something be done." Improvements in printing and better ways of reproducing photographs added greatly to the effectiveness of their writing.

Theodore Roosevelt, not intending to praise the authors who exposed the evils of the time, called them **muckrakers.** They were raking up muck, or dirt, in order to make people aware of it. Muckrakers exposed the corrupt activities of political bosses. They described the terrible living conditions of the slums. They showed children laboring in factories and sweatshops. They wrote about the sale of impure foods and drugs. There were even articles describing secret payments of money to college football players and other evils resulting from an "overemphasis" on college sports.

Among the best-known of the muckrakers were Lincoln Steffens, Ida Tarbell, and Upton Sinclair. Steffens specialized in exposing

Preview & Review

Use these questions to guide your reading. Answer the questions after completing Section 2.
Understanding Issues, Events, & Ideas. Evaluate the success of some of the reformers, using the following words: muckrakers, Golden Rule, Wisconsin Idea, direct primary, primary election, lobbyist, initiative, referendum, recall, Seventeenth Amendment, municipal socialism, socialist, free enterprise, Triangle Fire, minimum wage, Brandeis brief.
1. How did the Wisconsin Idea give voters more voice in selecting their candidates for public office?
2. Why did reformers believe states should make laws to protect workers?
3. What is the importance of the decision in *Muller v. Oregon*?
Thinking Critically. Imagine that you are a muckraker. What problem would you publicize? Why? How would you propose solving the problem or at least improving conditions?

Both, Brown Brothers

Lincoln Steffens and Ida Tarbell were two of the leading muckrakers of the early 1900s. Steffens examined city governments. Tarbell wrote a landmark study of Standard Oil.

HISTORY OF STANDARD OIL BY Ida M. Tarbell

MCCLURE'S MAGAZINE

NOVEMBER

PUBLISHED MONTHLY BY THE S. S. McCLURE CO., 141-155 E. 25th ST., NEW YORK CITY

10 Norfolk St., Strand, London, W. C., Eng. Copyright, 1902, by The S. S. McClure Co. Entered at N.Y. Post-Office as Second-Class Matter

The November 1902 issue of Mc-Clure's magazine contains stronger stuff than its cover would indicate. Inside is an installment of Ida Tarbell's History of Standard Oil.

Culver Pictures

corrupt city governments. In *McClure's* magazine, which was the most important muckraking periodical, he reported on conditions in St. Louis, Minneapolis, Cincinnati, and other "boss-ridden" cities. In 1904 Steffens published these articles in a book, *The Shame of the Cities*. He also wrote about corruption in state governments. But Steffens was not a mere scandal seeker. When he discovered well-run cities and honest officials, he praised them highly.

Ida Tarbell was one of the leading journalists of her day. She was also an important historian. Before she turned to muckraking, she wrote biographies of the French Emperor Napoleon as well as

Abraham Lincoln. But she specialized in business investigations. Her detailed study of the methods used by John D. Rockefeller's Standard Oil Company was published in 19 installments in *McClure's*. She claimed Rockefeller "employed force and fraud to obtain his end."

Sinclair, along with Frank Norris and Jack London, were primarily novelists. Sinclair's sensational novel *The Jungle* exposed the disgustingly unsanitary conditions in meat-packing plants. Norris' *The Octopus* described the railroads' control over the economic life of farmers. London's stories, such as *The War of the Class, The Iron Heel,* and *Revolution,* warned of a workers' uprising that could wipe out private capitalism.

Few muckrakers called attention to the plight of black Americans. The most important work was *Following the Color Line* by Ray Stannard Baker. In this series of magazine articles Baker reported on segregation and racial discrimination in America.

Some reformers used the camera to tell their story. As you have read, Jacob Riis made a study of life in the tenements of New York City. His photographs and essays captured the terrible conditions of the slums and tenements. Scenes of cramped conditions, dilapidated buildings, and filth shocked middle-class Americans who had never seen the slums. In *How the Other Half Lives,* Riis wrote:

Culver Pictures

Ray Stannard Baker, above, was one of the few muckrakers concerned with the plight of African Americans.

“ Go into any of the 'respectable' tenement neighborhoods . . . where live the great body of hard-working Irish and German immigrants and their descendants, who accept naturally the conditions of tenement life, because for them there is nothing else in New York. . . .

With the first hot nights in June police dispatches, that record the killing of men and women by rolling off roofs and windows-sills while asleep, announce that the time of greatest suffering among the poor is at hand. It is the hot weather, when life indoors is well-nigh [nearly] unbearable with cooking, sleeping, and working, all crowded into the small rooms together, that the tenement expands, reckless of all restraint. . . . In the stifling July nights, when the big barracks [buildings] are like fiery furnaces, their very walls giving out absorbed heat, men and women lie in restless, sweltering rows, panting for air and sleep. Then every truck on the street, every crowded fire-escape, becomes a bedroom, infinitely preferable to any the house affords. A cooling shower [rain] on such a night is hailed as a heaven-sent blessing in a hundred thousand homes.

Life in the tenements in July and August spells death to an army of little ones whom the doctor's skill is powerless to save. When the white badge of mourning [a white ribbon] flutters from every second door, sleepless mothers walk the streets in the gray of the early dawn, trying to stir a cooling

Both, Museum of the City of New York

Jacob Riis documented the slums of the cities with his camera as well as his pen. Two of his most famous scenes are "Baxter Street Alley—Rag Picker's Row" (left) and "Street Arabs in Night Quarters, Mulberry Street" (right). Describe in your own words what you think is happening in each photograph.

breeze to fan the brow of the sick baby. There is no sadder sight than this patient devotion striving against fearfully hopeless odds. Fifty 'summer doctors,' especially trained to this work, are sent into the tenements by the Board of Health, with free advice and medicine for the poor. Devoted women follow their track with care and nursing for the sick. ... but despite all efforts the grave-diggers in Calvary [a city cemetery] work over-time, and little coffins are stacked moutains high in the deck of the Charity Commissioners' boat that makes its semi-weekly trips to the city cemetery. ...[1]"

Riis also documented crowded and dangerous working conditions in sweatshops. Because of his active interest in helping the poor and the immigrants in the slums, Riis was called by many "the most useful citizen of New York."

[1]From *How the Other Half Lives* by Jacob Riis

Reforming City Governments

The struggle to rid cities of corrupt political bosses and their powerful machines was almost endless because more large cities were developing as the nation grew larger and more industrialized. By 1910 there were 50 American cities with populations of more than 100,000.

Among the notable reformer mayors of the Progressive Era was Samuel M. Jones. Jones was a poor farm boy who made a fortune drilling for oil. Then he sold out to Standard Oil and became a manufacturer of oil-drilling equipment in Toledo, Ohio.

During the depression of the 1890s Jones was shocked by the condition of the unemployed men who came to his plant looking for jobs. He set out to apply the **Golden Rule** in his factory: "Do unto others as you would have them do unto you." He raised wages. He reduced the workday to eight hours. He sold lunches to workers at cost. He created a park, gave picnics for his employees, and invited them to his home.

In 1897 "Golden Rule" Jones was elected mayor of Toledo. He held this office until his death in 1904. His election was a victory for honest government. He stressed political independence rather than party loyalty. He established the eight-hour day for many city workers. He built playgrounds and a city golf course. He provided kindergartens for young children.

Another progressive mayor, also from Ohio, was Tom L. Johnson of Cleveland. Johnson was less idealistic than Jones, but he got even more done. He forced the local streetcar company to lower its fares. He reduced taxes by cutting out wasteful city agencies and running others more efficiently. He improved the Cleveland parks. And he reformed the city prisons. After his investigation of Cleveland, Lincoln Steffens called Johnson "the best mayor of the best-governed city in the United States."

Other cities where important reform movements were organized by progressives included Philadelphia, Chicago, and Los Angeles. In San Francisco the corrupt machine of Boss Abraham Ruef was defeated by reformers led by Fremont Older, editor of the San Francisco *Bulletin,* and Rudolph Spreckles, a wealthy sugar manufacturer. In St. Louis a lawyer, Joseph W. Folk, headed the reformers.

And despite their problems, America's cities were a wonder. They were places of energy, industry, of progress. Most Americans were proud of their cities. Carl Sandburg's poem is an example.

Chicago

Hog Butcher for the World,
Tool Maker, Stacker of Wheat,
Player with Railroads and the Nation's Freight Handler;
Stormy, husky, brawling,
City of the Big Shoulders:

Point of View

Compare this fictional account, also from *Ragtime,* with Riis' description.

"This was early in the month of June and by the end of the month a serious heat wave had begun to kill infants all over the slums. The tenements glowed like furnaces and the tenants had no water to drink. . . . Families slept on stoops and in doorways. Horses collapsed and died in the streets. The Department of Sanitation sent drays around the city to drag away horses that had died. But it was not an efficient service. Horses exploded in the heat."
E. L. Doctorow, 1975

They tell me you are wicked and I believe them, for I
   have seen your painted women under the gas lamps
   luring the farm boys.
And they tell me you are crooked and I answer: Yes, it is
   true I have seen the gunman kill and go free to kill
   again.
And they tell me you are brutal and my reply is: On the
   faces of the women and children I have seen the marks
   of wanton hunger.
And having answered so I turn once more to those who
   sneer at this my city, and I give them back the sneer
   and say to them:
Come and show me another city with lifted head singing
   so proud to be alive and coarse and strong and cunning.
Flinging magnetic curses amid the toil of piling job on job,
   here is a tall bold slugger set vivid against the little soft
   cities;
Fierce as a dog with tongue lapping for action, cunning as
   a savage pitted against the wilderness,
      Bareheaded,
      Shoveling,
      Wrecking,
      Planning,
      Building, breaking, rebuilding.
Under the smoke, dust all over his mouth, laughing with
   white teeth,
Under the terrible burden of destiny laughing as a young
   man laughs,
Laughing even as an ignorant fighter laughs who has
   never lost a battle,
Bragging and laughing that under his wrist is a pulse, and
   under his ribs the heart of the people,
      Laughing!
Laughing the stormy, husky, brawling laughter of Youth,
   half-naked, sweating, proud to be Hog Butcher, Tool
   Maker, Stacker of Wheat, Player with Railroads and
   Freight Handler of the Nation.[1] **99**

Reforming State Governments

Progressives also tried to make state governments more responsive
to the wishes of the people. The most ''progressive'' state by far was
Wisconsin. The leading Wisconsin progressive was Robert M. La
Follette, who was elected governor of the state in 1900.

La Follette's program was known as the **Wisconsin Idea.** To give

Brown Brothers

Robert M. La Follette was the progressive governor and later senator from Wisconsin. His strongest adviser was his wife, Belle Case La Follette, who studied law and worked for women's suffrage.

[1]''Chicago'' by Carl Sandburg

voters more control over who ran for public office, he persuaded the legislature to pass a **direct primary** law. Instead of being chosen by politicians, candidates had to campaign for party nominations in **primary elections.** The people, not the politicians, could then select the candidates who would compete in the final election.

While La Follette was governor, the Wisconsin legislature also passed a law limiting the amount of money candidates for office could spend. Another law restricted the activities of **lobbyists**—those who urge legislatures to pass laws favorable to special interests.

La Follette had great faith in the good judgment of the people. If they were ''thoroughly informed,'' he said, they would always do what was right. La Follette also realized that state government had to perform many tasks which called for special technical knowledge that ordinary citizens did not have.

La Follette believed that complicated matters such as the regulating of railroads and banks and the setting of tax rates should *not* be decided by popular vote. Appointed commissions of experts ought to handle these tasks. This idea was not original with La Follette. There were state boards of education and railroad commissions in nearly every state long before 1900. But the spread of such organizations in the Progressive Era was rapid.

The Wisconsin Idea was copied in other states. Many passed direct primary laws. Some allowed ordinary citizens to sign petitions which would force the legislature to vote on particular bills. Others authorized the initiative, the referendum, and the recall. The **initiative** enables voters to initiate, or propose, laws when the state legislatures have not done so. Under the **referendum** a particular proposal could be placed on the ballot to be decided by the yes or no votes of the people at a regular election. The **recall** allowed voters to remove an elected official before the official's term expired.

Many states responded to the demands of women that they be allowed to vote. By 1915 two thirds of the states permitted women to vote in certain elections, such as for members of school boards. About a dozen states had given women full voting rights by that date.

The National American Women's Suffrage Association led this fight. The president of the association from 1900 to 1904 was Carrie Lane Chapman Catt. She was an intelligent person and certainly better informed about public issues than the average man. But she could not vote. She had become active in the fight for women's rights in her home state of Iowa in the 1880s and later in the national suffrage movement.

One further progressive effort to give the people more control over elected officials was the **Seventeenth Amendment** to the Constitution, which was ratified in 1913. Article I of the Constitution had provided that United States senators should be elected by members of the state legislatures. Sometimes, such as in the contest in Illinois between Abraham Lincoln and Stephen A. Douglas in 1858, the

Point of View

In *Richard Milhous Nixon,* his biographer sees a darker side of reform.

❝Intended as tools of popular participation in government, the new and exploitable levers of petition politics allowed well-financed special interest groups and other disciplined factions—those with the price of a public relations firm, the quarter-a-signature for petitions, the budget for advertising—to seize the legislative agenda or punish a foe.❞
                Roger Morris, 1990

National Portrait Gallery, detail

Carrie Lane Chapman Catt was painted in 1927 by Mary Foote. Remembered as the founder of the League of Women Voters, Carrie Lane was once the superintendent of schools in Mason City, Iowa (the model for River City in The Music Man, *a musical comedy).*

Reformers   791

Culver Pictures

To call attention to their cause, these women hiked from New York City to Washington, D.C. in 1913.

voters were able to make their wishes clear before the legislators acted. Often they were not. The Seventeenth Amendment changed the system. Thereafter, senators were to be "elected by the people" of the state.

Social and Economic Reforms

Progressives were making state and local governments more democratic. At the same time they were insisting that these governments do something about the social and economic problems of the times. Many city governments responded by taking over waterworks that had been privately owned. Some extended this policy, sometimes called **municipal socialism,** to the public ownership of streetcar lines and to gas and electric companies.

Not many progressives were **socialists.** Socialists favored government ownership of all the means of production. Most progressives believed in the **free enterprise** system—that is, the right of a business to take its own course without government controls. Its success or failure lay in how fit it was to survive, argued the Social Darwinists, whom we discussed earlier. But many progressives made an exception for local public utilities. To have more than one privately owned gas company or to set up competing streetcar lines would have been inefficient. Believers in municipal socialism thought the best way to protect the public against being overcharged was to have the people, through their local governments, own all public utilities.

The progressives continued the efforts to improve the health and housing of poor city dwellers begun by earlier reformers. In New York City, for example, an improved tenement house law was passed in 1901. Better plumbing and ventilation had to be installed in all new tenements. Older buildings had to be remodeled to meet the new standards. During the Progressive Era more than 40 other cities passed similar tenement house laws.

Conditions in factories also attracted much attention, especially after the terrible tragedy known as the **Triangle Fire.** In 1911 a fire in the Triangle Shirtwaist Company factory on the upper floors of a building in New York City caused the deaths of over 140 women. Some were burned to death. Others were overcome by smoke. Many died jumping from the windows in a desperate effort to escape the flames. After this disaster New York state passed 35 new factory

A policeman guards the broken bodies of some of the 140 women who died at their workplace in the Triangle Shirtwaist fire. These women died when they leaped from windows to escape the flames. Others were burned or overcome by smoke. What do you think of the camera when it becomes an eyewitness: do you want to turn away or do you look more closely at the picture?

Brown Brothers

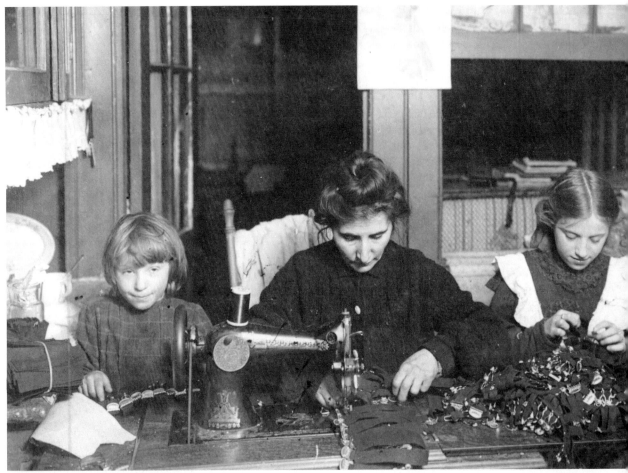

George Eastman House

Children who worked at home were safer than those who worked in factories, but the work was repetitive and tedious. And after such long days at the sewing machines, what could they know of the world beyond their tenement dwellings?

inspection laws. Other states also passed stronger laws to improve the safety of factories. Many began to require manufacturers to insure their workers against accidents.

Urged on by progressives, most states outlawed the employment of young children in factories. Many also limited the hours that women and older children could work. Most people agreed that states had the power to regulate child labor. But many employers and large numbers of workers claimed that laws regulating where or how long adults could work took away the right of individuals to decide such matters for themselves.

The Fourteenth Amendment, these people argued, says a state may not "deprive any person of life, liberty, or property." Laws that say women cannot work more than ten hours a day, or that coal miners cannot work more than eight hours a day, violate this amendment, they claimed. These employers and workers ignored the fact that the Fourteenth Amendment had been added to the Constitution to protect the civil rights of blacks in the southern states after the Civil War.

Those favoring reforms argued back by stressing the power of the state to protect the public. Despite the Fourteenth Amendment, criminals can be jailed or fined. Such actions must deprive them of liberty and property in order to protect the public against crime. By the same reasoning, laws that prevent people from working long hours or under unhealthy conditions protect their families and society in general, not only the workers themselves. Reformers even insisted that the state had the right to make laws setting a **minimum wage.** They argued that if workers did not earn a certain minimum wage, their families would suffer. Crime and disease and a general loss of energy would result. This would injure the entire society.

Reformers in the Courts

Both state and federal courts tried to resolve the conflict between the Fourteenth Amendment and the need for state governments to look after the common good. In the case of *Lochner v. New York* (1905) the Supreme Court decided that a New York law limiting bakers to a ten-hour workday was unconstitutional. Such laws were "meddlesome interference with the rights of the individual," the Court ruled. Bakers could work as long as they liked.

Three years later, however, the Supreme Court took the opposite position. This time the case involved an Oregon law that limited women laundry workers to a ten-hour workday. The Court decided that this law was a proper use of a state's power. Many women laundry workers are also mothers, the Court noted. If working too long injured their health, the health of any children they might have would suffer. Therefore, said the Court, "the well-being of the race" would be threatened.

This case, known as *Muller v. Oregon* (1908), is particularly important. For the first time the Supreme Court paid attention to economic and social evidence, not only to legal arguments. A lawyer for Oregon, Louis D. Brandeis, presented a detailed brief, or argument, showing that long hours of work in fact injured the health of women and thus the public health.

The research on which this **Brandeis brief** was based was done by two remarkable women, Florence Kelley and Josephine Goldmark. Kelley and Goldmark were officials of the National Consumers' League. They were deeply interested in many progressive reforms. The material they collected for Brandeis had a direct influence on the justices. More important, it changed the way future cases of this type were argued and decided.

Muller v. Oregon did not end the controversy about the power of a state to protect its weaker members. But by the end of the Progressive Era, many state laws had been passed to help workers and poor people. 🖮

Culver Pictures

Louis D. Brandeis was called "the people's attorney" after he persuaded the Supreme Court that limited work hours for women was reasonable. In 1916 he himself became a member of the Court.

Return to the Preview & Review on page 785.

Use these questions to guide your reading. Answer the questions after completing Section 3.
Understanding Issues, Events, & Ideas. Use the following words to describe Theodore Roosevelt's actions as a progressive: trust buster, restraint of trade, Northern Securities Case, Hepburn Act, Pure Food and Drug Act, conservation.
1. Why did some progressives want to break up supercompanies? Why did others believe corporations should be allowed to combine?
2. Why is Roosevelt described as an activist president?
3. Why was President Taft expected to carry on Roosevelt's policies?
Thinking Critically. 1. Do you think large corporations today are becoming too powerful? Why or why not? 2. You are J.P. Morgan. Write a memo to your employees at the Northern Securities Company, explaining why your company is being broken up and giving your view of Roosevelt.

3. GOVERNMENT VERSUS BIG BUSINESS

Progressives and Big Business

The "trust problem" of the 1880s and 1890s continued to be a matter of great concern in the early 1900s. All progressives looked with some alarm at large corporations—the supercompanies. They argued that supercompanies like U.S. Steel had too much power over important industries. Some sort of government check or control on these large corporations was necessary. But progressives did not agree as to how these giants should be regulated.

Some progressives favored using the Sherman Antitrust Act to break up large combinations into smaller competing businesses. Others argued that big businesses were more efficient than small ones. Competition between them would be dangerous and wasteful. Corporations in the same field should be allowed to combine or to cooperate with one another, these progressives believed. But the government should supervise and regulate their activities. They should not be allowed to use their great size and power to hold down small producers or take advantage of the consuming public.

Roosevelt and the Trusts

During Theodore Roosevelt's first term as president, he developed a reputation for being a **trust buster.** He charged a railroad combination, the Northern Securities Company, with violating the Sherman Antitrust Act.

The Northern Securities Company controlled three railroads—the Great Northern Railroad, which ran from St. Paul, Minnesota, to the West Coast; the Northern Pacific Railroad, another transcontinental line; and the Chicago, Burlington, and Quincy Railroad. These three lines carried most of the rail traffic between Chicago and the Pacific Northwest.

The Northern Securities Company was owned by J. P. Morgan and two railroad tycoons, E. H. Harriman and James J. Hill. Harriman also controlled the Union Pacific and Southern Pacific lines. Roosevelt charged that the Northern Securities Company was so powerful a combination that it caused **restraint of trade** and that it should be broken up.

The **Northern Securities Case** was decided by the Supreme Court in 1904. The Court agreed with Roosevelt. It ordered the combination dissolved. Roosevelt then brought antitrust suits against the meat-packers trust, the tobacco trust, and the Standard Oil trust.

But President Roosevelt did not want to break up all large combinations. There were, he insisted, "good" trusts and "bad" trusts.

Culver Pictures

Brown Brothers

Riehle Studios

(He tended to see things as all bad or all good.) Only the bad ones must be destroyed. Good trusts should be allowed to exist. But they must operate under rules laid down by the government.

In 1903 Roosevelt established a Bureau of Corporations. The bureau was to conduct investigations and issue reports indicating whether or not large corporations were being run properly. When "wrongdoing" was discovered, the bureau should call the evil to the attention of a corporation's executives. If they did not correct their errors voluntarily, their corporations could be broken up under the Sherman Act.

During his second term President Roosevelt became completely convinced that federal regulation was the only practical solution to the problems caused by the growth of big business combinations. In 1906 he persuaded Congress to increase the powers of the Interstate Commerce Commission. Under this law, the **Hepburn Act,** the Commission could inspect the business records of railroad companies to see how much money they were making. It also could fix the maximum rates the railroad lines could charge for moving freight and passengers.

At Roosevelt's urging, Congress also passed the **Pure Food and Drug Act** of 1906 as well as a meat inspection law. Roosevelt had read Sinclair's *The Jungle* and was revolted by its revelations. The Pure Food and Drug Act provided for federal control of the quality of most foods and drugs and for the supervision of slaughterhouses.

Roosevelt and the Presidency

In addition to expanding the government's regulation of businesses, Roosevelt strengthened the powers of the office of the president. His own personality had much to do with this. He was an activist by nature. He had to grit his powerful teeth to control himself whenever

These three giants of industry were owners of the Northern Securities Company. They are, from left to right, J. Pierpont Morgan, Edward Henry Harriman, and James Jerome Hill. The photographer of J. P. Morgan was Edward Steichen, who became an artist of the camera lens.

"Uncle Sam Unmasked" perfectly captures the popularity of President Teddy Roosevelt.

Culver Pictures

Theodore Roosevelt was an extremely popular president. People responded eagerly to his colorful personality. They admired his tremendous energy and his vivid imagination. There was a youthful, almost childlike quality to him. An English friend said of him: "You must always remember that the president is about six." Yet no one could doubt that he was also tough, brave, and public spirited.

"TR" was the first president to be affectionately referred to by his initials. He loved to make visitors go on long hikes with him in the woods around Washington, especially those who were overweight and unused to exercise. He invited the heavyweight champion of the world to the White House so that he could box with him.

Ordinary citizens read about events like these with glee. Newspaper reporters could count on Roosevelt to say something interesting or do something that was newsworthy almost every day. He made their work easy. They liked him and tended to write favorable stories about him.

Another Englishman said of Theodore Roosevelt: "Do you know the two most wonderful things I have seen in your country? Niagara Falls and the President of the United States, both great wonders of nature!" Some observers came to agree with the cartoon on page 797, "Uncle Sam Unmasked."

Point of View

Theodore Roosevelt's biographer explains what a peaceful presidency the Rough Rider had.

> **"Yet the extraordinary truth about this most pugnacious of Presidents is that his two terms in that office have been completely tranquil. . . . At the same time he has managed, without so much as firing one American pistol, to elevate his country to the giddy heights of world power."**
>
> From *The Rise of Theodore Roosevelt*, Edmund Morris, 1979

Congress or the courts or some state governor was dealing with an important problem.

Life in a large industrial country like the United States had become so complicated that Roosevelt believed decision making had to be centralized. The president was the logical person to make the decisions. Large elected legislatures like Congress were inefficient, he claimed. They could not "meet the new and complex needs of the times."

As early as 1902 Roosevelt involved himself in a national coal strike by forcing mine owners and miners into arbitration. Today presidents routinely bring pressure to bear on employers and workers when strikes threaten to disrupt the economy. But it had never been dealt with as Roosevelt did. Roosevelt threatened to take over the mines unless the owners agreed to a settlement. Then he appointed a special commission to work out the terms to end the dispute.

Because he was a great nature lover, Roosevelt was particularly interested in **conservation** of the nation's natural resources. He used his power as president very effectively in this area. He did not object to allowing lumber companies to cut down trees on government lands. But he believed in scientific forestry. Bypassing Congress, he placed large forest areas in federal reserves by executive order. Reserved land could not be claimed or purchased by special interests. But it could be leased to lumber companies. Their cutting, however, was strictly controlled by government experts.

Roosevelt applied the same principle to resources such as coal, waterpower, and grazing lands. He did a great deal to focus public attention on the importance of conserving natural resources and protecting the natural environment. In this respect he was a typical progressive. He assumed that when the people were informed, they would bring pressure on their representatives to do the right thing.

William Howard Taft

Roosevelt's views about federal regulation of business and about presidential power eventually caused a split in the Republican party. They also divided the Progressive Movement.

When he completed his second term as president, Roosevelt did not run again. Instead he used his influence to get the Republican nomination for his close friend William Howard Taft. Taft was easily elected, defeating William Jennings Bryan, who was running for president for the third and last time.

Taft was from Cincinnati, where he had been a federal judge. After the Spanish-American War he had moved from the court of appeals to the post of governor general of the Philippine Islands. In 1904 Roosevelt had appointed him secretary of war.

By the time he became president, Taft weighed over 300 pounds. He was good natured. He had an excellent sense of humor. When he laughed, his belly shook like the well-known bowlful of jelly. But Taft was not a success as president, and his great weight was partly to blame.

Taft found it hard to get all his work done. Because he was so overweight, he needed much rest and relaxation. Further, he was a poor politician. Theodore Roosevelt had often been able to keep both sides happy by taking a middle position on controversial questions. When Taft took a middle position, he usually made both sides angry with him.

Taft tried to continue the policies of the Roosevelt administration. He supported a new law to further increase the powers of the Interstate Commerce Commission. He added more forest lands to the national reserves. He also continued Roosevelt's policy of attacking "bad" trusts under the Sherman Act.

Taft allowed conservative Republicans to influence his policies in many ways. He bungled a well-meant attempt to get Congress to lower the tariffs on manufactured goods. There was a nasty fight within his administration over conservation policy between Secretary of the Interior Richard A. Ballinger and Gifford Pinchot, the chief forester of the department. The controversy was over Alaskan coal lands. Taft sided with Ballinger and dismissed Pinchot. He was probably correct in doing so. But Pinchot then persuaded ex-president Roosevelt that Ballinger and the president were not true friends of conservation. ▣

Copyright by the White House Historical Association; photograph by the National Geographic Society

William Howard Taft, like the other presidents of the United States, had his portrait painted while he was in the White House.

Return to the Preview & Review on page 796.

Government Versus Big Business   799

Preview & Review

Use these questions to guide your reading. Answer the questions after completing Section 4.

Understanding Issues, Events, & Ideas. Explain how President Wilson's program continued the spirit of reform, using the following words: Progressive party, Bull Moose party, New Nationalism, welfare state, New Freedom, Underwood Tariff, income tax, Sixteenth Amendment, Federal Reserve Act, Federal Reserve Board, Clayton Antitrust Act, Federal Trade Commission.

1. Why did ex-president Roosevelt form the Progressive party? What did Roosevelt mean by the New Nationalism?
2. How did Woodrow Wilson's New Freedom differ from Roosevelt's New Nationalism?
3. Why did Wilson win the presidency so easily?

Thinking Critically. Of the legislative acts passed under Wilson's New Freedom, which do you think is the most important? Why?

The Progressive Party

Roosevelt did not want to interfere with Taft's handling of the presidency. Nor did he want to second-guess him. As soon as Taft was inaugurated, Roosevelt went off to hunt big game in Africa. But when he returned to the United States in 1910, he quickly came into conflict with Taft. He soon decided that Taft was not really a progressive. Taft was not using the powers of his office forcefully, the way Roosevelt had. Roosevelt decided that Taft was a weak leader.

In particular Roosevelt objected to the president's antitrust policy. When Taft ordered an antitrust suit against the U.S. Steel Corporation, Roosevelt was furious. In his opinion U.S. Steel was a "good" trust. Its officers had cooperated faithfully with the Bureau of Corporations.

By 1911 all sorts of Republican leaders, conservatives as well as progressives, were telling Roosevelt that Taft was so unpopular that he could not be reelected in 1912. They urged Roosevelt to seek the nomination. Roosevelt finally agreed. He entered and won nearly all the Republican primaries.

However, there were far fewer presidential primaries in 1912 than there are today. In most states party professionals chose the convention delegates, and Taft got nearly all of them. When the Republican convention met in June, the Taft delegates were in the majority. The president was renominated on the first ballot.

Roosevelt was now ready for a fight. Large numbers of Republican progressives urged him to make the run for president. He agreed to form a new **Progressive party** and seek the presidency under its banner.

In his enthusiasm for the coming battle for the White House, Roosevelt announced that he felt "as strong as a bull moose." Cartoonists promptly began to use a moose as the symbol for the Progressive party to go along with the Republican elephant and the Democratic donkey. Soon people were referring to the party as the **Bull Moose party.**

Roosevelt's 1912 platform was ahead of its time. Corporations should be brought "under complete federal control," he said. Presidential candidates should be chosen by the people in primary elections, not by machine politicians at conventions. He also came out for a law to insure workers who were injured on the job, to assure a minimum wage for women, and to do away with child labor. He supported a Constitutional amendment giving women the right to vote.

Roosevelt called his program the **New Nationalism.** By nationalism he meant a stronger and more active national government. He

New York Public Library

was thinking of something similar to what we today call the **welfare state.** The government should be prepared to do "whatever . . . the public welfare may require," he said.

"Come Moosie," shows the Bull Moose of Roosevelt's third party. Why are both the Democrats and the Republicans eager that the bull moose eat their oats?

The Election of 1912

Roosevelt hoped to attract Democratic as well as Republican voters to the Progressive party. But since he had been a lifelong Republican, the new party was sure to draw most of its support from Republicans. This presented Democrats with a golden opportunity. With Republican voters split between Taft and Roosevelt, the Democrats' chances of winning the election were excellent. All they needed to nail down the victory was an attractive presidential candidate.

National Portrait Gallery, detail

Woodrow Wilson was a relative new-comer to politics. He had served as president of Princeton and governor of New Jersey. His slate was clean and therefore he had great appeal for pro-gressives. Do you think teaching is good preparation for the presidency?

The struggle for the nomination at the Democratic convention was hard fought. The person who won it was Woodrow Wilson, the governor of New Jersey.

Wilson was a newcomer to politics. He had been born in Virginia in 1856. After graduating from Princeton College and studying law, he studied political science and became a professor. Most of his teaching was done at Princeton, where he was very popular. In 1902 he had been elected president of Princeton. As president he intro-duced several important reforms in education. He hired more teach-ers and encouraged closer contacts between professors and students. He also added a large number of courses to the curriculum.

In 1910, however, Wilson resigned as president of Princeton to run for governor of New Jersey on the Democratic ticket. He was elected. He immediately proposed a number of progressive reforms. More important, he displayed remarkable political skill in getting the state legislature to enact his proposals into law. This success explains how he defeated the other Democratic presidential hopefuls in 1912.

The Democratic program was in the progressive tradition. Wil-son called it the **New Freedom.** The *objectives* of the New Freedom were quite similar to those of the New Nationalism. The *methods* proposed were quite different.

Wilson did not believe in close government regulation of big business. Instead he wished to rely on antitrust laws to break up monopolies. Unlike Roosevelt, who thought that competition was wasteful, Wilson thought competition made business more efficient. The federal government should pass laws defining fair competition, Wilson believed. Any company or individuals who broke those laws should be severely punished.

Wilson also disliked Roosevelt's New Nationalism because he thought it would make government too big and let it interfere too much in the affairs of citizens. He opposed federal laws that told large corporations how to manage their affairs. He also opposed laws that gave special privileges to labor unions or farmers or women or any other group.

In a way, Wilson wanted the federal government to act like the referee in a football game. The government should enforce the rules of the game strictly but evenhandedly. It should keep a sharp eye on the players and penalize any team that broke the rules. But it should not try to call the plays or choose sides.

A Victory for Reform

Wilson easily won the election of 1912. He received 435 electoral votes to Roosevelt's 88 and Taft's 8. However, he got less than 42 percent of the popular vote. Slightly over half the voters cast their ballots for either Roosevelt or Taft. In other words, Wilson was elected because of the breakup of the Republican party.

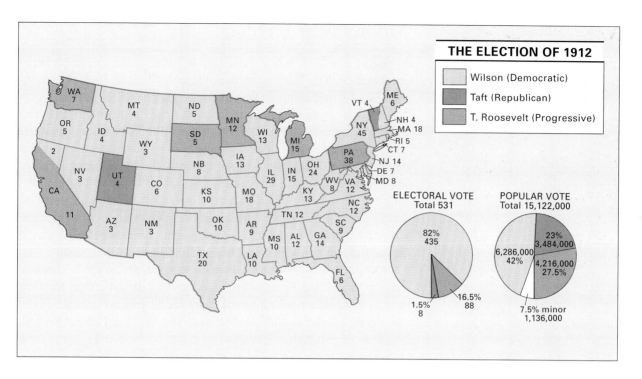

THE ELECTION OF 1912

- Wilson (Democratic)
- Taft (Republican)
- T. Roosevelt (Progressive)

WA 7 · MT 4 · ND 5 · MN 12 · VT 4 · ME 6 · NH 4 · NY 45 · MA 18 · RI 5 · CT 7 · NJ 14 · DE 7 · MD 8

OR 5 · ID 4 · WY 3 · SD 5 · WI 13 · MI 15 · PA 38

NV 3 · UT 4 · NB 8 · IA 13 · IL 29 · IN 15 · OH 24 · WV 8 · VA 12

CA 11 · AZ 3 · NM 3 · CO 6 · KS 10 · MO 18 · KY 13 · NC 12

OK 10 · AR 9 · TN 12 · SC 9

TX 20 · LA 10 · MS 10 · AL 12 · GA 14 · FL 6

ELECTORAL VOTE
Total 531

82% 435
16.5% 88
1.5% 8

POPULAR VOTE
Total 15,122,000

23% 3,484,000
4,216,000 27.5%
6,286,000 42%
7.5% minor 1,136,000

Nevertheless, the election was an overwhelming victory for progressivism and reform. Together, Wilson and Roosevelt received almost 70 percent of the popular vote. In addition almost 900,000 voters, about 6 percent of the total, cast their ballots for the Socialist party. The Socialists were demanding government ownership of railroads, banks, and "all large-scale industries."

The Socialist presidential candidate was Eugene V. Debs, the leader of the railroad workers who had been jailed for his role in the Pullman strike in 1894. While in prison, Debs had done a good deal of reading about government and politics. He became a socialist. He had run for president on the Socialist ticket in 1904 and in 1908, each time receiving about 400,000 votes. In 1912 his vote more than doubled. Clearly the American people were in a reform-minded mood.

Was the election a victory for Wilson's New Freedom philosophy? The answer to this question is unclear. The argument between Wilson and Roosevelt was the same one that Jefferson had with Hamilton in the 1790s about the role of the federal government. On the one hand, the large Socialist vote suggests increased support for the Hamilton (and Roosevelt) "big government" position. On the other hand, both Taft and Wilson believed, as Jefferson had, in competition rather than government regulations. Both promised to enforce the antitrust law strictly. When the Taft and Wilson votes are combined, they come to about 65 percent of the total.

Probably most citizens did not have a firm opinion about how reform should be accomplished. Most were voting for "a reformer" but not for a particular program.

LEARNING FROM MAPS. *Roosevelt's nomination by the Progressive party may have cost the Republicans the election of 1912. Roosevelt captured several states outright. How did the unit rule of the electoral college make the split of the Republican party that much more damaging?*

Wilson's New Freedom

As soon as he took office, President Wilson set out to put his ideas into practice. The Democrats had majorities in both houses of Congress, so he confidently expected to see his proposals passed.

He first urged Congress to lower the high protective tariff. The resulting **Underwood Tariff** of 1913 allowed food products, iron and steel, agricultural machinery—things that could be produced more cheaply in the United States than abroad—to enter the country without any tariff at all. For goods that needed some protection, the duties were lowered but not done away with. In addition, the Underwood Act provided for an **income tax.** This was possible because another progressive reform, the **Sixteenth Amendment** authorizing federal income taxes, had just been added to the Constitution.

Congress also passed the **Federal Reserve Act** in 1913. This law created 12 Federal Reserve Districts, each with a Federal Reserve Bank. These were banks for banks, not for businesses or individuals. The Federal Reserve Banks were supervised by the **Federal Reserve Board** in Washington. The board was not controlled by the federal government. It was an independent regulator of the money supply.

All national banks were members of the Federal Reserve system. All state banks that met certain requirements could also join. In times of depression when weak banks were on the brink of failing, Federal Reserve Banks could transfer money to prevent losses. The Federal Reserve system also made it possible to put more money into circulation to stimulate the economy or take some out to slow it down.

In practice the Federal Reserve system did not work quite so smoothly. It was not always easy to know whether to stimulate the economy or slow it down. Still, the Federal Reserve was a great improvement over the old national banking system established during the Civil War. It is still in operation today.

Then, in 1914, Congress passed the **Clayton Antitrust Act.** This law made it illegal for directors of one corporation to be directors of other corporations in the same field. It provided that the officers and managers of a company that violated the antitrust laws could be held personally responsible for the violations. It also stated that labor unions were *not* to be considered "combinations . . . in restraint of trade under the antitrust laws."

In 1914 Congress also created the **Federal Trade Commission.** This Commission conducted investigations of large corporations. If it found them acting unfairly toward competitors or the public, it issued "cease and desist orders," making them stop.

The Federal Trade Commission was closer in spirit to Theodore Roosevelt's New Nationalism than to the New Freedom. So was the Federal Reserve system. Wilson was not a rigid believer in old-style competition. Like Roosevelt, he was willing to use more than one technique in order to check the power of big business.

Return to the Preview & Review on page 800.

5. LIMITS OF PROGRESSIVISM

Restrictions on Immigration

By the end of 1914 the Progressive Movement had accomplished many political, social, and economic reforms. But the progressives had prejudices and blind spots that limited their achievements. Most were not very sympathetic to immigrants during a time of heavy immigration. Some years at the height of the progressive period, more than 1 million newcomers settled in the United States. In 1907 Americans demanded that the government stem the tide of Japanese immigration. In 1907 the United States and Japan reached what is known as the **Gentlemen's Agreement.** Japan promised not to allow unskilled workers to come to the United States.

Progressives who were alarmed about corruption in politics blamed the recent immigrants. These people cast a large proportion of the votes that kept corrupt bosses in power. Social workers and many others who were trying to help the poor thought that too many immigrants were crowding into the slums. They argued that the famous American **melting pot** could not absorb so many people so quickly. They were afraid that the character of American life would be undermined unless immigration was somehow limited.

Even Uncle Sam seems disturbed by the horde of new arrivals—"Anarchists in Chicago" and "Socialists in New York." What reveals the artist's prejudice?

The Granger Collection, New York

Use these questions to guide your reading. Answer the questions after completing Section 5.
Understanding Issues, Events, & Ideas. Explain the limits of progressivism, using these words: Gentlemen's Agreement, melting pot, Niagara Movement, National Association for the Advancement of Colored People, Great War.
1. Why were progressives not sympathetic to immigrants? What was the attitude of most progressives toward blacks? Why?
2. How did Booker T. Washington continue to work for black people? How did William E. B. Du Bois work for blacks?
3. What event slowed the pace of progressive reform?
Thinking Critically. Suppose you are a speaker at the Niagara Falls meeting of 1905. What demands would you make? How would you expect the government to meet those demands?

STRATEGIES FOR SUCCESS

COMPOSING PARAGRAPHS

You will often be asked to write a description or explanation. To do so effectively, you must organize your thoughts into paragraphs. A paragraph consists of several sentences that state a main idea and add an explanation or supporting details. For the paragraph to communicate your message, these sentences should be presented in a logical sequence.

How to Write a Paragraph

To write a paragraph, follow these guidelines.

1. **State a main idea**. Develop a clear statement of the main point you want your readers to understand.
2. **Support your main idea**. Include sentences that add detail or interest. These sentences should explain, support, or expand the main idea of the paragraph.
3. **Explain key terms**. Define or explain any special words you use in the paragraph. This can be done best in a separate sentence within the paragraph.
4. **Connect the sentences**. Make sure that your paragraph has a beginning and an end. Also make sure that all the information is tied logically together.

Applying the Strategy

Read the paragraph in the next column. The main idea is stated in the first sentence: *Progressives who were alarmed about corruption in politics blamed the recent immigrants.* This main idea is supported by the sentence: *These people cast a large proportion of the votes that kept corrupt bosses in power.* The other sentences in the paragraph expand on the situation faced by immigrants: *Social workers and many others who were trying to help the poor thought that too many immigrants were crowding into the slums. They argued that the famous American melting pot could not absorb so many people so quickly. They were afraid that the character of American life would be undermined unless immigration was somehow limited.* How would you restate the main idea of the paragraph?

Progressives who were alarmed about corruption in politics blamed the recent immigrants. These people cast a large proportion of the votes that kept corrupt bosses in power. Social workers and many others who were trying to help the poor thought that too many immigrants were crowding into the slums. They argued that the famous American melting pot could not absorb so many people so quickly. They were afraid that the character of American life would be undermined unless immigration was somehow limited.

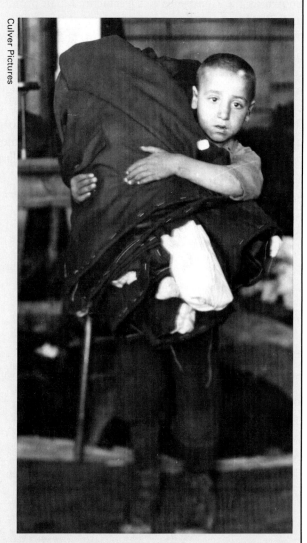

Culver Pictures

For independent practice, see Practicing the Strategy on page 812.

Equality in the Progressive Era

The most glaring weakness of the progressive reformers was their attitude toward racial problems. The Progressive Era was probably the low point in the history of racial relations after the Civil War.

There was no one progressive point of view on the racial question. A few progressives were strong believers in racial equality. Northern progressives tended to be less prejudiced against black people than southerners. But most progressives believed that blacks were entitled at best to second-class citizenship. The most common attitude was that of the Alabama progressive who said that blacks were meant "to be protected by Government, rather than to be the directors of Government."

Most progressives claimed not to be prejudiced and to want to help blacks. But being white and comfortably well off in most cases, they had little understanding of the effects of racial discrimination on black people. Theodore Roosevelt once invited Booker T. Washington to have a meal with him at the White House. When newspapers reported that the president had eaten with a black man, Roosevelt was flooded with complaints, many from progressives. Instead of defending his invitation, Roosevelt practically apologized for it. It had been a spur-of-the-moment act, he explained. Washington had just happened to be there on public business at mealtime. Roosevelt never invited another black person to dine at the White House.

Still, the early 20th century marked a turning point in the history of racial relations. Booker T. Washington remained an important figure. He raised a great deal of money for black schools. He worked cleverly behind the scenes to get political jobs for blacks and to fight racial discrimination cases in the courts. However, he was no longer the only significant black public figure. Younger leaders were beginning to reject his whole approach to the racial problem.

William E. B. Du Bois was the most important of the new black leaders. Du Bois was a historian and sociologist. Although he had very light skin, he was proud of being black. "Beauty is black," he said. He urged people to be proud of their African origins and culture. He set out to make other blacks realize that they must speak out for their rights. If they did not, they would actually be inferior, he warned. The trouble with Booker T. Washington is that he "apologizes for injustice," Du Bois wrote in 1903. Blacks will never get their "reasonable rights" unless they stop "voluntarily throwing them away," Du Bois said. He continued:

> ❝ While it is a great truth to say that the Negro must strive and strive mightily to help himself, it is equally true that unless his striving be not simply seconded, but rather aroused and encouraged, by the initiative action of the richer and wiser environing group [whites and wealthy African Americans], he cannot hope for success.

Culver Pictures

Booker T. Washington remained a powerful leader of African Americans as a younger generation joined the struggle for equality.

In his failure to realize and impress this last point, Mr. Washington is especially to be criticized. His doctrine has tended to make the whites, North and South, shift the burden of the problem to the Negro's shoulders and stand aside as critical and rather pessimistic spectators; when in fact the burden belongs to the nation, and the hands of none of us are clean if we bend not our energies to righting these great wrongs.[1] "

In 1905, at a meeting at Niagara Falls, Canada, Du Bois and a few other black leaders began the **Niagara Movement.** They demanded equality of economic and educational opportunities for blacks, an end to racial segregation, and protection of the right to vote. And they closed with this:

" *Duties:* And while we are demanding, and ought to demand, and will continue to demand the rights enumerated [listed] above, God forbid that we should ever forget to urge corresponding duties upon our people:

The duty to vote.
The duty to respect the rights of others.
The duty to work.
The duty to obey the laws.
The duty to be clean and orderly.
The duty to send our children to school.
The duty to respect ourselves, even as we respect others.

This statement, complaint, and prayer we submit to the American people, and Almighty God.[2] "

National Portrait Gallery

This portrait of Du Bois was made in 1925. What did Du Bois mean by "beauty is black?"

Then in 1909, Du Bois joined with seven white liberals to form the **National Association for the Advancement of Colored People** (NAACP). Du Bois became editor of the NAACP journal, *The Crisis.*

The NAACP's chief purpose in its early years was to try to put an end to lynching. Lynching was a terrible American problem. Ku Klux Klan mobs had killed many blacks during the Reconstruction period, and western vigilantes had hanged large numbers of gunslingers, horse thieves, and outlaws.

During the 1880s and 1890s about 150 to 200 persons a year were lynched. Many were white. Of 638 persons lynched between 1882 and 1886, 411 were whites. Throughout the Progressive Era about 100 persons were lynched each year in the United States. More than 90 percent of the victims were black. The NAACP crusade to end lynching followed the effort of African American journalist Ida B. Wells, who started her campaign against lynchings in 1901. She studied the records of hundreds of lynchings and found that most of the

[1]From *The Souls of Black Folk* by W.E.B. Du Bois
[2]From *The Niagara Movement Declaration of Principles* in *Afro-American History: Primary Sources,* edited by Thomas R. Frazier

Johnson Publications

Leaders of the Niagara Movement posed for this photograph in front of a studio backdrop after their meeting in 1905. W.E.B. Du Bois is second from right in the second row.

victims were killed for ''no offense, unknown offense, offenses not criminal, misdemeanors, and crimes not capital.''

The NAACP did not succeed in reducing the number of black lynchings, which remained high until well into the 1920s. Yet the organization grew rapidly both in members and in influence. By the end of the Progressive Era more and more blacks were speaking out strongly for their rights.

The Great War

After 1914 the pace of progressive reform slowed. President Wilson announced that the major goals of the New Freedom had been reached. Former president Roosevelt turned his attention to other matters.

This does not mean that the national mood that we call progressivism came to an end. Such movements rarely stop suddenly. Indeed, the basic beliefs of the progressives still influence American life. But in 1914 what was soon to be called the **Great War** broke out in Europe. After 1914 that war turned the thoughts of Americans from local problems to international ones.

Return to the Preview & Review o page 805.

Limits of Progressivism

LINKING HISTORY & GEOGRAPHY

IDENTIFYING GEOGRAPHIC REGIONS

In the vocabulary of geographers the word *region* is very important. It is used to describe parts of the earth that share certain specific features. These features may be physical, such as climate, soil, or vegetation. They may be cultural, such as language, economic activity, or cultural heritage. Or, the region may represent a combination of both. Whatever the qualities used to identify the region, it is the commonality of features that make an area a region. Understanding how regions are identified is an important geographic skill.

The American West

1. What are some of the common images of the American West?

One of the regions of the United States that Americans today are most familiar with is the one that is labeled "The West." The very word *west* conjures up an entire collection of images in the minds of Americans. These images usually include both physical features—mountains, deserts, bright blue skies, buffalo, cattle, and cactuses—and cultural features—Indians, hearty cowboys, villainous outlaws, long barbed-wire fences, waving fields of wheat, and gold mines.

You should note, however, that all these images of the geographic region we call the West are comparatively recent. Most are scarcely more than a century old. What, then, was "the West" to the first explorers and settlers who arrived on the shores of North America in the 1500s and 1600s?

The Importance of Point of View

2. Why has the geographic label "West" referred to so many different regions during America's history?

As the brave European explorers and settlers first turned their eyes toward the New World, even the Atlantic Ocean was the West to them. When they stepped off their ships on the eastern seaboard, the West must have been just a short distance inland or the not-so-distant horizon.

The West, then, like all regions, is really a mental function. A region is what and where we *think* it is, and its boundaries are the boundaries we place upon it. What makes up a region depends greatly on our point of view. As a result, through the centuries there have been many "Wests" in the minds of the American people.

The First American West

3. Where was the first area of America labeled "the West"?

The first of the Wests that colonists spoke about and labeled on maps was the territory just beyond the Appalachian Mountains. Settlers quickly filled the lands between the Atlantic and the Appalachians, looking across the mountainous spine to the frontier—the West. Rugged terrain, hostile Indians and French colonists, and British laws kept many from crossing the mountains until after the Revolutionary War. As soon as the war was over, settlers began pouring across the Appalachians, and Congress set about organizing these "western territories." In 1785 and 1787 laws established what they called the Northwest Territory (see pages 189-90).

A New "West"

4. What new area became the West?

As the westward movement of American people continued, the concept of the West moved with them. People pushed beyond the Northwest Territory and in time this first American west became known as "The Old Northwest." And for good reason. By the late 1830s and early 1840s another Northwest—the Oregon Territory—was being settled. This "new" Northwest, named for its geographic location, was soon labeled "The Pacific Northwest."

Actually the term "Old Northwest" never really did occupy a prominent place in the minds of its inhabitants or other Americans. More frequently another regional label was used—"The Middle West," or more simply stated, "The Midwest." As pioneers settled the lands west of the Mississippi, the "Old West" just beyond the Appalachians was now between the East and the frontier. Such labels demonstrate an important geographic concept: it is people, not the compass or the map, that create regional labels.

This concept is illustrated quite simply. What if the United States had been settled by explorers landing along the West Coast. What regional titles would have been applied to the land between the coasts? Would the region that we now call the Middle West have been called the Middle East? (If so, that would make the Rocky Mountain states the Near East!) All this shows that regional labels reflect a particular point of view.

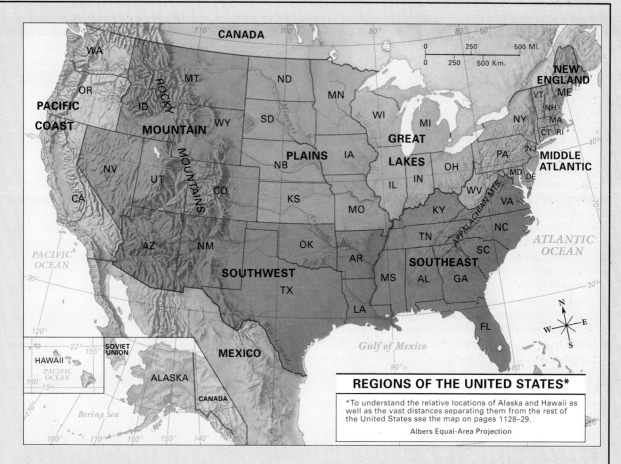

REGIONS OF THE UNITED STATES*

*To understand the relative locations of Alaska and Hawaii as well as the vast distances separating them from the rest of the United States see the map on pages 1128–29.

Albers Equal-Area Projection

The Concept of Regions

5. Why do regional labels depend on your point of view?

In the late 1840s and 1850s prospectors and entrepreneurs flocked to California, Colorado, and Nevada, adding still another "West" to the map of the United States! How could the same geographic term be applied to so many different areas? Because, like all regions, labeling depends on point of view. What was the West to colonists arriving along the East Coast was now *back East* to California miners!

So the term "the West"—confusing in its many uses—was applied to different areas as Americans settled the land. "The West" was a point just beyond the frontier. Americans soon learned that compass direction alone did not determine the limits and labels of regions. Instead, point of view, changing as the nation grew, became the most important element in labeling regions in America.

Regions of the United States Today

6. Into what regions do geographers divide the United States today?

Geographers use a variety of criteria to divide the United States into regions today. For that reason, not all regional divisions are identical. The map illustrates one of the most common regional divisions of the nation. What common features do you think were the basis for each of these regions?

Applying Your Knowledge

Your class will create a regional map of the United States that differs from the one on this page. After a class discussion identifies the new criteria for grouping the states, groups will recommend regional groupings. A volunteer from each group should then explain the group's reasoning. The class will then reach a consensus and create a map illustrating the new regional groupings.

CHAPTER 22 REVIEW

1890
Sherman Antitrust Act

1900
La Follette
elected in
Wisconsin

1901
More
form
U.S.

Chapter Summary

Read the statements below. Choose one, and write a paragraph explaining its importance.

1. Around the turn of the century a new progressive mood swept the country. Reformers hoped to make a better world.
2. Many of the problems attacked by progressives stemmed from rapid industrial and urban growth.
3. Investigative journalists called muckrakers helped publicize political, industrial, and social conditions that called for reforms.
4. Political reforms focused on city and state governments. Social reforms sought to improve the welfare of the people, particularly the poor and workers.
5. Reformers in government tackled the problem of big business. Many supercompanies had formed trusts and had eliminated competition. Led by Theodore Roosevelt, the government began to break the trusts.
6. Although Taft continued many of Roosevelt's reform programs, he was not as effective. With the Republican party split between Taft and Roosevelt, the Democrats won the election of 1912.
7. President Wilson's New Freedom continued the progressive direction in government.
8. Although the progressive spirit continued in America, the Great War in Europe ended the Progressive Era.

Reviewing Chronological Order

Number your paper 1–5. Then study the time line above and place the following events in the order in which they happened by writing the first next to 1, the second next to 2, and so on.

1. Morgan forms U.S. Steel
2. La Follette elected In Wisconsin
3. *The Shame of the Cities*
4. Progressive, Bull Moose, party formed
5. Pure Food and Drug Act

Understanding Main Ideas

1. What was the Progressive Movement?
2. What national problems did the progressives hope to solve?
3. How and why did Roosevelt strengthen the powers of the presidency?
4. How was the result of the election of 1912 a victory for reform?
5. What were the views of most progressives toward immigrants and blacks?

Thinking Critically

1. **Relating Past to Present.** If the muckrakers were investigating problems in American society today, what do you think would be the top five problems on their list?
2. **Synthesizing.** You are a progressive in the early 1900s. How do you propose to make local and state governments more responsive to society's needs?
3. **Evaluating.** Review the cases of *Lochner v. New York* and *Muller v. Oregon*. Do you think a feminist in 1908 would have supported the Court's decision regarding working women? Why or why not?

Writing About History

The progressive spirit continues in America. Newspapers and news magazines often carry articles about problems similar to those tackled by the progressives at the turn of the century. Choose a current issue that calls for reform. Write a letter to your representative in Congress stating your views and ask what stand he or she takes.

Practicing the Strategy

Review the strategy on page 806.
Composing Paragraphs. Reread Section 1 of this chapter on pages 780–84. Then write a paragraph of at least six sentences restating the main idea and supporting it.

	1905	1906	1908	1909	1911	1912	1914
3	Niagara	*The Jungle*	*Muller*	NAACP formed	Triangle	Progressive,	Clayton Antitrust Act
ɔell's	Movement	★	*v. Oregon*		Fire	or Bull Moose,	★
ɔry of		Pure Food	★			party formed	Federal Trade Commission
ɔdard Oil		and Drug Act	Taft			★	★
4			elected			Wilson elected	World War I ends
ɔ Shame			president			president	Progressive Era
ɔhe Cities							

1913
Sixteenth Amendment
★
Underwood Tariff
★
Federal Reserve Act
★
Seventeenth Amendment

ɔthern Securities Case

Using Primary Sources

Jack London was born in San Francisco, California, in 1876. Although he lived to be only 40 years old, his life was filled with adventure. His most popular novels, *The Call of the Wild* and *White Fang,* were set in the Klondike, which is part of Yukon Territory in northwestern Canada. There London spent time as a gold prospector. But on April 17, 1906, Jack London was in San Francisco. The following excerpt is from an article he wrote for a local newspaper. As you read, think about the effects of natural disasters on the people they strike.

On Wednesday morning at a quarter past five came the earthquake. A minute later the flames were leaping upward. In a dozen different quarters south of Market Street, in the working-class ghetto, and in the factories, fires started. There was no opposing the flames. There was no organization, no communication. All the cunning adjustments of a twentieth-century city had been smashed by the earthquake. The streets were humped into ridges and depressions and piled with debris of fallen walls. The steel rails were twisted into perpendicular and horizontal angles. The telephone and telegraph systems were disrupted. And the great water mains had burst. All the shrewd contrivances and safeguards of man had been thrown out of gear by thirty seconds' twitching of the earth crust.

1. From London's account, what seems to be the biggest problem faced by the city?
2. What effect will the damage caused by the earthquake have on the people who live in San Francisco?
3. What does the last sentence suggest about people and nature?

Linking History & Geography

Many people were horrified at the abuse the natural environment had taken. They became determined to conserve natural resources and protect the environment. To understand the situation the progressives found so shocking, answer these questions.

1. What effect had the booming Industrial Revolution on America's natural resources?
2. How was urbanization affecting the natural landscape of America?
3. Many business owners and builders claimed that resources were a God-given gift to the people who owned the land. The government countered by saying such gifts belonged to all Americans—especially future generations. To use them up or to destroy the natural setting was not fair to others. Which argument do you support? Explain your reasoning.

Enriching Your Study of History

1. **Individual Project.** Read further in your library and other American history books into the life of Theodore Roosevelt. Report on one of the following topics, or on a topic of your own:
   Roosevelt the Young Naturalist
   Roosevelt the Rancher
   Roosevelt the Rough Rider
   Roosevelt the Trust Buster
   Roosevelt the Conservationist
   Roosevelt the Family Man
2. **Cooperative Project.** Groups in your class will collect examples of contemporary journalism and classify them as objective or biased reporting. Your group will find stories in magazines and newspapers, then exchange them with the collections of another group. Compare your classifications, and reach a consensus.

Chapter 22 Review 8

UNIT SEVEN REVIEW

Summing Up and Predicting
Read the summary of the main ideas in Unit Seven. Choose one statement, then write a paragraph predicting its outcome or future effect.
1. In the late 1800s the United States began to acquire territories overseas.
2. For partly humanitarian and partly imperialistic reasons, the United States became involved in the Spanish-American War.
3. The United States secured trading rights in Japan and China, and built the Panama Canal, and issued the Roosevelt Corollary to the Monroe Doctrine.
4. As the progressive mood swept America around 1900, reformers attacked problems in industry, cities, politics, and society.
5. Muckrakers were journalists who called attention to areas needing reform.
6. Theodore Roosevelt was an active reformer, leading the way as a trustbuster.
7. Taft and Wilson followed in Roosevelt's footsteps as reformers.

Connecting Ideas
1. As you have learned, Filipinos and others who came under American control in the late 1800s protested that control. Why do you think they did not want the United States to take control? What were some benefits for those areas controlled by the U.S.?
2. What reforms begun by the progressives at the turn of the century are continuing today?
3. Scandals and corruption in government have been widely publicized in recent years, as they were in the early 1900s. Do you think there will always be corruption in government? Why or why not?

Practicing Critical Thinking
1. **Evaluating.** In 1977 the United States and Panama signed a treaty returning control of the canal zone to Panama in the year 2000. What are the risks of turning the canal zone over to Panama? Do you agree with this action? Explain your reasoning.
2. **Synthesizing.** You are a turn-of-the-century progressive who has been transported by a time machine into the 1990s. How would you solve the problem of homelessness in America?

3. **Drawing Conclusions.** Do you agree with Roosevelt, who thought competition in business was wasteful, or with Wilson, who thought it made business more efficient? Why?

Cooperative Learning
1. Working in groups, your class will assemble a notebook on the key people who helped build the Panama Canal. Include brief biographies of Theodore Roosevelt, Philippe Bunau-Varilla, Carlos Juan Finlay, Walter Reed, William Gorgas, George Goethals, David Galliard, and William Howard Taft. Donate your notebook to the school library.
2. You know that a spirit of reform swept the United States at the turn of the 20th century. Now another century approaches. Imagine you are filled with the spirit of the progressive movement. Write a letter to a classmate, telling why you are so optimistic, or pessimistic, about the events at the turn of the 21st century. Have your classmate respond, agreeing or disagreeing with you. Your teacher may post all pairs of letters in the classroom so that you can compare yours with others.

Reading in Depth
Antin, Mary. *The Promised Land.* Boston: Houghton Mifflin. Tells the story of a young immigrant's experiences.

Brau, M.M. *Island in the Crossroads: The History of Puerto Rico.* New York: Doubleday. Describes the importance of Puerto Rico's location.

Castor, Henry. *Teddy Roosevelt and the Rough Riders.* New York: Random House. Presents the exciting story of Americans in combat.

Cook, Fred J. *The Muckrakers: Crusading Journalists Who Changed America.* New York: Doubleday. Provides an inside look at investigative reporting in the progressive era.

Gluck, Sherna, ed. *From Parlor to Prison: Five American Suffragists Talk About Their Lives.* New York: Random House. Contains vignettes on the crusade for women's right to vote.

Reynolds, Robert L. and Douglas MacArthur, 2nd. *Commodore Perry in Japan.* New York: American Heritage. Describes Perry's landing and the events surrounding the opening of Japan.

J.S. Curry, *Tornado Over Kansas*, Hackley Picture Fund, Collection of The Muskegon Museum of Art. (Detail)

John Steuart Curry painted "Tornado over Kansas" in 1929.

A TROUBLED AMERICA

UNIT 8

In Unit 8 you will learn about World War I, the economic boom of the 1920s, and the Great Depression that followed in the 1930s. Here are some main points to keep in mind as you read the unit.

- Quarrels among the nations of Europe led to the outbreak of World War I in 1914.
- The United States was drawn into the conflict in 1917.
- At the peace conference following the war, President Wilson promoted the idea of peace without victory. But Britain and France wanted to punish Germany.
- A period of prosperity, the 1920s was a golden age for movies, radio, and the automobile.
- President Roosevelt's New Deal helped relieve the suffering of many, but it did not end the Depression.

The Great World War

The Great War that began in Europe in 1914 had been simmering since the late 19th century. Germany, France, Great Britain, Russia, and Austria-Hungary continually quarreled. Holding colonies in Africa and spheres of influence in China caused frequent disputes. While some European countries were expanding their influence abroad, others like Austria-Hungary and Germany had become unified nations, forged together in war by "blood and steel." The Slavic people—including Poles, Czechs, Slovaks, Serbs, and Croatians—resented being ruled by German-speaking Austria-Hungary. Complicated alliances prevented outright war for a time, but in 1914 the Allies (Great Britain, France, Russia, Serbia, and Belgium) began fighting against the Central Powers (Germany and Austria). How long could the United States resist entering what was becoming the largest war yet fought on the planet?

UPI/Bettmann Newsphotos

Guards drag Gavrilo Princip, assassin of the Archduke of Austria-Hungary and his wife, through the streets of Sarajevo. Explain why this assassination had such wide consequences.

1. THE SPARK IS LIT

War in Europe

The **Great War,** which Americans came to call World War I, began in Europe during the summer of 1914. It broke out following the assassination of an Austro-Hungarian prince, Archduke Ferdinand, and his wife in the city of Sarajevo in what later became Yugoslavia. The killer was a member of the Black Hand, a terrorist organization in the part of Yugoslavia that was then the nation of Serbia. Serbians wanted the southern Austro-Hungarian territories populated by Serbs. Austria declared war on Serbia. What had led to this explosive situation?

At first there seemed no reason why these murders would lead to a long and terrible war. However, several pressures were at work in Europe under the surface. The most important was **nationalism,** the feeling of pride and loyalty that people have for their country or for a shared language or customs. Nationalism helped unite Germany and brought many Slavic people closer together. However, some national groups such as the Serbians were ruled by other nations. Increasingly these people called for independence.

Another powerful force was **imperialism.** Some European nations had built great colonial empires in Asia and Africa. Others, such as Germany and Italy, envied these empires and wanted to build their own. Their attempts to do this brought them into conflict with the established imperialist nations. Empires brought power and prestige. So did military might. By 1900 the kaiser—the king of Germany—had built Germany's army into Europe's largest and best equipped. The other nations of Europe also began to strengthen their forces. Before long a dangerous arms race was underway.

To further increase their power, European nations had signed a complicated network of treaties. Two powerful groups called **alliances** had been created. European leaders claimed these alliances maintained a **balance of power.** That is, they kept the two groups of nations at nearly equal strength. These leaders hoped that a balance of power would preserve the fragile peace.

But alliances proved to be a grave danger. When a member of one alliance was threatened, the other members were pledged to support it. Austria and Serbia belonged to rival alliances. Austria held Serbia responsible for the assassinations. Quickly allies on both sides became involved, and their conflict resulted in a war that spread throughout Europe.

Germany and Austria were the principal members of one alliance. They were known as the **Central Powers** because they dominated the middle of Europe. Later they were joined in the war by Bulgaria and Turkey. Opposing them were a number of nations known as the **Allies.** Great Britain, France, and Russia were the

Preview & Review

Use these questions to guide your reading. Answer the questions after completing Section 1.
Understanding Issues, Events, & Ideas Using the following words, describe the events that led to war in Europe: Great War, nationalism, imperialism, alliance, balance of power, Central Powers, Allies.

Use the following words to explain how most Americans felt about going to war: arbitration treaty, peace movement, neutrality.

Describe Wilson's foreign policy in Mexico, using the following words: Mexican Revolution, military dictatorship, ABC Powers, mediate.

1. What did signers of arbitration treaties agree to do?
2. What did President Wilson believe should be the role of the United States in foreign affairs?
3. Why did the United States become involved in the Mexican Revolution?

Thinking Critically. Imagine that it is 1910, and you are a Mexican refugee who has crossed the Mexican border into New Mexico. Write a diary entry explaining why you have left Mexico and your hopes for the future.

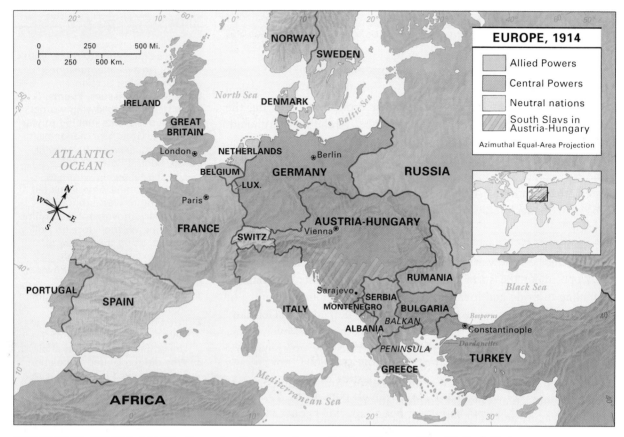

EUROPE, 1914

Allied Powers

Central Powers

Neutral nations

South Slavs in
Austria-Hungary

Azimuthal Equal-Area Projection

LEARNING FROM MAPS. *By 1914 Austria-Hungary had been unified into a huge country occupying central Europe. Many ethnic groups had been brought under its control. The struggles of these groups, seeking independence and the chance to form a nation of their own, helped cause the Great War. What countries made up the Central Powers? Why were they called that?*

leading members of this alliance. The United States was most concerned by the fighting between Great Britain and Germany.

American Neutrality

News of the outbreak of war caught Americans by surprise. There had not been a major war in Europe since the defeat of Napoleon at the battle of Waterloo in 1815. Prosperity and progress had encouraged people to hope that the nations of the world had become too "civilized" to resort to warfare to settle their disagreements.

Under Presidents Taft and Wilson the United States had negotiated **arbitration treaties** with a number of nations. The signers agreed in advance to discuss any differences during a "cooling off" period to last about a year. Only if a solution could not be found would they consider going to war.

In America the search for worldwide peace went even further. Both religious and secular groups became deeply involved in a **peace movement**. The Carnegie Endowment for International Peace, drawing upon funds provided by Andrew Carnegie's millions, mounted a campaign to promote peaceful solutions to international problems. William Jennings Bryan, Wilson's secretary of state, used both rational and religious arguments to further the quest for peace.

This American attitude helps explain why President McKinley

hesitated to ask Congress to declare war on Spain in 1898. Wars were to be fought only for a noble purpose and only after every reasonable effort had been made to negotiate a settlement.

Nearly all Americans felt the United States should not become involved in the war in Europe. Many persons of German or Austrian origin hoped that the Central Powers would win. So did large numbers of Irish Americans, who were anti-British because Great Britain still refused to grant Ireland its independence. People whose ancestors had come from the Allied nations tended to favor that side in the war. But for the vast majority of Americans the obvious policy for the United States was **neutrality.** Europe was far away. Its rivalries had always been viewed by Americans with distrust.

President Wilson expressed the general attitude clearly on August 18, 1914. Every American ought to "act and speak in the true spirit of neutrality," he said. This meant behaving with "impartiality and fairness and friendliness" to all the nations at war.

Wilson's Foreign Policy

As president of the United States, Woodrow Wilson had the chief responsibility for deciding the country's foreign policy. He had run for president, however, on the domestic issues of the Progressive Era. Foreign questions had not played much part in the 1912 campaign. Before 1912 Wilson had never been especially concerned with foreign affairs. Nevertheless, he had very strong opinions about what was morally correct in foreign affairs.

This is how Wilson reasoned: The United States did not need any more territory. It had no enemies. It did not want to injure any foreign country. Indeed, Wilson thought, being rich and powerful, the United States had a duty to help less fortunate nations, particularly its neighbors in Central and South America. America's destiny was not to control other countries but to encourage the spread of democratic ideas. After all, he felt no other country knew as much about democracy as the United States. The brief period of American imperialism had been a bad mistake, the president insisted.

Wilson thought the United States should help other nations and try to make life better for their people. His trouble was that he was convinced that he knew what was best for the rest of the world. He often tried to impose his ideas on people who did not agree with him.

Wilson did not seem to understand that nations with different cultures and traditions often saw things differently than he did. Even nations which sought the same goals as Wilson sometimes resented his efforts to assist them. Perhaps because he had been a teacher for so many years, the president had a tendency to lecture to the officials of other nations. His manner, rather than his actual words, created the impression that Wilson thought he knew better than foreign leaders what was best for their countries.

Culver Pictures

Victoriano Huerta became military dictator of Mexico in 1913. President Wilson said he headed a "government of butchers." Do you suppose such a display of medals was worn in the memory of fallen comrades or to impress those who opposed Huerta's heavy-handed rule?

Revolution in Mexico

Even before the war in Europe began, Wilson had to deal with an important foreign problem. This was the **Mexican Revolution.** This upheaval, which began in 1910, was against the dictator Porfirio Díaz who had ruled Mexico for many years and allowed foreign companies to exploit his country's resources. It was of concern to Wilson because United States investments in Mexico were threatened by the troubles. Also, many Mexican refugees from the fighting were crossing the border into Texas, New Mexico, Arizona, and California against U.S. wishes.

Before Wilson became president, the revolution had been led by Francisco Madero, a progressive-type reformer who had forced Díaz to resign and leave Mexico. Madero became president but early in 1913 was murdered by General Victoriano Huerta. Huerta set up a **military dictatorship** with all powers of government held by the generals. Wilson called this "a government of butchers." He refused to recognize Huerta as the legitimate leader of the Mexicans.

Many Mexicans agreed with Wilson. A new revolt broke out, led by Venustiano Carranza. Wilson was urged on by United States companies whose Mexican properties were in danger. He asked Huerta to order free elections and promise not to be a candidate himself. If he agreed, the United States would try to persuade the Carranza forces to stop fighting.

Wilson meant well. But even supporters of Carranza resented Wilson's interference. Mexico's problems were none of his business, insisted both sides. If we agreed to United States interference, said an official of the Huerta government, "all the future elections for president [of Mexico] would be submitted to the veto of any president of the United States."

Then, in April 1914, some American sailors on shore leave in Tampico, Mexico, were arrested. They were soon released, but by this time Wilson was so angry at Huerta that he used the incident to try to overthrow him. He sent a naval force to occupy the city of Veracruz.

Wilson did not intend to start a war. He expected his "show of force" would cause the downfall of Huerta. But 19 United States sailors and 126 Mexicans were killed before Veracruz was captured. Again, Carranza joined with his enemy Huerta in speaking out against the interference of the United States in Mexican affairs.

Fortunately, the ambassadors of the **ABC Powers**—Argentina, Brazil, and Chile—offered to **mediate** the dispute—that is, to act as neutral go-betweens to find a peaceful settlement. Wilson eagerly accepted their offer. The crisis ended. By summer Carranza had forced Huerta from power. The United States then withdrew its naval force from Veracruz.

Yet Wilson's troubles in Mexico were far from over. No sooner

Culver Pictures

To some Mexicans Pancho Villa and Emiliano Zapata were Robin Hood and Little John. To others they were bandits. In this photograph of the only meeting of the two leaders, they have taken over the presidential palace in Mexico City in 1914. Villa is seated at the center, and Zapata is to his left. Do these men seem at ease in the palace of the president?

1931, Fresco, 7'9 ¾" × 6'2", Collection, The Museum of Modern Art, New York. Abby Aldrich Rockefeller Fund.

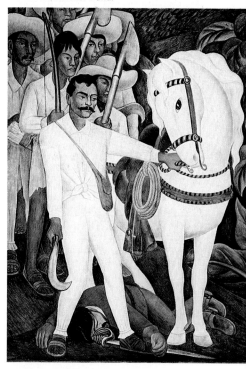

"¡Viva Zapata!" shouted supporters of Mexico's great fighter for land reform. The muralist Diego Rivera called his fresco of Zapata and his white horse "Agrarian Leader Zapata." With the slogan on his lips, "land and liberty," Zapata led an army of Indians in seizing plantations and villages. His movement called zapatismo had as its single purpose the breaking up of the large estates of the rich into small farms for the poor. How does this mural show that Rivera saw Zapata as a man of the people?

had Carranza defeated Huerta than one of his own generals, Francisco "Pancho" Villa, rebelled against him. Wilson supported Villa. He had resented Carranza's independence and refusal to follow United States advice. Villa seemed to be sincerely interested in improving the lives of poor Mexicans. Wilson also thought Villa could be more easily influenced by the United States.

Supporting Pancho Villa was probably the president's worst mistake. Villa was little better than a bandit, while Carranza was genuinely interested in improving the condition of the people of Mexico. From a practical point of view, Carranza had the stronger forces. His troops soon drove the Villistas, Villa's followers, into the mountains of northern Mexico.

At last, in October 1915, Wilson realized that the best policy for the United States was to keep hands off Mexico and let the people of that nation decide for themselves how they were to be governed. He then officially recognized the Carranza government.

This decision angered Pancho Villa. In January 1916 the Villistas stopped a train in northern Mexico and killed 17 citizens of the United States on board in cold blood. Then in March Villa and his men crossed the border and attacked the town of Columbus, New Mexico. They killed 17 more United States citizens and set the town on fire.

Wilson ordered troops under General John J. Pershing to capture Villa. This meant invading Mexico. Pershing was an experienced soldier. He had served during the Indian fighting of the 1880s, in Cuba during the Spanish-American War, and in the Philippine Islands. He earned the nickname "Black Jack" while commanding the 10th Cavalry regiment, which was made up entirely of black enlisted men. One of his first decisions when he was ordered to hunt down Villa was to include part of the 10th Cavalry in his expedition.

Pershing's men pursued Villa vigorously, but they could not catch him on his home ground. As had happened when Veracruz was occupied in 1914, United States interference angered Carranza. Wilson called off the invasion, which accomplished nothing.

Return to the Preview & Review on page 817.

2. WAR ON LAND AND SEA

Use these questions to guide your reading. Answer the questions after completing Section 2.
Understanding Issues, Events, & Ideas Describe the Great War, using the following terms: Eastern Front, Western Front, Battle of the Marne, no man's land, trench warfare, stalemate, U-boat, *Lusitania,* Sussex pledge.
1. What was the war on the Western Front like?
2. How did the U-boats break the rules of the high seas?
3. Why was Wilson unwilling to cut off trade with Great Britain?
Thinking Critically. Imagine that you are an American who has just learned about the torpedoing of the *Lusitania.* Write a letter to the editor of your local newspaper, describing your reaction and explaining what you think President Wilson should do about it.

The War on the Western Front

As early as 1915 the Great World War had become the bloodiest conflict ever fought. On the **Eastern Front** Russian troops clashed with Austrian and German armies in a series of seesaw battles. There was also fighting in Turkey and Serbia. In Africa and on the islands of the Pacific, Allied troops clashed with German colonial forces. In May 1915 Italy entered the war on the side of the Allies and attacked Austria-Hungary from the south.

The greatest interest of the United States at this time was in the fighting on the so-called **Western Front** in Europe—Belgium and France—and on the high seas. When the war began, the Germans marched into Belgium on their way to invade France. No matter that they had promised by treaty in 1870 to respect the neutrality of tiny Belgium in the event of war with France.

The Belgians resisted bravely, but they could not stop the invaders. By September 1914 the German armies had swept across Belgium and were within 20 miles (32 kilometers) of Paris. There, in the **Battle of the Marne,** they were checked by French and British troops.

The two armies then dug trenches to protect themselves from bullets and artillery shells. They put up mazes of barbed wire in front of their positions. Lines of these trenches ran all the way across

THE EASTERN FRONT

——— Farthest German-Austrian advance, Nov. 1918

——— Extent of Russian drive, Dec. 1914

```
0        200        400 Mi.
0     200    400 Km.
```

Azimuthal Equal-Area Projection

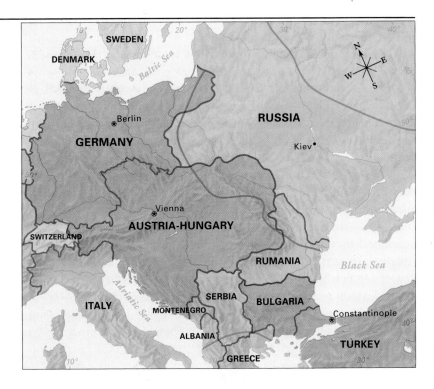

LEARNING FROM MAPS. *Russia invaded the Central Powers in 1914 in keeping with its alliance with Serbia. However, the Central Powers had soon pushed far into Russia. What ended the Russian war effort?*

Culver Pictures

northern France from the sea to Switzerland. Between the opposing trenches lay a narrow **no man's land.**

This was **trench warfare.** Soldiers ate and slept in the gravelike damp. First one side, then the other would try to break through at some point along the line. The artillery would begin the attack by firing exploding shells at the enemy trenches for hours. Soldiers would then climb from their trenches and rush "over the top" with fixed bayonets at the enemy line. The defender's artillery would rain shells upon them while sharpshooters and machine gunners from the trenches riddled the attackers with a hail of bullets. These attacks resembled the British attack at Breed's Hill in the first weeks of the American Revolution. But millions, not hundreds, of soldiers were involved. And their weapons were far more deadly.

The armies had reached a **stalemate**—neither side could win a decisive victory despite repeated attacks and counterattacks which cost hundreds of thousands of lives. No man's land came to look like the surface of the moon. No tree or house stood there. Scarcely a blade of grass could be found, so heavy was the bombardment. The surface, like the moon, was pockmarked by tens of thousands of craters where artillery shells had exploded.

The war on the Western Front was unlike any other war in

In the words of historian Barbara Tuchman, the soldiers who fought in these miserable trenches could do little more than "exchange one wet-bottomed trench for another." How was this kind of warfare like the early British attacks at Breed's Hill in the American Revolution? How was it far different?

War on Land and Sea   823

"Men could not sustain a war of such magnitude and pain without hope—. . . Like the shimmering vision of Paris that kept Kluck's° soldiers on their feet, the image of a better world glimmered beyond the shell-pitted wastes and leafless stumps that had once been green fields and waving poplars. Nothing less could give dignity or sense to the monstrous offensives in which thousands and hundreds of thousands were killed to gain ten yards and exchange one wet-bottomed trench for another. When every autumn people said it could not last through the winter, and when every spring there was still no end in sight, only the hope that out of it all some good would accrue to mankind kept men and nations fighting."
From *The Guns of August*, 1962

°Kluck was a German general.

history. The battle between the Union and Confederate armies around the city of Petersburg, Virginia, in the last stages of the Civil War comes closest to it. That battle lasted only a few months. The terrible struggle on the Western Front went on for years.

The War on the Atlantic

On the Atlantic Ocean a new kind of struggle developed in 1914-15. The British navy was far stronger than Germany's. It attempted to blockade all northern European ports in order to keep Germany from obtaining supplies from the United States and other neutral nations. The Germans, in turn, tried to keep supplies from the British by using swift submarines, which they called ''Undersea ships'' or **U-boats.**

All the major navies had submarines by 1914. Both Great Britain and the United States had more in operation at that time than Germany. Submarines were small, relatively slow vessels. Most naval authorities did not consider them important weapons. However, the German navy did not have enough surface ships to operate in the Atlantic against the Allied fleets. U-boats were the only naval weapon the Germans could use.

Like privateers during the American Revolution and the War of 1812, U-boats roamed the seas looking for unarmed merchant vessels to attack. When they sighted powerful enemy warships, they slipped away beneath the surface. These tactics worked so well that the Germans ordered that more U-boats be constructed as quickly as possible.

Both the British blockade and the German submarine campaign hurt American business interests. Both of these activities on the high seas also violated the rights of neutral nations according to international law. British warships stopped American ships and forced them to put into Allied ports for inspection. Goods headed for Germany were seized. The British even tried to limit the amount of goods shipped to neutral countries like Norway and Sweden. Otherwise, they claimed, those nations could import more American products than they needed for themselves and ship the surplus to the Central Powers.

The Germans refused to follow the international rules for stopping merchant ships in wartime. These rules provided that ships could be stopped and their cargoes examined. Enemy vessels and neutrals carrying war materials to enemy ports could be taken as prizes or sunk. Before destroying a merchant ship, the attacker was supposed to take the crew prisoner or give it time to get clear of the vessel in lifeboats.

It was extremely dangerous for submarines to obey these rules. If a submarine surfaced and ordered a merchant ship to stop, the merchant ship might turn suddenly and ram the submarine before it

With their hearts skipping a beat, the passengers on this Spanish steamer see the sleek German submarine surface from its prowls of the North Sea and ask to inspect their ship. Imagine such a close encounter at sea and describe it in your own words.

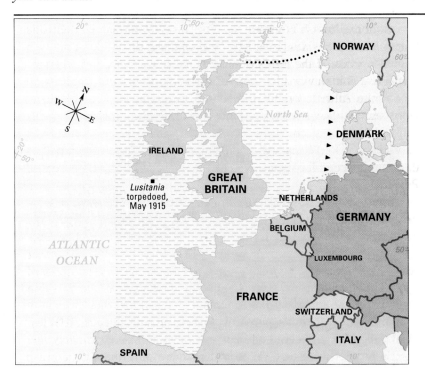

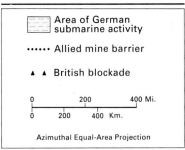

THE GREAT WAR IN THE ATLANTIC

▨	Area of German submarine activity
••••••	Allied mine barrier
▲ ▲	British blockade

0   200   400 Mi.

0   200   400 Km.

Azimuthal Equal-Area Projection

LEARNING FROM MAPS. *What was the purpose of each of the war strategies shown on this map?*

could react. Some merchant ships carried concealed cannon. A single cannon shell could send a submarine to the bottom in seconds. If an enemy warship should appear on the horizon while part of a U-boat's crew was examining the cargo of a merchant ship, the U-boat would almost certainly be blown out of the water before it could call back its men and submerge.

Therefore the U-boats attacked their targets from below the surface, firing torpedoes packed with TNT—a powerful explosive—without warning. Many sailors and passengers lost their lives when their ships went down.

Wilson on Neutral Rights

President Wilson protested strongly against both British and German violations of the international rules. If he had threatened to cut off trade with Great Britain as Jefferson had done in 1807, the British would undoubtedly have obeyed the rules. They could not fight the war without supplies from America. But Wilson was unwilling to go that far, in large part because the profitable trade with the Allies was extremely important to the United States.

Wilson took a much stronger stand against Germany. When U-boats began to sink ships without warning, he announced in February 1915 that Germany would be held to strict accountability for any American property destroyed or lives lost. In the language of diplomacy the phrase ''strict accountability'' was a polite way of saying, ''If you don't do what we ask, we will probably declare war.''

The danger of war over submarine attacks became suddenly critical on May 7, 1915, when the German *U-20* torpedoed the British liner *Lusitania* without warning. Technically this sinking could be defended. The *Lusitania* had deck guns. It was carrying a cargo of guns and ammunition. Its captain was guilty at least of carelessness, for a slow-moving submarine should never have been able to get close enough to a swift ocean liner to hit it with a torpedo.

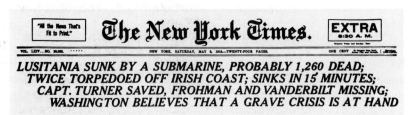

Brown Brothers

The *Lusitania* was crowded with civilian passengers. About 1,200 of them, including 128 American citizens, lost their lives in the sinking. The American public was shocked and furious. If Wilson had called for a declaration of war, Congress would probably have acted promptly. Instead, Wilson demanded only that the Germans

TORPEDO WARFARE

Brown Brothers

Aiming a torpedo accurately from a German U-boat was very difficult. Torpedoes were launched from tubes in the bow of the submarine. The submarine captain's vision was limited because he had to view the target through a periscope. He had to point the entire submarine in the direction he wanted to aim the torpedo.

The captain aimed ahead of his target the way a hunter "leads" a flying duck. He had to estimate the speed of the target and compare it to the speed of the torpedo, which traveled at about 30 miles (48 kilometers) an hour. Nowadays such calculations can be made accurately by computers. In 1915 such equipment was not available. Once fired, the torpedo traveled a fairly straight line. Its direction could not be changed by the captain, although waves and currents might cause it to veer off course.

The *Lusitania* had a top speed of about 25 miles (40 kilometers) per hour. If it had simply changed direction every few minutes, traveling in a zigzag course, it would have been prac-tically impossible for the slow-moving *U-20* to get close enough to aim a torpedo. If by great luck he did get within range, the captain, Lieutenant Walter Schwieger, would not have known where to aim a torpedo if the *Lusitania* were zigzagging. Between the time the torpedo was fired and the time its course intersected with the *Lusitania's,* the liner would have changed direction. Obviously, Captain William T. Turner assumed the *Lusitania* was in no danger and took no evasive action.

apologize, pay damages, and promise not to attack passenger ships in the future. Long negotiations followed. In March 1916, after another passenger vessel, the *Sussex,* was torpedoed with the loss of 80 lives, Germany finally gave in. It promised not to sink any more passenger or merchant ships without warning. This promise is known as the **Sussex pledge.**

Return to the Preview & Review on page 822.

Preview & Review

Use these questions to guide your reading. Answer the questions after completing Section 3.
Understanding Issues, Events, & Ideas Describe the importance of the following words: peace without victory, Zimmermann Note.
1. Which groups of people opposed Woodrow Wilson's reelection? Why did each group oppose his reelection?
2. Why did the Zimmermann Note alarm many Americans?
3. What did President Wilson mean by his statement, "The world must be made safe for democracy"?
Thinking Critically. If you had been able to vote in the presidential election of 1916, would you have voted for the reelection of Woodrow Wilson or not? Why?

The Election of 1916

By late 1916 some Americans, including ex-president Theodore Roosevelt, were arguing that the United States should enter the war on the side of the Allies. A larger number believed that the United States should at least prepare for war by building up the armed forces. Still, a majority of the people wanted to remain neutral. They appreciated Wilson's patient attempts to avoid involvement and his efforts to persuade the warring nations to make peace.

The depth of their feelings came out during the 1916 presidential campaign. One Democratic slogan, "He kept us out of war," proved to have enormous appeal. Wilson was not particularly popular in 1916. Many progressives who had voted for him in 1912 felt that he had not done enough for reform. African Americans considered him a racist, for he had actually increased the amount of segregation in government offices in Washington. Women found him reluctant to support their drive to obtain the right to vote. Yet the Progressive party, led by Theodore Roosevelt, had decided not to run a separate candidate in 1916. Instead the Progressives nominated the Republican candidate, Charles Evans Hughes, a justice of the Supreme Court.

Wilson tried to hold his progressive supporters in 1916 by backing a bill making child labor illegal and another making it easier for farmers to obtain low-interest loans. He approved a strong workman's compensation law. He appointed the liberal lawyer, Louis D.

This Wilson campaign van has at least one version of his popular slogan, "He kept us out of war." What else did Wilson do for the American people, according to the posters?

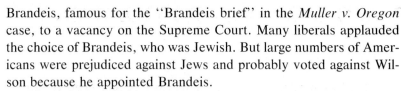

Brandeis, famous for the "Brandeis brief" in the *Muller v. Oregon* case, to a vacancy on the Supreme Court. Many liberals applauded the choice of Brandeis, who was Jewish. But large numbers of Americans were prejudiced against Jews and probably voted against Wilson because he appointed Brandeis.

The presidential election was very close. Wilson got 277 electoral votes to Hughes's 254. Nearly everyone agreed that the president's success in keeping out of the Great War saved him from defeat.

Wilson was too intelligent to take comfort from this fact. He knew that if the Germans ever decided to sink merchant ships again without warning, America could not stay neutral.

America Seeks Peace Without Victory

Wilson's fear of being forced into the war led him to make a strong effort to end it by negotiation. On January 22, 1917, he made a moving speech calling for **peace without victory.** If either side tried to profit from the war by taking land or money from the other, Wilson said, the only result would be hatred that would cause more wars. All the nations, including the United States, must try to make a peace based on "justice throughout the world."

Unfortunately, neither the Allies nor the Central Powers would settle for peace without victory. The cost in lives and money had been so great after two and one-half years of war that neither side could face the idea that all that expense had been wasted. At the very least each intended to make the other pay the entire monetary cost of the war. The German government already had secretly decided to resume submarine attacks on shipping without warning.

The Germans realized that unleashing their sharklike U-boats would probably cause the United States to declare war. Nevertheless, they expected that "ruthless submarine warfare" would keep food and munitions from reaching Great Britain. Then the British would have to surrender. The war would be over before the United States could raise and train an army and get its soldiers across the Atlantic to France.

Less than two weeks after Wilson's "peace without victory" speech, an American merchant ship was sunk by a U-boat. Wilson then broke diplomatic relations with Germany. He ordered the German ambassador out of the United States and recalled his own ambassador from Germany.

Late in February the president learned that German Foreign Relations Secretary Arthur Zimmermann was trying to make an alliance with Mexico. Zimmermann had sent a telegram to the German ambassador in Mexico with the following instructions:

❝ We intend to begin unrestricted submarine warfare on the first of February. We shall endeavor in spite of this to keep the United States neutral. In the event of not succeeding,

Courtesy of the Library of Congress

All eyes are upon President Wilson as he asks Congress to declare war on Germany. "The world," he said, "must be made safe for democracy."

we make Mexico a proposal of alliance on the following basis: Make war together, make peace together, generous financial support, and an understanding on our part that Mexico is to reconquer the lost territory of Texas, New Mexico, and Arizona. . . .

Inform the President [of Mexico] of the above most secretly as soon as the outbreak of war with the United States is certain. . . .[1] **"**

[1]From *The Zimmermann Telegram* by Barbara Tuchman

In the event of war with the United States, Germany wanted an alliance with Mexico. Americans would then send some troops to the Mexican border rather than sending them all to Europe. In return, Germany would help Mexico "reconquer" the "lost territory" of Texas, New Mexico, and Arizona. Nothing officially came from this **Zimmermann Note.** Yet when it was made public, it caused many Americans to call for war against Germany.

In February and March the number of merchant ships sunk by U-boats increased steadily. The *Housatonic,* the *Laconia,* the *Algonquin* were all torpedoed and sunk. Against this grim background the president took the oath of office for his second term. Almost a month later, on April 2, 1917, Wilson asked Congress to declare war. The reason, he said, was to make a just peace possible. "The world," he added in a famous sentence, "must be made safe for democracy."

Wilson did not mean by this that the purpose of the war was to make all nations democracies. Rather he meant that the world must be made a place where democracies could exist and flourish. He believed that if the United States did not help to bring the conflict to an early end, the losses and hatreds would be so great that no democratic government could survive. 🔲

Return to the Preview & Review on page 828.

4. THE WAR AT HOME AND ABROAD

Organizing Wartime America

Building an army and supplying it in a hurry was a huge task. Many changes had to be made in the way goods were manufactured and businesses run. The antitrust laws were suspended. In wartime Wilson agreed with Theodore Roosevelt's argument that large-scale organizations supervised by the government were more efficient than small competing firms. Because so many goods had to be moved, it became necessary to place all the nation's railroads under government management. Wilson appointed William G. McAdoo, the secretary of the treasury, to run the entire system.

The president also set up a **War Industries Board** to oversee the production and distribution of manufactured goods. The head of this board was Bernard Baruch, a millionaire stockbroker. Baruch was active in Democratic party politics at a time when most wealthy stockbrokers were Republicans. A friend and adviser of Wilson, he was a natural choice to head the War Industries Board. In this post he performed brilliantly.

Baruch's idea was to organize American industry as though it were one big factory. He decided what was to be made and where the raw materials were to come from. He controlled the distribution of scarce commodities and in some cases even set the price at which they were to be sold. His job was made easier because most producers were eager to cooperate with the War Industries Board. Profit and patriotism were pushing them in the same direction.

Both, Culver Pictures

Baruch's board had to supply both American needs and much of the war supplies, called **matériel,** and food for the Allied nations. Great Britain, in particular, depended on American wheat, meat, and other products for its survival. Wilson appointed Herbert Hoover as United States Food Administrator. It was Hoover's job to make sure

Preview & Review

Use these questions to guide your reading. Answer the questions after completing Section 4.
Understanding Issues, Events, & Ideas Explain the efforts of wartime America, using the following words: War Industries Board, matériel, American Expeditionary Force, Selective Service Act, propaganda, Industrial Workers of the World, Wobblies, Espionage Act, Sedition Act, Communist Revolution. Then describe the Great War overseas using these words: tanks, poison gas, dogfights, aces, machine guns, Verdun, Château-Thierry, Saint-Mihiel salient, Battle of the Argonne Forest, Hindenburg Line, armistice.

1. What were Herbert Hoover's main goals as United States Food Administrator?
2. How did the war affect African Americans? Women? Mexican Americans?
3. How did the war end?

Thinking Critically. 1. Do you think that the Espionage and Sedition Acts violated First Amendment rights? Why or why not? **2.** Imagine that you are an American soldier in Verdun in 1917. Write a letter home, explaining how the development of new weapons has changed the fighting in the Great War.

Preparing to fight a war 3,000 miles away are William G. McAdoo, left, who managed the nation's railroads, and Bernard Baruch, right, who organized American industry as if it were one big factory.

UPI/Bettmann Newsphotos

Herbert Hoover, another of Wilson's advisers for the war on the homefront, is shown at right inspecting a shipment of supplies to Europe. Hoover campaigned to persuade Americans to eat less. What slogans did he use?

that enough foodstuffs were produced and that they were distributed fairly.

Hoover had been head of the Commission for the Relief of Belgium early in the war. As Food Administrator he set out both to increase production and to reduce domestic consumption. At the same time it was important to keep prices from skyrocketing.

Hoover had little trouble increasing production. It was in the farmers' interest to grow more because the demand for their crops was increasing. For example, they raised 619 million bushels (218 million hectoliters) of wheat in 1917 and 904 million bushels (318 million hectoliters) in 1918.

Getting Americans to consume less was more difficult. Hoover organized a vast campaign to convince the public of the need for conservation. Catchy slogans carried his message. "Food will win the war" was the best known. Others included "When in doubt, eat potatoes," which was designed to save wheat, and "If you have a sweet tooth, pull it," to reduce sugar consumption.

Hoover also organized "Meatless Tuesdays" when no one was supposed to eat meat and "Wheatless Wednesdays" too. He even started a campaign to get every American family to raise a pig. Pigs could live on scraps and garbage and eventually be turned into bacon and pork chops. Hoover's rules could not be enforced. His technique was to depend on (and praise) voluntary cooperation. He made it clear that patriotic citizens were *expected* to obey the rules. The results were excellent.

National Archives

African American men could be drafted under the Selective Service System, but they could not fight side by side with their white colleagues. Blacks who were not drafted began a great migration to the North, where many found jobs in war plants.

Labor in Wartime

Organizing the human resources of the nation was also complicated. During the war the United States Employment Service directed almost 4 million people to new jobs. When war was declared, thousands of young men volunteered for military service. To raise the huge **American Expeditionary Force** (AEF) that was to fight in Europe, however, it was necessary to pass a draft law, the **Selective Service Act** of 1917.

For those men who were not drafted, and for women workers, the war brought many benefits. Wages rose. Unskilled workers got opportunities to move to better jobs. Union membership rose from about 3 million to over 4 million in a year.

It was important to prevent strikes from slowing down the production of vital goods. In December 1917 a National War Labor Conference Board was set up to try to settle disputes between workers and their employers. This board also tried to make sure that workers were not fired for trying to organize unions.

The American Federation of Labor grew to about 3 million members in 1918. AFL unions cooperated with the Conference Board in most cases. Samuel Gompers, president of the AFL, served as a presidential adviser. Gompers never promised that union members would not strike during the war. But he went along with the government's request that workers agree to arbitrate conflicts with their employers whenever possible.

The need for laborers especially helped African Americans, women, and other groups that had been discriminated against in the job market in the past. Thousands of descendents of slaves had already migrated from the South to northern cities before the war began. Half a million more followed between 1914 and 1919. Most of these newcomers earned far more in war plants than they could make raising cotton or tobacco in the South.

The Selective Service System drafted people of all races although soldiers were still segregated in the armed forces. African

The Granger Collection, New York

THE NAVY NEEDS YOU! DON'T READ AMERICAN HISTORY— MAKE IT!

U·S·NAVY RECRUITING STATION
34 EAST 23rd ST., NEW YORK

What message for readers of **The Story of America** *is found in the navy's recruiting poster?*

Americans soldiers were better treated and were given more opportunities than 20 years earlier during the Spanish-American War. About a thousand became officers. Emmett J. Scott of Tuskegee Institute was appointed an assistant to the secretary of war.

Of course, this did not amount to equal treatment. Yet while some African Americans protested, the strong-minded William E. B. Du Bois did not. "Fight for your rights but . . . have sense enough to know when you are getting what you are fighting for," Du Bois urged.

Women were not drafted under the Selective Service Act, although many served as army nurses and as volunteer workers overseas. Many others did volunteer work in hospitals and for such organizations as the Red Cross. Women from all walks of life, the wealthy of New York's Fifth Avenue and the poor immigrants from Grand Street, worked side by side preparing bandages for hospitals and first-aid stations. Most knew that it was only the war that threw such different people together. One American poet described her wartime experience.

> " I sat beside her, rolling bandages.
> I peeped. "Fifth Avenue" her clothes were saying.
> It's "Grand Street," I know well, my shirtwaist° says,
> And shoes, and hat, but then, she did not hear,
> Or she pretended not, for we were laying
> Our coats aside, as we were so near,
> She saw my pin like hers.
> And when girls are
> Wearing a pin these days that has a star°°,
> They smile out at each other. We did that,
> And then she didn't seem to see my hat.
>
> I sat beside her, handling gauze and lint,
> And thought of Jim. She thought of someone too;
> Under the smile there was a little glint
> In her eyelashes, that was how I knew.
> I wasn't crying—but I haven't any
> Pride in it; we've a better chance than they
> To take blows standing, for we've had so many.
> We two sat, fingers busy, all that day. . . .
>
> We're sisters while the danger lasts, it's true;
> But rich and poor's equality must cease
> (For women especially), of course, in peace.[1] "

Thousands of women also found jobs in factories and offices they could not have hoped to get before the war. "This is a woman's age!" the leader of the National Women's Trade Union League

°a type of dress
°°Women wore star-shaped pins to show they had loved ones in the war.
[1]From "Fifth Avenue and Grand Street" by Mary Carolyn Davies

Culver Pictures

The Salvation Army brought its good works to France, where kitchens were set up to feed the hungry soldiers.

announced in 1917. "Women are coming into the labor [movement] on equal terms with men." This was an exaggeration. Yet women workers did make important gains. Recognizing how necessary women were to the war effort, the Wilson administration established a Women's Bureau in the department of labor.

Mexican Americans also benefited from the labor shortage in the United States. Beginning in 1911, thousands had crossed the border

National Archives

Women would have been thought incapable of rolling these steel cables until the shortage of men during the Great War made it necessary for them to do so. Of course they had been capable of factory work all along, and many did very well. What chance had these women for employment when the soldiers returned from the war?

Courtesy of the Museum of New Mexico

Octaviano Larrazola was one of the thousands of Mexican Americans who came north for wartime jobs. Larrazola became the first Hispanic American governor of New Mexico and later represented New Mexico in the U.S. Senate.

to escape the disorder resulting from the Mexican Revolution. Even more came after the Great World War began. Most settled in the Southwest. Mexican American leaders worked hard to involve the new immigrants in American life. When New Mexico and Arizona became states in 1912, many Mexican Americans voted in their first United States election. In 1916 Octaviano Larrazolo was elected governor of New Mexico, the first Hispanic American governor. In 1928 he became the first Hispanic American in the United States Senate.

Besides working in the cotton fields of Texas and Arizona and on farms in Colorado and California, the Mexican Americans became railroad laborers, construction workers, and miners. Some settled in the northern cities, attracted by jobs in war plants. The jobs were mostly low paid and unskilled. Nevertheless, these workers could earn much more than they could by farming. By the end of the war there were communities of Mexican-born families in St. Louis, Chicago, Detroit, and several other northern cities. Many Mexican Americans served in the armed forces.

Propaganda and the Great War

From the beginning most Americans enthusiastically supported America's involvement in the war. But Wilson realized that other Americans opposed that involvement. So the government attempted to gain the cooperation of all Americans in the war effort. A week after war was declared, Wilson created the Committee on Public Information, headed by George Creel. The CPI used **propaganda** to influence people's opinions about the war. For example, it circulated millions of leaflets praising America's official war aims and criticizing the German government.

These releases portrayed the Germans as bloodthirsty Huns, willing to do anything to conquer the world. They even hinted that there were German spies in every office, factory, labor union, and university. And perhaps more importantly, they implied that any disagreement with the American war effort was unpatriotic.

Using propaganda also sold war bonds to raise money to pay for the war, convinced young men to join the armed forces, and even helped convert some doubters. Churches and religious groups, colleges, women's organizations, and civic groups joined in the government's efforts to "sell the war to the American people."

The Treatment of Protesters

The government's propaganda campaign failed to convince everyone of the rightness of United States actions. Despite the urgings of union leaders like Samuel Gompers, some workers were unwilling to go along with the government's labor policies. Radicals in the labor movement had founded a new organization, the **Industrial Workers of the World** (IWW), in 1905. According to the IWW, "the working class and the employing class have nothing in common." Workers should organize, "take possession of the earth and the machinery of production, and abolish the wage system."

One of the founders of the IWW was William D. Haywood. "Big Bill" Haywood had gone to work as a miner in Colorado at the age of 15. In 1896 he joined the Western Federation of Miners. A few years later he became a socialist. In 1904 he led a violent strike of miners in Cripple Creek, Colorado. The next year he was accused of planning the assassination of the governor of Idaho. He was successfully defended by the famous attorney Clarence Darrow. When the Great War broke out, Haywood was secretary-treasurer of the IWW, whose members were known as **Wobblies,** probably because of the way some mispronounced its initials.

Workers should stick together, Haywood said in 1915. They could

> ❝ stop every wheel in the United States . . . and sweep off your capitalists and state legislatures and politicians into the sea. ❞

In 1917 the IWW staged strikes in the lumber and copper-mining industries. The reaction of the government was swift. Federal agents raided IWW headquarters looking for evidence that the Wobblies were trying to slow war production. Over a hundred members, including Haywood, were arrested.

The Wobblies were revolutionaries. Their arrest when they deliberately interfered with the war effort was perfectly proper. But the times made people fearful and uncertain. This led the government to violate the civil rights of many radicals who did nothing but speak or write unpopular words. In 1917 Congress passed the **Espionage Act.** This law made it a crime to aid enemy nations or to interfere with the recruiting of soldiers. It also allowed the Postmaster General to censor mail. The next year a much stronger law, the **Sedition Act,** was passed. This law even cracked down on expressions of opinion. Heavy fines and prison sentences of up to 20 years could be imposed on persons who spoke or wrote anything critical of the government, the army or navy, or even the uniforms worn by soldiers and sailors.

One national political party—the Socialist party of America— also opposed the war, the only political party to do so. Surprisingly, the Socialists' stance helped them at the polls. Many non-Socialists voted for Socialist candidates as a way to express their disagreement with America's involvement in the war.

The government moved quickly to end this antiwar movement. In New York seven Socialists were expelled from the state legislature simply because they opposed the war. Victor Berger, a Socialist representative from Wisconsin, was denied his seat in the House.

Culver Pictures

Big Bill Haywood was a radical founder of the IWW. He headed a violent strike of miners in Cripple Creek, Colorado. When war came, Federal agents raided IWW meeting places and sometimes arrested IWW members, known as Wobblies. Why did the government think it was proper to make such raids and arrests?

The War at Home and Abroad   837

Even more notable was the arrest of Eugene V. Debs, leader of the Socialist party. Debs was jailed following a speech opposing the draft. At his trial in 1918 Debs spoke forcefully against the government's suppression of opinions it disagreed with. But Wilson and other government officials made it clear they would not tolerate opposition on the war issue.

An unreasoning hatred of anything German swept the country. Persons with German names were likely to be insulted by strangers. Schools stopped teaching the German language. Libraries took books by long-dead German authors off the shelves. German-born immigrants who had not become United States citizens were forced to register so that they could be watched closely.

The nation seemed to be in constant fear that radicals and spies would cause the country to lose the war. This was especially true after November 1917, when the **Communist Revolution** occurred in Russia. Americans were suspicious of the communists, and feared they would try to spread their revolution. The Russian communist government quickly made peace with Germany. That enabled the Germans to transfer troops from the Eastern Front to France just when large numbers of American soldiers were going into battle and convinced Americans that the communists were against them.

A sensible limit on freedom of speech in wartime was finally set by the Supreme Court in *Schenck v. United States* (1919), a case that questioned the constitutionality of the Espionage Act. The decision, written by Justice Oliver Wendell Holmes, Jr., one of the greatest of American legal thinkers, upheld the law.

The right of free speech is not an unlimited right, Holmes declared. No one has the right, for example, of "falsely shouting '*Fire!*' in a theater and causing a panic." If there is "a clear and present danger" that something said or written might hurt the war effort, the government may take action. The Supreme Court did not hand down this decision until after the war was over. Before it did so, local, state, and national officials frequently punished persons whose words had no effect on the war effort at all.

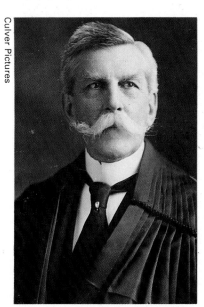

Culver Pictures

Oliver Wendell Holmes was known as the Great Dissenter for his carefully reasoned minority opinions as a justice of the Supreme Court. What did he say about the right of free speech?

Weapons of the Great War

After nearly four years of war, many new weapons had been developed. The fighting in Europe became more and more mechanized. The British and French were the first to use **tanks**—armored, truck-like vehicles that ran on treads rather than wheels. The first tanks were slow, clumsy, and unreliable. They were used to protect advancing troops rather than to attack enemy forces directly.

Another new weapon was **poison gas.** The Germans used gas first, but the Allies soon copied them. Gas was a horrible weapon, choking and blinding its victims. It was not very effective, however. If the wind shifted, it might blow back on those who released it.

Culver Pictures

Culver Pictures

Above, a British tank rolls through a devastated French village, where a horse lies dead near the road. The Great War was one of the last to use cavalry units but the first to use poison gas (left). This weapon choked and blinded its victims. Do you think chemical warfare should be banned? Explain.

Culver Pictures

Captain Edward V. Rickenbacker was America's most famous flying ace. Below, Norman Rockwell, a popular artist of several decades, pictures soldiers around the campfire for the songsheet of George M. Cohan's "Over There." The tune inspired all kinds of people to sing, "The Yanks are coming, the Yanks are coming."

Your Song—My Song—Our Boys' Song

OVER THERE

PHOTO © 1918
LIFE PUB. CO.

WORDS AND MUSIC BY
GEORGE M. COHAN

POPULAR EDITION
LEO. FEIST INC. NEW YORK

Culver Pictures

Airplanes were used increasingly as time passed. There were some bombing planes but none powerful enough to carry heavy loads of bombs for great distances. Mostly planes were used to locate enemy positions and signal artillery units where their shells were hitting so they could aim more effectively.

Yet control of the air was important. There were many exciting air battles called **dogfights** between Allied and German pilots. In this huge war of faceless fighters, pilots were individual heroes. Those who shot down five or more enemy planes were known as **aces.** Rene Fonck, a French ace, shot down 75 enemy planes. Edward Mannock, an Englishman, bagged 73. The most famous German ace, Baron Manfred von Richthofen, claimed 80 kills, but this was probably an exaggeration. Captain "Eddie" Rickenbacker was the leading American ace. He shot down 26 German planes.

But the deadliest weapons remained the artillery and **machine guns.** By 1917 each side had tens of thousands of cannon ranged behind the lines. To prepare for one offensive, the French fired 6 million shells into an area only 20 miles long (32 kilometers). The number of machine guns increased even more rapidly. Before the war American regiments were equipped with four machine guns. By the end of the war each regiment had 336.

Yet all these death-dealing weapons did not give either side enough advantage to end the long struggle quickly. Throughout the summer of 1918 the fighting continued with few movements in either direction. Day by day the number of Americans in the trenches increased from about 27,000 in early June to 500,000 by the end of August.

"Over There"

President Wilson put General Pershing in command of the American Expeditionary Force. The first units of the AEF reached Paris on Independence Day 1917 and took up positions on the front near **Verdun** in October. The AEF went into action in France just in the nick of time. In March 1918 the Germans launched a tremendous attack at the section of the Western Front nearest Paris. With the help of thousands of veterans transferred to France after the Russians left the war, the Germans advanced as far as **Château-Thierry,** a town on the Marne River northeast of Paris. There, in late May, American units were thrown into battle to reinforce French troops. The German advance was stopped.

The Americans who arrived at the front were shocked at the conditions. Soldiers spent weeks in muddy, rat-filled trenches. They faced steady artillery bombardment and the threat of poison gas attacks. One American soldier wrote home describing what it was like in an American artillery unit.

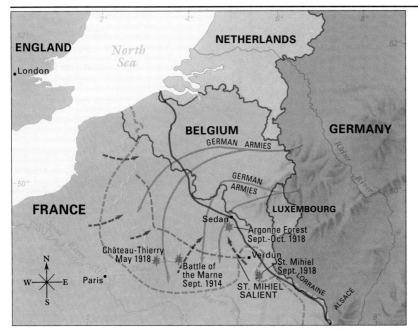

- - - -	Farthest German advance, Sept. 1914
- - - -	German advance, Summer 1918
- - - -	Hindenburg Line
- - ▶	Allied advance, Fall 1918
———	Armistice Line, Nov. 11, 1918
✷	Allied Victories

```
0          50        100 Mi.
|----+----|----+----|
0     50      100 Km.
```

Lambert Conformal Conic Projection

LEARNING FROM MAPS. *After marching through Belgium and deep into France, the German advance on the Western Front ground to a halt. When American troops arrived in late 1917 the tide of war turned in favor of the Allies. How close to Paris did the German armies push?*

CASUALTIES IN THE GREAT WAR		
Country	**Number of Casualties**	
	Dead*	Wounded
Allies		
Russia	1,700,000	4,950,000
France	1,357,800	4,266,000
Britain	908,371	2,090,212
Italy	650,000	947,000
United States	126,000	234,300
Rumania	335,706	120,000
Serbia	45,000	133,148
Belgium	13,716	44,686
Others	15,522	45,658
Total	**5,152,115**	**12,831,004**
Central Powers		
Germany	1,773,700	4,216,058
Austria-Hungary	1,200,000	3,620,000
Turkey	325,000	400,000
Bulgaria	87,500	152,390
Total	**3,386,200**	**8,388,448**
Total	**8,538,315**	**21,219,452**
*Estimated deaths from all causes		

Source: Encyclopedia Britannica

LEARNING FROM TABLES. *As this table of casualties in the Great War shows, the war had tremendous effects on the European population. Although American troops did not engage in combat until the last year, American casualty totals are quite high. Why do you think this is so?*

The War at Home and Abroad 841

Somewhere in France
July 8, 1918

My Dear Folks:

I believe I told you in another letter that because of the fine record we have made since we have been at the front, we have been chosen as "shock troops." Well, we sure are being shocked!

Try and picture the very worst thunderstorm you have ever heard. Then multiply it by about 10,000 and you will get some idea of the battle that has been and still is raging along this front and in which we are taking a very active part!

The battle started shortly after midnight a few days ago and had been raging ever since. It started with a very heavy bombardment all along the front, as the country here is very flat, you can see for a long way. I can tell you that it is some sight at night to see the blinding flashes of the guns all along the line. Even far off on the horizon you can see the pink glow flare up and die down and flare up and die down again—very much like a city burning in the distance. The roar and crash of the guns just seems to tear the air to pieces, and explosions shake the ground. To add to the confusion you have the whine and shriek of the shells, some coming and some going! . . .

Allied troops enter a devastated French village near Verdun, site of one of the major battles on the Western Front. At Verdun there were nearly 750,000 casualties. By the end of the war many villages and towns in northwestern France had been virtually destroyed.

National Archives

The Granger Collection, New York

Of course every so often the Germans send over poison gas. We have to be constantly on the alert for it and wear our gas clothes most of the time, and carry our gas masks all the time!

We all have cotton in our ears. Still, the noise of the guns has made us temporarily deaf. We have not taken off our clothes or gone to bed since the battle started. When it slows up a little we just lie down on the ground, right by the guns, and get what little rest and sleep we can. Our meals are brought to us, as we may not leave the position long enough to go and get them! . . .

This kind of warfare means a great many killed and wounded. But I prefer it, as it is the only way to end the war—just kill off all the Germans!

I have given you details and described disagreeable things, but I just wanted you to know what war is and what it means for us and for everyone!

But I think it's great sport and certainly am glad I'm here and taking part in this—one of the greatest battles the world has ever known.

Love,
E.J. Canright
Medical Artillery
149th Field Artillery
A.E.F.
A.P.O. No. 715[1]

The Rock of the Marne, *by Mal Thompson, illustrates warfare along the Marne River on the Western Front. Here soldiers from the 30th and 38th U.S. Infantry Regiments line a trench near Mezy, France, in July 1918 as German shells explode around them. U.S. troops such as these reinforced Allied defenses and then led the surge that turned the tide of war against the Central Powers.*

[1]From ''Some War-Time Letters'' by Eldon J. Canright in the *Wisconsin Magazine of History,* V: 192—195 (1921—1922)

These men wear masks in an attempt to protect themselves from the world-wide influenza epidemic that killed 20 million people, more than twice the number who died in the Great War.

Culver Pictures

Point of View

In his autobiography Charles Lindbergh recalls the end of the Great War.

❝I was attending a farm auction sale when the first announcement was made, on November 11, 1918. Word came by telephone. The auctioneer broke off his chant to tell us. Time was allowed for celebration before the sale continued. Men cheered, slapped each other on the back, and then, with nothing else to do, they simply stood about.❞

Charles A. Lindbergh, 1976

Return to the Preview & Review on page 831.

Finally the long stalemate began to break. In mid-September American and French forces pushed the Germans back from a wedge-shaped section of the front known as the **Saint-Mihiel salient.** Next came the long, desperate **Battle of the Argonne Forest.** The Argonne lay northwest of Saint-Mihiel. It was a rocky, hilly region crisscrossed by streams and blasted by constant shelling. Between September 26 and mid-October the Americans struggled through this hellish wilderness. German artillery rained high explosives upon them from the hills on their right flank.

Beyond the Argonne the Allies advanced against the **Hindenburg Line.** The line was actually three rows of trenches several miles apart. It bristled with machine gun nests and was guarded by mile after mile of rusty tangles of barbed wire. By this time over a million Americans were in combat. Another million had landed in France and more were arriving steadily.

On November 7 American units finally broke through the Hindenburg Line. They then advanced more swiftly toward Sedan, a city near the Belgian border. All along the front, French and British armies were also driving the Germans back, rapidly gaining ground. On November 11, 1918, the Germans gave up the hopeless fight. They signed an **armistice,** or truce, that was actually a surrender.

Some 126,000 Americans died during the Great War. Another 230,000 were wounded. About half the deaths were caused by disease, many by Spanish influenza. This world-wide epidemic killed 20 million people. America's war losses were much smaller than those of any of the other major nations. Still, during the last few months Americans bore their full share of the fighting and suffered their full share of the casualties. 🖎

5. THE SEARCH FOR PEACE

Preview & Review

Use these questions to guide your reading. Answer the questions after completing Section 5.

Understanding Issues, Events, & Ideas Use the following words to describe the end of the Great War: Fourteen Points, self-determination, League of Nations, Big Four, reparations, Versailles Peace Treaty, sanction, mandate.

1. How did President Wilson describe to Congress his plans for peace?
2. What was to be the purpose of the League of Nations?
3. What were some outcomes of the Treaty of Versailles? Of what was President Wilson most proud?

Thinking Critically. Wilson felt that the 14th of his 14 Points was the most important. Of the points described in the textbook, which do you think is the most important? Why?

Wilson's Plans for Peace

President Wilson had been preparing for making peace even before the United States entered the war. As we have seen, he wanted a peace without victory. Wilson believed the terms must not be so hard on the Central Powers as to cause them to begin planning another war to regain what was taken from them.

In January 1918, even before the end of the war, Wilson made a speech to Congress describing his plans for peace. "The world must be made safe for every peace-loving nation," he said. Unless all the nations are treated fairly, none can count on being treated fairly. In this respect "all the peoples of the world are in effect partners." The president then listed **Fourteen Points** that he said made up "the only possible program" for peace.

The first of Wilson's points promised that the peace treaty would

The National Gallery of Art

The flags of Great Britain, France, and the United States fly on Fifth Avenue. "Allies Day, May 1917" was painted by Childe Hassam in celebration of the alliance of these three nations.

The Search for Peace   845

not contain secret clauses. "Diplomacy shall proceed . . . in the public view." Another point called for freedom of the seas "in peace and in war." Restrictions like the ones the Germans and the Allies had imposed on neutral shipping must not be permitted. But this point, like urging disarmament and calling for the lowering of protective tariffs "so far as possible," was more hopeful than practical.

A more important point dealt with the future of colonies. In settling "all colonial claims," the interests of those who lived in the colonies must be taken into account, not merely the interests of the ruling powers.

Most of Wilson's other points concerned redrawing the boundaries of European nations. Belgium should get back all the territory occupied by Germany during the war. France should regain the province of Alsace-Lorraine on its eastern border. This region had been lost to Germany in an earlier war.

Elsewhere the boundaries should follow "lines of allegiance and nationality." Areas where the inhabitants thought of themselves as Italians should be part of Italy, Poles part of Poland, and so on. This became known as the right of **self-determination.** All peoples should be able to determine for themselves what nation they belonged to.

The 14th point was to Wilson the most important. It called for the creation of an "association of nations." The purpose of this international organization would be to guarantee the independence and the territory "of great and small nations alike." This **League of Nations,** as it was soon named, was to be a kind of international congress that would settle disputes between nations. When necessary, the League would use force against any nation that defied its rulings.

The "just peace" that Wilson was proposing appealed powerfully to millions of people all over the world. It helped to shorten the Great War by encouraging the Germans to surrender when their armies began to suffer defeats in the autumn of 1918.

After the signing of the armistice on November 11, 1918, Wilson became a world hero. Millions of people believed that his idealism, backed by the wealth and power of the United States, would bring about basic changes in international relations. A new era of peace and prosperity seemed about to begin.

The Versailles Peace Conference

In January 1919 representatives of the victorious Allies gathered at the Palace of Versailles, outside Paris, to write a formal treaty of peace. President Wilson headed the American delegation himself. No earlier president had ever left the nation while in office or personally negotiated a treaty. The chief British representative was Prime Minister David Lloyd George. The French premier, Georges Clemenceau, and the Italian prime minister, Vittorio Orlando, completed the

ANALYZING BOUNDARY CHANGES

Some national boundaries seem to change with amazing regularity while others remain the same for centuries. Recognizing why boundary changes take place will help you understand important events in history.

Boundary changes are usually the outcome of war or purchase, and are usually contained in the terms of a treaty. For example, as you read in Chapter 12, the United States acquired vast western lands as a result of the Treaty of Guadalupe Hidalgo at the end of the Mexican War. Other treaties are agreements of sale.

How to Analyze Boundary Changes

Before learning the steps for analyzing boundary changes, review Comparing Maps on page 517. Then to analyze boundary changes, follow these steps.

1. **Compare maps illustrating the changes.** Note where the differences in the boundaries are.
2. **Determine why the boundary changed.** Check if the change resulted from a war or a land purchase. If the change was an outcome of war, find out who won and why the boundary change was part of the treaty terms.

3. **Analyze the change.** Draw conclusions and form hypotheses about the new boundaries. Determine if the new boundaries solve a previous problem or create a new one. Consider how people in the area of the change feel about the change.

Applying the Strategy

The Treaty of Versailles, drawn up in 1919, ended the Great War. That treaty contained sweeping boundary changes in Europe. Compare the map below to the one on page 818. Note that some nations no longer exist—Serbia and Montenegro. Why? Several new countries now appear on the map. What are they? The delegates to the peace conference used such considerations as nationalism and self-determination to guide their redrawing of the map of Europe. Do you foresee any problems with creating new countries as the treaty did? Give some examples.

For independent practice, see Practicing the Strategy on pages 850–51.

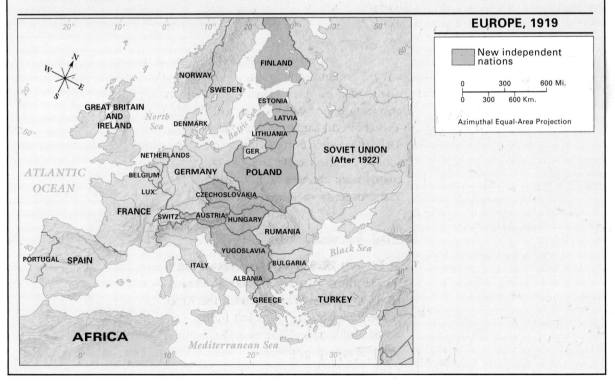

EUROPE, 1919

New independent nations

| 0 | 300 | 600 Mi. |

| 0 | 300 | 600 Km. |

Azimuthal Equal-Area Projection

Council of Four, popularly called the **Big Four.** Working under them were many hundreds of lawyers, mapmakers, economists, historians, military leaders, and all sorts of other experts.

Wilson had a difficult time persuading the other leaders to accept his idea of peace without victory. Clemenceau wanted to make Germany pay the entire cost of the war. France especially had been bled white. Most of the fighting had taken place on French soil. The northern part of the country was a vast no man's land. And almost 1.4 million French soldiers had been killed out of the country's total population of only about 40 million, including women, children, and elderly people.

Lloyd George and Orlando also put the interests of their own nations first. Wilson was forced to agree to a clause in the treaty stating that Germany alone had caused the war. He even accepted a clause making Germany pay "for all damage done to the civilian population of the Allies and their property."

This sum, called **reparations,** was so enormous that the Allies were not able to decide an actual amount. They made the Germans sign "a blank check" agreeing to pay whatever the victors finally demanded. The amount eventually named was $33 billion. This was far more than the Germans could possibly pay, whether or not they

The "Big Four" of the Great War are, left to right: Vittorio Orlando of Italy, David Lloyd George of Great Britain, Georges Clemenceau of France, and Woodrow Wilson of the United States.

Culver Pictures

were entirely responsible for the war. This was certainly not the peace without victory Wilson had promised.

Even if the Big Four had wanted to do so, putting all the 14 Points into practice would have been impossible. Self-determination was an excellent idea, but in many parts of Europe people of different nationalities were mixed together. There were villages of Germans living in Polish areas, Slavs in the midst of Italians or Hungarians.

Many agreements already in existence conflicted with the idea of self-determination. The victorious nations had made promises in order to win the war that violated this and other of Wilson's points. Britain and France had promised Italy parts of Austria-Hungary. The British had agreed to back an Arab nation in the Middle East and also to support a homeland for the Jews in the same region.

Yet, on balance, the final **Versailles Peace Treaty** did come close to the goal Wilson had aimed at in his 14 Points speech. Poland and Czechoslovakia became new states based on the principle of self-determination. The new map of Europe probably came closer to putting all the people of that continent under the flag of their choice than had ever been done before.

The treaty included what Wilson considered his most important point of all. This was the Covenant, or constitution, of the League of Nations.

The League consisted of a General Assembly of representatives of 42 Allied and neutral nations and a Council controlled by the Big Four and Japan. All League members were required to protect one another's territories against attack. All disputes between members were to be submitted to arbitration. Nations which did not obey League decisions could be punished by **sanctions.** These could take the form of a ban on trade with the offending country or even military force.

Furthermore, the former German colonies in Africa and the Far East and the parts of the Middle East that were taken from Turkey were made **mandates,** or dependencies, of the League as a whole. They were to be managed by individual Allied nations. Great Britain, France, and Japan held most of them. The entire League was made responsible for seeing that the interests of the local inhabitants were properly protected.

The League of Nations was Woodrow Wilson's proudest accomplishment. He believed that its founding marked the beginning of an era of permanent world peace. He knew that the Versailles Treaty was not the true "peace without victory" he had sought. Yet he was absolutely certain that the League would be able to deal with the problems the treaty had created. He believed that the entire arrangement made at Versailles depended on the acceptance and support of the League by all the powers. This was the message he brought when he returned to the United States from France. In July 1919 he submitted the treaty to the Senate. 🖳

Return to the Preview & Review on page 845.

CHAPTER 23 REVIEW

1910
Mexican Revolution

1914
American
capture Ve
★
Great War
★
First Battle
the Marne

Chapter Summary
Read the statements below. Choose one, and write a paragraph explaining its importance.
1. A variety of factors caused Europe to erupt into war in 1914. The conflict grew into the largest war in history.
2. The United States peace movement tried to end war, and most Americans felt the country should remain neutral.
3. Wilson's foreign policy was unsuccessful in dealing with the Mexican Revolution.
4. After a swift advance into France, German troops were battled to a stalemate. Trench warfare across a no man's land yielded no winner.
5. German U-boats eventually led the U.S. to declare war on the Central Powers in 1917.
6. At home the war effort led to special industrial and food programs. Women and minorities found increased job opportunities.
7. Modern weapons made the Great War especially deadly.
8. The Treaty of Versailles that ended the war was not the peace without victory Wilson felt was so essential to future peace.

Reviewing Chronological Order
Number your paper 1-5. Then study the time line above and place the following events in the order in which they happened by writing the first next to 1, the second next to 2, and so on.
1. Wilson reelected president
2. Great War starts
3. Battle of the Argonne Forest
4. Battle of the Marne
5. *Lusitania* sunk

Understanding Main Ideas
1. Why was the Mexican Revolution of concern to the United States? Why was Wilson's interference resented?
2. Describe trench warfare on the Western Front.

3. Give at least three reasons why the U.S. declared war on Germany in 1917.
4. How did Americans at home contribute to the war effort?
5. What was Wilson's Fourteen-Points plan? Why did he consider the League of Nations his most important point?

Thinking Critically
1. **Problem Solving.** Suppose that you were a close friend of President Woodrow Wilson. What personal advice would you give to help him deal more effectively with leaders of foreign nations? Explain your answer.
2. **Evaluating.** Do you think that President Wilson was justified in asking Congress to declare war in order to make the world safe for democracy? Why or why not?
3. **Synthesizing.** If you had been a patriotic American in 1917, believing Hoover's slogan, "Food will win the war," what would you have done to conserve food supplies?
4. **Drawing Conclusions.** You are to help the Allies negotiate the Versailles Peace Treaty. Do you think Germany should be held totally responsible for the cost of the Great War? Explain.

Writing About History
Imagine you and your classmates are war reporters. Each of you will phone in a report on one of the following: an aerial dogfight, trench warfare, the spotting of a U-boat. The "general editor" who receives the calls will write reports from the descriptions given over the phone. Use the information in Chapter 23 to help you develop your report. Reporters should hand in their "notes" and the general editor should submit their groups' reports.

Practicing the Strategy
Review the strategy on page 847.

Wilson's Presidency

THE GREAT WAR | 1920

	1916	1917	1918	1919
a announces "accountability"	American troops pursue Villa	Germans resume submarine warfare	Wilson issues 14 Points	Versailles Peace Treaty
	★	★	★	★
ia sunk	Sussex pledge	U.S declares war	Battle of Argonne Forest	League of Nations established
	★	★	★	
	Wilson reelected president	A.E.F. arrives in Europe	Armistice ends fighting	

Analyzing Boundary Changes. Study the maps on pages 422 and 442, and answer these questions.
1. Which river did Mexico insist was the southern boundary of the new state of Texas? Which river did the Americans claim was the boundary between the two countries?
2. How was that boundary dispute resolved?
3. What other large sections of land were acquired at about the same time? By what means did the United States gain possession of them?
4. How did the Texas boundary dispute with Mexico lead directly to the Mexican Cession?

Using Primary Sources
On April 2, 1917, only a month after his second inauguration, President Wilson knew that he had to make a formal request to Congress for a declaration of war. As you read the last paragraph of Wilson's message, note how Wilson appeals to the emotions of the American people.

> . . . we shall fight for the things which we have always carried nearest our hearts—for democracy, for the right of those who submit to authority to have a voice in their own governments, for the rights and liberties of small nations, for a universal dominion of right by such a concert of free peoples as shall bring peace and safety to all nations and make the world itself at last free. To such a task we can dedicate our lives and our fortunes, everything that we are and everything that we have, with the pride of those who know that the day has come when America is privileged to spend her blood and her might for the principles that gave her birth and happiness and the peace which she has treasured. God helping her, she can do no other.

1. Why do you think President Wilson says that "America is privileged to spend her blood"?
2. After reading this excerpt, what inference can you make about what President Wilson thought was important for the world?

3. President Wilson was famous for his speaking ability. In your opinion, what is the most moving phrase or sentence in this excerpt? Why?

Linking History & Geography
New weapons and tactics used in the Great War changed the geography of warfare. Many geographic barriers no longer offered protection. Distances no longer seemed so great. To understand how advances in technology helped shape the Great War, answer the following questions.
1. What weapon enabled Germany to break through British naval defenses?
2. How did airplanes help overcome certain geographic barriers? How did tanks? How did new, more powerful guns lead to trench warfare and vast spaces of no man's land?
3. How have advances in the technology of war almost completely eliminated geography as a factor of war?

Enriching Your Study of History
1. **Individual Project.** Create a series of posters (at least 3) to promote the war on the home front. You might develop posters for recruiting, for the war effort in the U.S., or for the Food Administrator (such as "Food will win the war" or the campaign for "Meatless Tuesdays"). Display your posters for the class.
2. **Cooperative Project.** Your group will use its historical imagination to present to the class a White House meeting between President Wilson and his advisers. The president is considering U.S. involvement in the Great War. One of your group will portray Wilson, and others will speak for each of the following positions: (a) remaining neutral, (b) protesting strongly to Great Britain and Germany for violations of international shipping rules, (c) holding Germany "strictly accountable" for attacks on American ships, and (d) declaring war on Germany.

Chapter 23 Review   851

The Twenties

When President Wilson returned to the United States with the Versailles Treaty, almost everyone believed the Senate would ratify it. Certainly everyone wanted the war to be officially over. And the idea of an organization like the League of Nations seemed a good one. A large majority of Americans probably favored the League, although few understood it entirely or were happy with its every detail. Now came the task of winning over the American Senate. But a difficult time lay ahead for the president.

Preview & Review

Use these questions to guide your reading. Answer the questions after completing Section 1.
Understanding Issues, Events, & Ideas. Explain Wilson's political troubles, using the following words: mild reservationists, strong reservationists, Lodge Reservations, Irreconcilables, Nineteenth Amendment.
1. What problem did the 1918 Congressional elections create for President Wilson?
2. How did Wilson's health influence the political situation in the United States?
3. Why was the voter turnout so large in 1920?
Thinking Critically. If you were a member of the Senate in 1919, would you have been a mild reservationist, a strong reservationist, or an Irreconcilable? Explain your answer.

1. THE TRAGEDY OF WOODROW WILSON

Republican Opponents

The Democrats had lost political power in the United States during the war. The Republicans gained in the Northeast by claiming that the heavy wartime income tax unfairly punished industrial areas. They gained in the Midwest and West, where farmers were angry over farm policies that seemed favorable to southern farmers. They also gained in urban areas, where laborers were unhappy with Democratic sponsorship of prohibition. As a result, in the 1918 Congressional elections the Republicans won majorities in both the House and the Senate. Wilson now needed the support of a large number of Republican senators to get the two-thirds majority necessary to ratify the Versailles Treaty.

Wilson had expected the Democrats would continue to control the Senate. He had campaigned for Democrats so that his peace policies would be carried out smoothly. After the election he made matters worse for himself by not including any Republican senators on the peace commission.

Why he did not is a mystery. Perhaps the president assumed the peace treaty would be so popular that senators would not dare vote against it. "The Senate must take its medicine," he said privately.

Wilson seemed to not realize that some parts of any complicated document like the Versailles Treaty were sure to displease many different people. When its details became known, various special interest groups demanded many changes in the treaty. But Wilson refused to agree to any changes whatsoever.

The most important criticism involved the League of Nations. The United States would be only one among many members. Suppose the League voted to use force against a nation. Was it not up to Congress to say when American troops were sent into battle? Old suspicions of tricky European diplomats now began to reappear. Senator William Borah, a leading foe of America's joining the League, stated the problem this way in a speech to the Senate:

❝ What is the result of this Treaty of Versailles? We are in the middle of all of the affairs of Europe. We have entangled ourselves with all European concerns. We have joined in alliance with all the European nations which have thus far joined the League, and all nations which may be admitted to the League. We are sitting there dabbling in their affairs and meddling in their concerns. In other words—and this comes to the question which is fundamental to me—we have surrendered, once and for all, the great policy of 'no entangling alliances' upon which the strength of this Republic has been based for 150 years.[1] ❞

National Portrait Gallery

The Senate Debate

In the Senate debate nearly all the Democrats supported the League without question. Many Republican senators also favored joining the League. Some of these, known as **mild reservationists,** were willing to vote for the treaty if a few minor changes were made. They had reservations about the League, but their reservations would not block American membership.

Other Republicans were willing to vote for the treaty—and the League—only if more important changes were made. These **strong reservationists** were led by Senator Henry Cabot Lodge of Massachusetts. He introduced what were called the **Lodge Reservations** to the treaty. The most important of these stated that American armed forces could not be sent into action by the League of Nations until Congress gave its approval.

If Wilson had been willing to accept the Lodge Reservations, the Versailles Treaty would have been ratified easily. Only a small group of senators, known as the **Irreconcilables,** refused to vote for it on any terms. The president could probably have gotten the two-thirds vote by making some small concessions to the mild reservationists alone. Yet he refused to budge. It had to be all or nothing.

Henry Cabot Lodge was the leading foe of President Wilson even before the fight over the Treaty of Versailles. Another of Lodge's Democratic enemies, Boston's legendary mayor John Fitzgerald (grandfather of President John Fitzgerald Kennedy), never forgot his first view of the Lodge wealth. A kindly cook for the Lodge family invited him to peek into the Beacon Street mansion where she worked. "That playroom was the most extraordinary sight," Fitzgerald later recalled, "filled with the most elaborate wooden toys you could ever imagine." Lodge's portrait is by John Singer Sargent.

[1]From *American Problems: A Selection of Speeches and Prophecies by William E. Borah,* edited by Horace Green

Brown Brothers

Partially paralyzed by the stroke he suffered in 1919, Woodrow Wilson is helped by a servant as he leaves his home in 1923. He has just made an Armistice Day broadcast. Critics claimed his mind was impaired, but decide for yourself after reading Wilson's remarks on this page.

A White House Invalid

For Wilson the basic issue of the treaty ratification was the idea of a truly international government. He argued that the United States must join the League on the same terms as all the other nations. His position was *reasonable* but not *realistic*. America had too long seen itself as "different" from the countries of Europe.

Americans were being asked to enter into the kind of "entangling alliances" that Jefferson had warned against in his first inaugural address in 1801. It was true that the United States had become an international power. But people needed to adjust gradually to modern conditions. "All or nothing" was not the way to educate them.

If the president had been in good health, he would probably not have taken such a rigid stand. But he was in very poor health. While in Paris, he had suffered a mild stroke—the breaking of a blood vessel in his brain. It had not been recognized as a stroke at the time by his doctor. The attack seriously affected Wilson's judgment.

Still Wilson took the debate to the American people. He went on a whirlwind tour of the United States, making 37 speeches in 29 cities in early September. At the beginning of the tour he stated what he felt was at the heart of the matter:

66 I wonder if some of the opponents of the League of Nations have forgotten the promises we made before we went to the peace table. We had taken men from every household, and we told mothers and fathers and sisters and wives and sweethearts that we were taking those men to fight a war to end all wars. If we do not end wars, we are unfaithful to the loving hearts who suffered in this war.

That is what the League of Nations is for—to end this war justly, and then to serve notice on other governments which might consider trying to do the same things that Germany attempted. The League of Nations is the only thing that can prevent another dreadful catastrophe and fulfill our promises. . . .

Now, look at what else is in the treaty. It is unique in the history of humankind, because the heart of it is the protection of weak nations. . . . If there is no League of Nations, the military point of view will win out in every instance, and peace will not last. . . .

If I were to state what seems to me to be the central idea of this treaty, it would be this: Nations do not consist of their governments but of their people. That is a simple idea. It seems to us in America to go without saying. But, my fellow citizens, it was never the leading idea in any other international congress made up of the representatives of governments. They were always thinking of national policy, of national advantage, of the rivalries of trade, of the

STRATEGIES FOR SUCCESS

COMPARING POINTS OF VIEW

Historical interpretations of an important event, person, or situation often vary widely. This is because people bring to their interpretations different points of view. One way you can better understand history is to compare historical points of view.

How to Compare Points of View

To compare points of view, follow these steps.
1. **Note the sources.** Find out about each author or speaker.
2. **Compare the main ideas expressed.** Note the similarities and differences. Some points will be quite similar. Others will be opposites.
3. **Compare supporting details.** Consider the amount of support and its logic as you make your comparison.
4. **Do research.** Find out as much as you can about the situation.
5. **Use your thinking skills.** Use your critical thinking skills to understand why people have different views of the event, person, or situation. Decide which point of view you think is most reliable, based on your study of the situation.

Applying the Strategy

As you have read, a lengthy debate over ratification of the Treaty of Versailles raged in the Senate in 1919. The main area of contention was the provision requiring the United States to join the League of Nations. President Woodrow Wilson fought long and hard in support of the United States joining the League. He thought that the League of Nations was "the only thing that can prevent another dreadful catastrophe" such as the Great World War. He also claimed that "the only country in the world that is trusted at this moment is the United States. The peoples of the world are waiting to see whether their trust is justified or not."

On the other hand, many Americans, including several influential members of Congress, opposed United States membership. Senator William E. Borah felt that joining the League would involve the United States in Europe's complex affairs and would mean "we have surrendered, once and for all, the great policy of 'no entangling alliances' upon which the strength of this Republic has been based for 150 years."

Now read and compare these other excerpts taken from the debate over American membership in the League.

Excerpt A

Our isolation ended twenty years ago. . . . There can be no question of our ceasing to be a world power. The only question is whether we refuse the leadership that is offered."
President Woodrow Wilson

Excerpt B

I object in the strongest possible way to having the United States agree, directly or indirectly, to be controlled by a League which may at any time . . . be drawn in to deal with internal conflicts in other countries. . . . It must be made perfectly clear that no American soldiers . . . can ever be engaged in war or ordered anywhere except by the constitutional authorities of the United States.
Senator Henry Cabot Lodge

Excerpt A is from a speech by President Woodrow Wilson urging the Senate to approve the treaty. Although he does not state it, Wilson's comments allude to the provision of the treaty which called for the United States to enter into the League of Nations.

What is Wilson's argument? He claims the United States is now a world power and must continue to assume that responsibility. What support did he use? He points out that the United States began overseas expansion, ending a period of isolation. It had annexed Hawaii, and had been involved in the Spanish-American War, events in Mexico, and the Great War. Why would Wilson hold the point of view he expresses—urging the Senate to ratify the treaty and join the League of Nations?

Excerpt B is taken from a speech against ratification by Senator Henry Cabot Lodge. As you have read, Lodge was a leading opponent of the treaty. His view is that the United States should not enter the League. What reasons does he give for his opposition?

As you know, the United States did not ratify the treaty or join the League of Nations. Why do you think Lodge's arguments were successful?

For independent practice, see Practicing the Strategy on page 893.

The Granger Collection, New York

After the U.S. Senate refused to ratify the Versailles Treaty, an American cartoonist in 1920 drew "The Accuser," showing the treaty stabbed by the Senate. What is this cartoonist's message? Why do you suppose editorial cartoonists of the time often portrayed their subjects as ancient Romans?

advantages of territorial conquest. There is nothing of those things in this treaty.[1] **99**

Then, in September 1919, while he was trying to rally support for the League, he suffered another stroke. This time there was no mistake about it. His left side was partially paralyzed.

For weeks Wilson was an invalid in the White House. As he slowly recovered, his advisers pleaded with him to compromise with the moderate Republicans. Otherwise the treaty was sure to be defeated. Wilson refused. It was better "to go down fighting," he told his friends.

On November 19, 1919, the treaty, with the Lodge Reservations attached, came to a vote in the Senate. It was defeated by Democratic votes. Then it was voted on without reservations. This time the Republicans defeated it. The following March, after further debate, the Senate again voted on the treaty with reservations. This time some Democratic senators refused to follow Wilson's urging. They voted for ratification. Not enough of them did so, however, and for a third and final time the treaty was rejected.

The Election of 1920

Wilson had hoped that the presidential election of 1920 would prove that the people of the United States wanted to join the League. The

[1]From *War and Peace: The Public Papers of Woodrow Wilson,* Vol. 1

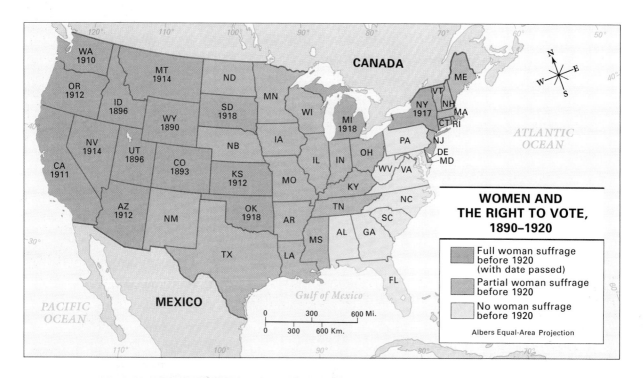

WA
1910

OR
1912

ID
1896

MT
1914

ND

MN

CANADA

ME

VT
NH
NY
1917
MA
CT RI

ATLANTIC
OCEAN

NV
1914

UT
1896

WY
1890

SD
1918

WI

MI
1918

PA

NJ
DE
MD

CA
1911

CO
1893

NB

IA

IL

IN

OH

WV VA

AZ
1912

NM

KS
1912

MO

KY

TN

NC

OK
1918

AR

SC

PACIFIC
OCEAN

MEXICO

TX

MS

LA

AL

GA

FL

Gulf of Mexico

0   300   600 Mi.
0   300   600 Km.

**WOMEN AND
THE RIGHT TO VOTE,
1890–1920**

Full woman suffrage
before 1920
(with date passed)

Partial woman suffrage
before 1920

No woman suffrage
before 1920

Albers Equal-Area Projection

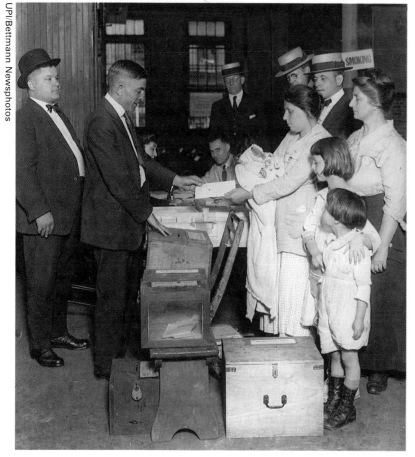

UPI/Bettmann Newsphotos

LEARNING FROM MAPS. *As you
can see from this map, women's right
to vote spread slowly between 1890
and the ratification of the 19th
Amendment in 1920. What four
states first granted women the right
to vote? Why do you think this movement started in the West?*

*The vote is theirs at last. After car-
rying the water, toting the firewood,
ironing the clothes, and keeping the
family together—these women have
come to claim what is rightfully theirs
as a result of the Nineteenth
Amendment.*

The Tragedy of Woodrow Wilson   857

Both, UPI/Bettmann Newsphotos

The 1920 presidential campaign was between Warren G. Harding and James M. Cox, both of Ohio. On the right Cox and his running mate Franklin D. Roosevelt (a year before he was crippled by polio). They lead a parade through Columbus, Ohio, after receiving official word of their nomination. Harding, below, campaigns from his front porch in Marion, Ohio. His wife, called Duchess, had great political aspirations for him, but his friends took advantage of his presidency with their shady schemes.

Return to the Preview & Review on page 852.

Democratic candidate, Governor James M. Cox of Ohio, campaigned on a platform which called for joining. The vice presidential candidate, Franklin D. Roosevelt, a distant cousin of Theodore Roosevelt, also supported the League strongly.

The Republican candidate, Senator Warren G. Harding, refused to take a clear position on the issue. Harding was an expert at avoiding controversial questions. During the presidential campaign he used a technique called "bloviating." This meant talking about a subject in a way that sounded intelligent but which actually made little or no sense. Citizens who favored the League could think that Harding favored it. Those who opposed it could interpret his statements the other way.

On Election Day, Harding won by a huge majority. The new **Nineteenth Amendment,** which gave women the vote in national elections, caused a large voter turnout in 1920. The vote for president was nearly nine million more than it had been in 1916. Harding got 61 percent of the total, over 16 million votes to Cox's 9.1 million.

Once elected, Harding stopped bloviating about the League. He made it clear that he did not want the United States to join it. Since the League could not be separated from the Versailles Treaty, Congress simply passed a resolution in the summer of 1921 declaring that the war was over.

2. AMERICAN REACTION TO THE WAR

Foreign Policy in the 1920s

The American people were not ready to assume the kind of international responsibilities that Wilson called for, but they really had little choice. The United States had become the leading industrial and financial power in the world. After the huge foreign loans made by the United States during the war, the rest of the world owed the United States $13 billion. America could not retreat into an isolated cocoon.

In practice the presidents of the 1920s tried to follow a middle road between the narrow view of **isolationism** and the broader view of **internationalism.** They wanted to enjoy the benefits of America's commanding economic position in the world. Yet they did not want to make binding promises to other countries. This attitude was clearly revealed in the way President Harding approached the question of reducing the size of the navy.

After the huge cost of the Great War the public was eager to avoid building still more warships. In 1921 Harding invited nine European and Asian nations to Washington to discuss **disarmament—** limiting the manufacture of weapons of war. Far Eastern issues were also discussed at this Washington Disarmament Conference.

Several treaties were negotiated by the delegates. The most important was the **Five-Power Naval Treaty.** In this treaty the United States, Great Britain, Japan, France, and Italy agreed to a ten-year

Culver Pictures

PUTTING HIS FOOT DOWN.

Preview & Review

Use these questions to guide your reading. Answer the questions after completing Section 2.
Understanding Issues, Events, & Ideas. Describe the postwar reaction in America using the following words: isolationism, internationalism, disarmament, Five-Power Naval Treaty, Open Door, postwar reaction, anarchists, Big Red Scare, Palmer raid, Emergency Quota Act, National Origins Act. Explain the major changes in American society after the war using these words: prohibition, dry state, Eighteenth Amendment, Volstead Act, bootlegger, repeal, Twenty-first Amendment, fundamentalism.

1. Why did American presidents in the 1920s try to find a middle ground between isolationism and internationalism?
2. What effect did peacetime have on industry? Why?
3. Why was prohibition difficult to enforce?
4. How was the fundamentalist movement a part of the postwar reaction in America? How was the Sacco-Vanzetti case a part?

Thinking Critically. **1.** You have read that after the Great War, Americans "wanted peace without the responsibility of maintaining it." Do you think that Americans still have that attitude? Give reasons to support your answer.
2. Write two editorials about the Scopes trial: one from the point of view of a person who favored the advances of science and technology being taught and the other from the point of view of a fundamentalist against teaching about them.

In this editorial cartoon, "Putting His Foot Down," Uncle Sam holds a copy of the "Trade Treaty with China" that began America's Open Door Policy. For a complete discussion of the Open Door Policy, see pages 768–69. What did the policy provide? Why did Americans consider such an agreement important in the 1920s?

> "Americans followed the leaders they chose, not those given to them by God or imposed by screaming and violent crowds. The leaders they freely chose, most of them anyway, who looked to me like Roman senators or Renaissance princes, were born on small farms, the sons of humble people. This free and easy flow of a whole nation toward the future seemed the enviable secret of America, a country where it was still possible to hope. But was that all there was, was it real or a creation of my imagination?"
>
> Luigi Barzini, 1977

"holiday" on the construction of battleships. They also agreed to maintain a fixed ratio, or balance, on all major warships. The United States and Great Britain were to have no more than 525,000 tons of such vessels. Japan's limit was 315,000 tons, France and Italy's 175,000 each. In another agreement all nine nations promised to uphold the principle of the **Open Door** in China. This was the policy which assured all nations equal trade rights with an independent China.

President Harding insisted that the Washington Conference treaties did not commit the United States "to any kind of alliance, entanglement, or involvement." This was true enough. The treaties were backed only by the good will of the nations that signed them. This satisfied most Americans. They wanted peace without the responsibility for maintaining it. They could accept the treaties and still believe that they could remain isolated in the old way from foreign "entanglements."

The Postwar Reaction

Isolation was an aspect of a larger **postwar reaction** in the United States. The Great War had been a Great Mistake, most people now thought. Millions of lives had been lost. Billions of dollars had been wasted. And for what purpose? The world had certainly not been made safe for democracy, as Wilson had promised.

In 1919 most Americans seemed more worried about making the United States safe for themselves. Many seriously believed that a communist revolution might break out in the United States at any moment. They were mindful that a tiny group of communists had taken over all of Russia in 1917. Now there were perhaps seventy thousand communists (called Reds) in the United States.

Communists wanted workers to raise the red flag of revolution, take up arms, and destroy the capitalist system. At the same time **anarchists,** who wanted all governments violently abolished, stirred up workers. But most workers were simply trying to keep their jobs. Going from war to peace had been difficult for American industry. Without contracts for war supplies, many plants shut down temporarily or slowed down their operations. Hundreds of thousands of wage earners were thrown out of work. Soldiers returning to civilian life found it almost impossible to get jobs. Many of the workers found their jobs had been filled by African Americans who had moved from the South during the war to work in factories. This added fuel to racial tensions that erupted in situations like the 1919 Chicago Race Riot.

As a result a wave of strikes spread over the land. At one time or another during 1919, 4 million workers were on strike. Seattle was paralyzed. In Boston even the police walked off their jobs. Strikes by police were unheard of at that time. With the streets of Boston

UPI/Bettmann Newsphotos

The Chicago Steel Strike of 1919 was one of the disturbing postwar walkouts. Even police went on strike in Boston. Most people blamed these strikes on "creeping Bolshevism"—a type of communism—as we see in the Red Scare cartoon below.

The Granger Collection, New York

unprotected, looters began breaking into stores. The governor of Massachusetts, Calvin Coolidge, finally called in troops to restore order in the city.

At the same time a series of bombings by terrorists took place. To this day no one knows who was responsible for most of the bombings. But the tendency was to blame "the Reds." A **Big Red Scare** swept over America.

President Wilson's attorney general, A. Mitchell Palmer, became convinced that a massive communist plot to overthrow the federal government was being organized. He ordered raids on the headquarters of suspected radical groups. These **Palmer raids** were often conducted without search warrants. Many suspected communists were held for weeks without formal charges. There was no evidence of a nationwide uprising. Yet in 1920 Palmer announced that such a revolution would take place on May 1, the communist Labor Day. When May 1 passed quietly, Americans realized that the danger of a revolution had been only in their minds. As quickly as it had begun, the Big Red Scare ended.

The nervous mood of the 1920s then took other forms. One was a revival of the Ku Klux Klan. Klan membership grew between 1920 and 1923 from about 5,000 members to several million. Unlike the Klan of Reconstruction days, this one spread into the northern states. It became a powerful but short-lived political and social force in the early 1920s and did much harm to many innocent people.

The postwar years brought despair for many African Americans. Aside from suffering at the hands of the Klan, they also faced hostility

Culver Pictures

The hooded figures are but a handful of the millions nationwide who joined the Ku Klux Klan in the 1920s. They burned crosses and lynched African Americans in the dead of night, some of their victims still wearing their uniforms from the Great War.

from middle-class Americans. They found it difficult to move up in the job market, where discrimination and segregation hindered their chances. At the same time, increasing numbers of southern blacks poured into northern cities. They were forced to live in ghettos, where life was vicious and degrading. Disease and crime rates soared.

Old prejudices resurfaced. Racial tensions sizzled. Mobs in the South lynched more than 60 African Americans, 10 of them Great War veterans still in uniform. Race riots erupted in Washington, D.C., and Chicago. To the surprise of many Americans, the NAACP now urged blacks to stand firm, to fight back. The violence increased throughout the country.

Some people blamed the communists for stirring up the racial trouble. Meanwhile black leaders and liberal whites pushed for anti-lynching laws. And many African Americans were attracted to the Universal Negro Improvement Association of Marcus Garvey. He appealed to the African American traditions and religious values. Garvey wanted African Americans to return to Africa where he hoped to create a kingdom with himself as the king. Although his plan failed, Garvey's movement boosted black pride and dignity and helped them deal with the frustrations of American society.

Garvey's ideas also had great influence in Central America, the Caribbean, and Africa. The leaders of independence crusades in countries such as Ghana and Kenya credited Garvey and his book, *Philosophy and Opinions,* for helping to fuel their fierce drive for freedom for their people. Even the African National Congress in southern Africa is a direct outgrowth of Garvey's movement.

At the same time the NAACP continued to battle for equal rights. Seeking to unify African Americans—in fact all Americans—the organization issued a national statement of its aims in 1919:

" 1. A vote for every Negro man and woman on the same terms as for white men and women.

2. An equal chance to acquire the kind of an education that will enable the Negro everywhere wisely to use this vote.

3. A fair trial in courts for all crimes of which he is accused, by judges in whose election he has participated without discrimination because of race.

4. A right to sit upon the jury which passes judgment upon him.

5. Defense against lynching and burning at the hands of mobs.

6. Equal service on railroad and other public carriers. This to mean sleeping car service, dining car service, Pullman service, at the same cost and upon the same terms as other passengers.

7. Equal right to use of public parks, libraries and other community services for which he is taxed.

8. An equal chance for a livelihood in public and private employment.

9. The abolition of color-hyphenation and the substitution of 'straight Americanism.'

If it were not a painful fact that more than four-fifths of the colored people of the country are denied the above

UPI/Bettmann Newsphotos

The flag passes by as a veteran of the 309th Colored Infantry pays his respects.

Cincinnati Art Museum, The Edwin and Virginia Irwin Memorial; © Estate of Grant Wood/VAGA New York 1990

Grant Wood was one of America's most popular 20th-century painters. Note that in this painting titled "Daughters of the Revolution" he posed the three subjects in front of a print of "Washington Crossing the Delaware."

named elementary rights, it would seem an absurdity that an organization is necessary to demand for American citizens the exercise of such rights. . . . Has not slavery been abolished? Are not all men equal before the law? Were not the Fourteenth and Fifteenth Amendments passed by the Congress of the United States and adopted by the states? Is not the Negro a man and a citizen?[1] **99**

The NAACP also made a strong statement of principles and observations of the plight of blacks in America. In part it said:

66 When the fundamental rights of citizens are so wantonly denied and that denial justified and defended as it is by the lawmakers and dominant forces of so large a number of our states, it can be realized that the fight for the Negro's citizenship rights means a fundamental battle for real things, for life and liberty.

This fight is the Negro's fight. 'Who would be free, himself must strike the blow.' But, it is no less the white man's fight. The common citizenship rights of no group of people, to say nothing of nearly 12,000,000 of them, can be denied with impunity [freedom from harm] to the State and the social order which denies them. . . . Whoso loves America and cherishes its institutions, owes it to himself and his country to join hands with the members of the National Association for the Advancement of Colored People to 'Americanize' America and make the kind of democracy we Americans believe in to be the kind of democracy we shall have in *fact,* as well as in theory.[2] **99**

[1] From "The Task for the Future—A Program for 1919" by the NAACP
[2] *Ibid.*

Despite these efforts, little progress was made in ending discrimination in America.

America's postwar mood was also reflected in new immigration laws. In 1921 Congress reacted to the isolationism of the times by taking steps to control the entry of foreigners into the United States. This made some sense at the time. The frontier had disappeared. In a machine age the nation no longer needed to import large numbers of unskilled laborers. The **Emergency Quota Act** limited the number of immigrants by nationality, reducing the number of newcomers from eastern and southern Europe. A still stiffer quota law, the **National Origins Act,** was passed in 1924. Beginning in 1929, a total of only 150,000 immigrants a year could enter the United States. In practice the number of actual immigrants fell below 100,000 every year from 1931 to 1946.

The Sacco-Vanzetti Case

Such xenophobia—the fear of foreigners—led to the Sacco-Vanzetti case. In April 1920 two men in Massachusetts killed a paymaster and a guard during a daring daylight robbery of a shoe factory. Shortly thereafter, Nicola Sacco and Bartolomeo Vanzetti were charged with the crime, and in 1921 they were convicted of murder. Sacco and Vanzetti were anarchists who believed that government was unnecessary and should be violently overthrown. They were also Italian immigrants. Their trial was a travesty of justice. There was little real evidence against them. Much of what was presented at the trial had been manufactured by the prosecution. In addition, the judge seemed prejudiced against the two, especially in his comments outside the courtroom.

Prominent people all over the world praised the dignity Sacco and Vanzetti showed throughout the trial. The noted lawyer Felix Frankfurter helped found the American Civil Liberties Union to fight for the two men. Other defenders of justice, including the novelist John Dos Passos and the poet Edna St. Vincent Millay, joined worldwide protests that for years kept Sacco and Vanzetti alive through efforts to obtain a new trial. Vanzetti's dignified words are still remembered:

❝ You see me before you, not trembling. I never commit a crime in my life. . . . I am so convinced to be right that if you could execute me two times, and if I could be reborn two other times, I would live again and do what I have done already. ❞

In August 1927 Sacco and Vanzetti were electrocuted. Historians now suspect that at least Sacco was guilty, but the truth and shame of the incident remain: at the time Sacco and Vanzetti paid with their lives for being radicals and foreigners as much as for any crime.

Whitney Museum of American Art

Were Nicola Sacco and Bartolomeo Vanzetti guilty of robbery and killing a paymaster? Or were they simply guilty of being foreigners at a time when xenophobia—fear of foreigners—swept America in the 1920s? Those who believed they were innocent may have hung Ben Shahn's lithograph, "The Passion of Sacco and Vanzetti," in their living rooms in protest against the death sentence.

Thomas Hart Benton depicts the dark side of prohibition in "The Bootleggers," painted in 1927. Planes, trains, and fast cars bring the customers to buy illegal liquor.

Reynolda House, Museum of American Art, Winston Salem, N.C.

Prohibition

During the Progressive Era there had been strong popular support for prohibiting the manufacture, transportation, and sale of alcoholic beverages. This temperance movement, like the one in the 1840s, was led by American religious groups who saw liquor as the devil's tool. By 1914 prohibition was in force in more than a quarter of the states, known as the dry states. Most of the dry states were in the South and rural areas, where many of the people were members of fundamentalist Protestant religious groups.

The outburst of moral and religious concern caused by the war gave energy to a national prohibition movement. Some saw it as an attack on the German custom of drinking beer; others as an attack on the drinking habits of European Catholics. What tipped the scales was a very effective campaign to protect young servicemen from the sale of alcohol on or near army bases. This fit closely with the prohibitionist charge that drinking was a cause of poverty and social disorder. As a result, in 1919 the **Eighteenth Amendment** was ratified. This amendment was enforced by the **Volstead Act,** which went into effect in January 1920, making the entire nation dry.

People who favored prohibition pointed to the sharp decline in arrests for drunkenness and to the lower number of deaths from alcoholism in the 1920s. Fewer workers spent their hard-earned dollars on drink. However, prohibition was impossible to enforce, even with the tough Volstead Act. Private individuals bought liquor smuggled by **bootleggers** or drank gin from teacups in "speakeasies"—secret bars or clubs.

Crime statistics soared in the 1920s. Most of the liquor was sold by gangsters such as "Scarface" Al Capone of Chicago. Hoodlums fought for territories with guns and bombs, killing innocent bystanders as well as their rivals. The scene was not much different from the one on some city streets today where drug deals are common. Dealers, like the bootleggers, fight over territory, often killing one another and innocent bystanders as well.

Still, in the 1920s powerful "dry" forces kept politicians in both parties from proposing that prohibition be lifted, or **repealed.** It remained in force until December 1933, when it was repealed by the **Twenty-first Amendment.**

The Fundamentalist Movement

America was rapidly changing in the postwar years. Over 19 million people moved from the farm to the city in the 1920s. Problems such as crime, gambling, and corruption seemed to be all too common, especially in the cities. The progressive spirit had died in the disillusionment following the Great War. Many Americans searching for a system of values in this time of rapid change found it in the

In this farming community, Protestants gather to witness a group baptism. White dresses are worn by the women who will participate by being dipped in a water trough. How does the artist, John Steuart Curry, show the feelings of the onlookers?

Whitney Museum of Art

In a rare moment of relaxation during the Scopes Trial, Clarence Darrow, left, and William Jennings Bryan appear friendly. Notice the fan. The courtroom was sweltering. This was the last public appearance for Bryan, a man of long public prominence. He died a few days after the trial. How had Bryan electrified another audience in 1896? How did he fare in the Scopes trial?

Culver Pictures

Protestant religious movement called **fundamentalism.** It was strongest on the farms and in the small towns of America. Many people in these rural areas blamed society's economic and social problems on modern urban culture. Fundamentalists believed that the King James translation of the Bible was God's truth. They took its words literally.

Fundamentalists thought that the science and technology of the machine age were challenging the traditional values and beliefs they held dear. Every year new discoveries seemed to question ideas held for centuries. As an example they seized on Charles Darwin's theory of evolution described in *The Origin of Species*. They campaigned vigorously for laws banning all mention of Darwin's theory, especially in textbooks and classrooms. Darwin, a British naturalist, had theorized that modern species of plants and animals had evolved from a few earlier ones. From Darwin's theory came the idea that human beings had slowly evolved from ape-like creatures, which of course had gradually evolved from even lower life-forms. This idea directly opposed the fundamentalist's view of God having created the heavens and the earth in six days. Didn't the Bible describe how and when God created each of his creatures, including humans?

In their battle against evolution, the fundamentalists found a leader in William Jennings Bryan, the forceful orator who had been Wilson's secretary of state. Bryan went about the country charging that modern Americans had "taken the Lord away from the schools." He even offered $100 to anyone who would admit in public that he was descended from an ape as he claimed Darwin had said.

In 1925 the fundamentalists won a victory when Tennessee passed a law forbidding instructors in the state's schools and colleges to teach "any theory that denies the story of the Divine Creation of man taught in the Bible." Many people were shocked at the law, which they felt restricted academic freedom, maybe even the freedom of speech. The American Civil Liberties Union, a nonprofit group whose stated purpose was to protect the basic freedom of the people, offered to defend any Tennessee teacher who would challenge the constitutionality of the law. A young biology teacher in the Tennessee mountain town of Dayton, John T. Scopes, agreed to violate the law and teach Darwin's theory. He was taken to court by the state. Clarence Darrow, perhaps the greatest lawyer of the time, headed Scopes' defense. Darrow put the issue this way:

> **66** Scopes isn't on trial. Civilization is on trial. The prosecution is opening the doors of a reign of bigotry equal to anything in the Middle Ages. No man's belief will be safe if they win. **99**

The prosecuting attorney was no less than William Jennings Bryan himself. Overnight the Dayton "Monkey Trial" attracted national attention. Sensing a story, big-city reporters like H. L. Mencken flocked to the trial.

The trial took place in a sweltering courtroom. The prosecution took every opportunity to state its view of creation. Bryan even testified as an expert witness on the Bible. On the stand he explained that he believed that the earth had been created in 4004 B.C., that a whale had swallowed Jonah, that Joshua had stopped the sun in its course, and that Eve had been created from Adam's rib, all as the Bible said. Under intense questioning by Darrow, Bryan showed an almost complete ignorance of modern scientific thought. And he doomed his own cause when he agreed that creation took hundreds of years, that a "day" in the Bible might actually be centuries.

This admission had no effect on the trial. The conviction of Scopes was a foregone conclusion. After rousing arguments from both sides, Scopes was found guilty and fined $100. That decision was soon overturned by the state supreme court. More important, Bryan had contradicted the fundamentalists' argument.

Still, the fundamentalism that prompted the trial had vigor throughout the country. Crusaders such as Billy Sunday found audiences over the airwaves.

And the vigor has not left the movement. Conservative church groups are the most rapidly growing segment of American Protestantism. Although their message and methods are different today, fundamentalists still seek to be heard by the American people. Through television they reach their widest audience ever. Many of the groups have become politically involved, taking active roles in a variety of movements.

The Scopes trial symbolized something larger than a controversy over Darwin's theory. It emphasized the divisions within American society—rural versus urban, traditional versus modern. The rising fortunes of the late 1920s made these divisions seem deeper. Business owners and urban laborers raked in the money. Yet prosperity seemed to pass by farmers and people in small towns, leaving many of them hostile to the new urban society. 🖅

Return to the Preview & Review on page 859.

Preview & Review

Use these questions to guide your reading. Answer the questions after completing Section 3.

Understanding Issues, Events, & Ideas. Describe the Roaring Twenties using the following words: jazz, Jazz Age, flappers, Harlem Renaissance, Golden Age of Sports, Harlem Globetrotters, expatriates.

1. What was the origin of jazz? How did jazz reflect the 1920s?
2. Name five heroes of the Golden Age of Sports and the sport for which each was famous.
3. How did movies influence people? What advantage did radio have over movies? Why did radio become a giant industry?
4. Who were the "lost generation?" Why does this name seem appropriate?

Thinking Critically. 1. Compose a poem or song about the changing values of women during the 1920s. 2. Why might someone want to become an expatriate? What reasons, if any, do you think are legitimate reasons to permanently leave America?

The Jazz Age

Not all Americans were so troubled in the 1920s. Many were finding new ways to enjoy life. Industry continued to grow, producing new wealth and providing more leisure time for many millions of people. Change was in the air, and the speed of change was increasing. People everywhere were casting off old ways and seeking new ways to express themselves.

Consider the typical music of the period. The music that most Americans listened to and danced to during the 1920s was called **jazz.** Jazz was created by African American musicians in New Orleans in the late 1800s. It grew out of the "blues"—music that reflected the hard life of most blacks in America and the tough-minded humor that many displayed in trying to cope with it. W. C. Handy of Alabama was the "father of the blues." His most famous composition was "St. Louis Blues" (1914).

Most of the early African American jazz musicians had little or no formal training in music. Yet they were superb performers. Their music was often the only outlet for their emotions. Bessie Smith, a leading singer of the 1920s, sang movingly about her own sorrowful experiences. Louis "Satchmo" Armstrong was the most famous jazz musician of the day. He won international fame as a trumpeter, a singer, and as an ambassador of goodwill to other countries.

Jazz musicians *improvised* much of their music. Taking a theme or musical idea, they chased a tune up and down the scales as they played. This gave musicians and listeners alike a sense of freedom.

Both, Brown Brothers

Bessie Smith and W.C. Handy are two of the great early jazz musicians who gave America its own special form of music. Bessie Smith lived only 40 years but is fondly remembered as the "Empress of the Blues." Handy composed "Memphis Blues" and "Beale Street Blues" and dozens of other standards. What made jazz spread quickly in the United States?

The New Britain Museum of American Art, Friends Purchase Fund

"Jazz" by Romare Bearden practically makes its own music with its rich colors and rhythmic composition. Notice how the artist combines all kinds of textures to make one unified image. How is that like jazz itself?

Jazz spread from New Orleans to Chicago and New York and then throughout most of the world. White musicians as well as black performed it. It became in its own way a powerful force for breaking down racial barriers, both among the players and for those who simply listened.

The decade of the 1920s is sometimes called the **Jazz Age.** In part the popularity of its music is enough to explain this. But jazz also symbolized the way many young people of the time felt about life in general. They sought to break away from rigid, conventional rules and traditions, just as jazz trumpeters and saxophonists departed from written notes in order to express themselves.

This new spirit of freedom also influenced the other arts. Isadora Duncan became world-famous for her beautiful and graceful free-form dancing. Frank Lloyd Wright expressed the same spirit in his architecture. Perhaps the most extreme expression of this break with the conventional was dadaism, an outrageous art movement started as a protest against all artistic and civilized standards.

Young women in particular seemed determined to free themselves from restricting ''out-of-date'' ideas and rules. They cast off uncomfortable (and unhealthy) corsets and thick petticoats in favor of short skirts and loose-fitting clothing. They cut their hair short. They wore makeup. They drank and smoked in public.

The behavior of these ''new women'' shocked older people deeply. They called them **flappers** and predicted they would come to a bad end. Actually most of these young women were just trying to liberate themselves. Not all of them were conscious feminists. Some were merely trying to keep up with the latest fads and fashions. Still, consciously or not, they were demanding the right to behave the same way men behaved.

Point of View

Two stanzas from ''Homage to the Empress of the Blues,'' show how much the poet admired Bessie Smith.

> **She came out on the stage in yards of pearls, emerging like a favorite scenic view, flashed her golden smile and sang.**
> . . . .
> **She came out on stage in ostrich feathers, beaded satin, and shone that smile on us and sang.**
> Robert Hayden, 1966

The Roaring Twenties 871

National Portrait Gallery

Langston Hughes, the most important poet of the Harlem Renaissance, also invented a character he called Jess B. Semple ("Simple" to his friends) who spoke out on life in Harlem in all its many aspects.

The Harlem Renaissance

The disappointments of the 1920s faced by African Americans produced the "New Negro," as they called themselves. These African Americans were determined to build pride and a better life for themselves and their children. Langston Hughes, one of the great poets of the era, expressed what life must have been like for African American children:

Merry-Go-Round

" *Colored child at carnival:*

> Where is the Jim Crow section
> On this merry-go-round,
> Mister, cause I want to ride?
> Down South where I come from
> White and colored
> Can't sit side by side.
> Down South on the train
> There's a Jim Crow car.
> On the bus we're put in the back—
> But there ain't no back
> To a merry-go-round!
> Where's the horse
> For a kid that's black?[1] **"**

Leaders like W.E.B. Du Bois and Marcus Garvey preached black pride and self-confidence. The ghetto was home, a black world where black men and women could be themselves. Black writers, musicians, and artists such as Aaron Douglas, William H. Johnson, Palmer Hayden, and Meta Warwick Fuller found in the ghettos an audience that unleashed their creativity. Harlem, a part of Manhattan cut off by racial suspicion, was in fact the largest "black city" in the world. Here was the center of a cultural revitalization called the **Harlem Renaissance.** Poets and writers like Hughes, James Weldon Johnson, and Countee Cullen put the black experience into words. Newspapers and magazines along with theater troupes and libraries owned and operated by African Americans flourished. Hughes captured the spirit of the renaissance when he said, "Harlem! I . . . dropped my bags, took a deep breath, and felt happy again."

The Golden Age of Sports

The 1920s had its full share of gangsters, corrupt politicians, and other villains. It also had its heroes. Athletes were among the most popular. Spectator sports boomed. Public relations ballyhoo and the magic of radio created larger-than-life performers who attracted thousands to sporting events. The 1920s was truly the **Golden Age of Sports.**

[1]From "Merry-Go-Round" by Langston Hughes

THE LONE EAGLE

The most popular American hero of the 1920s was Charles A. Lindbergh. On May 20, 1927, Lindbergh took off from a muddy, rain-drenched airfield near New York City in a tiny, one-engine plane, the *Spirit of St. Louis.* He was headed for France. Alone, hour after hour, he guided his plane eastward across the Atlantic. He flew with a map in his lap and only some coffee and a few sandwiches to keep up his strength. Staying awake called for a tremendous feat of willpower. If he dozed off, even for a minute, the *Spirit of St. Louis* might crash into the sea. But Lindbergh did not doze off. About 33 and a half hours after takeoff he landed safely at Le Bourget airport on the outskirts of Paris. He was the first aviator to fly nonstop across the Atlantic—and he had done it alone.

Lindbergh's achievement captured the imagination of the entire world. Here is how *The New York Times* described his landing at Le Bourget:

> PARIS, May 21—Lindbergh did it. Twenty minutes after 10 o'clock tonight suddenly and softly there slipped out of the darkness a gray-white air-

Culver Pictures

plane as 25,000 pairs of eyes strained toward it. At 10:24 the *Spirit of St. Louis* landed and lines of soldiers, ranks of policemen and stout steel fences went down before a mad rush as irresistible as the tides of the ocean.

Lindbergh returned home a grinning, modest hero. The idol of millions, he was given a tremendous ticker tape parade through New York City. The newspapers named him "The Lone Eagle." He was also known as "Lucky Lindy," but his success was due far more to courage and skill than luck.

Now that dozens of giant jets fly across the Atlantic every day, Lindbergh's flight may not seem very important. But his flight marked the coming of age of the airplane. Lindbergh himself is the perfect symbol of the Air Age. He was two years old when Wilbur and Orville Wright made the first successful airplane flights at Kitty Hawk, North Carolina, in 1903. Those flights lasted only a few seconds and covered only a few hundred yards at most. Yet before Lindbergh died, American astronauts had landed on the moon.

Some 91,000 boxing fans paid a total of more than $1 million in July 1921 to watch the heavyweight champion, Jack Dempsey, knock out Georges Carpentier of France. Every fall weekend thousands of people jammed football stadiums to cheer for players like Harold "Red" Grange, the "Galloping Ghost" of the University of Illinois. One Saturday afternoon in 1924 Grange took the University of Michigan's opening kickoff 95 yards for a touchdown. He scored three more touchdowns in the first quarter and another before the game ended, Illinois winning 39-14. Grange carried the ball 21 times and gained an incredible 402 yards.

The most famous football coach of the 1920s was Knute Rockne of Notre Dame's "Fighting Irish." He began the decade with an

Culver Pictures

Culver Pictures

Culver Pictures

UPI/Bettmann Newsphotos

Four of the greatest sports heroes of the 1920s were, clockwise from the bottom, Red Grange, Jack Dempsey, Helen Wills, and Babe Ruth.

undefeated season. For many the 1920 highlight was Notre Dame's defeat of Army, 27-17, owing largely to the 357 yards gained by the team's captain, George Gipp. Years later, at halftime of an important game, Rockne implored his team to "win one for the Gipper," who had died of pneumonia. The locker room speech, recreated in a popular movie starring Ronald Reagan as Gipp, would later serve as a metaphor for Reagan's enormous popularity as president.

In 1927 one of the most famous barnstorming, or traveling, basketball teams in the world was formed by Abe Saperstein. He recruited most of his players from the slums of Chicago's South Side, but he called his team of black athletes the **Harlem Globetrotters.** They became magicians with the basketball and drew fans throughout the world, as they continue to do today.

Baseball was the national game. Its most famous hero at the time was Babe Ruth, the "Sultan of Swat." Ruth was originally a pitcher—and a very good one. He was also a tremendous hitter. The Boston Red Sox quickly made him an outfielder so he could play every day. Thereafter, year after year, he was baseball's home run leader. In 1927 he hit 60, a record that stood until Roger Maris hit 61 in 1961. By the end of his career he had knocked out 714 home runs, most of them for the New York Yankees.

Americans were good at nearly all sports. Tennis players William "Big Bill" Tilden and Helen Wills both won many national and international championships. Johnny Weismuller held a dozen world swimming records. Gertrude Ederle became the first woman to swim across the English Channel.

Motion Pictures

Lindbergh's solo flight to Paris combined his own human abilities and the mechanical perfection of his plane. This combination was characteristic of the period. It explains the rapid growth of motion pictures, which, like the airplane, came of age in the 1920s.

Movies were popular even before the Great War. The early movie theaters were often installed in vacant stores. These "nickelodeons"—the usual admission charge was five cents—showed jerky, badly lit scenes. In the 1920s motion pictures became an important art form and one of the ten largest industries in the nation. In 1922, 40 million people a week went to the movies. By 1930 weekly attendance was averaging 100 million.

Every large city had its movie palaces—large, elaborate theaters seating several thousand people. Hollywood, California, became the motion picture capital of the world. The state's warm, sunny climate was ideal for outdoor movie making.

Americans in the 1920s flocked to every kind of film. There were historical pictures and the most durable of all movies—westerns. The leading actors and actresses were loved by millions. Movie fans followed the careers and personal lives of their favorites as though they were members of their families.

Movies influenced the way people dressed and talked. Women styled their hair like Greta Garbo or Mary Pickford. Men tried to copy Rudolph Valentino, the great lover of *The Sheik,* or Douglas Fairbanks, the sword-fighting hero of *The Three Musketeers.*

The greatest star of the 1920s was Charlie Chaplin. He wrote and directed his own films. In 1915 he created his world-famous character, the sad-looking "little tramp" who wore baggy pants and a battered derby hat and carried a springy bamboo cane. Chaplin

Millions of people flocked to the movies to see their favorite stars. Three of the most glittering were (below, left to right): swashbuckling Douglas Fairbanks, romantic idol Rudolph Valentino, and Charlie Chaplin, the most famous comic actor in the world. Why do you think sports and movies were popular in the 1920s?

All, Culver Pictures

was a marvelous slapstick comedian and a gifted mimic. He was also a superb actor, who could literally make audiences laugh and cry at the same time.

For years the movies were silent. Usually a pianist in each theater played mood music to accompany the action on the screen. Then, in 1927, Warner Brothers, a major film company, released the first "talkie," a film that projected the actors' voices as well as their movements. This film was *The Jazz Singer,* starring Al Jolson. He sang three songs and then told the film audience, "You ain't heard nothin' yet, folks." The next year Walt Disney made the first sound cartoon, *Steamboat Willie,* which introduced Mickey Mouse to the world.

Radio

Radio had an even more powerful hold on the public in the 1920s than movies. Like the movies, it could not have been developed without the remarkable scientific and technological advances of the times.

Everyone could enjoy and profit from radio, even sick and bed-ridden people who could not get to the movies. Radio could be listened to without admission cost and in the privacy of one's home. It was also "live." What people heard was taking place at that very moment: a politician making a speech, the crack of the bat when Babe Ruth hit another home run, the roar of the crowd at a football game, the sound of a jazz band or a symphony orchestra. More people than ever before became interested in sports and music.

The first commercial radio station was KDKA in Pittsburgh. It was operated by the Westinghouse Electric Company. KDKA began broadcasting in 1920. Two years later there were more than 500 commercial stations. The National Broadcasting Company (NBC) began combining local stations into a nationwide radio network in 1926. A year later the Columbia Broadcasting System (CBS) created a competing network. Thereafter, people all over the country could hear the same program at the same time. Audiences grew to the millions.

Radio became still another giant industry. Large companies sprang up to manufacture radio sets and broadcasting equipment. Department stores devoted entire floors to radios. Repairing radios became an important craft. By 1922, 3 million families already had radios. In the single year 1929, 5 million sets were sold.

Radio brought an enormous variety of information and entertainment into American homes. News, music, plays, political speeches, and sports events filled the airwaves. Radio also influenced what Americans bought in stores. Audiences were bombarded with commercials by manufacturers of all sorts. These advertisers paid large sums to broadcast their "sales pitches."

Postwar American Writers

The Great World War had shocked and disillusioned people all over the world. This was especially true of Americans who had resisted the war at first, only to be drawn in by promises of a better future, one made safe for democracy. It was Gertrude Stein, an **expatriate** writer who had left America to live permanently in Europe, who gave these young people a name. She told a young American writer, Ernest Hemingway, about a mechanic who took a very long time to repair her Model T. The owner of the garage reprimanded him: "You are a génération perdue! (lost generation!)." "That's what you are," Stein told Hemingway, "That's what you all are. All of you young people who served in the war, you are a lost generation." To these people progressive ideals that had been so important before the war seemed less so now. Many writers expressed this loss of values in their works.

Culver Pictures

The Metropolitan Museum of Art, Bequest of Gertrude Stein, 1946.

Ernest Hemingway survived a wound while driving an ambulance in Italy; was nearly gored by bulls running in Pamplona, Spain; and later walked away from an airplane crash in Africa. For all his adventures, he paid close attention to Gertrude Stein at her home in Paris. There she critiqued his writing and urged him to use only the "perfect word." Of her portrait by Pablo Picasso, left, she complained that it didn't look like her. The confident Picasso is said to have replied, "It will."

Culver Pictures

The Fitzgeralds, Zelda and Scott, pose with their daughter, Scottie. Fitzgerald wrote some of his best work in Paris, including his classic novel The Great Gatsby. *At the end of it, the narrator sees how America has changed: "And as soon as the moon rose higher the inessential began to melt away until gradually I became aware of the old island here [New York] that flowered once for Dutch sailor's eyes—a fresh, green breast of the new world."*

Ernest Hemingway spent much of his youth hunting and fishing with his father in northern Michigan and had been wounded in the Great War while driving an ambulance for the Red Cross. These Michigan memories and his wartime experiences were the subjects of his early writing.

Hemingway's style is probably the most widely imitated of all American authors. He took considerable pains to choose exactly the right word and no other, writing prose the way poets write poetry. He wanted very badly, he said, to write "one true sentence." In one of his first major novels, *A Farewell to Arms*, we can see the result of Hemingway's painstaking effort:

66 In the late summer of that year we lived in a house in a village that looked across the river and the plain to the mountains. In the bed of the river there were pebbles and boulders, dry and white in the sun, and the water was clear and swiftly moving and blue in the channels. Troops went by the house and down the road and the dust they raised powdered the leaves of the trees. The trunks of the trees too were dusty and the leaves fell early that year and we saw troops marching along the road and the dust rising and leaves, stirred by the breeze, falling and the soldiers marching and afterward the road bare and white except for the leaves.

The plain was rich with crops; there were many orchards of fruit trees and beyond the plain the mountains were brown and bare. There was fighting in the mountains and at night we could see the flashes from the artillery. In the dark it was like summer lightning, but the nights were cool and there was not the feeling of a storm coming.[1] 99

Hemingway gave the writing of fiction a new rhythm of action and simple, straightforward dialogue. He also developed the image of life as a battlefield on which a new type of hero suffers with grace and dignity and accepts gratefully life's few moments of pleasure. In 1954 Hemingway received the Nobel prize for literature for such works as *The Sun Also Rises, For Whom the Bell Tolls,* and *The Old Man and the Sea.*

Francis Scott Key Fitzgerald, more than any other author, gave a voice to the "lost generation." His greatest work—for many *the* great American novel—was *The Great Gatsby*. In it the American dream of wealth and power goes terribly and tragically wrong. Throughout the novel Fitzgerald used the glitter of Gatsby's life to symbolize the purposeless lives of the rich and powerful. Nick Carraway, the narrator, notes after a spectacular party at Gatsby's:

[1]From *A Farewell to Arms* by Ernest Hemingway

> "The caterwauling [noisy crying] of horns had reached a crescendo and I turned away and cut across the lawn toward home. I glanced back once. A wafer of a moon was shining over Gatsby's house, making the night fine as before, and surviving the laughter and the sound of his still glowing garden. A sudden emptiness seemed to flow now from the windows and the great doors, endowing with complete isolation the figure of the host, who stood on the porch, his hand up in a formal gesture of farewell.[1]"

[1]From *The Great Gatsby* by F. Scott Fitzgerald

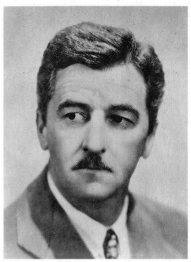

Culver Pictures

William Faulkner was the inventor of a fictional world called Yoknapatawpha County. He emerged into the real world to surprise and delight listeners with his acceptance speech in Stockholm, where he was awarded the Nobel Prize for literature.

Fitzgerald also wrote *Tender Is the Night,* an account of his own despair. He died in 1940 while writing *The Last Tycoon.*

While Fitzgerald and Hemingway wrote in Europe, William Faulkner in his native Mississippi invented a mythical county called Yoknapatawpha. He spent his life populating it with fallen southern aristocrats, new arrivals (all named Snopes), and the long-suffering blacks who tended what was left of the land. In this setting—the American South—he explored such universal themes as human suffering, the passions of the heart, and the destruction of the natural wilderness.

In Faulkner's novels the sudden shifts in time, frequent use of symbolism, and unusual syntax reveal the confused emotions of his characters and the disorder that surrounds them. His most noted works include *The Sound and the Fury, As I Lay Dying, Absalom, Absalom,* and *Light in August.*

Faulkner received a Nobel Prize for literature in 1950. In his acceptance speech at the ceremony in Stockholm, Sweden, he described his view of the writer:

> ". . . I decline to accept the end of man. It is easy enough to say that man is immortal simply because he will endure; that when the last ding-dong of doom has clanged and faded from the last worthless rock hanging tideless in the last red and dying evening, that even then there will still be one more sound: that of his puny inexhaustible voice, still talking. I refuse to accept this. I believe man will not merely endure: he will prevail. He is immortal, not because he alone among the creatures has an inexhaustible voice, but because he has a soul, a spirit capable of compassion and sacrifice and endurance. The poet's, the writer's, duty is to write about these things. It is his privilege to help man endure by lifting his heart, by reminding him of the courage and pity and sacrifice which have been the glory of his past. The poet's voice need not merely be the record of man, it can be one of the props, the pillars to help him endure and prevail."

Return to the Preview & Review on page 870.

4. AN AUTOMOBILE CIVILIZATION

Use these questions to guide your reading. Answer the questions after completing Section 4.
Understanding Issues, Events, & Ideas. Explain how the automobile changed America, using the following words: Model T, mass production, moving assembly line, Model A, tourism, suburb, air pollution.
1. How did Henry Ford change the automobile industry? How did the growth of the automobile industry affect the entire economy?
2. How did the automobile bring freedom to ordinary people?
3. What effects, both good and bad, did the automobile have on family life?
Thinking Critically. Write an obituary for Henry Ford that might have appeared in a newspaper or magazine; or compose an advertisement for Henry Ford's Model T.

Henry Ford's Automobile

Of all the forces reshaping American life in the 1920s, the automobile probably had the most influence. The first gasoline-powered vehicles were built in the 1890s. By the time the United States entered the Great War, over 1 million cars a year were being produced. In the 1920s an average of more than 3 million a year were turned out.

Henry Ford was the key figure in this new industry. Ford had come to Detroit, Michigan, because he hated farm work. He had talent for all kinds of mechanical projects. While working in Detroit for the Edison Illuminating Company in the 1890s, Ford designed and built an automobile in his home workshop. A little later he built a famous racing car, "999," which he drove to several speed records himself. In 1903 he founded the Ford Motor Company.

The first American automobiles were very expensive. They were toys for the rich. Henry Ford dreamed of producing cars cheaply so that ordinary people could own them. (The name of the well-known German automobile, the Volkswagen, or "people's car," expresses his idea exactly.) In 1908 he achieved his goal with his **Model T** Ford. It sold for only $850. And by 1916 Ford had reduced the cost of the new Model T's to $360.

Ford's secret was **mass production** achieved through the use of the **moving assembly line.** His cars were put together, or assembled, while being moved past a line of workers. Each worker or team performed only one fairly simple task.

This method of production was highly efficient. Prices were also held down by Ford's policy of keeping his cars simple and making the same basic model year after year. The Model T was not changed in any important way until 1928, when the **Model A** replaced it. According to a joke of the day, you could have a Model T in any color you wanted as long as you chose black.

Other automobile manufacturers copied Ford's methods. But most made more expensive cars. In prosperous times many customers were willing to pay for larger and more comfortable cars than the Model T. By the end of the 1920s Ford was no longer the largest manufacturer. The General Motors Company had taken the lead.

New Wealth from the Automobile

The automobile fueled an economic boom. The 3 million or more cars produced each year were worth about $3.5 billion even before the car dealers added their expenses and profits. This was only part of the new wealth the automobile created. A huge rubber industry sprang up to produce tires, belts, and hoses for cars. Manufacturers

Henry Ford is as spare as his famous Model T in this photograph. How did the Model T resemble the more recent German Volkswagen?

Culver Pictures

of steel, glass, paint, and dozens of other products greatly increased their output.

The automobile revolutionized the petroleum-refining industry. Before the war the most important petroleum product was kerosene. By 1919 ten times as much gasoline as kerosene was being refined. The total amount of petroleum refined in the United States soared from about 50 million barrels to 1 billion barrels a day.

Then there were the effects of the automobile on road building and on **tourism.** So long as people traveled no faster than a horse could pull a coach or wagon, the bumps and ruts of dirt and gravel roads did not matter much. By the 1920s, however, ordinary cars could speed along at 50 or 60 miles an hour or more. Such speeds were impossible on uneven surfaces. Hundreds of thousands of miles of smooth paved roads had to be built. Great amounts of asphalt and concrete were manufactured to surface them. New road-building machinery was designed and constructed. Thousands of new jobs were created in this road-building industry.

Better roads for cars meant more traveling, both for business and for pleasure. Gasoline stations appeared alongside each new highway. Roadside restaurants opened side by side with motor hotels—a new way of housing travelers, soon to be known as motels.

Point of View

Two of Henry Ford's biographers, Peter Collier and David Horowitz, tell of the first excursions in what Ford called the "baby carriage."

‶Seeing the strange little car coughing and wheezing along the narrow streets during the next few days, people would sometimes yell out the nickname his obsessive drive to build a horseless carriage had earned Ford—'Crazy Henry!' But whenever he stopped, crowds immediately surrounded his invention, examining it with such enthusiasm that he finally had to begin chaining it to lightposts for fear they would carry it off. 'Yes, crazy,' he sometimes said, tapping his temple with a forefinger. 'Crazy like a fox.'″

From *The Fords: An American Epic,* 1987

An Automobile Civilization   881

Culver Pictures

Plans for a Sunday drive have gone awry in this early traffic jam outside St. Louis, Missouri. Notice the large number of Model T's. How did the automobile bring Americans both freedom and dependence?

Automobiles and American Life

For thousands of years the power to move about freely and easily was a sign that a person had social status. That is why in ancient times and throughout the Middle Ages ownership of a horse meant that a person belonged to the upper class. Now, because of Henry Ford and the other pioneers of the auto industry, nearly everyone in the United States could afford a car. A *new* Model T could cost as little as $300 in the early 1920s. A secondhand Ford still capable of good service could be bought for $25 to $50.

Automobiles freed ordinary people. Cars let them travel far more widely and rapidly than medieval knights had traveled. They could live in **suburbs** outside the cities, surrounded by trees and green fields, and drive daily to jobs in the cities. They could visit places hundreds of miles away on weekends or cover thousands of miles on a two-week summer vacation.

Little wonder that automobiles became status symbols—objects associated with the upper classes of society—for many people. Owners spent Saturday mornings washing and polishing their cars the way a trainer grooms a racehorse or a pedigreed dog before a show. Car owners decorated their autos with shiny hood ornaments and put flowers in small vases on the inside.

The personalities of many car owners seemed to be affected by their vehicles. Once behind the wheel, drivers were in command of half a ton or more of speeding metal. They often became "roadhogs" who turned into cursing bullies when another driver got in their way or tried to pass them on the road.

Automobiles had both good and bad effects on family life. Family picnics and sightseeing trips brought parents and children closer together. However, crowding five or six people into a small space on a hot summer afternoon hardly made for family harmony. Quarrels developed about where to go and how to get there. People complained about "backseat drivers"—those passengers who made a habit of criticizing the driver.

The automobile also tended to separate family members. Once children were old enough to drive, they generally preferred to be off by themselves or with friends their own age. Soon "two-car" and "three-car" families came into being. In extreme cases the home became little more than a motel or garage. Family members rested there before zooming off again in their Fords and Chevrolets or, if they were wealthy, in their Packards and Pierce-Arrows.

The new automobile civilization had other unfortunate side effects. Between 1915 and 1930 the number of road accidents soared. By 1930 automobile crashes caused more than half the accidental deaths in the nation.

As the number of cars on the roads increased, traffic tie-ups became common. The exhaust fumes of millions of cars caused serious **air pollution** in some areas.

Because of the automobile, the oil resources of the nation were being used up at a rapidly increasing rate. Anyone who thought about the question realized that there was only so much petroleum in the ground. It had taken millions of years to be formed and could never be replaced. Still, the supply was so large that most people assumed that it would last practically forever. During the 1920s huge new oil fields were discovered in Texas and Oklahoma. Only a tiny percentage of the petroleum used in America then came from foreign sources. That percentage was actually declining in those years.

The nation was becoming more and more dependent upon gasoline and other petroleum products. Giant industries could not exist without oil in one form or another. Neither could the new life style that was developing in the United States. Yet in the 1920s few people worried about these matters. Gasoline was cheap. There was plenty of it. Let us enjoy life while we can, most people reasoned. 🖘

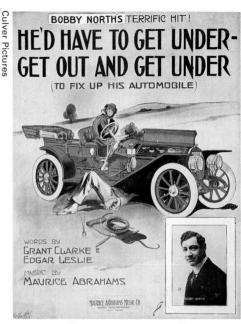

Culver Pictures

BOBBY NORTH'S TERRIFIC HIT!

HE'D HAVE TO GET UNDER-GET OUT AND GET UNDER
(TO FIX UP HIS AUTOMOBILE)

WORDS BY
GRANT CLARKE &
EDGAR LESLIE
MUSIC BY
MAURICE ABRAHAMS

MAURICE ABRAHAMS MUSIC CO
1570 BROADWAY

This song sheet cover takes a good-natured view of the plight of most car owners, who had to be their own mechanics. Scarcely a trip was made without at least patching a tire.

Return to the Preview & Review on page 880.

An Automobile Civilization   883

Preview & Review

Use these questions to guide your reading. Answer the questions after completing Section 5.

Understanding Issues, Events, & Ideas. Use the following words to describe American politics and the economy of the 1920s: Elk Hills, Teapot Dome, chain store, synthetic, sick industry, Farm Bloc, subsidy, Black Tuesday, Great Stock Market Crash.

1. How did the political mood of the 1920s differ from the way people behaved?
2. What changes took place in business in the 1920s? Which were the sick industries in the 1920s? Why were they sick?
3. Why did the Republicans win the election of 1928 so easily?
4. Why did people tend to adopt a "get-rich-quick" attitude in the 1920s?

Thinking Critically. 1. Imagine that you are a Wall Street reporter on October 29, 1929. Interview several people on the street and use their comments to write your newspaper article. 2. You are a farmer in the South in 1921. Write a letter to your congressman, a member of the Farm Bloc, explaining the troubles you are having.

Harding and Coolidge

The 1920s were a time when politics seemed to have little connection with how people lived and thought. While society was changing in dramatic and significant ways, most political leaders were conservative, slow moving, and lacking in imagination.

President Warren G. Harding looked like a statesman. He was friendly, good looking, firm jawed, and silver haired. He worked for conservative policies that favored big business. But he was not a creative leader. His programs included high protective tariffs on manufactured goods, lower taxes for the wealthy, and reducing the national debt, the same policies as earlier Republican presidents. Nor was he a strong leader. Harding was careless about the appointments he made to important public offices. Some people he appointed were incompetent. Others were plainly corrupt.

Harding died of a heart attack in 1923. Soon thereafter a series of government scandals was uncovered. Harding himself was not involved. It turned out that various members of his administration had stolen money intended for a veterans' hospital, mishandled government property, and accepted bribes.

The worst scandal involved Albert Fall, Harding's secretary of the interior. Fall leased government-owned land containing rich deposits of oil to private companies at very low rents. These included the **Elk Hills** reserve in California and the **Teapot Dome** reserve in Wyoming. In return the heads of the oil companies gave Fall bribes amounting to $400,000. When the facts were discovered by a government investigation in 1923, Fall was convicted and put in prison.

It was fortunate for the Republican party that Harding died before the scandals broke. His successor, Vice President Calvin Coolidge, had nothing to do with the corruption. Coolidge's personality was almost the exact opposite of Harding's. He was quiet and very reserved. He hated to spend money. Indeed, he was the only modern president who was able to save part of his salary while in office. He was thoroughly honest. His no-nonsense attitude made it difficult for the Democrats to take political advantage of the scandals.

In 1924 Coolidge easily received the Republican nomination for a full term. The Democratic nomination was decided only after a long and bitter struggle. The eastern wing of the party supported Governor Alfred E. Smith of New York. Most southern and western delegates favored William G. McAdoo, who had been President Wilson's secretary of the treasury.

Under the rules of the convention, a candidate needed a two-thirds majority to be nominated. Since neither Smith nor McAdoo could get two thirds, a deadlock developed. It lasted for days. Finally,

Both, National Portrait Gallery

At left is a portrait of Warren G. Harding by Margaret Lindsay Williams. Right is Calvin Coolidge, nicknamed "Silent Cal" because he was a man of few words. Once, at a White House dinner, a lady bet Coolidge that she could coax at least three words from him. "You lose," he replied. Howard Chandler Christy painted Grace Goodhue Coolidge, the popular first lady, with her collie, Rob Roy.

Copyright by the White House Historical Association; photograph by the National Geographic Society

on the 103rd ballot, the exhausted delegates nominated John W. Davis, a conservative lawyer from West Virginia.

The deadlock between Smith and McAdoo reflected the basic divisions within the Democratic party and within the nation itself. Smith was a Catholic. Many people were prejudiced against Catholics and would not vote for a Catholic for president. Some even feared that such a person would be a servant of the Pope rather than a servant of the American people.

Many rural people disliked Smith because he had been raised "on the sidewalks of New York." Yet the nation was becoming more and more urban. By the 1920s farmers no longer made up the majority of the population. Many farmers resented this fact. In Smith's candidacy they saw a symbol of the shift from a rural to an urban nation.

In addition to Coolidge and Davis, Senator Robert La Follette of Wisconsin ran for president in 1924. La Follette had been a leading progressive before the Great War. He found both the major parties too conservative for his taste after the war. He therefore formed a new Progressive party. La Follette campaigned on a platform calling for government ownership of railroads, protection of the right of workers to bargain collectively, aid for farmers, and other reforms. "The great issue before the American people," La Follette believed, was "the control of government and industry by private monopoly."

America Heads For a Crash   885

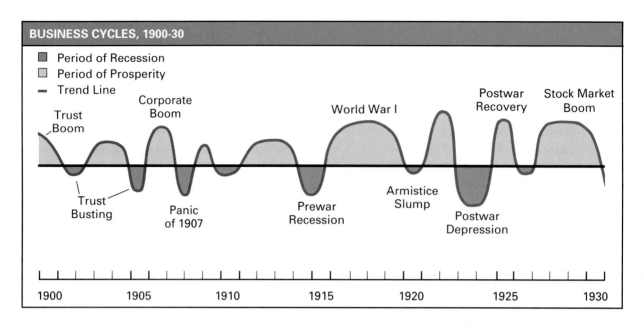

BUSINESS CYCLES, 1900-30

■ Period of Recession
□ Period of Prosperity
— Trend Line

Trust Boom
Trust Busting
Corporate Boom
Panic of 1907
World War I
Prewar Recession
Armistice Slump
Postwar Recovery
Postwar Depression
Stock Market Boom

1900   1905   1910   1915   1920   1925   1930

LEARNING FROM GRAPHS. *The graph above shows American business cycles between 1900 and 1930. What happened to the economy during the war? Why? What happened to the economy after the war ended? Why?*

Coolidge won the election easily. He received more than 15 million votes to Davis' 8.4 million and La Follette's 4.8 million. Clearly the national mood was politically conservative at a time when society was going through tremendous changes.

Business Growth in the 1920s

The policies of the federal government in the 1920s had large effects on the economy. These policies greatly influenced the lives of nearly everyone. President Coolidge believed that "the business of America is business." He also said, "The man who builds a factory builds a temple." His policies were designed to help business interests and other large investors.

Coolidge presided over one of the most business-minded administrations in American history. Its chief architect was Andrew Mellon, the secretary of the treasury. Mellon believed prosperity depended on the ability of Americans to invest and reinvest in business. He sponsored a tax cut that favored the wealthy and businesses by reducing the taxes for people making $60,000 a year or more. Within 3 years money was pouring into business investments.

To make up for the reduced revenues, the government raised tariffs and increased excise taxes slightly. The higher tariffs benefited businesses in two ways, allowing them to raise their prices while cutting down on their competition. The slight increases in excise taxes on consumer goods and a new tax on automobiles was paid primarily by the middle class.

The friendly attitude of the government encouraged businesses to make new investments. Once the switch back to peacetime production had been completed, the American economy certainly prospered. Many industries that had been established before the Great War expanded rapidly. Coolidge and his advisers expected this to create more jobs and a better standard of living for all.

Between 1915 and 1930 the number of telephone users in the United States doubled. Dial phones and improved switchboards speeded communication and cut costs. Electric light companies prospered. As more and more homes were hooked up for electricity, the electric appliance industry grew. Most families now had electric irons. Many had electric vacuum cleaners and washing machines and refrigerators as well. Electricity also became an important source of power for industry. By 1930 the United States was using more electricity than all the rest of the world *combined*.

Chain stores grew rapidly in the 1920s. The A&P grocery chain expanded from 400 outlets in 1912 to 15,000 in 1932. Woolworth "five and tens" were opened by the dozens in big cities and small towns. By the end of the decade Americans were buying more than 25 percent of their food and clothing in chain stores. With more and more people living in cities, sales of canned fruits and vegetables rose rapidly.

Even more impressive was the growth of entirely new industries. Chemical plants began turning out many **synthetics**—artificial substances such as rayon for clothing and Bakelite, a hard plastic, for radio cases. Other new mass-produced products included wristwatches, cigarette lighters, improved cameras, and Pyrex glass for cooking.

Some of the wonderful new labor-saving devices being advertised in the 1920s include the vacuum cleaner, refrigerator, and washing machine. Think how each made life a bit simpler.

All, The Granger Collection, New York

"Sick" Industries

Despite the general economic expansion of the 1920s, there were several weak areas in the economy. **Sick industries** like coal and textiles did not prosper at all. Coal was meeting stiff competition from oil, natural gas, and electricity. Over 1,000 coal mines were shut down in the 1920s, and nearly 200,000 miners lost their jobs.

Manufacturers of cotton and woolen cloth did not prosper either. Partly because of competition from rayon, the new synthetic textile, these manufacturers were soon producing more cloth than the public was buying. Their profits therefore shrank, and the number of unemployed textile workers rose.

American agriculture also suffered. Once the Great War was over, European farmers quickly recaptured their local markets. The price of wheat and other farm products fell sharply. Farmers' incomes declined, but their expenses for mortgage interest, taxes, tractors, harvesters, and supplies did not.

In 1921 a group of congressmen from the South and West organized an informal **Farm Bloc.** (A bloc is a common interest group.) Their purpose was to unite congressmen from farm districts behind legislation favorable to agriculture. The Farm Bloc pushed through a bill providing for **subsidies** for farmers through government purchase of farm surpluses. President Coolidge was not sympathetic to proposals to subsidize farm prices. He vetoed the bill.

But the tremendous growth of the 1920s also had a down side. Business owners pushed their factories to produce more, faster. New and improved products continued to attract buyers, and old models wore out and had to be replaced. But by the late 1920s businesses were producing more than the public demanded. By the end of the decade warehouses were full of consumer goods waiting to be purchased.

LEARNING FROM GRAPHS. *Early America was a nation of farmers. Even as late as 1879 more than half of the value of the gross national product came from agriculture. But what trend does the graph illustrate? Why do you think this happened?*

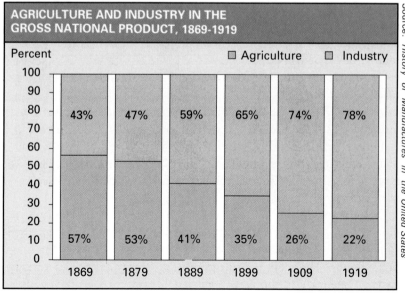

AGRICULTURE AND INDUSTRY IN THE GROSS NATIONAL PRODUCT, 1869-1919

Percent — Agriculture — Industry

Year	Agriculture	Industry
1869	57%	43%
1879	53%	47%
1889	41%	59%
1899	35%	65%
1909	26%	74%
1919	22%	78%

Source: *History of Manufactures in the United States*

UPI/Bettmann Newsphotos

The Election of 1928

President Coolidge played down the problems of farmers and workers in the "sick" industries. He believed the future was bright. In his 1928 State of the Union message he said:

Herbert Hoover, candidate for president in 1928, says "hello" to Elizabeth, New Jersey, where a large and enthusiastic crowd greets him. What made him so popular at the time?

❝ No Congress has met with a more pleasing prospect than that which appears at the present time. ❞

Most people agreed with Coolidge. Americans were enjoying the greatest period of prosperity in their history. Most were earning more money and working shorter hours than ever before. They had cars, radios, and household gadgets. Life was easy. It seemed likely to become easier still. The Republican party naturally took the credit for the good times.

In the 1928 presidential campaign, Herbert Hoover, the secretary of commerce, received the Republican nomination. The Democratic candidate was Alfred E. Smith. Smith had a record of solid accomplishment as governor of New York. He could not be denied the nomination. But his Catholic religion and his "big city" background hurt him in rural areas.

Hoover won the election with 21 million votes to Smith's 15 million. The electoral vote was 444 to 87. Smith even lost his own state of New York as well as several Democratic states in the once Solid South. The main cause of Smith's defeat was the prosperity issue. A majority of the American people had come to believe that the Republican party was the symbol of economic progress and the guardian of good times.

The Great Crash

Prosperity tended to make people ambitious and optimistic. A "get-rich-quick" attitude developed in the United States as the decade advanced. More and more people set out to make fortunes in the stock market. They followed the prices of stocks in the newspapers as closely as they followed Babe Ruth's batting average. By mid-1929 stocks had been climbing steadily in price for several months. The profits of most corporations were on the rise. By 1929 the companies listed on the New York Stock Exchange, one market where stocks were bought and sold, were paying out three times as much money in dividends as they had in 1920. A newspaper writer of the day made fun of the stock buying frenzy.

Culver Pictures

"Sold Out." These people could be two of thousands who lost their savings in the Stock Market Crash of 1929. What was the name given to the crash on October 29, 1929?

    " But nowadays the bores I find
    Are of a single, standard kind:
    For every person I may meet
    At lunch, at clubs, upon the street,
    Tells me, in endless wordy tales,
    Of market purchases and sales;
    Of how he bought a single share
    Of California Prune and Pear;
    Or how he sold at 33
    A million shares of T. & T.
    How McAvoy and Katzenstein°
    Told him to sell at 99;
    Of the thousands lost and millions made
    In this or that egregious°° trade;
    How bright he was to buy or sell
    EP, GM, X or GL.
    In herds, in schools, in droves, in flocks
    The men and women talk of stocks.[1] **"**

This boom could not go on forever. Speculation—investing money in hopes of making a profit—ran on the false belief that no matter how much a person paid for stock, someone would buy it from them. But once stock prices reached a certain level, there would be no more buyers. The market reached that peak in September. Nervous speculators realized prices could only come down.

Quite suddenly, on October 24, 1929, thousands of investors wanted to sell stocks instead of buy them. Investors jammed tele-

°A Wall Street investment firm
°°Notable
[1]From *Christopher Columbus and Other Patriotic Verses* by Franklin P. Adams

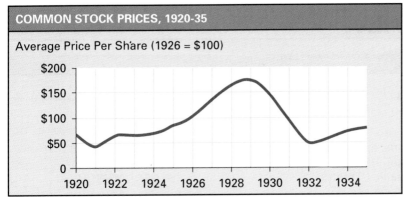

COMMON STOCK PRICES, 1920-35

Average Price Per Share (1926 = $100)

Source: *Historical Statistics of the United States.*

LEARNING FROM GRAPHS. *The graph shows the average price of a share of common stock for each year between 1920 and 1935. Because the graph shows the* average price, *remember that some stocks sold for much more and others for much less. What was the general trend in stock prices in the 1920s? What was the trend between 1930 and 1932? Why did the trend change?*

phone lines and crowded into brokers' offices, desperate to turn their stocks into cash. With many sellers and few buyers, the prices of stocks plunged. People even began to sell at a loss in order to get something before prices fell still lower. General Electric Company shares dropped from $315 to $283 in that one day. U.S. Steel skidded from $205 to $193.

Then, on October 29, a day known as **Black Tuesday,** came an even steeper decline. The **Great Stock Market Crash** reached panic proportions. Day after day the drop continued. By the middle of November General Electric stock was down to $168, U.S. Steel to $150.

The Granger Collection, New York

The prosperity of the 1920s was over. Overproduction and overspeculation—investing too much money in hopes of making a profit—had caught up with the American people. The country was about to enter the Great Depression.

Return to the Preview & Review on page 884.

CHAPTER 24 REVIEW

1917
America enters
the Great War

1918
The Great War
ends

1919
Treaty of Versailles
★
Palmer raids

1920
Prohibition begins
★
Senate rejects
Versailles Treaty
★
Nineteenth Amendment
★
First radio broadcast

1921
Emergency Quota Act

Chapter Summary

Read the statements below. Choose one, and write a paragraph explaining its importance.

1. Republican opposition to the Versailles Treaty, especially to the League of Nations, caused Wilson political troubles.
2. Wilson's failing health added to the problems of getting the treaty ratified. It was eventually rejected.
3. The Nineteenth Amendment gave women the vote in national elections. The large voter turnout in 1920 elected Warren Harding.
4. The United States steered a middle course between isolationism and internationalism in the 1920s.
5. At home, Americans worried about anarchists and communists. This led to a series of actions aimed at limiting foreign influences in the United States. Other examples of the American reaction to the war included prohibition, the fundamentalist crusade, and the Sacco-Vanzetti Case.
6. Most Americans enjoyed life during the "Roaring Twenties." Music, sports, motion pictures, and the radio began their golden ages. Writers of the Lost Generation produced works that gave a voice to both the despair and the dazzle of the postwar period.
8. America also became an "automobile civilization" during the Twenties.
9. Despite the prevalent "get-rich-quick" attitude, problems of farmers and "sick" industries slowed the economy. The bubble of speculation burst in October 1929 when the stock market crashed, causing panic throughout the American economy.

Understanding Chronological Order

Number your paper 1–5. Then study the time line above and place the following events in the order in which they happened by writing the first next to 1, the second next to 2, and so on.
1. Sacco and Vanzetti executed
2. Teapot Dome
3. Senate rejects Versailles Treaty
4. Stock market crash
5. Lindbergh flies across the Atlantic

Understanding Main Ideas

1. Why was the Versailles Treaty rejected? Who were the mild reservationists? The strong reservationists? The irreconcilables?
2. What was meant by the term "the Jazz Age?" Why was jazz music a symbol for the times?
3. What were some reasons the 1920s was the Golden Age of Sports?
4. What methods did Henry Ford use to produce automobiles that ordinary people could afford?
5. Which were the "sick" industries of the 1920s? Why were they called "sick"?
6. What caused the price of stocks to plunge after October 24, 1929?

Thinking Critically

1. **Resolving Issues.** If you were President Wilson, how would you have acted differently in order to be sure that the Senate would approve the United States joining the League of Nations?
2. **Imagining.** If you could be a celebrity during the Twenties, would you rather be a jazz musician, a poet living in Harlem, an athlete, an airplane pilot, a movie star, a radio comedian, or a writer living in Paris? Why?
3. **Evaluating.** You know that Henry Ford's Model T dominated the automobile market until the end of the 1920s, when General Motors gained the lead. What changes would you have advised Ford to make in 1925 in order to maintain his advantage?

Writing About History

Write a report on the great hero of the 1920s, Charles A. Lindbergh. You might wish to focus on topics such as a) Lindbergh's barnstorming days, b) the planning and building of the *Spirit of St. Louis,* c) the day before the transatlantic flight, d) the May 1927 flight itself, e) the reception in Paris, and f) Lindbergh's welcome home. Conclude your report by explaining how Lindbergh's flight was a triumph for both man and machine.

	1924	1925		1927	1928	1929
ng dies enly	National Origins Act	Scopes ''Monkey Trial''		Harlem Globetrotters formed	Hoover elected president	Stock market crash
idge eeds Harding	★ Teapot Dome			★ Ruth hits 60 home runs	★ Ford introduces Model A	★ Great Depression begins
	★ Coolidge elected president			★ Lindbergh's solo flight		
				★ Sacco and Vanzetti executed		

Practicing the Strategy

Review the strategy on page 855.

Comparing Points of View. Reread the comments of Senator Borah and President Wilson on pages 853-54. Then answer the following questions.

1. How does Wilson's statement about the League of Nations differ from Borah's?
2. Would you consider Borah an expert on American foreign affairs? Why? Do you consider President Wilson an expert? Why?
3. Which view of the League of Nations do you agree with? Why?
4. Use your historical imagination to explain how Americans in 1919 might have had a different view of an international peace-keeping organization than people today.

Using Primary Sources

The 1920s were a time of drastic social change. Two social scientists, Robert S. Lynd and Helen M. Lynd, wrote a book called *Middletown,* which was a study of the way people lived in a mid-sized American town. The following quotations from the book indicate how people felt about the automobile. As you read the comments, think about how the automobile transformed America.

'We don't have no fancy clothes when we have the car to pay for,' said another. 'The car is the only pleasure we have.'

'I'll go without food before I'll see us give up the car,' said one woman.

'Our daughters [eighteen and fifteen] don't use our car much because they are always with somebody else in their car when we go out motoring,' lamented one business class mother.

1. Why do you think someone would go without food or clothing before they would give up their car?

2. What does the last quotation suggest about how the automobile changed family life?
3. Do you think cars are as important to people today as they were in the 1920s? Why or why not?

Linking History & Geography

Throughout the nation's history, improvements in transportation and communication have helped bring Americans closer together. The automobile, the airplane, and the radio came of age in the 1920s. To understand how these developments reshaped Americans' sense of geography, answer the following questions.

1. How did the automobile affect the number and quality of roads, the distances between where people lived and worked, and the amount of the country the average person visited?
2. What advantages did the airplane have over other types of transportation? What disadvantages did it have?
3. What advantages did the radio have over the telegraph and the telephone?
4. What generalization can you state about the effects of the automobile, the airplane, and the radio on regional differences in the U.S.?

Enriching Your Study of History

1. **Individual Project.** Prepare a classroom display to show how the automobile changed American life.
2. **Cooperative Project.** Have your group use its historical imagination to prepare and present on tape a radio broadcast from the 1920s. Each of you should select one of the following topics: news of the day, music, interviews with famous persons, comedy routines, and commercials. Then combine your parts into a radio program. Research the 1920s carefully so that your broadcast seems true to the times.

Chapter 24 Review 893

The Great Depression and the New Deal

The stock market crash of 1929 was the first major event of what we call the Great Depression. There had been many earlier depressions in the United States, but the Great Depression lasted longer and was more severe than any before in the nation's history. Human suffering was widespread. Shopkeepers lost their businesses. Farmers lost their farms. Banks failed and investors lost their savings. Finally, in 1932, the nation turned to Franklin Delano Roosevelt, a man of wealth who understood suffering after his own struggle with the paralysis of polio he suffered in 1921. As president, could the popular FDR pull the nation from "the depths of depression"?

National Academy of Design

In this painting by Paul Starrett Sample titled "Unemployment," the city sidewalk and alley are crowded with people out of work. How do you think long-term mass unemployment might affect the nation? What would likely be some negative results?

1. THE COSTS OF DEPRESSION

The "Normal" Business Cycle

People had come to accept depressions as a regular part of the **business cycle.** This is how business cycles worked:

In good times economic activity tended to expand. More goods were produced. Prices rose. More workers were hired. Eventually output increased faster than goods could be sold. Surpluses then piled up in company warehouses and in retail stores. Manufacturers had to slow down their production. They let go some of their workers. These unemployed people had less money to buy goods. More manufacturers then had to reduce output and lay off more workers. Prices fell. Producers who were losing money began to go out of business. The general economy was in a state of **depression.**

People believed that depressions were self correcting. When output became very low, the surpluses were gradually used up. Then the efficient producers who had not gone out of business increased output. They rehired workers. These workers, with wages in their pockets, increased their own purchases. Demand increased. Prices rose. The economy entered the **recovery** stage. Recovery eventually led to **prosperity**—a time of high prices, full production, and almost no unemployment.

The Great Depression

A complete business cycle might last anywhere from two or three to five or six years. What made the **Great Depression** different was that it lasted for more than ten years. The economy declined steeply from late 1929 until the winter of 1932-33. Then it appeared to be stuck. Recovery was slow and irregular. The output of goods remained far below what it had been in 1929. Only in 1940, after the outbreak of the Second World War, did a strong recovery begin.

Throughout this long period at least 10 percent of the work force was unemployed. At the low point, early in 1933, about 25 percent of all Americans were without jobs. Americans spent $10.9 billion in food stores in 1929. But although the population increased in every year, Americans did not spend that much on food again until 1941. This was true also of money spent on furniture, clothing, automobiles, jewelry, recreation, medical care, and nearly all other items.

These cold figures tell us little about the human suffering and discouragement that the Great Depression caused. Shopkeepers who had worked for years to develop their businesses lost everything. People lost their savings in bank failures. Workers who had risen through the ranks to well-paid jobs found themselves unemployed. Those who had developed skills found that their skills were useless. Students graduating from schools and colleges could find no one willing to hire them.

Preview & Review

Use these questions to guide your reading. Answer the questions after completing Section 1.
Understanding Issues, Events, & Ideas. Use the following words to describe the depression: business cycle, depression, recovery, prosperity, Great Depression, soup kitchens and breadlines, public works, Bonus March.
1. How were depressions supposed to be self-correcting?
2. How did the Great Depression differ from other depressions in the nation's history?
3. How did President Hoover try to stimulate the economy?
4. Why did the Bonus Marchers come to Washington? How did Hoover respond to them? Why did Hoover's popularity suffer from that response?

Thinking Critically. Imagine you are a newspaper editor in 1932. Write an editorial in which you either criticize or praise Hoover's handling of the depression.

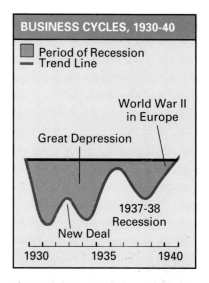

LEARNING FROM GRAPHS. *What effect did the New Deal have on the Great Depression? How can you tell?*

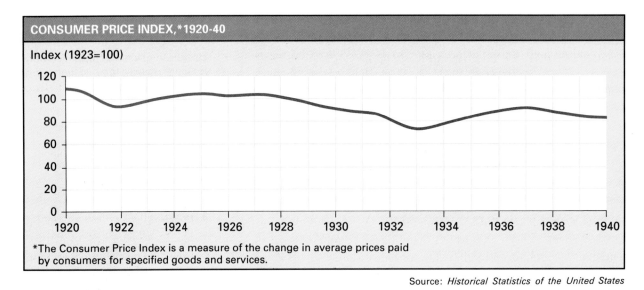

CONSUMER PRICE INDEX,*1920-40

Index (1923=100)

*The Consumer Price Index is a measure of the change in average prices paid by consumers for specified goods and services.

Source: *Historical Statistics of the United States*

LEARNING FROM GRAPHS. *The Consumer Price Index, or CPI, is a statistic that tells economists how much a typical American can afford. What happened to the CPI during the Great Depression? Why?*

The weakest and poorest suffered most. Many married women lost their jobs because employers thought they did not need to work. Unemployment was far higher among African Americans, Hispanics, and other groups than among whites. In the southwestern states thousands of Mexican-born farm laborers and their children born in the United States were gathered up by federal authorities and shipped back to Mexico when they were unable to find work. Officials excused this cruel policy by arguing that there was not enough relief money to care for them. Many Mexican-born workers who had *not* lost their jobs were also shipped back. In this case the excuse was that they were holding down jobs that United States citizens needed.

The term "depression" describes the mood of the people as well as the state of the economy. Until the middle of the 1930s there was no system of unemployment insurance and no national welfare assistance program to help the unemployed and their families. People in desperate need had no sure place they could turn to. One sufferer recalled:

    ❜ My first real memories come about '31. It was simply a gut issue then: eating or not eating, living or not living. My father was a coal miner, outside a small town in Illinois. . . .

      When the mine temporarily closed down in the early Thirties, my dad had to hunt for work elsewhere. He went around the state, he'd paint barns, anything. . . .[1]❝

Great efforts were made to assist the jobless. State and city governments and private charities raised money to feed the poor and provide them with a little cash for their other needs. Special "charity drives," many led by churches and religious groups, were conducted

[1]From *Hard Times: An Oral History of the Great Depression* by Studs Terkel

to collect clothing for the unemployed and their families. There were **soup kitchens** and **breadlines** where hungry people could get a free meal and lodging houses where the homeless could spend the night. One woman, a teenager during the Great Depression, recalled her experiences:

❝ My mother'd send us to the soup line. And we were never allowed to curse. If you happened to be one of the first ones in line, you didn't get anything but the water that was on top. So we'd ask the guy that was putting the soup into the buckets—everybody had to bring their own bucket to get the soup—he'd dip the greasy watery stuff off the top. So we'd ask him to please dip down to get some meat and potatoes from the bottom of the kettle. But he wouldn't do it. So we learned to curse.

Then we'd go across the street. One place had bread, large loaves of bread. Down the road just a little way was a big shed, and they gave milk. My sister and me would take two buckets each. And that's what we lived off for the longest time.

I can remember one time, the only thing in the house to eat was mustard. My sister and I put so much mustard on biscuits that we got sick. And we can't stand mustard till today. . . .

There was a feeling of together. . . . It's different today. People are made to feel ashamed now if they don't have anything. Back then, I'm not sure how the rich felt. I think the rich looked down on the poor as much as they do now.

Point of View

Unemployment struck every type of workplace—large and small, skilled and unskilled. One writer of the day put it in perspective.

❝The Ford Motor Company, in fact, serves as a good example of the devastating effect the crash had upon unemployment. In March of 1929, more than 129,000 people were on the Ford pay-roll. Two years later the number of employees had dropped to 84,000; by August of 1931 only 37,000 were employed by Ford. . . .❞

From *Years of Protest*

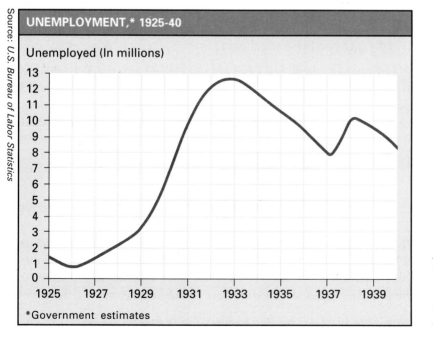

Source: U.S. Bureau of Labor Statistics

UNEMPLOYMENT,* 1925-40

Unemployed (In millions)

*Government estimates

LEARNING FROM GRAPHS. *Note the ups and downs of unemployment figures between 1925 and 1940. They are usually much more stable. What event caused them to soar in 1929–30? What helped bring them down in the mid-1930s?*

The Costs of Depression   897

UPI/Bettmann Newsphotos

These crowds have not come to see the latest movie by the popular Wallace Beery. They stand in line in the hope that there will be bread or soup when their turn comes. "We all had an understanding that it wasn't our fault," recalled one survivor of the Great Depression, but who was to blame?

But among the people that I knew, we all had an understanding that it wasn't our fault. It was something that had happened to the system. Most people blamed Hoover, and they cursed him—it was all his fault. I'm not saying he's blameless, but I'm not saying either it was all his fault. Our system doesn't run by just one person, and it doesn't fall by just one person, either.[1]

Many victims of the depression received help from relatives and friends. But others stood on street corners trying to sell apples or pencils. Some simply held out their hands, begging for a few pennies. Some became tramps, wandering aimlessly around the country, stealing rides on railroad freight cars. Some became thieves. And some people actually starved to death.

Hoover Fights the Depression

Herbert Hoover's work during the Great World War seemed good training for dealing with the depression. He had helped the Belgians after the Germans invaded their country. He had run the American food program after 1917. As secretary of commerce during the 1920s he had won the confidence of most business leaders.

[1] From *Hard Times: An Oral History of the Great Depression* by Studs Terkel

Dorothea Lange, *Woman of the High Plains*, Courtesy of the Dorothea Lange Collection, The City of Oakland,

This photograph titled "Woman of the High Plains, Texas Panhandle" was taken by Dorothea Lange in 1938. It is one of the most lingering images of the depression. Note that the woman's dress probably has been made from flour sacks.

Hoover also understood economics better than most politicians. When he realized that the nation had entered a serious depression, he tried to stimulate recovery quickly. He urged Congress to lower taxes so that people would have more money to spend on goods and services. He called for more government spending on **public works,** such as road construction or building dams. These measures would increase the demand for goods and put jobless people back to work, he said. Congress passed each of these measures. Unfortunately they were too limited to end the Great Depression.

Farmers in particular were hard hit by the depression. The price of most farm products fell sharply. Hoover urged farmers to form cooperatives and to raise smaller crops until prices rose. He also favored holding down interest rates so farmers and the businesses they supported could borrow money more easily. Neither bankers nor farmers were willing to follow these voluntary guidelines in the face of the crisis.

Above all, the president recognized that the American people

The Costs of Depression   899

Whitney Museum of American Art

"Home Relief Station" by the artist Louis Ribak reminds us that waiting and humiliation may be a part of charity. The victims of the Dust Bowl await their turn in front of the woman who will investigate their claims. Imagine what you would say to this person when your time came.

had lost confidence in the economic system. This was part of their psychological depression. He tried to encourage them to have faith in the future. "Prosperity," he said, "is just around the corner."

But Hoover's strength as an organizer in wartime proved to be a weakness during the depression. Voluntary cooperation would not solve the nation's problems this time. During the war people knew who the enemy was and what to do to protect themselves. In the depression they could not identify any particular enemy. Therefore they did not know how they could protect themselves.

Hoover displayed still another weakness. He believed that the federal government should not increase its authority just because times were hard. If the United States took over powers that normally belonged to state and local governments, it would become a "super-state." Even when city after city proved unable to raise enough money to take care of the unemployed, Hoover opposed federal grants for relief purposes. Such aid would destroy the "real liberty" of the people, he said.

Hoover supported federal assistance to banks and big industries. These loans were sound investments, he said. The money would be used to produce goods and earn profits. Then the loans could be repaid. Lending money to a farmer to buy pig feed or more seed or a tractor was also proper, according to Hoover's theory. But he opposed giving federal aid to farmers so that they could feed their children. That would be giving them something for nothing. He believed charity was the business of state and local governments and private organizations like the Red Cross and the Salvation Army.

As the Great Depression dragged on, Hoover became more and more unpopular. People began to think that he was hardhearted. He seemed not to care about the sufferings of the poor. His critics even claimed that he was responsible for the depression.

Both charges were untrue. Hoover cared deeply about the suffering the depression was causing. He sincerely believed that his policies were the proper ones. These policies had certainly not caused the depression. After all, every industrial nation in the world had high unemployment at the time. The Great Depression affected all of Europe and most of the rest of the world.

The economies of nations that depended on agriculture were badly depressed. There was a depression in wheat-growing Australia and in beef-raising Argentina. The price of Brazilian coffee fell so low that farmers there burned the coffee beans in cookstoves. Coffee made a cheaper fuel than coal or kerosene.

Still, even if he was not responsible for the long depression, Hoover's rigid policies were not working. He was in charge of the government. Therefore people tended to blame him.

The Bonus Army

Public opinion turned further against Hoover after the **Bonus March** of the summer of 1932. Some years earlier Congress had passed a law giving veterans of the Great World War an adjusted compensation bonus. Its purpose was to make up for the low pay that soldiers had received during the war while workers at home were earning high wages. The bonus money, however, was not to be paid until 1945.

During the depression veterans began to demand that the bonus be paid at once. As you can see in this excerpt from a letter to the veteran's committee, this issue was turning public opinion and anger against Hoover and the government.

66 Now that our income is but $15.60 a week (their are five of us My Husband Three little children and myself). My husband who is a world war Veteran and saw active service in the trenches, became desperate and applied for Compensation and was turned down and that started me thinking. . . . Oh why is it that it is allways a bunch of overley rich, selfish, dumb, ignorant money hogs that persist in being Senitors, legislatures, representatives Where would they and their possessions be if it were not for the Common Soldier, the common laborer that is compelled to work for a starvation wage, for I tell you again the hog of a Landlord gets his there is not enough left for the necessities if a man

Point of View

The editors of a collection of protest writings of the 1930s offer this introduction.

66The Great Depression, of course, did not begin with the collapse of the stock market in October 1929. For one thing, the prosperity enjoyed by many Americans in the twenties was not shared by Europeans. Europe spent the twenties first trying to restore the losses suffered as a result of World War I, and then trying to maintain the fiscal balance; it was a futile attempt . . . [This] had no more effect upon the optimism of America's leaders than did the cries of discontent which had for years been coming from rural America. America was prospering, and Europe was at peace; it was easy to ignore the signs of trouble.99

From *Years of Protest*, 1967

Brown Brothers

General Douglas MacArthur, above left, and his aide Dwight D. Eisenhower supervise federal troops (right), who use tear gas and bayonets in 1932 to clear the tent city set up by the Bonus Army. (MacArthur and Eisenhower would become leading commanders in World War II.) Were the Bonus Marchers dangerous radicals who needed to be driven from the capital?

Return to the Preview & Review on page 895.

UPI/Bettmann Newsphotos

has three or more children. . . . Oh for a few Statesmen, oh for but one statesman, as fearless as Abraham Lincoln, the amancipator who died for us. . . .[1] **99**

[1] From *Down and Out in the Depression: Letters from the "Forgotten Man,"* edited by Robert S. McElvaine

Then in July 1932 about 20,000 former soldiers marched on Washington to demonstrate before the Capitol. When Congress refused to change the law, some of the marchers settled down on vacant land on the edge of Washington. They put up a camp of tents and flimsy tar-paper shacks. They announced that they would not leave until the bonus was paid.

Hoover had opposed the bonus to begin with. Such giveaways threatened to destroy the "self-reliance" of the people, he said. He believed, wrongly as it turned out, that the Bonus Marchers were being led by dangerous radicals. When trouble broke out, Hoover ordered army units to assist police in driving out the veterans.

Troops commanded by General Douglas MacArthur went into action. Infantrymen backed by cavalry units and five tanks swiftly cleared the camp. No shots were fired and no one was killed. However, news film of steel-helmeted, rifle-bearing soldiers firing tear gas grenades at ragged, unarmed war veterans shocked millions of Americans. Hoover's popularity hit rock bottom. ▣

2. ROOSEVELT COMES TO POWER

Franklin D. Roosevelt

It is safe to say that in 1932 any Democratic presidential candidate could have defeated the Republican Hoover. Somewhere between 13 and 16 million workers were unemployed. The total income of all Americans had fallen from $87 billion in 1929 to $42 billion in 1932. All the shares of the stocks listed on the New York Stock Exchange were worth only a quarter of their value before the Great Crash.

The particular Democrat who profited from this situation was Franklin D. Roosevelt, the governor of New York. Roosevelt came from a wealthy family. He had graduated from Harvard College, studied law, and gone into politics. As we have seen, he had run for vice president in 1920 on the ticket with James M. Cox, who was defeated by Warren G. Harding.

The next year Roosevelt spent his usual vacation at his summer home in Campobello, Canada. One day in August 1921 he helped put out a brush fire while on an outing with his children. He returned home tired and chilled in his wet swimming suit. That night he burned with fever. Within a few days his legs were almost completely paralyzed. He had a severe case of polio. He recovered from the disease, but for the rest of his life he could walk only with the aid of metal braces and two canes. More often he was carried or used a wheelchair.

UPI/Bettmann Newsphotos

Preview & Review

Use these questions to guide your reading. Answer the questions after completing Section 2.
Understanding Issues, Events, & Ideas. Use the following words to trace Roosevelt's first moves to counter the depression: New Deal, relief, recovery, reform, Hundred Days, Bank Holiday, Federal Deposit Insurance Corporation, National Industrial Recovery Act, minimum wage, National Recovery Administration, Agricultural Adjustment Act, Tennessee Valley Authority, Federal Securities Act, Home Owner's Loan Corporation, Federal Emergency Relief Administration, Civil Works Authority, Civilian Conservation Corps.
1. Contrast the personalities of Herbert Hoover and Franklin Roosevelt.
2. How did the banking crisis turn out to be an advantage for the entire country?
3. What was the overall effect of the flood of laws passed during the Hundred Days?
Thinking Critically. Which do you think was the most important law passed during the Hundred Days? Why?

Well-wishers greet President Roosevelt at Warm Springs, Georgia. What words might you have used to describe the new president?

Roosevelt Comes to Power   903

Courtesy Vanity Fair, copyright 1934 (renewed 1962), Condé Nast Publications, Inc.

FEBRUARY 1934
PRICE 35 CENTS
CINE CONDE NAST
PUBLICATIONS, INC.

Vanity Fair, *a witty and popular magazine, offered this cover of FDR "breaking in" the rambunctious country in 1934. If the horse stands for the United States, how is Roosevelt doing?*

Roosevelt's usual high spirits sagged, but only briefly. He went on with his political career. In 1928, when Governor Alfred E. Smith of New York ran for president against Hoover, Roosevelt was chosen by the Democrats to run for governor. Hoover defeated Smith in the race for electoral votes in New York, but Roosevelt, the Democrat, was elected governor. Two years later he was reelected by a huge majority. This evidence of popular support won him the 1932 Democratic presidential nomination.

Roosevelt was almost the exact opposite of Hoover. Hoover was restrained, stiff, and by 1932, very glum. Roosevelt had a cheerful, relaxed, almost carefree personality. Indeed, in 1932 many observers thought he had more style than substance. He was no more radical than Hoover, but he was a much less rigid person. Hoover worked out careful theories and tried to apply them to the practical problems of government. Roosevelt mistrusted theories. Yet he was willing to apply any theory to any particular problem if there seemed a good chance it would work.

Roosevelt turned out to be a most popular political campaigner. He made excellent speeches. He had tremendous energy. Moreover, he was an optimist. At a time when most people were deeply depressed, his cheer encouraged and uplifted millions. The crowds that gathered when he campaigned seemed to inspire him as well. In November he defeated Hoover easily. His electoral majority was 472 to 59. The popular vote was 22.8 million to 15.8 million. The voters also gave the Democrats large majorities in both houses of Congress.

"Nothing to Fear but Fear Itself"

Roosevelt was elected in November, but he could not by law take his oath as president until March 4. Meanwhile, the economy seemed to drift downward aimlessly, like a falling leaf in a winter forest. Between December 1932 and February industrial production hit an all-time low. This, together with continuing news of bank failures, caused Americans to panic. Suddenly, in February, people all over the country began to rush fearfully to withdraw their savings from the banks. This banking panic forced even most of the soundest banks to close their doors.

The banking crisis turned out to be a great advantage for Roosevelt and indirectly for the entire country. It forced people to put politics aside and treat the depression as a great national emergency.

Inauguration Day in Washington was raw and damp. In this dark hour Roosevelt's speech came like a ray of summer sunshine. He said:

66 This great nation will endure as it has endured, will revive, and will prosper.

So, first of all, let me assert my firm belief that the only thing we have to fear is fear itself—nameless, unreasoning, unjustified terror which paralyzes needed efforts to convert retreat into advance. . . .

Happiness lies not in the mere possession of money; it lies in the joy of achievement, in the thrill of creative effort.

We face the arduous [hard] days that lie before us in the warm courage of national unity; with the clear consciousness of seeking old and precious moral values; with the clean satisfaction that comes from the stern performance of duty by old and young alike. . . .[1] **"**

Roosevelt spoke only generally about measures for fighting the depression. But he made his approach crystal clear. He was going to do something. "Action, and action now," was his theme. His first priority would be to put people back to work, he said.

The Hundred Days

In his inaugural address the president called upon Congress to meet in a special session on March 9 to deal with the emergency. From March 9 to June 16, when this special session ended, was 100 days. No one planned to have the session last exactly 100 days. The fact that it did dramatized how much that Congress accomplished.

In his campaign for president, Roosevelt had called for a **New Deal.** Roosevelt's New Deal had three general aims—relief, recovery, and reform. **Relief** came first and was aimed at all Americans in

The Bank Panic in 1933 brought lines of New Yorkers to see if their savings or deposits were safe in the American Union Bank. Even the soundest banks had to close their doors for protection. What event of the 1980s reminded many people of the panic?

[1]From *The Public Papers and Addresses, 1933* by Franklin D. Roosevelt

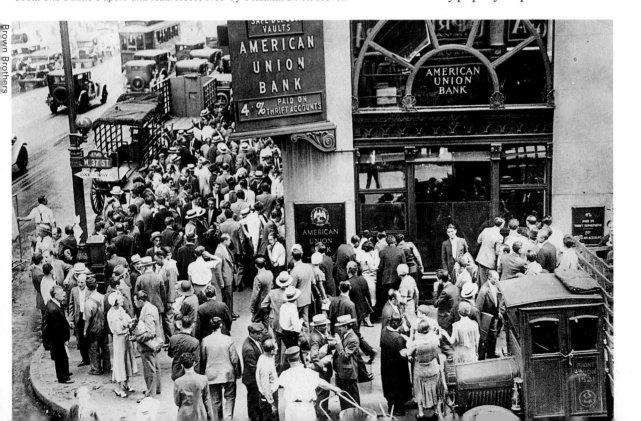

Brown Brothers

economic distress. **Recovery** would then spur the economy and get the country out of the depression. **Reform** would prevent another severe depression from happening. The flood of new laws passed during the **Hundred Days** had the effect of convincing people that old ways were indeed being tossed out, like a worn deck of cards. The country seemed to be making a fresh start.

Even before Congress met, Roosevelt declared a **Bank Holiday,** closing all the banks so that a general plan to protect the savings of the public could be developed. Congress then passed new banking laws, the most important being a measure which created the **Federal Deposit Insurance Corporation** (FDIC). The FDIC insured everyone's savings up to $5,000. Runs on banks stopped. Depositors knew that even if their bank failed, they would get their money back. Nothing did more than this measure to restore public confidence. As one of Roosevelt's advisers said:

> 66 The bank rescue of 1933 was probably the turning point of the Depression. When people were able to survive the shock of having all the banks closed, and then see the banks open up, with their money protected, there began to be confidence. Good times were coming. Most of the legislation that came after that didn't really help the public, the public helped itself, after it got confidence.
>
> It marked the revival of hope. . . .[1] 99

But new banking laws could not create jobs or cause farm prices to rise or stimulate business activity directly. So Congress quickly passed laws to accomplish these objectives. The most important and controversial measure was the **National Industrial Recovery Act** (NIRA).

The NIRA was supposed to stimulate private business by permitting manufacturers to cooperate with one another without fear of violating the antitrust laws. Firms in every industry were to draw up rules, called codes of fair competition. The firms were allowed to set limits on how much each could produce in order to avoid flooding markets with goods that could not be sold. They could also fix prices to avoid cutthroat competition.

In addition the codes provided certain benefits for workers. One was the right to freely join unions. Through these unions workers could bargain collectively with their employers. **Minimum wage** rates and maximum hours of work were also guaranteed under the codes. Each industrial code had to be approved, supervised, and enforced by the government through the **National Recovery Administration** (NRA). Roosevelt selected the enthusiastic Frances Perkins as his secretary of labor. She became the first woman cabinet member and an active advocate of workers' rights.

The Granger Collection, New York

VANITY FAIR

SEPTEMBER 1934
PRICE 35 CENTS
© THE CONDE NAST
PUBLICATIONS, INC.

In this Vanity Fair *cover, Uncle Sam is rescued by the Blue Eagle. Why was it a hopeful symbol?*

[1] From *Hard Times: An Oral History of the Great Depression* by Studs Terkel

Brown Brothers

Frances Perkins, the first woman cabinet member, greets workmen of Carnegie Steel. This is a far cry from the ugly scene of the Homestead Strike against Carnegie years earlier. How did the Great Depression bring a truce to labor, management, and government?

NRA officials made great efforts to persuade workers and employers to accept the new system. "We Do Our Part" was the slogan of the NRA. Its symbol was a picture of a Blue Eagle. Soon Blue Eagle stickers were being displayed in the windows of giant factories and small shops all over the country. This symbol was also printed on the labels of products of all kinds.

The NRA was expected to get the sluggish industrial economy moving again. Congress next dealt with the farm problem by passing the **Agricultural Adjustment Act** (AAA). During the depression farm prices had fallen even further than the prices of manufactured goods. The basic idea of the AAA was to push prices up by cutting down on the amount of crops produced.

Under this law the government rented some of the land that was normally planted in so-called basic crops, such as wheat, cotton, tobacco, and corn. No crops were planted on the land the government

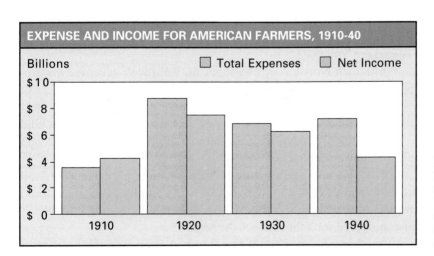

EXPENSE AND INCOME FOR AMERICAN FARMERS, 1910-40

Billings | ☐ Total Expenses | ☐ Net Income

LEARNING FROM GRAPHS. *The fortunes of American farmers had risen to new heights after the Great War, although expense still outdistanced income. What had happened to the difference between expense and income by 1940?*

UPI/Bettmann Newsphotos

Millie Wong, a ten-year-old girl in Brooklyn, received more Blue Eagles than any other individual. She wrote Washington to request ten Blue Eagles for her father, mother, and her seven sisters and brothers. She wanted to prove that all members of the Wong family were good citizens, although some were born in China and not naturalized. Her request was granted.

UPI/Bettmann Newsphotos

Senator George W. Norris of Nebraska was the "father" of the TVA, the program of flood control that brought electricity to the rural South.

rented. Farmers benefited in two ways. They got the rent money from the government, and they got higher prices for what they grew on the rest of their land because the total amount grown was smaller and therefore more valuable.

The AAA raised the money to rent the land taken out of production by what were called processing taxes. These were taxes paid by each business that processed, or prepared, the basic crops for general use—the miller who ground wheat into flour, the cotton manufacturer, and so on.

Congress also created the **Tennessee Valley Authority** (TVA) during the Hundred Days. This New Deal agency had no direct relation to the fight against the depression. Its "father" was Senator George W. Norris of Nebraska. During the 1920s, before the depression, Norris had fought efforts to get the government to sell to private interests the dam it had built at Muscle Shoals on the Tennessee River. He wanted the electricity produced at Muscle Shoals to be used as part of a broad plan to develop the resources of the entire Tennessee Valley.

Although Norris was a Republican, Roosevelt accepted his proposal. Under the TVA, Muscle Shoals was an efficient producer of electricity. The TVA had accurate information about how much electricity should cost consumers. The project therefore served as a kind of "yardstick" for measuring the fairness of prices charged by private electric power companies.

The TVA also manufactured fertilizers, built more dams for flood control, and developed a network of parks and lakes for recreation. It planted new forests and developed other conservation projects. It also provided jobs throughout the region.

Another achievement of the Hundred Days was the passage of

the **Federal Securities Act,** which regulated the way companies could issue and sell stock. Still another was the creation of the **Home Owners' Loan Corporation** (HOLC), which helped people who were unable to meet mortgage payments to hold on to their homes. Thousands of letters bombarded the president and officers of HOLC. Most showed tremendous loyalty and love for Roosevelt and begged for his help. One man wrote:

> ❝ I sincerely *hope* and *pray* you will come to my aid and help me save my home for my family, if I should loose it I don't know what I'll do as I have *no other place to go.* . . .
>
> I believe God will see us through some way but it has been the hardest thing I have had to go through, this may be His way so I'm writing to you asking and praying that you will do something to save our home.
>
> I am sure the President, if he only knew, would order that something be done, God Bless him. he is doing all he can to relieve the suffering and I am sure his name will go down in history among the other great men of our country. . . .[1]❞

These measures brought many benefits. Still, many people became homeless. Men left their families to find work. Whole families were forced out onto the street to search for shelter.

The greatest benefits of the New Deal came from what was done about the unemployed and the poor. The poor faced problems that

[1]From *Down and Out in the Great Depression: Letters from the "Forgotten Man,"* edited by Robert S. McElvaine

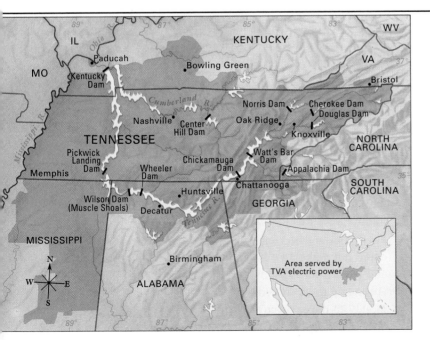

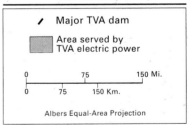

TENNESSEE VALLEY AUTHORITY

✐ Major TVA dam

▢ Area served by TVA electric power

| 0 | | 75 | | 150 Mi. |
| 0 | 75 | | 150 Km. | |

Albers Equal-Area Projection

LEARNING FROM MAPS. *One major aim of the Tennessee Valley Authority was flood control and river navigation. Which rivers were the heart of the TVA? The TVA stretched over vast areas in several southern states. What states were served by TVA electric power?*

Alexandre Hogue, *Drouth Stricken Area,* 1934, oil on canvas, Dallas Museum of Art, Dallas Art Association Purchase, 1945.6

Nature had seemed to smile upon the young nation in the 1830s. In the 1930s nature seemed particularly cruel. As times got harder, weather and even the land seemed to turn against the poor. Perhaps the hardest hit were the farmers of the high plains—the states from Texas and Oklahoma to South and North Dakota. This region rarely gets much rain. In the early 1930s almost none fell.

By 1934 the drought had become so bad that winds picked up powder-dry topsoil and blew it across the plains in dense, black clouds. The region came to be known as the Dust Bowl. It was impossible to grow anything on this shifting land.

Broke and discouraged, many Oklahoma farm families loaded

seemed almost overwhelming—no job, little food, no home. Yet many hoped and prayed that they could hold on to what they had and that better days were ahead. A woman wrote:

> Phila., Pa.
> November 26, 1934
>
> Honorable Franklin D. Roosevelt
> Washington, D.C.
> Dear Mr. President:
>
> I am forced to write to you because we find ourselves in *a very serious condition.* For the last three or four years we have had depression and *suffered* with my *family* and little children *severely.* . . . There has been unemployment in my house for more than three years. You can imagine that I and my family have suffered from lack of water supply in my house for more than two years. Last winter I did not have coal and the pipes burst in my house and therefore could not make heat in the house. Now winter is here again and we are suffering of cold, no water in the house, and we are facing to be forced out of the house, because I have no money to move or pay so much money as they want when after making settlement I am mother of little children, am

Silver Print, 12½ × 9⅞". Collection, The Museum of Modern Art, New York. Purchase.

into their secondhand Model T Fords and headed west toward California. There they became migrant workers, picking fruit, vegetables, cotton, and other crops. They followed the harvest in their overheated cars and spent their nights in roadside camps. Old people died alongside unfamiliar roads. Babies grew up hungry, their eyes big with suspicion.

One of the people who came to California was a young folk-

The human and physical consequences of the depression meet here. Alexandre Hogue painted "Drouth Stricken Area" with the thirsty cow, reduced to skin and bones, in the thin shadow of the windmill. The photograph of the migrant mother in California was taken in one quick ten-minute session by Dorothea Lange in 1936.

singer named Woodrow Wilson Guthrie, who arrived from Oklahoma in 1937. Californians

"needed more and more people to pick their fruits," Woody Guthrie said. "But they looked down for some reason on the people that came in there from other states to do that kind of work." The times were dangerous. "In most towns . . . it is a jailhouse offense to be unemployed," he wrote.

One of Woody Guthrie's songs put the plight of the migrant workers in this way:

California is a garden of Eden,
A paradise to live in or see.
But, believe it or not, you
*   won't find it so hot,*
If you ain't got the do-re-mi°[1]

°"do-re-mi" is money
[1]From "Do Re Mi," words and music by Woody Guthrie. TRO © copyright 1961 and 1963 Ludlow Music Inc., New York, N.Y. Used by permission.

TVA Information Office

A tenant farmer poses with his family during the Great Depression. Why would Americans of the 1830s have welcomed such a family?

Roosevelt Comes to Power 911

Brown Brothers

Civilian Conservation Corpsmen are clearing brush from scrubland in the western United States to lessen the risk of fire. Below is Harry Hopkins, a close friend of Roosevelt's, who conceived many of the attempts to remedy the Great Depression.

Culver Pictures

sick and losing my health, and we are eight people in the family, and where can I go when I don't have money because no one is working in my house. . . . Now I have *no money, no home* and *no wheres to go*. I beg of you to please help me and my family and little children for the sake of a sick mother and suffering family to give this your immediate attention so we will not be forced to move or put out on the street.

> *Waiting and Hoping that you will act quickly.*
> Thanking you very much I remain

Mrs. E.L.[1]

[1]From *Down and Out in the Great Depression: Letters from the "Forgotten Man,"* edited by Robert S. McElvaine

In response to such suffering Roosevelt rejected Hoover's ideas about what the federal government could and could not do about unemployment and poverty. Soon after Roosevelt took office, the **Federal Emergency Relief Administration** was created. This agency was headed by Harry Hopkins, a New York social worker. It distributed $500 million in federal grants among state organizations that cared for the poor. The following fall and winter another New Deal agency, the **Civil Works Authority,** also headed by Hopkins, found jobs for more than 4 million people out of work.

During the Hundred Days, Congress also created the **Civilian Conservation Corps** (CCC). This agency put unemployed young men from poor families to work on various conservation projects. CCC workers lived in camps run by the army. They cleared brush, planted trees, built small dams, and performed dozens of other useful tasks. The CCC provides a good example of how swiftly New Deal measures were put into effect. The law that created the program passed Congress on March 31, 1933. By July there were 300,000 corpsmen at work in 1,300 camps all over the country.

Return to the Preview & Review on page 903.

912   THE GREAT DEPRESSION AND THE NEW DEAL

3. THE NEW DEAL

Why the New Deal Was Popular

The New Deal was very popular. Democrats increased their majorities in Congress in the 1934 elections. When Franklin D. Roosevelt ran for a second term in 1936, against Alfred Landon of Kansas, he won every state in the Union except Maine and Vermont. He did so despite the fact that New Deal legislation had not ended the depression. Unemployment remained extremely high. Industrial production picked up, but only very slowly.

The personality of FDR, as the newspapers came to call him, had a great deal to do with the success of the New Deal. He was an optimist. His hope for better conditions was always cheerful and encouraging, but never silly or foolish. This excerpt from a popular song of 1936 tells how the people felt about their president:

❝ Just hand me my old Martin°, for soon I will be
    startin'
Back to dear old Charleston, far away.
Since Roosevelt's been reelected, we'll not be
    neglected.
We've got Franklin D. Roosevelt back again.
No more breadlines we're glad to say, the donkey won
    election day,
No more standing in the blowing, snowing rain;
He's got things in full sway, we're all working and
    getting our pay,
We've got Franklin D. Roosevelt back again.[1] **❞**

Roosevelt had a way of reaching people that was truly remarkable. He spoke frequently on the radio. These **fireside chats** were not speeches in the usual sense. The president seemed to come right into the room with his listeners. He explained what problems lay before the nation, how he proposed to deal with them, and what people could do to help him.

Roosevelt made great use of experts. His close advisers, mostly college professors, were known as the **Brain Trust.** Yet ordinary citizens never got the idea that Roosevelt was listening to theories that were not practical and down to earth.

The president never put all the nation's eggs in one basket. This made sense to most people. The economic mess was so complicated that no single plan or project was likely to untangle it. Roosevelt's way was to experiment with many things at once. This created the impression that the best minds in the country were hard at work

°A brand of guitar
[1]From "Franklin D. Roosevelt's Back Again," in *This Singing Land*, compiled and edited by Irwin Silber

Use these questions to guide your reading. Answer the questions after completing Section 3.
Understanding Issues, Events, & Ideas. Use the following words to explain the New Deal: fireside chat, Brain Trust, Rural Electrification Administration, Works Progress Administration, National Youth Administration, Second New Deal, Wagner Labor Relations Act, National Labor Relations Board, Social Security Act.

1. How did the New Deal help relieve much of the human suffering caused by the depression?
2. On what grounds did the Supreme Court rule that some New Deal measures were unconstitutional?
3. How did Roosevelt change his tactics in his battle against the depression?

Thinking Critically. Imagine that you are the owner of a large corporation in 1935. Write a letter to President Roosevelt explaining why you think that the New Deal will hurt your business. Cite specific measures in your letter.

COMPOSING AN ESSAY

You are often asked to prepare a written report or to answer an essay question on a test. An essay is a short composition on a specific topic. It should always contain three parts: an introduction, a body of information, and a closing.

You have already learned the preliminary steps to composing an essay: Writing About History (page xxiv) and composing paragraphs (page 806). Once you have mastered that strategy, the next step is the actual writing of an essay.

How to Compose an Essay

Before learning the steps for analzying economic statistics, review Composing Paragraphs on page 806. Then to compose an essay, follow these steps.

1. **Focus on the topic.** Make sure you understand what you are to write about. The topic should be broad enough to provide enough material for an essay but not too broad to be dealt with in a short composition.
2. **Organize your ideas.** Remember that your essay should have three parts. Organize your thoughts accordingly.
3. **Compose your essay.** Clearly state your topic in the introduction. Present your evidence and supporting details in the body of the essay. Your closing should briefly sum up what you have said in the essay.

Applying the Strategy

Suppose you were given an assignment to write an essay according to the following directive:

Explain briefly what the aims and outcomes of the three parts of the New Deal were.

Your first task is to identify the topic of your essay: *the aims and outcomes of the three parts of the New Deal.* You might organize your thoughts in a manner similar to the following outline:

The New Deal
I. Introduction
II. Three Parts of New Deal
  a. Relief
    1. Aims
    2. Outcomes
  b. Recovery
    1. Aims
    2. Outcomes
  c. Reform
    1. Aims
    2. Outcomes
III. Closing

For independent practice, see Practicing the Strategy on page 933.

Brown Brothers

President Roosevelt, originator of the "fireside chat" by radio, prepares for his message to be transmitted on all the major networks.

Point of View

In Robert Caro's biography of Lyndon Johnson, Caro discusses the Texas Hill Country and its poverty during the New Deal.

"The people of the Hill Country were grateful for what the New Deal had done for them; little as had been the help they realized from its programs, it was far more help than anyone had ever given them before. But their lives were not changed by the New Deal. The Hill Country was a country in which there was unbelievably little cash.

In 1937, as in 1932, the Johnson City High School nearly missed basketball season—because the school could not afford a basketball; after several weeks of fundraising, the *News* reported that 'collections are coming in too slow on the basketball.'"

Robert A. Caro,
The Path to Power, 1982

fighting the depression. They were not winning an immediate victory. But what seemed important was that *something* was being done.

The New Deal was also popular because it made large groups of people feel that the government was genuinely trying to improve their lives. This had little to do with the depression itself. For example, workers in industries like steel and automobiles were not organized in 1933. It was not the policy of the federal government to promote unions, but the spirit of the New Deal encouraged many workers to join unions. Roosevelt certainly wanted workers to be treated more fairly and with greater respect by their employers than had been common in the past.

President Roosevelt's greatest sympathy was for farmers. New Deal farm legislation was aimed at increasing their shrunken incomes and improving the quality of rural life. The **Rural Electrification Administration,** which brought electricity to remote farm districts, is a good illustration of how the lives of farmers could be improved.

Most important, the New Deal relieved much of the human suffering caused by the depression. The Civil Works Administration, and later the **Works Progress Administration** (WPA), found useful work for millions of idle men and women. Most of the jobs were of

The New Deal   915

Above is the work of a muralist in the Federal Arts Project. Below, many students had access to libraries for the first time under this WPA project. The advantages of such projects to society are numerous.

the pick-and-shovel type, but not all of them. Harry Hopkins insisted that the full skills of the unemployed be used whenever possible.

In the city of Boston, for example, New Deal work projects included building a subway, expanding the East Boston Airport, and improving a municipal golf course. Other Boston relief workers taught in nursery schools, cataloged books in the Boston Public Library, and read to blind people. College students employed by the **National Youth Administration** graded papers and did office chores in their schools. Singers performed in hospitals. Musicians gave concerts. Troupes of actors put on plays, including a revival of *Uncle Tom's Cabin*. Artists designed posters and painted murals on the walls of schools and libraries.

Criticism of the New Deal

The laws passed during the Hundred Days greatly increased the power of the federal government and particularly of the president. Many day-to-day decisions had to be made under these laws. The president and his appointees seemed the logical persons to make them. New Deal laws are full of such phrases as "The president is authorized . . ." and "The secretary of agriculture shall have the power to . . ." and "The Board shall have power, in the name of the United States of America, to . . ."

Some people found this trend alarming. Business leaders in particular objected to the new restrictions placed on how they conducted their affairs. The New Deal would destroy the free enterprise system, they charged. They therefore brought suits against the government in the courts, claiming that the new laws were unconstitutional.

In 1935 and 1936 the Supreme Court ruled that the National Industrial Recovery Act and the Agricultural Adjustment Act were indeed unconstitutional. The Court also declared unconstitutional some important state laws regulating economic affairs, such as a New York minimum-wage law. In the NIRA case, *Schechter v. U.S.* (1935), the Court decided unanimously that Congress had delegated too much of its law-making power to the boards that watched over industrial codes. In *U.S. v. Butler* it ruled that the AAA processing tax was not really a tax but a method of regulating farm production.

Conservatives charged that the New Deal was trying to do too much. Other critics argued that the government was not doing enough. As time passed, the excitement of the Hundred Days disappeared. Perhaps prosperity was "just around the corner," but the corner never seemed to be reached.

Courtesy of The Library of Congress

OLD RELIABLE!

Point of View

Roosevelt's biographer reminds us that the president *was* popular even when the New Deal was not.

"The decisive fact of 1938 was that most people *thought* Roosevelt had lost popular favor to a greater extent than he really had. . . . The popular attitude toward Roosevelt was marked by a deep ambivalence. On the one hand, almost everyone liked him as a person. Asked, "On the whole, do you like or dislike his personality?" eight out of ten Americans in the spring of 1938 answered "like" to only one who answered "dislike." Negroes, the poor generally, labor, the unemployed were enthusiastically for Roosevelt the person. The Southwest as a section delivered a resounding 98 percent for him, and other sections were not far behind. . . ."

From *Roosevelt: The Lion and the Fox,* James MacGregor Burns, 1956

With a wave of his wand, Roosevelt performs his trick "Old Reliable." What is this magic rabbit expected to do? Why does the cartoonist say it never fails?

All, UPI/Bettmann Newsphotos

Three very strong critics of President Roosevelt were, from left, Huey Long of Louisiana; Father Charles Coughlin; and Dr. Francis E. Townshend. Which one of their ideas is with us to this day?

Some people who had originally supported Roosevelt now turned against him. One was Senator Huey Long of Louisiana, who ruled like a king in his home state. The "Kingfish," as he was called, had great pity for the little person. He claimed that the president had become a tool of Wall Street investors. Long wanted to tax away all incomes of more than $1 million a year. With that money, he said, everyone would be guaranteed a large enough income to own a house, a car, and everything else needed to live decently. Long's Share-Our-Wealth organization had over 4.6 million members in 1935.

Francis Townshend, a California doctor, called for granting Old-Age Revolving Pensions to every American over 60. He attracted a very large following. A Catholic priest, Father Charles E. Coughlin, spoke to millions in his weekly radio broadcasts. He criticized various New Deal programs. Eventually he made bitter personal attacks on President Roosevelt.

There were even critics within the Roosevelt administration. Some were complaining by 1935 and 1936 that the president was not fighting the depression vigorously enough. They wanted the government to spend more money in order to stimulate the economy and put more people to work.

The Second New Deal

Roosevelt responded to the criticisms of the mid-1930s by proposing more reforms. We call his new program the **Second New Deal.**

After the Supreme Court struck down the National Industrial Recovery Act, Congress passed the **Wagner Labor Relations Act** of 1935. This law again gave labor unions the right to organize and bargain collectively. It set up a **National Labor Relations Board** (NLRB) to run union elections and settle disputes. When a majority of the workers in the plant voted to join a union in an NLRB election,

Courtesy of The Library of Congress

How could Roosevelt not have been a favorite for editorial cartoonists? "New Deal Remedies" shows how Roosevelt was able to try another approach if the first failed, but it hardly meant to pay him a compliment. How many remedies on the table can you identify?

that union became the representative of all the workers in the plant, not merely of those who had voted to join it.

In 1935 Congress also passed the **Social Security Act.** This law set up a system of old-age insurance, paid for partly by workers and partly by their employers. This system paid retired people 65 years of age and over a pension. The amount of the pension was based on the number of years a worker had paid into the system. The act provided for unemployment insurance too. This supplied money for workers who had lost their jobs and were looking for new ones. Many workers, such as farmhands and maids, were not covered by the original Social Security Act. Nevertheless, the law marked a great turning point for American society.

Other laws passed in 1935 included a "soak-the-rich" income tax and an act regulating banks more strictly. Another law was aimed at breaking up combinations among electric light and gas companies.

These measures marked a change of tactics in Roosevelt's battle against the depression. In 1933 he had tried to unite all groups and classes. By 1936 he had given up on holding the support of big business and rich people. During his campaign for reelection he attacked these people, whom he called "an enemy within our gates." He and his campaign managers turned instead to the labor movement; to women voters; and to blacks, Hispanics, and other such groups for support. Their efforts were successful. As we have already noted, Roosevelt was reelected by a landslide in 1936.

Return to the Preview & Review on page 913.

The New Deal   919

Use these questions to guide your reading. Answer the questions after completing Section 4.
Understanding Issues, Events, & Ideas. Use the following words to describe some of the effects of the New Deal: Black Cabinet, Urban League, Supreme Court Reform Plan, Commodity Credit Corporation, Fair Labor Standards Act, industrial union, Congress of Industrial Organizations, welfare state, deficit spending, federal deficit.

1. What accounted for the political shift that occurred among black voters between 1932 and 1936?
2. How did many New Deal programs discriminate against blacks and Hispanics either directly or indirectly? Why did many blacks and Hispanics continue to support the New Deal?
3. Why did the Supreme Court Reform Plan produce a bitter fight?
4. How did labor unions change during the New Deal?

Thinking Critically. 1. Imagine you are a young black artist in 1934. Write a diary entry explaining why you want to move to Harlem. 2. Do you think President Roosevelt took on too much power and responsibility during the New Deal years? Why or why not?

4. EFFECTS OF THE NEW DEAL

African Americans Vote Democratic

In 1936 a majority of African American voters cast their ballots for Roosevelt and other Democratic candidates. This marked one of the most significant political shifts of the 20th century. Before the New Deal most blacks had supported "the party of Lincoln." The Republicans had not done much to win or hold the loyalty of blacks since Lincoln's day. The southerners who dominated the Democratic party had usually offered blacks nothing at all.

During the 1920s African Americans lost many of the gains they had won during the Great World War when their labor had been so much in demand. The revived Ku Klux Klan was a constant source of worry. The migration of southern blacks to northern cities continued. Indeed, African Americans were the immigrants of the 1920s. They replaced the European immigrants, whose numbers had declined because of the new immigration laws.

So many African Americans moved to northern cities that they were crowded into slums, or ghettos. Harlem, in New York City,

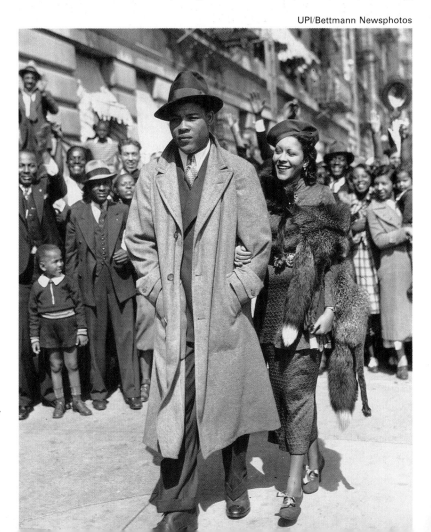

UPI/Bettmann Newsphotos

On his honeymoon with his wife, Marva, Joe Louis, the world heavyweight champion, strolls the streets of Harlem. Most blacks, like these onlookers, were proud rather than envious of his show of prosperity.

National Museum of American Art/Art Resource

One of the gentlest views of home and family life during the Harlem Renaissance is evident in "The Janitor Who Paints" by Palmer Hayden.

was the best known of the black ghettos. By 1930 165,000 blacks were crowded into Harlem's run-down row houses and decaying tenements.

Like the earlier immigrants, most black newcomers were able to get only the dirtiest, most exhausting, and lowest-paid work. Most labor unions shut out black members. This kept blacks from working in industries and crafts where organized labor was strong.

Yet, as you have read, even in segregated sections like Harlem, blacks were able to improve their situation. In such places they were actually the majority. They did not have to stand aside for white people. They could vote and elect black officials. Blacks came to have considerable influence on the larger politics of the city and state. They became more self-confident and more conscious of their rights.

Black writers, musicians, actors, and journalists had found audiences in Harlem. Black doctors and lawyers and other professionals practiced and prospered too. New York City blacks had experienced the Harlem Renaissance in the 1920s. Harlem had become the black intellectual and cultural capital of the nation. And it remained so throughout the depression. Ambitious young blacks from other states moved there, believing Harlem was the best place to develop their talents.

However, the Great Depression took much of the glitter from this revival of confidence. It struck African Americans with cruel force, as it did Hispanic Americans. As always in hard times, these workers were "the last hired and the first fired." By 1932 more than 30 percent of all black and Hispanic workers were unemployed.

Still, most African Americans voted the Republican ticket in 1932. In Chicago, for example, Hoover got 76 percent of the black vote. In Cincinnati he got 71 percent. But in 1936 most blacks in Chicago and Cincinnati voted for Roosevelt.

Black Support of the New Deal

Today it is hard to understand why African Americans and Hispanic Americans found Roosevelt and the New Deal so attractive. Many of the most important New Deal programs did little or nothing to help them. Most of the NRA industrial codes permitted employers to pay lower wages to black and Hispanic workers than to whites. New Deal farm policy badly hurt black tenant farmers and share-croppers in the South. The AAA payments went to land *owners*. They were paid for taking tobacco land out of production. The ten-ants and sharecroppers who had farmed these acres lost their jobs and often their homes as well. It did nothing to help Hispanic farmers in the Southwest. Unemployed blacks and Hispanics in all parts of the country rarely got a full share of federal relief money or jobs.

The social security program did not discriminate directly against African Americans or Hispanics. However, it left out farm laborers and household workers. The millions of blacks and Hispanics who did work of this kind received no share of the new pension and unemployment benefits.

Yet African Americans and Hispanic Americans liked the New Deal. Many became enthusiastic admirers of Franklin Roosevelt. Thousands of black and Hispanic parents in the 1930s named babies after the president. The reasons for such strong feelings are best understood by keeping in mind how white society treated these groups at that time. This is another example of the need to use historical imagination. For example, the Civilian Conservation Corps camps in the South were segregated. If black youths had *not* been sent to separate camps when they joined the CCC, the program could not have functioned in the southern states. More important, the program almost certainly would not have been created by Congress. Blacks realized this. Most blacks therefore accepted the segregation of the camps as a lesser evil than being without work.

Most African Americans and Hispanic Americans thought the

main point was that they were included in New Deal programs and that some effort to treat them fairly was being made by important officials. Because so many of the unemployed and poor were black or Hispanic, WPA and the federal relief programs were particularly important to them. President Roosevelt ordered state relief officials not to "discriminate . . . because of race or religion or politics" in distributing government aid. This order was not always obeyed, but Harry Hopkins and other key WPA officials tried hard to enforce it.

With the approval of Roosevelt, Harold L. Ickes, the secretary of the interior, appointed Clark Foreman to his staff. Ickes instructed Foreman to seek out qualified blacks and try to get them jobs in the Interior Department and other government bureaus. Foreman also served as a kind of watchdog, checking on cases of racial discrimination in various New Deal programs. Among distinguished African Americans whose government service began in New Deal agencies were Robert Weaver, who became the first head of the Department of Housing and Urban Development in the 1960s, and William Hastie, later a federal judge. These appointees made up what became known as Roosevelt's **Black Cabinet.**

National Portrait Gallery

One of the most prominent members of the Black Cabinet was Mary McLeod Bethune. She was the 15th child of former slaves. Some of her brothers and sisters had been sold away from her parents before the Civil War. Mary McLeod was fiercely independent. After completing her education in South Carolina, she taught at several schools for blacks in the South. In 1898 she married Albertus Bethune, also a teacher. She founded a school of her own in Florida during the Progressive Era.

In 1936 Mary McLeod Bethune was put in charge of the Office of Minority Affairs in the National Youth Administration. As with male black officials, her role was broader than her title indicated. She always had access to President Roosevelt. During the New Deal period, she later recalled, she conferred with him privately about six or seven times a year.

In a way their relationship points up the strengths and weaknesses of Roosevelt's way of dealing with his black supporters. His intentions were good, but he was unwilling to take the political risk. Once Mary Bethune asked him to act quickly on some important matter. He refused. "Mrs. Bethune, if we must do that now, we'll hurt our progress," he said. "We must do this thing stride by stride."

Mary McLeod Bethune worked strongly for equal rights for African Americans and other groups. She served as president of the National Association of Colored Women. She was a vice president of the two most important organizations in the United States that worked for racial equality—the NAACP and the **Urban League.** Yet she was not offended by Roosevelt's attitude. Indeed, she admired him enormously. Her reaction tells us a great deal about racial attitudes and the problems faced by minorities at that time.

Mary McLeod Bethune shows quiet dignity in this portrait by Betsy Groves Reyneau. What did Roosevelt think of Mary Bethune?

Effects of the New Deal   923

White House Historical Association

Eleanor Roosevelt, the first lady, had worked to improve the treatment of African Americans long before her husband became president. And no prominent white person in the United States worked harder than she during the New Deal in the struggle for racial equality. She was also a leader in women's rights organizations, a promoter of consumer protection, a friend of the working people, and a believer in the rights of young people. She constantly reminded and pleaded with her husband to remember the needs of the people who made up those groups.

As a young woman Eleanor Roosevelt attended exclusive private schools and spent holidays with her rich cousins in high society. Her uncle, President Theodore Roosevelt, gave her in marriage to her handsome distant cousin Franklin.

Eleanor had decided early to prepare herself for a life of social service. This was difficult for her. She was a shy person. She had five children to raise. She saw her husband through his crippling polio. But in the 1920s she began to timidly speak in public.

During the Great Depression Eleanor Roosevelt traveled throughout the country to find out the mood of the people. "You must be my eyes and ears," the president had told her. She seemed to be everywhere. A famous cartoon of the late 1930s showed two grime-covered coal miners looking up from their work as one said to the other, "For gosh sakes, here comes Mrs. Roosevelt."

The End of the New Deal

Despite his great victory in the election of 1936, President Roosevelt feared that much of the important New Deal legislation would be declared unconstitutional by the Supreme Court. These laws had greatly increased the powers of the federal government. The more conservative justices of the Supreme Court believed, for instance, that Congress had no right under the Constitution to control the negotiations of workers and their employers. Nor could it force workers to contribute to an old-age pension fund without their consent.

Roosevelt was not a constitutional expert. He felt that the election had proved that the people were behind the New Deal. Necessary reforms should not be held up by technical legal questions. He therefore proposed that Congress enable him to increase the number of Supreme Court justices. He would fill these new seats with his appointees. That way he could be sure that a majority of the Court would uphold key New Deal laws. This **Supreme Court Reform Plan** of 1937 produced a bitter, long, drawn-out fight. Roosevelt had misjudged the attitude of Congress and the public. The plan seemed to most people to threaten the independence of the Court. Roosevelt tried hard, but Congress rejected the plan.

However, the justices who had opposed New Deal laws eventually died or resigned. Roosevelt then appointed justices favorable to his program to replace them. The Wagner Labor Relations Act,

Brown Brothers

This 1937 cartoon recalls the biblical warning "It is easier for a camel to go through the eye of a needle than for a rich man to enter the Kingdom of God." What is the political inspiration for this cartoon?

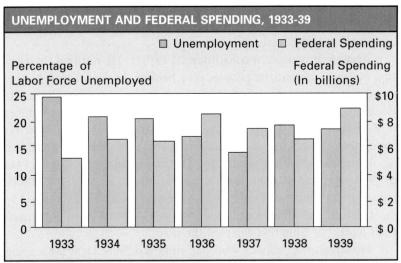

UNEMPLOYMENT AND FEDERAL SPENDING, 1933-39

☐ Unemployment ☐ Federal Spending

Percentage of Labor Force Unemployed

Federal Spending (In billions)

Source: *Historical Statistics of the United States*

LEARNING FROM GRAPHS. *Perhaps better than any other example, the results of New Deal programs showed the effects of government spending on employment. What happened to unemployment as government spending increased? Why do you think this happened? What happened to unemployment between 1937 and 1938? Why?*

the Social Security Act, and all other New Deal laws attacked in the courts were eventually declared to be constitutional. Nevertheless, the Court fight was a serious setback for Roosevelt.

Another setback soon followed. Roosevelt had never understood modern economics. When he was running for president in 1932, he had criticized President Hoover for spending federal money recklessly and unbalancing the budget. Roosevelt had never given up the hope of cutting government expenses and eventually reducing the national debt.

During 1936 and early 1937 the economy had been gradually improving. In June 1937 Roosevelt therefore decided to cut back sharply on federal money spent for relief.

The result was to bring the recovery to a sudden stop. Business activity fell off sharply. Unemployment increased. This recession in 1937 and 1938 was deeply discouraging. Just when prosperity appeared to be *really* around the corner, things turned again for the worse. Was the Great Depression going to last forever?

Roosevelt quickly agreed to increase government spending again. Congress provided money for a big new public works program to pick up the economy. At about this time Congress also passed a new Agricultural Adjustment Act. This established the **Commodity Credit Corporation.** It provided that when prices were low, producers of wheat, cotton, and certain other crops could store their crops in government warehouses instead of selling them. The Corporation would lend them money for their crops in storage.

When prices rose, the farmers could take their crops out of storage, sell them, and pay back the loans. This new system was called the ever-normal granary. (A granary is a storehouse for grain and other farm crops.) The new system raised prices by keeping surpluses off the market. Then, in years of bad harvests, there would be reserves to prevent shortages.

Another important law passed in 1938 officially outlawed child labor. This measure was the **Fair Labor Standards Act.** It also set the length of a normal work week at 40 hours and established a national minimum wage. Many New Dealers were uneasy with this law. It contained many loopholes "protecting" particular industries such as farming and family-operated businesses from having to meet "fair standards." Still, the principles the law established were important. Eventually most of the loopholes were closed.

The Fair Labor Standards Act was the last important New Deal law. In 1939 a new world war broke out in Europe. As during the Great World War (which now became known as World War I), European purchases caused the American economy to pick up.

Significance of the New Deal

All laws passed by Congress during the New Deal and all the new agencies and boards did not end the Great Depression. Why then is the New Deal considered so important? One reason is that it produced a revolution in relations between workers and their employers.

Under the National Recovery Administration and then under the National Labor Relations Board, industrial workers formed strong

John L. Lewis

national unions. The old-fashioned AFL unions had been organized along craft lines. Carpenters were in one union, plumbers in another, machinists in a third, and so on. This system made organizing the workers of a large industry, such as steel or rubber or farm machinery, very difficult. The New Deal laws encouraged workers to form new **industrial unions.** Industrial unions represented all the workers in a particular industry, regardless of their specialty. These unions joined together in a **Congress of Industrial Organizations** (CIO), which soon rivaled the AFL in importance.

There were some bitter strikes during the New Deal. In 1937 workers staged "sit-down" strikes in which they took over plants and refused to leave until their demands were met. New Deal legislation protected workers' rights and established orderly methods of settling labor-management disputes. Labor became a force that manufacturers could neither ignore nor hold back.

Culver Pictures

Vanity Fair, Copyright © 1935, 1963 by the Condé Nast Publications, Inc.

In Jonathan Swift's famous satire Gulliver's Travels, *Captain Lemuel Gulliver is staked to the ground by tiny people called Lilliputians. The same fate has here befallen Uncle Sam. New Deal agencies form the bonds, so we may assume that the artist thought the 'alphabet soup' of the New Deal had become a burden.*

Labor became a force in politics too. Unions made contributions to candidates for public office. Union leaders campaigned for candidates who supported policies favorable to organized labor. Union lobbyists put pressure on Congress to pass pro-labor legislation.

The New Deal also created what we think of as the **welfare state.** The popularity of New Deal relief programs and programs to create jobs was so great that it was impossible to depend only on state and local agencies after the depression was over. After the New Deal nearly all people agreed that the federal government ought to do whatever was necessary to advance and protect the general welfare. Later Republican administrations accepted this idea as enthusiastically as the Democrats, although Ronald Reagan, once a supporter and admirer of Roosevelt, was unrelenting in his efforts to dismantle much of the legacy of the New Deal.

Increasing the power of the federal government meant that state and local governments had less power. It also meant that the federal government had more control over individuals and over private organizations. Looking back, most Americans lost some freedom. Federal agencies became involved in more and more aspects of life. This seems to have been a necessary price to pay if such a complex society was to function smoothly. Still, the loss was large.

The New Deal years also saw a shift in the balance of power within the federal government. Congress came to have less power as the presidency grew stronger. Ever since it created the Interstate Commerce Commission in 1887, Congress had relied on special agencies and boards to carry out and enforce complicated laws. Since the presidents appointed the members of these organizations, the White House had gained more power and influence.

Under Franklin Roosevelt this trend became an avalanche. The crisis atmosphere of the times encouraged Congress to put more responsibility on the shoulders of Roosevelt and his appointees. Dozens of new agencies, each known by its initials, such as NRA, AAA, TVA, CCC, and NLRB, made up the confusing "alphabet soup" of the New Deal.

Roosevelt's great power and remarkable personal popularity made the presidency the strongest force in the government. At the time most liberals considered this both necessary and desirable. Conservatives such as Herbert Hoover were greatly alarmed by this trend. We shall see in a later chapter that both liberals and conservatives eventually changed their attitudes.

One more change that resulted from the New Deal was not fully clear until a number of years later. Economists and political leaders learned from their experiences during the Great Depression that the economy could be stimulated by unbalancing the federal budget.

The normal reaction of people during depressions had always been to cut down on their expenses. Most ordinary citizens believed that the government should also economize in hard times.

The long depression of the 1930s demonstrated that government economizing only made things worse. When the government spent more, even more than it received in taxes, called **deficit spending,** it put money into the pockets of citizens. When people spent this money, they encouraged producers to increase output. Indirectly they were causing employers to hire more workers. This was soon fairly obvious. However, most economists and political leaders hesitated early in the New Deal era to carry the technique far enough. Roosevelt's decision to reduce spending in 1937 illustrates this point very well. Greater government spending would probably have ended the depression sooner.

After their experience with unbalanced budgets during the Second World War, most governments got over their fear of the **federal deficit** which resulted from deficit spending. Everyone learned this lesson of the Great Depression. However, as we also shall see in a later chapter, attitudes on this subject would once again change with the passage of time. 🖳

Return to the Preview & Review on page 920.

Effects of the New Deal   929

LINKING HISTORY & GEOGRAPHY

DUST FROM THE GREENHOUSE

Half a century ago huge areas of the Great Plains blew away, leaving in the wake enormous human suffering and untold damage to the land. Many geographers and scientists wonder if we are heading in that direction again.

Breadbasket of America

1. Why had the Great Plains become a great farming region?

At the beginning of the 1900s the Great Plains was a region just starting to blossom. Rain fell in abundance, and farming techniques allowed farmers to turn the fields into the "breadbasket of America." No one foresaw a coming drought even though the region had had a history of drought and dust for centuries, even before the land was plowed. Indeed, many had come to believe that the more the land was plowed, the greater would be the rainfall.

Farmers poured into the region. The soil was broken, and just as forecasted, rain fell and wheat flourished. In the Texas panhandle some 82,000 acres had been planted in wheat in 1909. Twenty years later nearly 2 million acres were lush with ripening wheat.

This seeming miracle of agriculture was made possible by the tractor. Tractors enabled farmers to cultivate more and more of the grassland. As they moved westward, they came dangerously closer to the edges of the desert region. The plow that the tractor pulled pulverized the soil into powder. This to most farmers appeared ideal. They thought the layer of dust over the top of a hard-packed base would keep the moisture in the soil from evaporating. The tragedy of this, as we look back, is that it seemed to work. So by 1930 a layer of dust covered 5 million acres of wheat land stretching from Montana and the Dakotas in the north to Texas.

The Dust Bowl

2. What caused the Dust Bowl of the 1930s?

There have been many theories about the causes of the Dust Bowl of the 1930s. Certainly drought and wind were major physical factors. But they were aided by people and their greed.

Into the 1930s the rains continued to fall and the wheat thrived. In 1931 many plains farmers harvested as much as 50 bushels an acre. Then came the day of reckoning. Once-dependable rains suddenly stopped. Drought began to spread over the land. From 1933 to 1936, 20 states set records for dryness. (Those records still stand today.) Wheat withered. The carpeting of dust that covered the landscape was no longer held in place by moisture and a dense mantle of wheat. Dry winds lifted the dust from the fields in great clouds that swept across the sky.

This dust was so dense that people couldn't see. They had to string ropes from their barns to their houses to keep from getting lost in the swirling dust. It seemed like the whole landscape was on the move. Dust seemed to infiltrate everything. It covered dishes inside closed kitchen cabinets. It had to be scooped out of bathtubs before bathing. People slept with damp cloths over their faces to keep from choking.

Lessons of the Past

3. What can we learn from the tragedy of the Dust Bowl of the 1930s?

There are many lessons to be learned from that 1930s experience if we are to prevent its recurrence in the future. In the more than 50 years since those terrible days a great deal has been learned about managing land in areas subject to drought. Today's plows dig deeply into the soil, breaking it into large clods. This keeps the topsoil from blowing away. Marginal lands are not plowed. Many farmers do not plow at all but drill their seed into soil that is still covered by the stubble of last year's crop. Some plains farmers feel their techniques will prevent another dust bowl.

Many geographers disagree. The problem in the future, they admit, may not come from either the farmers or their agricultural practices. Rather, it is more likely to come from changes in the earth's atmosphere, changes that in the 1990s are well underway. The cause of these changes is the greenhouse effect.

The greenhouse effect is the name given to the process by which natural and humanmade gases trap solar heat in the earth's atmosphere. The process works like a greenhouse. In a greenhouse the sun's rays penetrate the glass but the glass keeps the heat from escaping. The sun's rays penetrate the earth's atmosphere like they do the glass of a greenhouse and strike the

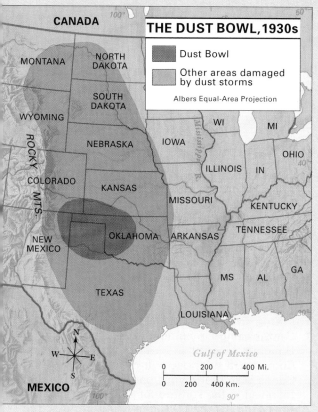

THE DUST BOWL, 1930s

Dust Bowl

Other areas damaged by dust storms

Albers Equal-Area Projection

CANADA

MONTANA

NORTH DAKOTA

SOUTH DAKOTA

WYOMING

ROCKY MTS.

NEBRASKA

IOWA

WI

MI

OHIO

ILLINOIS

IN

COLORADO

KANSAS

MISSOURI

KENTUCKY

TENNESSEE

NEW MEXICO

OKLAHOMA

ARKANSAS

Mississippi R.

TEXAS

MS

AL

GA

LOUISIANA

Gulf of Mexico

MEXICO

N
W E
S

0   200   400 Mi.

0   200   400 Km.

continues. Summers will be hotter and drier than they are today. Crops will wilt in the fields. Many areas will become unproductive. Can nothing be done? The answer is decidedly *yes,* if people are willing to pay the price.

The first and most useful step is to eliminate the production and use of chlorofluorocarbons (CFCs). CFCs are used primarily in air-conditioners and fast-food containers. In the atmosphere they trap 10,000 times as much heat as carbon dioxide. In 1990 President Bush called an international conference on CFCs. Most of the world nations agreed to totally stop the production of CFCs by the end of the 1990s. This should cut the greenhouse effect by 15 percent.

The biggest problem, however, will still be the amount of carbon dioxide pouring into the atmosphere as a byproduct of burning fossil fuels.

Unfortunately fossil fuels are comparatively cheap, and supplies are quite huge. It will be difficult and expensive to find alternatives to them. Certainly we could increase the use of solar power, hydroelectric power, and nuclear power. But these have drawbacks.

We also must stop burning the world's tropical forests to provide room for settlement and farming. Their destruction adds carbon dioxide to the atmosphere. In addition, trees naturally convert carbon dioxide into oxygen. Destroying the rain forests ruins this natural defense against the greenhouse effect.

Not all scientists and geographers agree on the extent of the greenhouse effect or the severity of its consequences. All do agree, however, that if we want to be sure to avoid the dust bowl conditions of the 1930s—which might be worldwide this time—people everywhere must awaken to the consequences of remaining ignorant of their environment.

APPLYING YOUR KNOWLEDGE

You will be organized into five groups. Each group will research and report on one of the following topics: the greenhouse effect, solar power, hydroelectric power, nuclear power, and the tropical forests. Reports should contain information on the most current research and prospects for the future. Your class will assemble the reports in a display for all the students in the school.

earth. Some of the heat is absorbed, but most is radiated back into the atmosphere. Carbon dioxide, a gas in the atmosphere given off by burning fossil fuels such as coal, oil, natural gas, and wood traps some of this heat, keeping it close to the earth's surface.

The greenhouse effect is a natural occurrence. Were it not for it, life on earth would be a nightmare of subzero temperatures. But since the Industrial Revolution there has been greatly increased use of fossil fuels, spewing more and more carbon dioxide in the atmosphere. Consequently, this atmospheric blanket is now capturing far more of the earth's radiated heat than at any time in the past. The result has been a gradual warming of the earth.

Future Effects

4. What can be done to slow or stop the greenhouse effect?

Droughts in the late 1980s showed Americans what they could expect if the warming trend

CHAPTER 25 REVIEW

1929
Hoover becomes president
★
Stock market crash
★
Great Depression begins

1932
Bonus March
on Washington
★
Roosevelt elected president

1933
New Deal begins
★
FDIC, NIRA, NRA, AAA, TVA, CCC

Chapter Summary
Read the statements below. Choose one, and write a paragraph explaining its importance.
1. A normal business cycle has periods of recession, depression, recovery, and prosperity.
2. The Great Depression lasted longer, was steeper, and had more severe consequences than other depressions.
3. Human suffering during the depression was great. People lost their jobs and their savings. Many were hungry. In general the poor suffered most.
4. Hoover attempted to stimulate the economy, but he believed that the federal government should not provide direct relief. This attitude and his handling of the Bonus Army ruined his public image.
5. Franklin D. Roosevelt defeated Hoover and was inaugurated in the midst of a banking panic.
6. Roosevelt's New Deal was aimed at relief, recovery, and reform.
7. Roosevelt's personality and the feeling of action made the New Deal popular with most Americans, including blacks and other disadvantaged groups.
8. Some critics complained that the president had not gone far enough to end the depression more quickly. Others claimed he had gone too far.
9. The New Deal produced a revolution in employer-employee relations, created a "welfare state," and changed thinking about deficit spending.

Reviewing Chronological Order
Number your paper 1-5. Then study the time line above and place the following events in the order in which they happened by writing the first next to 1, the second next to 2, and so on.
1. Social Security Act
2. Roosevelt elected president
3. National Industrial Recovery Act
4. New Deal begins
5. Stock Market Crash

Understanding Main Ideas
1. Describe how the business cycle works.
2. What were some of the actions taken by Congress during the Hundred Days?
3. Describe these New Deal agencies or laws: Civilian Conservation Corps (CCC), Agricultural Adjustment Act (AAA), Works Progress Administration (WPA).
4. How did the Second New Deal differ from the first?
5. Give examples to show how most blacks responded to the New Deal.
6. What was the "welfare state" created in the 1930s?

Thinking Critically
1. **Synthesizing.** Imagine that you are General Douglas MacArthur writing your memoirs. Compose a brief account of your view of the Bonus March and your part in the events that followed in the summer of 1932.
2. **Analyzing.** Of the FDIC, the NRA, the AAA, the TVA, the CCC, or the WPA, which program of the New Deal do you think raised American morale the most? Why?
3. **Relating.** The year is 1938. Write a letter to the president of the NAACP nominating Mary McLeod Bethune for Woman of the Year and explaining why you think she should be chosen for this honor.
4. **Evaluating.** In your opinion, what was the most important result of the New Deal? Explain your answer and support it with sound reasoning.

Writing About History
Use your historical imagination to write a series of at least ten diary entries to describe what you see and hear during the Great Depression. Describe how your family copes with hard times. Describe people both more fortunate and less fortunate than you. What are your thoughts about President Roosevelt and the New Deal? Use the information in Chapter 25 to help you write your entries. You also may wish to interview people who lived during the Great Depression.

35
:A, WPA

RA ruled
:constitutional

agner Act, Social Security Act
ssed; CIO established

1936
AAA ruled
unconstitutional
★
Roosevelt reelected

1937
Supreme Court
Reform Plan defeated
★
Recession slows
recovery

1938
New AAA is passed
★
Fair Labor Standards Act

1939
Second World War begins in Europe
★
Depression ends

Practicing the Strategy
Review the strategy on page 914.
Composing an Essay. Study the Chapter Summary on page 932. Choose one of the statements as your topic, then compose a short essay.

Using Primary Sources
Langston Hughes was one of the most famous writers of the Harlem Renaissance. Hughes greatly admired the work of Carl Sandburg, especially Sandburg's ability to capture the voice of the people. Hughes' "I, Too" is a response to a song millions of school children have sung: "My Country, 'tis of thee/Sweet land of liberty/Of thee I sing." As you read the following poem think about how the poet captures the voice of black Americans of the time.

I, Too

I, too, sing America.
I am the darker brother.
They send me to eat in the
kitchen
When company comes,
But I laugh,
And eat well,
And grow strong.
Tomorrow,
I'll be at the table
When company comes,
Nobody'll dare
Say to me,
"Eat in the kitchen,"
Then.
Besides,
They'll see how beautiful I am
And be ashamed—
I, too, am America.

1. To whom does the word *they* in line three refer? What do you think "the kitchen" symbolizes?
2. How does the last line differ from the first line?

Why do you think the poet changed the wording? Do you think Eleanor and Franklin Roosevelt would have agreed with the poet?
3. What prediction does the poet make? Do you think Hughes' prediction has come true? Explain your answer.

Linking History & Geography
In many ways the forces of nature were as hard on the American landscape as the economy was on the American people. Several of the programs of the New Deal were aimed at improving land use and conserving nature. To understand the impact of the New Deal on the geography of America, review President Roosevelt's first inaugural address and information on the CCC and TVA, especially the TVA map on page 909. Then answer these questions.
1. How does Roosevelt's inaugural address indicate he was concerned about the environment?
2. What did the CCC do to help conserve the nation's resources and natural environment?
3. Some critics claimed the TVA ruined rather than improved the environment. Why might they say this? Do you agree or disagree? Explain.

Enriching Your Study of History
1. **Individual Project.** Use an almanac to find unemployment figures, average income, or other economic statistics for the years 1929-39. Plot the numbers on a graph large enough to be seen by the entire class. Use the graph to illustrate how the economy changed in the 1930s.
2. **Cooperative Project.** Present-day historians sometimes record *oral history*. These are tape recorded (and sometimes video recorded) interviews that are later set down on paper. Oral history gives us the actual words of a person who recalls a period of history firsthand. Your group will prepare an oral history titled "The Great Depression: Personal Views." Group members will interview people in your community who lived through the events of 1929-39. You will then combine your interviews into a report, an audiotape, or a videotape and present it to the local library.

Chapter 25 Review   933

UNIT EIGHT REVIEW

Summing Up and Predicting

Read the summary of main ideas in Unit Eight below. Choose one statement, then write a paragraph predicting its outcome or future effect.

1. A variety of factors caused Europe to erupt in 1914 in the largest war in history.
2. The United States eventually declared war on the Central Powers in 1917.
3. The Treaty of Versailles reflected many of Wilson's 14 Points, including the League of Nations. But it was not the peace without victory he felt was so essential to future peace.
4. The United States rejected the Versailles Treaty and the League of Nations. American reaction to the war led to a series of actions aimed at limiting foreign influences in the United States.
5. Most Americans enjoyed the "Roaring Twenties." The automobile, jazz, sports, motion pictures, and the radio brought zest to life.
6. Despite the prevalent "get-rich-quick" attitude, problems of farmers and "sick industries" slowed the economy.
7. The Great Depression lasted longer and was steeper than other depressions, and human suffering was great, especially for the poor.
8. Roosevelt's New Deal was aimed at relief, recovery, and reform. It did not immediately end the depression, however.
9. The New Deal changed many things in American society, most importantly the role of government in business and everyday life.

Connecting Ideas

1. You know that radio became a powerful influence on American life in the 1920s. Do you think that television has less, the same, or more influence today than radio did then?
2. From what you have learned of the political ideas of Alexander Hamilton and Thomas Jefferson, how do you think each of them would have viewed President Roosevelt's use of power during the New Deal? In your answer cite some specific New Deal programs.
3. Choose any presidential election in this unit and either draw a political cartoon representing the point of view about an issue of the campaign or a candidate or create a campaign slogan for each party in that election.

Practicing Critical Thinking

1. **Analyzing.** As you have read, Oliver Wendell Holmes declared that if something said or written presents a "clear and present danger" to the war effort, the speaker or writer may be punished by law. Do you think this interpretation should also apply to peacetime crises such as the depression? Why or why not?
2. **Drawing Conclusions.** You know that during the 1920s American life was changed by the automobile. How do you think the widespread use of cars affected regional differences in the nation? Give specific examples.
3. **Synthesizing.** You are a reporter who can interview one of the following people: Herbert Hoover, Franklin Roosevelt, or Eleanor Roosevelt. Choose one, and make a list of five questions that you would ask during your interview.

Cooperative Learning

1. Your group will study the time lines at the end of each of the chapters in Unit Eight. Then you will create two time lines, one illustrating the most important domestic events in the unit and the other showing the major international events. Some group members may illustrate the time line by adding sketches or pictures. Display your time lines in the classroom.
2. Your group will create a chart to display in the classroom, showing the "alphabet soup" of the New Deal. Group members will research each agency and briefly describe its function. Others may illustrate the chart with appropriate symbols for the various agencies.
3. Your group will make a model of a battlefield on the Western Front, using clay or plaster of paris. Include trenches, barbed-wire mazes, and no man's land.

Reading in Depth

Allen, Frederick Lewis. *Only Yesterday.* New York: Harper & Row. Provides a highly readable account of life in the 1920s.

Hiebert, Roslyn and Ray Hiebert. *Franklin Delano Roosevelt, President for the People.* New York: Watts. Presents a closeup picture of the man who led America through the Great Depression.

Horan, James David. *The Desperate Years: A Pictorial History of the Thirties.* Portland, ME: Walch. Contains a dramatic visual portrayal of the decade through photographs and paintings.

Richards, Kenneth. *Babe Ruth.* New York: Children's Press. Traces the life and career of one of baseball's greatest stars.

National Air and Space Museum, Washington

The peaceful use of atomic power came with the race for space between the Soviet Union and the United States. Here Norman Rockwell, in "Apollo 11 Space Team", shows American astronauts with eager watchers, awaiting their expeditions into the unknown heavens.

A GLOBAL AMERICA

UNIT 9

I n Unit 9 you will learn about World War II and the conflict that followed, known as the Cold War. Here are some main points to keep in mind as you read the unit.

- World War II was the most savage war ever fought. Almost 40 million people died in the conflict.

- The war began with the German invasion of Poland in 1939. It ended after the United States dropped atomic bombs on Japan in 1945.

- The United States was forced into the war when Japan attacked the American naval base at Pearl Harbor.

- The Soviet Union and the United States, two victors in the war, quarreled. A "Cold War" began between them.

- In the 1950s, Dr. Martin Luther King, Jr. led a nonviolent movement to win equal rights for African Americans.

World War II

On September 1, 1939, an enormous German army of 1.7 million men invaded Poland. Two days later Poland's allies—Great Britain and France—responded to this attack by declaring war on Germany. The Second World War had begun. This great world conflict immediately affected the United States. It ended the economic depression. It forced President Roosevelt to direct nearly all of his attention to foreign affairs. And it caused the American people to look once again at their alliances in Europe and the Pacific.

"Il Duce," Benito Mussolini, and "the Führer," Adolf Hitler, ruled their countries with iron fists. Mussolini, here saluting his troops, wanted Italy to again have the greatness of ancient Rome. Hitler played on the emotions of the German people in their defeat after the Great War to forge a war machine fueled by hatred and prejudice. By 1945 both these leaders were dead, Mussolini hanged in a public square in Milan, Hitler a suicide in Berlin. Why do you think neo-Nazis and other such groups continue to express hatred for Jews and other ethnic and racial groups?

Culver Pictures

1. AMERICAN NEUTRALITY

Preview & Review

The Totalitarian States

The **Second World War** resulted from the efforts of three nations—Germany, Italy, and Japan—to conquer and control new territories. These nations developed what are called **totalitarian** governments. Their basic principle was that the state was everything, the individual citizen nothing. Totalitarian governments stamped out opposition. The only political party was controlled by the state. All power was in the hands of one leader, or **dictator.** The dictators allowed no criticism of their policies. They claimed absolute authority over the lives of their citizens.

Totalitarianism first developed in Italy in the 1920s. Benito Mussolini became the country's dictator. He called his political system **fascism.** The name came from the ancient Roman symbol of authority, the *fasces*, a bundle of rods tied tightly around an ax. The rods and ax represented the power of the state. Binding them closely together represented national unity. Mussolini, a swaggering, domineering leader, dreamed of controlling the entire Mediterranean region.

The Japanese system was somewhat different. The official head of the Japanese government was the emperor, Hirohito. He was considered to be a god, and he took no part in the day-to-day running of the government. In practice, however, the Japanese government was equally committed to the idea that the interests of the state were all-important.

The Japanese warlords who controlled the Japanese government in the late 1920s also dreamed of expansion and military glory. Seizing lands for raw materials for rapidly growing Japanese industries was the first step in a plan to control east Asia and the Pacific.

The Soviet Union witnessed the rise of a dictator during the 1920s too. Joseph Stalin replaced V.I. Lenin, founder of the Communist party in Russia and leader of the Communist Revolution in 1917. Stalin began a ruthless purge of all his opponents. He then openly showed his intention to spread communism throughout the world.

There were other dictators, including General Francisco Franco, who came to power in Spain in 1939 after a bloody civil war. Many Americans had watched the civil war closely, for it was the testing ground for the war machine of the European aggressors.

In Germany the National Socialists, or **Nazis,** led by Adolf Hitler, established a totalitarian government in 1933. In rousing speeches and rallies Hitler drew on the bitterness of the German people over the Versailles Treaty and the psychological effects of the postwar depression to captivate followers. Once in power he began ruthless expansion by conquest.

Hitler was a dictator who used terror and brute force to crush those Germans who opposed him. Democratic principles such as

Use these questions to guide your reading. Answer the questions after completing Section 1.
Understanding Issues, Events, & Ideas. Use the following words to describe the state-controlled governments of the 1930s: Second World War, totalitarian, dictator, fascism, Nazis, concentration camp, Holocaust, genocide, pacifist, conscientious objector, merchant of death, neutrality act, quarantine, collective security.
1. How did Hitler gain support for his rise to power?
2. Why did most Americans favor a policy of isolationism?
3. What events caused Congress to pass the neutrality acts?
4. Why did Roosevelt urge a quarantine of aggressor nations by peaceful nations?

Thinking Critically. 1. Imagine that you lived in a totalitarian nation such as Germany, Italy, or Japan during the 1920s-1930s. Write a letter to an American friend, describing what your life is like in that nation. **2.** If you had been a member of Hoover's cabinet when Japan invaded China, would you have recommended the policy of nonrecognition? Why or why not?

Culver Pictures

When Berlin hosted the 1936 Olympic Games, African American Jesse Owens won four gold medals. Hitler, in a sulk, refused to award the medals as was the custom for the leader of the host nation.

freedom of speech and the press were destroyed in Germany and wherever the Nazis were victorious in the war.

Hitler believed that the Germans belonged to a special breed of humans, a "master race" that was supposed to be superior to all others. When Jesse Owens, an African American athlete from the United States, began winning gold medals in the 1936 Olympics held in Berlin, Hitler stopped attending the games. But he reserved most of his hatred for Jews, whom he considered to be morally and physically inferior. He seized Jewish property, denied Jews the right to higher education, and threw tens of thousands of Jews into horrifying **concentration camps.**

Hitler intended to round up the millions of Jewish people in the conquered countries of Europe, force them to work in concentration camps until they dropped, and then kill them in cold blood. This was the **Holocaust.** About 6 million Jews—men, women, and children alike—were murdered on Hitler's orders.

The Holocaust is an example of **genocide,** the deliberate elimination of a people, its heritage and traditions. Throughout history, madmen of one sort or other have tried to eliminate whole races of people. During the early part of the 20th century millions of Armenians were exterminated by the Turks. Many of the Armenians who escaped came to make new lives in America; many others remained behind in Armenia.

Japanese Aggression

In 1931 a Japanese army marched into Manchuria, a province in northern China. This action gave Japan control of rich coal, oil, and iron ore deposits and blocked Soviet designs on the region. Although the attack challenged the Open Door policy, President Herbert Hoover refused to take either military or economic measures against Japan. He instead announced that the United States would not recognize Japan's right to any Chinese territory seized by force.

This policy of nonrecognition had no effect on Japan. In 1932 the Japanese navy attacked the Chinese port of Shanghai. Early the following year, before Franklin D. Roosevelt took his oath of office as president, the Japanese marched into Jehol, a province in northern China.

American Isolationism

Totalitarian ideas had little appeal to Americans. Totalitarian states silenced their political opponents and stormed over the borders of weaker nations during the 1930s. This shocked and angered nearly everyone in the United States. When a totalitarian nation attacked another country, the danger of war spreading was on everyone's mind. Americans nearly always sympathized with the victims of the

Wide World Photos

invaders. But they did not want to become involved in another foreign war. Most Americans once again favored a policy of isolationism. Charles Lindbergh voiced their sentiments:

66 No one can make us fight abroad unless we ourselves are willing to do so. . . . Over one hundred million people in this nation are opposed to entering the war. If the principles of democracy mean anything at all, that is reason enough for us to stay out. If we are forced into a war against the wishes of an overwhelming majority of our people, we will have proved democracy such a failure at home that there will be little use fighting for it abroad.[1] 99

Also urging isolation were a large number of American **pacifists.** These people believed war for any cause was wrong. Throughout American history pacifists had objected to United States involvement in war. Many based their beliefs in religious teachings. Among the most notable pacifists were the Quakers. Most Quakers had refused to enter the armed forces during the Great War. War was against their religion, they said. These **conscientious objectors** had served in the medical corps in the war. The human suffering they witnessed further strengthened their belief that war was wrong.

Never has the "civilized" world known such hatred as that of Hitler for the Jews of Eastern Europe. His deadly policy was genocide—the systematic elimination of 6 million Jews and their ancient culture. Here, Nazi soldiers drive terrified women and children from the Warsaw ghetto. Most of them will be sent to Treblinka, a death camp. Hitler's soldiers also rounded up thousands of political enemies and members of other outcast groups to be hauled off to prisons.

[1]From a speech by Charles A. Lindbergh, Jr., in *The New York Times,* April 24, 1941

In Elsa Morante's powerful novel of World War II, a poor widow, Ida, witnesses the train that will take its Jewish occupants to the concentration and death camps.

66 Perhaps ten paces from the entrance she began to hear, at some distance, a horrible humming sound, but for the moment she couldn't understand precisely where it was coming from.

The invisible voices were approaching and growing louder, . . . as if they came from an isolated and contaminated place. The sound suggested certain dins of kindergartens, hospitals, prisons; however all jumbled together. . . . At the end of the ramp on a straight, dead track, a train was standing which to Ida seemed of endless length. The voices came from inside it.

There were perhaps twenty cattle cars. . . . The cars had no windows except a tiny grilled opening up high. At each of these grilles two hands could be seen clinging, or a pair of staring eyes. 99

From *La Storia (History)*, 1974

The movement for disarmament and antiwar feelings were quite strong throughout the 1930s. When the ten-year naval holiday negotiated after the Great World War expired in 1932, Dorothy Dexler and the Women's International League for Peace and Disarmament doggedly insisted that Americans negotiate another. Antiwar groups spread the word in every way possible, as the following excerpt from an antiwar song shows:

66 I'll sing you a song, and it's not very long
It's about a young man who never did wrong
Suddenly he died one day
The reason why no one could say
     . . . Only one clue as to why he died
     —A bayonet sticking in his side.[1] 99

In fact, fighting the Great World War to make the world safe for democracy now seemed a terrible mistake. The totalitarian governments that arose after the war were enemies of democracy. America's allies had failed to pay back the money that the United States had lent them in their hour of desperate need. Looking back, the only Americans who appeared to have profited from the war were the manufacturers of guns and other munitions. It became popular to refer to these manufacturers as **merchants of death.**

The Neutrality Acts

Japan's attacks in China worried Roosevelt. Still, he could not ignore the strong isolationist and antiwar sentiment in the United States. On the 18th anniversary of America's entrance into the Great World War, 50,000 veterans paraded through Washington in a march for peace. A few days later some 175,000 college students across the country staged a one-hour strike against war. The government should build "schools not battleships," they claimed.

In August 1935 Congress responded by passing the first of a series of **neutrality acts.** This law prohibited the sale of weapons to either side in any war. Later neutrality acts directed the president to warn American citizens that if they traveled on the ships of warring nations, they did so at their own risk.

The idea behind the neutrality laws was to keep the country from repeating what now seemed to be the mistakes of the 1914–17 period. At that time, it will be remembered, President Wilson had insisted on American neutral rights. American ships, citizens, and goods, he stated, had the right to travel without interference on the high seas. That policy had led to the deaths of Americans in submarine attacks and eventually to America entering the war.

[1]From an antiwar song by the Almanac Singers, cited in *America in the Twentieth Century* by James T. Patterson

Roosevelt's Strategy

Soon after the passage of the first neutrality act, Italian troops invaded the African nation of Ethiopia. Roosevelt immediately applied the neutrality law. Nearly all Americans sympathized with the Ethiopians, who had done nothing to provoke Italy. Yet because the Ethiopians had few modern weapons to use against the heavily armed Italians, the neutrality act hurt them far more than their enemy.

Therefore, when Japan launched an all-out attack against China in 1937, Roosevelt refused to apply the neutrality law. Using the technicality that Japan had not formally declared war, he allowed the Chinese to buy weapons from American manufacturers.

Roosevelt was looking for a way to check the totalitarian nations without getting involved in a shooting war. In a speech in October 1937 he warned that "mere isolation or neutrality" was no protection. Peaceful nations must work together to isolate, or **quarantine,** aggressor nations. He was talking about what was called **collective security.** Safety required that democratic countries cooperate in the effort to prevent the aggressors from seizing whatever they wanted. However, Congress took no action, and Roosevelt let the matter drop.

Roosevelt's annual message to Congress in January 1939 shows how difficult the situation was becoming. Americans knew the actions of the aggressors were wrong and that they must be prepared. But officially they must remain neutral. Roosevelt said:

“ There comes a time in the affairs of men when they must prepare to defend not only their homes alone but the tenets of faith and humanity on which their churches, their governments, and their very civilizations are founded. The defense of religion, of democracy, and of good faith among nations is all the same fight. To save one we must now make up our minds to save all. . . .

The world has grown so small and weapons of attack so swift that no nation can be safe in its will for peace so long as any other single powerful nation refuses to settle its grievances at the council table.

For if any government bristling with implements of war insists on policies of force, weapons of defense give the only safety. . . .

Obviously we must proceed along practical, peaceful lines. But the mere fact that we rightly decline to intervene with arms to prevent acts of aggression does not mean that we must act as if there is no aggression at all. Words may be futile, but war is not the only means of commanding a decent respect for the opinions of mankind. . . .[1] ”

[1]From "Message of the President of the United States," January 4, 1939, *Congressional Record,* Vol. 84, Part 1

Return to the Preview & Review on page 937.

Preview & Review

Use these questions to guide your reading. Answer the questions after completing Section 2.

Understanding Issues, Events, & Ideas. Use the following words to explain American attempts to help battle totalitarianism while remaining neutral: cash-and-carry policy, Dunkirk, Battle of Britain, internationalist, Four Freedoms, Lend-Lease Act, wolf pack, Battle of the Atlantic, Atlantic Charter, convoy.

1. What was Poland's fate in 1939? What had Hitler done before the invasion of Poland?
2. What was Roosevelt's destroyers-for-bases trade?
3. What promise about the war did President Roosevelt make during his campaign for a third term?
4. What were Roosevelt's Four Freedoms?
5. What was the purpose of the Atlantic Charter?

Thinking Critically. 1. Imagine that it is the fall of 1940, and you are Edward R. Murrow. Write an outline for a radio news report to broadcast from London to the United States. **2.** Construct a time line of the events that led to America's undeclared war with Germany. Start your time line with the Battle of Britain.

2. THE EUROPEAN WAR

Western Europe Falls to Hitler

After 1933 Hitler systematically violated the Versailles Treaty. His troops occupied the Rhineland and he annexed Austria. A famous American journalist had this to say about the German aggressions:

66 Write it down. On Saturday, February 12, 1938, Germany won the world war, and . . . Nazism started on the march across all of Europe east of the Rhine.

Write it down that the world revolution began in earnest—and perhaps the world war. . . .

Why does Germany want Austria? For raw materials? It has none of any importance. To add to German prosperity? Austria is a poor country with serious problems. But strategically it is the key to the whole of central Europe. Czechoslovakia is now surrounded. The wheat fields of Hungary and the oil fields of Rumania are now open. Not one of them will be able to withstand the pressure of German domination.

It is horror walking. Not that 'Germany' joins with Austria. We are not talking of 'Germany.' We see a new Crusade, under a pagan symbol, worshiping 'blood' and 'soil,' preaching the holiness of the sword and glorifying conquest. It hates the Slavs, whom it thinks to be its historic 'mission' to rule. It subjects all life to a militarized state. It persecutes men and women of Jewish blood. . . .

Today, all of Europe east of the Rhine is cut off completely from the western world. . . .[1] 99

Then in the summer of 1939 Germany invaded Poland. Great Britain and France immediately declared war on Germany. The Soviet Union, which had signed a nonaggression treaty with Germany

[1]From *Let the Record Speak* by Dorothy Thompson

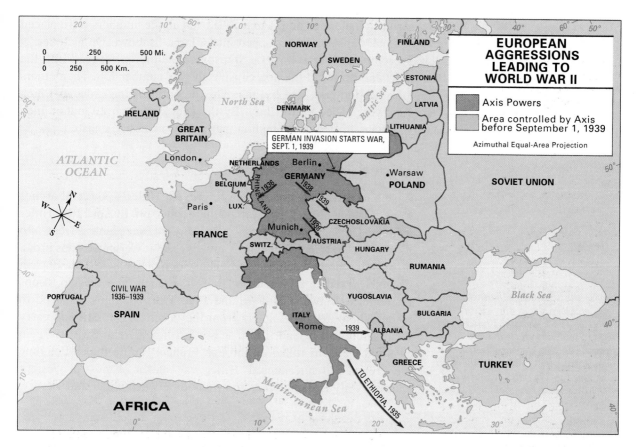

EUROPEAN
AGGRESSIONS
LEADING TO
WORLD WAR II

Axis Powers

Area controlled by Axis
before September 1, 1939

Azimuthal Equal-Area Projection

GERMAN INVASION STARTS WAR,
SEPT. 1, 1939

guaranteeing it would not interfere in German expansion, seized the
eastern part of Poland. The motorized and well-equipped German
army crushed its Polish opponents. In a little more than a month,
Poland was swallowed up. The Second World War, also called World
War II, had officially begun, although Japanese, Italian, and German
armies had been on the move throughout the 1930s.

In September President Roosevelt called Congress into special
session to revise the neutrality laws. After several weeks of debate
Congress agreed to allow warring nations to purchase arms and other
goods provided that they paid for them in cash and transported their
purchases in foreign ships. This **cash-and-carry policy** favored the
Allies. As in the Great World War, now called the First World War
or World War I, the British and French navies controlled the Atlantic
Ocean. German merchant ships could not reach American ports.

The Draft Lottery

As the United States moved closer to war, Congress voted to draft
men between the ages of 21 and 35 for military service. In September
1940 Congress authorized a draft to be made by a lottery.

On October 16 more than 16 million men reported to their local
draft boards to register for a possible call to military duty. Each was

LEARNING FROM MAPS. *German and Italian actions eventually brought on World War II. Italy hoped to claim an empire in Africa. What country did they attack there? Why do you think the first German aggressions were in the areas shown on the map? Which action was the immediate cause of World War II?*

The European War   943

assigned a number from 1 to 8,500. Then all the numbers were placed in small capsules and dropped into a large fishbowl. On October 29 Secretary of War Henry L. Stimson, blindfolded, reached into the bowl and drew out the first capsule. It was number 158. Then others took out the rest, one by one. This determined the order in which men were called up for duty. By the end of the war 10 million men had been drafted and 6 million men and women had enlisted.

Hitler's War Machine Rolls On

Cash and carry was not enough to prevent Hitler's powerful armies from crushing Poland. His war machine rolled on. In April 1940 Hitler invaded Denmark and Norway. On May 10 Nazi tanks swept into the Netherlands and Belgium. A few days later German troops broke through the French defenses at Sedan. Soon they reached the English Channel, trapping thousands of British, French, and Belgian troops at **Dunkirk.** Between May 26 and June 4 British ships managed to rescue about 340,000 soldiers from the beach at Dunkirk and carry them safely to England. But it was a crushing defeat. Swift German armored divisions rolled on through France. Before the end of June the French had surrendered. Hitler was master of most of western Europe. Only Britain and its navy stood between Hitler and victory.

Across the English Channel come boats of every shape and size in the spring of 1940. British, French, and Belgian soldiers had their backs to the channel as the Germans advanced. France was lost, but 340,000 men were saved by the courage and mettle of the British at Dunkirk.

Imperial War Museum

Nearly everyone in the United States was horrified by the thought of such a victory. Hitler was both cruel and power mad. If he conquered Great Britain, would the United States be safe from his mighty armies? Without massive American aid, Great Britain seemed in danger of being invaded and overwhelmed. German U-boats and bombers had sunk many British destroyers needed to protect Atlantic shipping and prevent a German invasion of England. In July 1940 British Prime Minister Winston Churchill appealed to President Roosevelt for help. He needed 40 or 50 American destroyers. These vessels were not being used because the United States had replaced them with more modern ships.

Roosevelt wanted to help the British. He knew that it would take time to get Congress to act. Therefore he issued an executive order turning over 50 destroyers to the British in exchange for 99-year leases on several naval and air bases in the British West Indies. This destroyers-for-bases trade was acceptable to those people who would have objected to simply giving the ships to Great Britain.

The Election of 1940

Hitler expected to crush British resistance with massive air raids and then invade the shattered island. The Nazi bombings brought the war uncomfortably close to the United States. In the fall of 1940 an American news commentator, Edward R. Murrow, began a series of radio broadcasts from London.

> 66 *September 13, 1940*
> This is London at 3:30 in the morning. This has been what might be called a 'routine night'—air-raid alarm at about nine o'clock and intermittent bombing ever since. I had the impression that more high explosives and fewer incendiaries [fire bombs] have been used tonight. . . .
>
> *September 18, 1940*
> You can have little understanding of the life in London these days—the courage of the people, the flash and the roar of the guns rolling down the streets where much of the history of the English-speaking world has been made, the stench of air-raid shelters in the poor districts. These things must be experienced to be understood. . . .
>
> *September 22, 1940*
> I'm standing again tonight on a rooftop looking out over London, feeling rather large and lonesome. . . . At the moment there's an ominous silence hanging over London. But at the same time a silence that has a great deal of dignity. . . .[1] 99

[1]From *In Search of Light* by Edward R. Murrow

Photo Researchers

Hitler is the Grim Reaper in this political cartoon, slaughtering all who oppose his takeover of Europe by force.

Bettmann Newsphotos

Edward R. Murrow's broadcasts held Americans spellbound as they leaned closer to their radios to hear news of the war from London. He became America's most distinguished broadcaster and fighter for truth.

St. Paul's Cathedral, the masterpiece of famed architect Sir Christopher Wren, was so badly damaged by the nightly bombings and fires that it was not fully restored for twenty years.

The English, even school children, went about their business in spite of the deadly German bombings. In London, children learned how to use gas masks and to find the nearest shelters. In the countryside, farm children wait in a trench for the German planes to fly home once more.

John Topham/Black Star

The **Battle of Britain** formed the background of the presidential election of 1940. Republicans could not decide between Senator Robert A. Taft, the son of former president William Howard Taft, and Thomas E. Dewey of New York. After six ballots the convention turned to a dark horse, Wendell Willkie of Indiana. Willkie, a former Democrat, was the head of a large public utility corporation. He had led the opposition to the creation of the Tennessee Valley Authority in 1933. Willkie was a strong supporter of aid to Britain. His nomination was a victory for the Republican **internationalists** over the isolationist wing of the party, led by Senator Taft.

When the Democratic convention met in Chicago, not even Roosevelt's closest advisers knew if he would seek renomination. No president had ever run for a third term. However, Roosevelt felt he was needed because of the critical international situation. He won the nomination easily.

Roosevelt ran on his record. Willkie tried to play up the third-term issue and the failures of the New Deal to get the economy moving. Late in the campaign he also accused the president of planning to involve the United States in the war. "If you reelect him," Willkie told one audience, "you may expect war in April 1941."

Roosevelt responded quickly. "I have said this before, but I shall say it again and again and again: your boys are not going to be sent into any foreign wars." In the November election Roosevelt received 449 electoral votes, Willkie only 82.

The Lend-Lease Act

Roosevelt interpreted his reelection as an endorsement of his policy of aiding Great Britain. The British were now running desperately short of money to pay for American supplies. Therefore Roosevelt proposed lending them the weapons and goods they needed to continue the struggle against Hitler. In a fireside chat he told the people that the United States "must become the great arsenal of democracy." He asked them to support increased aid to Great Britain even at the risk of becoming involved in the war.

In January 1941 Roosevelt called for support for those who were fighting in defense of what he called the **Four Freedoms**—freedom of speech and religion, freedom from want and fear. A few days later he asked Congress to pass his program for aid to Britain, the **Lend-Lease Act.** This measure gave the president authority to sell or lend war supplies, or matériel, to any nation whose defense was essential to America's security.

The Lend-Lease bill aroused fierce opposition. "Lending war equipment is a good deal like lending chewing gum," said Senator Taft. "You don't want it back." But the public was behind the president. One poll showed that 70 percent of those questioned supported aid to Britain—even at the risk of war. Congress passed the Lend-Lease Act in March.

The Battle of the Atlantic

To stop the flow of supplies to Britain, swarms of German U-boats, called **wolf packs,** ranged the Atlantic. Hitler also shifted part of his air force to attack Atlantic shipping. The **Battle of the Atlantic** was a desperate struggle. During the first half of 1941, U-boats sank ships faster than the British could build them. Roosevelt authorized the United States naval yards to repair damaged British ships, and he transferred ten Coast Guard cutters to the British navy.

In April the United States set up bases in Greenland. American naval vessels began to patrol the Atlantic. These American ships did not try to sink German submarines. Their purpose was to track the submarines and radio their location to British planes and destroyers.

On June 22, 1941, Hitler broke his 1939 nonaggression agreement with Joseph Stalin and invaded the Soviet Union. Roosevelt quickly

Point of View

In *V Was for Victory,* a scholar of the war makes these comments about Roosevelt.

"Circumstances overcame his hesitancies. When the Nazis swept across western Europe in the spring of 1940, the President, who was eager to aid the British, confronted the bankruptcy of the American armed forces. He confronted, too, the need for greater national unity at the very moment of a national political campaign. Beginning then, moving more rapidly after his re-election and the ensuing passage of the Lend-Lease Act, continuing thereafter as American involvement in the war in the Atlantic grew, he created one defense agency after another...."
John Morton Blum, 1976

Frank Scherschel/Life Picture Service

To cover the war in Europe—and later in the Pacific—magazines such as Life *sent artists as well as photographers. This painting shows what the camera at night might not show so well: the* Campbell, *training its searchlights on a U-boat being shelled. The U-boat was sunk, but the* Campbell *was so badly damaged that it had to be towed 800 miles to safety.*

announced that lend-lease aid would be extended to the Soviet Union. In July he ordered 4,000 Marines to Iceland. This move pushed the area under American protection farther into the Atlantic.

The Atlantic Charter

In August 1941 President Roosevelt met with Prime Minister Churchill aboard the destroyer *Augusta* at Argentia Bay in Newfoundland. There the two leaders outlined their aims for the postwar world. This **Atlantic Charter,** as it became known, is an inspiring statement of eight democratic principles. In the conclusion the president and the prime minister called for gradual disarmament:

❝ Eighth, they [the United States and Great Britain] believe that all of the nations of the world, for realistic as well as spiritual reasons, must come to the abandonment of the use of force. Since no future peace can be maintained if land, sea, or air armaments continue to be employed by nations which threaten, or may threaten, aggression outside of their frontiers, they believe, pending the establishment of a wider and permanent system of general security, that the disarmament of such nations is essential. They will likewise aid

Wide World Photos

and encourage all other practicable measures which will lighten for peace-loving peoples the crushing burden of armaments.[1] **"**

[1]From *The Atlántic Charter* by Franklin D. Roosevelt and Winston S. Churchill, August 14, 1941

Franklin Roosevelt and Winston Churchill, leaders of the free world, met at sea in 1941 to plan for the postwar world and to declare the Atlantic Charter. What did they mean when they wrote, "lighten for peace-loving peoples the crushing burden of armaments"?

The Undeclared War

In September 1941 a German submarine fired a torpedo at the United States destroyer *Greer* off Iceland. The destroyer had been trailing the U-boat and relaying its position to a British plane, which had dropped four depth charges. Although the *Greer* provoked the attack, Roosevelt called the attack "piracy legally and morally." He compared Hitler to a rattlesnake. He ordered naval vessels to escort, or **convoy,** merchant ships carrying lend-lease goods across the Atlantic. And he ordered naval vessels to "shoot on sight" any German submarines they encountered.

After a submarine sank the destroyer *Reuben James* on October 30, killing over 100 sailors, Congress authorized the arming of merchant ships. All restrictions on American commerce were removed. The United States was now engaged in an undeclared war with Germany. 🔳

Return to the Preview & Review on page 942.

Use these questions to guide your reading. Answer the questions after completing Section 3.
Understanding Issues, Events, & Ideas. Use the following words to describe the situation in America at the outbreak of World War II: Tripartite Pact, Rome-Berlin-Tokyo Axis, Pearl Harbor, National War Labor Board, withholding system, G.I. Bill of Rights, internment camp, Fair Employment Practices Committee, bracero.
1. What economic steps did Roosevelt take to check Japan?
2. What was the extent of the damage done by the Japanese attack on Pearl Harbor? How did the United States react?
3. How did the war finally bring the Great Depression to an end?
4. What problems were there for black and Hispanic Americans in the military during the war? in labor? What advances were there?
Thinking Critically. 1. Write an eyewitness account of the attack on Pearl Harbor. **2.** Imagine that you are a young Japanese American who will soon be placed in an internment camp. Explain why you think the government's reasons for this treatment are unfair.

3. THE PACIFIC WAR

Negotiations with Japan

Meanwhile Japan continued to increase its control in east Asia. In September 1940 Japanese troops had conquered part of French Indochina, now Southeast Asia. Later that month Japan, Germany, and Italy signed a mutual defense treaty, the **Tripartite Pact.** This treaty created what was called the **Rome-Berlin-Tokyo Axis.**

Roosevelt hoped to check Japanese aggression with economic weapons. In July 1940 he stopped the export of aviation gasoline and scrap iron to Japan. To prevent a total breakdown of communications with Japan, he did not cut off oil, which Japan needed most. Japan depended upon the United States for 80 percent of its oil.

In July 1941, after Hitler invaded Russia, Japanese troops moved into French Indochina (now Vietnam), obviously preparing to attack the Dutch East Indies, where there were important oil wells. Roosevelt then cut off all oil shipments to Japan.

The oil embargo stunned the Japanese. Japan had no oil supply for their rapidly growing industries. They would either have to come to terms with the United States or strike for an independent supply. Since the United States insisted that Japan withdraw from China and Indochina, Japan decided to attack the United States.

Attack on Pearl Harbor

The Japanese planned a surprise air attack to destroy the American fleet stationed at **Pearl Harbor** in Hawaii. They believed that by the time the United States could rebuild its Pacific forces, Japan would have further expanded its control of the Far East. Then it would be able to defeat any American counterattack. The attack date was set for Sunday, December 7.

American intelligence experts had broken Japan's diplomatic code. Decoded radio messages indicated that war was near. As early as November 22 one dispatch from Tokyo revealed that "something was going to happen" if the United States did not lift the oil embargo and stop demanding that Japanese troops leave China.

On November 27 all American commanders in the Pacific were warned to expect a "surprise aggressive move" by Japan. The Americans thought the attack was coming in southeast Asia, possibly in the Philippines. Hawaii seemed beyond the range of Japanese forces. The commanders at Pearl Harbor, Admiral Husband E. Kimmel and General Walter C. Short, took precautions only against sabotage by Japanese secret agents in Hawaii.

By the early morning hours of December 7 the Japanese naval task force was in position about 200 miles (320 kilometers) north of the Hawaiian Islands. The aircraft carriers' crews sent their planes

Wide World Photos

off with shouts of "Banzai! Banzai!"—the Japanese battle cry which means "10,000 years!" The first wave of 183 planes headed for Pearl Harbor.

The lead pilots reached their target about 7:30 on a peaceful and quiet Sunday morning in Honolulu. On the ships some sailors were still asleep. Others were getting breakfast or lounging on deck. Many were on their way to church services. Some were getting ready to go ashore for a swim at Waikiki Beach. Admiral Kimmel and General Short had a date to play a game of golf.

At 7:55 the Japanese struck. Screaming dive bombers swooped down for the kill. Explosions shattered the air. Fortunately, the American aircraft carriers were all at sea. But seven battleships were lined up on Battleship Row in the harbor. The bombers came so low over these ships that sailors could see the faces of Japanese pilots as they released their bombs.

The destruction was terrible. The worst blow came when the

Never was the United States so surprised as by the Sunday morning attack on Pearl Harbor by the Japanese. Now the U.S. had to enter the war. Apparently the attack was anticipated, but no one knew when it would come—or with what force. Read on and then report on the extent of the destruction.

On December 9, the day after the president had asked for a declaration of war, he spoke to the nation in perhaps his saddest "Fireside Chat."

❝We are now in this war. We are all in it—all the way. Every single man, woman, and child is a partner in the most tremendous undertaking of our American history. We must share together the bad news and the good news, the defeats and the victories—the changing fortunes of war.❞

Franklin D. Roosevelt

U.S.S. *Arizona* blew apart and sank, trapping more than a thousand men inside. The Japanese planes rained bombs on every ship in the harbor. They ranged up and down the coast, attacking airfields and barracks. In less than two hours 19 warships were sunk or disabled. Three others were damaged. One hundred and fifty planes were destroyed, most of them on the ground. Then the Japanese returned to their carriers. The task force sped back to Japanese waters. The attack on Pearl Harbor was by far the worst defeat the United States navy has suffered in all its history.

Americans were shocked and angered by the attack on Pearl Harbor. President Roosevelt went before Congress on December 8 to ask that war be declared on Japan. He called December 7, 1941, "a date which will live in infamy." He had the whole country behind him. Germany and Italy, in turn, carried out the terms of their Tripartite Pact and, on December 11, declared war on the United States.

The Home Front

The United States was much better prepared to fight World War II than it had been to fight the Great World War. Long before the attack on Pearl Harbor, Roosevelt had established councils to oversee the production and distribution of war matériel. After war was declared, similar boards were given broad powers to control the distribution of raw materials to manufacturers and to stop the production of many nonessential goods. The government rationed scarce foods, such as meat, butter, and sugar, to make sure that all citizens got their fair share.

The demand for weapons and supplies finally ended the Great Depression. American industry had slowly been climbing out of the depression, helped by European war needs. Now greatly expanded production was needed. Suddenly steel, aluminum, rubber, and other raw materials needed to make weapons were in extremely short supply. There was no serious shortage of gasoline, but gas was rationed in order to discourage unnecessary travel. Gasoline rationing also saved rubber by keeping drivers from wearing out their tires.

Many manufacturers shifted their plants from the production of consumer goods to weapons. A typical example was the producer of orange juice squeezers who made bullet molds during the war. The automobile companies, of course, turned out tanks and trucks, and airplanes too. The output of airplanes increased from less than 6,000 in 1939 to 96,000 in 1944.

Hundreds of thousands of new workers were needed to produce the tools of war. Unemployment ceased to be a national problem for the first time since 1929. Men and women flocked from farms, towns, and great cities to the East Coast shipyards, to the steel plants and former automobile factories of the Midwest, and to the aircraft plants of the West.

Margaret Bourke-White/Life Magazine © Time Warner, Inc.

The famous photographer Margaret Bourke-White composed unique and striking images of the war. Note the angle she used to show these women helping to build tanks in 1943. The women enjoyed knowing they could handle this "man's work."

About 6 million women were employed during the war. Songs like "Rosie the Riveter" helped persuade women to take jobs traditionally held only by men. One woman remembered her job as a riveter and the pride and confidence it brought her:

❝ I loved working at Convair [an aircraft factory]. I loved the challenge of getting dirty and getting into the work. I did one special riveting job, hand riveting that could not be done by machine. I worked on that job for three months, ten hours a day, six days a week, and slapped three-eighths- or three-quarter-inch rivets by hand that no one else would do. I didn't have that kind of confidence as a kid growing up, because I didn't have that opportunity. Convair was the first time in my life that I had the chance to prove that I could do something, and I did.[1] ❞

[1]From *The Homefront: America During World War II* by Mark Jonathan Harris, et al.

The role of American air force personnel was crucial to Allied victory in World War II. Among those who contributed to the defeat of the Axis powers were African Americans known as the Tuskegee Airmen. Their record of achievement during the war is particularly impressive in view of the special difficulties they faced. They had to fight not only the enemy but another tough foe as well: racial prejudice.

Since World War I, African Americans in the armed forces had been segregated from whites and given low-level work. Many military leaders and officials in the War Department thought blacks incapable of mastering highly skilled jobs. They doubted the ability of blacks to perform bravely under fire. This prejudice was widespread at the time. But African American leaders, newspapers, and organizations such as the NAACP spoke out against racial bias in the armed forces. They won supporters in Congress who pressured the military to treat blacks fairly. Gradually, African Americans were given opportunities to prove themselves.

The air force experimented with training African Americans to fly fighter planes. The first unit was the 99th Fighter Squadron. The experiment took place at a base near Tuskegee Institute in Alabama, where an airfield already existed to train civilian pilots.

To the surprise of many top air force officials, the experiment succeeded. The 99th Fighter Squadron saw combat in Africa, France, Italy, Poland, Romania, Greece, and Germany. In its more than 200 escort missions in Europe, the squadron never lost a U.S. bomber to enemy fighters. Partly because of the 99th's example, schools for bombardiers and navigators were opened to blacks in 1943.

In 1944, the 99th became part of the newly formed 332nd Fighter Group, equipped with long-range fighter-bombers. Immediately, this unit began making a record for itself, in one month downing five German planes over Munich and sinking an enemy destroyer. They proved that blacks were capable of performing highly technical jobs under stress and of showing great courage in air battle.

In March 1945, the 332nd Fighter Group was awarded the Distinguished Unit Citation (the highest unit decoration) for its 1,600-mile roundtrip air attack on Berlin. By that time the group had flown 1,578 combat missions and had destroyed 261 enemy aircraft. Group members had received 95 Distinguished Flying Crosses, a Silver Star, a Legion of Merit, 2 Soldier Medals, 14 Bronze Stars, 744 Air Medals and Clusters, and 8 Purple Hearts. On May 6, 1988, a statue of a Tuskegee airman was erected to honor the men of the unit. Today it stands at the U.S. Air Force Academy in Colorado Springs. It was sculpted by Clarence L. Shivers, a former Tuskegee airman.

Permission by Branden Publishing, Boston

Movies pictured the wives and sweethearts of servicemen working at these jobs while their loved ones fought against the Germans and the Japanese. It was all so new and exciting for many. One woman, who was only 18 at the time, recalled her experience as a machinist in an airplane engine plant:

> " I was very unsophisticated at the time, but I was very zealous, probably overzealous. I remember some of the older guys who had been there for years used to say, 'Hey kid, don't be in such a hurry!'
>
> But I'd get into the thing and geared up for it and I'd just keep plugging away, measuring and grinding, measuring and grinding, and they'd say, 'Hey kid, take it easy.' . . .[1] "

The wartime labor shortage cemented the gains that organized labor had made under the New Deal. A **National War Labor Board** was established in 1942 to regulate wages and prevent labor disputes.

Farmers experienced boom times. The demand for food to feed American and Allied troops was enormous. Farm income more than doubled during the war. Farmers who had suffered during the 1920s and 1930s were soon able to pay off their mortgages, improve their property, and put aside savings too.

During the war Congress adopted the **withholding system** of payroll deductions for collecting income taxes. Employers withheld a percentage of their workers' pay and sent the money directly to the treasury. The withholding system made paying taxes a little less painful. It also supplied the government with a steady flow of funds and made evading taxes almost impossible.

High taxes on personal incomes (up to 94 percent) and on the profits of corporations helped persuade Americans that no one was benefiting too much from the war while soldiers were risking their lives overseas. To boost the morale of those in uniform, Congress passed the Serviceman's Readjustment Act of 1944. This **G.I. Bill of Rights** made low-cost loans available to veterans who wished to buy houses or start new businesses. It also provided money for expenses such as tuition and books for those who wished to resume their education after the war.

Suspicion of Japanese Americans

World War II had great popular support. Almost no one questioned the decision to fight the Axis powers. Assured of the solid backing of the people, the Roosevelt administration adopted a relaxed attitude toward freedom of speech in wartime. There was little persecution of German Americans as had occurred during the Great World War.

The one blot on the Roosevelt record of civil liberties was the

[1]From *Americans Remember the Home Front: An Oral History* by Roy Hoopes

National Archives

Along with most Japanese Americans, these two generations of the Mochida family, tagged for evacuation from their home in Hayward, California, would be interned until the war ended—even though many were U.S. citizens. Read some of the accounts by these victims on this page and the next.

treatment of Japanese Americans. About 112,000 lived on the West Coast. They were forced to move to **internment camps** in barren sections of the country. The government was afraid that some were disloyal and would try to interfere with the war effort and help Japan. Others were placed in the camps for their own protection.

The white population of the American West had always been suspicious of the Chinese and Japanese who settled there. Partly this was the typical dislike of immigrants with different customs. Partly it was a matter of racial prejudice. The suspicion was greatly increased by the sneak Japanese attack on Pearl Harbor. Many people were convinced that unless everyone of Japanese origin was cleared out of the Pacific Coast region, the Japanese would soon be bombing San Francisco.

There was absolutely no evidence that the Japanese Americans were less loyal than other Americans. Most of them had been born in the United States. Immigration from Japan had been ended by the so-called Gentlemen's Agreement of 1907. Nevertheless, all were forced to sell their homes and property and leave for the camps. One woman, a college student in Seattle, Washington, at the time of her internment, described a relocation camp:

66 Camp Minidoka was located in the south-central part of Idaho, north of the Snake River. It was a semidesert region. When we arrived I could see nothing but flat prairies, clumps of greasewood shrubs, and jack rabbits. And, of

course, hundreds and hundreds of barracks, to house 10,000 of us.

Our home was one room in a large army-type barracks, measuring about 20 by 25 feet [6 by 7.5 meters]. The only furnishings were an iron pot-belly stove and cots.

Our first day in camp we were given a rousing welcome by a dust storm. We felt as if we were standing in a gigantic sand-mixing machine as the gale lifted the loose earth up into the sky, hiding everything. Sand filled our mouths and nostrils and stung our faces and hands like a thousand darting needles. . . .

Idaho summer sizzled on the average of 100 degrees [43 degrees Celsius]. For the first few weeks I lay on my cot from morning to night, not daring to do more than go to the mess hall three times a day. . . .

Winter in Minidoka was as intense an experience as summer had been. . . .[1]"

Another victim of the internment remembered his confusion over what was happening to him and his family.

" I remember the pain of being labeled a 'dirty Jap' and a 'dangerous enemy.' For me, a Los Angeles teenager of 17, it was a time when my entire value system was thrown out of kilter. If we, good Christians and loyal American citizens, could be stripped of our civil rights, it seemed that all of the values and ideals I held most dear would need to be reexamined. . . .[2]"

After the war many Americans regretted their treatment of Japanese Americans. In 1948 Congress passed an act to help those interned to recover part of the losses. Court decisions in the 1980s further awarded retribution to the families sent to the camps.

African Americans and Hispanic Americans in Wartime

African Americans also had a difficult time during the war. About 1 million enlisted or were drafted. Black servicemen were expected to risk their lives for the country. Still they were kept in segregated units and frequently treated with disrespect by both officers and enlisted men. Yet by comparison with their treatment during earlier wars, there was some improvement. More black officers were commissioned. A number of blacks became pilots in the air force.

As during the Great World War, the labor shortage benefited

[1]From *Nisei Daughter* by Monica Stone
[2]From "Point of View: A Sorry Part of Our History" by Daniel Kuzuhara, from *The Chicago Tribune*, August 26, 1981

Point of View

Roosevelt's biographer writes of the decision to intern Japanese Americans.

"During January the climate of opinion in California turned harshly toward fear, suspicion, intolerance. Clamor arose for mass evacuation and other drastic action. The causes of the change have long been studied and defy easy explanation. Partly it was the endless Japanese advance in the Pacific, combined with a spate of false alarms . . . of attacks on the coast, stories of secret broadcasting equipment, flashing signals, strange lights and the like. . . . But the main ingredient that fired and fueled the demand for "cleaning out the Japanese" was starkly obvious. The old racism— economic, social, and pathological—toward the Japanese on the West Coast simmered a few weeks after Pearl Harbor and then burst into flames."
James MacGregor Burns, 1970

Gordon Coster/Life Magazine © Time Warner, Inc.

Asa Philip Randolph was a writer and editor of the Messenger. *He had planned a march on Washington in 1941 to demand jobs for blacks in defense industries. Roosevelt persuaded him not to protest because it would disrupt the war effort. After reading further and using historical imagination, determine which man you think had the stronger argument.*

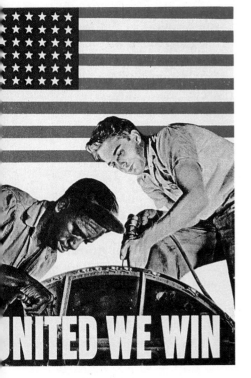

NITED WE WIN

Return to the Preview & Review on page 950.

black workers. Thousands got a chance to learn new skills and therefore earn higher wages. Yet racial discrimination did not end. For this reason, early in 1941 a black leader, A. Philip Randolph, decided to organize a march on Washington to protest the way blacks were being treated.

President Roosevelt feared that such a march would split public opinion at a time when national unity was essential. To persuade Randolph to cancel the march, he issued an executive order prohibiting racial discrimination in defense plants. This rule was enforced by a **Fair Employment Practices Committee.** Randolph then called off the march.

This did not mean that African Americans were satisfied with their treatment after 1941. Many whites resented the concessions Roosevelt had made. There was a good deal of racial trouble in the armed services and in industrial plants throughout the war years. In 1943 it erupted in riots involving attacks on blacks in New York City and Detroit. More and more African Americans were demanding their rights as members of a democratic society. It was clear that when the war ended, demands by blacks for fair treatment were sure to increase.

The situation for Hispanic Americans was similar. Almost 400,000 of them served in the armed forces during the war. A higher percentage saw combat duty overseas than any other ethnic minority. They also received more military medals. Yet like black soldiers and sailors, Hispanic Americans suffered discrimination. On the other hand, for many it was their first chance to experience life outside their neighborhoods. When they returned home, Hispanic Americans were determined to fight for a better life.

The war brought many new opportunities for Hispanic Americans on the home front despite a vicious riot against them in Los Angeles in 1943. Hispanic American women gained jobs in many industries, especially in the West and Southwest. In July 1942 the United States and Mexico signed a treaty that allowed **braceros,** Mexican farm workers, to enter temporarily and work in the United States. Their efforts helped keep up vital food production during the war.

A Move Toward Religious Toleration

The war had an important effect on religion in America. American society moved toward religious pluralism, or the acceptance of different religions. People from all denominations found themselves supporting the war. The open hatred for Jews led by Adolf Hitler and his Nazi followers shocked all Americans. People of various faiths sang *God Bless America* as they united in the struggle to win against their common enemy. By the end of the war the various religions had grown more tolerant of each other.

4. THE ALLIES REGAIN EUROPE

The Invasion of North Africa

The nations that fought the Axis powers in World War II were known as the **Allies.** Chief among the Allies were the United States, Great Britain, France, the Soviet Union, China, Australia, and Canada. Joint planning among the Allies eventually led to an overall war strategy. Stated simply it was "Europe first, then the Far East." Allied military strategists hoped to hold the line against further Japanese advances in the Pacific. Their first major effort would be to defeat Germany. By early 1942 Hitler controlled nearly all of Europe and most of North Africa as well.

In June 1942 President Roosevelt put General Dwight D. Eisenhower in command of American troops in Europe. "Ike" was a first-rate military planner. He also got on well with all kinds of people. Managing and directing the huge and complicated Allied war machine required diplomacy as much as military talent.

Use these questions to guide your reading. Answer the questions after completing Section 4.
Understanding Issues, Events, & Ideas. Use the following terms to describe the Allied victory in Europe: Allies, Operation Torch, Battle of Kasserine Pass, Sicily, Operation Overlord, D-Day, Normandy, Battle of the Bulge, Bastogne, Berlin, V-E Day.

1. What was the Allies' overall war strategy?
2. In what ways was Operation Overlord a massive military operation?
3. Why did Roosevelt run for a fourth term?
4. What did the Germans hope to accomplish at the Battle of the Bulge? Why were they not successful?
5. Which allied nations marched on Berlin to end the war?
Thinking Critically. 1. Why do you think the author says that Churchill was mistaken when he called Italy "the soft underbelly of Europe"? Give reasons to support your answer. **2.** Imagine that you are a member of the American Third Army. Write a letter to your family, describing your impressions of General Patton.

Frank Scherschel/Life Picture Service

The commanders of the Allied troops in North Africa, Eisenhower of the U.S., and Montgomery of Britain— "Ike" and "Monty"—showed the stuff generals are made of by presenting a united front to their troops despite personal differences. Why is this particularly important in all team efforts?

The Allies Regain Europe   959

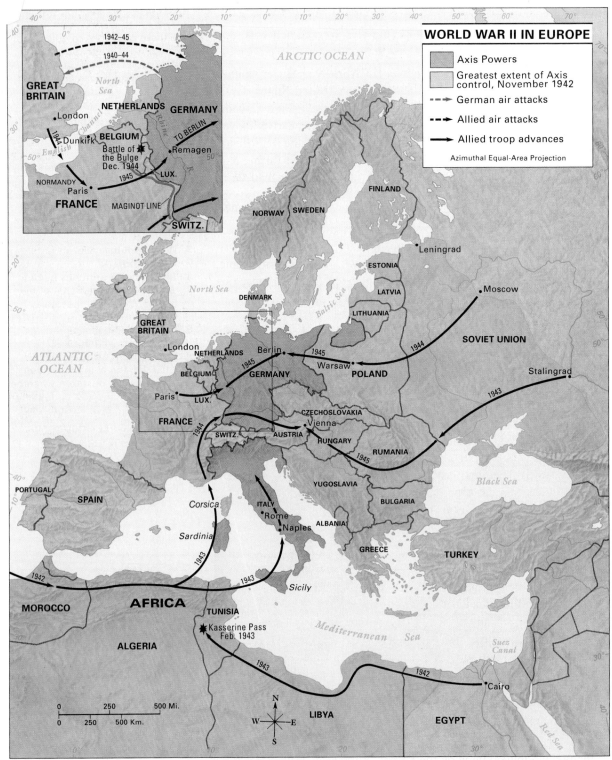

WORLD WAR II IN EUROPE

▨	Axis Powers
▨	Greatest extent of Axis control, November 1942
⇢	German air attacks
⇢	Allied air attacks
→	Allied troop advances

Azimuthal Equal-Area Projection

ARCTIC OCEAN

North Sea

GREAT BRITAIN
• London
NETHERLANDS
BELGIUM
Dunkirk
Battle of the Bulge Dec. 1944
NORMANDY
Paris •
FRANCE
GERMANY
• Remagen
TO BERLIN
LUX.
MAGINOT LINE
SWITZ.
Rhine
English Channel

1942–45
1940–44

NORWAY
SWEDEN
FINLAND

DENMARK

Baltic Sea

ESTONIA
LATVIA
LITHUANIA

• Leningrad

• Moscow

SOVIET UNION

GREAT BRITAIN
• London
NETHERLANDS
BELGIUM
Paris •
LUX.
FRANCE
SWITZ.
AUSTRIA
GERMANY
Berlin •
1945
Warsaw •
POLAND
1944
CZECHOSLOVAKIA
• Vienna
HUNGARY
RUMANIA
1945
1944
Stalingrad •
1943

ATLANTIC OCEAN

North Sea

PORTUGAL
SPAIN

Corsica

Sardinia

ITALY
• Rome
Naples •

Sicily

1943

1943

1943

AFRICA
MOROCCO
1942
ALGERIA
TUNISIA
Kasserine Pass Feb. 1943
1943
LIBYA

ALBANIA
YUGOSLAVIA
BULGARIA
GREECE
TURKEY

Black Sea

Mediterranean Sea

Suez Canal

• Cairo
1942
EGYPT

Red Sea

N
W   E
S

| 0 | 250 | 500 Mi. |
| 0 | 250 | 500 Km. |

LEARNING FROM MAPS. *Allied plans called for the defeat of Germany first. German defenses were strong, but the Allies eventually won. What countries were under Axis control by November 1942?*

Allied leaders did not feel an invasion of Europe was possible until more troops and supplies had gathered in England. So the first major campaign that Eisenhower directed was **Operation Torch,** an attack on Morocco and Algeria in North Africa. On November 8, 1942, three separate forces, one from America, two from England, landed at three points in North Africa. About 110,000 troops, mostly American, were put ashore quickly and efficiently. There was little resistance, and Morocco and Algeria were soon in Allied control.

Then, in February 1943, the first real battle between the Americans and the Germans in North Africa took place at Kasserine Pass in Tunisia. The brilliant German general, Erwin Rommel, deployed his *Afrika Korps* tanks against American tanks in desert warfare. This **Battle of Kasserine Pass** ended in a standoff. But soon the Germans were driven out of the rest of North Africa.

The Italian Campaign

In July 1943 Eisenhower's forces invaded the Italian island of **Sicily,** the first step in an attack on what Prime Minister Churchill mistakenly called ''the soft underbelly of Europe.'' In a little more than a month Sicily was conquered. The Italians then revolted against the dictator Mussolini and tried to surrender. Unfortunately, the German army in Italy simply took over control of the country. The Americans made a successful landing on the Italian mainland. But the conquest of Italy against fierce German resistance was a long and bloody process.

War correspondents kept Americans informed about the day-to-day events of the war, including the horrors of the battlefield. Ernie Pyle, one of the most outstanding war correspondents, spent months at the front with American troops, as did the famous photographer Margaret Bourke-White, the first woman war correspondent accredited by the U.S. army. American novelist John Steinbeck was also a war correspondent. He had this to say about the job:

> 66 What the correspondent really saw was dust and the nasty burst of shells, low bushes and slit trenches. He lay on his stomach, if he had any sense, and watched ants crawling among the little sticks of the sand dune. . . .
>
> Then he saw an advance. Not straight lines of men marching into cannon fire, but little groups scuttling like crabs from bits of cover to other cover, while the deep chatter of machine guns sounded, . . .
>
> He might have seen the splash of dirt and dust that is a shell burst, and a small Italian girl in the street with her stomach blown out, and he might have seen an American standing over a twitching body, crying. He probably saw many dead mules, lying on their sides, reduced to pulp. He saw the wreckage of houses, with torn beds hanging like shreds out of the spilled hole in a plaster wall. There were

Heinrich Hoffmann/Life Magazine © Time Warner, Inc.

"The Desert Fox," German General Erwin Rommel, *effectively used his* Afrika Korps *to stall the Allies for months and keep them from landing on the European mainland.*

red carts and stalled vehicles of refugees who did not get away.

The stretcher-bearers come back from the lines, walking in off step, so that the burden will not be jounced too much, and the blood dripping from the canvas, brother and enemy in the stretchers, so long as they are hurt. And the walking wounded coming back with shattered arms and bandaged heads, the walking wounded struggling painfully to the rear.

He would have smelled the sharp cordite [gunpowder] in the air and the hot reek of blood if the going has been rough. The burning odor of dust will be in his nose and the stench of men and animals killed yesterday and the day before. . . .[1]"

D-Day

Now the long-awaited invasion of France, **Operation Overlord,** was about to begin. For months the United States and British air forces had been bombing industrial targets and railroad yards in Germany in preparation for the invasion. Now, on **D-Day**—June 6, 1944—4,000 landing craft and 600 warships carried 176,000 soldiers across the English Channel. They went ashore at several beaches along the coast of **Normandy,** a province in northern France. Naval guns and 11,000 planes bombarded the German defense positions. By nightfall 120,000 men were ashore. The reconquest of Europe had begun.

The Germans fought skillfully and bravely, but the Allies held the beaches. Reinforcements were brought over. In a single week 326,000 men, 50,000 tanks and trucks, and over 100,000 tons of supplies were ferried across the Channel. By the end of July more than 1 million Allied soldiers were safely landed and established on French soil.

The opening of this second front was truly the beginning of the end for the Germans. Until D-Day they had been able to concentrate their forces in eastern Europe, driving deep into the Soviet Union. Millions of Soviet soldiers and citizens died in the onslaught. Stalin became more and more frustrated as the Americans and British planned the assault. Each hesitation led to tremendous losses by Soviet forces and opened a rift among the Allies. But after D-Day the Germans had to fight on two fronts.

The Allies Enter Paris

In August, after fierce fighting, the American Third Army under General George S. Patton broke through the German defenses and raced toward Paris. Patton was a colorful and controversial general. He wore ivory-handled pistols more suitable to a cowboy than a

Eliot Elisofon/Life Magazine © Time Warner, Inc.

"God help me, but I love it," said General George S. Patton of war. What emotions he must have felt during Operation Overlord, shown in panorama on the facing page. In this huge military operation the Allies, on D-Day, June 6, 1944, invaded Normandy to begin their advance on Berlin.

[1]From *Once There Was a War* by John Steinbeck

lieutenant general. He insisted that all his soldiers, in or out of combat, wear a combat helmet and tie. He once slapped one battle-weary soldier because he thought he was a coward seeking to avoid combat. But Patton had a first-rate military mind. He was a master of tank warfare. Troops under General Patton's command moved quickly and decisively. They won victories.

Allied troops entered Paris amid great rejoicing in late August. By the end of September almost all of France was liberated. Everyone expected that the invasion of Germany would soon follow.

The Election of 1944

With victory in sight Roosevelt had to decide whether to run for a fourth term in 1944. He should not have done so because he was in very poor health. He had a bad heart, high blood pressure, and other physical ailments. Still, he was determined to bring the war to a victorious conclusion. The need for a new world organization to replace the League of Nations was also on his mind.

The president was renominated by the Democrats without opposition. Senator Harry Truman of Missouri was chosen as his running mate. The Republican candidate was Governor Thomas E. Dewey of New York. Dewey was not a particularly effective campaigner, but no one could have defeated the popular Roosevelt on the eve of victory in the war. The election was never in doubt. The popular vote was 25.6 million for Roosevelt, 22 million for Dewey. The electoral count was 432 to 99.

The Battle of the Bulge

In December 1944 the Allied armies were poised along the German border from Holland to Switzerland. On December 16, before the Allies could march, Hitler threw his last reserves—250,000 men—into a desperate counterattack. The Germans hoped to break through the Allied line and drive on to the Belgium port of Antwerp. That would split the Allied force in two.

The German attack was a total surprise. Within ten days the Germans had driven a wedge, or bulge, 50 miles (80 kilometers) deep into the Allied lines. This attack was called the **Battle of the Bulge.** American troops of the 101st Airborne Division were surrounded at the important road junction of **Bastogne.** The Germans demanded that the American commander, General Anthony C. McAuliffe, surrender his troops. "Nuts!" replied the general. Bastogne was held and the German advance stopped.

Elsewhere along the bulge every available American soldier, including platoons of black volunteers, were thrown against the German surge. For the first time white and black soldiers fought side by

Robert Capa/Magnum Photos

side, breaking the barriers of segregation that still existed in the armed services. By January the bulge had been flattened. The Allies were now ready to storm into Germany.

Victory in Europe

The Battle of the Bulge shattered Hitler's hope of winning the war. The end came swiftly. In March 1945 Allied forces crossed the Rhine River into Germany. By the middle of April American, British, and French troops were within 50 miles (80 kilometers) of **Berlin,** the German capital. Russian armies were approaching the city from the east. On April 25 American and Russian troops met at the Elbe River. Five days later Adolf Hitler killed himself in his bombproof air raid shelter in Berlin. On May 8 Germany surrendered. This became known as **V-E Day**, for Victory in Europe.

American joy at the ending of the war was restrained, for President Roosevelt was dead. On April 12, while working on a speech at his winter home in Warm Springs, Georgia, he had died of a massive stroke. The burdens of the presidency were now upon the shoulders of Harry S Truman.

The Battle of the Bulge was Hitler's last attempt to break through Allied lines in Belgium. His troops succeeded in driving a wedge, or bulge, in the lines, but the Allies held.

Return to the Preview & Review on page 959.

The Allies Regain Europe   965

Preview & Review

Use these questions to guide your reading. Answer the questions after completing Section 5. **Understanding Issues, Events, & Ideas.** Describe the Allied victory in the Pacific, using the following words: Philippine Islands, Battle of the Coral Sea, Battle of Midway, island-hopping, Guadalcanal, Battle of Leyte Gulf, Iwo Jima, Okinawa, kamikaze, atomic bomb, Manhattan Project, Hiroshima, Nagasaki, V-J Day.

1. What had General MacArthur pledged in 1942? When did he keep his pledge?
2. What was the American strategy in the Pacific? What was General MacArthur's role? What was Admiral Nimitz's role?
3. How did Japanese troops in the Pacific resist the American advance?
4. How did the Second World War bring home the horrors of war to people around the world?

Thinking Critically. Write a conversation between two people. One person should argue in support of the atomic bombing of Hiroshima and Nagasaki. The other person should argue against the bombing.

The War in the Pacific

The war against Japan was slowly approaching its climax. The strategy, it will be recalled, was first to prevent further Japanese advances. After Pearl Harbor the Japanese had conquered the **Philippine Islands,** capturing large numbers of American troops. An army nurse described the last days before the Japanese took over:

❝ Conditions at Hospital Number 1 were not too good during the last few weeks we spent there. Patients were flooding in. We increased from 400 to 1,500 cases in two weeks time. Most of them had serious wounds, but nine out of ten patients had malaria or dysentery besides.

We were out of quinine [a drug to fight malaria]. There were hundreds of gas gangrene cases, and our supply of vaccine had run out months before. There were no more sulfa drugs. There weren't nearly enough cots, so triple-decker beds were built from bamboo, with a ladder at one end so we could climb up to take care of the patients. They had no blankets or mattresses.

There was almost no food except carabao [water buffalo]. We had all thought we couldn't eat carabao, but we did. Then came mule, which seemed worse, but we ate that too. . . .[1]❞

General Douglas MacArthur, the commander in the Philippines, was evacuated by submarine on the order of President Roosevelt before his troops surrendered. "I shall return," he promised.

Japan, confident of victory, next prepared to invade Australia. But in the great naval **Battle of the Coral Sea** in May 1942 the Japanese fleet was badly damaged. The Japanese were forced to give up their planned invasion.

Then, in June 1942, a powerful Japanese fleet advanced toward American-owned Midway Island west of Hawaii. The plan was to force a showdown with the American Pacific fleet. But the Japanese ships never reached Midway. The Americans broke their secret codes and spy planes spotted their movements. On June 4 dive bombers from American aircraft carriers pounded the Japanese vessels. They sank four Japanese aircraft carriers and destroyed 275 Japanese planes. Again the Japanese fleet had to withdraw. This **Battle of Midway** gave the United States control of the central Pacific.

[1]From "An Army Nurse at Bataan and Corregidor," as told by Annalee Jacoby in *History in the Writing* by Gordon Carroll

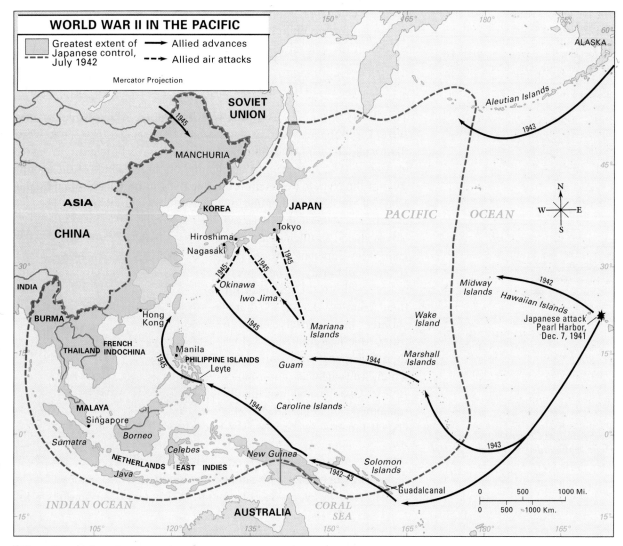

WORLD WAR II IN THE PACIFIC

Greatest extent of Japanese control, July 1942
Allied advances
Allied air attacks

Mercator Projection

The Pacific Campaign

As victory in Europe seemed assured, the Allies turned their full attention to Japan. To defeat Japan, the strategists believed, the Japanese islands must be invaded. But how to get there? The Japanese controlled thousands of small islands in the Pacific—the Bismarcks, the Carolines, the Gilberts, the Solomons, the Marshalls, and others. Capturing all these islands would be too costly, both in lives and in time.

General MacArthur, the commander of the army forces in the Pacific, was set on returning to the Philippines. He favored a sweep through the Bismarck Islands to the Philippine Sea. The Philippines could then be regained and the captive American soldiers set free.

Admiral Chester W. Nimitz, commander of the Pacific fleet,

LEARNING FROM MAPS. *After defeating the Germans, the Allies turned their full attention to the Pacific. To defeat the Japanese, the Allies had been using a tactic called "island hopping." This called for driving the Japanese from some islands while bypassing others. Why does this seem like a good strategy in the Pacific?*

argued for advancing directly toward Japan itself. The military planners in Washington, the Joint Chiefs of Staff, decided on a two-pronged campaign. MacArthur was to clean out the Bismarcks and then head for the Philippines. Nimitz would attack the Japanese-held islands in the central Pacific and press on toward Japan.

From Guadalcanal to Leyte

The Allied strategy was called **island hopping.** Allied forces would seize key Japanese-held islands while bypassing others that were then isolated. First the Solomon Islands had to be captured. Early in August 1942 American troops landed on three islands of the group. Two of the islands were captured quickly. But on **Guadalcanal** Island some of the hardest fighting of the Pacific war took place. For six months the Americans struggled slowly ahead through dense jungles. The Japanese troops resisted stubbornly. They were ready to die to the last man for their country. Japanese sharpshooters tied themselves high in trees. Machine gun teams set up their weapons in caves from which retreat was impossible. Before Guadalcanal was finally reclaimed in February 1943, 20,000 Japanese were killed.

As Nimitz's forces advanced, every island they attacked was defended with equal determination. The Japanese fought desperately for every inch of ground. When American marines went

Culver Pictures

Fleet Admiral Chester W. Nimitz was made commander of the Pacific Fleet after Pearl Harbor.

LEARNING FROM TABLES. *Most people believed there would never be a war as destructive as the Great War. They were wrong. How do the statistics in this table compare with those from the Great War in the table on page 841?*

MILITARY DEATHS IN WORLD WAR II					
ALLIES			**AXIS**		
Soviet Union	7,500,000		Germany	3,500,000	
China	2,200,000		Japan	1,219,000	
United States	405,399		Italy*	307,448	
Great Britain	329,208		Others	912,000	
France	210,671				
Others	300,000				
Total	10,945,278		Total	5,938,448	
	Total		16,883,726		

*Italian losses: 294,297 as member of Axis;
13,151 against Germany after Sept. 8, 1943

ashore on the island of Tarawa, they were opposed by 4,500 troops. Only 17 of these Japanese soldiers were taken prisoner. All the rest died in battle.

To the south MacArthur's army was carrying out its part of the plan. In October 1944 it recaptured the Philippines. In the **Battle of Leyte Gulf** the navy destroyed the last major Japanese fleet. Now the United States had complete control of Philippine waters.

Iwo Jima and Okinawa

The Allies next secured the bases needed for the invasion of Japan. The marines first fought hard to capture the tiny island of **Iwo Jima,** 750 miles (1,200 kilometers) south of Japan. The fight to capture Iwo Jima was bitter. On February 23 the victorious marines reached the top of Mount Suribachi, a volcano on the southern tip of the island.

Island-hopping forces moved determinedly across the Pacific as they closed in on Japan. Here American fighters signal the conquest of this small island by hanging an American flag between tropical palm trees.

Associated Press

The Allies Win in the Pacific   969

Carl Mydans/Life Picture Service

Driven from the Philippines early in the war, in 1944 Douglas MacArthur returned as he had promised. Soon the U.S. had complete control of the Philippines and surrounding waters.

As they crawled toward the rim of the crater, they came under fire from Japanese soldiers dug in on the other side of the mountain. A fierce fight developed. To rally his men one marine picked up an iron pipe, bound a small American flag he was carrying to it, and held it for the men to see. Later another marine arrived with a larger flag and pole. The victorious marines proudly planted it at the top of the mountain. A photographer took a picture of this famous second flag raising over Iwo Jima. That picture has become the most reproduced image—in paintings and sculptures—of the Second World War.

Two weeks after taking Iwo Jima, American troops went ashore on **Okinawa,** a much larger island only 350 miles (560 kilometers) from Japan. Before the battle for Okinawa ended in June 1945, the Japanese had suffered over 100,000 casualties, the Americans over 11,000.

The United States now had complete control of both air and sea. From airfields throughout the Pacific, American planes bombed Japan mercilessly. American battleships and cruisers moved in closer to pound industrial targets with their heaviest guns. Soon every important Japanese city was a smoking ruin.

As American forces neared Japan, they were repeatedly pestered by **kamikaze** attacks. These suicide pilots, who crashed their planes

Joe Rosenthal/Wide World Photos

into the approaching American fleet, had pledged their lives to protect Japan. They took their name from a divine wind believed to have foiled an invasion of Japan centuries before.

All Americans take pride in this moment as the flag is raised on Mt. Suribachi on the island of Iwo Jima. Associated Press photographer Joe Rosenthal won a Pulitzer Prize in 1945 for this picture. It served as a model for the United States Marine Corps War Memorial in Washington, D.C.

The Atomic Bomb

Victory was now certain. Although Japanese leaders had begun trying to arrange a surrender, progress was extremely slow. Military experts expected that Japan would have to be invaded, at tremendous cost. Japanese soldiers had demonstrated repeatedly that they would fight every battle to the last man. Some authorities believed that the United States would suffer 1 million more casualties before Japan was conquered.

This was the situation President Truman faced when he learned that American scientists had produced a new and terrible weapon—

STRATEGIES FOR SUCCESS

EVALUATING DECISIONS

Many key decisions made by world leaders have worldwide consequences, both at the time and for the future. Such decisions are debated endlessly by historians. By using historical imagination to understand the situation at the time and analyzing the consequences, it is possible to evaluate the decision. This evaluation will help you learn to make better decisions.

How to Evaluate Decisions

To evaluate decisions, follow these steps.

1. **Determine the nature of the decision to be made.** Use research and historical imagination to take into account the conditions that existed at the time the decision was made.
2. **Identify the alternatives available.** Note the possible choices the decision maker had.
3. **List the risks and benefits of each alternative.** Note the short-term and long-term effects of each choice.
4. **Weigh the costs and benefits of each alternative.** Compare the possible benefits and costs. Don't overlook possible future benefits or costs.
5. **Evaluate the decision.** Determine if, all things considered, the decision was a good one or a bad one. Remember that the long-range effects may not have been evident at the time the decision was made.

Applying the Strategy

Read the following paragraphs about Truman's decisions concerning the end of World War II.

Victory was now certain. Still, military experts expected that the cost of invading Japan would be enormous. Japanese soldiers had demonstrated repeatedly that they would fight every battle to the last man. Some authorities believed that the United States would suffer 1 million more casualties before Japan was conquered.

This was the situation President Truman faced when he learned that American scientists had produced a new and terrible weapon—the atomic bomb. . . . President Truman had to make an extremely difficult decision. Dropping an atomic bomb on a Japanese city would kill thousands of innocent civil-

ians. He also feared use of the terrible force would turn international sentiment against the United States. Yet Truman felt that he had no choice. Without the atomic bomb far more people would be killed before the war was over. He believed that the only way to convince the proud Japanese that further resistance was useless was to use this revolutionary bomb against them.

Let's evaluate Truman's decision making. What was the nature of the decision to be made? Truman had to decide how to end the war as quickly and with as few losses as possible. What were his alternatives? He could invade Japan. Or he could use the terrible new atomic bomb. What were the risks and benefits of each alternative? Invading Japan might cost 1 million more American casualties. But it followed the practices of conventional warfare. Using the atomic bomb might end the war much more quickly, sparing hundreds of thousands of lives on both sides. But unleashing the horrible destruction might turn international furor against the United States. How do the risks and benefits of each alternative compare? Truman chose to use the bomb to end the war quickly, thus avoiding a bloody invasion of Japan. The following paragraphs describe the situation further.

On August 6, 1945, in one blinding flash 75,000 people died. Another 100,000 were injured. Another atomic bomb was dropped on the city of Nagasaki. The radioactivity released by the explosions caused hundreds of persons to die horrible, lingering deaths. Later many children were born deformed because of radioactive damage suffered by their parents. Was there no way that the Japanese could have been shown the power of the bomb without using it on human beings?

On the other hand, the bomb may have saved lives— Japanese as well as American. Far more people would have died in an all-out invasion than died in the atomic blasts. There was also the hope that a demonstration of the horrors of atomic warfare would convince the entire world that such a weapon must never be used again. So far none has.

Do you think President Truman made the correct decision? Support your position.

For independent practice, see Practicing the Strategy on pages 976–77.

the **atomic bomb.** On orders from President Roosevelt, scientists had been working on the top-secret **Manhattan Project** since early 1942. Now they had produced a weapon with the explosive force of 20,000 tons of TNT. This tremendous power was released by the breaking of the chemical bonds that held together the atoms of uranium and plutonium, two highly radioactive elements.

President Truman had to make an extremely difficult decision. Dropping an atomic bomb on a Japanese city would kill thousands of innocent civilians. He also feared use of the terrible force would turn international sentiment against the United States. Yet Truman felt that he had no choice. Without the atomic bomb far more people might be killed before the war was over. He believed that the only way to convince the proud Japanese that further resistance was useless was to use this revolutionary bomb against them.

The mushroom cloud of nuclear destruction rose twice over wartime Japan. Such a sight recalls the address to the UN by Pope Paul VI: "Ne jamais plus la guerre": "Never again war."

Bettmann Newsphotos

The Allies Win in the Pacific   973

J.R. Eyerman/Life Picture Service

The aftermath of the bombing of Nagasaki shocked all who saw it. Is it any wonder that the Japanese surrendered when they witnessed such terrible destruction?

On August 6, 1945, an American bomber dropped the first atomic bomb on Hiroshima, a city of 344,000. In one blinding flash 75,000 people died. Another 100,000 were injured. John Hersey collected accounts such as the following from the survivors of the explosion.

❝ Then a tremendous flash of light cut across the sky. Mr. Tanimoto has a distinct recollection that it traveled from east to west, from the city toward the hills. It seemed a sheet of sun. . . . Mr. Tanimoto took four or five steps and threw himself between two big rocks in the garden. He . . . did not see what happened. He felt a sudden pressure, and then splinters and pieces of board and fragments of tile fell on him. . . .

As Mrs. Nakamura stood watching her neighbor, everything flashed whiter than any white she had ever seen. . . .

The reflex of a mother set her in motion toward her children. She had taken a single step . . . when something picked her up and she seemed to fly into the next room over the raised sleeping platform, pursued by parts of her house.

Timbers fell around her as she landed, and a shower of tile pommelled her; everything became dark, for she was buried. The debris did not cover her deeply. She rose and freed herself. She heard a child cry, ''Mother, help me!,'' and saw her youngest—Myeko, the five-year-old—buried up to her breast and unable to move. As Mrs. Nakamura started to frantically claw her way toward the baby, she could see or hear nothing of her other children.[1] ""

[1] From *Hiroshima* by John Hersey

When the Japanese still hesitated to surrender, another atomic bomb was dropped on the city of **Nagasaki.** This convinced the Japanese. On September 2, **V-J Day** (Victory in Japan), the Japanese signed terms of surrender. World War II was finally over.

The terrible destruction caused by the atom bombing of Hiroshima and Nagasaki has resulted in a long controversy about President Truman's decision. Even today, people disagree on whether or not the president did the right thing. Aside from the immediate loss of so many lives, the radioactivity—emissions harmful to humans—released by the atomic explosions caused hundreds of people to die horrible, lingering deaths. Later many children were born deformed because of radioactive damage suffered by their parents. Was there no way that the Japanese could have been shown the power of the bomb without using it on human beings?

The bomb may have saved lives—Japanese as well as American. Most people thought that far more Americans would have died in an all-out invasion. There was also the hope that a demonstration of the horrors of atomic warfare would convince the entire world that such a weapon must never be used again. So far none has.

The final judgment on President Truman's decision lies in the future. It depends upon what all of us and all our descendants do with our knowledge of the atomic bomb and the dreadful consequences of atomic explosions.

The Horrors of War

The Second World War made Americans see how horrible war really is. Photographs of survivors of the Bataan Death March in the Philippines, of the liberation of the concentration camps of the Holocaust, and of the barren landscapes of Hiroshima and Nagasaki made the point clearer than ever before. People around the world began to feel that the world could not survive another global war. 🖃

Point of View

A joint study by Japanese and Americans a few months after World War II revealed the extent of the atomic bombing of Hiroshima.

"In the case of an atomic bombing . . . a community does not merely receive an impact; the community itself is destroyed. Within 2 kilometers of the atomic bomb's hypocenter all life and property were shattered, burned, and buried under ashes. The visible forms of the city where people once carried on their daily lives vanished without a trace. The destruction was sudden and thorough; there was virtually no chance to escape. . . . Citizens who had lost no family members in the holocaust were as rare as stars at sunrise. . . .**"**

From *The Making of the Atomic Bomb,* Richard Rhodes, 1986

Return to the Preview & Review on page 966.

CHAPTER 26 REVIEW

1922
Mussolini takes power in Italy

1931
Japan seizes Manchuria

1932
Roosevelt elected preside

1933
Hitler becomes dictator
of Germany

Chapter Summary
Read the statements below. Choose one, and write a paragraph explaining its importance.
1. Despite the rise of totalitarian governments, most Americans believed in isolationism.
2. Hitler insisted Jews were an inferior people. He set up concentration camps for the Jews and murdered nearly 6 million of them. This genocide is called the Holocaust.
3. Roosevelt sought ways to check the aggressors without becoming involved in a shooting war.
4. Hitler's war machine invaded Poland, starting World War II.
5. Japanese bombing of Pearl Harbor brought the United States into World War II.
6. Allied efforts focused on Europe first. By early 1945 Allied armies had retaken Europe and Germany had surrendered.
7. In the Pacific the Allies then island-hopped toward Japan. Atomic bombs dropped on Japan in 1945 ended the war.
8. The horrors of World War II made many people realize that global war must now be avoided.

Reviewing Chronological Order
Number your paper 1-5. Then study the time line above and place the following events in the order in which they happened by writing the first next to 1, the second next to 2, and so on.
1. V-E Day
2. Lend-Lease Act
3. Germany invades Poland
4. V-J Day
5. Atomic bomb dropped on Hiroshima

Understanding Main Ideas
1. What was the reaction of most Americans to the aggressions of the 1930s? How were the neutrality acts part of this reaction?
2. Describe U.S. actions that showed the step-by-step movement away from the neutrality of the 1930s to open aid for the Allies by 1941.
3. By 1942 which were the major Axis and Allied countries?
4. How were minorities affected by World War II, including Japanese Americans?

5. Explain the importance of Operation Overlord and the battles of the Coral Sea and Midway.

Thinking Critically
1. **Synthesizing.** You are either a pacifist or a conscientious objector during World War II. Write a handbill explaining why you think war is wrong.
2. **Creating.** Create a poster, poem, song, or short story about the historic raising of the American flag on the island of Iwo Jima.
3. **Evaluating.** Choose either the topic of Japanese internment or the use of the atomic bomb. Discuss whether you think the correct decision was made by the United States. If you think the decision was incorrect, suggest an alternate course of action. Support your position.

Writing About History
With your classmates, use historical imagination to write letters about the war. Some of you might write letters home to your families from the front. Tell of your experiences and describe one of the U.S. generals. Other classmates might write letters to you from home telling of their work in the U.S. for the war effort. Use the information in Chapter 26 to help you write your letters.

Practicing the Strategy
Review the strategy on page 972.
Evaluating Decisions. Study the sections titled "Negotiations with Japan" and "Attack on Pearl Harbor" on pages 950–52, then answer the following questions.
1. Why did Japan attack Pearl Harbor?
2. What response did the United States make to the attack on Pearl Harbor? Do you think that the Japanese expected the United States to respond in this way? Why or why not?
3. What alternate course of action, if any, could Japan have taken? What alternate course could the U.S. have taken? If you do not think that there were alternate courses, explain why.

1939
Germany invades Poland
★
Second World War begins

1940
Battle of Britain
★
U.S. institutes draft
★
Roosevelt elected to third term

1941
Lend-Lease Act
★
Japanese attack Pearl Harbor
★
U.S. declares war on Japan

1942
Battles of Coral Sea, Midway, and Guadalcanal
★
Operation Torch

1943
Italian campaign

1944
Operation Overlord
★
MacArthur returns to Philippines
★
Roosevelt wins fourth term

1945
Roosevelt dies, Truman takes over
★
Germany surrenders (V-E Day)
★
Hiroshima and Nagasaki
★
Japan surrenders; the war ends (V-J Day)

---

4. Evaluate the decisions made by Japan and by the United States. Support your position.

Using Primary Sources

During World War II the American people were asked to show their loyalty to the United States. If families worked together to help the war effort, they earned a V-Home certificate, which they received from their local Defense Council and which they could place in their windows. As you read the following text of the V-Home certificate, think about how the war changed people's lives.

THIS IS A V-HOME!

We in this house are fighting. We know this war will be easy to lose and hard to win. We mean to win it. Therefore we solemnly pledge all our energies and all our resources to fight for freedom and against fascism. We serve notice to all that we are personally carrying the fight to the enemy, in these ways:

I. This home follows the instructions of its air-raid warden, in order to protect itself against attack by air.

II. This home conserves food, clothing, transportation, and health, in order to hasten an unceasing flow of war materials to our men at the front.

III. This home salvages essential materials, in order that they may be converted to immediate war uses.

IV. This home refuses to spread rumors designed to divide our nation.

V. This home buys War Savings Stamps and Bonds [stamps and bonds sold by the U.S. government to help finance the war] regularly. We are doing these things because we know we must to Win This War.

1. In what ways did the war change the everyday lives of ordinary people?

2. Do you think that the war emergency justified these changes?

3. Why do you think that it was necessary for people to conserve their health?

Linking History & Geography

The conflict that began in the 1930s erupted into the Second World War. Many nations were involved, and fighting raged throughout the world. To understand the global nature of the war and the tremendous distances involved, with your classmates prepare a world map showing the United States and the areas of North Africa, Europe, and the Pacific involved in the fighting. Then create two large maps to show the war in Europe and in the Pacific. Label the sites of the major battles and give short reports on each.

Enriching Your Study of History

1. Individual Project. On April 12, 1945, Franklin D. Roosevelt died suddenly in Warm Springs, Georgia. The new president, Harry S Truman, told reporters, "I felt like the moon, the stars, and all the planets had fallen on me." Use historical imagination to interview Truman on his first day in the White House. Discuss with him some of the major decisions he must make, such as his plans for ending the war.

2. Cooperative Project. Your group will create an oral history of one of the following: a person who fought in World War II or a person who worked on the home front. Each person in your group should prepare five questions that will lead the interview in a purposeful way. Get permission from the subject to tape the interview. Play your taped oral history for the class.

Chapter 26 Review   **977**

America in the Cold War

The Cold War began before World War II was over. The United States and the Soviet Union, marching toward Berlin to crush Hitler's capital, already distrusted each other. Like master chess players each side played up the other's weaknesses and for the next half century they held one another in wary check. Americans criticized the Soviets for building the Berlin Wall and for violations of human rights. The Soviets challenged America to resolve its racial inequalities and to redistribute its great wealth more fairly among the people. Sympathy for communist satellite countries such as Poland, Hungary, and Czechoslovakia was strong in America. Would this Cold War rivalry erupt into a global war?

Preview & Review

Use these questions to guide your reading. Answer the questions after completing Section 1.
Understanding Issues, Events, & Ideas. Describe world politics in the late 1940s, using the following words: San Francisco Conference, United Nations, Big Three, Yalta Conference, puppet government, communist, Cold War, capitalism.
1. What was the result of the San Francisco Conference?
2. How was the United Nations created?
3. Why did the Big Three meet at Yalta in 1945?
Thinking Critically. What do you think is the most important sentence in the preamble to the United Nations Charter? Why?

1. THE UNITED NATIONS

The Search for World Peace

Any war as widespread and destructive as World War II was bound to cause difficulties and conflicts that would not disappear simply because the shooting had stopped. President Roosevelt had realized this. During the war he prepared to face postwar problems. In particular he hoped to avoid the mistakes that Woodrow Wilson had made after World War I. Wilson's policies had led to the rejection of the Versailles Treaty by the Senate.

In 1943 Congress had agreed to commit to American participation in an international peace-keeping organization. In July 1944 the United States, Great Britain, the Soviet Union, and China met to outline plans for such an organization. Then in 1945 delegates from 50 nations met in San Francisco to draft a charter for the organization to be called the United Nations.

Roosevelt succeeded in avoiding Wilson's mistake of not consulting the opposition party about the peace treaty. He made Senator Arthur Vandenberg of Michigan, who was the leading Republican on the Foreign Relations Committee, a delegate to the **San Francisco Conference** to draft the **United Nations** (UN) charter. As a result the

UPI/Bettmann Newsphotos

Flanked by the flags of 50 nations, Secretary of State Edward Stettinius signs the United Nations Charter on behalf of the United States. President Truman stands to his right. With your classmates, name some of the actions taken and programs sponsored by the United Nations since its founding in 1945.

Senate approved the treaty that made the United States a member of the UN by a vote of 87 to 2.

The new international organization was created to replace the League of Nations. The United Nations did not have the power to make the United States or any other major power do anything it did not want to do. Under the UN charter the United States, Soviet Union, Great Britain, France, and China all had the right to block any UN Security Council action by their veto power.

The United Nations had wide appeal in America. Politicians, scholars, even religious figures such as evangelist Billy Graham, Rabbi Joshua Loth Liebman, and Monsignor Fulton J. Sheen, supported it. All conducted enormously popular television programs. They urged Americans to accept their place as leaders of the world community.

The United Nations Charter

The delegates in San Francisco represented three fourths of the people on the planet. Long weeks of discussion and debate were necessary for the delegates to agree on the wording of the charter. It was then ratified by the separate nations. On October 24, 1945, the world organization officially came into being.

John Isaac, UN Photo

Olive branches—traditional symbols of peace—surround a map of the world on the United Nations flag.

The preamble to the charter is a fine statement of the hopes of the postwar world:

" We the peoples of the United Nations, determined to save succeeding generations from the scourge of war, which twice in our lifetime has brought untold sorrow to mankind, and

To reaffirm faith in fundamental human rights, in the dignity and worth of the human person, in the equal rights of men and women and of nations large and small, and

To establish conditions under which justice and respect for the obligations arising from treaties and other sources of international law can be maintained, and

To promote social progress and better standards of life in larger freedom,

And for these ends

To practice tolerance and live together in peace with one another as good neighbors, and

To unite our strength to maintain international peace and security, and

To ensure, by the acceptance of principles and the institution of methods, that armed force shall not be used, save in the common interest, and

To employ international machinery for the promotion of the economic and social advancement of all peoples,

Have resolved to combine our efforts to accomplish these aims.[1] "

The Yalta Conference

President Roosevelt and Prime Minister Churchill worked closely together on military and diplomatic problems during the war. Both also consulted frequently with the Soviet dictator Joseph Stalin. The most important meeting of the **Big Three,** as they were called, took place at the Soviet seaside resort of Yalta in February 1945.

At the time of this **Yalta Conference** the war in Europe was almost over. The war had started back in 1939 when Germany had invaded Poland. The Allies had entered the war with the intention of restoring an independent Polish government. Yet by 1945 Poland had been entirely occupied by the Soviet troops who were driving the Germans out. Roosevelt and Churchill hoped to prevent the Soviet Union from keeping too much territory in Poland.

Stalin, however, was determined to prevent any government unfriendly to the Soviet Union from controlling Poland. The Germans had invaded his country from Poland in 1941. Many times in the past other enemies had crossed Poland to attack the Soviet Union.

[1]From the preamble to *The United Nations Charter*

UPI/Bettmann Newsphotos

From this meeting at Yalta on the Crimean Sea in the Soviet Union came the compromises of the Cold War. Left to right are Winston Churchill, soon to lose power in England; Franklin Roosevelt, gravely ill after twelve years as president of the United States; and the ruthless Soviet dictator Joseph Stalin. These "Big Three" worked out the plan that allowed most of Eastern Europe to remain under Soviet control. Why do you think the United States and Great Britain allowed the Soviets to dominate Eastern Europe?

The difficulty was that no freely elected Polish government was likely to be friendly to the Soviet Union. After all, the Soviet Union had joined Germany in dividing up Poland before the Great World War and again in 1939. Soviet troops had treated the Poles brutally. Thousands of Polish officers had been murdered in cold blood by the Soviets in the Katyn Forest Massacre of 1940.

After considerable discussion the Big Three worked out a compromise. The Soviet Union was to add a large part of eastern Poland to its territory. In the rest of Poland free elections were to be held. The Poles could choose whomever they wished to govern them.

The trouble was that Stalin did not keep his promise.to permit free elections in the new Polish republic. Instead he set up a **puppet government,** one that he could control as completely as a puppeteer controls a puppet. This government was bitterly resented by the vast majority of the Polish people.

Probably nothing could have prevented the Soviet Union from dominating Poland. Soviet troops had already occupied the country. The Allies could have driven them out only by going to war. And war with the Soviet Union at that time was unthinkable. Rather, the Allies hoped to convince the Soviets to join them in defeating Japan, a nation the Soviets were not at war with.

The United Nations   981

During the siege of Leningrad by the Germans and what Napoleon once called "General Winter," a woman pulls firewood across a snowy square. The poster behind her says "Death to the Murderers of Children!" Why would the Soviets choose such a subject to rally the people during the terrible siege?

Sovfoto

Most Americans admired and respected the Soviets in 1945, even though the Soviet Union was a **communist** society in which the government controlled the economy and was ruled by a dictator. The Soviets had defended their country bravely and had contributed their full share to the Allied destruction of the Nazi armies. Indeed, more than 7 million—perhaps as many as 20 million—Soviets died in the war, many of them civilians who starved during the two-year Siege of Leningrad by the Germans.

General Eisenhower referred at this time to the long record of "unbroken friendship" between the United States and the Soviet Union. He said, "The ordinary Russian seems to me to bear a marked similarity to what we call an 'average American.'"

However, the seeds of what was called the **Cold War** were planted in these broken promises and suspicions. It became a standoff between western **capitalism,** in which individuals control the economy, and communism, between democracy and totalitarianism. ▱

Return to the Preview & Review on page 978.

2. TRUMAN IN THE COLD WAR

Getting Back to "Normal"

President Roosevelt died a few weeks after returning from Yalta. Less than a month later Germany surrendered. The Soviets then declared war on Japan, keeping a promise Stalin had made to Roosevelt at Yalta. However, their contribution to the defeat of Japan was not needed because the United States ended the war by dropping the atomic bomb.

The new president, Harry S Truman, was more suspicious of Soviet motives than Roosevelt had been. He believed that the Soviets expected the United States to suffer a serious postwar economic depression. They were "planning to take advantage of our setback," he later wrote.

Truman was eager to frustrate Soviet plans by preventing a depression. But could he handle the complicated task of converting the economy from wartime to peacetime production?

Truman had grown up on a Missouri farm. He had been an artillery captain in World War I. During the 1920s he got involved in Missouri politics. He served as a local judge, and in 1934 he was elected to the United States Senate. He received the 1944 Democratic vice presidential nomination because party leaders needed a likable candidate without any enemies to replace Vice President Henry A. Wallace, whom they considered too radical.

Truman had a reputation for being honest and reasonably liberal, but he seemed a rather ordinary politician. Yet no one had ever accused him of being unwilling to accept responsibility. When he became president, he put a sign on his desk in the White House that said, "The Buck Stops Here." However, many people, including Truman himself, wondered whether he would be "big enough" to fill Franklin Roosevelt's shoes.

The depression that Truman feared never occurred. War contracts were canceled and thousands of war workers lost their jobs. However, millions of consumers had saved money during the war when there were few civilian goods to buy. The demand for all sorts of products from houses and automobiles to washing machines and nylon stockings was enormous. No automobiles had been manufactured for civilian use since 1941. Millions of people wanted to replace their worn-out cars. Returning soldiers and laid-off war workers quickly found new jobs.

Unfortunately, the huge demand for goods could not be satisfied quickly. Shortages developed. A period of confusion and bickering followed. After four years of going without and paying high taxes, people wanted to enjoy themselves. They believed that they had sacrificed enough for the common good and the national interest. Now they hoped to concentrate on their own interests. Workers

Preview & Review

Use these questions to guide your reading. Answer the questions after completing Section 2.
Understanding Issues, Events, & Ideas. Use the following words to discuss Truman's domestic programs: Fair Deal, wage and price controls, Twenty-second Amendment, Taft-Hartley Act, closed shop, "cooling-off period."

Explain Truman's foreign policy, using these words: Iron Curtain, Truman Doctrine, Marshall Plan, satellite nation, Republic of West Germany, Berlin Airlift, North Atlantic Treaty Organization, Warsaw Pact, containment policy.

1. Why didn't a postwar depression occur?
2. How did Truman respond to the Taft-Hartley Act?
3. What caused the communist parties in Europe to grow stronger?
4. What effect did the Marshall Plan have on the economy of Europe? On the politics?
5. What agreements were made by signers of the NATO treaty?

Thinking Critically. Define each word in the phrase "Iron Curtain." Then explain why you think Churchill used this phrase to describe the political division between Western and Eastern Europe.

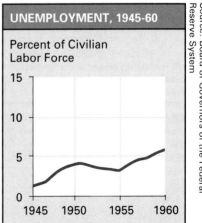

Source: Board of Governors of the Federal Reserve System

UNEMPLOYMENT, 1945–60

Percent of Civilian Labor Force

LEARNING FROM GRAPHS.
Why did unemployment rise between 1945 and 1950?

The CIO Political Action Committee sponsored this 1944 poster by Ben Shahn, an artist who portrayed important social issues.

for full employment after the war
REGISTER • VOTE
C I O POLITICAL ACTION COMMITTEE

For Full Employment After War Register Vote. Offset lithograph, 30 × 39⅞. Collection, Museum of Modern Art, New York. Gift of CIO Political Action Committee.

Source: *Historical Statistics of the United States*

PURCHASING POWER*, 1940-60

$2.20
$2.00
$1.80
$1.60
$1.40
$1.20
$1.00
$0.80
$0.60
$0.40
$0.20
0

1940   1950   1960

*Purchasing power is computed using the average prices of specific goods and services.

LEARNING FROM GRAPHS. *Statistics on purchasing power are often a good measure of the value of money and the overall effects of inflation on consumers. For statistical purposes, 1957 was chosen as the base year. In that year the value of $1.00 was $1.00. The purchasing power of all the other years are compared to that year. How much was $1.00 worth in 1960? You may wish to find what it would buy today.*

demanded higher wages but protested angrily against increases in consumer prices. Manufacturers wanted all controls lifted and their taxes reduced.

President Truman tried to resist these demands. He proposed a group of reforms he called the **Fair Deal** to balance national and personal interests. It called for larger social security benefits, a national health insurance plan, a higher minimum wage, money for public housing, and a continuation of the Fair Employment Practices Committee. At the same time the president resisted efforts to do away with **wage and price controls**—limits the government had set during the war.

Congress refused to pass most of the laws Truman requested. Few workers or employers supported any of Truman's proposals except those that benefited them directly. The president became more and more frustrated and less and less popular.

Finally, in late 1946 nearly all wartime economic controls were removed. Prices then rose sharply. Workers responded by demanding higher wages. When they got them, their increased spending caused prices to go up again. An upward spiral of wages and prices was set in motion, one that has continued almost without interruption to the present day.

Turning Out the Democrats

By the fall of 1946 even large numbers of Democrats had decided that Truman was incompetent. "To err is Truman," became a commonly heard wisecrack. "Had enough?" Republican candidates asked during the 1946 Congressional campaign, "Vote Republican."

A majority of the voters in 1946 did just that. The Republican party won control of both houses of Congress for the first time since the 1920s.

This new Congress set out to reverse the trend toward liberal legislation that had begun with the election of Franklin Roosevelt. First it passed the **Twenty-second Amendment** to the Constitution, limiting future presidents to two terms. This was a slap at Roosevelt's memory. The Congress also reduced appropriations for many social welfare programs. It tried to lower the income taxes of people with large incomes, but Truman vetoed that bill.

The most controversial measure of the session was the **Taft-Hartley Act,** passed in June 1947. The Wagner Labor Relations Act of 1935 had banned unfair labor practices by employers. The new Taft-Hartley law prohibited unfair practices by unions. It outlawed the **closed shop**—the clause in many labor contracts that required job applicants to join the union before they could be hired. It also gave the president the right to get court injunctions which would force striking unions to call off their strikes for an 80-day **"cooling-off" period.** The president could only seek these injunctions when strikes threatened the national interest. Yet judges seldom refused to issue injunctions when the president asked for them. Truman vetoed the Taft-Hartley bill, but Congress repassed it over his veto.

Senator Robert Taft was known throughout Washington as "Mr. Republican." He was the son of the 27th president of the United States and sponsor of the Taft–Hartley Act.

The Truman Doctrine

Truman's domestic difficulties did not prevent him from developing a determined foreign policy. Because he was suspicious of Stalin's motives, he worried a great deal about the danger of Soviet expansion and the spread of communism.

In Europe the change from war to peace had not been easy. While the American economy had expanded during the war, in Europe the reverse was true. More than 30 million Europeans had been killed. The loss of so many potential workers was a terrible blow to the economies of every nation. More millions were homeless and hungry. Such people could not produce very effectively. In every country railroads had been wrecked, bridges blown up, factories smashed. About 25 percent of all the wealth of Great Britain was destroyed during the war. In Germany there were shortages of everything. A package of American cigarettes cost as much as a German laborer could earn in a month.

These conditions caused a rapid increase in the strength of communist parties in several Eastern European countries. Whether or not the Soviet government had anything to do with this trend, it was certainly willing to take advantage of it. Truman reasoned that once the communists got control of a government, as they had in Russia in 1917, they would do away with free elections. Then their opponents could get back into power only through revolt and bloodshed.

Harry S Truman's oil portrait was painted by Martha Kempton. Behind the president is the Capitol. What did Truman's famous sign, "The Buck Stops Here," tell visitors to the Oval Office in the White House?

Truman in the Cold War   985

Johnny Florea/Life Magazine © Time Warner, Inc.

Robert Capa/Magnum Photos

Above are two images of postwar Germany: At left, a woman with all her belongings sits not far from the badly bombed cathedral in Cologne. At right is the Brandenburg Gate in Berlin, later closed by the famous wall built to separate East and West Germany.

It therefore seemed absolutely necessary to Truman that the spread of communism in Europe be checked. But how could this be done without starting another war? The question became urgent in early 1947. Greece seemed about to fall behind what Churchill described as the **Iron Curtain**—the striking image he used to show the political division between democratic and communist territories in western and eastern Europe. Communist guerrillas in Greece were seeking to overthrow the conservative Greek government. Great Britain had been providing aid to that government. In February 1947 the British informed President Truman that because of their own economic problems they could no longer afford to help Greece.

Truman believed that if Greece became communist, its neighbor, Turkey, might also fall under Soviet influence. He thought this would give the Soviets the confidence to move against Italy and perhaps France. He apparently believed this even though the Soviets were not supporting the Greek guerrillas. Truman was sure the communists would then seize American businesses in these countries, ruining American economic interests in Europe. The president therefore asked Congress for $400 million to aid Greece and Turkey. He said:

“ It must be the policy of the United States to support free peoples who are resisting . . . outside pressures. . . . I believe that we must assist free peoples to work out their destinies in their own way. . . . Our help should be primarily through economic and financial aid. . . .[1] ”

[1]From speech to Congress by Harry S Truman, March 12, 1947

986   AMERICA IN THE COLD WAR

STRATEGIES FOR SUCCESS

ANALYZING HISTORICAL INTERPRETATIONS

How and why did the Cold War begin? Historical interpretations of how and why it began are varied. A historical interpretation is an explanation by a historian about why an event happened as it did. One historian may emphasize a different cause or effect than another, or they may disagree completely. This difference occurs, in part, because historians bring different points of view to their interpretations. To effectively interpret historical accounts, you must analyze historical interpretations and evaluate their supporting evidence.

How to Analyze Historical Interpretations

Before learning the steps for analzying historical interpretations, review Comparing Points of View on page 855. Then to analyze historical interpretations, follow these steps.

1. **Identify the main points of the interpretation.** Determine the main points and conclusions.
2. **Determine the historian's point of view.** Identify circumstances that might have influenced the historian's interpretation. Note whether the historian was a participant or observer, or wrote a later interpretation.
3. **Assess the evidence and reasoning.** Study the information provided. Check the logic of the historian's reasoning.
4. **Compare the interpretation with other interpretations of the event.** Note similarities and differences among interpretations. If there are differences, ask yourself why such differences exist.
5. **Evaluate the interpretation.** Based on your analysis of the interpretation, assess its reliability. Accept or reject its main points.

Applying the Strategy

Read the following excerpts that offer different interpretations of how and why the Cold War began. Excerpt A is from an article written in 1947 by George Kennan, at the time Counsellor of the United States Embassy in Moscow. Excerpt B is from *The Holy Crusade: Some Myths of Origin* written in 1969 by Michael Parenti.

Excerpt A

Belief is maintained in the basic badness of capitalism, in the inevitability of its destruction, and in the obligation . . . to assist in that destruction [and in

an] antagonism between capitalism and socialism.

Basically, the antagonism remains. . . . And from it flow many of the phenomena which we find disturbing in . . . foreign policy: the secretiveness, . . . the wary suspiciousness and the basic unfriendliness.

This means that we are going to continue for a long time to find the Russians difficult to deal with.

Excerpt B

It was Harry Truman who succeeded to the Presidency before the war's end, and no reading of his opinions or actions would uphold the view that the United States was motivated by a sincere intention to extend friendly cooperation, only to be taken by surprise by Russian aggressiveness. If Truman brought anything to the White House, it was an urgency . . . "to get tough" with the Kremlin. "Unless Russia is faced with an iron fist and strong language, another war is in the making," he concluded, "The Russians would soon be put in their places" and the United States would then "take the lead in running the world in the way that the world ought to be run. . . ." What is overlooked is the probability that Truman's own belligerent, uncompromising, and ungracious approach was a major factor in actualizing [causing] the struggle and in preventing the kind of accommodation [agreement] between the United States and the Soviet Union that is just beginning to emerge today.

Note that these historians differ greatly in their interpretations. Kennan stated that the Cold War resulted from communist antagonism toward capitalism. This caused the Soviets to see Americans as the enemy. What in Kennan's background influenced his point of view? He was a high-ranking official of the United States embassy in the Soviet Union, writing in 1947 as the Cold War began. He was considered an authority on Soviet-U.S. relations.

How does Parenti's interpretation differ? He claims the Cold War started with Truman's "get-tough" policies. Parenti's point of view differs almost as much as his interpretation. He is a political analyst writing in 1969, more than 20 years after the event. What other information would help you analyze these interpretations to allow you to assess their reliability?

For independent practice, see Practicing the Strategy on pages 1024–25.

This idea became known as the **Truman Doctrine.** Of course, Truman's reference to outside pressures, namely the Soviets, was either mistaken or a deliberate falsehood. But in the mood of the day Congress appropriated the money and the communist threat to Greece and Turkey was checked.

The Marshall Plan

The Truman Doctrine was popular in the United States because it appealed to both liberals and conservatives. Liberals liked the idea of helping the people of other countries defend their independence and rebuild their war-torn economies. Conservatives liked the idea of resisting communism and thus preserving the free enterprise system. Nearly everyone took pride in the great influence and prestige that came to the United States in other parts of the world.

Critics of the Truman Doctrine argued that it was a disguised form of imperialism. They saw it as a revived form of dollar diplomacy, similar to the old technique of encouraging American investments in nations like Nicaragua and Haiti before World War I. They also thought that the doctrine aimed too much at attacking communism and not enough at helping people in need.

National Portrait Gallery

In 1953 General George C. Marshall was awarded the Nobel Peace Prize. How did this selection pay tribute to the Truman Doctrine as well as the Marshall Plan?

To counter these objections, George C. Marshall, whom Truman had appointed secretary of state, proposed his **Marshall Plan** in a speech at Harvard University in June 1947. All the nations of Europe, including the Soviet Union, needed American help in rebuilding their war-damaged societies, Marshall said. But they also had to help themselves. The plan could not be imposed on the Europeans from the outside. The United States would provide money once the European nations had developed a European recovery plan.

Marshall's offer to include the Soviet Union was a bluff, or at least a gamble. If the Soviets had accepted it, Congress would probably not have provided the money to make the plan work. But Marshall did not think the Soviets would accept this plan, and he was right. They also forced the countries under its control to pull out of the meeting. The communists had no desire to contribute to the revival of the capitalist nations.

While the Soviet Union and the countries of eastern Europe under its control rejected the Marshall Plan, western Europeans adopted it eagerly. They soon created the Committee for European Economic Cooperation (CEEC) to decide what needed to be done and how much it would cost. Over the next few years the United States gave CEEC about $13 billion to carry out its plans.

The Marshall Plan was a brilliant success. By 1951 the economies of the participating nations were booming. Still, the plan had further divided Europe into two competing systems. When Czechoslovakia showed signs of accepting Marshall Plan aid, the local communist party seized power with Soviet support. Democracy was destroyed.

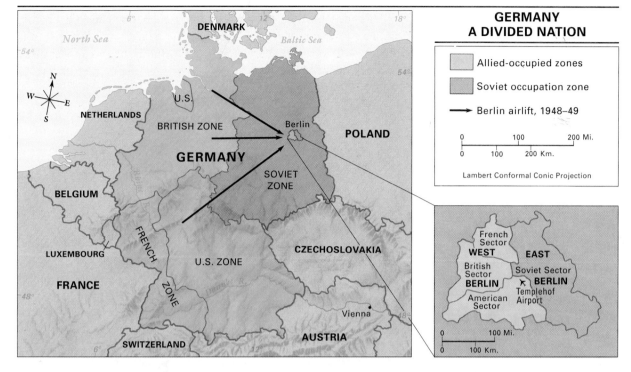

Allied-occupied zones

Soviet occupation zone

→ Berlin airlift, 1948–49

0   100   200 Mi.

0   100   200 Km.

Lambert Conformal Conic Projection

French Sector

WEST

British Sector

BERLIN

American Sector

EAST

Soviet Sector

BERLIN

Templehof Airport

0   100 Mi.

0   100 Km.

Czechoslovakia, like Poland, Hungary, and the other states of eastern Europe, fell into the Soviet orbit. The countries dominated by the Soviet Union became known as **satellite nations.**

The Berlin Airlift

After the war the victors had divided Germany into four zones. One zone was controlled by the United States, one by Great Britain, one by France, and one by the Soviet Union. Berlin, the capital city, was located in the Soviet zone. Because of Berlin's large size and importance, however, the western nations were unwilling to let the Soviets control it all. It too was divided into four zones.

In 1948 the United States, Great Britain, and France announced plans to create an independent **Republic of West Germany** from the part of Germany they controlled. This step led the Soviets to close all the roads leading across their zone to Berlin. They could not block the formation of the West German republic. But they might force the Allies to give up their zones in the capital city.

The Soviet action caused a serious crisis. If the Americans tried to ship supplies to Berlin by truck or train, they would run into a Soviet roadblock. Then they would either have to turn back or start a fight. Truman therefore decided to *fly* supplies to Berlin. Fortunately, Tempelhof Airport lay within the United States zone, in the heart of the city.

Truman's **Berlin Airlift** turned the tables on the Soviets. There was no way to block the air lanes. Now the Soviets would have to

LEARNING FROM MAPS. *The victorious Allies—the United States, Great Britain, France, and the Soviet Union—divided defeated Germany for purposes of administration. Soon after the war, however, the iron curtain clanged down across the country, separating western Germany from Soviet-dominated eastern Germany. The situation was even graver within the divided city of Berlin. West Berliners, surrounded by Soviet-controlled eastern Germany, felt seriously threatened as a result.*

Truman in the Cold War   989

Walter Sanders/Life Picture Service

Through the clouds over Berlin a C-47 swoops down with its supplies to keep the 2 million residents of West Berlin alive. Why had the Soviets blocked all highways and railroads to Berlin?

decide whether to allow the supplies to reach West Berlin or start fighting.

The Soviets chose to do nothing. They probably believed that it would be impossible to keep the 2 million residents of West Berlin supplied with food and other necessities by air alone.

The Berlin Airlift was assigned to the United States air force. Bulky products usually shipped by river barge or freight car had to be flown in on military planes. At one point General Lucius D. Clay, who had charge of the airlift, telephoned an American air force general in Frankfurt, Germany, "Have you any planes that can carry coal?" he asked.

"We must have a bad phone connection," the air force general replied, "It sounds like you are asking if we have any planes for carrying coal."

"Yes, that's what I said—coal."

"The air force can deliver anything," the astonished general then responded. And he proved that it could indeed. Over the next 11 months American and British planes flew some 277,000 missions into Berlin. Their cargoes kept West Berliners fed and working.

In May 1949 the Soviets gave up trying to squeeze the western powers out of Berlin. They lifted the land blockade. The city, however, remained divided into Soviet and Allied zones.

Containment

The United States and its western European friends responded to the communist takeover of Czechoslovakia and the blockade of Berlin by strengthening their own alliance. In April 1949 the United States, Great Britain, France, Italy, and eight other nations signed a treaty creating the **North Atlantic Treaty Organization** (NATO). The signers agreed to defend one another in case of attack and to form a unified military force for this purpose. By the time the NATO force was organized, the Soviet Union had exploded its first atomic bomb. The American monopoly on nuclear weapons had been broken. Soon after the Soviet Union and its satellites signed the **Warsaw Pact,** pledging mutual defense as NATO members had.

Rivalry between the communist and capitalist worlds grew steadily more intense. Neither side dared risk open warfare in the atomic age. Instead they waged the Cold War. For American leaders the main objective of the Cold War was to prevent the expansion of Soviet influence in every way possible short of all-out war. In 1947 George F. Kennan, a professional diplomat who had served for many years at the American embassy in Moscow, explained how the Cold War could be won. America must build up its armed forces and be prepared to *contain* Soviet expansion wherever it was attempted.

This **containment policy,** according to Kennan, President Truman, and most other Americans, was purely defensive in purpose. The Soviets, on the other hand, felt that the containment policy,

COLD WAR IN EUROPE, 1950s

- NATO members*
- Soviet Union and satellites
- Nonaligned nations
- Independent communist state

*North Atlantic Treaty Organization; other members: U.S., Canada, Iceland.

0   300   600 Mi.
0   300   600 Km.

Azimuthal Equal-Area Projection

LEARNING FROM MAPS. *Soviet refusal to leave the Eastern European countries it had liberated from Germany in World War II helped trigger the Cold War. What countries in Eastern Europe became Soviet satellites? Which have moved away from Soviet domination in recent years?*

Have you ever been involved in a disagreement which lasted so long that you could not remember who started it? If so, you will understand why historians have been unable to agree about who started the Cold War between the Soviet Union and the United States. It was called a "Cold War" because it was a war without direct military conflict. Yet it was bitterly contested.

The two superpowers engaged in this Cold War for more than 40 years after World War II. It began after the Yalta Conference, when the United States and the Soviet Union were still allies. It intensified in the 1950s with wars in Korea and Vietnam.

Historians agree that there was a Cold War but they have disagreed about which nation started it and why. In 1950, Thomas A. Bailey claimed in *America Faces Russia* that the Soviet Union was completely responsible. To historian William Appleman Williams, author of *American Relations* (1952), the Cold War was not a struggle between communism and democracy. Rather, it was a conflict brought about by the supposed need of American businesses for markets in other parts of the world, especially in the nations that were not industrialized.

In his 1965 book, *Atomic Diplomacy*, Gar Alperovitz insisted that the United States had started the Cold War in an effort to contain the spread of Soviet influence. Alperovitz claimed that President Truman's decision to drop the atomic bomb on Japan was part of this attempt to convince the Soviets that the United States had superior armed forces.

In the 1970s, several historians argued that the United States and the Soviet Union shared the blame. More recently, in *A Preponderance of Power* (1992), Melvyn P. Leffler attempted to explain the full significance of the Cold War, now that it is over. He argued that after the end of World War II, conditions around the world were so chaotic that American leaders felt Soviet communism was a threat to democracy everywhere. United States officials wished to stop the rise of communism in Europe and to integrate Germany and Japan into an American alliance system.

According to Leffler, some American policies like the Marshall Plan were wise. Other policies, however, were foolish, even dangerous. For example, the belief that if one developing nation went communist so would its neighbors was clearly incorrect. On balance, Leffler assigned "as much of the responsibility for the origins of the Cold War to the United States as to the Soviet Union." He reminds us, however, that a final judgment is impossible without a study of Soviet archives.

How will historians of the future explain the Cold War? Does the weakness of today's Russia indicate that American worries and fears all these years were needless? Does the ending of the conflict prove that America's foreign policy of trying to stop communism was correct? Does the Cold War's end after half a century of repeated crises mean that the atomic bomb is as much a force for peace among nations as a threat of destruction? Time will tell.

---

particularly the NATO force, would provoke war. Each side suspected the other of preparing all kinds of threatening schemes. In part the tensions of the Cold War were caused by poor communications between the communist and noncommunist diplomats. For this the secretive and overly suspicious Soviets were chiefly to blame.

The containment policy worked well for the United States and its allies. It enabled the western European nations to rebuild their economies and preserve their democratic political systems. It may even have helped prevent a major war. The chief difficulty with containment, from anyone's point of view, was that it tended to prolong the Cold War. A policy of negotiation and compromise might have ended it or at least avoided some of the tension and crises it produced. 🔳

Return to the Preview & Review on page 983.

3. TRUMAN SURVIVES HIS CRITICS

Preview & Review

Use these questions to guide your reading. Answer the questions after completing Section 3.

Understanding Issues, Events, & Ideas. Use the following words to describe the Cold War atmosphere at home and abroad in the early 1950s: Progressive party, Civil Rights Committee, States' Rights party, McCarthyism, North Korea, South Korea, Inchon, Yalu River, Korean War, McCarran Internal Security Act.

1. Who were the four candidates for president in 1948? For what reasons was Truman elected?
2. What events in 1949 and 1950 prompted a widespread fear of communism among the American people?
3. What kinds of accusations did Joseph McCarthy make? Why did many Americans believe him?
4. What provoked the Korean War? How did Truman respond?

Thinking Critically. Imagine that you witnessed a speech by Truman during his whistle-stop campaign. Explain why you would or would not vote for Truman in the election of 1948.

The Election of 1948

While the success of the Berlin Airlift was still in doubt, the 1948 presidential election campaign took place. The Democratic party was badly divided. Almost none of its leaders wanted to renominate Truman. Some supported Henry A. Wallace, who was running as the candidate of a new **Progressive party.** Wallace had been Truman's secretary of commerce. He believed that the Soviets' intentions were good—they wanted to help the countries of Eastern Europe as well as themselves—and that Truman's aggressive Cold War strategy was likely to lead to a real war. When Wallace criticized the Truman Doctrine, the president had forced him to resign. Wallace went on to attack the Marshall Plan and fight every aspect of Truman's containment policy.

Conservative southern Democrats opposed Truman because of his civil rights policy. In 1947 his **Civil Rights Committee** recommended laws protecting the right of African Americans to vote and banning segregation on railroads and buses. It also called for a federal law punishing lynching and the creation of a permanent Fair Employment Practices Committee.

Truman had urged Congress to adopt all these recommendations. He issued executive orders ending segregation in the armed forces and prohibiting job discrimination in all government agencies. After much discussion and a fruitless search for another candidate, the Democratic convention nominated Truman and made his proposals part of the party platform. Southern Democrats who were known as Dixiecrats then organized a **States' Rights party** and nominated Strom Thurmond, the governor of South Carolina, for president.

With three Democrats running, the Republican candidate, again Thomas E. Dewey, seemed sure of victory. Dewey's strategy was to avoid taking stands on controversial issues while the Democrats fought among themselves. But Truman conducted a hard-hitting campaign. In his exhausting whistle-stop tour by train he attacked the record of the "do-nothing" Republican-controlled Congress. The Republican party, he claimed, wanted to "turn the clock back" and do away with all the reforms of the New Deal era.

These tactics worked well. Organized labor supported Truman because of his veto of the Taft-Hartley Act. African Americans backed him because of his civil rights stand. Many farmers were persuaded by his argument that Congress had refused to provide adequate storage space for surplus farm products. Former New Dealers responded to his charge that the Republicans intended to repeal important New Deal laws.

UPI/Bettmann Newsphotos

President Truman was given such a slim chance of being elected in 1948 that he took great glee when the Chicago Tribune *incorrectly proclaimed Dewey the winner. For what reasons did the newspaper's editors believe Truman had lost?*

Still, nearly all the experts continued to predict that Dewey would be elected. How could Truman win with two other candidates competing with him for Democratic votes? The editor of the *Chicago Tribune* was so sure that Dewey would win that he approved the headline "DEWEY DEFEATS TRUMAN" and went to press on election night before all the votes had been counted.

But the experts were wrong. Truman received over 2 million more votes than Dewey and won a solid majority in the electoral college. The States' Rights ticket won in only four southern states. Wallace's Progressive party was swamped everywhere. Truman had proved himself a clever politician. His energy, courage, and determination in fighting so hard when his cause seemed hopeless was part of the reason for his success. Another reason was that a majority of the voters wished to continue the policies of the New Deal.

The New Red Scare

Despite his remarkable victory, Truman was unable to get much of his Fair Deal program passed by Congress during his second term. More and more, the Cold War was occupying everyone's attention. A number of events in 1949 and 1950 produced widespread fear of communism similar to the Red Scare of 1919-20. One was the sensational trial of Alger Hiss, the president of the Carnegie Foundation for International Peace. Hiss had been a state department official before and during World War II. Whittaker Chambers, a former associate, charged that Hiss had been a member of the Communist party and had given him secret state department documents to pass on to the Soviets. When Hiss denied this, he was tried and found guilty of lying. He was sentenced to five years in prison.

Next came the arrest and conviction of several Americans accused of turning over secret information about the manufacture of atomic bombs to the Soviets. People panicked. Some believed that Soviet spies were hiding in every pumpkin patch and that the American government was a nest of traitors.

Then came what many called the loss of China to communism. In 1949 Chinese communists, called the Red Chinese, had defeated the armies of General Chiang Kai-shek. Chiang and his supporters were forced to flee to the island of Formosa (Taiwan). China, with its hundreds of millions of people, was now part of the communist world.

In the feverish atmosphere caused by the spy trials, many Americans believed that conspiracy lay behind the communists' victory in China. During the Chinese civil war state department experts had reported that the Chiang government was hopelessly corrupt and inefficient. Now these same experts were accused of being secret communists who helped cause the Chiang government's overthrow by cautioning against giving Chiang more money. The fact that their

Culver Pictures

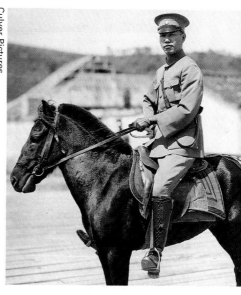

Above, Generalissimo Chiang Kaishek sits astride his Mongolian pony. His followers (below left) are in retreat from mainland China to the island of Formosa.

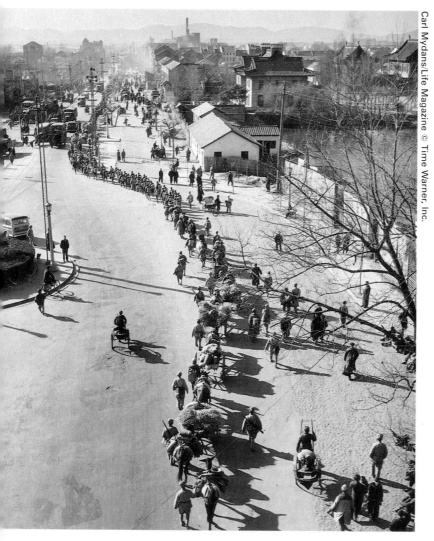

Carl Mydans/Life Magazine © Time Warner, Inc.

When the playwright Lillian Hellman was asked to testify to the House Committee on Un-American Activities, she wrote these lines.

❝I am not willing, now or in the future, to bring bad trouble to people who, in my past association with them, were completely innocent of any talk or any action that was disloyal or subversive. I do not like subversion or disloyalty in any form and if I had ever seen any I would have considered it my duty to have reported it to the proper authorities. But to hurt innocent people I knew many years ago is, to me, inhuman and indecent and dishonorable. I cannot and will not cut my conscience to fit this year's fashions, even though I long ago came to the conclusion that I was not a political person and could have no comfortable place in any political group. . . .❞

From *Scoundrel Time,*
Lillian Hellman, 1976

The "Whispering Gallery" was what some called the almost continual conferences of Senator Joseph McCarthy (left) and his lawyer Roy Cohn during the Army-McCarthy hearings. Why did people believe McCarthy at first?

reports had been accurate did not protect them. If the United States had given more military and economic aid to Chiang, the critics claimed, he could have defeated the Red Chinese forces.

The Rise of McCarthyism

Early in 1950 a Republican senator, Joseph R. McCarthy of Wisconsin, charged that the state department was riddled with traitors. He claimed to know the names of 205 communists who held policy-making posts in the department.

This accusation naturally caused a sensation. McCarthy had been almost unknown outside Wisconsin. Suddenly he was making headlines in newspapers all over the country. He quickly took advantage of his new fame by making even more astonishing charges. For example, General Marshall had for a time been a special ambassador to China. Now McCarthy accused him of being part of the conspiracy to turn that country over to the communists.

McCarthy was a total fraud. His charges were false. One of the first Americans to see through McCarthy was Edward R. Murrow, the news commentator who described the Battle of Britain. Another early critic was one of McCarthy's fellow senators, Margaret Chase Smith, who in June 1950 questioned McCarthy's tactics:

❝ I think it is high time that we remembered that we have sworn to uphold and defend the Constitution. I think it is high time that we remembered that the Constitution, as amended, speaks not only of freedom of speech but also of trial by jury instead of trial by accusation. . . .

Wide World Photos

The American people are sick and tired of being afraid to speak their mind lest they be politically smeared as Communists or Fascists by their opponents. Freedom of speech is not what it used to be in America. It has been so abused by some that it is not exercised by others. . . .[1]"

Still, thousands of Americans assumed that no high public official would make such serious charges without evidence. Politicians often exaggerated. Sometimes they deliberately misled people. But flagrant lying was a different matter. If McCarthy announced that he had a list of 205 or 81 or even 57 communists, people thought surely there must be *some* truth in what he was saying.

In this atmosphere McCarthy did not have to prove his charges. He never showed anyone the 205 names or told anyone where he had obtained this information. The people whom he accused of being "soft on communism" found their careers in government ruined. This was **McCarthyism.** When he attacked other politicians who tried to expose his lies, he was believed, not they. For a time McCarthy became one of the most powerful men in the entire United States.

The Korean War

McCarthy's rise came at a time when war broke out in Korea, a nation on the east coast of Asia. Japan had absorbed the Kingdom of Korea, a nation with a long history and a distinct and unique culture, in 1910. After World War II Korea was freed from Japanese control and divided in two. **North Korea** was supported by the Soviet Union, **South Korea** by the United States.

Efforts to reunify Korea after the war were unsuccessful. The Soviet Union blocked free elections because two thirds of the people lived in the South, which would easily control the elections. The Soviets apparently hoped for a unified Korea they could dominate as a check on the growing prestige of Communist China.

The two Korean governments exchanged serious threats. Although the United States supported South Korea, official policy considered Korea too far away to be essential to American defense. Soon South Korean leaders began mobilizing their troops. In June 1950 the North Korean army reacted to these troop movements by invading South Korea.

President Truman assumed that the Soviet Union was behind the invasion. It is possible that he was incorrect and that the North Koreans acted on their own. Truman was intent on maintaining United States prestige in the face of growing communist threats and felt he had no time to investigate the situation in detail. He decided to apply the containment policy to the situation. In the name of the

[1]From *Congressional Record*, 81st Congress, 2nd Session, June 1, 1950

Carl Mydans/Life Magazine © Time Warner, Inc.

Above is five-star General Douglas MacArthur. At right, a helicopter picks up American marines in the harbor of Inchon.

Wide World Photos

United Nations he ordered American forces stationed in Japan into Korea. General MacArthur was put in command of the campaign.

Truman did not ask Congress to declare war. Truman's power to send American troops to Korea was challenged by Robert Taft, the leading Republican in Congress. He claimed Truman had "usurped," or illegally seized, Congress' power to declare war. However, Congress took no further action. Perhaps if it had, circumstances in Vietnam 14 years later would have been different.

The North Koreans had the advantage of surprise. By September they had conquered nearly all of South Korea. Then the UN army, which consisted mainly of Americans and South Koreans, managed to check their advance. Next General MacArthur planned and executed a brilliant counterattack. He landed troops at **Inchon,** far behind

Point of View

American Caesar was the title General Douglas MacArthur's biographer gave to him.

"He was a great thundering paradox of a man, noble and ignoble, arrogant and shy, the best of men and the worst of men, the most protean, most ridiculous, and most sublime. No more baffling, exasperating soldier ever wore a uniform. . . . He carried the plumage of a flamingo. . . . Yet he was also extraordinarily brave. His twenty-two medals—thirteen of them for heroism—probably exceeded those of any other figure in American history.**"**
William Manchester,
1978

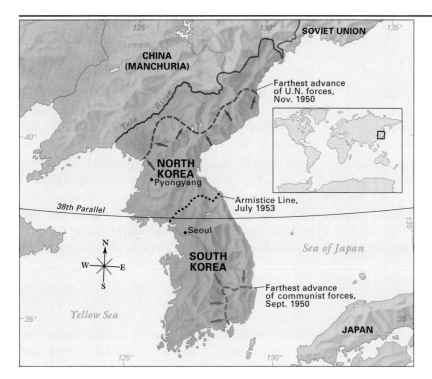

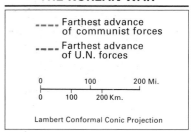

- - - - Farthest advance
of communist forces

- - - - Farthest advance
of U.N. forces

| 0 | 100 | 200 Mi. |

| 0 | 100 | 200 Km. |

Lambert Conformal Conic Projection

LEARNING FROM MAPS. *The division of Korea after World War II left North Korea with most of Korea's mineral resources and heavy industry, but with scarce agricultural resources. South Korea, on the other hand, found itself with most of the country's people, commerce, farmland, and food production but almost no industrial raw materials. Since the Korean War, almost no trade between the two countries has crossed the 38th parallel. How does North Korea's relative location seem to assure that it would become communist?*

the North Korean lines. The tide of battle turned swiftly. The North Koreans, attacked from two sides, retreated. Soon MacArthur's troops had driven the invaders out of South Korea.

However, instead of stopping at this point, MacArthur obtained permission from Truman to invade North Korea. By November his troops were approaching the **Yalu River,** the boundary between North Korea and China. This action caused the Chinese to enter the war. Striking suddenly and with tremendous force, they routed MacArthur's army, driving it back into South Korea. Finally, in the spring of 1951, the battle line was stabilized along the original border between the two Koreas.

MacArthur then requested permission to bomb China and to use anticommunist Chinese troops from Taiwan in Korea. President Truman refused to allow this expansion of the war. Still, MacArthur continued to argue for his plan. Truman was forced to remove him from command. The fighting in Korea continued.

The **Korean War** added to the public's worry about communist spying and therefore to the influence of Senator McCarthy. Early in the war Congress passed the **McCarran Internal Security Act.** This law required all communist organizations to register and open their financial records to the government. A special board was set up to investigate organizations that might be subversive—that is, out to overthrow the government. By 1952 Senator McCarthy was describing the Roosevelt and Truman administrations as "20 years of treason." 🖎

Return to the Preview & Review on page 993.

Preview & Review

Use these questions to guide your reading. Answer the questions after completing Section 4.

Understanding Issues, Events, & Ideas. Use the following words to describe the key events of the Eisenhower years: massive retaliation, brinksmanship, Army-McCarthy Hearings, East Germany and Hungary, Vietnam, Israel, Suez Canal, Summit Meeting, U-2 Affair, St. Lawrence Seaway, Federal Highway Act, Interstate System, Warren Court, *Brown v. Board of Education of Topeka,* Little Rock, Montgomery Bus Boycott, nonviolent resistance, sit-in.

1. Why did Stevenson have little chance of defeating Eisenhower in the 1952 election?
2. Why did the Eisenhower-Dulles foreign policy tend to prolong the Cold War?
3. How was Eisenhower's domestic policy conservative? How was it liberal?
4. Why was it important that the decision of the Warren Court in *Brown v. Board of Education* be unanimous?
5. What prompted the Montgomery Bus Boycott? What was its outcome?

Thinking Critically. 1. Argue either for or against President Eisenhower's response to various world trouble spots in the 1950s. **2.** Imagine that you are one of the nine black students attending the previously all-white high school in Little Rock. Write a poem or short story describing your feelings on your first day of school.

The Election of 1952

Although the Twenty-second Amendment did not apply to him, President Truman decided not to seek reelection in 1952. Instead he gave his support at the Democratic convention to Governor Adlai Stevenson of Illinois. Stevenson was an excellent speaker, witty and thoughtful at the same time. He had the courage to attack McCarthy head-on during the campaign, something few Democrats dared do.

Yet Stevenson had little chance of being elected. Many people thought he was too intellectual. More important, a majority of the voters seemed to be ready for a change. After all, the nation had not elected a Republican president since Hoover's victory in 1928. The Republican candidate was Dwight D. Eisenhower, the outstanding hero of World War II.

Aside from his fame as a general, Eisenhower had the advantage of never having been involved in party politics. Because he did not have a long association with the Republican party, thousands of normally Democratic citizens could vote for him without feeling that they were voting for a Republican. As a matter of fact, before deciding to back Stevenson, President Truman had tried to persuade Eisenhower to run on the Democratic ticket!

In addition, Eisenhower's warm, easygoing personality appealed to millions. The campaign slogan "I like Ike" perfectly expressed the general reaction. Liberals of both parties who were worried about

The opponents in the 1952 presidential election, Adlai Stevenson, left, and Dwight Eisenhower, right, share a friendly handshake after the heat of the campaign.

Dwight D. Eisenhower Presidential Library

A biographer of the Dulles family wrote these lines.

During all but the final months of the Eisenhower era it was the Dulles family which managed and manipulated the foreign affairs of the United States, and, in consequence, decidedly influenced the policies of the rest of the world. John Foster Dulles was at the peak of his powers, a Secretary of State so powerful and implacable that no government in what was then fervently referred to as the Free World would have dared to make a decision of international importance without first getting his nod of approval. . . .

Leonard Mosley, 1978

Senator McCarthy voted for Eisenhower in hopes that he would be able to silence or control the senator. Further, Eisenhower announced during the campaign that if elected he would go to Korea to negotiate a settlement of the war there. Any last doubts about his victory evaporated. Eisenhower won by more than 6 million votes.

When asked how he felt after being so badly beaten, Stevenson said that he felt like a small boy who had stubbed his toe—too grown-up to cry but too hurt to laugh. These were the same words used to concede defeat in 1858 by another candidate from Illinois, Abraham Lincoln.

Eisenhower's Foreign Policy

President Eisenhower made no basic changes in the containment policy. But he was under great pressure from conservative Republicans to reduce government spending. He and his secretary of state, John Foster Dulles, developed a strategy called **massive retaliation.** In simple terms, massive retaliation meant threatening to respond to Soviet aggression anywhere in the world by dropping nuclear bombs on Moscow and other Soviet cities. It meant being willing to go "to the brink" of all-out war to contain communism. This policy came to be known as **brinksmanship.**

Atom bombs were replacing "what used to be called conventional weapons," Dulles said. There was no need, he argued, to spend huge amounts on tanks, battleships, and other expensive "military hardware."

Dulles' policy was pure bluff. By 1953 both the Soviets and the United States had made hydrogen bombs hundreds of times more deadly than the bomb that destroyed Hiroshima. Neither Dulles nor

John Foster Dulles

Eisenhower ever seriously considered dropping a nuclear bomb on anyone. It would have been suicidal to do so because a nuclear strike would almost surely have caused the world to erupt in nuclear war.

The warlike language Dulles used tended to keep Cold War tensions high at a time when the Soviets were taking a less aggressive position. Joseph Stalin died in 1953. The new Soviet leaders claimed to favor "peaceful coexistence and competition" with the western nations. This gave them an advantage in the worldwide competition to influence public opinion, for Dulles seemed unable to back off from his policy of brinksmanship.

The Eisenhower-Dulles foreign policy also increased Senator McCarthy's influence in the United States because it focused attention on the danger of a clash with the communist powers. The popular President Eisenhower detested McCarthy and his tactics, but he was unwilling to criticize the senator openly.

Eisenhower stiffened the already harsh loyalty program that Truman had set up to clean out possible communist sympathizers in the government. Employees found to be "security risks" were to be fired even if they had not actually done anything wrong. For example, persons who had been convicted of crimes in the past might be classified as security risks. The idea was that communist agents might threaten to expose such people's pasts unless they turned over secret information. Under this program about 3,000 employees were fired.

Joseph Welch, seated at left, represented the Army in the Army-McCarthy hearings. After a vicious smear of a young aide of Welch's by McCarthy, millions of television viewers heard Welch exclaim, "Have you no decency left, sir?" How was McCarthy's spell broken?

Robert Phillips/Black Star

An even larger number resigned. Yet almost none of these people had actually done anything disloyal.

McCarthy finally went too far. Early in 1954 one of his assistants was drafted into the army. McCarthy tried unsuccessfully to get him excused from service. Out of spite he then announced an investigation of "subversive activities" in the army. These **Army-McCarthy Hearings** were televised. They destroyed McCarthy's prestige completely. Day after day the emptiness of his charges and his snarling cruelty and insensitivity were seen by millions of viewers. The people he attacked were aware that they were being watched and judged by this enormous audience. They *had* to fight back. When they fought and survived, McCarthy's spell was broken.

The hearings produced no specific political or legal results. Later, in August 1954, the Senate voted to investigate McCarthy's behavior. In December the Senate voted to censure him. By a vote of 67 to 22 the Senate resolved "that the conduct of the Senator from Wisconsin, Mr. McCarthy, is contrary to senatorial traditions and is hereby condemned." McCarthy's power to do harm was gone. He remained in the Senate until his death in 1957, ignored if not forgotten.

Eisenhower and the Cold War

During his campaign Eisenhower had promised to go to Korea. Soon after his victory, and before becoming president, he flew to Korea to meet with U.S. commanders to discuss strategy. Eisenhower and Dulles decided on a "peace or else" policy. Early in 1953 the U.S. increased air attacks on North Korea while hinting to the Chinese that if peace talks did not start soon they would send bombers across the Chinese border—perhaps carrying nuclear weapons. Finally in July 1953 a truce was signed. Although peace talks have continued, no final treaty has ever been signed. Armies continued to face each other across a narrow demilitarized zone near the 38th parallel. The United States has refused to remove its soldiers until a final settlement has been reached. United States soldiers still guard the border.

Elsewhere President Eisenhower avoided military solutions to international problems. Dulles had spoken of "liberating" the people of eastern Europe who had been forced to accept communist governments after World War II. There were revolts against these governments in **East Germany** in 1953 and in **Hungary** in 1956. But Eisenhower did not intervene.

When the French, who had colonized Southeast Asia in the 1860s, were being driven out of **Vietnam** by local communists in 1954, Eisenhower rejected the suggestion that the air force bomb communist positions. Instead the United States supported the division of Vietnam into a northern, procommunist section and a southern, pro-Western government. This United States position was contrary to the Geneva Accords signed in 1954 by the French and the leaders of

John Sadovy/Life Magazine © Time Warner, Inc.

A young Hungarian freedom fighter stands guard in Budapest. Behind him are burned-out Soviet tanks and anti-tank guns. But what sad lesson did supporters of a free Hungary learn in 1956? How many years did it take to win true freedom?

rival Vietnamese groups. That agreement called for a unified and independent Vietnam by 1956.

Another example of Eisenhower's restraint occurred in 1956 in the Middle East. In 1948 the state of **Israel**, which had formerly been the British mandate, or colony, of Palestine, declared its independence. Many Jews who had escaped Hitler's Holocaust flocked to Israel after the war to start a new life. So did thousands of Jews from all over the world, many of them former residents of the United States.

However, the Arab nations surrounding Israel took up arms to prevent what they considered an invasion of their territory. A series of wars resulted. Although outnumbered, the Israelis overcame the Arabs. Nearly 1 million Arabs who had lived in the area when it was Palestine fled to neighboring regions. They then conducted raids and terrorist attacks on Israel, determined to recover their homeland and drive the Jews from the Middle East.

A crisis erupted in 1956 when Egypt stepped up its raids against Israel and seized control of the **Suez Canal,** which was an international waterway. Israel fought back, joined by Great Britain and France, who wanted to reopen the canal.

Eisenhower faced a serious dilemma. The United States had supported the independence of Israel from the start. Most Americans felt that the Jews were entitled to a country of their own after their terrible suffering during World War II. In addition, Great Britain and France were also allies of the United States. But Eisenhower objected to their using force to regain the canal. He demanded that the invaders pull back. So did the Soviets, who threatened all-out war. As a result the allies withdrew, and Egypt kept control of the Suez Canal.

By 1954 Nikita Khrushchev had become the head of the Soviet government. Khrushchev was a difficult person to understand. At one moment he was full of talk about peace, at the next he was threatening to use nuclear bombs. One historian described Khrushchev as a mixture of Santa Claus and a "wild, angry Russian bear."

Eisenhower and the heads of the British and French governments met with Khrushchev in Geneva, Switzerland, in July 1955. They accomplished little at this Geneva **Summit Meeting,** or gathering of world leaders, but their discussions were friendly. Experts spoke hopefully of a possible end of the Cold War. Yet, little more than a year later, Khrushchev threatened to bomb Great Britain and France if they did not pull back from their war with Egypt over the Suez Canal.

Soviet scientists then shocked the world on October 4, 1957, when they sent into orbit around the earth a small satellite called *Sputnik.* (Sputnik is the Russian word for "traveling companion.") In November they launched a larger satellite, *Sputnik II,* which carried a dog. These amazing feats shattered American self-confidence and provided a great propaganda boost for the Soviet Union and communism. Soon "rocket fever" swept the United States. After repeated embarrassing failures the Americans hurled a grapefruit-sized satellite into space in January 1958. The United States and the Soviet Union were now in the space race.

The success of *Sputnik* sent shock waves through American society. Americans felt they led the world in science and technology. Now many people blamed the educational system for falling behind the Soviets in the space race. Courses in science and mathematics were added to school and college curriculums, and valuable scholarships were awarded to promising students in these fields. America was determined to "catch up."

Perhaps the most serious Cold War test of Eisenhower was the **U-2 Affair.** In 1960 the Soviets scored a second propaganda victory over the United States when they shot down an American U-2 "spy plane" which was illegally taking photographs high over Soviet territory. President Eisenhower at first denied that the plane had been on a spying mission. Later, when Premier Khrushchev revealed that the pilot had survived the plane crash, the president was forced to admit the truth about the U-2 mission.

MINIMUM HOURLY WAGE RATES 1950-91	
Year	Minimum Hourly Wage Rate
1950	$0.75
1955	$0.75
1960	$1.00
1965	$1.25
1970	$1.60
1975	$2.10
1980	$3.10
1985	$3.35
1990	$3.80
1991	$4.25

Source: Statistical Abstract of the United States, 1989

LEARNING FROM TABLES. *The minimum hourly wage rate, set by the government after studying statistics on inflation, purchasing power, and other economic indicators, influences the wages of both hourly and salaried employees. What might explain the unusually large increase in the rate between 1975 and 1980?*

Eisenhower's Domestic Policies

President Eisenhower stood halfway between the conservative domestic policies of the Republicans of the 1920s and the liberal policies of the New Deal. He was eager to reduce government spending. He favored measures designed to help private enterprise. He hoped to turn over many federal programs to the individual states.

Yet Eisenhower was unwilling to do away with most of the social welfare legislation of the 1930s. He agreed that it was the government's job to try to regulate economic growth and stimulate the economy during hard times.

While Eisenhower was president, 11 million more workers were brought into the social security and unemployment system. The minimum wage was raised. A start was made in providing public housing for low-income families. Eisenhower also established the new cabinet-level Department of Health, Education, and Welfare. The first head of this important department was Oveta Culp Hobby, the former director of the Women's Army Corps.

Although Eisenhower genuinely wished to hold federal spending to a minimum, he approved two very large new projects. One was the construction of the

Myron Davis/Life Magazine © Time Warner, Inc.

Oveta Culp Hobby

LEARNING FROM GRAPHS. *As you can see from the graph, the business cycle entered strong periods of prosperity during World War II and the Korean War. What economic problem troubled both Truman and Eisenhower, and had a negative effect on the business cycle as well?*

BUSINESS CYCLES, 1940-60

- Period of Recession
- Period of Prosperity
- Trend Line

World War II

Postwar Recovery

Korean War

Postwar Conversion of Industry

1940   1945   1950   1955   1960

St. Lawrence Seaway, which deepened the channel of the St. Lawrence River so that ocean-going ships could sail directly into the Great Lakes. The other was the **Federal Highway Act** of 1956. This measure authorized the construction of an enormous network of superhighways, the **Interstate System.** Eisenhower considered both these projects necessary for defense in case of war. Yet it was also Eisenhower who in his Farewell Address warned against the rising power of the "military-industrial complex." By this he meant the economic power and prestige of defense industries that had developed during World War II and had grown during the Cold War.

While Eisenhower was president, the last of the 50 states were added to the Union. Alaska became a state in January 1959 and Hawaii was admitted in August of the same year.

School Desegregation

In 1956 Eisenhower again defeated Adlai Stevenson for president. His margin was even larger than in 1952. Clearly a majority of the voters approved of his middle-of-the-road philosophy.

Yet Eisenhower's most important action during his first term produced radical social changes. Eisenhower himself strongly disapproved of some of these changes. No better modern example exists of how difficult it is to understand the historical significance of events until long after they have occurred.

The action in question was Eisenhower's appointment of Governor Earl Warren of California as Chief Justice of the United States in 1953. Warren had served three terms as governor. He had also run for vice president in 1948 on the ticket with Thomas E. Dewey.

Although Warren had never been a judge before, he quickly became the most important member of the Supreme Court. Under his leadership the Court became a solid unit, at least where civil rights cases were concerned.

In 1954 this **Warren Court** made one of the most important decisions in the history of the Supreme Court. It decided in the case known as **Brown v. Board of Education of Topeka** (Kansas) that it was unconstitutional for states to maintain separate schools for black and white children. This case overturned the "separate but equal" doctrine established in *Plessy v. Ferguson* in 1896. The decision said:

❝ Today, education is perhaps the most important function of state and local governments. Compulsory school attendance laws and the great expenditures for education both demonstrate our recognition of the importance of education in a democratic society. It is required in the performance of our most basic public responsibilities, even the armed forces. It is the very foundation of good citizenship. Today, it is a principle instrument in awakening the child to cultural values, in preparing him for later professional training, and

Yousuf Karsh/Woodfin Camp

Chief Justice Earl Warren, who had been the Republican governor of California, was appointed by President Eisenhower. But the Warren Court's growing liberalism and strong stance against segregation scattered the American landscape with "Impeach Earl Warren" signs. Eisenhower was not as strongly criticized when he enforced the Court's decision to integrate schools in Brown v. Board of Education. *Explain how the president proved to be a defender of the Constitution in this action.*

The American flag of fifty stars and thirteen stripes has gone through many changes. The early colonies had a variety of flags depicting patriotic themes, such as one showing Benjamin Franklin's advice: "Join, or Die." Others showed rattlesnakes with the warning "Don't tread on me." By the 1750s many of the flags were using 13 alternating stripes, usually red and white, to symbolize the 13 colonies.

As conflicts with England drew the colonies closer together, the desire for a colonial flag grew. The 1775 Continental Colors was the first national flag. It had 13 alternating red and white stripes (7 red, 6 white) and the British flag in the upper left. After the Declaration of Independence, the Continental Congress acted to remove the British flag from the American flag. In 1777 Congress resolved that "the Flag of the united states be 13 stripes alternate red and white, and the Union be 13 stars white on a blue field representing a new constellation." This was the original American flag.

No one knows for sure who designed this flag, or who made the first one. Soon after it was adopted, Congressman Francis Hopkinson of Pennsylvania said he was its designer. In 1870 William J. Canby claimed that his grandmother, Betsy Ross, a Philadelphia seamstress and flag maker, had designed and sewn the first flag. Historians are unable to support either claim.

The stripes were probably taken from the most popular patriotic flag of the Revolution, the flag of the Sons of Liberty. On it the stripes represented the 13

America's strong young navy showed a rattlesnake ensign in 1775. Its warning seems perfectly clear.

This early flag of the revolutionary period, with twelve stars in a wreath and one in the center, was first adopted by the famed Third Maryland Regiment and flown by them at the Battle of Cowpens, South Carolina, in 1781.

"Beautiful as a flower to those who love it, terrible as a meteor to those who hate it." This unique "Great Flower" flag was made in 1861.

All six flags from the Mastai Collection of Antique American Flags, Amagansett, N.Y. / Photography by Boleslaw Mastai

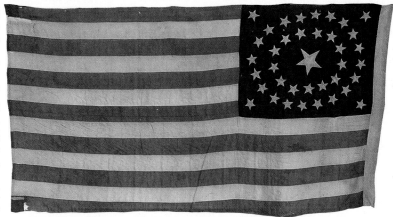

This ensign has 38 stars displayed in a "double-wreath" pattern, 13 in the inner ring and the balance for states joining the Union until 1877.

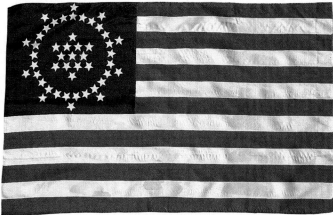

The Whipple Flag of 48 stars has a central six-pointed "Great Star" for the 13 colonies and was designed by Wayne Whipple.

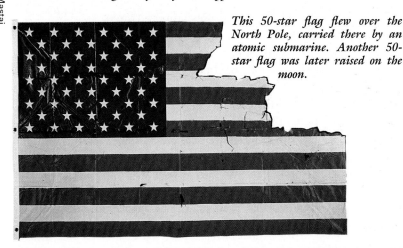

This 50-star flag flew over the North Pole, carried there by an atomic submarine. Another 50-star flag was later raised on the moon.

original colonies. This part of the flag's design has changed little over the years. The first flags after independence added stripes as well as stars for new states. The flag of 1795, for example, had 15 of each. But the flag of 1818 went back to 13 stripes, the standard for all flags afterward.

The stars in the first design stood for the states. The Continental Congress in 1777 stated there should be 13 of them. But it did not indicate how they should be arranged. The most common arrangement of the time was alternating rows of three stars, two, three, two, and three. Another flag had twelve stars in a circle around the 13th star. And still another had all thirteen stars in a circle. In 1818 Congress ordered that a new star be added on the July 4th after a state joined the Union. It still did not say how the stars should be arranged. So many arrangements were seen until 1912. Since then presidential orders have fixed the positions of the stars as new ones are added.

The Continental Congress also never stated why red, white, and blue were chosen for the flag's colors. But later when designing the nation's seal— also red, white, and blue—they listed the following meanings: *red* for courage and hardiness, *white* for purity and innocence, *blue* for justice, vigilance, and perseverance.

The flag is saluted by the Pledge of Allegiance:

"I pledge allegiance to the flag of the United States of America and to the Republic for which it stands, one Nation under God, indivisible, with liberty and justice for all."

The Eisenhower Legacy   1009

in helping him adjust normally to his environment. In these days, it is doubtful that any child may reasonably be expected to succeed in life if he is denied the opportunity of an education. Such an opportunity, where the state has undertaken to provide it, is a right which must be made available to all on equal terms.

We come then to the question presented: Does segregation of children in public schools solely on the basis of race, even though the facilities and other 'tangible' factors may be equal, deprive the children of the minority group of equal educational opportunities? We believe it does. . . .

We conclude that in the field of public education the doctrine [idea or principle] of 'separate but equal' has no place. Separate educational facilities are inherently [by nature] unequal. . . .[1]"

The Court ruled that a separate education was by its very nature an unequal education. This would be true even if the conditions in the separate schools were identical. Segregation, in other words, suggests that the people kept out are inferior. As Chief Justice Warren wrote, segregation had harmful effects on all children, white as well as black.

In 1954 all the southern states had separate school systems for whites and blacks. Many northern schools were also segregated in fact if not by law. Putting the *Brown v. Board of Education of Topeka* decision into effect was bound to be time consuming and difficult. Therefore, a year later the Court announced that the states must go ahead "with all deliberate speed." This actually meant that they could change slowly. Still, they must begin to change promptly and move steadily toward single, racially integrated school systems.

The *Brown* decision was a unanimous one. This was extremely important. If even one of the nine justices had written a dissenting opinion arguing against the ruling, opponents of desegregation could have used his reasoning to justify resisting the law.

Even in the face of a unanimous Court, many southern whites were unwilling to accept school integration, no matter how slowly carried out. There was talk of "massive resistance." This was not mere bluff as in the case of Dulles' "massive retaliation." In 1957 the school board of **Little Rock,** Arkansas, following a court order to integrate schools, voted to admit nine black students to a high school for whites. Governor Orville Faubus called out the Arkansas National Guard to prevent the children from entering the school.

President Eisenhower was not personally opposed to school integration. He believed, however, that it was "just plain *nuts*" to force white parents to send their children to integrated schools be-

[1]From *Brown v. Board of Education of Topeka,* Supreme Court of the United States, 347 U.S. 483, 1954

Burt Glinn/Magnum Photos

cause of the problems such a move would cause. But Faubus' act was a direct challenge to federal authority. The president promptly sent 1,000 soldiers to Little Rock. With this force behind them, the black children were admitted to the school. The president of the Arkansas chapter of the NAACP described the day:

66 At 9:22 A.M. the nine Negro pupils marched solemnly through the doors of Central High School, surrounded by twenty-two soldiers. An army helicopter circled overhead. Around the massive brick schoolhouse 350 paratroopers stood grimly at attention. Scores of reporters, photographers, and TV cameramen made a mad dash for telephones, typewriters, and TV studios. Within minutes a world that had been holding its breath learned that the nine pupils, protected by the might of the United States military, had finally entered the 'never-never land.'

When classes ended that afternoon, the troops escorted the pupils to my home. . . .

I asked if they had a rough day. Not especially, they said.

President Eisenhower ordered U.S. troops to escort nine black students into Central High School in Little Rock, Arkansas. Why had they been denied admission to the school? What effect did photographs such as this one have on the American public in the late 1950s?

In *Parting the Waters* the Montgomery Bus Boycott is seen in two perspectives.

❝ Only the rarest and oddest of people saw historical possibilities in the bus boycott. Of the few people who bothered to write the *Advertiser* at first, most were women who saw it as a justifiable demand for simple decent treatment. One woman correspondent did speculate that there must be a Communist hand behind such strife, but the great mass of segregationists did not bother to address the issue. . . . As for the boycotters themselves, the religious fervor they went to bed with at night always congealed by the next morning into cold practicality, as they faced rainstorms, mechanical breakdowns, stranded relatives, and complicated relays in getting from home to job without being late or getting fired. . . .❞

Taylor Branch, 1988

'Then why the long faces?' I wanted to know.

'Well,' Ernest [Green] spoke up, 'you don't expect us to be jumping for joy, do you?'

Someone said, 'But, Ernest, we *are* in Central. . . .'

'Sure we're in Central,' Ernest shot back, somewhat impatiently. 'But how did we get in? We got in, finally, because we were protected by paratroops. Some victory!' he said sarcastically.

'Are you sorry,' someone asked him, 'that the President sent the troops?'

'No,' said Ernest. 'I'm only sorry it had to be that way.'[1] ❞

Photographs and motion pictures showed the nine black youngsters being taunted by crowds of angry adults or walking beside army paratroopers in battle dress. These scenes had a powerful impact on millions of people, southerners as well as northerners.

The Struggle for Equal Rights

African Americans had been fighting for their rights long before *Brown v. Board of Education*. After the Supreme Court declared

[1] From *The Long Shadow of Little Rock* by Daisy Bates

UPI/Bettmann Newsphotos

Rosa Parks sits at the front of a Montgomery, Alabama, bus one year after she refused to give up her seat to a white man. What emotions do you suppose she felt when this picture was taken?

school segregation unconstitutional, African Americans began to speak out even more vigorously against all forms of racial discrimination. In December 1955, Rosa Parks, a black woman in Montgomery, Alabama, was arrested because she refused to give up her seat on a city bus to a white man. Her arrest led the blacks of Montgomery to refuse to ride the buses until the rule requiring blacks to sit in the rear was changed. This boycott was a heavy financial loss for the city's bus system.

The **Montgomery Bus Boycott** lasted for nearly a year. It ended with a victory for the African Americans. The Supreme Court ruled that the Alabama segregation laws were unconstitutional. It was in leading the strike that a young African American clergyman, Martin Luther King, Jr., first became well known. When asked why Rosa Parks had refused to move, he explained how she and many African Americans felt:

❝ No one can understand the action of Mrs. Parks unless he realizes that eventually the cup of endurance runs over, and the human personality cries out, 'I can take it no longer.' Mrs. Park's refusal to move back was her intrepid affirmation [brave statement] that she had had enough. It was an individual expression of a timeless longing for human dignity and freedom. . . .[1]❞

[1]From *Stride Toward Freedom* by Martin Luther King, Jr.

Throughout the long contest he advised blacks to avoid violence no matter how badly provoked by whites.

King believed in **nonviolent resistance,** what he called nonviolent direct action, for basically religious reasons. He argued that love was a more effective weapon than hate or force. There were also practical reasons for nonviolence. African Americans were a minority in the United States. To obtain fair treatment, they needed the help of white moderates. They were more likely to get that help by appeals to reason and decency than by force.

By the end of Eisenhower's second term real progress had been made. School desegregation was moving ahead slowly. Other forms of segregation were being ended. In 1960, African Americans began an attempt to desegregate lunch counters and similar facilities by staging **sit-ins.** A group would enter a place that served only whites, sit down quietly, and refuse to leave. They were either served or arrested. In either case their actions attracted wide attention and strengthened the drive for fair treatment. By 1960, new organizations such as the Southern Christian Leadership Conference, founded by Reverend King, and the Student Nonviolent Coordinating Committee (SNCC) had sprung up to organize and direct the campaign for equal rights. 🖘

Wide World Photos

"Say I was a drum major for justice," said the Reverend Martin Luther King, Jr., seen here marching in Montgomery in 1956. What philosophy did he preach and practice?

Return to the Preview & Review on page 1000.

Understanding Issues, Events, & Ideas. Use the following words to discuss the Kennedy years: New Frontier, Cuba, Central Intelligence Agency, Bay of Pigs, Peace Corps, Alliance for Progress, Berlin Wall, Cuban Missile Crisis, "hot line," Camelot.

1. What were Nixon's strengths and weaknesses as a candidate for president in 1960? What were Kennedy's strengths and weaknesses?
2. Why did President Kennedy hesitate to allow the CIA to carry out its invasion of Cuba? What happened to his prestige after the invasion failed?
3. Why did Khrushchev build the Berlin Wall?
4. What provoked the Cuban Missile Crisis? What was Kennedy's response? What was Khrushchev's response?

Thinking Critically. 1. Nixon and Kennedy were the first presidential candidates to hold a televised debate. Suppose you were a member of the studio audience. List five topics that you would have liked to hear the candidates debate. **2.** Imagine that you had been able to interview President Kennedy. What three questions would you have wanted to ask him?

5. A YOUTHFUL COLD WARRIOR

The Election of 1960

In 1960 the Republicans nominated Richard M. Nixon for president. Nixon was Eisenhower's vice president. Before that he had been a congressman and a senator from California.

In Congress Nixon had been a leading communist-hunter. Long before most people took the charges against Alger Hiss seriously, Nixon was convinced of Hiss' guilt. He worked closely with Senator McCarthy in his search for traitors in the government. He was almost as reckless in his charges as McCarthy. While running for vice president in 1952, for example, Nixon claimed that Adlai Stevenson was "soft on communism."

Nixon was a clever politician, but victory was more important to him than fair play. He was an intelligent and hard-working legislator. He sympathized with the civil rights movement, and he had strongly supported President Truman's foreign policy. While vice president he had toned down his talk about traitors in the government. He tried to act more like a statesman. This "new Nixon" persuaded Eisenhower and other Republican leaders to back him for president.

Still, many people did not trust Nixon. Nixon tried hard to explain his controversial reputation. "I believe in battle," he said. "It's always been there, wherever I go." He wrote that his life had been a series of crises. In each one, he claimed, he had triumphed by being "cool and calm" and working hard. But he may have appeared quarrelsome along the way, he admitted.

The Democratic candidate for president in 1960 was Senator John F. Kennedy of Massachusetts. Kennedy was young, handsome, intelligent, and rich. He was a war hero, seriously injured in a rescue mission in the Pacific. He was a Pulitzer prize-winning author and a shrewd politician. And he was an excellent campaigner. Kennedy appealed to liberals because he seemed imaginative and forward looking. Many conservatives supported him too because his policies were moderate.

Kennedy's major handicap was his Catholic religion. Al Smith's crushing defeat by Herbert Hoover in 1928 suggested that the anti-Catholic prejudices of voters in normally Democratic states might be difficult to overcome.

During the campaign Kennedy argued that Eisenhower had been too cautious and conservative. The economy was not growing rapidly enough. The nation needed new ideas. He called his program the **New Frontier.** He would open up new fields for development by being imaginative and vigorous. Nixon, on the other hand, defended Eisenhower's record and promised to follow the same lines. In the election the popular vote was extremely close. Kennedy won by only

UPI/Bettmann Newsphotos

100,000 votes out of a total of more than 68 million. But in the electoral vote his margin was 303 to 219.

In his inaugural address on January 20, 1961, the president stirred the nation with these words:

66 We observe today not a victory of party but a celebration of freedom—symbolizing an end as well as a beginning—signifying renewal as well as change. For I have sworn before you and Almighty God the same solemn oath our forebears prescribed nearly a century and three quarters ago.

The world is different now. For man holds in his mortal hands the power to abolish all forms of human poverty and all forms of human life. And yet the same revolutionary beliefs for which our forebears fought are still at issue around the globe—the belief that the rights of man come not from the generosity of the state but from the hand of God.

We dare not forget that we are the heirs of that first revolution. Let the word go forth from this time and place, to friend and foe alike, that the torch has been passed to a new generation of Americans—born in this century, tempered by war, disciplined by a hard and bitter peace, proud of our ancient heritage—and unwilling to witness or permit the slow undoing of those human rights to which this nation has always been committed, and to which we are committed today at home and around the world.

Crowds press forward to see John F. Kennedy during his campaign for president in 1960. Both Kennedy and his opponent, Richard Nixon, traveled widely between Labor Day, when campaigns traditionally began, and election day. Kennedy's presidential portrait below is by Aaron Shikler.

Copyright by the White House Historical Association; photograph by the National Geographic Society

A Youthful Cold Warrior 1015

Let every nation know, whether it wishes us well or ill, that we shall pay any price, bear any burden, meet any hardship, support any friend, oppose any foe to assure the survival and success of liberty. . . .

And so, my fellow Americans: Ask not what your country can do for you—ask what you can do for your country. . . .

With good conscience our only sure reward, with history the final judge of our deeds, let us go forth to lead the land we love, asking His blessing and His help, but knowing that here on earth God's work must truly be our own.[1] **"**

Close listeners could hear behind such golden rhetoric the old challenges of the Cold War hurled down by this young leader.

The Bay of Pigs

President Kennedy had stressed domestic economic issues in the 1960 campaign. But shortly after he took office, foreign problems began to occupy most of his time. During President Eisenhower's second term there had been a revolution in **Cuba** led by Fidel Castro. Castro set up a communist-type government on this island just 90 miles (144 kilometers) off the tip of Florida. Americans had invested heavily in Cuba, and Castro now claimed that property for Cuba. The Eisenhower administration had cut off trade with Cuba. Castro took an increasingly unfriendly attitude toward the United States and established close ties with the Soviet Union.

Meanwhile, the **Central Intelligence Agency** (CIA), a government bureau created in 1947, began to train a small army of Cuban refugees. The plan was to have this force invade Cuba from Central America in order to overthrow Castro. Of course this was done in complete secrecy.

When Kennedy learned of the plan, he hesitated to allow the CIA to put it into effect. He had criticized Eisenhower for supporting conservative governments in Latin America only because they were anticommunist. Should he now encourage the overthrow of a government only because it was procommunist?

Kennedy decided to go ahead with the CIA scheme. But he altered the plan. He encouraged the Cuban patriots to invade the island, but he withheld American air cover for them. On April 17, 1961, the Cuban force was put ashore in southern Cuba, at a place known as the **Bay of Pigs.** The invaders hoped to be joined by other Cubans. Instead they met only Castro's army. All were captured or killed.

The Bay of Pigs dealt a terrible blow to the prestige of the United States and to Kennedy in particular. Was the youthful new president

Andrew St. George/Magnum Photos

Fidel Castro, the communist leader of Cuba, is surrounded by flags of his country as he speaks in Havana. What is the connection between Castro and President Kennedy?

[1]From *Public Papers of the Presidents of the United States: John F. Kennedy,* 1961

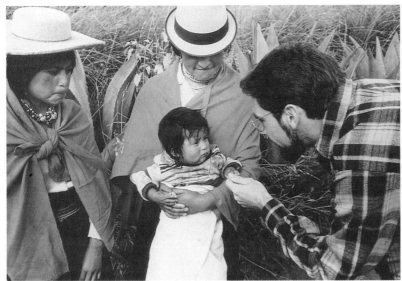
P. Meyer/Black Star

A Peace Corps volunteer in Ecuador tries making friends with a child, who appears curious about the American.

a reckless adventurer? Could he stand up to his clever communist opponents? Citizens who had voted for Kennedy because they did not trust Nixon were especially shocked by the mission's secrecy. Everyone was shocked by its failure.

The disaster in Cuba all but hid the fact that Kennedy was eager to develop good relations with Latin American countries and to help them improve the lives of their poor. In early 1961 he created the **Peace Corps,** an organization that sent volunteers to help the people of needy countries. It earned tremendous worldwide goodwill for the U.S. as it still does today. Kennedy also proposed what he called an **Alliance for Progress** to provide economic aid for Latin American countries.

The Berlin Wall

The Soviets had taken advantage of Eisenhower and the United States with the publicity of the U-2 Affair. They had pointed their finger at the United States, claiming it was the aggressor, not the Soviet Union. Now Khrushchev decided to take advantage of the Bay of Pigs Affair and test Kennedy's will to resist Soviet pressure.

Without consulting the western authorities in Berlin, Khrushchev suddenly had a wall built across the city, sealing the Soviet zone off from the three western zones. This **Berlin Wall** was actually a sign of communist weakness. Thousands of people from East Germany had fled to the West by way of Berlin since the end of World War II. They went in search of greater personal freedom and the higher wages they could earn there.

The wall reduced this flow to a trickle. But it also reminded the world that large numbers of people in the eastern European countries were captives of communism.

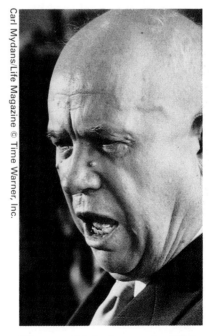
Carl Mydans/Life Magazine © Time Warner, Inc.

The powerful Soviet premier Nikita Khrushchev is shown here at the time of the U-2 Affair. Who could believe that with trembling lip he would soon leave his condolences at the U.S. Embassy upon the death of President Kennedy?

A Youthful Cold Warrior   **1017**

Flip Schulke/Black Star

President John F. Kennedy watches
Air Force fighter planes in 1962.

The Cuban Missile Crisis

The United States let the Berlin Wall stand. Khrushchev then apparently decided to test Kennedy still further. The Soviets began to build bases in Cuba from which rocket-powered missiles could be fired. When Kennedy inquired about the purpose of these weapons, the Soviets assured him that only defensive, antiaircraft missiles were being installed.

This was a bald-faced lie, and Kennedy knew it. American U-2 planes had secretly photographed the new installations. The Soviets were preparing longer-range offensive missile bases from which they could fire nuclear warheads at American targets.

Now came the most dangerous moment in the long Cold War. If the United States destroyed the missile bases, a third world war might result. If the Americans did nothing, they risked destruction.

On October 22, 1962, Kennedy appeared on television to tell the public about the **Cuban Missile Crisis.** He demanded that the Soviets remove all their offensive weapons from Cuba and close down the new missile bases. The United States navy would stop and search all ships approaching Cuba to make sure that no more weapons were brought in. If atomic missiles were fired from Cuba, the United States would launch an all-out attack on the Soviet Union.

For three days the world held its breath. Then Khrushchev agreed to remove the missiles. Kennedy won a great personal victory. More important, the possibility of a nuclear war between the United States and the Soviet Union seemed less likely. Both sides had finally come to the brink that John Foster Dulles had foreseen but never actually faced in the 1950s. Both sides had stepped back rather than risk the destruction of the whole world. The United States pledged never to invade Cuba and to remove some missile bases in Turkey, pledges it kept.

Following the Cuban Missile Crisis, a **"hot line"** telephone connection was set up between Washington and Moscow. In any future crisis American and Soviet leaders could talk to each other directly. In the summer of 1963 the two nations took a small first step toward disarmament. They agreed to stop testing nuclear weapons above ground, where the explosions would release dangerous radioactivity into the atmosphere.

Triumph and Tragedy

His success in dealing with the missile crisis made Kennedy seem sure of being reelected in 1964. After years of wartime austerity and the modest styles of the Trumans and the Eisenhowers, Americans were captivated by the style of the new administration. French chefs now prepared their specialties at White House dinners for dazzling people from the arts and sciences who mingled with world leaders, listening to musicians such as the great cellist Pablo Casals. This side of the Kennedy administration later came to be known as **Camelot,** a reference to the mythical Court of King Arthur. In his travels to France with his wife Jacqueline and to Berlin, Kennedy proved what a popular international figure he had become. But at their summit meeting in Vienna in 1961 Kennedy had his ears boxed by the wily Khrushchev who treated the president like a young boy who still had much to learn about international politics. Determined to regain his forceful image, Kennedy prepared more carefully for the international stage. In divided Berlin he electrified the huge crowd:

“ All free men, wherever they may live, are citizens of Berlin. And therefore, as a free man, I take pride in the words *'Ich bin ein Berliner'* ['I am a Berliner']. **”**

Before his famous speech in Berlin, President Kennedy gazed into the world enslaved by communism beyond the Berlin Wall.

John Dominus/Life Magazine © Time Warner, Inc.

Nevertheless, Kennedy was not able to get Congress to enact much of his domestic program into law. For example, in 1963 he supported a large tax cut. Reducing taxes would stimulate the economy, he claimed. If people paid lower taxes, they would have more money left to spend on goods. Their purchases would cause producers to increase output. More workers would be hired. Unemployment would go down. Personal and business incomes would rise.

In the long run, the president argued, the lower tax rates would actually produce more income for the government. But conservative members of Congress in both parties objected to lowering taxes while the government's budget remained in the red.

Kennedy also introduced a strong civil rights bill in 1963. His proposal outlawed racial discrimination in all places serving the public, such as hotels, restaurants, and theaters. Like the tax reduction, it failed to pass Congress.

Kennedy tried repeatedly to inspire the stubborn Congress. In a typical Cold War challenge, the president told Congress on May 25, 1961:

“ I believe that this nation should commit itself to achieving the goal, before this decade is out, of landing a man on the moon and returning him safely to earth. ”

Congress agreed to fund this venture and two presidents later, in July 1969—six months before Kennedy's deadline—American ingenuity prevailed. Apollo 11 with its crew of three astronauts—Neil Armstrong, Edwin ''Buzz'' Aldrin, and Michael Collins—settled into orbit around the moon. While Collins remained in the command module, Armstrong and Aldrin landed on the moon in an area known as the Sea of Tranquillity. Millions watching on TV saw them step from the lunar lander and heard Armstrong say:

“ That's one small step for a man, one giant leap for mankind. ”

To try to smooth local political matters before the election of 1964, the president and his wife visited Texas in November of 1963. On November 22, 1963, while riding through Dallas in an open car, President Kennedy was shot dead. The deed was done so quickly that onlookers scarcely saw the president slump into his wife's lap. The governor of Texas, riding in the front of the car, was wounded. Vice President Johnson, two cars behind in the motorcade, was safe. He was sworn in as president two hours later on *Air Force 1* as it carried the slain president's body home for burial in Arlington National Cemetery. Millions saw the orderly transfer of power on television, as well as the stately funeral procession of world heads of state led by the president's widow Jacqueline.

The man accused of assassinating the president was Lee Harvey Oswald, a mysterious figure who, it turned out, had at one time lived

Fred Ward/Black Star

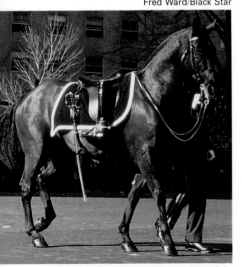

The riderless horse, boots reversed in the stirrups, symbolizes a leader's death in President Kennedy's funeral procession.

NASA

In its way, this photograph is as important as Columbus' journal describing the first sighting of the Americas. To report "Man Walks on Moon," The New York Times *had to make special headline type large enough for the biggest story of the 20th century.* Neil Armstrong took this picture of Edwin Aldrin, his fellow walker on the moon. Note Armstrong's reflection in Aldrin's face mask.

in the Soviet Union. Before Oswald could be properly questioned, *he* was murdered while being transferred from one jail to another. This amazing incident caused many people to believe that Oswald had been killed to keep him from confessing that he was acting with a group of enemies of the president. There have been many investigations of the assassination and many theories put forth to explain it. But none have ever been proved.

Return to the Preview & Review on page 1014.

A Youthful Cold Warrior   1021

LINKING HISTORY & GEOGRAPHY

POLITICAL GEOGRAPHY: UNCLE SAM'S ISLANDS

Political geographers have long been interested in the connections between mother countries and their colonies, especially their locations and the movements between them. The aftermath of World War II and the accompanying tide of independence movements all but ended colonialism. Yet, surprisingly, the United States found itself in possession of an "empire."

An American Empire

1. How did the United States find itself in control of an "empire"?

Few Americans actually like the idea of colonies. After all, our nation once held that status, and we fought a war over 200 years ago to end it. Military conquest and strategic needs have created an American Empire that is a collection of island colonies.

Most American islands have their own governments and fly their own flags. But they are not independent countries. They use American currency, but are not actually part of the United States. They have no direct say in the decisions made for them by Congress. So, while the U.S. has never officially labeled its possessions as colonies, they are precisely that politically.

The total population of Uncle Sam's islands is just a little under four million persons. The total amount of land they occupy is a modest 4,000 square miles [10,360 square kilometers], less than the area of our third-smallest state, Connecticut. These islands stretch from the Pacific to the Caribbean.

Colonial Status and Benefits?

2. What advantages does colonial status provide for islanders?

The five largest American island colonies—Puerto Rico, the Virgin Islands, Samoa, the Northern Marianas, and Guam—are democracies in the sense that they all have locally elected governors and legislators. But they are definitely not independent, self-governing political entities. To varying degrees each possession answers to some branch of the federal government in Washington, D.C., and each is subject to American laws. Although considered citizens of the United States, islanders cannot vote in presidential elections. They elect as their representative in Washington one *non-voting* delegate to the United States House of Representatives.

The United States does not collect federal income taxes from the residents of its possessions. Instead, it allows the local governments of the islands to claim these monies. In addition, islanders do enjoy the opportunity to travel, live, and work in the states. More than 2 million Puerto Ricans have moved to the mainland, especially to New York, although many return to Puerto Rico when they retire. Some 85,000 Samoans, more than twice the population of American Somoa itself, now reside in Hawaii, California, and the state of Washington.

American Islands in the Caribbean

3. What islands in the Caribbean does America control?

Puerto Rico is both the largest and most populous of Uncle Sam's islands. Its people are American citizens, and they are generally proud of it. Many would like to see Puerto Rico become the 51st state. A small but vocal minority would rather see it become an independent nation.

Puerto Rico enjoys a key economic benefit in its relationship with the U.S. Tax laws give American companies exemptions from United States taxes on business done in Puerto Rico. These laws also allow the profits earned in Puerto Rico to go back to mainland offices without incurring taxes. Such laws are powerful incentives for American companies to build plants in Puerto Rico and to employ large numbers of Puerto Rican workers.

In 1917, during World War I, the United States bought some of Puerto Rico's neighboring islands, the Virgin Islands, from Denmark. The purpose of the purchase was to protect the Panama Canal from possible German submarine attack. The American Virgin Islands consist of 50 small islands and three larger ones—St. Thomas, St. Croix, and St. John.

Although poor in many natural resources, the American Virgin Islands are all rich in natural beauty and climate. Virgin Islanders have made the most of these. Each year nearly two million tourists visit the islands. The money they spend equals half the islands' total income.

The Pacific Possessions

4. Why do these islands welcome their present colonial status?

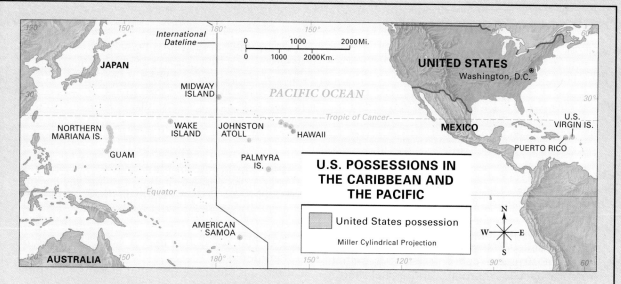

U.S. POSSESSIONS IN THE CARIBBEAN AND THE PACIFIC

United States possession

Miller Cylindrical Projection

Far to the west, in the South Pacific Ocean, is American Samoa. Its 38,000 people have been generally satisfied with how the American government has administered the island. Although many Samoans have left the island, they keep close ties to home. They send money home to supplement local incomes, most of which are earned from U.S. businesses. And even though the average income earned by American Samoans is less than that of Puerto Ricans or Virgin Islanders, it is three and one-half times that of residents of independent Western Samoa just 80 miles away. This is a powerful incentive to retain its current colonial status.

Guam is the most populous and largest American possession in the Pacific. Most Guamanians are proud to be Americans. Yet they are not entirely happy with the present relationship. In particular Guam would like the opportunity to operate more like Puerto Rico in encouraging American businesses to open in Guam.

Guam is an important military base. Much of its income is from military spending. But tourism is growing. Half a million tourists a year now visit the island, most of them from Japan. Meeting the needs of this booming industry is spurring development on Guam, which seems headed for a more secure economic future.

Few Americans have even heard of the Northern Mariana Islands. After being liberated from the Japanese in World War II, many of the islands in the Pacific were turned over to the United States. Most of these territories have

since voted for independence. The Northern Marianas, a group of 16 islands, on the other hand, feel they benefit from their status. The United States department of the interior is responsible to the United Nations for the islands' finances, communications, education, public health, agriculture, and legal problems. The islands receive about $33 million dollars a year for development. And they, like Guam, are attracting large numbers of Japanese tourists. Their sun-drenched beaches are just 1,400 miles (2,240 kilometers) south of Tokyo.

Beyond these larger possessions, the American empire consists of a handful of sparsely populated dots in the Pacific, most of which are important as military bases. Wake Island is a base for the air force. The Midway Islands and Kingman Reef are naval bases. Johnston Atoll is property controlled by the Defense Nuclear Agency, and Palmyra, about 1,000 miles (1,600 kilometers) south of Hawaii, is privately owned. Thus, in the 1990s, the United States is actually one of the few nations in the world retaining colonies. Interestingly, our "colonies" seem unlikely to want this to change in the near future!

APPLYING YOUR KNOWLEDGE
Your class will work in groups to report on U.S. possessions. Each group's report will include maps, pictures, and information on the people, geography, and economy of the possession. Display the reports in the school library.

CHAPTER 27 REVIEW

1945
World War II ends
★
United Nations is formed

1947
Truman Doctrine
★
Taft-Hartley Act

1948
Marshall Plan enacted
★
Berlin Airlift begins
★
Truman elected president

1949
NATO is formed
★
Communists control China

1950
McCarran Internal Security Act
★
Korean War begins

1951
Twenty-second Amendment

1952
Eisenhower elected president

1953
Department of Health, Education, and Welfare created
★
Truce halts the Korean War

1954
Brown v. B of Educatio
★
Communis attack in Vietnam

1955
Montgome Bus Boyco

Chapter Summary

Read the statements below. Choose one, and write a paragraph explaining its importance.

1. After World War II the search for world peace led to the establishment of the United Nations, with the United States as a leading member.
2. President Truman concentrated on getting America back to "normal," and established a program called the Fair Deal. Congress, however, refused to pass most of the legislation.
3. Despite the help of the Marshall Plan to war-ravaged countries, communists gained power in Europe and China, leading the United States to adopt a policy of containment and involvement in the Korean War. It also led to Mc-Carthyism at home.
4. The Cold War between capitalism and communism caused widespread tension.
5. President Eisenhower's foreign policy threatened massive retaliation based on brinksmanship, but avoided direct conflict.
6. Eisenhower's domestic policies were moderate, sometimes liberal, sometimes conservative. He supported the Constitution after *Brown v. Board of Education of Topeka* and sent troops to enforce school integration in Little Rock.
7. John Kennedy's victory in 1960 brought the nation to a New Frontier. He was more assertive toward the communists than either Truman or Eisenhower. Kennedy's leadership, however, was cut short by an assassin's bullet.

Reviewing Chronological Order

Number your paper 1-5. Then study the time line above and place the following events in the order in which they happened by writing the first next to 1, the second next to 2, and so on.

1. Berlin Airlift
2. Korean War erupts
3. Cuban Missile Crisis
4. Fighting in Vietnam erupts
5. Kennedy elected president

Understanding Main Ideas

1. What major decision about Poland did the Big Three make at Yalta? How did the Soviet Union come to dominate Poland?
2. Explain how the Truman Doctrine and the Marshall Plan were intended to stop the spread of communism.
3. Describe the three-way split in the Democratic party in the election of 1948.
4. Why did President Truman order U.S. troops into Korea? Why did he remove General MacArthur from command?
5. Explain the case of *Brown v. Board of Education*. What did the Supreme Court direct in its unanimous decision?

Thinking Critically

1. **Resolving Issues.** Imagine that you are a delegate to the United Nations when it is first created. What three world problems would you most like to see resolved?
2. **Analyzing.** President Truman was not affected by the Twenty-second Amendment. Read the amendment and explain why the amendment did not apply to him.
3. **Synthesizing.** You are a magazine reporter who has been assigned to cover the meeting at Yalta in 1945. Write an article describing the meeting and explaining its historical significance.

Writing About History

Use historical imagination to write a thank you letter from a Berliner for the airlift of 1948-49. Use the information in Chapter 27 and other accounts of the airlift to help you write your letter.

Practicing the Strategy

Review the strategy on page 987.
Analyzing Historical Interpretations. Read the following passage by historian John Lewis Gaddis on the origins of the Cold War. Then answer the questions that follow.

·56
ungarians revolt against Soviets
★
gypt seizes Suez Canal
★
senhower reelected
·57
vil Rights Act passed

1959
Castro comes to power
in Cuba
★
Alaska and Hawaii
become states
1960
Kennedy elected president

1961
Alliance for Progress
established
★
Peace Corps established
★
Bay of Pigs invasion fails
1962
Cuban Missile Crisis

1963
Kennedy is assassinated

Historians have debated at length the question of who caused the Cold War. . . . Too often they view that event only as a series of actions by one side and reactions by the other. . . . officials in Washington and Moscow brought to the task of policy making a variety of fixed ideas, shaped by personality, ideology, political pressures, even ignorance and irrationality, all of which influenced their behavior. . . . it becomes clear that neither side can take complete responsibility for the Cold War.

1. Do you agree with Gaddis' reasoning that brings him to the conclusion that neither side was completely responsible for the Cold War? Why or why not?
2. Would you say that Gaddis' analysis was biased? Why or why not?

Using Primary Sources

The following excerpt is from an interview with Diane Nash, who led the movement to desegregate lunch counters in Nashville's department stores. The interview was published in *Eyes on the Prize: America's Civil Rights Years, 1954–1965.* As you read the excerpt, think about how the civil rights movement accomplished social change.

I think it's really important that young people today understand that the movement of the sixties was really a people's movement. The media and history seem to record it as Martin Luther King's movement, but young people should realize that it was people just like them, their age, that formulated goals and strategies, and actually developed the movement. When they look around now, and see things that need to be changed, they should say: "What can I do?"

1. How does Diane Nash offer encouragement to young people today?
2. What do you see that needs to be changed? How could you help to make that change?
3. The civil rights movement used nonviolent direct action. Why do you think the movement chose this strategy?

Linking History & Geography

Geographers often study the earth by dividing it into regions that share similar features, including similar political goals. During the Cold War in Europe, three separate regions developed—NATO members, communist nations of the Warsaw Pact, and neutral nations. Study the map on page 991 and similar maps in reference atlases. Then on an outline map of Europe show the members of NATO and the Warsaw Pact. You may also wish to create a map that illustrates the European Community, the Council for Mutual Economic Assistance, and the European Free Trade Association.

Enriching Your Study of History

1. **Individual Project.** Complete one of the following projects: Listen to recordings of the Army-McCarthy Hearings of 1954 and prepare a class report; prepare a report on the life of Martin Luther King, Jr., and his long struggle for equal rights; prepare a large version of the map on page 991 to show Europe during the Cold War. Use the map to illustrate a series of written reports on major events of the Cold War. Topics should include the Marshall Plan, containment, Churchill's Iron Curtain speech, the Berlin Airlift, uprisings in East Germany and Hungary, the establishment of NATO and of the Warsaw Pact, the brinksmanship of John Foster Dulles, and the 1955 Geneva Summit Conference.
2. **Cooperative Project.** Your class will use library periodicals and reference books to find out how meetings of the Security Council of the United Nations are conducted. Some of your class will represent the members of the council and discuss a matter of current world interest. Try to bring the matter to some resolution. The permanent council members are: the United States, China, Great Britain, France, and the U.S.S.R. Other members of your class will represent African and Asian countries, Eastern Europe, Latin America, and Western Europe.

Chapter 27 Review **1025**

UNIT NINE REVIEW

Summing Up and Predicting
Read the summary of the main ideas in Unit Nine below. Choose one statement, then write a paragraph predicting its outcome or future effect.

1. Most Americans believed in isolationism after the Great World War.
2. Totalitarian governments in Italy, Japan, and Germany began aggressive actions in both Europe and Asia. President Roosevelt sought ways to check them without becoming involved in a shooting war.
3. Hitler's war machine invaded Poland, touching off World War II. Japanese bombing of Pearl Harbor brought the U.S. into the war.
4. The Allies first defeated Hitler in Europe. They then turned their full attention on the Japanese. Atomic bombs dropped on Hiroshima and Nagasaki ended the war.
5. The horrors and inhumanity of the Second World War made people realize that war must now be avoided at all costs.
6. After World War II the search for world peace led to the establishment of the United Nations, with the United States as a leading member.
7. At home after the war, American presidents—Truman and Eisenhower—concentrated on getting America back to "normal."
8. Meanwhile communists gained power in Europe and China, leading to a Cold War between capitalism and communism.
9. John Kennedy's victory in 1960 brought the nation to a New Frontier. Kennedy's leadership, however, was cut short by an assassin's bullet.

Connecting Ideas
1. If you could have been a member of the White House staff during the Roosevelt, Truman, Eisenhower, or Kennedy administrations, which would you have chosen to work for? Why?
2. Describe the incident at Little Rock High School in constitutional terms. Explain the conflict between state and federal powers. How was the conflict resolved? Cite the part of the Constitution that explains how conflicts of this nature should be solved.

Practicing Critical Thinking
1. **Predicting.** What do you think might have happened if Germany had developed the atomic bomb before the United States?
2. **Analyzing.** One of the arguments for the internment of Japanese Americans was that the constitutional rights of citizens are suspended during wartime. Do you think that the constitutional rights of all citizens should be suspended during wartime? Why or why not?
3. **Evaluating.** The Cuban Missile Crisis brought the United States to the brink of war with the Soviet Union. Do you agree with Kennedy's decision to stand tough? Support your view.

Cooperative Learning
1. Your group will prepare a multimedia presentation on one of the following: the *Brown* decision and school desegregation, Martin Luther King, Jr.'s, struggle for equal rights, the assassination of John Kennedy, or the fears and reactions in America during the height of the Cold War. Reports should include pictures and recordings when possible.
2. On April 12, 1945, President Franklin Roosevelt died suddenly. The new president, Harry Truman, told reporters, "I felt like the moon, the stars, and all the planets had fallen on me." One member of your group will play the part of Truman, and the rest of your group will act as reporters. Stage a press conference for the class. The reporters will interview President Truman on his first day in office. Reporters should ask the president about some of the major decisions he will have to make.

Reading in Depth
Barker, Elisabeth. *The Cold War.* New York: Putnam. Contains a description of the beginnings of tensions between the United States and the Soviet Union.

Frank, Anne. *Diary of a Young Girl.* Garden City, NY: Doubleday. Provides a vivid account of a Jewish girl and her family as they hide from the Nazis.

Hichiya, M. *Hiroshima Diary.* Chapel Hill, NC: University of North Carolina Press. Presents eyewitness accounts of the devastation caused by the atomic bomb.

Litz, Richard. *Many Kinds of Courage: An Oral History of World War II.* New York: Putnam. Contains interviews with the men and women who took part in the Second World War.

Savage, Katherine. *The Story of the United Nations.* Portland, ME: Walck. Provides accounts of the international movement for peace and the beginnings of the UN.

Larry Downing/Woodfin Camp

Mikhail Gorbachev and Ronald Reagan meet in one of their several summits.

MODERN AMERICA UNIT 10

I n Unit 10 you will learn about the Vietnam War, the Watergate Affair, and the Reagan-Bush Era. Here are some main points to keep in mind as you read the unit.

- Medicare and the Voting Rights Act were among the successes of President Johnson's Great Society program.

- As the United States grew more involved in the Vietnam conflict, millions of Americans began to oppose the war.

- 1968 was a tragic year in American history. Martin Luther King, Jr., and Robert Kennedy both were assassinated.

- President Nixon had many successes in foreign policy, such as improving relations with China and the Soviet Union.

- Nixon's involvement in the coverup of the Watergate burglary forced him to resign the presidency.

- President Reagan in the 1980s moved the nation in a more conservative direction.

- The Soviet Union collapsed in the early 1990s. Russia and Ukraine were the two most important successor nations.

The Great Society

Lyndon Johnson's first address to Congress as president.

❝ No memorial oration or eulogy could more eloquently honor President Kennedy's memory than the earliest possible passage of the civil rights bill for which he fought so long. We have talked enough in this country about equal rights. We have talked for one hundred years or more. It is time now to write the next chapter—and to write it in the books of law.

I urge you again, as I did in 1957 and again in 1960, to enact a civil rights law so that we can move forward to eliminate from this nation every trace of discrimination and oppression that is based upon race or color. . . .❞

Lyndon Johnson, 1963

Lyndon B. Johnson takes the oath from Judge Sarah T. Hughes, Lady Bird and Jacqueline Kennedy at his side.

Once again an assassin's bullet claimed an American president when John F. Kennedy was shot in 1963. And again the transfer of power to the vice president, clearly outlined in the Constitution, was orderly as Lyndon Baines Johnson succeeded to the presidency.

Perhaps no man has come to the presidency with greater qualifications than Johnson. He had served President Kennedy faithfully. Now he would be an active president. No one knew Washington more intimately. He decided to try to get President Kennedy's legislation passed by Congress as a memorial. He would build a Great Society to improve the lives of all people, but especially the poor and the powerless. And Lyndon Johnson, a Son of the South, would preside over the passage of the Civil Rights Act. The Johnson presidency reminded some people of the early days of Johnson's hero Franklin Delano Roosevelt. Could Johnson truly build a great society where others had failed?

Wide World Photos

1. THE JOHNSON PRESIDENCY

A Whirlwind of Energy

Before becoming vice president Johnson served for many years in the House and Senate. A lifelong Democrat, he worshipped Franklin Roosevelt and admired Harry Truman. Yet as majority leader of the Senate he had worked with President Eisenhower, a Republican, on most legislative matters. His years in Washington taught him much about government and how to get things done.

In personality and style Johnson resembled Andrew Jackson more than any other president. He was both warmhearted and hot-tempered. And like Jackson, he was energetic. He seemed to be everywhere—inspecting offices, signing bills, greeting tourists, settling disputes.

Johnson's first goal as president was to make sure there was no disruption in leadership. He was also determined to get Kennedy's program adopted by Congress. This would honor Kennedy's memory and establish Johnson's own reputation. Here Johnson's long service in Congress was an enormous advantage. He bullied, wheedled, and bargained. He had a way of brushing aside or smothering other people's objections and doubts. He would call in a hesitating lawmaker, rise intimidatingly to his full height of nearly six and a half feet, grab him by the lapels of his suitcoat, and say, "Come, let us reason together." More often than not the legislator would do what Johnson wanted, moved by a combination of awe and fear.

Wide World Photos

Preview & Review

Use these questions to guide your reading. Answer the questions after completing Section 1.
Understanding Issues, Events, & Ideas. Use the following words to describe the economic and social programs proposed by Lyndon Johnson: Civil Rights Act, Economic Opportunity Act, Head Start, Job Corps, VISTA, Great Society, Medicare, Immigration Act of 1965, Housing Act, Highway Safety Act, Voting Rights Act.
1. Why was Lyndon Johnson considered highly qualified for the presidency?
2. For what reasons was Johnson determined to get President Kennedy's programs adopted by Congress?
3. What was contained in the Civil Rights Act of 1964?
4. What were some Great Society measures passed by Congress?
Thinking Critically. 1. Imagine that you are an American citizen who has benefited from one of the Great Society programs. Write a letter to a friend in which you describe how this program has improved your life. **2.** If you had been a voter in 1964 would you have supported Johnson or Goldwater for president? Explain your answer.

With a stroke of his pen Lyndon Johnson, a Son of the South, signs into law the Civil Rights Act of 1964. Johnson was such a forceful personality that Washington still debates whether the act passed as a memorial to President Kennedy or because of Johnson's sheer willpower. Which do you think?

Photo Researchers

A volunteer for VISTA—Johnson's domestic program to parallel the Peace Corps—consoles a child at school.

As a result of Johnson's hard work, Congress passed in 1964 a bill reducing taxes by over $10 billion and a **Civil Rights Act** prohibiting racial discrimination in restaurants, theaters, hotels, hospitals, and public facilities of all sorts. This Civil Rights Act also made it easier and safer for southern blacks to register and vote.

Congress also passed the **Economic Opportunity Act** of 1964 at Johnson's urging. This law sought to help poor people improve their ability to earn money. It attacked the problem at every level. It set up the **Head Start** program to give extra help to children at risk even before they were old enough to go to school. There was a **Job Corps** to train school dropouts as well as an adult education program. The law also founded **VISTA,** a domestic parallel to the overseas Peace Corps.

Johnson wanted to leave his own legacy as well. He tended to dislike the "Harvard intellectuals" left over from the Kennedy presidency and was particularly suspicious of Robert Kennedy, the attorney general and former president's brother. He gradually replaced most of them with people he trusted.

The Great Society

Lyndon Johnson easily won the Democratic nomination for president in 1964. Although there had been great popular support for choosing Robert Kennedy for vice president, Johnson chose Hubert Humphrey, a liberal senator from Minnesota. His Republican opponent was Senator Barry Goldwater of Arizona. Even people who disliked Goldwater's ideas tended to like him personally. He was sincere and frank, not the kind of politician who adjusts positions to the mood and the prejudices of the voters. Goldwater was extremely conservative. He spoke critically of such basic policies as the social security system. He favored selling all the facilities of the Tennessee Valley

Authority to private companies. He wanted to cut back or eliminate many other long-established functions of the federal government.

In his acceptance speech at the Republican National Convention, Goldwater frightened many of his listeners when he said:

66 Extremism in the defense of liberty is no vice. And . . . moderation in the pursuit of justice is no virtue. 99

Most voters found Goldwater's ideas *too* extreme. Johnson defeated him easily. The Democrats increased their majorities in Congress as well.

Johnson then proposed what he called the **Great Society** program. With typical energy he sent Congress 63 messages calling for legislation in a single year. He stated his vision of the Great Society:

66 The Great Society is a place where every child can find knowledge to enrich his mind and to enlarge his talents. It is a place where leisure is a welcome chance to build and reflect, not a feared cause of boredom and restlessness. It is a place where the city of man serves not only the needs of the body and the demands of commerce but the desire for beauty and the hunger for community.

It is a place where man can renew contact with nature. It is a place which honors creation for its own sake and for what it adds to the understanding of the race. It is a place where men are more concerned with the quality of their goals than the quantity of their goods.

But most of all, the Great Society is not a safe harbor, a resting place, a final objective, a finished work. It is a challenge constantly renewed, beckoning us toward a destiny where the meaning of our lives matches the marvelous products of our labor.[1] 99

[1]From *History of U.S. Political Parties* by Arthur M. Schlesinger

Paul Slade/Globe Photos

Senator Barry Goldwater became the chief spokesman for the conservative wing of the Republican party. In the early 1960s his firm stand against communism earned him national prominence. His widely read 1960 book The Conscience of a Conservative *was a statement of his views on American foreign policy and the use of force against communism. How did Goldwater's ideas differ from Johnson's?*

Congress approved nearly everything Johnson asked for. It created **Medicare,** providing health insurance for people over 65. It supplied huge grants to improve elementary and secondary education. The **Immigration Act of 1965** abolished the system of favoring immigrants from the nations of northern and western Europe. Future admission to the United States was to be based on the skills and abilities of the newcomers, regardless of nationality.

There was also a **Housing Act** to help pay the rent of poor people and a **Highway Safety Act.** Another civil rights measure, the **Voting Rights Act,** was passed. This law appointed new federal officials called registrars in districts where local white officials were refusing to allow African Americans to register to vote. These federal officials made sure there were no problems or irregularities in voter registration in those districts. Within a year and a half a million southerners were added to the voter lists.

Return to the Preview & Review on page 1029.

The Johnson Presidency 1031

Preview & Review

Use the questions to guide your reading. Answer the questions after completing Section 2.

Understanding Issues, Events, & Ideas. Explain America's progress in the 1950s and 1960s, using the following words: standard of living, Affluent Society, factors of production, AFL-CIO, nuclear energy, synthetic textile, transistor, antibiotic, polio vaccine, white-collar worker, blue-collar worker, television, computer, fiscal policy, monetary policy.

1. What was the standard of living in America by the mid-1960s? What is meant by the Affluent Society?
2. What were some of the reasons that Americans were so optimistic after World War II?
3. What peacetime use of nuclear energy began in the 1950s?
4. What were some products developed after World War II?

Thinking Critically. Americans were optimistic about the future of their society in the 1950s and 1960s. Do you think that Americans in the 1990s still have this feeling of optimism about their country's future? Give reasons to support your answer.

The Affluent Society

The 1950s had seemed settled and comfortable. Americans were enjoying the great prosperity that had developed after World War II. Yet some who looked forward, like folksinger Bob Dylan, warned, "A hard rain's gonna fall." The Cold War and the space race had placed new and greater demands on American science, technology, and education. Not all Americans shared equally in the nation's prosperity, and the rising protests of African Americans and others against discrimination and poverty called for government action.

The election of the vigorous and energetic John F. Kennedy in 1960 had signaled that the nation was ready to take up the challenges of change. Kennedy had promised a bold new course for the nation. Lyndon Johnson's first actions as president showed he planned to follow a similar course.

In the mid-1960s the United States seemed to be entering a new Golden Age. Looking back over the 20 years since the end of World War II, most observers were struck by the tremendous advances that had been made. The **standard of living** of the nation as a whole—the measure of the necessities, comforts, and luxuries available—had never been so high. The percentage of poor people had fallen sharply and would probably be further reduced by President Johnson's Great Society program. The worst tensions of the Cold War with the Soviet Union seemed over. Science and technology had produced many new marvels and promised still further advances. America was the most productive country in the world. The question now, wrote the economist John Kenneth Galbraith in 1958, was how to use the abundant wealth created by this **Affluent Society.**

The dominant mood of the 1950s and early 1960s was one of optimism. This does not mean that everyone was satisfied with the state of American society. On the contrary, optimism made many people dissatisfied. They felt that society had serious weaknesses, especially the unequal distribution of wealth. But because they were optimistic, they believed that these weaknesses could be eliminated.

This hopeful, forward-looking mood had many roots. Victory in World War II was certainly one of the most important. Millions of soldiers and sailors came home confirmed optimists, if only because they had survived amid the death and destruction of battle. They and other millions who had not actually fought in the war found that victory strengthened their belief that the American way of life was superior to all others. The contrast between the United States and war-torn Europe further strengthened this belief, as did the dependence on American aid of both the Allies and the defeated Germans and Japanese.

Loomis Dean/Life Magazine © Time Warner, Inc.

So optimistic were the times that some people believed the Great Society would eliminate poverty from America altogether. The resources to do so existed.

Although it may look like a foreclosure and bankruptcy auction of the 1980s, this 1950s family displays every item purchased with the new easy credit available in the Affluent Society.

The Growing Economy

The unprecedented period of prosperity the United States had created by 1960 was built on what economists call "an economy of abundance." This meant that American businesses were able to produce more goods and services than Americans could consume. In the late 1950s a group of distinguished economists described the growing economy:

66 America today has the strongest, most productive economic system in human history. . . . The United States, with little more than 6 percent of the world's population and less than 7 percent of the land area, now produces well over one third of the world's goods and services and turns out nearly half of the world's factory-produced goods. 99

There were many reasons for America's remarkable prosperity. The United States had the key **factors of production**—the resources used to produce goods and services. The nation enjoyed abundant natural resources, an excellent transportation network, and a large and skilled labor force. In addition, businesses and industries became more highly organized and efficiently managed. More effective methods of distribution overcame problems of getting products to customers. Advertising created new ways to convince Americans they needed more and better goods and services. And American capitalism

Point of View

In *Henderson the Rain King,* a Nobel Prize-winning novelist wrote of the desire for more.

66 There was a disturbance in my heart, a voice that spoke there and said, *I want, I want, I want!* It happened every afternoon and when I tried to suppress it it got even stronger. . . . It never said a thing except *I want, I want, I want!*99

Saul Bellow, 1958

The American Federation of Labor merged with the Congress of Industrial Organizations in 1955. What do you think the illustration on the seal is meant to symbolize?

Walter Sanders/Life Magazine © Time Warner, Inc.

The latest in 1950s clock-radios did more than wake you up. It also could turn on the electric coffeepot in the morning.

and the new prosperity rewarded both individual effort and teamwork.

The steadily improving relations between labor and management also helped spur economic growth. Naturally the labor force grew in size as the population increased. The two major branches of the labor movement—the American Federation of Labor (AFL) and the Congress of Industrial Organizations (CIO)—united to form the **AFL-CIO,** with George Meany, head of the AFL Plumbers Union, as president. The new union had 16 million members. American workers were convinced unions would protect their rights, and management showed a willingness in many instances to negotiate. Politicians eagerly sought union backing.

The Wonders of Science

New scientific and technological advances caused America's economy to boom. Increasingly efficient and complex power-driven machinery became common in almost every business and industry. Farms, mines, offices, even homes benefited. New goods and services poured out of American factories and businesses in ever-increasing quantities.

Scientific advances caused American farm production to soar. Fertilizers and insecticides and other applications of science to agriculture as well as advances in farm management provided Americans with the abundant and varied diet that made them among the best-fed people in the world. The United States exported huge amounts of farm products each year.

Many industries experienced explosive growth. The aircraft industry became a multibillion-dollar industry. Thousands of men and women were employed in plants producing huge new jets. Thousands more were employed by airlines as pilots, ticket agents, maintenance workers, and flight attendants. The electronics industry expanded in similar fashion. It had been spurred by the need during World War II for radio transmitters, radar, and other military equipment. After the war it continued to grow. The production of radios, phonographs, and countless new appliances for homes and offices made electronics one of the fastest-growing American businesses. Then in the 1950s the industry skyrocketed with the popularity of television and demand for television sets.

The products of the new technology that these discoveries made possible added to the general optimism. One of the most exciting was **nuclear energy.** The same laws of physics that had led to the atom bomb could be used to produce controlled nuclear reactions instead of violent explosions. The enormous energy released by these reactions could be converted into electricity. Some experts predicted that energy would soon be almost as plentiful as water and air. What

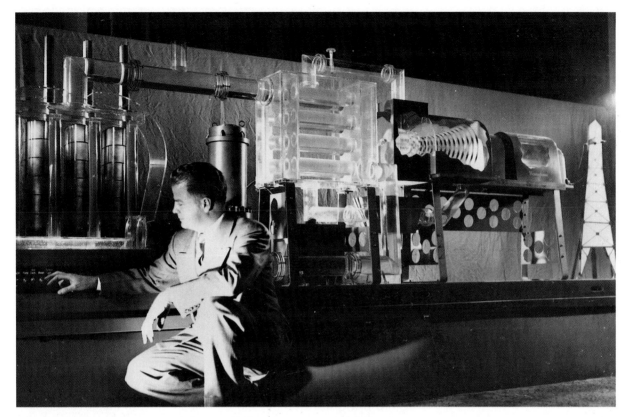

Charles H. Weaver, manager of the Westinghouse atomic power division, explains a station's workings.

this would mean in more wealth and leisure for everyone was easy to imagine. The United States had launched the nuclear-powered submarine *Nautilus* in 1954. By 1956 nuclear power plants could make and distribute electricity, and they began to do so in the United States in 1957. Few people then understood the problems that the nuclear age could bring.

Dozens of products and techniques that made life more comfortable and interesting were introduced in the years after World War II. Television and jet airliners and home air conditioners changed the way people used their spare time and where they lived and worked. New products included such **synthetic textiles** as Orlon and Dacron, water-based latex paint, small portable radios, and even smaller hearing aids. These radio, hearing aids, and a host of other devices used tiny **transistors** instead of bulky vacuum tubes.

Medical advances contributed to the general optimism. Penicillin, first used in military hospitals during World War II, became available to everyone. Along with other new **antibiotics,** penicillin practically eliminated many infectious diseases as major causes of death. The discovery by Dr. Jonas Salk of a **polio vaccine** virtually eliminated infantile paralysis, a particularly frightening crippler of children and some adults, like Franklin D. Roosevelt.

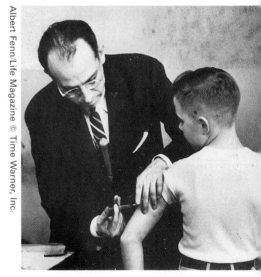

Albert Fenn/Life Magazine © Time Warner, Inc.

Dr. Jonas Salk gives 10-year-old Randy Bazilausakas his first innoculation of polio vaccine. How was the vaccine a godsend?

LEARNING FROM TABLES. *As you can see from the table, both the number and the percentage of women in the labor force have increased greatly over the last 100 years. What are some of the reasons for this increase? During what decade was the increase the greatest? Why do you think the increase was largest at that time?*

WOMEN IN THE LABOR FORCE, 1890-1990		
Year	Number of Women Employed Outside the Home	Percentage of the Total Labor Force
1890	3,600,000	16.8
1900	5,000,000	17.0
1910	7,700,000	19.5
1920	8,300,000	20.0
1930	10,600,000	20.4
1940	13,800,000	27.1
1950	18,300,000	29.6
1960	23,200,000	33.4
1970	32,500,000	38.1
1980	45,400,000	42.4
1990	53,479,000	45.4

Source: *U.S. Bureau of Labor Statistics*

A Changing Labor Force

The labor force that created the products of this period of American prosperity was significantly different from the American labor force before World War II. Many more women were now employed outside the home. In 1940 about 25 percent of the employees were women. By 1960 the percentage had risen to about 35 percent.

This rapid rise, the largest ever to that point, was the result of several developments. The demand for workers on the home front during World War II had helped break down prejudices against women, and it allowed women to show they could handle the same tasks as men in many jobs. Even more importantly, the rapidly growing economy created many more and new jobs. Most did not require sheer muscle. Because labor-saving devices had freed many women from household chores, they filled a large portion of these new jobs.

There was also a striking increase in the number of white-collar workers. In 1956 **white-collar workers**—teachers, doctors, lawyers, sales persons, secretaries, clerks, and others who worked in offices—for the first time outnumbered **blue-collar workers**—those who worked in factories or did other types of manual labor. Many of these workers held jobs in government. By 1960 nearly one of every seven workers was employed by the federal, state, or local government.

The Impact of Television and Computers

Even before World War II inventors had developed a way to transmit pictures similar to the way sound is transmitted by radio. As you know, this technique was called **television.** Only in the late 1940s, however, did manufacturers first offer reliable television sets—appliances to receive television signals—at prices that many people could afford. The demand for television sets proved to be tremendous. Throughout the 1950s television sets were sold at a rate of about 7 million a year. By 1960 nearly every family in America had at least one set. Television was one modern advance that even the poorest people seemed able to afford.

Television combined the virtues of radio and motion pictures. Techniques for broadcasting realistic sound combined with the newest visual techniques from the movies to make television an instant hit. Sports events such as baseball and football games were popular from the start. So were musical programs, comedy hours, and serial dramatic shows. Serials were known as soap operas because many of them were sponsored by manufacturers of soap and similar household products. News programs kept viewers informed and used pictures and maps to illustrate their reports. For the first time people could watch images of the news of the day.

Television soon became a force that influenced public opinion and events as well as one that reported them. For example, televised hearings exposed Senator McCarthy for the bully he was. Many observers believed that John F. Kennedy won the 1960 presidential election because he made a better impression before the TV camera than Richard Nixon. It was even suggested that if Nixon had used better makeup, the election might have gone to him. This was almost certainly an exaggeration. Still, the fact that people could think it was so shows how important television had become. And, as we shall see in the next chapter, when live television began bringing into American homes the war in Southeast Asia and inner cities torn with riots and looting, ordinary people were shocked to see this dark side of America.

The power of television and its almost hypnotic effect on viewers quickly became apparent. Critics warned of the potential hazards of watching what they called "the one-eyed monster." They claimed people would read less, even socialize less, as they locked themselves

TELEVISIONS IN AMERICA		
Year	Number of Households with Televisions	Percentage of American Homes with Televisions
1945	5,000	Less than 0.1
1950	3,880,000	9.0
1955	30,700,000	64.5
1960	45,750,000	87.1
1970	59,550,000	95.2

Source: *Bureau of the Census*

LEARNING FROM TABLES. *Americans soon fell in love with television. In which five-year period did television "come of age"?*

Ed Clark/Life Magazine © Time Warner, Inc.

The Thomas Knox family of Cornelius, North Carolina, watches with delight "The Ed Sullivan Show"—a popular program that brought vaudeville to television. Here Elvis Presley and the Beatles were introduced to the American television-viewing public. Why did the Chairman of the FCC call television "a vast wasteland"?

in with their "TV dinners" to watch "the tube." The head of the Federal Communications Commission (FCC) challenged broadcasters in these early days to improve the quality of television. Would his review be much different today?

    ❝ I am the Chairman of the FCC. I am also a television viewer and the husband and father of other television viewers. I have seen a great many television programs that have seemed to me eminently worthwhile. When television is good, nothing—not the theater, not magazines or newspapers—nothing is better.

    But when television is bad, nothing is worse. I invite you to sit down in front of your television set when your station goes on the air and stay there without a book, magazine, newspaper, profit-and-loss sheet or rating book to distract you—and keep your eyes glued to that set until the station signs off. I can assure you that you will observe a vast wasteland.

    You will see a procession of game shows, violence, audience participation shows, formula comedies about totally unbelievable families, blood and thunder, mayhem, violence, sadism, murder, Western badmen, Western good men, private eyes, gangsters, more violence, and cartoons. And most of all boredom. True, you will find a few things you will enjoy. But they will be very, very few. . . .[1]❞

[1]From *Equal Time: The Private Broadcaster and the Public Interest* by Newton N. Minnow, edited by Lawrence Laurent

Perhaps equal to the impact on American life of the television was that of the electronic **computer.** People began to refer to the computer revolution. The first computers were huge, cumbersome, and slow. But advances in computer technology were startlingly rapid, and by 1960 there were 5,000 computers in use in the United States. In a fraction of a second these computers performed tremendously complex calculations. By the 1960s they could perform nearly 360,000 additions or subtractions or 180,000 multiplications in one second. Laboratories used them to analyze complex technical information. Computers took over many of the mental and manual tasks once performed by men and women. They measured, counted, filed, and stored information—usually more efficiently than humans. Banks and businesses used them for bookkeeping and billing. The government used them to collect statistics and to check income tax returns. And there were many other business uses for these fantastic machines. The flights into space would have been unthinkable before the computer came of age.

Eventually the United States would become a computerized society. Schools, businesses, laboratories, hospitals, banks, government offices, hundreds of other organizations, even private homes would come to rely on computers.

Advances in computer technology also led to developments such as robots which seemed straight out of science fiction. Robots—machines that perform the tasks usually done by humans—became commonplace in some factories. These industrial robots worked on assembly lines run by computers. Scientists and engineers have worked to develop robots for every setting in which humans work—even the home. In 1983 one science writer foresaw the development of household robots that seemed somewhat humanlike.

  “ Times change fast, especially on the technological landscape. . . . The development of the microcomputer [a very small computer] bolstered [supported] the belief that intelligent machines, able to work and act as well as ponder, could be built.

    Today they are with us. . . . The Japanese are calling it a ''robolution,'' a revolution that extends from factory spot welders to devices that slice sushi [cold rice cakes usually topped with raw fish] for overworked chefs to piano-playing home robots (available, with many other talents and a price tag of $42,000, from a leading Tokyo department store).

    Robotics is breeding a new generation of machines that we may soon meet as pets. . . . BOB, short for Brain On Board . . . scuttles across the room, relying on ultrasonic detectors to avoid walls. When it senses a warm body with infrared detectors, it stops, swaying ever so slightly. BOB does get disoriented, a feature that makes it slightly human.

A bop on the head and it speaks—20 words with a mild robot accent.[1] "

Household robots have not yet become common. But who knows what the future holds?

Of course, the wonders of science are the result of human effort and creativity. As one robotics engineer told the science writer of the *Smithsonian* article:

" BOB is cute, a delightful gimmick, but even among those robotics engineers working on more serious problems, there is a singular awe and admiration of the human organism. . . . 'The only ones who really appreciate how smart people are, are those who try to do some of these things [get them to perform human tasks] with a robot.'[2] "

[1]From "Robots are playing new roles as they take a hand in our affairs" by Jeanne McDermott in *Smithsonian*, November 1983
[2]*Ibid.*

J. R. Eyerman/Life Magazine © Time Warner, Inc.

This photograph shows one consequence of the computer revolution. A single operator in the foreground does the work of the 31 clerks in the background. Why did computers make many people apprehensive?

Oliphant, © 1986, United Press Syndicate, reprinted by permission. All rights reserved.

Fine-tuning the Economy

In another important advance economists seemed to have figured out a way to prevent depressions. When business activity began to slow down, they said, the government should stimulate it. There were two ways to do this. One, called **fiscal policy,** involved the federal budget. The government must increase spending and lower taxes. Its spending would increase the demand for goods and services through direct purchases by the government and through increased buying by businesses and individuals who received government money. Lower taxes would leave consumers with more money to buy goods.

The other method for preventing economic recessions or depressions involved **monetary policy.** It called for having the Federal Reserve Board lower interest rates. Then businesses and consumers could borrow money more easily in order to expand business output and increase consumer consumption.

If the economy began to grow too rapidly, causing prices to rise, fiscal and monetary policies could be reversed. If that happened, economists said, the government should reduce its expenditures, increase taxes, and raise interest rates. Economists claimed that it was possible to "fine-tune" the economy by shifting these policies back and forth. A steady rate of economic growth would follow.

For the most part in the 1950s and 1960s these methods worked. The Federal Reserve Board and government economic analysts kept an eye on indicators of business activity such as the rate of inflation, unemployment, and the prime rate—the rate of interest banks charged on loans to their best customers. They then worked to coordinate fiscal and monetary policies to keep the economy growing steadily.

The popular cartoonist Oliphant takes a dimmer view than the Federal Reserve Board of efforts to fine-tune the economy. Is this cartoon critical of fiscal policy or monetary policy?

Return to the Preview & Review on page 1032.

3. A SOCIETY OF MANY MEMBERS

Use these questions to guide your reading. Answer the questions after completing Section 3.
Understanding Issues, Events, & Ideas. Use the following words to explain the direction of American society in the 1950s and 1960s: Sun Belt, National Aeronautics and Space Administration, suburb, development, shopping center, public housing project, shopping mall, Elementary and Secondary Education Act.

1. What were some of the reasons for the shift in population to the Sun Belt?
2. What changes did the shift to the suburbs bring in housing and shopping? How did this shift put a strain on the finances of city governments?
3. Why did suburban schools benefit from the education boom? Why did city schools suffer?
4. What caused college enrollments to jump between 1946 and 1960?
5. What were some of the ways that Americans used their leisure time in the 1950s and 1960s?

Thinking Critically. Imagine that you are living in a major U.S. city in the early 1960s. Your city is suffering from urban decay and you are very concerned about this situation. Write a letter to the mayor and city council suggesting ways to keep middle class families and businesses from moving to the suburbs.

The Population Explosion

One result of prosperity and public optimism was a rapid increase in the population of the United States. During the Great Depression many people had been too poor to marry and have children. During the war millions of men were overseas. Between 1929 and 1946 the population rose quite slowly, from about 122 million to about 145 million. This was a rate of a little more than 1 million people a year.

In 1946 the depression was over and soldiers had returned home from the war. In that year the population increased by nearly 3 million. The new trend continued for about 20 years. By the end of 1965 the population of the United States had reached 195 million.

The Sun Belt

After World War II the entire population distribution of the United States shifted. The American population had been moving westward since the first colonists arrived. But the shift in the 1950s and 1960s was as dramatic as that of the westward movement 100 years before. The territories of Alaska and Hawaii were admitted to statehood in 1959. This was a sign of their population growth and economic development. All the western states grew rapidly during these years. There was a similar population shift to the South. Florida and other southern states soon had population growth rates that rivaled those of western states.

The South and Southwest came to be called the **Sun Belt** because so many people were being drawn there by the warm climate. Retired people in particular moved to Florida and the Southwest to avoid the harsh northern winters. Home air conditioners, which became available in the 1950s, made the hot southern summers more bearable. By the late 1960s nearly 20 million homes were air conditioned.

There were other reasons for the migration to the West and South. Many firms in the aircraft and electronics industries tended to locate in these regions where lower taxes and living costs meant reduced production costs. Thousands of young families followed, attracted by the high wages and pleasant working conditions in specially designed and newly built offices and factories these industries provided. The new federal highway network made it possible for people to move long distances easily.

The federal government encouraged the shift by establishing huge new facilities in the Sun Belt. The best known were the John F. Kennedy rocket-launching base at Cape Canaveral in Florida and the headquarters of NASA—the **National Aeronautics and Space Administration** in Houston, Texas.

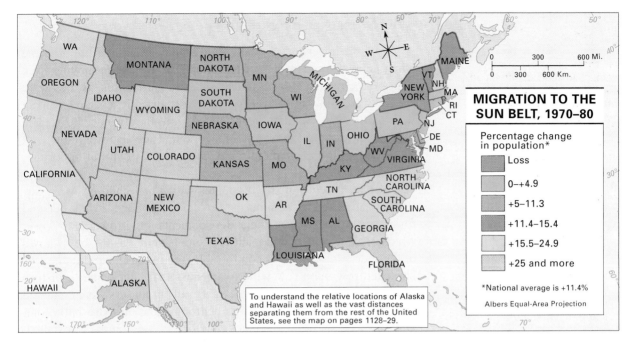

MIGRATION TO THE SUN BELT, 1970–80

Percentage change in population*

	Loss
	0–+4.9
	+5–11.3
	+11.4–15.4
	+15.5–24.9
	+25 and more

*National average is +11.4%

Albers Equal-Area Projection

To understand the relative locations of Alaska and Hawaii as well as the vast distances separating them from the rest of the United States, see the map on pages 1128–29.

LEARNING FROM MAPS. *What parts of the United States gained population during the 1970s? Why?*

Below is a colorful view of a blast-off from Cape Canaveral.

NASA

Point of View

From the book *Cities on a Hill* comes this observation:

❝In a sense, the residents of Sun City Center and their peers across the United States are living on a frontier. Not a geographical frontier but a chronological one. Old age is nothing new, of course, but for an entire generation to reach old age with its membership almost intact is something new. . . . In seventeenth-century France, for example, a quarter of all human beings died before the age of one, another quarter died before the age of twenty . . .❞
Frances Fitzgerald, 1986

The Shift to the Suburbs

A second major change in the nation's population distribution came when people in every part of the United States began moving from cities to their surrounding **suburbs.** These suburbanites, as they were called, were looking for the space, fresh air, privacy, and contact with nature that country life provided. Still they needed to remain near the cities where most of them worked. They also wanted to take advantage of the excitement, conveniences, and cultural opportunities of city life.

Young, recently married couples with small children were particularly attracted to the suburbs. Builders responded to their demand for homes by constructing huge **developments.** Levittown, New York, which became a suburb in itself on Long Island, was the best known of these developments. Its comfortable, relatively cheap tract houses stretched row upon row with a sameness that later came to disturb many Americans. But at the time nearly all purchasers were delighted with the houses. Most had three bedrooms and an extra bathroom. Dishwashers, washing machines, and dryers were already installed. Between 1950 and 1960 nearly a million new homes and apartments were built each year. The construction of schools, hospitals, roads, and offices accompanied this housing boom.

In and around the developments **shopping centers** sprang up, complete with supermarkets, department store branches, movie theaters, and dozens of small shops. The shopping centers were surrounded by acres of paved parking lots, for suburbanites traveled everywhere by automobile. Almost any product that local residents might want could be purchased in these shopping centers. Bulldozers busily cleared an estimated 3,000 acres (1,200 hectares) of land a day for these developments.

Joe Schershel/Life Magazine © Time Warner, Inc.

Jumping rope and counting-out songs will be found wherever there are children. The game below is in Levittown, one of the first planned suburbs in the United States. On the opposite page children play in front of their Chicago housing project. How might the lives of the schoolchildren in each of these groups differ?

Fritz Goro/Life Magazine © Time Warner, Inc.

Few poor people lived in the new suburbs. The poor could not afford even the smallest tract homes. There were almost no apartment houses or other places to rent. In other words, suburbs were mostly for members of the middle class—office workers, shopkeepers, teachers and other government employees—and well-paid blue-collar wage earners such as carpenters, electricians, and automobile assembly-line workers.

The government tried to improve the living conditions of poor people in the cities by putting up large **public housing projects.** These nonprofit apartments were rented at relatively low rates. Usually the rents were based on the income of the tenants.

The problem was that when the percentage of poor people in the cities increased, more and more middle-class people moved out to the suburbs. This seriously strained the finances of city governments because when the well-to-do left, income from taxes collected by cities fell off. Sales tax receipts dwindled as less and less money was spent on goods and services in cities, and property tax collections sagged as residents vacated more expensive city housing. Because cities had less money, public housing projects were largely neglected and soon become unsafe places to live and raise children.

Many manufacturers shifted to the suburbs to find room to expand and because property taxes were lower. This shift caused many of their employees to become suburbanites. Stores built suburban branches—**shopping malls**—and followed their customers to the suburbs. Each of these moves from the city to the suburbs also meant decreased city tax revenues.

Since many of the poor who remained in the cities were non-whites, a new kind of segregation developed. The worst effects of this segregation were not felt until after 1965. Until then well-meaning people had high hopes that President Johnson's Great Society programs would solve this problem along with others.

A Society of Many Members

Jan Branneis/Life Magazine © Time Warner, Inc.

Graduates celebrate commencement at the University of California at Berkeley in 1962. There is no sign here of the protest movements that would temporarily shut down this university in the 1970s.

The Education Boom

With so many children being born after the war, thousands of new schools had to be built. Most schools in the suburbs were low, light, and airy brick buildings. In addition to ordinary classrooms, space was provided for teaching arts and crafts and for sports activities. Teachers' salaries rose, for the increased enrollments created a teacher shortage.

As wealthy and middle-class residents moved out of cities, schools there suffered when the tax revenues that supported them declined. The **Elementary and Secondary Education Act** of 1965 supplied large amounts of federal money to improve these schools.

Changes in higher education were even more dramatic in the affluent society of the 1950s. College enrollments jumped from 1.6 million in 1946 to 3.5 million in 1960. Clearly, many young people, whose parents had not had the opportunity, were going to college. Making a college education available to so many more people had important economic and social effects. There was a close relationship between the amount of education people got and the kinds of lives they led when their training was completed.

In business and in many other fields people with intelligence, imagination, and energy often succeeded brilliantly with little formal schooling. Education helped, but it was not essential. College training, however, was required for entry into the professions such as

USING THE CENSUS

April 1, 1990 marked the bicentennial of the first census of the population of the United States, taken in 1790. In that year 17 U.S. marshals and 200 assistants went door-to-door to count the number of people in the brand-new American nation. The Constitution, ratified in 1788, called for a census within three years of the first Congress and every tenth year thereafter. The 1990 Census was the 21st such survey.

The most important reason for taking a census then (and now) was to ensure that citizens were fully represented in the federal government. Under the one person, one vote principle, states must redraw their Congressional election districts to reflect population shifts. (By law the number of representatives is set at 435.)

The census provides a wealth of other information about the American people. The 1990 census included questions about race and ethnic backgrounds, the disabled population, income and medical costs, energy use, housing, and much more. All the information is closely studied by various groups, especially those who work in various local, state, and federal government agencies.

The census contains an amazingly rich resource about trends in American society. Using the census data will give you a picture of the nation's people and insights into changes the nation and its people are undergoing.

How to Use the Census

To use the census, follow these steps.

1. **Select a topic.** Because the information collected by the census is almost overwhelming, it is necessary to focus on a specific body of information.
2. **Study the census data.** Check all the data about your topic. Remember that information may be provided in a variety of forms—in narrative descriptions, on maps, charts and tables, and on graphs.
3. **Note the trends.** Study the changes reflected by the data.
4. **Use the census information.** Draw conclusions and form hypotheses based on census figures. Remember that the statistics portray American society.

Applying the Strategy

Study the table of census data below. It illustrates information for the years 1970 and 1980 in three categories: land area, population, and population density. By how much did the urban population increase between 1970 and 1980? As you can see, it increased by over 17 million people. By how much did the rural population increase between 1970 and 1980? It increased by over 5 million. What is one conclusion you can draw from the data in this table?

For independent practice, see Practicing the Strategy on page 1059.

CHANGES IN URBAN AND RURAL POPULATION DENSITIES, 1970-80						
	1970			1980		
	Land Area (sq. mi.)	Population (in millions)	Density (per sq. mi.)	Land Area (sq. mi.)	Population (in millions)	Density (per sq. mi.)
Total	3,540,023	203,212	57	3,539,289	226,546	64
Urban	54,103	149,325	2,760	73,930	167,051	2,260
Rural	3,485,920	53,887	15	3,465,360	59,495	17

Tears rolled down the cheeks of young boys and old men alike the day the decision was announced—the Dodgers were leaving Brooklyn. The team led by Jackie Robinson and Duke Snider was moving west. The fabled and successful franchise—five National League championships and one World Series crown in the 1950s—was moving to Los Angeles in 1958. And to add to the shock of New Yorkers their Giants were heading for San Francisco that same year. Why were these teams leaving their loyal fans?

Teams had moved throughout baseball's history. Usually a team moved when attendance sagged sharply. New cities meant more fans—baseball's life blood. But before World War II these moves were limited to the East Coast and the Middle West. Most western cities were not as large and the West Coast was just too far away. It would take too long for opposing teams to travel there to play.

But the same changes that swept the rest of American society after the war affected baseball. Large numbers of people were moving to booming cities in the West and the Sun Belt, creating huge markets for sports franchises. Technology was producing rapid modes of transportation that pulled the widespread parts of the country more closely together. With the coming of television baseball entered the homes of millions of viewers who quickly became fans. Soon television revenues became a major source of income for a team. Suddenly the West Coast didn't seem so far away—or such a bad investment for team owners.

The Boston Braves had moved to Milwaukee in 1953 and the Philadelphia Athletics to Kansas City in 1955. (Both would move again—the Braves to Atlanta and the Athletics to Oakland—in search of fans and dollars.) But the Dodgers and Giants took the biggest step, moving across the continent to bring baseball to California and the West. Soon major league baseball had spread to all the corners of the nation—and the continent. Teams now play in Seattle in Washington, Denver in Colorado and Miami in Florida, even Montreal and Toronto in Canada.

Other sports have followed baseball's lead. Major league sports teams now represent San

Los Angeles Dodgers on parade

Wide World Photo

medicine, law, and teaching. Easier access to a college education after World War II opened the professions to a much broader section of the population than ever before.

Leisure Time

Advances in technology created an unexpected benefit for many workers: shorter workweeks. Between 1940 and 1960 the average workweek decreased from 44 to 40 hours. In some of the skilled trades it actually dropped to 35 hours. At the same time the average paid vacation increased from one to two weeks.

Americans began to look for ways to spend their increased free time and money. Millions bought new cars—nearly 50 million during the 1950s. By 1960 nearly 75 percent of all American families owned at least one car, and more than 15 percent owned two or more.

Antonio, Salt Lake City, San Diego, Portland, and Phoenix.

Technology has continued to influence baseball. In 1965 the Houston baseball team—then called the Colt .45's—moved into the engineering masterpiece of its day, an indoor stadium called the Astrodome. Baseball and football teams now play in huge indoor arenas in such places as Minneapolis, New Orleans, and Seattle. Several other teams, along with many college and university teams, play on the artificial surface created to replace the grass that simply would not grow under the Astrodome's roof. Most of those same college teams now use aluminum bats, which have replaced breakable wood bats on every level below the highest minor and major leagues.

Baseball, all America's traditional game, is part of American culture. As such it reflects many of the changes that influence society—the shifting populations, technological advances, and social changes.

The Astrodome with its artificial turf

These families climbed into their cars and headed for vacations at the beach, the mountains, or the country. More and better roads were needed to handle the growing traffic. The Highway Act in 1956 provided funding for the construction of 42,500 miles (68,400 kilometers) of new superhighways. State and local funds paid for thousands of miles of roads and streets. Motels, fast-food restaurants, and service stations soon lined these roads and highways.

Hundreds of golf courses and bowling alleys were built and were soon crowded. People bought boats of all descriptions. These soon appeared on lakes and harbors throughout the country. Attendance at spectator sports grew tremendously as well. Baseball and football teams built new stadiums to hold the crowds that numbered in the tens of thousands.

At home families gathered around their wonderful new television sets. By 1960 the television was turned on for at least 5 hours a day

Point of View

From *God's Country and Mine:*

> Whoever wants to know the heart and mind of America had better learn baseball, the rules and realities of the game—and do it by watching first some high school or small-town teams.
>
> Jacques Barzun, 1954

TRANSCONTINENTAL TRAVEL*	
Vehicle	**Time It Took To Make Journey**
Covered wagon	5 months
Steamship through Panama Canal	30 days
Overland stagecoach	23 days
Railroad, 1875	7 days
Railroad, 1900	4 days
Railroad, 1945	2.5 days
Airplane, propeller	7.5 hours
Airplane, jet	4 hours
*From east coast to west coast	

LEARNING FROM TABLES. *As you can see from the table, the changing technology of travel has made the United States "smaller." Now you can travel coast to coast in a few hours. How long did it take by covered wagon? What changes do you think more rapid transportation has brought to America?*

in the average home. But television did not claim all of Americans' new leisure time. Sales of magazines, books, records, and audio tapes climbed steadily in the 1950s and early 1960s.

The New Generation

A major concern of many Americans in the midst of all these changes was the direction being taken by the young men and women reaching adulthood in the 1950s and early 1960s. Their goals appeared to be having plenty of money, a good job, a house in the suburbs, and comfortable retirement. Critics accused them of a lack of concern about politics and the issues confronting the United States and the world.

Critics even went so far as to claim that this tendency to avoid controversy and to conform was not confined to young people. They said that all age groups, men and women alike, seemed to share the same attitude of conformity. Among other critics, John Kenneth Galbraith and Rachel Carson warned Americans that they were neglecting the poor, causing the environment to deteriorate, and permitting cites to decay. In *Silent Spring*, Carson said,

66 As the tide of chemicals born of the Industrial Age has arisen to engulf our environment, a drastic change has come about in the nature of the most serious health problems.[1] 99

She challenged people to protect the earth from the hazards

66 created by radiation in all its forms, born of the never-ending stream of chemicals of which pesticides are a part, chemicals now pervading the world in which we live, acting upon us directly and indirectly, separately and collectively.[2] 99

[1]From *Silent Spring* by Rachel Carson
[2]*Ibid.*

It is a challenge Americans still face.

Alfred Eisensteadt/Life Magazine © Time Warner, Inc.

Rachel Carson wrote so movingly of the natural environment that not all her readers realized at first that she was warning America to change its ways before the environment deteriorated and cities decayed. Explain the title Silent Spring.

Return to the Preview & Review on page 1042.

4. MOVEMENTS FOR EQUAL RIGHTS

Women Seek Equal Rights

Women in the 1960s continued their long struggle for equal rights. The 1964 Civil Rights Act had banned discrimination on the basis of sex as well as race. Still, women's organizations pressed for a Constitutional amendment that would guarantee their equality under law.

Tens of thousands of women from relatively poor families had always had to work. Middle-class women, however, had tended to work in the home after marriage. In the 1950s more and more of these women took jobs outside the home. They discovered that in nearly every field the wages and salaries paid to women were lower than those earned by men doing the same work. Moreover, the best jobs were rarely open to women. It was much harder for women to gain admission to law schools and medical colleges. In the business world women were rarely promoted to important positions, especially to those where they might be issuing orders to men.

Most male employers justified their practice by claiming that women usually worked only while waiting to be married. There was no use in promoting women, they said, because most would soon leave in order to marry and raise a family. When it was pointed out that more and more married women were working away from home, employers shifted their argument. They claimed that it was all right to pay married women less than men because married women did not have to support a family on their own!

Women naturally resented being discriminated against in the job market. When their numbers increased in the 1950s and 1960s, their resentment burst forth in the **Women's Liberation Movement.** The movement first attracted widespread public attention with the publication in 1963 of *The Feminine Mystique* by Betty Friedan. By "feminine mystique" Friedan meant the image of women society holds and the specific attributes of femininity.

Friedan had become interested in the problems of well-educated women after she made a study of graduates of Smith College, one of the nation's leading women's colleges. She discovered that a large percentage of these women were unhappy. Why, she wondered, were so many intelligent women so dissatisfied with their lives?

The answer, Friedan concluded, was that women felt held back by family responsibilities. They did not see themselves as individuals. In her own mind the typical woman was "Mrs. Jones" or "Billy Jones' mother." Not even her name could she call her own.

Most women thought that they *ought* to be completely satisfied with their roles as wives and mothers, Friedan wrote. Were not popular magazines like the *Ladies' Home Journal* full of articles describing the satisfactions of raising a large family?

Preview & Review

Use these questions to guide your reading. Answer the questions after completing Section 4.
Understanding Issues, Events, & Ideas. Discuss the movements for equal rights that took place in the 1960s, using the following words: Women's Liberation Movement, consciousness-raising, National Organization for Women, Red Power, Indian Rights Act, American Indian Movement, Wounded Knee, poverty line, nonviolent direct action, Birmingham, March on Washington.
1. What did Betty Friedan discover in her survey of women?
2. What were some of the goals of the National Organization for Women?
3. How did the Indian Rights Act of 1968 cause problems for tribal governments?
4. What did Dr. Martin Luther King, Jr., hope to accomplish by his policy of nonviolent direct action?
5. How did Dr. King share in the optimism that was typical of the early 1960s?
Thinking Critically. 1. Imagine that you are one of the founders of the National Organization for Women or the American Indian Movement. Write a list of goals which you would like to see the organization carry out in order to help the people for whom it was founded. 2. Write an eyewitness account of the March on Washington. Include a description of how you felt hearing Dr. King's speech as well as the reaction of the crowd to his famous words.

Steve Northrup/Time Magazine © Time Warner, Inc.

Among the marchers for women's rights are Bella Abzug, in hat, and Betty Friedan, far right.

Point of View

In *The Feminine Mystique* we read:

" Who knows what women can be when they are finally free to become themselves? Who knows what women's intelligence will contribute when it can be nourished without denying love? . . . The time is at hand when the voices of the feminine mystique can no longer drown out the inner voice that is driving women on to become complete."

Betty Friedan, 1963

Many women who read *The Feminine Mystique* experienced what has come to be called **consciousness-raising.** They became aware that their personal doubts and dissatisfactions were shared by others.

Betty Friedan was not a radical. She did not argue that caring for a family was a bad thing. While she was writing her book, she was also bringing up three children of her own. But she insisted that the way to have a satisfying life was the same for women as for men: they must find some sort of "creative work."

In 1966 Friedan helped found the **National Organization for Women** (NOW). Its purpose was to end legal restrictions on women and see that they got equal employment opportunities in all fields. The government should provide day-care centers and other assistance for working women with small children, NOW officials argued. What would come of all this we shall see in a later chapter.

The American Indian Movement

Other American groups also struggled for equal rights, among them American Indians. During the New Deal period the federal government had given up the effort begun with the Dawes Act of 1887 to force Indians to copy white ways and adopt white values.

Instead, the Indian Reorganization Act of 1934 encouraged the revival of tribal life. Indians should choose their own leaders and run their own affairs, supporters of the new policy believed. Many Indians did so.

Indian schools began to teach Indian languages and history. Ancient arts and crafts were relearned and developed. A National Indian Youth Council, founded in 1961, pressed for the return of Indian lands in many parts of the nation. Some Indians coined the term **Red Power** to rally supporters.

In 1968 Congress passed the **Indian Rights Act.** This law was intended to protect Indians against discrimination and mistreatment. But it had the unintended effect of weakening the governments the tribes had set up under the Indian Reorganization Act. These were often dominated by powerful chiefs who did not respect the needs and opinions of other tribe members. Many Indians used the new law to have these chiefs removed.

In 1972 a new organization, the **American Indian Movement** (AIM) began to use more radical tactics. The most dramatic of AIM's actions occurred in 1973 at the town of **Wounded Knee**, South Dakota. AIM leaders chose to publicize their demands at Wounded Knee because white soldiers had massacred Indian women and children there in 1890. The Indians held the town for weeks before laying down their arms.

The Struggle Continues

African Americans did not receive their fair share of the new affluence. As late as 1960 about half were still either poor or barely keeping their heads above the so-called **poverty line.** But in 1965 the economic condition of the average black seemed to be improving. More opportunities were opening up. The new AFL-CIO labor federation had promised "to encourage all workers without regard for color" to join their organization. Although some unions shut out black workers, the leaders of the AFL-CIO spoke out strongly against this practice. The United Automobile Workers and a number of other big unions achieved excellent records in promoting harmony between black and white workers. Perhaps even more promising, Jackie Robinson became the first black player in major league baseball. This quickly opened opportunities for blacks in many sports.

Jim Cartier/Photo Researchers

Seminole children in Big Cypress, Florida, work with their teacher at the Ahfachkee School. Note that they are learning their native American language as well as English.

> **❝ You suddenly find your tongue twisted and your speech stammering as you seek to explain to your six-year-old daughter why she can't go to the public amusement park that has just been advertised on television, and see tears welling up in her little eyes when she is told that Funtown is closed to colored children. . . .❞**
> Martin Luther King, Jr., 1963

"Injustice anywhere is a threat to justice everywhere," said Martin Luther King, Jr., who was killed by an assassin. Try to listen to King's famous speeches on records or tapes.

Martin Luther King, Jr.

The greatest leadership for blacks was provided by a Baptist minister, the Reverend Martin Luther King, Jr. After his success in leading the Montgomery bus boycott, King became a national figure. Everywhere he preached the idea of **nonviolent direct action,** as the best way to achieve racial equality. "Nonviolent resistance is not a method for cowards," he said. One must "accept blows from the opponent without striking back." Love, not hate or force, was the way to change people's minds.

The movement also used songs to tell its aim and hopes—songs of protest, adaptations of spirituals, and newly composed songs.

C. Ray Moore/Black Star

These expressed what King felt was fundamental to the movement's success: determination. The unofficial theme song of the movement was "We Shall Overcome," which was adapted from a version of an old spiritual by the staff at the Highland Folk School in Tennessee. It was sung everywhere the movement went. Here are the first three verses:

> ❝ We shall overcome, we shall overcome,
> We shall overcome someday.
> Oh, deep in my heart, I do believe,
> We shall overcome someday.
>
> We are not afraid, we are not afraid,
> We are not afraid today.
> Oh, deep in my heart, I do believe,
> We shall overcome someday.
>
> We are not alone, we are not alone,
> We are not alone today.

Charles Moore/Black Star

Oh, deep in my heart, I do believe,
We are not alone today.[1] 🙶

Protesters in Birmingham, Alabama, were assailed by firemen with powerful hoses.

In April 1963 King led a campaign against segregation in **Birmingham,** Alabama. The police turned fierce dogs on the peaceful demonstrators and drove them from the streets with jets of water from powerful fire hoses. King was thrown into jail. Yet this incident proved the value of King's approach. Millions of Americans who saw reports of the events on television were impressed by the demonstrators' courage and outraged by the brutality of the police. They reacted strongly on the behalf of the blacks, writing letters to the editors of their local newspapers and even joining protest marches.

Later in 1963, 200,000 people gathered in Washington to demonstrate peacefully in favor of President Kennedy's civil rights legislation. During the proceedings King made his famous "I Have a Dream" speech. He dreamed of a time, he told the huge audience who had come to this **March on Washington,** when all white and black Americans could live together in peace and harmony. The printed page can scarcely do justice to the moving and powerful speech King delivered. But part of it is reproduced on the following pages:

[1] New words and music arrangement by Zilphia Horton, Frank Hamilton, Guy Carawan, and Pete Seeger. TRO Copyright © 1960 and 1963 by Ludlow Music, Inc.

Movements for Equal Rights   1055

Fred Ward/Black Star

The crowd of more than 200,000 that assembled around the reflecting pool in Washington, D.C., marched to support President Kennedy's civil rights legislation. The speech Dr. King delivered that day seemed particularly inspired.

“ Five score years ago, a great American, in whose symbolic shadow we stand today, signed the Emancipation Proclamation. This momentous decree came as a great beacon light of hope for millions of Negro slaves who had been seared in the flames of withering injustice. It came as a joyous daybreak to end the long night of their captivity.

But one hundred years later the Negro is still not free. One hundred years later, the life of the Negro is still badly crippled by the manacles of segregation and the chains of discrimination. One hundred years later, the Negro lives on a lonely island of poverty in the midst of a vast ocean of material prosperity. One hundred years later, the Negro is still languishing in the corners of American society and finds himself an exile in his own land. So we have come here today to dramatize a shameful condition. . . .

I say to you today, my friends, even though we face the difficulties of today and tomorrow, I still have a dream. It is a dream deeply rooted in the American dream. I have a dream that one day this nation will rise up and live out the true meaning of its creed: 'We hold these truths to be self-evident, that all men are created equal. . . .'

I have a dream that one day on the red hills of Georgia, the sons of former slaves and the sons of former slaveowners will be able to sit down together at the table of brotherhood.

I have a dream that one day, even the State of Mississippi, a state sweltering with the heat of oppression, will be transformed into an oasis of freedom and justice. . . .

I have a dream that one day, down in Alabama, with its vicious racists . . . little black boys and black girls will be able to join hands with little white boys and white girls as sisters and brothers.

I have a dream today!

I have a dream that one day every valley shall be exalted, every hill and mountain shall be made low, the rough places will be made plain and the crooked places will be made straight and the glory of the Lord shall be revealed and all flesh shall see it together.

This is our hope. This is the faith that I go back to the South with. With this faith we will be able to hew out of the mountain of despair a stone of hope. With this faith we will be able to transform the jangling discords of our nation into a beautiful symphony of brotherhood. With this faith we will be able to work together, to pray together, to struggle together, to go to jail together, to stand up for freedom together, knowing that we will be free one day. . . .

From every mountainside, let freedom ring. And when we let freedom ring, when we let it ring from every village and every hamlet, from every state and every city, we will be able to speed up that day when all of God's children, black men and white men, Jews and Gentiles, Protestants and Catholics, will be able to join hands and sing in the words of the old Negro spiritual: 'Free at last! Free at last! Thank God almighty, we are free at last!'[1]**"**

[1]From Martin Luther King, Jr.'s "I Have a Dream" speech. Copyright © 1963 by Martin Luther King, Jr. Reprinted by permission of Joan Daves.

King was an exceptional person, but his optimism was typical of the times. "The believer in nonviolence has deep faith in the future," he once said.

No one knew better than Martin Luther King, Jr., that American society was far from perfect. Yet he believed sincerely that the nation was making progress toward the goals that he was seeking. Millions of other Americans, black and white alike, faced the future in the mid-1960s as hopefully as he did. 🖎

Return to the Preview & Review on page 1051.

CHAPTER 28 REVIEW

1957
Nuclear
power plants
begin to
generate electricity

1958
The Affluent Society published

1963
March on Wash
and "I Have a
Dream" speech
★
*The Feminine
Mystique* publi
★
Kennedy
assassinated;
Johnson becom
president

1964
Civil Rights Act
★
Johnson electe
president

Chapter Summary

Read the statements below. Choose one, and write a paragraph explaining its importance.

1. Lyndon Johnson used forceful personality and his experience in government to accomplish many of his goals as president.
2. As a result of Johnson's hard work, Congress passed the laws which enacted his domestic program called the Great Society.
3. The unprecedented period of prosperity in the 1950s and early 1960s led to a mood of optimism in the United States.
4. There was a difference in the labor force following World War II as the percentage of women and the number of white collar workers increased greatly.
5. Television and the computer had a significant impact on American life in the 1950s and 1960s.
6. A dramatic shift in population occurred following World War II when many Americans moved to the Sun Belt and from the cities to the outlying suburbs.
7. The Women's Liberation Movement gained momentum following the publication of *The Feminine Mystique* in 1963.
8. Red Power became a rallying point for Indian Rights activists in the 1960s.
9. Dr. Martin Luther King, Jr., gained support for the civil rights movement in the early 1960s by a campaign in Birmingham and the March on Washington.

Reviewing Chronological Order

Number your paper 1–5. Then study the time line above and place the following events in the order in which they happened by writing the first next to 1, the second next to 2, and so on.

1. American Indian Movement founded
2. National Organization for Women founded
3. Johnson elected president
4. March on Washington
5. Elementary and Secondary Education Act passed

Understanding Main Ideas

1. Explain why the United States was called the Affluent Society in the mid-1960s.
2. What were some wonders of science that were developed after World War II?
3. Explain the difference between monetary policy and fiscal policy. Tell how economists planned to use each to prevent future depressions.
4. What were the good and bad effects of the growth of the suburbs following World War II?
5. Describe the efforts of African Americans, women, and Indians in the 20 years following World War II to secure equal rights.

Thinking Critically

1. **Evaluating.** Television began to greatly influence public opinion in the United States in the 1950s, and it continues to do so today. Discuss whether you think television has had a positive or negative effect on society. If you think its effect has been negative, suggest several ways that the television industry could improve its programming.
2. **Problem Solving.** Imagine that you are an African American in 1963 and have just participated in the March on Washington. You heard Dr. King's "I Have a Dream" speech which has greatly inspired you. Make a list of some of the problems faced by African Americans in the early 1960s and suggestions for how these problems may be solved.
3. **Comparing Ideas.** A major concern of many adult Americans in the 1950s and early 1960s was the direction taken by many young people who were becoming adults during this period. Their goals appeared to be having plenty of money, a good job, a house in the suburbs, and comfortable retirement. They were accused of

Society program
sed and passed

gration Act

entary and Secondary Education Act

nal Organization for Women formed

1973
Wounded Knee

conforming and lacking in concern for the poor and the environment. Would you say that this description could be used to describe America's youth today? Why or why not?

Writing About History
America's Affluent Society is discussed in this chapter. Write a newspaper editorial in which you outline how America's abundant wealth and resources can be put to better use so that all of its people benefit from them. Conclude your editorial by mentioning which of America's riches you most appreciate and how they have benefited you and your family.

Practicing the Strategy
Review the strategy on page 1047.
Using the Census. Study the census data on page 1047 and answer these questions.
1. Did the total of square miles increase or decrease in urban areas between 1970 and 1980?
2. Did urban density increase or decrease from 1970 to 1980?
3. What conclusion can you draw from the information you found regarding square miles and density?

Using Primary Sources
In 1963 during an attempted nonviolent campaign against segregation in Birmingham, Alabama, Dr. Martin Luther King, Jr., was arrested. He drew severe criticism from local white clergymen, who accused Dr. King of being an outside agitator. They claimed his demonstrations ignited violence by forcing a confrontation between demonstrators and police. In answer to these accusations Dr. King wrote his now famous "Letter from a Birmingham Jail" while imprisoned in that city. As you read the following excerpt from Dr. King's letter, think about the wisdom of his words and the impact they had on those who continued using nonviolent methods in their campaign for civil rights.

In your statement you assert that our actions, even though peaceful, must be condemned because they precipitate [cause] violence. But is this a logical assertion [statement]? Isn't this like condemning a robbed man because his possession of money precipitated the evil act of robbery? . . . We must come to see that, as the federal courts have consistently affirmed, it is wrong to urge an individual to cease his efforts to gain his basic constitutional rights because the quest may precipitate violence. Society must protect the robbed and punish the robber.

1. Who do you think Dr. King is referring to when he uses the term "robber?"
2. What is it that Dr. King implies is being stolen by the robber?
3. Do you agree or disagree with Dr. King that it is wrong to tell people not to seek their constitutional rights because it "may precipitate violence?" Explain your answer.

Linking History & Geography
People moved from rural to urban areas in ever-increasing numbers in the decades following World War II. To better understand the dramatic impact of this population shift, study the map on page 1043. Then with your classmates prepare a map of the United States showing the major urban areas in 1940 and in 1980. You may need to refer to an historical atlas, the *Statistical Abstract of the United States*, or other reference books for the years 1940 and 1980 to complete your maps.

Enriching Your Study of History
1. **Individual Project.** Prepare an oral report on one of the following changes or trends that occurred in the 1950s and 1960s: advances in science and technology; population growth and shifts; higher standard of living. Tell how these changes affected American life in the 1950s and 1960s.
2. **Cooperative Project.** Your group will make a collage that illustrates leisure time activities enjoyed by Americans today. Each of you should contribute to the collage by bringing in as many pictures from magazines and newspapers as you can find on the subject or subjects chosen by your group.

Chapter 28 Review   1059

The Vietnam Era

In August 1964 President Johnson announced that North Vietnamese gunboats had attacked the American destroyer *Maddox* in the Gulf of Tonkin, off the coast of Southeast Asia. He called upon Congress to approve and support in advance "the determination of the president, as commander in chief, to take all necessary measures to repel any armed attack against the forces of the United States." Congress voted for this resolution almost unanimously. As we shall soon see, this is another example of how an event that seems unimportant at the time can have far-reaching and unexpected historical significance. What consequences would commitment to the war in Vietnam have for America and its people?

Larry Burrows/Collection

American troops land at Da Nang to pit their sophisticated weaponry against the tunnels and jungle hideouts of the Viet Cong. What vehicle did the United States commonly use to move troops during the war? This picture give you a hint. After reading about the war in this section, explain why this vehicle was used.

1. WAR IN VIETNAM

The Domino Theory

In the summer of 1964 the former French colony of Vietnam was torn by war. Vietnam had been divided into two countries in 1954. Communist North Vietnam was supplying aid to pro-communist South Vietnamese guerrillas, who were known as the **Viet Cong.** The Viet Cong had been seeking to overthrow the government of South Vietnam, which was pro-American. They controlled large parts of the country, especially the rural regions.

While Dwight Eisenhower was president, a small number of American military advisers had been sent to South Vietnam to help train the South Vietnamese army. The United States also gave South Vietnam large sums of money for military supplies and economic aid. President Kennedy continued this policy.

The president of South Vietnam, Ngo Dinh Diem, was incompetent and unpopular. Many of the men around him were openly corrupt. Shortly before President Kennedy was assassinated, a group of Vietnamese army officers overthrew the Diem government and killed Diem. Unfortunately, they proved no better than he at defeating the Viet Cong.

President Johnson did not change American policy toward Vietnam until the Gulf of Tonkin affair. Even then, he was mainly interested in *appearing* to be more aggressive. His Republican opponent in the 1964 presidential election, Senator Barry Goldwater, demanded that the United States make a bigger effort to ''check communism'' in Vietnam. Johnson hoped that the **Tonkin Gulf Resolution,** which gave him broad war powers, would convince the voters that he was pursuing that objective vigorously. But he made a special point of not getting *too* involved in Vietnam. He insisted that he ''would never send American boys to do the fighting that Asian boys should do themselves.''

After winning the election, however, Johnson decided to step up American military activity in Vietnam. This would restore morale to the South Vietnamese. President Eisenhower had warned of a ''falling domino'' effect if communist expansion were allowed to go unchallenged. He had said in 1954:

66 You have a row of dominoes set up, you knock over the first one, and . . . the last one . . . will go over very quickly. 99

According to this **domino theory,** if South Vietnam were controlled by the communists, its neighbors, Laos and Cambodia, would also become communist. Then all Southeast Asia, and perhaps even India with its hundreds of millions of people, would follow.

Use these questions to guide your reading. Answer the questions after completing Section 1.
Understanding Issues, Events, & Ideas. Use the following words to describe American involvement in Vietnam: Viet Cong, Gulf of Tonkin Resolution, domino theory, escalation, doves, hawks, Saigon, Tet offensive.
1. How did Johnson respond to communist expansion in Southeast Asia after the Tonkin Gulf Resolution?
2. How was Johnson's Vietnam policy different from the policies of Eisenhower and Kennedy?
3. Why did President Johnson and his advisers believe they were acting with restraint in Vietnam?
4. What effect did the Tet offensive have on Americans?
Thinking Critically. 1. Why do you think Congress passed the Tonkin Gulf Resolution so easily? **2.** What do you think the American officer meant when he said that ''we had to destroy it in order to save it?'' Imagine that you are Vietnamese. How would you react to such a remark?

Point of View

A priest and an army sergeant come to tell Gene and Peg Mullen that their son has been killed in Vietnam.

"Gene looked beyond Father Shimon to the sergeant and asked again, "Is my boy *dead?*"

"Let's go into the house, Gene," Father Shimon said. "I want to talk to you there."

"No!" Gene said, not moving. "I want to *know!* Tell me, *is my boy dead?*"

"I can't tell you here," Father Shimon said, his hand fluttering up toward Gene's shoulder. "Come into the house with us please?"

Gene spun away before the priest's pale fingers could touch him.

Peg Mullen heard the back door open, heard Gene rushing up the stairs into the kitchen, heard him shouting, "It's Mikey! It's Mikey!" his voice half a scream. . . ."

From *Friendly Fire,*
C.D.B. Bryan, 1976

Recent events in Korea and the Cuban Missile Crisis seemed to show that the way to check communist expansion was by firmness and force. President Johnson, urged on by a military with unprecedented power and prestige, felt he could not waver. He said:

" We could tuck our tails between our legs and run for cover. That would just whet the enemy's appetite for greater aggression and more territory, and solve nothing."

The assumption behind this reasoning was that the fighting in South Vietnam was between local Vietnamese patriots and "outside" communists. If the outsiders were allowed to conquer the country, the argument ran, they would be encouraged to press farther. In reality the struggle in South Vietnam was a civil war between supporters of the government and the Viet Cong. "Outside" communists from China and the Soviet Union were supplying the Viet Cong with weapons and advice, just as the United States was helping the anticommunist government of South Vietnam. The communist government of North Vietnam was deeply involved too. Its objective was to unite the two Vietnams under a communist regime.

America Escalates the War

In February 1965 Johnson made a fateful decision. After Diem's assassination in late 1963, the Viet Cong had gained control of more and more South Vietnamese villages. The war now became a test of the president's will. "I will not be the President who saw Southeast Asia go the way China went," he said, referring to the communist takeover in China in 1949. He ordered the air force to bomb selected targets in North Vietnam. In March he sent two battalions of marines to Vietnam. Their job was to protect the air base from which the bombers were operating. Soon more troops had to be sent in to reinforce the marines!

A few months later the American forces in Vietnam were given permission to seek out and attack Viet Cong units. Still, many restrictions on how American troops could fight the war remained. Nonetheless, more troops were shipped to Vietnam. By the end of 1965 there were 185,000 American fighting men in the country.

This steady **escalation,** or increase, in American military strength and involvement in Vietnam went on for three years. Each increase brought more North Vietnamese into the conflict in support of the Viet Cong. By 1968 more than half a million Americans were fighting in Vietnam. Yet Congress never officially declared war. Johnson instead waged war by the authority of the Tonkin Gulf Resolution, which had seemed to have little historical significance when it was passed by Congress in 1964.

The president and his advisers thought they were acting with great restraint. The enormous difference in size and wealth between

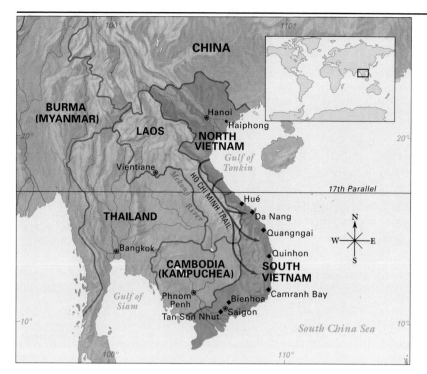

→ Ho Chi Minh Trail

◆ U.S. base

```
0          200        400 Mi.
0    200       400 Km.
```

Mercator Projection

LEARNING FROM MAPS. *Compare this map to the one of Korea on page 999. Note that the geography of Vietnam is similar to that of Korea. Describe how the geography of the two is similar. After reading about President Nixon's decision to extend U.S. bombing into Cambodia, study this map. What was the geographic reasoning behind Nixon's decision?*

the United States and North Vietnam lulled them into believing that the United States could win the war whenever it chose. How, asked the advisers, could a tiny country like North Vietnam successfully resist the United States? They wanted to risk the lives of as few Americans as possible. When each escalation proved to be not enough, they hoped just one more increase would do the job.

But North Vietnam was successful because the war in Vietnam was like no other war Americans had fought. Much of it was guerrilla warfare. The enemy, the Viet Cong, wore no uniforms and fought by ambush and by night. By day they blended with the rest of the population. Much of the war was fought in dense jungles and rugged mountains where tanks, even jeeps, were almost useless. Small squads of American soldiers slowly worked their way through vegetation so thick they could see only a few feet in any direction. The enemy could be hiding anywhere. Snipers would pick off one or two men and then disappear. One soldier recalled an attack in the jungle:

❝ Men all around me were screaming. The fire [shooting] was now a continuous roar. We were even being fired at by our own guys. No one knew where the fire was coming from, and so the men were shooting everywhere. Some were in shock and were blazing away at everything they saw or imagined they saw. . . .[1] ❞

[1]From "Death in the Ia Drang Valley" by Jack Smith in the *Saturday Evening Post*, January 28, 1967

Larry Burrows/Life Magazine © Time Warner, Inc.

The United States became mired in a land war in Southeast Asia, just as the French had before them. Critics sharply opposed the war. Much of the antiwar sentiment focused on American soldiers. Later came a time of reconciliation. Many efforts today are directed at helping Vietnam veterans reestablish their place in American society. Do you think the government has this responsibility after a war?

Mines and booby traps—hidden explosive devices—made movement through the countryside terrifying. Added to these difficulties were the limits placed on American troops. Often, they could not fire until fired upon, could not pursue the enemy in many places, could not bomb certain areas. And while American forces struggled in Vietnam, large numbers of people at home turned against the war, focusing much of their opposition on the soldiers fighting the war under the orders of others.

Time passed without victory. Large numbers of Americans began thinking that the war was a terrible mistake. Some claimed that keeping in power the government of South Vietnam, which was weak and very unpopular with the South Vietnamese people, was not worth the cost in American lives and money. Others argued that it was wrong for Americans to be killing people in a small country that was quite literally on the other side of the world.

The fighting in Vietnam was savage. Both sides showed a capacity for cruelty. Prisoners were sometimes tortured and killed. Hundreds of civilians died in air raids. Peaceful villages were burned to the ground to root out Viet Cong sympathizers. Local South Vietnamese officials were murdered by Viet Cong terrorists.

Americans who wanted to stop the war were called **doves,** after the traditional bird of peace. Those who insisted that the war must be fought until it was won were known as **hawks.** For a long time the hawks were in the majority. National pride and hatred of communism made many hawks believe that it would be cowardly and shameful for the United States to pull out of South Vietnam.

Both sides grew more vocal as escalation proceeded. President Johnson expressed the determination of the United States government to see victory in Vietnam. Early in 1965 he said:

> " Tonight Americans and Asians are dying for a world where each people may choose its own path to change.
>
> Why must we take this painful road?
>
> Why must this nation endanger its ease, and its interest, and its power for the sake of a people so far away?
>
> We fight this war because we must fight if we are to live in a world where every country can shape its own destiny [fate]. And only in such a world will our own freedom be secure. . . .
>
> Why are we in South Vietnam?
>
> We are there because we have a promise to keep. Since 1954 every American president has offered support to the people of South Vietnam. We have helped to build, and we have helped to defend. Thus over many years have we made a national pledge to help South Vietnam defend its independence.
>
> And I intend to keep that promise.
>
> To dishonor that pledge, to abandon this small and brave nation to its enemies, and to the terror that must follow, would be an unforgivable wrong. . . .[1] "

Equally determined opponents spoke out against American involvement in the war. One opponent, Senator J. William Fulbright of Arkansas, chairman of the Senate Foreign Relations Committee, said:

> " We [the United States] are in a war to 'defend freedom' in South Vietnam. . . .
>
> One wonders how much the American commitment to Vietnamese freedom is also a commitment to American pride—the two seem to have become part of the same package. When we talk about the freedom of South Vietnam, we may be thinking about how our pride would be injured if we settled for less than we set out to achieve. We may be thinking about our reputation as a great power, fearing that a compromise settlement would shame us before the world, marking us as a second-rate people with failing courage and determination.
>
> Such fears are senseless. They are unworthy of the richest, most powerful, most productive, and best educated people in the world. . . .[2] "

[1]From "Peace Without Conquest," a speech by Lyndon B. Johnson on April 7, 1965
[2]From *The Arrogance of Power* by J. William Fulbright

DRAWING CONCLUSIONS

One of the most important ways to use the information you read and study is as a basis to draw conclusions. A conclusion is a reasoned judgment arrived at by studying evidence. Historians draw conclusions based on evidence from primary and secondary sources, maps, charts and graphs, the census, and many other sources.

How to Draw Conclusions

To draw conclusions, follow these steps.

1. **Study the evidence carefully.** Note all trends and other relationships.
2. **Read "between the lines."** Make inferences by using your reasoning abilities to look for implied or suggested meanings. (But be sure to treat all inferences with caution. Use them carefully to support or refute the solid evidence you collect.
3. **Continually test your conclusions and revise if necessary.** Collect additional evidence. Refine your conclusion to fit the additional information. The more supporting facts you have, the more likely the conclusion you have drawn is correct.
4. **Use your conclusions.** Apply the conclusions you draw to the topic you are studying to help you understand the topic.

Applying the Skill

Read the following excerpt. It contains conclusions by a historian. See if you can identify one of the conclusions.

President Johnson did not change American policy toward Vietnam until the Gulf of Tonkin Affair. Even then he was mainly interested in appearing to be more aggressive. His Republican opponent in the 1964 presidential election, Senator Barry Goldwater, demanded that the United States make a bigger effort to "check communism" in Vietnam. Johnson hoped that the Tonkin Gulf Resolution would convince the voters that he was pursuing that objective vigorously. But he made a special point of not getting too involved in Vietnam. He insisted that he "would never send American boys to do the fighting that Asian boys should do themselves."

The most obvious conclusion stated by the historian in the excerpt is that President Johnson only wanted to appear more aggressive. The historian has reached this conclusion based on his research into this situation. Now read the following except and draw at least two conclusions based on your reading.

After winning the election, however, Johnson decided to step up American military activity in Vietnam. . . . In February 1965 Johnson made a fateful decision. He ordered the air force to bomb selected targets in North Vietnam. In March he sent two battalions of marines to Vietnam. Their job was to protect the air base from which the bombers were operating. Soon more troops had to be sent in to reinforce the marines!

A few months later the American forces in Vietnam were given permission to seek out and attack Viet Cong units. More troops were shipped to Vietnam. By the end of 1965 there were 185,000 American fighting men in the country.

This steady escalation, or increase, in American military strength in Vietnam went on for three years. Each increase brought more North Vietnamese into the conflict in support of the Viet Cong. By 1968 more than half a million Americans were fighting in Vietnam. Yet Congress never officially declared war. Johnson instead waged war by the authority of the Tonkin Gulf Resolution, which had seemed to have little historical significance when it was passed by Congress in 1964.

The president and his advisers thought they were acting with great restraint. The enormous difference in size and wealth between the United States and North Vietnam lulled them into believing that the United States could win the war whenever it chose. How, asked the advisers, could a tiny country like North Vietnam successfully resist the United States? They wanted to risk the lives of as few Americans as possible. When each escalation proved to be not enough, they hoped just one more increase would do the job.

What conclusions can you draw from this information? You might conclude that Johnson took his election victory as a sign that the American people supported escalated American involvement in Vietnam. Another conclusion you might draw is that Johnson's advisers did not portray an accurate picture of what it would take to win the war. What are some other conclusions you can draw from this excerpt?

For independent practice, see Practicing the Strategy on page 1086.

Charles Gatewood/Magnum Photos

In New York's Washington Square Park, protesters of the war light candles in a moratorium. What does the word moratorium *mean?*

Point of View

The author of *A Bright Shining Lie* brings a historical perspective to the Tet offensive.

❝Yet to turn the war decisively in [the Viet Cong's] favor they had to achieve a masterstroke that would have the will-breaking effect on the Americans that Dien Bien Phu had had on the French. The masterstroke was Tet, 1968. . . . In cities and towns all across South Vietnam, tens of thousands of Communist troops were launching . . . a 'panorama of attacks.' . . . The goal was to collapse the Saigon regime with these military blows. . . . Ho Chi Minh and his confederates hoped to knock the prop out from under the American war, force the United States to open negotiations under disadvantageous conditions, and begin the process of wedging the Americans out of their country. . . .❞
Neil Sheehan, 1988

Early in 1968 the American commander in Vietnam, General William C. Westmoreland, announced that victory was near. Soon the Viet Cong would be crushed. But on January 30, the Vietnamese New Year's Day (*Tet*), the Viet Cong suddenly attacked cities all over South Vietnam. They even briefly gained control of parts of **Saigon,** the capital. They held a number of important cities for weeks.

The American and South Vietnamese troops fought back, as one historian has put it, "with the fury of a blinded giant." Eventually they regained control of the cities. In doing so, however, they destroyed even more of Vietnam. In a remark that soon became famous, an American officer justified the smashing of the town of Ben Tre. "We had to destroy it in order to save it," he said.

The American counterattack crushed the **Tet offensive.** Viet Cong and North Vietnamese losses were enormous. Still, the American public was profoundly shocked at the strength shown by the communists after so many years of war. The tide of opinion turned against the war. When General Westmoreland asked for another 200,000 men, President Johnson turned him down. 🖅

Return to the Preview & Review on page 1061.

2. A YEAR OF TRAGEDY

Use these questions to guide your reading. Answer the questions after completing Section 2.

1. How did Lyndon Johnson acknowledge that his Vietnam policy had failed?
2. How did many Americans react to the assassination of Martin Luther King, Jr.?
3. What caused the riots at the 1968 Democratic convention?
4. Why did many Americans think Nixon would never be president? How did he get another chance in 1968?
5. Why was the selection of Agnew as Nixon's running mate a key to the 1968 election?

Thinking Critically. 1. Imagine you are a delegate to the Democratic National Convention in 1968. Write an article for your local newspaper explaining who you are supporting and why. 2. Imagine that Martin Luther King, Jr., and Robert Kennedy had not been assassinated in 1968. How might this have changed events in the years after 1968?

1968 Shocks Americans

In March 1968 President Johnson acknowledged that his Vietnam policy had failed. He had been planning to run for a second full term in 1968. Senator Eugene McCarthy of Minnesota had announced that he would oppose Johnson for the Democratic nomination. McCarthy was a leading dove. Before the Tet offensive no one gave him any chance of defeating Johnson.

After Tet, however, the situation changed. McCarthy almost defeated Johnson in the New Hampshire presidential primary. Then Robert F. Kennedy, brother of the slain president, declared that he too was a candidate. Faced with a difficult fight that would probably divide the country still further, Johnson announced that he would not seek reelection.

On April 4, less than a week after Johnson's withdrawal, came another shock. Martin Luther King, Jr., was murdered in Memphis, Tennessee, where he had gone to support a strike of garbage collectors. King had foreseen the price he might have to pay for his leadership. In a speech delivered in Memphis just before his assassination he observed:

66 Well, I don't know what will happen now. We've got some difficult days ahead. But it really doesn't matter with me now, because I've been to the mountaintop. And I don't mind. Like anybody, I would like to live a long life. Longevity has its place. But I'm not concerned about that now. I just want to do God's will. And He's allowed me to go up to the mountain, and I've looked over, and I've seen the promised land. I may not get there with you. But I want you to know tonight, that we as a people will get to the promised land. And so I'm happy tonight. I'm not worried about anything. I'm not fearing any man. Mine eyes have seen the glory of the coming of the Lord.[1] 99

King's murder caused an explosion of anger in black communities all over the country. Riots broke out in 125 cities in 28 states. Whole sections of Washington were aflame in the shadow of the Capitol.

Robert Kennedy was among those who tried to calm the waters. In an impromptu speech in an Indiana ghetto, he announced King's assassination with these words:

66 Martin Luther King dedicated his life to love and to justice for his fellow human beings, and he died because of that effort.

[1] From *Bearing the Cross* by David J. Garrow

Senator Eugene McCarthy in his Children's Crusade—so called because his supporters were young and had yet to vote for president—was the first candidate to challenge President Johnson. How did the Tet offensive make McCarthy's candidacy a serious challenge?

Leonard McCombe/Life Magazine © Time Warner, Inc.

Declan Haun/Black Star

Flip Schulke/Black Star

In this difficult day, in this difficult time for the United States, it is perhaps well to ask what kind of a nation we are and what direction we want to move in. For those of you who are black—considering the evidence there evidently is that there were white people who were responsible—you can be filled with bitterness, with hatred, and a desire for revenge. We can move in great polarization—black people amongst black, white people amongst white, filled with hatred toward one another.

Or we can make an effort, as Martin Luther King did, to understand and to comprehend, and to replace that violence, that stain of bloodshed that has spread across our land, with an effort to understand with compassion and love. . . .

What we need in the United States is not division; what we need in the United States is not hatred; what we need in the United States is not violence or lawlessness, but love and wisdom, and compassion toward one another, and a feeling of justice towards those who still suffer within our country, whether they be white or they be black. . . .

Martin Luther King, Jr., received a traditional African American funeral procession. In the photograph above left, his mourners march through the streets of Atlanta behind a wagon drawn by mules. How was this a reminder of King's heritage? King's widow, Coretta Scott King, and his daughter Yolanda are pictured above at his funeral service.

A Year of Tragedy   1069

B. Glinn/Magnum Photos

Robert Kennedy became nearly as popular as his presidential brother when he campaigned for the Democratic nomination in 1968. What chance had he of winning the nomination?

We've had difficult times in the past. We will have difficult times in the future. It is not the end of violence; it is not the end of lawlessness; it is not the end of disorder.

But the vast majority of white people and the vast majority of black people in this country want to live together, want to improve the quality of our life, and want justice for all human beings who abide in our land.

Let us dedicate ourselves to what the Greeks wrote so many years ago: to tame the savageness of man and to make gentle the life of this world.

Let us dedicate ourselves to that, and say a prayer for our country and for our people.[1] **"**

In June Robert Kennedy himself was assassinated by an Arab immigrant who objected to the support the United States was giving the country of Israel. Kennedy had just won the California presidential primary. He had seemed likely to win the nomination at the Democratic national convention in Chicago. After his death, Vice President Hubert H. Humphrey became the favorite.

Humphrey loyally supported Johnson's policy in Vietnam. (If

[1]From *Robert Kennedy and His Times* by Arthur M. Schlesinger, Jr.

he had not, Johnson would not have supported him for president.) When the convention met, large numbers of antiwar protesters, many of whom favored Senator McCarthy for president, flocked to Chicago to demonstrate. Mayor Richard Daley, a Humphrey supporter, packed the area around the convention hall with city police.

Radicals among the demonstrators insulted and taunted the police. They called them "pigs" and other vulgar names. The police responded by rushing into the crowd, clubs swinging. Millions of television viewers who had tuned in to watch the convention debates saw instead helmeted policemen repeatedly hitting the demonstrators with their nightsticks and herding them dazed and bloody into police wagons.

Not many people at the time realized that the protests in Chicago were a continuation of the antiwar and free-speech movements spreading across the land. At the University of California, students burned draft cards, and at Columbia University they took over many campus buildings.

The Election of 1968

Humphrey won the Democratic nomination easily. But thousands of Democrats blamed him, quite unfairly, for the police riot in Chicago. Most of these same Democrats resented his support of the war in Vietnam.

This split in the Democratic party helped the Republican candidate, Richard M. Nixon, the former vice president whom Kennedy had defeated in 1960. Few had expected Nixon to get a second chance to run for president. In 1962 he had run unsuccessfully for governor of California. At the time he seemed a sore loser, blaming reporters for his defeat.

However, Nixon had worked hard for the Republican party during the Kennedy and Johnson administrations. Hundreds of local Republican officials felt that he deserved a second chance for the presidency. When the 1968 Republican convention met, he had a majority of the delegates in his camp and was easily nominated.

Governor George C. Wallace of Alabama, an outspoken foe of racial integration, also ran for president in 1968 on an independent ticket. For this reason, Nixon chose Spiro T. Agnew of Maryland as his running mate. Agnew had taken a tough stand against black activists, urban crime, and protesters of all kinds. He was not well known nationally, but his record on several issues made him acceptable to many voters who might otherwise have supported Wallace.

In the three-way contest for president, Nixon won. He got only about 43 percent of the popular vote, less than 1 percent more than Humphrey. But he received a solid majority (56 percent) of the electoral vote. 🖃

Fred Ward/Black Star

Bettmann Newsphotos

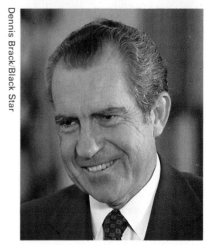

Dennis Brack/Black Star

From top: 1968 presidential candidates Hubert Humphrey, George Wallace, and Richard Nixon.

Return to the Preview & Review on page 1068.

Use these questions to guide your reading. Answer the questions after completing Section 3.
Understanding Issues, Events, & Ideas. Use the following words to discuss key events during Nixon's first term in office: wage-and-price freeze, antiwar movement, Vietnamization, Cambodia, Ho Chi Minh Trail, Kent State and Jackson State, Strategic Arms Limitation Treaty, détente, Hanoi, Six Days' War, Arab Oil Crisis, shuttle diplomacy.
1. What was a major cause of the inflation that President Nixon set out to check? How did he attempt to check it?
2. Why did Nixon order American troops into Cambodia? What was the response in the United States to this move?
3. What diplomatic moves did President Nixon make in 1972? What effect did they have on the American people?
4. What were some reasons that Nixon was reelected by such an overwhelming majority?
5. What were the terms of the first Vietnam War peace agreement negotiated by Henry Kissinger? What reasons were given for its failure?
Thinking Critically. 1. Why do you think the United States, with its far greater wealth and technology was unable to win the war in Vietnam? What other lessons do you think Americans can learn from the Vietnam War? 2. Why might it have been easier for Nixon to visit China and initiate regular diplomatic relations than it would have been for Eisenhower or Kennedy?

3. NIXON AS PRESIDENT

Nixon and the Economy

The new president favored moderation. He sought to please middle-income voters and persons who were neither radicals nor reactionaries. (Politically, radicals favor extreme change; reactionaries resist change or want to return to old-fashioned ways, an extreme change in itself.) These moderates and middle-income people were worried about high taxes and rising prices. Inflation in particular seemed the most alarming economic issue of the times. President Nixon set out to end it.

President Johnson was partly responsible for the inflation. Each time he ordered an escalation of the war in Vietnam, the government had to spend billions of additional dollars on weapons and other supplies. Government purchases put huge sums of money into the economy, but the economy was not producing more consumer goods. So people had money but a limited supply of goods to spend the money on. The prices of goods rose sharply. In addition, Johnson had not asked Congress to increase taxes to pay for the war, partly because he feared that his domestic programs would be cut back if he did so. (He also wished to avoid the congressional debate on the war that asking for a tax hike would cause.) A popular expression of the day was, "He refused to choose between guns and butter," or between spending money on the war and on domestic programs. As a result, the federal budget was badly unbalanced.

Nixon used fiscal and monetary policies to check inflation. He reduced government spending and persuaded the Federal Reserve Board to raise interest rates to discourage borrowing. The economy slowed down. These policies caused unemployment to go up. Plants cut back production, and people were laid off as consumer buying dropped off. But for some reason prices continued to go up too. Economists were as puzzled by the trend as the president. Throughout 1969 and 1970 the trend continued.

Finally, in August 1971, Nixon took a drastic step. He suddenly ordered a **wage-and-price freeze.** During a 90-day period, he set up new government boards to supervise wages and prices. Then he announced guidelines that placed maximum limits on future increases in wages and prices. This program did not stop inflation, but it did slow it down.

Nixon and the War

Nixon also sought a middle-of-the-road solution to the war in Vietnam. He was unwilling to give up the American goal of keeping the communists from conquering South Vietnam. Yet every report of

Robert Ellison/Black Star

This Vietnamese army nurse attends a fallen soldier as American fighters look on. The picture was taken during the Vietnamization of the war. Why was there doubt from the start about this policy?

new American casualties in Vietnam increased the strength of the American **antiwar movement**—the organized effort to stop the war. Nixon's problem was how to reduce the casualties without losing the war in Vietnam.

He decided to shift the burden of fighting the Viet Cong and North Vietnamese to the South Vietnamese army. Gradually, as that army grew stronger, American troops could be withdrawn. This was called the **Vietnamization** of the war.

Whether Vietnamization would work was doubtful from the start. After all, the escalation of the American effort in Vietnam had

"We are people of this generation, bred in at least modest comfort, housed now in universities, looking uncomfortably at the world we inherit."

Tom Hayden, 1962

been necessary because the South Vietnamese had not been able to defeat the communists on their own. At best, Vietnamization would take a long time. The first reduction of American strength amounted to only 25,000 out of an army of more than 540,000.

As time passed, however, Nixon was able to reduce the size of the American force in Vietnam considerably. By the spring of 1970 it was down to 430,000. Nixon proudly announced that he intended to pull out another 150,000 men within a year.

Instead, only a few days later, on April 30, the president suddenly announced an expansion of the war. He was sending American troops into **Cambodia,** the nation on the western border of Vietnam. The reason for this invasion, Nixon said, was that the North Vietnamese were using Cambodia as a sanctuary, or safe base of operations, from which to launch attacks on South Vietnam. The Americans were going to destroy these bases.

For years, the North Vietnamese had been moving soldiers and supplies into South Vietnam along the **Ho Chi Minh Trail** in Cambodia and Laos. (Ho Chi Minh had been the president of North Vietnam.) The Americans had responded by bombing the trail. Since Cambodia was a neutral country, this bombing was done secretly. And like so much in this frustrating war, the bombings were in vain. No large bases were ever found in Cambodia.

Nixon's public announcement of the invasion of Cambodia set off a new storm of protest in the United States. In November 1969 250,000 people had staged a protest demonstration in Washington against the war. But the antiwar movement had become less vigorous as Nixon reduced the number of American soldiers in Vietnam. It now suddenly revived. If Vietnamization was a success, why was it necessary to send Americans into Cambodia?

College students in particular reacted angrily to news of the invasion. Throughout the spring of 1970 there were demonstrations on campuses all over the country. Much property was destroyed. The worst trouble occurred at **Kent State** University in Ohio. Rioting there led the governor of Ohio to send National Guard troops to the campus to preserve order. After several days of troubles in May, an overly tense guard unit opened fire on protesting students. Four students were killed and nearly a dozen more were wounded. Some of the victims had merely been walking across the campus on their way to classes when the guardsmen began shooting.

Several days later two students were shot down by Mississippi state police at **Jackson State.** The killings at Kent State and Jackson State caused still more student protests. Some colleges were forced to close down for the remainder of the school year. Parents were shaken by the spectacle of their children under fire. They had thought such things could never happen in the United States.

The Cambodian invasion did not lead immediately to much heavy fighting. Nixon depended increasingly on air attacks on North

John Paul Filo

Americans were deeply shocked by this picture taken in 1970 at Kent State University. There, National Guardsmen opened fire on students during a campus protest. What announcement by President Nixon prompted this demonstration?

Vietnam to weaken the communists. Soon the American troops in Cambodia were ordered back into South Vietnam. Nixon continued the troop withdrawals. By the end of 1972, fewer than 100,000 Americans were fighting the war, and the number was declining steadily.

Nixon Visits China and the Soviet Union

As American soldiers withdrew from Vietnam, President Nixon tried to end the war by diplomacy. His chief foreign policy adviser, Henry Kissinger, entered into secret discussions with North Vietnamese leaders in Paris. In February 1972, Nixon himself made a dramatic trip to China, a nation that supported North Vietnam.

The United States had never officially recognized the communists as the legal rulers of China. At the time of the 1949 civil war that brought the communists to power in China, Nixon had been a leader of the group in Congress that opposed recognizing the new government. Like Senator Joseph McCarthy, Nixon had blamed the state department for the loss of China to the communists. Over the years he had opposed having any dealings with the "Red Chinese."

Now Nixon reversed himself completely. He no longer saw the need for containment. Instead he hoped to establish a balance of power. "It will be a safer world and a better world if we have a

John Dominis/Life Picture Service

In Beijing, President and Mrs. Nixon were greeted by Mao Tse-tung, communist leader of China. This was one of two historic visits made by the Nixons. What was the other?

strong, healthy United States, Europe, Soviet Union, China, Japan—each balancing the other, not playing one against the other, an even balance,'' he said in 1971. America's withdrawal from Vietnam—where it had been involved since the Eisenhower administration in the early 1950s—also helped open the way.

His visit to China was his boldest step towards a balance of power, and it was a great success. The Chinese leaders greeted him warmly. He agreed to support the admission of Red China to the United Nations in place of Taiwan, which had represented China since 1949. Important trade agreements were worked out. It was clear that the two nations would soon establish regular diplomatic relations.

A few months later Nixon made another important diplomatic move. This time he went to the Soviet Union. Again he was given an extremely friendly welcome. This happened despite the fact that the Soviet Union, like China, was supporting the North Vietnamese in the war. Out of this visit came the first **Strategic Arms Limitation Treaty** (SALT). This treaty placed limits on the use of nuclear weapons by the two powers. The two powers seemed to be entering a period of **détente,** or reduction of tensions between them.

The Election of 1972

President Nixon rose in popularity after his successful diplomatic visits and his sincere efforts to wind down the war in Vietnam. The

Republicans nominated him for a second term without opposition. The Democrats, however, had no obvious leader in 1972. Hubert Humphrey hoped to face Nixon again. Senator Edmund Muskie of Maine had many supporters. But the nomination went to Senator George McGovern of South Dakota, who had campaigned hard in the primaries on an antiwar platform.

McGovern's campaign was bungled from the start. His running mate, Senator Thomas Eagleton of Missouri, was discovered to have been hospitalized in the past for psychiatric treatment. At first McGovern announced that he would stand behind Eagleton "one thousand percent." Then he changed his mind. He asked Eagleton to withdraw. Sargent Shriver, a brother-in-law of John F. Kennedy, was chosen instead. This incident made McGovern seem both indecisive and unfaithful to a loyal supporter.

Bettmann Newsphotos

In *White House Years* Secretary of State Henry Kissinger describes the banquet hall where the leaders of China and the U.S. met.

> **"The banquets in the capital took place in the gigantic Great Hall of the People that commemorates the Communist takeover. . . . [It] faces the vermilion walls of the Forbidden City across Tien An Men Square. . . . The banquet protocol throughout my visits was unvarying. One reached the banquet hall by a grand staircase that rose steeply through various levels to seemingly distant heights. No visitor with a heart condition could possibly make it to the top alive. . . ."**
>
> Henry Kissinger, 1979

Henry Kissinger, left, Nixon's tireless national security adviser and later secretary of state, announced "Peace is at hand" shortly before Nixon stood for reelection in 1972. What happened instead?

Shortly before the election, Nixon's negotiator, Henry Kissinger, announced that he had reached an agreement with North Vietnamese leaders. "Peace is at hand," he said. As a result, Nixon won an overwhelming victory on election day. He won more than 60 percent of the popular vote and carried every state but Massachusetts.

America Leaves Vietnam

After Kissinger's "peace is at hand" announcement, Nixon stopped the bombing of North Vietnam. The agreement Kissinger had negotiated called for a cease-fire, joint North and South Vietnamese administration of the country, and free elections. Then the last of the

American troops would go home and the American prisoners of war held by the North Vietnamese would be released.

After the presidential election this agreement fell through. According to the Americans, the Vietnamese communists backed away from terms they had accepted earlier. But perhaps the main reason the talks ended was the refusal of South Vietnamese president Thieu to cooperate because his government objected to parts of the agreement. President Nixon then resumed the air strikes.

This time the president sent B-52 bombers, the largest in the air force, to strike at **Hanoi,** the capital of North Vietnam. These were far heavier attacks than any launched on Germany in World War II.

Nixon halted the bombing in December; peace negotiations resumed in Paris. Finally, in January 1973, an agreement was signed. So far as the United States was concerned, the war was over. But American policy had been a failure. The United States had lost the war. By the time the last Americans were airlifted out of Saigon (which was later renamed Ho Chi Minh City) the war had cost more than $100 billion and the lives of more than 58,175 Americans and a much larger number of Vietnamese. No one then anticipated how great would be the adjustment for the returning veterans, many of whom were deeply shocked by the war. There were few parades for them, few joyous public celebrations. Some Americans saw them as the symbol of all that was wrong with the war. Yet had they not been drafted and sent to that war by the American government, just as soldiers had been sent to previous wars? The veterans deeply resented the treatment they received.

What did the Vietnam War teach us? One of the most important lessons of the war in Vietnam was the effect a truly divided nation has on the war effort and the people fighting it. Antiwar sentiments focused first on government leaders and then on the soldiers themselves. Perhaps just as important is the lesson learned from fighting a war without going "all out." As one article on the war said:

> " Viet Nam veterans argue passionately that Americans must never again be sent to die in a war that 'the politicians will not let them win.' And by win they clearly mean something like a World War II-style triumph ending in unconditional surrender.[1] "

The aftermath of the Vietnam War brought another point to light. It proved the domino theory was wrong. The communist victory in Vietnam did not lead to the long-feared communist control of East and Southeast Asia. The countries of the region, such as Vietnam and Cambodia (also called Kampuchea), began fighting among themselves. The dominoes, instead of falling one after the other against Western democracy, seemed to crash angrily into each other.

[1]From *Time* magazine, April 15, 1985

THE VIETNAM VETERANS MEMORIAL

Etched in the polished black granite are 58,175 names. They are the names of the Americans who died in the Vietnam War. The names are listed in order of death, showing the war as a series of personal sacrifices and giving each person a special place in history.

To most Americans, the Vietnam Veterans Memorial is a symbol of long-overdue public recognition of the Americans who fought in the controversial war. The nation's commitment to this war had never been as intense as it had been to previous wars that involved American troops. In fact, public opinion about America's involvement in the war was sharply divided. Even many of those who fought in Vietnam came to question why they were there and how the war was being fought.

In other times war-weary veterans were greeted by cheering crowds and parades. Vietnam veterans returned instead to indifference, and sometimes hostility. Many buried their memories of the war and kept silent. Some had a difficult time readjusting to life after the stress of combat and their reception at home. Others returned successfully to civilian life. Gradually Vietnam veterans organized and began to insist on public recognition of their war efforts.

In July 1980, Congress selected a site for a Vietnam memorial in the Constitutional Gardens near the Lincoln Memorial in Washington, D.C. The memorial's design would be chosen through a national competition open to all American citizens 18 years of age or older. The only criterion set by the committee was that the memorial must display the names of the Americans who had died in the war.

In May 1981 a jury of eight internationally famous artists, designers, and architects announced their unanimous first choice from the 1,421 entries. The winning entry had been submitted by Maya Ying Lin of Athens, Ohio. At the time she was a 21-year-old student at Yale University. In March 1982 ground was broken and construction began. The memorial was dedicated on November 13, 1982.

Maya Lin's design creates a park within a park—a quiet and peaceful place. The mirrorlike surfaces of the polished black granite reflect the surroundings—trees, flowers, and the faces of the people who search the memorial for names. The memorial's walls point to the Lincoln Memorial and the Washington Monument.

Flowers, pictures, and other mementos cover the ground at the base of the walls. They are remembrances brought by parents, friends, and loved ones. But the most striking feature of the memorial is the list of names. As Lin had planned, the names became the memorial. They are the ultimate honor to those who died in America's most controversial war.

Christopher Morris/Black Star

Source: World Book Encyclopedia

THE COSTS OF AMERICA'S WARS		
War	Military Deaths	Financial Costs
Revolutionary	25,324*	$101,100,000
War of 1812	2,260	$90,000,000
Mexican	13,283	$71,400,000
Civil	529,332	$5,183,000,000
Spanish-American	2,446	$283,200,000
The Great War	126,000	$18,676,000,000
World War II	405,399	$263,259,000,000
Korean	54,246	$67,386,000,000
Vietnam	58,132*	$150,000,000,000
Persian Gulf	268	$31,500,000,000
*Estimated		

LEARNING FROM TABLES. *This table contains the number of military deaths and financial costs of each of America's wars. In which war did the most Americans die? Why? Why do you think the expenditures for World War II and the Vietnam War were so high?*

Middle Eastern Diplomacy

Vietnam was not the only trouble spot to attract America's attention. The Arab states of the Middle East continued to present perplexing problems, mostly because they remained opposed to the very existence of Israel. In 1967 Israel had won a smashing victory over Egypt in the **Six Days' War.** A precarious peace, broken by Arab raids and Israeli reprisals, had held until October 6, 1973. On that day, Yom Kippur, the Jewish holy day of atonement, Egypt and Syria again attacked Israel. While the war raged, the Arab-controlled Organization of Petroleum Exporting Countries (OPEC) banned all oil shipments to the United States in retaliation for its support of Israel. The Netherlands, Portugal, and South Africa also suffered the oil embargo.

The impact surprised many Americans. Petroleum products, most notably gasoline, were rationed. Long lines of cars waited at gas pumps all over America.

This **Arab Oil Crisis** caused Americans to realize that an extended ban would threaten the American economy and life-style. They had known petroleum was a limited and nonrenewable resource since the automobile boom of the 1920s. They had learned to conserve petroleum during the emergency of World War II. Now they began to conserve petroleum in their everyday lives. People were encouraged to use carpools or mass transit. Gasoline prices were raised, in part to discourage extra driving. Schools and public buildings closed on the coldest or hottest days to conserve the electricity or oil needed to heat or cool the building.

Nixon realized that America's two Middle Eastern interests—Israel and oil—created a complex situation. He sent his master negotiator, Henry Kissinger, into action. Kissinger visited the Middle East nearly every month. His **shuttle diplomacy,** so-called because of his frequent diplomatic trips, brought Egypt and Israel to a cease-fire. He kept the region from erupting into the flames of war and reestablished the flow of Middle Eastern oil to the United States.

Return to the Preview & Review on page 1072.

4. THE WATERGATE AFFAIR

Preview & Review

Nixon's Power Begins to Crumble

The ending of the war and his landslide victory in the 1972 election made Richard Nixon seem one of the most powerful of American presidents. He used his power to cut back sharply on various New Deal and Great Society programs designed to help poor people, blacks, and other disadvantaged groups. He hoped the cut in government spending would slow inflation. He also announced that it was time to crack down hard on crime. He criticized what he called the "permissiveness" of many Americans.

Yet, at the very moment of his great election success, Nixon's power began to crumble. The cause was the **Watergate Affair,** one of the strangest episodes in the entire story of America.

On the night of June 17, 1972, shortly before the presidential nominating conventions, five burglars were arrested in the headquarters of the Democratic National Committee in Washington, D.C. The headquarters were located in the Watergate, a modern office building and apartment house complex on the Potomac River.

The burglars had large sums of money in new $100 bills in their wallets when they were arrested. They were carrying two expensive cameras, 40 rolls of film, and a number of tiny listening devices, or "bugs." They had obviously intended to copy Democratic party records and attach the bugs to the office telephones.

Suspicion naturally fell on the Republican party. One of the men arrested was James W. McCord, a former CIA employee who was working for Nixon's campaign organization, the Committee for the Reelection of the President (CREEP). Soon it was discovered that two other campaign officials had been involved in the break-in. Other CREEP techniques came to light. CREEP workers had joined the campaign of Senator Muskie in 1972 and disrupted it by spreading damaging and false rumors to the press and mixing up schedules so that Muskie and his supporters missed several important appearances and appointments.

Both Nixon's campaign manager, former Attorney General John Mitchell, and the president himself denied that anyone on the White House staff had anything to do with Watergate. Nixon's press secretary described it as a "third-rate burglary." Vice President Spiro Agnew suggested that the Democrats might have staged the affair to throw suspicion on the Republican party. Most people accepted the president's denial. The Watergate Affair had no effect on the election.

The Cover-up

Early in 1973 the Watergate burglars were put on trial in Washington. Most of them pleaded guilty. This meant that they could not be

Use these questions to guide your reading. Answer the questions after completing Section 4.
Understanding Issues, Events, & Ideas. Use the following words to explain Nixon's fall from power: Watergate Affair, executive privilege, Saturday Night Massacre, Twenty-fifth Amendment, articles of impeachment.
1. What three articles of impeachment were passed by the House Judiciary Committee against Nixon?
2. How was the Supreme Court involved in the case against Nixon?
3. Why were the transcripts of the White House tapes unable to prove the president's claim of innocence?
4. In your opinion, should the president be allowed to resign to avoid impeachment? Explain your view.
Thinking Critically. Do you think that President Ford should have offered Nixon a pardon? Why or why not?

Gjon Mili/Life Magazine © Time Warner, Inc.

All of Washington sought passes to the Watergate hearings held to determine whether or not the president of the United States should be impeached. Here John Dean, the president's lawyer, is sworn in.

questioned about the case. But one of them, James McCord, told the trial judge, John Sirica, that a number of important Republican officials had been involved in planning the burglary.

McCord's charges were found to be true. The Justice Department renewed its efforts to locate the people behind the break-in. One by one, important members of the Nixon administration admitted that they had known about the incident. The head of the FBI confessed that he had destroyed documents related to the affair. Clearly there had been a cover-up of evidence, which is a crime—obstruction (blocking) of justice. The Senate began an investigation.

John Dean, the president's lawyer, provided particularly damaging evidence to investigators. The president fired Dean, whom he considered a traitor. Nixon's two closest aides, H. R. Haldeman and John Ehrlichman, were forced to resign. Still, Nixon insisted that they were loyal public servants who had done nothing wrong.

As the Senate investigation proceeded, witnesses brought out more and more details about Watergate and other illegal activities connected with Nixon's campaign for reelection. Evidence suggested that many large corporations had made secret contributions to the campaign fund. Such gifts were illegal. John Dean testified that the president had helped plan the cover-up from the beginning. When he had gone on television to deny that anyone in the White House was involved, the president had lied, Dean said.

Dean's testimony was extremely important because it so directly involved the president. He appeared to be telling the truth. When details of his testimony could be checked against other sources, they proved to be correct. But Nixon denied the charges. It seemed to be his word against Dean's.

Then another witness revealed to the startled investigators that Nixon had been secretly recording all the conversations that had taken place in his office. These tape recordings would show whether or not Dean had told the truth! At once the Senate investigators demanded that the president allow them to listen to these and other White House tapes that might reveal important information.

Nixon refused to allow anyone to listen to the tapes. He claimed what he called **executive privilege**—the right to keep information secret when it related to presidential business.

More and more people came to the conclusion that Nixon was lying. Charges that he had cheated on his income taxes while president by claiming large illegal deductions further turned public opinion against him. Yet how could the full truth be discovered while people Nixon had appointed ran the Justice Department? To end the criticism, Nixon agreed to the appointment of a distinguished law professor, Archibald Cox, as a special prosecutor for the Justice Department to take charge of the case. Cox was promised a free hand and told to pursue the truth wherever the facts led him.

Professor Cox also demanded that the White House tapes be turned over to his investigators for study. Again Nixon refused. A federal judge then ordered him to give Cox the tapes. Instead of doing so, Nixon ordered Attorney General Elliot L. Richardson, head of the Justice Department, to fire Cox!

Richardson resigned rather than carry out this order. So did the assistant attorney general. But Nixon persisted and finally a third member of the Justice Department, Robert G. Bork, discharged Cox. These events occurred on the evening of Saturday, October 20, 1973. The affair was called the **Saturday Night Massacre.**

Nixon's entire administration seemed riddled with scandal. Only ten days before the Saturday Night Massacre, Vice President Spiro Agnew admitted that he had been cheating on his income taxes. He resigned from office. Actually, the official record of his case revealed that he had also accepted $200,000 in bribes while serving as a public official in Maryland. To avoid the national shame of having a vice president in prison, government lawyers had allowed him to admit guilt by pleading nolo contendere (no contest) to the charge of income tax evasion. Agnew was fined and placed on probation.

The **Twenty-fifth Amendment** of the Constitution, ratified in 1967, includes a provision that when the vice presidency falls vacant, the president shall appoint a new vice president. Nixon chose Congressman Gerald R. Ford of Michigan. The appointment was approved by Congress and Ford became vice president.

Nixon Falls from Power

The Saturday Night Massacre led many people to demand that Nixon be impeached. (*Impeachment* is the legal process of charging a high

The House Judiciary Committee left little doubt how they felt about Nixon's behavior during the Watergate investigation.

Article I
" . . . Richard M. Nixon, has prevented, obstructed, and impeded the administration of justice. . . .

Article II
. . . Richard M. Nixon . . . has repeatedly engaged in conduct violating the constitutional rights of citizens, . . . contravening [blocking] the laws of governing agencies. . . .

Article III
. . . Richard M. Nixon . . . has failed without lawful cause or excuse to produce papers and things, as directed by duly authorized subpoenas [writs commanding a person to turn over evidence or to testify]. . . .

Wherefore, Richard M. Nixon, by such conduct, warrants impeachment and trial, and removal from office."

From *Articles of Impeachment*, July 30, 1974

official with wrongdoing.) To quiet those demanding his impeachment, Nixon promised to cooperate with Cox's successor as Watergate prosecutor, Texas lawyer Leon Jaworski. Nevertheless, the Judiciary Committee of the House of Representatives began an investigation to see if there were grounds for impeaching Nixon.

While the Judiciary Committee studied the evidence of Nixon's involvement, prosecutor Jaworski proceeded against the others involved in CREEP's illegal activities. One after another, men who had been involved in Nixon's campaign for reelection were charged and convicted of crimes. Some had lied under oath, others had obstructed justice, and one had raised money for the campaign in an unlawful manner.

Late in April 1974 Nixon released edited transcripts of some of his taped conversations. These, he said, would prove his innocence. However, important parts of conversations were left out in these printed versions. At many places the typescripts contained blanks because, Nixon claimed, the tapes had not recorded what was said clearly enough to be understood. Still he refused to let others check on the editing by listening to the tapes.

Both what the transcripts revealed and what they left out led to increased demands that the president allow investigators to listen to the key tapes themselves. Nixon still refused. He would not turn them over to either the House Judiciary Committee or to special prosecutor Jaworski.

Jaworski therefore asked the Supreme Court to order the president to give him the tapes of 64 specific conversations known to have taken place in the White House. While the Court considered the matter, the Judiciary Committee decided to allow its sessions to be broadcast and televised. In July 1974 the committee passed three **articles of impeachment,** or charges against the president. One accused Nixon of obstructing justice. Another accused him of misusing the powers of the presidency. The third concerned his refusal to let the committee listen to the tapes.

Under the Constitution, the Judiciary Committee's report would be submitted to the full House of Representatives. If the report was accepted, the House would then impeach Nixon by presenting the articles of impeachment to the Senate. The Senate would act as a court hearing the charges. If two thirds of the senators voted in favor of any of the three articles, Nixon would be removed from office.

While the Judiciary Committee was still debating, the Supreme Court ruled that Nixon must turn the tapes over to prosecutor Jaworski. Nixon hesitated. If he defied the Court's order, it was difficult to see how it could be enforced. But Nixon's advisers convinced him that if he refused to obey the court order, the Senate was certain to remove him from office. At last he gave up the tapes.

The tapes proved conclusively that Nixon had known about and even ordered the Watergate cover-up from the start. Only one day after he had said on television that no one in the White House had anything to do with the affair, he had ordered his chief assistant, H. R. Haldeman, to persuade the FBI not to investigate the break-in too vigorously. The FBI could be told that national security was involved, the president had suggested.

Meanwhile the Judiciary Committee voted on their recommendation to impeach the president. It was a somber evening as committee members cast their votes. One writer recalled:

“ The room is utterly still except for the call of the roll and the sound of cameras clicking. The moment has taken over the members; they know what they are doing, and they are physically, mentally, and emotionally spent [drained]. They have been through a long period of strain. . . . One can barely hear the members as they respond to the clerk.

The clerk announces, 'Twenty-seven members have voted aye, eleven members have voted no.' All twenty-one Democrats—including three Southerners—and six Republicans have voted to impeach the President for the cover-up. . . .

The room is utterly silent, and then, at a few minutes after seven, Rodino [committee chairman Peter Rodino] announces, 'Article I . . . is adopted and will be reported to the House.'[1] ”

[1]From *Washington Journal: The Events of 1973–1974* by Elizabeth Drew

Nixon now had the choice of resigning before the House voted to impeach him or going on trial in hopes that the Senate might not remove him. He resigned. On August 9, at noon, he officially surrendered his powers. Gerald R. Ford then took the oath of office and became president of the United States.

One of President Ford's first actions was to offer Nixon a pardon for any crimes he may have committed. He offered the pardon, he said, because Nixon would have a difficult time getting a fair trial. It would also save America the embarrassment of having an ex-president on trial. "My conscience tells me clearly and certainly that I cannot prolong the bad dreams that continue to reopen a chapter that is closed. My conscience tells me that only I, as President, have the constitutional power to firmly shut and seal this book." Thus Ford "shot himself in the foot" as far as his future political plans went. Nixon promptly accepted the pardon.

Here we close this sad chapter with the full truth about the Watergate Affair still not known. While many Americans look on the incident with shame, others point out that it showed that the American system of government worked: a powerful president was forced to resign when he betrayed the faith of the people. 🖅

Dennis Brack/Black Star

After Gerald Ford took the oath as president, he and his wife, Betty, escorted Patricia and Richard Nixon from the White House. How would you summarize President Nixon's strengths and weaknesses as a national leader?

Return to the Preview & Review on page 1081.

CHAPTER 29 REVIEW

1964
Johnson elected
President
★
Tonkin Gulf
Resolution

1965
American involvement in Vietnam escala
1967
Twenty-fifth Amendment ratified

Chapter Summary
Read the statements below. Choose one, and write a paragraph explaining its importance.
1. The Tonkin Gulf Resolution gave President Johnson the power to escalate American involvement in Vietnam. By 1968 more than 500,000 Americans were in Vietnam.
2. At home, antiwar sentiments grew rapidly after the 1968 Tet offensive.
3. Americans were shocked in 1968 when President Johnson admitted his Vietnam policy was a failure, Martin Luther King, Jr., and Robert Kennedy were murdered, riots scorched American cities, and violence disrupted the Democratic National Convention in Chicago.
4. Richard Nixon began the withdrawal of American troops. Finally, in 1973, a treaty was signed and the war was over.
5. Nixon improved foreign relations with the Soviets, the Chinese, and in the Middle East.
6. The Watergate Affair caused Nixon's power to crumble. He eventually resigned rather than face impeachment proceedings.

Understanding Chronological Order
Number your paper 1–5. Then study the time line above and place the following events in the order in which they happened by writing the first next to 1, the second next to 2, and so on.
1. Burglars break into the Watergate
2. Vietnam War ends
3. Shootings at Kent State and Jackson State
4. Tet offensive
5. Martin Luther King, Jr., murdered

Understanding Main Ideas
1. What role did each of the following play in the Vietnam War: South Vietnam, North Vietnam, and the Viet Cong?
2. What events made 1968 a year of tragedy for the United States?
3. What was Vietnamization? Why did Nixon send American troops into Cambodia? What reaction did this set off in the United States?

4. What was the extent of President Nixon's victory in his reelection in 1972? How was the Democratic campaign bungled?
5. What was the Watergate Affair?

Thinking Critically
1. **Using Historical Imagination.** Suppose you are an adviser to President Johnson. Write him a memorandum recommending either escalation of American involvement in the war or American withdrawal from it.
2. **Citing Historical Significance.** Imagine you are a historian. Explain the historical significance of Nixon's visit to the Soviet Union to events in Eastern Europe today.
3. **Evaluating Ideas.** You are a personal friend and adviser to President Nixon. Write him a letter in which you encourage him to surrender the Watergate tapes.

Writing About History
As secretary of state under President Nixon, Henry Kissinger won the Nobel Peace Prize in 1973. Research one of these secretaries of state: John Quincy Adams (pages 316-17, 323-24), John Hay (762, 768, 771), John Foster Dulles (1001–03), or Henry Kissinger (1075, 1077, 1080) and write a report on their activities as secretary.

Practicing the Strategy
Review the strategy on page 1066.
Drawing Conclusions. Read "America Escalates the War" on pages 1062–67. Then answer the following questions.
1. What conclusion does the author draw about how the president and his advisers viewed their actions in fighting the Vietnam War?
2. What evidence does the author present to support this conclusion?
3. What information in this section suggests some Americans disagreed with this conclusion?

58
offensive

1970
Nixon decides to
bomb Cambodia

★

Shootings at Kent State
and Jackson State

1971
Wage-and-price
freeze

1972
Nixon reelected

★

Nixon travels to
China and
Soviet Union

★

Watergate Affair
begins

1973
Agnew resigns;
Nixon appoints
Gerald Ford

★

Final U.S. troops
leave Vietnam

OPEC announces oil embargo

1974
Kissinger's shuttle diplomacy
in Middle East

★

Nixon resigns

★

Ford pardons Nixon

rtin Luther King, Jr., murdered

bert F. Kennedy killed

xon elected president

i9
etnamization and American withdrawal begins

Using Primary Sources

While many people the world over applauded the new détente between the United States and the Soviet Union, others cautioned Americans to beware of Soviet tricks. One was famous Soviet writer Aleksandr Solzhenitsyn, who had spent many years in detention and labor camps for writings that were critical of Stalin and later Soviet leaders. Finally in 1974 he was forced to leave the Soviet Union and live in exile. As you read the excerpt from a 1975 speech by Solzhenitsyn, consider his warning in light of more recent events in the Soviet Union.

America—in me and among my friends and among people who think the way I do over there [in the Soviet Union], among all ordinary Soviet citizens—brings forth a mixture of admiration and compassion. You're a country of the future; a young country; a country of still unused possibilities; a country of tremendous geographical distances; a country of tremendous spirit; a country of generosity. But these qualities—strength and generosity—usually make a person and even a whole country trusting. This already has done you a disservice several times.

I would like to call upon America to be more careful with its trust and prevent those people who are falsely using the struggle for peace and social justice to lead you down a false road. They are trying to weaken you. They are trying to disarm your strong and magnificent country.

1. According to Solzhenitsyn, what makes Americans particularly trusting?
2. Do you agree with Solzhenitsyn that being trusting has done America a disservice several times? Give examples to support your answer?
3. What do you think Solzhenitsyn is warning Americans against?

Linking History & Geography

The Middle East has been an area of concern for the United States since World War II. To better understand its relative location and the countries of the region, create two maps. On an outline map of the world, label the Mediterranean Sea, the Nile River, Egypt, Israel, and the Middle East. Then draw or use an outline map of the Middle East to label all the countries, their capitals, major bodies of water, and the Suez Canal.

Enriching Your Study of History

1. **Individual Project.** Create a map of the Vietnam War. Your map should show the two Vietnams and the surrounding countries, major cities and towns, battle sites, and physical features. Display your map on the bulletin board or use it to illustrate a discussion of the war.
2. **Cooperative Project.** As an oral history project, have members of your group ask family members to describe their reactions to major events of the late 1960s and early 1970s. Topics should include the Vietnam War and the antiwar movement; the assassinations of Martin Luther King, Jr., and Robert Kennedy in 1968; the Chicago riot between antiwar demonstrators and police; the opening of China by President Nixon; and the Watergate Affair and Nixon's resignation. Compile the responses into a group report, either written or on tape. Combine members' reports into a single commentary on the late 1960s and early 1970s.

CHAPTER 30

Modern Times

All the recent presidents of the United States have had to grapple with extremely complex domestic problems. How will the famous American melting pot accommodate all the newcomers to the United States? How can the crisis in America's cities be resolved if decaying housing and conditions bred by poverty drive working-class and middle-class residents out into the suburbs? How can America cope with pollution—smog, oil spills, acid rain—and preserve its fragile environments? How will Americans cope with growing energy needs? What is the future of nuclear energy? How can the treatment of women in the workplace be made equal to that of men? And, finally, with the pace of world affairs quickened by the collapse of the Soviet Union, the liberation of Eastern Europe, the reunification of Germany, and the end of the Cold War, what will be the future role of the United States in the world community?

Cross/Miami Herald/Black Star

Flags fly in this celebration of citizenship in Miami. Cuban immigrants swear to uphold the Constitution. Even though they are relative newcomers, Cubans have contributed greatly to the nation's culture and prosperity.

1. THE FORD PRESIDENCY

A Different Style

Before he became president, Gerald Ford was known as an honest, hardworking politician. Nearly everyone in Congress liked him. He got along easily with people. But he had never been noted for vision or originality. When he became president, he announced that he would work closely with Congress. Because both Ford and his vice president, Nelson Rockefeller, had been appointed rather than elected by the people, Ford's style seemed the proper one to adopt.

Dennis Brack Black Star

Economic Slowdown

Ford's biggest problem was the economy. By 1974, business activity had slowed down. Unemployment was increasing and the inflation rate was rising. Democrats wanted to increase government spending in order to speed recovery. Most Republicans, however, feared the economic slump less than they feared inflation. Even when the economy was slowing down, prices had continued to rise. Republicans predicted that more government spending would push prices still higher.

Use these questions to guide your reading. Answer the questions after completing Section 1. **Understanding Issues, Events, & Ideas.** Use the following words to describe important events that occurred during the presidency of Gerald Ford: stagflation, Bicentennial, Operation Sail.

1. Why did President Ford's style seem a proper one for him to adopt when he assumed the presidency?
2. What were some of the bills passed by the Democratic-controlled Congress during Ford's administration? How did President Ford react to them?
3. What helped to end the economic stagflation that occurred in the mid-1970s?
4. In what ways did the tall ships symbolize pride and hope?

Thinking Critically. Imagine that you are present at one of the following events on July 4, 1976: the swearing in ceremony in Miami Beach; the president's speech in either Valley Forge or at Independence Hall; the celebration at the Mall in Washington, D.C.; Operation Sail in New York Harbor; a ceremony in your community or anywhere in the U.S. Write a brief eyewitness account of what you see going on around you. Include a description of your participation, and how you feel as an American on this day.

Cartoon by S.C. Rawls, reprinted by permission of N.E.A., Inc.

Gerald Ford was a popular president. Much was made of his days as a college football player. Hence the cartoon, "Bad Tackle, Jer," showing the override of Ford's veto of spending bills by Congress.

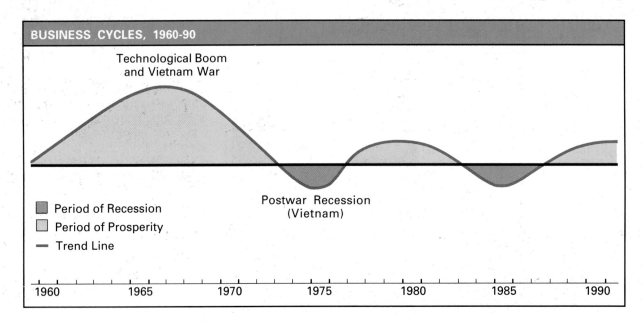

BUSINESS CYCLES, 1960-90

Technological Boom
and Vietnam War

Postwar Recession
(Vietnam)

■ Period of Recession
□ Period of Prosperity
— Trend Line

1960   1965   1970   1975   1980   1985   1990

LEARNING FROM GRAPHS. *How would you describe the rise and fall of the business cycle since 1975? What factors might account for such behavior?*

Charles Gatewood/Magnum Photos

Hopes for a rollback in the costs of food during the stagflation of the Ford administration were dashed by presidential vetoes. How was the recession finally ended?

In the 1974 congressional elections, voters, still stung by Watergate, expressed their dislike of scandals by voting many Republicans out of office. As a result, the Democrats increased their majorities in both houses of Congress. When the new Congress met, it passed bills designed to help poor people and to create new jobs. Measures providing for construction of public housing, aid to education, and health care were sent to President Ford. He vetoed all of them. Spending more money, he argued, would lead to greater inflation. In most cases the Democrats were not able to get the two-thirds majorities needed to override the president's vetoes.

The recession continued. Economists began to describe the country as passing through a period of **stagflation**—a word coined by combining "*stag*nation," which means not developing or advancing, and "in*flation*." Finally, in the spring of 1975, Ford reluctantly signed a bill reducing taxes, a step he had avoided for fear it would fuel greater inflation. The cut put more money in circulation and helped to end the downturn. By early 1976 the recession was over.

The Bicentennial

American spirits were lifted by the recession's end. In 1976 the United States also celebrated its **Bicentennial,** the 200th anniversary of the signing of the Declaration of Independence. The celebration was carried out in grand style. Communities all over the country organized and carried out hundreds of special programs.

In Miami Beach, Florida, 7,000 immigrants were sworn in as citizens of the United States in a mass ceremony at Convention Hall. A man in Oro Grande, California, unfurled a giant American flag measuring 102 by 67 feet (about 30 by 20 meters). There was a balloon

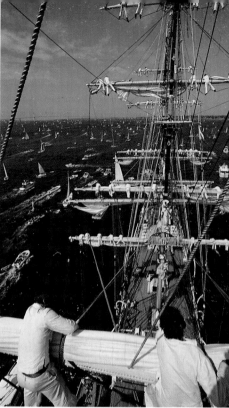

Kenneth Garrett/Woodfin Camp

A burst of fireworks over New York Harbor and the Statue of Liberty salute the nation's Bicentennial in 1976. At right, crew members secure the rigging of a tall ship as it enters the Hudson River. What did the tall ships symbolize?

race to celebrate the occasion in San Antonio, Texas, and a cherry-pie eating contest in Traverse City, Michigan. In other cities and towns there were parades, fireworks, and reenactments of Revolutionary War battles.

President Ford spoke at Valley Forge, where Washington's army had spent the hard winter of 1777–78, and at Independence Hall in Philadelphia, where the Declaration had been signed.

The highlight of the Bicentennial was **Operation Sail,** a majestic procession of gaily decorated ships in New York Harbor. No fewer than 16 great, high-masted sailing ships from different nations participated. Millions of people lined the New York waterfront and crowded the windows of skyscrapers to watch these "tall ships" and the hundreds of other craft that accompanied them.

Somehow the tall ships became a symbol of pride and hope. They had come to New York from all over the world, sent by nations with close ties to the United States as well as those with not-so-close ties to help celebrate the anniversary. This was a recognition of the importance of the United States and even more of what America had meant over the centuries to the people of other nations.

And the tall ships had endured, just as the United States had endured, through a time of enormous change. They were old but still strong, sound, and very beautiful. Although dwarfed by the great Verrazano Bridge across the harbor entrance and by the skyscrapers of Manhattan, they seemed to tower over their surroundings. They had a quiet dignity in contrast to the noise and bustle of the tugs, ferries, and other craft that swarmed about them. They stood for the value of tradition, for past achievements, for history. Better than any military parade or other display of modern power, they reflected the strength of the American people. 🖅

Return to the Preview & Review on page 1089.

The Ford Presidency   1091

Cambodian refugees leave Phnom Pehn in their 1975 exodus after the city fell to the Khmer Rouge. Some of these refugees eventually reached the United States, setting out on boats that were not seaworthy. Report on the "boat people" who reached America.

Borrell/Sipa Press

Preview & Review

Use these questions to guide your reading. Answer the questions after completing Section 2.

Understanding Issues, Events, & Ideas. Use the following words to describe immigration and social changes in American society from the 1960s to the 1990s: National Farm Workers Association, barrios, Black Power, Equal Rights Amendment.

1. For what reasons did immigrants come from Korea and Vietnam after 1965?
2. By whom and why was the NFWA formed?
3. How were the Puerto Rican immigrants similar to the European immigrants before World War I?
4. How did older African American leaders respond to the race riots of the 1960s?
5. What were some of the problems faced by Indians on reservations in the 1980s?
6. How did the status of women improve in the 1970s and '80s?

Thinking Critically. Imagine that you are a member of the United Farm Workers during the great *huelga* against the California grape growers. Write a newspaper editorial explaining why you are striking, what you hope to achieve by the strike, and why you support Cesar Chavez as your leader.

2. AMERICA'S CHANGING FACE

Immigration and Social Change

The composition of the population of America at the time of the Bicentennial was changing rapidly because of the passage of the Immigration Act of 1965. Europeans no longer accounted for the majority of new immigrants. In their place were people from Mexico, the Caribbean, Central and South America, and Asia. Under the old regulations, the entire continent of Asia was allowed only 20,000 immigrants to America in a 40-year period. In the single year 1973, almost 120,000 Asians entered this country.

The tensions left over from the Korean War and the stern policies of the South Korean government led thousands of South Koreans to migrate to the United States. Most of them settled in California and Hawaii, but considerable numbers came to New York and other eastern cities. Still larger numbers of Filipinos moved to the United States. When the islands became independent after World War II, immigration slowed to a trickle. After the 1965 immigration act, it soared again. Many Filipino immigrants were skilled workers and professional people dissatisfied with prospects in their homeland.

After the Vietnam War, large numbers of South Vietnamese who had worked with the Americans during the war came to the United States to escape persecution by the victorious communists. The United States government helped these refugees settle in this country.

The growth of the Asian American population has been dramatic. Although Asian Americans currently make up only about 3 percent of the population, experts expect their numbers to approach 10 million by the year 2000, about ten times as many as in 1970. Why are people attracted to the United States? Studs Turkel, who has interviewed hundreds of recent immigrants, observed:

Nina Barnett

“ New immigrants are trying all over again to integrate themselves into the system. They have the same hunger. . . .

The Vietnamese boat people [who fled Vietnam after the communist takeover in 1975] express it as well as anyone. They don't know if they're gonna land, if the boat's gonna sink. They don't know what's gonna happen to 'em, but they've a hunch they might make it to the U.S. as the 'freedom place.'

There is the plain hard fact of hunger. In order to eat, a person will endure tremendous hardship.[1]”

Mexican Americans Increase Their Numbers

During the 1980s, the Hispanic population of the United States grew by 40 percent, more than four times as fast as the rest of the population. Census experts estimate that by the year 2025, Hispanic Americans may constitute as much as 20 percent of the nation's population.

By far the largest group among the new immigrants has come from Mexico. When the United States entered World War II, the demand for labor in the Southwest soared. The United States and Mexico signed an agreement allowing Mexicans to work temporarily in this country. These workers were called *braceros,* a name that comes from the Spanish word for "arm." Between 1942 and 1964, almost 5 million *braceros* came to the United States under the program. They came north to harvest crops, and most of them returned to Mexico when the harvest season ended. But each year, many stayed rather than return to Mexico.

Many of the Mexicans who settled found the United States a true land of opportunity. Some obtained farms of their own. Others found good jobs in manufacturing. Their success caused thousands of other Mexicans to want to come to the United States. After the 1965 immigration law put a limit on the number of newcomers from the Western Hemisphere, many Mexicans entered the United States illegally.

Throughout the postwar years, Mexican-born workers harvested most of the crops grown in the Southwest. Cesar Chavez emerged as their leader. Chavez had grown up in the migrant camps of California. He founded the **National Farm Workers Association** (NFWA), a labor union.

The NFWA worked hard to improve wages and the poor conditions in migrant camps. Most workers received less than half the minimum wage, which at the time (1965) was $1 per hour. Their camps were usually no more than rough cabins, often without running water. To attract attention to these problems, Chavez called for a great *huelga,* or strike, against the California grape growers.

The strikers won a great deal of public sympathy. Chavez's

[1]From *American Dreams: Lost and Found* by Studs Terkel

Proudly displaying his drawing of the flag of his country, this Chinese American boy celebrates democracy with his parents. Below is Cesar Chavez, whose fasts for the National Farm Workers drew worldwide attention.

Paul Fusco/Magnum Photos

personal dedication was almost as important in winning support as was the public's realization of the plight of the poorly paid workers. Eventually the grape growers recognized the union and settled the strike. Chavez inspired migrant workers with a sense of their own worth. "We . . . stood tall outside the vineyards where we had stooped for years," the grape pickers stated proudly.

Michael Rougier/Life Picture Services

The plentitude of food on your family's kitchen table comes in part from these Mexican-born harvesters called **braceros.** *When this photo was taken, many Mexicans had to cross the border illegally to find work until a public amnesty program was approved by Congress.*

Yo Soy Joaquín	I am Joaquín
. . . Y en todos los terrenos fértiles	And in all the fertile farmlands,
los llanos átidos,	the barren plains,
los pueblos moñtaneros	the mountain villages,
cuidades ahumadas	smoke-smeared cities
empezamos a AVANZAR.	we start to MOVE.
La Raza!	La Raza!
Mejicano!	Mejicano!
Español!	Espanol!
Latino!	Latino!
Hispano!	Hispano!
Chicano!	Chicano!
o lo que me llame yo,	or whatever I call myself,
yo parezco lo mismo,	I look the same
yo siento lo mismo	I feel the same
yo lloro	I cry
y	and
canto lo mismo	sing the same
Yo soy el bulto de mi gente y	I am the masses of my people and
yo renuncio ser absorbida.	I refuse to be absorbed.
Yo soy Joaquín	I am Joaquín
Las desigualdades son grandes	The odds are great
pero mi espíritu es firme	but my spirit is strong,
mi fé impenetrable	my faith unbreakable
mi sangre pura.	my blood is pure.
Soy príncipe Azteca y Cristo cristiano	I am Aztec Prince and Christian Christ
YO PERDURARE!	I SHALL ENDURE!
YO PERDURARE!	I WILL ENDURE![1]

Other Hispanic Newcomers

Another major group of Hispanic immigrants came from Puerto Rico. Because Puerto Rico was a commonwealth of the United States, Puerto Ricans were already American citizens. Immigration laws did not apply to them. Hundreds of thousands of Puerto Ricans settled in New York City, which soon had a larger Puerto Rican population than San Juan, the capital of Puerto Rico.

In many ways the Puerto Ricans were like the European immigrants of the years before World War I. Most of them were poor farm laborers unaccustomed to city life. Few could speak English. In New York they were crowded into **barrios,** or Hispanic neighborhoods, in neglected pockets of the city.

Yet many Puerto Ricans did very well for themselves. Herman

[1] From "I am Joaquín" by Corky Gonzales

Badillo came to New York from Puerto Rico in the early 1940s, when he was eleven. He worked washing dishes and setting up pins in a bowling alley. Later he earned a college degree and a law degree. In 1970 he was elected to Congress.

Since 1960, more than 2 million people from other Latin American nations have immigrated to the United States. After the Cuban revolutionary leader Fidel Castro made an alliance with the Soviet Union, many Cubans were admitted to the United States under laws that allowed refugees from communist countries to come. About half of them settled in southern Florida. For the next 20 years, Castro made it almost impossible for Cubans to leave their country. In 1980, however, he changed his mind. When he did, more than 100,000 Cubans flocked to the United States. Even more Hispanic people have immigrated from Central and South America.

As the graph on this page shows, Hispanic Americans have not shared equally in America's wealth. The average Hispanic American has fewer years of schooling, and the average Hispanic family has a lower-than-average income. Yet great variations exist within the Hispanic American population. Cuban Americans have reached levels close to non-Hispanic Americans in average years of schooling and average family income. Puerto Rican Americans, on the other hand, have a poverty rate that is nearly four times that of non-Hispanics.

This smiling girl is a marcher in New York City's Puerto Rican Day Parade. She is holding the flag of Puerto Rico. Do you think Puerto Rico should become the 51st state? Explain.

Source: *Current Population Reports, Series p-20, No. 416, 1987*

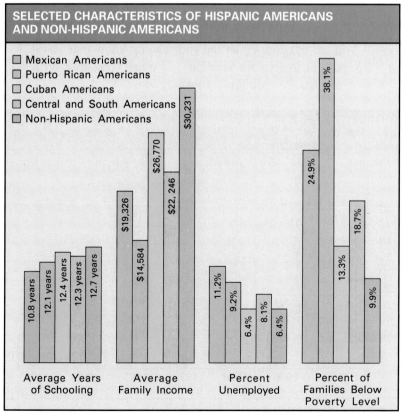

SELECTED CHARACTERISTICS OF HISPANIC AMERICANS AND NON-HISPANIC AMERICANS

- Mexican Americans
- Puerto Rican Americans
- Cuban Americans
- Central and South Americans
- Non-Hispanic Americans

Average Years of Schooling
- 10.8 years
- 12.1 years
- 12.4 years
- 12.3 years
- 12.7 years

Average Family Income
- $19,326
- $14,584
- $26,770
- $22,246
- $30,231

Percent Unemployed
- 11.2%
- 9.2%
- 6.4%
- 8.1%
- 6.4%

Percent of Families Below Poverty Level
- 24.9%
- 38.1%
- 13.3%
- 18.7%
- 9.9%

LEARNING FROM GRAPHS. *The label* Hispanic American *encompasses people from many different backgrounds. This graph shows certain characteristics of the largest groups of Hispanic Americans. Compare the data on the graph. Then state a comparison of the four Hispanic American groups. How do these groups compare to non-Hispanic Americans?*

America's Changing Face 1095

V. S. Naipaul, who grew up in Trinidad, observed this about the American South today.

66'Nearly sixteen millions of hands will aid you in pulling the load upward, or they will pull against you the load downward. We shall constitute one-third and more of the ignorance and crime of the South, or one-third of its intelligence and progress; we shall contribute one-third to business and industrial prosperity of the South; or we shall prove a veritable body of death, stagnating, depressing . . . the body politic.'

The words read like special pleading. They come from the speech Booker T. Washington made in Atlanta in 1895, when he was only thirty-nine: a famous speech that . . . calmed white people down and offered hope to black people at a time of near hopelessness. . . . Those words now read like prophecy.99
From *A Turn in the South,* 1989

LEARNING FROM GRAPHS. *This graph shows the number of white Americans and African Americans below the poverty level. What trend do you note for African Americans? Is the trend the same for white Americans? Explain any differences you find.*

African Americans Continue the Struggle

Increased awareness of past injustices made African Americans even more determined to gain respect and equal treatment. In the 1960s, Martin Luther King, Jr.'s policy of persuasion and nonviolent direct action no longer satisfied some black activists. Leaders such as Stokely Carmichael advocated what they called **Black Power**, a more radical approach to the struggle for equal rights that advocated the use of force when necessary. King's movement had taken the first steps, but it seemed obvious to Carmichael and others that white people "cannot understand the black experience."

Other blacks, such as Malcolm X, went even further. Some joined the Black Muslims, who believed in separating themselves entirely from white society. Malcolm X, broke with the Black Muslims in 1964 and called for "a working unity among all peoples, black as well as white." But before he could embark on this new direction, he was murdered in 1965, apparently as a result of his break with the Black Muslims. Malcolm X and Carmichael both spoke of action for African Americans. In a speech Malcolm X put it this way:

66 Whether you like it, or I like it, or they like it, or not, you will see that there is a generation of black people becoming mature to the point where they feel that they have no more business in being asked to take a peaceful approach than anybody else takes, unless everybody's going to take a peaceful approach. . . .

You get freedom by letting your enemy know that you'll do anything to get your freedom. . . . When you stay radical long enough . . . you'll get your freedom.¹99

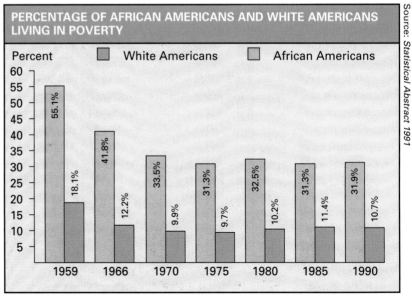

PERCENTAGE OF AFRICAN AMERICANS AND WHITE AMERICANS LIVING IN POVERTY

Source: Statistical Abstract 1991

¹From *Malcolm X Speaks,* edited by George Breitman

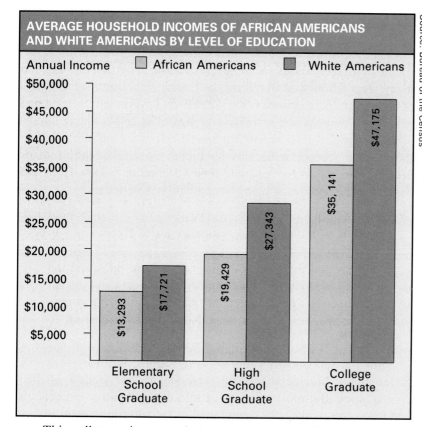

AVERAGE HOUSEHOLD INCOMES OF AFRICAN AMERICANS AND WHITE AMERICANS BY LEVEL OF EDUCATION

Annual Income — African Americans — White Americans

Elementary School Graduate: African Americans $13,293; White Americans $17,721

High School Graduate: African Americans $19,429; White Americans $27,343

College Graduate: African Americans $35,141; White Americans $47,175

Source: Bureau of the Census

LEARNING FROM GRAPHS. *Years of schooling completed has a dramatic effect on income, as this graph shows. How much more on average does a white college graduate make than a white American who only completed elementary school? What is the difference for African Americans in the same categories? Why do you think this is true?*

This call to action appealed to many young African Americans. They met white aggression and violence with their own. Between 1965 and 1967, riots scorched cities such as Los Angeles, Chicago, Tampa, Detroit, and Newark. Many people, including African Americans, thought the riots and violence had gone too far. Older leaders continued to emphasize peaceful means. They warned that violence only leads to more violence. They were sure that black pride and working within the political and economic systems would pay off in the long run.

To many American blacks, their African heritage was a source of pride. They preferred to be known as African Americans. An increasing number of schools and colleges offered courses in African history and culture. Voter-participation drives resulted in an upswing in the number of African American elected officials. By the early 1990s there were approximately 450 blacks elected to state and national legislatures, up from a mere 182 in 1970.

Problems for Native Americans

Like African Americans, native Americans continued to search for ways to revive their culture. But the violence of the confrontation at Wounded Knee in 1973 drained some of the public's sympathy for the American Indian movement.

The frustration of African Americans was demonstrated by marchers and picketers in the 1960s. Study the sign carried by the young mother below. What are her complaints?

Eli Reed/Magnum Photos

Ernest Haas/Magnum Photos

This young Crow in beaded tribal headdress helps us recall the past. Yet what does the speaker quoted on this page say about the past of native Americans?

In the late 1970s, courts began to award millions of dollars in damages to tribes who sued the government over broken treaties. These rulings provided some small sense of justice. But by the 1980s, Indians on reservations faced several disastrous problems. Life on many reservations had deteriorated. Unable to recapture past ways of life, many Indians were forced to rely on government welfare and help from religious and charitable groups. The demoralizing effects of this situation led to alcoholism and suicide at far higher rates than the national average, especially for Indian teenagers. Many Indians dropped out of school and left their reservations. One Hopi girl described the feelings of many young native Americans:

&& We would like to leave the reservation. We wouldn't mind seeing how Indians live in cities. A lot of Hopis say you stop being a Hopi when you go into a city and live in big buildings and forget about our land, and our hills, and the sky over us. Maybe. I don't know. The Indian can't just sit and think of his past. My mother says it's a pity; our people were happy here for so long. Now, a lot of us want to leave.[1] &&

For Indians who were not on reservations, life was somewhat better. Many became successful professionals and leaders in their communities. But most still felt the loss of their culture. In schools and in the job market, they continued to face discrimination.

Women Fight for Equality

"I am woman, hear me roar," went a popular song of the 1970s. The roar continues to grow louder. Census reports predict that by the year 2000, women will outnumber men in the United States by 6 million. Women continue to fight to maintain the gains they have made in the political arena, in business, and on the domestic front since World War II.

After much debate, Congress passed an **Equal Rights Amendment** (ERA) to the Constitution in 1972 and sent it on to the states for ratification. The ERA provided that "equality of rights under the law shall not be denied or abridged by the United States or any state on account of sex." The proposed amendment was controversial. Opponents believed it was unnecessary because, they said, women were protected against discrimination by laws that already existed. They also claimed that the ERA would eliminate existing laws that provided special benefits to female workers. Supporters of the ERA said that it would simply make equality for women legal. The ERA did not receive the approval from the needed three-fourths of the state legislatures and consequently failed to become part of the Constitution.

[1]From *Eskimos, Chicanos, Indians: Volume IV of Children in Crisis* by Robert Coles

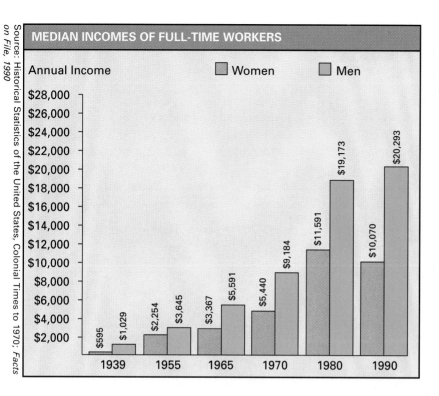

Source: Historical Statistics of the United States, Colonial Times to 1970; Facts on File, 1990

MEDIAN INCOMES OF FULL-TIME WORKERS

Annual Income | ☐ Women ☐ Men

	1939	1955	1965	1970	1980	1990
Women	$595	$2,254	$3,367	$5,440	$11,591	$10,070
Men	$1,029	$3,645	$5,591	$9,184	$19,173	$20,293

LEARNING FROM GRAPHS.
Although women have begun to claim more higher-paying jobs than ever before, a gap between the average salary for women and men still exists. What was that gap in 1990? How would you explain the difference?

More and more people became concerned about the inequality of women in American society. As a result, administrations from the 1970s onward have increasingly recognized the contributions of women and appointed many to top positions in the federal government. Yet by 1991, women held only two seats in the Senate and 27 in the House of Representatives. Democrat Geraldine Ferraro's campaign for the vice presidency in 1984, though unsuccessful, was a first: a woman as a candidate on a major party ticket.

From the 1970s through the early 1990s, women entered the American workforce by the millions. "Equal pay for equal work" was a feminist slogan of the 1970s. Today, that ideal is still far from realized, although women who work outside the home make up more than 45 percent of the total workforce. In 1989, statistics showed that on the average, an American woman earned only about 68 percent of a man's income. This figure had risen only 6 percentage points since 1955. This "disparity gap" also includes representation in various fields of work. Minority women, for example, disproportionately hold poor-paying part-time jobs. These inequalities indicate that the trend continues: low status and low pay go hand in hand with female-dominated occupations.

In recent decades, social critics have also noted the "glass ceiling" felt by many women who could advance only to a certain level in business or government. The top positions seemed reserved exclusively for men. Perhaps partly as a reaction to this situation, many women bought or started their own businesses in the 1970s and

Uniphoto Picture Agency

In 1991, Clarence Thomas (top right) replaced Justice Thurgood Marshall after controversial confirmation hearings. The other justices of the Supreme Court are, left to right, (back row): David Souter, Antonin Scalia, Anthony Kennedy; (front row) John Paul Stevens, Byron White, Chief Justice William Rehnquist, Harry Blackmun, and Sandra Day O'Connor, the first female justice.

1980s—5.4 million by 1987. In fact, the Small Business Administration has predicted that by the year 2000, half the businesses in the United States will be owned by women.

With more mothers working, child-care issues moved into the national spotlight. Providing more resources, public and private, for early childhood programs, including child care, is regarded by supporters of women's rights as one of the major goals for the 1990s. Census data from the mid 1980s showed that a large number of working mothers used some kind of day care. But by 1987, only 18 states had created new child-care programs and increased the number of children served since 1981. Demographics indicate that the number of children will increase dramatically because the post-World War II baby boomers are having more children than the generation preceding them. A sharp increase in the employment of mothers will likely produce a demand for more high-quality, affordable child care.

In 1991, a relatively new women's issue received national attention: sexual harassment in the workplace. The subject arose during the confirmation hearings by the Senate Judiciary Committee of Clarence Thomas, an African American judge nominated to the Supreme Court by President George Bush. Professor Anita Hill of the University of Oklahoma charged Thomas with having sexually harassed her earlier when she had worked for him. When Thomas was cleared of all allegations and given a seat on the country's highest court, many women were angered. Sexual harassment became an important issue for women.

Return to the Preview & Review on page 1091.

3. THREE AMERICAN CHALLENGES

Crisis in America's Cities

By the 1970s, about three-quarters of the American people were living in cities and their surrounding suburbs. As these metropolitan areas expanded, they began to meet one another to form super metropolitan areas. One such **megalopolis** (Greek for "great city") stretched from Portland, Maine, through Boston, New York City, Philadelphia, Baltimore, and Washington, D.C., to Richmond, Virginia. It became known as BosWash. Another, ChiPitt, reaches from Chicago to Pittsburgh. A third, SanSan, extended from San Francisco to San Diego along the California coast. The central areas, or **inner cities**, of these regions wasted away as well-to-do and middle-class residents moved to the suburbs. Poor city dwellers, many of them African Americans, Puerto Ricans, and Mexican Americans, remained behind.

A vicious cycle of decay resulted from this population shift. When the people with money to spend began to leave an area, retail stores and other businesses followed. This meant that there were fewer jobs for inner-city residents. It meant also that city tax collections fell off.

Preview & Review

Use these questions to guide your reading. Answer the questions after completing Section 3.
Understanding Issues, Events, & Ideas. Use the following words to explain three major problems that faced the American people in the 1970s and 1980s: megalopolis, inner cities, dropouts, urban decay, pollution, smog, acid rain, greenhouse effect, Environmental Protection Agency, nuclear energy, Three Mile Island, Chernobyl.
1. What causes a megalopolis to develop?
2. Describe the vicious cycle of decay that developed when the urban population shifted to the suburbs.
3. What development added to the problem of homelessness?
4. Why was it necessary to establish the Environmental Protection Agency?
5. Why was the construction of nuclear power plants halted?
Thinking Critically. 1. Imagine that you have just become the mayor of a large American city. Outline plans for how you intend to help the homeless in your city. **2.** Write a letter to your senator or representative, suggesting ways for coping with the problems of pollution.

Michael Weisbrot/Black Star

"East Side, West Side, All Around the Town." Songs sung in what seemed more innocent times would today mask the urban decay and blight that has spread through whole areas of America's cities.

The Reverend Jesse Jackson presented this view of environmental concern.

> "The question is not, 'will we start treating our environment better?' The question is, 'will we start treating ourselves better by not contaminating the environment that we live in and are part of?'
>
> This is, at its very heart, a spiritual question. Ultimately we must decide how much respect and love we have for other human beings. . . .
>
> The environment is, in the final analysis, a political question. That means we must organize across and against lines of race, class, gender, nation and geography in order to save the earth. . . . If we can take down the Berlin Wall, we can take down the wall that prevents us from seeing what must be done to leave our children a livable world."
>
> *Greenpeace,* 1990

Public services then declined. If the city governments raised tax rates to make up for the loss, more middle-income citizens moved away. Higher property taxes also made it difficult for landlords to make a profit. In their efforts to do so, they skimped on maintaining their buildings. Heating systems broke down in winter. Roofs leaked. Corridors were dark and littered with refuse. Buildings soon deteriorated beyond repair, and what had been decent neighborhoods became slums. As the population of the inner cities fell, whole neighborhoods were abandoned.

This decline made life harder for the people who had to remain in the inner cities. Many of these were discriminated against because of their race or color. Poverty and dreadful living conditions commonly resulted in the breakup of inner-city families. Bitterly discouraged, some people sought escape in alcohol and various illegal drugs. Those who became drug addicts were even more desperate. Because they were without work, many addicts resorted to robbery and mugging to get money to support their habits.

Because the city governments had less money, the schools began to suffer too. Classes were overcrowded. Teachers were underpaid. Supplies were inadequate. Equipment broke down. Faced with such conditions, many students lost interest in school. They learned few skills and had little hope of getting decent jobs when they completed their schooling. They were called "dropouts" because they left school (dropped out) before receiving their diplomas.

Unable to find jobs because they were poorly trained or not trained at all, many of these dropouts hung idly around, causing trouble. Hopeless and resentful, some of them turned to crime. For example, many of the children of drug addicts were badly neglected or even abused. Many young people were left to roam the streets unsupervised. Others turned to drug dealing, where they could make considerable sums of money—at the risk of going to prison or losing their lives. Some also turned to violent crime.

One of the worst examples of this **urban decay** was the section of New York City called the South Bronx. Many of the buildings in the South Bronx became fire-blackened, empty shells. Such places were sometimes the scene of violence and rioting. In Los Angeles in 1991, Rodney King, a black motorist, was arrested for speeding after a hectic chase by several white policemen. When they caught up with King, the angry officers beat him mercilessly. Unknown to the policemen, a bystander recorded the scene with a video camera. The pictures of the brutal beating were soon played repeatedly on television and printed in newspapers all over the country. The policemen were charged with assault, but, to the surprise of many, an all-white jury found them not guilty.

The jury's decision caused a terrible outburst of violence in inner-city Los Angeles. Rioters put buildings to the torch, looted shops, and beat innocent passersby. The violence was inexcusable but understandable. It reminded the white majority that despite desegregation and equal rights legislation, much remained to be done before true equality and justice for all could be achieved.

Another example of urban decay in the 1980s was the astonishing increase in the number of homeless people. These people wound up living on the streets and in parks with only shopping bags to hold their meager belongings. Visitors to America were shocked. The problem was compounded when many nonviolent mental patients were "deinstitutionalized," that is, released from mental hospitals on the theory that they would be better off "free" and supplied with shelter and medication locally. But no one seemed able to devise a system that would allow the homeless to retain their dignity and human rights while receiving the assistance that many of them needed.

Riots in Los Angeles' predominately African American neighborhoods followed the outcome of the Rodney King case. Millions of dollars worth of property went up in smoke amid angry violence, destruction, and looting.

Ken Biggs/After Image

Los Angeles, "The City of Angels," lies smothered in the smog created in part by the movement of traffic along the freeways. But environmentalists with activities such as Earth Day, below, have fought for 20 years to awaken the consciences of polluters.

Werner Wolff/Black Star

Coping with Pollution

Beginning in the 1960s, the crowding of people and manufacturing into metropolitan areas caused serious **pollution**—substances that harm the environment. Millions of automobiles, buses, and trucks poured harmful exhaust fumes into the air. The furnaces of factories and utility companies released clouds of smoke and cinders. Denver, Colorado, the "mile-high city" once famous for its pure air, was veiled in haze. At certain times in Los Angeles, polluting substances called **smog** (a term coined by combining the words *smoke* and *fog*) made venturing outside actually dangerous. Some people with heart trouble, allergies, or lung diseases began wearing gas masks outdoors to protect themselves! Air-borne wastes from American factories were carried by winds to Canada, where they fell back to earth as **acid rain**, or rain that contains a high concentration of industrial chemicals and falls as pollution. Acid rain caused much damage to forests, lakes, and human beings. Also, accidents involving offshore oil wells or huge oil tankers released tons of thick, black crude oil into the oceans. The oil smothered birds and fish and covered miles of beaches with tar and grease.

Chemicals used to kill insects and to fertilize the soil proved harmful too. Scientists claimed that the gases used in spray cans caused damage in the upper atmosphere by weakening the ozone layer that protects the earth from dangerous radiation from the sun. According to weather experts, increased burning of coal, oil, and other fuels in homes, factories, and automobiles was raising the amount of carbon dioxide in the atmosphere. This was causing a **greenhouse effect**: The increased amount of carbon dioxide was preventing heat from escaping into space, thereby raising the average temperature on Earth.

In 1970, Congress established an **Environmental Protection Agency** (EPA) to monitor pollution and seek ways to eliminate it. But the EPA's efforts were seldom successful. The cost of cleanup was high, and auto makers and other manufacturers often resisted obeying EPA directives.

Coping with Energy Shortages

The soaring price of oil in the 1970s forced Americans to cut back on their consumption of petroleum products. They turned down the thermostats in their homes during winter, for example, and bought smaller automobiles to replace the "gas guzzlers" they had previously favored. Eventually, conservation and the discovery of new oil fields in non-OPEC nations caused the price to fall considerably—but not nearly as low as it had been in 1973.

Meanwhile, the search for other sources of energy went on. One source, **nuclear energy**, was already producing large amounts of electricity. Nuclear plants make electricity by splitting atoms of uranium, the same element used in atomic bombs. But instead of exploding, in nuclear plants the uranium is split under controlled conditions in reactors. The process results in enormous amounts of heat. The heat turns water into steam, just as the heat of coal or oil fires does in conventional power plants. The steam turns the turbines that create electricity.

Nuclear power plants are efficient, but if an accident caused the uranium to "overheat," it might explode, releasing deadly radioactive particles over large areas. In 1979, an accident at the **Three Mile Island** nuclear plant in Pennsylvania did great damage to the plant and caused a near panic in surrounding communities. In 1986, the explosion of a Soviet plant at **Chernobyl,** near Kiev, spewed huge amounts of radiation into the air. Its effect was felt over thousands of miles. After Chernobyl, plans to construct more nuclear power plants in the United States ground to a halt. 🖅

Return to the Preview & Review on page 1101.

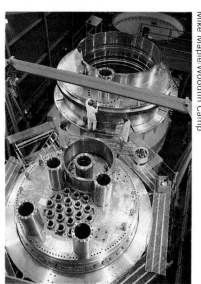

This pair of photos shows a nuclear power plant from cooling tower to the central core. Explain briefly how nuclear energy is produced.

Chris Harris/Gamma-Liaison

Mike Maple/Woodfin Camp

Use these questions to guide your reading. Answer the questions after completing Section 4.
Understanding Issues, Events, & Ideas. Use the following words to describe Jimmy Carter's election to the presidency and his term in office: Twenty-Sixth Amendment, Camp David Accords.

1. What was Carter's strategy in his campaign against Ford for the presidency in 1976?
2. What was a major factor in Carter's victory at the polls?
3. How did Carter manage to alienate himself from Congress and the American people? Why were many African Americans dissatisfied with Carter?
4. In what way did Carter help to bring peace to the Middle East?

Thinking Critically. 1. If you had been a voter in 1976 would you have supported Ford or Carter for president? Explain your answer.
2. Imagine that you are a newspaper reporter and have just interviewed President Carter. Write an account of your impressions of him, including a description of some of his characteristics, such as his mannerisms and style.

4. THE DEMOCRATS TAKE A TURN

The Election of 1976

In the mid 1970s, the United States was beginning to face those three challenges. As a result of the Watergate affair, many Americans lost faith in their country's leadership. The Democrats nominated James Earl Carter, Jr., for president. Jimmy Carter, as he preferred to be known, had been a little-known governor of Georgia, peanut farmer, and businessman. At the Republican nominating convention, President Ford won a narrow victory over Ronald Reagan, a former Hollywood actor who had served two terms as governor of California.

During the campaign, Carter's strategy was to present himself as an outsider, one who had no connection with the corruption and scandal that surrounded Washington in the Watergate era. He stressed his sincerity, his honesty, and his deep religious faith. He would run the federal government efficiently, he said, and he would balance the budget. In one campaign speech, he voiced the concerns of many Americans and his vision of the nation:

    66 Can our government in Washington, which we love, be decent? Is it possible for it to be honest and truthful and fair and idealistic, compassionate, filled with love? Is it possible for our government to be what the American people are, or what we would like to be? Can it once again be a source of pride instead of apology and shame and embarrassment?

    A lot of people think the answer is no. I think the answer is yes. . . . We still have a system of government that's the best on earth. The vision that was ours 200 years ago is still there. Our Constitution still says the same thing. Equality, equity, fairness, decency, are still aspects of our government. Freedom, liberty, individualism, are still integral aspects of our government. We have a nation of which we ought to be proud. . . .

    We ought to be searching for a way to make our nation more decent and more fair.[1] 99

By comparison, President Ford emphasized his political experience. He compared his more than 25 years in national politics to Carter's brief stint at the state level. Neither candidate presented imaginative solutions to the nation's problems, and people took little interest in the campaign. Barely half of the eligible voters went to the polls. Actually, this was part of a continuing trend. But it was worrisome that relatively few of the people aged 18 to 20 bothered to cast ballots. They had only recently been given the right to vote by the **Twenty-Sixth Amendment**, ratified in 1971.

[1]From *A Government as Good as Its People* by Jimmy Carter

The election was close. Carter won in the electoral college by 297 votes to 240. He carried the northern industrial states and the South. A major reason for his victory was the support he received from Mexican Americans, particularly in south Texas, and from African Americans. Almost 95 out of every 100 African American voters cast their ballots for Carter.

The election of Carter, who publicly affirmed his religious convictions, also represented a change that had developed in American society since World War II. He symbolized the reawakening of an American religious spirit, especially among conservative Protestants. Despite radical movements and unprecedented scientific breakthroughs, the tide of popular religion had continued to rise. Many people—including political candidates and even Catholic priests—described experiences something like a traditionally Protestant "rebirth."

These "born again" Americans spread the experience, publicly and privately. Some born-again Protestant ministers made effective use of radio and television to attract converts and raise money. The Reverend Jimmy Swaggart, for example, was said to have more than 2 million followers. (In the 1980s, however, some of the most popular of these preachers would be convicted of misusing money they had collected. Others would be exposed for committing scandalous personal behavior. By 1990, the movement would experience a decline.)

The Carters appear at one of the inaugural balls celebrating the return of the Democrats to the White House. Report to your classmates on the most recent evaluations of the Carter presidency. Predict for whom the woman registering to vote below cast her ballot: Carter or Ford?

Carter at Home

In office Carter stressed an informal style. He tried to make himself more available to ordinary people than most recent presidents. Instead of riding to the White House in a limousine after his inauguration, he and his wife and small daughter walked down Pennsylvania Avenue at the end of the inaugural parade, waving and smiling to the crowd. He appeared on television wearing a cardigan sweater instead of a suit coat. He had a "call in" program in which he answered questions phoned in by citizens.

As time passed, however, Carter often displayed a kind of peevishness—he seemed almost arrogant and acted in a haughty manner, especially in dealing with Congress. And though he was a good orator, he often spoke to the people about things they could not feel or understand. Carter claimed there was "a growing *malaise* of the American spirit." By this French word he meant a vague uneasiness, a discomfort that would be difficult to treat. This pessimism could hardly console troubled Americans who were hoping that the economy would improve and that foreign tensions would ease. Carter also stressed that with citizenship came certain obligations, such as obeying the law and striving for the common good. How bright the future would be depended in large part on how actively each American worked toward creating a just and prosperous society.

D. B. Owen/Black Star

The triumph of the Carter presidency was bringing together the leaders of two ancient rivals: Egypt, represented by Anwar Sadat, and Israel, represented by Menachem Begin. What agreement did they reach at Camp David before this handshake?

Return to the Preview & Review on page 1106.

As the months passed, critics began to claim that Carter was a poor leader. His economic policies were not achieving results, and his civil rights measures were not strong enough. Within his own party some Democrats insisted that to stimulate the economy and reduce unemployment, Carter should urge Congress to increase government spending.

Instead, the president attempted to slow inflation by cutting government spending. He set out with zeal to protect the environment, the workplace, the consumer, and the nation's highways. But each new regulation brought protests from businesses, which feared losing profits if they complied with the new laws. Carter named three women to his cabinet, and more women, African Americans, and Hispanics received federal jobs and judgeships than ever before. Some African Americans complained bitterly, however, that President Carter had not appointed enough of their members to posts in his administration.

Carter and Foreign Relations

Although Carter's intentions were good, his inexperience in foreign relations caused problems. He bravely set the tone for his foreign policy in his inaugural address:

> ❝ Because we are free we can never be indifferent to the fate of freedom elsewhere. . . . Our commitment to human rights must be absolute.[1] ❞

[1] From his inaugural speech by Jimmy Carter, January 20, 1977

Securing these rights for people in other countries, however, proved difficult. Pressure for human rights weakened American ties with anticommunist nations such as Iran and Nicaragua and undermined their autocratic governments, which regularly violated the human rights of their citizens. For the same reasons, it threatened detente with the Soviets. Then Carter's firm stand against the Soviet invasion of Afghanistan in 1979 sent detente into a tailspin and led the president to withdraw the important Strategic Arms Limitation Treaty (SALT II) that had just been negotiated with the Soviets.

Yet President Carter did win much praise for his efforts to bring peace to the troubled Middle East. He invited Israel's premier, Menachem Begin, and Egypt's president, Anwar Sadat, to Camp David, the presidential retreat outside Washington. With Carter's help, Begin and Sadat hammered out an agreement known as the **Camp David Accords**. Israel withdrew from all captured Egyptian territory, and Egypt extended formal recognition to Israel. As a result of their efforts toward ending the Arab–Israeli conflict, Begin and Sadat shared the 1978 Nobel Peace Prize. 🖥

Bettmann Newsphotos

Even his sharpest critics concede that Ronald Reagan, shown here with his wife, Nancy, was a very popular president.

5. THE REPUBLICANS TRIUMPHANT

The Election of 1980

The energy crisis of the 1970s aggravated the problem of inflation. The skyrocketing price of gasoline, heating oil, and everything made from petroleum helped push the **inflation rate** to about 13 percent by 1979. With prices rising much more rapidly than wages, inflation became the main issue in the 1980 presidential election.

President Carter won the Democratic nomination after a hard campaign against Senator Edward M. Kennedy, a younger brother of President John F. Kennedy. During the primaries, Carter faced an international crisis that had broken out in November 1979. A mob in Teheran, the capital of Iran, had broken into the American embassy and held as hostages the Americans in the building. The leaders demanded that the United States turn over to the Iranian government the former shah, or king, of Iran, who had been deposed a year earlier and who was receiving treatment for cancer in the United States.

The United States refused to return the shah, and a stalemate resulted. For months, the Iranians held more than 50 Americans prisoner in the embassy in Teheran. In desperation, President Carter in April 1980 ordered a team of marine commandos flown into Iran by helicopter to rescue the hostages. The mission had to be called back after several of the helicopters developed mechanical problems. Then, eight commandos died when two helicopters collided during a refueling stop in the desert. The Iranians shocked the world with a ghoulish display of the dead.

The effort earned Carter a mixture of blame, because it failed, and praise for having at least tried to free the hostages, but they remained in captivity. This was a severe blow to Carter and to the prestige of the United States.

Preview & Review

Use these questions to guide your reading. Answer the questions after completing Section 5.
Understanding Issues, Events, & Ideas. Use the following words to describe the presidential elections of 1980 and 1984, as well as the Reagan years: inflation rate, supply-side economics, Sandinistas, Income Tax Act of 1986, Contras, Boland Amendment, *glasnost, perestroika,* strategic defense initiative.
1. What international crisis helped cause the defeat of Jimmy Carter in the 1980 presidential election?
2. What is supply-side economics?
3. Why did Reagan send aid to the El Salvador government and anti-government Nicaraguans?
4. What was a major difference in policy between Reagan and Mondale?
5. What were some of the alarming changes occurring in American society at the end of the 1980s?
Thinking Critically. Imagine that you are a member of Congress in the early 1980s. Write a press statement in which you either defend or attack Reagan's policy of sending military and economic aid to the Contras in Nicaragua.

The Republicans Triumphant   1109

Patrick Siccoli/Gamma-Liaison

The Republicans nominated Ronald Reagan, who had lost the nomination four years earlier by only a narrow margin. In the election, Reagan won a sweeping victory, 43.9 million popular votes to 35.5 million for Carter. A third party candidate, John Anderson, received 5.7 million popular votes. Reagan's majority in the electoral college was even more stunning: 489 to Carter's 49. The Republican party also made large gains in seats in both houses of Congress.

On January 20, 1981, Reagan took the oath of office as president. At a luncheon immediately afterward, he announced that the hostages in Iran had been freed.

After leaving office, Jimmy Carter devoted himself to world peace and to sheltering the poor and homeless. Eventually, many of his former critics would see him in a new light. Yet he seemed unequal to many of the challenges during his term as president.

Reagan as President

A committed conservative, President Reagan believed that the federal government had grown too big and was involved in too many aspects of everyday life. "It is my intention to curb the size and influence of the Federal establishment," he announced in his inaugural address. He hoped that by 1988, many major federal programs would have been taken over by the states. He called his plan "The New Federalism."

Reagan was determined to increase the amount of money spent on defense but to cut back on other government spending. He also wished to reduce taxes. He argued that the budget could be balanced despite the lower taxes. He said it would work this way: Americans would invest the money they saved on taxes in new business enterprises, which in turn would cause the economy to boom. More jobs would be created, and profits would increase. With more people working and businesses earning more money, tax revenues would go up, even though tax rates were lower. This theory was known as **supply-side economics**, also called "trickle-down economics" by its opponents.

Reagan proved to be an extremely skillful politician. By midsummer 1981, the Reagan budget and bills reducing the federal income tax by 25 percent over three years had been enacted into law.

Despite Reagan's economic policies, the nation's economic problems persisted, and a serious recession developed. Business activity lagged. Unemployment rose to more than 10 percent, and interest rates remained high. With tax revenues down and the government spending billions on defense, the deficit rose to nearly $200 billion in 1983.

The recession did have one good result: The inflation rate tumbled from more than 12 percent to less than 4 percent by early 1984.

The hostages held in Iran, shown above upon their arrival on free soil, were given a boisterous ticker tape parade a few days later in New York (below).

Jake Rajs/Life Magazine © Time Warner, Inc.

With that, business began to pick up. Thousands of idle workers found new jobs.

But the huge budget deficit remained. Some advisers urged Reagan to reduce it by cutting military spending. He refused to do so because he believed that the Soviet Union was out to dominate the globe. He said that it was "the focus of evil in the modern world." The president wanted the Soviets to know that the United States was stronger than they were and would resist aggression. Then the Soviets would restrain themselves, he said.

This policy caused Reagan to take a strong stand against possible Soviet "penetration" of Central America. Some years earlier, rebels in Nicaragua known as **Sandinistas** had overthrown the country's reactionary dictator. The Sandinistas had set up a government that was friendly to the Soviet Union. They were also supporting rebel forces in the neighboring nation of El Salvador. Reagan provided advisers and military and economic aid to the government of El Salvador and ordered the CIA to organize antigovernment Nicaraguans who were seeking to defeat the Sandinistas.

The Election of 1984

Reagan's Central American policy was controversial, but he remained popular. In 1984 the Republican convention unanimously nominated him for a second term as president. For the first time, an African American—the Reverend Jesse Jackson—waged a serious campaign for the Democratic nomination. He attracted wide support by denouncing Reagan's economic policies as harmful to the poor. But the nomination went to Walter Mondale, who had been Carter's vice president.

Mondale electrified the country by selecting a woman, Representative Geraldine Ferraro of New York, as his running mate. He also announced that if elected he would ask Congress to raise taxes in order to reduce the budget deficit. This was a direct challenge to President Reagan, who had sworn not to increase taxes under any circumstances.

The election resulted in a landslide for Reagan. He won nearly 60 percent of the popular vote and carried the electoral college by 525 to 13. African Americans were one of the few traditionally loyal Democratic groups to support Mondale. The Democratic tactic of nominating a woman for vice president was a failure. Far more women voted for Reagan than for Mondale.

The Reagan "Revolution"

In his second term, President Reagan continued attempts to cut back government spending on social welfare projects and to lower taxes still further. The **Income Tax Act** of 1986 relieved 6 million low-income

Griffiths/Magnum Photos

The Mondale/Ferraro ticket failed to capture the imagination of most American voters. In spite of Geraldine Ferraro's presence on the Democratic ticket, for whom did most women vote?

Cynthia Johnson/Time Picture Syndication

people from paying income taxes and lowered the maximum rate for anyone else to 28 percent. The taxes paid by corporations also were reduced.

The president also pursued his policy of appointing and promoting as many conservatives as possible in public office. When Chief Justice Warren Burger resigned from the Supreme Court in 1986, Reagan nominated Associate Justice William Rehnquist, an extremely conservative justice, to the top post. Rehnquist's position was filled by Antonin Scalia, another conservative. The next year, when another justice retired, Reagan named Robert Bork, a judge so extremely conservative that the Senate refused to confirm him. It did confirm Reagan's next choice, however, the more moderate conservative Anthony Kennedy.

The composition of the high court was especially important to those on both sides of the issue of abortion. "Right to life" advocates argued that all life is sacred, and that only in the most extreme cases should an unborn child be aborted. They were challenged by the pro-choice movement, which claimed that a woman had the constitutional right to control her own body, and thus to end an unwanted pregnancy during the early stages, if she chose to do so. The Court was drawn into the argument by the 1973 landmark case, *Roe v. Wade,* which ruled that a woman's constitutional right to privacy included the right to have an abortion during the first three months of pregnancy. Later Supreme Court decisions, however, authorized the states to limit the circumstances under which abortions might be performed. (The pro-choice versus pro-life debate continued heatedly, well into the 1990s.)

President Reagan's success in having many of his programs adopted was the result partly of his personal popularity. His appointments of federal office holders were also moving the government in

Cynthia Johnson/Time Picture Syndication

Top: marchers for Women's Equal Rights come to Washington. Above is Norma McCorvey, who used the name "Jane Roe" to protect her identity in the case of Roe v. Wade.

STRATEGIES FOR SUCCESS

EXPRESSING A POINT OF VIEW

You may often be called upon to express and defend your point of view on a topic—in class discussions, essay tests, research papers, or debates. At such times you need to clearly state your positions and provide support.

How to Express a Point of View

To express a point of view, follow these guidelines.

1. **Research the issue.** Make sure you know what you are talking about. Find out what the opposing points of view are.
2. **Decide on your position.** Study the evidence and evaluate the situation. Decide how you stand on the issue. Begin to collect support for your position.
3. **State your position simply and clearly.** Prepare an introduction that identifies the issue and states your position in simple and clear terms.
4. **Support your position.** When writing your point of view, develop additional paragraphs that provide support for your position. End with a concluding paragraph briefly restating your position and reasoning.

Applying the Skill

Today the issue of gun control raises a controversy in many parts of the United States. The basic question is: To what degree should the government regulate and limit the sale and ownership of guns? Those who are against gun control point for their defense to a portion of the Second Amendment which guarantees a "right of the people to keep and bear arms." However, those who favor gun control cite the rise in violent, gun-related crimes to support their call for legislation regulating the sale and ownership of guns, particularly handguns and semi-automatic weapons. State your point of view on gun control. Be sure to support your position.

For independent practice, see Practicing the Strategy on page 1125.

The Granger Collection, New York

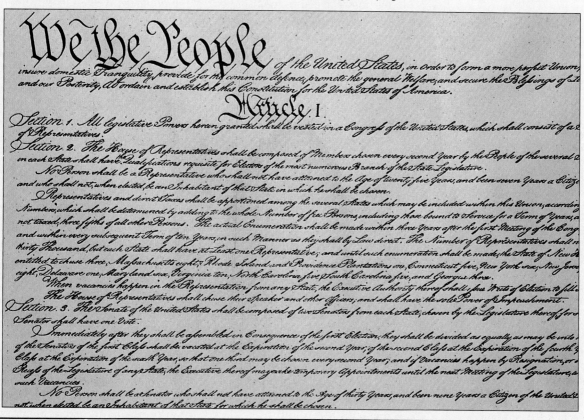

The Republicans Triumphant   1113

Chiaisson/Gamma–Liaison

Realization that mothers could pass the deadly AIDS virus to their unborn children came slowly. The children who contracted the disease were sometimes abandoned. Mother Hale, pictured above, cares for such children. The disease has no cure nor vaccine. Your families, schools, and churches can help you understand how the AIDS virus is spread.

the conservative direction that he favored. But at the same time, serious social problems were changing the face of America. Despite efforts to get tough with criminals, crime rates were rising. Illegal, habit-forming drugs flooded the country. "Crack," a particularly habit-forming type of cocaine, became especially troublesome because it was relatively cheap, widely available, and potentially lethal.

Equally, if not more, disturbing was the sudden appearance of a deadly new disease, acquired immunodeficiency syndrome, or AIDS. AIDS was caused by a virus that prevents the body from fighting off pneumonia and other diseases. Because there was no known cure for AIDS, almost everyone who contracted it eventually died.

Although the economy was booming in the late 1980s, few people were sharing in the wealth being produced. Many of the rich were getting richer, but many of the poor were getting poorer. Many Americans became victims of technological unemployment. That is, computers and automated machinery were replacing human workers at the lower end of the wage scale.

Reagan's policy of eliminating government restrictions on business resulted in a great deal of healthy competition. But competition hurt inefficient producers, who were swallowed up by the more successful. Ending government regulation also encouraged recklessness. Savings banks and savings-and-loan associations (S&Ls) in particular, freed from strict control, sometimes invested in extremely risky ventures. Additionally, when falling oil prices caused a severe depression in Texas and other oil-producing states, many companies were unable to repay their loans. Area banks and S&Ls went "belly up" by the dozens.

Another problem resulted from the flood of imports from Japan and other Asian countries such as South Korea and Taiwan. The imports were eagerly sought by American consumers, but American businesses that competed with the imports suffered.

The Iran-Contra Scandal

In two foreign areas, Reagan pursued policies that made his last years in office unhappy. One involved the Central American nation of Nicaragua. In 1981 Reagan persuaded Congress to provide weapons and other supplies to the **Contras** (counter-revolutionaries), who were seeking to overthrow the pro-communist Sandinistas. But the Contra revolt made little progress. In 1984, fearing that continued military assistance might lead to "another Vietnam," Congress passed the **Boland Amendment**, which banned such aid in the future.

Meanwhile, a savage war had broken out in the Middle East between Iran and Iraq. Like most Americans, President Reagan had no love for the Iranians because of their anti-American policies and the 1979 attack on the American embassy in Teheran. Additionally, a number of Americans had been held captive for years at secret

John Ficara/Woodfin Camp

locations in Lebanon by radicals supported by Iran. Reagan was eager to obtain their release. In 1986, despite his stated opposition to bargaining with hostage takers, he authorized the secret sale of American arms to Iran, expecting that Iran would arrange the release of the hostages in exchange.

The man who managed this Iranian arms deal was Oliver North, a marine colonel assigned to the White House. After Congress' ban on aid to the Contras, North had been given the job by administration officials of persuading foreign countries and well-to-do individuals to contribute money to the Contras' cause. North, with the knowledge of his immediate superiors, used the profits of the arms sale to Iran ($12 million) to supply the Contras in Nicaragua. This, of course, was against the law. When the secret sales became known in late 1986, during a series of hearings by a Senate investigating committee, North and Reagan's national security adviser were forced from office. Most Americans disapproved of the Iran-Contra deal and did not believe that President Reagan was telling the truth when he denied knowing anything about it. In any case, his final term was ending.

The End of an Era

The most important event that occurred abroad during Reagan's second term was the dramatic change in the Soviet Union after Mikhail Gorbachev became the Soviet leader in March 1985. Because of the problems undermining the Soviet economic system, a failure that also affected the Soviet satellite nations in Eastern Europe, Gorbachev decided to impose some drastic reforms. First he encouraged the Soviet people to discuss public issues and even to criticize government actions (the policy called *glasnost*). He then tried

The Iran-Contra hearings began with the swearing in of Colonel Oliver North, whose performance impressed many television watchers but not the members of the committee. Name another of the Washington hearings you've read about in **The Story of America** *that attracted wide interest.*

The magazine *Vanity Fair* published this profile of Mikhail Gorbachev after the collapse of the communist governments in Russia's eastern satellites.

"The eyes. Everyone is struck by the gleam that blazes behind his dark eyes. Presidents, Soviet-ologists, resident C.I.A. psychologists, Wall Street deal makers—all come away talking about some strange chemical reaction, as if with the intensity of his belief Mikhail Gorbachev had burned his image of a new world onto their own retinas and they will never be the same.

'His eyes convey an intensity that is slightly abnormal,' muses a senior analyst . . . 'It's as though his temperature is a little higher than normal, and he's running a little faster than anybody else.'"

Gail Sheehy, 1990

Return to the Preview & Review on page 1109.

Arm in arm in the Kremlin are Ronald Reagan, Raisa Gorbachev, Mikhail Gorbachev, and Nancy Reagan.

to stimulate the Soviet economy by encouraging individual enterprise. This was called *perestroika*.

At first Reagan was suspicious of these new Soviet policies. He urged Congress to appropriate large sums to build a **strategic defense initiative** (referred to by the press as "Star Wars"), a complicated and expensive computerized system of nuclear-armed missiles designed to destroy incoming missiles while they were still in outer space. Such a system would only be needed in case of a Soviet attack. But by 1986 it was clear that Gorbachev was really interested in reducing international tensions. Disastrously small harvests had forced the Soviets to sign trade agreements with many nations, including the United States. Other breakdowns in the Soviet economic system followed soon after. Gorbachev announced that the Soviet Union wanted to be readmitted to the world community, on which it had turned its back at the outbreak of the Cold War.

At a summit meeting in 1987, Reagan and Gorbachev finally signed a treaty eliminating medium-range nuclear missiles, a major step toward reducing the danger of nuclear war. People all over the world cheered the efforts of the two world leaders.

Bill Fitzpatrick/The White House

Bettmann Newsphotos

6. TOWARD A NEW CENTURY

Preview & Review

Use these questions to guide your reading. Answer the questions after completing Section 6.

Understanding Issues, Events, & Ideas. Use the following word in describing an important event that occurred during the Bush presidency: apartheid.

1. How was Bush able to beat Dukakis, even though Dukakis was favored to win at the beginning of the race?
2. What were the important world political events viewed as positive by the Bush administration?
3. Why were some Americans unhappy with the results of the war in the Persian Gulf?
4. What factors contributed to President Bush's defeat in the 1992 election?

Thinking Critically. Imagine that you are a newspaper columnist. Write a column for the day after the 1992 election, analyzing the ups and downs of the campaign and giving what you think are the reasons for the election results.

The Election of 1988

Reagan was a very popular president. He was, as his show-business friends would say, "a tough act to follow." To succeed him, the Republicans chose the logical candidate, Reagan's vice president, George Bush. There were so many lesser-known candidates battling for the Democratic nomination that some political writers referred to them as "the Seven Dwarfs." Eventually, the field shrank to two: the Reverend Jesse Jackson and Governor Michael Dukakis of Massachusetts. Jackson, who ran another exciting campaign, attracted more white support than he had in 1984. But Dukakis had a solid majority of the delegates at the convention and was nominated on the first ballot. Dukakis presented himself as the efficient governor of a prosperous state. At the start, he seemed the likely winner, as Bush appeared overshadowed by Reagan.

But the race did not turn out as expected. Bush attacked Dukakis at every turn, while Dukakis was slow to respond in defense of himself. Neither candidate aroused much popular enthusiasm. But Bush's campaign made skillful use of television advertising to depict Dukakis as irresponsible and frighteningly liberal. Although President Reagan threw very little support behind his vice president, by election day it was clear that most of the voters preferred Bush. He won easily, carrying the electoral college by 426 to 112.

Steve Liss/Time Picture Syndication

Rivals for the Democratic nomination in a friendly moment, above, are the Reverend Jesse Jackson and Michael Dukakis. Both had a formidable opponent in George Bush, who promised to continue much of the Reagan legacy. The Bush inaugural and the grandeur of the Capitol are pictured at top.

Eric Bouvet/Gamma-Liaison

The people, not their leaders, decided the Wall separating West and East Germany must come tumbling down. The celebration at the reconciliation of East and West drew millions to the Brandenburg Gate in Berlin.

Diana Walker/Time Picture Syndication

George Bush and Mikhail Gorbachev met in Malta in 1989, just before the communist bloc of eastern countries began to tumble.

Into the 1990s

Bush's presidency began well. Encouraged by Gorbachev's policies, the satellite countries of Eastern Europe—Poland, East Germany, Czechoslovakia, Hungary, Romania, and Bulgaria—turned out their communist leaders. Even republics within the Soviet Union, such as Lithuania and Georgia, demanded independence. Meanwhile, the Berlin Wall was torn down by East and West Germans, who were eager to reunite their country. Then the central committee of the Soviet Union itself, under Gorbachev's prodding, called for a popular election of a president and announced that the communist party would no longer be the only legal political party. Other political parties would be encouraged. The committee made these changes in hopes of reversing the economic collapse that threatened the nation and in hopes of preventing revolts that such a collapse might cause.

In February 1990, the ruling Sandinistas were defeated in democratic elections in Nicaragua. Violeta Barrios de Chamorro became president. In Africa, after the United States and many other nations had applied economic sanctions, South Africa moved to ease its policy of **apartheid**—separation of the races.

These heartening developments were not repeated elsewhere. In China, after taking part in peaceful demonstrations in Tiananmen Square in Beijing calling for democracy, dozens of students were mowed down by tanks and government troops, untold numbers of others were imprisoned, and all criticism of the communist authorities was ruthlessly suppressed.

Uniphoto Picture Agency.

© Misha Erwitt/Magnum

In Central America, drug dealers often controlled the leaders of their countries through force and violence, making the war on drugs difficult to wage. Panama was ruled by a notorious leader with drug-dealer connections, Manuel Noriega. After Noriega was indicted in the United States for drug dealing, Bush mounted a successful invasion of the country to capture him. Unfortunately, some American soldiers and many innocent Panamanians were killed during the fighting. Noriega was captured, brought to the United States, tried, and convicted. Other Latin American nations were alarmed by Bush's use of military force in the area. Nevertheless, Bush remained popular in the United States.

Above left: American soldiers prepare for "Operation Desert Storm" in Saudi Arabia. Above, Colin Powell, chairman of the U.S. Joint Chiefs of Staff, appears at a press conference with General Norman Schwarzkopf, commander of the mostly American United Nations forces in the Persian Gulf War. Below is Iraq's Saddam Hussein, whose invasion of Kuwait triggered the war.

The War in the Persian Gulf

President Bush's popularity further increased when he acted decisively after President Saddam Hussein of Iraq invaded and occupied Kuwait, Iraq's tiny oil-rich neighbor. This gross act of aggression led the United Nations to impose a total ban on trade with Iraq. At the invitation of Saudi Arabia, which Saddam also threatened to attack, the United States and several other UN member nations sent troops and warships to the area. When Saddam refused to withdraw his troops from Kuwait, the United Nations authorized the use of forces to drive them out.

In January 1991, the mostly American UN force, commanded by General Norman Schwarzkopf of the United States Army, was unleashed. For one month, planes bombed Iraqi targets. Finally, when Saddam still refused to pull out of Kuwait, hundreds of thousands of UN ground troops swept into Kuwait and Iraq. In three days Kuwait was liberated, Iraq's army was smashed, and many

Claude Salhani/Gamma-Liaison

© Misha Erwitt/Magnum

BUSINESS STINKS $ALE 20-50%

Rising unemployment and slow economic growth hurt retail sales during the Bush administration. To stay in business, some merchants were forced to cut prices drastically in order to sell goods.

AP/Wide World Photos

Boris Yeltsin had to confront the terrible economic problems in Russia after the fall of communism. Many people in western countries feared he might fail and be overthrown by the Russian military.

thousands of Iraqi soldiers were killed. Saddam then agreed to United Nations terms, which included paying Kuwait for damages.

President Bush expected that Saddam's opponents in Iraq would force him from office, and Bush urged them to do so. However, the overwhelming defeat of Saddam's forces did not lead to his overthrow. Saddam used what was left of his army to crush his Iraqi opponents, and he refused to carry out many of the terms of the peace agreement. Bush's critics in the United States began to complain that he should have captured Baghdad, the Iraqi capital, and arrested Saddam just as he had arrested Noriega.

Bush had predicted that the American economy would boom after the Gulf War. Instead, growth slowed almost to a stop. Unemployment rose to more than 7 percent in 1992. As a result of the economic problems, Bush's standing in opinion polls began to fall.

At the same time, the world situation seemed less encouraging. In August 1991, hard-line communists in the Soviet Union tried to seize power by arresting Gorbachev. Their coup failed and they were imprisoned. The Soviet Union was then dissolved, replaced by a loose federation of republics.

During this period, Boris Yeltsin was the leader of Russia, the largest of the republics. He courageously defied the hard-liners during the coup and emerged as the most powerful leader in the federation. With the end of the Soviet Union, Gorbachev went into retirement.

The Election of 1992

The overwhelming American victory in the Gulf War of January and February 1991 had increased President Bush's already high standing in public opinion polls. Because his reelection seemed almost certain, many prominent Democrats were discouraged from seeking their party's presidential nomination. The best organized of the Democrats who did enter the primaries was Governor Bill Clinton of Arkansas. Although charged with misrepresenting facts about how he had avoided being drafted during the Vietnam War, Clinton won most of the primaries and was nominated at the convention on the first ballot.

Despite resentment from many conservative Republicans over President Bush's breaking his campaign promise "No new taxes," he won solid victories in the Republican primaries. For a time, an independent candidate, H. Ross Perot, a billionaire businessman from Texas, entered the race as an independent. Perot was ready, he said, to spend $100 million of his own money on his campaign. While he attacked Bush's handling of the economy and other domestic issues, his main argument was that the Democrats and Republicans alike were out of touch with "the people."

Perot was strong in Texas and the Southwest, a traditionally Republican region, so he seemed a greater threat to Bush than to

Marcy Nighswander/Wide World Photos, Inc.

John Swart/Wide World Photos, Inc.

Clinton. He lost many supporters, however, when he withdrew from the race, then reentered it only eleven weeks later. At the Republican convention, President Bush and Vice President Quayle were nominated without opposition.

In the campaign, Clinton accused Bush of failing to deal effectively with the lingering economic recession. He promised to create jobs, to encourage private investment, and to improve the nation's education and health insurance systems. Bush played down the seriousness of the recession and national debt, and he emphasized the need for "family values."

Most polls showed Bill Clinton well ahead as the fall campaign progressed, even after Ross Perot reentered the race in October. Late in the campaign, President Bush, worried by his consistently poor standing in the opinion polls, launched personal attacks on his opponent, charging that Clinton was untrustworthy and lacked experience in world affairs.

On election day, however, Clinton won an easy victory. The popular vote was more than 43 million for Clinton, 38 million for Bush, and 19 million for Perot. Because of Perot's large vote, nearly 20 percent of the total, Clinton did not gain a majority. On election night, however, his electoral college victory was substantial, 370 to Bush's 168. Perot did not win the electoral votes of any state.

Experts agreed that a political turning point had been reached. Clinton and his running mate, Senator Albert Gore of Tennessee, represented a new, younger generation of political leaders—energetic, optimistic, and ambitious. With the Democrats controlling both branches of the new Congress, Clinton was determined to make good on his campaign promises to put an end to the recession and reduce the national debt. Whether he would succeed remained to be seen. Meanwhile, we draw the curtain on our story of America. 📧

The three-way campaign for the presidency made 1992 an exciting election year. Above left are Democrats Al Gore and Bill Clinton, victors in the race for vice president and president, respectively. Above, George Bush and Dan Quayle accept the Republican party's nomination for their reelection. H. Ross Perot, below, delivers some homespun wit at a press conference during his campaign.

© 1992 Ben Van Hook/Black Star

Return to the Preview & Review on page 1117.

FATAL ERROR: OIL ON WATER

Prince William Sound is an emerald jewel, one of Alaska's scenic wonders. It is a bay with 1,000 miles of shoreline. Its waters teem with fish. It is the playground of hundreds of thousands of sea otters, seals, sea lions, and whales. Sea birds and bald eagles nest along its rocky shores. Surrounding the sound are snow-capped peaks and enormous glaciers that send icebergs floating off into the crystal-clear water. This is how it had been for centuries. Then, a little after midnight, on March 24, 1989, a fatal error was made.

The Disaster Begins

1. What caused the *Exxon Valdez* to snag on the rocks in the sound?

Late Thursday night, March 23, the *Exxon Valdez,* a supertanker as long as three football fields, left the port of Valdez filled with crude oil. There was nothing unusual about the impending voyage. Since 1977 some 8,700 loaded tankers had made the trip out of Valdez with virtually no incidents. Visibility was 10 miles or more and the seas were calm that night. All electrical and mechanical systems aboard the ship were working perfectly.

The captain radioed the Coast Guard for permission to cross from the outbound lane to the inbound lane to avoid some small icebergs. It was a routine request. The Coast Guard gave permission. Within 10 minutes the huge ship had swung into the inbound lane. But instead of following the lane to the southwest, it headed due south. Fifteen minutes later it had completely crossed the inbound lane and had sailed into waters closed to oil tankers.

Half an hour later the *Exxon Valdez* passed close to Busby Island, far outside the well-established and clearly marked tanker lanes. Suddenly the unlicensed third mate commanding the ship realized that an error had been made. He frantically gave orders to turn sharply to the west to reenter the traffic lanes. Meanwhile, the captain was asleep in his cabin.

But the mate's orders came too late. At four minutes after midnight the *Exxon Valdez* scraped the rocks of Bligh Reef. The enormous tanker crunched to a halt, balanced on a pinnacle of rock. From its ripped hull 10.1 million gallons of thick crude oil gushed into the pristine waters of Prince William Sound.

The Disaster Grows

2. Why did emergency plans fail?

In 1973, when Congress approved the Alaska pipeline, all of the oil companies involved made solemn promises in writing to do everything possible to protect Alaska's fragile environment. Yet on that tragic night, Alyeska Pipeline Service Company had no emergency crew on hand and little equipment ready for use. It did virtually nothing for three days. During those first few critical days the sound's waters were flat calm, there was almost no wind, and it was unseasonably warm and sunny. Conditions for clean-up were ideal. The spill spread to cover only a five-square mile area, and it was entirely manageable.

Then, 66 hours after the accident, rapidly rising winds and seas sent the main mass of oil racing southwestward. It surged forward at more than a mile per hour, churning the sound into a foamy mixture of oil and water.

By the second week the oil had sunk to depths of more than 90 feet, making the water hazardous even for bottom-feeding marine life. It had spread across more than 3,000 square miles of water. In the cold water, the surface of the spill had weathered into a heavy, tar-like substance. Under this coating was a 6- to 18-inch layer of oil with the consistency of peanut butter. The annual spring migration of salmon and herring was on a collision course with black, oily death.

Fourteen days after the ship hit the reef just 630,000 gallons out of 10.1 million gallons of oil had been picked up. The western beaches along the sound were covered with oozing, stinking tar. The poisoned bodies of otters and seabirds lay matted and almost unrecognizable in the gooey mess. Five weeks after the accident the spill covered an area the size of Massachusetts.

The Disaster's Effects

3. What human and environmental toll did the spill take?

The sound's fishing industry had been among Alaska's most productive. It had yielded about $100,000,000 annually. Now it was ruined.

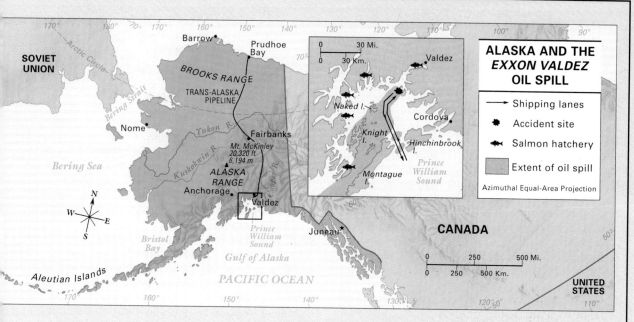

ALASKA AND THE *EXXON VALDEZ* OIL SPILL

- → Shipping lanes
- ✳ Accident site
- 🐟 Salmon hatchery
- ▦ Extent of oil spill

Azimuthal Equal-Area Projection

Despair tore at the hearts of the residents of tiny fishing villages. Their way of life was disappearing before their eyes. Not only were millions of fish dying, but there was danger that toxins in the oil might become embedded in the still-living fish, making them unfit to eat. The public would fear eating fish, shrimp, or crab from the sound. They knew it would be years before they could rebuild their industry, if ever.

Lessons to be Learned

4. What lessons can we learn from this disaster? One of things that makes the situation difficult to analyze is that the issues are so loaded with emotion. Oil spills and dying animals make a powerful case against current methods of transporting dangerous materials.

But it should be remembered that for 12 years oil had flowed safely through the pipeline and had been safely transported out of Prince William Sound. Also for 12 years the oil industry had assured the public that through technological feats it could handle any emergency.

For 12 years few people worried. A large number of Alaskans make their living from the oil industry. The state's economy rests comfortably on the money received in taxes from the oil industry. Many schools, symphonies, and museums were handsomely financed by donations from large oil companies. Oil was good for Alaska!

Perhaps the most valuable long-term lesson to be learned is that alertness, when untested for too long, deteriorates into complacency. Human failing is the thing to attack, not oil exploration or oil transportation. The world needs oil.

History shows clearly that the oil-shipping industry is basically safe. There have been amazingly few spills considering the enormous volume of oil that has been transported around the world. But the industry seemed so safe that responsible people forgot that they are still required to run it properly. Environmental protection demands constant vigilance. Powerful incentives must keep that protection on task. Human errors must be made harder to repeat and too expensive and too dangerous to be tolerated.

APPLYING YOUR KNOWLEDGE

Your class will study environmental concerns in your local community. Each group will select or will be assigned a concern to research. The group will then create a display or presentation that informs others about the concern. Donate your display to the local library or perform your presentation for the city or county council.

CHAPTER 30 REVIEW

1971
Twenty-Sixth
Amendment ratified

1973
Roe v. Wade

1974
Nixon resigns;
Ford becomes
president

1976
U.S. Bicentennial
★
Carter elected president

1979
Three M
Island
★
Hostage
seized
in Iran

Chapter Summary
Read the statements below. Choose one, and write a paragraph explaining its importance.
1. In 1976 people throughout the United States celebrated the nation's Bicentennial.
2. Jimmy Carter brought the leaders of Egypt and Israel together to sign the Camp David Accords.
3. During the 1970s and 1980s Americans had to cope with the problems of urban decay, pollution, and energy shortages.
4. Many of the immigrants of the 1970s came from Asia and Latin America.
5. Many modern blacks were eager to recover their lost heritage and preferred to be known as African Americans.
6. The problem of searching for ways to revive their lost culture continued to plague many American Indians in the 1980s.
7. In 1972 Congress passed the Equal Rights Amendment, but it was not ratified by the states.
8. President Reagan proved to be a determined leader and a skillful politician.
9. In the 1990s, America faced difficult problems with difficult solutions, such as a rising crime rate, drug abuse, and the devastating AIDS virus.
10. Under George Bush, American forces helped liberate Kuwait from Iraqi occupation.

Reviewing Chronological Order
Number your paper 1–5. Then study the time line above and place the following events in the order in which they happened by writing the first next to 1, the second next to 2, and so on.
1. Sandra Day O'Connor becomes first woman on the Supreme Court
2. Eastern European countries begin to allow free elections
3. Iran Contra deal becomes known
4. George Bush becomes the forty-first president of the United States
5. Twenty-Sixth Amendment ratified

Understanding Main Ideas
1. Why did President Ford veto spending projects approved by Congress in the mid-1970s? What action did he later take to end stagflation?
2. Why do you think the United Farm Workers won public sympathy in their strike against California grape growers?
3. In what ways did the civil rights movement transform the United States?
4. What economic actions did Reagan take after his 1980 election? What happened as a result of the decrease in tax revenues and the increase in government spending on defense?
5. What were the cause and the outcome of the Persian Gulf War?

Thinking Critically
1. **Hypothesizing.** Throughout *The Story of America* you have been encouraged to use your historical imagination. You have also been asked to think about historical significance. Two good examples of historical significance are the Monroe Doctrine and the Tonkin Gulf Resolution. Neither seemed particularly important when first announced. Yet 35 presidents have based Latin American policy on the Monroe Doctrine. And Lyndon Johnson waged war in Vietnam under the Tonkin Gulf Resolution. What government actions in recent years do you think might have historical significance? Explain.
2. **Analyzing.** Prepare a brief essay in which you describe what you think is the most important challenge facing America today. Include a paragraph in which you tell how you think our sense of American history can help us meet the challenge.
3. **Evaluating Ideas.** If you were a member of Congress would you have voted for the Reagan budget? The Income Tax Act of 1986? The Boland Amendment? Why or why not?

Writing About History
Imagine that it is the year 2040. Write a letter to your grandchildren describing what it was like

| The Reagan Presidency | | | | | | | | | |

80	MODERN TIMES								1990	

| **80**
agan
ected
esident | **1981**
Hostages in Iran freed
★
Sandra Day O'Connor
becomes first woman
Supreme Court Justice | **1984**
Reagan
reelected
as president | **1985**
Gorbachev
becomes
Soviet leader | **1986**
Iran-Contra
deal
becomes
known | **1988**
Bush elected
president | **1989**
Berlin Wall comes
down; democratic
movements in
Eastern Europe | **1992**
Clinton
elected
president |

growing up in the 1980s and 1990s in America. Include descriptions of your family life, school, leisure-time activities, and styles in clothes and music. It might be interesting to save your letter and read it in the year 2040.

Practicing the Strategy
Review the strategy on page 1113.
Expressing a Point of View. Reread the section titled "Women Fight for Equality" on page 1098. Then write an essay in which you answer the following questions.
1. What is your position on the Equal Rights Amendment?
2. Why do you take that position?
3. How would American society have changed if the ERA had been ratified? What were the effects of its being rejected?

Using Primary Sources
Like his hero, Dr. Martin Luther King, Jr., African American leader Reverend Jesse Jackson also has a dream for a better America. The following is an excerpt from Jackson's autobiography, *Straight from the Heart,* in which he implores young people to dream.

I am more convinced than ever that we can win. We'll vault up the rough side of the mountain—we can win. But I just want the youth of America to do me one favor. Exercise the right to dream. You must face reality— that which is. But then dream of the reality that ought to be, that must be. Live beyond the pain of reality with the dream of a bright tomorrow. Use hope and imagination as weapons of survival and progress. Use love to motivate you and obligate you to serve the human family. . . .

Young people, dream a new value system. . . . Dreams of authentic leaders who will mold public opinion against a headwind, not just ride the tailwinds of opinion polls. Dream of a world where we measure character by how much we share and care, not by how much we take and consume. Preach and dream. Our time has come.

We must measure character by how we treat the least of these, by who feeds the most hungry people, by who educates the most uneducated people, by who cares and loves the most, by who fights for the needy and seeks to save the greedy. We must dream and choose the laws of sacrifice, which lead to greatness, and not the laws of convenience, which lead to collapse.

1. What does Reverend Jackson mean when he says, "We'll vault up the rough side of the mountain?"
2. Do you agree with Reverend Jackson that we need "a new value system?" Explain.
3. Do you find Reverend Jackson's words inspirational? Why or why not?

Linking History & Geography
As the American population continued its shift to urban areas, major metropolitan regions expanded to the point where they met one another. To comprehend the size and to identify the location of these supercities, with your classmates prepare a map of a megalopolis mentioned in this chapter. On your map you should label the most important city or cities, suburbs, and transportation links. You may need to use an atlas or gazetteer to prepare your map. Discuss with your classmates the impact that these supercities have had on America.

Enriching Your Study of History
1. **Individual Project.** Prepare a classroom display to show various forms of energy in use today, and those proposed for tomorrow. Prepare an oral report to go along with the display in which you describe the strengths and weaknesses of each.
2. **Cooperative Project.** Your group will make a collage on the theme that America is a country of many peoples and special interest groups. Each group member should participate in preparing the collage by bringing in as many pictures from magazines and newspapers as he or she can find on this subject.

Chapter 30 Review   **1125**

UNIT TEN REVIEW

Summing Up and Predicting
Read the summary of the main ideas in Unit Ten below. Choose one statement, then write a paragraph predicting its outcome or future effect.
1. Among the successes of the Great Society were Medicare and the Voting Rights Act.
2. By the 1960s the United States was called the Affluent Society because no nation in the world had ever been so productive.
3. Movements for equal rights by women, Indians, and African Americans continued.
4. The belief in the domino theory led to U.S. involvement in South Vietnam.
5. The year 1968 was a tragedy because of the Tet offensive in Vietnam, the assassinations of Dr. Martin Luther King, Jr., and Robert Kennedy, and the riots at the Democratic convention in Chicago.
6. The Watergate cover-up led to the resignation of President Nixon.
7. Presidents Ford, Carter, Reagan, and Bush struggled with the economy.
8. By the early 1990s the Cold War ended after the Soviet Union collapsed.
9. American forces helped liberate Kuwait from its Iraqi conquerors in a short war in 1991.

Connecting Ideas
1. The author says that by 1960 the impact of computers was beginning to be felt in the United States. He said that "Eventually the United States would become a computerized society." Do you think the author was correct in his prediction and that we have become a "computerized society?" What are some of the ways that we rely on computers?
2. The Twenty-Sixth Amendment to the Constitution, which lowered the voting age to 18, was ratified in 1971. However, in every national election since ratification the voter turnout for 18- to 20-year-olds has been relatively low. How would you account for this? What can be done to encourage 18- to 20-year-olds to vote?

Practicing Critical Thinking
1. **Analyzing.** In his acceptance speech as Republican presidential candidate in 1964 Barry Goldwater said, "Extremism in the defense of liberty is no vice. And . . . moderation in the pursuit of justice is no virtue." Do you agree or disagree with Goldwater? Why do you think many voters were frightened by this statement?
2. **Predicting.** What do you think might have happened if President Nixon had not resigned and had been put on trial by the Senate?
3. **Evaluating.** During the hostage crisis in Iran in 1979-80 President Carter, acting out of desperation, sent a team of marine commandos to Iran in an attempt to rescue the hostages. Tragically the plan failed. Do you agree with the way that President Carter handled the crisis? How might he have handled it differently?

Cooperative Learning
1. Your group will prepare a pictorial essay of either a major event that occurred or a policy that was enacted in the United States from 1964 to the present. Your group will prepare an oral report to go along with the essay and choose a member of the group to present the report.
2. Working in two groups, your class will research and then prepare a debate on a current controversial topic. A speaker from each side should be chosen to present the case. After the speakers have finished, each side should present a rebuttal or final argument defending their side's point of view. Present your debate before a civic or community group.

Reading in Depth
Greene, Laura. *Computer Pioneers.* New York: Franklin Watts/First Books. Presents an account of men and women of the electronic age.

Harlan, Judith. *American Indians Today: Issues and Conflicts.* New York: Franklin Watts/Impact Books. Focuses on the problems of Native Americans today.

Lasky, Kathryn. *Home Free.* Soquel, Ca.: Four Winds Press. Contains the story of a fifteen-year-old boy and his valiant effort to protect endangered bald eagles whose home is being threatened by a developer.

Thomas, Joyce Carol. *Water Girl.* New York: Avon Books/Flare Books. Provides an account of an African American teenage girl who unwittingly comes across a piece of her own history.

Woods, Geraldine, and Harold Woods. *The Right to Bear Arms.* New York: Franklin Watts. Provides a better understanding of the debate over gun control.

REFERENCE
SECTION

T he Reference Section contains a variety of features designed to enhance your understanding of the story of America. The atlas includes a world map and several United States maps that illustrate absolute and relative locations and other geographic themes. The section of graphs and charts presents statistical profiles of major social and economic changes in American society. The glossary lists boldfaced words and their definitions. The index provides page references for the topics discussed in *The Story of America*. Source citations for the Points of View identify the work from which each excerpt was taken. Acknowledgments list the title and publisher of the primary sources used in *The Story of America*.

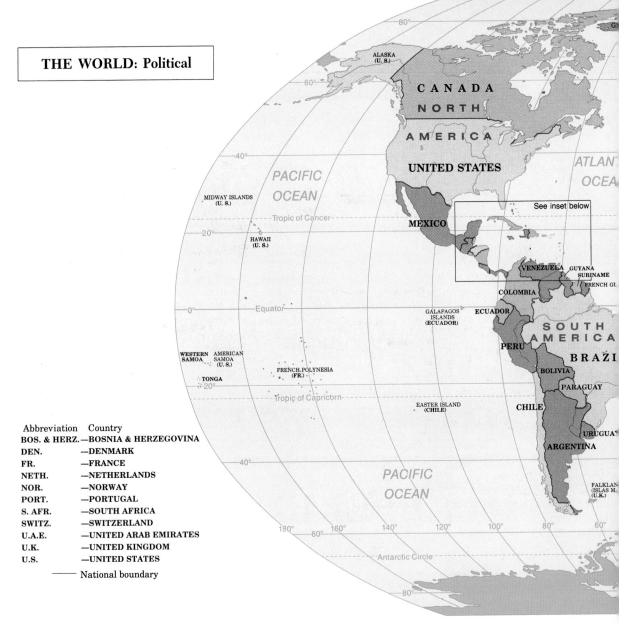

THE WORLD: Political

ALASKA (U. S.)

CANADA

NORTH

AMERICA

UNITED STATES

PACIFIC OCEAN

MIDWAY ISLANDS (U. S.)

Tropic of Cancer

MEXICO

HAWAII (U. S.)

See inset below

VENEZUELA   GUYANA
SURINAME
FRENCH GU

COLOMBIA

Equator

GALAPAGOS ISLANDS (ECUADOR)   ECUADOR

ATLAN OCEA

SOUTH
AMERICA

BRAZI

WESTERN SAMOA   AMERICAN SAMOA (U.S.)

PERU

FRENCH POLYNESIA (FR.)

BOLIVIA

TONGA

PARAGUAY

Tropic of Capricorn

EASTER ISLAND (CHILE)

CHILE

URUGUA

Abbreviation	Country
BOS. & HERZ.	—BOSNIA & HERZEGOVINA
DEN.	—DENMARK
FR.	—FRANCE
NETH.	—NETHERLANDS
NOR.	—NORWAY
PORT.	—PORTUGAL
S. AFR.	—SOUTH AFRICA
SWITZ.	—SWITZERLAND
U.A.E.	—UNITED ARAB EMIRATES
U.K.	—UNITED KINGDOM
U.S.	—UNITED STATES
——	National boundary

ARGENTINA

FALKLAN (ISLAS M. (U.K.)

PACIFIC OCEAN

Antarctic Circle

Central America and West Indies

Gulf of Mexico

FLORIDA (U.S.)

BAHAMAS

Tropic of Cancer

CUBA

ATLANTIC   OCEAN

MEXICO

BELIZE

HAITI   DOMINICAN REPUBLIC

VIRGIN ISLANDS (U.S., U.K.)

JAMAICA

PUERTO RICO (U. S.)

ANTIGUA & BARBUDA

Caribbean

ST. KITTS & NEVIS

GUADELOUPE (FR.)

GUATEMALA   HONDURAS

Sea

N

DOMINICA

EL SALVADOR

NICARAGUA

NETHERLANDS ANTILLES (NETH.)

ST. LUCIA

MARTINIQUE (FR.)

ST. VINCENT AND THE GRENADINES

BARBADOS

PACIFIC OCEAN

GRENADA

COSTA RICA

VENEZUELA

TRINIDAD & TOBAGO

PANAMA

COLOMBIA

GUYANA

0   200   400 Miles

0   200   400 Kilometers

MERCATOR PROJECTION

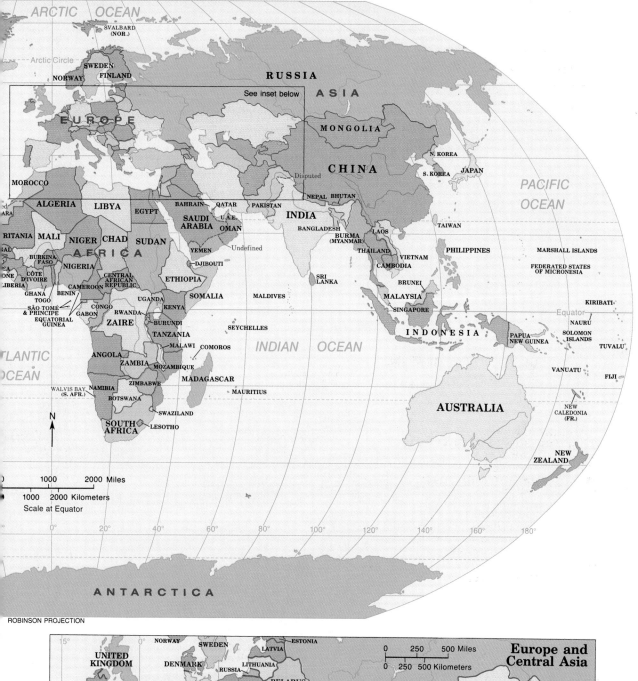

ROBINSON PROJECTION

MERCATOR PROJECTION

PACIFIC TIME

MOUNTAIN TIME

CENTRAL TIME

• Seattle
River
Olympia
WASHINGTON

RANGE

Columbia
• Portland
★ Salem

CASCADE

OREGON

IDAHO

★ Boise

Snake   *River*

Helena ★

MONTANA

• Billings

ROCKY

WYOMING

NORTH DAKO

★ Bismarck

BLACK HILLS

SOUTH DAK

• Pierre

Si

NEBRASKA

COASTAL

SIERRA

• Carson City

NEVADA

★ Sacramento
• San Francisco

NEVADA

RANGE

CALIFORNIA

Great Salt Lake

Salt Lake City ★

UTAH

Cheyenne ★

MOUNTAINS

★ Denver

COLORADO

KANSA

W

Las Vegas

River

• Los Angeles

Colorado

ARIZONA

• San Diego

Santa Fe ★

Albuquerque •

NEW MEXICO

• Amarillo

Ok

OKLA

• Lubbock

★ Phoenix

• Tucson

PACIFIC

OCEAN

30°

120°

110°

• El Paso

TEXAS

HAWAII TIME

Kauai
160°
Nihau   Oahu ● Honolulu
              Molokai
H A W A I I   Lanai   Maui
PACIFIC
OCEAN   20°   Hawaii
160°
0   100 Miles
0   100 Kilometers

150°

ARCTIC OCEAN

70°

Arctic Circle

ALASKA

Yukon   *River*
          • Fairbanks

Mt. McKinley
20,320 ft
6,194 m

• Anchorage

30°

60°

60°

Aus

San Antonio •

Rio

Grande

Bering Sea

50°   0   250   500 Miles
170° 0   250   500 Kilometers

170°

PACIFIC OCEAN

50°

ALEUTIAN   ISLANDS

150°

Juneau ★

Gulf of Alaska

ALASKA TIME

130°

100°

EASTERN
TIME

MAINE
★ Augusta

VERMONT
★ Montpelier

NEW
HAMPSHIRE
★ Concord

Albany ★
• Boston

MASSACHUSETTS
Hartford ★ ★ Providence
RHODE
CONNECTICUT ISLAND

Duluth •
ESOTA

Lake Superior

MICHIGAN

Lake Huron

Lake Michigan

Lansing ★

Detroit •

Lake Erie

Rochester •
Buffalo •

NEW YORK

New York •

40°

•apolis • ★ St. Paul
Mississippi
WISCONSIN

Milwaukee ★
Madison

Chicago •
Gary •

OHIO

Columbus •

Cleveland •

PENNSYLVANIA

Pittsburgh •

Harrisburg ★

Philadelphia •
NEW
JERSEY
★ Trenton

Wilmington •
★ Dover
DELAWARE

70°

IOWA

• Des Moines

ILLINOIS

Springfield ★

INDIANA

★ Indianapolis

Cincinnati •

Baltimore •
Washington ◉ ★ Annapolis
**WEST
VIRGINIA**

MARYLAND

Kansas
City •

St. Louis •

★ Frankfort
Louisville •

Charleston ★

Richmond ★

Chesapeake Bay

Norfolk •

ATLANTIC

Jefferson
City ★

Ohio River

KENTUCKY

VIRGINIA

OCEAN

MISSOURI

★ Nashville

TENNESSEE

Raleigh ★

**NORTH
CAROLINA**

ARKANSAS

Memphis •

Tennessee River

Charlotte •

Little ★
Rock

Mississippi River

Birmingham •

Atlanta ★

SOUTH

★ Columbia

CAROLINA

Charleston •

UNITED STATES: PHYSICAL

⊛ National capital
★ State capital
• Other city
—— National boundary
—— State boundary

★ Jackson

ALABAMA

★ Montgomery

GEORGIA

Savannah •

Standard time zones are indicated by
clocks. (When it is 2 P.M. in western
Alaska, it is 6 P.M. along the eastern
coast of the United States.)

MISSISSIPPI

Red River

Mobile •

Jacksonville •

30°

Albers Equal-Area Projection

LOUISIANA

★ Baton Rouge

New Orleans •

•ouston

★ Tallahassee

FLORIDA

Orlando •

Gulf of Mexico

N

Tampa •

Miami •

0   250   500 Miles
0   250   500 Kilometers

90°

80°

1131

This photograph of North America taken by a satellite in space gives you an interesting perspective of the continent and the United States. Large physical features such as the Great Lakes are easily identifiable.

1133

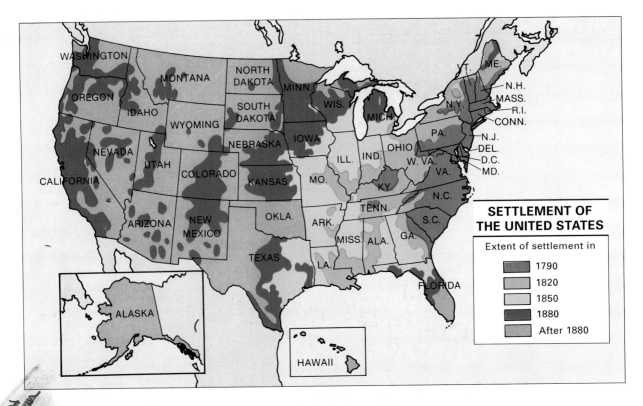

SETTLEMENT OF THE UNITED STATES

Extent of settlement in

- 1790
- 1820
- 1850
- 1880
- After 1880

ALASKA

HAWAII

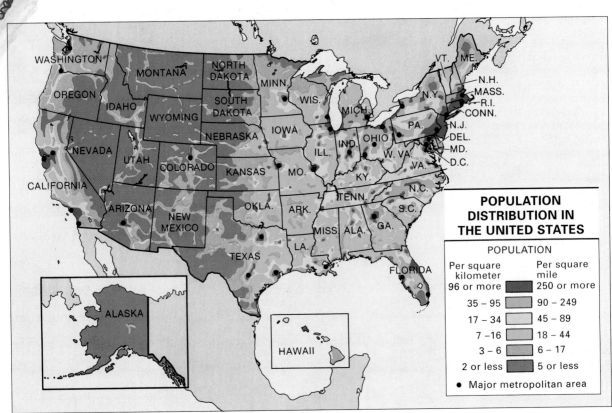

POPULATION DISTRIBUTION IN THE UNITED STATES

POPULATION

Per square kilometer	Per square mile
96 or more	250 or more
35 – 95	90 – 249
17 – 34	45 – 89
7 – 16	18 – 44
3 – 6	6 – 17
2 or less	5 or less

● Major metropolitan area

ALASKA

HAWAII

FACTS ABOUT THE STATES

State	Year of Statehood	1990 Population	Reps. in Congress	Area (Sq. mi.)	Population Density (Sq. mi.)	Capital	Largest City
Alabama	1819	4,040,587	7	51,705	79.6	Montgomery	Birmingham
Alaska	1959	550,043	1	591,004	1.0	Juneau	Anchorage
Arizona	1912	3,665,228	6	114,000	32.3	Phoenix	Phoenix
Arkansas	1836	2,350,725	4	53,187	45.1	Little Rock	Little Rock
California	1850	29,760,021	52	158,706	190.8	Sacramento	Los Angeles
Colorado	1876	3,294,394	6	104,091	31.8	Denver	Denver
Connecticut	1788	3,287,116	6	5,018	678.4	Hartford	Bridgeport
Delaware	1787	666,168	1	2,045	340.8	Dover	Wilmington
District of Columbia	—	606,900	—	69	9,882.8	—	Washington
Florida	1845	12,937,926	23	58,664	239.6	Tallahassee	Jacksonville
Georgia	1788	6,478,216	11	58,910	111.9	Atlanta	Atlanta
Hawaii	1959	1,108,229	2	6,471	172.5	Honolulu	Honolulu
Idaho	1890	1,006,749	2	83,564	12.2	Boise	Boise
Illinois	1818	11,430,602	20	56,345	205.6	Springfield	Chicago
Indiana	1816	5,544,159	10	36,185	154.6	Indianapolis	Indianapolis
Iowa	1846	2,776,755	5	56,275	49.7	Des Moines	Des Moines
Kansas	1861	2,477,574	4	82,277	30.3	Topeka	Wichita
Kentucky	1792	3,685,296	6	40,410	92.8	Frankfort	Louisville
Louisiana	1812	4,219,973	7	47,752	96.9	Baton Rouge	New Orleans
Maine	1820	1,227,928	2	33,265	39.8	Augusta	Portland
Maryland	1788	4,781,468	8	10,460	489.2	Annapolis	Baltimore
Massachusetts	1788	6,016,425	10	8,284	767.6	Boston	Boston
Michigan	1837	9,295,297	16	58,527	163.6	Lansing	Detroit
Minnesota	1858	4,375,099	8	84,402	55.0	St. Paul	Minneapolis
Mississippi	1817	2,573,216	5	47,689	54.9	Jackson	Jackson
Missouri	1821	5,117,073	9	69,697	74.3	Jefferson City	Kansas City
Montana	1889	799,065	1	147,046	5.5	Helena	Billings
Nebraska	1867	1,578,385	3	77,355	20.5	Lincoln	Omaha
Nevada	1864	1,201,833	2	110,561	10.9	Carson City	Las Vegas
New Hampshire	1788	1,109,252	2	9,279	123.7	Concord	Manchester
New Jersey	1787	7,730,188	13	7,787	1,042.0	Trenton	Newark
New Mexico	1912	1,515,069	3	121,593	12.5	Santa Fe	Albuquerque
New York	1788	17,990,455	31	49,108	381.0	Albany	New York City
North Carolina	1789	6,628,637	12	52,669	136.1	Raleigh	Charlotte
North Dakota	1889	638,800	1	70,702	9.3	Bismarck	Fargo
Ohio	1803	10,847,115	19	41,330	264.9	Columbus	Columbus
Oklahoma	1907	3,145,585	6	69,956	45.8	Oklahoma City	Oklahoma City
Oregon	1859	2,842,321	5	97,073	29.6	Salem	Portland
Pennsylvania	1787	11,881,643	21	45,308	265.1	Harrisburg	Philadelphia
Rhode Island	1790	1,003,464	2	1,212	960.3	Providence	Providence
South Carolina	1788	3,486,703	6	31,113	115.8	Columbia	Columbia
South Dakota	1889	696,004	1	77,116	9.2	Pierre	Sioux Falls
Tennessee	1796	4,877,185	9	42,144	118.3	Nashville	Memphis
Texas	1845	16,986,510	30	266,807	64.9	Austin	Houston
Utah	1896	1,722,850	3	84,899	21.0	Salt Lake City	Salt Lake City
Vermont	1791	562,758	1	9,614	60.8	Montpelier	Burlington
Virginia	1788	6,187,358	11	40,767	156.3	Richmond	Virginia Beach
Washington	1889	4,866,692	9	68,139	73.1	Olympia	Seattle
West Virginia	1863	1,793,477	3	24,232	74.5	Charleston	Charleston
Wisconsin	1848	4,891,769	9	56,153	90.1	Madison	Milwaukee
Wyoming	1890	453,588	1	97,809	4.7	Cheyenne	Cheyenne

PRESIDENTS OF THE UNITED STATES

No.	Name	Born–Died	Years in Office	Political Party	Home State	Vice President
1	George Washington	1732–1799	1789–97	None	Va.	John Adams
2	John Adams	1735–1826	1797–1801	Federalist	Mass.	Thomas Jefferson
3	Thomas Jefferson	1743–1826	1801–09	Republican*	Va.	Aaron Burr
						George Clinton
4	James Madison	1751–1836	1809–17	Republican	Va.	George Clinton
						Elbridge Gerry
5	James Monroe	1758–1831	1817–25	Republican	Va.	Daniel D. Tompkins
6	John Quincy Adams	1767–1848	1825–29	Republican	Mass.	John C. Calhoun
7	Andrew Jackson	1767–1845	1829–37	Democratic	Tenn.	John C. Calhoun
						Martin Van Buren
8	Martin Van Buren	1782–1862	1837–41	Democratic	N.Y.	Richard M. Johnson
9	William Henry Harrison	1773–1841	1841	Whig	Ohio	John Tyler
10	John Tyler	1790–1862	1841–45	Whig	Va.	
11	James K. Polk	1795–1849	1845–49	Democratic	Tenn.	George M. Dallas
12	Zachary Taylor	1784–1850	1849–50	Whig	La.	Millard Fillmore
13	Millard Fillmore	1800–1874	1850–53	Whig	N.Y.	
14	Franklin Pierce	1804–1869	1853–57	Democratic	N.H.	William R. King
15	James Buchanan	1791–1868	1857–61	Democratic	Pa.	John C. Breckenridge
16	Abraham Lincoln	1809–1865	1861–65	Republican	Ill.	Hannibal Hamlin
						Andrew Johnson
17	Andrew Johnson	1808–1875	1865–69	Republican	Tenn.	
18	Ulysses S. Grant	1822–1885	1869–77	Republican	Ill.	Schuyler Colfax
						Henry Wilson
19	Rutherford B. Hayes	1822–1893	1877–81	Republican	Ohio	William A. Wheeler
20	James A. Garfield	1831–1881	1881	Republican	Ohio	Chester A. Arthur
21	Chester A. Arthur	1830–1886	1881–85	Republican	N.Y.	
22	Grover Cleveland	1837–1908	1885–89	Democratic	N.Y.	Thomas A. Hendricks
23	Benjamin Harrison	1833–1901	1889–93	Republican	Ind.	Levi P. Morton
24	Grover Cleveland		1893–97	Democratic	N.Y.	Adlai E. Stevenson
25	William McKinley	1843–1901	1897–1901	Republican	Ohio	Garrett A. Hobart
						Theodore Roosevelt
26	Theodore Roosevelt	1858–1919	1901–09	Republican	N.Y.	
						Charles W. Fairbanks
27	William Howard Taft	1857–1930	1909–13	Republican	Ohio	James S. Sherman
28	Woodrow Wilson	1856–1924	1913–21	Democratic	N.J.	Thomas R. Marshall
29	Warren G. Harding	1865–1923	1921–23	Republican	Ohio	Calvin Coolidge
30	Calvin Coolidge	1872–1933	1923–29	Republican	Mass.	
						Charles G. Dawes
31	Herbert Hoover	1874–1964	1929–33	Republican	Calif.	Charles Curtis
32	Franklin D. Roosevelt	1882–1945	1933–45	Democratic	N.Y.	John Nance Garner
						Henry Wallace
						Harry S Truman
33	Harry S Truman	1884–1972	1945–53	Democratic	Mo.	
						Alben W. Barkley
34	Dwight D. Eisenhower	1890–1969	1953–61	Republican	Kans.	Richard M. Nixon
35	John F. Kennedy	1917–1963	1961–63	Democratic	Mass.	Lyndon B. Johnson
36	Lyndon B. Johnson	1908–1973	1963–69	Democratic	Texas	
						Hubert H. Humphrey
37	Richard M. Nixon	1913–	1969–74	Republican	Calif.	Spiro T. Agnew
						Gerald R. Ford
38	Gerald R. Ford	1913–	1974–77	Republican	Mich.	Nelson A. Rockefeller
39	Jimmy Carter	1924–	1977–81	Democratic	Ga.	Walter F. Mondale
40	Ronald Reagan	1911–	1981–89	Republican	Calif.	George H.W. Bush
41	George H.W. Bush	1924–	1989–1993	Republican	Texas	J. Danforth Quayle
42	Bill Clinton	1946–	1993–	Democratic	Ark.	Albert Gore, Jr.

*The Republican party of the third through sixth presidents is not the party of Abraham Lincoln, which was founded in 1854.

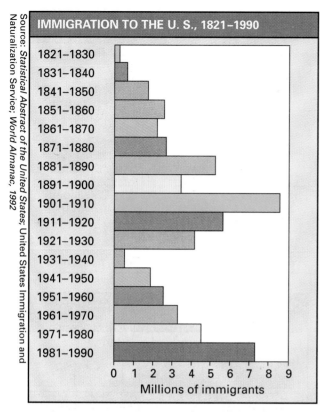

IMMIGRATION TO THE U. S., 1821–1990

Source: Statistical Abstract of the United States; United States Immigration and Naturalization Service; World Almanac, 1992

1821–1830	
1831–1840	
1841–1850	
1851–1860	
1861–1870	
1871–1880	
1881–1890	
1891–1900	
1901–1910	
1911–1920	
1921–1930	
1931–1940	
1941–1950	
1951–1960	
1961–1970	
1971–1980	
1981–1990	

Millions of immigrants

As the graphs on this page indicate, the United States has a rich and varied racial and cultural heritage. This rich heritage is due in large part to immigration. Prior to World War II the majority of immigrants to the United States came from Europe. The Immigration Act of 1965, however, made it easier for non-Europeans to enter the United States. As a result, people from Central and South America, the Caribbean, and Asia now make up the majority of new immigrants.

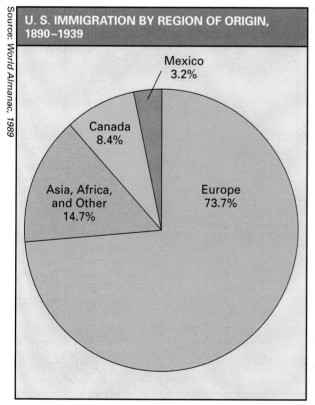

U. S. IMMIGRATION BY REGION OF ORIGIN, 1890–1939

Source: World Almanac, 1989

Mexico 3.2%
Canada 8.4%
Asia, Africa, and Other 14.7%
Europe 73.7%

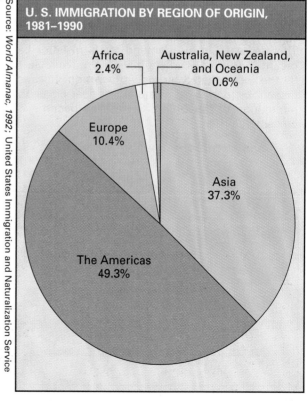

U. S. IMMIGRATION BY REGION OF ORIGIN, 1981–1990

Source: World Almanac, 1992; United States Immigration and Naturalization Service

Africa 2.4%
Australia, New Zealand, and Oceania 0.6%
Europe 10.4%
Asia 37.3%
The Americas 49.3%

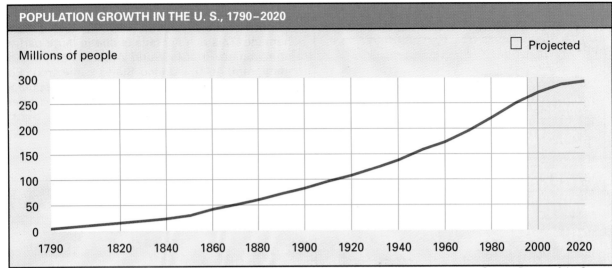

POPULATION GROWTH IN THE U. S., 1790–2020

☐ Projected

Millions of people

Source: Bureau of the Census

Technology also has helped shape American society. The graphs on this page illustrate some of the social consequences of new technologies. Advances in medicine and public sanitation, for instance, have increased the number of years most people live. As a result, the population of the United States has grown. More efficient farming methods have reduced the number of farmers needed to produce food for the American people. This decrease in the demand for farm labor has meant that more workers have been available to fill the jobs created by industrialization. Because these jobs tend to be located in or near cities, the population of the United States has become increasingly urban.

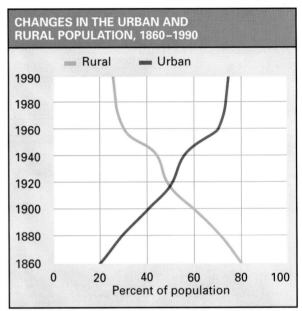

CHANGES IN THE URBAN AND RURAL POPULATION, 1860–1990

Rural   Urban

Percent of population

Source: Bureau of the Census

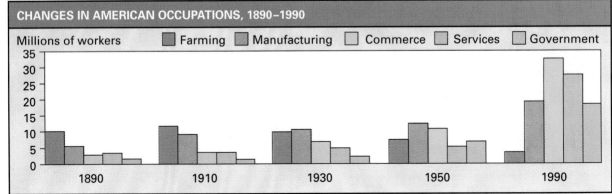

CHANGES IN AMERICAN OCCUPATIONS, 1890–1990

Millions of workers   ■ Farming   ■ Manufacturing   ☐ Commerce   ■ Services   ■ Government

Source: U.S. Dept. of Agriculture; *Monthly Labor Review*

Over its history the United States has enjoyed strong economic growth. Not everyone in society, however, has shared equally in this prosperity. This is evident when one examines the graphs on family income and unemployment on this page. On average, white Americans have enjoyed the highest family incomes and the lowest rates of unemployment.

Social Security and other government programs have made the retirement years more secure for most older Americans. As the graph on the over-65 population indicates, however, the number of elderly is expected to increase over the next few decades. This increase will place new pressures on the government to develop ways to meet the needs of older Americans.

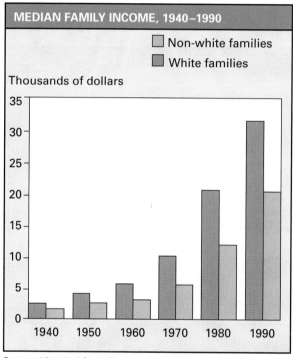

MEDIAN FAMILY INCOME, 1940–1990

Source: *Historical Statistics of the United States; Statistical Abstract of the United States, 1988*; Bureau of the Census, 1990

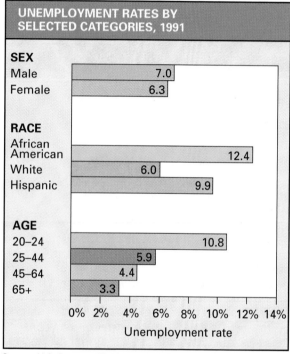

UNEMPLOYMENT RATES BY SELECTED CATEGORIES, 1991

Source: U.S. Bureau of Labor Statistics

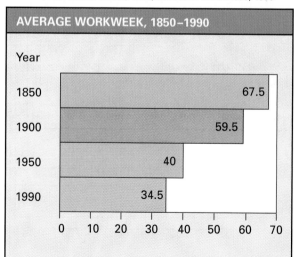

AVERAGE WORKWEEK, 1850–1990

Source: *Statistical Abstract of the United States, 1989*; U.S. Bureau of Labor Statistics

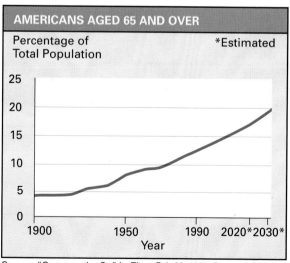

AMERICANS AGED 65 AND OVER

Source: "Grays on the Go" in *Time*, Feb.22, 1988; Bureau of the Census, 1990

The federal government must have enough money to finance its programs and activities. The money the government collects for this purpose is called receipts. Most government receipts are in the form of taxes. The money the government spends is referred to as outlays. As can be seen from the graph at the top left, in recent decades the federal government has spent more than it has taken in. This shortfall is called a budget deficit. When the federal government experiences a budget deficit, it must borrow money to finance its spending. This borrowed money is called the national debt. As the graph on the top right shows, paying the interest on the national debt is a major outlay for the federal government.

In recent years, the United States also has experienced a trade deficit. A trade deficit occurs when a nation imports more than it exports. The graph at the bottom of the page shows the relationship between United States import and export values since 1950. The inset traces the rise and fall of United States tariffs.

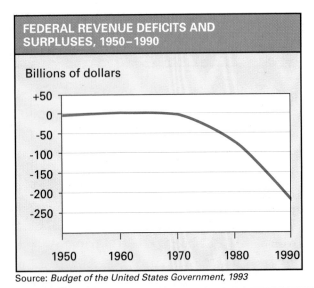

FEDERAL REVENUE DEFICITS AND SURPLUSES, 1950–1990

Billions of dollars

Source: *Budget of the United States Government, 1993*

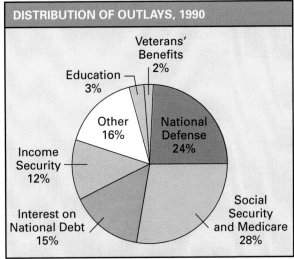

DISTRIBUTION OF OUTLAYS, 1990

- Veterans' Benefits 2%
- Education 3%
- Other 16%
- National Defense 24%
- Income Security 12%
- Interest on National Debt 15%
- Social Security and Medicare 28%

Source: *Statistical Abstract of the United States, 1991*

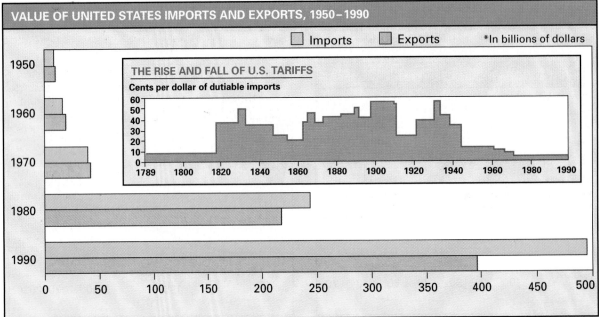

VALUE OF UNITED STATES IMPORTS AND EXPORTS, 1950–1990

Imports   Exports   *In billions of dollars

THE RISE AND FALL OF U.S. TARIFFS

Cents per dollar of dutiable imports

Source: *Statistical Abstract of the United States, 1991*

All societies must face the fact that the resources needed to produce goods and services are limited. Thus each society must decide how best to use its limited resources. A society makes this decision by answering three basic economic questions: (1) What goods and services should be produced? (2) How should these goods and services be produced? (3) For whom should these goods and services be produced?

In the United States these three questions are answered in a free-market environment. By free market, we mean that people are free to produce, sell, and buy whatever they wish and to work for whomever they want. What goods and services are actually produced, however, is determined by the forces of supply and demand. Producers supply those goods and services that are demanded by consumers.

Over time, changes in technology and in the types of goods and services available from other markets around the world have altered the nature of business and industry.

MAJOR ADVANCES IN AMERICAN BUSINESS AND INDUSTRY

	1607–1783	1783–1850	1850–1900	1900–1920	1920–Present
Power	Human muscles Animals' muscles Wind and water power	Steam power	Electric power Internal combustion engines		Atomic energy Geothermal energy
Manufacturing Materials	Copper, bronze, iron Wood Clay Plant and animal fibers	Large-scale production of iron	Large-scale production of steel Development of combustion fuels: coal, oil, gas	Large-scale production of light metals and alloys Development of plastics and synthetics	Large-scale production of plastics and synthetics
Factory Methods	Handforges and tools Hand-powered equipment	Machinery powered by water and steam Interchangeable parts	Mass production, with centralized assembly of interchangeable parts	Conveyor-belt assembly line	Automation Computer-operated machinery
Agriculture	Wooden plows Spades and hoes Axes and other hand tools	Iron and steel plows Cotton gin Mowing, threshing, and haying machines	McCormick reaper Barbed-wire fencing	Scientific agriculture	Large-scale mechanized agriculture Corporation farms
Transportation	Horses Animal-drawn vehicles Sailing vessels	Canals Clipper ships Development of railroads and steamships	Large-scale steamship and railroad lines City trolleys, elevated trains	Automobiles, trucks, and buses Development of propeller-driven aircraft	Space exploration Monorail trains Supersonic airplanes
Communication	Hand-operated printing presses Newspapers	Mechanized printing pressess Telegraph Mass-circulation books and magazines	Transatlantic cable Telephones Phonographs Typewriters Cameras	Motion pictures Radios	Television Transistors Computers Compact discs Lasers Satellite transmissions FAX machines
Merchandising and Business Organization	Small shops Peddlers	Individual and family-owned factories and mills General stores	Chain stores Mail-order houses Growth of corporations Trusts	National advertising Holding companies	Shopping malls Conglomerate corporations Multinational corporations

OUR LIVING HERITAGE

One of the best ways to use your historical imagination is by visiting the sites of important events or the homes of famous people. The places listed here are but a few of the many historic sites in the United States. For more information about sites in your community or state, write your county or state historical society.

Many of the sites listed below are under the care of the federal government. These national historic locales are abbreviated **NMP** for military parks, **NHP** for historic parks, **NHL** for landmark, **NHB** for battlefields, **NHS** for sites, and **NM** for national monuments. Page references are included to help you review the importance of the sites described in this book. For further information write the appropriate regional office of the National Park Service.

Western Region, 450 Golden Gate Avenue, San Francisco, CA 94102; **Midwest Region,** 1709 Jackson, Omaha, NB 68102; **North Atlantic Region,** 15 State Street, Boston, MA 02109; **National Capital Region,** 1100 Ohio Drive, SW, Washington, DC 20242; **Southeast Region,** 75 Spring Street, SW, Atlanta, GA 30303; **Rocky Mountain Region,** 655 Parfet Street, PO Box 25287, Denver, CO 80225; **Southwest Region,** PO Box 728, Santa Fe, NM 87501; **Pacific Northwest Region,** Westin Building, Room 1920, Seattle, WA 98121; **Alaska Area,** 540 West 5th Avenue, Room 202, Anchorage, AK 95501.

ALABAMA
Horseshoe Bend NMP north of Dadeville is the site of Andrew Jackson's victory over the Creek nation in 1814. The visitor center has exhibits of Creek culture and frontier life. **307**

Tuskegee Institute NHS in Tuskegee is the site of the pioneer school founded for blacks in 1881 by Booker T. Washington. **617**

Alabama Space and Rocket Center in Huntsville features exhibits including simulated travel to the moon and tours of the Marshall Space Flight Center. **1005**

The First White House of the Confederacy and the **Alabama State Capitol** in Montgomery commemorate the role of Jefferson Davis as president of the Confederacy. **544**

ALASKA
Alaskaland-Pioneer Park in Fairbanks is a 40-acre park recreating a gold rush town and an Indian village. **The University of Alaska Museum** in Fairbanks has displays on Eskimo culture as well as on Russian and gold rush history of the state.

Sitka NHP north of Sitka is a memorial to the Tlingit Indians. The visitor center also has exhibits on life during the time Russia owned Alaska. **740**

ARIZONA
Tombstone NHS preserves this silver rush town of the 1880s. Visitors can see exhibits of the town's history at Schieffelin Hall and the Wells Fargo Museum and tour the underground silver mines.

The Heard Museum of Anthropology and Primitive Art in Phoenix displays arts and crafts of southwestern Indians and Mexicans. It has exhibits on South American cultures and Spanish colonial days.

Casa Grande Ruins in Casa Grande, **Montezuma Castle** east of Prescott, and the **Navajo National Monument** east of Kaibab all have ruins of prehistoric Indian cultures.

ARKANSAS
Arkansas Territorial Restoration in downtown Little Rock is one of the nation's finest, consisting of 13 buildings dating from the 1820s and 1830s.

Ozark Folk Center at Mountain Valley is an 80-acre living museum that features arts, crafts, music, and Ozarks lore.

Fort Smith NHS features Indian and pioneer artifacts in the commissary building, all that remains of a fort that was famous as a gateway to the West.

CALIFORNIA
Hearst San Simeon State Historic Park south of Monterey contains the castle built by publishing tycoon William Randolph Hearst and designed by Julia Morgan. **753**

Marshall Gold Discovery State Historic Site at Coloma, near Sacramento, is where the Gold Rush began in 1848. Attractions include Sutter's Mill, Marshall's cabin, a museum, and the Wah Hop store, which explains the role of the Chinese in the Gold Rush. **432**

Sutter's Fort NHL in Sacramento is a recontruction of that early settlement. The **State Indian Museum** is also located in Sacramento. **431**

Santa Barbara Mission NHL at Santa Barbara is one of the 21 missions founded by Father Junípero Serra. It has a fine collection of original mission treasures. **426**

Bodie NHL near Bridgeport is a ghost town of 170 buildings, reminders of its Gold Rush days. **432**

Fort Ross NHL near Jenner is a restoration of a Russian fort used by seal and otter hunters on the Pacific. **376**

COLORADO
Central City is the site of Colorado's first important gold discovery in 1859. **Cripple Creek, Telluride,** and **Georgetown** are other restored mining towns. **639**

Mesa Verde National Park near Cortez contains hundreds of dwellings inhabited by Indians between 400 and 1300 A.D. **6**

Bent's Old Fort NHS near La Junta preserves a fort and trading post on the Santa Fe Trail. **430**

CONNECTICUT
Old New-Gate Prison in East Granby was originally a copper mine opened in 1707. It was used during the

Revolutionary War to house prisoners of war. Attractions include the prison yard with its scaffold, a museum, and tours of the restored mine and dungeons.

Mystic Seaport and Museum is one of the oldest shipbuilding and whaling ports in the U.S. The seaport preserves the atmosphere of a mid-19th century New England maritime village. At berth is the *Charles W. Morgan*, the last of the 19th-century wooden whaleships.

DELAWARE

Henry Francis du Pont Winterthur Museum in Winterthur contains almost 200 period rooms and displays devoted to American furniture and decorative arts.

The Delaware State Museum in Dover has exhibits on state history, the plantation home of Revolutionary War leader John Dickinson, and the Octagonal School House, a restored school house built in 1836.

Fort Christina NHL in Wilmington marks the landing place of Swedish colonists in 1638. **63**

DISTRICT OF COLUMBIA

The White House, home of every president but Washington, has tours of its splendid public rooms. **270**

The Smithsonian Institution includes the National Air and Space Museum, showing the history of aviation and space travel, the National Collection of Fine Arts; the National Portrait Gallery, from which many portraits in this book were obtained; and the National Museum of History and Technology.

The Library of Congress began with the purchase of Thomas Jefferson's library. On display are Jefferson's rough draft of the Declaration of Independence and Lincoln's drafts of the Gettysburg Address.

The National Archives displays the original Declaration of Independence, the Constitution, and the Bill of Rights.

The U.S. Capitol, seat of Congress, features murals of historic events and statues of presidents and other famous Americans. **270**

Vietnam Veterans Memorial NM in the Congressional Gardens features a black granite wall with the names of those Americans who died in the Vietnam War. **1079**

The Supreme Court Building, seat of the Supreme Court, features murals of the chief justices and other exhibits detailing Court history. **273**

FLORIDA

Cape Canaveral Air Force Station and **John F. Kennedy Space Center,** both near Titusville, are the launching sites of the U.S. manned space flights and the space shuttle. There are tours of the Moon Launch Pad, Vehicle Assembly Building, Mission Control Center, and the Air Force Museum. **1043**

St. Augustine NHL reflects the Spanish heritage of the oldest city in the U.S. The city has many restored buildings and ships. **117**

GEORGIA

New Echota in Calhoun is a restoration of the Cherokee capital. It explains the Cherokees' efforts to establish a republican form of government. **393**

Fort Benning in Columbus has exhibits of U.S. history from the Revolutionary War to the present.

Andersonville NHS preserves this infamous Civil War prison camp.

HAWAII

Pu'uhonua o Honaunau (City of Refuge) NHP features exhibits on life in Hawaii before outsiders arrived in the 1700s.

U.S.S. *Arizona* NM at Pearl Harbor on Oahu is the site of the Japanese bombardment on December 7, 1941. **950**

IDAHO

Massacre Rocks State Park west of American Falls marks an 1862 ambush on a wagon train on the Oregon Trail.

Nez Perce NHP near Spaulding contains 23 historic sites showing the tribe's history and culture. **634**

Fort Hall NHL north of Pocatello is a reconstruction of a fort that was important in the westward migration.

ILLINOIS

Nauvoo Restoration was a Fox Indian village until the Mormons arrived in 1839. **427**

Among Chicago's great museums are the **Chicago Historical Society,** which recreates the Great Chicago Fire, and the **Art Institute,** with its splendid American art.

The Ulysses S. Grant Home is in Galena, once the wealthiest city in Illinois. **580**

Springfield has memorials to Abraham Lincoln including the **Lincoln Home** and the **Old State Capitol** NHL where Lincoln served in the state legislature. Nearby is **New Salem State Park,** a reconstruction of the town as Lincoln knew it in the 1830s. **531**

INDIANA

Lincoln Boyhood National Memorial south of Lincoln City and **Lincoln Pioneer Village** in Rockport preserve the childhood residences of Abraham Lincoln. **377**

The Benjamin Harrison Home NHL in Indianapolis features many of the original furnishings in the home of the 23rd president. **712**

Vincennes, the oldest town in Indiana, has many historic sites, including George Rogers Clark NHP and Grouseland, the home of William Henry Harrison. **173**

The Tippecanoe County Historical Museum in Lafayette has relics of the Battle of Tippecanoe. **299**

IOWA

Herbert Hoover NHS in West Branch features the two-room cottage where the 31st president was born and his presidential library. **889**

The Living History Farm near Des Moines is a working pioneer farm with an 1870 mansion.

Amana Village NHL west of Iowa City gives a view of life in this ideal community founded in the 19th century. **490**

KANSAS

Dodge City, founded in 1872, features Boot Hill; Old Fort Dodge Jail, which houses a museum; and a replica of Old Front Street. **647**

Pawnee Indian Village in Belleville features Pawnee earth lodges from the early 1800s and a museum. **623**

Dwight D. Eisenhower Home in Abilene is the boyhood home of the 34th president and site of his library. **1001**

The John Brown Memorial Park and **John Brown Cabin** in Osawatomie commemorate the abolitionist in Kansas. **522**

KENTUCKY

Cumberland Gap NHP south of Middlesboro marks this pathway to the West first blazed by Daniel Boone. The park includes parts of Boone's Wilderness Road and Hensley Settlement, a reconstructed mountain community. **349**

The Appalachian Museum in Berea features a smokehouse, blacksmith shop, and a country store.

Ashland NHL, a reconstruction of Henry Clay's mansion, is in Lexington. His law office may also be visited. **379**

LOUISIANA

New Orleans Jazz Museum traces the history of jazz and honors jazz greats like Louis Armstrong. **870**

The Vieux Carre Historic District in New Orleans preserves the flavor of the city when it was Spanish and French. Among landmarks are the Cabildo and Jackson Square, where the U.S. flag was first raised over Louisiana Territory. **277**

Chalmette NHP near New Orleans marks the site of the Battle of New Orleans. **310**

MAINE

Shaker Village near Poland is maintained as a living museum of life in this religious community. **490**

Boothbay Railway Museum, the **Grand Banks Schooner Museum,** and the **Boothbay Regional Museum** are all in Boothbay.

The Old Conway House Complex in Camden is an 18th-century farmhouse and restored community.

The Bath Maritime Museum honors the state's ties to the sea. Several grand mansions also stand in Bath.

Roosevelt Campobello International Park on Campobello Island features the summer home of Franklin and Eleanor Roosevelt. **903**

MARYLAND

The U.S. Frigate *Constellation* NHL, the nation's oldest warship, is in Baltimore. **Mount Clare Station** is the nation's first railroad station and the **Baltimore & Ohio Transportation Museum** has a collection of antique railroad engines and cars. **The Peale Museum** NHL features paintings by the Peales, several of which appear in this book. **302**

Fort McHenry NM in Baltimore is the site where Francis Scott Key composed "The Star-Spangled Banner" during the War of 1812. **310**

Antietam National Battlefield near Sharpsburg marks the site of a decisive but costly battle of the Civil War. **568**

MASSACHUSETTS

Lexington Green NHL commemorates the Battle of Lexington and Concord. Nearby are the Buckman Tavern, where the Minute Men gathered before battle, Hancock-Clarke House, where Sam Adams and John Hancock stayed, and Monroe Tavern, headquarters of the British troops. **143**

Freedom Trail in Boston takes visitors past many historic sites, including Faneuil Hall, Paul Revere's House, Old North Church, and the Old State House. At the Boston Naval Shipyard is the U.S.S. *Constitution.* **302**

Among the numerous restored, recreated, or preserved historic towns are **Old Deerfield** (117), **Hancock, Shaker Village** near Pittsfield (490), **Plymouth Plantation** at Plymouth (53), **Quincy** with the Adams NHS (256), **Salem,** and **Old Sturbridge Village.**

Lowell NHP features seven mills, a canal, and the 19th-century buildings of a factory town. **339**

MICHIGAN

Greenfield Village in Dearborn is a recreated American community of the early 19th century. The Henry Ford Museum includes exhibits on American arts and crafts.

The International Afro-American Museum in Detroit tells the history of blacks in America. Also in Detroit are the **Historical Museum** and **Fort Wayne Military Museum.**

Mackinaw Island NHL features many historic buildings, including one of the oldest existing forts in the U.S.

The Gerald R. Ford Museum in Grand Rapids has presidential papers. **1089**

MINNESOTA

Winona is an old steamboat town which features an 1898 Mississippi riverboat at the **Steamboat Museum,** the **Bunnell House,** a pioneer home, and a country museum.

Old Mendota, the oldest permanent settlement in the state, has historic buildings that recall the days when Mendota was a trading post village.

Fort Snelling State Park NHL has been restored near Minneapolis and St. Paul. **The Gibbs Farm Museum** in St. Paul features the farm's original equipment.

MISSISSIPPI

Natchez features many historical sites, including a number of ante-bellum mansion, reflecting its steamboat days. Attractions include Connelly's Tavern, Stanton Hall, and Longwood.

Beauvoir near Biloxi was the home of Jefferson Davis after the Civil War. **544**

Vicksburg National Military Park features extensive remains of breastworks and gun emplacements. **579**

Old Natchez Trace Museum is near Tupelo. The trace was a road used by people who floated their goods down the Mississippi.

MISSOURI
The Trail of Tears State Park near Cape Giradeau contains part of the trail taken by the Cherokees in 1838. 394

Among the many sites in St. Louis is the sweeping arch of the Jefferson National Expansion Memorial. Within the park, site of the original French village, is the Old Courthouse, where the Dred Scott case was heard. 527

Harry S Truman Memorial Library, with its presidential memorabilia, is in Independence. 985

Sainte Genevieve, the oldest permanent settlement in Missouri, has many buildings in the French style.

MONTANA
Custer Battlefield NM on the Crow reservation marks the site where Sioux and Cheyenne defeated Custer. 632

Fort Benton Museum features dioramas recalling the days when the site was a stopping point for the Lewis and Clark Expedition and later a trading post. 281

Virginia City, home of Montana's 1863 gold strike, has restored buildings and museums.

The Grand-Kohrs Ranch NHS near Deer Lodge recaptures life on a large 19th-century cattle ranch. 643

The C. M. Russell Gallery in Helena holds a good collection of Russell's work, which appears frequently in this book; dioramas; and a recreated 1880 street scene.

NEBRASKA
Buffalo Bill Ranch State Historic Park near North Platte was the ranch of Buffalo Bill Cody. 635

Brownville, a steamboat town founded in 1854, features a museum with exhibits on pioneer life.

The Stuhr Museum of the Prairie Pioneer in Grand Island recreates a prairie town of the 19th century.

The Bryan House NHL in Lincoln was the home of William Jennings Bryan. 726

NEVADA
The Nevada State Museum in Carson City features Indian and pioneer history and an underground mine tour.

Virginia City NHL near Carson City is the mining boom town that made fortunes. 639

NEW HAMPSHIRE
Old Fort No. 4 in Claremont, a replica of a 1744 fort, has exhibits and demonstrations of early means of defense.

The Historic Information Center in Portsmouth, housed in a grand 1784 mansion, can provide information on many buildings of historic interest including the Strawberry Banks restoration.

NEW JERSEY
Waterloo Village near Morristown has been restored as a pre-Revolutionary village. Morristown NHP was winter headquarters for Washington. The park includes the Ford Mansion, where the Washingtons stayed, Fort Nonsense, and Jockey Hollow. 164

Edison NHS in West Orange is a complex of buildings in which Thomas A. Edison worked. 667

Monmouth Battlefield NHL near Freehold is the site of Washington's battle in 1778 that boosted American morale. 170

NEW YORK
Among the many museums in New York City is Castle Clinton NM, a restored fort built to protect New York City during the War of 1812. The Statue of Liberty NM, off the tip of Manhattan, features the American Museum of Immigration. 685

Richmondtown Restoration on Staten Island is a group of 40 buildings that show the evolution of the American village.

The Black History Museum in Hempstead traces the history of American blacks from colonial times. Also on Long Island are Old Bethpage Village restoration and Sagamore Hill NHS, home of the Theodore Roosevelt family. 798

The Vanderbilt Mansion NHS and the Franklin D. Roosevelt Home and presidential library are in Hyde Park. 903

Washington's Headquarters NHL at Newburgh is the site where the Washingtons lived in 1782–83. Also at Newburgh are the Knox Headquarters and the Windsor Cantonment, a military village planned by General von Steuben. 164

Saratoga NHP near Stillwater marks the site where General Burgoyne surrendered his British army. 167

West Point NHL is the site chosen by Washington for the U.S. Military Academy. 173

NEW MEXICO
The Indian Pueblo Cultural Center in Albuquerque explains the Pueblo culture through demonstrations and tours. 6

Los Alamos Scientific Laboratory has exhibits at Bradbury Science Hall on the uses and applications of nuclear energy. 1106

The Taos Pueblo NHL, two large five-story pueblos that are still inhabited, and the Mission of St. Francis of Assisi, built in the early 1700s, are both near Taos.

Impressive Indian village remains are at Aztec Ruins NM near Farmington, Gila Cliff Dwellings NM, Chaco Canyon NM, and Bandelier NM.

NORTH CAROLINA
Oconaluftee Indian Village near Cherokee is a replica of an 18th-century Cherokee village with a museum. 394

Wright Brothers NM south of Kitty Hawk is the site of the first successful flight in 1903. 873

Fort Raleigh NHS on Roanoke Island is a reconstruction of the Lost Colony of Roanoke. 43

Guilford Court House NMP near Greensboro is the site of the Revolutionary War battle that sent Cornwallis in retreat to the coast. **171**

NORTH DAKOTA
Fort Abercrombie State Historic Site near Wahpeton contains reconstructed blockhouses, a stockade, and a museum.

Bonanzaville, U.S.A. near Fargo is a recreated village in the Red River Valley, where gigantic farms flourished. **653**

Frontier Museum and Pioneer Village near Williston has two museums and a reconstructed village.

Fort Mandan State Historic Site near Washburn is a reconstruction of the fort where the Lewis and Clark Expedition spent the winter of 1804–05. **281**

OKLAHOMA
Cherokee National Capitol NHL in Tahlequah was the site of the capital city of the Cherokee Nation. **394**

Indian City U.S.A. near Anadarko is a reconstruction of villages of the Plains Indians.

The National Cowboy Hall of Fame and Western Heritage Center outside Oklahoma City has exhibits on the Old West, including a sod house and an Indian village. **623**

OHIO
Mound City Group NM near Chillicothe is an excavation of a cultural center of the prehistoric Hopewell Indians. **8**

Harriet Beecher Stowe House in Cincinnati is a museum dedicated to the author of *Uncle Tom's Cabin*. **512**

Au Glaize Village near Defiance, **Geauga County Historical Society Century Village** at Burton, **Hale Farm** and **Western Reserve Village** at Bath and **Zoar Village** at Zoar are all 19th-century villages.

Fort Recovery is a state memorial near Fort Recovery and includes a partially restored fort and museum with exhibits on the Indian Wars of the 1790s.

OREGON
Fort Clatsop National Memorial near Astoria is a replica of the fort erected by Lewis and Clark in 1805. **280**

Collier Memorial State Park near Klamath Falls has a logging museum and pioneer village.

Jacksonsville Historic District is a restored 1880s gold rush town.

PENNSYLVANIA
In Philadelphia a visitor center provides maps and information about **Independence** NHP, which includes the Liberty Bell, Independence Hall, Congress Hall, and buildings dating from 1732 to 1834. **180**

Gettysburg NMP is the site of a major battle of the Civil War fought in 1863. Here Lincoln later delivered his famous address. **574**

Valley Forge NHP is the place where the American army spent the hard winter of 1777–78. **169**

Fort Duquesne and **Fort Pitt** are landmark sites on the Ohio River. **119**

PUERTO RICO
San Juan NHS contains the Spanish fortresses Castillo El Morro and Castillo San Cristobal, the San Juan Gate, and La Fortaleza, the governor's palace built in 1530.

RHODE ISLAND
Old Slater Mill in Pawtucket consists of restored buildings of the 1793 mill built for early mass production. **335**

Bowen's Wharf of Newport has been restored to show houses and public buildings dating from 1675 to 1820.

Mount Zion Black Museum in Newport exhibits black history and culture in a pre-Civil War church.

SOUTH CAROLINA
In or near Charleston are the sites of **Old Charles Towne,** a restoration of the state's first permanent settlement (66), **Fort Sumter** NM (548), and the **Old Slave Mart Museum.** This beautiful city preserves many gracious homes.

Historic Camden is a restoration of the town the British burnt during the Revolutionary War. **171**

King's Mountain NMP near Spartansburg is the 4,000-acre site of the decisive American victory in 1780. **171**

The Calhoun House (also known as Fort Hill) on the campus of Clemson University in Clemson is the plantation house of John and Floride Calhoun. **374**

Lexington County Homestead Museum, near Columbia, honors Swiss-German settlers.

SOUTH DAKOTA
Wounded Knee Battlefield NHL near Hot Springs is a museum and mass grave commemorating the last important battle between Plains Indians and U.S. army soldiers. **637**

Prairie Village at Madison is a reconstructed late 19th-century town.

Deadwood near Rapid City preserves buildings of a mining town of the Old West. **641**

TENNESSEE
The American Museum of Atomic Energy in Oak Ridge has tours explaining atomic energy and its uses. **1106**

Cades Cove near Gatlinburg is a living museum of pioneer homesteads along an 11-mile stretch of road.

The Hermitage NHL near Nashville is the beautiful home of Andrew and Rachel Jackson, kept as it was when Jackson died in 1845. **382**

Shiloh NMP, the Civil War site, is near Savannah. **578**

TEXAS
The rich historical heritage of San Antonio includes the **Alamo** NHL; **La Villita,** a restoration of San Antonio's earliest community, and the **Spanish Governor's Palace. The San Antonio Mission** NHP includes four of the finest missions in the United States. **406**

Square House Carson County Historical Museum near Amarillo is an 1893 ranch with displays on life in the West. **643**

The NASA Lyndon B. Johnson Space Center in Houston has a visitor center and self-guiding tours. **1042**

The Sam Houston Memorial Museum in Huntsville has exhibits on Texas Pioneers and the Texas Revolution. **408**

The Lyndon B. Johnson Presidential Library in Austin has a replica of the Oval Office and excellent displays. **1029**

UTAH

Pioneer Museum near Provo has a fine collection of regional pioneer artifacts and a pioneer village.

The Golden Spike NHS at Promontory marks the spot where the last spike was driven to lay tracks for the first transcontinental railroad. **628**

Salt Lake City Temple Square NHL commemorates achievements of the Mormons. **The Utah Pioneer Village** recreates their pioneer life. **426**

VERMONT

The President Coolidge Homestead near White River Junction is the home where Coolidge was sworn in as president. A museum exhibits 19th-century tools. **884**

The Outdoor Shelburne Museum at Shelburne includes 18th- and 19th-century houses and a 1903 side-wheel steamboat.

VIRGINIA

Williamsburg NHL, with its over 100 restored buildings in the colonial capital, is a living demonstration of colonial life. **72**

Colonial NHP includes Jamestown Island, site of the Jamestown Colony, and Yorktown, the site where Cornwallis surrendered to Washington in 1781. **47**

Mount Vernon is the lovely home of George and Martha Washington. **236**

Monticello near Charlottesville is the elegant and functional home designed by Thomas Jefferson. **266**

The Appomattox Court House NHP at Appomattox was the scene of Lee's surrender to Grant in 1865. **584**

Manassas National Battlefield Park commemorates the Civil War battles of Bull Run and Richmond. **556**

WASHINGTON

The U.S.S. *Missouri* in the Naval Shipyard at Bremerton was the scene of the Japanese surrender in 1945. **975**

The Whitman Mansion NHS near Walla Walla depicts missionary activity in the West. **412**

The Willis Carey Historical Museum near Wenatchee features a typical 19th-century community and many Indian artifacts.

Point Defiance Park at Tacoma holds a replica of the first fort built by the Hudson Bay Company on the Pacific Coast, an old logging camp, and a pioneer home.

WEST VIRGINIA

Lewisburg near White Sulphur Springs features a restoration of the colonial town.

Harpers Ferry NHP preserves the town as it was at the time of John Brown's raid in 1859. **532**

Fort New Salem at Salem is a reconstruction of a settlement founded in 1792.

WISCONSIN

Historic Galloway House and Village in Fond du Lac is a replica of an 1890 village, including a 30-room Victorian mansion.

Stonefield at Cassfield includes a 19th-century frontier village, the home of a gentleman farmer, and a museum.

La Follette Home NHL in Maple Bluff was the home of Robert and Belle Case La Follette. **790**

WYOMING

Fort Laramie NHS near Torrington was an important stop for travelers on the Oregon Trail. **626**

South Pass City near Lander offers a museum and restoration of this gold rush town.

The Oregon Trail Ruts NHL near Guernsey shows the ruts made by wagons on the Oregon Trail, some six feet deep. **413**

Glossary

This glossary contains the words you need to understand as you study American history. After each word there is a brief definition or explanation of the meaning of the word as it is used in *The Story of America*. The page number(s) refer to the page(s) on which the word first appears in the textbook.

Phonetic Respelling and Pronunciation Guide

Many of the key terms in this textbook have been respelled to help you pronounce them. The following Phonetic Respelling and Pronunciation Guide offers the simplest form of usage, and for this Glossary is adapted from *Webster's Ninth New Collegiate Dictionary, Webster's New Geographical Dictionary,* and *Webster's New Biographical Dictionary.* The letter combinations used in the respellings are explained below.

MARK	AS IN	RESPELLING	EXAMPLE
a	alphabet	a	*AL·fuh·bet
ā	Asia	ay	AY·zhuh
ä	cart, top	ah	KAHRT, TAHP
e	let, ten	e	LET, TEN
ē	even, leaf	ee	EE· vuhn, LEEF
i	it, tip, British	i	IT, TIP, BRIT·ish
ī	site, buy, Ohio	y	SYT, BY, oh·HY·oh
	iris	eye	EYE ·ris
k	card	k	KARD
ō	over, rainbow	oh	oh·vuhr, RAYN·boh
u̇	book, wood	ooh	BOOHK, WOOHD
ȯ	all, orchid	aw	AWL, AWR·kid
ȯi	foil, coin	oy	FOYL, KOYN
au̇	out	ow	OWT
ə	cup, butter	uh	KUHP, BUHT·uhr
ü	rule, food	oo	ROOL, FOOD
yü	few	yoo	FYOO
zh	vision	zh	VIZH·uhn

*A syllable printed in small capital letters receives heavier emphasis than the other syllable(s) in a word.

A

ABC Powers The countries of Argentina, Brazil, and Chile. **820**

Abilene (AB·uh·leen) Kansas meeting place for Western cattle ranchers and Eastern buyers. **643**

abolitionist (ab·uh·LISH·uh·nists) Person who wanted to end slavery in the U.S. **465**

abominable Hateful or offensive. **385**

absolute monarch Ruler who has complete control. **742**

accommodation Going along with the desires of others. **617**

account Description of facts, conditions, or events. **27**

accountability Responsibility or having to answer for something. **827**

acid rain Rain containing a high concentration of industrial chemicals that falls as pollution. **1104**

ace Pilot in the Great War who shot down five or more enemy airplanes. **840**

adobe (uh·DOH·bee) Building material made of sun-baked brick plastered with mud. **6**

adventure school School for girls that focused on the arts and handicrafts. **485**

advice and consent Senate approval required by the Constitution for major presidential appointments or treaties. **224**

advocate One who supports or defends a cause. **906**

Affluent (AF·loo·unt) **Society** Economist's term to describe the wealthy America of post-World War II. **1032**

AFL-CIO. Organization of labor unions formed when the American Federation of Labor and the Congress of Industrial Organizations merged in 1955. **1034**

aftermath Period immediately following a devastating event such as a war. **1078**

Age of Realism Literary and artistic movement characterized by works that portrayed life and people as they really were. **706**

Age of Reform Period in America between about 1830 and 1850 of social concern and improvement. **476**

Agricultural Adjustment Act (AAA) New Deal legislation passed in 1933 that aided farmers by paying them subsidies for land taken out of production. This reduced the crop surplus and helped raise prices for farm goods. **907**

air pollution Exhaust fumes and other pollutants that harm the earth's atmosphere. **828**

Alamo (AL·uh·mo) San Antonio fort where 187 Texans died fighting for independence. **410**

Alaskan Purchase Land deal by which the United States acquired Alaska from Russia for $7.2 million in 1867. **740**

Albany Plan of Union First plan for uniting the colonies drafted by Benjamin Franklin in 1754. **100**

Alien and Sedition (si·DISH·uhn) **Acts** Four 1798 laws aimed at foreigners and others in the U.S. who were supposedly undermining the government by helping France. **261**

Alliance for Progress President Kennedy's program to provide economic assistance for Latin American countries. **1017**

alliance Agreement made between nations to support each other, especially in times of attack. **817**

Allies (AL·eyez) Nations which fought together in World War I, including the U.S., Great Britain, Italy, and Russia; and those that fought together in World War II, including the U.S., Great Britain, France, and the Soviet Union. **817**

almshouse Home for poor people. **499**

alphabet soup Term referring to the many New Deal agencies that were known by their initials. **929**

Amana (uh·MAN·uh) **community** Shaker settlement founded by Christian Metz in early 1800s. **490**

ambush Trap or surprise attack. **631**

amendment. Change or addition to a bill or law such as to the Constitution. **237**

America Name given to the lands discovered in New World—later North, Central, and South America; after explorer Amerigo Vespucci. **27**

American Colonization Society Group that offered to help former slaves resettle in Africa. **449**

American expansionism Belief that North and South America and the islands of the Pacific should be under the control of the U.S. **738**

American Expeditionary (ek·spuh·DISH·uh·ner·ee) **Force** U.S. military forces that fought in Europe during the Great War. **833**

American Federation of Labor (AFL) National labor union of skilled workers founded in 1886. **681**

American Indian Movement (AIM) Organization founded in 1968 to work for fairer treatment of Native Americans. **1053**

American System Plan developed by Henry Clay in early 1800s for sectional cooperation on legislation. **379**

Amistad **mutiny** Shipboard revolt by African slaves who were then jailed in America but finally freed when the Supreme Court declared their mutiny legal. **526**

amnesty (AM·nuhs·tee). Official pardon for crimes committed against the government. **593**

Amnesty Act of 1872 Law that reversed the decision to bar former Confederate officials and soldiers from holding public office. **611**

anarchist (AN·uhr·kuhst). One who opposes all government. **767**

anguished (AN·gwisht) Distressed or full of sorrow. **497**

annexation (an·ek·SAY·shuhn) Addition of territory to a country. **405**

anthropologist (an·thruh·PAHL·uh·juhst) Scientist who studies the physical, social, and cultural development of people. **9**

antibiotic (ant·ih·by·OHT·ik) Substance such as penicillin which is produced to kill disease-carrying organisms. **306**

anticipating Looking forward to or expecting. **1035**

Antifederalist Person who supported

strong state governments and opposed ratification of the U.S. constitution. **226**

anti-imperialist Person opposed to imperialism or owning colonies. **762**

antitrust movement Organized effort to regulate business practices that restrained free trade. **676**

antiwar movement Campaign in the United States to end war, especially the Vietnam War. **1073**

Apache (uh·PAACH·ee) Plains Indian tribe that lived in Texas and New Mexico. **623**

apartheid (uh·PAR·teyt) South African policy of separation of the races. **1118**

apocalyptic Forecasting disaster; prophetic. **935**

Appeal to the Colored Citizens of the World Essay by David Walker urging African Americans to fight for freedom. **471**

appellate (uh·PEL·uht) **court** Lower federal appeals court. **224**

Appomattox (ap·uh·MAT·uhks) **Court House** Virginia town where Lee surrendered to Grant ending the Civil War. **584**

appropriate (ah·PRO·pre·ayt) Set money aside for a specific use. **741**

appropriations Funds designated for a specific purpose or program. **985**

Arab Oil Crisis Shortage of petroleum products in the United States in 1973 created by an Arab-controlled OPEC ban on the shipment of oil to countries that supported Israel. **1080**

Arapaho (uh·RAP·uh·ho) Indian tribe that occupied the central region of the Great Plains. **623**

arbitration (ahr·buh·TRAY·shun) Hearing on and settlement of a dispute between two parties by a neutral third party. **745**

arbitration treaties Agreements between nations to try and settle their differences and avoid war. **818**

arch Chief or principal (as in arch-rival). **513**

archaeologist (ahr·kee·AHL·uh·juhst) Scientist who studies history and

culture by examining the remains of early human cultures. **9**

archipelago (ahr·kuh·PEL·uh·go) Group of islands. **741**

ardent Very strong. **237**

armistice Truce or agreement between countries to stop fighting. **844**

Army-McCarthy Hearings Senator Joseph McCarthy's investigation of subversive activities in the army. **1003**

Army of Northern Virginia Confederate army commanded by Robert E. Lee. **559**

Army of the Potomac Union army near Washington, D.C., during the Civil War. **557**

arsenal Storehouse of weapons. **195**

Articles of Confederation Agreement under which the thirteen original colonies established a government of states in 1781. **185**

article of impeachment Charge of wrongdoing against the president or other government official. **1084**

artifact (AHRT·i·fakt) Objects made by humans, such as jewelry, tools, or weapons. **9**

assassination (uh·sas·uhn·AY·shuhn) Murder of a public figure. **592**

assay. Test or analyze for content. **639**

assembly Lawmaking body elected by the people. **110**

asset Advantage or helpful resource. **730**

assimilate To absorb into the culture tradition. **686**

astrolabe (AS·truh·layb) Instrument used to measure a ship's latitude or distance from the equator. **19**

Atlanta Major southern city in Georgia that was captured and burned to the ground by General Sherman (1864). **582**

Atlanta Compromise Proposal by Booker T. Washington that blacks and whites both honor the separate-but-equal principle. **617**

Atlantic Charter Agreement between Great Britain and the U.S. to work for a world free of war, signed by Roosevelt and Churchill on August 14, 1941. **948**

atomic bomb Powerful explosive

used by the United States to destroy two Japanese cities during World War II. **971**

atonement Being forgiven or reconciled for past sins. **1080**

atrocious (uh·TROH·shus) Horrifying or disgusting. **518**

attainment Accomplishment of a goal. **1097**

attorney general Chief law officer of the nation and legal advisor to the president. **235**

austerity Simple and unadorned. **1019**

autocratic Ruled by a government with absolute authority over all aspects of life. **1109**

Aztecs (AZ·teks) Power Indian rulers of Central Mexico at the time of the Spanish invasion in 1519. **29**

B

Bacon's Rebellion Revolt of Virginia colonists led by Nathaniel Bacon in 1676 which resulted in the killing of Indians, the burning of Jamestown, and the removal of the governor. **105**

balance of power Equal military and economic strength among nations. **817**

Bank Holiday Order by Franklin Roosevelt closing all banks for several days in 1933 while a program to protect the savings of the public was developed. **906**

bank note Paper money supported by gold or silver. **242**

Bank of the United States Central banking system created by Congress in 1791 to support American industries. **242**

bankrupt Out of funds or unable to pay debts. **389**

Barbary pirate Seaman from the North African states who in the early 1800s helped seize and rob ships traveling on the Mediterranean Sea. **275**

barnstorming Traveling from place to place, especially through rural areas, making brief stops. **874**

barrio Hispanic neighborhood in a city. **1094**

base metal Non-precious metal that lies under a coating of gold or silver. **683**

Bastogne (ba·STOHN) French town where Allied forces held back a German advance during World War II. **964**

Battle of Antietam (an·TEET·uhm) (1862) Bloody Civil War clash that caused Confederate troops to withdraw from Maryland. **568**

Battle of Britain Germany's attempt to break Britain spirit and destroy its air force by massive bombings in 1940. **946**

Battle of Buena Vista (bway·nuh·VEE·stuh) American victory by General Taylor in 1847 in Northern Mexico. **420**

Battle of Bunker Hill (1775) First major battle of the Revolutionary War; British suffered heavy losses in defeating patriots. **149**

Battle of Chancellorsville (CHAN·suh·luhrz·vil) Brilliant 1863 Confederate victory in which Stonewall Jackson was killed. **574**

Battle of Cold Harbor Last major victory for Lee and third clash against Union forces led by Grant (1864). **581**

Battle of Cowpens Defeat in 1781 of British in South Carolina. **171**

Battle of Fallen Timbers Decisive fight in 1794 in the Northwest Territory in which Wayne defeated Indians led by Blue Jacket. **248**

Battle of Fredericksburg Victory in 1862 by Confederate forces under Lee that left 12,000 Union soldiers dead. **573**

Battle of Gettysburg Defeat in 1863 of Lee's invasion of the North. **575**

Battle of Horseshoe Bend Defeat of Creek Indians by Andrew Jackson in 1814. **307**

Battle of Kasserine (kas·uh·REEN) **Pass** Tank warfare in 1943 between Americans and Germans in North Africa in World War II. **961**

Battle of Leyte (LAYT·ee) **Gulf** World War II fight in 1944 in the Pacific in which the U.S. navy defeated the Japanese. **968**

Battle of Long Island Revolutionary War conflict in which British General Howe defeated Washington's forces (1776). **164**

Battle of Midway Naval defeat of the Japanese that gave the U.S. control of the central Pacific during World War II (1942). **966**

Battle of Monmouth Court House British defeat by George Washington in 1778. **170**

Battle of New Orleans Major fight won by Jackson after the War of 1812 was officially over (1815). **312**

Battle of Princeton (1776) Revolutionary War battle in which Washington defeated two British regiments. **165**

Battle of Put-in-Bay Perry's defeat of the British navy on Lake Erie in 1813. **305**

Battle of Saratoga Important 1778 American victory in Revolutionary War after which France recognized American independence. **168**

Battle of Seven Pines Civil War clash in which Confederate Commander Johnston was wounded and succeeded by Robert E. Lee. **559**

Battle of Shiloh Costly 1862 Union victory in Mississippi. **579**

Battle of the Argonne Forest Site of 1918 Great War fight in which American forces drove back German troops. **844**

Battle of the Atlantic. Naval war waged between German submarines and the British navy and air force from 1941 to 1943. **947**

Battle of the Bulge. Major German counterattack in 1944 that created a bulge in the Allied line of advance in Europe during World War II. **964**

Battle of the Coral Sea. World War II naval contest in which heavy damage to the Japanese fleet stopped Japan's planned invasion of Australia (1942). **966**

Battle of the Little Big Horn Fight between U.S. Calvary led by Custer and Sioux led by Sitting Bull in which Custer and his men were all killed (1876). **632**

Battle of the Marne. Great War conflict in which French and British troops stopped German advance toward Paris (1914). **822**

Battle of the Thames (TEMZ) Fight in which Harrison won back the Great Lakes region from the British and Tecumseh was killed (1813). **306**

Battle of the Wilderness Clash of Lee's and Grant's forces in the forests southwest of Washington, D.C., resulting in heavy losses on both sides (1864). **581**

Battle of Tippecanoe Fight with the Indians in 1811 that made William Henry Harrison a hero. **299**

Battle of Trenton (1776) Revolutionary War victory during which George Washington defeated Hessian mercenaries. **165**

Bay of Pigs. Site in Cuba of a failed invasion by exiles trained by the U.S. (1961). **1016**

Bear Flag Revolt Defeat of Mexican forces in California by American settlers in 1847. **420**

Beecher's Bibles Name given to guns bought with money raised by abolitionist minister Henry Ward Beecher of New York and sent to antislavery forces in Kansas in the 1850s. **519**

Berlin Capital of Germany that was divided into East and West Berlin after World War II. **965**

Berlin airlift Rescue mission during the Cold War in which the U.S. flew supplies to West Berlin after the Soviets blocked roads. **990**

Berlin Wall Wall built in 1961 to close off communist-controlled East Berlin from West Berlin. **1017**

besieged Under attack or surrounded by the enemy. **547**

Bessemer (BES·uh·muhr) **converter** Invention by Henry Bessemer that made the mass production of steel possible. **661**

bias (BY·us) Prejudice. **267**

Bicentennial Nationwide celebration in 1976 of the 200th anniversary of the Declaration of Independence. **1090**

"big business" Term applied to large

companies with political and social influence. **783**

Big Four Leaders of the Versailles Peace Conference after the Great War; British Prime Minister Lloyd George, French premier Clemenceau, Italian prime minister Orlando, and President Wilson. **848**

Big Red Scare Widespread fear of a communist takeover that swept the U.S. after World War I. **861**

Big Three During World War II, British Prime Minister Churchill, U.S. President Roosevelt, and Soviet dictator Stalin. **980**

Bill of Rights Name given to the first ten amendments to the Constitution. **182**

Birmingham Alabama site of 1963 protest led by Reverend Martin Luther King, Jr., in which local police used dogs and fire hoses against demonstrators. **1055**

Black Cabinet African Americans appointed to government jobs under Roosevelt's New Deal. **923**

Black Codes Regulations passed by southern governments after Reconstruction to restrict the rights of African Americans. **594**

"black gold" Another name for oil. **664**

Black Power Movement in the 1960s by African Americans that supported the use of force and political and economic power in the struggle for equal rights. **1096**

"Black Republican" Name given to the post-Civil War governments in the South. **602**

Black Tuesday Day the stock market crashed, October 29, 1929. **891**

blacklist List of workers in unions who were denied employment. **682**

Bladensburg Village in Maryland taken by the British in 1814 just before their march on Washington. **308**

Bland-Allison Act Law that authorized the purchase and coinage of from $2 to $4 million worth of silver each month (1878). **719**

"Bleeding Kansas" Name given in eastern newspaper accounts to

fighting in Kansas in the 1850s between proslavery and antislavery forces. **522**

blockade runner Small, fast ship used during the Civil War. **563**

blot Bad mark on one's reputation or record. **955**

blue-collar worker Generally an industrial worker or one whose job involves manual labor. **1036**

board of directors Group that makes the decisions for a corporation. **661**

Boland Amendment Law passed in 1984 that prohibited U.S. aid to foreign revolutionary groups. **1116**

bolstered Supported or reinforced. **581**

bonanza (buh·NAN·zuh). Rich deposit of ore. **639**

Bonus March March of Great War veterans on Washington in July 1932 to protest the government's decision to not pay early their compensation for their low pay as soldiers in the war. **901**

boom Period of thriving business activity. **392**

boom town Town that grows suddenly near a gold or silver strike. **641**

boot hill Cemetery for cowboys who "died with their boots on." **647**

bootlegger Person who produces, sells, or transports liquor illegally, especially during Prohibition. **866**

border state State such as Maryland, West Virginia, Kentucky, Delaware, and Missouri that held slaves but did not leave the Union during the Civil War. **536**

borer Tool used to make holes. **334**

borough Administrative district in which a city is divided. **1096**

boss Leader of political machine. **699**

Boston Massacre Incident between British soldiers and Americans in 1770 Boston in which several Americans were killed. **131**

Boston Tea Party Protest in 1773 against British tax on tea during which colonists dumped three shiploads of tea into Boston harbor. **141**

bound Under legal or moral obligation; required. **15**

Boxer Rebellion Uprising in 1900 in China during which foreign property was destroyed and foreign missionaries and business people were held captive. **769**

boycott (BOY·kaht) Refusal to buy certain goods or services as a protest. **128**

Bozeman Trail Route across the Great Plains marked by John M. Bozeman. **630**

bracero (brah·SER·oh) Mexican farm laborer allowed to enter the United States temporarily to do seasonal work. **958**

Brain Trust Advisers of Franklin Roosevelt who were mostly college professors. **913**

brand Mark burned on an animal's hide with a hot iron to show ownership. **645**

Brandeis (BRAN·dys) **brief** Argument presented by Louis D. Brandeis before the Supreme Court that long work hours injured the health of women and children; research for the brief was done by Florence Kelley and Josephine Goldmark. **795**

bread-and-butter issue Concern of labor such as higher wages, shorter hours, and better working conditions. **681**

breadbasket of America Name for the wheat-growing region of the Great Plains. **653**

breadline People waiting to be given free food during the Great Depression. **897**

breadwinner Primary wage earner in a family. **480**

breechcloth Clothing worn by American Indian braves that hung from the waist. **625**

brief Outline of a lawyer's argument or case. **795**

brink Edge. **804**

brinksmanship Policy under President Eisenhower promoted by Secretary of State Dulles to risk all-out war to contain communism. **1001**

bristle Stiffen to show anger or defiance. **614**

British Being of Great Britain, which in colonial days was England, Scotland, Wales, or Ireland. **86**

Brooklyn Bridge Span between Brooklyn and Manhattan that, at the time of its completion in 1883, was the longest bridge in the world. **693**

Brown v. Board of Education of Topeka Landmark 1954 Supreme Court decision that schools must be integrated, overturning "separate but equal" ruling of *Plessy v. Ferguson.* **849**

bugler (BYOO·gler) Person who sounds signals with a bugle or trumpet. **414**

Bull Moose party Nickname for the Progressive party when Theodore Roosevelt ran for president in 1912. **800**

Bull Run Site in Virginia of first battle between Union and Confederate armies, a Confederate victory (1861). **557**

bungled Mishandled. **799**

business cycle Economic trends that move through periods of prosperity and recession. **894**

bust Complete failure or disappointment. **630**

busybody Nosy person who interferes in someone else's business. **500**

C

cabinet Officials who head government agencies and are appointed by and advise the president. **235**

cable car Trolley car pulled up a steep hill by a moving cable. **692**

The Calhouns of South Carolina Wealthy southern family headed by plantation owner and statesman John C. Calhoun. **374**

Cambodia (kam·BOH·dee·uh) Country bordering Vietnam where American troops were sent in 1970 causing widespread protest in the U.S; also called Kampuchea (kam·poo·CHEE·uh). **1073**

Camelot (CAM·uh·laht) Legendary site of King Arthur's court which was noted for its faith in human goodness; often applied to the years of the Kennedy administration. **1019**

Camp David Accords Peace agreement between Israel's Premier Begin and Egypt's President Sadat initiated by President Carter in 1979. **1109**

Canal Zone Strip of land leased to the U.S. by Panama that extends five miles on each side of the Panama Canal. **771**

canal Waterway dug (especially in the 1800s) for transportation, to link rivers and lakes, and for irrigation. **351**

capitalism Economic system in which individuals own and control the factors of production and government intervention is limited. **982**

captor Person who takes someone prisoner. **636**

carbon-14 dating Process used to determine the age of an ancient object by measuring its radioactive content. **9**

Carpetbagger Northerner who went to the South after the Civil War to profit financially from confused and unsettled conditions. **602**

cash-and-carry policy Plan that allowed the United States to sell weapons to warring nations that paid cash and transported the goods in foreign ships. **943**

cash crop Product raised to be sold rather than consumed on the farm. **90**

cattle baron Wealthy and powerful cattle rancher. **644**

cattle kingdom Grasslands of the High Plains that stretched from Texas to Canada and from the Rockies to eastern Kansas used to graze hundreds of thousands of cattle. **643**

cattle town Western town where cattle were bought and sold. **643**

censure (SEN·shur) Officially condemn or disapprove of. **1003**

Central Intelligence Agency (CIA) U.S. organization created in 1947 to gather and analyze political, economic, and military information about other countries. **1016**

Central Powers Germany, Austria, and later Hungary, Turkey, and Bulgaria during the Great War. **817**

Cerro Gordo (ser·uh·GAWRD·oh) Mexican town where Americans won an important battle in 1847 in the War with Mexico. **420**

chain store Store with a number of outlets in different areas. **888**

Challenger U.S. space shuttle that exploded after takeoff in 1986. **869**

championed Defended or upheld. **462**

charter Official government document granting special rights and privileges to a person or company. **42**

Château-Thierry (sha·TOH·ty·ree) French town where American and French forces stopped the German advance in the Great War (1917). **840**

Chattanooga (chat·uh·NOO·guh) Important railway center in Tennessee around which several Civil War battles were fought. **580**

chauvinist (SHOW·vuh·nuhst) Person who has an attitude of superiority toward the opposite sex. **163**

checks and balances. System in which the three branches of government have powers to limit the other branches so that no branch will become too powerful. **224**

Chernobyl (chuhr·NOH·buhl) Soviet nuclear power plant that exploded in 1986 and released massive amounts of radiation over a widespread area. **1105**

Cherokee (CHER·uh·kee) **Nation** Large group of Indian tribes united under Cherokee law. **395**

Cheyenne (shy·AN) Indian tribe of the Central Great Plains. **623**

Chicago Illinois city that is a major railway and meatpacking center. **643**

Children's Aid Society Group founded to help homeless children by relocating them to farm families and lodging houses. **500**

Chilean Crisis Tension in 1891–92 between Chile and the U.S.

started by a fight in Valparaiso between U.S. sailors and Chileans. **744**

Chinese Exclusion Act Law passed in 1882 that barred Chinese laborers from entering the United States for 10 years. **689**

Chisholm Trail One main route over which Texans drove cattle to market. **643**

Chivington Massacre Slaughter of Cheyenne that provoked Indian attacks on settlers; also called the Sand Creek Massacre. **630**

cholera (KOL·er·uh) Deadly intestinal disease. **347**

church school Early American school taught by the minister and his wife. **484**

Circular Letter Plea issued by the Massachusetts legislature to other colonial assemblies that all colonists act together to resist taxation without representation. **130**

circumnavigate (suhr·kuhm·NAV·uh·gayt) To sail completely around the world. **29**

citizenship Legal membership in a country or state; a citizen is granted rights by the country or state and in return has certain duties and obligations, such as obeying the law. **1109**

civic Of or relating to citizens and citizenship. **600**

Civil Rights Act of 1866 Law that made African Americans citizens of the United States. **595**

Civil Rights Act of 1875 Law that prohibited segregation of public places. **614**

Civil Rights Act of 1964 Law that made it easier and safer for southern African Americans to vote and that prohibited racial discrimination in public facilities. **853**

Civil Rights Cases Lawsuits concerning the constitutional rights of black Americans. **614**

Civil Rights Committee Group appointed by Truman in 1947 to recommend laws to protect the rights of African Americans. **993**

Civil Rights Movement Campaign in the 1960s to achieve equality for Black Americans. **856**

Civil Service Commission Agency established in 1883 to design and administer examinations for certain government positions. **705**

civil service reform Effort to improve government service by adopting an employment system based on skill and merit rather than on politics. **704**

Civil War (1861–1865) Conflict between the northern (Union) and southern (Confederacy) states over the issues of slavery and states' rights. **548**

Civil War Amendments Three constitutional amendments (13th, 14th and 15th) guaranteeing civil rights to African Americans. **600**

Civil Works Authority New Deal agency created in 1934 to help the unemployed find jobs. **912**

Civilian Conservation Corps (CCC) New Deal agency that put some 3 million young men to work on conservation and rural improvement projects. **912**

clan Social or family group. **5**

Clayton Antitrust Act Law that prohibited a person from serving as a director in more than one corporation and which exempted labor unions from antitrust laws (1914). **804**

Clayton-Bulwer Treaty Agreement in 1850 between Great Britain and America that neither would take exclusive control of a canal between the Atlantic and Pacific oceans. **770**

clipper ship Sailing ship of the 19th century built for speed. **432**

close state State neither strongly Republican or strongly Democratic where either party might win a national election. **698**

closed shop Business that hires only members of a labor union. **985**

clout Influence or power. **686**

Coercive (ko·UHR·siv) **Acts** Series of laws passed by the British to punish the colonists for the Boston Tea Party; also called Intolerable Acts. **142**

Cold War Tensions between the U.S. and Russia after World War II. **982**

collective bargaining Right of a labor union to bargain for all workers employed by a business. **682**

collective security World security guaranteed by an agreement among all nations to join in action against a nation that attacks any one of them. **941**

Columbian Exchange Exchange of material things and ideas between Europe and America. **36**

Comanche (kuh·MAN·chee) Plains Indians of Texas and New Mexico. **623**

commandos Small force of soldiers who specialize in raids in enemy territory. **532**

commenced Began. **133**

Commercial Revolution Economic expansion in Europe that occurred from 1450 to the 1700s. **18**

commissioned Awarded a military rank and the authority that goes with it. **958**

commission Committee formed for a specific purpose and with specific powers to act. **101**

Committee of Correspondence Group formed by radicals in colonies to spread the protest of British rule. **143**

Commodity Credit Corporation Organization created in 1938 that paid farmers money for surplus crops kept in storage, resulting in higher prices because there were fewer crops on the market. **926**

commodities (kuh·MAH·duht·ees) Goods. **831**

common man Ordinary American rather than a representative of the rich and wealthy. **383**

commonwealth Territory in which there is self-government. **58**

communications revolution More rapid, long-distance communication made possible by the inventions of the telegraph and telephone. **665**

communist Economic system in which the government owns or controls almost all the means of production. **982**

Communist Revolution Rebellion in 1917 in Russia in which the communist party took control. **838**

compass Instrument used to tell direction. **19**

compelled Forced or driven. **86**

compensated Given payment to make up for a loss or shortage. **569**

component Part or ingredient. **893**

Compromise of 1850 Resolution that temporarily settled disputes between the North and South over slavery issues. **443**

Compromise of 1877 Concessions made by Republicans and Democrats that settled disputed election of 1876 by which Hayes became president. **612**

compulsive Having the power to compel or force. **197**

computer (kohm·PYOO·ter) Electronic machine that can store, retrieve, and process information rapidly. **1039**

Comstock (KAHM·stahk) **Lode** Extremely rich silver deposit in Nevada. **639**

conceive To think of. **86**

concentration System of separating and thereby controlling the Indian tribes of the Great Plains by placing them on reservations. **626**

concentration camp Nazi prison were prisoners of war, especially the Jews, are held. **938**

concept Thought or idea. **59**

concession Something given in a compromise. **223**

conclusively Without a doubt. **1084**

Concord One of two Massachusetts towns (along with Lexington) where the first battles of the Revolutionary War were fought (1775). **144**

Conestoga (kahn·uh·STOH·guh) **wagon** Sturdy covered wagon used by many of the pioneers who moved westward. **374**

confederacy Alliance of independent states. **544**

Confederate States of America Association of 11 independent southern states formed after their secession from the Union in 1860–61. **544**

confederation Union of groups for a common cause. **9**

conferring Giving or bestowing

upon; as in an honor or award. **1111**

conform To go along with the majority or to behave according to rules or standards set by society. **1050**

Congress Legislative, or lawmaking, branch of government made up of the House of Representatives and the Senate. **220**

Congress of Industrial Organizations (CIO) National labor union formed in 1935 to organize all the workers in mass production industries. **927**

conquest Something that has been taken over or conquered. **2**

conquistador (kawn·KEES·tuh·dawr) Spanish soldier who helped conquer Mexico and Peru. **31**

Conscience Whigs. Northern members of the Whig party who were against slavery (see **Cotton Whigs**). **523**

conscientious Behaving according to what is right or honest. **234**

conscientious objector. One who refuses to serve in the military because of moral or religious beliefs. **939**

consciousness-raising Increasing awareness, usually about a social or political issue. **1052**

conscript To draft people by law to serve as soldiers. **565**

conservation Protection or preservation from waste or loss, such as natural resources. **798**

conservative Tending to go by established methods; slow to change. **182**

consolidated Joined together into one or under one system. **781**

constitution Written plan of government that includes its laws and principles. **182**

Constitutional Convention Meeting of 12 states (all but Rhode Island) in Philadelphia in 1787 to draft the U.S. Constitution. **197**

Constitutional Unionist Party Political party formed in 1860 that ignored the slavery issue in hopes of preserving the Union. **536**

consumption Using up of, as of goods or services. **560**

containment policy U.S. strategy in the 1950s aimed at limiting the spread of communism. **991**

contempt Disrespect or scorn. **119**

contend Struggle or compete. **273**

continental divide Ridge of the Rocky Mountains that separates rivers flowing generally east from those flowing generally west. **281**

Continental dollars Paper money printed by Congress after the Revolutionary War to pay its debts. **196**

contraband (KAWN·truh·band) Slave who crossed Union lines during the Civil War. **565**

contrary Opposite or not in agreement with. **465**

Contras (KAWN·truhs) Nicaraguan counter-revolutionaries who received aid from the U.S. in their effort to overthrow the ruling Sandinista government. **1114**

cooperatives Farms or other enterprises owned and operated jointly by members who share in the benefits. **899**

covenant Formal and binding agreement. **849**

Convention of 1800 Treaty that prevented war between France and the United States in 1799. **269**

convoy Fleet of ships that is accompanied or escorted by a protective force. **286**

"cooling-off" period Time that a union could be forced to delay a strike if that strike threatens national interest. **985**

co-op (KOH·ahp). Group formed through the Farmers' Alliance in order to sell crops and to purchase goods at better prices for members. **720**

Copperhead Northerner who opposed the Civil War. **561**

corporation Business owned by stockholders and run by a board of directors. **661**

Corps of Discovery Group chosen by Lewis and Clark to help them explore the Louisiana Territory. **280**

cotton boll (bol) Seed pod of a cotton plant that grows into a fibrous ball. **450**

cotton diplomacy Belief that England

and France would support the Confederacy to insure their supply of cotton. **564**

cotton gin Machine invented by Eli Whitney in 1793 that separated cotton fibers from the seeds. **451**

"Cotton Is King" Southern slogan which meant that cotton, and therefore slavery, was essential to the region. **463**

county court Local government in the southern colonies. **110**

court Official gathering to rule on legality of an action. **182**

Coxey's Army Band of unemployed workers who, led by Jacob Coxey, marched on Washington to protest the plight of the unemployed (1894). **724**

cradle Tool used to cut grain. **561**

Creek War Indian attacks in 1813 in Alabama in which more than 400 settlers were killed. **306**

Crime of 1873 Name given by farmers and miners to the law that discontinued the mining of silver. **718**

crop-lien (KRAWP·leen) **system** Agreement in which supplies were lent to a farmer by merchants or landowners in exchange for portions of the crops. **608**

Cross of Gold speech William Jennings Bryan's stirring appeal for the free coinage of silver that got him the Populist Party's nomination for president (1896). **728**

crucial (KREW·shuhl) Extremely important. **184**

Crusade One of a series of religious wars between 1100 and 1300 undertaken by the Christians in Europe to regain the Holy Land from the Moslems. **16**

Cuba Island with a communist government about 90 miles south of Florida. **1016**

Cuban Missile Crisis Tense confrontation in 1962 between the U.S. and the Soviet Union over the building of Soviet missile bases in Cuba. **1018**

culminated Reached the end or resulted in. **363**

culture Special characteristics of the people who make up a society, such as their language, govern-

ment, how they make a living, family relationships, and how they educate their children. **4**

Cumberland Road First road built linking East and West from Maryland to Illinois; also called the National Road. **350**

cumbersome Hard to handle because of weight or bulk. **152**

curriculum Courses offered by a school. **450**

cutbacks Reductions or decreases. **889**

D

D-Day Beginning of the Allied invasion of France on June 6, 1944, to drive out Hitler's occupying armies. **963**

dadaism Art movement of the 1920s that was a protest against traditional artistic values. **871**

dame schools Urban school in early America taught by women. **484**

dark horse Political candidate who unexpectedly wins a party's nomination. **405**

Dawes Severalty (SEV·uh·ruhl·tee) **Act** Law that divided reservations into quarter sections of land owned by individual Indian families (1887). **638**

deadlock Standstill created when opposing sides are unable to break a tie. **885**

Declaration of Independence Document adopted by the Second Continental Congress in 1776 that declared American independence from Great Britain and listed the reasons for this action. **157**

Declaratory (di·KLAR·uh·tawr·ee) **Act** Law passed in 1766 by the British parliament that declared the American colonies subject to British law. **128**

deep-seated Firmly established or hard to remove. **85**

Deerfield English settlement in Massachusetts destroyed by the French during Queen Anne's War. **117**

defame To speak badly of or ruin a reputation. **261**

deficit (DEF·uh·suht) **spending** Paying out more public funds than are raised in taxes. **834**

deflation (de·FLAY·shun) Decline in prices caused by a decrease in money supply or spending. **703**

deliberate Slow and careful in acting. **546**

demand Amount of a product or service that the public is ready and able to buy. **875**

demilitarized Not controlled or used by the military. **1003**

Democrat Member of the political party begun in the early 1800s that supported strong states' rights and government made up of many classes of people. **382**

Democratic-Republican Member of one of the first two political parties; its members favored policies of Jefferson such as restricting the powers of federal government over the states. **255**

democracy Form of government in which power is vested in the people and exercised by them through a system of free elections. **79, 162**

demoralizing Weakening the spirit. **1100**

denounced Stated disapproval of or condemned. **503**

department of state Government bureau that advises the president on foreign relations. **234**

department store Large store selling a variety of goods arranged in different sections. **669**

depressed Period of low economic activity. **895**

depression Period of severe decline in business activity, usually marked by high levels of unemployment. **191**

descendant Offspring. **9**

desist Stop or cease to act. **804**

destined Intended or determined beforehand. **404**

destiny Something to which a person or group is destined; a predetermined course. **819**

détente (day·TAHNT) Reduction of or tensions between two countries, particularly the United States and the Soviet Union. **1076**

deteriorate (dee·TIHR·ee·ohr·ayt) To grow worse or decline in quality or condition. **1050**

detonated. Set off or caused to explode. **843**

development Generally a suburban neighbrhood in which a number of similar houses have been built. **1044**

dickering Bargaining to reach an agreement or compromise. **316**

dictator (DIK·tayt·uhr) Ruler with absolute power. **269**

dignified Calm, reserved, or noble. **237**

diplomacy Art of handling negotiations between nations. **827**

direct primary Preliminary election within the parties to choose candidates to run for public office. **791**

disallow Refuse permission. **110**

disarmament (dis·AHRM·uh·ment) Reduction or limitation in the number of weapons of war. **859**

disrepair In need of repair. **890**

dissent Judge's statement of disagreement with the opinion or decision of the majority. **616**

distinct Clearly different or distinguishable. **4**

distortion Twisting or stretching of the true facts. **367**

district court Lower federal trial court in each specified U.S. region. **224**

District of Columbia Federal area designated as the permanent capital of the United States. **255**

diversified (duh·VUHR·suh·fyd) **economy** Type of economy that depends on both manufacturing and agriculture. **330**

divide and conquer Military strategy to weaken an opponent by scattering its forces. **626**

division of labor Separation of the manufacturing steps into specialized tasks to speed and increase production. **663**

doctrine Statement of principles, system of beliefs, or government policy. **97**

doctrine of nullification (nuhl·uh·fuh·KAY·shun) Theory put forth in 1798 that because the United States Constitution limited power of the federal government over the states, a state had the right to refuse to accept a national law it disagreed with. **268**

Dodge City Kansas cattle town famous as a rowdy entertainment center for cowboys. **647**

dogfight Battle between fighter planes, usually at close range. **840**

doggedly In a stubborn, persistent manner. **940**

dollar diplomacy U.S. policy in the early 1900s of investing money in Latin American countries in hopes that more stable governments would result. **777**

domineering Controlling or ruling with arrogance or tyranny. **937**

dominate Control or rule over. **2**

Dominion of New England Territory created by King James II of England in 1686 in an attempt to unify the British colonies. **111**

domino theory Idea that if a country fell to communism, the countries on its borders would also fall; key principle of U.S. foreign policy from the 1950s to the 1970s. **1061**

Dorchester Heights Site near Boston of General Washington's first victory against the British in the Revolutionary War. **155**

dormant Not actively growing but protected from the environment (as in the life cycle of plants.) **2**

dove Person opposed to war. **1064**

"Drake's Folly" Nickname for the first oil well, drilled by E. L. Drake of Titusville, Pennsylvania (1859). **664**

Dred Scott v. Sandford Supreme Court ruling in 1857 that Scott, a former slave who sued for his freedom, was still a slave despite living in a free state for a time. **527**

dredged. Widened or made deeper by removing dirt. **772**

drought Long period of dry weather that stunts crop growth. **651**

drudgery Dull and tiresome work. **596**

dry farming Technique used to raise crops in areas with little rainfall. **651**

dry states States that adopted prohibition. **866**

dumbfounded Surprised to the point of being speechless. **278**

Dunkirk. French town where German troops forced a major evacuation of Allied forces during World War II. **944**

duty Tariff or tax placed on foreign goods brought into the country. **124**

dwindled Grew less and less. **1045**

dynamic Energetic, forceful or powerful. **97**

E

East Germany Country under communist control created when Germany was divided between Allied powers after World War II. **1003**

East India Company British company; given assistance in selling tea in the colonies by the parliament in 1773, leading to the Boston Tea Party. **138**

Eastern Front Combat zone in Eastern Europe during the Great War. **822**

Economic Opportunity Act Law passed in 1964 that attacked poverty in the U.S. through programs such as Head Start, the Job Corps and VISTA. **1030**

economy System of producing, distributing, and consuming goods or services. **35**

egalitarian Marked by the belief in equal social and political rights for all people. **385**

Eighteenth Amendment Constitutional change that prohibited the manufacture and sale of alcoholic beverages (1919). **866**

El Caney (el·kuh·NAY) Site of major 1898 battle in Cuba during Spanish-American War. **756**

elaborate Complicated or very detailed. **7**

elastic clause "Necessary and proper" clause of the Constitution often used to expand the powers of Congress. **243**

elderly People approaching old age. **888**

elector Person selected in a state to cast an electoral vote for president. **223**

electric light Invention by Edison that makes light by passing electricity through a fine wire housed in a bulb. **667**

electric trolley System of streetcars propelled along tracks by electric currents from overhead wires. **692**

electrified Excited or thrilled. **1019**

Elementary and Secondary Education Act Law passed in 1965 that provided federal money to support school programs in low-income areas. **1046**

eligible Meeting the requirements or being qualified. **698**

elite (uh·LEET) Small privileged group. **505**

Elk Hills Government-owned oil reserve in California. **884**

emancipate To free. **569**

emancipation (i·man·suh·PAY·shun) Freedom. **466**

Emancipation Proclamation Decree issued by Abraham Lincoln in 1863 freeing slaves in the South. **570**

Embargo Act Law passed in 1807 prohibiting all exports from the U.S. in response to the impressment of American sailors by the British. **288**

embodied Represented. **199**

Emergency Quota Act Law passed in 1921 limiting by nationality the number of United States immigrants. **865**

empresario Mexican word to describe businessmen who brought settlers into Texas. **408**

enclosure movement Period when British landowners fenced in their fields and began raising sheep. **44**

endeavor Effort or attempt to accomplish something. **449**

endorsement Public statement of approval. **947**

enlightened Informed. **222**

Enlightenment Intellectual movement in the 1750s characterized by a belief in the power of human reason and marked by many scientific discoveries and inventions. **98**

enterprise Project or undertaking. **48**

entrepreneur (ahn·truh·pruh·NUHR) Person who develops a business. **670**

enumerated (i·NOOH·muh·rayt·uhd) **articles** Goods produced in the American colonies that could be sold only within the British empire. **114**

environment Everything in people's surroundings that affects them in any way; nature. **6**

Environmental Protection Agency (EPA) Department established in 1970 to monitor pollution and seek ways to reduce it. **1098**

Equal Rights Amendment Failed Constitutional amendment proposed in 1972 to provide that equal rights for women. **1101**

"Era of Good Feelings" Period from 1817 to 1821 when the country was prosperous and at peace under President Monroe. **364**

Erie Canal New York waterway completed in 1825 that connected the Hudson River to Lake Erie. **351**

escalation Increase in military involvement. **1062**

escapades Wild adventures. **41**

Espionage Act Law passed in 1917 that made it a crime to help enemy countries or to interfere with military recruitment. **837**

ethical Behaving according to what is considered moral or right. **238**

ethics Code of morals of a particular society, religion, or group. **708**

ethnic neighborhood City community made up of immigrants from the same country. **686**

even-handed Fair or just. **253**

ever-normal granary System of storing grain in government granaries rather than selling it to help regulate prices and keep surpluses off the market. **926**

evolution Theory that all living species and animals developed from simpler lifeforms. **867**

excavate To uncover objects underground by digging. **280**

excerpts Selected or quoted sections of a book or other source. **117**

executive Person or branch of the government responsible for enforcing or carrying out the laws. **182**

executive privilege Right to keep information about presidential matters secret. **1083**

exempted Released or freed from duty. **565**

expatriate Person who leaves his or her native country permanently. **877**

expeditionary force Name given to American troops sent to foreign countries. **754**

exploit (EK·sploit) Heroic and daring act. **303**

exploitation Unfair use of another person or situation for one's own advantage. **738**

extorted Took by force. **142**

extremist Person who holds radical ideas or supports radical measures. **245**

F

faction Group within a group that has its own goals. **535**

factors of production Resource used to produce goods and services. **1033**

Fair Deal President Truman's proposals to extend New Deal programs. **984**

Fair Employment Practices Committee Commission created in 1941 to prevent job discrimination against racial and ethnic groups and women. **958**

Fair Labor Standards Act. Act that outlawed child labor and set a 40-hour work week (1938). **927**

far-flung Widely spread or distributed. **108**

Farm bloc Group of U.S. representatives from heavily agricultural states organized to support the interests of farmers (1921). **889**

Farmers Alliance Social organization that became a political force to represent farm interests. **720**

fascism (FASH·iz·uhm) Political movement that stresses nation and race; begun in Italy in 1919 under Mussolini. **937**

fateful Having important conse-quences. **1062**

favorable balance of trade Situation in which a country exports more than it imports, or sells more than it buys. **112**

federal deficit Shortage in federal in-come. **929**

Federal Deposit Insurance Corpora-tion (FDIC) Federal agency cre-ated to protect savings deposits in banks. **906**

Federal Emergency Relief Adminis-tration Department created in 1933 to distribute money to agen-cies that helped the poor. **912**

Federal Highway Act Law passed in 1956 that provided federal funding for construction of interstate highways. **1007**

Federal Reserve Act Law passed in 1913 that created a national bank-ing system of 12 Federal Reserve Banks. **804**

Federal Reserve Board Government agency that oversees the opera-tion of the Federal Reserve Sys-tem. **804**

Federal Securities Act Law passed in 1933 that regulated the way com-panies issue and sell stock. **908**

Federal Trade Commission Agency-created in 1914 to help eliminate unfair business practices and to enforce antitrust laws. **804**

federalism Sharing of power by the national and state governments. **198**

Federalist Papers Series of newspa-per articles written in 1787-88 that explained and defended the U.S. Constitution. **228**

Federalists One of the first two po-litical parties; its members sup-ported a strong central govern-ment and a powerful executive branch. **226**

feudal system Structure of society in medieval Europe in which peas-ants were bound to a lord who, in turn, owed service or payments to a higher ruler. **15**

Fifteenth Amendment Constitutional amendment that guarantees all citizens the right to vote. **600**

Fifty-Niner Nickname given to a

prospector who went to Colorado in 1859 in search of gold. **630**

figurehead Leader in name only, wih little or no power. **222**

filament Fine, threadlike wire that glows when heated by electric current. **667**

fireside chat Informal presidential speech given by Franklin Roose-velt in the 1930s. **913**

First Amendment Constitutional amendment that guarantees free-dom of speech, religion, and the press, and the right to assemble peacefully. **266**

First Continental Congress. Meeting of colonial delegates in 1774 at which the colonies demanded re-peal of the Intolerable Acts. **143**

fiscal (FIS-kuhl) **policy** Means of stimulating the economy through government spending and taxa-tion. **1041**

Five Nations League of Iroquois tribes that inhabited the eastern woodlands of the Northern United States. **9**

Five-Power Naval Treaty Agreement in 1922 between the U.S., Great Britain, Japan, France, and Italy to a ten-year ban on the construc-tion of warships. **859**

five themes of geography Basic con-cepts—location, place, relation-ships within places, movement, and region—considered by many geographers as key to the under-standing of geography. **860**

fixed cost Regular expense involved in running a business. **673**

flagrant Obviously wrong. **997**

flagship Ship that carries the com-mander of a fleet. **752**

flank Right or left edge of an army. **171**

flappers Young women whose bold actions and dress expressed a new spirit of freedom after World War I. **871**

fleet Swift. **622**

fluently With an easy command of the language. **246**

folk tale Story that has been passed down from generation to genera-tion. **9**

foothold Secure position that can be

used as a base for further ad-vance. **519**

forge Furnace or shop where iron products are made. **114**

forged Formed or shaped, usually with great effort. **593**

Fort Donelson Confederate fort n Tennessee taken in 1862 by Grant sson after his capture of Fort Henry. **578**

Fort Henry Confederate fort in Ten-nessee captured by Grant in 1862. **578**

Fort McHenry Fort in Baltimore harbor where Americans stopped a British attack in 1814; this battle was the inspiration for "The Star-Spangled Banner." **310**

Fort Pitt French Fort Duquesne captured and renamed by the British during the French and In-dian War. **121**

Fort Sumter Federal fort in Charles-ton, South Carolina, harbor where an attack by southern forces began the Civil War. **543**

Forty-Niner Nickname given to a prospector who went to California in 1849 in search of gold. **432**

Four Freedoms Freedom of speech and religion, freedom from want and fear, mentioned in 1941 Franklin Roosevelt speech. **947**

Fourteen Points Peace program out-lined by President Wilson in 1918. **845**

Fourteenth Amendment Constitu-tional amendment that made Af-rican Americans citizens of their states as well as of the U.S., guar-anteed their civil rights, and gave them equal protection of the laws. **597**

Fourth of July American Indepen-dence Day celebrating the anni-versary of the signing of the Dec-laration of Independence. **157**

framer Author of a document. **254**

franchise (FRAN-chyz) Right to do business granted by the govern-ment. **699**

frayed Ragged or torn. **273**

free coinage Act of turning all avail-able silver into coins. **720**

free enterprise Economic system in which there is limited government control over business practices. **677**

free soiler Person opposed to slavery who could go to Kansas and vote to keep slaves out. **519**

Free-Soil party Political party founded in 1848 by northern Democrats who were opposed to popular sovereignty. **437**

free state State that did not allow slavery. **436**

freedmen Former slaves. **594**

Freedmen's Bureau Organization run by the army to care for protect southern blacks after the Civil War. **595**

freeman Person who has all the political and civil rights of citizebship in a city, state, or nation. **58**

Freeport Doctrine Stephen Douglas' statement that the people have the ultimate power to decide if slavery should or should not exist in a location. **531**

French Revolution Rebellion beginning in 1789 of the poor French lower classes against the monarchy that resulted in the establishment of a Republic. **244**

frenzy State of wild excitement. **980**

frigate American warship of the early 1800s. **302**

frontier Edge of a settled region. **79**

Fulton's Folly Name skeptics gave the *Clermont*, Fulton's first steamboat. **354**

functional illiteracy Not being able to read or write well enough to hold a job or function in a complex society. **891**

Fundamental Orders First written form of government in America; drafted by representatives of the first settlements along the Connecticut River. **58**

fundamentalism. Conservative religious beliefs. **867**

fur trade Early American industry involving the sale of hides and furs to Europe. **92**

G

Gadsden Purchase Land along the southern borders of New Mexico and Arizona purchased from Mexico in 1853 to allow construction of the Southern Pacific Railroad. **515**

galleon Heavy sailing ship used as a commercial vessel or a warship in the 15th to 18th centuries. **41**

generalization Broad statement based on loosely associated facts. **5**

genocide Deliberate and planned destruction of a race or cultural group. **938**

Gentlemen's Agreement Deal in 1907 in which Japan promised not to allow laborers to come to the United States. **805**

geography Study of the the physical and cultural features of the earth. **22**

Gettysburg Address Speech containing a classic expression of American democratic ideals delivered by President Lincoln in 1863. **575**

ghetto Section of a city where members of racial or ethnic groups live because of economic or social pressures. **862**

ghost town Abandoned mining town. **435**

ghoulish (GOOL·ish) Horrible or disgusting. **1110**

G.I. Bill of Rights Program under established in 1944 which enabled veterans to obtain low-cost loans to buy homes or start businesses. **955**

Gilded Age Period between 1865 and 1900 that was marked by growth in industry and the availability of consumer goods but also by business corruption, greed and materialism. **683**

glasnost (GLAS·nohst) Spirit of openness and freedom in the Soviet Union begun under Gorbachev. **1115**

Glorious Revolution English uprising in 1688 in which the Catholic king James II was replaced by the Protestant monarchs William and Mary. **111**

Gold Rush Surge of 80,000 miners to California to look for gold in 1848. **432**

gold standard Monetary system that used only gold to mint coins and to back bank notes. **723**

Golden Age of Sports Period during the 1920s when the radio, increased leisure time and money, and public relations efforts caused spectator sports to become very popular. **873**

Golden Rule Principle of conduct that states,"Do unto others as you would have them do unto you" followed by reform mayor Samuel M. Jones. **789**

Goliad Texas town where 350 Texans were killed by Mexican troops in 1836. **410**

government bond Interest-bearing certificate sold by the government to raise revenue. **241**

governor Chief executive of an English colony or American state. **109**

grandfather clause Law which eliminated literacy tests and poll taxes for persons who had voted before 1867 and their descendants. This meant only white men qualified to vote. **613**

graphic Showing realistic or lifelike detail. **709**

grappled Grab hold of. **273**

"Great American Desert" Nickname given to the Great Plains by early explorers. **623**

Great Awakening Time in the 1740s of widespread religious fervor; a force for toleration in the colonies. **95**

Great Compromise Agreement made at the Constitutional Convention in 1787 to create a House of Representatives elected by the people on the basis of population and a Senate elected by the state legislatures, two members from each state. **220**

Great Depression Economic crisis from 1929 to 1940. **895**

Great Plains Geographic region that extends from western Texas north to the Dakotas and into Canada and west to the foothilss of the Rockies. **623**

Great Society Social and economic programs of President Lyndon Johnson. **1031**

Great Stock Market Crash Disastrous fall in the stock prices in 1929 that signaled the end of the prosperity of the 1920s. **891**

Great War Name given to World War I, which broke out in Europe in 1914. **809**

greenback Paper money which was not exchangeable for gold or silver coins. **702**

greenhouse effect Warming of the earth's surface caused by air pollution in the earth's atmosphere. **1104**

Guadalcanal (gwahd·uhl·ka·NAL) Pacific island that was the scene of heavy fighting during World War II. **968**

Guam (GWAHM) Pacific island that became U.S. territory after the Spanish-American War. **761**

guano (GWAHN·oh) Manure of sea birds or bats used as fertilizer. **369**

guerrilla (guh·RIL·uh) Fighter who commits sabotage or surprise attacks. **522**

guerrilla warfare Fighting by ambush and surprise raids, often behind enemy lines. **747**

Guilford Court House Site in South Carolina of an American victory in 1781. **171**

gunboat diplomacy Name for the policy of the Roosevelt Corollary, which said the U.S. would make a show of force to prevent European interference in events in the Western Hemisphere. **777**

H

haggled Argued about terms or price. **745**

hail Relentless showering. **312**

Hanoi (ha·NOY) Capital of North Vietnam. **1078**

haphazard Without any plan or order. **690**

hard-hitting Forceful. **785**

hard money Gold or silver coins, or paper money that could be exchanged for gold or silver. **193**

Harlem Globetrotters Traveling team of African American basketball players famous for its skill and fancy ball-handling. **874**

Harlem Renaissance (ren·uh·SAHNS) Period during the 1920s when New York City's Harlem became an intellectual and cultural capital for African Americans. **872**

Harpers Ferry Site of a government arsenal raided in 1859 by John Brown and his commandos. **532**

Hartford Convention Meeting of New England states in 1814 to discuss separation from the Union. **313**

havoc Great damage or ruin. **755**

Hawaiian Islands Group of islands in the Pacific Ocean that the United States annexed in the 1890s. **741**

hawk Person who supports war. **1064**

Hay-Bunau-Varilla Treaty Agreement with Panama granting the U.S. a 10-mile canal zone through Panama (1903). **772**

Haymarket bombing Incident during an 1886 Chicago strike in which a bomb exploded, turning public opinion against unions. **681**

Hay-Pauncefote (PAHNS·fooht) **Treaty** Agreement in 1901 between Great Britain and the U.S. giving the U.S. sole right to build and control a canal between the Atlantic and Pacific oceans. **770**

headright Agreement by colonists to pay their way or that of others to Virginia in exchange for 50 acres of land for each "head" transported from England. **50**

Head Start Program created in 1964 to give disadvantaged children a better start in school and life. **1030**

heartened Encouraged. **525**

heavy-handed Harsh. **64**

Hepburn Act Law giving the Interstate Commerce Commission the power to inspect the business records of railroad companies and to regulate rail rates (1906). **797**

heralded Proclaimed or announced with enthusiasm. **330**

hereafter Life after death. **19**

Highway Safety Act Law passed in 1966 that established safety standards for vehicles and roadways. **1031**

Hindenburg Line Line of trenches on the Western Front from which German forces launched attacks in the Great War. **844**

Hiroshima (hir·uh·SHEE·muh) Japanese city that was site of the first atomic bombing by the U.S. in August 1945. **974**

Hispaniola (his·puhn·YOH·la) First island settled by Columbus and his crew in 1492; today the site of the Dominican Republic and Haiti. **25**

historical imagination Ability to look at past events objectively by recognizing what people knew and did not know at a particular time. **3**

historical significance Importance of an event to other events. **325**

Ho Chi Minh (HO·CHEE·MIN) **Trail** Path running from North Vietnam through Cambodia and Laos to South Vietnam that was used by the North Vietnamese as a supply trail during the Vietnam War. **1074**

Holocaust (HO·luh·kawst) Hitler's program to exterminate the Jews. **938**

Holy Land Palestine; important to Christians as the birthplace of Jesus and site of biblical events. **16**

Home Owners' Loan Corporation (HOLC) Organization created in 1933 to help people meet house payments by refinancing home mortgages at lower rates. **908**

home schools Educational system in which children are taught at home by parents or other relatives. **484**

Homestead Act Law passed in 1862 that granted free public land to farmers who agreed to cultivate the land for a given period of time. **535**

Homestead Strike Violent 1892 AFL strike in Homestead, Pennsylvania, during which steel workers and Pinkerton detectives were killed. **682**

hotbed Fertile starting place. **1120**

"hot-line" Direct emergency telephone line set up in 1963 between Moscow and Washington, D.C., to reduce the risk of accidental war. **1019**

House of Burgesses First elected

government body in America, in Virginia in 1619. **50**

house of refuge Place built to house delinquent and homeless children and separate them from adult criminals. **500**

House of Representatives House of Congress in which states are represented according to their population. **220**

Housing Act Law passed in 1961 that helped poor people pay their rent. **1031**

Hull House Chicago settlement house founded in 1889 by social worker Jane Addams which became a model for others throughout the country. **691**

human right Privilege belonging to all human beings. **238**

Hundred Days First part of Franklin Roosevelt's first term during which Congress passed many New Deal programs. **906**

Hungary Eastern European nation in which a revolt against communist control took place in 1956 and the 1980s. **1003**

I

Ice Age Period when icecaps and glaciers covered large parts of the earth's surface. **2**

ideal community. Settlement established far from other communities in which residents could live as they wished. **490**

ideology Opinions or theories that make up a social or political program. **1120**

ill-advised Unwise or without sound advice. **129**

immigrant Person who comes to another country to live. **343**

Immigration Act of 1965 Law that changed admission quotas to the U.S. based on nationality. **1031**

immoral Wicked or morally wrong. **440**

immunity Resistance to a disease. **35**

impartial Not favoring one side. **746**

impartiality Fairness or objectivity. **819**

impeachment Formal charge of

wrongdoing brought against a official of the federal government. **225, 598**

imperialism Practice of establishing and controlling colonies. **762, 817**

imposed Established or applied by authority. **837**

impressment Practice used by the British in the early 1800s of forcing sailors of British ancestry to serve in the British navy. **287**

impromptu Without preparation. **1068**

improvised Composed, invented, or arranged on the spur of the moment. **871**

inadmissable Not allowed. **470**

Incas (ING-kuhs) Highly civilized nation of people who lived in the mountains of Peru at the time of the Spanish invasion. **34**

Inchon (IN-chawn) Korean port from which American forces launched a successful attack against the North Korean army during the Korean War. **998**

income tax Tax upon a person's earnings. **804**

Income Tax Act Law passed in 1986 that lowered income taxes, especially for the poor. **1111**

inconclusively Done without settling anything or reaching a definite result. **294**

indentured servant Laborer who signed a contract agreeing to work for a period of time without wages in return for passage to America. **50**

Independent Treasury System System in the 1840s where debts to government were paid in gold and silver and stored in vaults. **400**

Indian Rights Act (1968) Law passed to protect the rights of American Indians. **1053**

Indies Islands off the east coast of Asia. **18**

indifference Lack of interest. **163**

indigo (IN-dug-goh) Plant that produces a dark blue dye used in manufacturing cloth. **91**

indirect tax Tax on imports that were collected from shippers and paid by consumers in the form of higher prices. **130**

Industrial Revolution Change in production methods in the early 1800s from human to machine power. **335**

Industrial Workers of the World (IWW) A radical organization of laborers who wanted to put industry under the control of the workers. **837**

industrial technology Tools and machines used to produce goods. **333**

industrial unions Organization of all the laborers involved in a particular industry. **927**

inequity Lack of fairness or objectivity. **1100**

infamy Extreme disgrace or dishonor. **952**

infant mortality rate Annual number of children under one year of age that die for every 1,000 that live. **886**

infested Overrun or swarming with. **47**

inflamed Intensely excited or angered. **749**

inflation Rise in price levels resulting from an increase in the amount of money or a decrease in the amount of goods available for sale. **193**

inflation rate Amount of inflation or the degree to which inflation affects the economy. **1100**

inflationary (in-FLAY-shuh-ner-ee) **spiral** Continuous rise in prices that occurs when the higher cost of one product or service causes the prices of other goods and services to rise. **392**

inhumanity The quality or state of being cruel or brutal. **458**

initiative (in-ISH-uht-iv) Procedure allowing voters to propose a law to the legislature. **791**

injunction Court order that prohibits an individual or group from carrying out a given action. **985**

inner city Usually an older, run-down and densely populated central section of a city. **1101**

insight Clear understanding of the inner or true nature of something. **504**

installation Military camp, fort or base. **1018**

interchangeable (in·tuhr·CHAYN·juh·buhl) **parts** Production advance involving parts that can be substituted one for the other; an essential process for mass production. **334**

interlocking Connected so that each part is dependent on another to operate. **673**

internal improvements Parts of the transportation network such as roads and canals built at public expense. **380**

Internationalism A policy of cooperation among nations. **859**

internationalists Those who support political and economic involvement with other nations. **946**

internment (in·TUHRN·muhnt) **camps** Enclosed compounds in a barren section of the U.S. where Japanese-Americans were held during World War II. **956**

interstate commerce Business transactions between residents or companies in different states. **676**

Interstate Commerce Act Law passed in 1887 to regulate railroad freight rates and business practices and which set up a commission to oversee railroad affairs. **676**

Interstate System Network of superhighways begun in 1956 under President Eisenhower. **1007**

intimately In a very personal or familiar way. **1028**

Intolerable Acts Name colonists gave to the Coercive Acts passed by the British government in 1774 to punish the colonists for the Boston Tea Party. **142**

Iran Country in the Middle East where 53 Americans were held hostage during the Carter administration and which fought a long war with Iraq. **866**

Iron Curtain The term Winston Churchill used to describe the barrier of censorship and secrecy between communist countries and the rest of the western world. **986**

ironmaster Manufacturer of iron. **663**

Irreconcilables Group of senators who refused to approve the WWI Versailles Peace Treaty under any condition. **853**

Islam Muslim religion founded by the prophet Mohammed. **16**

island hopping Military strategy used in World War II where important consecutive islands were seized and used as bases. **968**

isolationism A national policy of maintaining a nation's interests without being involved in alliances with other countries. **859**

isthmus Narrow strip of land connecting two larger segments of land. **28, 770**

isolationism (eye·suh·LAY·shuh·niz·uhm) Policy that stresses freedom from foreign alliances and national self-sufficiency. **737**

Israel Country in the Middle East formed in 1948 for Jews. **1016**

Iwo Jima (EEH·woh·JEE·muh). Small Pacific island captured by the Americans in World War II after heavy fighting with the Japanese. **968**

J

Jackson State Mississippi university where two students were killed in 1970 by state police during a protest of the Vietnam War. **1074**

Jacksonian Follower of Andrew Jackson who believed in the rights and abilities of typical Americans or the common man. **384**

Jamestown First successful English colony in America. **47**

Jay's Treaty Treaty in which the British agreed to withdraw troops from western ports and give shipping and trading concessions to the United States. **250**

Jazz Music created by African American musicians in New Orleans in the late 1800s that became popular during the 1920s. **870**

Jazz Age Nickname for the 1920s. **871**

Jim Crow law Any law that promoted segregation. **614**

Job Corps A Great Society program to train poor, unskilled workers. **1030**

joint-stock company Group of investors formed to outfit colonial expeditions in the early 1600s. **44**

jokester Comedian or one who cracks jokes. **194**

junta (HOON·tah) In this case, committee established in the U.S. by Cuban revolutionaries to gather support in the late 1890s. **749**

justice of the peace Chief official of county courts in the South. **110**

juvenile delinquency Problem of children and teens breaking the law. **499**

K

kamikaze (kom·i·KAH·zee) Japanese pilots who committed suicide with honor by crashing their planes into enemy targets. **971**

Kansas-Nebraska Bill Law that allowed the question of slavery in the Nebraska Territory to be decided by popular sovereignty and which created the Kansas and Nebraska territories. **516**

keelboat Shallow covered riverboat that is towed, poled or rowed. **281**

Kent State Northern Ohio university where four students were killed in 1970 during a riot protesting the Vietnam War. **1074**

Kentucky and Virginia Resolutions Statements written in 1798 by Jefferson and Madison to question the power of the federal government over the states **267**

kickbacks Illegal practice of receiving back part of the money paid for a job. **699**

King George's War Third conflict between the French and English in America from 1744 to 1748. **117**

King William's War (1689–97) First in a succession of colonial conflicts between the English and French. **116**

kingpin Leader in a group or undertaking. **76**

King's Mountain Site of Tory defeat in South Carolina (1780). **171**

Knights of Labor Union of skilled and unskilled workers founded in 1869. **680**

Know-Nothings Name given to members of the Native American party during the 1850s. **523**

Korean War War in 1950-52 between North and South Korea in which South Korea was supported by U.N. troops, mainly from the U.S. **999**

Ku Klux Klan (koo·kluhks·KLAN) Secret organization which terrorized African Americans. **610**

L

Lancasterian (lan·KAS·tree·ahn) **system** Educational system where teachers taught older pupils who then taught younger students. **489**

Land Ordinance of 1785 Law that setup a method for surveying and selling western territories by townships. **189**

Land Ordinance of 1787 Plan for governing the lands in the Northwest Territory as they grew to statehood (also Northwest Ordinance). **189**

lathe (LAYTH) Machine that shapes wood by holding and turning it against a cutting tool. **334**

Latin America Countries in Central and South America settled by Spain and Portugal. **323**

Law of Prior Appropriation Law that states that rights of water use belong to the person who first uses the water, as long as it is for beneficial purposes such as farming. **430**

Law of Riparian Rights Law that states that all property owners along whose land borders a river or stream have equal right to the water; they may not increase or decrease its flow or change its quality. **429**

League of Nations International organization established in 1920 to seek world peace; dissolved in 1946 when many of the League's functions were taken over by the United Nations. **846**

Lecompton Constitution Proposed Kansas state constitution that would have allowed slavery. **528**

legacy (LEG·uh·see) Something left or handed down by a predecessor. **1030**

legal right Privilege given to people by law. **238**

legislature Elected body given the responsibility of making laws. **110**

Lend-Lease Act Law passed in 1941 that allowed for the sale or lease of war supplies to any country whose defense was important to the security of the United States. **947**

Lexington One of two Massachusetts towns (along with Concord) where the first battles of the American Revolution were fought. **144**

liberal Openminded and supportive of individual freedom. **929**

Liberia (ly·BIR·ee·ah) Country on West Coast of Africa where some formers slaves settled. **449**

lien (leen) Claim on property as security for a debt. **608**

life chance Possibility for a person to share in the in the opportunities and benefits society has to offer. **878**

likening Comparing or pointing out as similar. **727**

limited liability One advantage of corporations; investors risk only the amount of money they have invested. **661**

The Lincolns of Indiana Rugged pioneer family in which President Abraham Lincoln was raised. **377**

Line of Demarcation (dee·mahr·KAY·shahn) Agreement in 1493 that dividing the Atlantic Ocean gave claim to all lands west of the line to Spain and all lands east to Portugal. **25**

literacy test Proof of a person's ability to read and write as a requirement for voting. **613**

Little Rock Arkansas capital where U.S. soldiers were sent in 1957 to escort black students to a high school for whites to achieve court-ordered segregation. **1010**

livelihood Means of support. **328**

lobbyist Person representing a special interest group who tries to influence legislators. **791**

lockout Refusal by an employer to allow employees to come to work unless they agree to his terms. **682**

lock Canal chamber where ships are raised and lowered from one water level to another. **772**

lode Deposit of mineral ore. **639**

Lodge Reservations A series of changes to the WWI Versailles Peace Treaty supported by Senator Henry Cabot Lodge. **853**

The Lodges of Boston Wealthy Boston family who began a political dynasty in the 1800s. **372**

Log Cabin Campaign Whig strategy to win votes for William Henry Harrison based on his reputation as a rugged man of the people. **400**

long drive. Two-month journey that brought cattle from Texas to the railroads. **643**

Long Night Period of racial segregation after the Civil War. **613**

loophole Omission or unclear statement in a document such as a law or contract through which the intent of the document can be evaded or negated. **927**

Lost Generation American writers whose works expressed the disillusionment felt after World War I. **828**

lot One's fate in life. **336**

lottery Process of drawing lots to choose or decide something. **943**

Louisiana Purchase Acquisition from France made by the United States in 1803 of all the land between the Mississippi River and the Rocky Mountains for $15 million. **278**

Lowell system Method of employing young women to operate power looms first used in 1813 to recruit laborers for factories in Lowell, Massachusetts. **339**

Loyalist American during the Revolution who remained loyal to the king of England; also called a Tory. **155**

lush Growing thick and rich. **643**

Lusitania British passenger ship sunk by German U-boats in May 1915 during the Great War; 128 Americans were among the more than 1,200 people who died. **826**

M

machine gun Automatic weapon that fire a rapid, continuous stream of bullets. **840**

Macon's Bill Number Two (1810) Law that removed restrictions on trade with France and Britain and promised American support to either nation that stopped attacks on American ships. **291**

Maine Free state created through the Missouri Compromise of 1820 to keep a balance of slave and free states in Congress. **437**

mainland Continent or main body of a continent. **543**

mainstay Chief means of support. **7**

malice (MAHL·us) Hatred toward or the desire to hurt others. **593**

mandate Wishes of the people expressed to a candidate as an authorization to follow campaign proposals; also a territory or colony under the management of the League of Nations. **712**

Manhattan Project Code name for the top-secret plan to develop the atom bomb. **973**

manifest destiny Belief popular in the 1840s that the obvious future role of the U.S. was to extend its boundaries to the ocean. **412**

Manila (mah·NIL·ah) **Bay** Site in the Philippines of Commodore Dewey's victory over the Spanish fleet in the first battle of the Spanish-American War (1898). **752**

manor Land and village ruled over by a feudal lord. **15**

Marbury v. Madison Legal case that established the power of the Supreme Court to declare an act of Congress unconstitutional. **273**

March on Washington (1963) Huge civil rights demonstration in Washington, D.C., during which Martin Luther King delivered his famous "I Have a Dream" speech. **1055**

market Economic term for the buying and selling of goods and services. **875**

marl Crumbly soil of sand and clay rich in calcium carbonate and used as fertilizer. **369**

Marshall Plan United States program for the economic recovery of Europe after World War II. **988**

Mason-Dixon line Boundary between Maryland and Pennsylvania, traditional line separating North and South. **101**

masonry Stone or brickwork. **65**

mass production Manufacture, usually by machinery, of goods in large quantities. **333**

Massachusetts Bay Company American colony established by the Puritans in 1630. **58**

massive retaliation (ri·tal·ee·AY·shun) U.S. policy under Eisenhower that threatened to respond to Soviet aggression with nuclear weapons. **1001**

materialistic Caring more about money and material things than spiritual things. **867**

matériel (mah·TEER·ee·el) Equipment and supplies used by a military force. **831**

matrilineal Descendants or kinship traced down through the mother's side. **5**

Mayflower Compact Document drawn up by the Pilgrims in 1620 that provided a legal basis for self-government. **53**

McCarran Internal Security Act 1950 law that required Communists to register with the government and made it illegal for communists to work for the government. **999**

McCarthyism Use of American suspicion of communists in the 1950s by Senator Joseph McCarthy to gain power by presenting charges of communist infiltration in the State Department. **997**

McKinley Tariff Act in 1890 that lifted the tariff on raw sugar imports causing Hawaii's sugar industry to suffer. **742**

meager Small amount; scanty. **65**

mechanical reaper Machine invented by Cyrus McCormick to harvest wheat. **560**

mediate (MEE·dee·ayt) To be the impartial party that helps settle a dispute between two parties in disagreement. **820**

Medicare A Great Society program that provided health insurance for people over 65. **1031**

megalopolis Continuous heavily-populated urban area connecting a number of cities. **1101**

melting pot Idea that immigrants of various racial and cultural backgrounds eventually become adapted to American ways. **805**

mercantilism Economic policy in which a country tries to maintain a favorable balance of trade by producing goods and services for export and limiting imports in every way possible.

mercenary (MUHRS·uhn·er·ee) Soldier hired to fight for money. **165**

merchant adventurer English merchant in the early 1600s who backed exploration and colonization. **44**

merchants of death Nickname given to companies that profited from the manufacture of weapons used during WWI. **940**

merit system Policy adopted by the U.S. Civil Service to make government appointments and promotions on the basis of ability rather than politics. **704**

Mesabi (muh·SAH·bee) **Range** Region in Minnesota where rich deposits of iron ore were found in the 1890s. **662**

Mexican Revolution Rebellion beginning in 1910 which ended the dictatorship of Porfirio Diaz and led to a constitutional government begun in 1917. **820**

Mexico City Capital of Mexico where Mexican forces surrendered to Americans in 1847. **420**

middleman Trader who buys products from one person and sells them at higher prices to a merchant or directly to the consumer. **20**

Middle Passage Slaves' voyage across the Atlantic. **88**

Midway Islands Islands northwest of Hawaii occupied by the United States navy in 1867; site of an important U.S. naval victory in World War II. **738**

midwife Woman who assists in childbirth. **336**

mild reservationist Republican senator who could accept the WWI Treaty of Versailles with only a few minor changes. **853**

militant Aggressive or ready to fight. **482**

military dictatorship Control of a country by the leaders of the military. **820**

military-industrial complex Phrase used by Eisenhower to describe the special interest groups representing the military and defense industries that had risen to unprecedented power during and after World War II. **1007**

mindful Being aware or bearing in mind. **239**

minimum wage Least pay a worker can receive by law. **795**

mining camps Village formed by miners working a strike. **434**

Minute Men Revolutionary War civilian-soldiers who were trained to fight on short notice. **144**

mission Task for which a person feels called or destined. **33**

Missouri Compromise Act passed in 1820 which allowed Missouri to become a slave state and Maine a free state and attempted to settle the question of slavery's spread by allowing slavery only in territories south of 36 30°N **437**

Model A Ford car that made after the Model T that introduced different colors and body styles. **880**

Model T First mass-produced car that made automobile transportation affordable for many Americans; introduced by Henry Ford in 1908. **880**

moderate Person who avoids extreme political views. **593**

moderation State of being reasonable and temperate. **1072**

monetary (MAHN·uh·ter·ee) **policy** Plan that dictates the coinage, printing and circulation of money; also method of stimulating business activity by lowering interest rates on loans to business owners and consumers. **702**

monopoly (muh·NAHP·uh·lee) Exclusive control of a product or service that results in fixed prices and elimination of competition. **139, 673**

Monroe Doctrine Important statement of foreign policy that said the United States would not tolerate European interference in the Western Hemisphere. **324**

Montgomery Bus Boycott 1955 protest by African Americans against Montgomery Alabama's segregation of city buses. **1013**

monumental Enormous and long-lasting. **814**

Mormon Trail Route to Utah used by Mormon pioneers. **429**

Mormons Religious group begun in the 1920s Society by Joseph Smith. **427**

Moslems Followers of the Islamic faith. **16**

motivated Supplied the reason or desire for acting. **670**

Mound Builders Prehistoric American Indians who buried their dead in elaborate earthen mounds. **8**

moving assembly line Method of mass production used by Henry Ford in which each worker or team performed only one simple task as the product moved past. **880**

muckraker (MUHK·rayk·uhr) Author who exposed corruption in the early 1900s. **785**

multinational Corporation that has branches in a number of countries. **876**

municipal socialism Plan which transferred private ownership of streetcar lines and gas and electric companies to city governments. **792**

mutual (MYOO·choo·ahl). Shared in common. **539**

N

Nagasaki (nah·gah·SAH·kee) Japanese city, site of the second atomic bombing by the U.S. in 1945 which ended the war. **974**

National Aeronautics (ar·oh·NAH·tiks) **and Space Administration** (**NASA**) Government agency responsible for space research programs. **1042**

National Association for the Advancement of Colored People (**NAACP**) Civil rights organization formed in 1909. **808**

National Farm Workers Association Labor union of Mexican-born farm workers founded by migrant leader Cesar Chavez. **1093**

national government Level of government with jurisdiction over all people and all other levels of government. **197**

National Grange (GRAYNJ) Farmers' organization that became politically active during the 1870s. **715**

National Industrial Recovery Act (**NIRA**) New Deal law that allowed industry to set fair codes of competition, guaranteed the right of workers to join unions, and set minimum wage rates. **906**

national judiciary Highest level courts in a country. **220**

National Labor Relations Board (**NLRB**) Board created by the Wagner Labor Relations Act to settle union disputes and guarantee fair union elections. **918**

National Organization for Women (**NOW**) Association founded by Betty Freidan in 1966 to promote equal opportunities for women. **1052**

National Origins Act. (1924) Law that severely restricted immigration from certain countries to the United States **865**

National Recovery Administration (**NRA**) Government body organized to supervise the industrial codes created under the National Industrial Recovery Act in 1933. **906**

National Road First road built linking East and West from Maryland to Illinois; also called the Cumberland Road. **350**

National Trades' Union Organization formed in 1834 by groups of skilled workers to promote better wages and working conditions. **503**

National War Labor Board Board created during World War II to stabilize wages and settle labor disputes. **955**

National Youth Administration New Deal agency that helped people between 16 and 25 years of age find employment. **916**

nationalism Patriotic feelings for one's country. **197**

Native American Party Political organization formed by native-born Americans to oppose immigration and immigrants. **523**

native sons Political candidate from a key state who is nominated in hopes of carrying that state in a national election. **698**

nativist Former whig who favored strict immigration controls. **343**

natural rights Privilege of all people defined by what is instinctively felt to be moral or good. **238**

Nauvoo (naw·voo) City in Illinois settled by Mormons in the 1800s. **427**

naval stores Product produced from the pine forests of the South, such as pitch used to make ships watertight. **91**

navigation Science of charting the position or course of a ship, aircraft, or similar vehicle. **22**

Navigation Acts British laws that were a key aspect of mercantile policy and that restricted the production of goods by American colonies and forbade trade with countries other than England between 1651 and 1733. **113**

Nazis (NAHT·seez) Members of the National Socialists party that controlled Germany from 1933 to 1945 under the dictatorship of Adolf Hitler. **937**

necessary and proper clause Section of the Constitution often used to expand the powers of Congress; also called the "elastic clause." **243**

Negro Fort Florida fort controlled by runaway slaves that was destroyed by American troops in 1816. **314**

Negro Hill Site of rich gold deposit discovered by two African-Americans. **435**

neutrality Policy of avoiding permanent ties with other nations. **253**

neutrality acts Laws passed in the 1930s to prevent United States involvement in another war. **940**

New Deal Franklin Roosevelt's program to revive the country from the Great Depression. **905**

New England Name given in the early 1600s to the northeastern-most colonies; still used as a label for that section of the United States. **57**

New Freedom Woodrow Wilson's progressive program proposed in 1912. **802**

New Frontier John F. Kennedy's social and economic programs of the early 1960s. **1014**

New Immigration Wave of immigration between 1880 and the 1920s that brought millions of people from Eastern and Southern Europe to America. **683**

New Jersey Plan Design for Congress presented by William Peterson during 1787 Constitution Convention that favored a one-state, one-vote system. **220**

New Nationalism Theodore Roosevelt's progressive platform in 1912. **800**

New Netherland Name given to the colony in the Hudson River area claimed and settled by the Dutch. **63**

New Spain Areas in North and Central America, and the Caribbean claimed and settled by the Spanish. **65**

New Sweden Colony along the Delaware River founded by Swedish settlers. **64**

New World Name given in the early 1500s by explorer Amerigo Vespucci to the lands in Central and South America. **27**

Nez Perce (NEZ·PUHRS) Indian tribe routed out of Western Idaho and eventually moved to reservations in Oklahoma. **634**

Niagara (ny·AG·ruh) **Movement.** Effort begun in 1905 by prominent African American leaders to fight racial segregation. **807**

nickelodeon Early movie houses where admission was five cents. **875**

Nineteenth Amendment Constitutional amendment in 1920 that gave women the right to vote. **858**

no man's land Devastated area between the trenches on the Western Front during the Great War. **1016**

nominal Very small or insignificant. **484**

nominating convention Meeting of party members to choose presidential and vice presidential candidates. **384**

Non-Intercourse Act Law passed in 1809 permitting trade with all countries except Britain and France. **291**

nonviolent direct action Method proposed by Martin Luther King for protesting without violence against discrimination. **1054**

nonviolent resistance Showing opposition or resistance to something without the use of violence. **1013**

normal school Teacher training school. **489**

Normandy Northern French province that was the site of the D-Day invasion during World War II. **963**

North Atlantic Treaty Organization (NATO) Agreement made in 1949 to stand firm against Soviet military threats, made between the U.S., Great Britain, France, and eight other nations. **991**

North Korea Korea north of the 38th parallel and under Soviet control since World War II. **997**

Northern Securities Case Antitrust lawsuit in which the Supreme Court dissolved the combination of three major railroads. **796**

Northwest Ordinance Plan of government for the lands in the Northwest Territory: also Land Ordinance of 1787. **189**

Northwest passage Shipping route from the Atlantic to the East Indies through North America. **44**

nuclear energy Energy released by controlled nuclear reactions; developed in the twentieth century as an alternative energy source to fossil fuels. **1034**

Nueces (nooh·AY·suhs) **River** Texas River Mexicans claimed was the boundary between Mexico and Texas. **418**

Nullification (nuhl·uh·fuh·KAY·shuhn) **Crisis** Episode in 1832 in which South Carolina nullified, or refused to follow, a tariff law causing the government to threaten force if the law was not followed. **387**

nullify (NUHL·uh·fy) To cancel the legal force of a law. **267**

O

oil refining Removing the impurities from crude oil. **664**

Okinawa (ohk·i·NAH·wa) Japanese island captured by American forces in World War II after heavy losses on both sides. **970**

"Old Ironsides" Nickname for the American warship *Constitution* used in the War of 1812. **303**

Olive Branch Petition Plea sent in 1775 to King George III requesting protection of the American colonies from the British Parliament. **151**

one person, one vote Principle of electing legislators from districts with populations of approximately the same size. **104**

Oneida (oh·NYD·uh) **community** Ideal settlement in New York. **490**

onslaught An especially fierce attack. **962**

Open Door An 1899 U.S. policy that assured all nations equal trade rights with China. **860**

Open Door Note Note sent in 1889 by John Hay requesting nations to accept the Open Door Policy in China. **768**

open-minded Willing to listen to new ideas. **73**

open range Government-owned grazing land used by ranchers to feed their herds. **643**

Operation Overlord British and American invasion of France that began the Allied conquest of Europe during World War II. **963**

Operation Sail Procession of decorated ships in New York Harbor in honor of the American Bicentennial. **1091**

Operation Torch Allied occupation of French North Africa led by Eisenhower during World War II. **961**

oppressed Burdened or kept down by a harsh and unjust authority. **407**

optimist One who always sees the bright side or expects the best to happen. **913**

oratory The art of fine public speaking. **634**

ordeal Severe trial or painful experience. **28**

ordinance Public act or law. **387**

ordinance of nullification Legal proposal made by John C. Calhoun that described an orderly way for a state to cancel a federal law it believed unconstitutional. **387**

Oregon Trail Route followed by pioneers to the Northwest. **414**

Organization of Petroleum Exporting Countries (OPEC) Oil cartel founded in 1960 to control oil prices that included Venezuela, Saudi Arabia, Iran, Kuwait, and Iraq. **863**

orrery Mechanical model that illustrates the movement of the sun and planets. **100**

Ostend (ahs·TEND) **Manifesto** Secret proposal that stated that the United States would be justified to take Cuba from Spain by force if Spain refused to sell it; news of the manifesto outraged northerners, who saw it as an attempt by southerners to gain more territory. **518**

outpost Pioneer settlement on the frontier. **306**

outraged Shocked and angered by a serious or terrible offense. **511**

overemphasis Too much stress on or attention to. **785**

overhead Fixed costs. **673**

override Constitutional power of Congress to overrule a presidential veto by a two-thirds vote. **225**

overseer Person who supervises other workers. **374**

P

Pacific Ocean Largest ocean; west of North and South America; first European sighting by Balboa in 1513 and named by Magellan in 1520. **28**

Pacific Railway Act Law passed in 1862 authorizing construction of a railroad from Nebraska to the Pacific Coast. **627**

pacifist Person who is against violence and war. **939**

Palmer raids Raids on radical groups ordered by Attorney General A.Mitchell Palmer during the Big Red Scare. **861**

Pan American Conference (1899) Meeting with representatives of Latin American countries sponsored by the U.S. with the hopes of bringing the nations of the Western Hemisphere closer together. **744**

"Pancho" Villa (PAHN·choh·VEE·yah) Mexican bandit and revolutionary who helped overthrow the Diaz dictatorship but failed to win the presidency for himself. **820**

Panic of 1837 Economic collapse caused by reckless lending and too much paper money in circulation. **392**

parallel Counterpart or something that is similar in nearly every way. **1030**

paraphrased Put into one's own words something that has been stated or written before. **783**

parcel Section or plot of land. **644**

Parliament Law-making body of England. **109**

partnership Business organization of two or more people who share the profits and losses. **661**

Pasha Title of rank or honor in Turkey and North Africa. **275**

passive resistance Method of demonstrating nonviolent opposition to a policy or program considered unjust. **856**

patriot During the American Revolution, a person who favored independence for the American colonies. **144**

patronage Awarding of government positions to political supporters by office holders. **705**

patroon Landholder who controlled a huge estate in colonial Dutch New York and New Jersey. **64**

Pawnee (paw·NEE) Indian tribe that occupied western Nebraska. **623**

Peace Corps Program established by President Kennedy that sent trained American volunteers to needy countries. **1017**

peace movement Efforts made by organized groups to promote peace among nations. **818**

Peace of Ghent Treaty signed in 1814 that ended the War of 1812. **313**

Peace of Paris Agreement in 1783 between Great Britain and the United States that ended the Revolutionary War. **188**

peace without victory Topic of a speech by President Wilson calling for the Allies and Central Powers to end the war. **829**

Pearl Harbor Port in the Hawaiian Islands where the American Pacific fleet was destroyed in a Japanese surprise attack in 1941. **950**

peculiar institution Name some gave to slaveholding. **86**

Pendleton Act (1883) Law which created a Civil Service Commission to administer exams for applicants seeking government jobs. **705**

People's party Third party formed in 1892 that represented the interests of farmers and labor unions; also called the Populist Party. **721**

peppered Fired shots at repeatedly. **145**

perestroika (per·uh·STROY·kuh) Plan to improve and broaden the Soviet economy initiated by Mikhail Gorbachev. **1116**

Perkins Institution School for the blind founded in 1830s by Samuel Gridley Howe. **498**

perplexing Complicated or puzzling. **1080**

persistent Continuing steadily despite interference. **2**

pervading Spreading throughout. **1050**

"pet bank" State banks chosen by President Jackson to receive deposits or funds removed from the Bank of the United States in 1833. **391**

Petersburg Town in Virginia where Grant's army kept up a nine-month attack against Lee's army. (1865). **581**

petulance Show of irritableness or rudeness in speech and behavior. **1108**

Philippine Islands Group of islands in the South Pacific that became a battleground for Japanese and U.S. forces during World War II. **966**

phonograph Machine that reproduced sound from tracings made on a cylinder or disk. **667**

picaroons (pik·ah·ROONS) French merchant ships that seized cargo from American merchant ships in the 1790s. **257**

piety Devotion to religious duties. **56**

Pilgrims Community of people who settled in Massachusetts in the 1620s to practice their religion freely; also called Separatists. **53**

Pinckney's Treaty Agreement between Spain and the United States that gave Americans shipping access to the Mississippi and recognized Florida boundary line set by Americans. **251**

Pinkerton Armed guard who worked as an agent for the Pinkerton Detective Agency. **682**

pious Having or showing religious devotion. **70**

Plains Indian Member of an Indian tribe that lived on the grasslands between the Rocky Mountains and the Mississippi River. **7**

Plattsburg New York city where Americans defeated the British during the War of 1812. **306**

Plessy v. Ferguson. Supreme Court case concerning civil rights that legalized the "separate-but-equal" rule. **615**

plodded Walked slowly and heavily. **351**

plunder Rob or take by force. **622**

Plymouth Site in Massachusetts where the Pilgrims first landed in America in 1620. **55**

pockmarked Covered with pits or indentations as in the scars left by smallpox. **823**

poison gas A chemical weapon first used by the Germans during World War I. **838**

polio vaccine (vak·SEEN) An inoculation developed by Dr. Jonas Salk which protected people from the polio virus. **1035**

political equity Principle that all citizens have the right to vote regardless of wealth. **79**

political machines Big city organization run by bosses who won elections by controlling poor and immigrant voters. **698**

poll tax Fee charged for voting. **613**

pollution Harmful substances that affect the quality of the environment. **1104**

polygamy (puh·LIG·uh·mee) Practice of having more than one wife or husband. **427**

pommel Rounded knob at the top of a saddle. **647**

pomp Showy or grand display. **273**

Pontiac's Rebellion Indian uprising in 1763 led by Chief Pontiac. **123**

pool Agreement between businesses to charge the same rates and share available markets. **673**

popular sovereignty (SAHV·uh·ruhn-tee) System that allowed settlers in each territory to decide whether or not they would have slavery. **437**

popular vote Vote of the people. **384**

Populist party Third party formed in 1892 that represented the interests of farmers and labor unions; also called People's party. **721**

Port Hudson Mississippi River stronghold in Louisiana captured by Union forces in 1862 to split the Confederacy in two. **580**

postwar reaction Response to the horrors of the Great War felt by many young people; characterized by xenophobia, disillusionment, and a return to fundamental values. **860**

Pottawatomie (paht·uh·WAHT·uh-mee) **Massacre** Murder of five people at Pottawatomie Creek, Kansas, by John Brown and his followers in revenge for pro-slav-ery attack on Lawrence, Kansas (1856). **522**

potent Strong or powerful in effect. **1116**

poverty line Level of income below which one is classified as poor according to the federal government. **1053**

Preamble Introduction to the Constitution that explains its purpose. **197**

precedent Guide for later action. **234**

president Elected head of the executive branch of government. **220**

presidio Fort in which Spanish soldiers were stationed. **406**

pressing Calling for immediate attention; urgent. **123**

prestige High standing or reputation based on achievement or character. **76**

prevail Triumph or succeed. **98**

price system Economic system where the cost of items determines the amounts and types of goods produced. **875**

primary elections Process for selecting candidates to run for public office. **791**

privateer (pry·vuh·TIR) U.S. merchant ship or crew who flew the French flag and attacked unarmed British ships in the early 1800s. **246**

Privy (PRIV·ee) **Council** Advisers to the King of England who set policies for governing the American colonies. **109**

Proclamation of 1763 Decision by the British to close to colonial settlers the area west of the Appalachians. **123**

productivity Amount of goods or services a worker produces. **876**

profoundly Deeply or intensely. **222**

Progressive Movement Period in the early 1900s marked by social reforms and a general feeling of hope and optimism. **781**

Progressive party Third party formed to support Roosevelt in his 1912 bid for the presidency; and party formed in 1948 to support Wallace's bid for presidency against Truman. **800**

progressives People who sought to improve life American society. **781**

prohibition Act of forbidding the manufacture, transportation, and sale of alcoholic beverages. **500**

Promontory Utah city where the Union Pacific and Central Pacific Railroads met to complete the first American transcontinental railroad. **628**

propaganda Information or ideas spread in order to gain public support for a cause or to damage an opposing cause. **836**

proprietary (pruh·PRY·uh·ter·ee) **colony** Colony granted by the British crown to an individual owner who had all the governing rights. **60**

prospective Likely to be or become. **478**

prospector One who searched for gold or silver. **432**

prosperity Economic term for a time of high production and low unemployment. **895**

protective tariff Tax on imports to increase their cost, helping American manufacturers compete with foreign producers. **330**

Protestant Reformation Religious movement in the 16th century aimed at reforming the Catholic church and resulting in the formation of several Protestant religions. **53**

provided Made the condition or established. **185**

proviso Special clause in any document that introduces a condition. **438**

public housing project Housing development for low-income families that is made affordable by public funds. **1045**

public school Free school funded by taxes and open to all children. **74**

public servant Government official. **183**

public works Roads, railways, bridges and other structures that are built for public use at public cost. **899**

Puebla (poo·EB·luh) Site of an important American victory in 1847 in the Mexican War. **420**

pueblo (poo·EB·loh) Indian village of the Southwestern U.S.; from the Spanish word for town. **6**

Puerto Rico (pohrt·uh·REE·koh) Island east of Cuba and southeast of Florida ceded to the United States after the Spanish-American War; now a self-governing commonwealth of the U.S. **756**

Pullman Strike Major railway work stoppage in 1894 begun by workers of the Pullman Palace Car Company that resulted in a violent clash with federal troops. **725**

puppet government Government whose actions are dictated or controlled by another nation. **981**

Pure Food and Drug Act Law passed in 1906 that provided for the inspection of food and drugs and the supervision of slaughterhouses. **797**

purge To get rid of someone or something undesirable such as a political opponent. **937**

Puritans English Protestants who wished to purify the Church of England and who came to America in the early 1600s for religious freedom. **58**

putting-out system Method of production in which workers wove cloth on looms in their own homes from thread "put out" by the manufacturer. **336**

Q

quadruplex (kwah·DROO·plehx) **telegraph** Edison's first major invention, a machine that could send four messages over one wire at the same time. **667**

Quaker Member of a Pacifist religious sect which came to America seeking religious freedom. **67**

quarantine (KWAHR·un·teen) Policy of isolating aggressor nations in the 1930s. **941**

quartered Housed or sheltered. **130**

Quebec (kwi·BEK) First permanent French settlement in North America founded in 1608. **62**

Queen Anne's War French and English conflict after which England gained control of Nova

Scotia, Newfoundland and the Hudson Bay (1702–1713). **117**

R

radiated Shone brightly as if sending out rays from a center. **95**

radical Person who favors sudden or extreme changes. **53**

railroad baron Person who made a fortune through railroads, often by using illegal or unfair methods. **660**

ramrod Marked by rigidity or stiffness. **383**

ranchero (ran·CHER·oh) Mexican landholder who owned a *rancho*. **405**

rancho (RAN·cho) Vast estate with cattle grazing lands owned by a Mexican citizen. **405**

range right Claim in dry areas to the water of a stream which allowed control of the lands around it. **643**

range war Battle in the 1880s between sheep and cattle ranchers for control of grasslands. **648**

rangy (RAYN·gee) Tall and long-limbed. **643**

rank-and-file Enlisted men or common soldiers as distinguished from the officers. **557**

ratify To approve. **186**

ratifying convention Meeting held in a state for the purpose of approving the Constitution. **226**

ravaged Violently destroyed. **594**

reactionary Person who wants to oppose political or social change. **255**

rebate (REE·bayt) Illegal kickback, or money returned, to preferred shippers by the railroads in the 1870s. **673**

recall Process of removing an official from office by public vote. **791**

reckoning Figuring or calculating. **302**

reclusive Withdrawn from society. **497**

reconcentrado (ree·kawn·sen·TRAH·doh) Concentration camp in Cuba in the 1890s. **749**

Reconstruction Process after the Civil War, of bringing the southern states back into the Union. **595**

Reconstruction Act Four-part measure passed in 1867 that ordered a military occupation of the South and ordered Southerners to give African Americans constitutional rights. **598**

recovery Part of the New Deal plan aimed at boosting the economy. **906**

Red Power Term used by American Indians in the '60s to rally support for the Indian rights movement. **1053**

Red Stick Confederacy Alliance of all Indian tribes east of the Mississippi formed by Tecumseh to resist white expansion. **298**

referendum (ref·uh·REN·duhm) Legal procedure by which the people can revoke a law passed by the legislature. **791**

refined Polished and well-mannered. **30**

reform Part of the New Deal plan aimed at preventing another depression. **906**

regime (ruh·ZHEEM) Form of government. **1062**

regulatory (REG·yuh·luh·tohr·ee) **agency** Government group that supervise business operations. **676**

relatively Somewhat or to a relative extent. **15**

relentless Unwilling to be less harsh or to show pity. **663**

relief Aim of Roosevelt's New Deal to relieve the poverty of many Americans following the Depression. **905**

reminiscent Suggestive of or tending to remind one of. **1120**

Removal Act Law passed in 1830 that provided money to help Indian tribes move west. **396**

reparations (rep·ah·RAY·shunz) Money given by defeated nations as payment for wrongs, damages, or injuries suffered by other nations during a war. **848**

repeal To reject or revoke a law. **268**

repel To drive back. **1060**

Republic of California Name that Californians gave to their country after declaring independence from Mexico. **420**

Republic of Panama Nation formed in 1903 after Panamanians revolted, with U.S. support, against the Republic of Columbia. **771**

Republic of Texas Country formed after Texans declared independence from Mexico in 1836. **410**

Republic of West Germany. Nation formed by combining the zones of Germany controlled by Britain, France and the U.S. after World War II. **989**

Republican Type of government in which power is held by representatives elected by the people. **190**

Republican party Political party formed in 1854 by Northern Whigs and Democrats who opposed slavery. **523**

rescind. To cancel. **130**

reservations Limiting conditions or specific objections. **856**

restrained Quiet or controlled in behavior and manner. **464**

restraint of trade Interference with the free flow of goods or with fair competition. **796**

restraint A control that prevents extreme behavior or activity. **224**

retribution Reward or compensation for good done; can also mean punishment for evil done. **957**

revitalization The giving of new life or restoring energy to. **872**

revived Brought back to life or renewed. **313**

Revolutionary War War for American independence fought by the American colonies against Great Britain (1775-83); also called the War for American Independence. **147**

rhetoric Eloquent but insincere speech. **1016**

Rhode Island system Labor force of children who operated spinning machines in Rhode Island mills. **337**

riddled Pierced with many holes as in rapid gunfire. **823**

rift Split or a drawing apart. **962**

rigging The ropes used to work the sails on a ship. **303**

right of deposit Right to load and unload cargo, especially at New Orleans in the early 1800s. **250**

right of way Strip of land granted by the government to railroad companies laying down tracks. **627**

rigorous Harsh or severe. **50**

Rio Grande (ree·oh·GRAND·ee) "Great River" that forms the border between Texas and Mexico. **418**

Roanoke (ROH·uh·nohk) Island off the coast of North Carolina where two English settlements failed. **43**

Romantic Age Movement in art and literature in the 19th century marked by an interest in nature and an emphasis on natural feelings, emotions and imagination over logic. **495**

Rome-Berlin-Tokyo Axis Alliance formed by Italy, Germany and Japan during World War II. **950**

Roosevelt Corollary Policy that extended the Monroe Doctrine and said that the United States had the right to force countries in the Western Hemisphere to pay their debts in order to prevent European interference. **776**

Rosa Parks Black woman arrested in Alabama in 1955 because she refused to give up her seat on a bus to a white man. **1013**

rotation in office Replacing of government jobholders with other members of the political party in power. **385**

Rough Rider Member of Theodore Roosevelt's regiment sent to Cuba during the Spanish-American War. **754**

round-up Bringing together cattle scattered over the open range. **645**

rubble Broken pieces of masonry or rock; usually associated with the destruction of houses or buildings. **606**

runaway inflation Uncontrollable rise in prices due to a high circulation of paper money. **718**

Rural Electrification Administration New Deal agency that helped bring electricity to remote areas. **915**

Rush-Bagot Agreement Agreement between Great Britain and the United States not to allow naval forces on the Great Lakes. **314**

S

saga Traditional Scandinavian story form that tells about legendary figures and events. **14**

Saigon (sy·GON) Capital of South Vietnam. **1067**

St. Lawrence Seaway Waterway created by deepening the St. Lawrence River from the Atlantic Ocean to the Great Lakes. **1007**

Saint-Mihiel salient (san·mee·YEL SAYL·yahnt). Point on the Western Front where U.S. forces defeated the Germans in WWI. **844**

Salt Lake City City in Utah where the Mormons settled and prospered. **428**

San Francisco Conference The meeting held in 1945 to draft the United Nations Charter. **979**

San Jacinto (san·juh·SINT·oh) Texas town where 1836 defeat of Santa Anna's forces led to Texan independence from Mexico. **410**

San Juan (san·WAHN) **Hill** Site in Cuba of a key victory by Roosevelt's Rough Riders during Spanish-American War (1898). **756**

San Salvador (san·SAL·vuh·dawr) Island where in 1492 Christopher Columbus first landed in the Americas. **24**

sanction Penalty for violating a treaty. **849**

Sandinistas (san·duh·NEES·tuhs) Rebels in Nicaragua who set up a government friendly to the Soviets. **1111**

Santiago (sant·ee·AHG·oh) Cuban seaport captured by American forces during Spanish-American War. **755**

satirize Ridicule or make fun of. **497**

satellite nation Country that is politically or economically controlled by a larger, stronger country. **989**

Saturday Night Massacre The resignations and discharge, in one evening, of top officials in the Justice Department who refused to aid President Nixon in the Watergate cover-up. **1083**

Savannah Georgia city captured by Sherman during Civil War (1863). **583**

scalawag (SKAL·i·wag) Southern white in the Republican party during Reconstruction. **602**

scavenger (SKAV·en·juhr) Animal or organism that feeds on garbage. **347**

Schenectady (skuh·NEK·tuhd·ee) New York town attacked by French and Indians at the start of King Williams' War in 1689. **116**

sea dog Nickname given to English sea captains in the l6th century. **41**

Sea Island cotton Type of Cotton that grew well only on the Sea Islands along the coasts of Georgia and South Carolina. **450**

seaboard Part of the country by the sea. **342**

seaports Harbor town whose economy depends upon the sea. **80**

secede (si·SEED) To withdraw from, as a state leaving the union. **440**

secession (si·SESH·uhn) Withdrawal from an association or group. **278**

Second Bank of the United States National Bank founded in 1816. **388**

Second Battle of Bull Run Confederate victory in Northern Virginia in 1862 that preceded Lee's invasion of Maryland. **568**

Second Continental Congress Meeting of colonial delegates in 1776 at which the Declaration of Independence was written and approved. **150**

Second Great Awakening. Period of religious revival in the 1820s. **494**

Second New Deal New program of reforms introduced by President Roosevelt in 1935 after many of his original New Deal reforms were declared unconstitutional. **918**

Second Open Door Note Second half of U.S. Open Door policy which declared opposition to foreign occupation of China. **769**

Second World War Conflict provoked in 1939 by Germany's invasion of Poland which caused

England and France to declare war on Germany; the United States became involved after the bombing of Pearl Harbor. **937**

sectional conflict Disagreements between the Northeast, South and West over government policies. **371**

secular Pertaining to worldly matters or things not religious or sacred. **818**

secure In this case, to get or obtain. **450**

security Something given as a promise or guarantee of payment. **242**

Sedition Act Law passed in 1918 that made it illegal to oppose the government and its policies. **837**

seepage Pool of oil that has oozed up from the ground. **664**

seethed Boiled with anger. **521**

segregation Separation of people on the basis of racial, religious, or social differences. **511**

Selective Service Act Law passed in 1917 that provided for the draft of men into military service for World War I. **833**

self-determination Principle that all people should be able to decide for themselves which nation they belong to. **846**

self-sufficient Able to take care of oneself. **19**

semiarid Partially dry or getting only light rainfall. **429**

Senate House of Congress in which each state is represented by two senators. **220**

Seneca (SEN·i·kuh) **Falls Declaration** Statement issued by delegates to the 1840 women's rights convention that demanded that women be given the same rights and privileges as men. **483**

separate-but-equal Argument which supported the legality of segregation when races were separated in supposedly equal public schools. **616**

separatist Person who withdrew or separated from the Church of England; also called a Pilgrim. **53**

serf Peasant who under the feudal system was bound to work a master's land. **15**

serial (SIHR·ee·uhl) Story told or TV show shown in continuing parts or sequences. **1037**

servitude Slavery. **613**

settlement house Community center in an urban neighborhood. **690**

Seven Days Before Richmond Series of 1862 Civil War battles during which McClellan's Union forces failed to take Richmond, the Confederate capital. **559**

Seven Years' War European conflict from 1756 to 1763 between England, France and their allies; called the French and Indian War in America. **121**

Seventeenth Amendment Constitutional amendment that provided for the election of senators by popular vote. **791**

"Seward's Folly" Nickname Americans gave the purchase of Alaska in 1867 by Secretary of State William Seward. **741**

shady Not honest or trustworthy. **257**

Shaker Member of a religious group founded in England in 1747 that established several communities in America. **490**

shaman Religious leader in an American Indian tribe who used magic or rituals to heal sickness or control events. **393**

sharecropping System in which landowners provided laborers with the supplies needed for farming in exchange for a portion of their crops. **606**

Shays' Rebellion Uprising in 1787 in Massachusetts protesting high state taxes. **195**

Sherman Antitrust Act Law enacted in 1890 to prevent monopolies by banning trusts and other business combinations that restricted competition. **676**

Sherman Silver Purchase Act Law passed in 1890 that increased the amount of silver bought to 4.5 million ounces a month. **719**

ship of the line During the War of 1812 a British ship armed with 70 or more cannons. **302**

shirker One who avoids his or her duties. **165**

shopping center Stores, restaurants and other businesses grouped together and sharing one parking lot. **1044**

shopping mall Large enclosed building that houses a number of stores, restaurants and other service establishments. **1045**

shrewd Cunning or clever. **44**

shuttle diplomacy Negotiations between two nations carried out by a diplomat who travels back and forth between the two countries; used most often to describe Henry Kissinger's role in seeking peace in the Middle East in the 1970s. **863**

Sicily (SIH·suh·lee) Italian island in the Mediterranean taken by Allied prior to the occupation of Italy during World War II. **961**

sick industry Business such as coal and textiles which did not prosper during the 1920s. **888**

sidled Moved sideways in a sly manner. **641**

Siege of Vicksburg Union attack led by General Grant in 1863 on a key port in the Mississippi River. **580**

Sioux (SOO) Plains Indians who occupied the Dakotas; also called the Dakota. **623**

sit-in Form of protest where a group sits down in a public place and refuses to leave. **1013**

sitting on the fence Political term for not taking a strong stand on a political issue. **701**

Six Days' War Conflict in 1967 between Egypt and Israel quickly won by Israel. **1080**

Sixteenth Amendment Constitutional amendment that gave Congress the power to levy an income tax. **804**

skimped Spent too little money. **1104**

skyscraper Very tall building. **668**

slapstick Crude type of comedy in which the humor depends on horseplay or rough physical activity. **876**

slave state State that permitted slavery. **436**

slave Person who is owned and forced to work for others either by capture, purchase or birth. **86**

sluggish Slow in movement or growth as in a sluggish economy. **907**

smelt To melt away impurities in ore to obtain metal. **662**

smog "Smoke" plus "fog" produced by smoke and chemical fumes. **1104**

sniper Sharpshooter who harasses the enemy by shooting at individuals from a hidden position. **145**

Social Security Act Law passed in 1935 that created a system to provide old-age insurance and unemployment compensation. **919**

socialists Person who believes in public ownership and operation of all means of production and distribution of goods. **792**

society Group of people who live and work together and share similar values and patterns of behavior. **4**

sod house Home made of chunks of grassy soil built by the pioneers of the Great Plains. **650**

soldier of fortune Professional fighter who is willing to fight for any country or group that will pay him. **47**

Solid South Term applied to the southern states who as a group supported the Democratic party after the Civil War. **697**

somber Gloomy or depressing. **1085**

Sons of Liberty Patriot groups who fought against British authority in the American colonies. **128**

soup kitchen Places where food was served to the needy during the Great Depression. **897**

South Korea Korea south of the 38th parallel and backed by U.S. support since World War II. **997**

southern hospitality Term for the friendly welcome given strangers by southerners. **75**

southern regionalism Loyalty to the South, its way of life, and its values. **539**

Spanish-American War (1898) War between Spain and the United States over Cuban independence. **752**

Spanish Armada Large Spanish war fleet defeated by the British in 1588. **42**

Spanish influenza Disease that killed 20 million people worldwide in 1918. **844**

spar Pole used to support the sails of a ship. **80**

special interest group Organization that seeks to influence the government to support its own specific cause. **252**

specialization (spesh·luh·ZAY·shun) Concentration on the manufacture of a particular product; division of labor in which each person does one specific part of the whole process. **369**

speculator Person who invests money where there is a considerable risk but also the possibility of large profits. **241**

spheres of influence Area controlled in large part by a more powerful country, such as parts of China in the 19th century that were influenced by various European nations. **768**

spinning jenny Mechanical spinning wheel invented by James Hargreaves in 1765. **335**

spite Petty ill will or hatred. **422**

spoils of office Term for the dividing up of political rewards by the party that wins. **385**

spoils system Practice by an elected party of rewarding party supporters with appointments to government offices. **385**

Spotsylvania Court House Site of a bloody 1864 Civil War clash between Grant and Lee. **581**

squatters Person who clears and settles a tract of land that he or she does not own. **79**

squeamish Easily shocked or overly sensitive. **221**

stagflation Word coined by combining parts of "*stag*nation" and "in*flation*" which means inflation that is not improving. **1090**

stake a claim To declare ownership of an area by marking it with wooden stakes; especially during the Gold Rush. **434**

stalemate (STAYL·mayt) Deadlock in which neither opposing side can act effectively. **823**

Stamp Act British law that placed a tax on all printed matter in the colonies. **127**

standard of living Average quantity and quality of goods, services, and comforts available in a society. **1032**

Standard Oil Company Business founded in 1870 and built into a monopoly by John D. Rockefeller. **674**

standoff Tie or draw in a contest. **982**

starving time Period of severe hunger in Jamestown that lasted from 1609 to 1611. **48**

states' rights Doctrine that holds that the states not the federal government have the ultimate power. **268**

States' Rights party Political party formed by Southern Democrats (Dixiecrats) in 1948. **993**

Statue of Liberty Statue of the Goddess of Liberty in New York Harbor that was given to the United States by France. **685**

status Position or standing. **470**

steam engine Motor driven by steam patented by James Watt in 1769. **369**

steel plow Farming tool manufactured by James Oliver in 1868 that helped make farming of the hard, dry soil of the Great Plains possible and profitable. **653**

stemmed Stopped or checked a flow. **523**

stint Period of time spent at a particular activity. **1107**

stock certificate Document that shows ownership of stock in a corporation. **661**

stockholder Person who buys shares in a corporation. **661**

Stone Age Early period of human cultural development when stone was used to make tools and weapons. **5**

stovepipe hat Tall silk hat worn during the 1800s. **546**

straggling Wandering from the direct course or from the main group. **724**

strait Narrow water passage connecting two larger bodies of water. **28**

Strait of Magellan Water passage between the Atlantic and Pacific Oceans at the tip of South America. **28**

straitlaced Morally strict or prudish. **69**

Strategic (struh·TEE·jik) **Arms Limitation Treaty** (SALT) Agreement between the U.S. and the Soviet Union to limit nuclear weapons. **1076**

strategic defense initiative (''Star Wars'') Complex, computerized anti-missile system that president Reagan urged Congress to support with large sums of money. **1116**

strategy Military plan made to gain an advantage over the enemy. **542**

strife Struggle or conflict. **876**

strike Refusal of employees to work until their demands for better wages or working conditions are met; sudden discovery of gold or silver. **680**

strong reservationist Republican senator who would not support the Treaty of Versailles unless it underwent major changes. **853**

stronghold In this case an area dominated by a particular group such as a political party. **364**

subordinate Under the control of another. **128**

subsidy (SUB·suh·dee) Financial aid provided by the government for programs that benefit the public. **889**

substantial Of a large size or amount. **79**

suburb Residential area located outside a city. **882**

suburbanite One who lives in a suburb. **1044**

subversive Having the intention to undermine or overthrow a government by secretly working from within. **999**

Suez Canal International waterway in the Middle East seized by Egypt in 1956. British, French, and Israeli troops unsuccessfully attempted to end Egyptian control. **1004**

Sugar Act. Law passed in 1764 which taxed the colonists' im-

ports of sugar, wine, and coffee. **124**

summit meeting Conference between the heads of governments to settle political issues. **1005**

Sun Belt Warm weather states in the South and Southwest where population is increasing. **1042**

sunshine patriot Term used by Thomas Paine to describe an American who supported independence only when things were going well. **165**

superstate Government or state having complete power over other subordinate states. **900**

supply Quantity of products and services offered for sale at a certain time or at one price. **875**

supply-side economics Policy followed by President Reagan that lowered tax rates in order to increase spending, which would thereby increase tax revenues. **1110**

Supreme Court Highest U.S. court of appeals, composed of nine justices. **220**

Supreme Court Reform Plan President Roosevelt's unsuccessful plan to add New Deal supporters to the Supreme Court. **925**

suspension bridge Roadway held up by chains or cables anchored on either sides. **668**

Sussex pledge Promise made by the Germans during WWI not to sink passenger or merchant ships. **827**

Sutter's Fort Fortified town built by John Sutter on California's American River in 1839. **413**

swashbuckler Swaggering, boasting soldier. **47**

sweatshop Factory in which workers toil in bad working conditions for low pay. **679**

synthetic Artificial substance or material. **888**

synthetic textile Cloth made from artificial substances. **1035**

T

Taft-Hartley Act Law passed in 1947 to regulate labor union activities

and outlaw unfair practices by labor unions as well as employers. **985**

Tammany (TAM·uh·nee) **Hall** Political machine run by New York City Democrats. **698**

Tanks Heavily armed vehicles that move on metal belts first used during WWI. **838**

Tariff of Abominations Act of 1828 that placed a high tariff on imports and was bitterly opposed by Southern states. **385**

tariff question Disagreement between northeastern and southern states in 1830s over tariffs on foreign imports. **385**

tariff Tax on imports; in some countries also placed on exports. **130**

taskmaster A stern boss. **169**

taunted Teased or pestered. **131**

taxation without representation Argument by colonists that they were taxed by the British without being represented in Parliament. **125**

Tea Act Laws passed on 1773 that gave the East India Company exclusive rights to sell tea directly to American retailers. **138**

Teapot Dome Rich government oil reserve in Wyoming that was the subject of a scandal involving the illegal leasing of federal lands during President Harding's administration. **884**

telegraph Machine invented by Morse in the 1840s that transmitted messages through electronic signals sent over wire. **665**

telephone Instrument invented by Bell in 1876 that sends speech over distances by turning sound into electrical current. **665**

television Process of transmitting pictures by radio or wire. **1037**

Teller Amendment Resolution adopted on the eve of the Spanish-American War stating that the United States would not take control of Cuba. **752**

temperance (TEM·puh·ruhns) Movement to restrict the drinking of alcoholic beverages. **500**

tenement (TEN·uh·muhnt) Building in which several families live crowded together, often in unsafe and unsanitary conditions. **348**

tenet Principle or belief outlined in a doctrine or held in common by an organization or group. **539**

Tennessee Valley Authority (TVA) Federal agency established in 1933 to develop the water-power resources of Tennessee River valley. **908**

Tenure (TEN·yuhr) **of Office Act** Law passed in 1867 that prohibited the president from removing appointed officials with the consent of Congress. **598**

territory Area of land under the jurisdiction of the United States government but not yet a state. **190**

Tet offensive Major attack in 1968 on South Vietnamese cities by the North Vietnamese. **1067**

Texas longhorn Type of cattle with low, wide horns that once grazed freely in Texas. **643**

Thanksgiving Day American holiday tradition begun when the Pilgrims gave thanks for the help of the Indians and their first harvest in America. **56**

theory An abstract idea or hypothetical set of facts, principles or circumstances. **606**

third party Political group organized to compete against the two major political parties, usually in a national election. **712**

Thirteenth Amendment Constitutional amendment that abolished slavery. **594**

three-dimensional Having depth or being described in well-rounded completeness, as the characters in a book. **706**

Three-Fifths Compromise Agreement made by the writers of the Constitution to include three fifths of slaves in counting a state's population. **221**

Three Mile Island Nuclear power plant near Harrisburg, Pennsylvania that was the site of an accident in 1979. **1105**

Three R's Fundamental subjects of early American schools—reading, writing, and 'rithmetic. **489**

ticket List of candidates nominated by a political party. **387**

tidewater Name given southern coastal areas where rivers were affected by the ocean tides. **91**

tinkerer One who works on something in an unskilled, clumsy or experimental manner. **667**

Toleration Act Maryland law passed in 1649 that granted freedom of religion to all Christians. **61**

Tom Thumb First steam-driven locomotive, built by Peter Cooper in 1830. **355**

Tonkin Gulf Resolution Authority granted by Congress to Lyndon Johnson in 1964 to approve and support in advance "the determination of the President, as Commander in Chief, to take all necessary measures to repel any armed attack against the forces of the U.S." **1060**

Tory Colonist who remained loyal to England during the Revolutionary War. **155**

total abstinence (AB·stuh·nuhns) Drinking no alcohol. **500**

total war Strategy of war such as that used in the Civil War that calls for the destruction of resources of the enemy's civilian population as well as the army. **583**

totalitarian (toh·tal·uh·TER·ee·uhn) Type of government in which the state has absolute control over all citizens and no opposition to the government is allowed. **937**

tourism Traveling or sightseeing for pleasure. **881**

Townshend Acts (TOWN·zuhnd) Tariff of 1767 that taxed things in everyday use that were not produced by Americans. **130**

tow path Track along the bank of a canal used by men or animals in towing boats. **351**

town common Park-like square in the center of a New England village where the church, meeting house and school were located. **74**

town meeting Gathering of townspeople to act upon town business; early form of government, especially in New England. **110**

township Section of land equalling 36 square miles. **189**

trade deficit Economic situation in which the value of a country's imports is greater than the value of its exports. **877**

Trail of Tears Name expressing the sadness and hardships of the forced removal of Cherokee Indians from Georgia in 1838. **394**

transcendentalism (trans·en·DENT·uhl·is·uhm) Philosophy promoted by a group of New England idealists that people could rise above reason by having faith in themselves. **492**

transcontinental railroad Railway that extends across North America from coast to coast. **628**

Transcontinental Treaty Agreement in 1818 between the U.S. and Spain that extended America's southern boundaries to the Pacific Coast. **311**

transfer payment Money distributed through government programs that provide financial aid to individuals in need. **878**

transistor Miniature electronic device used to control and increase an electronic current. **1035**

Transportation Revolution Advances during the mid-1800s in the speed and ease of transportation systems which joined people in the West with those in the East. **357**

travesty Mockery or grossly inferior imitation. **865**

tread To walk or step. **234**

treasury Department of the government that manages the nation's finances. **234**

treaty of alliance Agreement among countries of support in case of attack. **168**

Treaty of Dancing Rabbit Creek Treaty of 1830 under which Choctaw Indians agreed to move West of the Mississippi. **397**

Treaty of Greenville Agreement in 1795 in which Indians turned over the Southern half of Ohio to American settlers. **250**

Treaty of Guadalupe Hidalgo (GWAHD·uhl·OOP·ay·hi·DALL·goh)

Agreement that ended the Mexican war and arranged the sale of vast territories to the United States. **422**

trench warfare Fighting during World War I that took place in trenches that ran across northern France from the sea to Switzerland. **823**

trend General direction or line of development especially with social change. **502**

Triangle Fire. New York factory fire that killed 140 women and prompted the passing of factory inspection laws. **793**

triangular trade Name given to the profitable trade between the northern colonies, the West Indies, and England although trade did not always flow in a simple triangular fashion. **93**

tribute In this case, any forced payment of money. **276**

Tripartite Pact Mutual defense treaty signed by Germany, Italy and Japan during World War II. **950**

Truman Doctrine U.S. policy to give financial and military aid to nations so they could resist communist rule. **988**

trust Group of corporations formed by a legal agreement and organized especially for the purpose of reducing competition. **674**

trust buster Person who wants to dissolve an established trust. **796**

trustee Person who is entrusted with the management of another person's property. **69**

turbine Rotary engine driven by a pressure of steam, water, or air against the vanes of a wheel; often used to generate electricity. **1106**

turbulent Causing disorder, violence or disturbance. **28**

turnover Shift or change in a company's personnel. **713**

turnpike Road on which tolls are collected. **349**

Tuskegee (tuhs·KEE·gee) **Institute** School for African Americans located in Alabama and founded by Booker T. Washington in 1881. **617**

Twelfth Amendment Constitutional amendment that clarified the electoral process by separating votes for the president and vice president. **271**

Twenty-fifth Amendment Constitutional amendment that said if the president is removed from office the vice president shall become president and that a vacancy in the vice president's office shall be filled by a presidential appointment. **1083**

Twenty-first Amendment Constitutional amendment that ended prohibition by repealing the Eighteenth Amendment. **867**

Twenty-second Amendment Constitutional amendment that said no one could hold the office of president for more than two terms. **985**

Twenty-sixth Amendment Constitutional amendment that gave 18- to 20-year-olds the right to vote. **1106**

two-party system Political system with two major parties of similar strength; in the U.S. these are now the Democratic and Republican parties. **254**

tyranny (TIR·uh·nee) Oppressive and unjust government. **156**

U

U-boats German submarines or "undersea ships" used during World War II. **824**

ultimate Final goal or the maximum point possible. **181**

ultimatum (uhl·tuh·MAYT·uhm) Final offer or demand. **752**

unassuming Not forward or arrogant; modest. **420**

unconditionally Absolutely, without any reservations or restrictions. **974**

unconstitutional Not in keeping with or supported by the laws of the Constitution. **194**

Underground Railroad System by which escaping slaves were secretly helped to reach Canada. **472**

undermine Weaken or hurt by unfair means. **608**

Underwood Tariff Act passed in 1913 that created an income tax and reduced tariffs on imports where American goods controlled the market. **804**

United Farm Workers Organizing Committee Labor union for migrant farm workers formed when the National Farm Workers Association and an organization of Filipino-born laborers merged. **1094**

United Nations International organization of nations formed in 1945 to promote world peace; replaced the League of Nations. **979**

United States of America Country formed by the 13 British colonies in North America who declared independence from Great Britain in 1776. **155**

unprecedented Never been done before. **1033**

unrelenting Determined or persistent. **928**

upheaval Sudden, violent change or disturbance in affairs. **820**

upland cotton Variety of cotton that withstands cold temperatures, making it hardy enough to grow almost anywhere in the southern states. **451**

uppity Arrogant or acting superior. **611**

urban center Area with a population of at least 2,500 persons. **347**

urban decay Decline in prosperity or ruining of a city area caused by a population shift to the suburbs. **1102**

urban frontier Western cities that developed on the edge of settled areas and were used as outposts and depots from which settlers spread. **346**

Urban League Organization founded in 1910 to work for equal rights for African Americans. **923**

usurped Seized power or authority illegally or by force. **998**

U-2 Affair Incident in 1960 when an American spy plane was shot down during a mission over the Soviet Union. **1005**

V

V-E Day Allied victory in World War II when Germany surrendered to the Allies on May 8, 1945. **965**

V-J Day Allied victory in the South Pacific in World War II when Japan surrendered to the U.S. on August 14, 1945. **974**

vagrant Tramp or beggar who wanders from place to place.**154**

vain Thinking too highly of oneself; conceited. **270**

Valley Forge General Washington's winter camp in Pennsylvania where in 1777 the Continental army lost thousands of men to harsh weather and desertion. **169**

vaquero (vah·KAH·roh). Spanish cowhand; they invented almost all the tools of the cowhand's trade. **645**

Venezuela Boundary Dispute Disagreement between Great Britain and Venezuela over boundary between British Guiana and Venezuela that was settled by United States arbitration in 1899. **746**

Veracruz (ver·uh·KROOZ) Mexican seaport captured by Americans in 1847 in War with Mexico. **420**

Verdun French city and site of one of the longest World War I battles. **840**

verge Brink or edge. **522**

Versailles (vuhr·SY) **Peace Treaty** Agreement ending World War I that placed the blame for the war on Germany; also created the League of Nations. **849**

veto Presidential power to reject bills passed by Congress. **225**

viceroy Spanish colonial ruler appointed by the King. **65**

Viet Cong South Vietnamese guerrilla soldiers who are procommunist. **1061**

Vietnam Southeast Asian country where United States and South Vietnam forces fought a war against the communist North Vietnamese. **1003**

Vietnamization Policy of building up the South Vietnamese army so that American troops could be withdrawn. **1073**

vigilance committee Group of volunteers organized to keep watch over a town. **642**

vigilante Volunteer crime fighter; member of a vigilance committee. **642**

Viking. Scandinavian sailor who traveled the seas between the 8th and 10th centuries. **14**

Vincennes (vin·SENZ) Site in the present-day Indiana of 1778 Revolutionary War battle where Clark's forces defeated the British, securing the Northwest in 1778. **173**

Vinland Name for North America used in ancient Viking sagas. **14**

Virginia City Famous Nevada mining boom town. **641**

Virginia Plan Proposal presented at the Constitutional Convention that recommended a government with three separate branches and representation based on population. **220**

virtue Quality of goodness. **400**

void Law no longer in force. **527**

volley Firing of many shots at once. **145**

Volstead Act Law passed in 1919 that declared beverages containing one-half of one percent of alcohol intoxicating. **866**

Volunteers in Service to America (VISTA). Organization similar to the overseas Peace Corps but operating on a domestic level. **1030**

voter participation rate Percentage of eligible voters who vote. **1108**

Voting Rights Act Law passed in 1965 that greatly increased the number of African American voters by putting an end to literacy tests and other practices used to keep African Americans from registering. **1031**

vulcanization Heat and chemical process for hardening rubber. **369**

W

wadding Soft padding material; in colonial days used in packing a bullet in a rifle barrel. **152**

wage and price controls Economic controls set by the government during World War II. **984**

wage and price freeze Controls imposed for 90 days by President Nixon in 1971 to regulate the economy. **1072**

Wagner Labor Relations Act Law passed in 1955 that gave labor unions the right to organize and bargain collectively. **918**

wake Track or path left by a moving ship in the water. **324**

war department Bureau of government in charge of military affairs. **234**

war hawk People from the West and South who favored the War of 1812 against England. **295**

War Industries Board Group that reorganized American industry to support the war effort during WWI. **831**

War of 1812 Conflict from 1812 to 1814 between the U.S. and Great Britain over Indian agitation and freedom of the seas. **301**

warlords Military leaders who controlled the government of an area or country. **937**

Warren Court Supreme court that passed important civil rights legislation under the liberal leadership of Chief Justice Warren from 1953 to 1968. **1007**

Warsaw Pact Twenty-year mutual defense agreement signed in response to NATO by most of the communist nations of Eastern Europe. **991**

wary Cautious or carefully suspicious. **978**

Washita (WAHSH·uh·taw) Site in present-day Oklahoma where Arapaho and Cheyenne were defeated by U.S. army in 1868. **630**

water-frame Spinning machine invented in 1768 by Richard Arkwright; one of the first inventions of the Industrial Revolution because it used a power source other than human or animal muscle. **335**

Watergate Affair Government scandal that began in 1972 and led to the resignation of President Nixon in 1974. **1081**

watershed Important turning point in history. **593**

welfare state Situation in which the government assumes a large measure of responsibility for the social well-being of the people. **801**

well-meaning Having good intentions. **1045**

wended Went or proceeded on one's way. **542**

Western Front WWI combat zone between the Allied states of Belgium, France and Italy and the Central Powers of Germany and Austria-Hungary. **822**

wheedled Coaxed or flattered to get something. **1029**

whet Sharpen or stimulate. **1062**

Whig American who believed in patriotic resistance to King George III; member of a major political party of the 1830s and 1840s. **155**

whirlwind Fast or rushed. **744**

whistle-stop Brief, personal appearance by a political candidate in the course of a tour. **993**

white-collar worker Generally a professional whose job does not involve manual labor. **1036**

wildcatter Name given to oil prospectors in the 1860s. **664**

Willamette Valley Fertile area in Oregon where missionaries began a settlement in the 1830s. **412**

Wilmot Proviso (pruh·vy·zoh) Failed proposal presented in 1846 to prohibit slavery in any land gained from Mexico. **438**

Wisconsin Idea Program of progressive reforms by Robert M. La Follette of Wisconsin in the early 1900s. **790**

withholding system System of paying income taxes where the employer withholds part of an employee's wages to be paid to the government. **955**

Wobblies Nickname for members of the Industrial Workers of the World. **837**

wolf packs Groups of German U-boats that attacked convoys in the Atlantic during WWII. **947**

Women's Liberation Movement Campaign of political action and demonstrations begun in the late 1960s aimed at attaining equal rights for women. **1051**

Women's Rights Convention Meeting in Seneca Falls, New York, in 1840 to seek equal rights for women. **482**

Works Progress Administration (WPA) New Deal agency that found useful work for millions of unemployed persons. **915**

world market International demand for goods and services. **608**

Wounded Knee Site in South Dakota where Sioux Indian families were massacred by United States troops in 1891; also site of 1973 Indian protest. **638**

X

XYZ Affair Scandal in the 1790s in which the French sought bribes from American diplomats. **92**

xenophobia Fear of foreigners or strangers. **865**

Y

Yalta Conference Meeting in 1945 at Yalta in the Crimea between Churchill, Stalin and Roosevelt to plan the defeat and occupation of Germany and German-occupied territories. **980**

Yalu (YOL·oo) **River** River that marks the border between China and North Korea. **999**

Yankee ingenuity (in·juh·NOO·uht·ee) Nickname for American knack for solving difficult problems in clever ways. **92**

yellow journalism Writing style of newspapers that played up the Spanish-American war as well as crime and scandal during the 1890s. **753**

yellow-dog contract Agreement signed by an employee that the employee will not join a union. **682**

Yorktown Battle site in Virginia where in 1871 British general Cornwallis surrendered to George Washington ending the Revolutionary War. **173**

Z

zest Keen enjoyment. **706**

Zimmermann Note Document which showed that Germany was trying to make an alliance with Mexico in 1917 and which prompted the U.S. to declare war on Germany. **830**

Index

Page numbers in *italics* that have a *p* written before them refer to pictures or photographs; *c,* to charts, graphs, tables, or diagrams; and *m,* to maps.

A

AAA. *See* Agricultural Adjustment Act

ABC Powers, 820

Abilene, Kans., 643

abolitionism, 465-67, 470-73, 477, 480, 482, 512, 519, 526, 527, 532, 535

abortion, 1114

absolute monarch, 742

accommodation, 617

acid rain, 1104

ACLU. *See* American Civil Liberties Union

Adams, Abigail, 162-63, 215, 237, *p237*

Adams, John: Boston Massacre and, 133; Declaration of Independence and, 157; election of 1796, 256-57; 1800, 269-71; presidency of, *p256*, 257, 259-61, 266, 268-69, 273, 275, 286; at Second Continental Congress, 150; Treaty of Paris and, 187, *p188;* as vice president, 231; view on conquering the West, 412

Adams, John Quincy: *p399; Amistad* mutiny and, 526; manifest destiny and, 318; presidency of, 380-81, *p380;* as presidential candidate, 379, 382-83; during Revolutionary War, 316; as secretary of state, 316-17, 323-24, 379; and Transcontinental Treaty, 316-17

Adams, Samuel, *p130,* 131, 133, 135, 140, 141, 144, 150, 197, 227

Addams, Jane, 690, *p690,* 762

adding machine, 668

adobe, 6

Adventists, 494

adventure schools, 485

advertising, 669, 876, *887*

advice and consent, 224

Affluent Society, 1032-33

Afghanistan, 1108, *m1128-29*

AFL. *See* American Federation of Labor (AFL)

Africa, *p81-84, m81,* 86, 87-88, 176, 449, 470-71, 822, 849, 862, 941, 959, 961, 1120

African Americans: abolitionists, 470-73, *p471-73;* in Civil War, 570-71, *p571;* after Civil War, 594-98, 601-04, 606-17; cowhands, 646; current status of, 1096-1097, *c1098, p1099, c1100;* Democratic party and, 920, 922, 1107, 1111; Depression of 1893 and, 723; discrimination against, 449-50, 511, 613-16, 805, 807, 833-34, 861-65, 922, 993, 1013, 1030, 1053-55, 1096-1097; draft riots during Civil War and, 572; education of, 449, 450, 601-02, *p602,* 616, 617, *p617,* 807, 1007, 1010-12, *c1097;* employment of, 958; equality for, 807-08, 862-64, 872, 923, 924, 958, 993, 1007, 1010-13, 1025, 1030, 1031, 1053-57, *p1054-56,* 1096-97, *p1097;* as farmers, 717; free African Americans before Civil War, 449-50, 566-67; Gold Rush and, 435, *p435;* in government, 270, 602-04, *p604,* 923; Great Depression and, 896, 922; after the Great War, 860, 861-65; during the Great War, 833-34; Harlem Renaissance and, 872; heritage of, *p81-84, m81;* income of, *c1096, c1100;* inventors, 668; in labor unions, 680; Lewis and Clark expedition and, 281; literature of, 872, 933; lynching of, 617, 808-09, 862; migration to northern cities, 862, 920-21; in the military, 163, 570-71, *571,* 833-34, *p863,* 957-58, 964-65; music of, 870-71, *p870, p871;* New Deal and, 922-23; during 1920s, 920-22; population of, *c463;* during Progressive Era, 787, 805, 807-09, *p807, p808;* race riots and, 860, 862, 1068, 1097; during Reconstruction, 602-12, *p602, p604, p607, p609, p610,* 619; Republican party and, 698, 920, 922; during Revolutionary War, 163; in Spanish-American War, 756; in sports, 874, 938, *p938;* in the Twenties, 870-72, *p870, p871;* voting rights of, 214, 613; in War of 1812, 306; on Woodrow Wilson, 828; during World War II, 957-58, *p958. See also* Africa; National Association for the Advancement of Colored People; slavery

African National Congress, 862

Afrika Korps, 961

Age of Discovery, 20-26, *p20, p22, p23, m24, p26,* 36

Age of Realism, 706-11, *p710-11*

Age of Reason, 98-99

Age of Reform, 476-94,498-05

Agee, W. H. R., 614

Agnew, Spiro T., 1071, 1081, 1083

Agricultural Adjustment Act (AAA), 907-908, 917, 922, 926

agriculture. *See* farming and farmers

agriculture, department of, 703

Aguinaldo, Emilio, 762, *p762,* 767

AIDS (Acquired Immune Deficiency Syndrome), 1114

AIM. *See* American Indian Movement (AIM)

airplanes, 840, *p840,* 873, 952, 954, 1034, *c1050*

Carteret, Sir George, 66, 67
Cartier, Jacques, 62
cartoons, interpretation of editorial, 775
Cartwright, Peter, 494
Casals, Pablo, 1019
Cascade Mountains, *m444*, 445, *m1130-31*
cash-and-carry policy, 943
cash crops, 90
Cass, Lewis, 437, 438
Cassatt, Mary, 711, *p711*
Castro, Fidel, 1016, *p1016*, 1095
Cather, Willa, 651, *p652*, 651-53
Catholics, in America, 60-61, 64-65, *p65*, 343-44, *p344*, 406, 523, 866, 885, 889, 1014
cattle, 37, 642, 647-48. *See also* ranches and ranching
cattle baron, 644
cattle kingdom, 643-48, *m644*, *p645*, *p646*, *p647*
cattle towns, 643, *m644*
Catton, Bruce, 556, 593
cause-effect relationships, 132
Cayuga Indians, 9, *m10*
CBS. *See* Columbia Broadcasting System (CBS)
CCC. *See* Civilian Conservation Corps (CCC)
census, 1047
Central America. *See* Latin America; names of specific countries
Central Intelligence Agency (CIA), 1016, 1111
Central Pacific Railway Company, 627-28, *p628*
Central Powers, in Great War, 817, *c841*
Cerro Gordo, Battle of, 421
Cervera, Pascual, 755, 756
Chaco Canyon, N. M., *p6*
chain stores, 669, 887
Chambers, Whittaker, 994
Chamorro, Violeta Barrios de, 1118
Champlain, Samuel de, 62, *m63*
Chancellorsville, Battle of, *m570*, 573-74
Chandler, Mrs. Samuel, *p80*
Channing, William Ellery, 493
Chapin, Thomas B., 459
Chaplin, Charlie, 875-76
Chapman, Carrie Lane, 791, *p791*
Charbonneau, Toussaint, 281
Charles I (king of England), 52, 60, 66

Charles II (king of England), 64, 66, 68, 108, 111
Charles V (king of Spain), 28, 30
Charles VIII (king of France), 23
Charleston, S.C., 66, 80
charter, 42
Chase-Riboud, Barbara, 526
Chateau-Thierry, Battle of, 840, *m841*
Chattanooga, Battle of, *m577*, 580
Chavez, Cesar, 1093-94, *p1093*
checks and balances, 224-25, *c225*
Chernobyl accident, 1105
Cherokee Indians, 8, *m10*, 393, 394, *p394*, 395
Cherokee Nation, 394, 395
Chesapeake, U.S.S., *p287*, 302
Chesnut, Mary Boykin, 606
Cheyenne Indians, 7, *m10*, 623-24, 630
Chiang Kai-shek, 995-96, *p995*
Chicago, Ill., 643, 669, 679, 683, *m684*, 688, 690, 724-25, 789-90, 836, 860, *p861*, 922, 1070-71, 1097
Chicago Race Riot, 860
Chickasaw Indians, 8, *m10*
child labor, 337-38, 503, 794, *p794*, *p806*, 927
children: in colonial America, 73, 74-75, *p75*; 87; in Mexico, 408; 19th-century reform movement and, 499-500, *p500*; women's role in child-rearing, 480
Children's Aid Society, 500
Chile, *m325*, 744, 820, *m1128-29*
China, 18, *p757-760*, 768-769, *p768*, *p769*, *p859*, 860, 938, 940, 941, 959, 978, 979, 995-96, 999, 1003, 1062, 1075, 1076, 1118, *m1128-29*
Chinese Americans, 435, *p435*, 627, *p627*, 689
Chinese Exclusion Act, 689
Chisholm Trail, 643, *m644*
Chivington, John M., 630
Chivington Massacre, 630, *m636*
Choctaw Indians, *m10*, 396-98, 398, 400
church schools, 484
churches. *See* names of specific churches
Churchill, Winston, 945, 948, *p949*, 961, 975, 980-81, *981*
CIA. *See* Central Intelligence Agency (CIA)
Cincinnati, Ohio, *p189*, *m684*, *c688*, 922

Cinqué, Joseph, 526, *p526*
CIO. *See* Congress of Industrial Organizations (CIO)
circle graphs, reading of, 78
Circular Letter, 130, 131
circumnavigation, 29
cities and towns: African American migration to, 833, 862, 920-21; in colonial America, 80; current problems of, 1101-04; eastern cities, 346; farmers moving to, 690, 867; on frontier, 346; government of, 789-90; rise in early 1800s, 343-48; late 19th-century growth of, 683-93, *m684*; immigrants in, 343-45, 683-87, 689; inner cities, 1101-03, *p1101*; land values in, 691; life in mid-19th century, 345-55, *p346*, *c347*; megalopolis, 1101; Mexican Americans in, 836; municipal socialism and, 792-93; population from 1790 to 1840, 328, 343-48, *c347*; population from 1860 to 1900, *m684*, *c688*, 691; population in early 20th century, 658; problems in, 690-693, 781, 783; reform movement in, 789-90, 793; suburbs, 882, *p882*, 1044-45, *p1044*; tenements in, 348, 690-92, 787-88, *p788*, 793; urban decay, 1102; in the West, 377. *See also* names of specific cities and towns
citizenship, 213-14, 1107
civil rights: and Eisenhower administration, 1007, 1010-13; and Johnson administration, 1030, 1031; Kennedy administration and, 1020, 1055; and F. Roosevelt administration, 958; and Truman administration, 993
Civil Rights Act of 1866, 595-96
Civil Rights Act of 1875, 614
Civil Rights Act of 1964, 1030, 1051
Civil Rights Cases, 614
Civil Rights Committee, 993
civil rights movement, 598, 600, 1012-13, 1025, 1053-57, *p1054-56*, 1059, 1068-70, 1096-97, *p1097*
Civil Service Commission, 705
civil service reform, 703-05
Civil War: African Americans and, 570-71, *p571*; aftermath of, 593-94; armies of, 549-56, *p553*, *p555*; battles of, 556, 558, 568-69, *m570*, 572-84, *m577*, *m582*, *m587*; begin-

m818; casualties and costs of, *p841,* 844, 848, *c1080;* Eastern Front of, 822, *m822;* end of, 844, 846; European boundaries after, 846, *m847,* 849; postwar reaction in U.S., 852-65; propaganda during, 836; protest during, 836-38; time line of, *c850-51;* U.S. activities at home during, 831-38, *p832-33, 835;* U.S. entry into, 830, 851; U.S. involvement in, 840, 842-44; U.S. neutrality at beginning of, 818-19; Versailles Peace Conference, 846, 848-49, *p848;* war on the Atlantic, 824-27, *m825, p825;* weapons used during, 826-27, 838, *p839,* 840; Western Front of, 822-24, 840, *m841,* 842-44; Wilson's peace plans, 829-30, 845-46, 848
Greece, *m943, m960,* 986, *m991, m1128-29*
Greek Americans, 683
Greeley, Andrew M., 343-44
Greeley, Horace, 633
Green Mountain Boys, 147
Greenback party, 712
greenbacks, 702-03
Greene, Nathanael, 171
greenhouse effect, 930-31, 1104
Greenville, Fort, 248
Grenville, George, *p109,* 124, 127, 128
Grimké, Angelina, 466, *p466,* 482
Grimké, Sarah, 466, *p466,* 482
Guadalcanal, Battle of, 968, *m967*
Guam, 761, *m767,* 1022, 1023, *m1023*
guerrillas, 522
Guilford Court House, Battle of, 172
Guinn v. U.S., 613
Guiteau, Charles,
Gulf of Mexico, 77, *m177, m1130-31*
Gulf Stream,
gun control, 1113
gunboat diplomacy, 777
Gutenberg, Johann, 19
Guthrie, Woody, 911

H

habeas corpus, right of, 562
Haldeman, H. R., 1082, 1085
Hale, Sara Josepha, 480
Hallidie, Andrew S., 692

Hamilton, Alexander: Bank of the United States and, 204, 242-43, 256, 273, 388; at Constitutional Convention, 196; death of, 279, *p279;* disagreements with Jefferson and, 255-56; Federalist Papers and, 228-29; Federalists and, 255; national debt and, 240-41, 252, 273; as secretary of treasury, 235, *p235,* 236, *p240;* support for war, 261, 269; view of Adams, 257, 269-70; view of government, 784; view of Senate, 224
Hampton, Wade, 611
Hancock, John, 144, 150, 227
Hancock, Winfield Scott, 712
Handy, W. C., 870, *p870*
Hanna, Marcus, 729
Hanoi, *m1063,* 1078
hard money, 193, 388, 702
Harding, Warren G., 858, 859-60, 884, *p885,* 903
Hargreave, James, *p334,* 335
Harkins, George M., 397
Harlan, John Marshall, 616, *p616*
Harlem, 920-22
Harlem Globetrotters, 874
Harlem Renaissance, 872, *p872,* 921-22
Harmar, Joseph, 247
Harpers Ferry, Va., 532-35, *p534*
Harriman, E. H., 796, *p797*
Harris, Joel Chandler, 706
Harrison, Benjamin, 712, *p712, p713,* 743, 744
Harrison, William Henry, 297, 298, *p298,* 299, *p299,* 305-06, 400-01, 404
Harte, Bret, 641
Hartford Convention, 313
Hastie, William, 923
Hawaii, 741-43, *m649, m655, m715, m742, p743, p757-60,* 762, *m767,* 779, 950-52, *p951,* 1042, 1092, *m1130-31*
hawks, 1064
Hawthorne, Nathaniel, 495-96, *p496,* 706
Hay, John, 762, 768, 771
Hay-Bunau-Varilla Treaty, 772
Hay-Pauncefote Treaty, 770
Hayden, Tom, 1074
Hayes, Rutherford B., 611-12, *p611,* 698, 704-05
Haymarket bombing, 681
Haywood, William D., 837

Head Start, 1030
headright, 50
health, education and welfare department, 1006
Hearst, George, 640
Hearst, William Randolph, 750, 753
Hellman, Lillian, 996
Hemingway, Ernest, 877-78, *p877*
Henry, Fort, *m577,* 578
Henry, Patrick, 150-51, 173
Henry the Navigator (Prince), 22, *p22*
Henry VII (king of England), 23, 40, 62
Henry VIII (king of England), 53
Hepburn Act, 797
heritage, cultural: portfolios of: American Indian, *p10-14;* Hispanic, *p81-84;* Pacific, *p757-60;* West African, *p81-84*
Hernandez, Joseph, 400
Hessians, 165
Hicks, Edward, 101, *p102*
Hidalgo y Costilla, Miguel, 323, 407
Hill, Anita, 1100
Hill, James J., 660, 796, *p797*
Hillsborough, Lord, 130, 133
Hindenburg Line, *m841,* 844
Hirohito (Emperor), 937
Hiroshima, 974, *m967*
Hispanic Americans: in Civil War, 571; culture of, 407-09, 423-26, 717-18; current status of, 1093-95, *p1093, p1094, p1095, c1095;* Depression of 1893 and, 723; discrimination against, 1093-94; elected officials, 400, 836; farmers, 717; Great Depression and, 896, 922; heritage of, 319, *p319-22,* 1093-95; New Deal and, 922-23; during World War II, 958. *See also* Mexican Americans; Cuban Americans
Hispaniola, 25
Hiss, Alger, 994, 1014
historical significance, 325
Hitler, Adolf, *p936,* 937-38, 942, 944-45, 947, 949, 959, 965
Ho Chi Minh, 1074
Ho Chi Minh City, 1078
Ho Chi Minh Trail, *m1063,* 1074
Hoar, George F., 762
Hobart, Garret A., 767
Hobby, Oveta Culp, 1006, *p1006*
Hodgdon, Mary, 339
Hodgdon, Sarah, 339-40

Raleigh, Sir Walter, 42-43, *p42, m46,* 52
rancheros, 425-26, *p425*
ranches and ranching, 406, 408, 424-26, *p425,* 643-48, *m644, p645, p647*
ranchos, 425-26, *p425*
Randolph, A. Philip, 958
Randolph, Edmund, 220, 235
range rights, 643-45
range wars, 648
ratification: of Articles of Confederation, 186; of Constitution, 210, 226-29, 231
rationing, 952, 1080
Rawlins, Kentura, *p75*
Reagan, Nancy, *p1109, p1116*
Reagan, Ronald, 206, 874, 1106, 1110-12, 1114-16, *p1109, p1116*
Realism, Age of, 706-11
Reason, Age of, 98-99
recall, 791
Reconstruction, 595-604, 606-17, 619
Reconstruction Acts, 597-98, 600
Red Cloud, Chief, 630-31, *p630*
Red Cross, 834
Red Eagle, 306-07, *p307*
Red Power, 1052
Red Scare, 860-61, *p861,* 862, 994-97, 1002-03
Red Shirts, 611
Red Stick Confederacy, 298-99, 306-07
Reed, Walter, 772
referendum, 791
Reform, Age of, 476-94, 498-05
reforms: during Age of Reform, 476-94, 498-505; business and, 796-97; in child care, 499-500; city government, 789-90; and the courts, 795; for the disadvantaged, 498-99; economic reforms, 502, 792-94; in education, 484-89; muckrakers and, 785-88, *p785, p786, p788;* political corruption and, 699-701; during Progressive Era, 780-04; prohibition of alcohol, 500-02; religion and, 490-94; social reforms, 792-94; state government, 790-92; women and, 477-83; for workers, 503-04, 793-95
regional differences. *See* New England; North; sectional conflicts; South; West
regions, geographic, 810-11, *m811*

regulatory agencies, 676
Rehnquist, William, 1114
relative location, on maps, 46, 274
religion: abolitionism and, 465; revitalization during the 1970s and 1980s, 1107; fundamentalism, 866, 867-69, *p867;* gospel of wealth, 671; Great Awakening in colonial America, 95-98, *p95, p96;* ideal communities, 490-91; of Indians, 393, 637; Judeo-Christian influences on democratic institutions, 180-81; political and social issues concerning, 836-37, 893; Second Great Awakening, 492-94, *p493, p494;* of slaves, 469-70; toleration during World War II, 958; transcendentalism, 491-92, *p492. See also* names of specific individuals, groups, and churches
religious freedom, 61, 68, 211, 237
religious persecution, 53, 59-60
Remington, Frederic, 750
Remond, Charles, 471
Removal Act, 396
Rensselaer, Kiliaen Van, 64
reparations, 848
repeal (of laws), 268
republic, 190, 272
Republic of West Germany, 989, *m991, m1128-29*
Republican party: African Americans and, 698, 920, 922; beginnings after Kansas-Nebraska Act, 523-24; bloody shirt oratory and, 697; economic progress and, 889-90; election of 1856, 524; election of 1860, 535-36; election of 1876, 611-12; election of 1896, 726, 729-31; election of 1912, 800-01; Moderate Republicans after Civil War, 593; monetary policy and, 726; in North, 697-97; political machines and, 701; Radical Republicans after Civil War, 593; Reconstruction and, 593, 595-96, 598, 600, 602-04, 611; sitting on the fence and, 701; symbol of, *p696;* tariff and, 702; Watergate Affair and, 1081-82
restraint of trade, 796
Revere, Paul, *p129, p130,* 131, *p131,* 144, 227
Revolutionary War, 143-55, 164-75, *m166, m171, m173, c178-79,* 179, 189-88, 191, *c1080*
Rhine River, 176, *m817, m840, m960*

Rhode Island, 193-94, *p194,* 196, 198, 210, *p328, m649, m655, m715, m1130-31;* as colony, 60, *c68, m91*
Rhode Island system, 337-38
rice production, 91, *m91,* 372, 451
Richardson, Elliot L., 1083
Richmond, Va., *p549,* 559, 568, 573, 583, *p583,* 693
Rickenbacker, "Eddie," 840
Riedesel, Baron von, 167
Riedesel, Frederika von, 167
Riegal, Robert E., 633
right of deposit, 250, 276
right-of-way, 627
Riis, Jacob, 348, 690, 787-88, *p788*
Rillieux, Norbert, 450
Rio Grande, 285, 316, 407, *m411,* 418, *m422, m1130-31*
Rittenhouse, David, 100, *p100,* 101, *p101*
Rivera, Diego, 424
rivers, in colonial America, 73-74. *See also* names of specific rivers
roads, 74, 349-51, *m349, p350,* 881, *p882*
Roanoke colony, 43
Roaring Twenties, 870-79
Robinson, Harriet, 525
Robinson, Jackie, 1048
Robinson, Sallie J., 614
robots, 1039-40
Rochambeau, Count, 168, 174
Rochester, N.Y., 679
Rockefeller, John D., 670, 673-74, *p674,* 675-76, 787
Rockefeller, Nelson, 1089
Rockne, Knute, 873-74
Rocky Mountains, 176, 281-82, 283, 317, 412, 414, *m444,* 445, 623, 647, *m1130-31*
Roe v. Wade, 1112
Roebling, John A., 693
Roebling, Washington, 693
Rolfe, John, 52
Rölvaag, O. E., 648
Roman Catholics. *See* Catholics
Romania, *m991,* 1118, *m1128-29*
Romantic Age, 495-97, *p495-97*
Rome-Berlin-Tokyo Axis, 950
Rommel, Erwin, 961, *p961*
Roosevelt, Eleanor, 924, *p924*
Roosevelt, Franklin Delano: advisors of, 913, 923; African Americans and, 922-23, 958; Atlantic Charter and, 948-49, *p949;* atomic

Acknowledgments

For permission to reprint copyrighted material, grateful acknowledgment is made to the following sources:

American Federation of Labor and Congress of Industrial Organizations: Adapted from ''America, We Beg You to Interfere'' by Aleksandr I. Solzhenitsyn in the *AFL-CIO American Federationist,* July 1975. Copyright © 1975 by AFL-CIO.

Anchor Books, an imprint of Doubleday, a division of Bantam, Doubleday, Dell Publishing Group, Inc: From ''The Immigrant Experience'' from *The Ordeal of Assimilation: A Documentary History of the White Working Class,* edited by Stanley Feldstein and Lawrence Costello. Copyright © 1974 by Stanley Feldstein and Lawrence Costello.

Atheneum Publishers, an imprint of Macmillan, Inc.: From ''The Vast Wasteland'' from *Equal Time: The Private Broadcaster and The Public Interest* by Newton N. Minow, edited by Lawrence Laurent. Copyright © 1964 by Newton N. Minow.

Atlantic Monthly Press: From ''A New Hopi Girl'' from *Eskimos, Chicanos, Indians: Volume IV of Children of Crisis* by Robert Coles, M.D. Copyright © 1977 by Robert Coles.

Beacon Press: Adapted from *The Broken Spears, The Aztec Account of the Conquest of Mexico,* edited by Miguel Leon-Portilla. Copyright © 1962 by Beacon Press.

Laura Benet: ''Fifth Avenue and Grand Street'' by Mary Carolyn Davies.

Columbia University Press: From ''Conclusion'' from *The United States and the Origins of the Cold War, 1941–1947* by John Lewis Gaddis. Copyright © 1972 by Columbia University Press.

Crisis Publishing Company, Inc.: From ''The Task for the Future—A Program for 1919'' by the NAACP. Copyright 1919 by Crisis Publishing Company, Inc.

The Dial Press/James Wade, an imprint of Bantam, Doubleday, Dell Publishing Group, Inc: From ''The Man Upstairs'' from *Dulles: A Biography of Eleanor, Allen, and John Foster Dulles and Their Family Network* by Leonard Mosley. Copyright © 1978 by Leonard Mosley.

Fortress Press, a division of Augsburg Fortress Publishers: From *Straight from the Heart* by Reverend Jesse L. Jackson, edited by Roger D. Hatch and Frank E. Watkins. Copyright © 1987 by Jesse L. Jackson.

Rodolfo Gonzáles: From *I Am Joaquín/Yo Soy Joaquín: An Epic Poem* by Rodolfo Gonzáles. Copyright © 1967 by Rodolfo Gonzáles.

Greenpeace: From ''Jesse Jackson'' from ''How We Can Save It'' from *Greenpeace,* vol. 15, no. 1, January/February 1990. Copyright © 1990 by Greenpeace.

Greenwood Press: From ''God's Country and Mine'' by Jacques Barzun.

Harcourt Brace Jovanovich, Inc.: From "War Lords and Vassals" from *V was for Victory: Politics and American Culture During World War II* by John Morton Blum. Copyright © 1976 by John Morton Blum. From *The Constitution: Foundation of Our Freedom* by Warren E. Burger. Copyright © 1990 by Warren E. Burger; additional material copyright © 1990 by Harcourt Brace Jovanovich, Inc. From "Defeat: The Endless Battlefields" from *Roosevelt: The Soldier of Freedom* by James MacGregor Burns. Copyright © 1970 by James MacGregor Burns. From "The East Side" from *World of Our Fathers: The Journey of the East European Jews to America and the Life They Found and Made* by Irving Howe. Copyright © 1976 by Irving Howe. From "Apple of Knowledge" from *Autobiography of Values* by Charles A. Lindbergh. Copyright © 1978 by Harcourt Brace Jovanovich, Inc. and Anne Morrow Lindbergh. From "Using Leisure" from "Inventions Re-Making Leisure" from *Middletown: A Study in Contemporary American Culture* by Robert S. Lynd and Helen Merrel Lynd. Copyright 1929 by Harcourt Brace Jovanovich, Inc.; copyright renewed © 1957 by Robert S. and Helen M. Lynd. From two songs by the left-wing, antiwar Almanac Singers, 1940–41 from "Nonintervention to War 1929–1941" from *America in the Twentieth Century: A History,* Second Edition by James T. Patterson. Copyright © 1976, 1983 by Harcourt Brace Jovanovich, Inc. "Chicago" from *Chicago Poems* by Carl Sandburg. Copyright 1916 by Holt, Rinehart and Winston, Inc.; copyright renewed 1944 by Carl Sandburg. "Song for a Youth Temperance Group" from *A History of the American People, Volume One: To 1877* by Stephan Thernstrom. Copyright © 1984 by Harcourt Brace Jovanovich, Inc.

Harper & Row, Publishers, Inc.: From *O America: When You and I Were Young* by Luigi Barzini. Copyright © 1977 by Luigi Barzini. From *The Day Lincoln was Shot* by Jim Bishop. Copyright © 1955 by Jim Bishop. From *In the Days of McKinley* by Margaret Leech. Copyright © 1959 by Margaret Leech Pulitzer. From *Andrew Jackson and the Course of American Empire, 1767–1821* by Robert V. Remini. Copyright © 1977 by Robert V. Remini. From "Toward the Sunset" from *Giants in the Earth* by O. E. Rölvaag. Copyright 1927 and copyright renewed © 1955 by Harper & Row, Publishers, Inc.

Harvard University Press and the Trustees of Amherst College: "This is my letter to the world" from *The Poems of Emily Dickinson,* edited by Thomas H. Johnson: The Belknap Press of Harvard University Press. Copyright 1951, © 1955, 1979, 1983 by the President and Fellows of Harvard University.

Louise Levitas Henriksen: From "How I Found America" from *Hungry Hearts* by Anzia Yezierska. Copyright 1920 by Anzia Yezierska; copyright © 1948 by Louise L. Henriksen.

Hill and Wang, Inc., a division of Farrar, Straus & Giroux: From *How the Other Half Lives: Studies Among the Tenements of New York* by Jacob Riis. Copyright © 1957 by Hill and Wang.

Houghton Mifflin Company: From "The Shimerdas" from *My Ántonia* by Willa Cather. Copyright 1918 and copyright renewed 1946 by Willa Sibert Cather; copyright 1926 by Willa Sibert Cather and copyright renewed 1954 by Edith Lewis; copyright 1949 by Houghton Mifflin Co. and copyright renewed © 1977 by Bertha Handlan. From "Write It Down" from *Let the Record Speak* by Dorothy Thompson. Copyright 1939 by Dorothy Thompson Lewis.

V. Annette Grant: Adapted from "Johnny Reb and Billy Yank" by Alexander Hunter from *The Blue and the Gray: The Story of the Civil War as Told by Participants,* Volume I, edited by Henry Steele Commager. Copyright 1950 by Henry Steele Commager.

Alfred A. Knopf, Inc.: From "Reaping" from *The Years of Lyndon Johnson: The Path to Power* by Robert A. Caro. Copyright © 1982 by Robert A. Caro, Inc. "I, Too" from *Selected Poems of Langston Hughes.* Copyright 1926, 1948 by Alfred A. Knopf, Inc.; renewed 1954 by Langston Hughes. "Merry-

Go-Round" from *Selected Poems of Langston Hughes*. Copyright 1942 by Langston Hughes; copyright renewed © 1970 by Arna Bontemps and George Houston Bass. From *History: A Novel* by Elsa Morante, translated from Italian by William Weaver. Translation copyright © 1977 by Alfred A. Knopf, Inc. From "September 13, 1940," "September 18, 1940," and "September 22, 1940" from *This Is London* by Edward R. Murrow. Copyright, Murrow. Edward R. Murrow, copyright © 1967 by the Estate of Edward R. Murrow. Originally published in *This Is London*. From " 'I Am the Sire of the Century by The Dynasty" from *A Distant Mirror: The Calamitous 14th* by Barbara W. Tuchman. Copyright © 1978 by Barbara W. Tuchman.

Lerner Publications: "Farewell to thee" from *The Irish in America* by James E. Johnson. Copyright © 1967 by Lerner Publications.

Little, Brown and Company: From *The Longhorns* by J. Frank Dobie. Copyright 1941 by Little, Brown and Company. From *The House Years* by Henry Kissinger. Copyright © 1979 by Henry Kissinger. From "Reville" from *American Caesar: Douglas MacArthur 1880–1964* by William Manchester. Copyright © 1978 by William Manchester.

Little, Brown and Company in association with The Atlantic Monthly Press: From "A New Hopi Girl" from *Eskimos, Chicanos, Indians: Volume IV of Children of Crisis* by Robert Coles, M.D. Copyright © 1977 by Robert Coles. From "Henry's Wedding and a Most Curious Tea Party" from *Nisei Daughter* by Monica Sone. Copyright 1953 by Monica Sone.

Ludlow Music, Inc.: From "Do Re Mi," words and music by Woody Guthrie. TRO, Copyright © 1961 (renewed) and 1963 by Ludlow Music, Inc. New York, NY. From "We Shall Overcome," new words and music arrangement by Zilphia Horton, Frank Hamilton, Guy Carawan, and Pete Seeger. TRO, Copyright © 1960 (renewed) and 1963 by Ludlow Music, Inc., New York, NY.

Macmillan Publishing Company: From "Two Motherlands" by José Martí from *The Yellow Canary Whose Eye Is So Black*, edited and translated by Cheli Durán. Copyright © 1977 by Cheli Durán Ryan. From "Afterward" from *The Guns of August* by Barbara W. Tuchman. Copyright © 1962 by Barbara W. Tuchman.

David McKay Co., Inc. From *The Long Shadow of Little Rock: A Memoir* by Daisy Bates. Copyright © 1962 by Daisy Bates.

Music Sales Corporation: From "Franklin D. Roosevelt's Back Again" from *This Singing Land*, compiled and edited by Irwin Silber. Copyright © 1965 by AMSCO Music Publishing.

The New York Times Company: From "The Text of Colonel Lindbergh's Address at Rally of the America First Committee Here" from *The New York Times*, April 24, 1941. Copyright 1941 by The New York Times Company. From "Aviators Save Him From Frenzied Mob of 100,000" by Edwin L. James from *The New York Times*, May 22, 1927. Copyright 1927 by The New York Times Company.

North Point Press: From *Son of the Morning Star* by Evan S. Connell. Copyright © 1984 by Evan S. Connell.

October House, Inc.: Excerpt from "Homage to the Express of the Blues" by Robert Hayden from *Robert Hayden: Selected Poems*. Copyright © 1966 by Robert Hayden.

Oxford University Press, Inc.: From "Schoolhouses and Scholars" from *The Culture Factory: Boston Public Schools*, 1789–1860 by Stanley K. Schultz, pp. 69–92. Copyright © 1973 by Oxford University Press, Inc.

Pantheon Books, a division of Random House, Inc: From *Hard Times: An Oral History of the Great Depression* by Studs Terkel. Copyright © 1970 by Studs Terkel. From "The Stream" by Leonel I. Castillo from *American Dreams: Lost and Found* by Studs Terkel. Copyright © 1980 by Studs Terkel.

Pathfinder Press: From "To Mississippi Youth" from *Malcolm X Speaks:*

Selected Speeches and Statements, edited by George Breitman. Copyright © 1965 by Merit Publishers.

Putnam Publishers, Inc.: From "The League of Nations" from *American Problems; A Selection of Speeches and Prophecies* by William E. Borah, edited by Horace Green. Copyright 1924 by Duffield & Company. From *The Home Front: America During World War II* by Mark Jonathan Harris, et al. Copyright © 1984 by The Putnam Publishing Group.

Ramparts Magazine, Inc.: From "The Organizer's Tale" by César Chávez from *Ramparts,* vol. 5, no. 2, July 1966. Copyright © 1966 by Ramparts Magazine.

Random House, Inc.: From *Washington Journal: The Events of 1973–1974* by Elizabeth Drew. Copyright © 1974, 1975 by Elizabeth Drew. From *The Arrogance of Power* by J. William Fulbright. Copyright © by J. William Fulbright. From *A Bright Shining Lie: John Paul Vann and America in Vietnam* by Neil Sheehan. Copyright © 1988 by Neil Sheehan.

Marian Reiner for Joan Daves: From "I Have a Dream" by Martin Luther King, Jr. Copyright © 1963 by Martin Luther King, Jr. From *Stride Toward Freedom: The Montgomery Story* by Martin Luther King, Jr. Copyright © 1958 by Martin Luther King, Jr. From "Letter From Birmingham Jail" by Martin Luther King, Jr. Copyright © 1963, 1964 by Martin Luther King, Jr.

Saturday Evening Post Company: From "I Saw Lee Surrender" by Seth M. Flint from *The Saturday Evening Post,* July/August 1976, vol. 248, no. 5. Copyright © 1976 by The Saturday Evening Post Company. From "Death the Ia Drang Valley" by Jack P. Smith from *The Saturday Evening Post,* January 28, 1967, 240th year, no. 2. Copyright © 1967 by The Curtis Publishing Company.

Charles Scribner's Sons, an imprint of Macmillan Publishing Company: From *The Great Gatsby* by F. Scott Fitzgerald. Copyright 1925 by Charles Scribner's Sons; copyright renewed 1953 by Frances Scott Fitzgerald Lanahan. From *A Farewell to Arms* by Ernest Hemingway. Copyright 1929 by Charles Scribner's Sons; copyright renewed © 1957 by Ernest Hemingway.

Simon & Schuster, Inc.: From "The Montgomery Bus Boycott" from *Parting the Waters* by Taylor Branch. Copyright © 1989 by Taylor Branch. From "I Intend to Win" from "Toward the Nomination/1975–1976" from *A Government as Good as Its People* by Jimmy Carter. Copyright © 1977 by The Carter Foundation for Governmental Affairs, Inc. From "Sun City—1983" from *Cities on a Hill* by Frances Fitzgerald. Copyright © 1981, 1983, 1986 by Frances Fitzgerald. From *The Making of the Atomic Bomb* by Richard Rhodes. Copyright © 1986 by Richard Rhodes.

Smithsonian Institution: From "Robots are Taking a Hand in Our Affaris" by Jeanne McDermott from *Smithsonian,* November 1983. Copyright © 1983 by Smithsonian Institution.

State Historical Society of Wisconsin: Adapted from "Documents: The Letters of Eldon J. Canright" from "Some War-Time Letters" from *The Wisconsin Magazine of History,* vol. V, 1921–1922. Copyright 1921 by The State Historical Society of Wisconsin.

Summit Books, a division of Simon & Schuster, Inc.: From *The Fords: An American Epic* by Peter Collier and David Horowitz. Copyright © 1987 by Peter Collier and David Horowitz.

Texas Folklore Society: From "Shelling Corn by Moonlight" by Jovita González from *Tone the Bell Easy,* edited by J. Frank Dobie. Copyright 1932 by Texas Folklore Society. Published by Southern Methodist University Press.

Time, Inc.: From "Lessons from a Lost War" from *Time,* April 15, 1985. Copyright © 1985 by Time, Inc. From "Hospital Number 1, As Told to Annalee Jacoby" from *History in the Writing* by the Foreign Correspondents of Time, Life & Fortune, selected and edited by Gordon Carroll. Copyright 1945 by Time, Inc. Adapted from *Memoirs: Volume One, Year of Decisions*

by Harry S Truman. Copyright © 1955 by Time, Inc. From "For Pres[...]
Kennedy: An Epilogue" by Theodore H. White from *Life,* vol. 55, no. 2[...]
December 6, 1963. Copyright © 1963 by Time, Inc.

University of Nebraska Press: From *Black Elk Speaks: Being the Life Story of a Holy Man of the Oglala Sioux,* as told through John G. Neihardt (Flaming Rainbow). Copyright 1932, 1959, 1972 by John G. Neihardt; copyright © 1961 by the John G. Neihardt Trust; copyright © 1979 by the University of Nebraska Press.

The University of North Carolina Press: Adapted from *Down & Out in the Great Depression: Letters from the "Forgotten Man",* edited by Robert S. McElvaine. Copyright © 1983 by The University of North Carolina Press.

University of Oklahoma Press: From *The Mining Frontier: Contemporary Accounts from the American West in the Nineteenth Century,* collected and edited by Marvin Lewis. Copyright © 1967 by the University of Oklahoma Press.

University Press of New England: "The First Modern War" from *America Goes to War* by Bruce Catton. Copyright © 1958 by William B. Catton.

Viking Penguin Inc., a division of Penguin Books USA: "American Bores Common, Ex Div." from *Christopher Columbus and Other Patriotic Verses* by Franklin P. Adams. Copyright 1931 by Franklin P. Adams. From *Henderson The Rain King* by Saul Bellow. Copyright © 1958, 1959 by Saul Bellow. From "Italy" from *Once There Was a War* by John Steinbeck. Copyright © 1943, 1958, by John Steinbeck, From *Eyes on the Prize: America's Civil Right Years, 1954–1965* by Juan Williams, with the Eyes on the Prize Production Team. Copyright © 1987 by Blackside, Inc.

A.P. Watt Limited: From *The Outline of History: Being a Plain History of Life and Mankind* by H. G. Wells. Copyright 1920, 1931, 1940 by H. G. Wells; copyright 1949 by Doubleday & Company, Inc.

Wylie, Aitken & Stone, Inc.: From "The Truce with Irrationality—I" from *A Turn in the South* by V. S. Naipaul. Copyright © 1989 by V. S. Naipaul.

Picture Credits

TABLE OF CONTENTS. Page: v (l), © Tony Linck; v(r), The Granger Collection, New York; vi(tl), John Greenwood, *Abigail Gerrish with her grand-mother, Abigail (Flint) Holloway Gerrish,* c 1750 Courtesy of The Essex Institute, Salem, MA. Accession No. 105,416; vi(tr), John Trumbull, *Surrender of Lord Cornwallis* Yale University Art Gallery; vi(bl), Photo by Gabor Demjen/ Benjamin Franklin Institute, Boston; vii(t), The Granger Collection, New York; vii(tr), Rembrandt Peale, *Thomas Jefferson.* Copyrighted by the White House Historical Association. Photograph(s) by the National Geographic Society; vii(bl), William Birch, *Third and Market Streets.* Courtesy of the John Carter Brown Library at Brown University; vii(br), Field Museum of Natural History; viii(tl), George Tattersail, English, 1817-1849, *Highways & Byeways of the Forest.* Sketch in brown and white wash on gray paper. 8 1/2 x 11 3/4 in. M. & M. Karolik Collection of American Watercolors & Drawings. Courtesy, Museum of Fine Arts, Boston; viii(tr), San Jacinto Museum of History Association; viii(bl), Thomas Coke Ruckle, *Fairview Inn or Three Mile House on Old Frederick Road,* 1829(?). Watercolor on paper. Collection of the Maryland Historical Society, Baltimore; viii(br), The National Portrait Gallery, Smithsonian Institution (NPG.74.45); ix(tl), The Granger Collection, New York; ix(tr), Picture Collection, The Branch Libraries. The New York Public Library; ix(bl), The Granger Collection, New York; ix(br), Edward Lamson Henry, *Kept In,* 1888. New York State Historical Association, Cooperstown; x(tl), Albert Bierstadt, *The Last of the Buffalo.* In The Corcoran Gallery of Art, Gift of Mrs. Albert Bierstadt, 1909.; x(tr), The Granger Collection, New York; x(b), Winslow Homer, *The Croquet Game.* © The Art Institute of Chicago. All Rights Reserved.; xi(t), The British Library; xi(c), Culver Pictures; xi(b), The Granger Collection, New York; xii(tl), Romare Bearden, *Jazz.* Photograph by E. Irving Blomstrann. From the Collection of the New Britain Museum of American Art, Connecticut. Friends Purchase Fund; xii(tr), Anton Otto Fischer, *Campbell.* Photograph by Frank Scherschel. Life Picture Service; xii(bl), Dorothea Lange, *Migrant Mother* 1936. Silver Print, 12 1/2 x 9 7/8″. Collection, The Museum of Modern Art, New York, Purchase.; xii(br), NASA; xiii(t), Chris Morris/ Black Star; xiii(c), Wide World Photos; xiii(b), Eric Bouvet/ Gamma-Liaison; xiv, Science Photo Library/ Photo Researchers, Inc.

UNIT ONE—CHAPTER ONE Page: 4, Photo by Lee Boltin/Courtesy Department of Library Services, American Museum of Natural History. Neg./Trans No. 1979(2); 5(t), Courtesy Department of Library Services, American Museum of Natural History. Neg./Trans. no. 3178(2); 5(b), The Peabody Museum of Archeology and Ethnology. The Museums Council of Harvard University; 8(t), Courtesy Department of Library Services, American Museum of Natural History. Neg./Trans no. 1429(2); 10, The Peabody Museum of Archeology and Ethnology. The Museums Council of Harvard University; 11(tr), The National Portrait Gallery, Smithsonian Institution (NPG.65.61); 11(c), Courtesy Department of Library Services, American Museum of Natural History. Neg./Trans. No. 2056(2); 12(bl), National Museum of Canada, Ethnology Division/Canadian Museum of Civilization; 12(c), The University Museum, University of Pennsylvania, (neg# T4-128 40707); 13(tr), From *Edward Sheriff Curtis: Visions of a Vanishing Race* © 1976 by Florence Curtis Graybill and Victor Boesen; 13(b), George Catlin, Black Rock, *A Two Kettle Chief,* 1832. National Museum of American Art, Smithsonian Institution, Gift of Mrs. Joseph Harrison, Jr.; 16, Inizio Buoncosiglio, *Month of August.* Scala/Art Resource, N.Y.; 18, "Marco Polo in the costume of a Tartar". Venice, Correr. Mus. SEF/Art Resource; 19(b), National Maritime Museum, Greenwich, London; 20, National Maritime Museum, Greenwich, London; 22(b), Musei Civici DiComo; 23, MAS, Barcelona, Spain; 28(t), MAS, Barcelona, Spain; 30, Courtesy of Department of Library Services, American Museum of Natural History. Neg.1412(3); 37(l), (C) Norm Thomas/ Photo Researchers, Inc.; 37(r), (C) Michael Gadomski/Photo Researchers, Inc.; **CHAPTER TWO** Page: 45, Breviary Grimany, *July, Wheat Harvest and Sheep Sheering.* Giraudon/Art Resource, NY; 49, John Gadsby Chapman, *Good Times in the New World (The Hope of Jamestown),* 1841. Virginia Museum of Fine Arts, Richmond. Collection of Mr. Paul Mellon; 56, Courtesy of the Pilgrim Society, Plymouth, Massachusetts; 58, Harvard University Portrait Collection, Cambridge, Massachusetts. Given to Harvard College in 1835 by Thomas L. Winthrop; 61, Emanuel Leutze, *Founding of Maryland* (depicts 1634), oil on canvas. Collection of the Maryland Historical Society, Baltimore; 62, George Catlin, *Chief of the Taensa Indians Receiving La Salle, March 1682,* 1847/1848. National Gallery of Art, Washington; Paul Mellon Collection; 67, Benjamin West, *Penn's Treaty with the Indians.* Courtesy of The Pennsylvania Academy of The Fine Arts, Philadelphia. Gift of Mrs. Sarah Harrison. **CHAPTER THREE** Page: 75, John Greenwood, *Abigail Gerrish with her grand-mother, Abigail (Flint) Holloway Gerrish''*, c. 1750. Courtesy of The Essex Institute of Art, Salem, MA; 76, Washington/Custis/Lee Collection, Washington and Lee University, Lexington, VA; 79, W.J. Bennett (after George Harvey), *Spring #2: Burning Fallen Trees in a Girdled Clearing*. Copyright Yale University Art Gallery, The Mabel Brady Garvan Collection; 80, Winthrop Chandler, *Mrs. Samuel Chandler* c. 1780. National Gallery of Art, Washington. Gift of Edgar William and Bernice Chrysler Garbisch; 84(tr), Abby Aldrich Rockefeller Folk Art Center. The Colonial Williamsburg Foundation; 84(bl), Abby Aldrich Rockefeller Folk Art Center. The Colonial Williamsburg Foundation; 84(br), Romare Howard Bearden, SHE-BA, 1970. Collage on composition board. Wadsworth Atheneum, Hartford. The Ella Gallup Sumner and Mary Catlin Sumner Collection; 85, Thomas Coram, *View of Mulberry Plantation* oil on paper, 10.17.6 cm. The Gibbes Museum of Art, Carolina Art Association; 88, National Maritime Museum, Greenwich, London; 90, Courtesy of the John Carter Brown Library at Brown University; 96, Courtesy of the New-York Historical Society, NYC; 99(l), Harvard University Portrait Collection, Cambridge, Massachusetts. Bequest of Dr. J.C. Warren, 1856; 104, Anonymous, *Quaker Meeting* British, 4th quarter, 18th century or 1st qtr 19th century. Oil on canvas, 25 1/4 x 30in. Courtesy, Museum of Fine Arts, Boston. Bequest of Maxim Karolik. **CHAPTER FOUR** Page: 120, Washington/Custis/Lee Collection, Washington and Lee University, Lexington, VA; 122, Benjamin West, *The Death of General Wolfe*. The National Gallery of Canada, Ottawa; 130(t), John Singleton Copley, American, 1738-1815, *Samuel Adams*. Oil on canvas, 50 x 40 1/4 in. Deposited by the City of Boston. Courtesy, Museum of Fine Arts, Boston; 130(b), John Singleton Copley, American, 1738-1815, *Paul Revere*. Oil on canvas, 35 x 28 1/2 in. Gift of Joseph W., William B. and Edward H.R. Revere. Courtesy, Museum of Fine Arts, Boston.

UNIT TWO—CHAPTER FIVE Page: 148, *Attack on Bunker's Hill, with the Burning of Charles Town,* 1783 or later, National Gallery of Art, Washington; Gift of Edgar William and Bernice Chrysler Garbisch; 151(b), Courtesy, The Henry Francis du Pont Winterthur Museum; 152, Anne S. K. Brown Military Collection, Courtesy of the John Hay Library at Brown University; 153, Howard Pyle, *The Battle of Bunker Hill*. Oil on Canvas. Acc#2025. Delaware Art Museum, Wilmington; 154(r), Picture Collection, The Branch Libraries, The New York Public Library; 156, The National Portrait Gallery, Smithsonian Institution. (L/NPB.2.80); 158, John Trumbull, *The Declaration of Independence*. Copyright, Yale University Art Gallery; 165, John Trumbull, *The Death of General Mercer at the Battle of Princeton*. Yale Univeristy Art Gallery; 173, The National Portrait Gallery, Smithsonian Institution. **CHAPTER SIX** Page: 181, William Birch, *The Arch Street Ferry, The City of Philadelphia*. Rare Book Department, Free Library of Philadelphia/Photo by Joan Broderick; 188, Courtesy, The Henry Francis du Pont Winterthur Museum; 192, Courtesy of the John Carter Brown Library at Brown University; 220, Mrs. B.S. Church, *Portrait of William Paterson (1745-1806)*, oil on canvas, 36 1/8 x 26 1/8 in. The Art Museum, Princeton University **CHAPTER SEVEN** Page: 240, Photo by Bradley Smith/Laurie Platt Winfrey,Inc./The Historical Society of Pennsylania; 244, Cliche des Musees Nationaux—Paris; 248, Courtesy, The Henry Francis du Pont Winterthur Museum; 256, John Singleton Copley, American, 1738-1815, *John Adams*. Oil on canvas, 20 x 13 1/2 in. Seth Kettell Sweetser Residuary Fund; Courtesy, Museum of Fine Arts, Boston

UNIT THREE—CHAPTER EIGHT Page: 265, Jules Tavernier, *Indian Village*. From The Collection of The Gilcrease Museum, Tulsa; 267(b), Gilbert Stuart, *James Madison*. Bowdoin College. Museum of Art, Brunswick, Maine; 269(t), Copyrighted by the White House Historical Association. Photograph(s) by the National Geographic Society; 269(b), John Vanderlyn, *Aaron Burr*, 1802. Oil on canvas, 22 1/4 x 16 1/2. Courtesy of The New-York Historical Society, N.Y.C.; 270, Picture Collection, The Branch Libraries, The New York Public Library; 276(t), W.A. Martin, *Decatur at Tripoli*. Courtesy, United States Naval Academy Museum; 282, From The Collection of The Gilcrease Museum, Tulsa; 283(t), Courtesy, Amon Carter Museum, Fort Worth; 288, Thomas Jefferson Memorial Foundation, Monticello. Charlottesville, VA. **CHAPTER NINE** Page: 294, Alfred Jacob Miller, *Shoshone Encampment at Green River Rendezvous*. From The Collection of The Gilcrease Museum, Tulsa; 297, Field Museum of Natural History; 298(t), The National Portrait Gallery, Smithsonian Institution (NPG.75.27); 298(b), George Catlin, *The Open Door, Known as the Prophet, Brother of Tecumseh* (1830). The National Museum of American Art, Smithsonian Institution; 304, The National Archives Trust Fund Board; 305, William Powell, *Battle of Lake Erie*. United States Capitol Historical Society. Photograph(s) by the National Geographic Society; 308(t), Anne S.K. Brown Military Collection, Courtesy of the John Hay Library at Brown University; 308(b), Bass Otis, *Mrs. James Madison* ca. 1817. Oil on canvas, 29 x 24. Courtesy of The New-York Historical Society, N.Y.C.; 310, Collection of the Maryland Historical Society, Baltimore; 311(tr), National Museum of American History, Smithsonian Institution; 312, Hyecinth Laclotte, *Defeat of the British Army (Battle of New Orleans)*. Yale University Art Gallery, The Mabel Brady Garvan Collection; 316, John Singleton Copley, American 1738-1815, *John Quincy Adams*. Oil on canvas, 30 x 25 in. Bequest of Mrs. Charles Francis Adams. Courtesy, Museum of Fine Arts Boston; 318, Thomas Birch, *Conestoga Wagon on a Pennsylvania Pike in 1814*. Shelburne Museum, Shelburne, Vermont; 319(l), Diego Rodriquez de Silva y Velazquez, *Las Meninas*, Giruadon/Art Resource, N.Y.; 319(r), Frenando Botero, *Princess Margarita after Velazquez*. Courtesy of Christie's of New York; 321(t), MAS, Barcelona, Spain; 321(br), Artist Unknown, *Atahualpa*. From The Collection of The Gilcrease Museum, Tulsa; 322(tl), Amelia Pelaez del Casal, *Fishes*. 1943. Collection, The Museum of Modern Art,

New York; 323, Museum of Modern Art of Latin American, Organization of American States; 324(t), The National Portrait Gallery, Smithsonian Institution. 324(b), Copyrighted by the White House Historical Association; Photograph(s) by the National Geographic Society. **CHAPTER TEN** Page: 332, Artist Unknown, *The Yankee Pedlar*, 1830. Oil on canvas, 24 x 31 inches. Collection IBM Corporation, Armonk, New York; 333, William Giles Munson, *The Eli Whitney Gun Factory*. Yale University Art Gallery. The Mabel Brady Garven Collection; 342, *Barfoot for Darton: Progress of Cotton #6, Spinning*. Yale University Art Gallery. Mabel Brady Garvan Collection; 346, Francis Guy, *Tontine Coffee House*. Oil on canvas, 42 1/4 x 64 1/4. Courtesy of The New-York Historical Society, N.Y.C.; 350, George Tattersail, English, 1817-1849, *Highways and Byeways of the Forest*. Sketch in brown & white wash on gray paper, 8 1/2 x 11 3/4 in. M.& M. Karolik Collection of American Watercolors & Drawings. Courtesy, Museum of Fine Arts, Boston; 352, Print Collection, Miriam & Ira D. Wallach Division of Art, Prints and Photographs. The New York Public Library. Astor, Lenox and Tilden Foundations; 363, Albert Bierstadt, *The Oregon Trail*. The Butler Institute of American Art, Youngstown, Ohio.

UNIT FOUR—CHAPTER ELEVEN Page: 365, John Lewis Krimmel, *Fourth of July in Centre Square*. Courtesy of The Pennsylvania Academy of The Fine Arts, Philadelphia. Pennsylvania Academy purchase (from the Estate of Paul Beck,Jr.); 367, John W. Jarvis, *James Fenimore Cooper*. Yale University Art Gallery. Gift of Edward S. Harkness; 373, Joshua Tucker, *South East View of Greenville, South Carolina*. Abby Aldrich Rockefeller Folk Art Center. The Colonial Williamsburg Foundation; 374(t), The National Portrait Gallery, Smithsonian Institution (NPG 65.58); 375, Thomas Coke Ruckle, *Fairview Inn or Three Mile House on Old Frederick Road*, 1829 (?). Watercolor on paper. Collection of the Maryland Historical Society, Baltimore; 376, Oriana Day, *Mission San Gabriel Arcangel*. The Fine Arts Museums of San Francisco, Gift of Eleanor Martin; 378, Karl Bodmer, *Settler's Farm in Indiana*. Joslyn Art Museum, Omaha, Nebraska; 380, The National Portrait Gallery, Smithsonian Institution (NPG.70.12); 382, Thomas Sully, *Andrew Jackson*, 1845. National Gallery of Art, Washington, Andrew W. Mellon Collection; 397, John M. Stanley, *International Indian Council*, 1843. National Museum of American Art, Smithsonian Institution, Gift of the Misses Henry, 1908.; 399(br), The National Portrait Gallery, Smithsonian Institution. **CHAPTER TWELVE** Page: 404, The National Portrait Gallery, Smithsonian Institution (NPG.70.23); 411, San Jacinto Museum of History Association; 413, 419, Picture Collection, The Branch Libraries, The New York Public Library; 421, Anne S.K. Brown Military Collection, Courtesy of the John Hay Library at Brown University; 425, Julio Michaud, *Hacendado y Su Mayordomo*. From The Collection of The Gilcrease Museum, Tulsa; 427., C.C.A. Christensen, *Handcart Pioneers*. ©1989 by The Church of Jesus Christ of Latter-Day Saints. Reprinted by Permission; 428, Christian Inger, *View of Great Salt Lake City*, lithograph, 1867. Courtesy, Amon Carter Museum, Fort Worth; 432(t), Olaf C. Seltzer, *Prospector*. From the Collection of The Gilcrease Museum, Tulsa; 432(b), Frank Vining Smith, *Flying Cloud*. From the Marine Art Collection of The Seamen's Bank for Savings; 433, Charles C. Nahl & Frederick August Wenderoth, *Miners In The Sierras*, 1851-1852. National Museum of American Art, Smithsonian Institution, Gift of The Fred Heilbron Collection; 434, Charles Christian Nahl, American, 1818-1878, *Sunday Morning In The Mines*, 1872. Oil on canvas Crocker Collection, Crocker Art Museum.; 436, The Philbrook Museum of Art, Tulsa, Oklahoma; 437, 441, 443, The National Portrait Gallery, Smithsonian Institution; 447, Texas State Archives. **CHAPTER THIRTEEN** Page: 450, Picture Collection, The Branch Libraries, The New York Public Library; 451, Samuel F.B. Morse, *Eli Whitney*. Yale University Art Gallery. Gift of George Hoadley, B.A. 1801.; 460, E. Crowe *Slave Auction at Richmond*. Private Collection. Photograph courtesy of Kennedy Galleries, Inc. New York; 473, The National Portrait Gallery, Smithsonian Institution (NPG.74.45). **CHAPTER FOURTEEN** Page: 477, Jerome B. Thompson, American, 1814-1886, *A "Pic Nick," in the Woods of New England*. Oil on canvas 41 x 62 in. Gift of Maxim Karolik for the Karolik Collection of American Paintings, 1815-1865. Courtesy, Museum of Fine Arts, Boston; 478, Anonymous, *Girls Evening School*, American. Pencil and watercolor, 13 1/2 x 18 1/8 in. Gift of Maxim Karolik for the M. & M. Karolik Collection of American Drawings and Watercolors, 1800-1875. Courtesy, Museum of Fine Arts, Boston; 483(b), The National Portrait Gallery, Smithsonian Institution (NPG.74.72); 485, The National Portrait Gallery, Smithsonian Institution (NPG.67.31); 488, The National Portrait Gallery, Smithsonian Institution; 492(r), The National Portrait Gallery, Smithsonian Institution (NPG.72.119); 492(c), The National Portrait Gallery, Smithsonian Institution (NPG.78.6); 496(t), Charles Osgood, *Nathaniel Hawthorn*, 1840. Oil on canvas. Courtesy of The Essex Institute, Salem, MA; 496(b), Berkshire Athenaeum, Herman Melville Memorial Room; 500, Thomas LeClear, *Buffalo Newsboy*, 1953. Oil on canvas, 24 x 20". Albright-Knox Art Gallery Buffalo, New York. Charlotte A. Watson Fund, 1942.

UNIT FIVE—CHAPTER FIFTEEN Page: 509, *Gettysburg Cyclorama*, Photography by Henry Groskinsky. Gettysburg National Military Park, United States Department of the Interior; 511(t), Eastman Johnson, *A Ride for Liberty—The Fugitive Slaves*, 1862. The Brooklyn Museum, Gift of Miss Gwendolyn O.L. Conkling; 511(b), Picture Collection, The Branch Libraries, The New York Public Library; 512, The National Portrait Gallery, Smithsonian Institution (NPG.68.1); 516, The National Portrait Gallery, Smithsonian Institution (NPG.65.49); 519, The National Portrait Gallery, Smithsonian Institution (NPG 76.68); 522, F.O.C.Darley, *Border Ruffians Invading Kansas*. Yale University Art Gallery. The Mabel Brady Garvan Collection; 524(t), The National Portrait Gallery, Smithsonian Institution. Transfer from The National Gallery of Art. Gift of Andrew W. Mellon, 1942 (NPG.65.48); 524(b), The National

Portrait Gallery, Smithsonian Institution (NPG 72.17); 526, Nathaniel Jocelyn *Cinque*, 1839. Oil on canva~ ~0 1/4 x 25 1/2. New Haven Colony Historical Society; 530, The National Portrait Gallery, Smithsonian Institution (NPG77.163); 534, Thomas Hovenden, *The Last Moments of John Brown*. Copyright Hovenden 1884. The Metropolitan Museum of Art, Gift of Mr. and Mrs. Carl Stoeckel, 1897 (97.5); 536, Thomas Cole, *Home in the Woods*. Reynolda House, Museum of American Art. Winston-Salem, North Carolina. **CHAPTER SIXTEEN** Page: 542, E.B. & E.C. Kellogg, *The Eagle's Nest*. The Connecticut Historical Society; 544, John Robertson, *Jefferson Davis* (portrait 1863). Photography by Katherine Wetzel. The Museum of the Confederacy, Richmond, Virginia; 548, Picture Collection, The Branch Libraries, The New York Public Library; 549, *Richmond, From the Hill above the Waterworks*, Colored Aquatint, Stokes Collection -1833-E-58. Miriam and Ira D. Wallach Division of Art, Prints and Photographs. Astor, Lennos & Tilden Foundatons. The New York Public Library; 553, Picture Collection, The Branch Libraries, The New York Public Library; 555, Winslow Homer, *Young Soldier*. Oil, gouache, graphite on canvas, 36 x 18.2 cm. Gift of Charles Savage Homer. Courtesy of the Cooper Hewitt Museum, Smithsonian Institution/ Art Resource, NY. Photo by Scott Hyde; 563, Conrad Wise Chapman, *Quaker Battery*. Photography by Katherine Wetzel. The Museum of the Confederacy, Richmond, Virginia; 571(r), The National Portrait Gallery, Smithsonian Institution (NPG 76.101); 578, The National Portrait Gallery, Smithsonian Institution. Gift of Mrs. Harry Newton Blue, 1966 (NPG76.8); 579, William Heysham Overend, *An August Morning with Farragut: the Battle of Mobile Bay, August 5, 1864*, 1883. Wadsworth Atheneum, Hartford. Gift of Citizens of Hartford by Subscription; 581, Charles Hoffbauer, *Summer*. Photographer, Richard Cheek. Collections of the Virginia Historical Society; 583(b), The Brady Collection, The National Archives Trust Fund Board; 585, Louis M.D. Guillaume, *Surrender of General Lee to General Grant*. Photography by Russ Finley. Appomattox Court House National Historical Park. **CHAPTER SEVENTEEN** Page: 600, The National Portrait Gallery, Smithsonian Institution, Transfer from the National Museum of American Art. Gift of Mrs. Ulysses S. Grant, Jr.; 601, Richard Norris Brooke, *A Pastoral Visit*, In the Collection of The Corcoran Gallery of Art, Museum Purchase, Gallery fund; 602, Rufus and S. Willard Saxton Papers, Manuscripts and Archives, Yale University Library; 604, Robert B. Elliott, *The Shackle Broken by the Genius of Freedom (detail)*, 1874. Lithograph, published by E. Sachs & Co., Baltimore. Chicago Historical Society; 607(t), Winslow Homer, *Cotton Pickers*, 1876, oil on canvas. The Los Angeles County Museum of Art, Acquisition made possible through Museum Trustees: Robert Anderson, R. Stanton Avery, B. Gerald Cantor, Edward W. Carter, Justin Dart, Charles E. Ducommun, Mrs. Daniel Frost, Julian Ganz, Jr., Dr. Armand Hammer, Harry Lenart, Dr. Franklin D. Murphy, Mrs. Joan Palevs, Richrd E. Sherwood. Maynard J. Toll and Hal B. Wallis; 610, Picture Collection, The Branch Libraries, The New York Public Library; 611(t), The National Portrait Gallery, Smithsonian Institution. (NPG 76.1); 615, Edward Lamson Henry, *Kept In*, 1888. New York State Historical Association, Cooperstown; 621, William Hahn, *Sacramento Railroad Station*, 1874. The Fine Arts Museums of San Francisco, Gift of the M.H. de Young Endowment Fund.

UNIT SIX—CHAPTER EIGHTEEN Page: 622, Albert Bierstadt, *The Last of the Buffalo*, 1889. In The Corcoran Gallery of Art, Gift of Mrs. Albert Bierstadt, 1909; 626, Alfred Jaboc Miller, *Fort Laramie*. Beinecke Rare Book and Manuscript Library, Yale University; 627, Joseph Becker, *Snow Sheds on the Central Pacific Railroad in the Sierra Nevada Mountains*. From The Collection of The Gilcrease Museum, Tulsa; 630, Henry H. Cross, *Red Cloud and His Granddaughter, Burning Heart*. From The Collection of The Gilcrease Museum, Tulsa; 632, Henry H. Cross, *General George A. Custer*. From The Collection of The Gilcrease Museum, Tulsa; 633, Henry H. Cross, *Sitting Bull*. From The Collection of The Gilcrease Museum, Tulsa; 634, The National Portrait Gallery, Smithsonian Institution (NG68.19); 645, Charles Marion Russell, *Jerked Down*. From The Collection of The Gilcrease Museum, Tulsa; 647, Montana Historical Society, Helena. **CHAPTER NINETEEN** Page: 666, J.J. Fogerty, *Broadway and Maiden Lane*, 1880. Lithograph, colored. Courtesy of The New-York Historical Society, N.Y.C.; 667, U.S. Department of the Interior, National Park Service, Edison National Historic Site; 681(t), Robert Koehler, *The Strike*, 1886. Private Collection, Lee Baxandall. Laurie Pratt Winfrey, Inc.; 681(b), The George Meany Memorial Archives. Official Archives of the Americn Federation of Labor and Congress of Industrial Organizations. **CHAPTER TWENTY** Page: 703, Courtesy of the Cooper-Hewitt Museum, Smithsonian Institution; 705(t), 705(b), Copyrighted by the White House Historical Association. Photograph(s) by the National Geographic Society; 709(tr), George Arents Research Library for Special Collections. Syracuse University Library; 710(b), Winslow Homer, *The Croquet Game*. © The Art Institute of Chicago. All Rights Reserved; 711(r), Mary Cassatt *The Bath*, 1891-92. Oil on canvas, 39 1/2 x 26 in. Robert A. Waller Fund, 1910.2. © 1989 The Art Institute of Chicago. All Rights Reserved; 712(r), The National Portrait Gallery, Smithsonian Institution; 729, Copyrighted by the White House Historical Association. Photograph(s) by the National Geographic Society; 731, Frederick Childe Hassam, American, 1859-1935, *Boston Common at Twilight*. Oil on canvas, 42x60". Gift of Miss Maude E. Appleton. Courtesy, Museum of Fine Art, Boston. **CHAPTER TWENTY-ONE** Page: 742, The Bernice P. Bishop Museum, The Liliuokalani Trust; 754, Courtesy Frederic Remington ~ensburg, New York; 758-759 (tr), Fernand Bourges/Life Picture Service; 768, Hubert Vos, *Portrait ~press Dowager of China, Tz'u-Hsi*, 1905-1906, oil on canvas. The Fogg Art Museum, Cambridge, Grenville L. Winthrop (1943.162); 776, Copyrighted by the White House Historical Association. ~ the National Geographic Society. **CHAPTER TWENTY-TWO** Page: 780, William Glackens, *The* ~rk*, 1905. Oil on Canvas. Purchase from the J.H. Wade Fund, 39.524. The Cleveland Museum of

Art; 782, John Sloan, *Women's Work*, c. 1911. Oil on Canvas. Gift of Amelia Elizabeth White, 64.160. The Cleveland Museum of Art; 791, The National Portrait Gallery (detail), Smithsonian Institution. Transfer from the National Museum of American History, Gift of the National American Woman Suffrage Association through Mrs. Carrie Chapman Catt, 1939 (NPG 71.31); 799, Copyrighted by the White House Historical Association. Photograph(s) by the National Geographic Society; 801, Picture Collection, The Branch Libraries, The New York Public Library; 802, National Portrait Gallery (detail), Smithsonian Institution. Transfer from the National Museum of American Art. Gift of the City of New York through the National Art Committee, 1923 (NPG 65.42); 808, The National Portrait Gallery, Smithsonian Institution; 815, John Steuart Curry, *Tornado over Kansas*, 1929. Courtesy of the Muskegon Museum of Art, Muskegon, Michigan.

UNIT EIGHT—CHAPTER TWENTY-THREE Page: 821(b), Diego Rivera, *Agrarian Leader Zapata*, 1931. Fresco, 7' 9 3/4: x 6' 2". Collection, The Museum of Modern Art, New York. Abby Aldrich Rockefeller Fund; 833(t), 835, 842, The National Archives Trust Fund Board; 845, Childe Hassam, *Allies Day, May 1917*, 1917. National Gallery of Art, Washington. Gift of Ethelyn McKinney in memory of her brother, Glenn Ford McKinn. **CHAPTER TWENTY-FOUR** Page: 853, The National Portrait Gallery, Smithsonian Institution; 864, Grant Wood, *Daughters of Revolution*. Cincinnati Art Museum, The Edwin and Virginia Irwin Memorial. © Estate of Grant Wood/VAGA New York 1990.; 865, Ben Shahn, *The Passion of Sacco and Vanzetti*. 1931-32. Tempera on Canvas. 84 1/2 x 48 inches. Collection of Whitney Museum of American Art. Gift of Mr. & Mrs. Milton Lowenthal in memory of Julian Force. (#49.22); 866, Thomas Hart Benton, *The Bootleggers*, 1927. Reynolda House, Museum of Amerian Art. Winston-Salem, North Carolina; 867, John Steuart Curry, *Baptism in Kansas*, (1928). Oil on Canvas, 40 x 50 inches. Collection of Whitney Museum of American Art. Gift of Gertrude Vanderbilt Whitney. #31.159; 871, Romare Bearden, *Jazz*. Photo by E. Irving Blomstrann. From the collection of the New Britain Museum of American Art, Connecticut. Friends Purchase Fund; 872, Photography by Edward Weston (C) 1981, Arizona Board of Regents. Center for Creative Photography/National Portrait Gallery, Smithsonian Institution (NPG 77.264);877(b), Pablo Picasso (1881-1973), *Gertrude Stein*, 1906. Oil on canvas, 39 1/8 x 32 in. The Metropolitan Museum of Art, New York: Bequest of Gertrude Stein, 1946; 885(tl), The National Portrait Gallery, Smithsonian Institution (NPG66.21); 885(tr), The National Portrait Gallery, Smithsonian Institution (NPG65.13); 885(b), Copyrighted by the White House Historical Association. Photograph(s) by the National Geographic Society. **CHAPTER TWENTY-FIVE** Page: 894, Paul Starrett Sample, *Unemployment*, 1931. Oil on canvas, 36 x 40 1/4 inches. National Academy of Design, New York City; 899, Dorothea Lange, *Woman of the High Plains*. Courtesy of the Dorothea Lange Collection. © The City of Oakland, The Oakland Museum, 1992; 900, Louis Ribak, *Home Relief Station*, (1935-36). Oil on canvas, 28 x 36 inches. Collection of Whitney Museum of American Art. #36.148; 910, Alexander Hogue, *Drought Stricken Area*. The Dallas Museum of Art, DMA 1945.6; 911(t), Dorothea Lange, *Migrant Mother*, 1936. Silver Print 12 1/2 x 9 7.8 in. Collection, The Museum of Modern Art, New York. Purchase; 921, Palmer Hayden, *The Janitor Who Paints*, 1937. National Museum of American Art, Smithsonian Institution, Gift of The Harmon Foundation; 923, The National Portrait Gallery, Smithsonian Institution (NPG 67-78); 924, Copyrighted by the White House Historical Association; Photograph(s) by the National Geographic Society.

UNIT NINE—CHAPTER TWENTY-SIX Page: 935, National Air and Space Museum, Washington, D.C./Printed by permisson of the Estate of Norman Rockwell. Copyright © 1969 Estate of Norman Rockwell; 944, Charles Cundall, *The Withdrawal From Dunkirk, June 1940*. The Imperial War Museum, London; 945(t), AKG/Photo Researchers, Inc.; 948, Anton Otto Fischer, *Campbell*. Photograph by Frank Scherschel. Life Picture Service; 956, The National Archives Trust Fund Board; 959, Frank Scherschel/Life Magazine © Time Inc.; 969, Associated Press/Wide World Photos. **CHAPTER TWENTY-SEVEN** Page: 984, *For Full Employment after the War Register—Vote*, 1944. Offset lithograph, 30 x 39 7/8 inches. Collection, The Museum of Modern Art, New York. Gift of the CIO Political Action Committee; 985(b), Copyrighted by the White House Historical Association. Photograph(s) by the National Geographic Society; 988, The National Portrait Gallery, Smithsonian Institution. Transfer from the National Museum of American Art. Gift of the International Business Machines Corporation to the Smithsonian Institution, 1962 (NPG 66.64); 995, 1001, Carl Mydans/Life Magazine © Time Inc.; 1004, John Sadovy/Life Magazine © Time Inc.; 1008(t,c,b), 1009 (t,c,b), Flags from Mastai Collection of Antique American Flags, Amagansett, New York/Photography by Boleslaw Mastai. From *The Stars and The Stripes—The American Flag as Art and As History, From the Birth of The Republic to The Present* by Boleslaw and Marie Louise d'Otrange Mastai (Alfred Knopf), New York, 1973; 1015(b), Copyrighted by the White House Historical Association. Photography(s) by the National Geographic Society.

UNIT TEN—CHAPTER TWENTY-EIGHT Page: 1030, © Bruce Roberts/Photo Researchers, Inc.; 1046, Jon Brenneis/Life Magazine © Time Inc.; 1053, © Jim Cartier/Photo Researchers, Inc. **CHAPTER TWENTY-NINE** Page: 1070, Burt Glinn/Magnum Photos; 1073, Paul Stephanus/R. Ellison/Black Star; 1082, Gjon Mili/Life Magazine © Time Inc **CHAPTER THIRTY** Page: 1089(b), Cartoon by S.C. Rawls, Palm Beach Post, 1974. Reprinted by Permission NEA, Inc.

REFERENCE SECTION Page: 1127, 1132, Science Photo Library/Photo Researchers, Inc.